Small animal surgery

Warning:
Veterinary science is constantly evolving, as are pharmacology and the other sciences. Inevitably, it is therefore the responsibility of the veterinary clinician to determine and verify the dosage, the method of administration, the duration of treatment and any possible contraindications to the treatments given to each individual patient, based on his or her professional experience. Neither the publisher nor the author can be held liable for any damage or harm caused to people, animals or properties resulting from the correct or incorrect application of the information contained in this book.

This book has been published originally in spanish under the title:
La cirugía en imágenes, paso a paso. La parte posterior

ISBN spanish edition: 84-932921-7-6

For this english edition:

Plaza Antonio Beltrán Martínez nº 1, planta 8 - letra I
(Centro empresarial El Trovador)
50002 Zaragoza - Spain

2nd print run, September 2012

Translators/Proofreaders:
Karin de Lange DVM MRCVS
Mette Bouman DVM
Ian Neville BVSc MRCVS

Design and layout:
Servet editorial - Grupo Asís Biomedia, S.L.
www.grupoasis.com

Printing:
Gráficas Lizarra S.L.
Ctra. Tafalla, km 1
31132 Villatuerta
Navarra, Spain

ISBN: 978-84-92569-46-5
D.L.: Z 1771-2012

Printed in Spain

Small animal surgery

José Rodríguez Gómez

Jaime Graus Morales

María José Martínez Sañudo

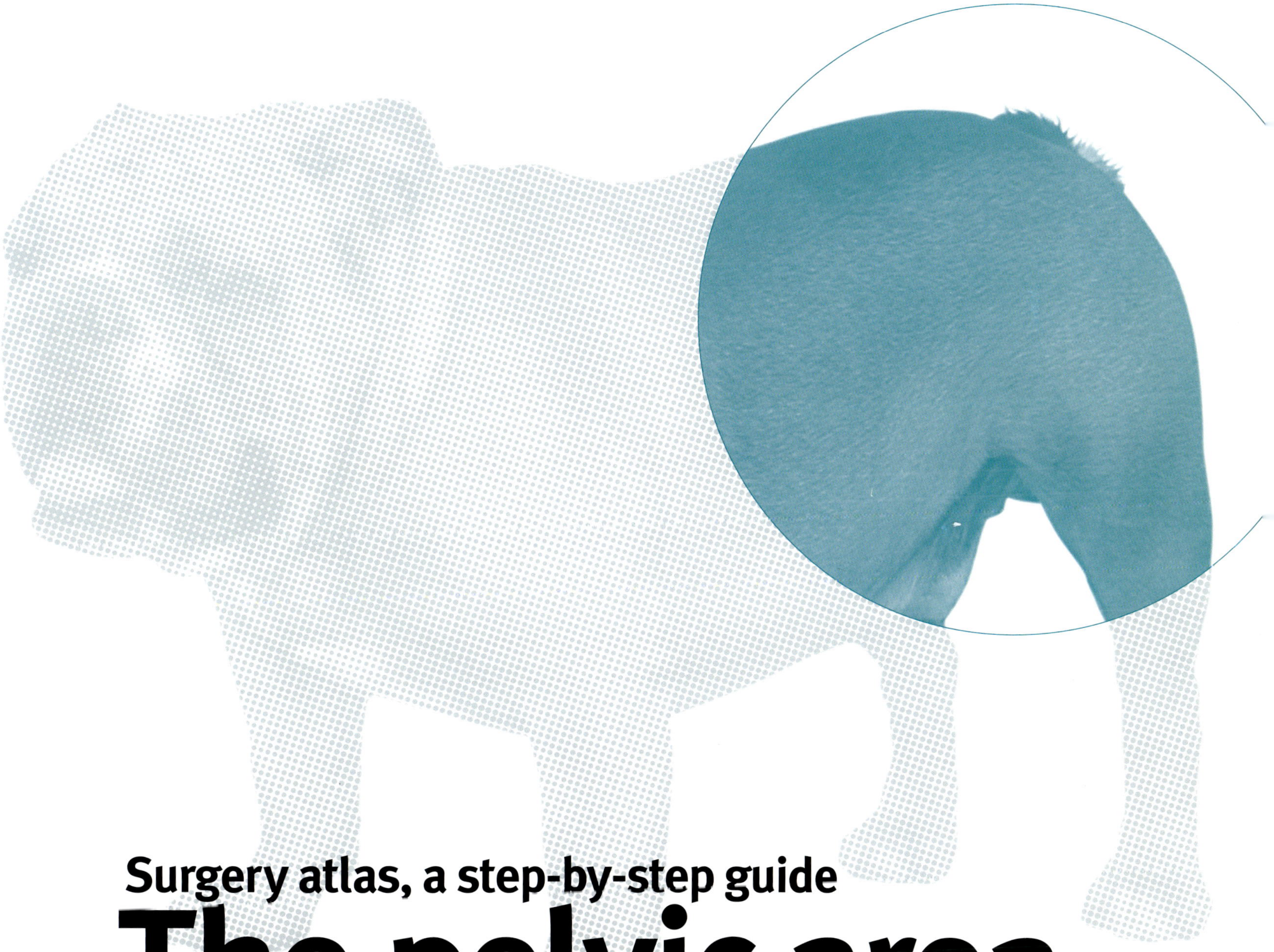

Surgery atlas, a step-by-step guide

The pelvic area

SERVET

Authors

From left to right; Jaime Graus, Associate Professor of Veterinary Surgery of the Clinical Veterinary Hospital of the Zaragoza Faculty of Veterinary Medicine (HCVZ), Maria José Martínez, Professor of Clinical Medicine and Surgery and Assistant Director of the HCVZ, and José Rodríguez, Professor of Clinical Medicine and Surgery and Director of the HCVZ.

Foreword

The recent abundance of publications on veterinary surgery and the high quality of their content demonstrates the increasing interest in this area of clinical practice. In certain ways, we might say that veterinary surgery is coming of age.

There is a natural predisposition to practise surgery, but it is of vital importance to have good learning methods and continuing education, and for the surgeon to familiarise himself with new techniques that allow progress, thereby assuming a certain risk – as knowledge or progress cannot be achieved without risk.

Surgery comes naturally to many people; however, a good learning process, including continuing education, as well as the drive to keep learning new techniques are very important for progress, which always carries a certain risk. Without taking risks, nothing is learned and no progress is made.

This book is a great compendium of clinical cases, well-documented and using real images of excellent quality, confirming the saying that a picture is worth a thousand words. Beyond the process of obtaining and selecting the pictures, we can appreciate the amount of effort and work, which only authors with great professionalism and sense of responsibility can offer. The approach of this book, based on the authors' experience, is highly practical and visual. This allows the reader to rapidly recognise the cases that are presented and the successive steps of the techniques that are used. Some are easy and can be carried out by novice surgeons. Other, more complex cases, require a little more experience.

I consider this book to be a must for every veterinary surgeon's library, together with a good anatomical atlas, a reference book on physiology and a detailed compendium of surgical pathology and small animal surgery. Although the latter offer the theoretical support for practical surgery, the present book offers immediate, hands-on information, which is of great use.

It is an easy-to-read book that will help the clinician to progress at his own speed in the area of surgery without too much effort. With the help of this book, the reader may take the risk of making progress.

Jordi Cairó
Veterinary Surgeon
CANIS, Veterinary Hospital. Girona

Anyone wanting to jump for the first time into a swimming pool to enjoy the water should think twice before diving in headfirst. We all more or less know how to swim, but can we do an entire length, or ten, or will we be exhausted after the first four strokes? Do we know the depth of the pool before plunging in?

I can see a lifeguard close-by and an increasing number of swimmers! This is a relief because, although normally nothing will happen to me, I know I will have help if needed. And of course there's always the pool ladder nearby and the bathrobe at hand. When everything is ready and nothing has been left to chance, we only need to change our clothes, don our surgical cap, mask, gown and gloves and proceed to the operating theatre.

Preface

This book is dedicated to surgery, perhaps the most spectacular activity of a veterinary clinician: probably because it is a direct therapy, carried out by hand, and it confers a kind of magical power on the surgeon, aided by the fact that a disorder can often be solved very rapidly in the operating theatre.

The art of surgery is an 'acid test' for the novice surgeon, with successes that can be spectacular and greatly add to the prestige of the surgeon, but failures that can be dramatic too.

Either way, the mythical aura that surrounds both surgery and the surgeon force us to plan each surgical intervention in detail, in order to obtain the best results in the shortest time and with the least possible trauma. All this will not only be of benefit to the patient but will also ensure that the clinician enjoys being in the operating theatre, as surgery can and should be a pleasure.

This is a book without pretensions, which aims to be a companion to the veterinarian in the operating theatre; it is a faithful reflection of routine clinical work and the experience that has been gathered over the years, including successes and failures. It also mirrors the pride the authors take in their work, and the hope of doing things well, and improving every day.

The core of this book is the photographic material that has been collected over past years. The initial purpose was different, namely to use it for undergraduate teaching at our faculty. To a large extent, this book came about by chance. One afternoon, when we were discussing clinical cases together, one patient led to another, and that one to yet another, until we had so much material on the table that we were surprised ourselves.

We then thought that maybe the amount of material, accumulated with care, could be of use to others besides our own students. We decided to use a format that makes it easy for the veterinary clinician to recognise the content straight away when presented with a similar case.

This volume compiles the main pathological processes of the pelvic area of the dog and cat, from the perineal hernia and anus to the glans and the prepuce, including the external genitals of the female.

The clinical cases described in each chapter are those that we consider important to illustrate certain disorders, with a special emphasis on the case-specific aspects and relevant points that should be taken into consideration.

For each case, the treatment is also presented, in particular the surgical treatment, without trying to turn this book into a manual of surgical techniques. The described procedures are those that we carry out routinely on our patients. In our opinion we believe they work well and they were chosen for that reason, but we are well aware that others exist, which can also lead to good results.

Before finishing, we would like to apologise to photography buffs. The images shown are snapshots, taken by us in the consulting room or the operating theatre, we are vets, not photographers, and it shows. Often, it is not the best image possible from a technical viewpoint. Nevertheless, we trust that, from a clinical point of view, they are sufficiently interesting and that this makes up for their shortcomings.

If we can contribute as colleagues ideas that may be of assistance to you in your daily practice, we will be satisfied. It would be wonderful if, in addition, we are able to transmit some of the pleasure that surgery gives us. In any case: thank you for your attention.

Acknowledgements

To all dear members of the small "great family" of the Veterinary Clinical Hospital of Zaragoza:

Thank you very much for your assistance, collaboration and support, without which we would, no doubt, not have come this far.

Thanks to the teaching, administrative and support staff, both clinical and non-clinical, as all tasks are equally important.

Thanks also, of course, to the clinicians who entrusted us with the treatment of their patients.

A special thanks to the veterinary interns past and present, because their hard work is one of the best incentives for us who are not that young anymore. Thanks to Amaya, Susana y Maitane, to María Eugenia, Ana and Gorka, to Alicia and to Olga, to Ana, María, Ainara and José. Your everyday commitment and dedication make you deserving of excellent careers.

And of course our sincerest recognition to the team of the Servet Publishing Company which has helped to present our work in the best possible way.

Dr. José Rodríguez Gómez
Dr. Jaime Graus Morales
Dra. María José Martínez Sañudo
Clinical Veterinary Hospital. Zaragoza.

How this book works

"The pelvic area" is divided into nine chapters. The first chapter of the book, "General considerations on rectal, anal and perineal surgery", gives an introduction to the main aspects to consider before carrying out an operation in this area.

The next seven chapters are dedicated to different anatomical areas. They give step-by-step, detailed explanations of the surgical procedures aimed at resolving the most common disorders.

The last chapter, "General techniques" includes a series of basic techniques that complement those described throughout the book.

In the contents, there is a clear distinction between the description of surgical techniques on the one hand and the clinical presentation of disorders and medical treatments on the other.

The chapter openings

On each double page, schematic diagrams offer an anatomical review of the area.

Name of the chapter.

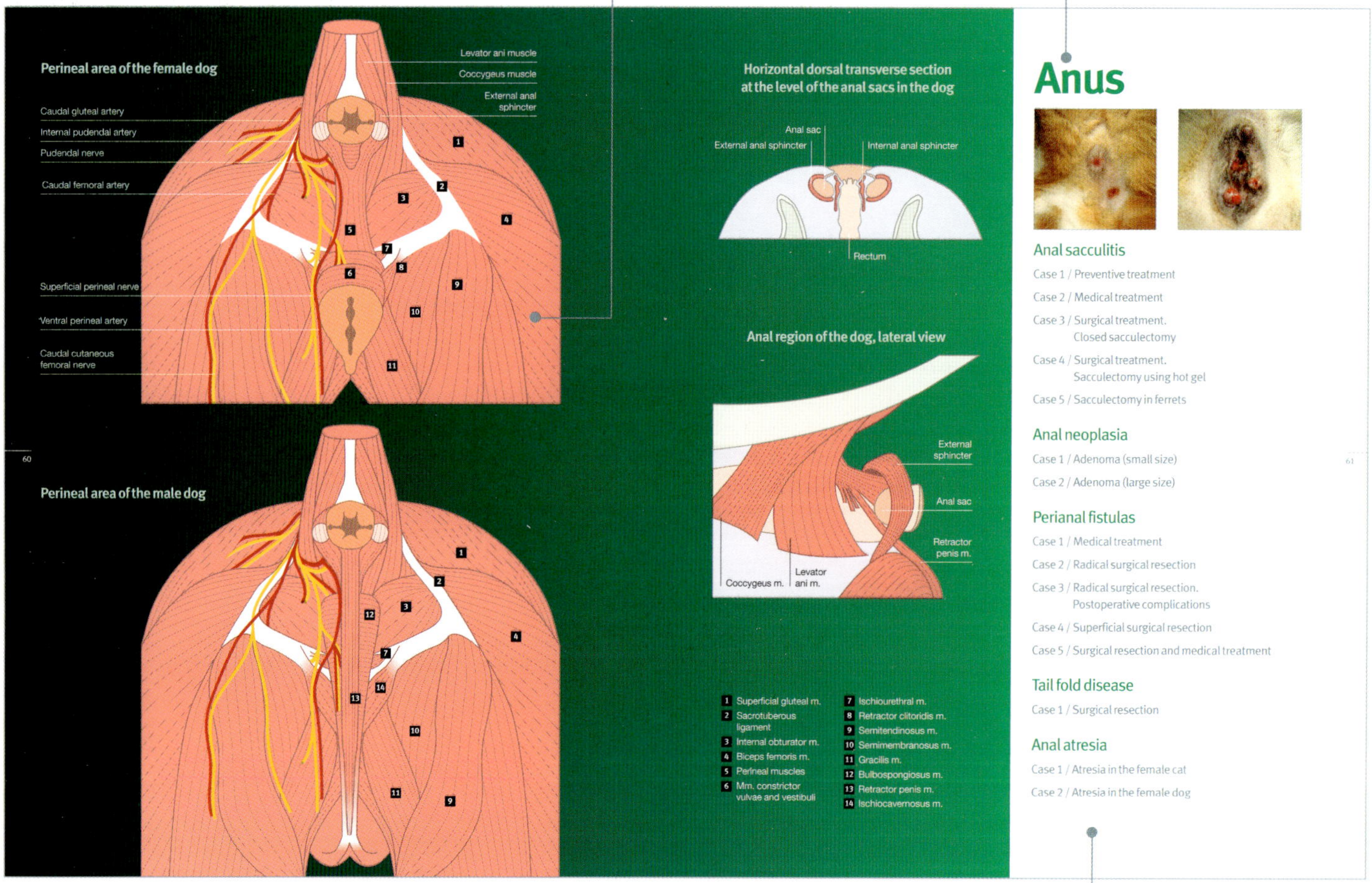

Index for easy reference to find a clinical case or a surgical technique.

The contents

On certain pages, a box supplies information about the technical difficulty of the procedure used and the prevalence of the described disorder (from 1 to 5).

Reference to other techniques or explanations in the book are clearly indicated to facilitate decision making during consultations.

Step-by-step explanation of the surgical technique used.

The pelvic area

Rectal prolapse. Case 2 / Colopexy

Prevalence	
Technical difficulty	

Colopexy aims to create a stable fixation of the colon to the abdominal wall, which prevents caudal movement and prolapse of the rectum.

Colopexy is indicated to prevent the recurrence of rectal prolapse.

The technique starts with an infraumbilical laparotomy and identification of the descending colon.

See infraumbilical laparotomy → *page 282*

- Draw the descending colon towards the abdominal cavity in order to reduce the prolapse.
- Abrade the non-mesenteric wall of the descending colon close to the pelvis over an area of 5 to 10 cm. A gauze swab can be used for this (fig. 1).

24

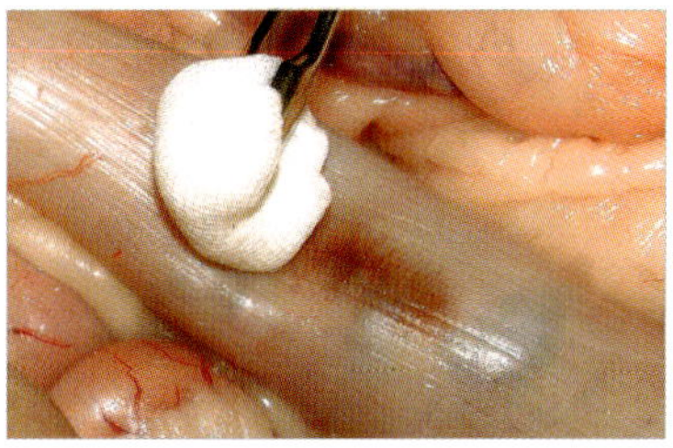

Fig. 1. The anti mesenteric border (opposite the mesenteric side) of the colon is rubbed with a gauze swab until irritation and hyperaemia of the covering peritoneal lining is observed.

- The same procedure is repeated on the left abdominal wall, some 3 cm from the laparotomy incision (fig. 2).
- Next, the colon is sutured to the abdominal muscle, using synthetic absorbable 3/0 suture material (figs. 3 and 4).
- The operation is concluded by closing the laparotomy as described in the corresponding section.

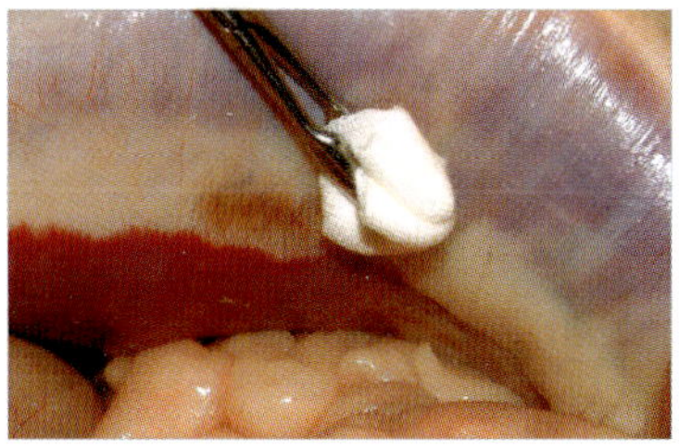

Fig. 2. Irritation of the peritoneal wall to increase the adhesion of the colon to the abdominal wall.

The coloured strip indicates the description of a surgical technique.

Introduction of the clinical case or disorder.

These notes indicate a risk in the intervention or a phase requiring particular attention.

The procedures are illustrated, step by step, by means of excellent photographs.

The clear strip describes the disorder or a medical treatment.

The operation is illustrated, step by step, by means of excellent photographs.

Anus / Anal sacculitis

Anal sacculitis. Case 1 / Preventive treatment

A simple impaction can be treated by emptying the anal sacs by manual pressure.
In dogs, the third (middle) finger is inserted in the anus to carry out rectal palpation, focusing on the sides of the anal sphincter (at 4-5 and 7-8 o'clock) (fig. 1). Both sacs are emptied by squeezing the sacs in direction of the anal opening (fig. 2).

Do not squeeze too hard, as the sac may rupture.
Take care that the content does not end up on your coat.

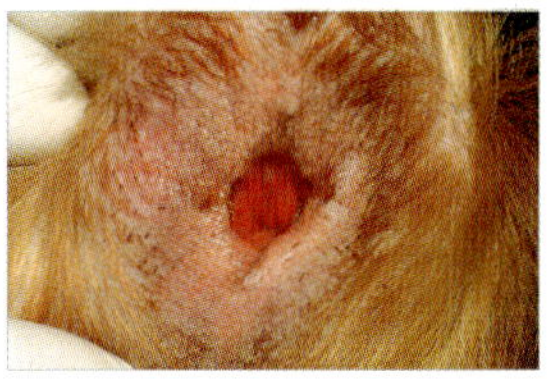

Fig. 1. Identification of the orifices of the anal sacs. In this case, their opening is more dorsal than usual.

In miniature breeds, in cats and in animals in which rectal palpation is not possible, apply pressure to empty the sacs from the outside, squeezing the sac through the skin (fig. 3).
It is also indicated to flush the sacs with saline at room temperature in order to clean them mechanically. In case of infection and intense local inflammation, besides emptying the anal sacs, they should be flushed using lukewarm saline and a 10% iodine povidone or a 0.5% chlorhexidine solution.
In case of an abscess, a local antibiotic/anti-inflammatory ointment should be prescribed, and in severe cases, systemic treatment should also be given. Recommend increasing the fibre in the diet to facilitate the emptying of the anal sacs.

63

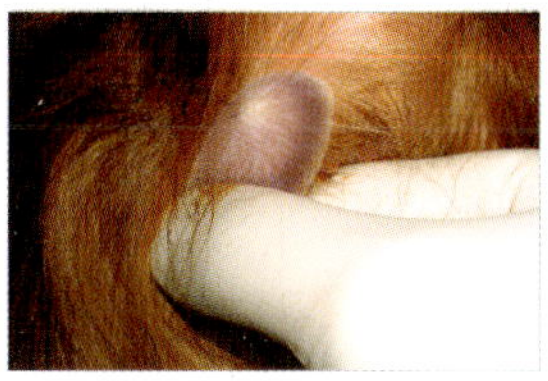

Fig. 2. Emptying the anal sac by squeezing from its most internal part.

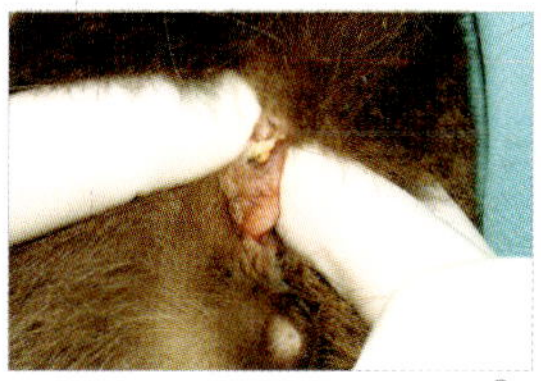

Fig. 3. Emptying the right anal gland using external digital pressure.

Name of the chapter and the disorder described.

Boxes highlight useful tips.

The captions describe each step in a concise but complete manner.

Table of contents

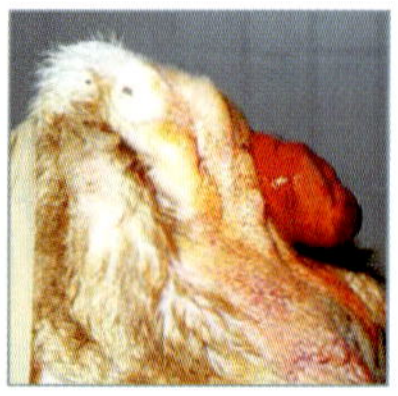

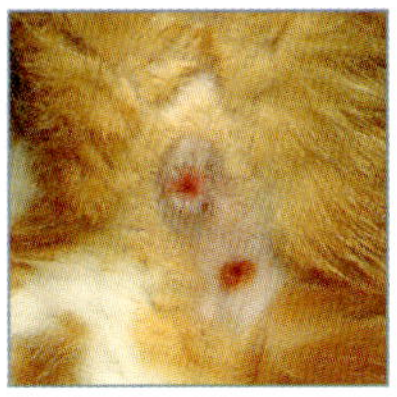
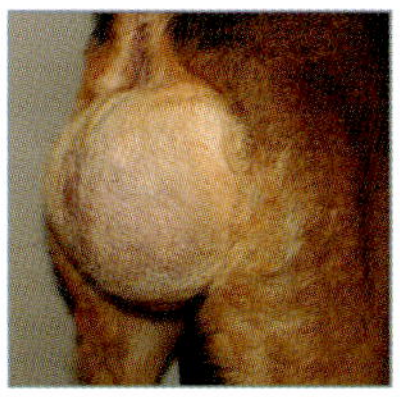
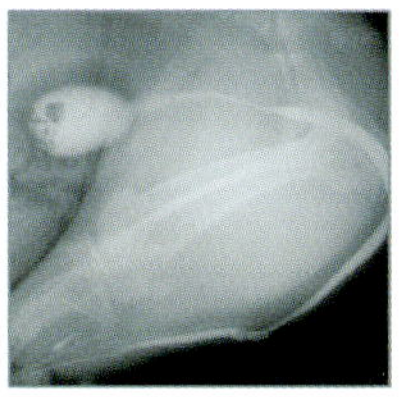
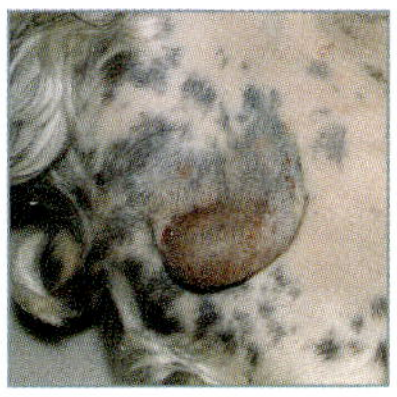
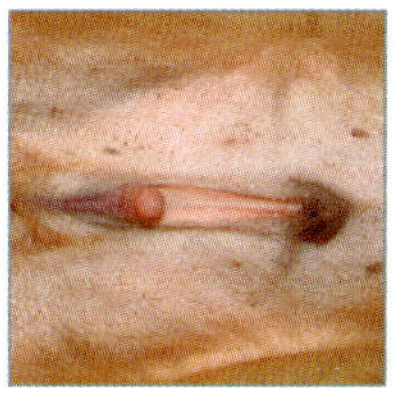
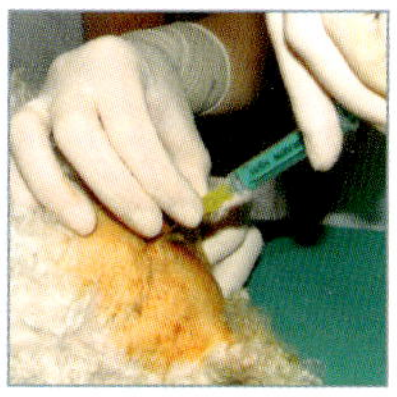

General considerations
for rectal, anal and perineal surgery

General rules for surgery in the perineal area

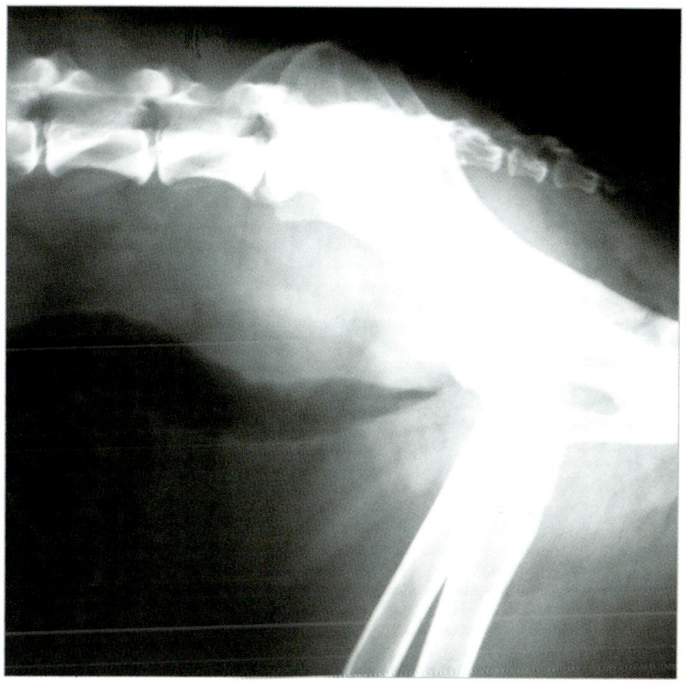

General rules for surgery in the perineal area

The **perineum** is the part of the body wall that closes the caudal opening of the pelvis, surrounding the anal and urogenital tract.
Operations in this area have a high rate of postoperative complications and relapses, a reason why many veterinarians are reluctant to carry them out.
It is necessary to have a good **anatomical knowledge** of this area, to reach the best possible pathological diagnosis and to follow an appropriate surgical protocol.
The **diagnosis** of the changes in this area should be based on the history, clinical signs, physical examination – rectal palpation is of particular importance (fig. 1) – and on complementary diagnostic tests.
If a **neoplasm** is observed in this area, an abdominal X-ray should be taken to check for metastases in the regional lymph nodes (fig. 2).

> ***Take your time when examining the rectal tract. When withdrawing your finger you should be sure whether the patient has the suspected lesion or not.***

Blood testing rarely supplies relevant data, unless the patient has neoplasia and paraneoplastic signs (anaemia, hypercalcaemia...) or if there is a difficulty in urine elimination (urinary tract obstruction).

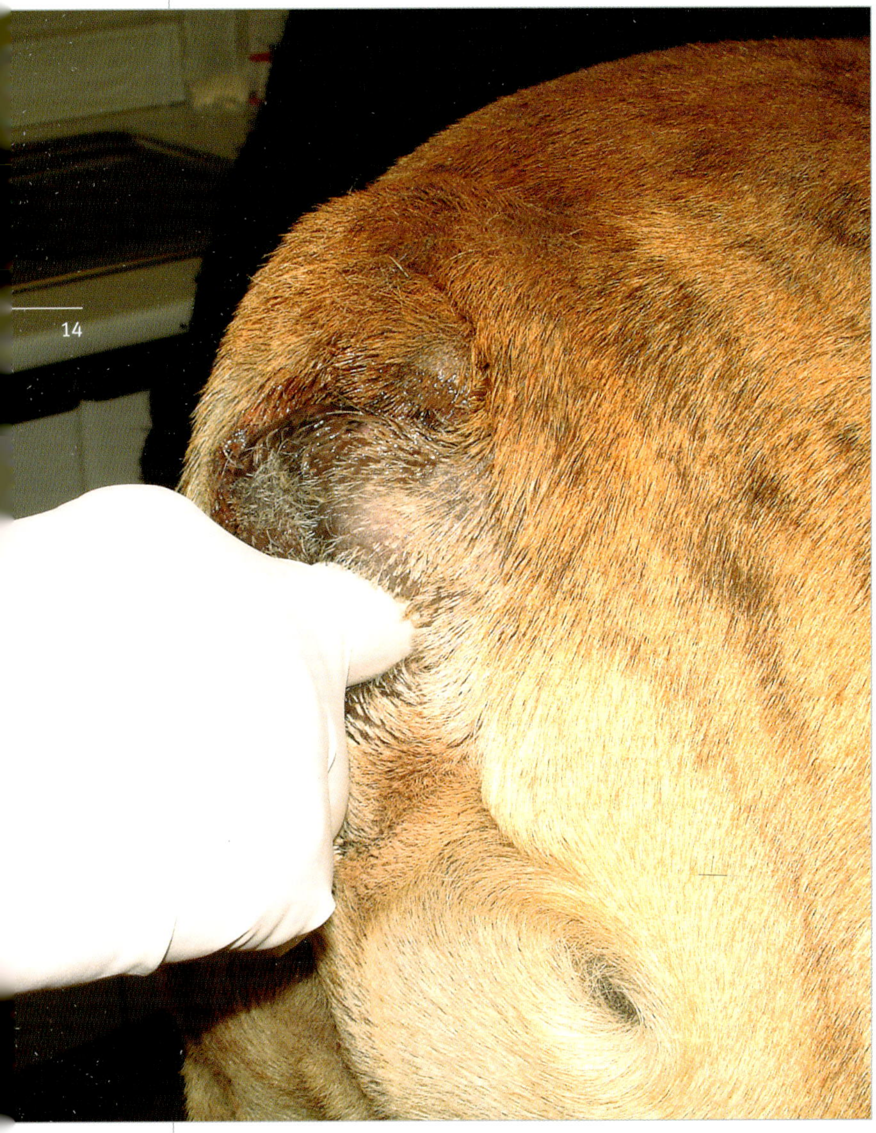

Fig. 1. The rectal tract should be examined manually in all cases where an alteration of the rectum, anus or perineum is suspected. Always use the 3rd finger (middle finger) of your dominant hand.

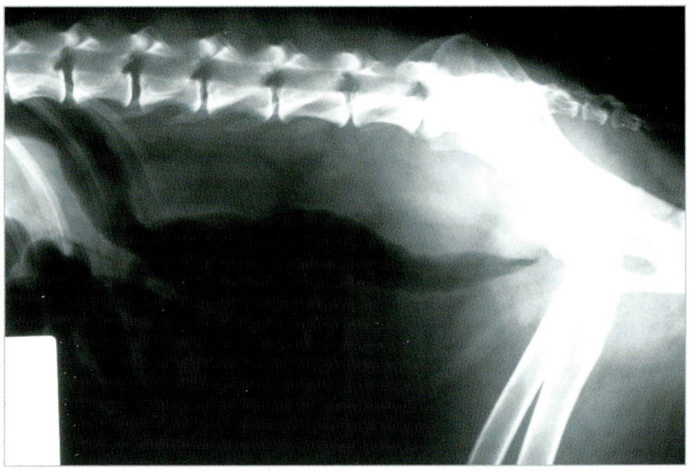

Fig. 2. Tumour metastases in the sublumbar lymph nodes in a patient with a perianal adenocarcinoma. Note the ventral displacement of the colon due to the lumbar lymphadenopathy.

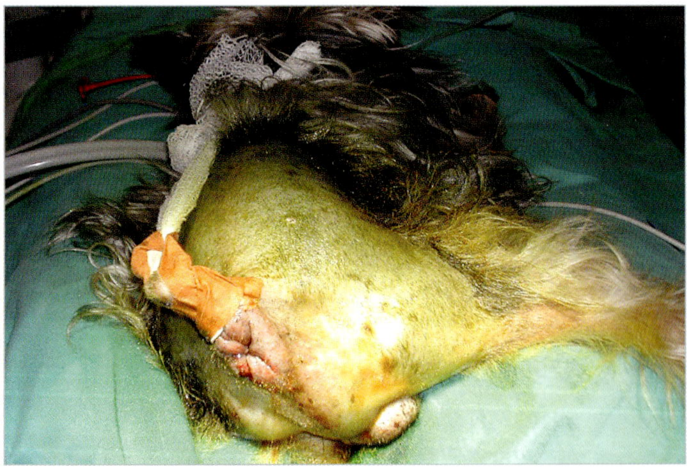

Fig. 3. Position the patient in sternal recumbency, with the hind legs over the edge of the operating table.
A purse string suture avoids the expulsion of faeces during the operation and prevents soiling of the operating field.

The highest bacterial concentration in the entire digestive tract is found in the colon and rectum. For this reason, the patient should be prepared with great care prior to the intervention, and the technique to be used should be chosen carefully.

Important aspects to consider in a case of perineal surgery:

- Feed a low-residue diet for the three days prior to the operation (different companies supply this type of diet, or alternatively, minced meat with white rice can be given).
- No solids by mouth for 24 hours prior to the operation. Drinking is allowed up to 4 hours before.
- Laxatives such as bisacodyl (5-20 mg PO in dogs, 2.5-5 mg PO in cats). Contraindicated in case of intestinal obstruction.
- Isotonic enemas at least 24-36 hours before and never on the day of the operation.

It is contraindicated to give an enema on the day of the operation. The liquid intestinal content cannot be retained during the intervention and will contaminate the operating field.

- Preoperative antibiotic prophylaxis against Gram negative aerobic and anaerobic bacteria. Use one of the following combinations, to be administered intravenously during anaesthesia:
  - Cefazolin: 20 mg/kg IV.
    Metronidazole: 10 mg/kg IV.
  - Enrofloxacin: 5-10 mg/kg IV.
    Amoxicilin + clavulanic acid: 20 mg/kg IM.
- Place the patient in a comfortable position for you and the animal, avoiding injuries to the patient's hind legs (fig. 3).

See patient positioning → *page 248*

- Avoid the expulsion of faeces during the operation (fig. 4).

See purse string suture → *page 252*

- Maximize hygiene measures during the intervention.
- Use monofilament, synthetic, absorbable material for the internal sutures.
- Use monofilament, synthetic, non-absorbable material for the skin sutures.
- Prevent the patient from licking or chewing the area. The use of an Elizabethan collar is recommended.
- Examine the patient regularly to check post-operative progress, at least after 24 hours, 3 and 6 days...

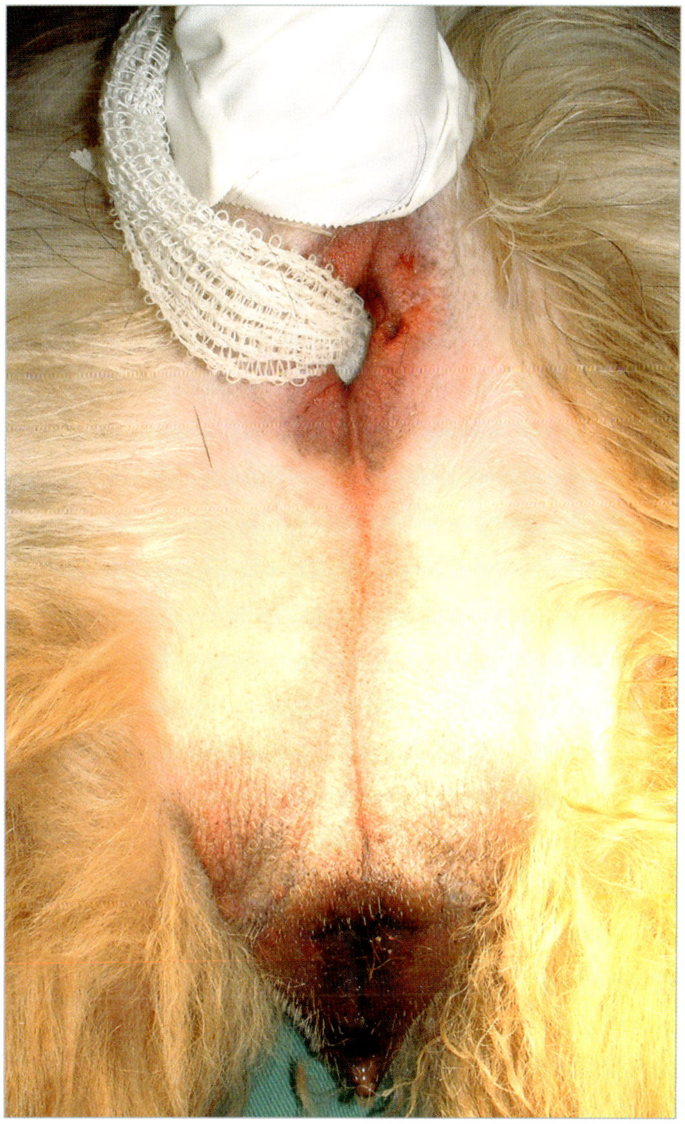

Fig. 4. Occlude the rectum with a gauze bandage to avoid contamination of the operating field with faeces that may be expelled from the anus during surgery.

Muscles of the urogenital region in the female dog

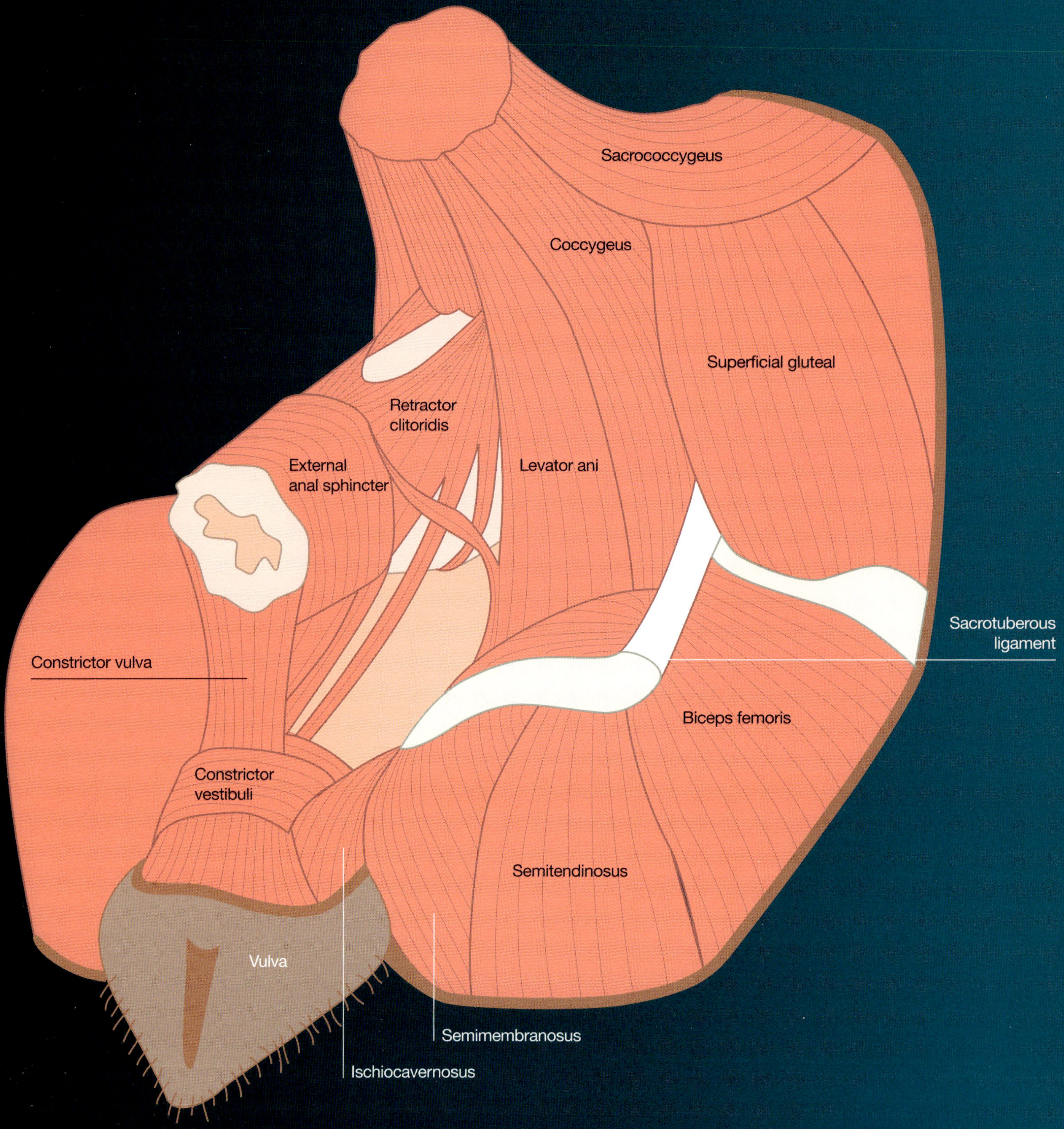

Arteries of the pelvic region

Female dog

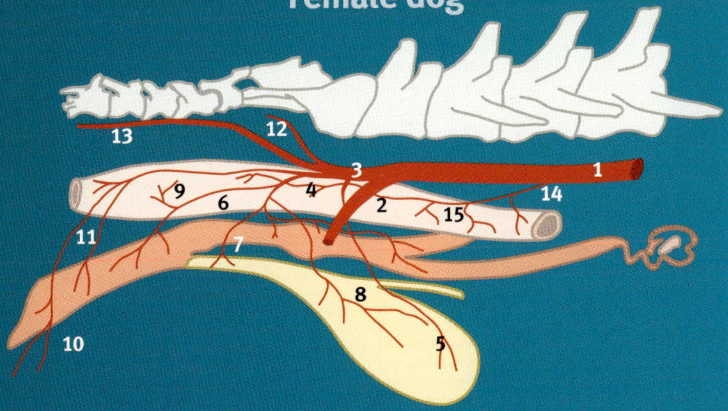

Male dog

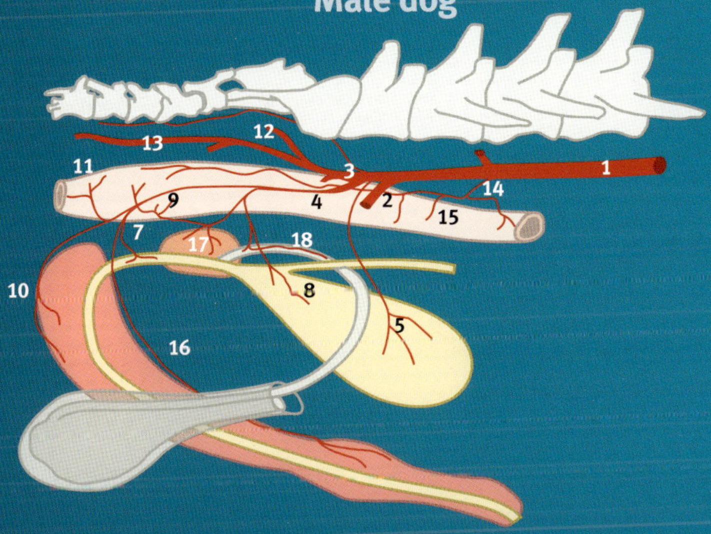

1 Aorta
2 External iliac a.
3 Internal iliac a.
4 Internal pudendal a.
5 Umbilical a.
6 Vaginal a.
7 Urethral a.
8 Caudal vesical a.
9 Middle rectal a.
10 Ventral perineal a.
11 Caudal rectal a.
12 Caudal gluteal a.
13 Lateral caudal a.
14 Caudal mesenteric a.
15 Cranial rectal a.
16 Dorsal artery of penis
17 Prostatic a.
18 Artery of ductus deferens

Rectum

Rectal prolapse

Case 1 / Rectal amputation

Case 2 / Colopexy

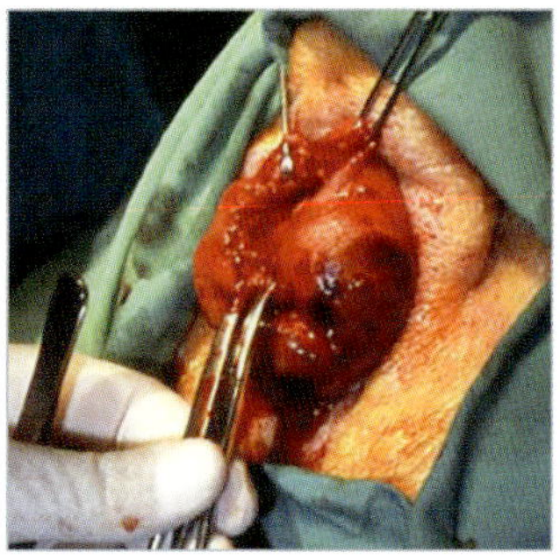

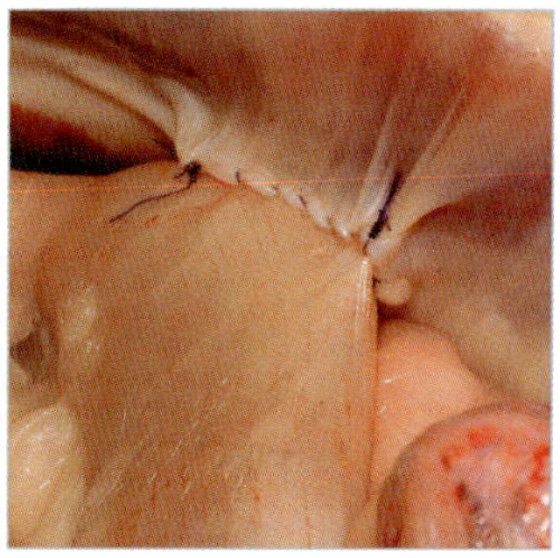

Stenosis

Case 1 / Transanal rectal resection

Case 2 / Abdominal colectomy

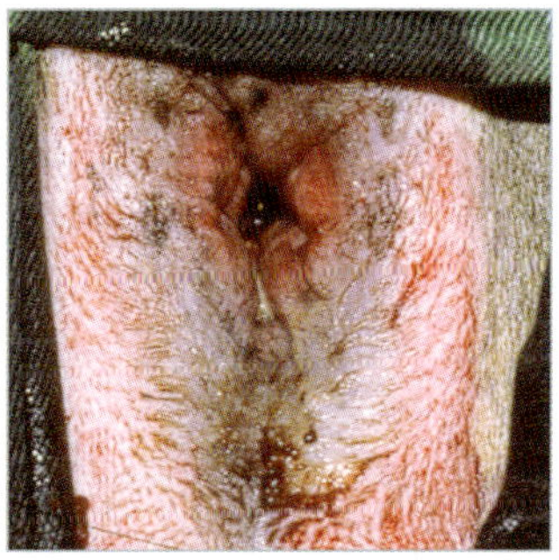

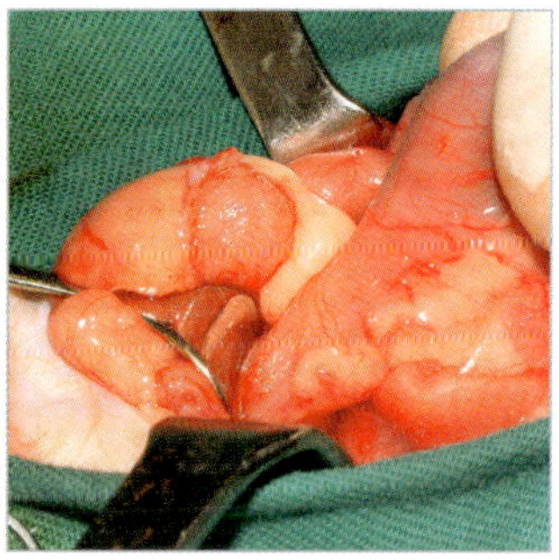

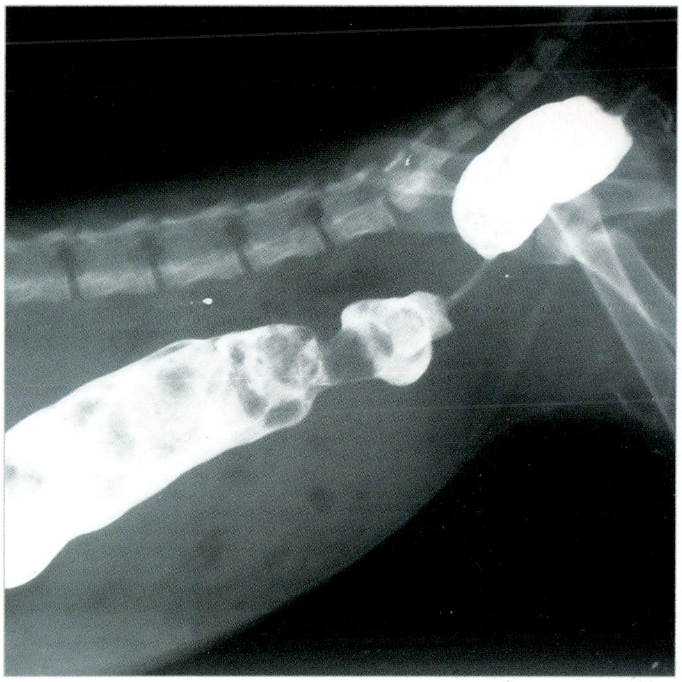

Rectal prolapse

Prevalence

Rectal prolapse occurs in young animals with a parasite burden or diarrhoea (fig. 1), and in adult animals with intestinal tenesmus (associated with polyps, fig. 2) it can also be a post-operative complication of perineal herniorraphy (fig. 3).

> *In a case of rectal prolapse in a puppy, think of intestinal parasites.*
> *In adult animals, consider differential diagnoses for intestinal tenesmus.*

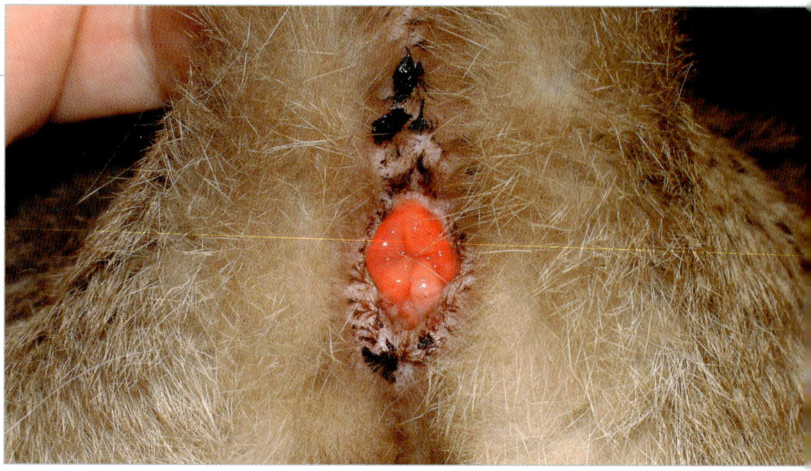

Fig. 1. Prolapse of the rectal mucosa in a cat with diarrhoea secondary to intestinal parasites.

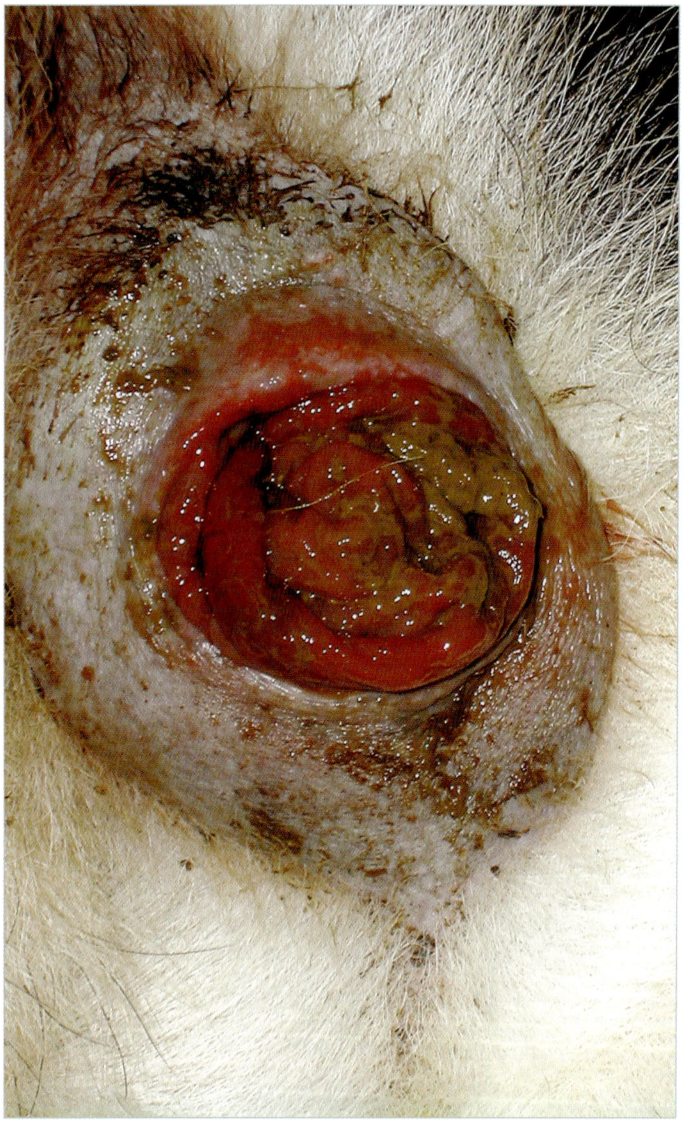

Fig. 2. Rectal prolapse in an adult dog that had difficulty defecating for 4 days. A rectal tumour was diagnosed.

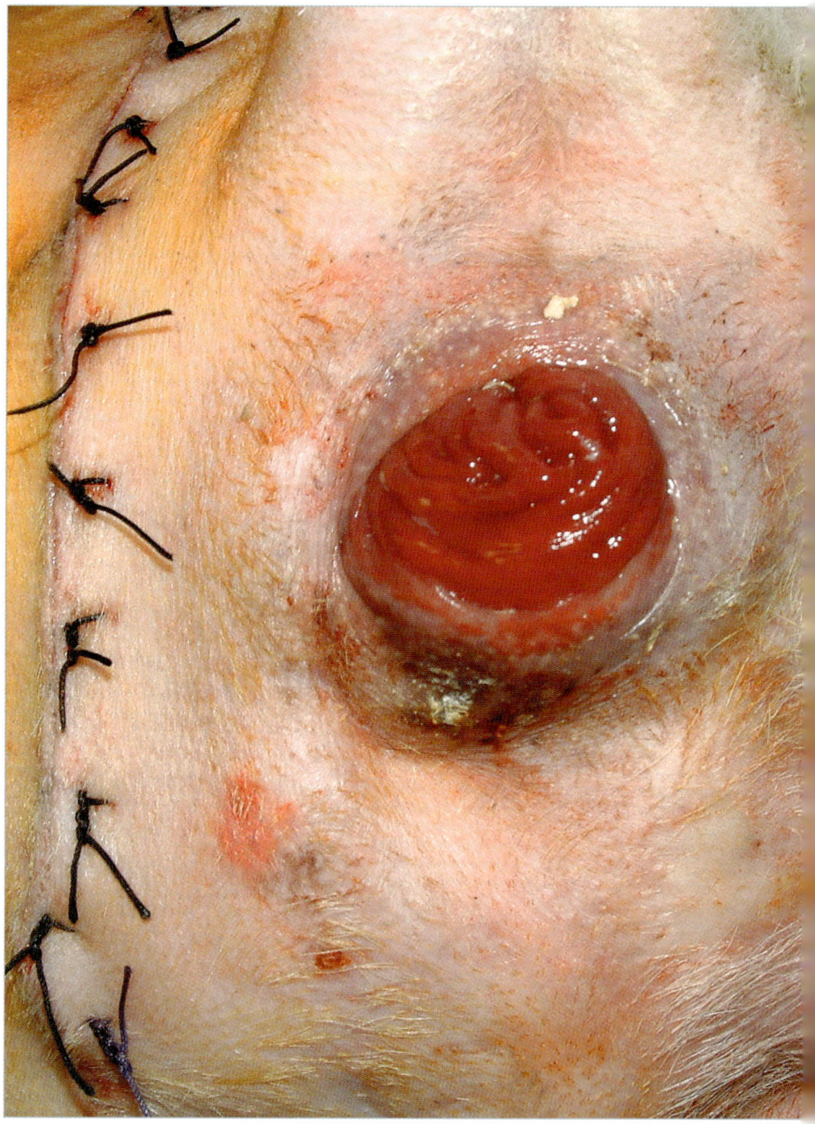

Fig. 3. After carrying out a perineal herniorraphy, a rectal prolapse can occur, particularly if the rectum is deviated.

Rectal prolapse can affect only the mucosa (fig. 1) or the entire rectal wall (fig. 4).
It is important to differentiate a "true" rectal prolapse from a prolapsed intestinal intussusception. To do so, insert a thermometer between the anus and the prolapsed mass; if the thermometer can be introduced easily, it is an intussusception (fig. 5a), if it cannot, it is blocked by the mucosa of the prolapsed rectum (fig. 5b).

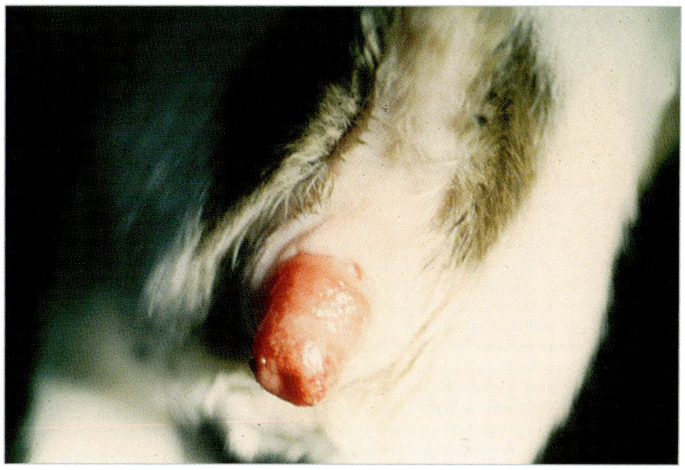

Fig. 4. Complete rectal prolapse in a cat that suffered from intense tenesmus. This is a good candidate for manual reduction.

a

b

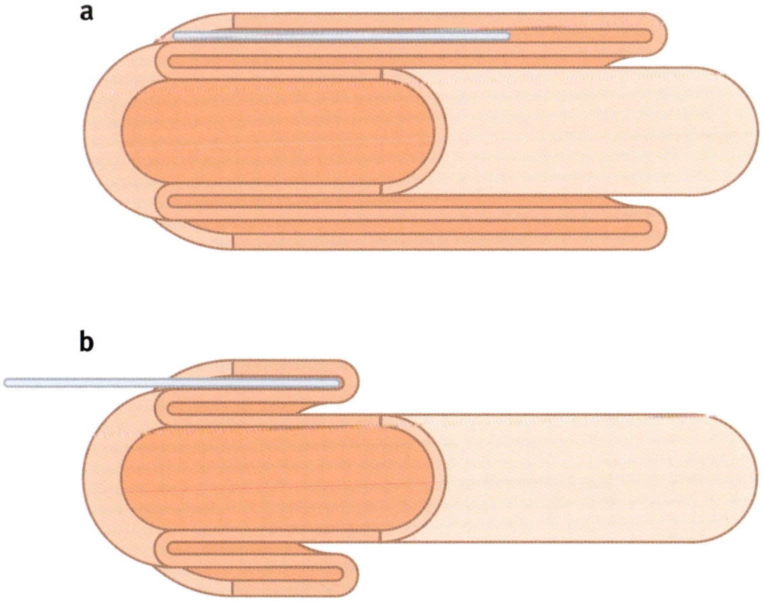

Fig. 5. a. Prolapse of an intestinal intussusception. b. Prolapsed rectum.

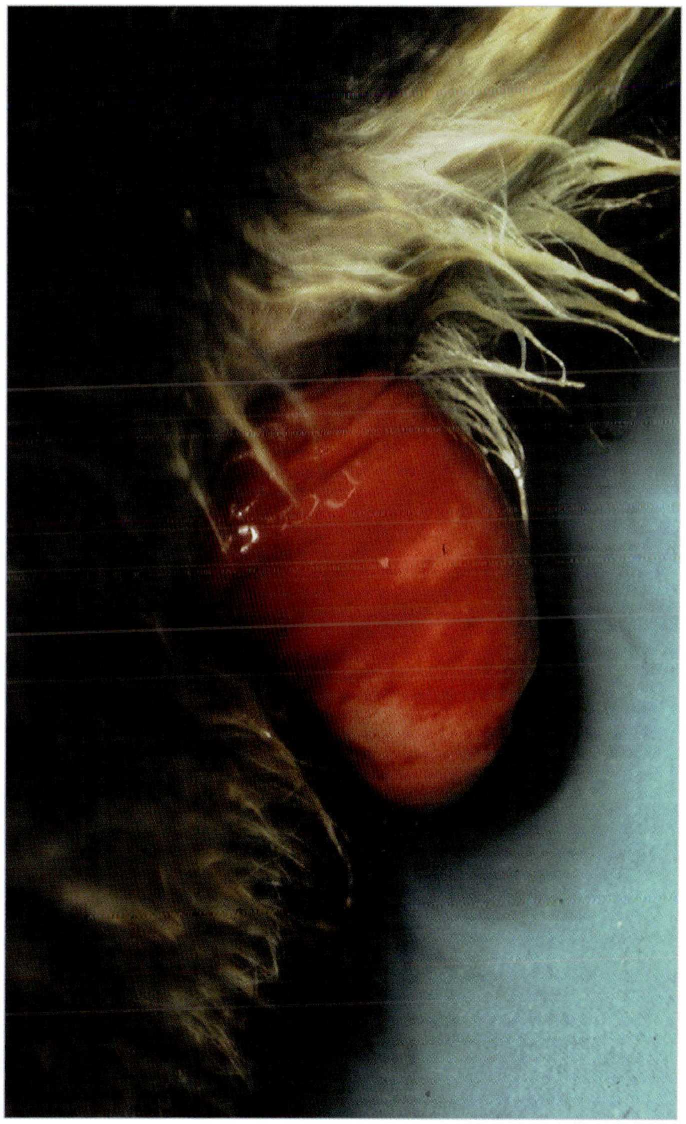

Fig. 6. Recurrent rectal prolapse in a German Shepherd puppy. The prolapsed tissue becomes congested and inflamed. In time, this problem becomes worse, making manual reduction more difficult.

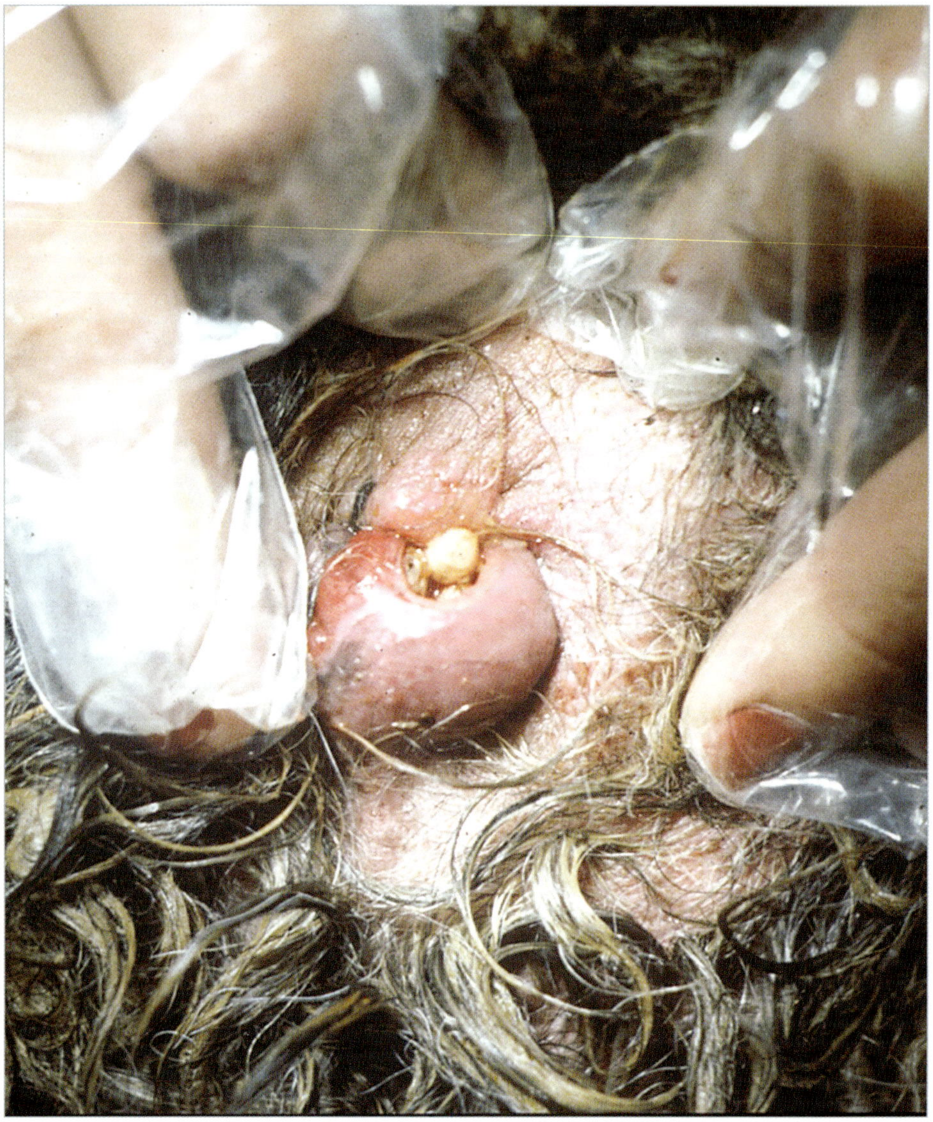

Fig. 7. The rectal prolapse in this case has undergone necrosis in the lower part, and has become infested with fly eggs and larvae. In this patient, surgical resection is indicated.

The everted tissue becomes inflamed due to vascular damage. Later, the tissue will dry out, and haemorrhagic and necrotic areas will appear (figs. 6 and 7).

Possible causes of a rectal prolapse		
Intestinal irritation	Tenesmus	Surgery
Parasites Enteritis/ colitis Foreign bodies	Prostatic disease Rectal neoplasia Constipation Dystocia Urolithiasis	Perineal hernia Perianal surgery

Treatment

Try to locate the origin of the problem and treat it.

Manual reduction

Indicated when the prolapse is small or when the mucosa does not present any major lesions (figs. 1-4).

- Apply gauzes soaked in a hypertonic solution, or, failing that, sugar, for 30 minutes to reduce the rectal oedema to a minimum.
- Manually compress the prolapsed mass towards the anus with moderate and continuous pressure.
- Place a purse string suture around the anus to avoid recurrence. In order to prevent complete closure of the anus, the suture should be tied after insertion of an object (approximate diameter 9 mm) in the anus.
- Prescribe laxatives (lactulose, approximately 0.3 ml/kg to effect) in order to facilitate faecal elimination.

Surgical treatment

- Amputation.

In cases of a severely traumatised prolapse or one that cannot be reduced.

See Case 1 / Amputation ➔ *page 21*

- Colopexy.

In cases of repeated recurrence after manual reduction or amputation.

See Case 2 / Colopexy ➔ *page 24*

Rectal prolapse. Case 1 / Rectal amputation

Prevalence	■□□□□
Technical difficulty	■■■□□

A 2-year-old Chow-Chow was referred by its veterinarian for rectal amputation, as repeated attempts to reduce the rectal prolapse proved unsuccessful.

The technique is based on the simultaneous resection and an end-to-end anastomosis of the rectal prolapse.

- After induction of general anaesthesia and preparation of the operating field, the patient is placed on the operating table and the operating field is disinfected (fig. 1).

See positioning of the patient ➜ *page 248*

✱ ***Rectal amputation is indicated if a prolapse cannot be reduced manually, or it is severely traumatised.***

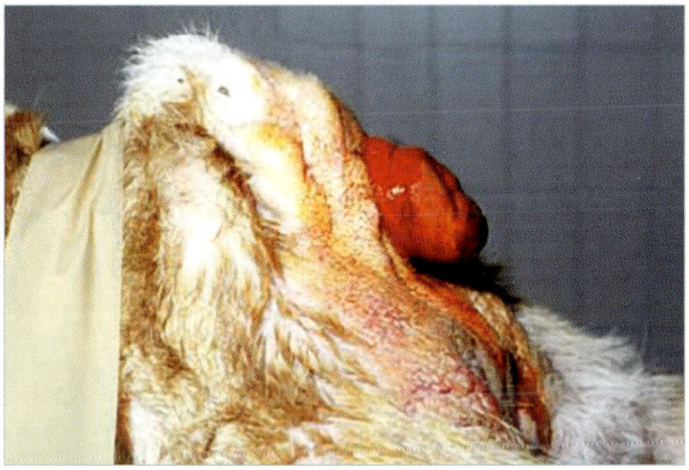

Fig. 1. The patient is positioned as described, with exposure of the anal region in a way that is comfortable for the surgeon. Note the congestion and damage to the prolapsed rectum.

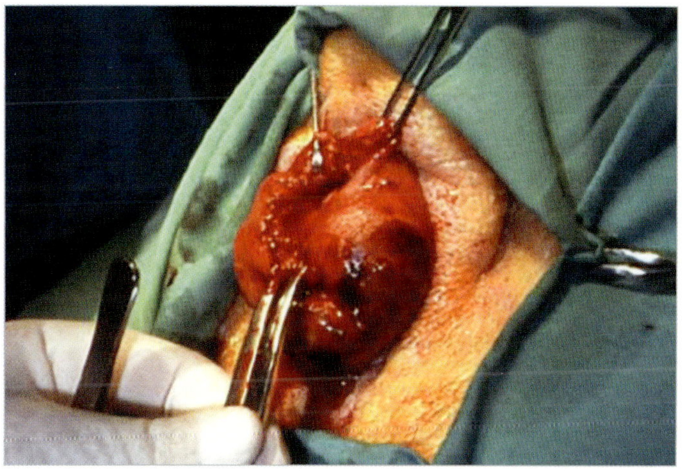

Fig. 2. This picture shows the initial fixation of the distal part of the rectum with Allis forceps.

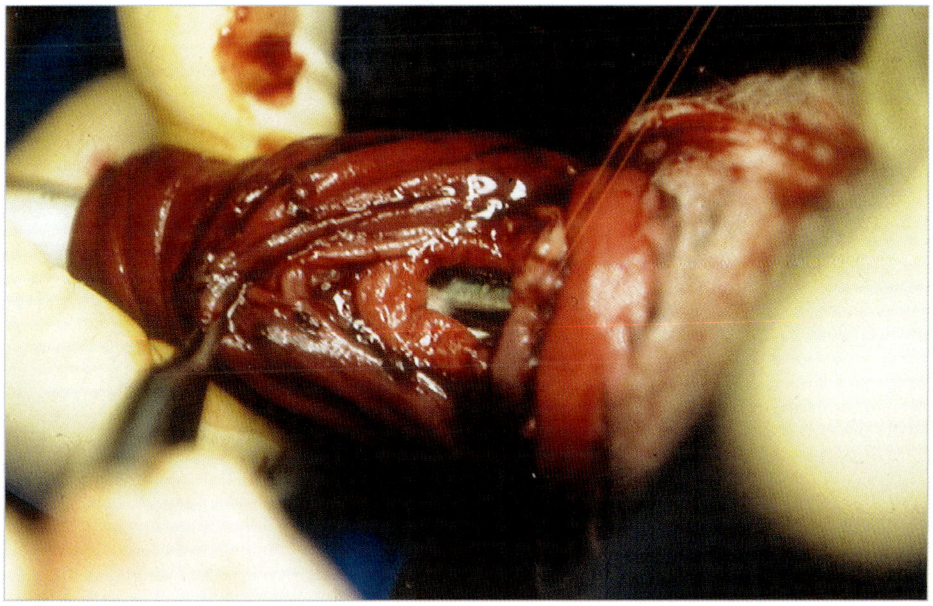

- Three holding sutures are placed (at 12, 4 and 8 o'clock) near the anus to maintain a view of the rectum during anastomosis (figs. 2 and 3).

Fig. 3. Some surgeons recommend placing a test tube in the rectal lumen to facilitate the placement of the holding sutures, as well as the amputation of the traumatised area at a later stage.

- Next, the prolapsed rectum is resected and an end-to-end anastomosis is carried out, using simple interrupted sutures of synthetic 3/0 or 4/0 absorbable material (figs. 4-8).

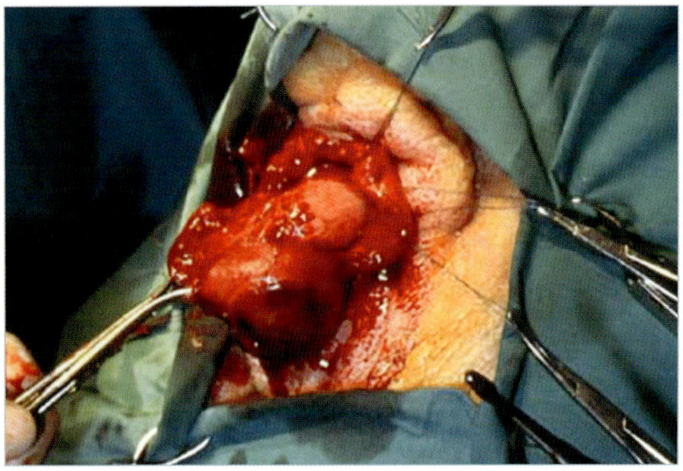

Fig. 4. The positioning of the holding sutures ensures the correct exposure of the distal rectum.
This picture shows the resection of the dorsal external area of the prolapsed rectum.

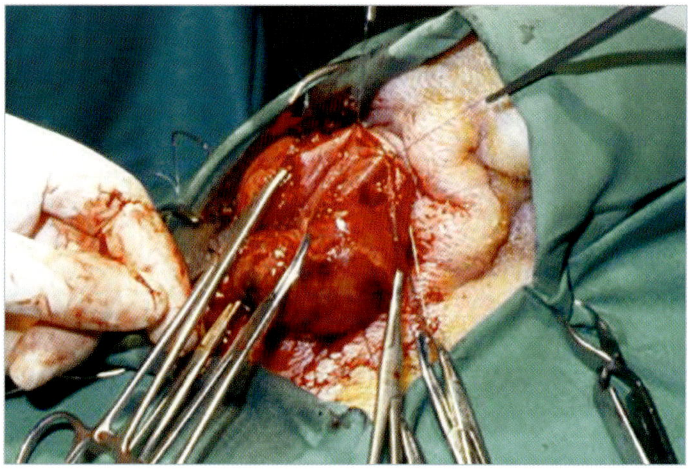

Fig. 5. Next, the proximal area of the rectum is incised, followed by end-to end anastomosis, using interrupted sutures of absorbable material at intervals of approx. 2 mm.

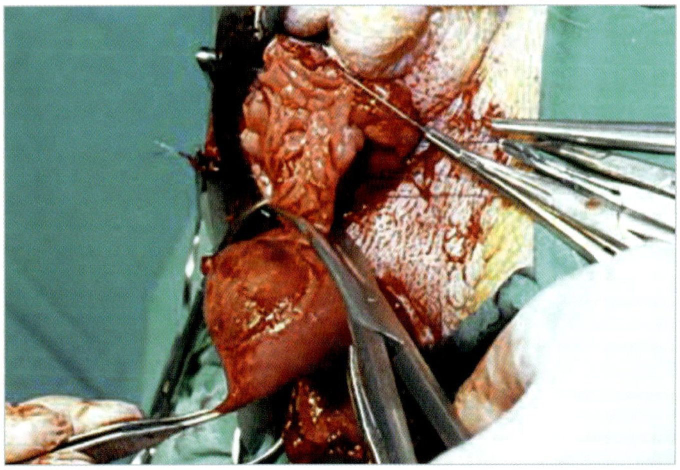

Fig. 6. At this stage of the operation, two thirds of the rectal circumference has been sutured. Next, the ventral area of the traumatised rectum will be sectioned followed by anastomosis.

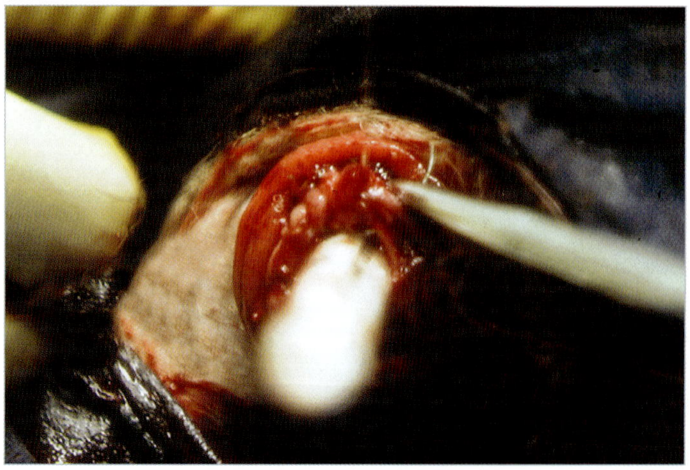

Fig. 7. In this picture, which belongs to another case, the finished anastomosis is shown. In this case, a test tube was maintained in the rectal lumen.

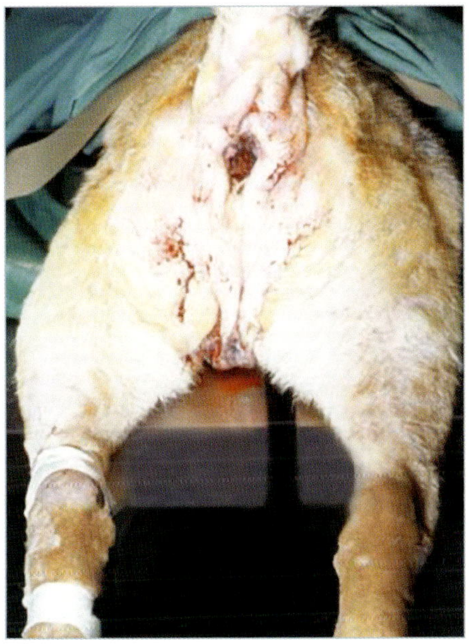

Fig. 8. The holding sutures are removed and the anastomosed rectum is replaced in the pelvic canal. End result of the operation.

In some cases, it is advisable to place a purse string suture around the anus for 1 or 2 days in order to prevent recurrence of the prolapse.

See purse string suture ➜ page 252

To prevent the rectum from accidentally inverting into the pelvic canal during anastomosis, only a small part is sectioned and sutured at a time. This procedure is repeated in small sections over the entire circumference of the prolapse.

After surgery

- Continue with prophylactic antibiotic therapy, started preoperatively, for 3 or 4 days.
- Give low-residue food.
- Give mild laxatives to facilitate defaecation for two weeks (lactulose 0.3 ml/kg TID PO until the desired effect is obtained).

Prognosis is good if the primary cause of tenesmus or the irritation is controlled.

Possible complications

- Rectal stenosis due to the inclusion of an excessive amount of tissue in the anastomosis.
- Dehiscence of the anastomosis due to secondary infection and poor suturing technique.
- Faecal incontinence due to trauma of the anal sphincter or its nerves.

With thanks to Dr. Cairó (Canis Veterinary Clinic. Girona) for the kind supply of the images for this chapter.

Rectal prolapse. Case 2 / Colopexy

Prevalence	■□□□□
Technical difficulty	■■■□□

Colopexy aims to create a stable fixation of the colon to the abdominal wall, which prevents caudal movement and prolapse of the rectum.

✱ ***Colopexy is indicated to prevent the recurrence of rectal prolapse.***

The technique starts with an infraumbilical laparotomy and identification of the descending colon.

See infraumbilical laparotomy ➜ *page 282*

- Draw the descending colon towards the abdominal cavity in order to reduce the prolapse.
- Abrade the non-mesenteric wall of the descending colon close to the pelvis over an area of 5 to 10 cm. A gauze swab can be used for this (fig. 1).

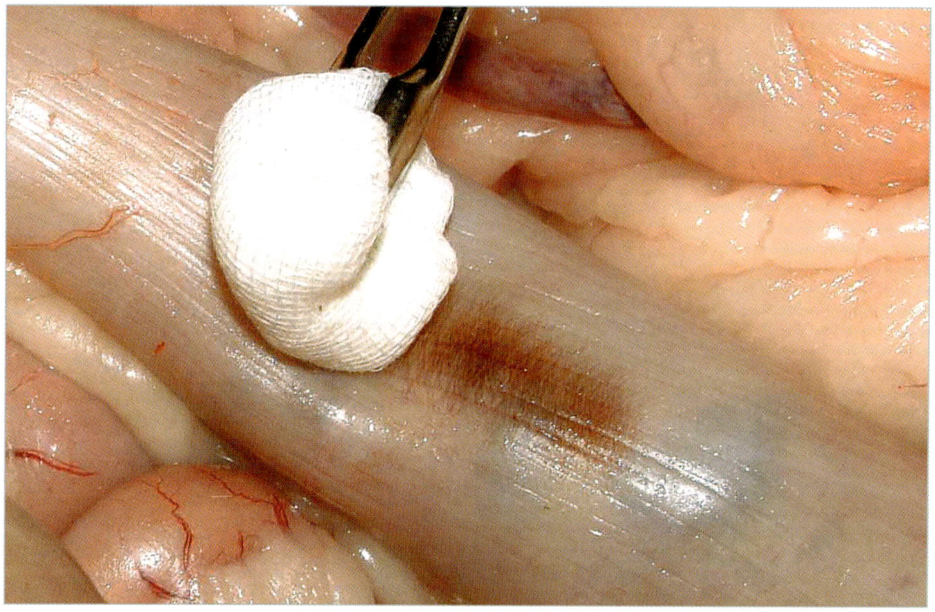

Fig. 1. The anti-mesenteric border (opposite the mesenteric side) of the colon is rubbed with a gauze swab until irritation and hyperaemia of the covering peritoneal lining is observed.

- The same procedure is repeated on the left abdominal wall, some 3 cm from the laparotomy incision (fig. 2).
- Next, the colon is sutured to the abdominal muscle, using synthetic absorbable 3/0 suture material (figs. 3 and 4).
- The operation is concluded by closing the laparotomy as described in the corresponding section.

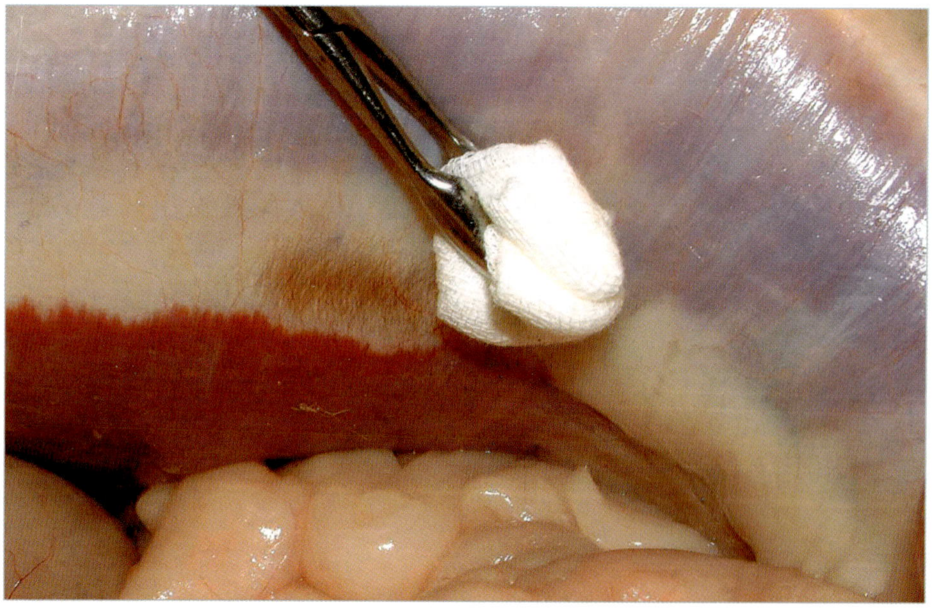

Fig. 2. Irritation of the peritoneal wall to increase the adhesion of the colon to the abdominal wall.

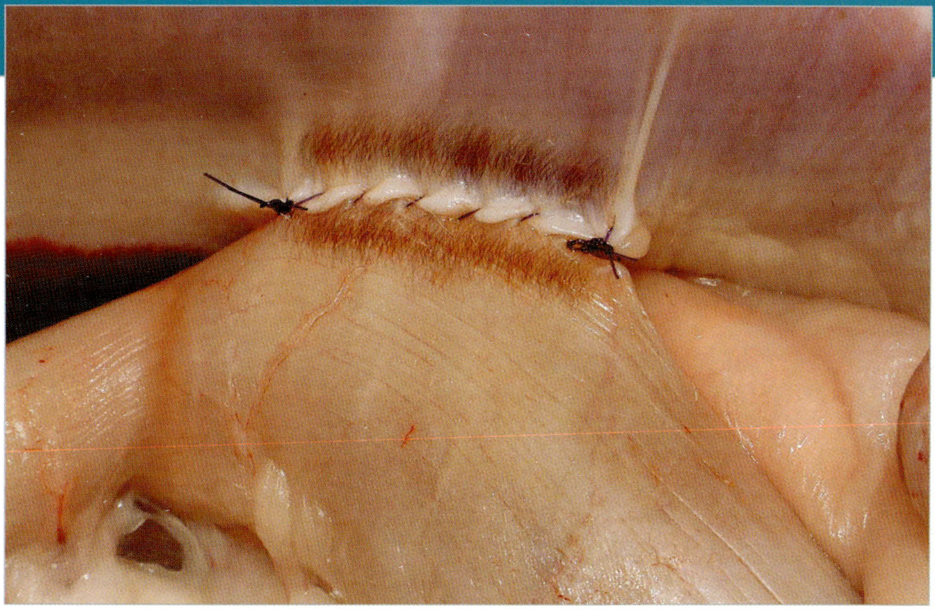

Fig. 3. Each suture should include the submucosa, the most resistant layer of the intestine, while avoiding penetration of the colonic mucosa.

Use atraumatic round needles in order to minimise trauma to the intestine during suturing.

If the colon is not handled correctly, if it is accidentally perforated or if multifilament suture material is used, infectious peritonitis may develop as a complication.

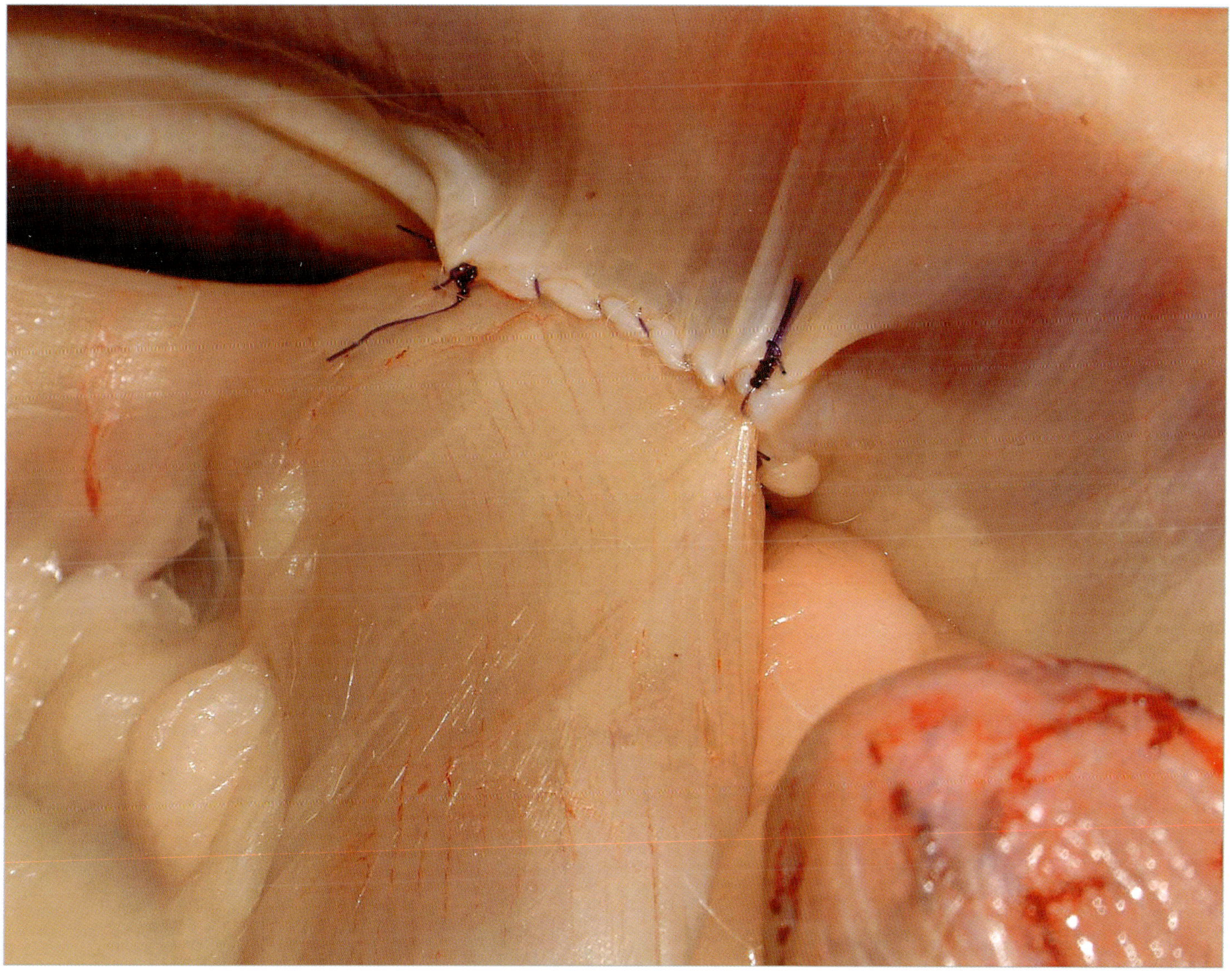

Fig. 4. Colopexy is carried out with two separate rows of monofilament absorbable sutures to ensure the fixation of the colon to the abdominal wall.

Stenosis

Prevalence	■	□	□	□	□

The rectum can develop stenosis secondary to neoplasia of the intestinal wall or secondary to fibrosis following a local inflammatory process (fig. 1).

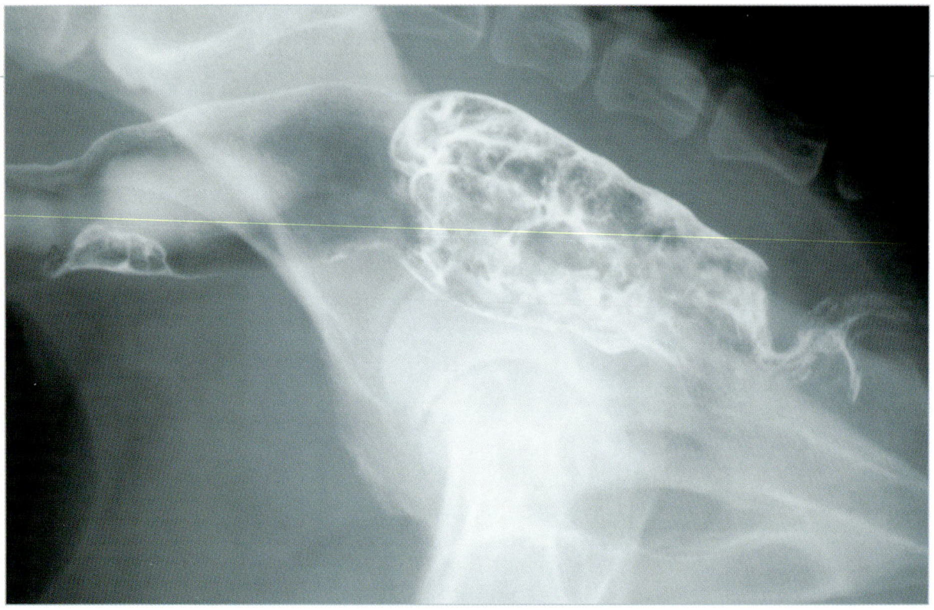

Fig. 1. Dorsal rectal stenosis, making defecation difficult.

These patients present with tenesmus, dyschezia and/or haematochezia, as well as thin faeces (in the shape of a tape).

> ✱ ***Adenocarcinomas of the colon can be circumferential and produce significant stenosis of the intestine. A correct differential diagnosis should be carried out.***

These problems can be tackled in different ways, depending on their location (fig. 2).

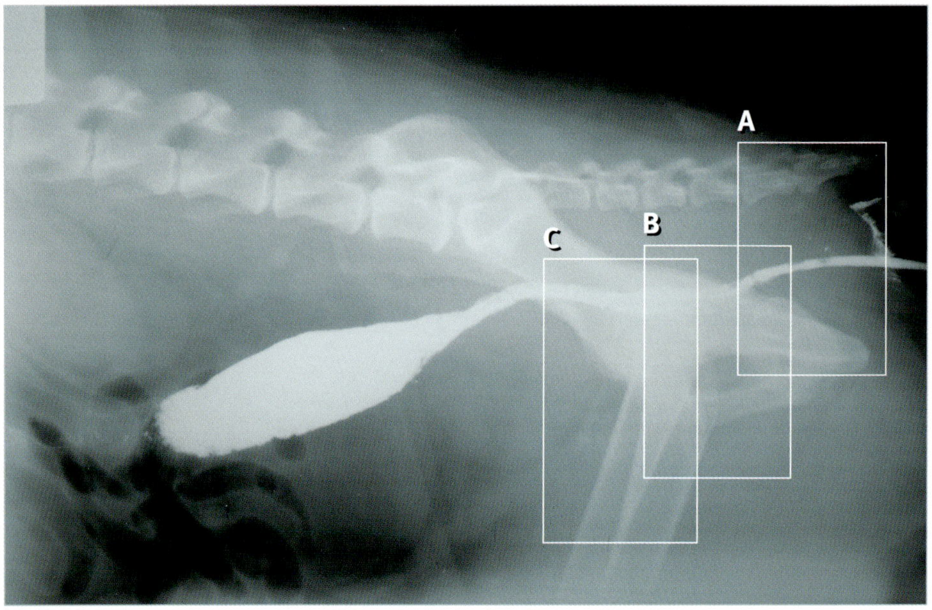

Fig. 2 Zone A: Transanal resection.
Zone B: Pubic osteotomy.
Zone C: Suprapubic laparotomy.

Stenosis. Case 1 / Rectal transanal resection

Prevalence	■□□□□
Technical difficulty	■■■■□

Indications for rectal resection

- Neoplasia.
- Trauma and necrosis.
- Perforations and lacerations.
- Stenosis.

A patient is presented for consultation with difficulty defaecating as the only clinical sign. A general examination shows no changes but in the rectal tract, stenosis is noted approximately 4 cm from the anus (figs. 1 and 2).
Results of blood tests are normal.

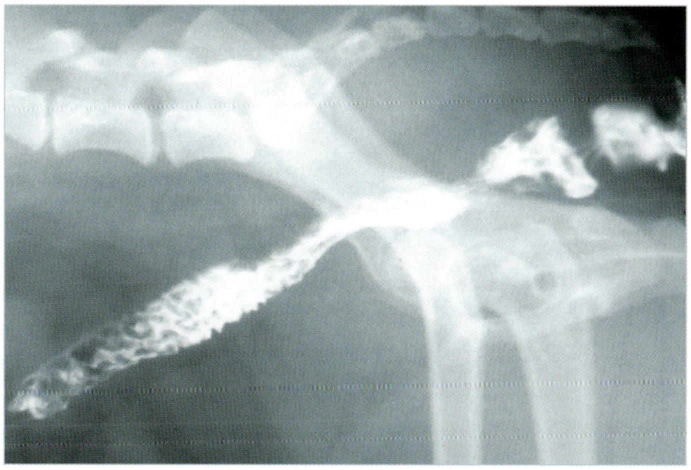

Fig. 1. By administering a barium enema, the stenosis is clearly demonstrated. Also, X-rays confirm that there are no sublumbar adenopathies.

Prior to surgery

- Low-residue diet (white rice and mince meat) for 3 days.
- No solids for 24 hours.
- Warm water enema the day before.
- Enema containing povidone iodine (10%) 4 hours prior to surgery.
- Antibiotic prophylaxis (2nd generation cephalosporin).

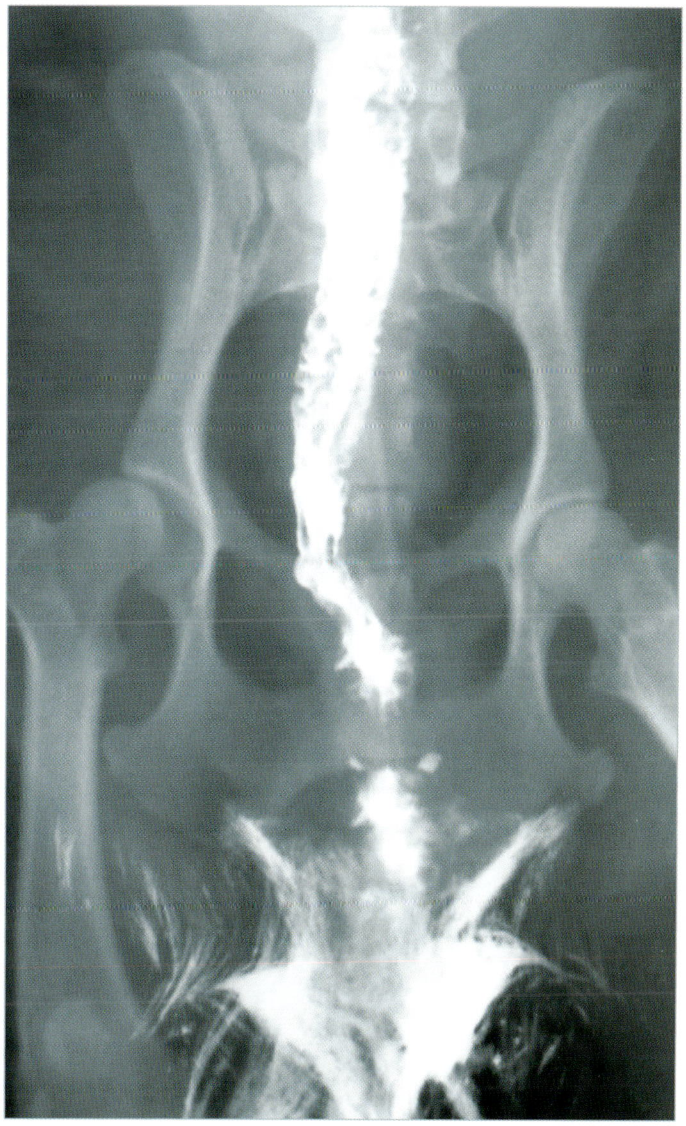

Fig. 2. The stenosis is clearly seen in a ventrodorsal radiograph.
As it is located near the anus, a rectal resection can be carried out through the anus.

Surgical technique

This technique is indicated for the excision of a lesion that is too distal to be approached by laparotomy, and too far cranial to be exteriorised by anal eversion.

See patient positioning ➔ page 248

- Dilatation of the anal sphincter in order to manipulate the rectum (fig. 3).
- Place holding sutures in the distal rectum to evert it (fig. 4).
- Next, holding sutures are placed in the rectal wall, cranial to the previous ones (fig. 5).
- The rectum is sectioned over 360° and the rectum is mobilised by blunt dissection of its external wall (figs. 6 and 7).
- The rectum is sectioned lengthwise to check if the lesion has (already) been reached (fig. 8).
- When healthy tissue is located cranial to the lesion, the rectum is resected over a third of its circumference (fig. 9).
- Following resection of the rectum, it is anastomosed with an interrupted suture using synthetic absorbable monofilament material (figs. 10-12). The rectum should be cut and sutured in sections using synthetic absorbable monofilament material.

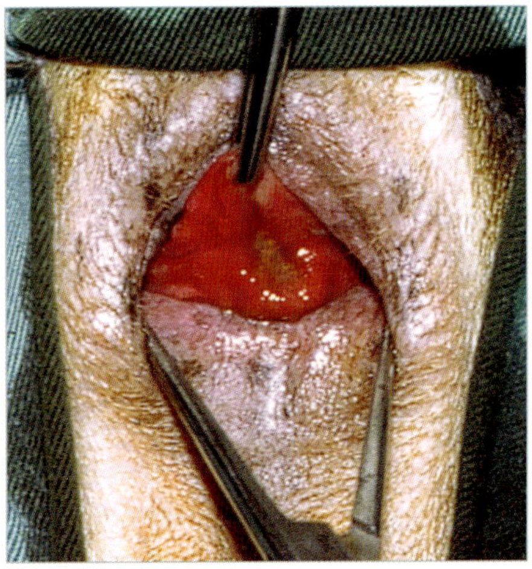

Fig. 3. Using forceps and separators, the anal sphincter is dilated in order to access the distal rectum.

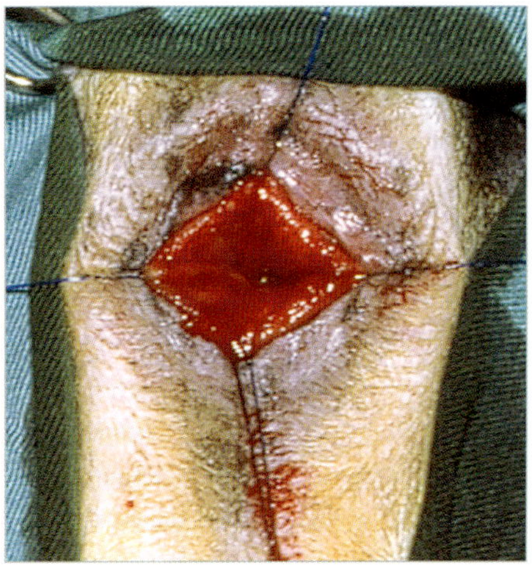

Fig. 4. Holding sutures are placed approximately 1 cm from the anal sphincter. This ensures the location of the caudal part of the future anastomosis.

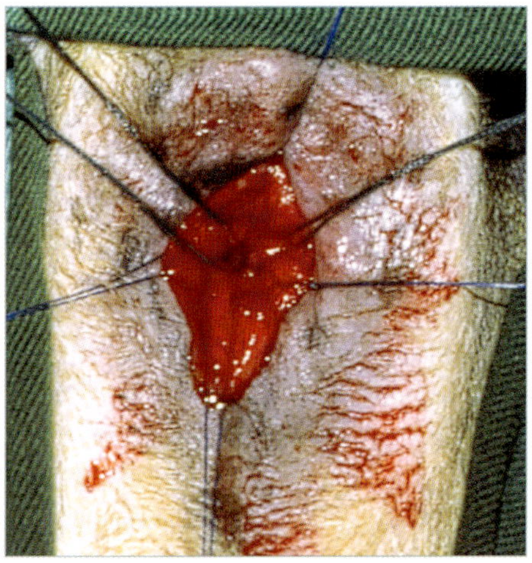

Fig. 5. In the cranial area of the rectum, two to three traction sutures are placed, and between these and the holding sutures (previously placed), the rectum is sectioned.

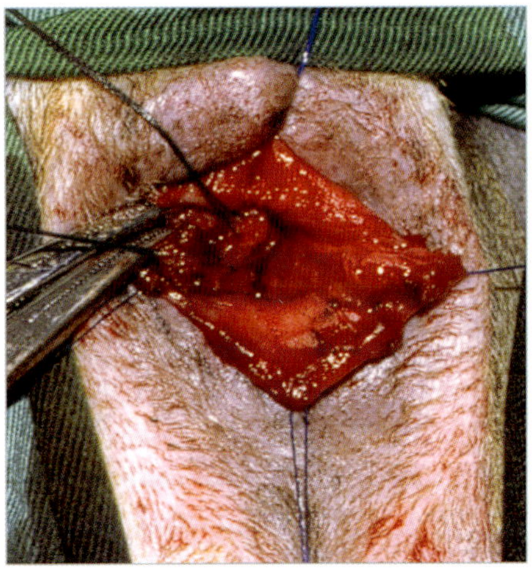

Fig. 6. After the circumferential section of the rectum, it is bluntly dissected through the incision.

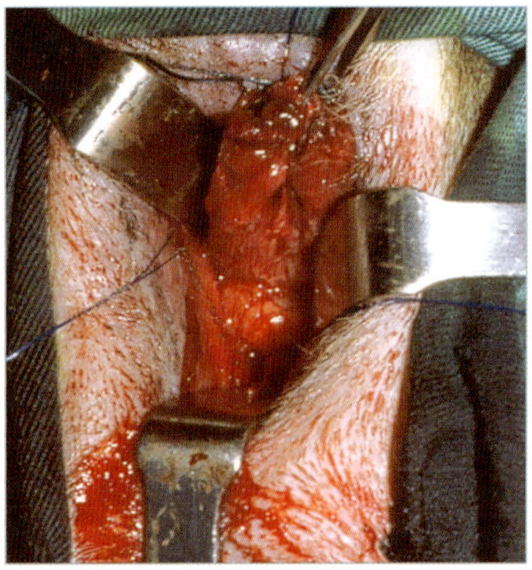

Fig. 7. External dissection of the rectum allows it to move externally. The rectal blood vessels should be tied off or coagulated as necessary.

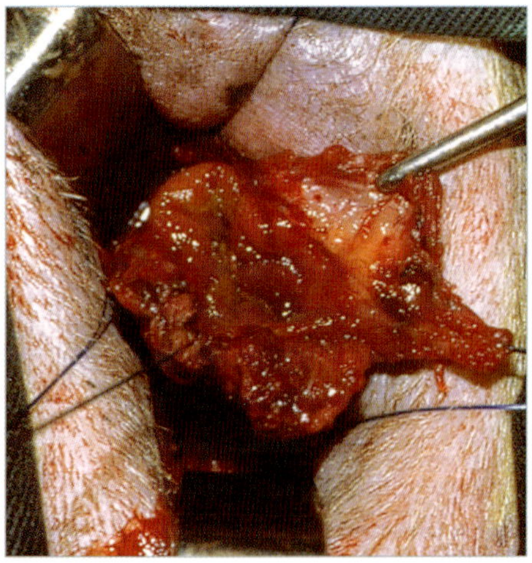

Fig. 8. The rectum is sectioned lengthwise in order to identify the affected area and the healthy tissue cranial to it.

Complications

- Tenesmus.
- Haematochezia.
- Temporary faecal incontinence due to anal dilatation.
- Permanent faecal incontinence due to a lesion of the rectal nerves or extensive dissection.
- Stenosis due to scar tissue.

In order to avoid these complications, use absorbable suture material, do not resect too large a tract, control the infection and avoid excessive tension.

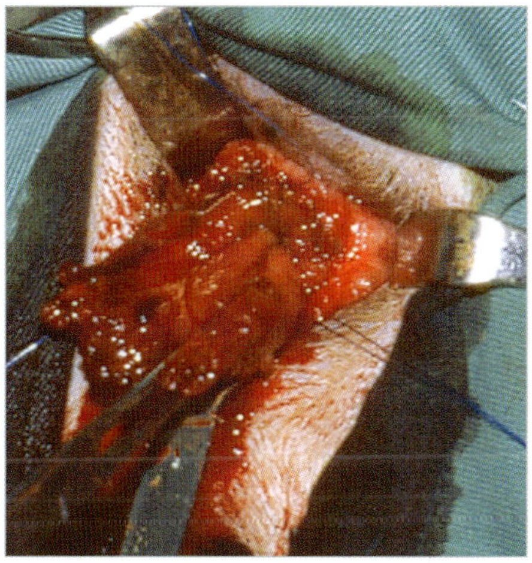

Fig. 9. The healthy rectum is sectioned 1 cm from the lesion and is sutured to the anal sphincter with absorbable 3/0 or 4/0 monofilament suture material. The sutures between 12 o'clock and 3 o'clock can be seen.

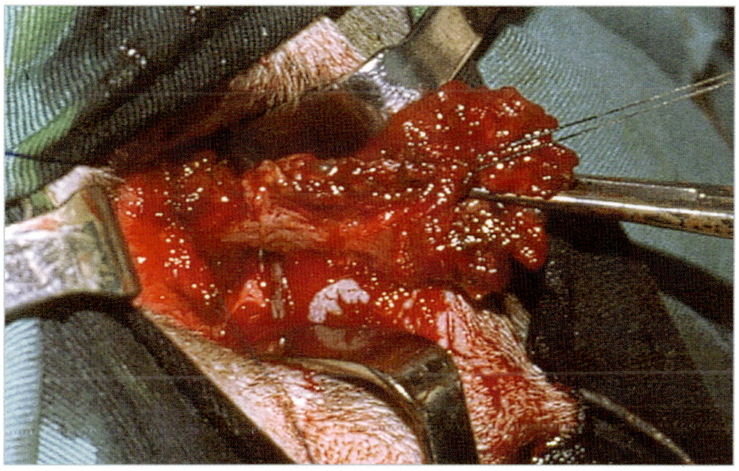

Fig. 10. This image shows the area to be sectioned and sutured (6 – 9 o'clock). The area of fibrosis can be seen in the exteriorised rectal segment.

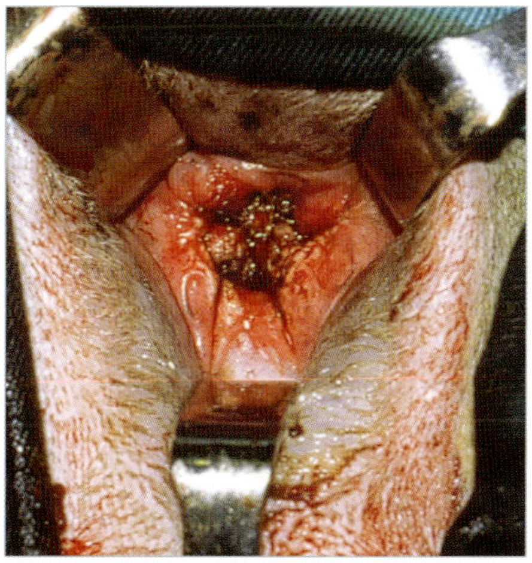

Fig. 11. Completion of the end-to-end anastomosis after resection of the rectal tissue affected by stenosis.

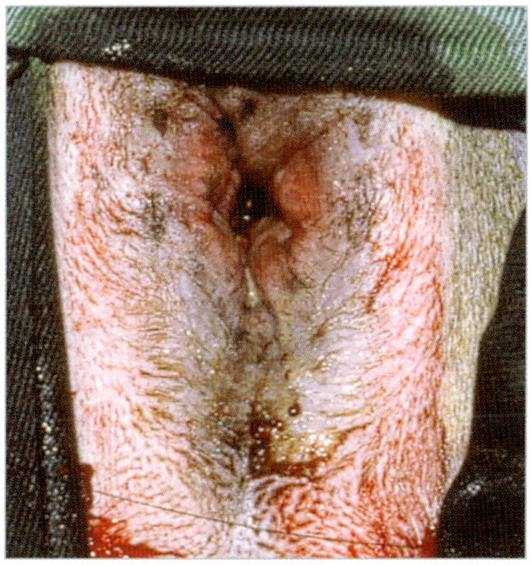

Fig. 12. End of the operation.

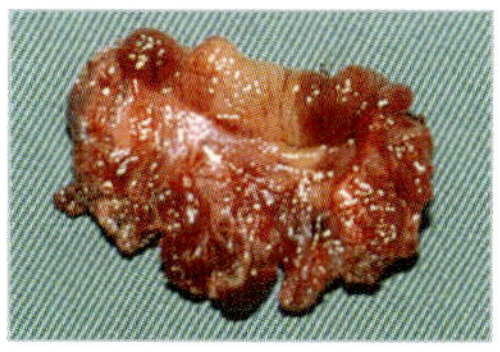

Fig. 13. Resected gut segment. Note the area of central fibrosis, which caused the patient's clinical signs.

Stenosis. Case 2 / Abdominal colectomy

Prevalence	■	□	□	□	□
Technical difficulty	■	■	■	■	□

The owner of "Campanilla" (fig. 1) took her to the veterinarian because the cat had shown very soft and thin, tape-like faeces since birth.

Fig. 1. "Campanilla" is a two-month-old cat that has always had problems defaecating.

The contrast radiograph showed stenosis in the proximal rectum (figs. 2-4).

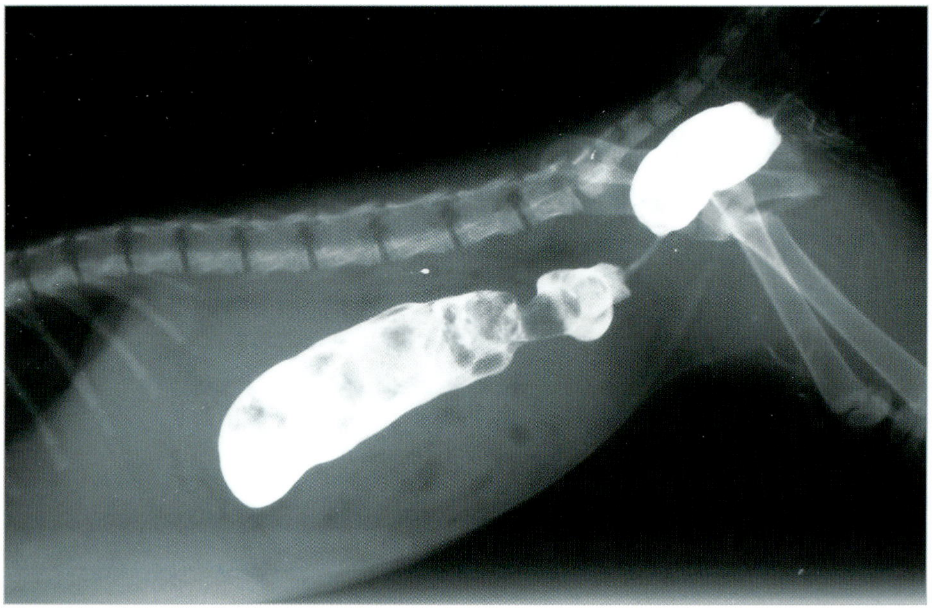

Fig. 2. In the first radiograph, taken after the administration of a barium enema, a clear filling defect of the rectum can be seen just in front of the pelvis.

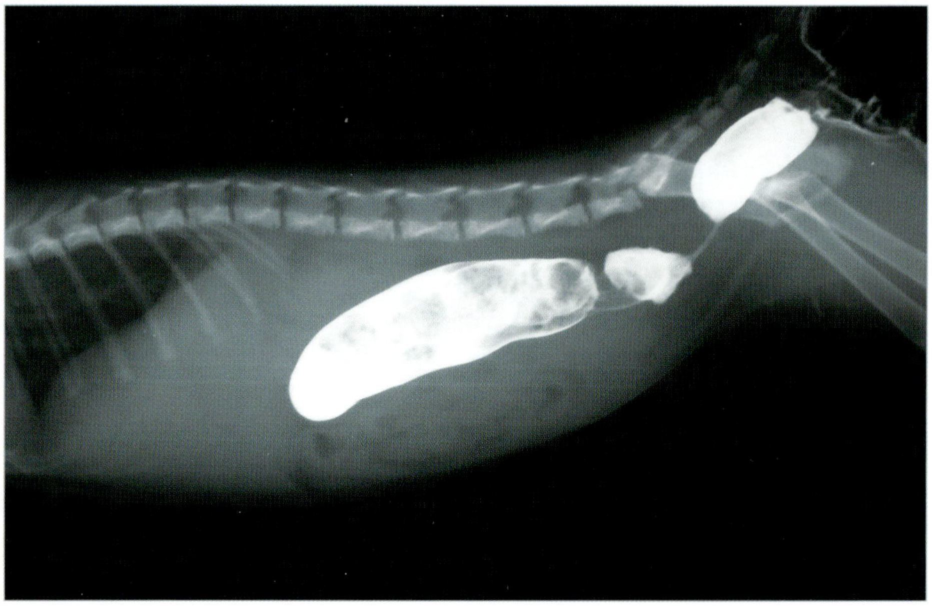

Fig. 3. The second radiograph, taken 30 minutes later, shows very little movement. This confirms the suspected diagnosis of intestinal stenosis.

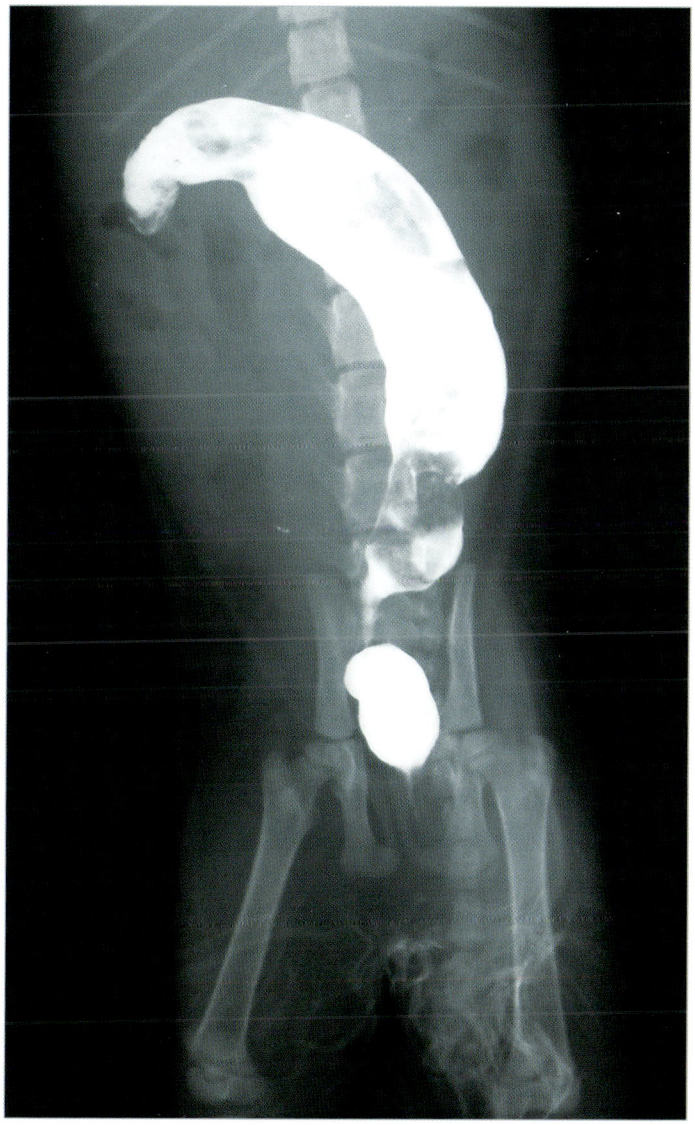

Fig. 4. The ventrodorsal view shows that the stenosis affects the entire circumference of the rectum.

In this case, since the stenosis is located cranial to the pelvic rim, it was decided to resect the intestinal segment (colectomy) by means of a suprapubic laparotomy.

See infraumbilical laparotomy page 282

Prior to surgery

- Low-residue diet (white rice and mince meat) for three days.
- No solids for 24 hours.
- Warm water enema the day before.
- Enema containing povidone iodine (10%) 4 hours prior to surgery.
- Antibiotic prophylaxis (2nd generation cephalosporin).

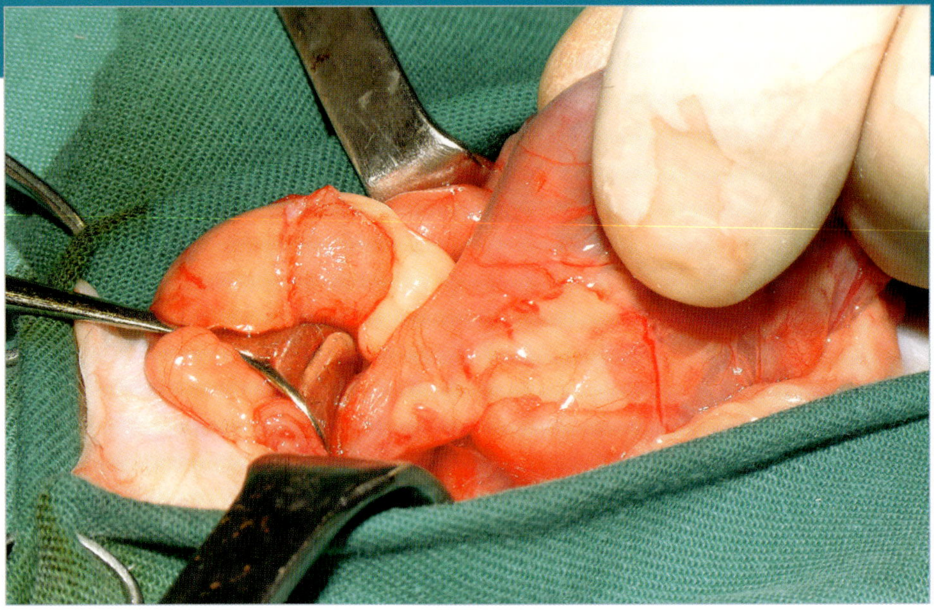

Fig. 5. After midline laparotomy, the pelvic rectum is dissected to facilitate its movement into the abdominal cavity.

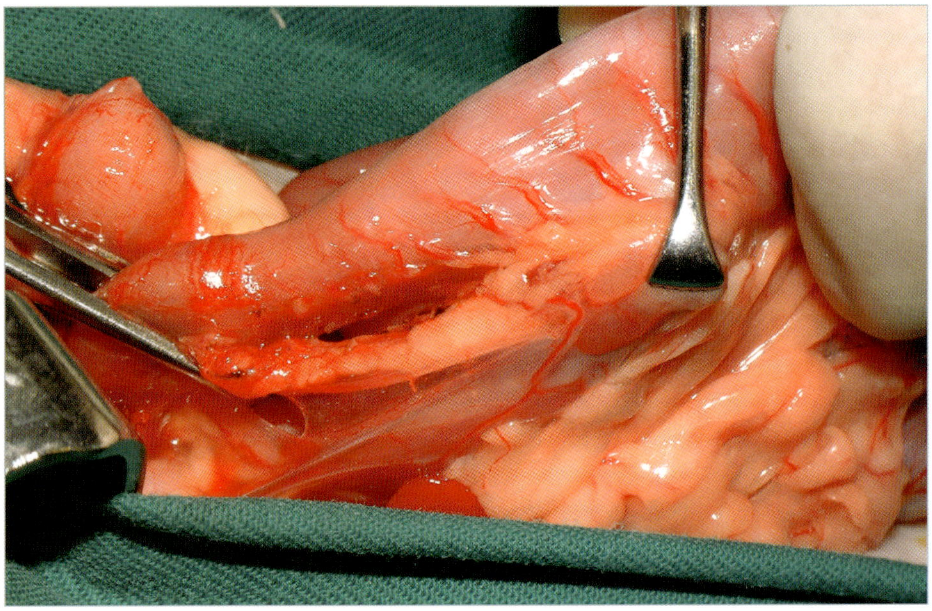

Fig. 6. In order to maintain vascularisation of the rectum by the cranial rectal artery, the branches of the artery that supply the area affected by the stenosis are sealed off using bipolar coagulating forceps.

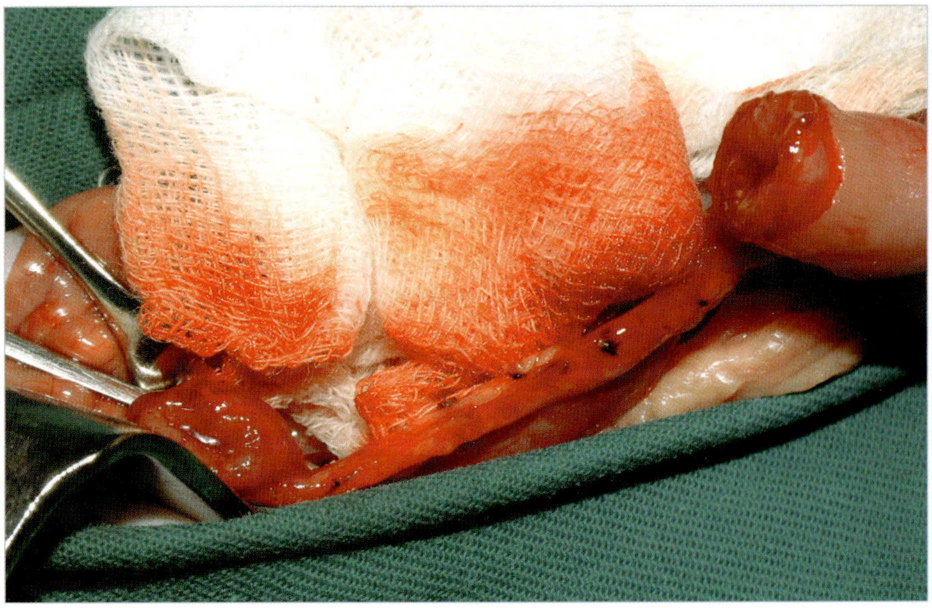

Fig. 7. After clamping the intestines with modified Allis forceps, the stenotic segment is resected. Due to the low mobility of the rectum and the difficulty of exteriorising it, measures taken to avoid faecal contamination of the peritoneum should be maximised.

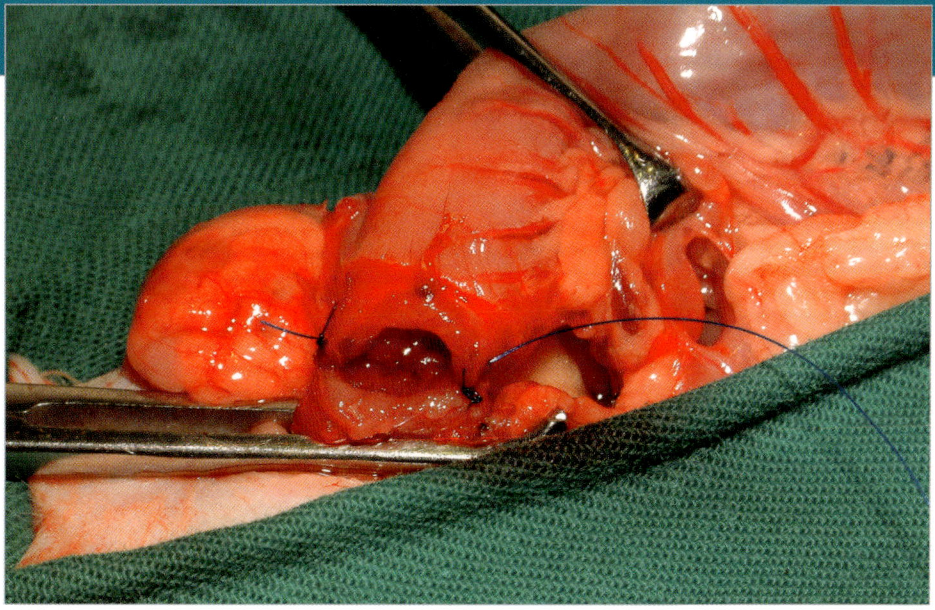

Fig. 8. The end-to-end anastomosis is carried out with interrupted sutures of monofilament suture material starting at the posterior side.

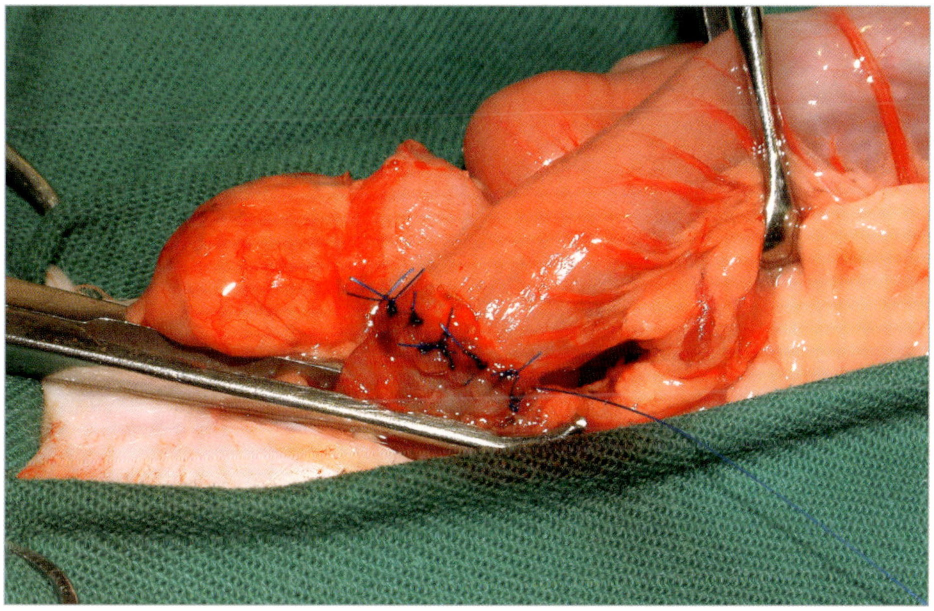

Fig. 9. Next, the anterior side is sutured. When completing the anastomosis, it is essential to check that it is watertight by injecting saline into the intestine; it should not leak through the sutures. Before closing the laparotomy wound, rinse the abdominal cavity well using lukewarm sterile saline solution.

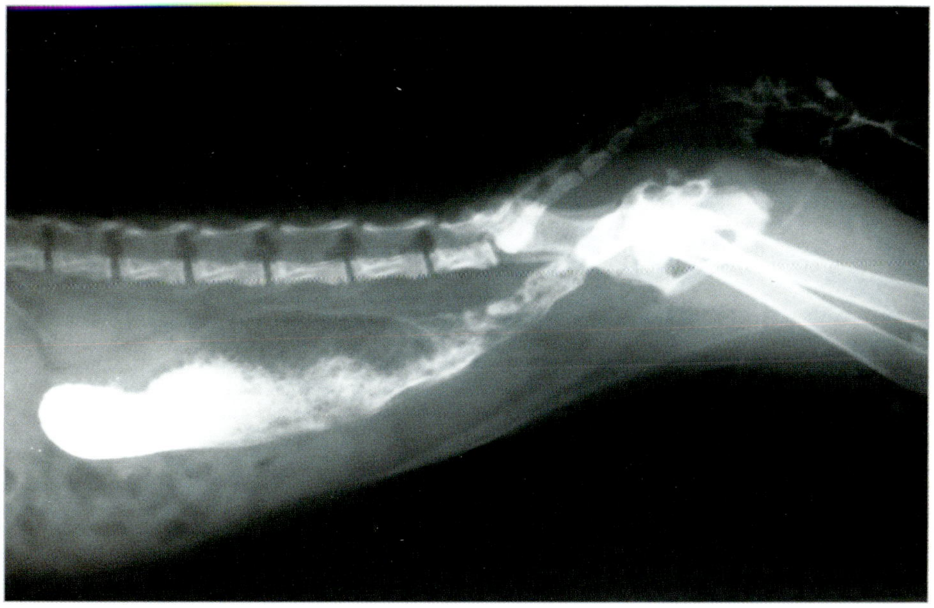

Fig. 10. Two months after the operation, the result is checked.
The stenosis has disappeared. However, the cat still presents a proximal megacolon.

The intestinal mucosa should not protrude through the anastomosis sutures, as this would lead to fistulas and secondary peritonitis.

Dorsal view of the gluteal muscles

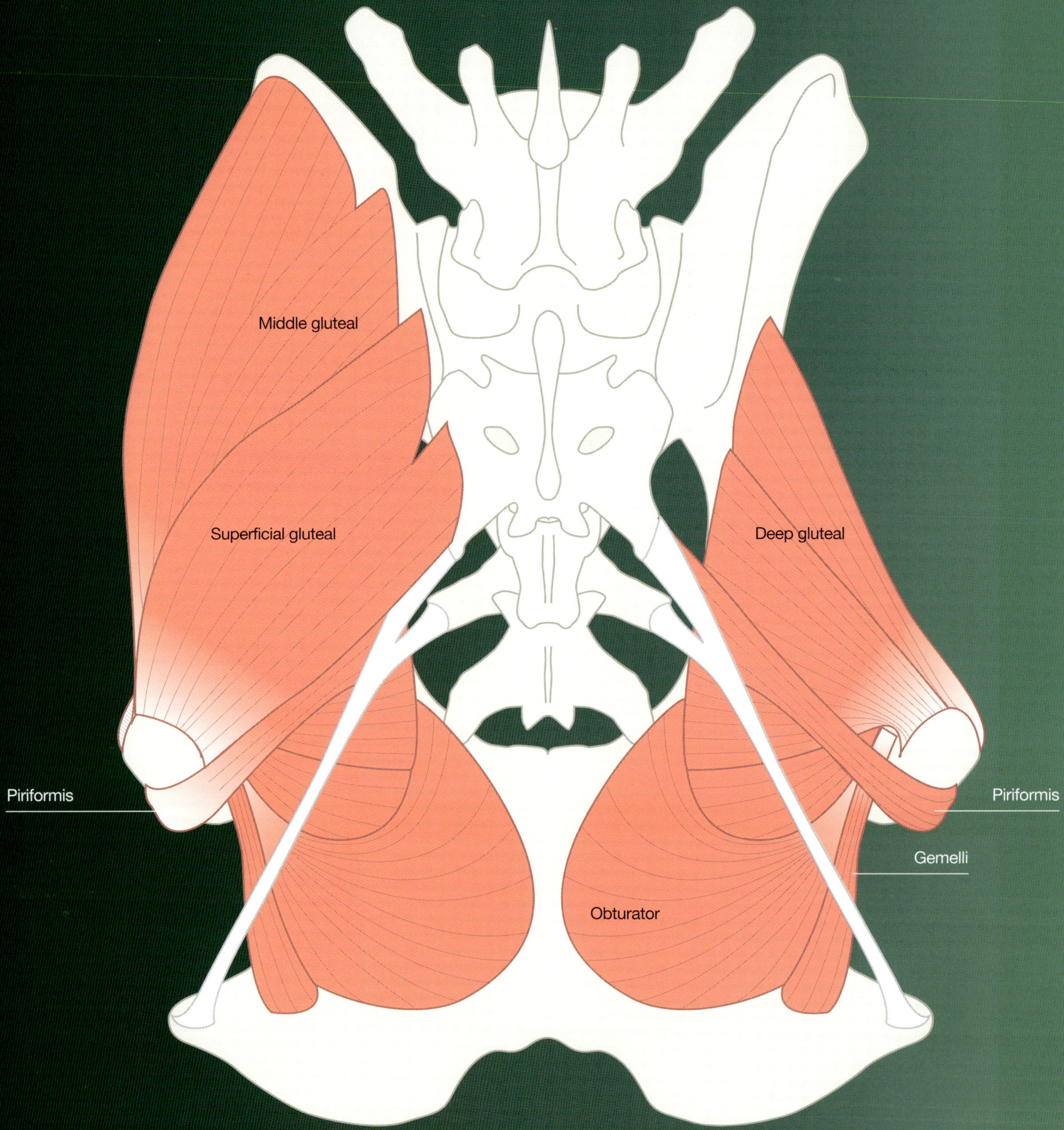

Hernias

Perineal hernia

Case 1 / Simple herniorraphy

Case 2 / Mesh implant

Case 3 / Transposition of the superficial gluteal muscle and elevation of the obturator internus muscle

Case 4 / Double muscular transposition (internal obturator and superficial gluteal)

Case 5 / Deferensopexy

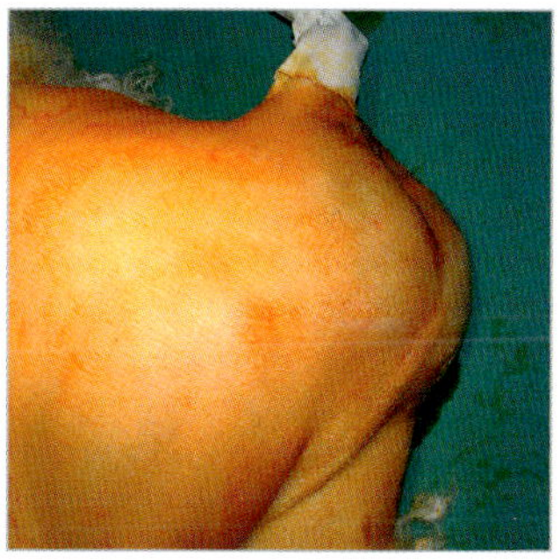

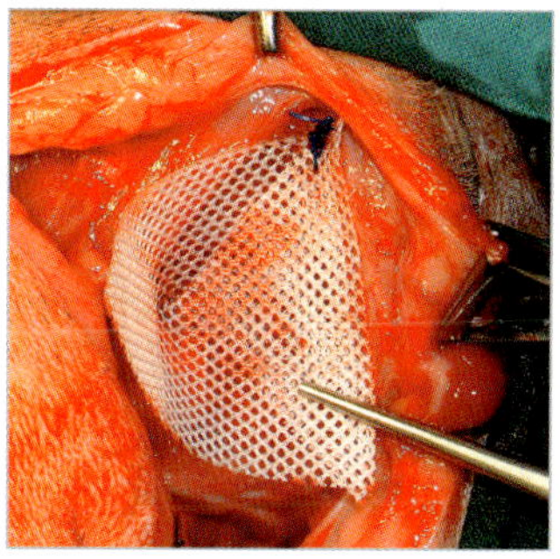

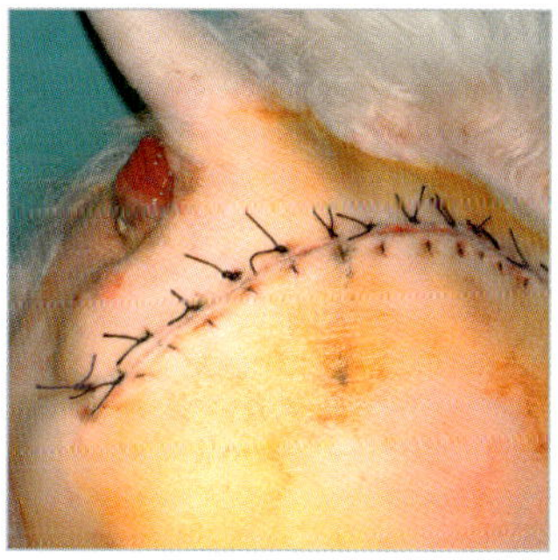

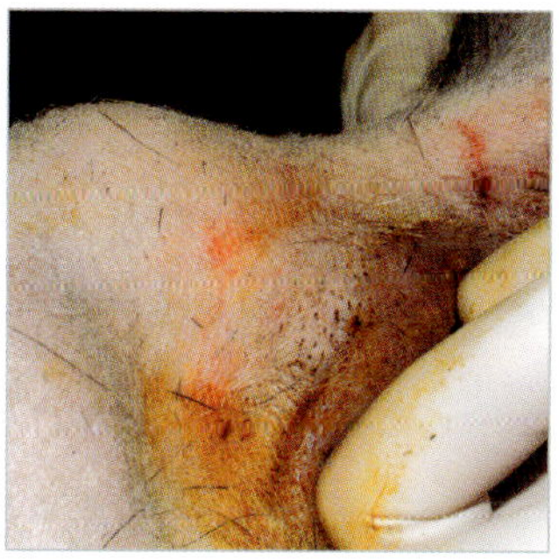

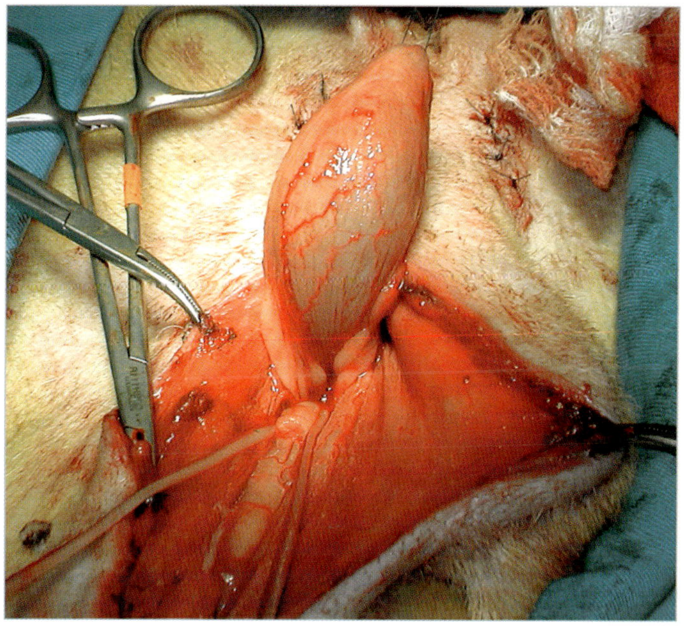

Pelvic diaphragm

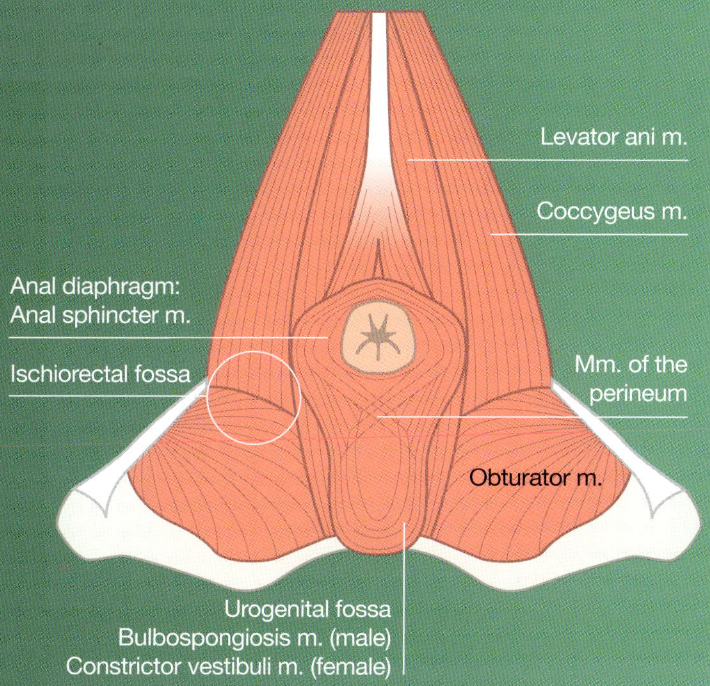

Pelvic muscles of the dog

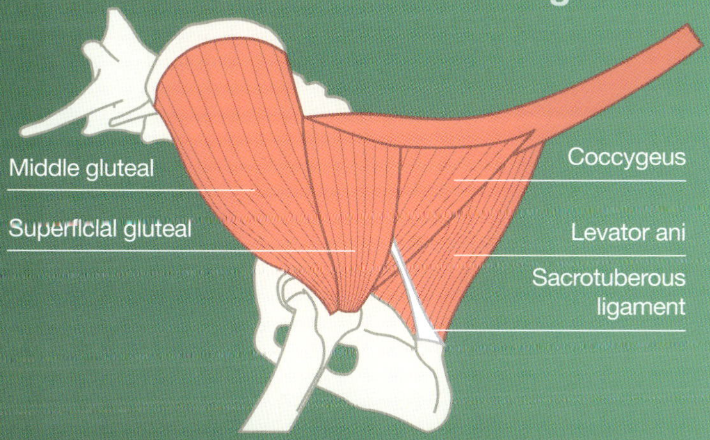

Peritoneal pouches in the dog

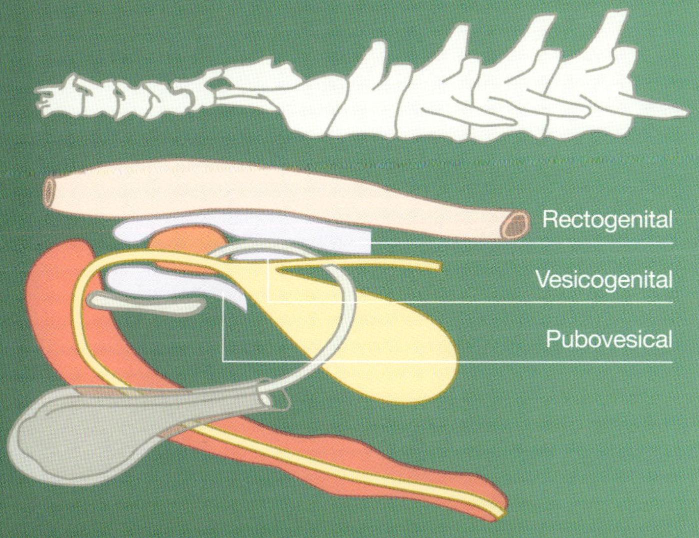

Perineal hernia

Prevalence

Perineal hernias almost exclusively appear in middle-aged or old, entire male dogs. They occur only anecdotally in the cat and female dogs. The breeds that are most commonly affected are: Boxer, Boston Terrier, Pekingese, Collie, Dachshund and the Old English Sheepdog. They are also common in small mixed breeds of the Terrier type.

Hernias originate from deterioration of the pelvic diaphragm due to weakening of the muscles. Perineal atrophy or degeneration is often multifactorial. Those that should be highlighted include: neurogenic atrophy caused by the stretching of the motor neurons of the perineal area in patients with chronic constipation and tenesmus, senile atrophy, atrophy of the coccygeal muscles in dogs with docked tails, myopathies due to endocrine disorders of the sex hormones and prostatic disease. In all cases, the result is reduced support of the rectal wall, so that the terminal portion of the digestive tract is pushed sideways, forming a pouch or a diverticulum.

The herniation is usually located lateral to the external anal sphincter. The herniated contents can slip between the sphincter and the levator ani muscle. Often, the levator ani is atrophied, leaving space for the contents to slip out of the abdomen between the anal sphincter and the coccygeus muscle (fig. 1).

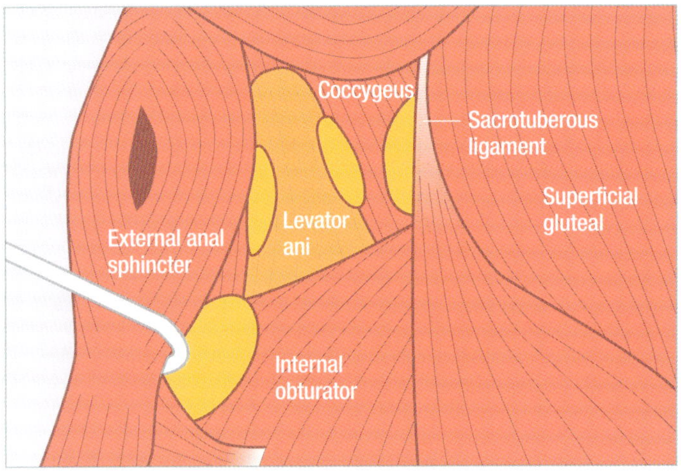

Fig. 1. Anatomical diagram of the perineum showing the possible sites of herniation.

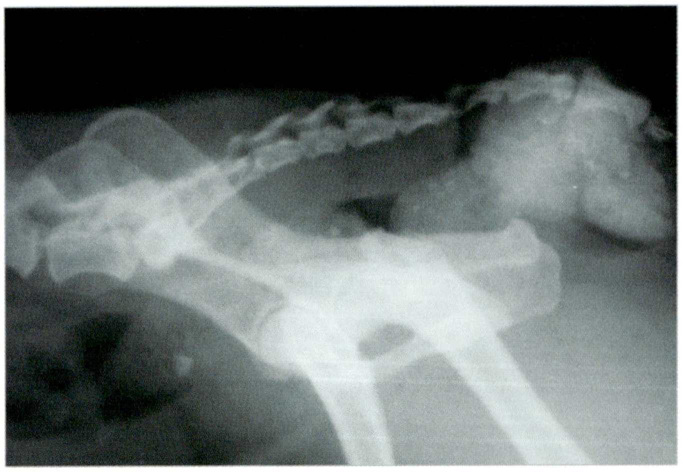

Fig. 2. Lateral radiograph of the abdomen, showing a unilateral perineal hernia. The content of the hernia is a rectal pouch filled with faeces.

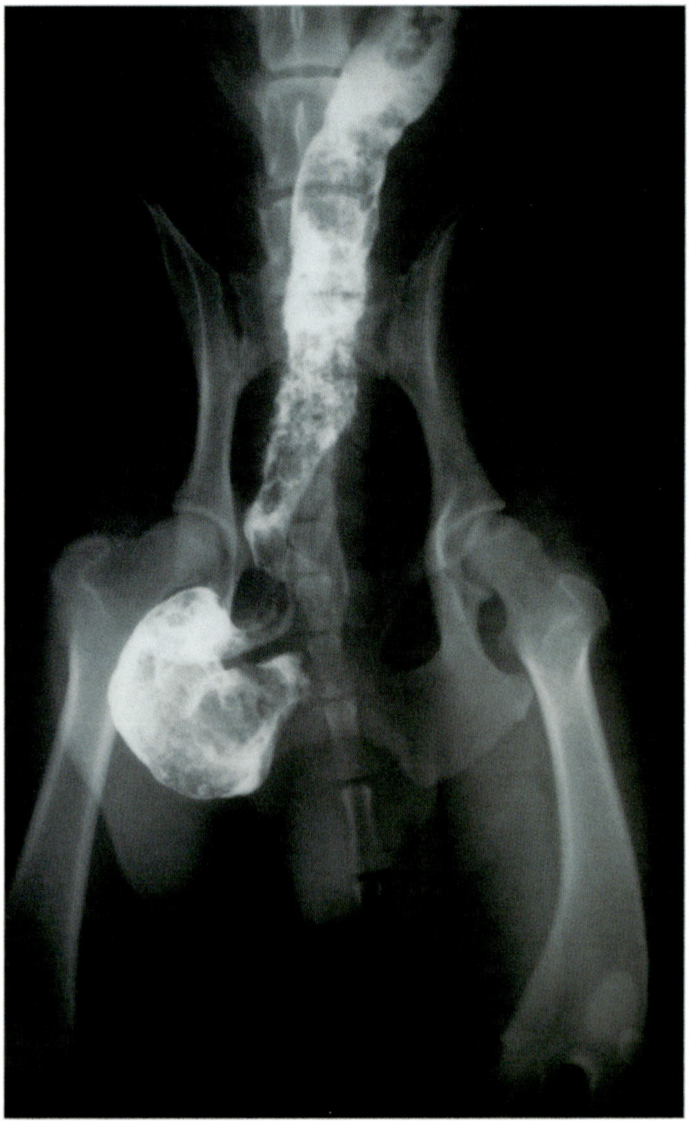

Fig. 3. Ventrodorsal contrast radiograph of the abdomen, showing a unilateral perineal hernia, containing the deviated rectum.

The most common content of a perineal hernia is intestines or fatty tissues of abdominal origin. As a result of the defective muscular function of the pelvic diaphragm, the rectum is often deviated laterally, forming a loop in the herniated content. In some cases, a rectal pouch is formed following chronic constipation, and it is the pressure exerted on the perineum by the retained faeces that produces the hernia (figs. 2 and 3).

The bladder and/or the prostate can also herniate. Sometimes, the bladder retroflexes and herniates on its own, and sometimes it is dragged along by the prostate. (figs. 4 and 5).

Clinical signs include a swelling, generally reducible, of the perineum on one or both sides of the anus, depending on whether the hernia is bilateral or not (fig. 6). Other signs include constipation, tenesmus and dyschezia, sometimes alternating with diarrhoea or faecal incontinence. If the bladder is included in the hernia and is retroflexed, the clinical picture can worsen to the point when urination becomes impossible, which in turn leads to postrenal azotemia.

A complete diagnostic approach should include the identification of the anatomical structures included in the hernia, based on radiography and rectal palpation. Only in this way will it be possible to anticipate the possible surgical difficulties and to select the most appropriate treatment. For this, an X-ray should be taken with or without contrast media in the bladder and/or the rectum.

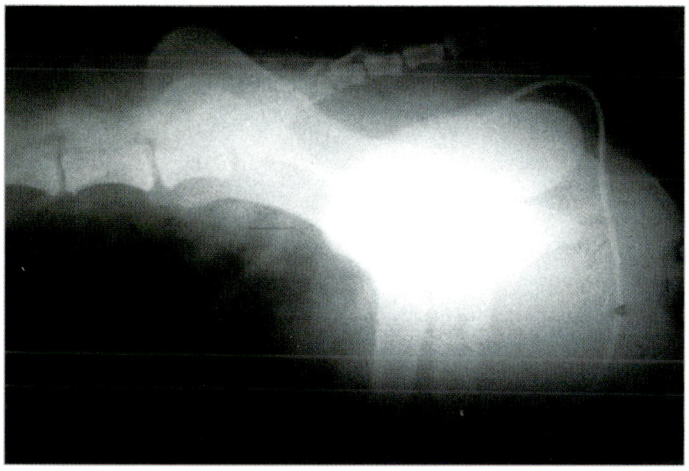

Fig. 4. Contrast radiograph, using an iodinated medium, of a cystocoele with the bladder located in the perineal area.

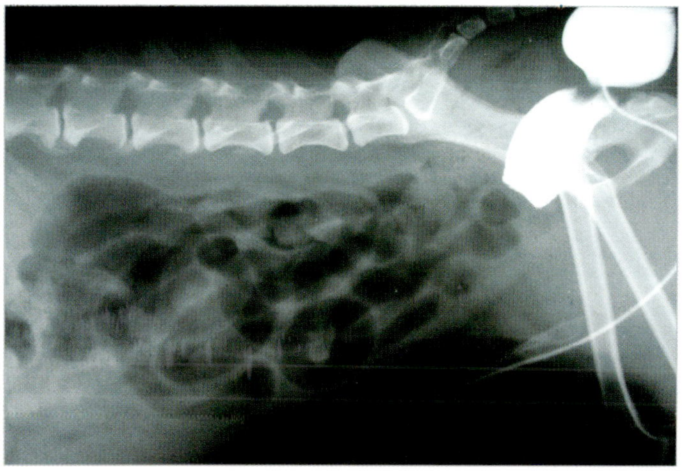

Fig. 5. This cystogram shows a caudally displaced bladder. Part of it is located in the pelvic canal, part in the hernia.

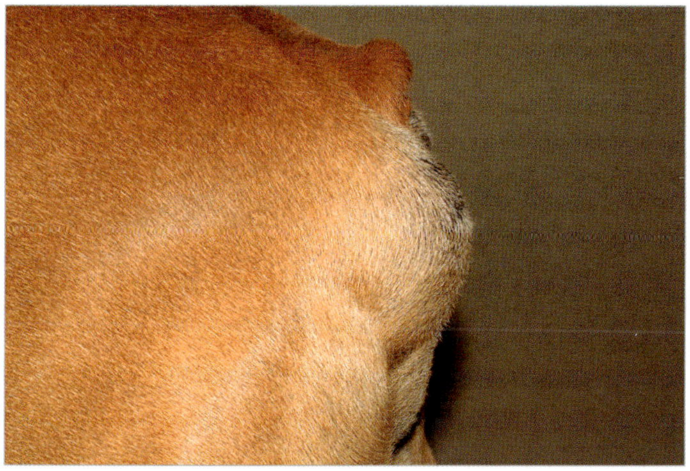

Fig. 6. Swelling of the perineal area corresponding to a unilateral perineal hernia. Note that the animal has a docked tail.

Medical and dietary treatment is aimed at defaecation and the production of soft faeces. It is based on the combination of a moist diet high in fibre and bulk-producing laxatives and/or stool softeners. Hormonal therapy or castration can be added in cases of prostratic hypertrophy. The outcome of these treatments is relatively poor and it is generally necessary to perform surgery in order to solve the problem.

If the radiological examination has shown that the bladder is included in the hernia, surgery must be performed as soon as possible. There is a risk that urine retention will lead to postrenal azotemia.

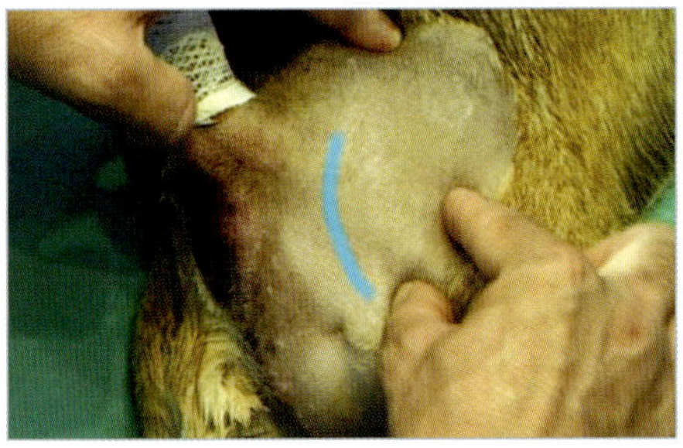

Fig. 7. Incision line for a simple herniorraphy.

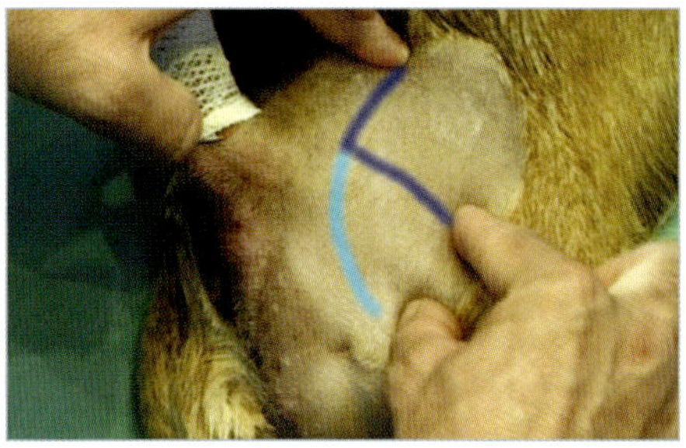

Fig. 8. Extension and side incision in order to carry out a muscular transposition of the superficial gluteal and/or internal obturator muscle.

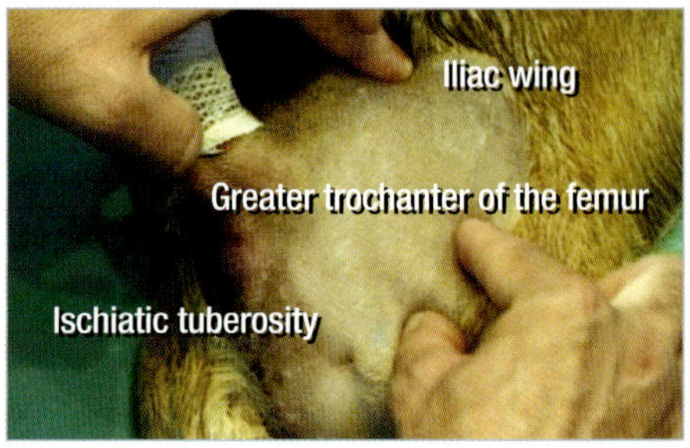

Fig. 9. Landmarks used for the approach to a perineal hernia.

Prior to surgery

- Withhold food from the patient for 24 hours to ensure emptying of the digestive tract in order to avoid contamination of the operative field.
- Administer an enema with the same objective.
- If the hernia includes the bladder, urine should be removed using a catheter or cystocentesis.
- Patients with dehydration or uraemia due to urine retention should be stabilised prior to surgery.
- Prepare the surgical field and position the patient as for any other operation of the perineal area.

The perineal hernia can be repaired surgically by a number of techniques. The most suitable approach for each case depends on:

- The state of the perineal musculature (size and location of the hernia, degree of muscular atrophy...)
- The herniated content (intestines, bladder...)
- The surgeon's experience with each technique.

Surgical techniques for the repair of perineal hernias include:

- Simple herniorraphy.
- Elevation or transposition of the internal obturator muscle.
- Transposition of the superficial gluteal muscle.
- Transposition of the semintendinosus muscle.
- Placement of a mesh prosthesis.
- Cystopexy.
- Deferensopexy.
- Colopexy.

The skin incision will vary depending on the surgical technique used for repairing the hernia. For a simple herniorraphy or for the placement of a mesh, it is sufficient to make an incision lateral to the anus, over the herniated pouch, extending from the base of the tail in a ventral direction to the ischium (fig. 7). If transposition of the superficial gluteal muscle is required, the incision should be prolonged dorsally and/or a second incision, perpendicular to the first, should extend towards the major trochanter of the femur (fig. 8). The ischiatic tuberosity, the greater trochanter of the femur and the iliac wing are the landmarks for these approaches (fig. 9).

After surgery

- Fit the patient with an Elizabethan collar and leave it on during the entire postoperative period.
- Administer laxatives in order to avoid straining during defaecation.
- Prescribe a soft diet in order to avoid constipation.
- Advise the owner about the importance of good hygiene of the area (which should be cleaned every time the animal defecates).

Complications are rare. They include: wound infection, faecal incontinence, dysuria, tenesmus, rectal prolapse and paralysis of the sciatic nerve.
On the other hand, recurrences are relatively common, with an incidence varying between 10 and 40% according to the literature. This percentage is largely dependent on the experience of the surgeon and the technique used. Some studies indicate that castration reduces these figures by a third, and also reduces the occurrence of a contralateral hernia.

If a hernia of this type is repaired surgically, simultaneous castration of the dog should always be recommended to the owner.

Perineal hernia. Case 1 / Simple herniorraphy

Technical difficulty

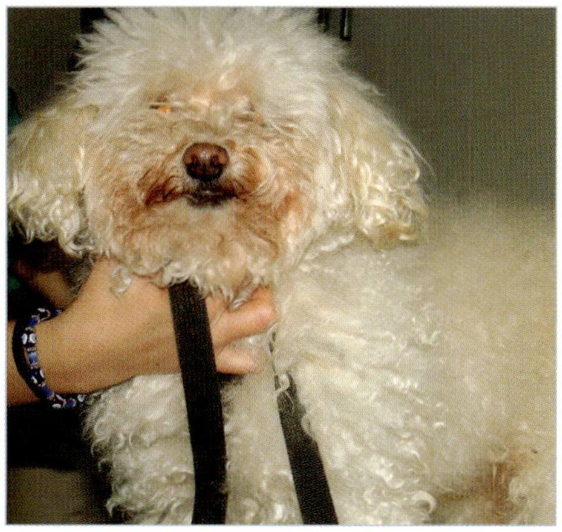

Fig. 1. The patient on the day of the first consultation.

Whenever it is possible to perform a simple herniorraphy, this technique is preferable as it is the easiest, and consists of closing the hernial ring with interrupted sutures. The success of the technique depends on the state of the perineal muscles adjacent to the hernial ring, which will need to support the tension of the sutures. Another determining factor is the size of the hernial ring, which will dictate the tension on the sutures.

A male, 10-year-old Poodle is presented with a swelling in the perineal area (fig. 1). The patient shows no signs of tenesmus or faecal retention. A bilateral perineal hernia is diagnosed by rectal exploration. The rectum is not affected, which is confirmed by a contrast radiograph (fig. 2). It is decided to operate.

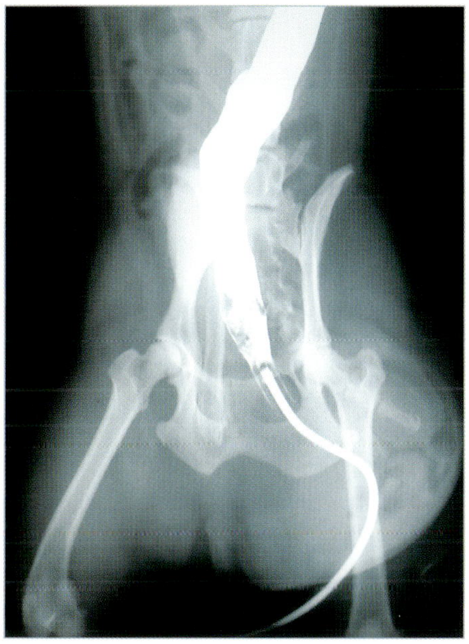

Fig. 2. Ventrodorsal contrast radiograph showing that, in this case, the rectum is not included in the hernia.

Fig. 3. Operating field prepared in the usual way, showing the swelling on both sides of the anus.

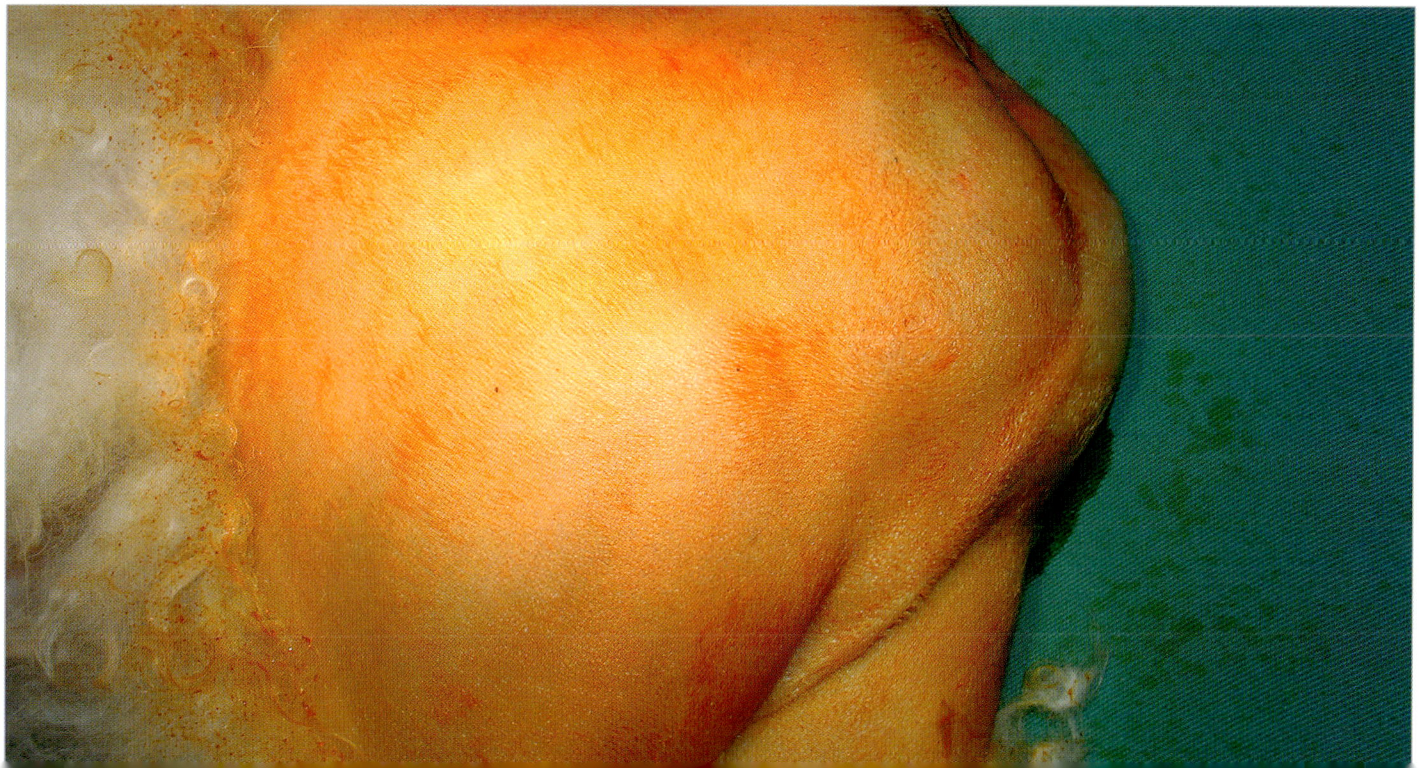

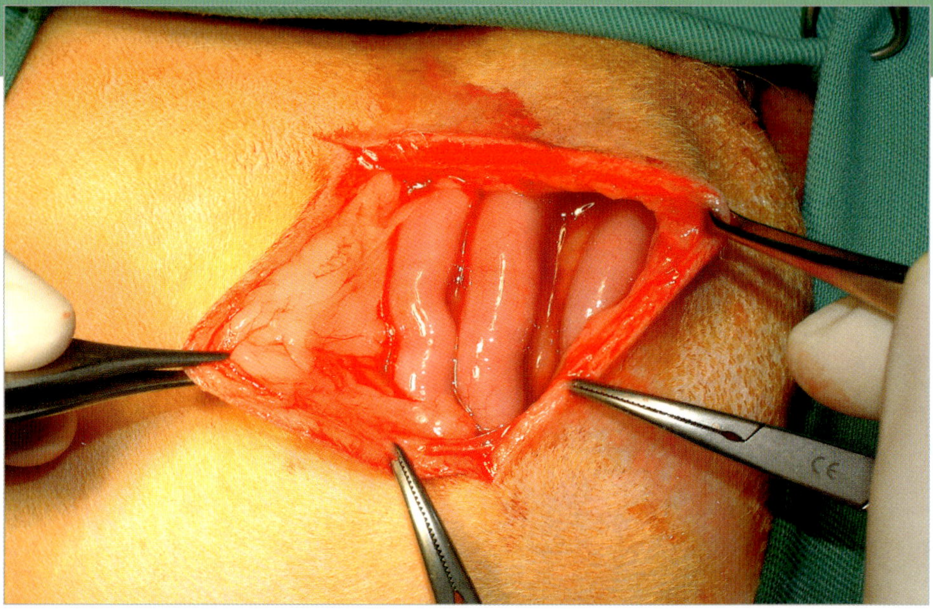

Fig. 4. After opening the hernial pouch, its contents consisting of healthy intestinal loops, can be seen.

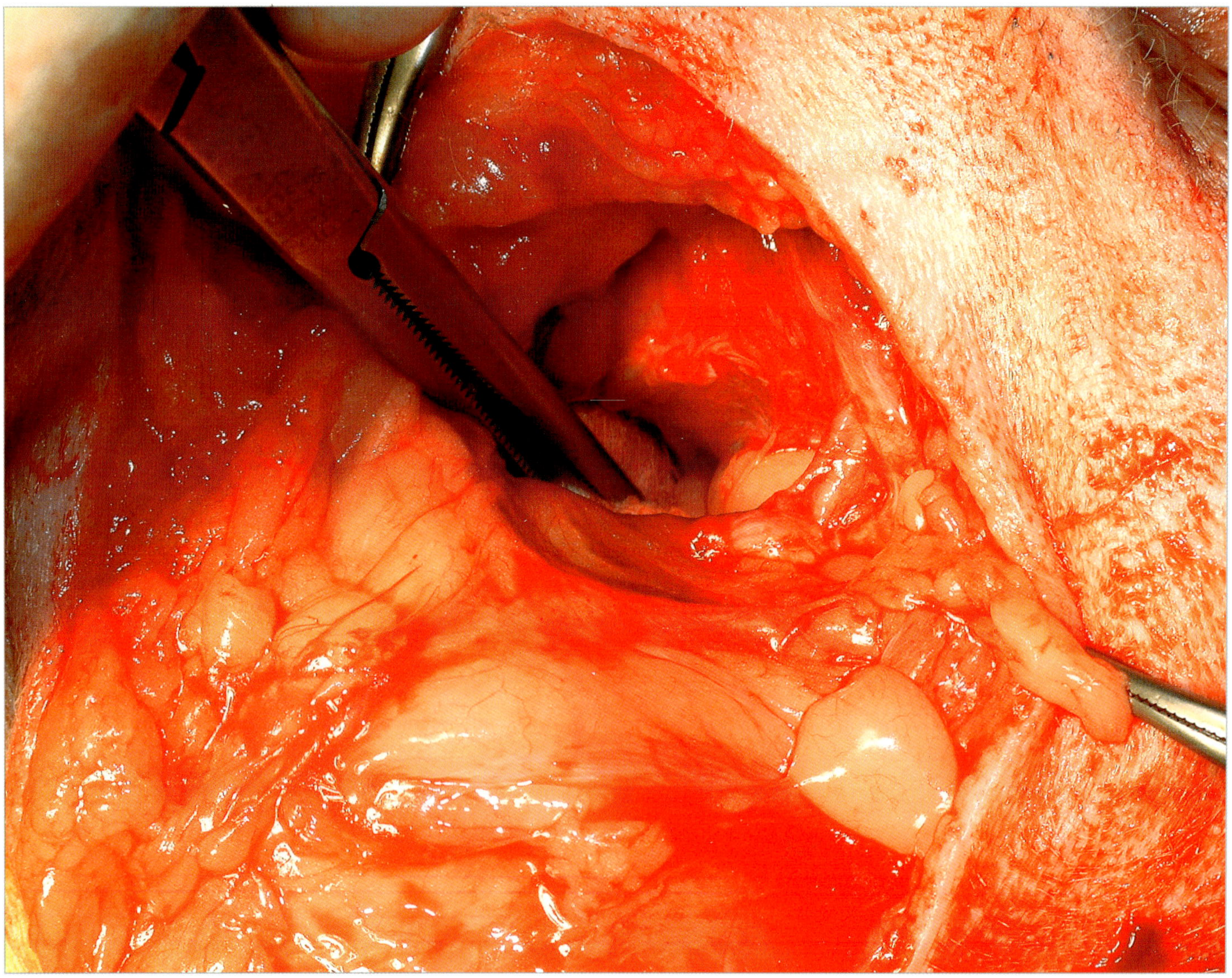

Fig. 5. The content of the hernia is reduced using gauze swabs held in long forceps, which help to keep it in place during suture placement. The photograph shows that the defect is not too large, with good integrity of the coccygeus and the external anal sphincter, surrounding the hernia. It was therefore decided to perform a simple herniorraphy.

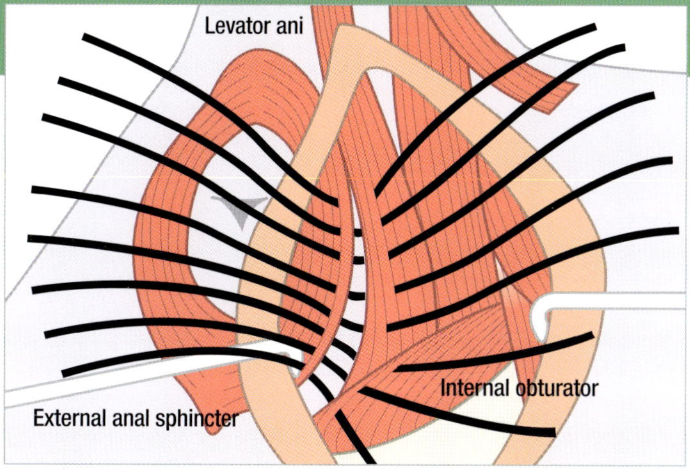

Fig. 6. Schematic drawing of a perineal hernia, showing the position of the interrupted sutures between the anal sphincter and the levator ani and coccygeus muscles and the sutures between those muscles and the internal obturator.

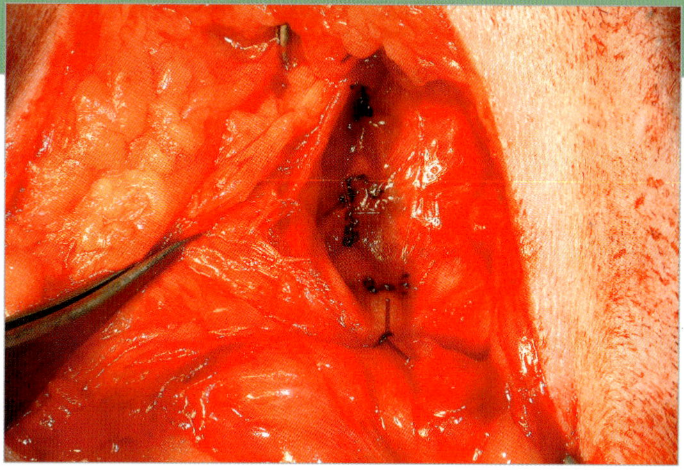

Fig. 7. Note the hernial ring after closure with simple absorbable sutures.

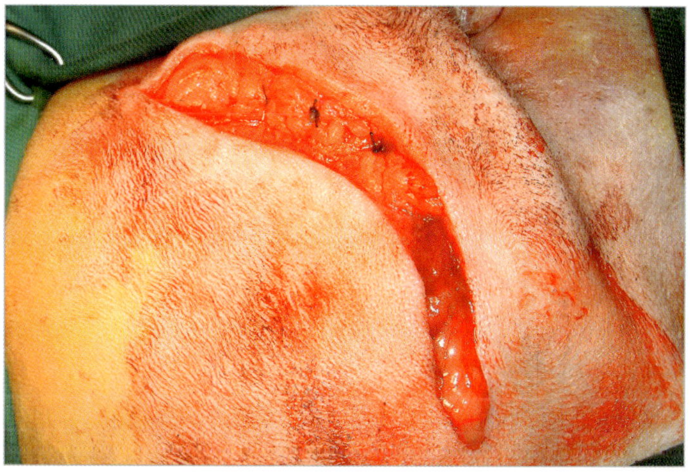

Fig. 8. After the herniorraphy, it is important to suture the subcutaneous tissue with care, to obtain the best possible apposition of a tissue that has been stretched by the hernia.

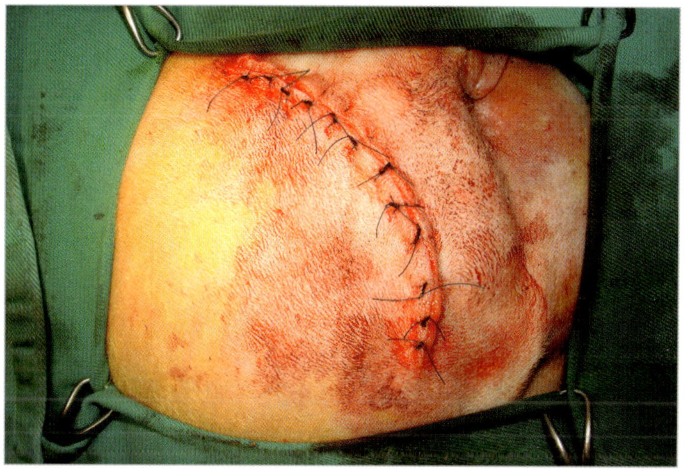

Fig. 9. Final appearance of the wound after subcutaneous suturing. During the same operation, contralateral herniorraphy was performed, as well as compulsory castration.

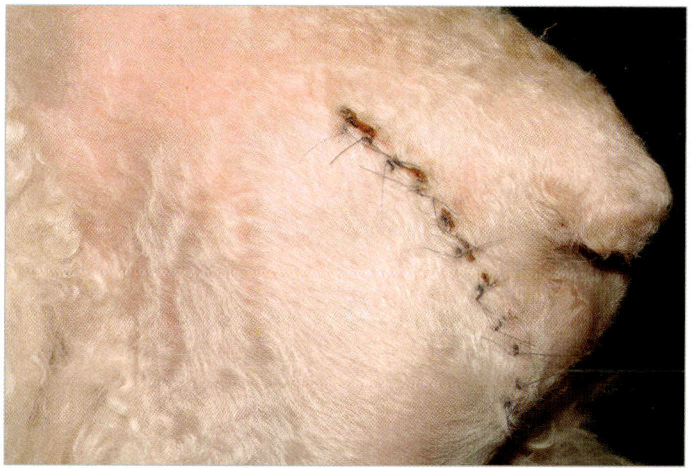

Fig. 10. Surgical result at the time of suture removal. Note the normal appearance of the perineum and the disappearance of the postoperative inflammation common in this area.

If the state of the perineal muscles allows it, and the hernial defect is not too big, simple herniorraphy is the technique of choice because of its simplicity.

See castration → page 264

Perineal hernia. Case 2 / Mesh implant

Technical difficulty	■	■	□	□	□

If the perineal muscles are not strong enough to support sutures under tension, an alternative to simple herniorraphy is to implant a surgical polypropylene mesh. The disadvantage of this technique is the cost of the mesh.

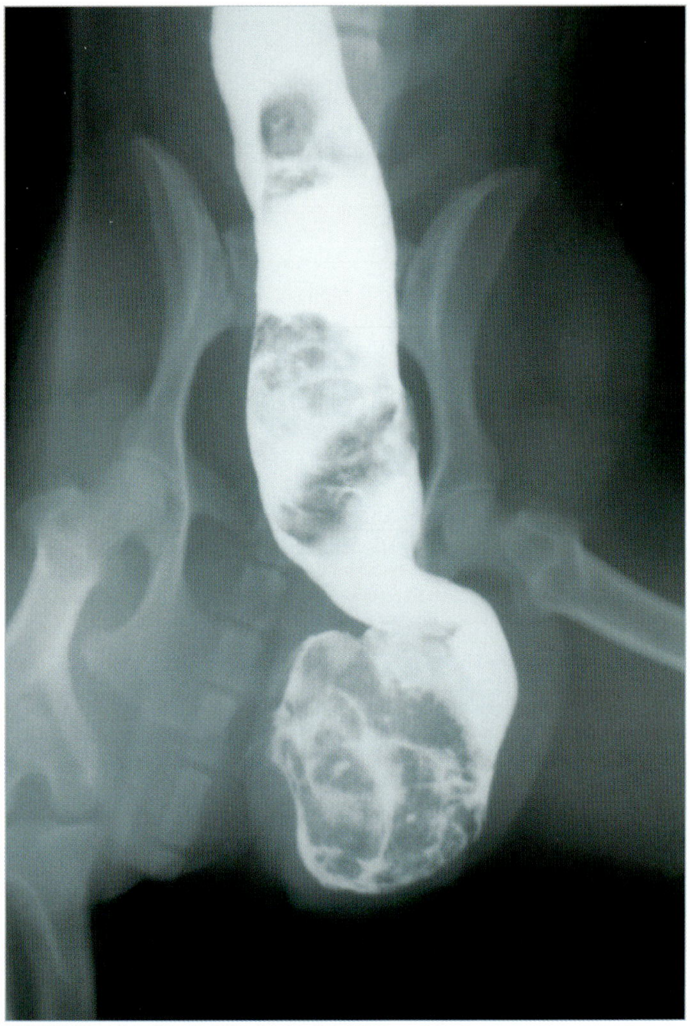

Fig. 1. Ventrodorsal radiograph of a dog showing a large perineal hernia on the left, which includes a rectal pouch.

✱ ***Do not forget to place a purse string suture around the anal sphincter and to remove it at the end of the operation!***

See purse string suture ➔ ***page 252***

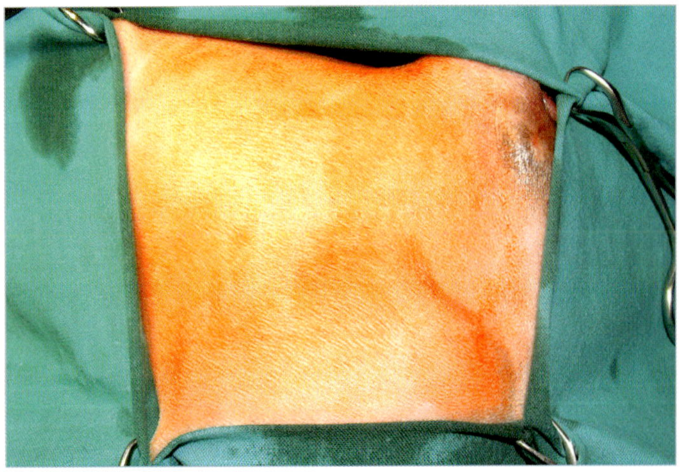

Fig. 2. Preparation of the surgical field. The patient is placed in sternal recumbency, with a raised pelvis and the tail fixed to the back. The incision is made as for the simple herniorraphy, oblique and over the herniated pouch.

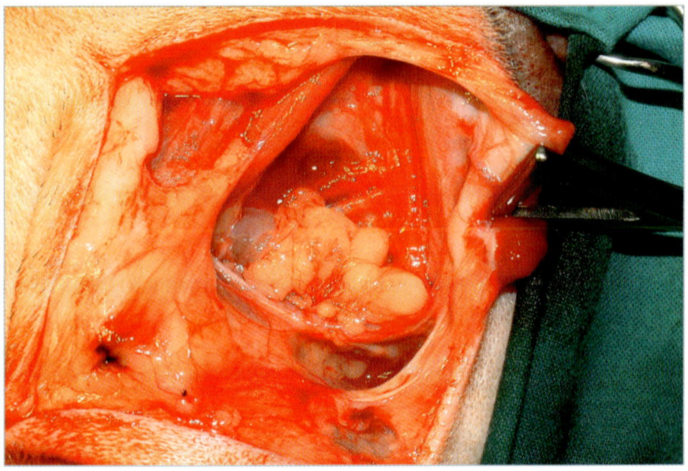

Fig. 3. Once the hernia is reduced and the hernial ring is dissected, the size of the defect and the muscular weakness can be appreciated. For this reason, it was decided to place a surgical mesh implant.

When choosing a mesh for the repair of a perineal hernia, cone-shaped meshes are the most appropriate.

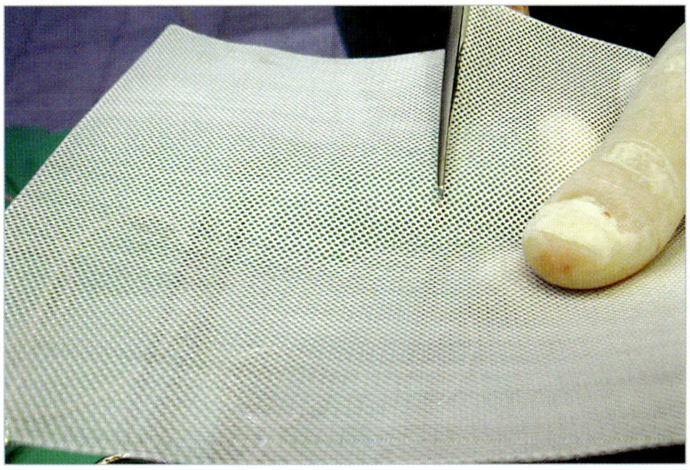

Fig. 4. The surgical mesh is made of polypropylene, a non-absorbable material that serves as a support for the scar tissue. This consists of fibroblasts which invade the mesh.

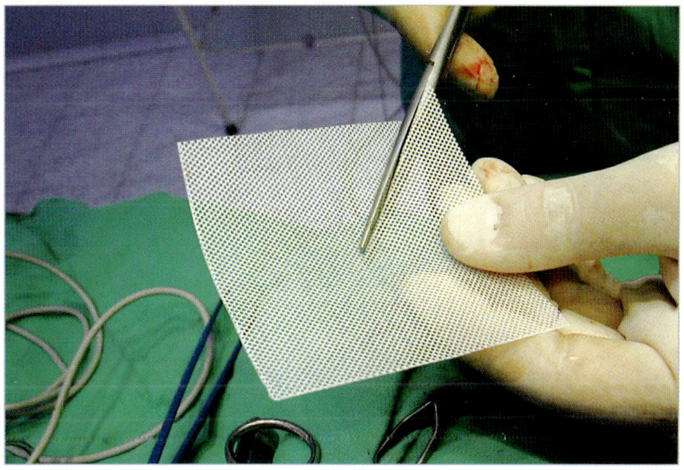

Fig. 5. Considering the depth of the anatomical defect causing the perineal hernia, it is practical to create a cone shape with the mesh, as shown in the picture.

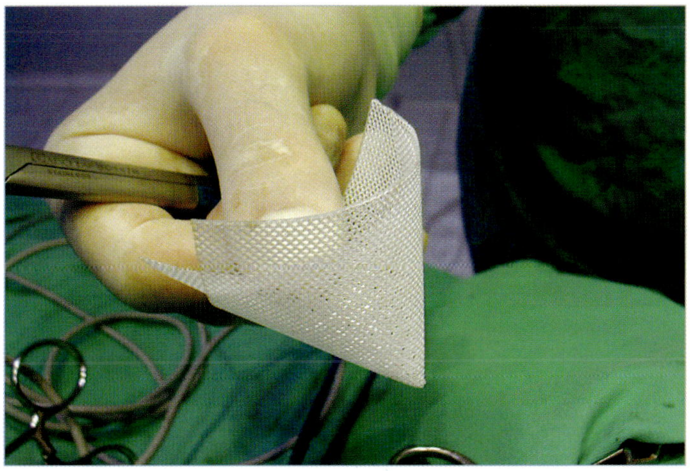

Fig. 6. Once the cone has been made, it is placed with the vertex in the deepest part of the defect.

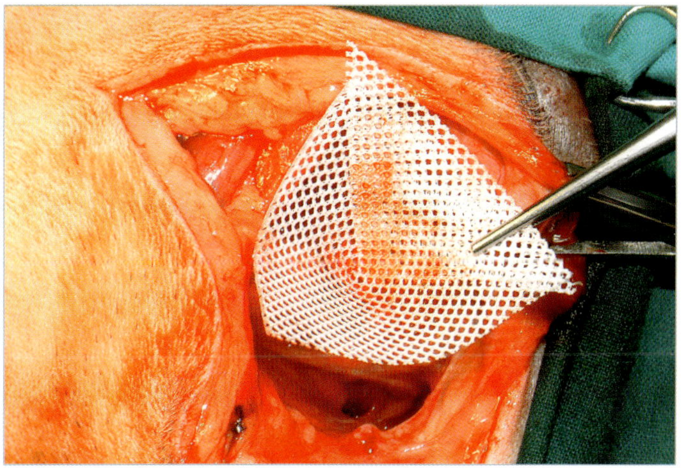

Fig. 7. The mesh cone is placed over the defect and its size adjusted, until the base of the cone covers the hernial ring.

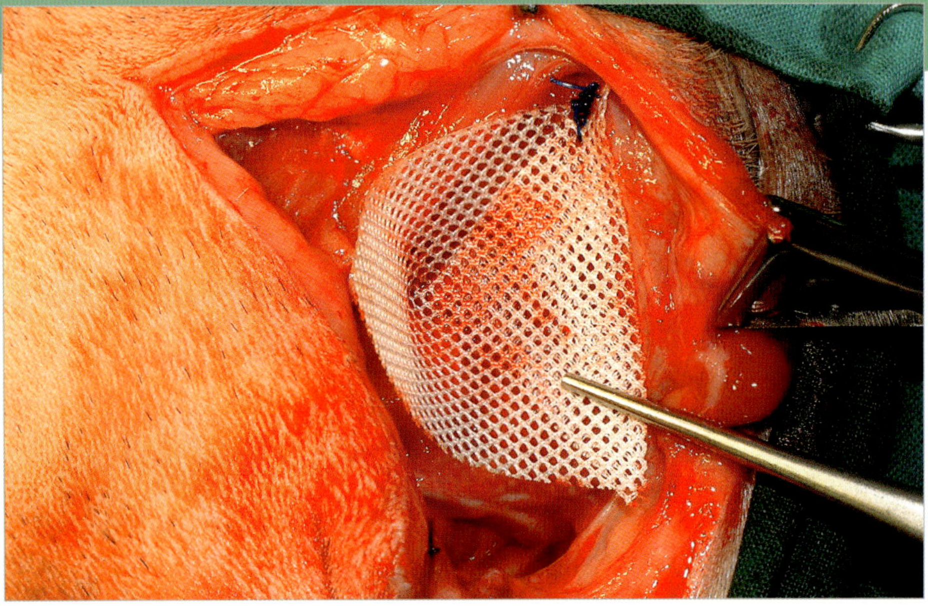

Fig. 8. Next, the circumference of the cone base is sutured to the muscles that delimit the hernial ring. Ensure that the sutures are placed in healthy muscle and take care to avoid excessive tension on the sutures.

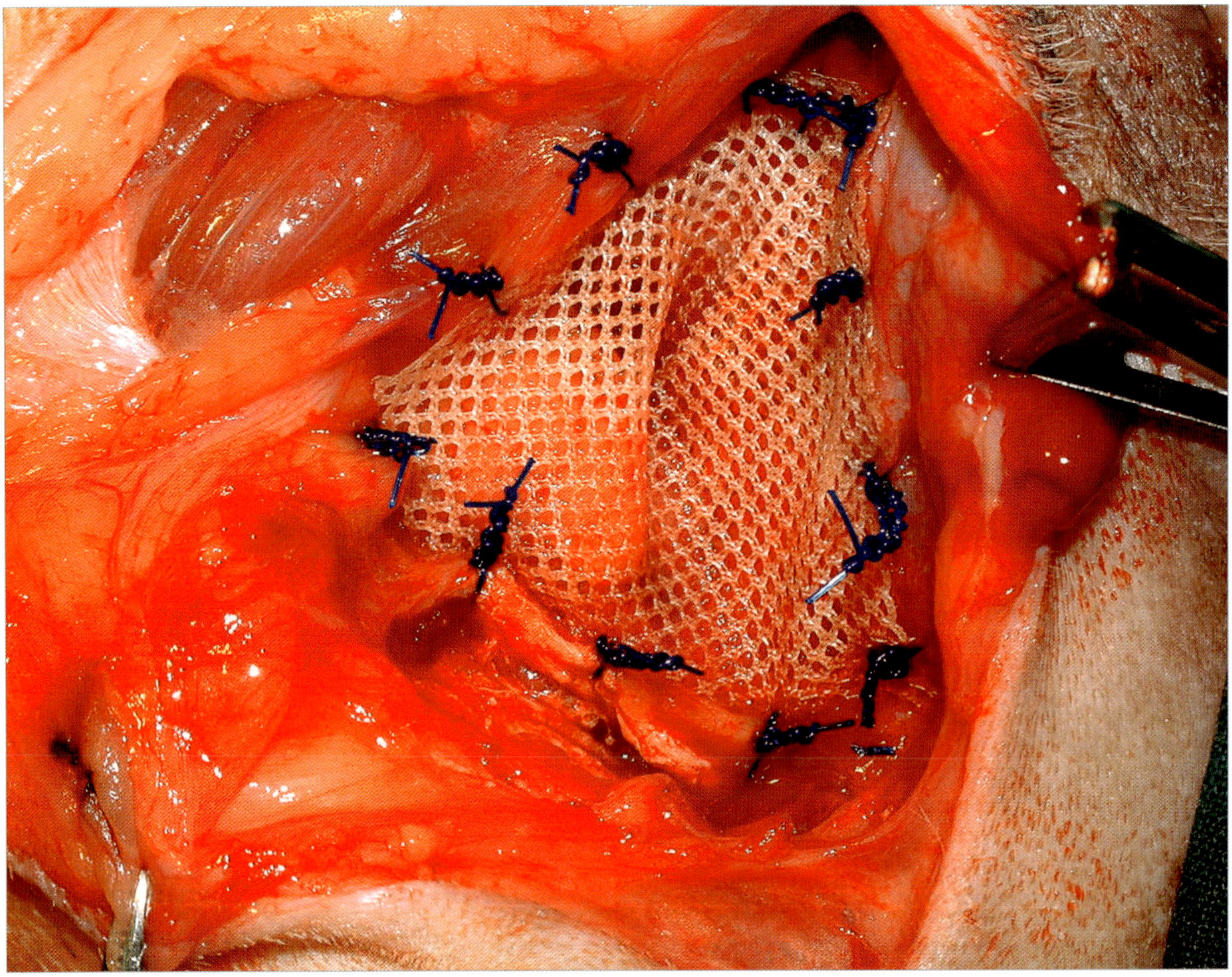

Fig. 9. To fix the mesh, simple, interrupted sutures of non-absorbable monofilament material are placed around the circumference.

Perineal hernia. Case 3 / Transposition of the superficial gluteal muscle and elevation of the internal obturator muscle

Technical difficulty

In cases where the hernial ring is too wide to perform simple herniorraphy, muscle transposition techniques are an alternative to polypropylene mesh implants. These are technically more demanding, but less expensive. Of the available techniques, the one that offers the best results in the authors' experience, is a combination of the elevation of the internal obturator muscle and transposition of the superficial gluteal muscle. The obturator effectively covers the ventral part of the hernial ring, while the gluteal muscle closes the dorsal area of the defect.

Fig. 1. "Monday" on the day of the initial consultation.

✱ *Cases like these, where the bladder is included in the hernia, constitute an emergency.*

"Monday", an 8-year-old male Samoyed cross was presented for consultation (fig. 1). The owner commented that the animal had been making continuous effort to urinate for the last two days and that he had observed a swelling next to the anus. Examination reveals the presence of an apparently reducible perineal hernia, which, in view of the clinical picture, probably includes the urinary bladder in retroflexion. Blood tests show a mild uraemia with otherwise normal parameters.

Radiological examination is carried out after introducing an iodinated contrast medium into the bladder (fig. 2), showing that the bladder is indeed within the hernia, in retroflexion. A situation like this carries the risk of postrenal uraemia and requires immediate action. The first measure is to empty the bladder by catheterisation.

After reducing the hernia, a new radiograph is taken, which shows that the bladder is no longer retroflexed, but is still displaced caudally, together with the prostate (fig. 3).

In order to complete the study of the herniated content, a barium enema is given to the patient and a new radiograph is taken, showing a deviation of the rectum (fig. 4).

The decision is made to repair the hernia surgically.

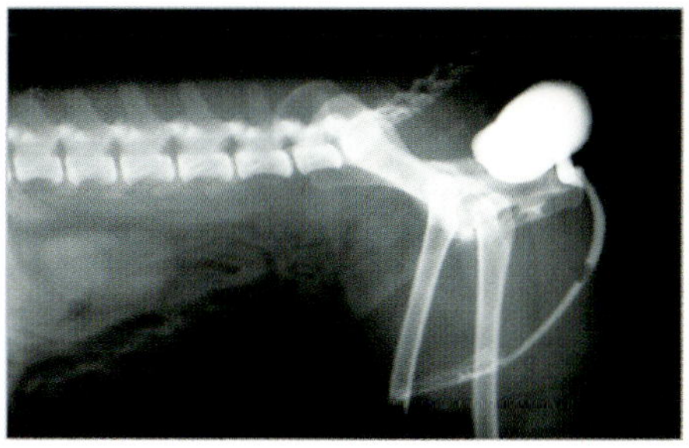

Fig. 2. Lateral contrast radiograph showing the bladder in retroflexion, included in the hernia.

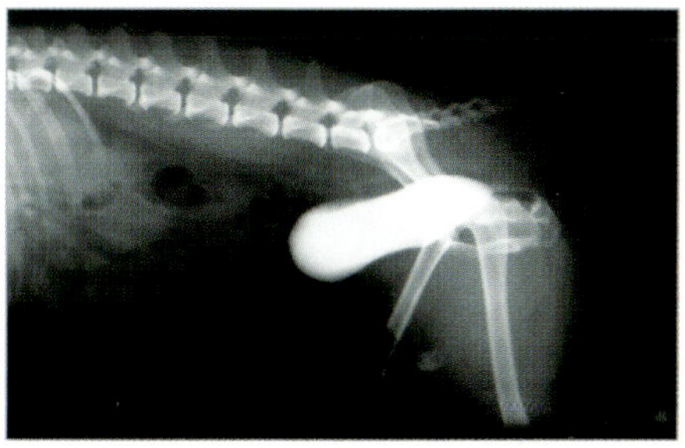

Fig. 3. Lateral image of the repositioned bladder, which is still in the pelvic canal.

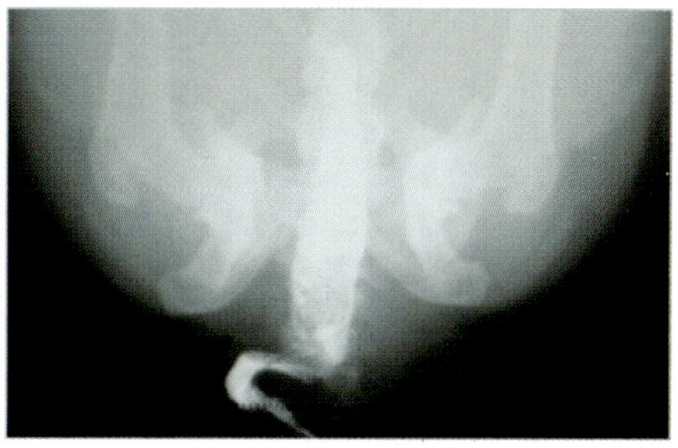

Fig. 4. Ventrodorsal radiograph after inserting contrast medium in the rectum, showing a deviation of the rectum inside the hernial pouch.

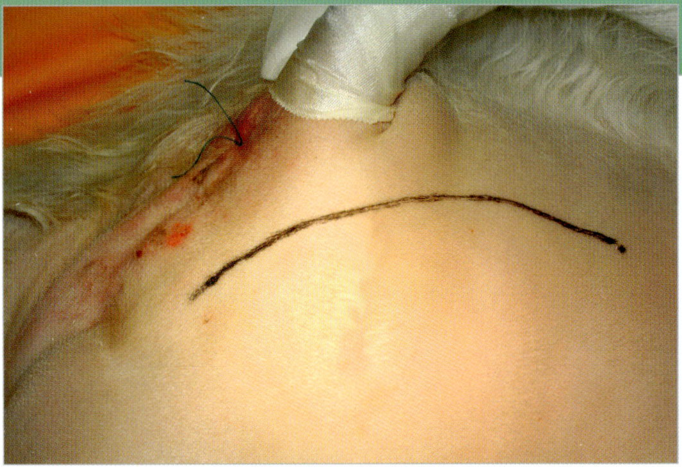

Fig. 5. The patient is prepared as usual. The line of incision should be a wide arc starting dorsal to the greater trochanter of the femur and ending below the ischiatic tuberosity. Place a purse string suture around the anus and fix the tail to the back.

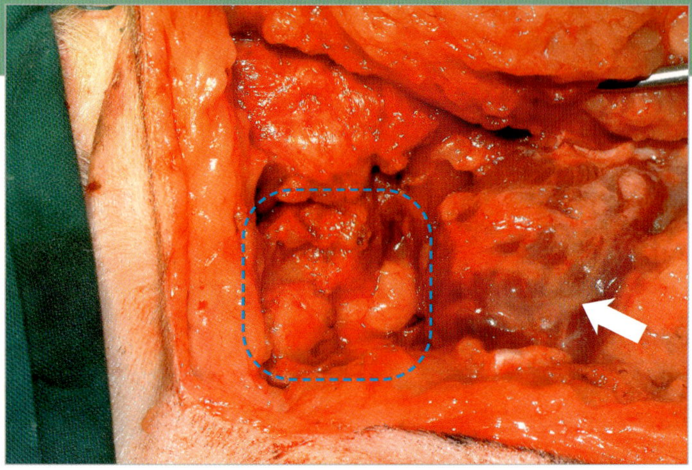

Fig. 6. View of the surgical area showing, on the left, the hernial defect (blue line), and on the right, the superficial gluteal muscle (white arrow). Given the size of the defect, it is decided in this case to perform a transposition of the superficial gluteal muscle and an elevation of the internal obturator muscle.

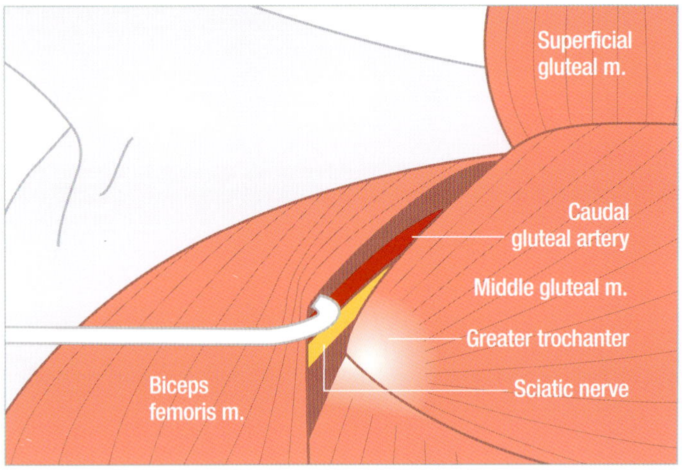

Fig. 7. Schematic anatomical drawing of the area after detaching the tendon of the superficial gluteal muscle from the greater trochanter of the femur.

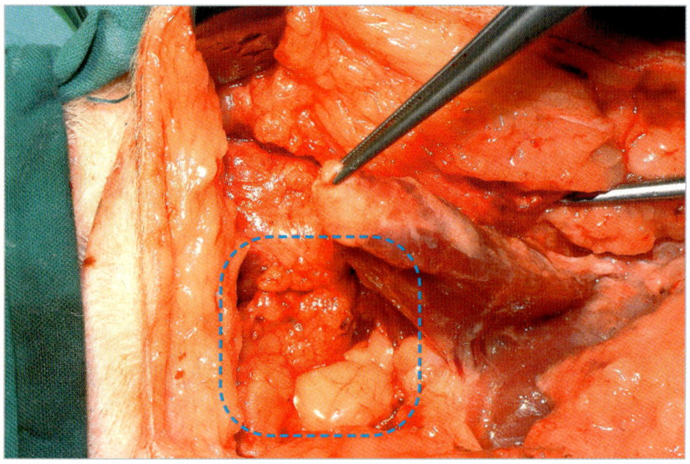

Fig. 8. Once the gluteal muscle has been detached, taking care not to damage its medial blood supply, it is transposed towards the hernial defect. This transposition normally permits coverage of the dorsal part of the hernial ring, but not the ventral part the hernial defect as delimited by the blue line.

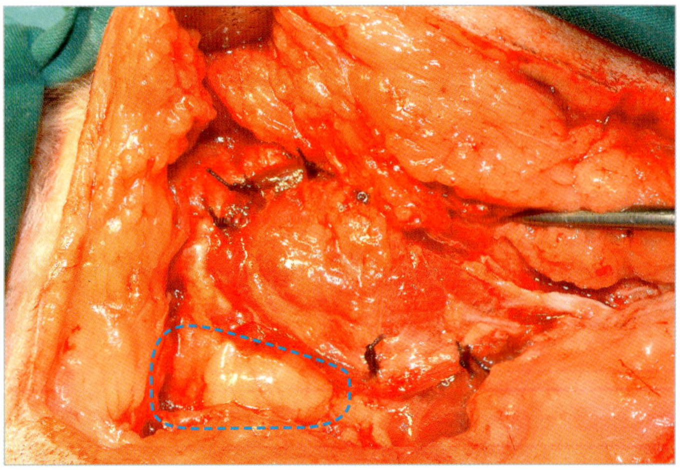

Fig. 9. This image shows how the gluteal muscle covers a large part of the defect, leaving only a small open part. The image shows fatty tissue in this ventral area. The hernial defect is delimited by the blue line.

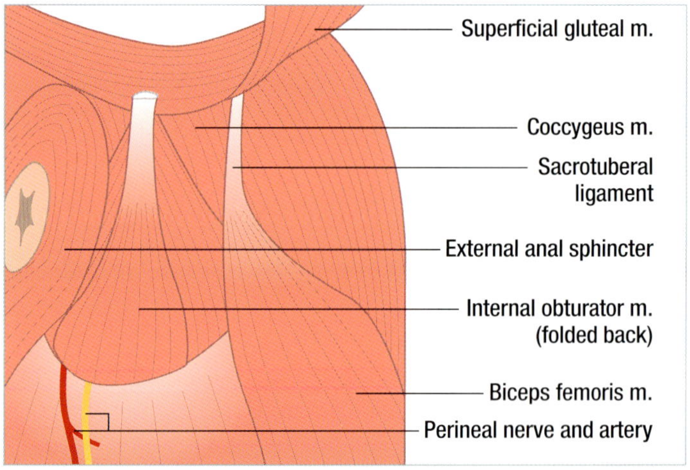

Fig. 10. Schematic anatomical drawing showing the internal obturator. Note that this muscle is attached with a thin aponeurosis at the caudal limit of the ischiatic plane. It is this same aponeurosis that should be severed as close as possible to the ischial arch in order to preserve the fibrous tissue that gives strength to the suture in the obturator, once elevated.

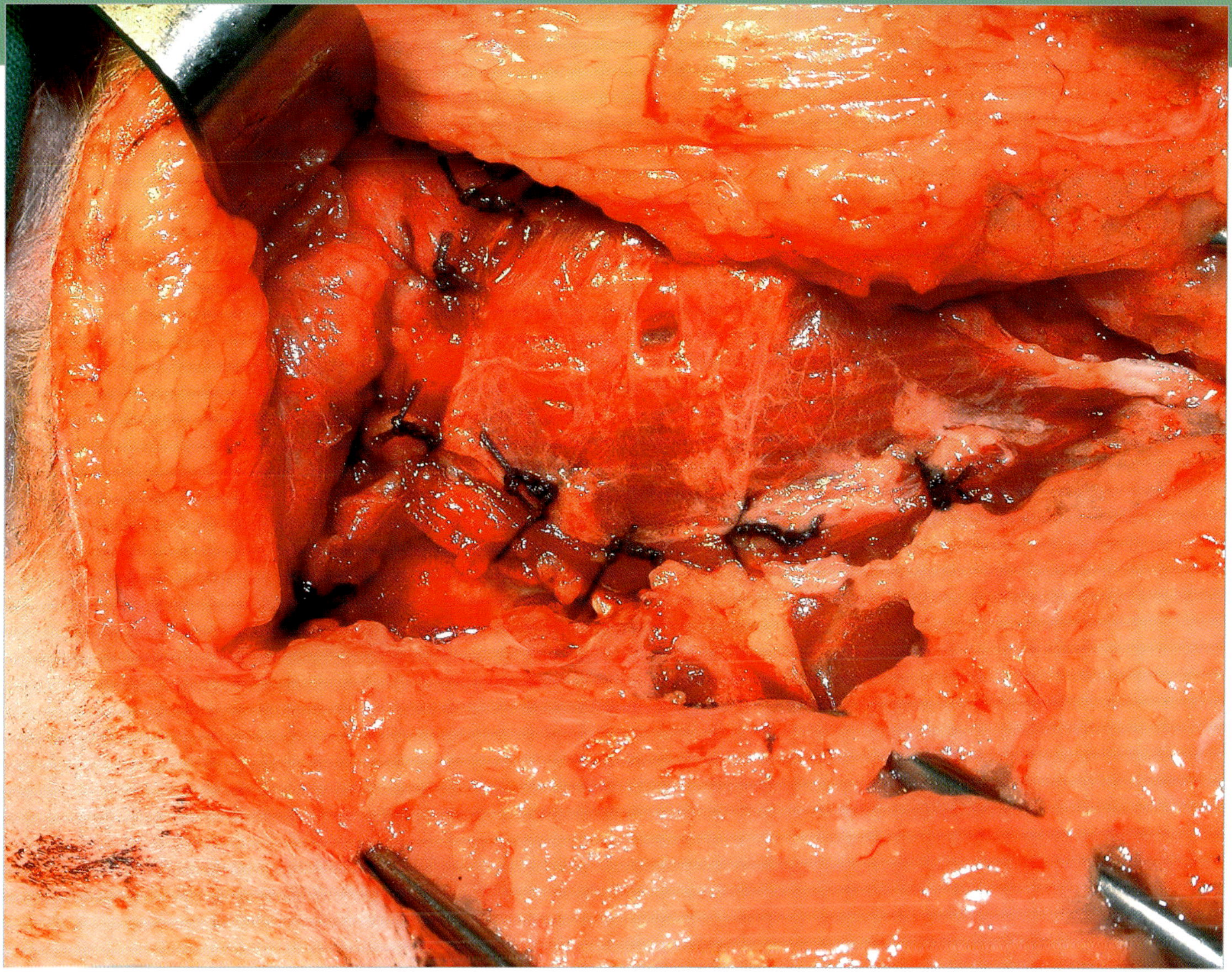

Fig. 11. Final view of the operative area, showing the anal sphincter to the left, the transposed superficial gluteal muscle dorsally to the right and the elevated internal obturator ventrally. By suturing these three muscles together, the hernial ring can be closed. In this case, it was not necessary to sever the tendon of the internal obturator, which simplified the technique.

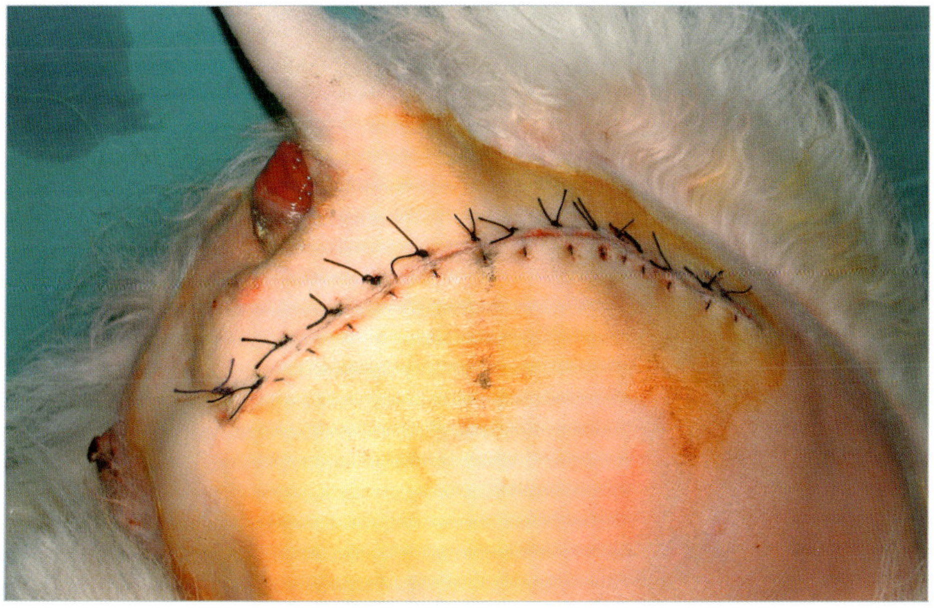

The combination of the transposition of the superficial gluteal muscle and elevation of the internal obturator is a technique that solves the majority of large perineal hernias.

Fig. 12. As in this image, it is not unusual for the patient to develop a certain degree of rectal prolapse, which generally resolves without intervention in a few days.

Perineal hernia. Case 4 / Double muscular transposition (internal obturator and superficial gluteal muscle)

Technical difficulty

"Satan", a 9-year-old entire male German Shepherd is presented because the owner has observed a swelling in the left perineal area (fig. 1). Upon examination, a perineal hernia is diagnosed, containing a rectal loop (fig. 2). It is decided to operate.

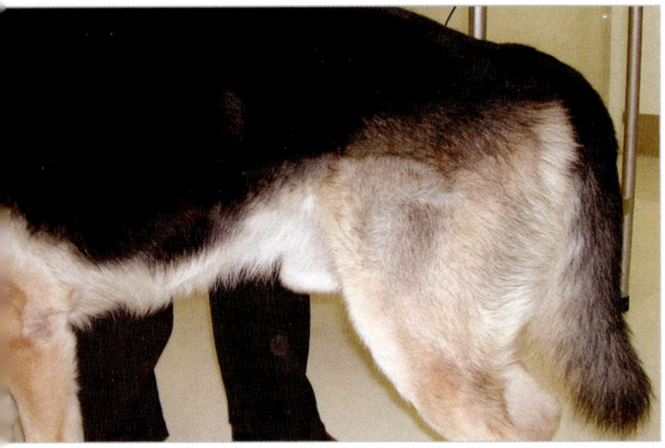

Fig. 1. The patient on the day of the initial consultation. The tail is displaced laterally away from the hernia.

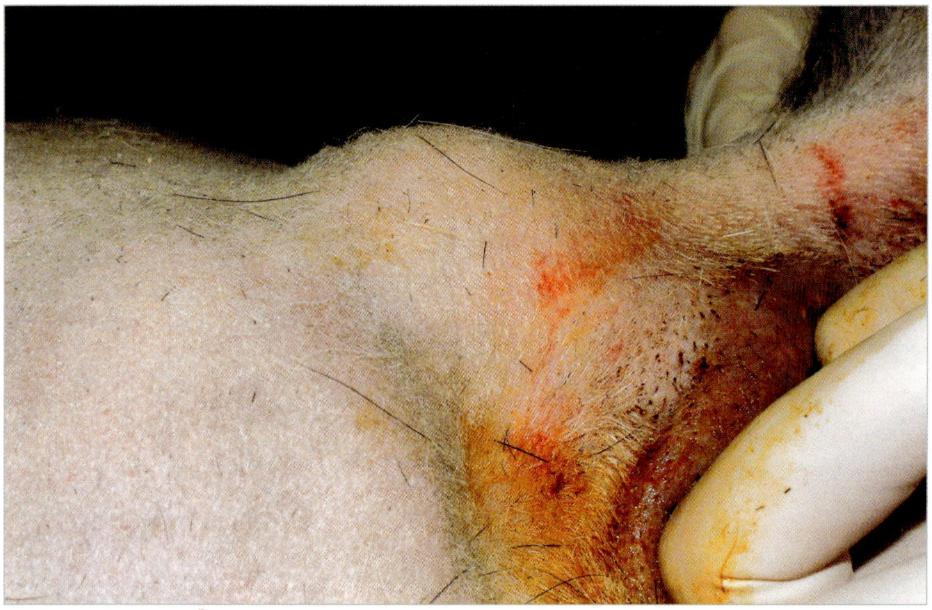

Fig. 2. Rectal palpation immediately prior to the operation. Note the bulge of the finger in the herniated area.

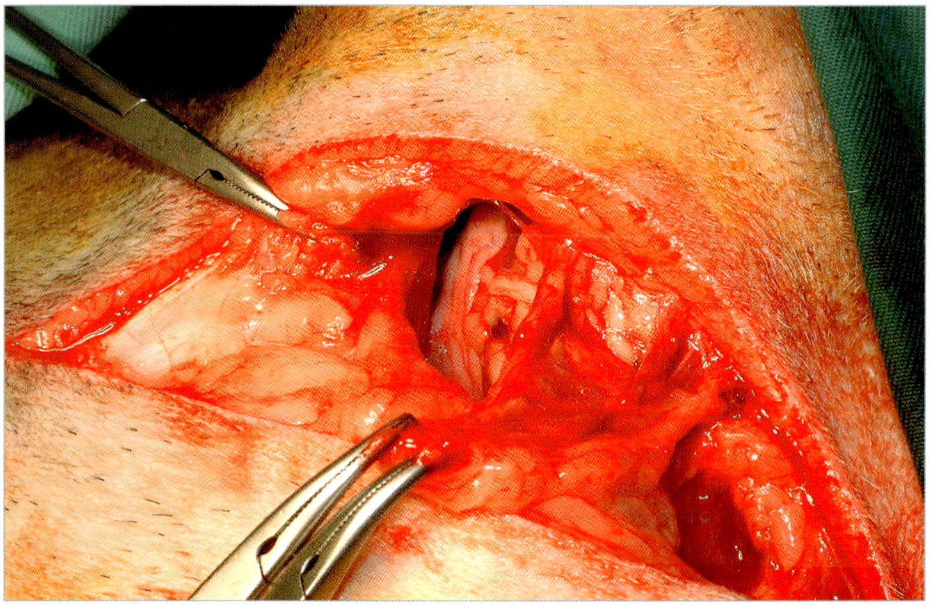

Fig. 3. After skin incision and dissection of the subcutaneous tissue, the wide hernial ring can be seen, and beyond it, the rectum and fatty tissue. It was decided to carry out a double transposition of the internal obturator and superficial gluteal muscles.

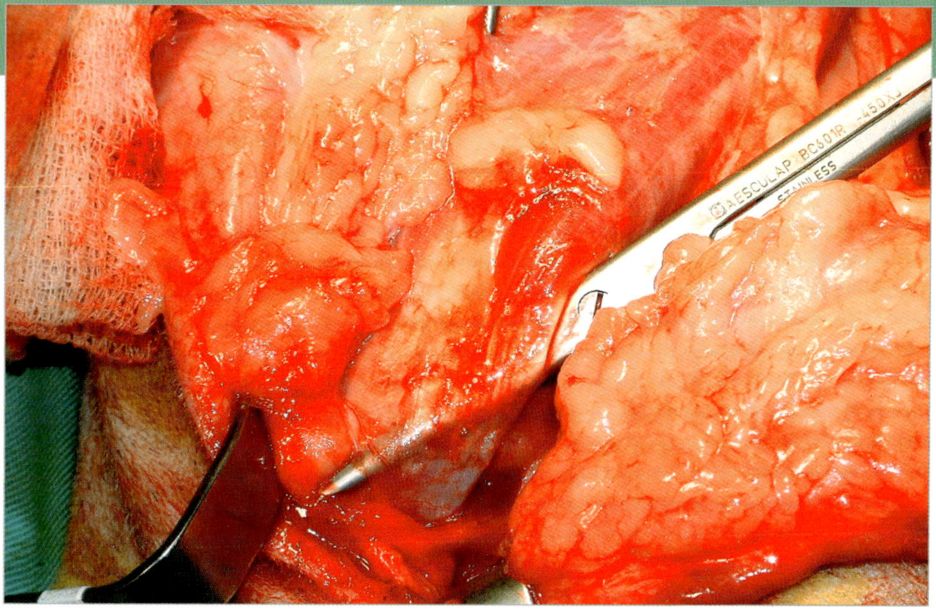

Fig. 4. Start by locating the insertion of the superficial gluteal tendon on the greater trochanter of the femur. For this, a second skin incision, perpendicular to the first, can be made in the direction of the greater trochanter.

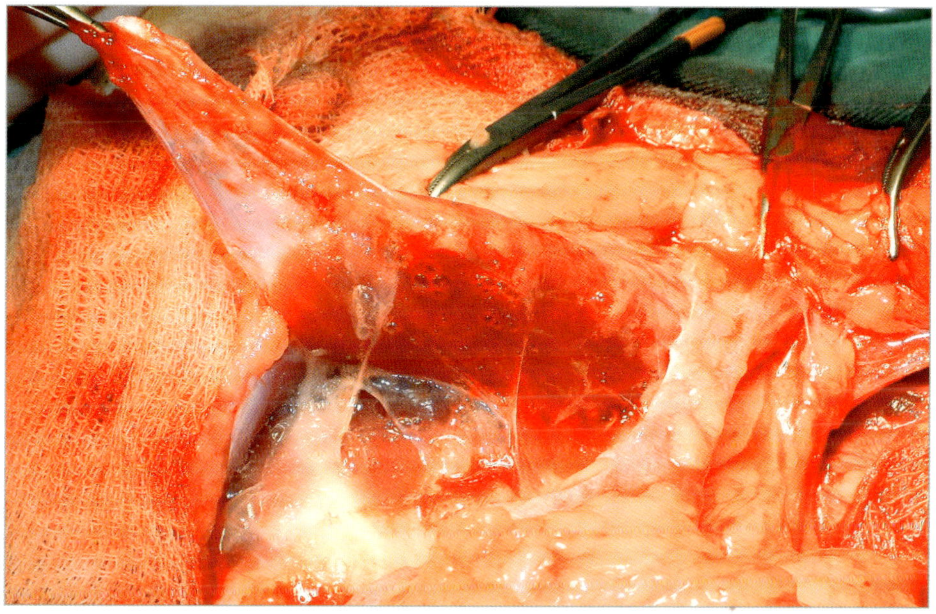

Fig. 5. Once the tendon of insertion of the superficial gluteal muscle has been sectioned, the muscle is transposed towards the perineum. During its dissection and manipulation, the blood supply that enters through the medial side should not be touched.

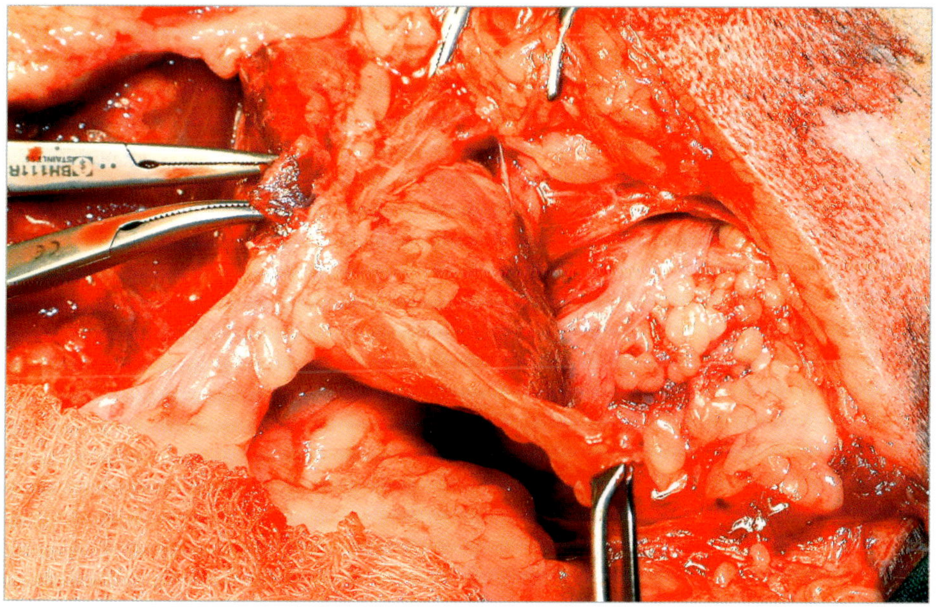

Fig. 6. The gluteal is lifted caudally and medially in order to cover the most dorsal part of the hernial defect.

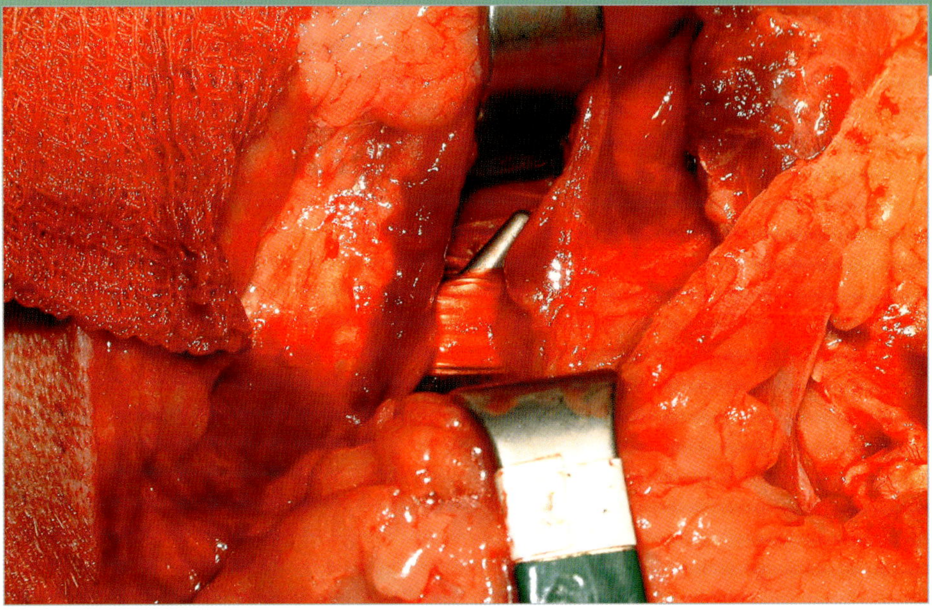

Fig. 7. Next, the tendon of the internal obturator should be located on the caudomedial side of the femur. For this, we medially rotate the leg.

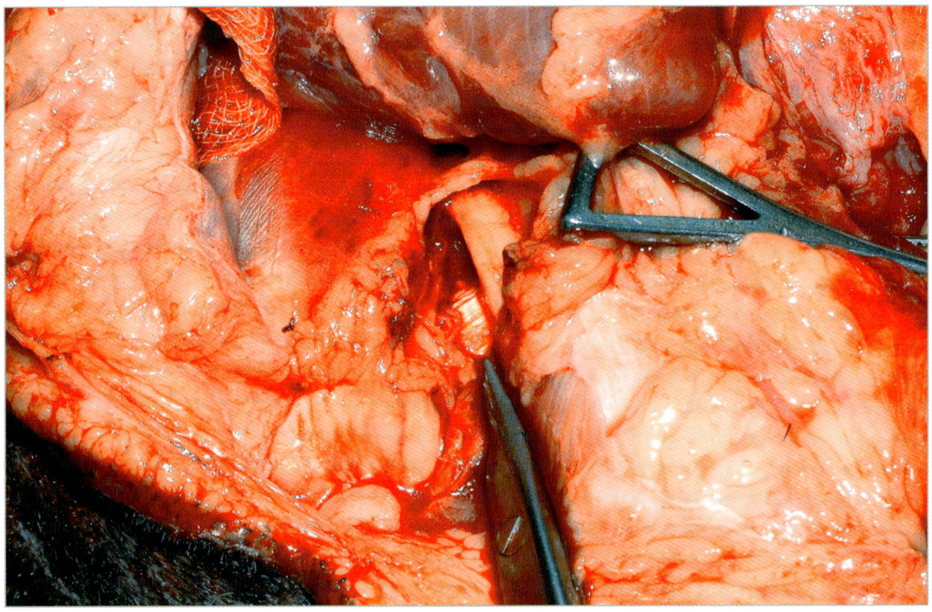

Fig. 8. When sectioning the tendon of the obturator, special attention should be paid to the sciatic nerve that runs over it.

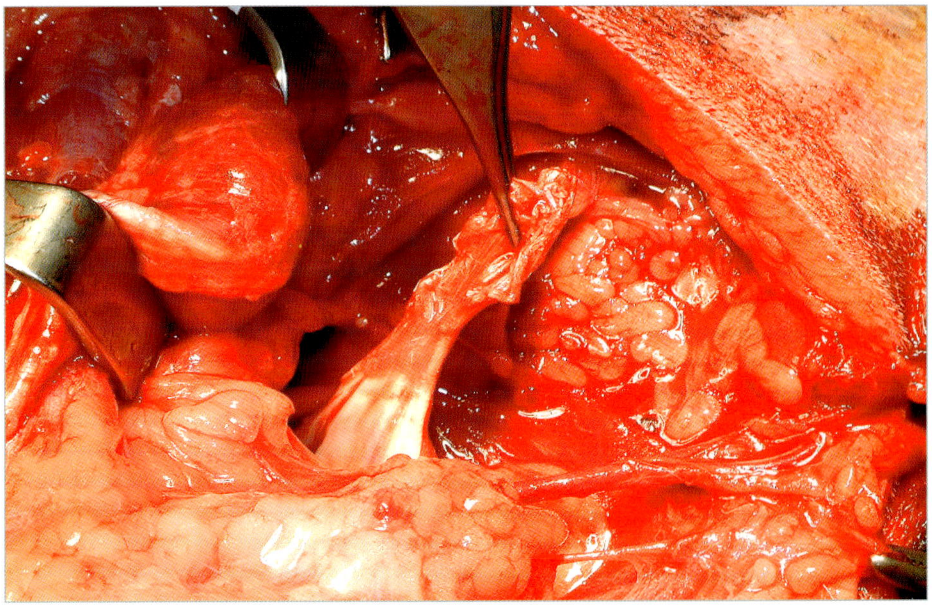

Fig. 9. Once the tendinous insertion and the insertion on the ischial plane have been severed, the obturator tendon is lifted up to cover the ventral part of the herniated defect. Note the proximity of the pudendal vessels.

✱ *When transposing the internal obturator, care should be taken to avoid damaging vascular and nervous structures like the pudendal vessels or sciatic nerve.*

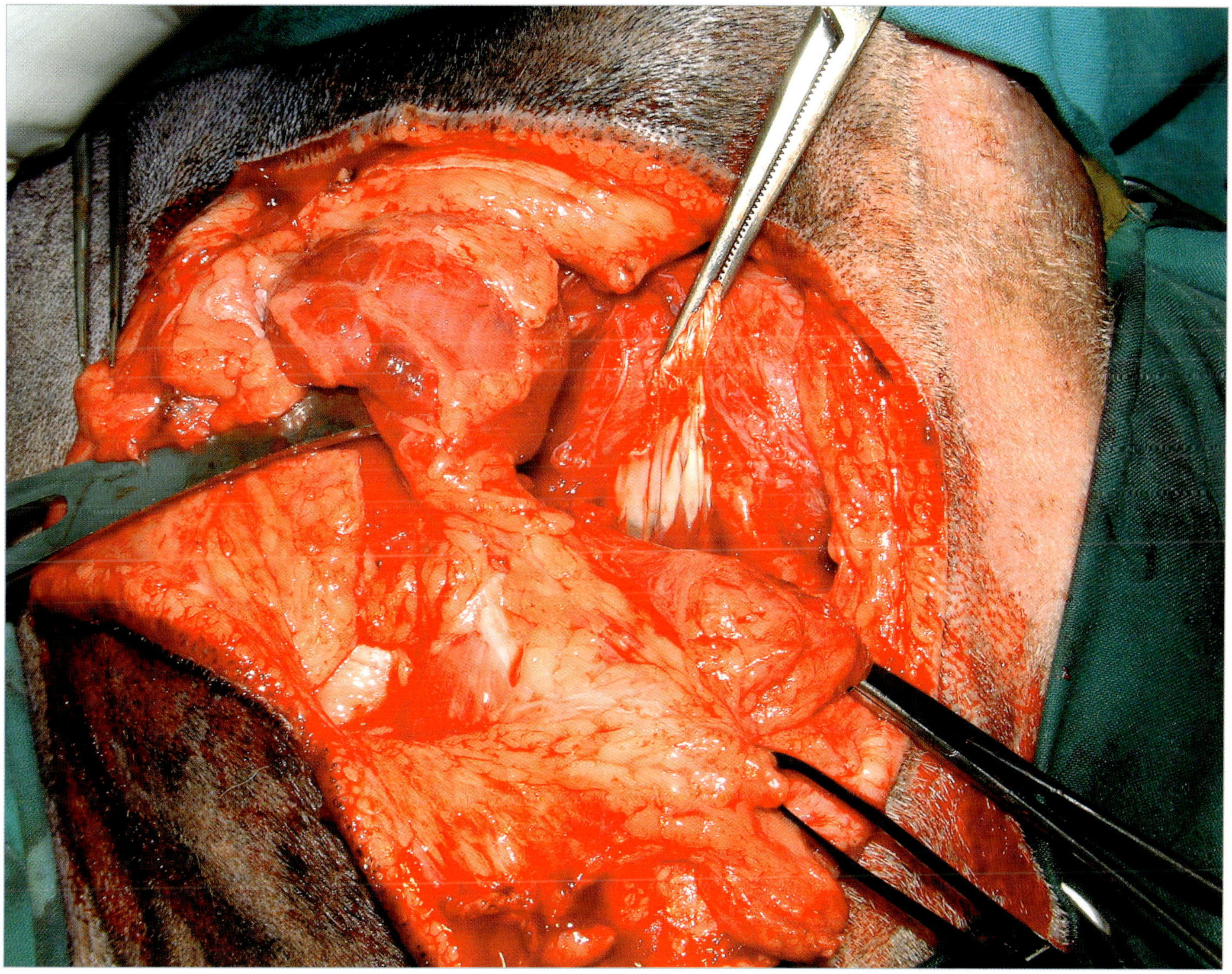

Fig. 10. The part of the obturator muscle dissected from the ischial plane is lifted in the same direction.

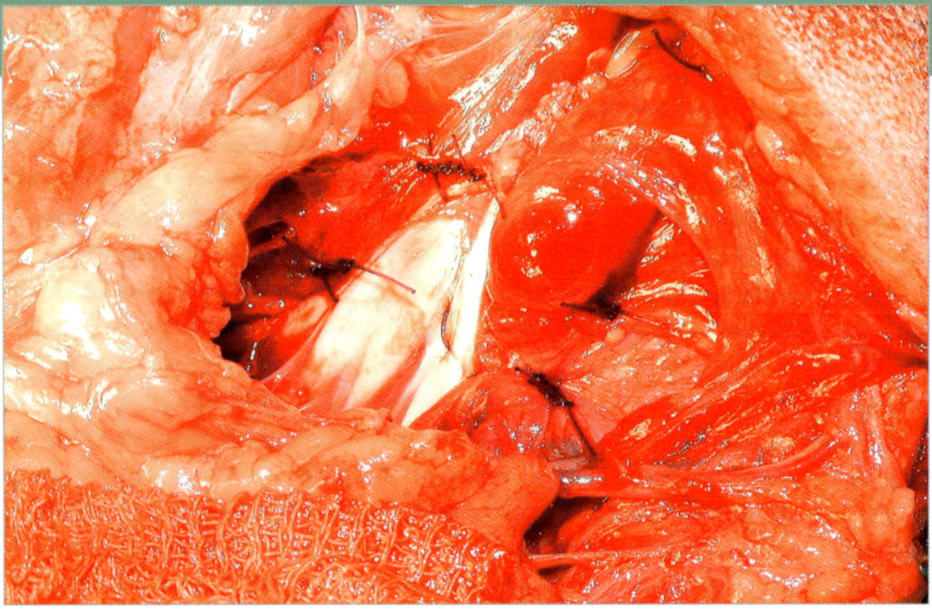

Fig. 11. Both parts of the internal obturator muscle are sutured to the anal sphincter and to the coccygeus muscle.

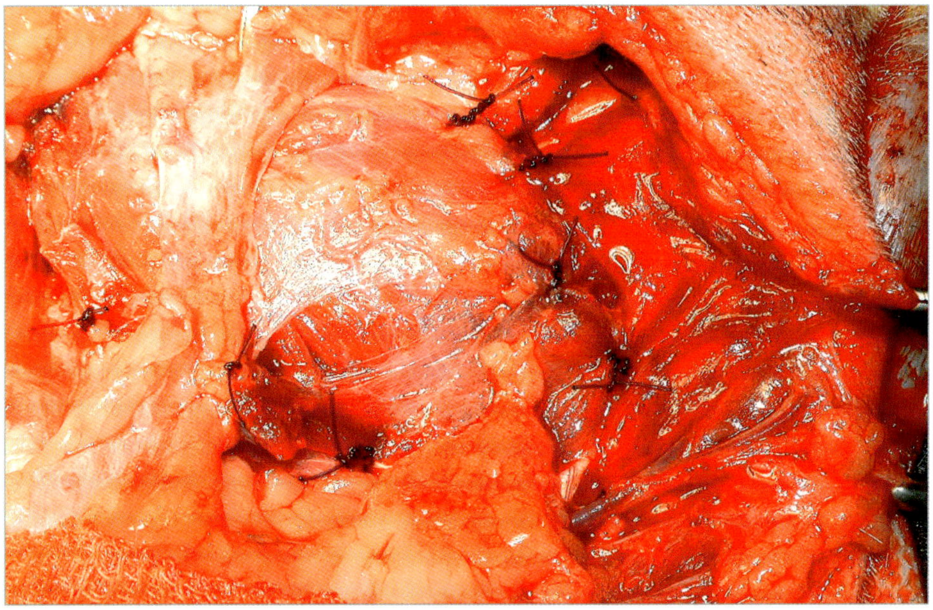

Fig. 12. Next, the superficial gluteal muscle is sutured to the most dorsal part of the external anal sphincter and ventrally, to the transposed obturator muscle.

In order to transpose the internal obturator, it is necessary to section its tendon of insertion. This increases the technical difficulty but allows the closing of large hernial defects.

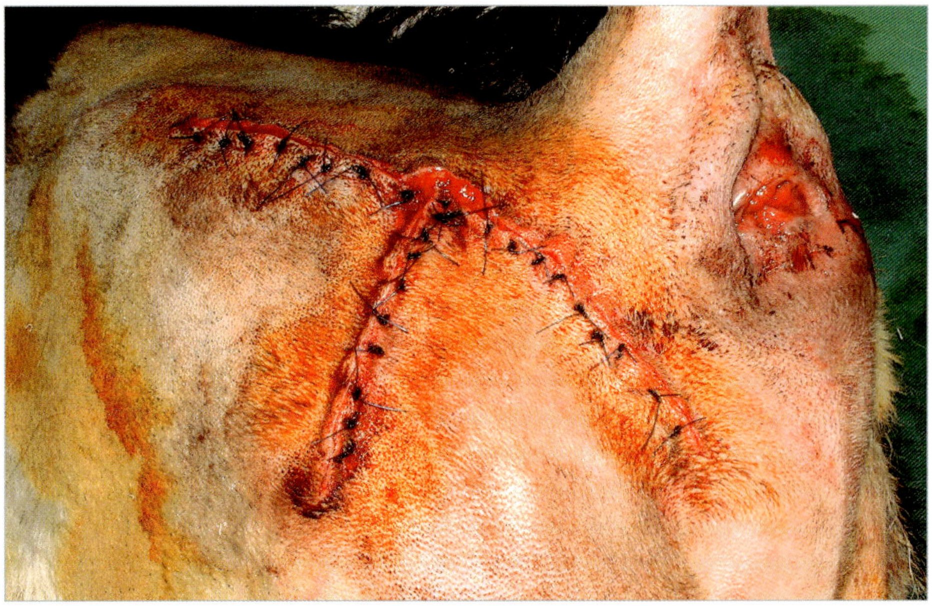

Fig. 13. View of the surgical wound after suturing, showing the T-shaped incision that gives access to the insertion point of the superficial gluteal muscle on the greater trochanter of the femur.

Perineal hernia. Case 5 / Deferensopexy

Technical difficulty	■	■	■	□	□

Hypertrophy of the prostate, a common finding in older dogs, can be a mechanical hindrance to defecation when it is displaced into the pelvis by abdominal straining. As a result, the patient shows tenesmus and chronic constipation. The prostate acts like a battering ram on the pelvic diaphragm during defaecation efforts, thereby contributing, along with other causes already mentioned, to the weakening of the perineal muscles, leading to herniation.

In these cases, the prostate moves into the pelvic canal, dragging the bladder along, a reason why both structures can be contained in the hernia (fig. 1). Reduction of the hernia and repair of the hernial ring are insufficient in these cases to fully prevent recurrence.

On the next pages, the technique of deferensopexy is described. The aim of this technique is to fix the prostate and the bladder in the abdominal cavity, thus preventing their displacement towards the pelvis and recurrence of the hernia.

This technique is complementary to the earlier described techniques of herniorraphy, mesh implantation and muscular transpositions.

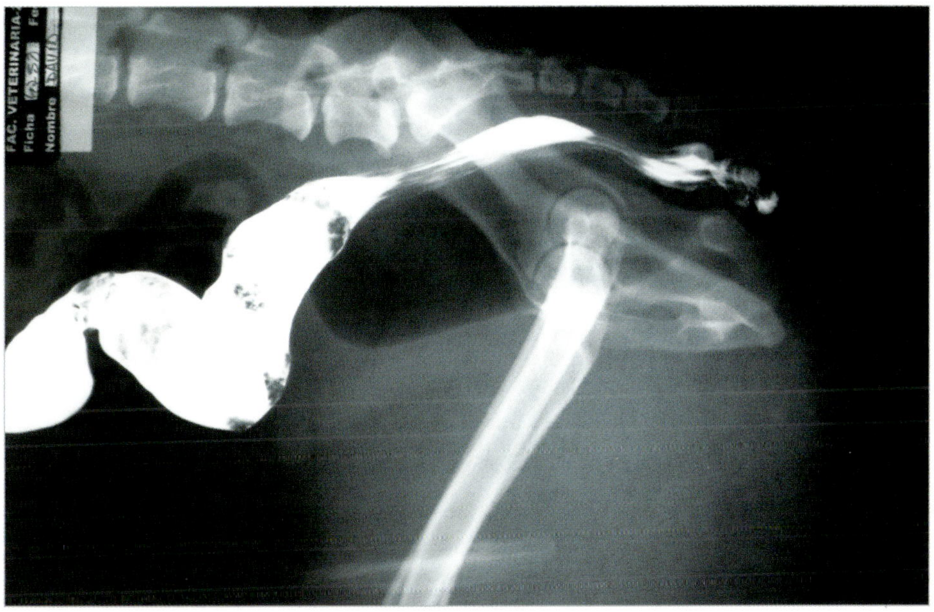

Fig. 1. Lateral radiograph of the abdomen of the patient, showing that the herniated content includes the prostate, which has dragged the bladder in a caudal direction into the pelvic canal. Radiographic examination includes a barium enema and a pneumocystogram.

Deferensopexy is a complementary surgical technique, particularly indicated for perineal hernias that involve the bladder and/or the prostrate.

See castration ➔ *page 264*

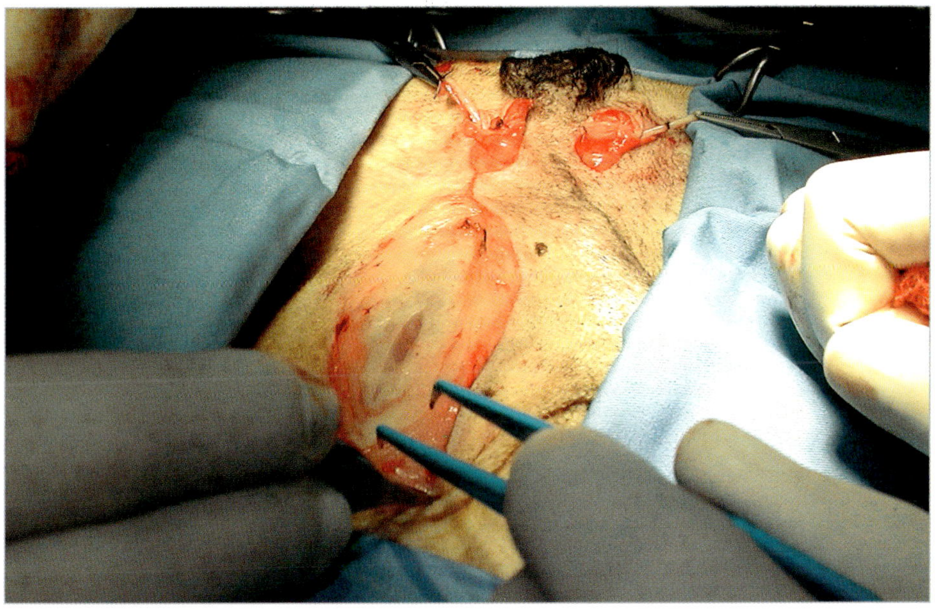

Fig. 2. First, castration is performed, leaving the patient with forceps on the vasa deferentia. Both incisions are left momentarily without sutures. Next, a parapenile laparotomy is performed.

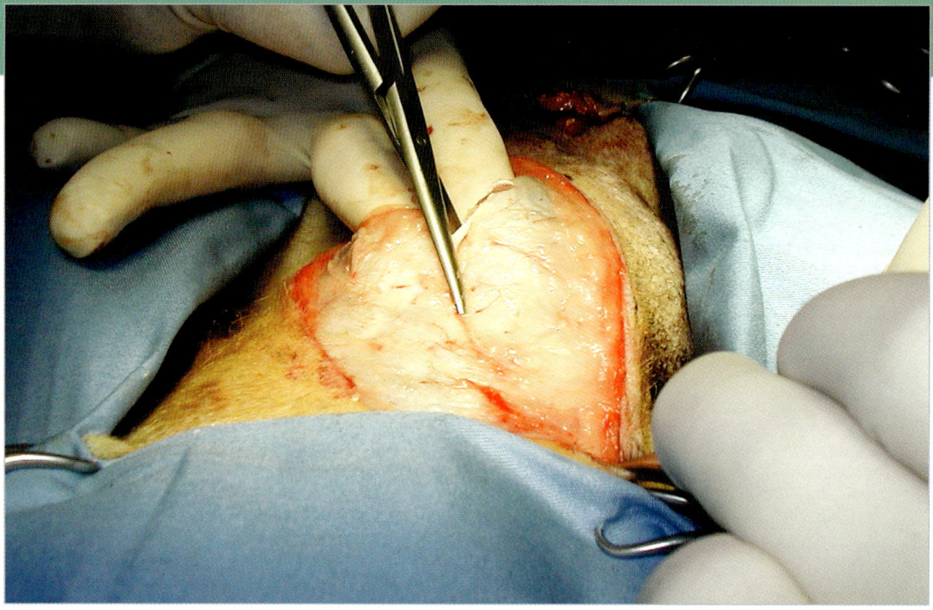

Fig. 3. Laparotomy is performed in the usual way after lateralisation of the penis: via the linea alba and taking care to protect the abdominal organs.

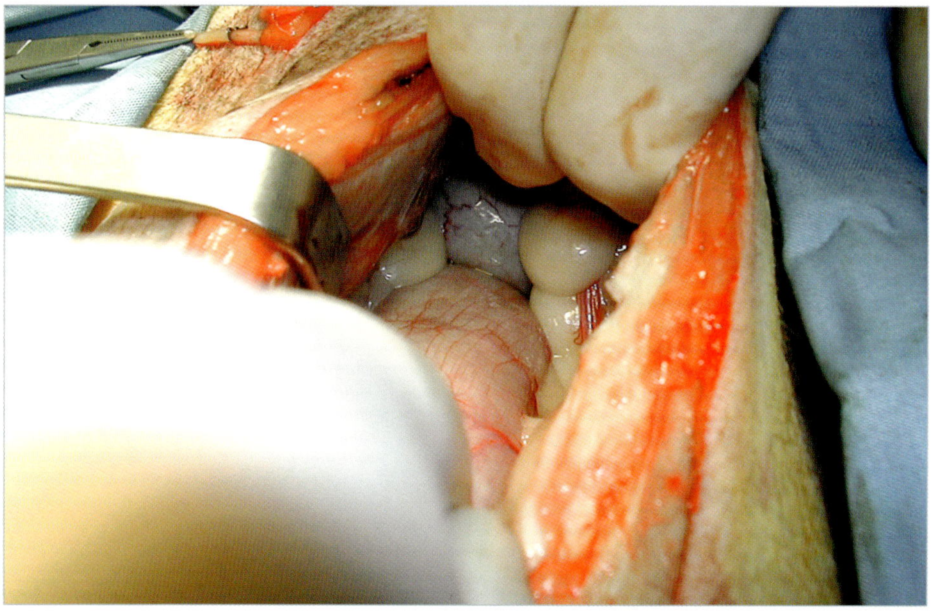

Fig. 4. Once the abdomen is opened, the bladder can be seen. After moving the intestines cranially, the colon can be identified.

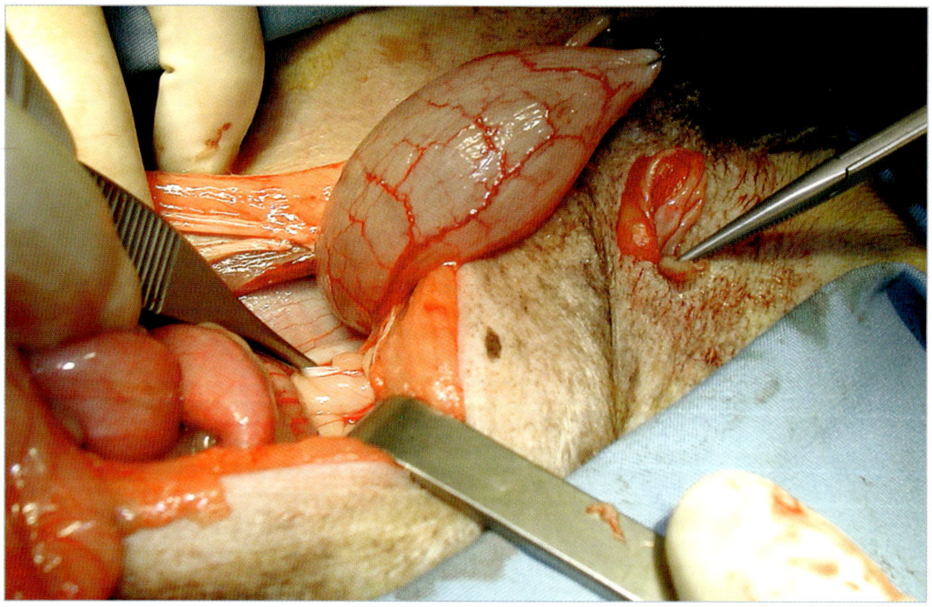

Fig. 5. The bladder is moved caudally in order to locate the vasa deferentia leading to the prostate, crossing the ureters.

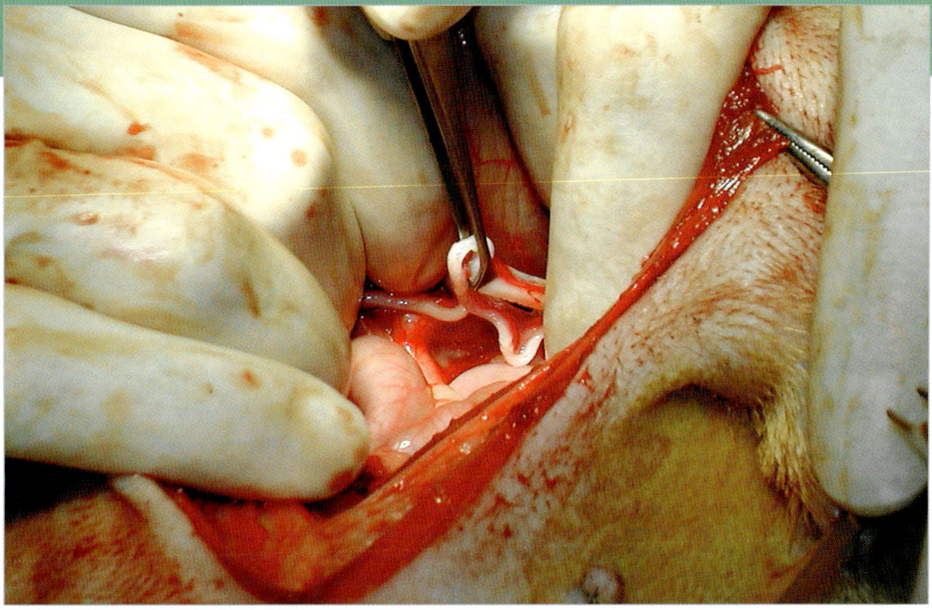

Fig. 6. Once the vasa deferentia are located, the forceps placed during castration are loosened, and one of the ducts is pulled back into the abdominal cavity through the inguinal ring.

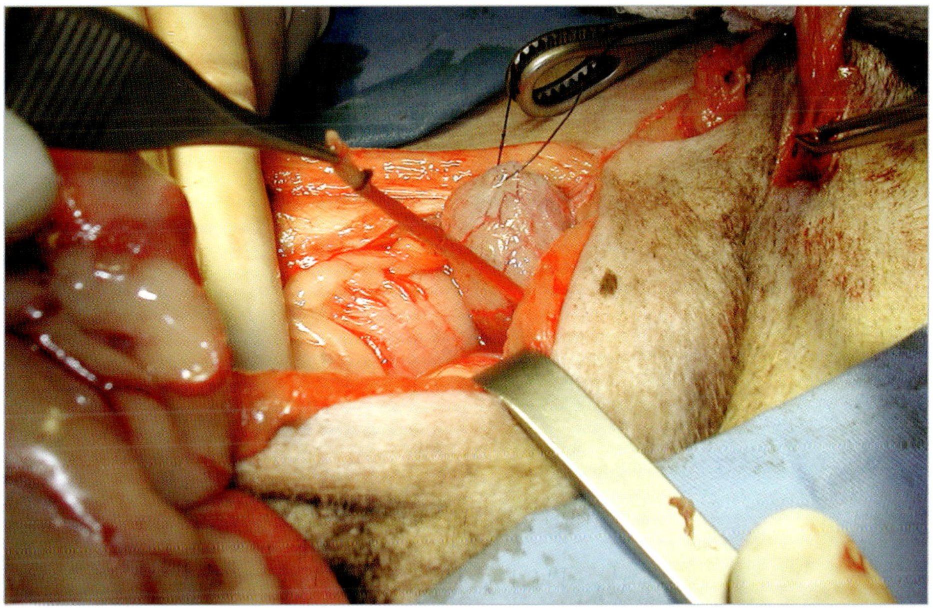

Fig. 7. This picture shows one of the vasa deferentia back in the abdominal cavity. The bladder is kept back with the help of a holding suture and an atraumatic clamp.

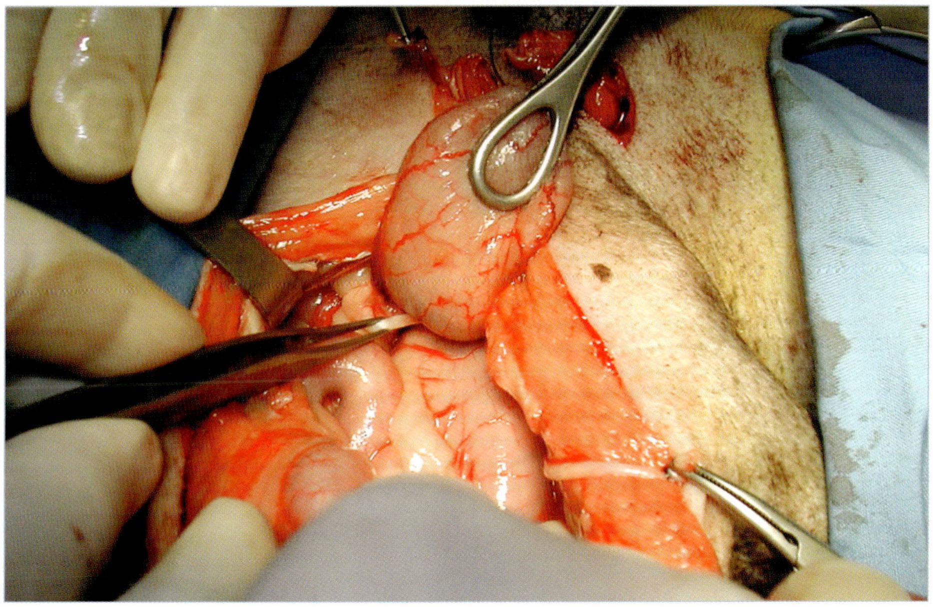

Fig. 8. The first duct is held by forceps to check its location. The same is done with the other duct.

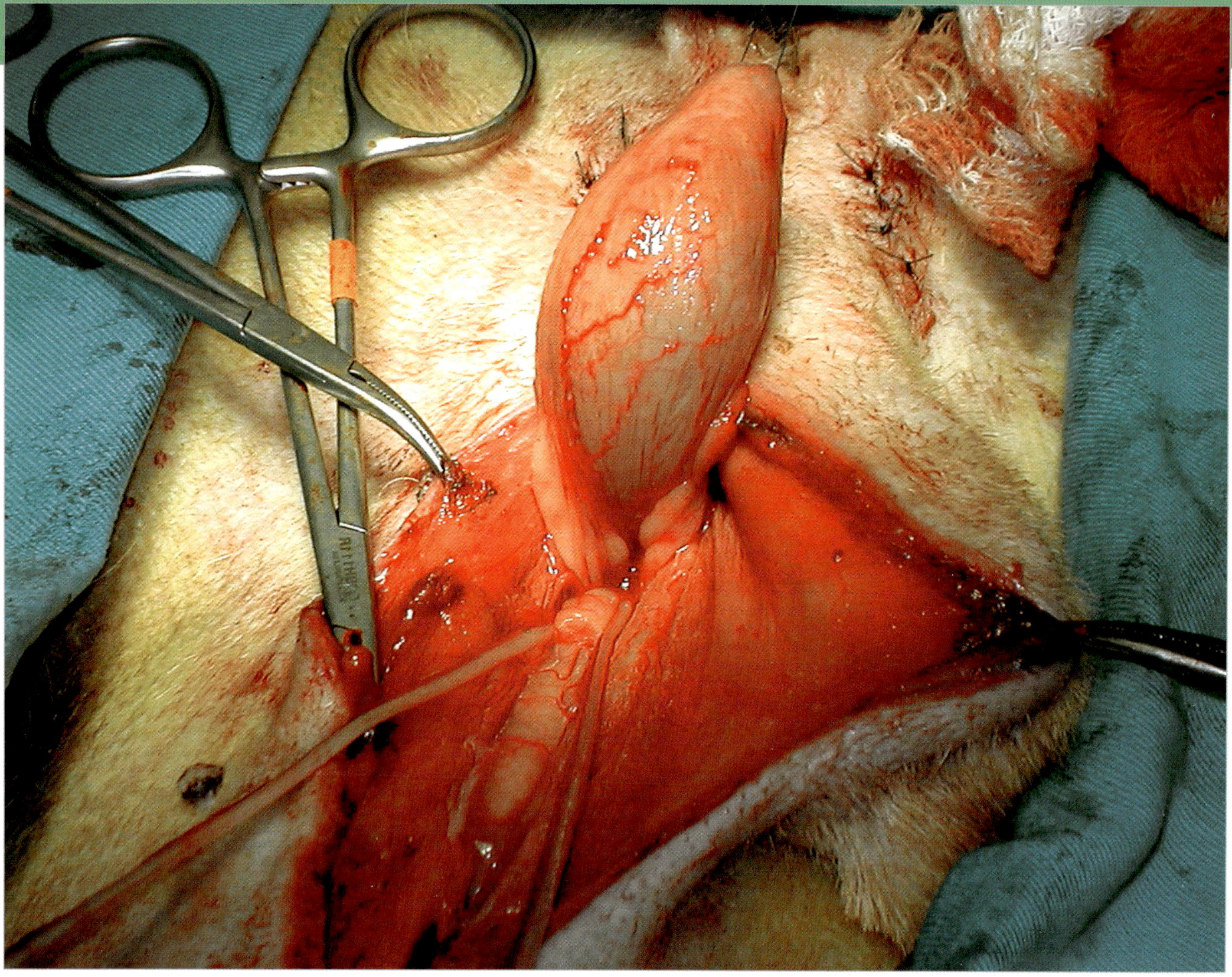

Fig. 9. Both vasa deferentia are clearly visible in the abdomen, attached to the prostate.

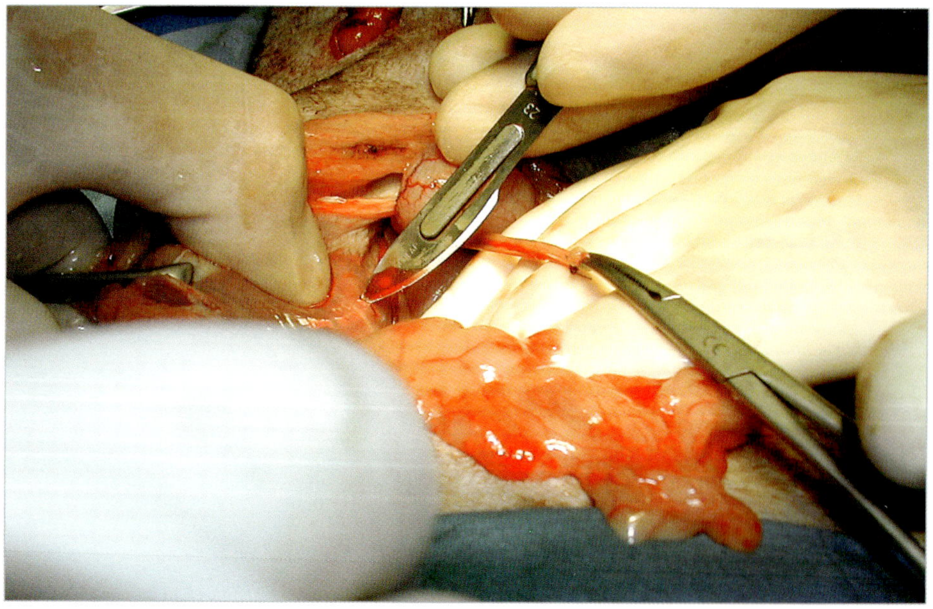

Fig. 10. The aim is to use the two vasa deferentia to fix the prostate in the abdomen, by anchoring them in a tunnel in the abdominal wall. In order to do so, a small incision is made in the lateral abdominal wall, cranial to the bladder.

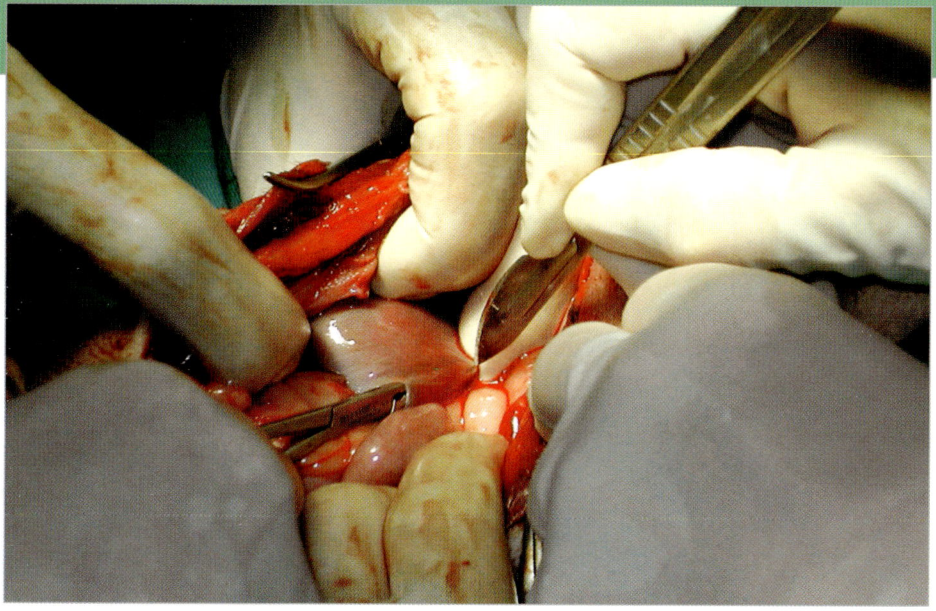

Fig. 11. Mosquito forceps are passed through the incision, thus creating a 1-cm-long tunnel, just under the fascia of the transverse abdominal muscle. The exit point of the mosquito forceps is opened using a scalpel.

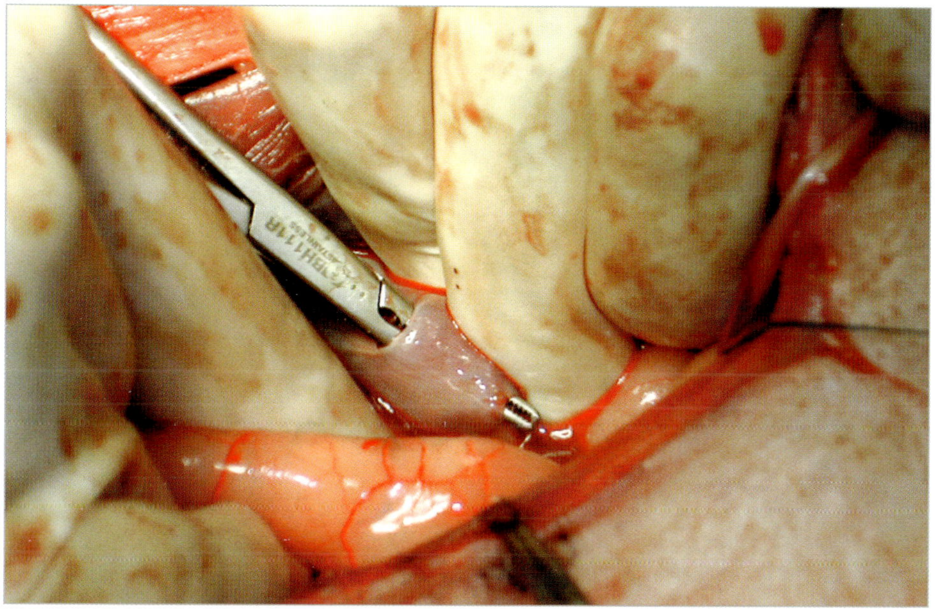

Fig. 12. This picture shows the tunnel, prepared for passage of the vas deferens.

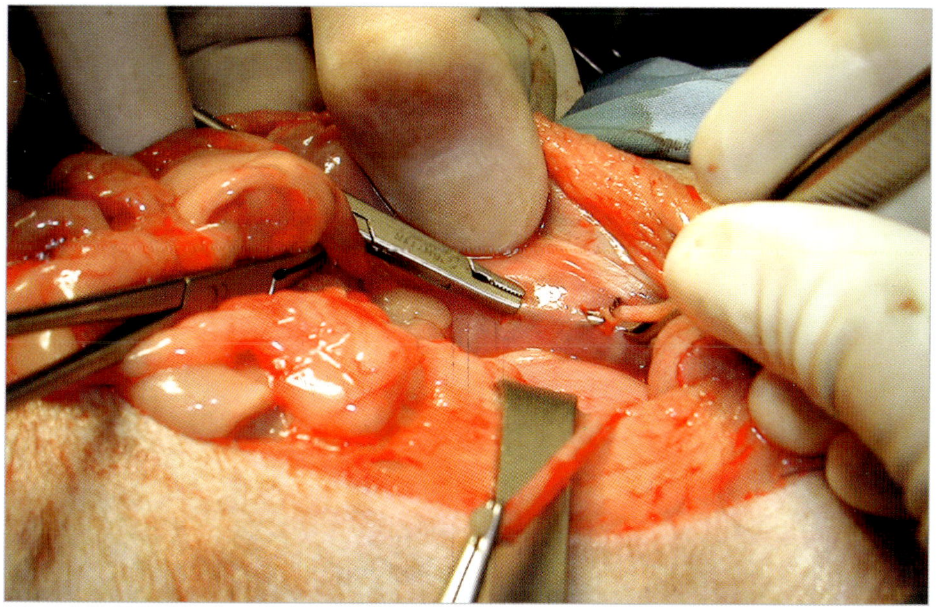

Fig. 13. Using a second pair of mosquito forceps, the vas deferens is passed through the tunnel.

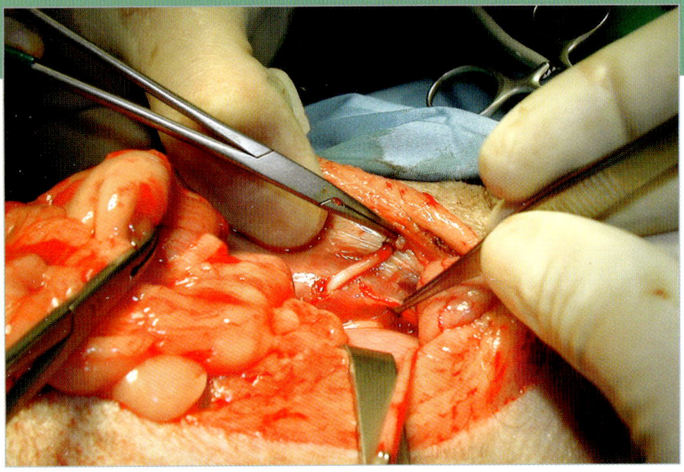

Fig. 14. The vas deferens is pulled in a cranial direction and tightened until the prostate is fixed in the abdominal cavity. Then, the duct is folded back on itself and is attached with a suture.

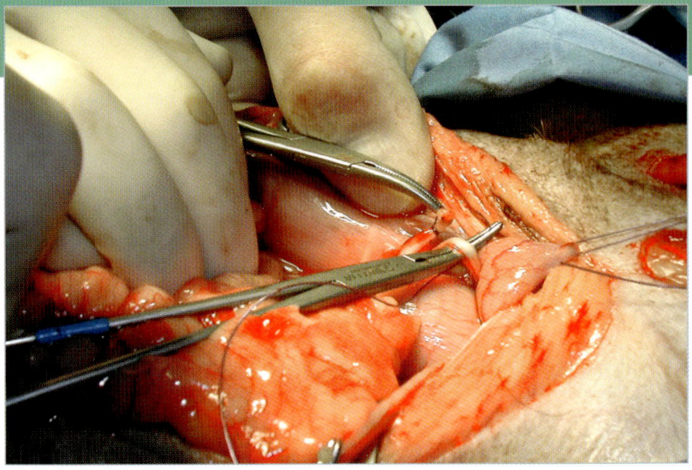

Fig. 15. After folding and fixing the vas deferens, another suture is tied around both segments.

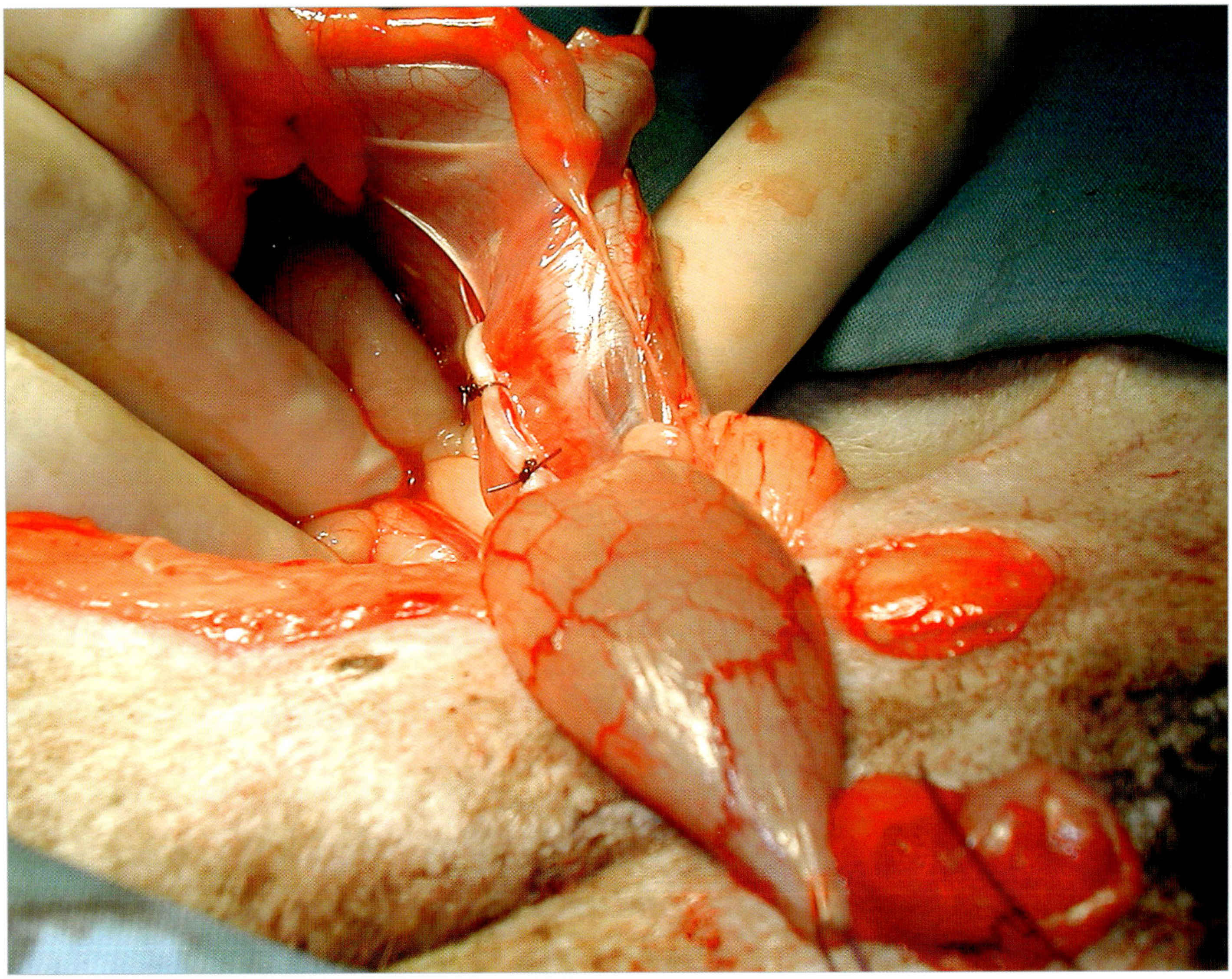

Fig. 16. View of the vas deferens fastened on itself with two sutures. The same technique is used for the duct on the other side.

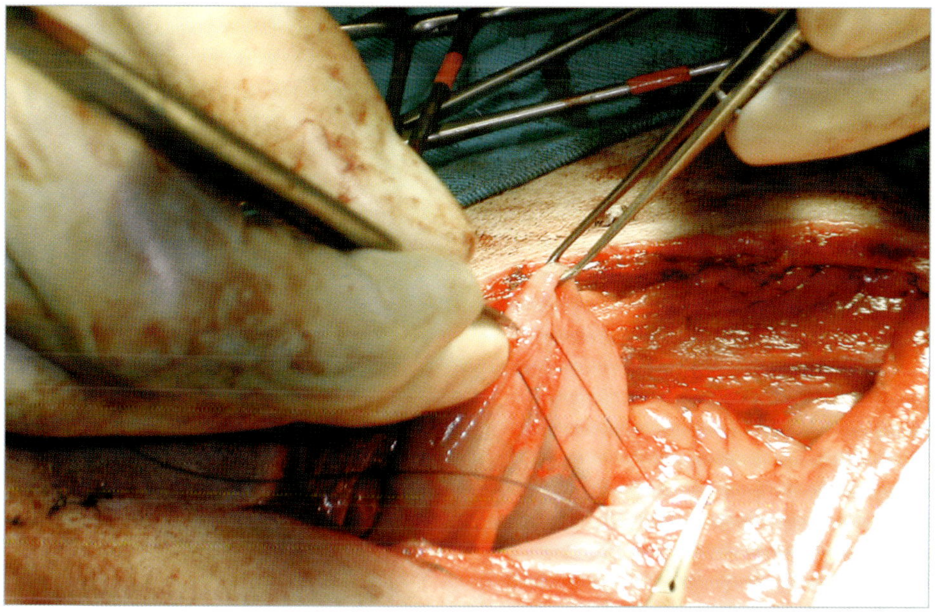

Fig. 17. Deferensopexy ensures that the prostate cannot be displaced into the pelvic canal or drag the bladder with it, but it does not prevent the bladder from retroflexing. To avoid this possibility, a cystopexy can be performed.

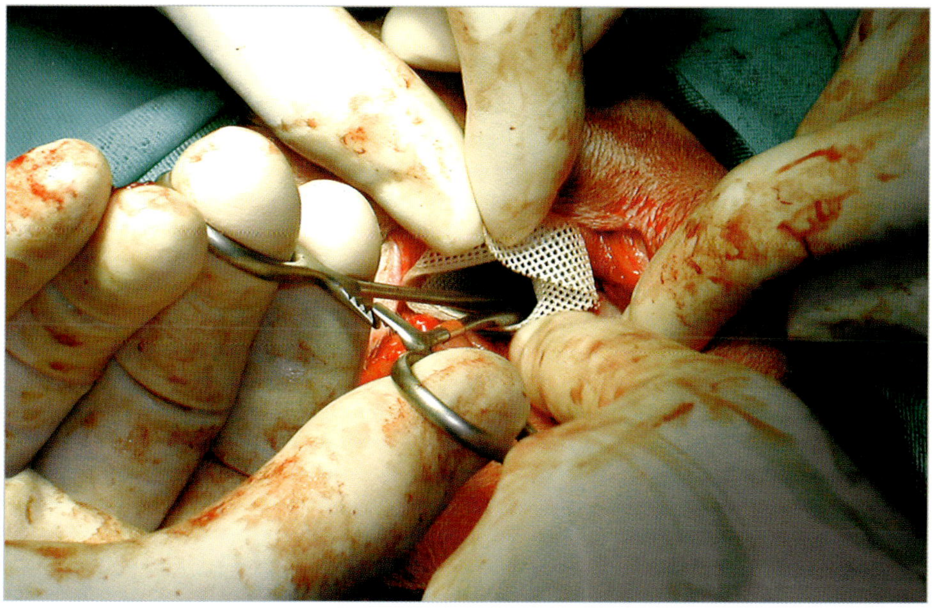

To complement deferensopexy, it may be advisable to perform a cystopexy, which fixes the bladder in its anatomical position and prevents retroflexion.

Fig. 18. Once the abdominal cavity is closed, the patient is placed in sternal recumbency, with the rear end elevated in order to close the hernial ring with one of the techniques described.
In this case, it was decided to use a cone-shaped polypropylene mesh implant.

Perineal area of the female dog

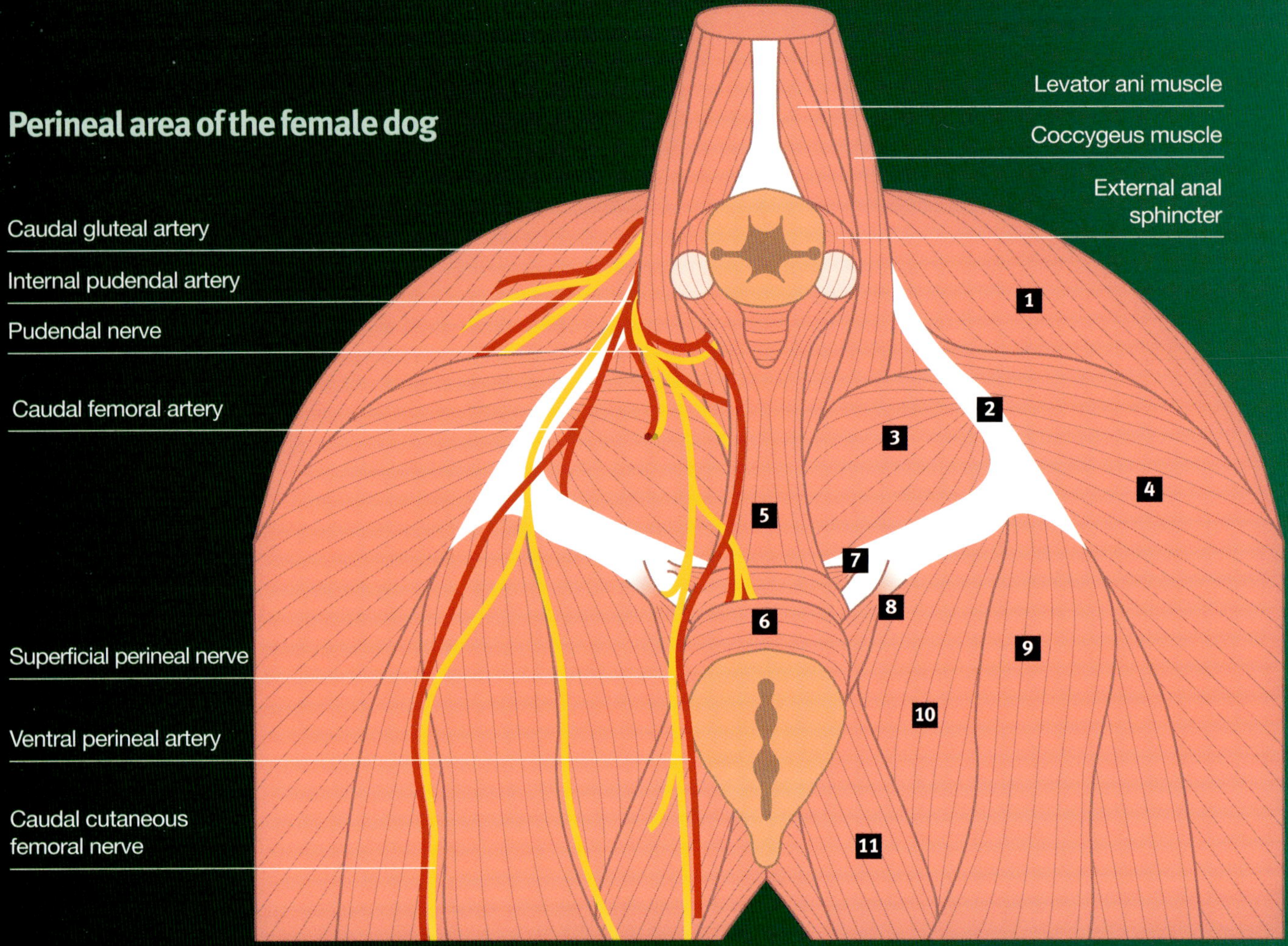

Perineal area of the male dog

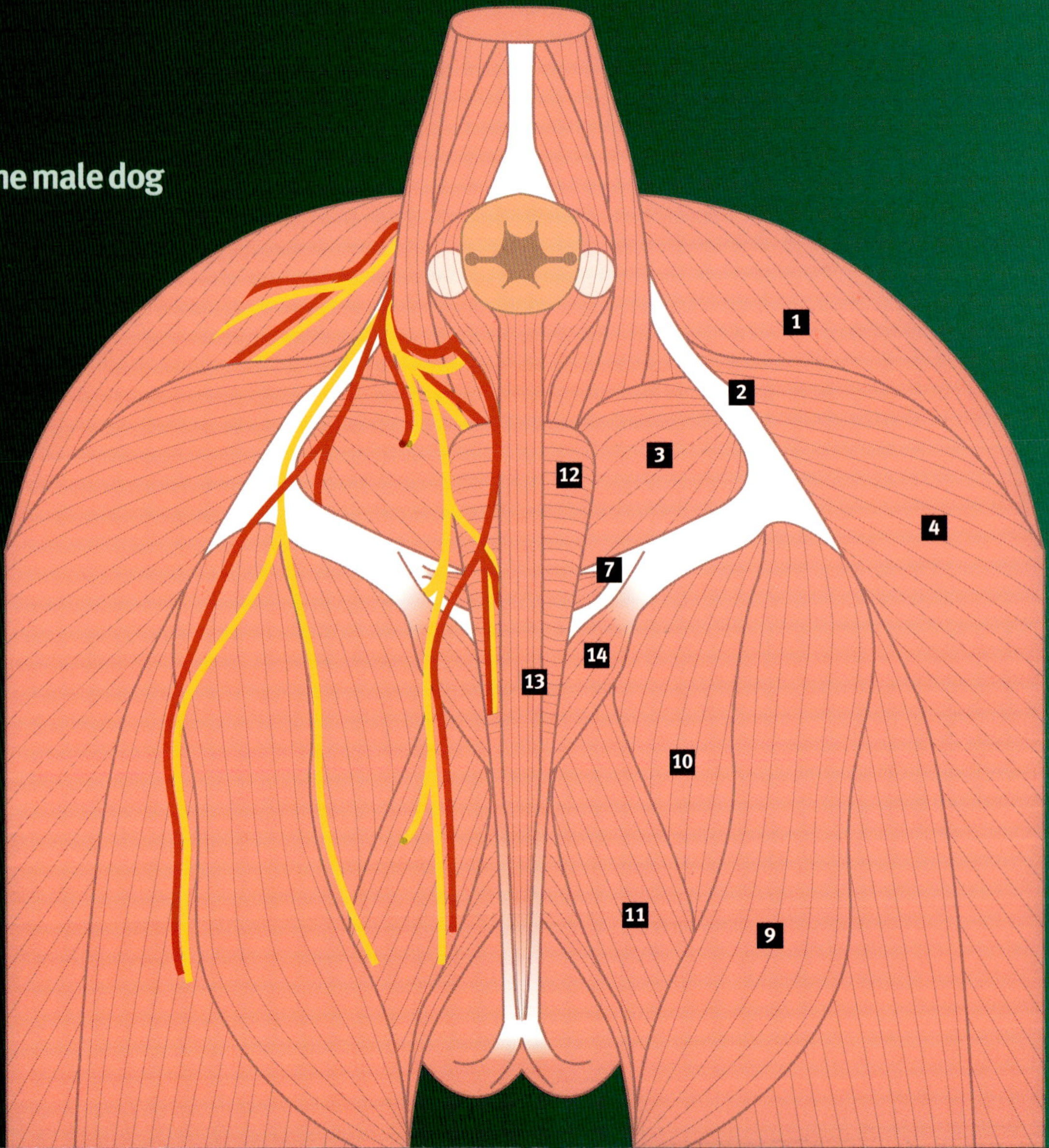

Horizontal dorsal transverse section at the level of the anal sacs in the dog

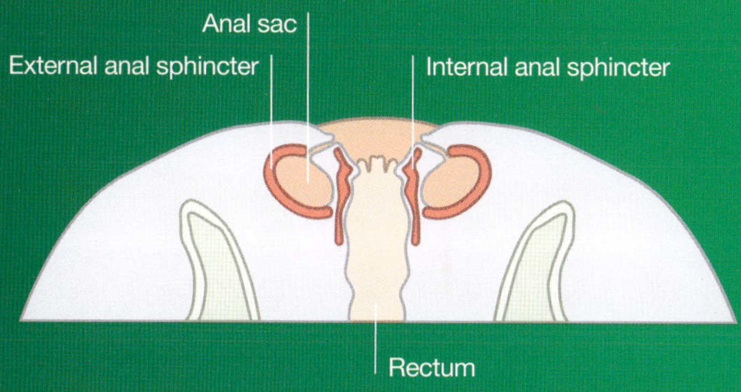

Anal region of the dog, lateral view

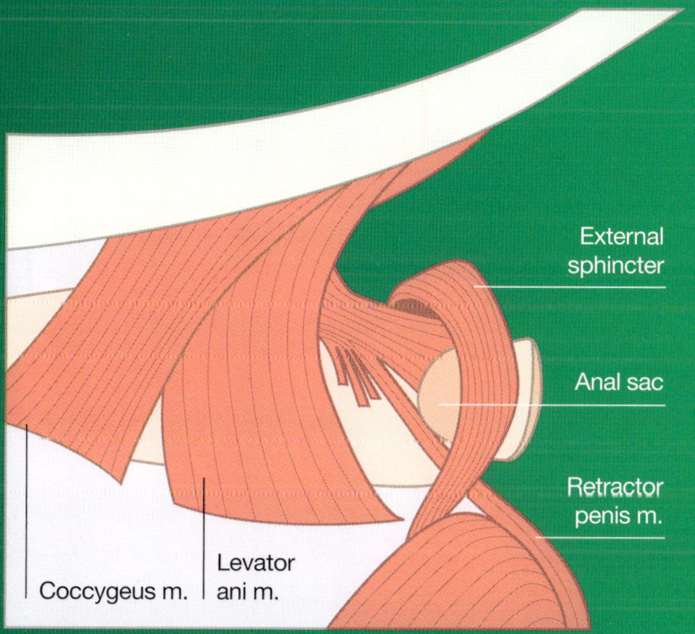

1 Superficial gluteal m.
2 Sacrotuberous ligament
3 Internal obturator m.
4 Biceps femoris m.
5 Perineal muscles
6 Mm. constrictor vulvae and vestibuli
7 Ischiourethral m.
8 Retractor clitoridis m.
9 Semitendinosus m.
10 Semimembranosus m.
11 Gracilis m.
12 Bulbospongiosus m.
13 Retractor penis m.
14 Ischiocavernosus m.

Anus

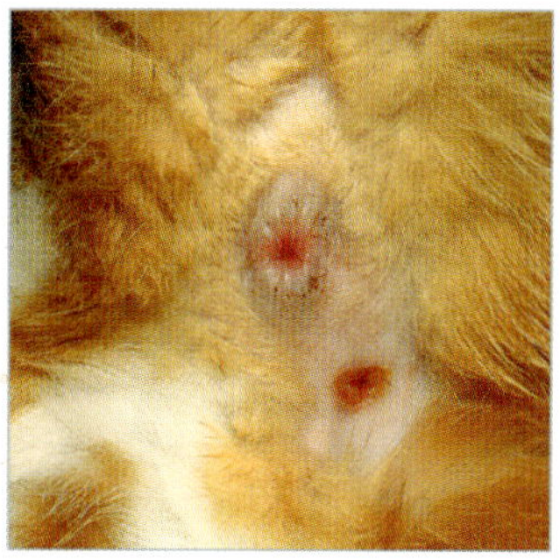

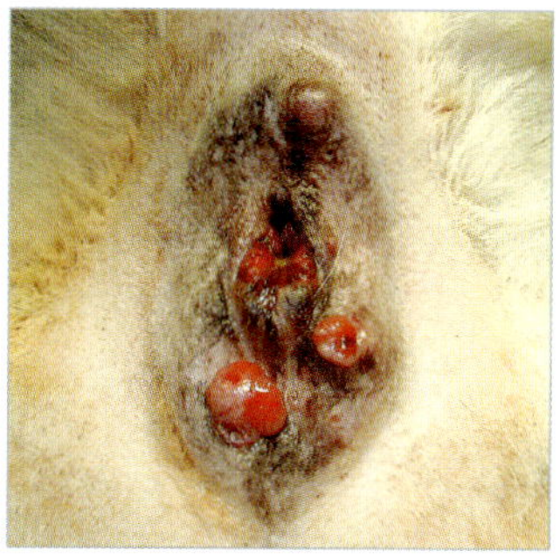

Anal sacculitis

Prevalence

Sacculitis is the inflammation and infection of the anal sacs.
It is a very common disorder, affecting around 10% of dogs, small breeds in particular.

The anal sacs are located at either side of the anus, between the internal and external anal sphincters. They act as reservoirs for the secretions of the apocrine and sebaceous glands.

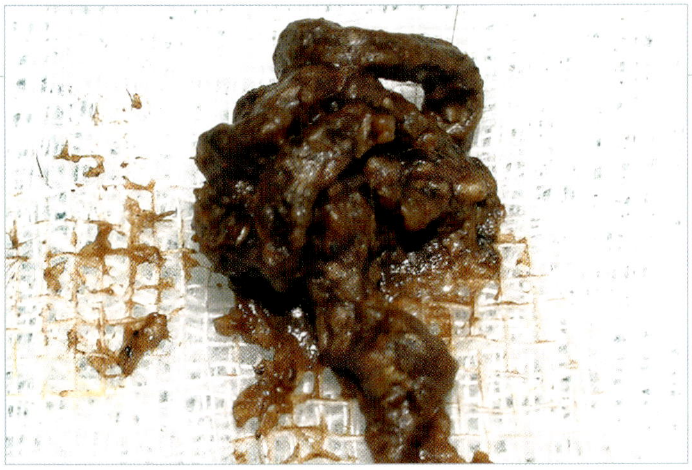

Fig. 1. Manually expressed contents from the anal sac of a cat with typical signs of sacculitis.

Aetiology

The aetiology of sacculitis is not clearly defined. It is associated with inappropriate food, soft stools, lack of exercise, functional changes of the anal sphincter, perianal fistulas... In fact, any situation where there is incorrect emptying of the anal sacs during defaecation will lead to infection of the contents.

Clinical signs

- Pruritus of the area:
  - Scooting, rubbing the anus against the floor.
  - Licking and even self-mutilation of the anal area.
- Pain.
- Tenesmus.
- Dyschezia.
- Haematochezia.
- Perianal inflammation.
- Thick, malodorous, haemorrhagic or purulent content (fig. 1).
- Perianal fistula(s) (figs. 2 and 3).

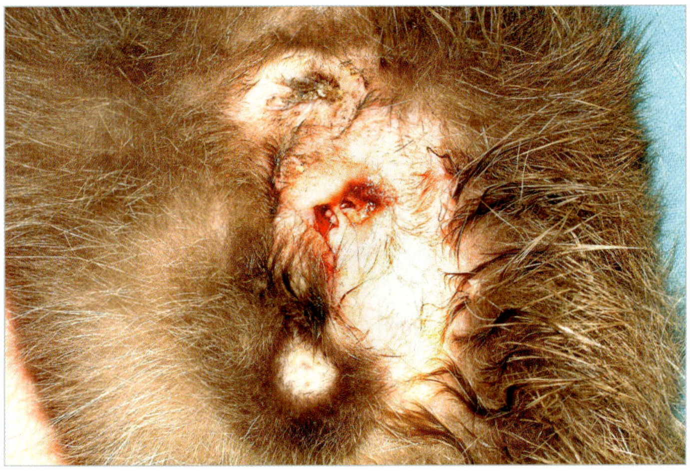

Fig. 2. Perianal fistula at 5 o'clock due to an abscess of the right anal sac.

Anal sacculitis could be one of the causes of perianal fistulas in breeds like the German Shepherd.

The anal sacs should be palpated and emptied during any routine physical examination, allowing the detection of any changes at an early stage.

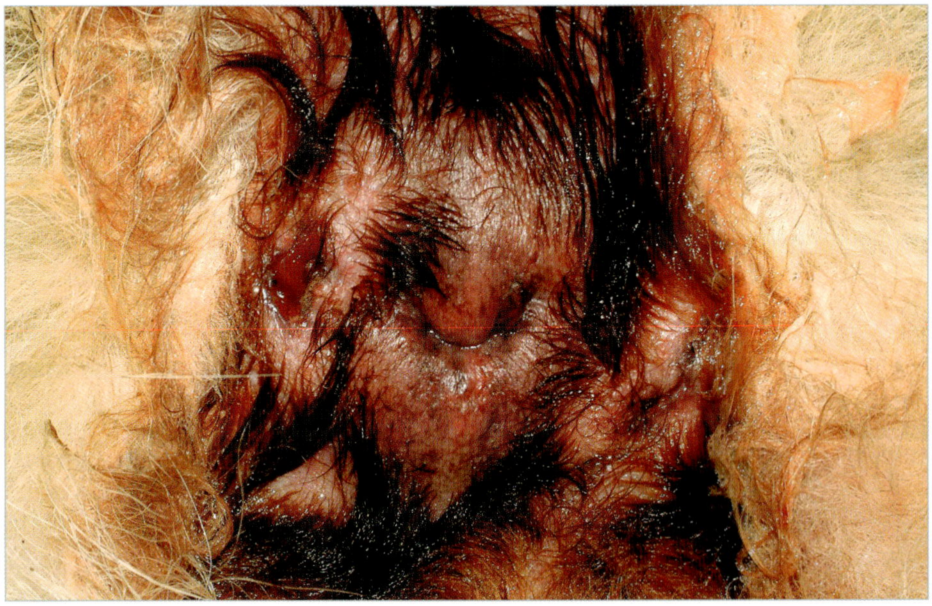

Fig. 3. In certain large breeds, the anal sacs are located deeper. If these become infected and rupture, they cause a diffuse cellulitis around the anus and several fistular tracts.

Anal sacculitis. Case 1 / Preventive treatment

A simple impaction can be treated by emptying the anal sacs by manual pressure.
In dogs, the third (middle) finger is inserted in the anus to carry out rectal palpation, focusing on the sides of the anal sphincter (at 4-5 and 7-8 o'clock) (fig. 1). Both sacs are emptied by squeezing the sacs in the direction of the anal opening (fig. 2).

> ***Do not squeeze too hard, as the sac may rupture.***
> ***Take care that the content does not end up on your coat.***

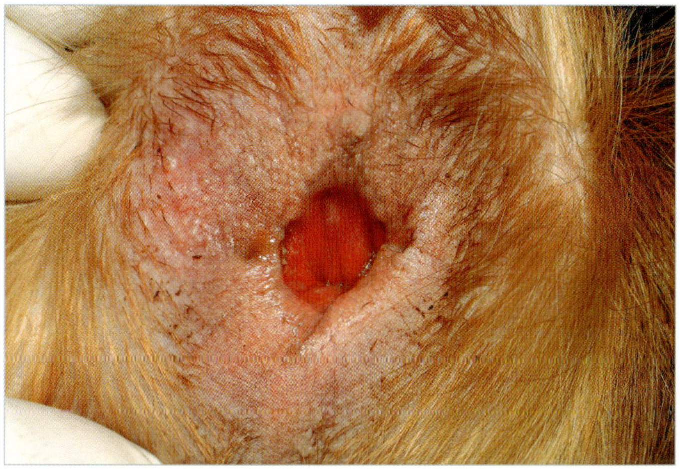

Fig. 1. Identification of the orifices of the anal sacs. In this case, their opening is more dorsal than usual.

In miniature breeds, in cats and in animals in which rectal palpation is not possible, apply pressure to empty the sacs from the outside, squeezing the sac through the skin (fig. 3).
It is also indicated to flush the sacs with saline at room temperature in order to clean them mechanically. In case of infection and intense local inflammation, besides emptying the anal sacs, they should be flushed using lukewarm saline and a 10% povidone iodine or a 0.5% chlorhexidine solution.
In case of an abscess, a local antibiotic/anti-inflammatory ointment should be prescribed, and in severe cases, systemic treatment should also be given. Recommend increasing the fibre in the diet to facilitate the emptying of the anal sacs.

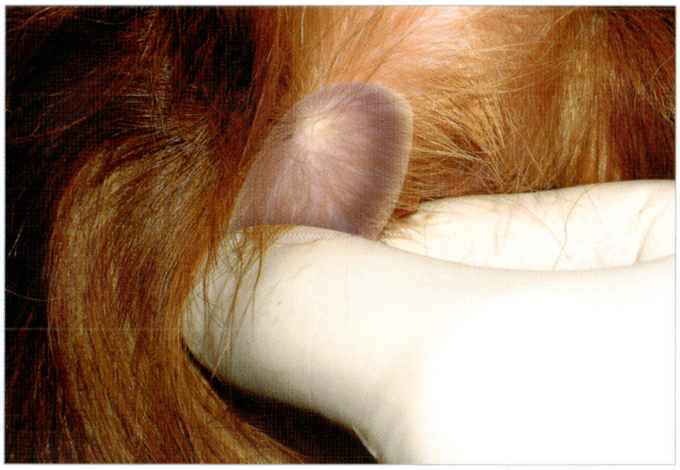

Fig. 2. Emptying the anal sac by squeezing from its most internal part.

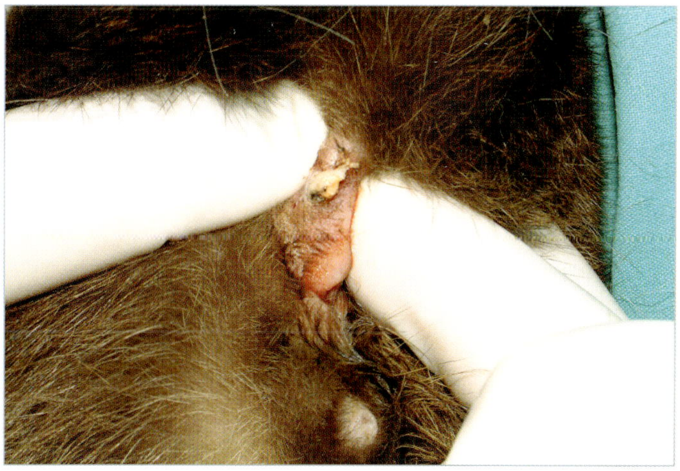

Fig. 3. Emptying the right anal gland using external digital pressure.

Anal sacculitis. Case 2 / Medical treatment

"Sam" is a castrated male European cat, brought for consultation because he cannot stop licking his rear end, which is also bleeding.
During the clinical examination, no systemic changes are found, but in the perineal area, a discharge can be seen to the lower right of the anus (fig. 1).

The patient is sedated and the area is cleaned mechanically with saline and a watery solution of povidone iodine diluted to 50%.
An antibiotic/anti-inflammatory ointment is prescribed, to be applied by the owner twice daily, first in the fistula and then in the anus.
In this case, no systemic antibiotics were necessary.

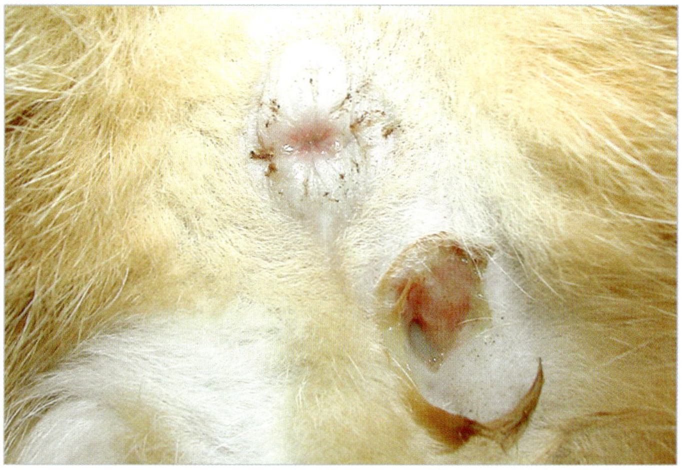

Fig. 1. To the lower right of the anus, there is a large fistulous area, with a purulent secretion.

Don't forget to remind the owners that the patient must wear an Elizabethan collar to prevent licking of the area.

Follow-up

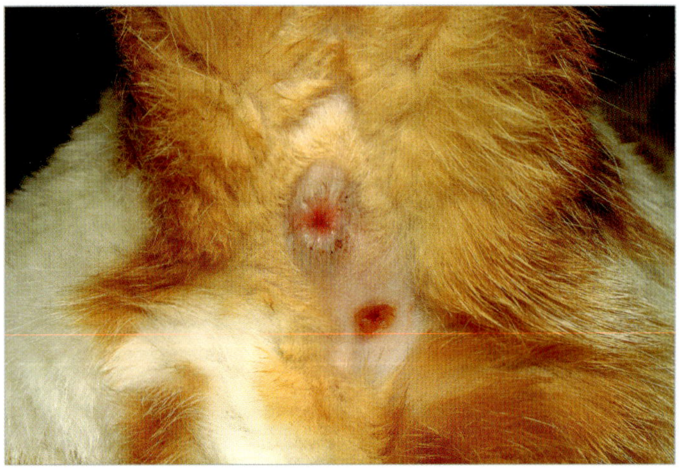

Fig. 2. After seven days of treatment, the prognosis is favourable.
The infection is under control and healing of the area is satisfactory.

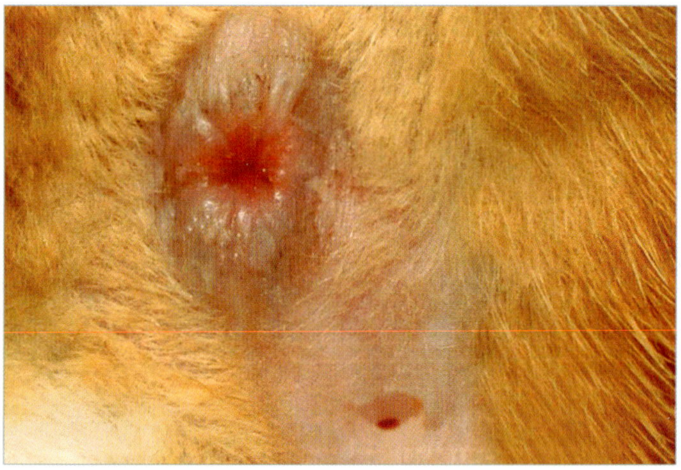

Fig. 3. After 10 days of treatment, the fistula is closed and the ointment no longer needs to be applied.

Anal sacculitis. Case 3 / Surgical treatment: closed sacculectomy

Technical difficulty

Sacculectomy, resection of the anal sacs, is performed in cases of recurrent sacculitis.

The patient documented on the following pages suffered from recurrent bilateral sacculitis and the owner elected surgery to solve the problem once and for all.

Anatomical reminder

The anal sac is located between the muscular fibres of the anal sphincter, near the rectum, with branches of the caudal rectal artery and vein medially, and in close proximity to the branches of the pudendal nerve that innervate the anus.

Before surgery

- Empty the rectum.
- Do not use laxatives in the 24 hours prior to surgery.
- Empty the anal sacs.
- Shave and prepare the surgical area aseptically.

Surgical technique

In order to minimize postoperative complications with this technique, it should not be performed while the sacs are inflamed and infected.

Even if the problem is unilateral, removal of both anal sacs is recommended to prevent similar problems developing on the other side in the future.

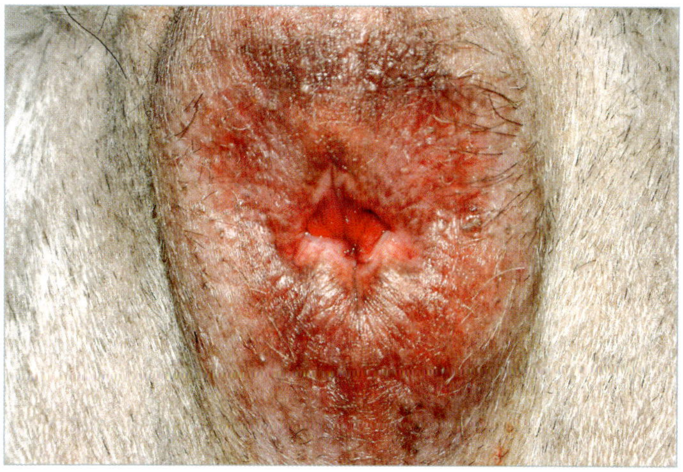

Fig. 1. Preparation of the operative field

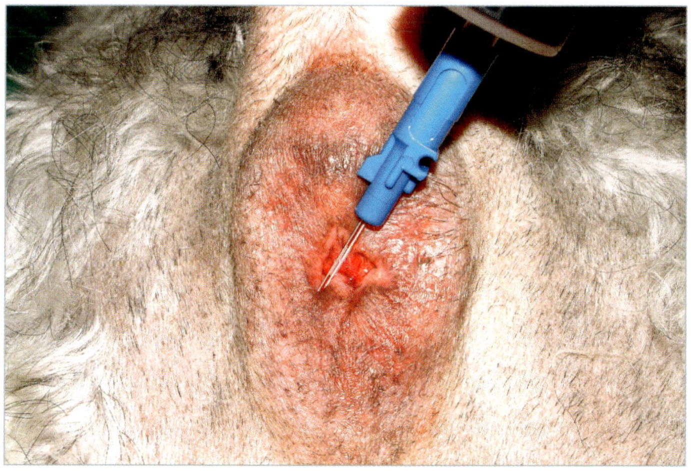

Fig. 2. After emptying the anal sacs, they should be flushed with an antiseptic solution (povidone iodine or chlorhexidine), to avoid secondary contamination in case the sac ruptures during dissection.

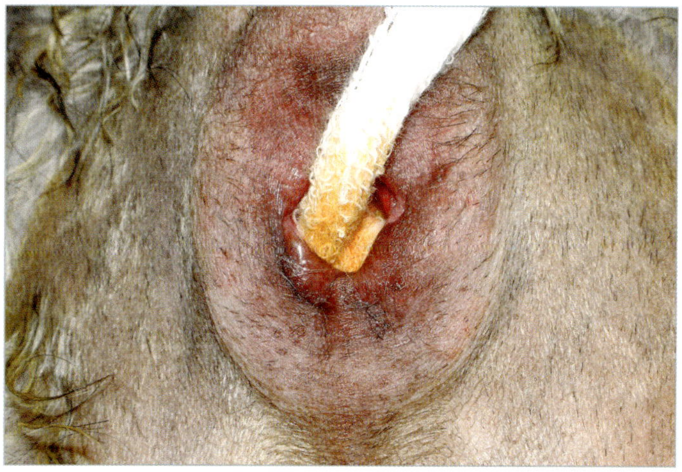

Fig. 3. A plug of gauze soaked in antiseptic is placed in the rectum to disinfect the area and to avoid the expulsion of faeces during surgery. The patient is placed in sternal recumbency on the operating table.

See positioning of the patient → page 248

During surgery

- Proceed in the least traumatic way and take extreme care, in particular in the deep areas, to avoid trauma to the vessels and nerves that supply and innervate the anus.
- Flush the tissues regularly with saline to stop them from drying out.

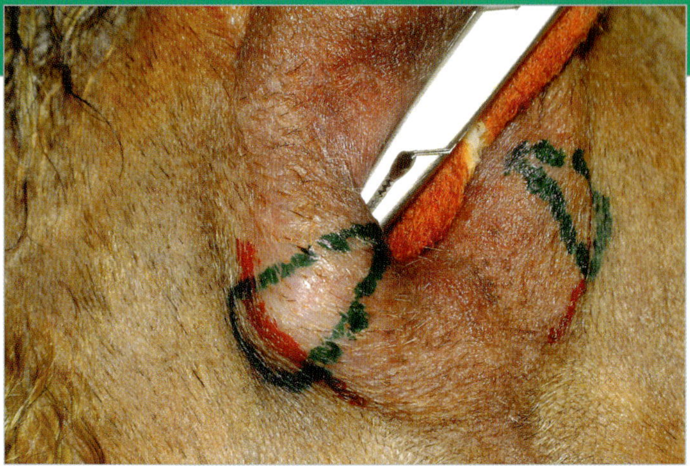

Fig. 4. The anal sacs are marked in green and the incision in red. In this case, haemostatic forceps have been introduced to demonstrate the left sac.

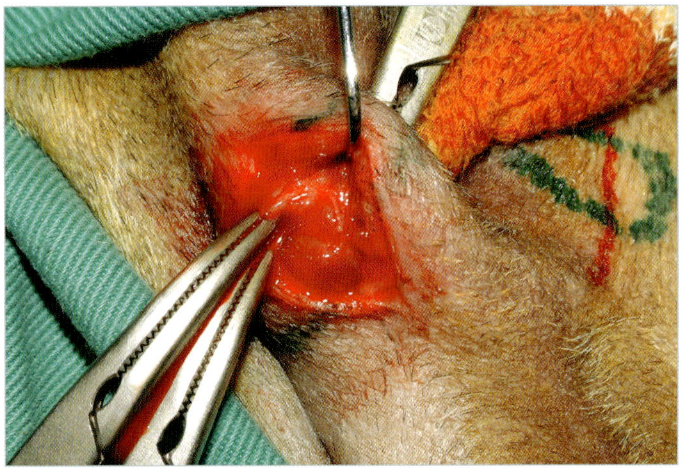

Fig. 5. The skin incision is parallel to the fibres of the anal sphincter. Haemostasis is achieved by clamping bleeding vessels with haemostats or by bipolar coagulation.

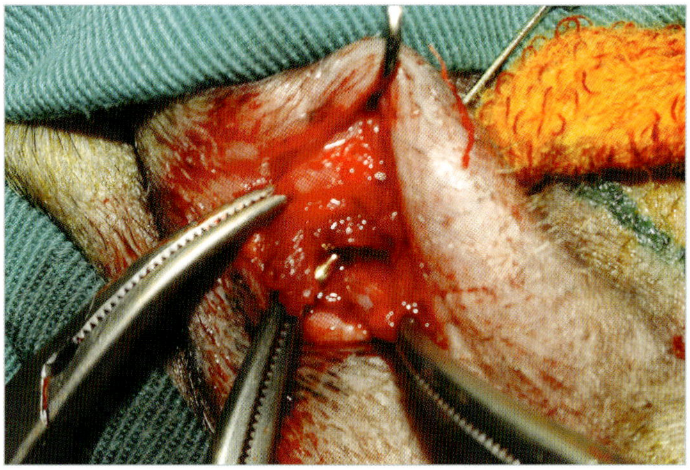

Fig. 6. During dissection of the anal sac, accidental rupture is possible. If the sac ruptures, great care should be taken to remove all tissue as any remaining sac tissue could produce recurring fistulas.

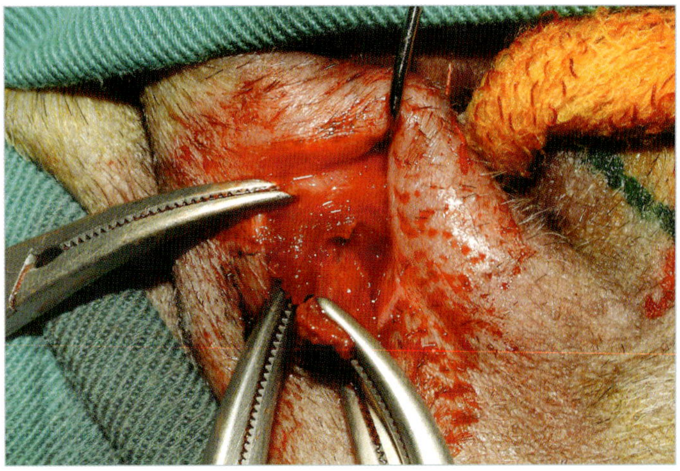

Fig. 7. Handle the anal sac gently and dissect it from the muscular fibres until it is only attached by its duct.

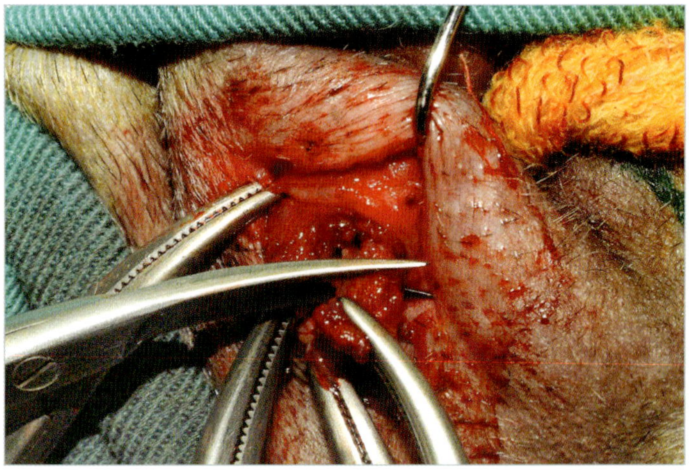

Fig. 8. Once the anal sac is isolated, its duct should be ligated with absorbable suture material, as close as possible to the anal orifice. It is then sectioned with scissors and removed.

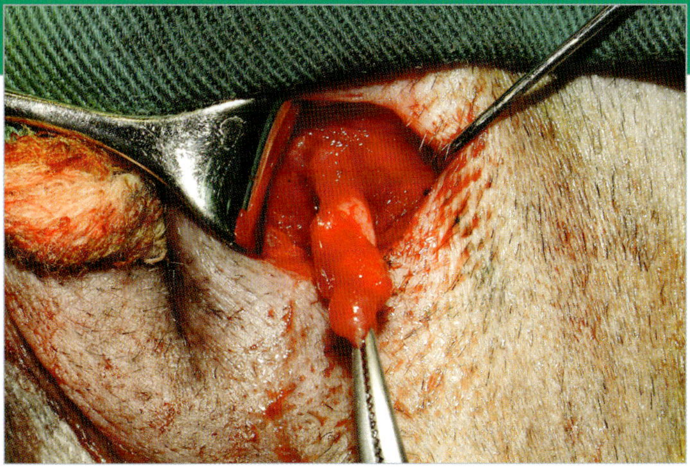

Fig. 9. Repeat the same steps on the other side. In this case, the right anal sac was less attached to the anal sphincter, and its resection was easier and quicker.

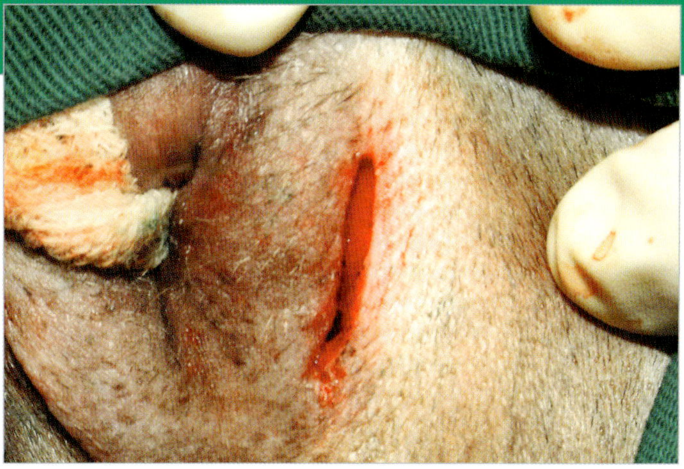

Fig. 10. The incisions are rinsed with saline and the sectioned muscles are closed with a continuous suture using absorbable 4/0 suture material.

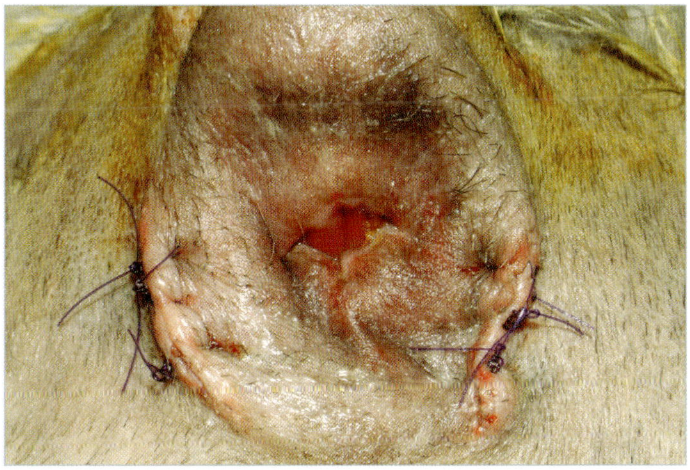

Fig. 11. The skin wound is closed with vertical mattress sutures of monofilament non-absorbable 3/0 suture material.

Avoid monopolar coagulation, which can cause significant tissue damage and excessive scar fibrosis.

Inflammation and recurrent infections of the anal sacs lead to extensive fibrosis and adhesions within the fibres of the anal sphincter. This makes dissection more difficult and increases the risk of perforation.

Extreme care is required when dissecting the cranial part of the sac, since it should be remembered that this area contains vessels and nerves that are important for the correct functioning of the anus.

After surgery

- Elizabethan collar to prevent the patient licking the area.
- Systemic antibiotic treatment for 3 or 4 days if there are no infectious complications.
- Regular cleaning of the area with soap and water.
- Prescribe medication that softens the stools to facilitate defaecation.

Inform the owner that temporary faecal incontinence may occur (lasting less than a week).

Laxatives	Dog	Cat
Lactulose	1 ml/4.5 kg/8 h PO	5 ml PO
Bisacodyl	5-20 mg PO 1 to 3 times daily	2.5-5 mg PO 1 to 3 times daily

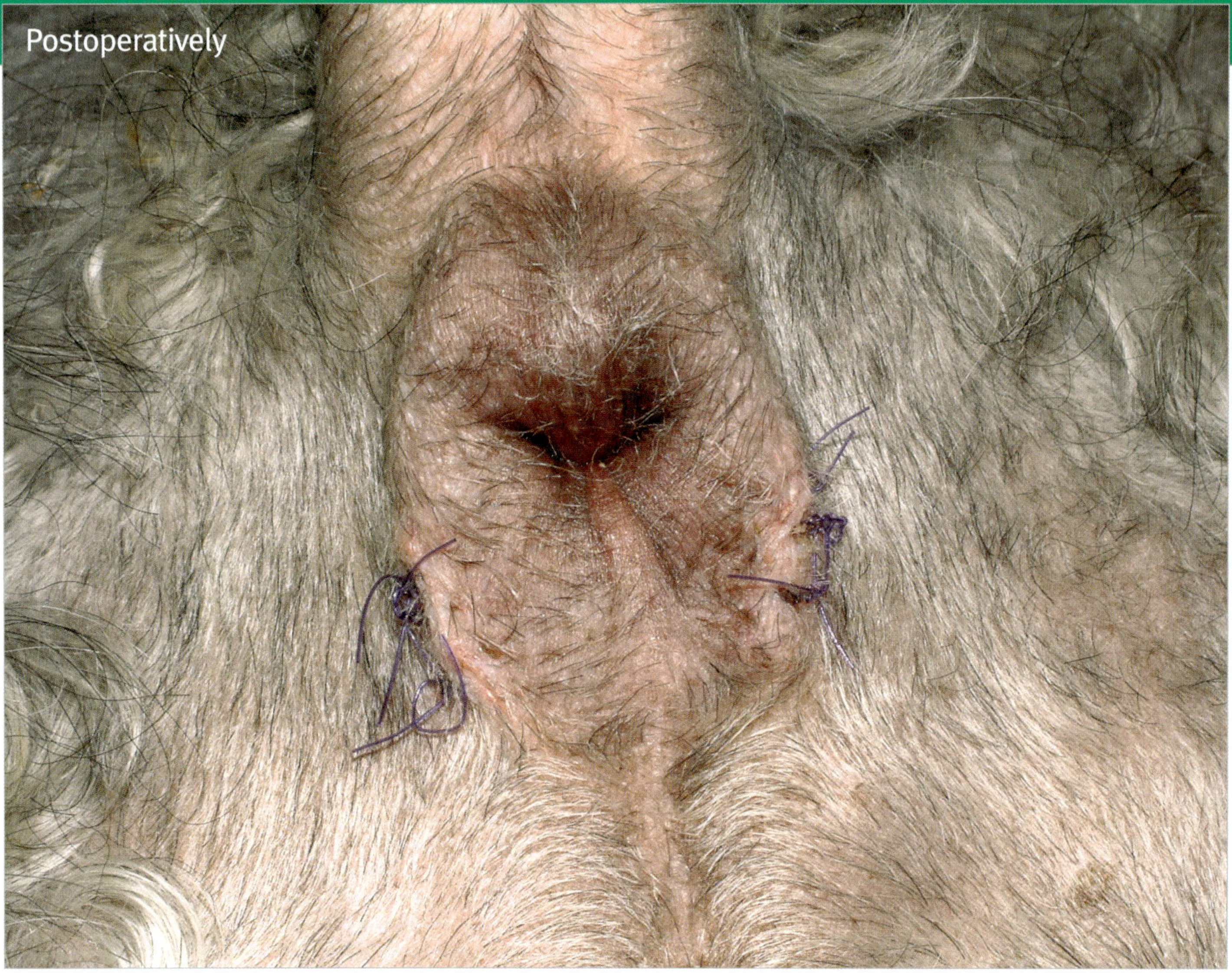

Fig. 12. If these steps and recommendations are followed, postoperative inflammation and infection, if any, will be minimal. On day 8, the sutures are removed and the treatment is complete.

Complications are common in the case of inexperienced or excessively aggressive surgeons.

Complications

- **Faecal incontinence.** This is a relatively common complication, due to excessive trauma of the anal sphincter. Normally, this is no cause for concern, and the owner should be reassured, because it only lasts a few days. If it persists, it is possible that there has been irreversible damage to the nerves (anal branch of the pudendal nerve), and a medical-nutritional or surgical treatment should be considered.
- **Tenesmus and dyschezia.** These two problems can occur in the initial postoperative period if there is local infection. If they appear in the medium-term, they can be due to stenosis of the anus as a result of excessive scar tissue formation. In the first case, correct antibiotic treatment should be prescribed, while the second requires medical treatment facilitating faecal elimination or surgical resection of the scar tissue causing the signs.
- **Recurrence of the fistula.** This is associated with incomplete resection of the sac. Take care to place the ligature on the duct as close as possible to its exit, so that no sac or glandular tissue remains.
- **Local infection and appearance of fistulas.** If the duct is not ligated correctly, pathogens may pass from the anus into the subcutaneous tissue.

Anal sacculitis. Case 4 / Surgical treatment: sacculectomy using hot gel

Technical difficulty

If it is anticipated that resection of the anal sacs will be difficult because of perianal fistulas, recurrent chronic infections or due to the lack of experience of the surgeon, a special gel is used to facilitate the procedure.

The gel expands the anal sac and makes it easier to identify during surgery and the heat dissolves the fibrotic adhesions, facilitating dissection. No additional postoperative problems have been encountered using this gel.

A 4-year-old mixed-breed dog is presented with perianal fistulas that do not heal in spite of medical treatment of the primary sacculitis.

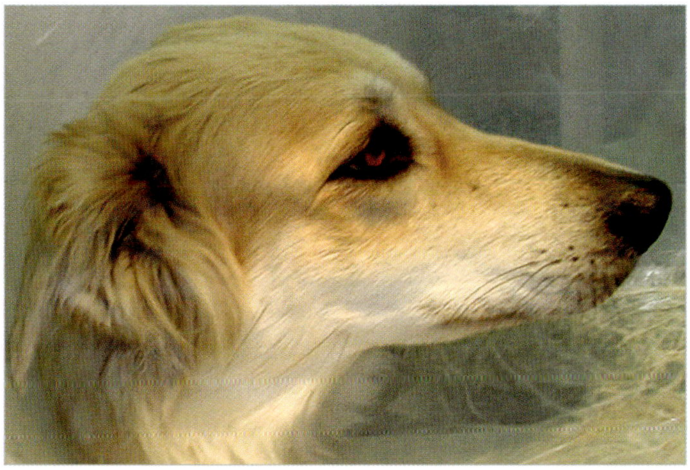

Fig. 1. “Figo” is suffering from perianal fistulas as a result of bilateral sacculitis with secondary complications.

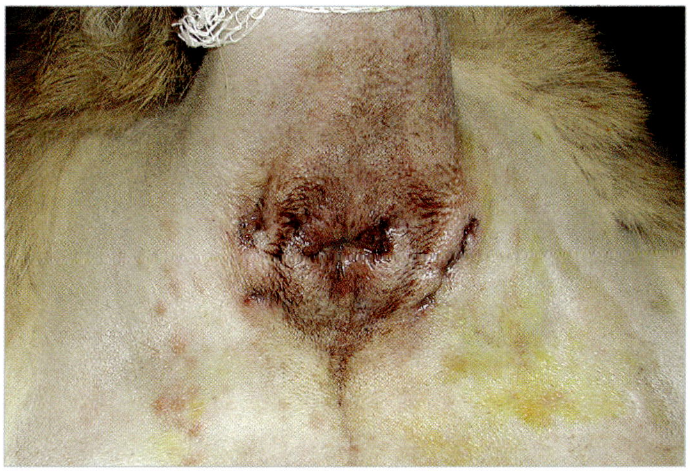

Fig. 2. After shaving the area, the fistulas can be seen clearly on both sides of the anus. They are due to infection of the anal sacs.

For this type of surgery, specific equipment is required, consisting of a special gel cartridge, an applicator syringe and a blunt needle for insertion into the anal sacs (figs. 3-5).

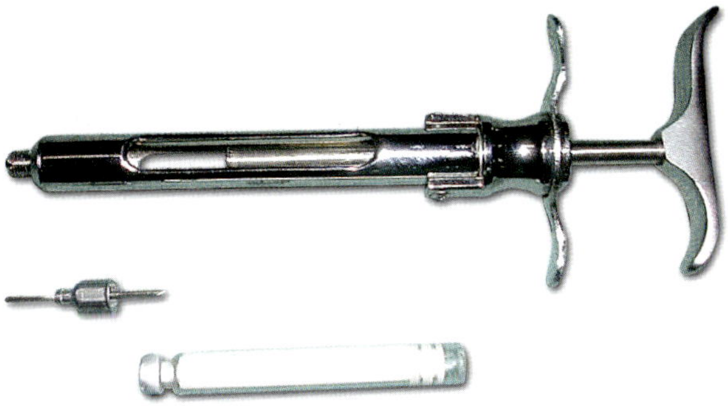

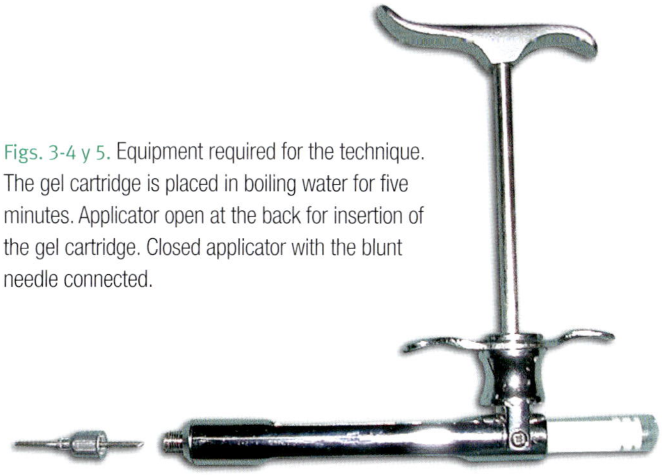

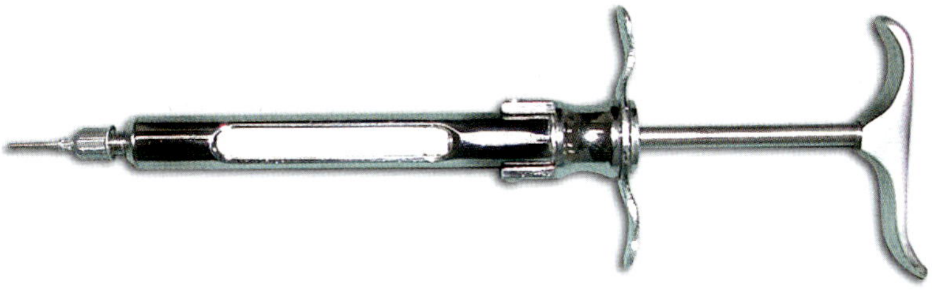

Figs. 3-4 y 5. Equipment required for the technique. The gel cartridge is placed in boiling water for five minutes. Applicator open at the back for insertion of the gel cartridge. Closed applicator with the blunt needle connected.

Before surgery

- Remove faecal content from the rectum.
- Do not use laxatives during 24 hours prior to surgery.
- Empty the anal sacs and flush them with an antiseptic solution.
- Shave and disinfect the surgical field.

See positioning of the patient ➔ page 248

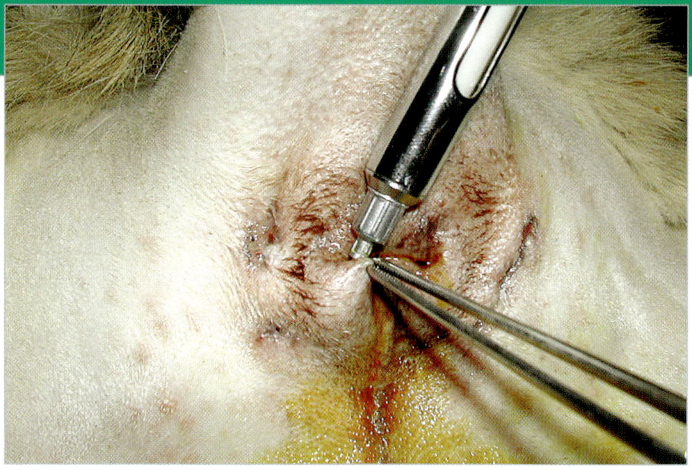

Fig. 6. By inserting the gel into the anal sacs, the antiseptic solution used to flush the sacs is expelled.
In small breeds, half a cartridge is inserted in each sac, while in large breeds, an entire cartridge should be used for each side.

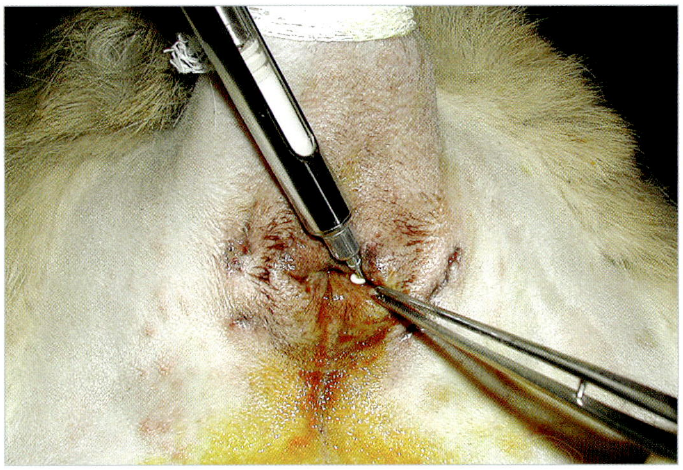

Fig. 7. Injection of the hot gel in the right anal sac.
Note that the needle does not prevent the gel from flowing out when the sac is full. This avoids rupturing of the sac due to excessive distension.

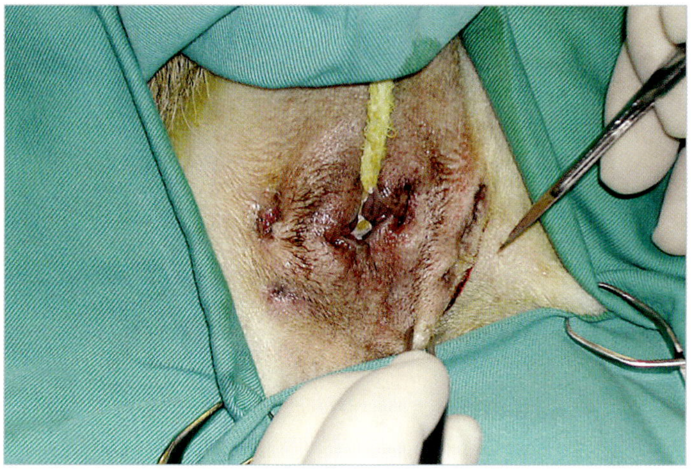

Fig. 8. After preparation of the surgical field and plugging the anus, an elliptical skin incision is made around the fistula.

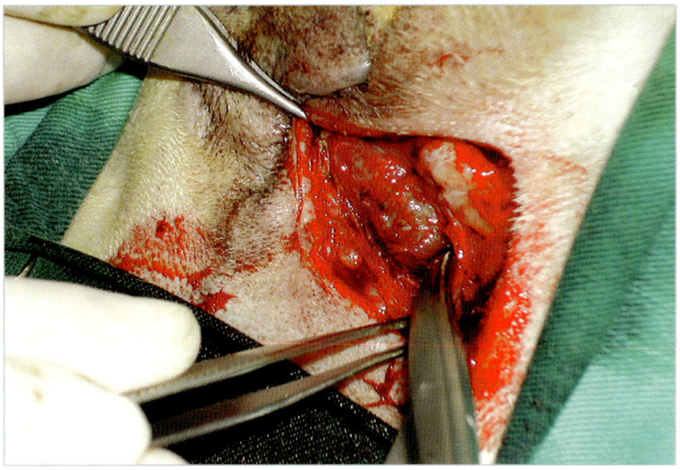

Fig. 9. Thanks to the gel, which has hardened, the sac can easily be identified between the muscular fibres of the anal sphincter.
This makes dissection of the sac easier, minimising the risk of accidental perforation.

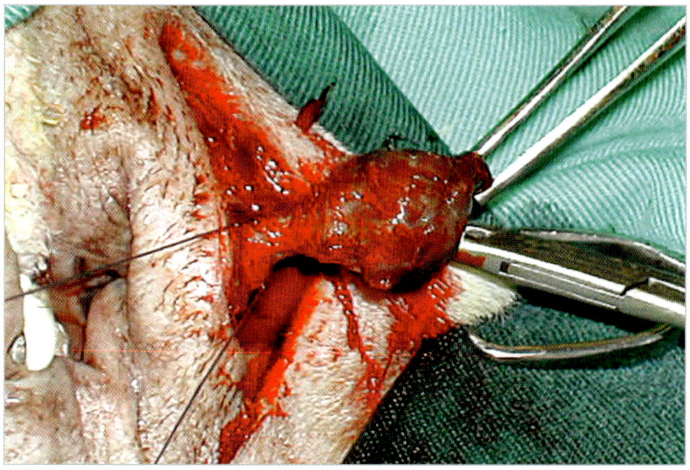

Fig. 10. Complete dissection of the anal sac. It is now only attached by its duct. Next, the duct is ligated as close as possible to the anal wall. For this ligature, synthetic absorbable 3/0 material is used.

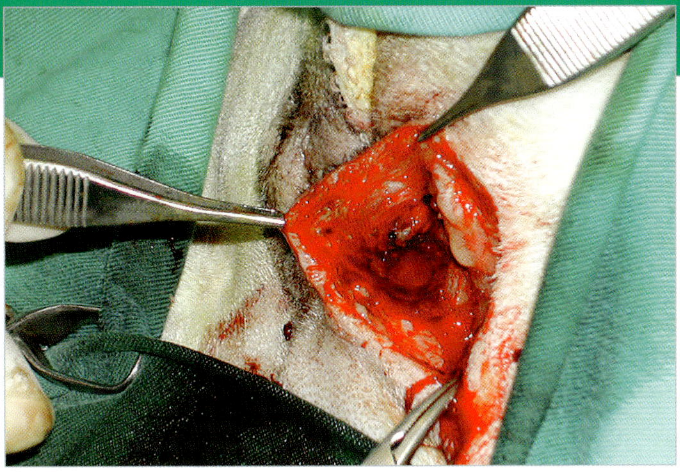

Fig. 11. The cavity that remains is irrigated with lukewarm saline to eliminate tissue remnants, clots and bacteria.

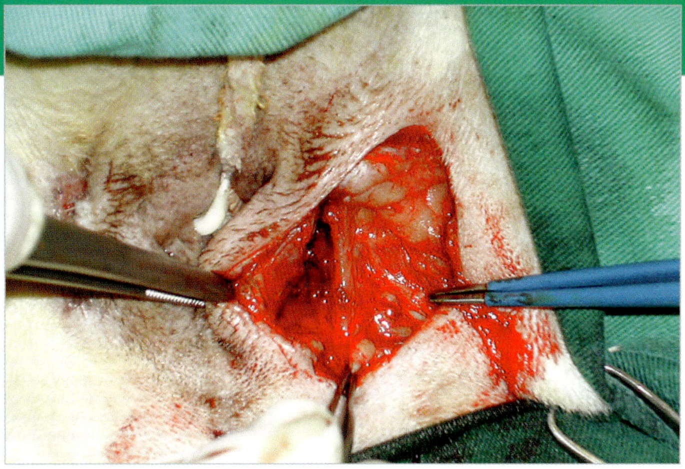

Fig. 12. To control haemorrhage, haemostatic forceps or bipolar coagulation are used. We recommend the latter option.

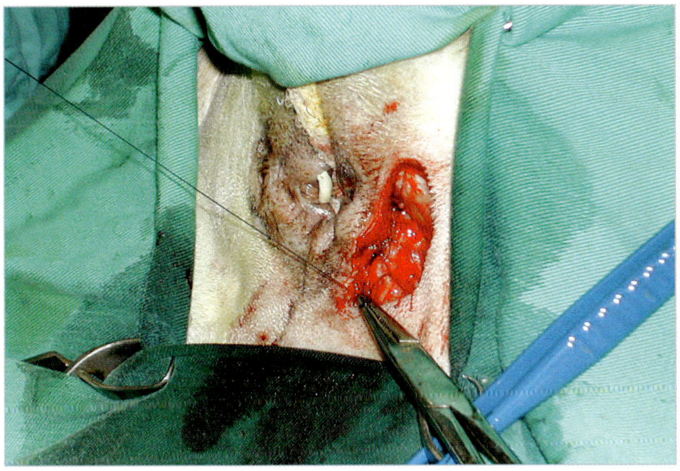

Fig. 13. The muscular layer and subcutaneous tissue are closed with absorbable monofilament 4/0 suture material. The same steps are carried out on the left.

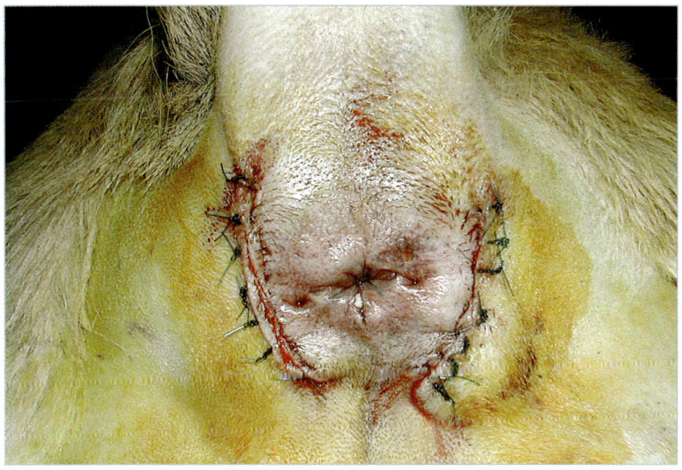

Fig. 14. The skin wound is closed with interrupted, vertical mattress sutures, using monofilament non-absorbable material, making sure the knots are placed on the outer edge to avoid contact with faeces during defecation.

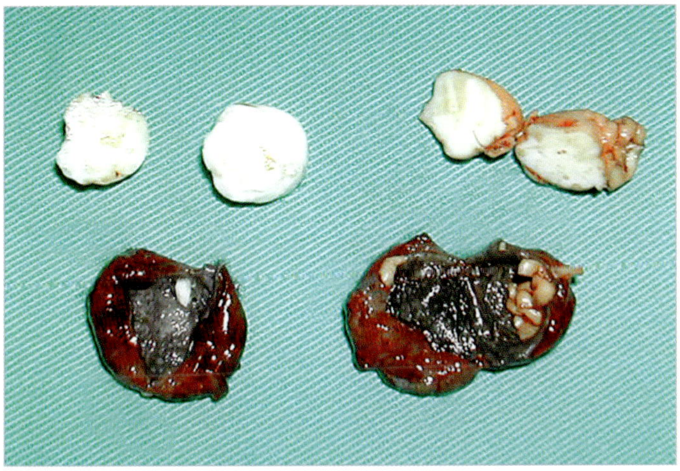

Fig. 15. Both anal sacs have been completely removed. Incisions into each sac reveal the gel that was used to facilitate their dissection.

In case of sacculitis, the sac can rupture during the introduction of the gel. In order to avoid this, the gel should be injected slowly, making sure the needle does not completely seal off the opening of the duct, so that the gel can escape easily in case of high intraluminal pressure.

Postoperatively

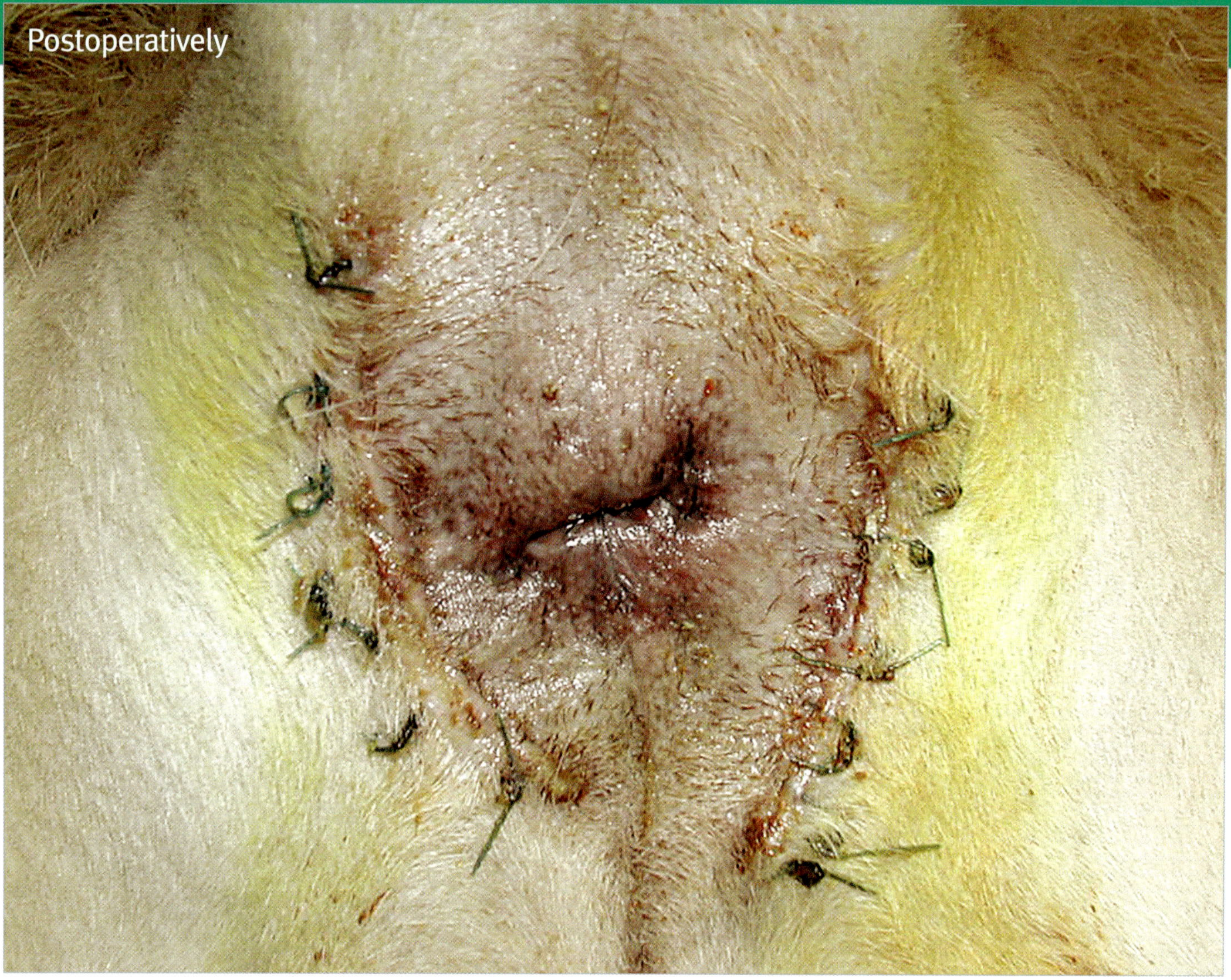

Fig. 16. After three days, healing has progressed normally. There are no signs of infection.

After surgery

- Systemic antibiotic therapy for 4 to 5 days, if there are no infectious complications.
- Clean the anal area every 12 hours with water and a neutral soap.
- Place an Elizabethan collar to avoid self-mutilation.

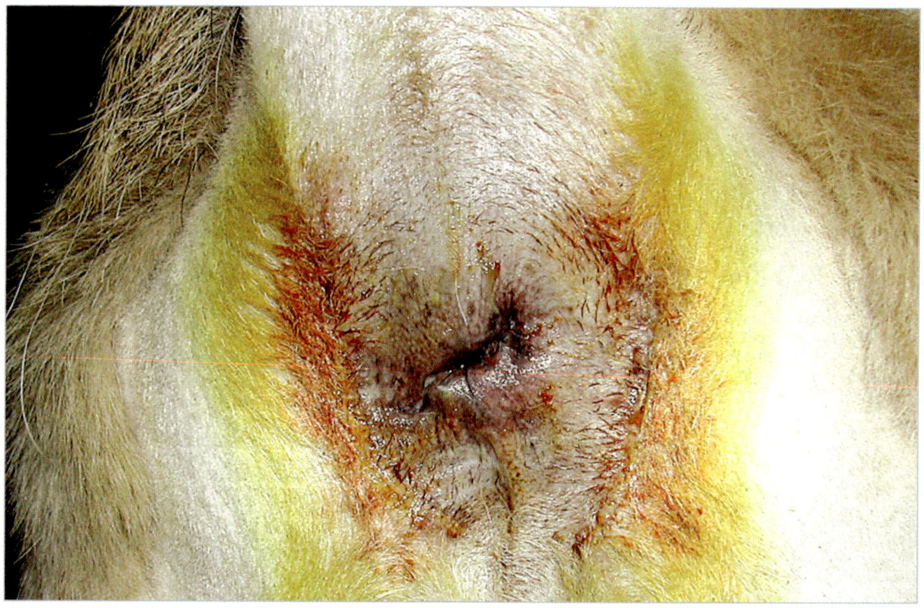

Fig. 17. Ten days after surgery, the sutures are removed and Figo's treatment is finished.

Anal sacculitis. Case 5 / Sacculectomy in ferrets (Descenting)

Prevalence	■■□□□
Technical difficulty	■■□□□

Ferrets enjoy increasing popularity as pets. However, their great drawback is the odour of the secretions of their anal glands. As in other carnivores, the anal sacs are located on both sides of the anus, between the fibres of the external and internal anal sphincters.

It is recommended to perform this surgery in ferrets of both sexes between 6 and 8 months of age.

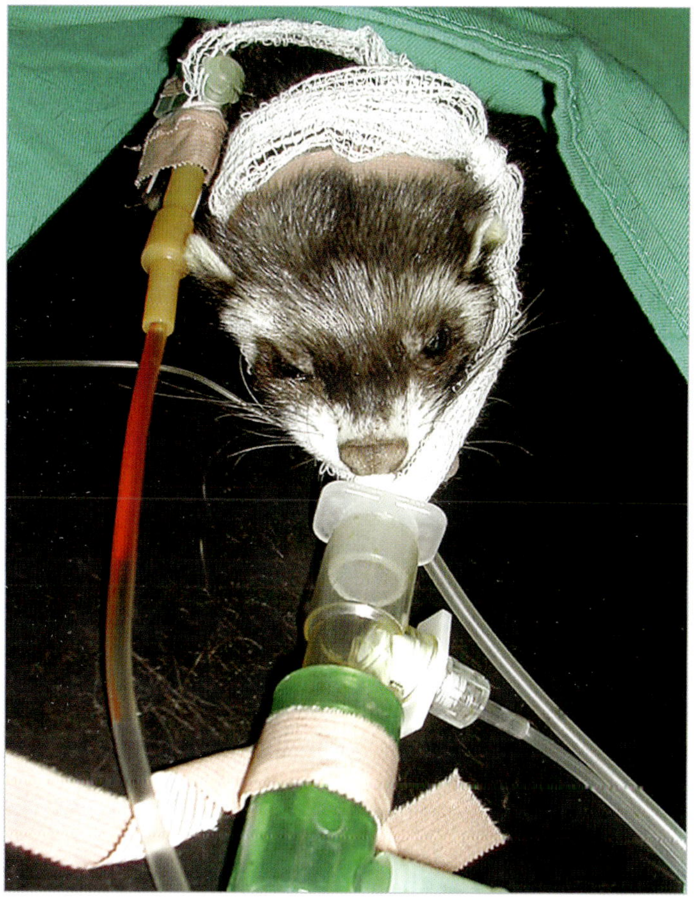

Fig. 1. Anaesthetic maintenance with isoflurane using tracheal intubation and an open circuit with an Ayre's T-piece.

Sacculectomy in ferrets eliminates the smell of the anal sacs, but it does not avoid the odour of the sebaceous and apocrine glands in the perianal area.

It is also recommended to neuter ferrets in order to avoid future odours, and in particular to prevent the development of aplastic anaemia in non-breeding females (secondary to high levels of oestrogen due to prolonged oestrus).

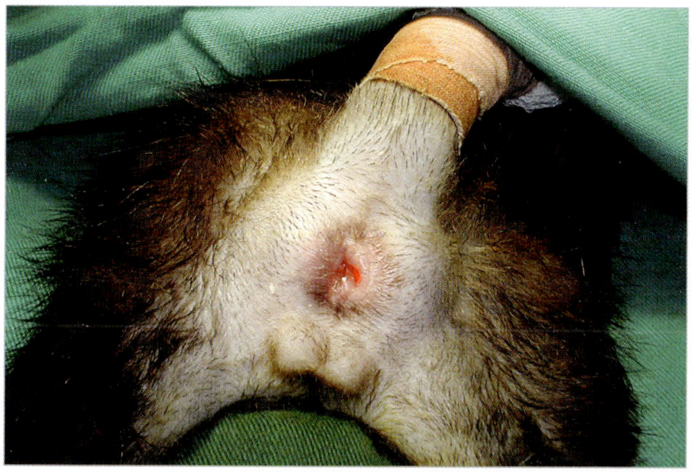

Fig. 2. Preparation of the operative field, with the tail fixed to the back of the patient. Good asepsis is very important, in particular if castration is carried out at the same time.

Before surgery

Measure the haematocrit (normal: 52.4%) and the level of serum protein (6.0 g/dl).

Premedication of the ferret is based on low doses of acepromazine (0.1-0.3 mg/kg), diazepam (2 mg/kg) and xylazine (1 mg/kg) via the intramuscular or subcutaneous route. Induction and maintenance of anaesthesia should be performed using isoflurane[1] (fig. 1).

An alternative to inhalation anaesthesia is the use of a combination of ketamine (15 mg/kg), butorphanol (0.2 mg/kg) and xylazine (2 mg/kg) given intramuscularly.

The patient is placed in sternal recumbency at the edge of the operating table, on a cushion in order to avoid trauma to the extremities. This also avoids hypothermia due to excessive loss of body heat (fig. 2).

It is very important to control hypothermia in these animals.

[1] Protocol used by the University of Zaragoza.

Closed sacculectomy is carried out as described earlier (figs. 3-6). This surgical technique usually has very few complications.

Ligation of the duct, using absorbable material, should be achieved as close as possible to the skin of the anus.

See purse string suture ➜ *page 252*

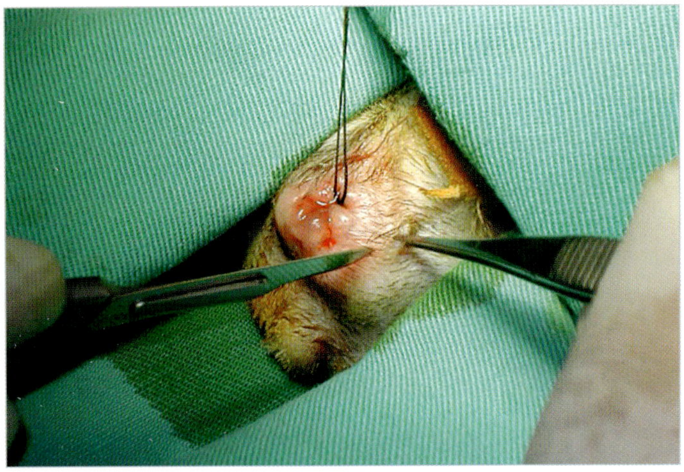

Fig. 3. After placing a purse string suture around the anus, an incision is made over the anal sac (right).

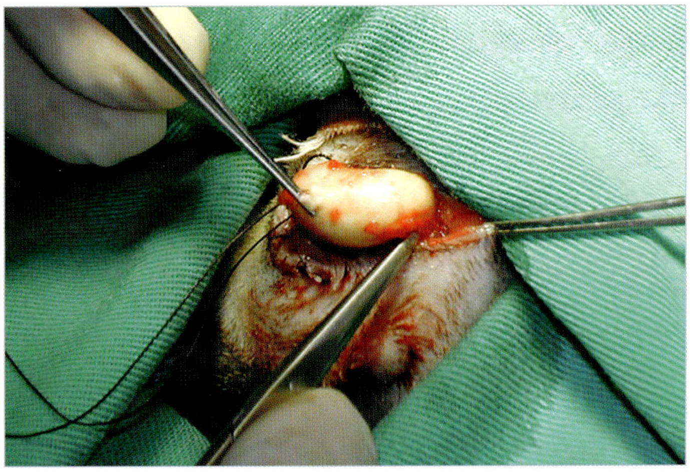

Fig. 4. The anal sac is easily identified by its whitish colour (and even easier if hot gel is used).
The dissection of the external anal sphincter is not very difficult. Special care should be taken not to perforate or tear the anal sac.

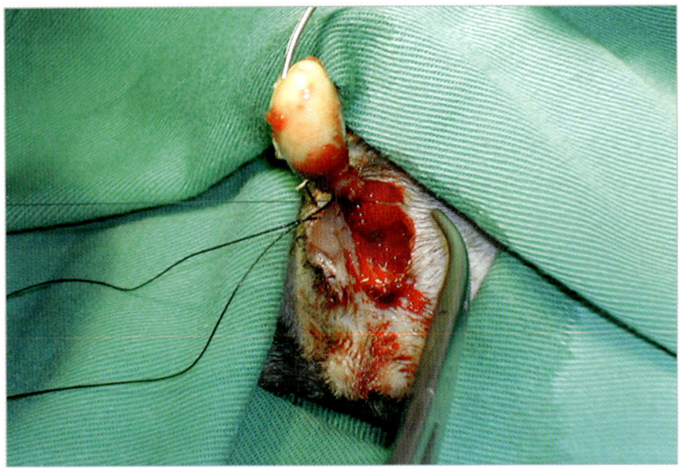

Fig. 5. Bleeding should be controlled with gauze swabs or bipolar coagulation. The duct should be dissected up to its exit in order to ensure removal of the accessory glands that feed into it.

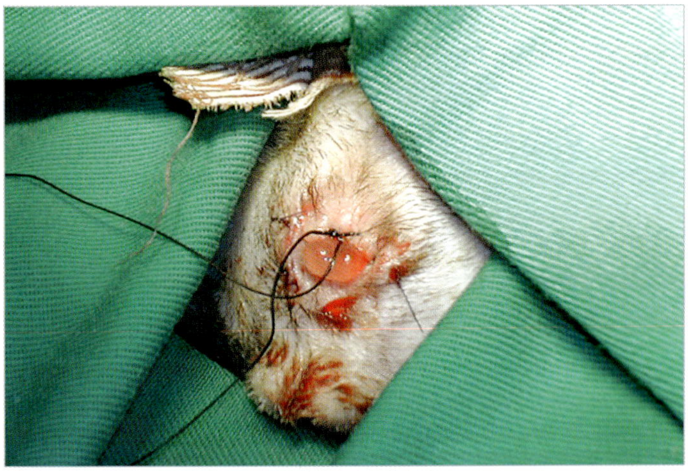

Fig. 6. Next, the skin is sutured using synthetic absorbable monofilament material. Some surgeons do not suture these wounds, leaving them to heal by secondary intention.

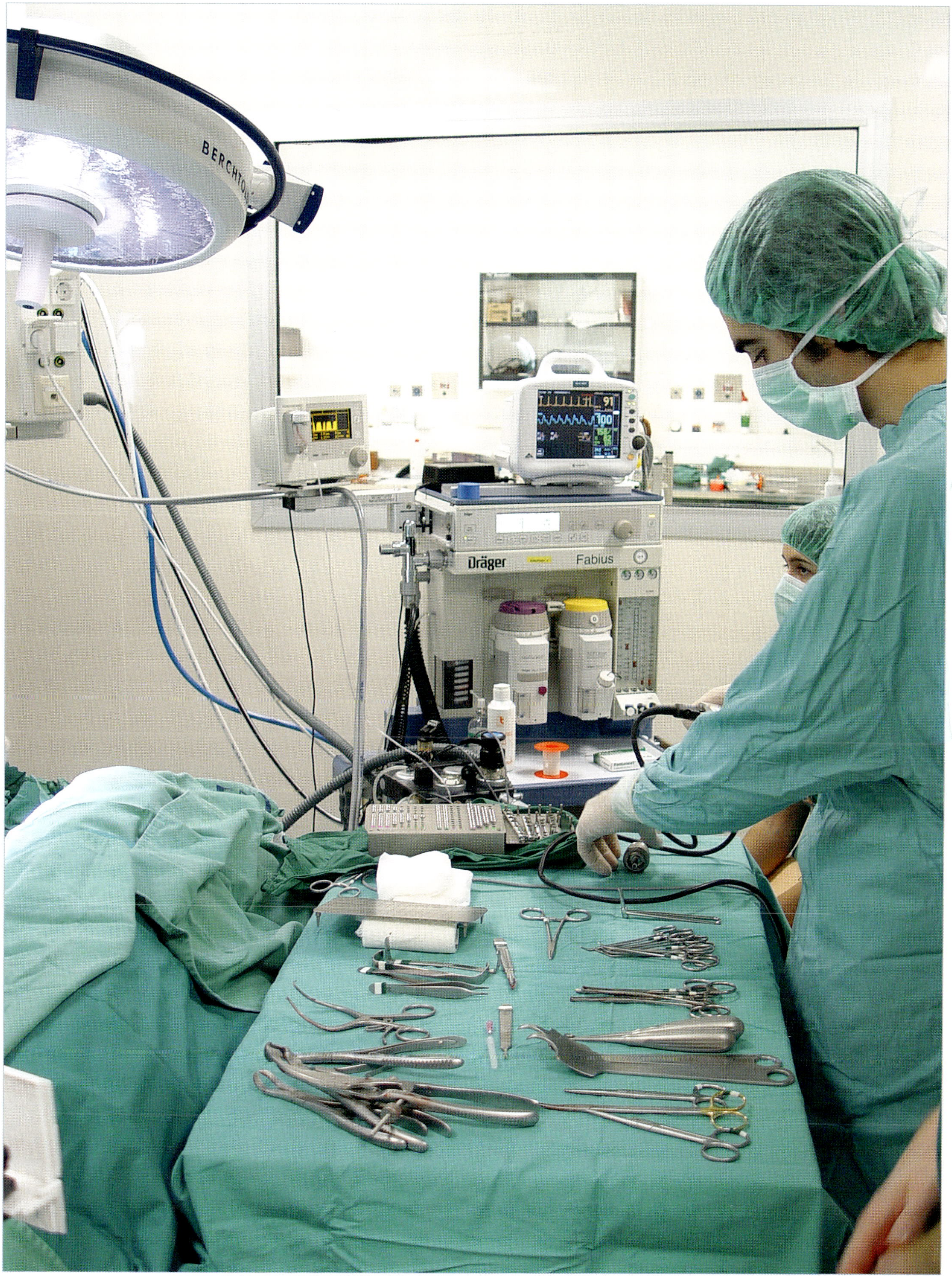
BERCHTOLD
Dräger
Fabius

Anal neoplasia

Prevalence

Tumours located around the anus tend to be either adenomas and carcinomas of the perianal glands, or adenocarcinomas of the apocrine glands located in the anal sacs.

Perianal adenomas are the most common neoplasms found in this area (80%). They can also be found in other locations like the prepuce, the tail or the lumbosacral area.

They are hormone-dependent neoplasms and a large number of patients also have interstitial cell testicular tumours (Leydig cell tumour). Normally, they are small, smooth, multiple, well-defined and ulcerated tumours (fig. 1). However, they can also be solitary and large (fig. 2). Their growth is slow.

Perianal adenomas are stimulated by an imbalance of the sex hormones. It is therefore recommended to castrate affected male dogs.

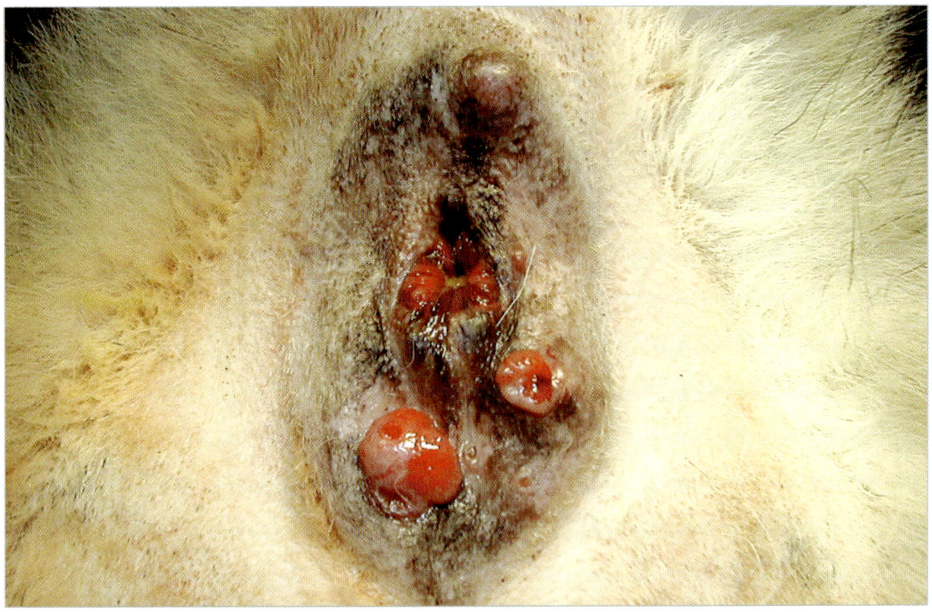

Fig. 1. Circumanal tumours in an 8-year-old dog with a testicular Leydig cell tumour.

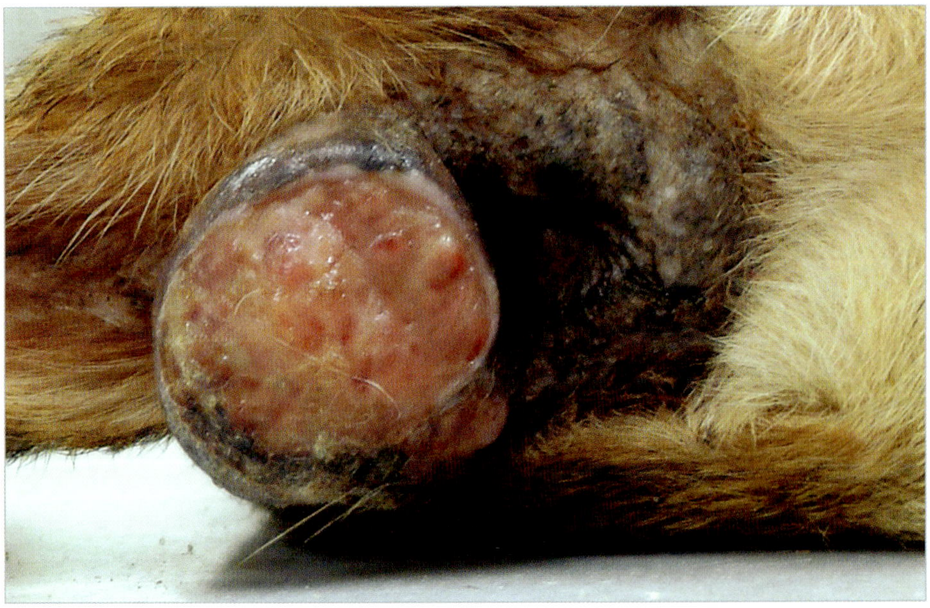

Fig. 2. Large perianal adenoma located between the anus and the base of the tail.

Carcinomas of the perianal glands cannot be differentiated macroscopically from adenomas.

Usually, they are solitary, ulcerated and locally invasive (fig. 3). In addition, their growth is faster than that of the adenomas.

These neoplasias are not hormone-dependent.

They mainly metastasise to the intrapelvic and sublumbar lymph nodes (fig. 4).

Adenocarcinomas of the apocrine glands arise from the anal sacs. They are usually unilateral and their growth is slow. Initially, they only affect the anal sacs but later can invade neighbouring tissues.

They are highly malignant and metastasise to multiple organs. They also cause hypercalcaemia, anorexia, vomiting, constipation, muscle weakness, polydipsia and polyuria.

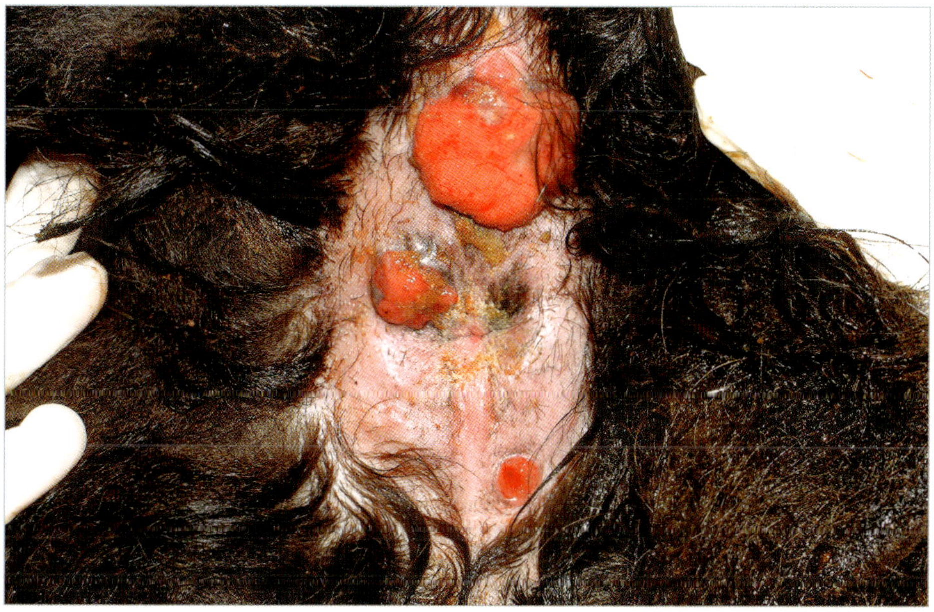

The prognosis for patients with hypercalcaemia is worse than those with normal calcium levels.

Fig. 3. Ulcerated and infected circumanal carcinomas. The smaller masses can be confused with perianal fistulas.

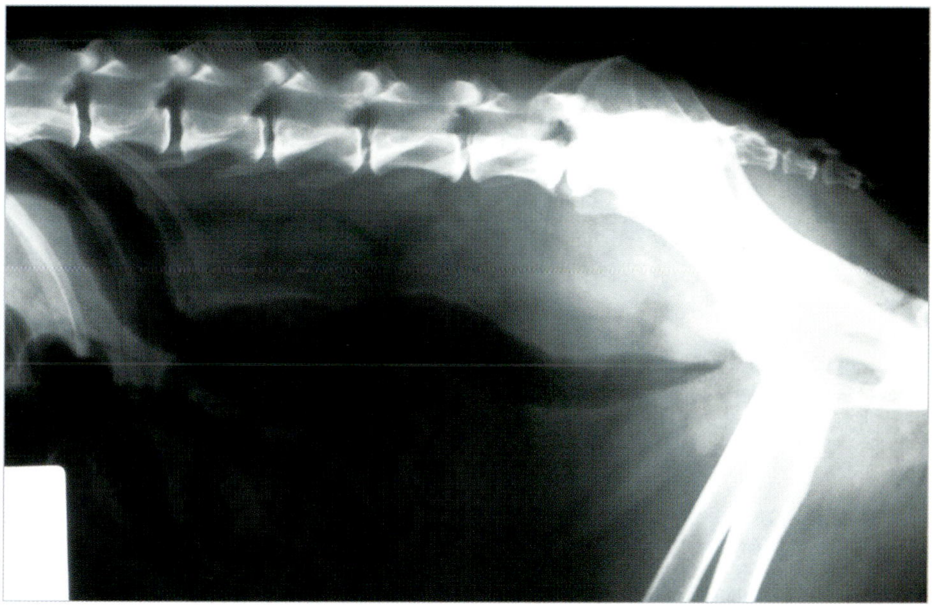

Fig. 4. In these patients, radiographic or ultrasound examinations should be carried out to detect any metastases.
This radiograph of the previous case shows metastasis in the sublumbar lymph nodes.

Anal neoplasia. Case 1 / Adenoma (small size)

Technical difficulty ■□□□□

This patient presents with various perianal neoplasias of different sizes, some of which are ulcerated (fig. 1). During physical examination, the right testis was found to be much smaller than the left one. No metastases were detected and the blood tests were normal.

After preparation of the operative field, the patient is placed on the table in sternal recumbency, and a purse string suture is placed around the anus (fig. 1).

✱ *Do not use enemas on the day of the operation, as this may contaminate the operative field with liquid faeces.*

See positioning of the patient ➜ *page 248*

See purse string suture ➜ *page 252*

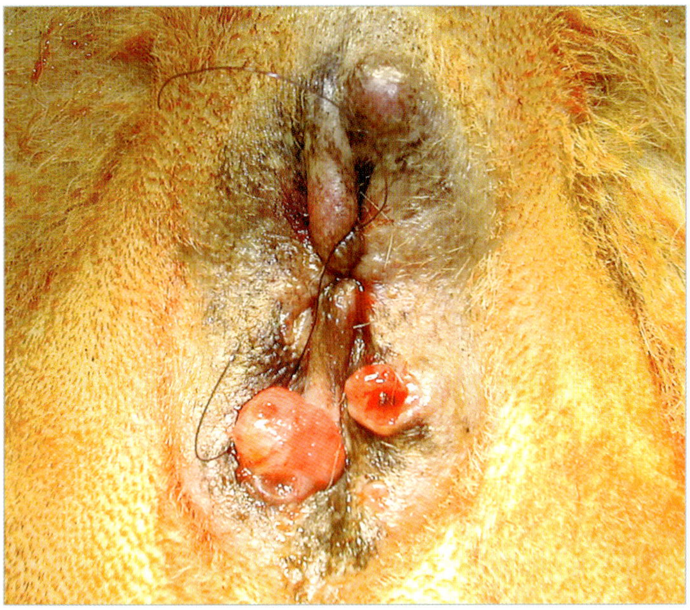

Fig. 1. The operative field after shaving, disinfection and placement of a purse string suture to avoid faecal contamination.

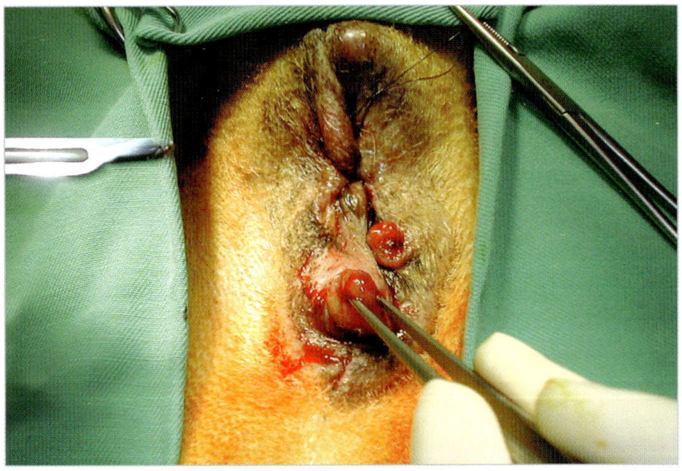

Fig. 2. The skin around each of the neoplasms is incised with a scalpel, and the subcutaneous tissue is dissected. It is a simple technique as the tumours are normally not invasive.

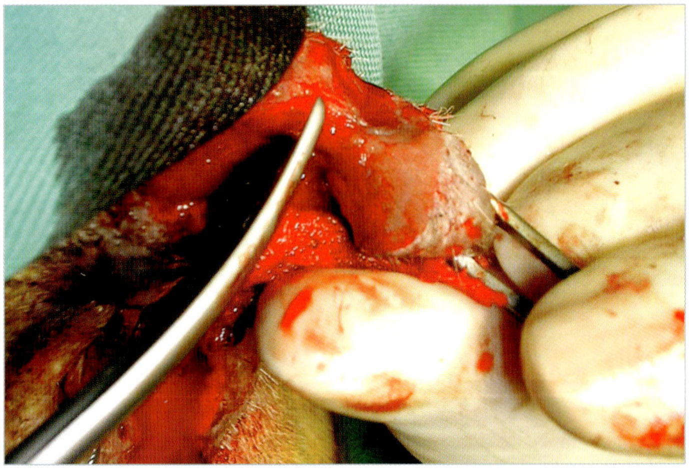

Fig. 3. Adenomas of the perianal glands are easily dissected and the external anal sphincter rarely needs to be incised.

Avoid overusing monopolar coagulation as this may cause excessive fibrosis and iatrogenic anal stenosis.

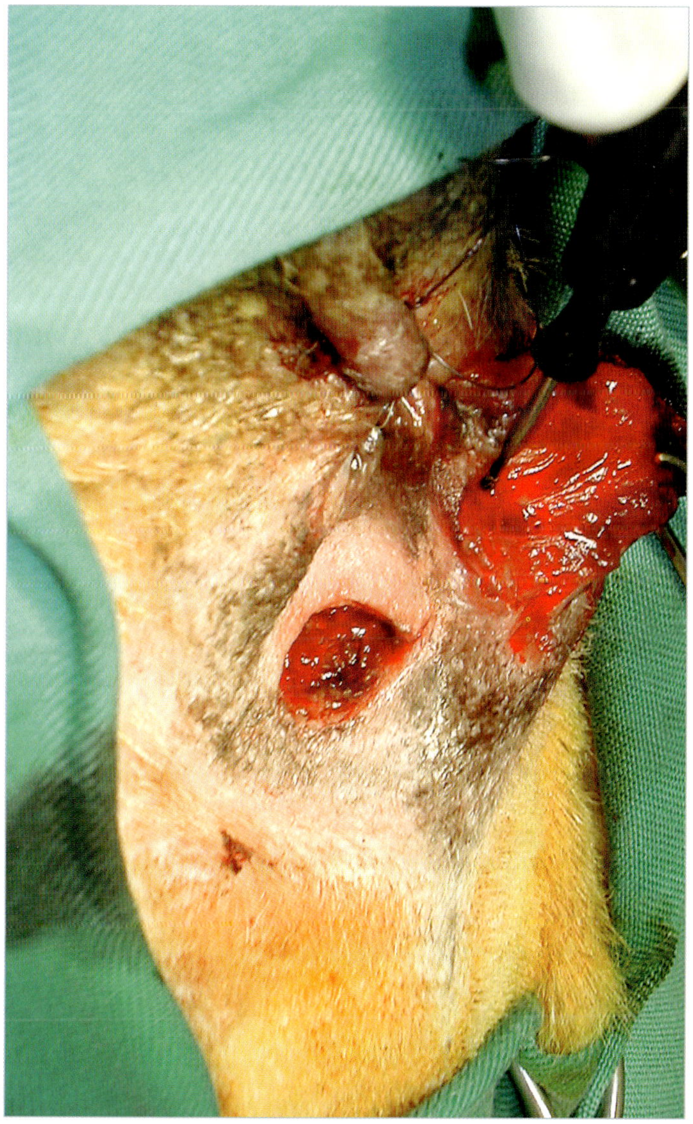

Fig. 4. This area is well-vascularised so it is necessary to control bleeding during surgery by applying pressure with swabs. Only if the bleeding is intense, should electrocautery, preferably using a bipolar coagulator, be performed.

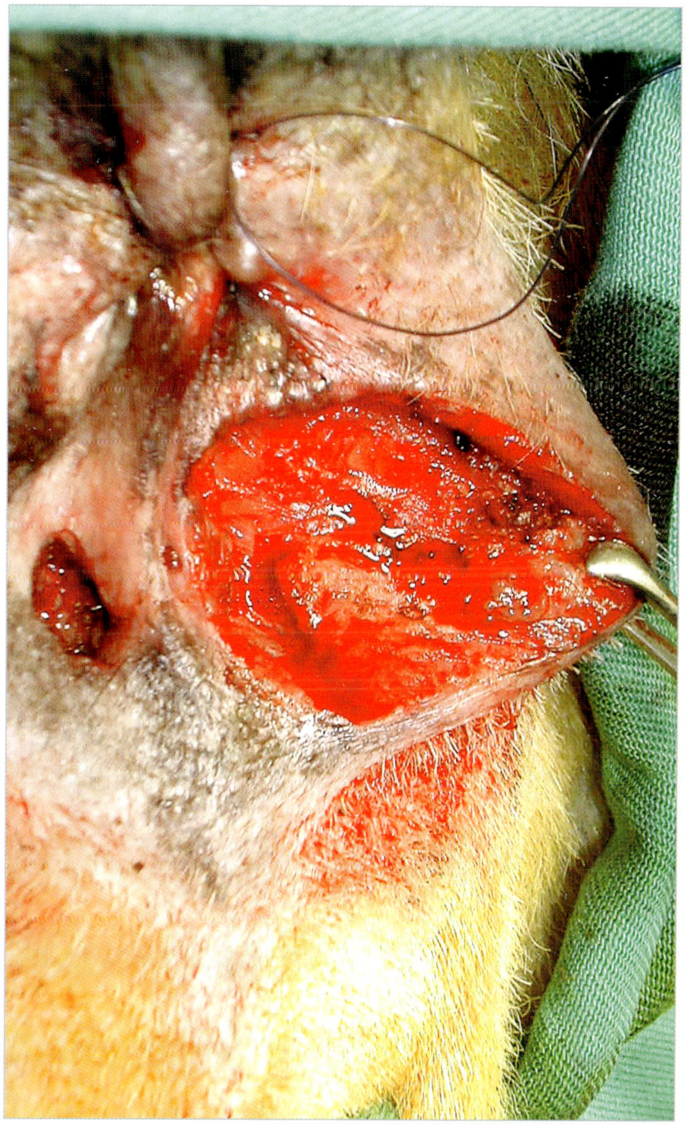

Fig. 5. After checking that there is no active bleeding in the bed of the resected area, the subcutaneous tissue should be closed using 3/0 absorbable suture material.

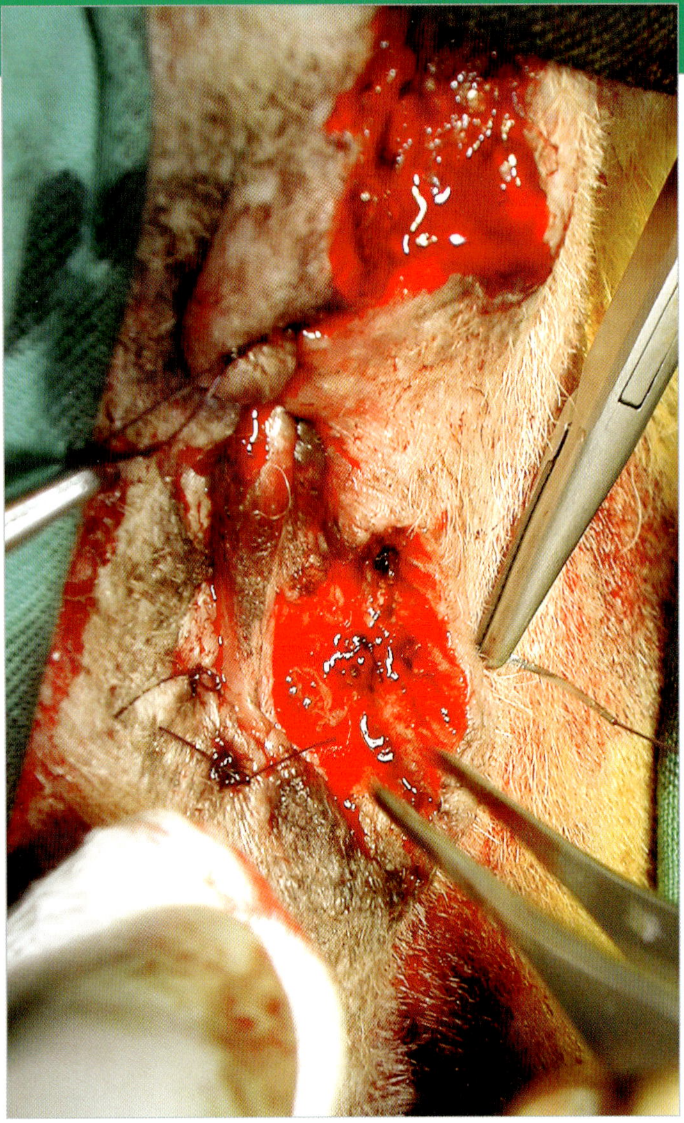

Fig. 6. The skin is closed with vertical mattress sutures using 3/0 non-absorbable monofilament material.

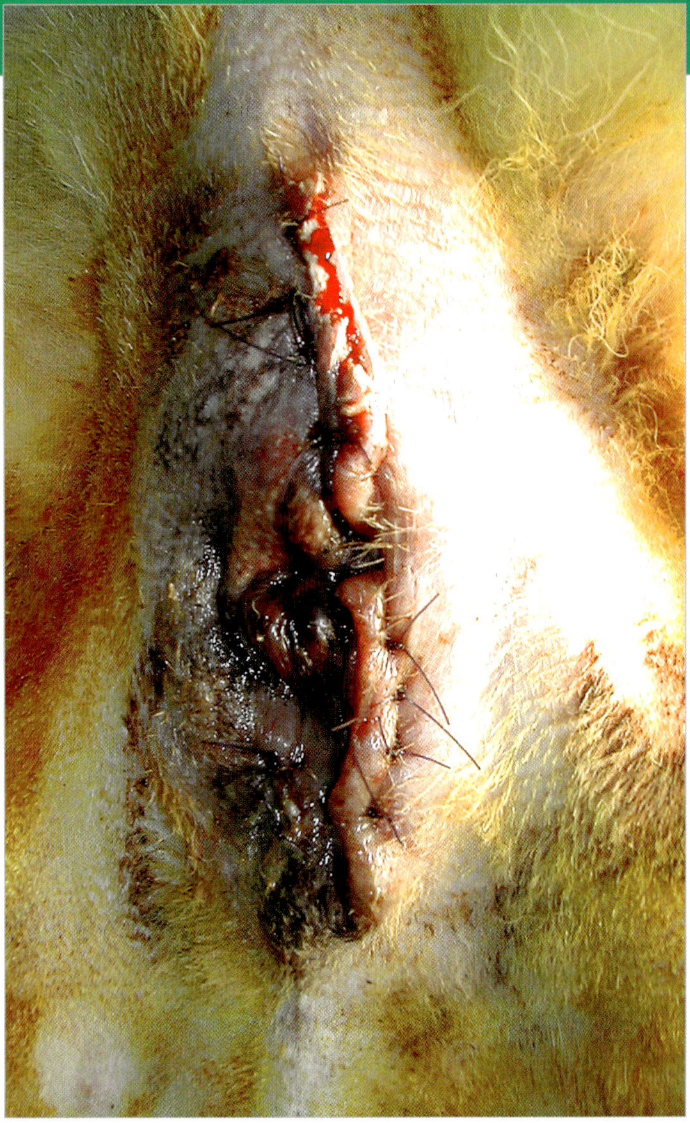

Fig. 7. The skin sutures near the anus should be perpendicular to the anus to avoid interfering with the lumen and function post-operatively.

In order to reduce the risk of recurrence, bilateral castration performed.

See castration ➜ *page 264*

Histopathological examination of this case confirmed the presence of a Leydig cell tumour in the right testis.

After surgery

- Continue with antibiotic therapy for several days if contamination has taken place during surgery.
- Prescribe mild laxatives to avoid straining during defaecation.
- Ensure the dog wears an Elizabethan collar, and observe strict hygiene in the area (wash the perianal area several times daily with water and soap, in particular after defaecation).
- Regularly check the progress of wound healing.
- Recheck the patient 6 weeks later for possible recurrence.

Some authors recommend castration is carried out prior to the resection of the neoplasms in order to reduce the tumour size.

Anal neoplasias. Case 2 / Adenoma (large size)

Technical difficulty	■	□	□	□	□

"Papu" (fig. 1) is a 10-year-old mixed breed dog presented for examination because of constant anal irritation and difficulty defaecating. Also, a mass is observed in the area (fig. 2).

Fig. 1. "Papu" has shown tenesmus for several weeks, is rubbing his anus frequently, staining the owner's carpet with blood.

Abdominal and thoracic radiographs are normal. The blood test results show no changes.

As in all similar cases, castration is carried out to reduce the risk of recurrence.

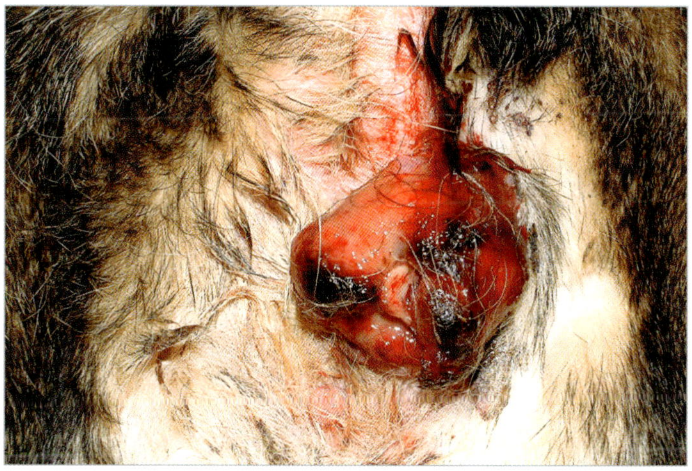

Fig. 2. In this case, a solitary mass is seen to the lower right of the anus, with several ulcerated areas. The base is not infiltrating the anus but its large size occludes the anus, making the elimination of faeces difficult.

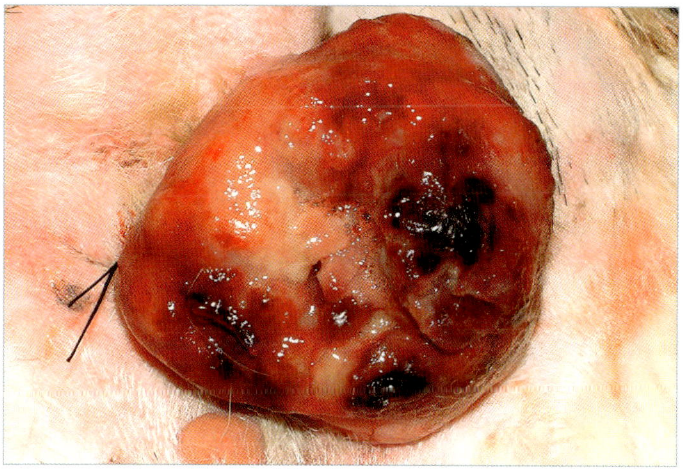

Fig. 3. The operation is based on superficial resection of the tumour. The surgical field is prepared and a purse string suture is placed around the anus.

Postoperatively

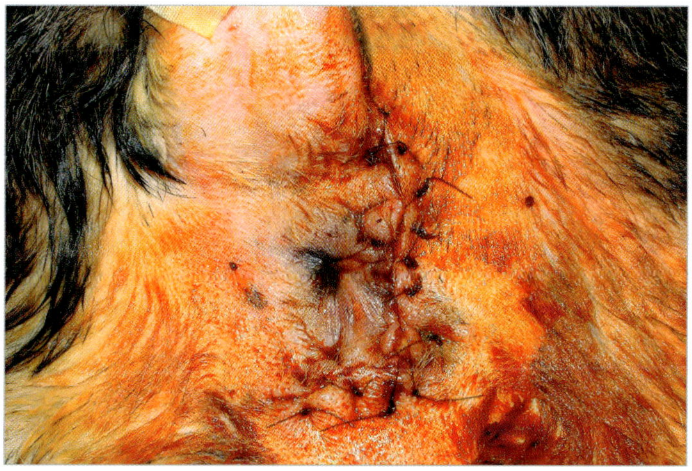

Fig. 4. The superficial resection of the neoplasm does not affect the anal sphincter and the skin wound is closed with vertical mattress sutures with non-absorbable monofilament material.

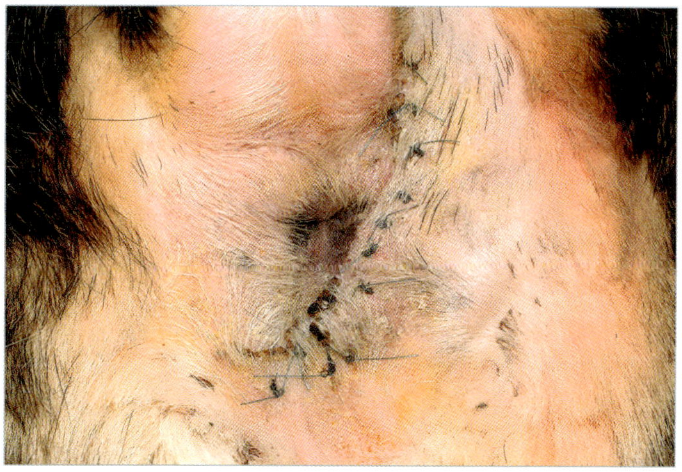

Fig. 5. If the operation is carried out correctly, healing is rapid. On the 9th day after surgery, the sutures are removed and no further treatment is needed.

Perianal fistulas

Prevalence ■■■□□

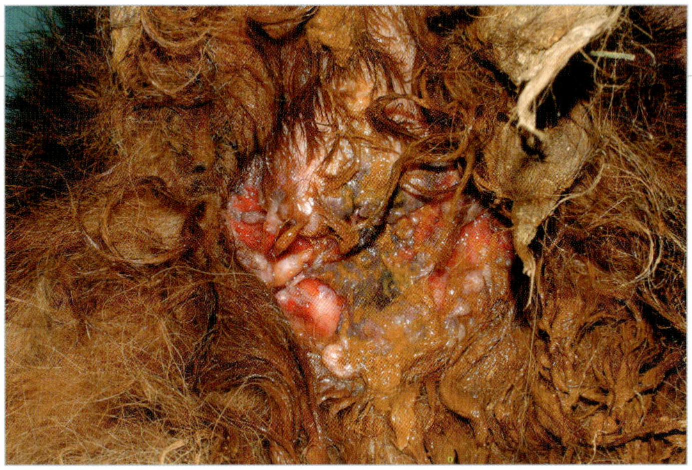

Fig. 1. Image showing the perianal fistulas of a 6-year-old male German Shepherd. The patient had intense pain in the area and difficulty defaecating.

Perianal fistulas are characterised by a chronic inflammatory, purulent ulcerated lesion with multiple interconnecting fistular canals and a severe infection around the anus (fig. 1). It mainly affects male dogs of certain breeds like the German Shepherd and the Irish Setter.

Clinical history

- Pain in the perianal area.
- Foul smell.
- Constant licking of the perineal area.
- Digestive problems (constipation, diarrhoea, tenesmus, dyschezia...).
- Ulceration, haemorrhagic or purulent discharge.

Clinical signs

- Very intense pain of the area, becoming worse when an attempt is made to lift the tail.
- Fistulas around the anus (figs. 2 and 3).
- Ulcerations and necrotic tissue around the anus (figs. 4-6).
- Anal stenosis due to excessive post-inflammatory fibrosis.

> *Take care when examining the perineal area, a calm animal can become aggressive due to the pain.*

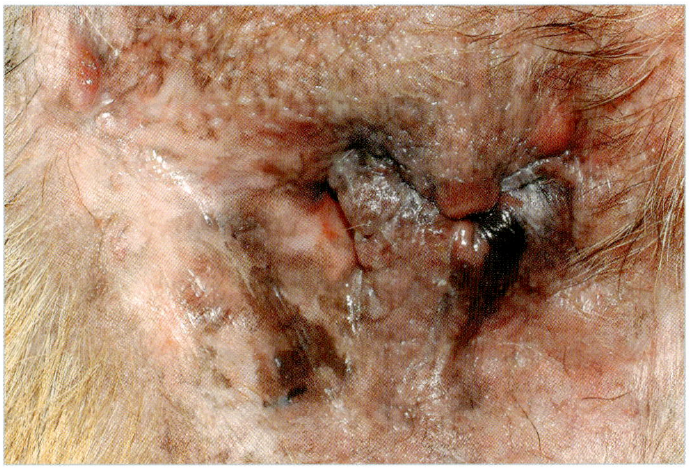

Fig. 2. Small fistulous openings in a German Shepherd bitch on the left side of the anus.

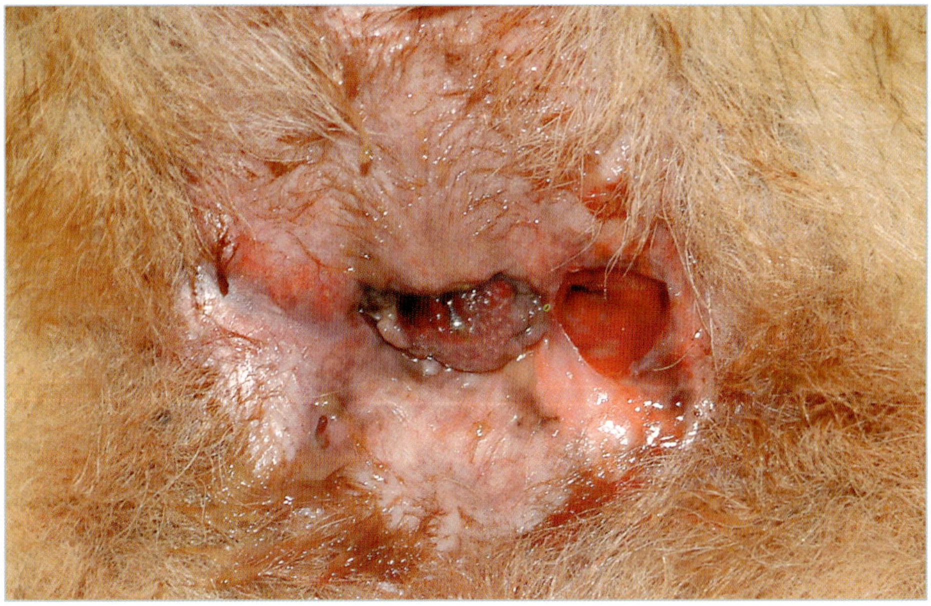

Fig. 3. Patient with recurring perianal fistulas. Note the small fistulous openings on the left and the ulceration on the right.
Secondary anal stenosis is also present in this case.

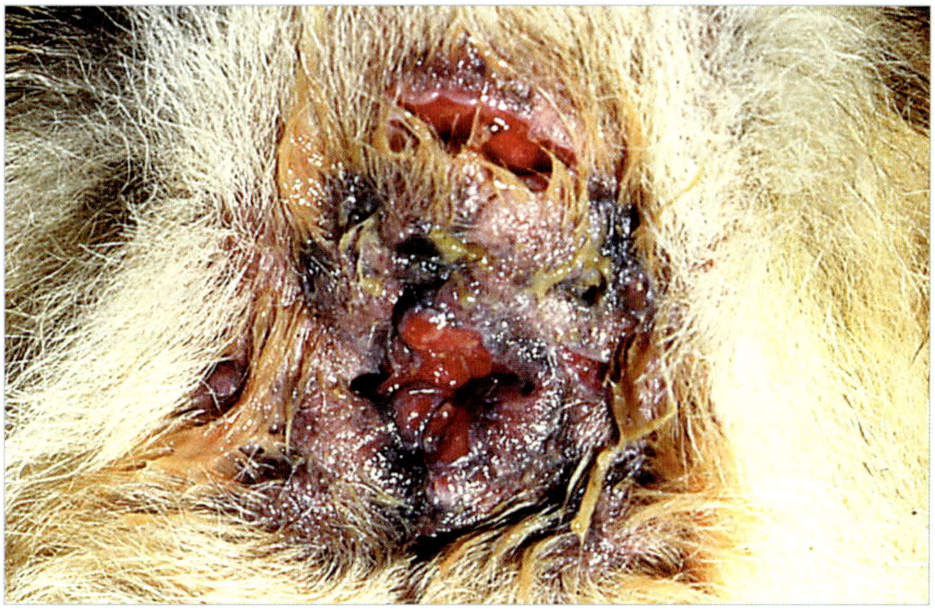

> *Some patients need to be sedated or even anaesthetised to permit examination of the perineal area.*

Fig. 4. Large ulcerated areas appear when several fistulous tracts coalesce. There is intense pain and a considerable local infection.

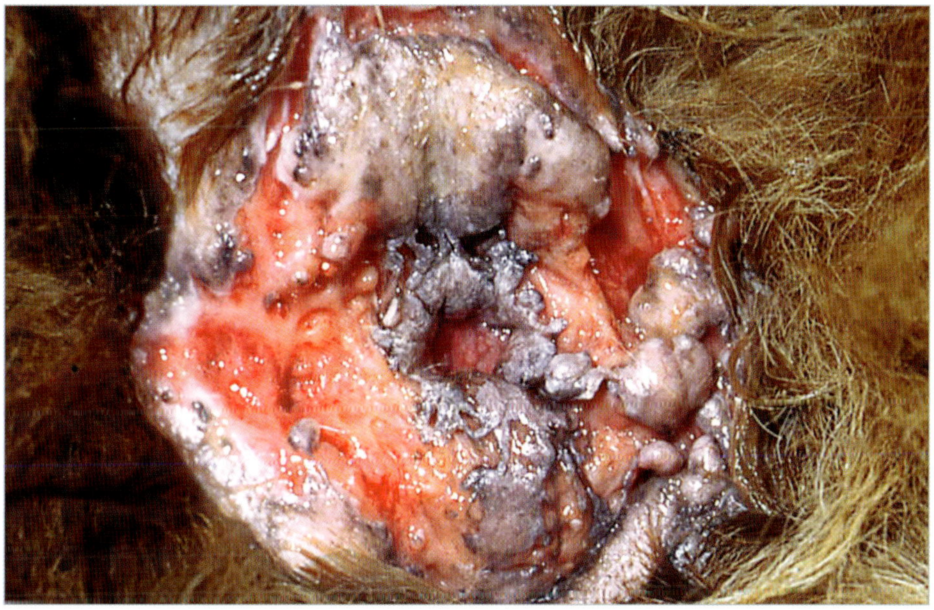

The owner should be informed about the severity of the condition, the treatment to be carried out, the expected results and, most importantly, the need for co-operation and long-term commitment during the postoperative period.

> *Recurrence is common, irrespective of the treatment.*

Fig. 5. Perianal fistulas in an 8-year-old German Shepherd. Together they have affected the entire circumference of the anus.

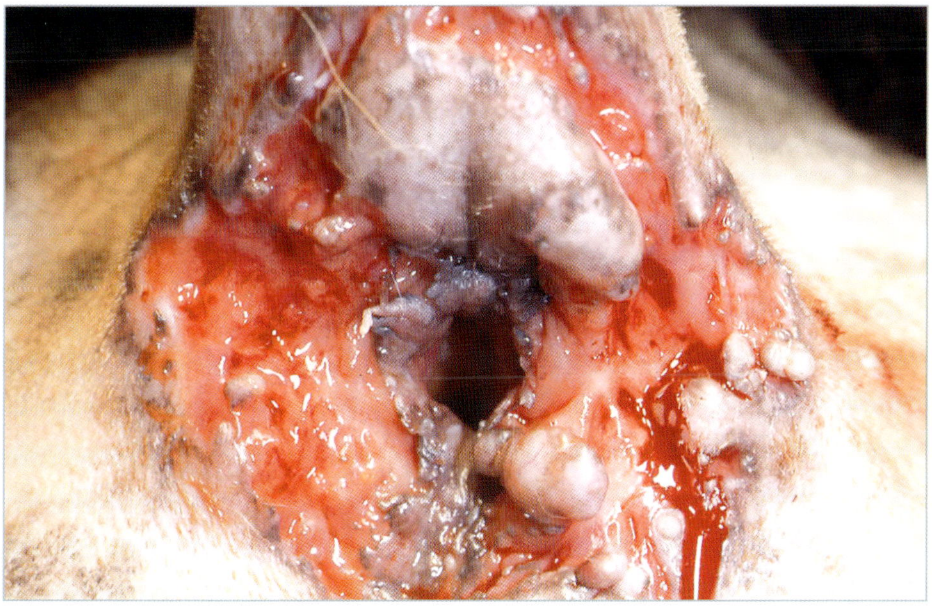

Fig. 6. The perianal lesions are extensive, the patient is in great pain, has problems defaecating, is licking the area and it is bleeding. This patient will undergo surgical treatment.

Perianal fistulas. Case 1 / Medical treatment

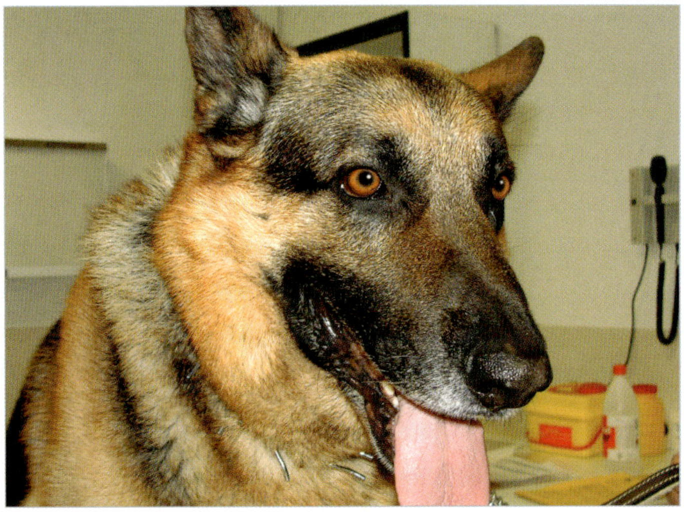

"Zar", a 6-year-old male German Shepherd (fig. 1), is presented for a problem in the anal area. The area is reddened, the dog has difficulty defaecating and is licking himself continuously (fig. 2).

Fig. 1. "Zar" during consultation, waiting for a general examination and inspection of the perineal area.

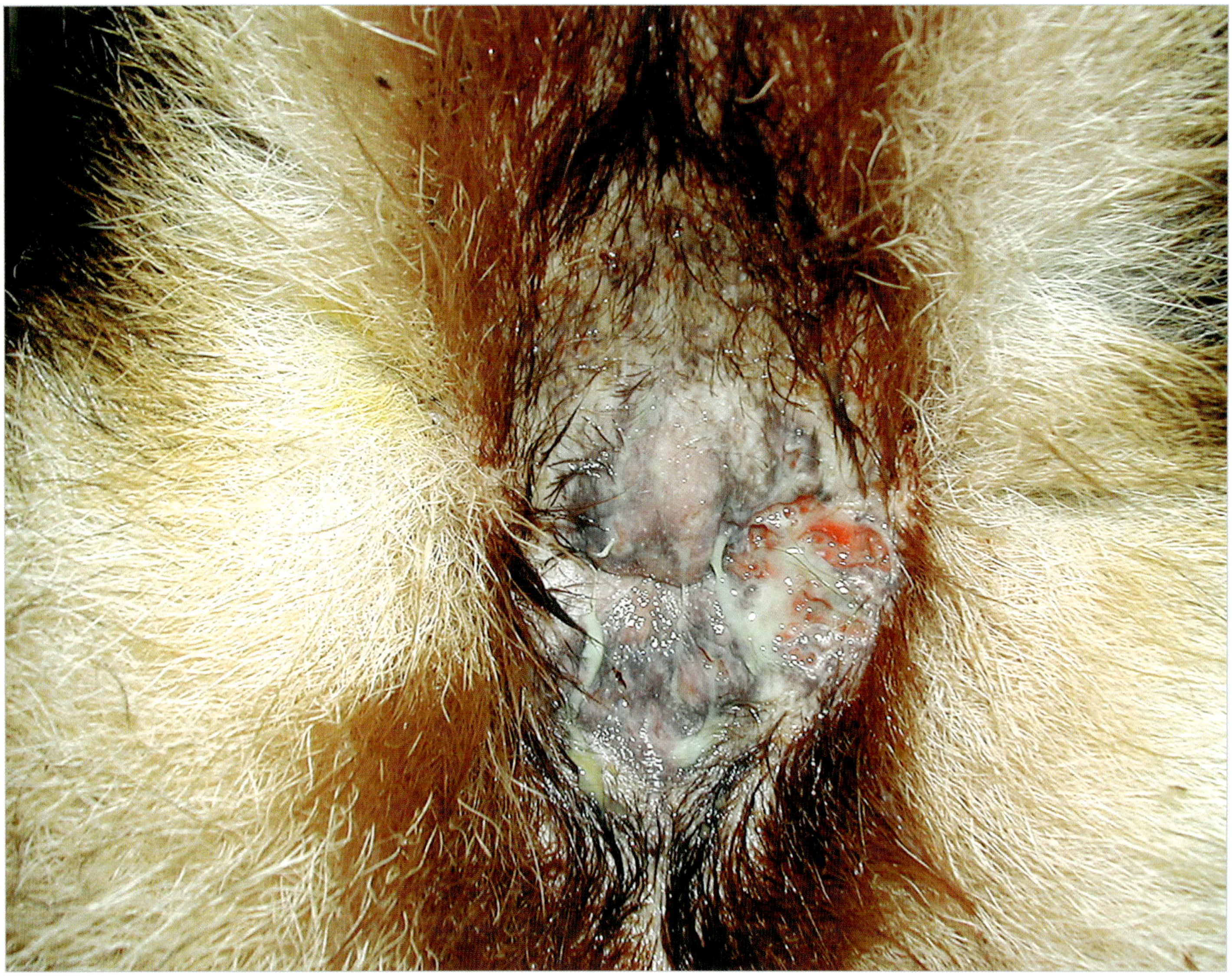

Fig. 2. The perianal area is inflamed and infected.

The general examination is normal, as are the results of the blood tests. The examination of the perineal area is apparently not painful and the patient allows us to lift the tail, clean the area and inspect the perianal fistulas (fig. 3).

The owner is informed about the condition his dog is likely to be suffering from and medical treatment is initiated, based on:

- Checking the ease of defaecation and, in the presence of tenesmus or dyschezia, administering lactulose per os (1 ml/5 kg) several times a day until the desired effect is achieved.
- Daily mechanical cleaning of the area with neutral soap and water, particularly after defaecating.
- Antibiotic ointment (bacitracin-neomycin-polymixin B) three times daily.
- Ointment with 0.1% tacrolimus twice daily (treatment with this ointment can prove expensive).

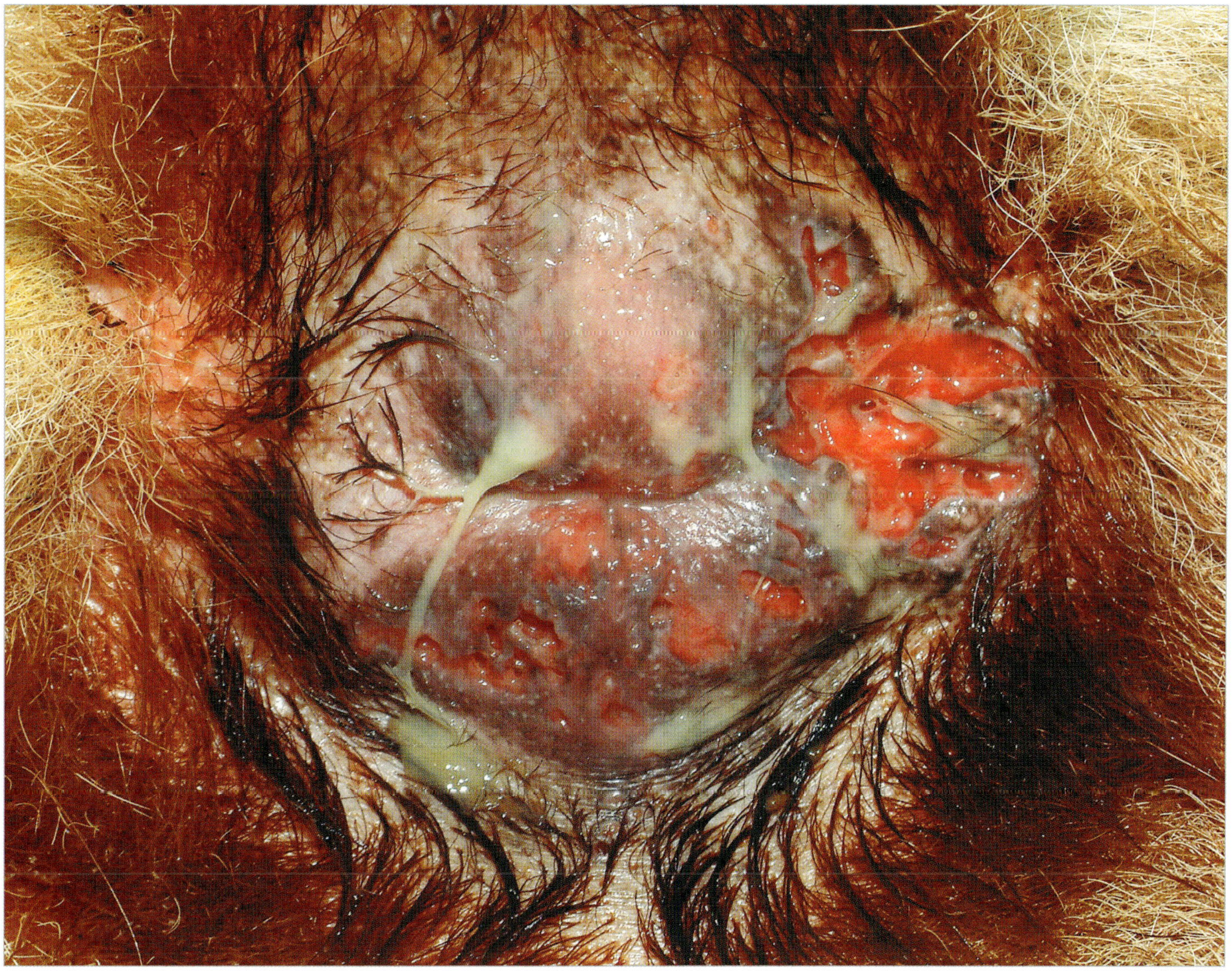

Fig. 3. After cleaning the area, different fistulous openings can be identified in the area ventral to the anus, and a large ulcerated area to the right.

Postoperatively

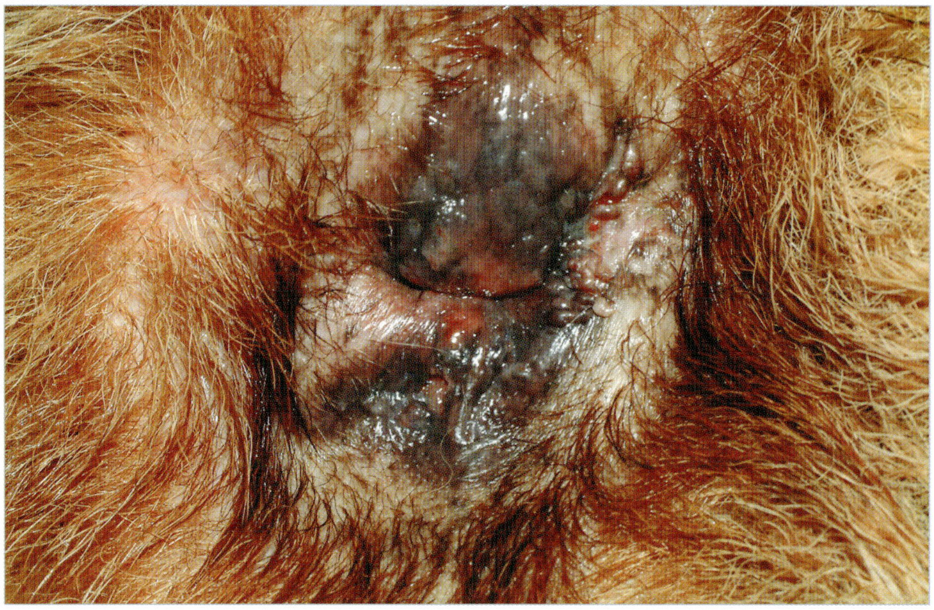

Fig. 4. During the first month of treatment, progress is satisfactory, the lesions are reducing in size and severity. The owner comments that the dog is happier and that his demeanour has improved.

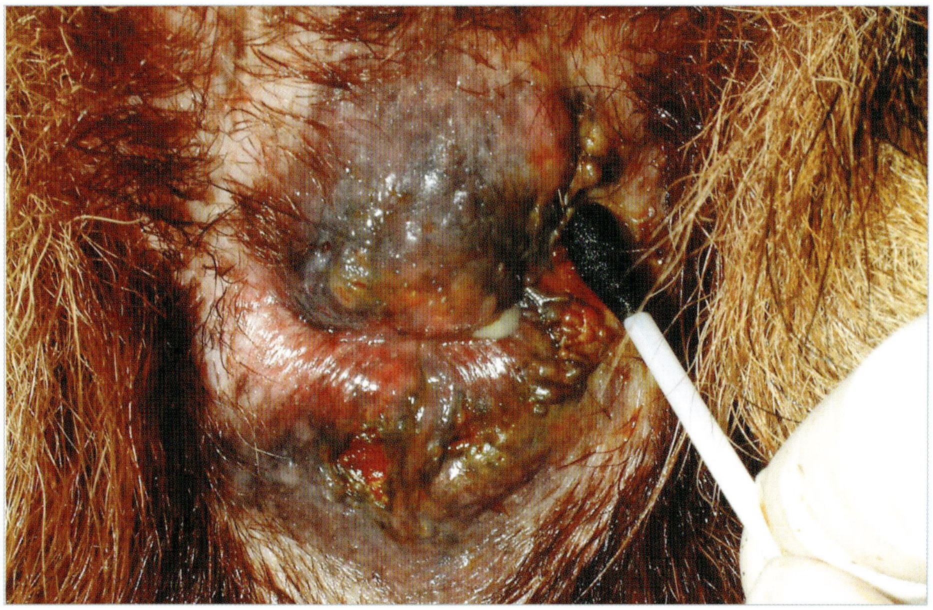

Fig. 5. Fifty days after treatment. Improvement does not continue at the same rate as in previous days, the small fistulous canals are not completely healed. To reactivate the healing process, the lesions are cauterised with a 7% iodine solution.

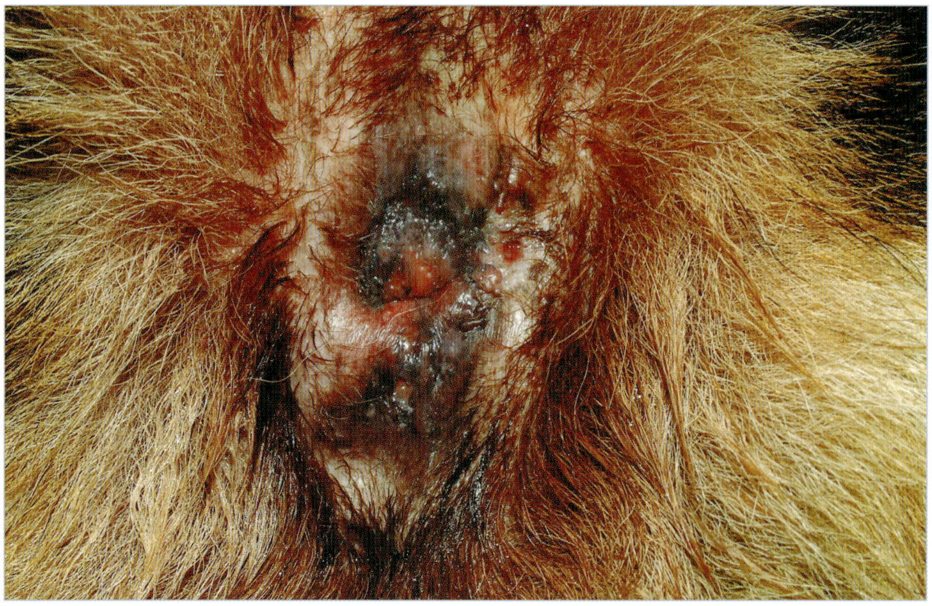

Fig. 6. Four days later, a slight improvement is noticed. The iodine solution is applied every 4 days. The tacrolimus ointment is applied once daily.

Treatment should be maintained for several months and the progress of the patient should be assessed regularly.

Other approaches to medical treatment:

- Mild laxatives to facilitate defaecation (fig. 8). The faeces should be soft but not pasty so that they do not stick to the anus and contaminate the area.
- Clean the perineal area with soap and water, in particular after defaecation. Remember that the area should be dried after cleaning to reduce the risk of a secondary dermatitis.
- Topical and systemic antibiotic therapy in advanced cases.
- Systemic immunosuppressants:
  - Cyclosporin A (1.75-5 mg/kg/12 h PO). This can be given with ketoconazole (12-15 mg/kg/24 h PO) to slow metabolism of cyclosporin, allowing its dose to be reduced, lowering the cost of treatment. Treatment should be continued for 2 weeks after resolution of the fistulas.
  - Azathioprine (50 mg/24 h PO) in combination with metronidazole (400 mg/ 24 h PO) is indicated 3-4 weeks before and after surgery.

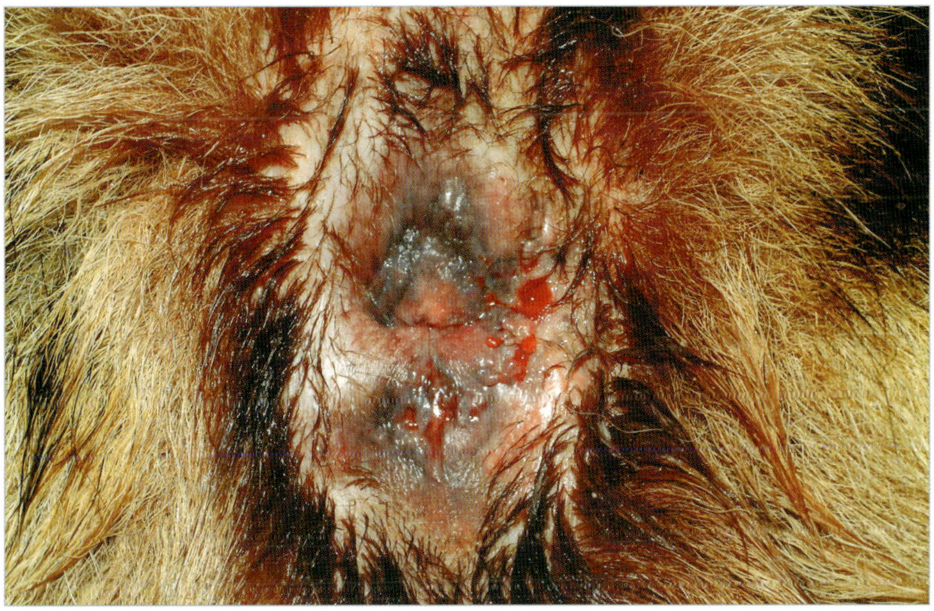

Medical treatment is long, expensive and requires commitment from the owner, but in all cases faecal continence is preserved.

Fig. 7. Four weeks later, the lesions are much reduced, the patient has no difficulty defaecating. The topical treatment is changed to tacrolimus ointment at a lower concentration (0.03%).

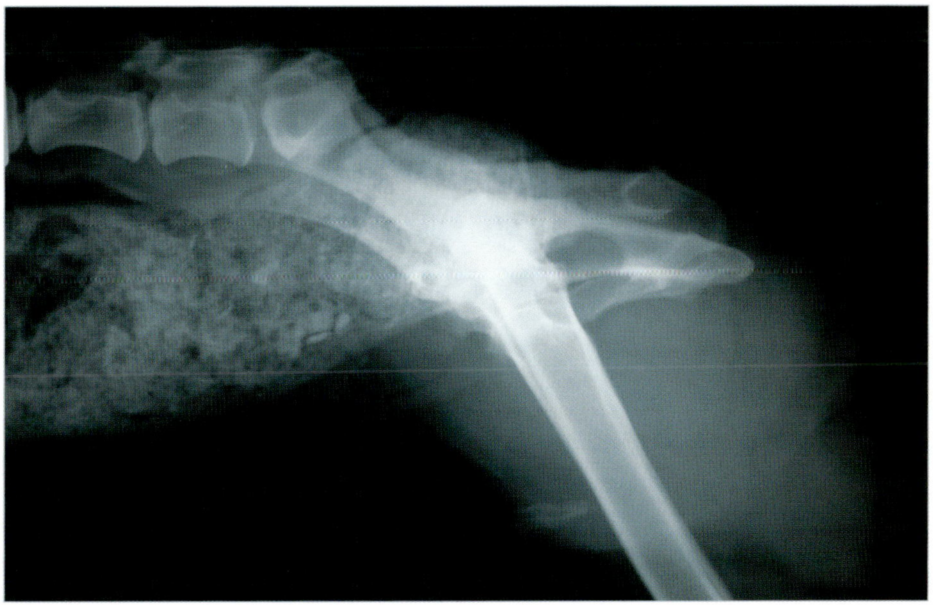

Fig. 8. Many patients have difficulty defaecating due to the intense pain in the perianal area. Secondary digestive problems, which may have systemic consequences, should be avoided by administering mild laxatives and non-hypertonic enemas.

Perianal fistulas. Case 2 / Radical surgical resection

Technical difficulty

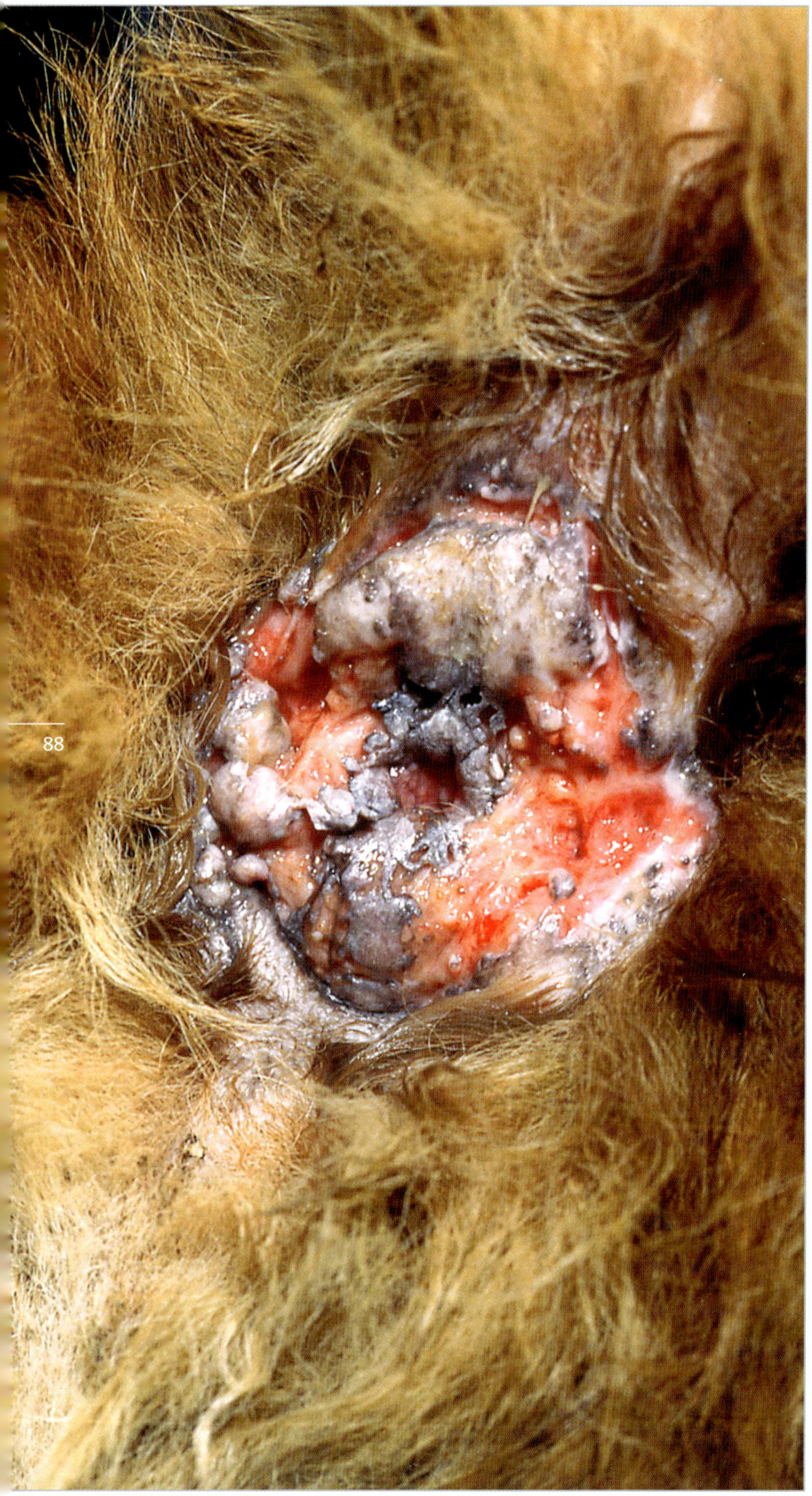

Fig. 1. The perianal lesions are severe, and affect 360° of the area. Medical treatment has improved the clinical signs and has reduced the lesions, but has not achieved complete healing.

Radical resection is based on the excision of the entire affected perianal area, eliminating the fistulous and ulcerated tissue.

"Kaiser" is an 8-year-old male German Shepherd with severe clinical signs of perianal fistulas that do not respond well to medical treatment (fig. 1). The owner is informed about surgical intervention, as well as the possible complications that may arise. The owner accepts these warnings and is committed to giving the immediate and long-term postoperative care that "Kaiser" will need.

Before surgery

- Mild laxatives for several days before the operation.
- Rectal enema 48 hours before.
- Thorough cleaning with antiseptic soap and water.
- Antibiotic prophylaxis (against Gram negative and anaerobic bacteria).

Do not use enemas in the 24 hours prior to surgery. The faeces may become very liquid and contaminate the surgical field.

See positioning of the patient ➔ page 248

Try to preserve the anal sphincter as much as possible to reduce the risk of faecal incontinence.

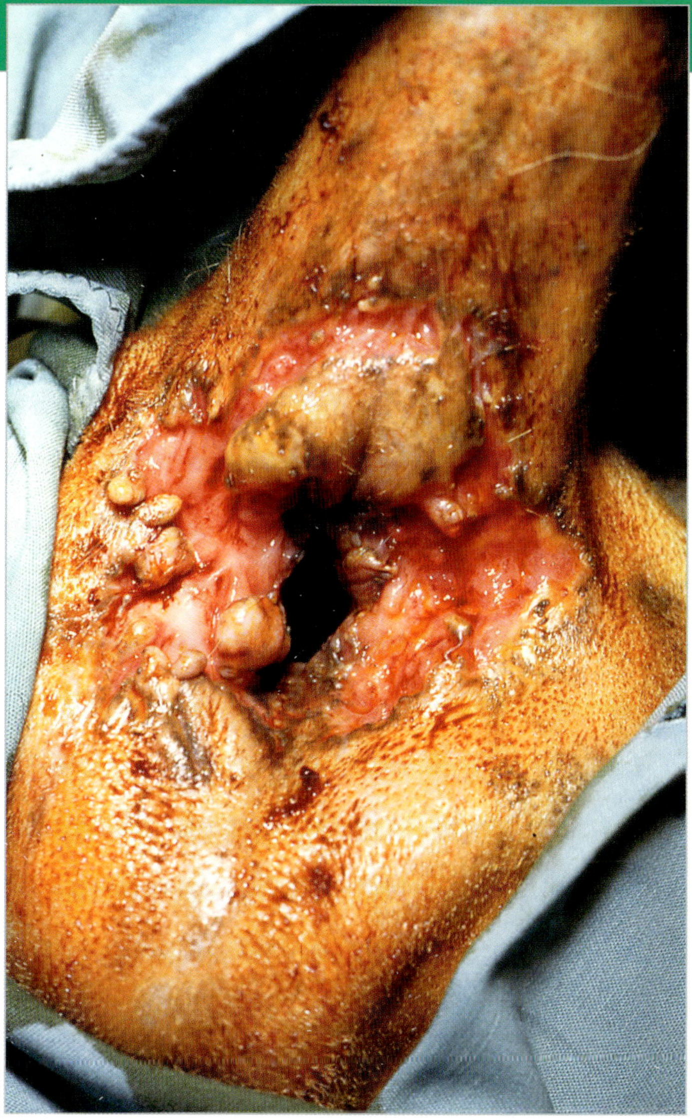

Fig. 2. Note the large area of affected tissue, which includes the anal sphincter. Using a scalpel, incise the skin on the outside and the anal sphincter on the inside. Resect the entire affected area: skin, subcutaneous tissue, muscle, fascia and the majority of the anus.

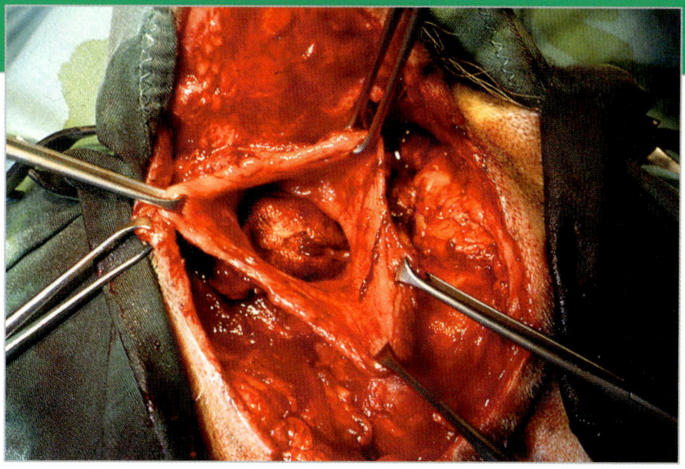

Fig. 3. After resection of all affected tissue, the rectum is sutured to the skin. Keep the rectal plug in place to avoid faecal contamination of the surgical field.

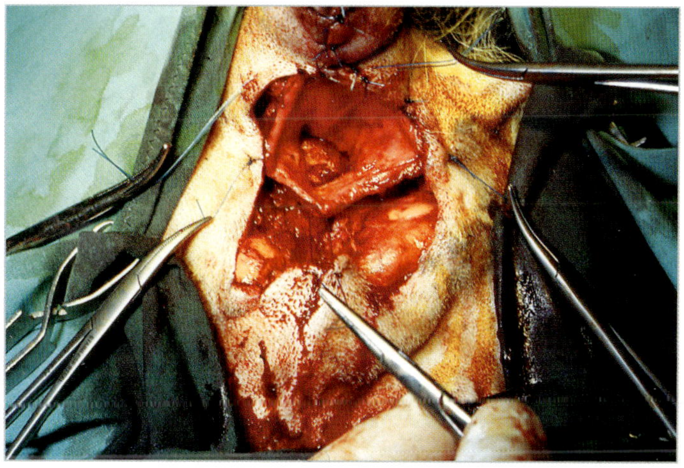

Fig. 4. Interrupted simple sutures are placed, using non absorbable monofilament material.

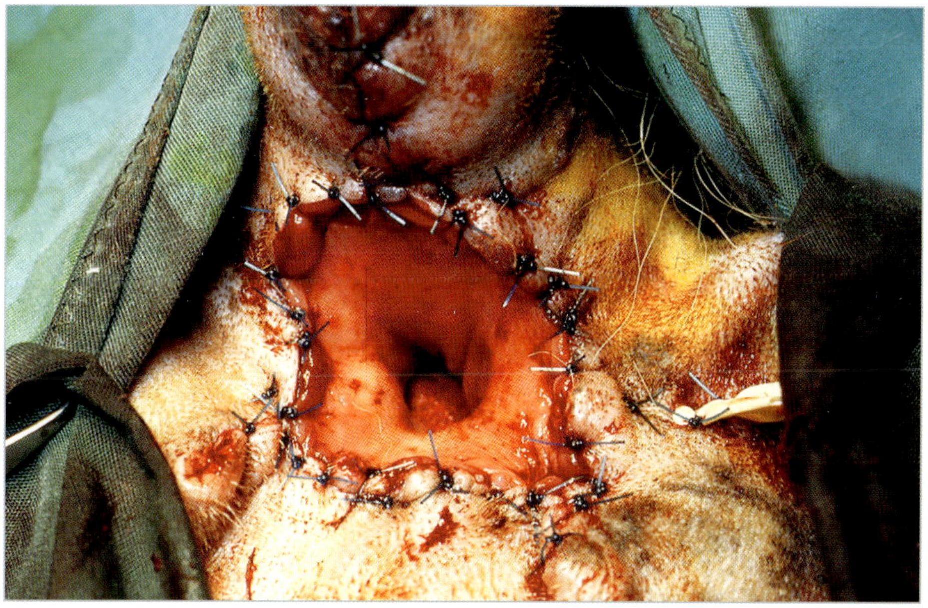

Fig. 5. Before finishing suturing, place one or two Penrose drains to avoid seromas forming postoperatively.

After surgery

- Elizabethan collar.
- Systemic analgesics.
- Cleaning of the anal area several times a day, particularly after defaecation.
- Mild laxatives for 3 to 4 weeks. Faeces should be eliminated easily, but should not become excessively pasty.
- Systemic antibiotics.
- Check-up every 2 days until complete healing, then once a month.

Possible complications

- Faecal incontinence (24-28%).
- Recurrence (17-33%).
- Anal stenosis (14%).
- Diarrhoea.
- Tenesmus.
- Dyschezia.
- Constipation.

Postoperatively

Regular check-ups are required to asses the progress of the patient.

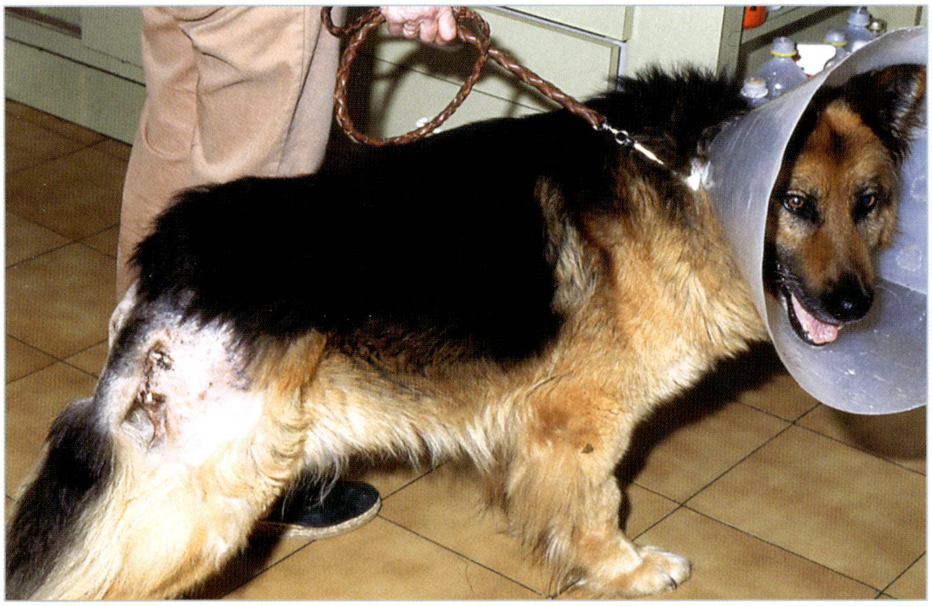

Fig. 6. The evolution after 36 hours is satisfactory. It is very important that the patient wears an Elizabethan collar at all times.

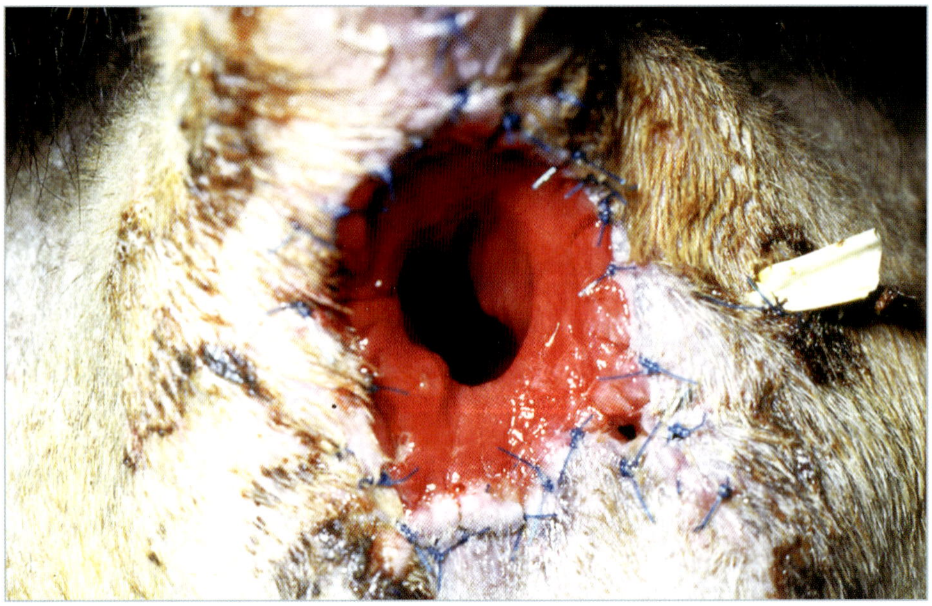

Fig. 7. Four days after the operation, the surgical area is healing satisfactorily, apart from the small dehiscence of a suture in the lateral area.
The drains are removed and their exit wounds are allowed to heal by secondary intention.

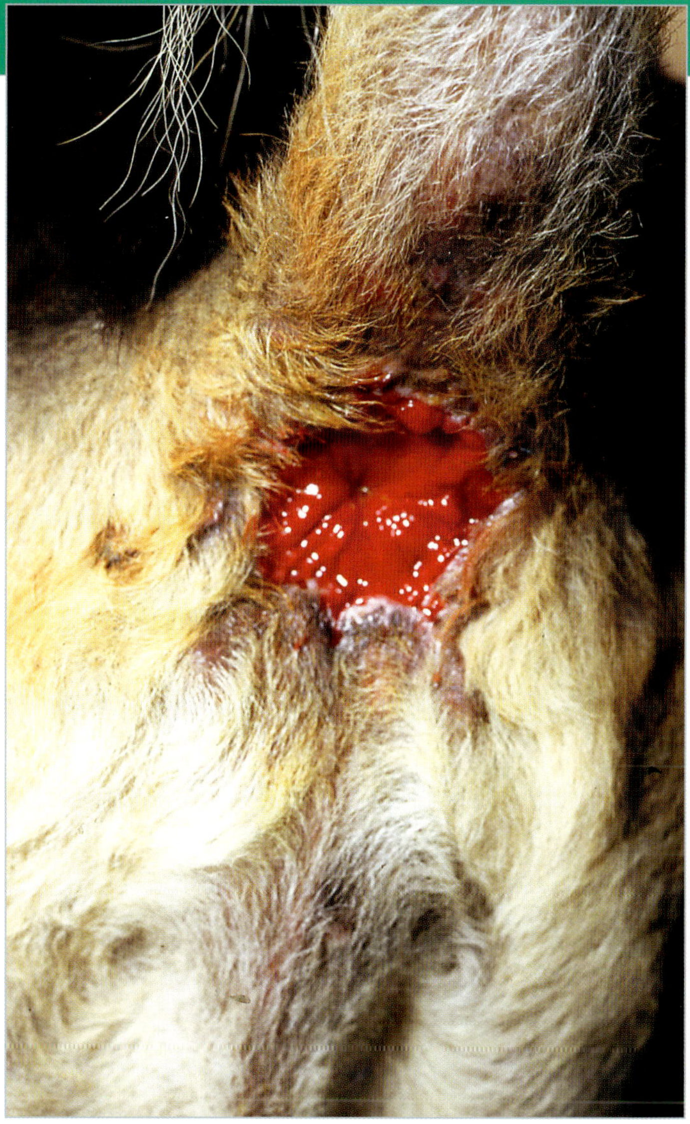

Fig. 8. Fifteen days after the operation, healing is progressing well. "Kaiser" is defaecating normally and shows no pain in the area. During initial postoperative period, no infection has been observed as the wound edges have progressively retracted.

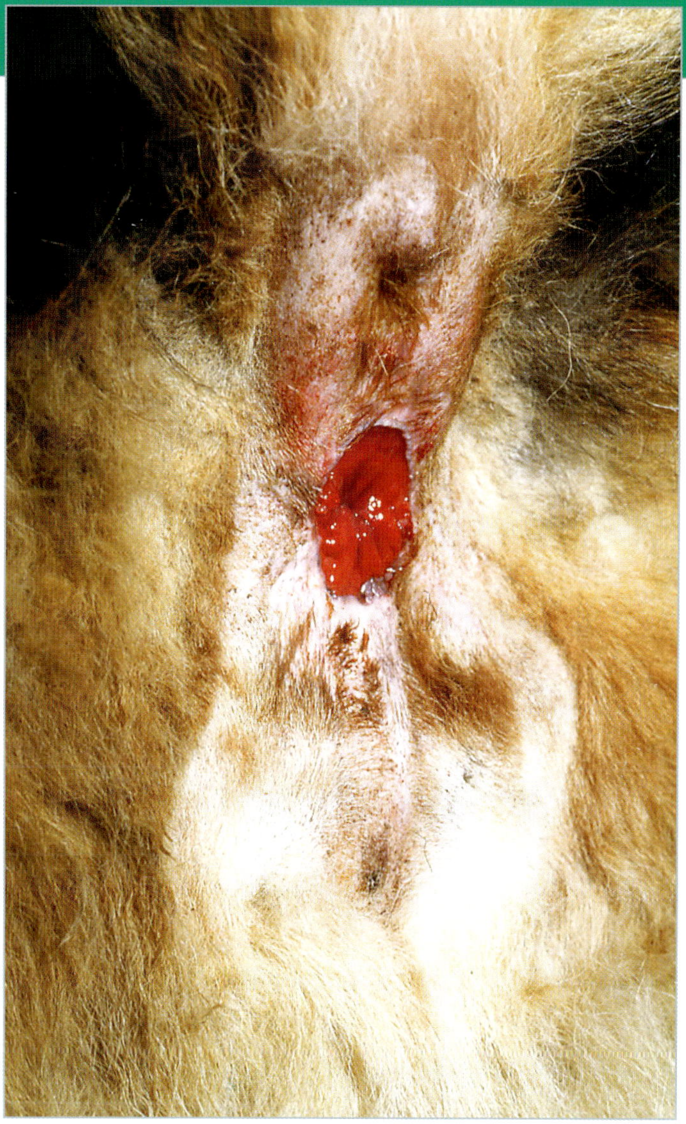

Fig. 9. After three months, the patient has regained weight, leads a completely normal life and there are no signs of recurrence of the perianal fistulas. Scar tissue contraction does not cause stenosis or defaecation problems.

From now on, monthly check-ups are recommended to monitor for recurrence. If any lesions appear, they should be dealt with promptly with cauterising substances.

Cauterising substances

- Silver nitrate.
- Phenol (5% solution).
- Iodine (7% solution).

Faecal incontinence is the most common postoperative complication of this kind of surgery.

This case was supplied by Dr. Cairó, of the Canis Veterinary Clinic, Girona (Spain).

Perianal fistulas. Case 3 / Radical surgical resection. Postoperative complications

Technical difficulty

A 4-year-old male German Shepherd is presented to the clinic with signs of perianal fistulas (fig. 1).

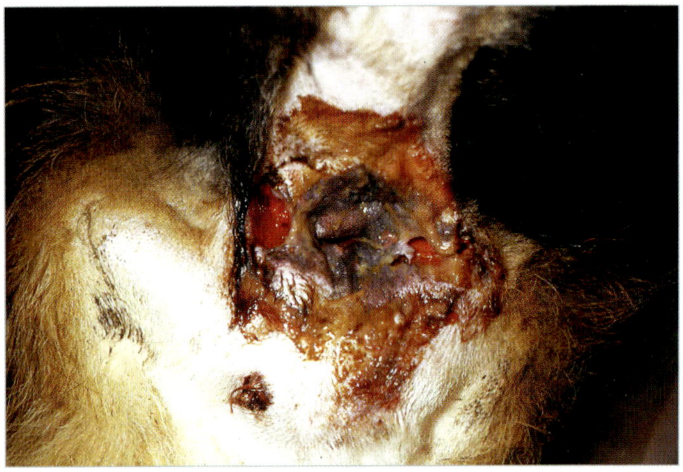

Fig. 1. Ulceration and infection of the entire perianal region.

Medical management based on cleaning the area, topical and systemic antibiotic therapy and systemic immunosuppressants is initiated. Given the high cost of the medical treatment, a radical resection of the affected area, as described in case number 2, is carried out; the owner is informed of the possible complications of this surgical intervention (fig. 2).

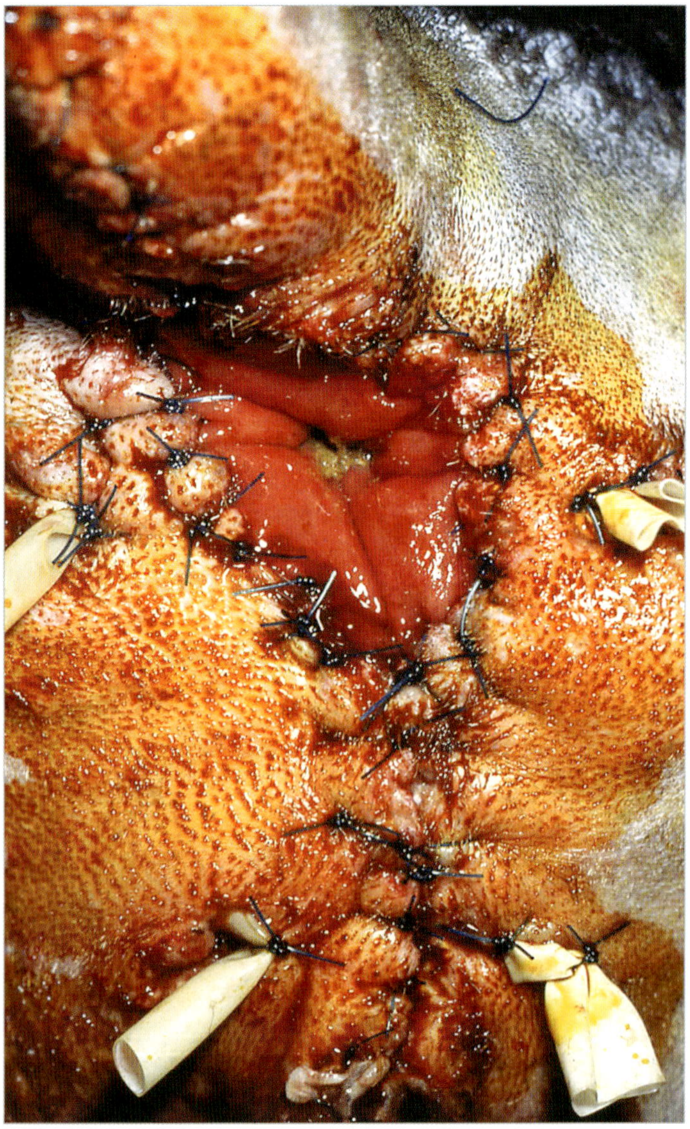

Fig. 2. Radical resection of the perianal area, suturing the rectum to the skin. In this case, two Penrose drains were placed on each side.

Postoperatively

24 hours after the operation healing is progressing favourably, but at the 48 hour post-operative check, the appearance is disastrous (fig. 3). The patient was not monitored correctly, did not wear its Elizabethan collar and has developed diarrhoea which the owner has not noticed.

> ✱ *Postoperative care is essential in this type of condition.*

Medical treatment is initiated, based on the following:

- Washing, once daily, with lukewarm water under pressure (for example by using a hand shower) and neutral soap to remove contaminating material.
- Cleaning and disinfection of the perianal area with a commercial iodine solution diluted 1:1 with saline, each time it defaecates.
- Systemic antibiotics. Amoxicillin + clavulanic acid (20 mg/kg) and enrofloxacin (5 mg/kg).

The lesions are left to heal by secondary intention.

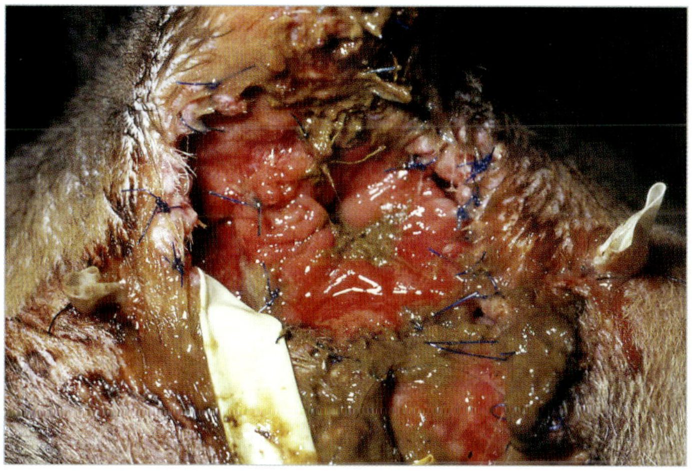

Fig. 3. Self-mutilation and infection have lead to the dehiscence of most sutures.

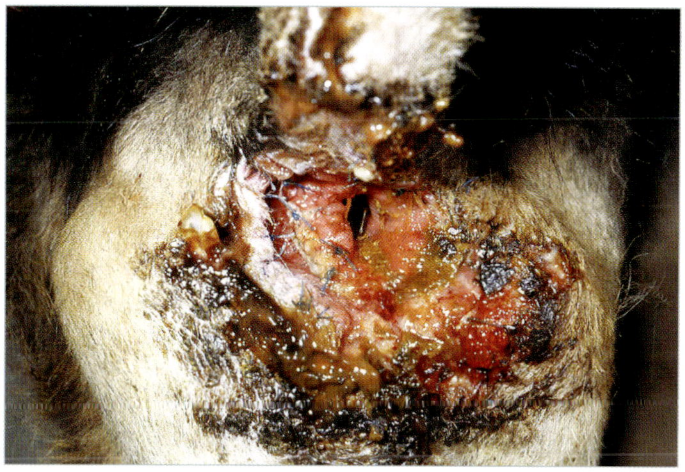

Fig. 4. Two days later, the infection is diminishing and the general appearance has improved. The drains are left in place and the medical management is continued.

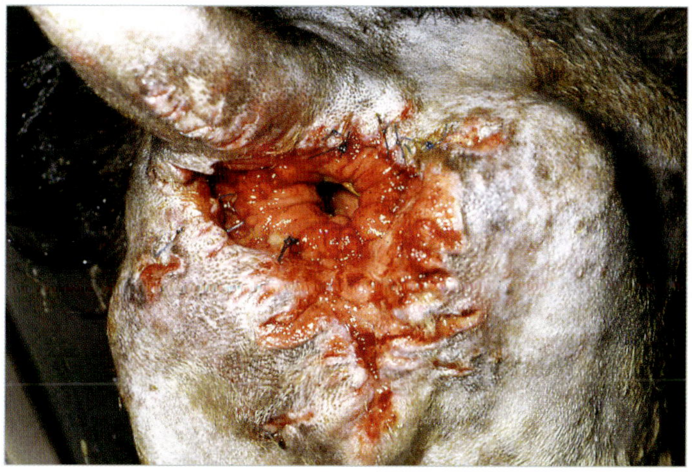

Fig. 5. On day 6, the infection is under control and the wounds are healing by secondary intention. The drains are removed at this stage. From this point, clinical signs improved progressively, and the lesions healed correctly.

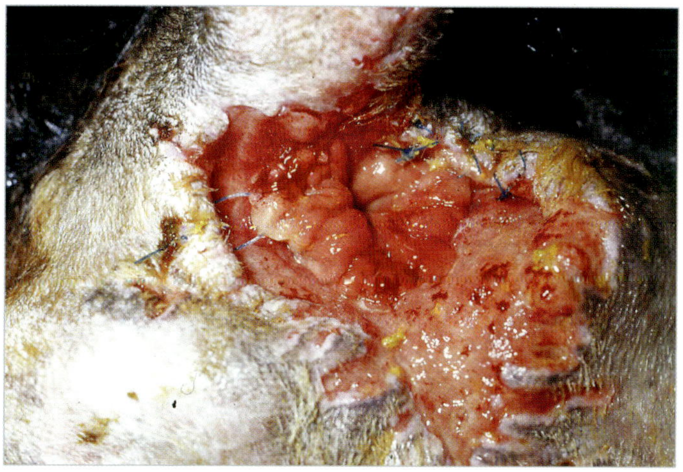

Fig. 6. 13 days after the operation.

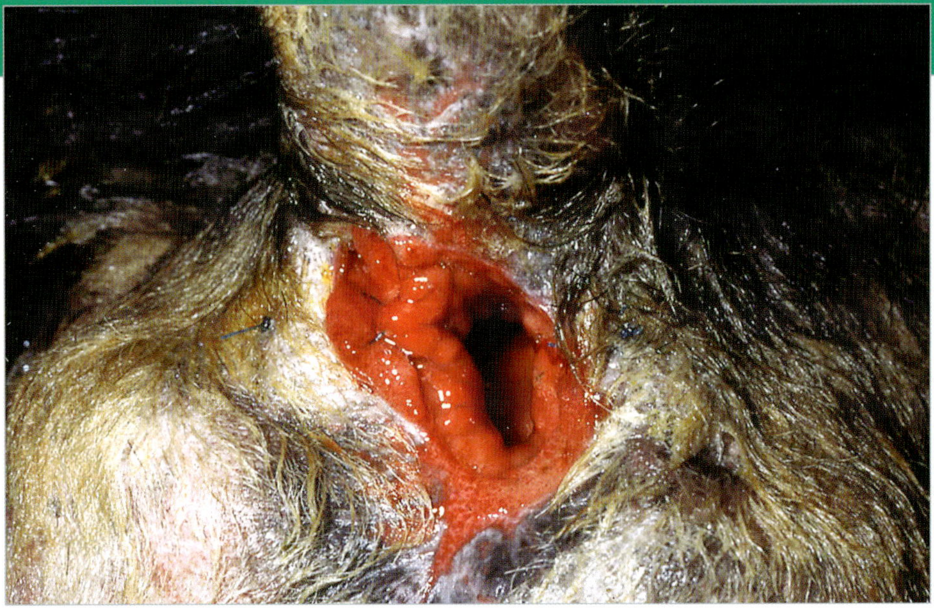

Fig. 7. 17 days after the operation.

The patient's initial lesions have resolved and, thanks to the perseverance and determination of the owner, the secondary complications of the postoperative infection have also healed.
The patient should have regular check ups to monitor for recurrence of the perianal fistulas.

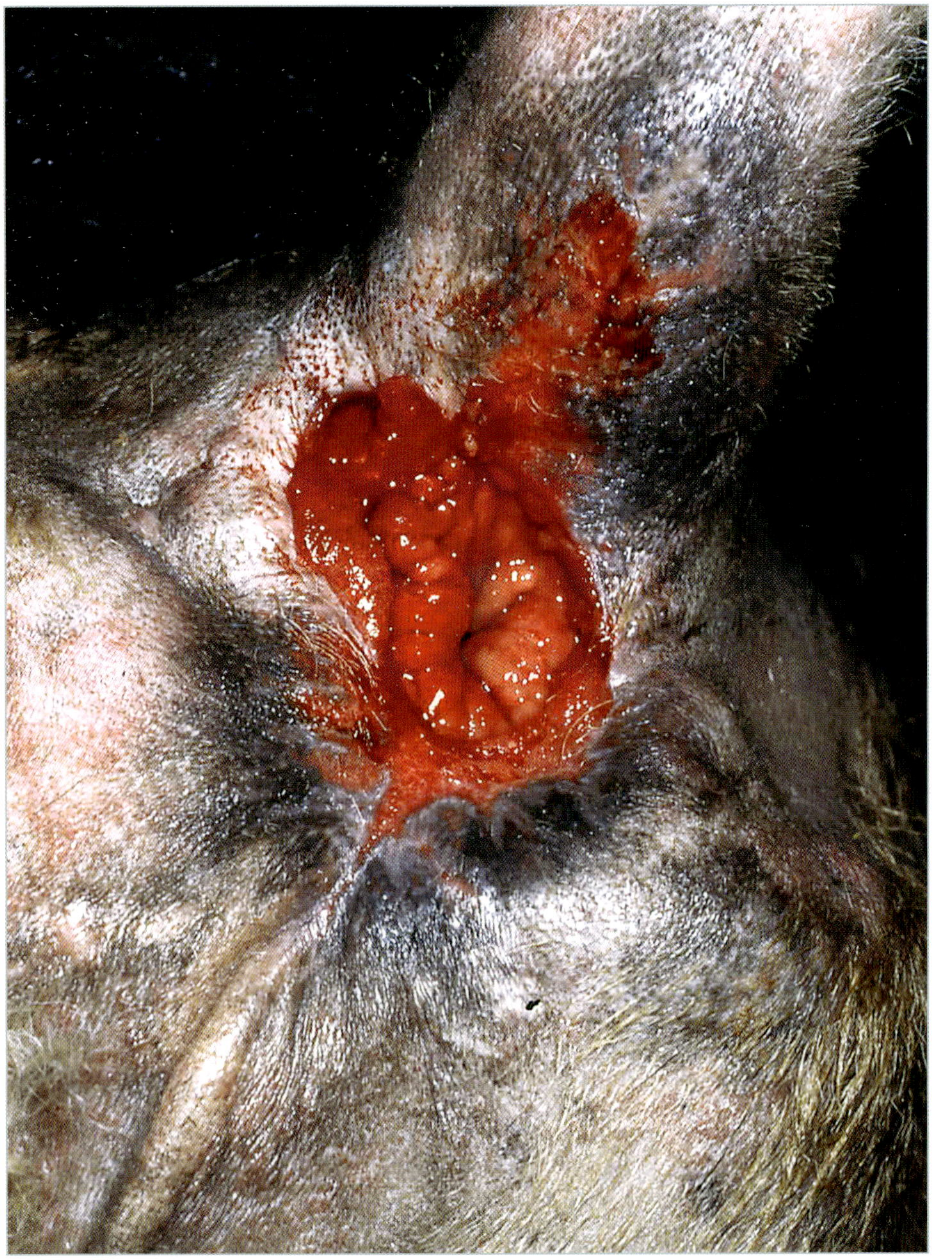

Fig. 8. 20 days after the operation.

This case was submitted by Dr. Cairó, of the Canis Veterinary Clinic, Girona (Spain).

Perianal fistulas. Case 4 / Superficial surgical resection

Technical difficulty

"Linda" (fig. 1) is a 5-year-old German Shepherd bitch. She was referred to the hospital by her veterinarian for fistulas on the left side of the anus (fig. 2).

In the German Shepherd, the anal sacs are located deeper than in other breeds. For this reason, if they rupture following an infection, the purulent material will infiltrate the muscle fibres, thereby creating fistular tracts to the outside.

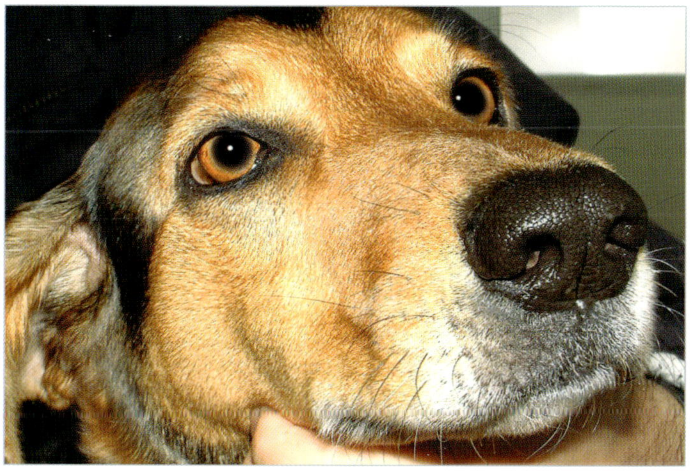

Fig. 1. "Linda" on the day of consultation. She is very apprehensive and shows great aversion to her tail being lifted for examination of the perianal area.

The case history supplied by the referring veterinarian reveals that, a few months earlier, the patient underwent bilateral sacculectomy for recurring sacculitis.

Two weeks after the intervention, fistulas appeared on both sides of the anus. They were resected surgically.

Three weeks later, fistulas appeared again on the left side of the anus, but not on the right.

The owners are informed of the most likely cause of the fistulas: remnants of glandular tissue that continue to secrete material into the perianal tissue, and that the dog will need to undergo surgery again to remove this.

The owners opt for medical management before subjecting the dog to surgery again.

An alcohol-iodine solution (7%) is introduced in the fistular openings. Following this, an antibiotic cream is prescribed for topical application every 8 hours.

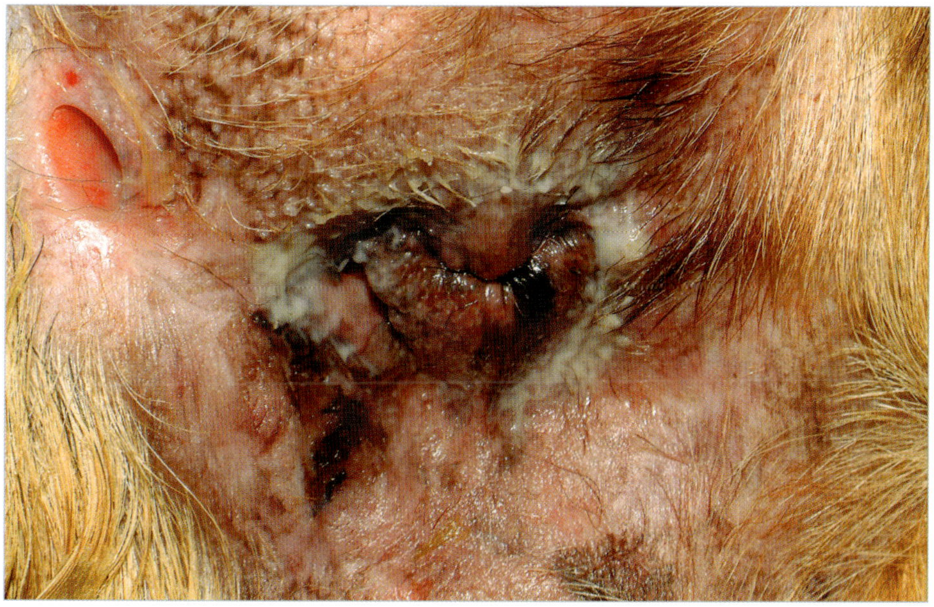

The patient must wear an Elizabethan collar to avoid licking the anal area.

Fig. 2. On the left side of the anus, two fistular orifices are visible, one next to the anal sphincter and the other in the dorsolateral area, adjacent to the tail base.

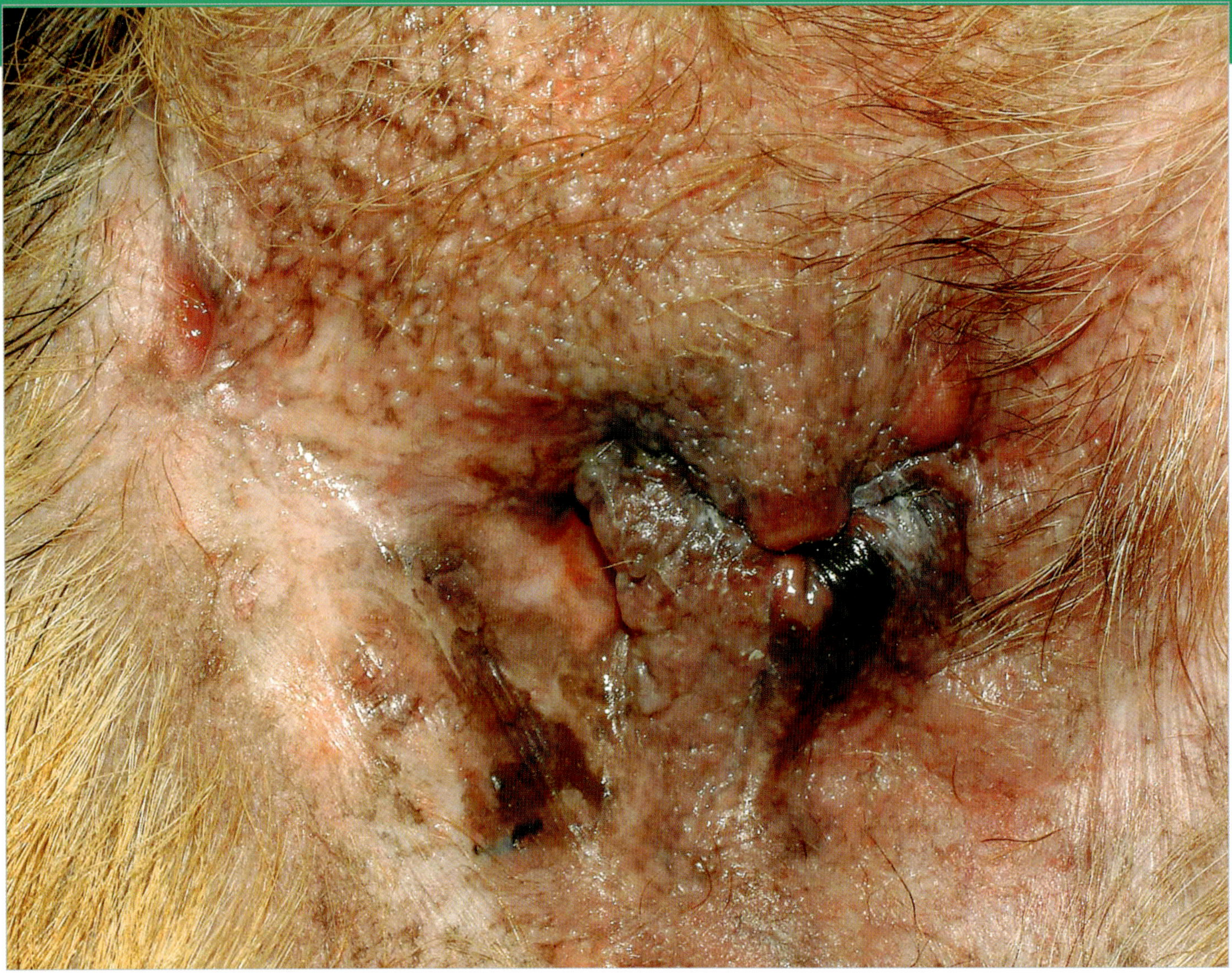

Fig. 3. Five days later, the fistular openings have become smaller and there is hardly any discharge. After 10 days of medical treatment, the lesions are the same, and have not continued to heal.

After ten days, the lesions have not improved, the owners agree to further surgical intervention.

See patient positioning ➔ page 248

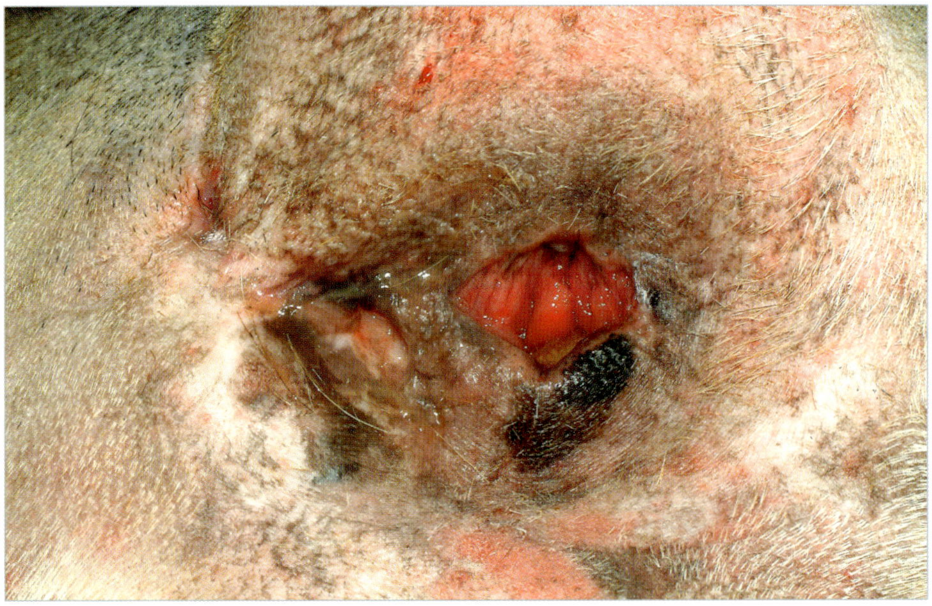

Fig. 4. After preparing the surgical field, the fistular openings on the left of the anus are clearly visible.

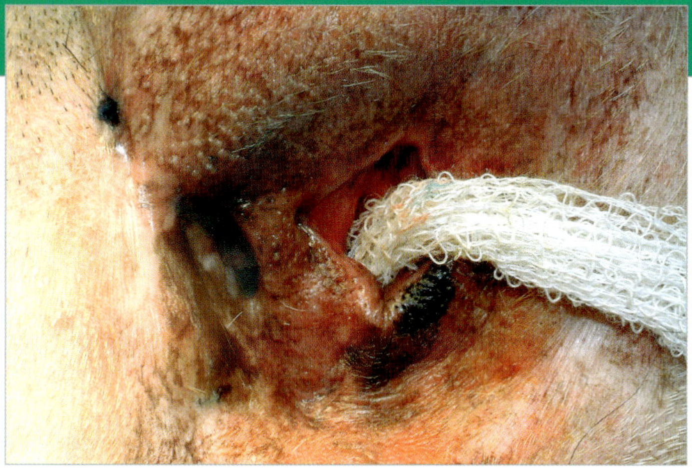

Fig. 5. In order to clearly identify the fistular tracts, a biological dye (methylene blue) is injected into the upper and middle fistular openings.

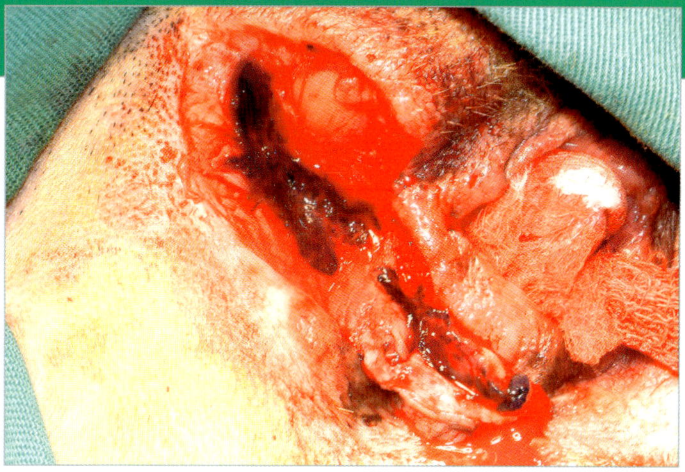

Fig. 6. The skin around the fistular tracts is resected. The tracts are visible due to the dye.

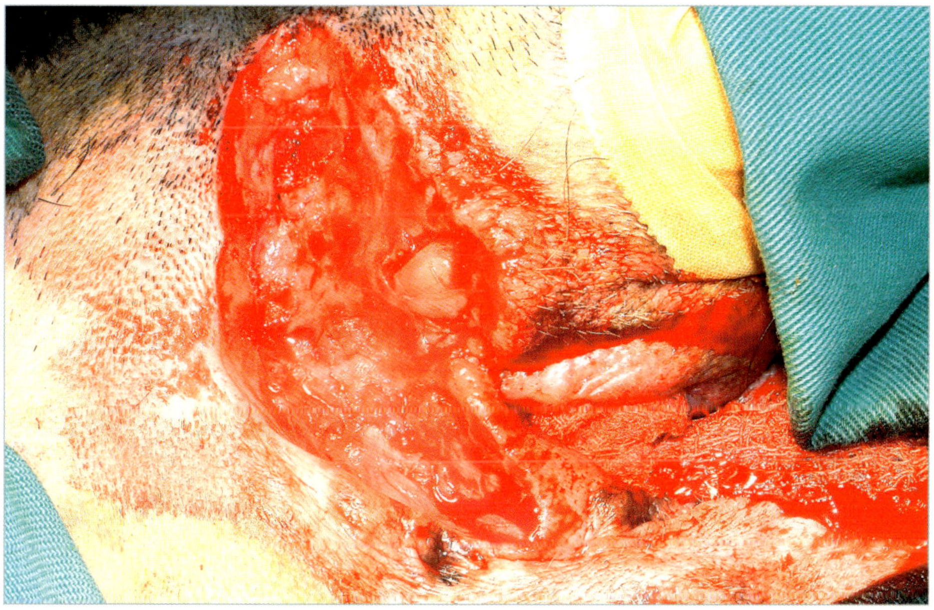

Fig. 7. All affected and dyed tissue is resected and removed.

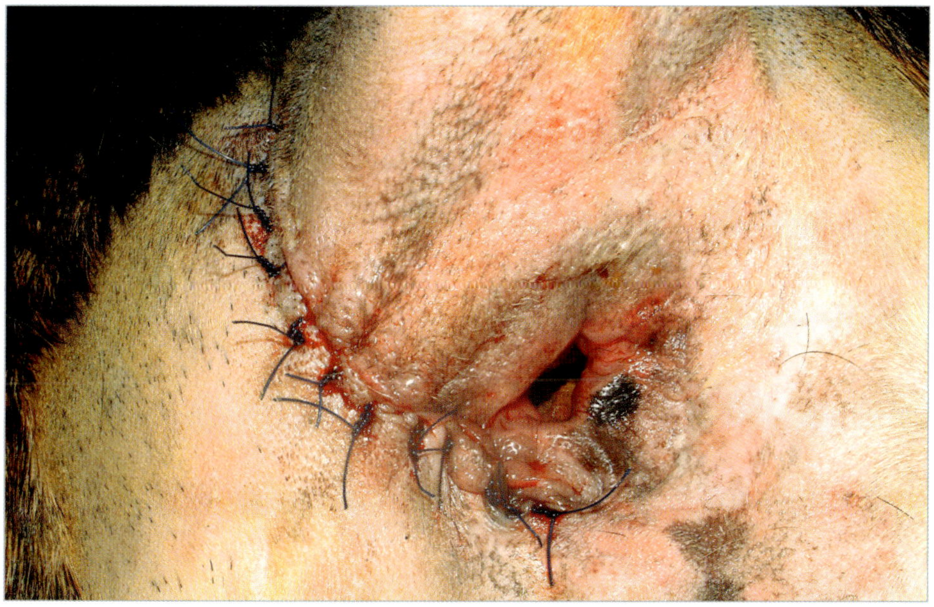

Fig. 8. The subcutaneous tissue is closed with interrupted sutures using absorbable monofilament material.
The skin is closed with vertical mattress sutures using non-absorbable monofilament material.
The anus is pulled towards the sutures, but resumes its original position in the following days.

After surgery

Postoperative treatment involves daily cleaning of the area, systemic antibiotics and a mild laxative for two weeks.

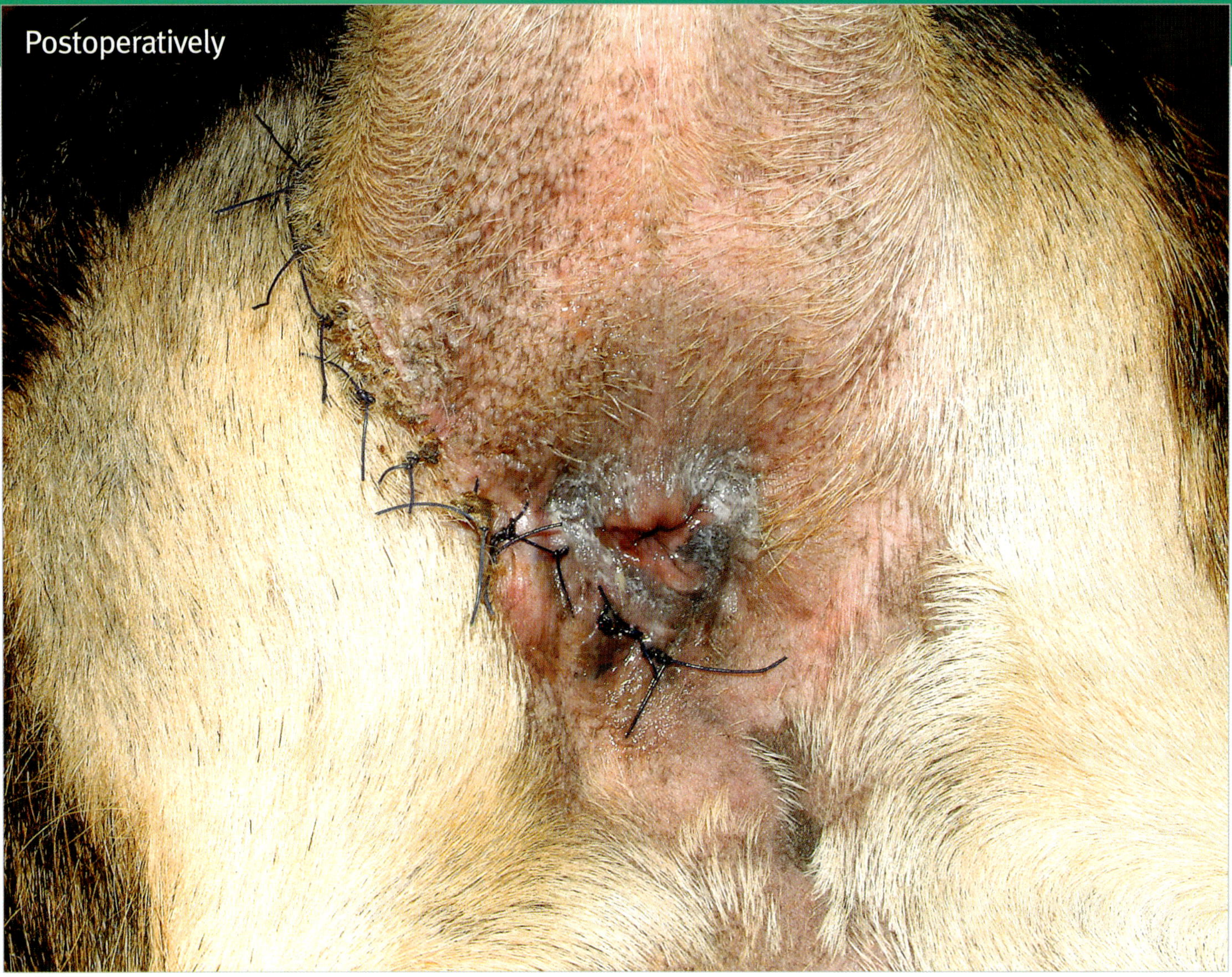

Fig. 9. Ten days after surgery, healing is progressing well and there are no signs of recurring fistulas. The sutures are removed.

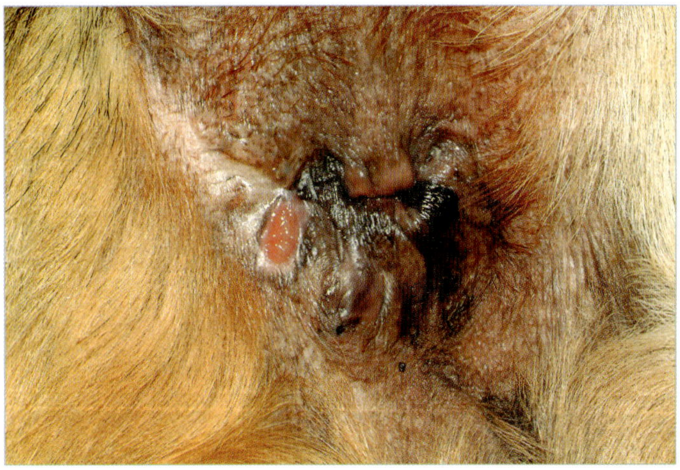

Fig. 10. One month after the operation, healing is complete, apart from a small ulcer that can be seen on the left side of the anus.
Ongoing treatment consists of painting the ulcers with a 7% iodine solution every three days for three treatments.

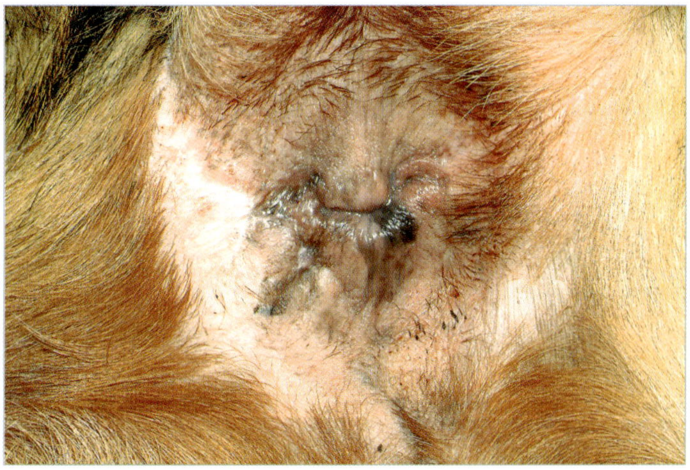

Fig. 11. On re-examination 23 days later, the area has healed completely with no further recurrence of fistulas. "Linda" has finished her treatment.

Perianal fistulas. Case 5 / Surgical resection and medical treatment

Technical difficulty	■	■	■	□	□

A 9-year-old male German Shepherd (fig. 1) is presented with perianal fistulas (fig. 2).

> ***The smaller the fistular lesions, the higher the success rate of their surgical resection.***

As the lesions are not very extensive, surgical intervention (figs. 3-7) is suggested to the owner.

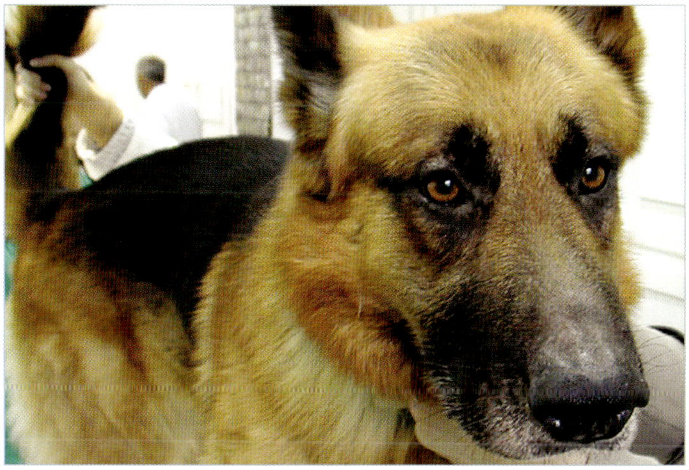

Fig. 1. "Larry" is a very well-behaved dog but does not like his tail being lifted for examination of the perianal area.

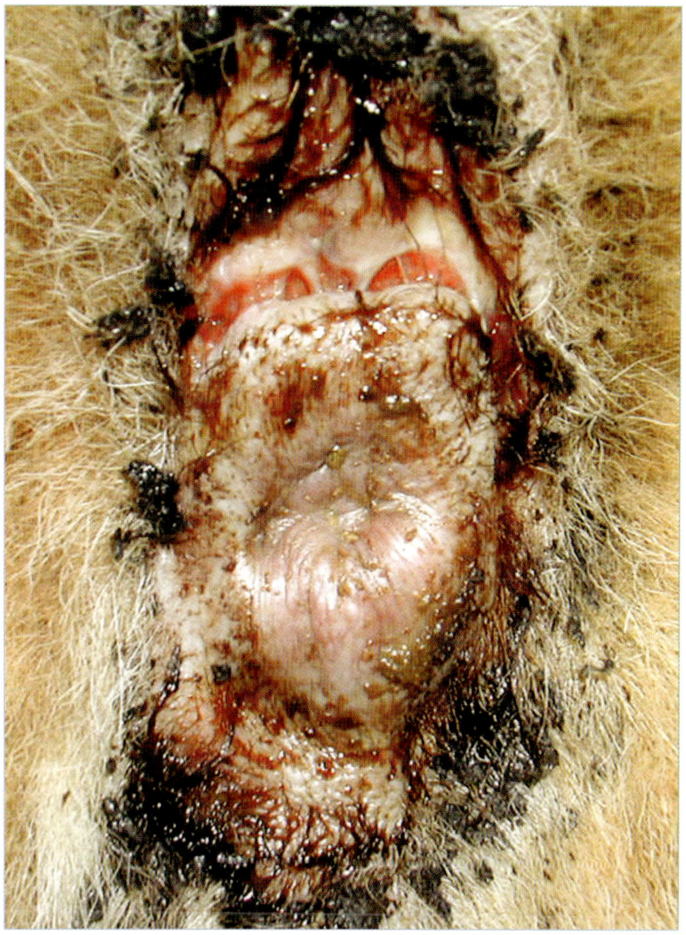

Fig. 2. The lesions are mainly situated in the area dorsal to the anus. Another fistula can be found in the left ventrolateral area.

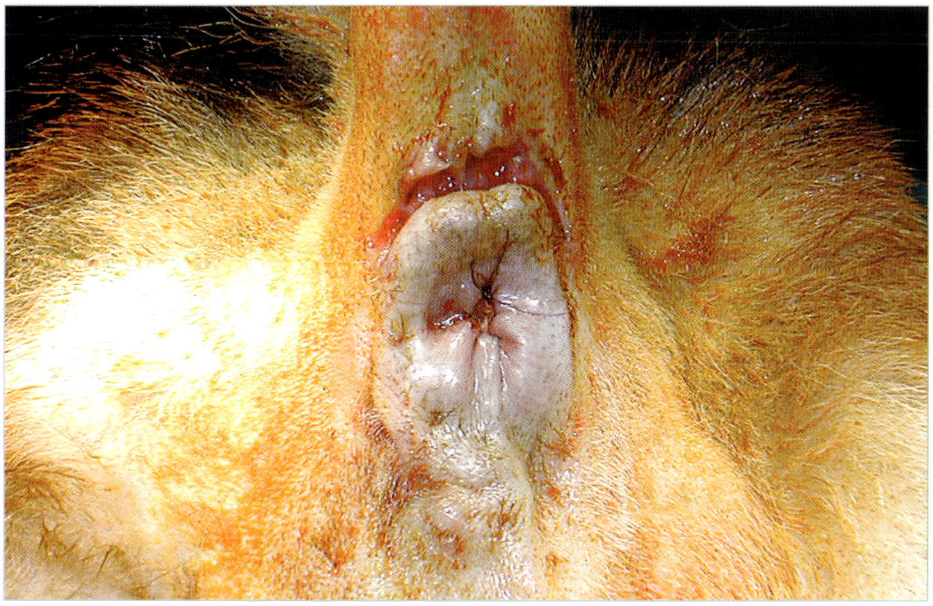

Fig. 3. Three days before surgery, systemic and topical antibiotic treatment is initiated, combined with cleaning of the area with water and soap. This image shows the patient in sternal recumbency and prepared for the operation.

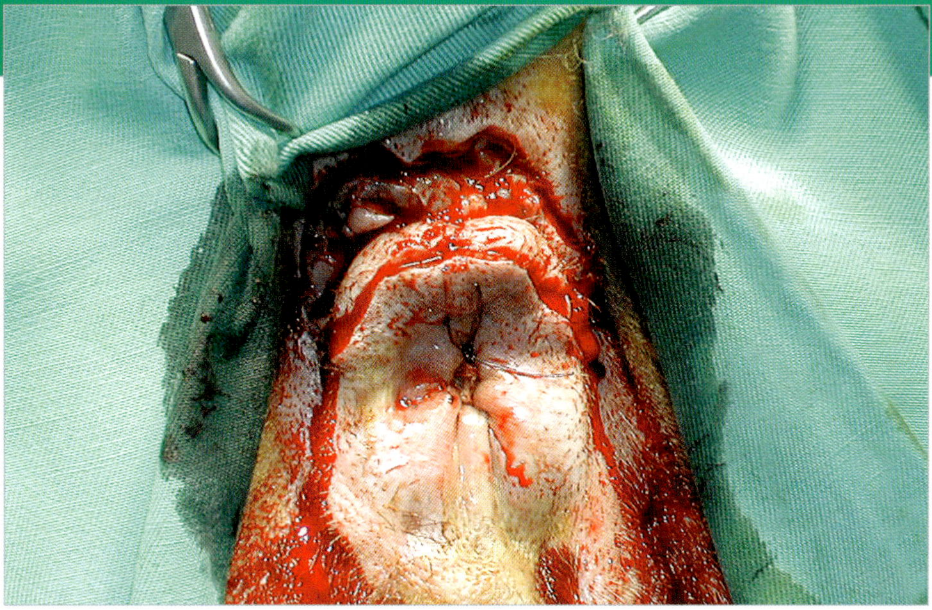

Fig. 4. There is copious bleeding in this area as a result of considerable superficial vascularisation. Monopolar coagulation should be used as little as possible to minimise the risk of secondary fibrosis.

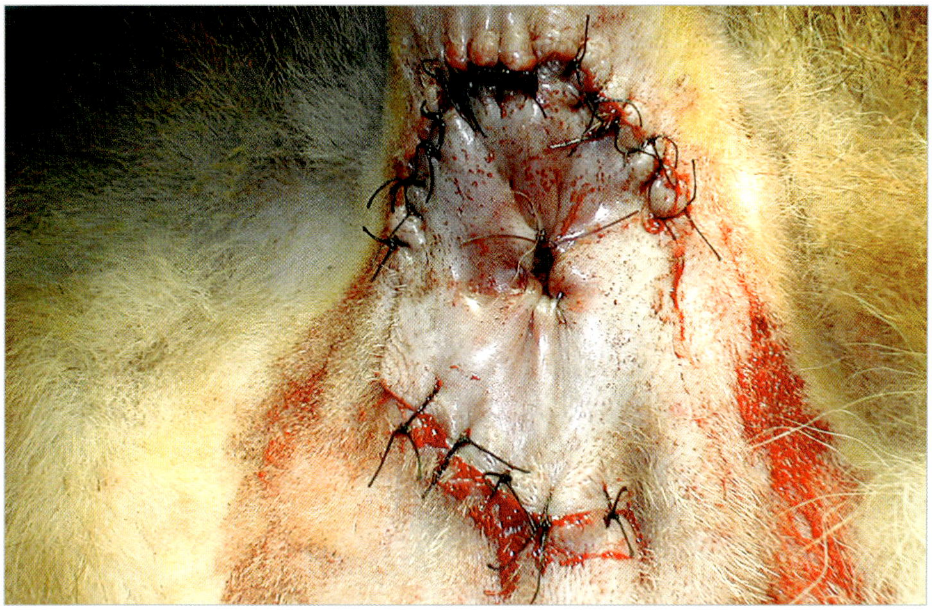

Fig. 5. After resection of the affected tissue, the subcutaneous tissue is closed using interrupted sutures with absorbable 3/0 material. The skin is closed with interrupted sutures of non-absorbable monofilament material.

Postoperative care

Systemic antibiotic treatment is continued for 7 days postoperatively, with strict attention to local hygiene and antiseptic measures.

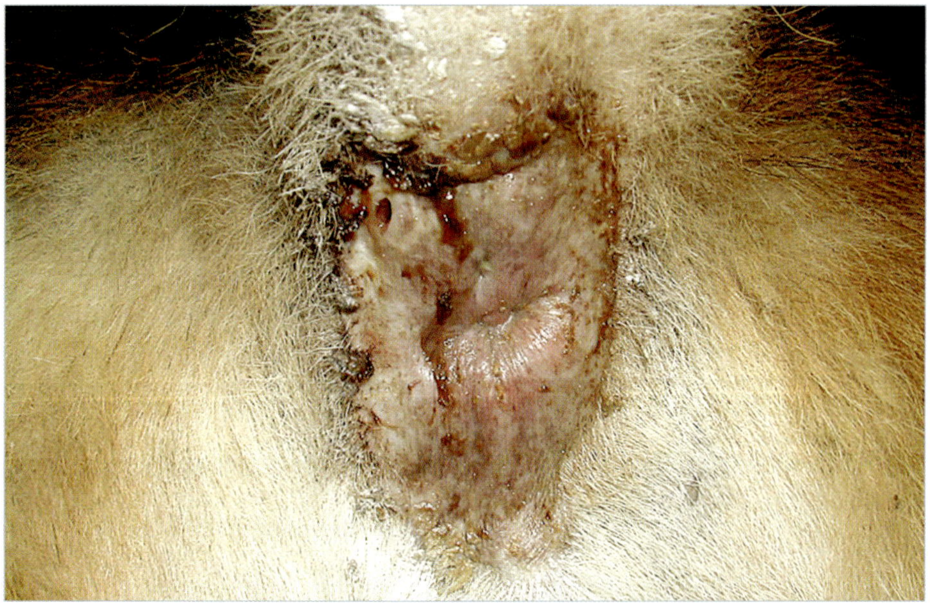

Fig. 6. During the first days after the operation, the progression is favourable and healing is normal. However, on day 20, a recurrence is observed in the dorsal area of the anus. Local hygiene measures are applied again, and a 0.03% tacrolimus topical cream is applied twice daily.

The time interval between tacrolimus ointment applications will increase according to the healing of the lesions. Check regularly for small fistular lesions and treat them as soon as possible.

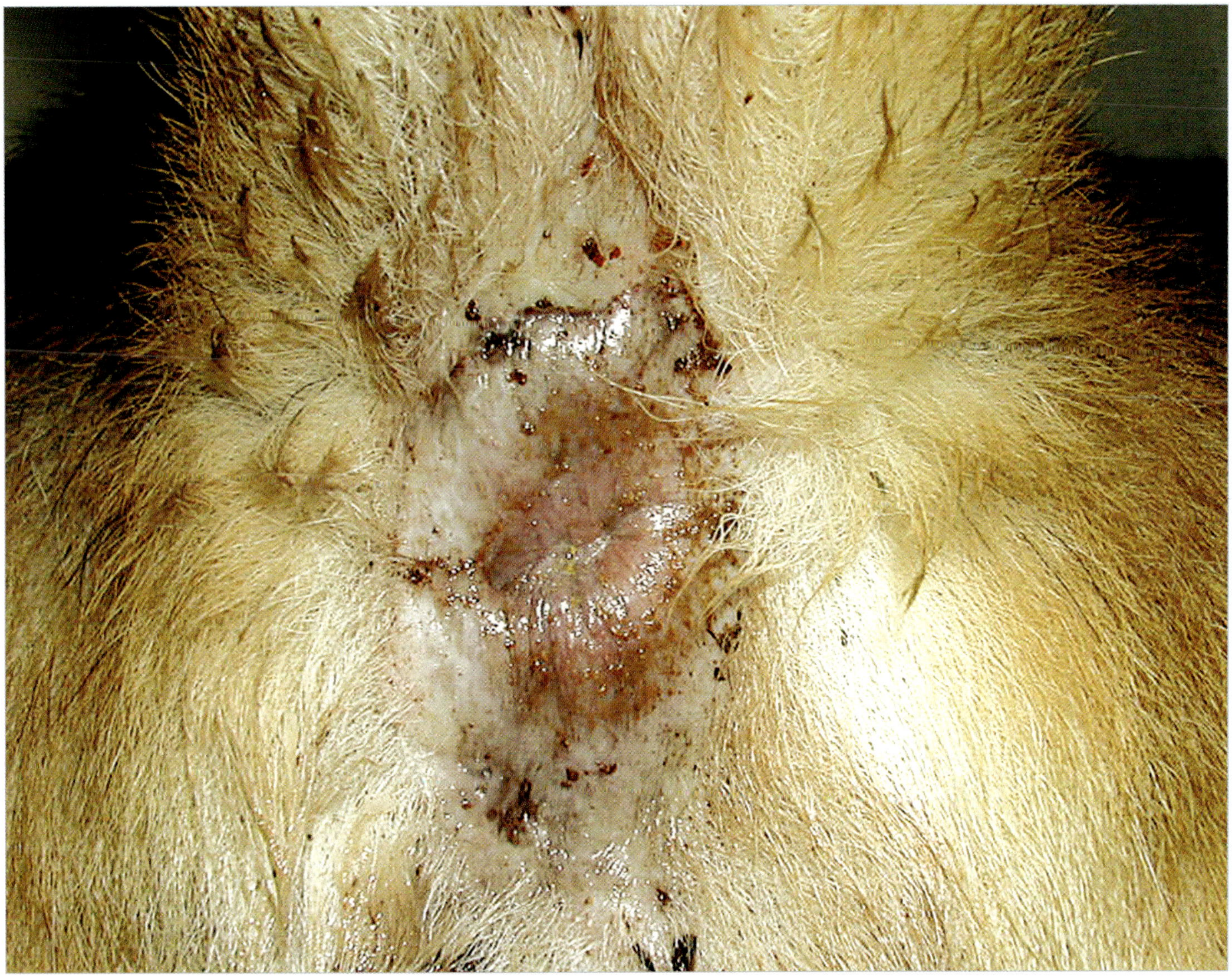

Fig. 7. Perform regular check-ups to monitor progress. This image shows the perianal region of the patient two months after surgery.

Tail fold disease

Prevalence	■				

Many dogs and cats with a short tail may have a sideways deviation of the coccygeal vertebrae ("corkscrew" tail), which forms skin folds on the lateral and ventral sides of the tail (figs. 1 and 2).
Inside these folds, fat secretions of the apocrine glands and faecal material may accumulate, leading to severe infections of the area.

Surgical treatment is based on the resection of the skin folds, with or without amputation of the coccygeal vertebrae.

Pyoderma that occurs in the tail fold does not respond to medical treatment. The only effective solution is surgery.

Depending on the country, this surgical treatment may bar the patient from any future dog shows, and the owner should be informed of this prior to surgery.

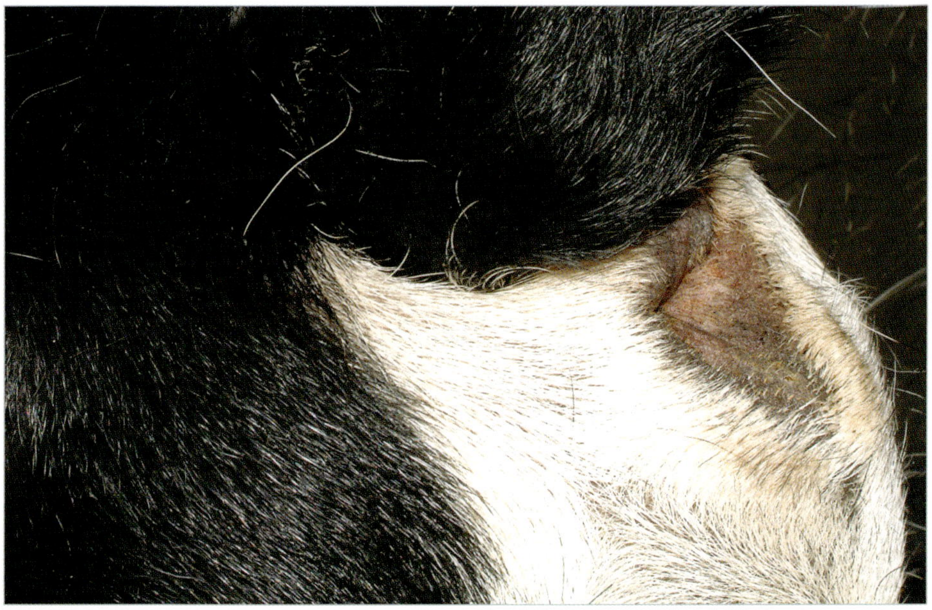

Fig. 1. "Corkscrew" tail in a 3-year-old male Bulldog. This patient presents no clinical signs.

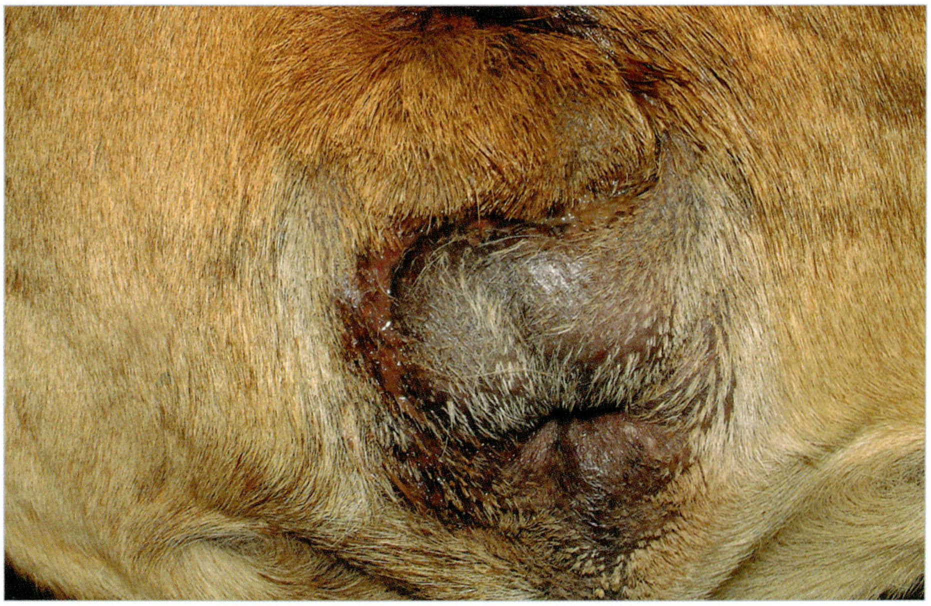

Fig. 2. This patient suffers from severe moist pyoderma of the tail. Note the purulent material discharging the left ventral area.

Tail fold disease. Case 1 / Surgical resection

Technical difficulty	■ ■ ■ ■ ■

Fig. 1. "Christopher" on the first day of his surgical consultation.

"Christopher" is a 6-year-old male Bulldog that was brought to the hospital for a severe infection of the skin folds of the tail, which non-responsive to medical management (figs. 1-3).

The main problem for the owner is the smell of the dog due to the infection.

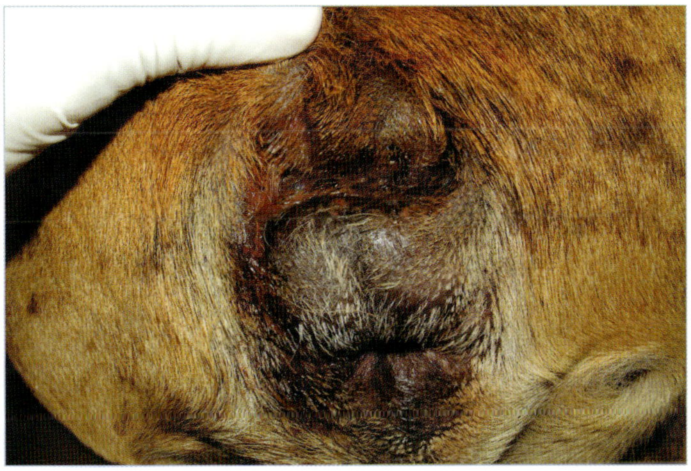

Fig. 2. The deviation of the tail to the right has caused deep skin folds. The discharge of purulent material from the lower fold is clearly visible.

Surgical technique

Surgery is based on the resection of the skin folds while trying to preserve the coccygeal vertebrae.

Before surgery

- Antibiotic prophylaxis starting 3 days before surgery.
- Antiseptic cleaning of the area with iodine soap in an attempt to eliminate the contaminated material in the skin folds.

See patient positioning ➔ *page 248*

See purse string suture ➔ *page 252*

✱ *This surgery can be time-consuming, so plan for this.*

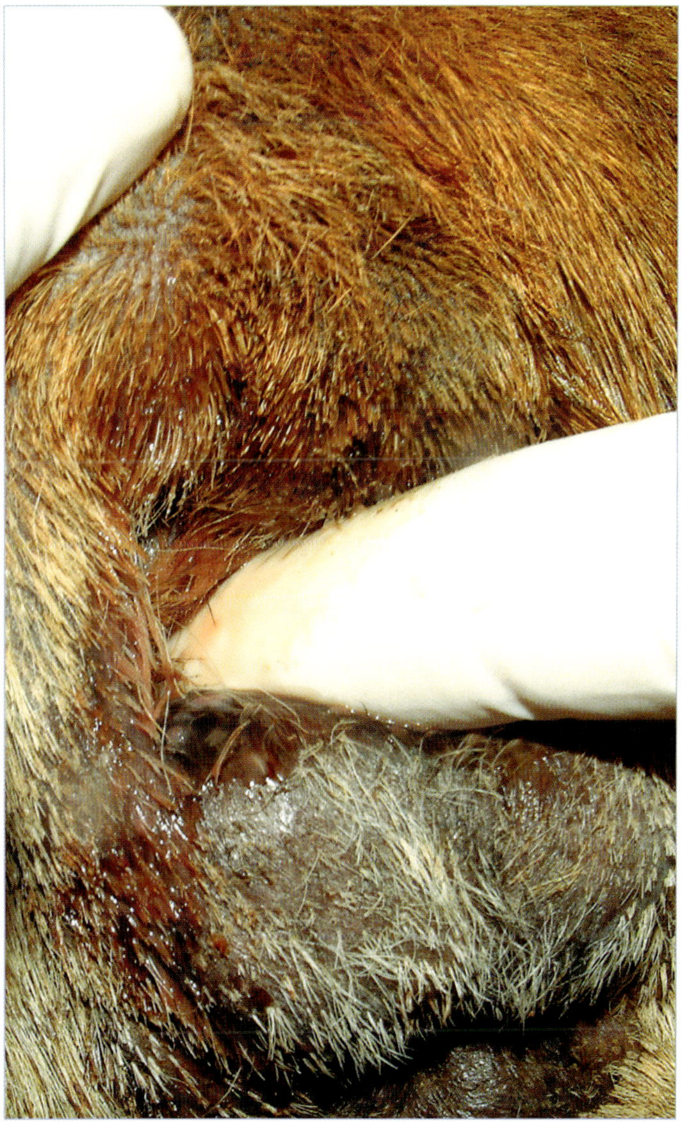

Fig. 3. The skin fold is very deep. Note that a finger is introduced up to the second phalanx.

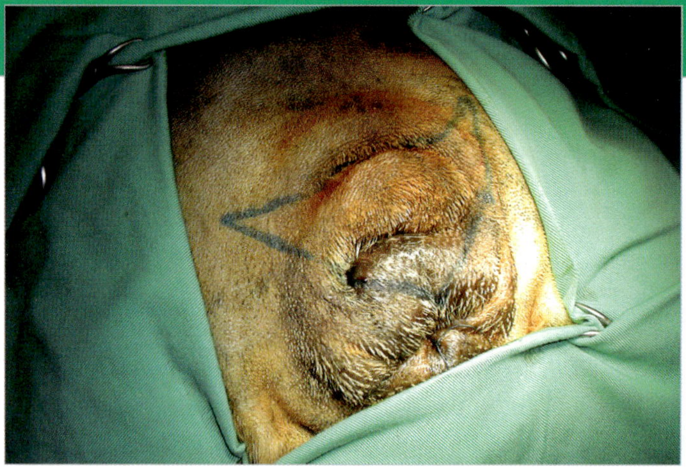

Fig. 4. Preparation of the operative field and marking of the skin incision that is required to remove the skin folds.

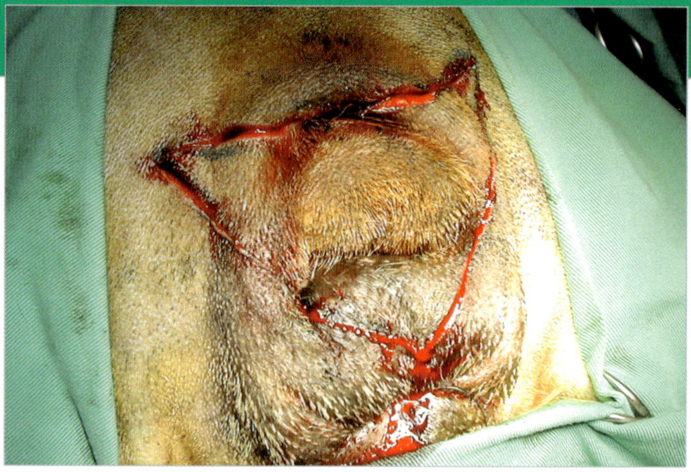

Fig. 5. Skin incision following the marked lines.
The triangular resection of the skin and its suturing in a T-shape will achieve a satisfactory aesthetic result, with minimal change to the anal sphincter.

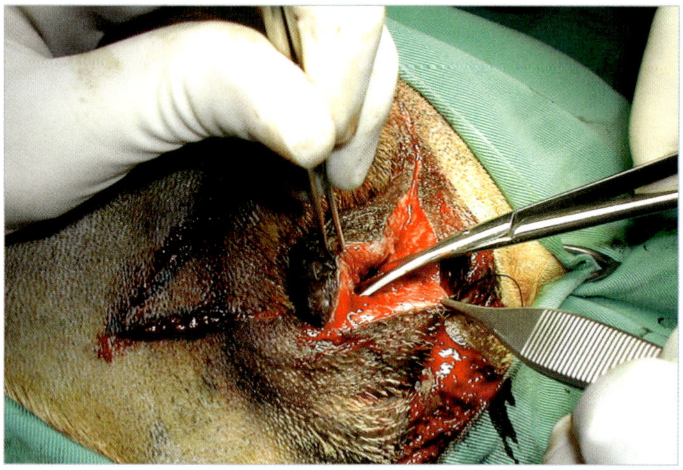

Fig. 6. The dissection is carried out through the subcutaneous tissue, following a line parallel to the skin folds.

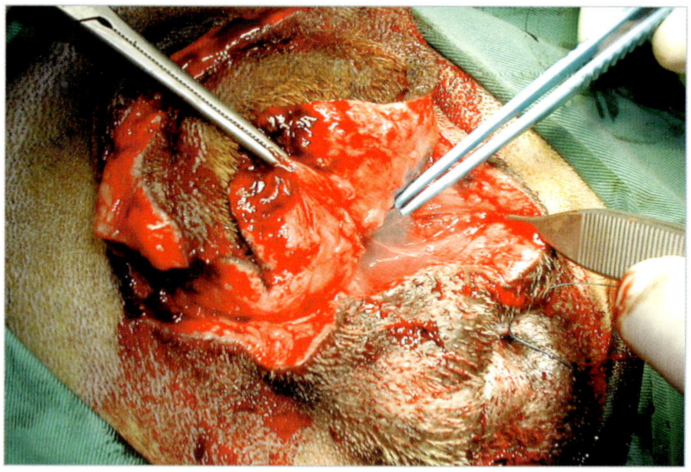

Fig. 7. Bleeding will be copious as the area is highly vascularised. Use a bipolar coagulator to minimise tissue damage.

Remember that the rectum is located just underneath. Take care to avoid trauma to the rectum.

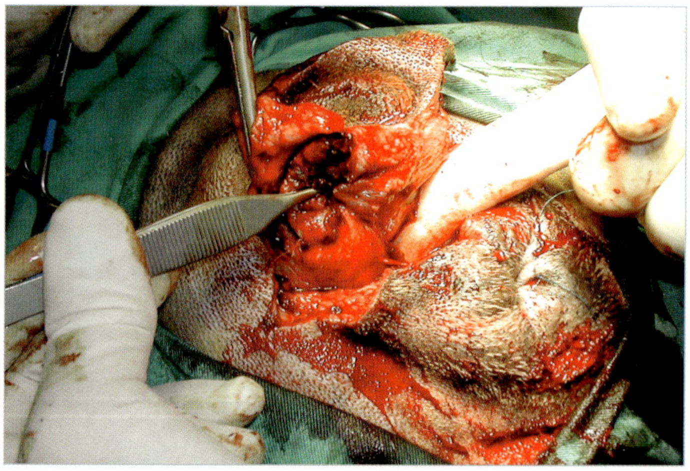

Fig. 8. The skin lies close to the vertebrae and its dissection is more difficult in this area. Some authors recommend amputation of the coccygeal vertebrae at this level with a Gigli saw.
The surgeon is palpating the coccygeal vertebrae with his finger.

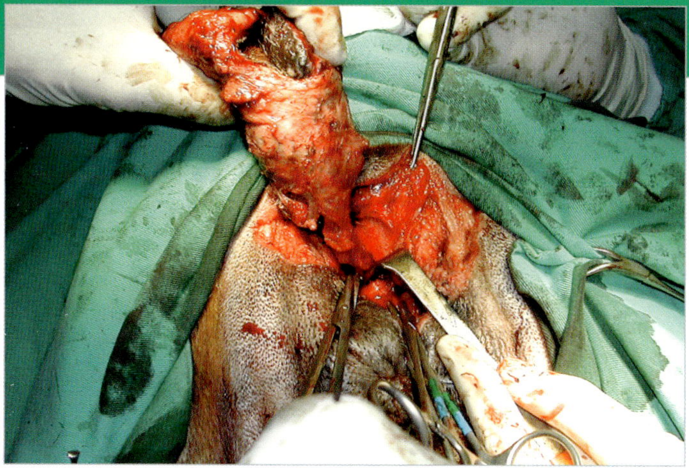

Fig. 9. Final stage of the procedure, resecting the deep part of the ventral fold.

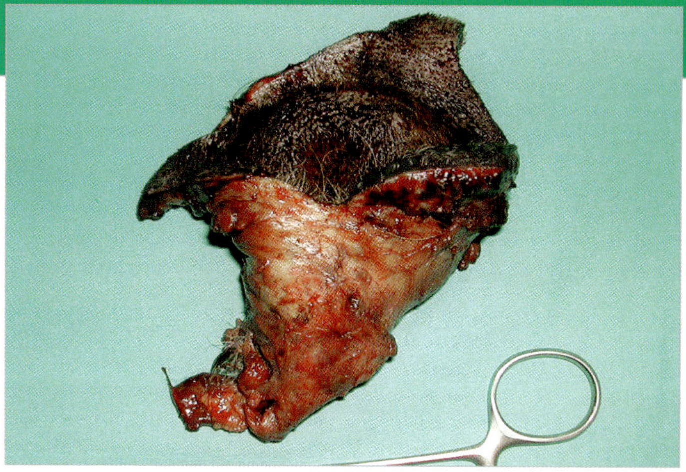

Fig. 10. This image clearly shows the total amount of resected skin as well as the depth of the skin folds.

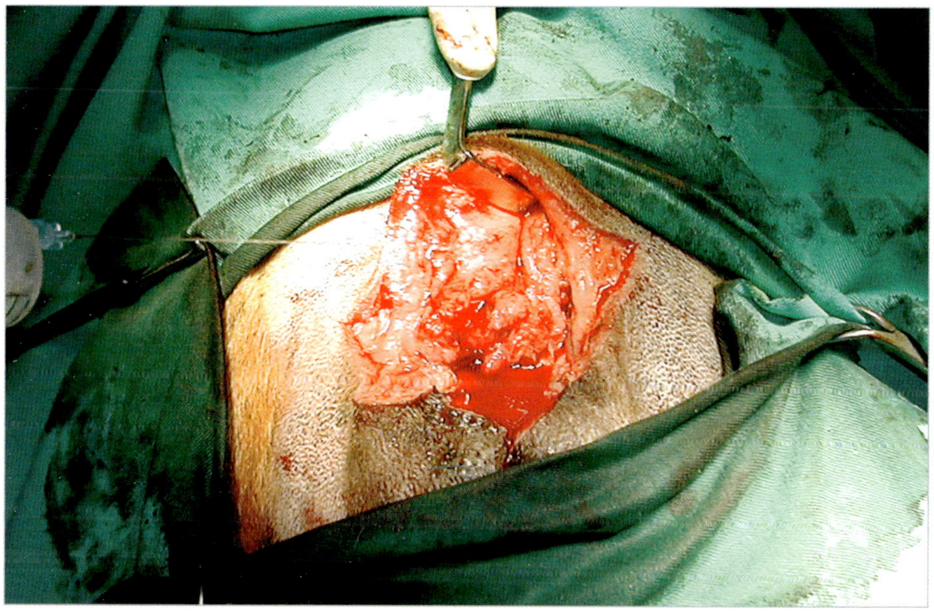

Fig. 11. Before closing the skin, it is recommended to flush copiously with saline under pressure to remove any necrotic remnants and bacteria that could have entered the operating field.

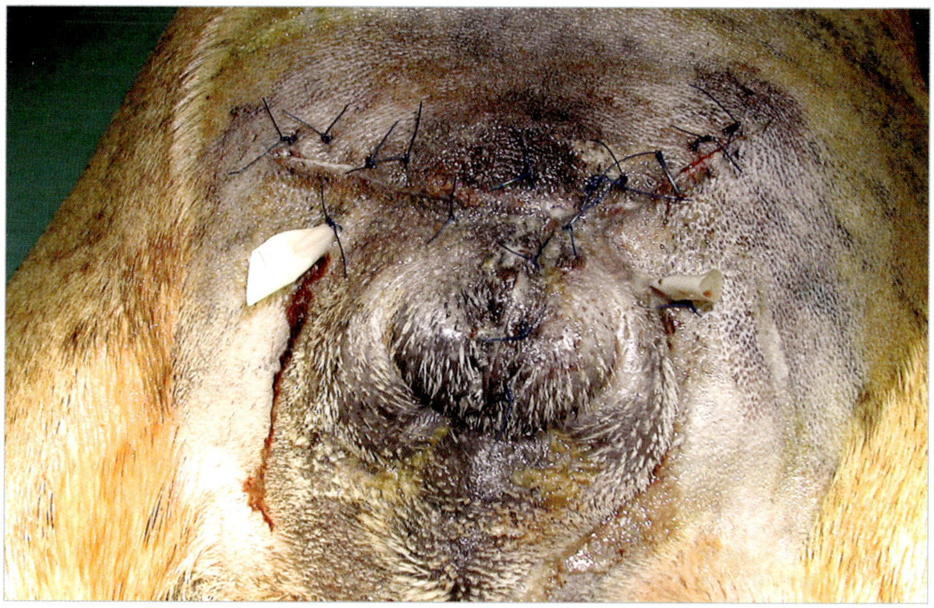

Fig. 12. Considering the size of the resected area and the tissue trauma, two Penrose drains are placed. The subcutaneous tissue is closed with interrupted sutures using absorbable 3/0 monofilament material. The skin is closed with vertical mattress sutures using non-absorbable monofilament material.

After surgery

- Continue the antibiotic therapy that was initiated prior to surgery.
- Clean the area to avoid faecal contamination via the drains.

Postoperatively

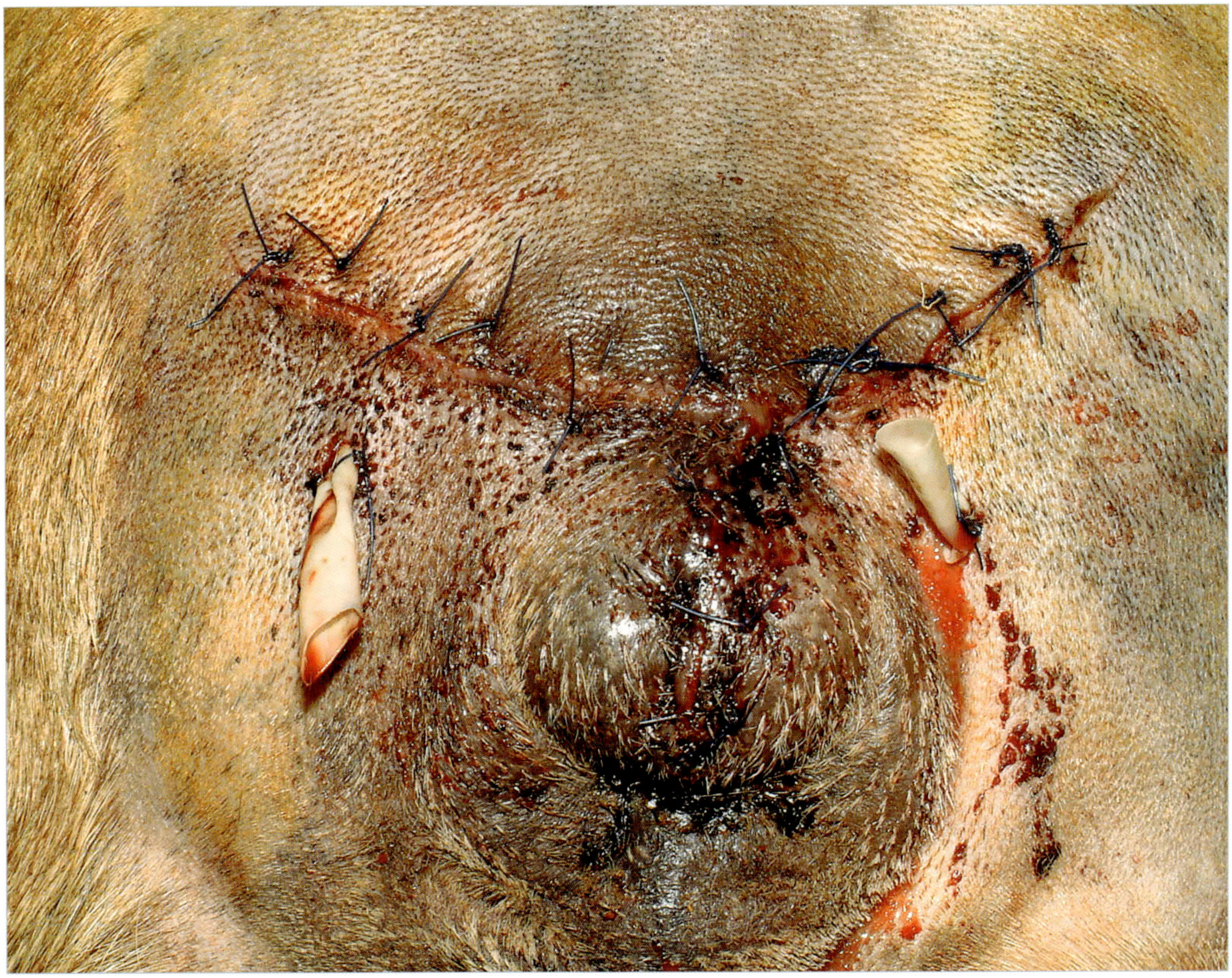

Fig. 13. 24 hours postoperatively, the progress is satisfactory. 48 after the operation, discharge from the drains is minimal and they are removed.

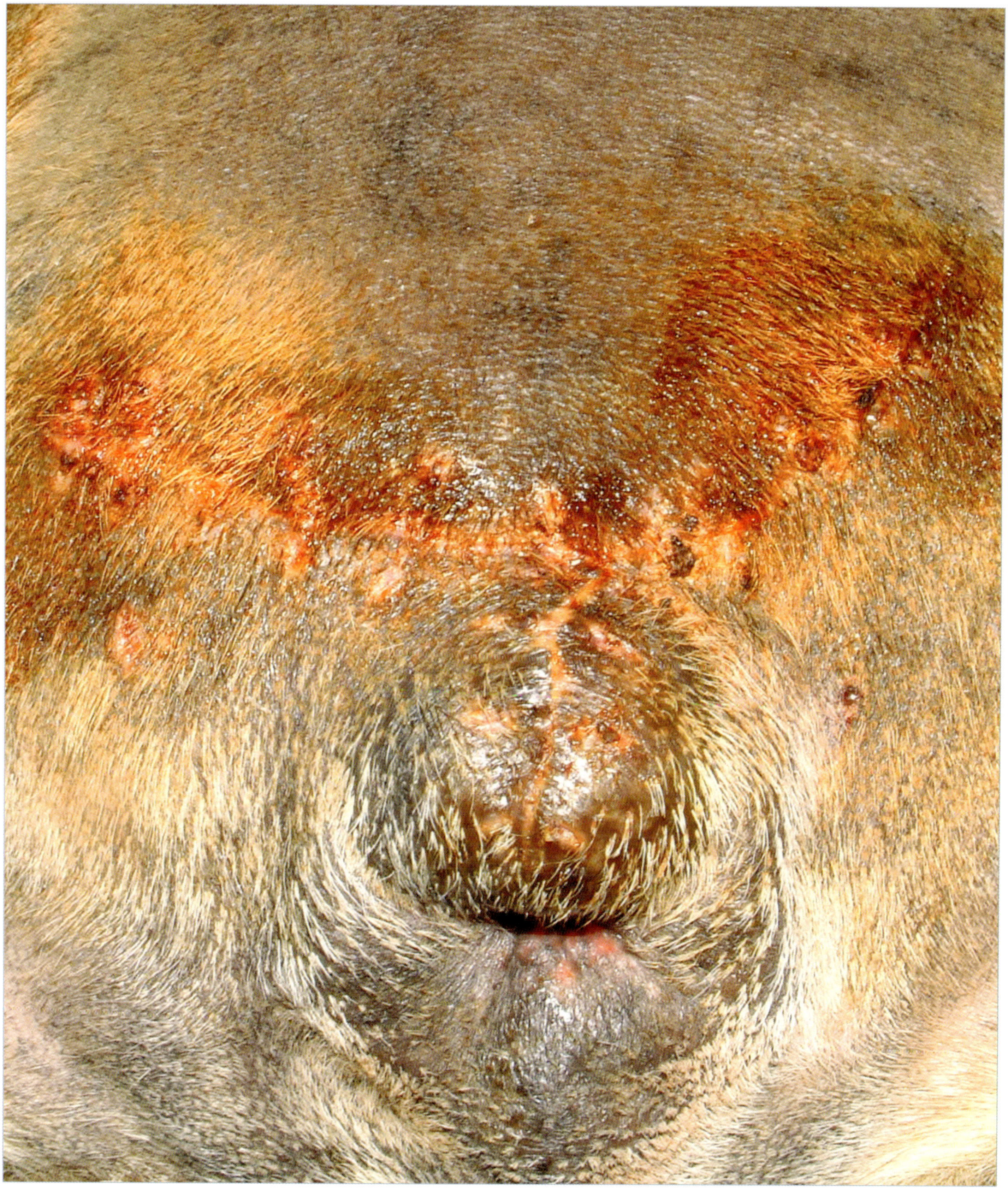

Fig. 14. 10 days later, the sutures are removed and treatment is complete.

Anal atresia

Prevalence

Non-development of the anus is a rare anomaly in small animal practice. It can be classified into four types:

- **Type I.** Congenital anal stenosis.
- **Type II.** Persistence of an anal membrane occluding the anus.
- **Type III.** The anus is not perforated and the rectum is separated from the anus.
- **Type IV.** The anus is developed but the rectum ends in a sac in the pelvic canal.

In these animals, the faeces exit through a recto-vaginal fistula in females (figs. 1 and 2).

Treatment is surgical and aims to widen or open the anus or to attach it to the rectum, depending on the type of disorder. The prognosis is guarded due to the initial poor condition and malnutrition of the patient, secondary megacolon that may develop and possible postoperative complications (anal stenosis, infection, suture dehiscence…).

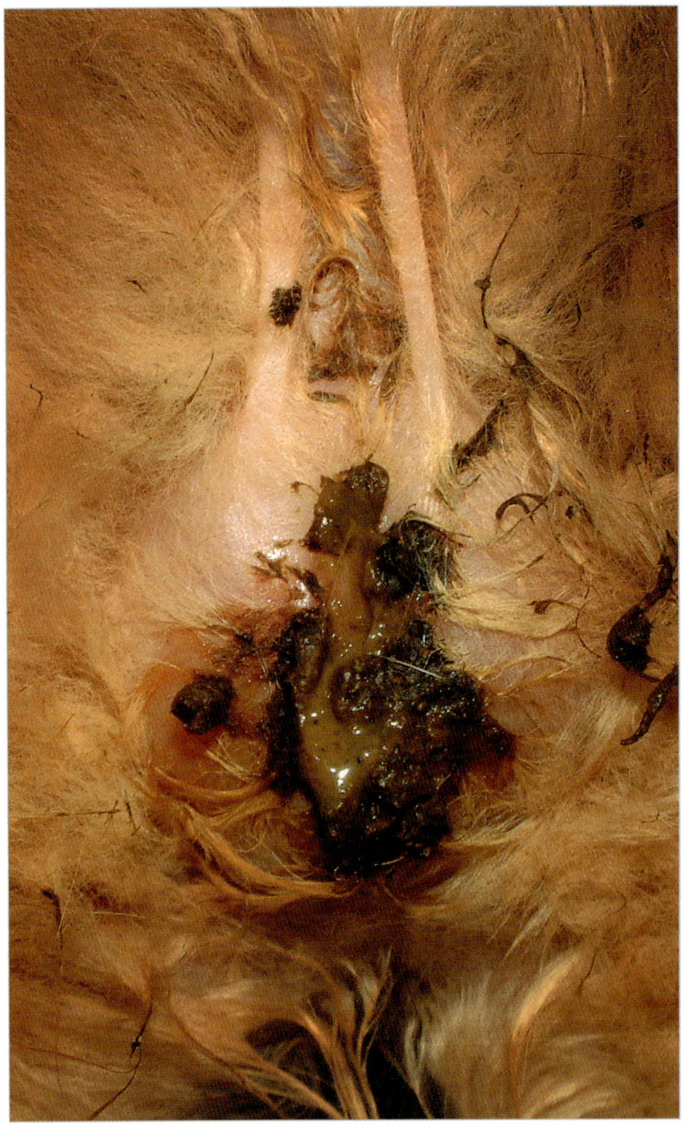

Fig. 1. Expulsion of pasty faeces through the vulva in a 2-month-old female Persian kitten.

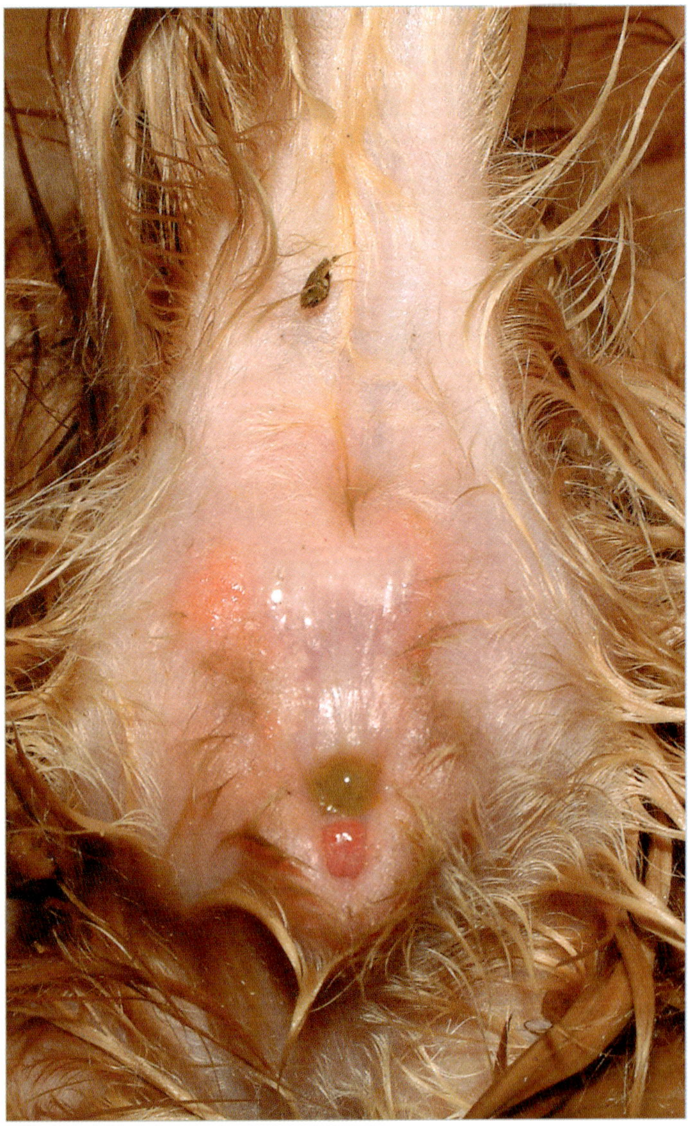

Fig. 2. Non-perforation of the anus with faeces visible between the labia.

Anal atresia. Case 1 / Atresia in the female cat

"Zara" is a two-month old female European kitten (fig. 1), presented because she was not defaecating normally. Elimination was difficult and the faeces were ribbon-like.

Fig. 1. "Zara" on the day she was brought to the hospital.

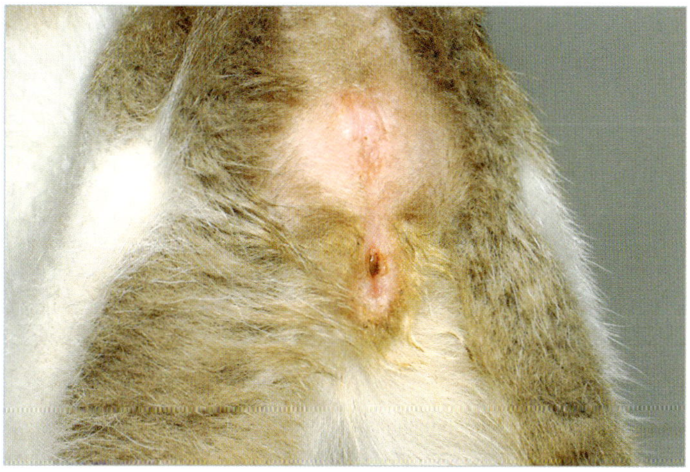

Fig. 2. During clinical examination, a build-up of faecal material was detected in the distal digestive tract. In the perineal area, an absence of the anal opening was noted.

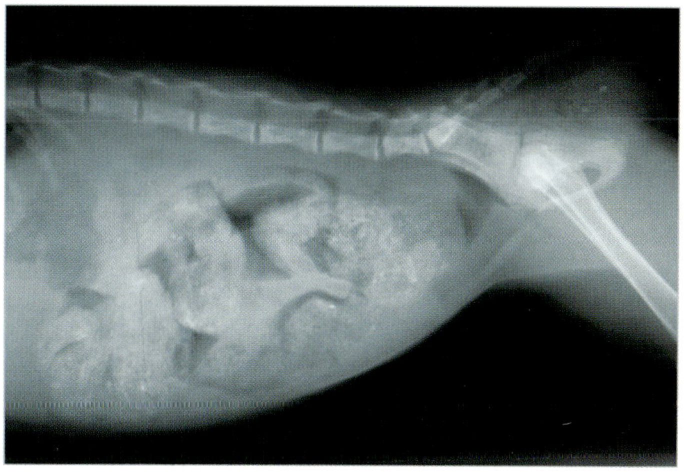

Fig. 3. A plain radiograph shows retention of faeces in the colon.

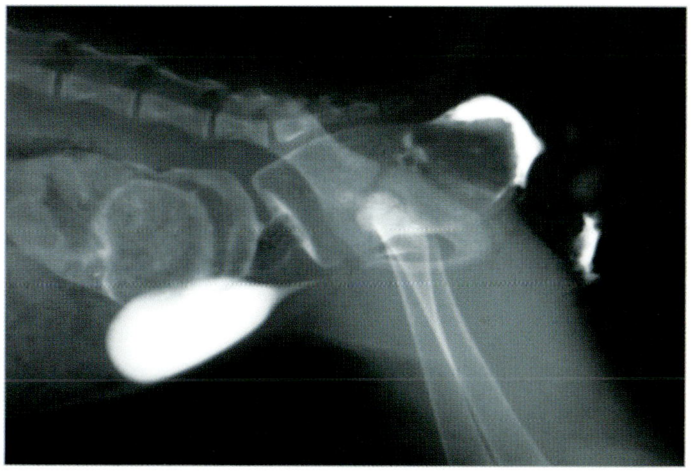

Fig. 4. Introduction of an iodine contrast medium into the vagina, confirms that the ureters and bladder are normal.
In the radiograph, a recto-vaginal fistula (ventral to the distal rectum) and the end of the rectal sac (adjacent to the internal anal sphincter) are visible.

Surgical treatment

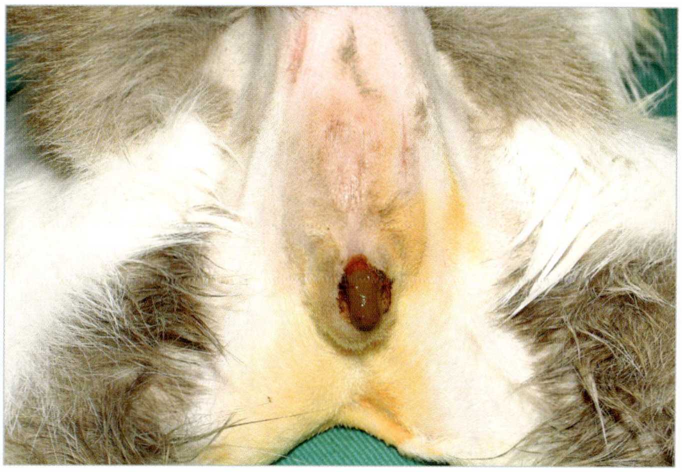

Fig. 5. Under anaesthesia with relaxation of the muscles, the expulsion of faeces through the vagina is visible.
The patient is placed in sternal recumbency and the surgical field is prepared.

See patient positioning page 248

Closing the rectovaginal fistula

Technical difficulty	■	■	□	□	□

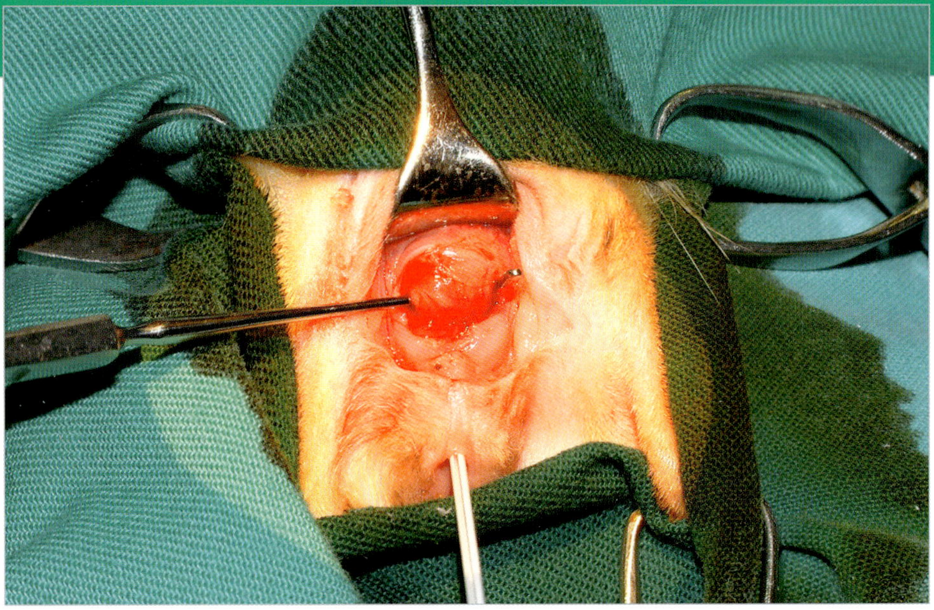

Fig. 6. A probe is inserted into the vagina and the skin is incised between the anal area and the vulva, permitting location and closure of the rectovaginal fistula.
Via blunt dissection of the space between the vagina and rectum, the rectovaginal fistula is located. It is surrounded by a large quantity of fibrous tissue.

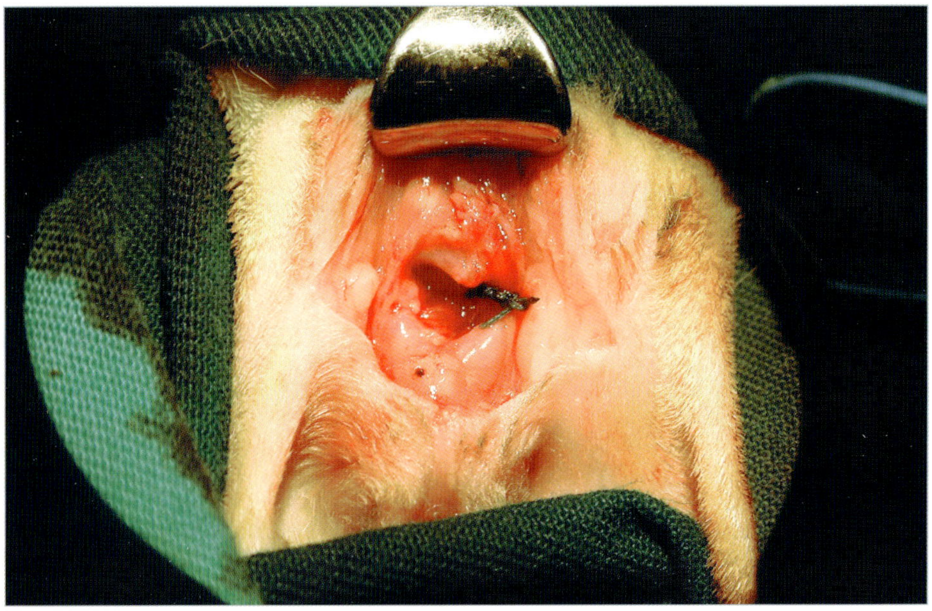

Fig. 7. The fistula can be ligated or sutured and cut, the choice depends on the size of the patient and the size of the available operative field.
In this case, a ligature was placed using 3/0 non absorbable material.

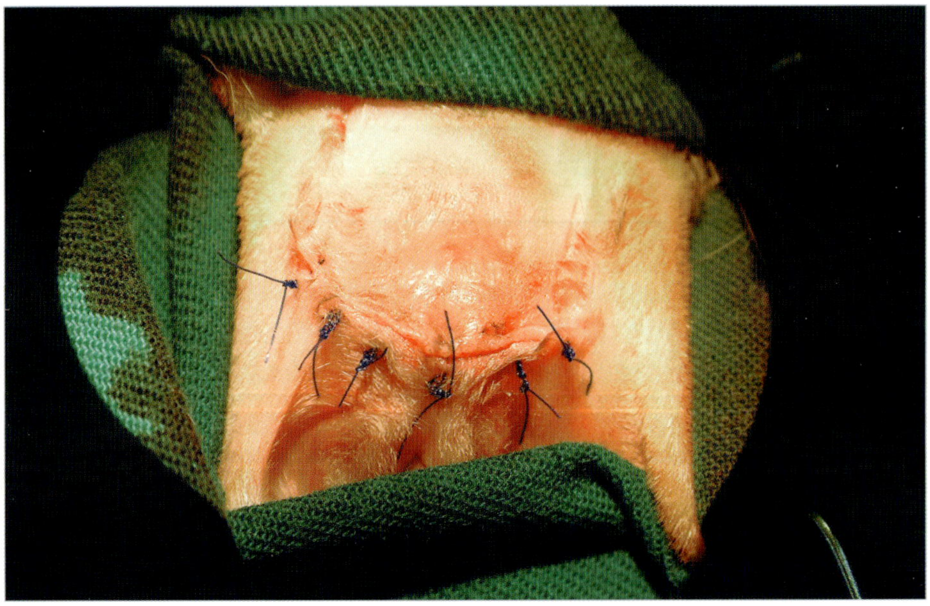

Fig. 8. After ligating the fistula, the skin is closed with interrupted sutures using non-absorbable 4/0 monofilament material.

Opening the anus

Technical difficulty	■	■	■	□	□

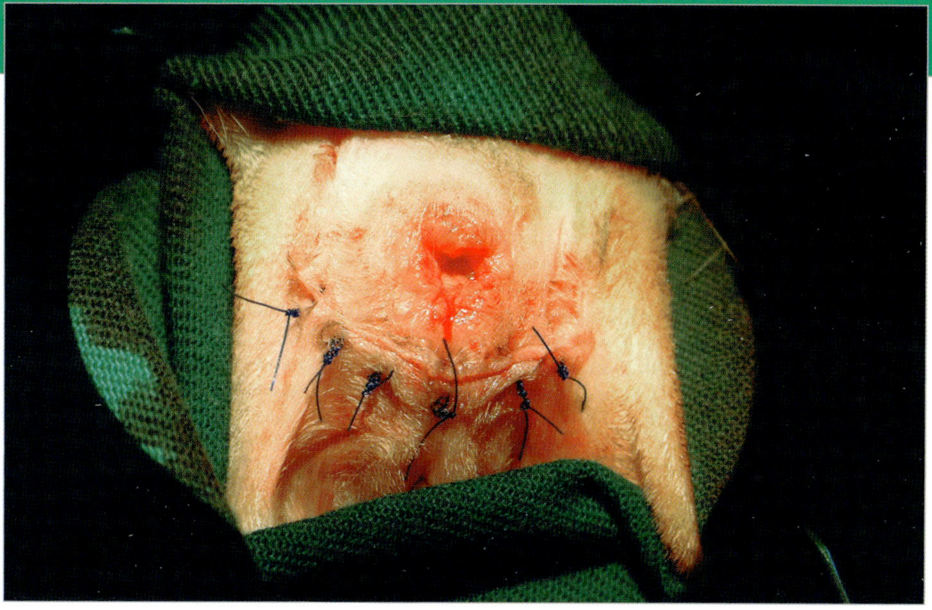

Fig. 9. The external anal sphincter is located and a vertical Y-shaped incision is made in order to obtain the largest possible diameter for the anastomosis. Note where the anal sacs are located to avoid damaging them.

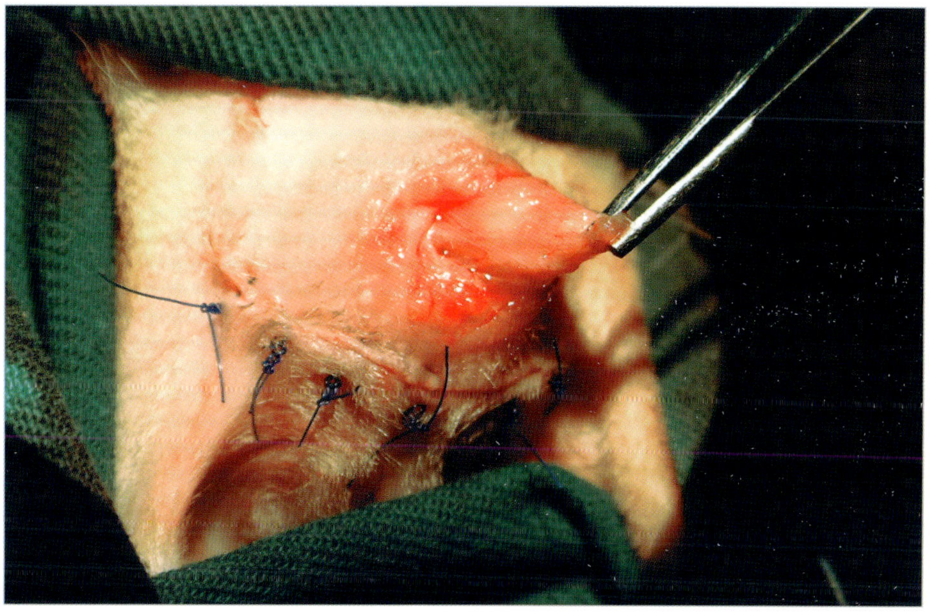

Fig. 10. Next, dissection is carried out in cranial direction to locate the distal end of the rectal sac, which is then loosened and gently repositioned caudally.

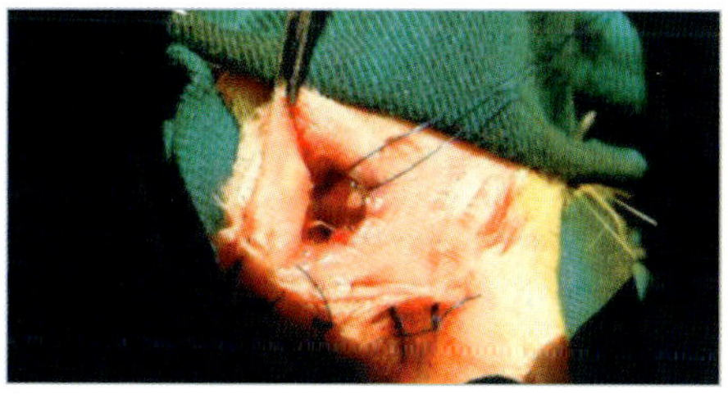

▲ Fig. 11. In the next phase, the bottom of the sac is resected and the rectum is attached to the inner side of the anal sphincter using interrupted sutures of synthetic absorbable 4/0 or 5/0 monofilament material. Use as few sutures as possible to achieve a leak-free anastomosis.

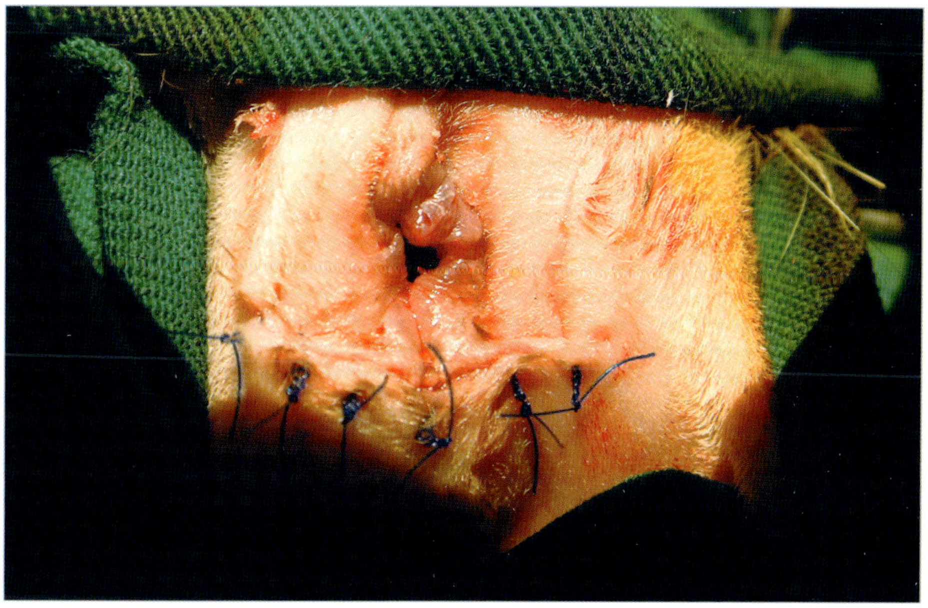

Fig. 12. End of the recto-anal anastomosis. The skin incision in a Y has created a lumen that is wide enough for faecal elimination.

Colotomy

Technical difficulty	■	■	■	□	□

The prognosis of these patients is relatively guarded due to the possible loss of colonic function following distension caused by retained faeces.

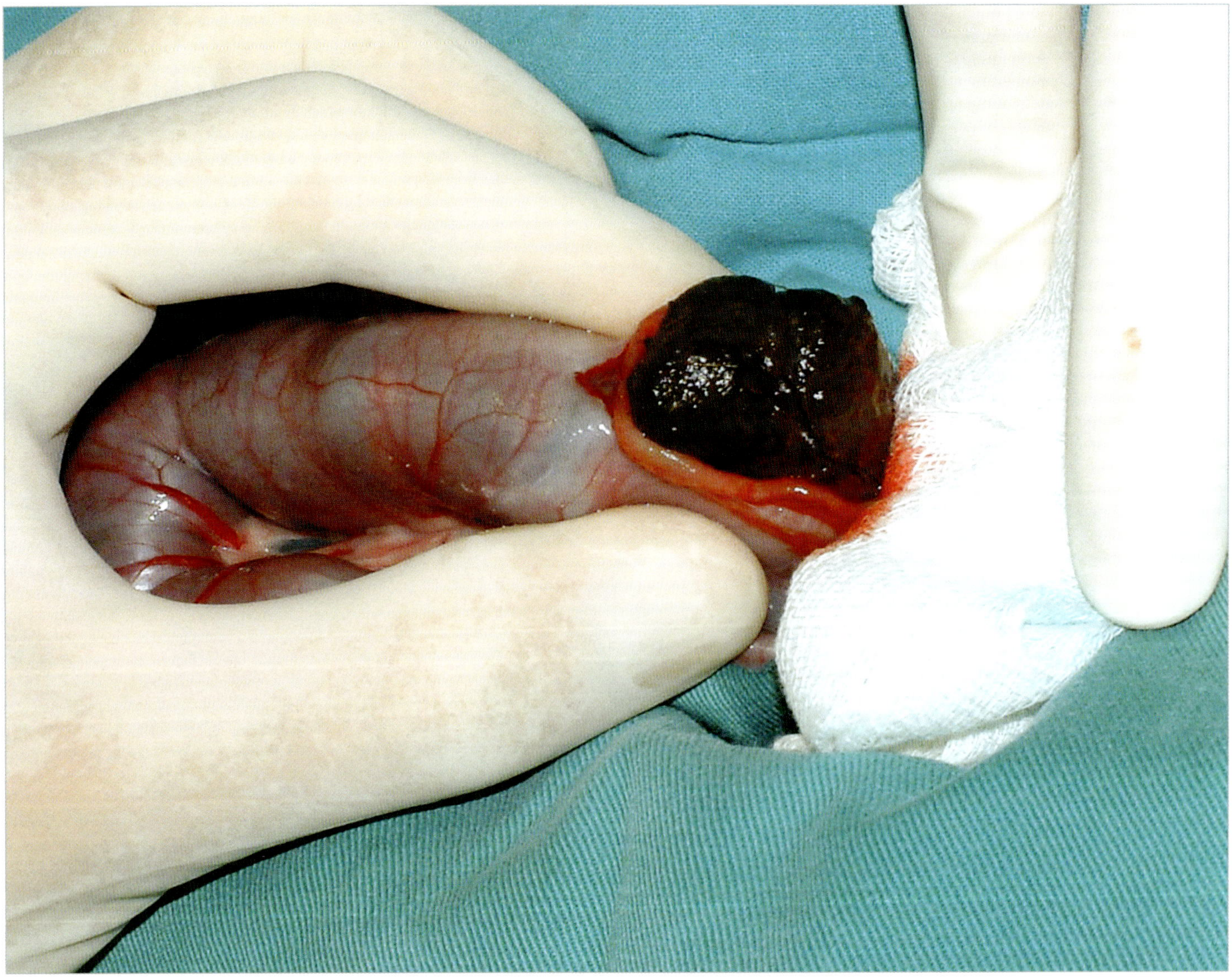

Fig. 13. Finally, an infraumbilical laparotomy is performed, the descending colon is exteriorised and a colotomy is carried out to extract the retained faeces from this intestinal segment.

Postoperative care

From the day after surgery, "Zara" was fed a low-residue diet. Mild laxatives were administered orally to facilitate defaecation and the owner carried out abdominal massage to aid intestinal evacuation.

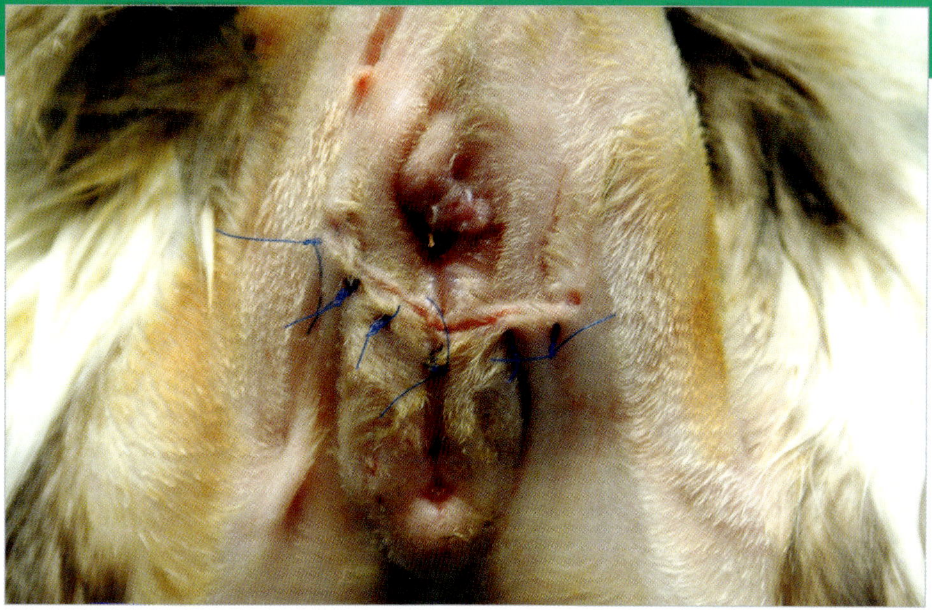

Fig. 14. Photograph from the day after surgery. As with all surgeries in this area, strict hygiene is essential.

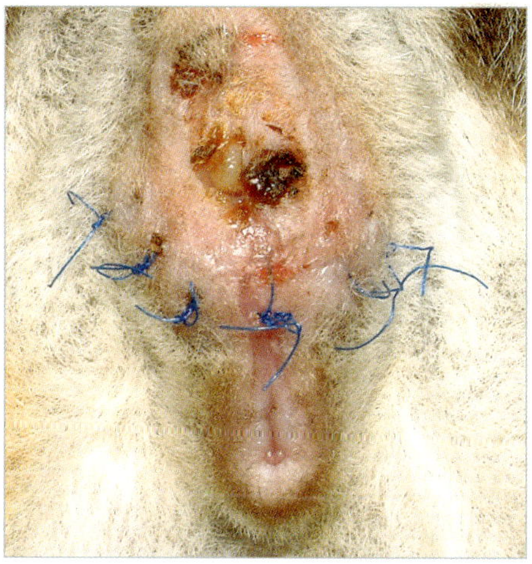

Fig. 15. Three days after surgery, the patient was eating normally but did not defaecate and had to be helped with isotonic enemas.
Ten days after the operation, faecal elimination was slow and faeces started to accumulate in the colon.

Seventeen days after the operation, "Zara" was unable to defaecate normally. She had developed a secondary megacolon. The owner did not want to subject her to further surgery and elected to euthanasia (fig. 16).

> ***This type of operation should be carried out as early as possible, in order to avoid secondary and irreversible damage to the nerves of the colon.***

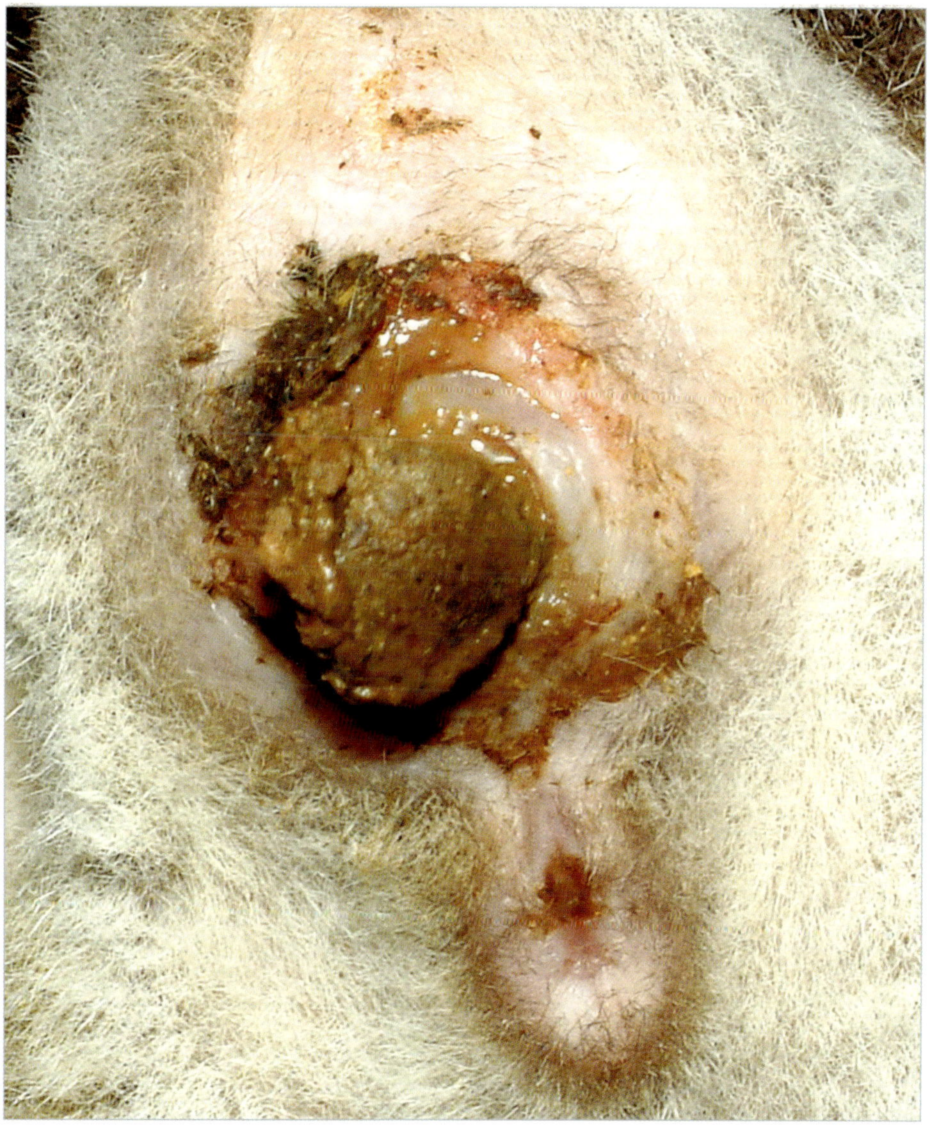

Fig. 16. After euthanasia, when the muscles were relaxed and pressure was exerted on the abdomen, it was possible to examine the functionality of the anus. From a technical viewpoint, the surgery was successful, but the functional result was disappointing due to the lack of peristaltic movements in the colon.

Anal atresia. Case 2 / Atresia in the female dog

Technical difficulty

A two-month-old female Yorkshire Terrier puppy was presented because she was smaller than her littermates and was having defaecation problems (figs. 1 and 2).

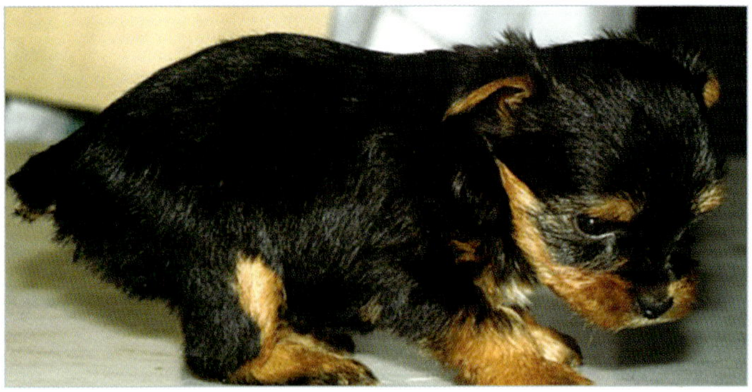

Fig. 1. She also presented with tenesmus and very soft faeces.

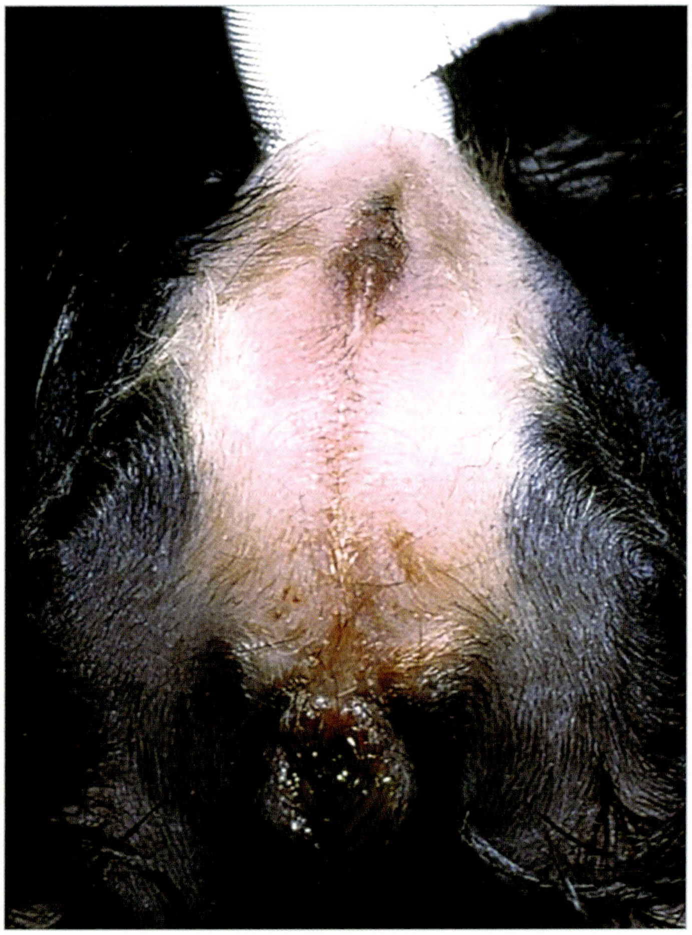

Fig. 2. Examination of the perineal region reveals an imperforate anus with faeces being voided through the vulva.

Surgical technique

Procedure that includes the closure of a rectovaginal fistula and the opening of the anus, with anastomosis to the rectum.

See patient positioning → page 248

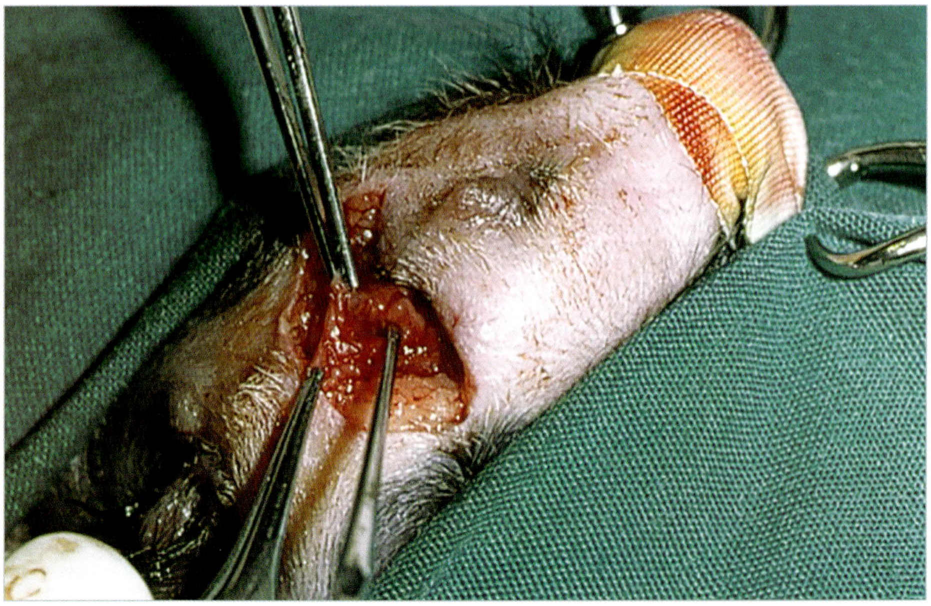

Fig. 3. A skin incision across the perineum and below the anus gives access to the space between the rectum and the vagina.

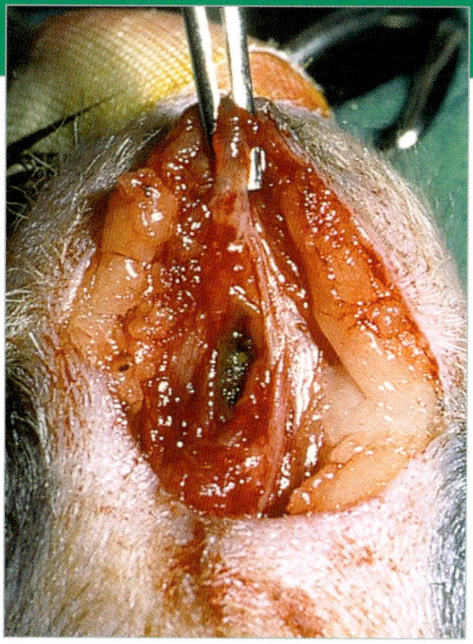

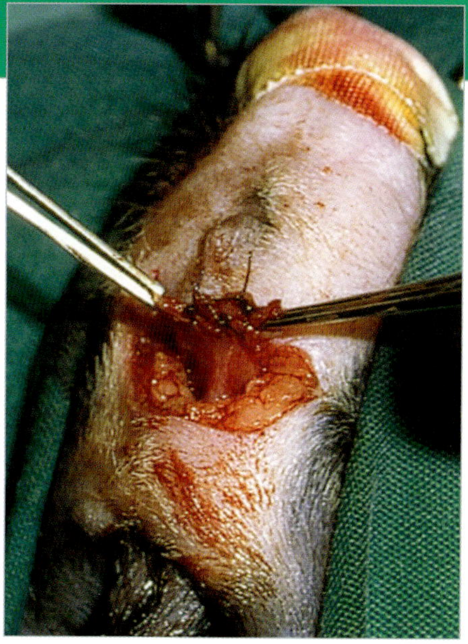

Fig. 4 (left). In this case, it was decided to cut the recto-vaginal fistula and to suture the rectum and vagina independently.

Fig. 5 (right). This image shows the closure of the vaginal roof with interrupted sutures using absorbable 4/0 material.

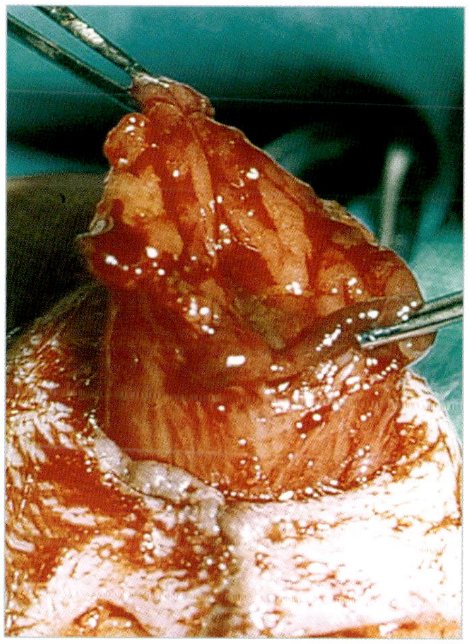

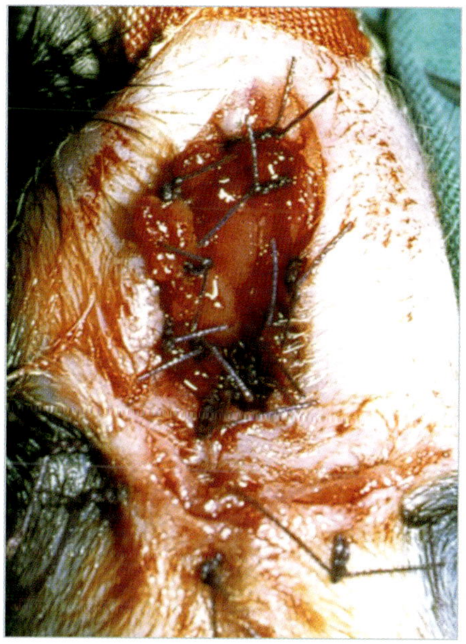

Fig. 6 (left). Next, the anal area is incised, followed by rectal dissection and opening.

Fig. 7 (right). In this case, the anal sphincter could not be identified, the opening of the rectum was attached directly to the skin, using synthetic 4/0 non-absorbable material.

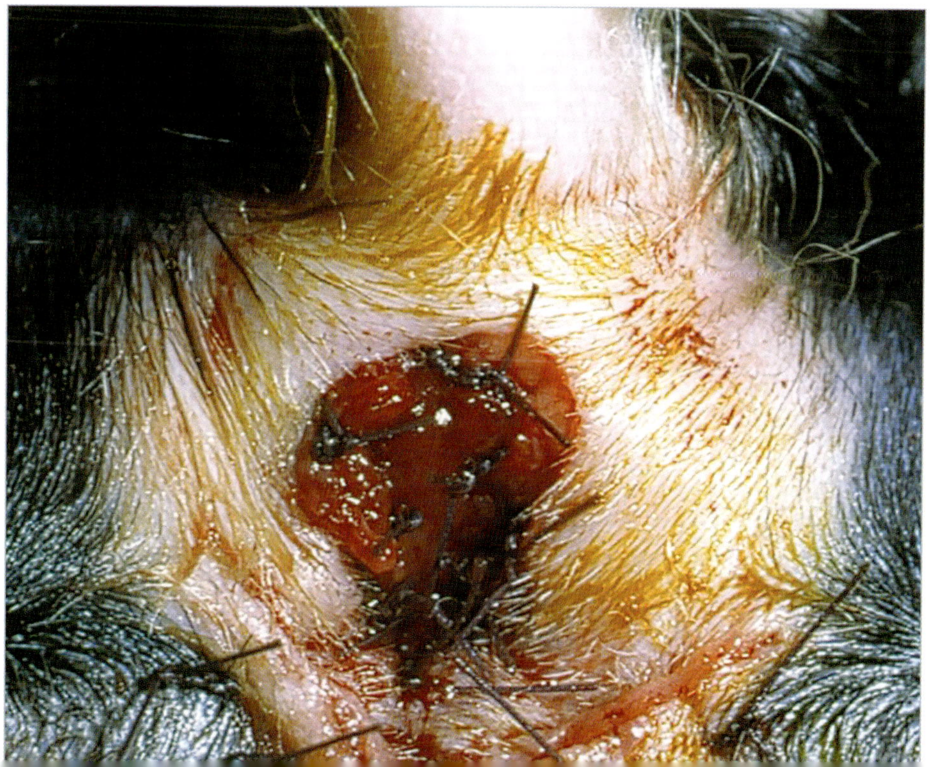

Fig. 8. 48 hours after surgery, the patient has recovered well, and is eating and defaecating without difficulty.

After surgery

- Observe strict antiseptic and hygiene measures.
- Initiate suitable antibiotic therapy.
- Clean the area well during the postoperative period.
- Monitor the animal closely.
- Prevent the patient from licking the area by using an Elizabethan collar.

Schematic drawing of a cross-section of the vagina, vestibule and vulva

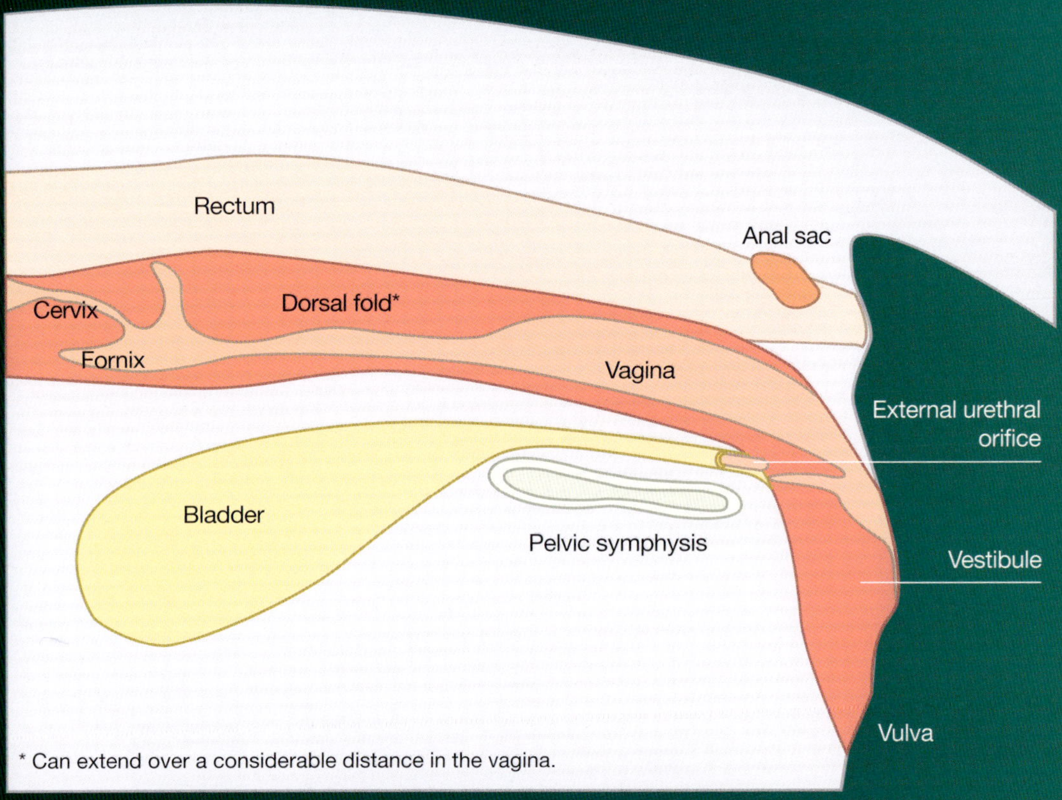

* Can extend over a considerable distance in the vagina.

Muscles of the genital apparatus of the bitch

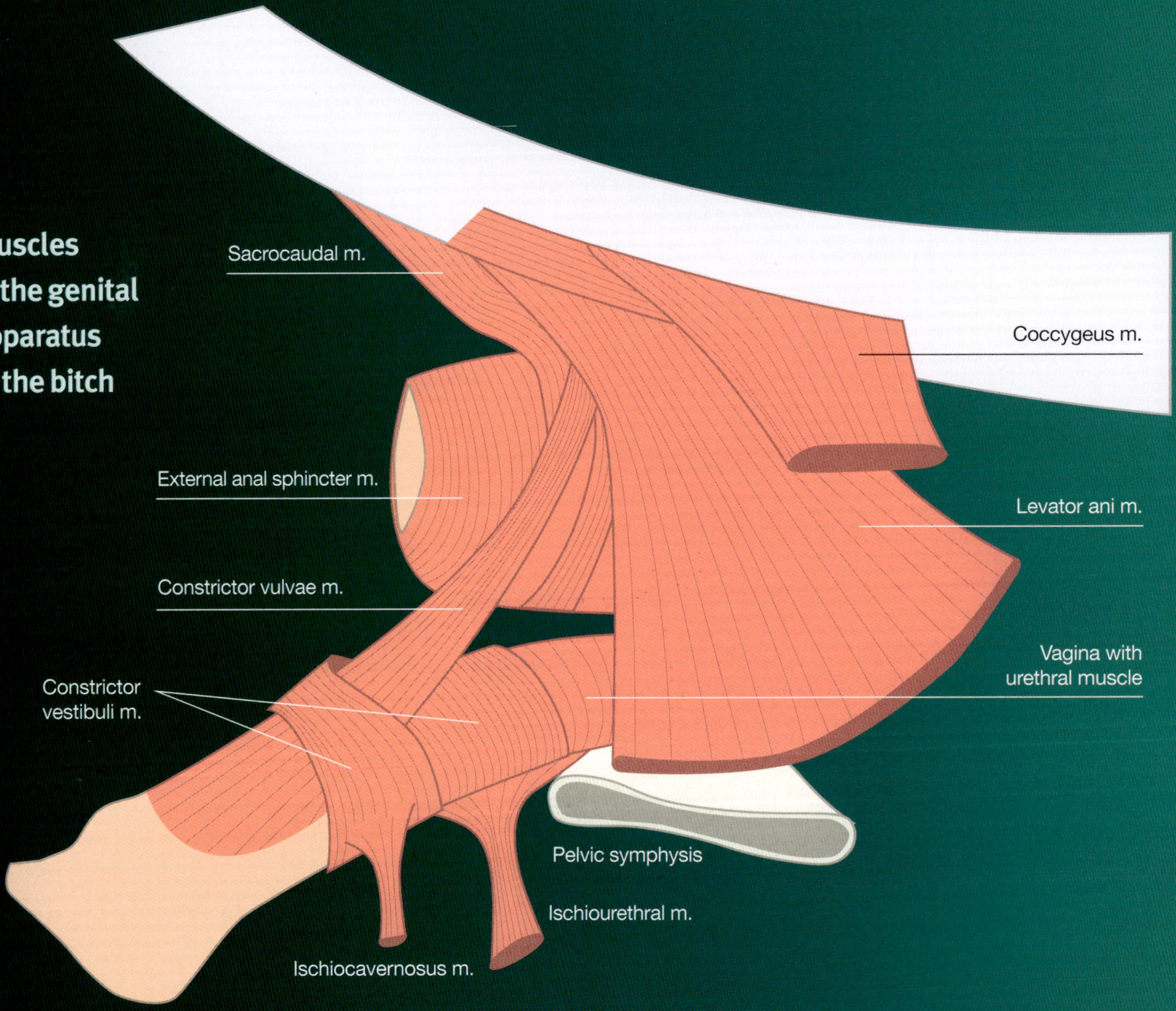

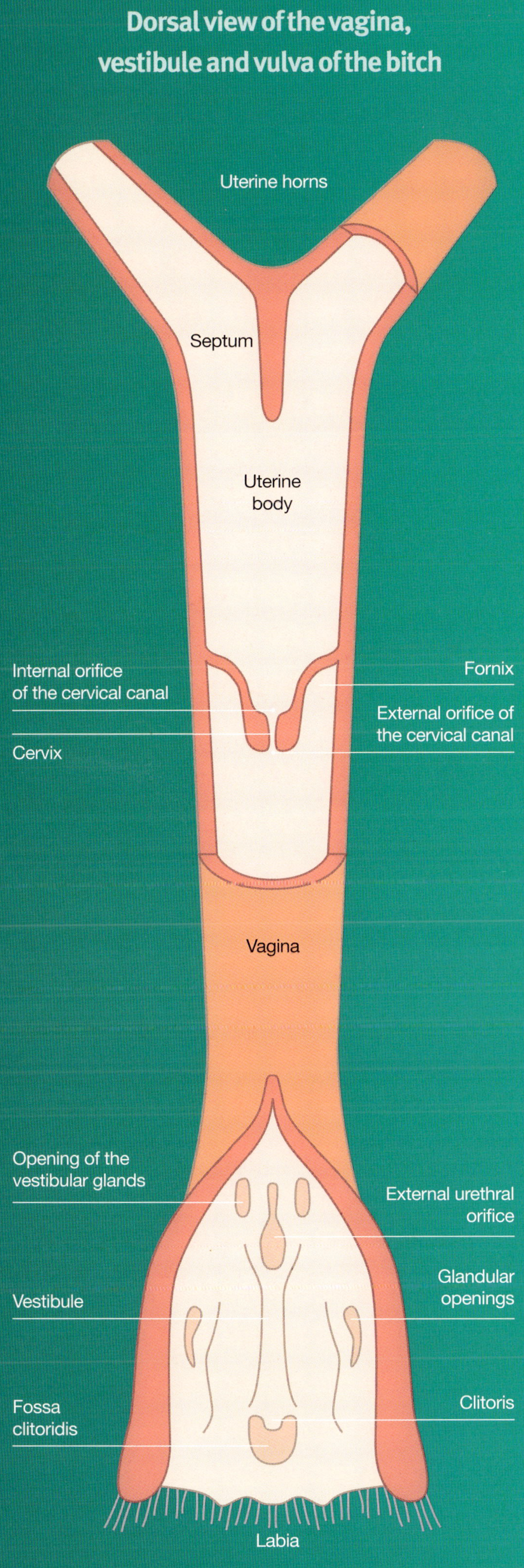

Vulva-vagina

Neoplasia

Case 1 / Tumour of the labium

Case 2 / Transmissible venereal tumour

Case 3 / Tumour of the vaginal floor

Case 4 / Tumour of the vaginal roof

Case 5 / Vulvar polyps

Case 6 / Vaginal tumour

Case 7 / Subcutaneous lipoma

Persistent hymen

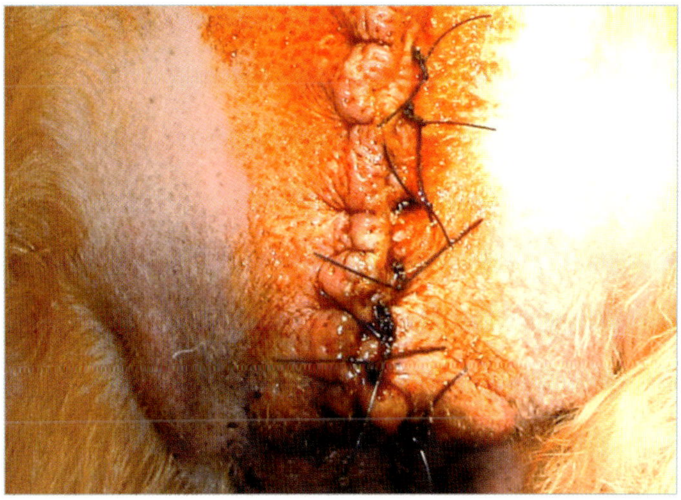

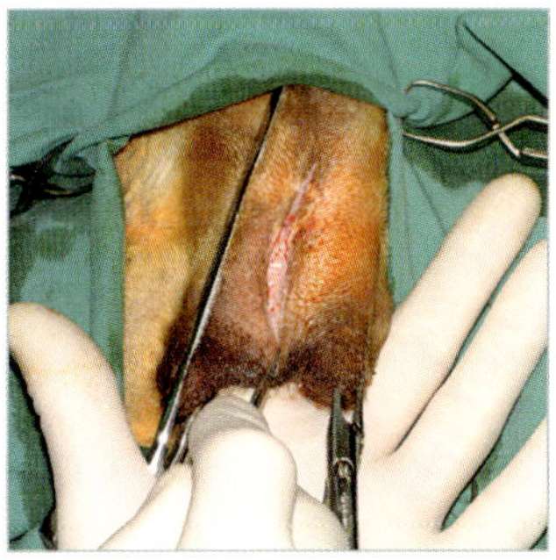

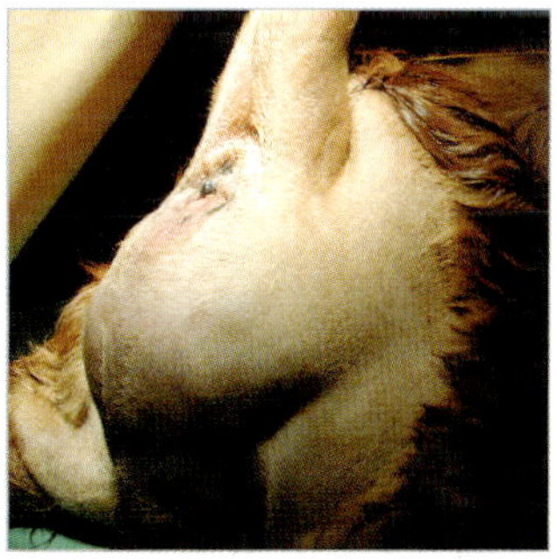

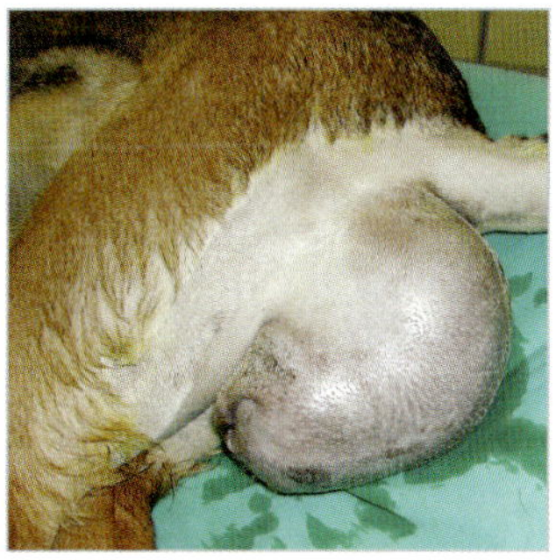

Neoplasia

Tumours of the vulva and vagina are the second most common in the bitch after mammary tumours. In the queen, they are very rare. Vulval and vaginal tumours are common in middle-aged and old dogs. 70-80% of these tumours are benign.

The majority of tumours in this area are benign and respond to surgery. However, they can be spectacular.

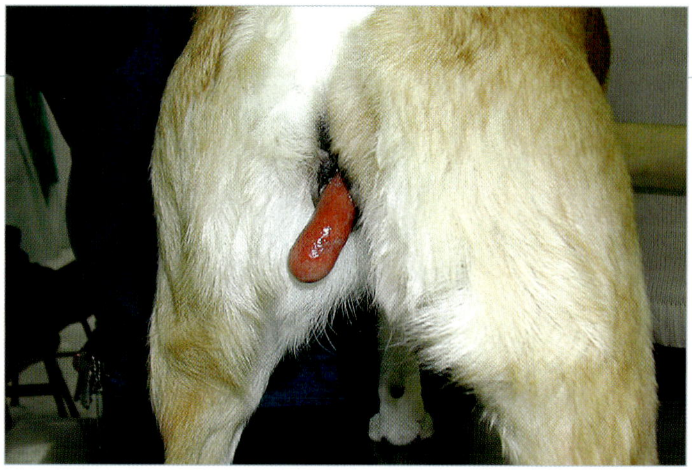

Fig. 1. Vaginal polyp.

Fibromas, lipomas and leiomyomas occur most commonly in this region. These three tumour types cannot be distinguished macroscopically. They are firm, rounded, often pedunculated masses with a smooth surface. **Leiomyosarcoma** is the most common malignant vaginal tumour, while **transmissible venereal tumour** has become rare in our environment but is still seen in rural areas where dogs run free. The latter, also called Sticker's lymphosarcoma, has an irregular, haemorrhagic, often ulcerated surface and can be solitary or multiple. It has a cauliflower form and is more or less pedunculated. Other malignant tumours include the **mastocytoma** and **squamous cell carcinoma**. Metastasis of vaginal tumours is very rare.

On examination, it is common to find protrusion of tumour-like tissue through the vulva or a swelling of the perineal region. Haemorrhagic or purulent discharge may also be present.

Diagnosis is completed by rectal and vaginal palpation. Thoracic and abdominal radiographs will detect possible metastases. Special attention is required to detect invasion of the inguinal, iliac and sacral lymph nodes. For this reason, an abdominal ultrasound examination can be useful. Cytology will indicate the nature of the tumour, which will be confirmed by histopathology of the resected tissue.

The differential diagnoses include vaginal hyperplasia and uterine prolapse. The first is seen in young dogs, in association with oestrus and originates from the vaginal floor, cranial to the urethral orifice. Uterine prolapse is linked to parturition and is more common in cats.

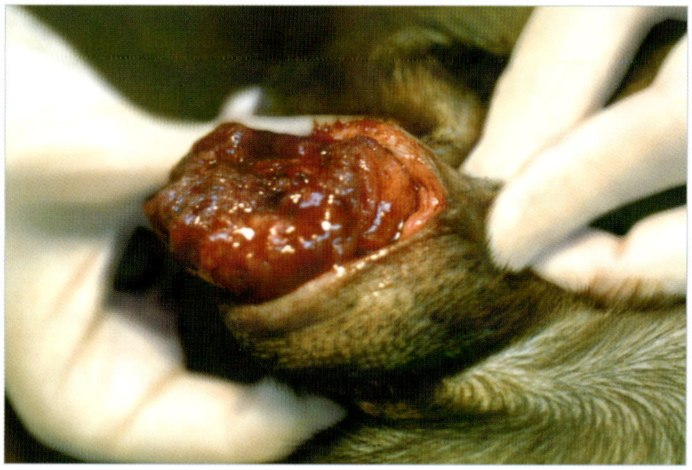

Fig. 2. Transmissible venereal tumour.

A vaginal mass is most probably a tumour if the patient is an adult female dog. If the patient is young and in oestrus, it is most likely vaginal hyperplasia.

Treatment is mainly surgical; transmissible venereal tumours can also be treated with vincristine.

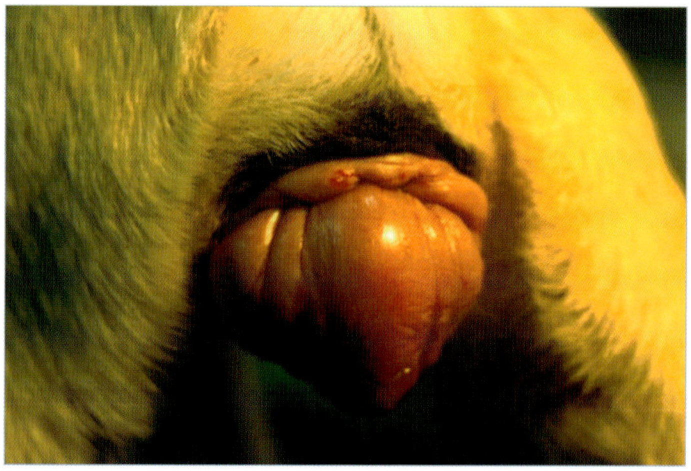

Fig. 3. Vaginal hyperplasia.

Neoplasia. Case 1 / Tumour of the labium

A 7-year-old female Boxer was presented with a round mass at the vulva. Upon examination, the mass was found to be peduncular and attached to the labium at the mucocutaneous junction. Cytology indicated a diagnosis of fibroma and it was decided to remove the mass (fig. 1).

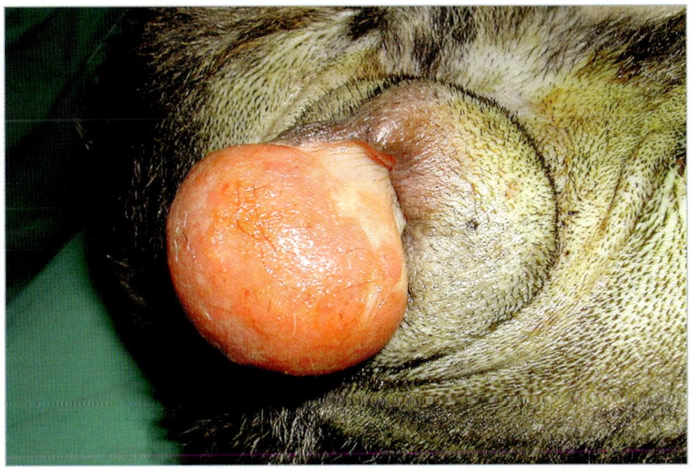

Fig. 1. View of the neoplastic mass located on the right labium.

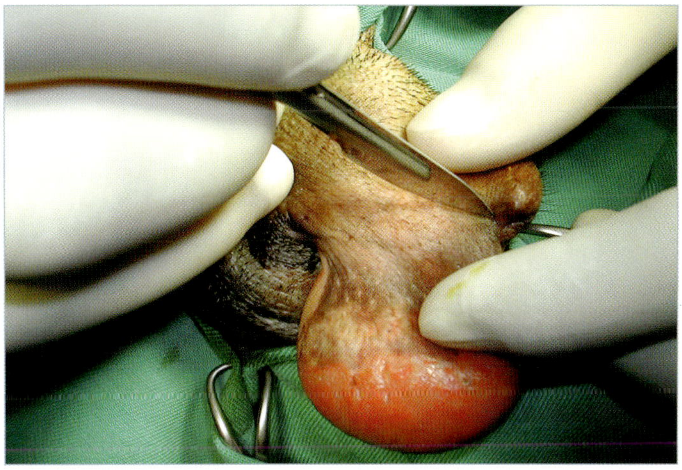

Fig. 2. After preparing the operative field, the pedicle is incised with a scalpel.

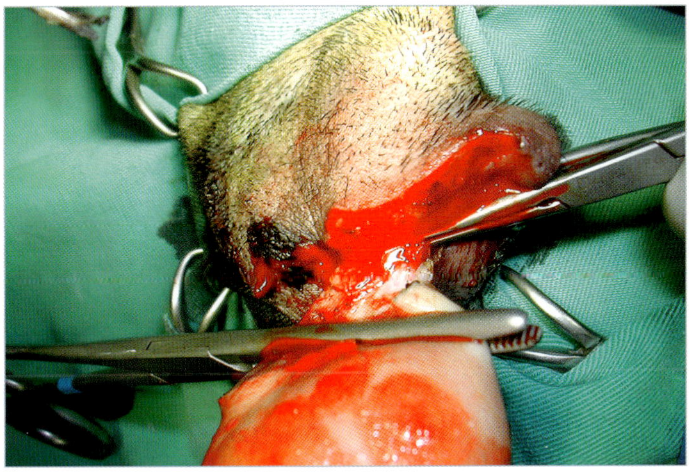

Fig. 3. Haemostatic forceps are used to control haemorrhage and dissection of the pedicle is completed with scissors or a scalpel.

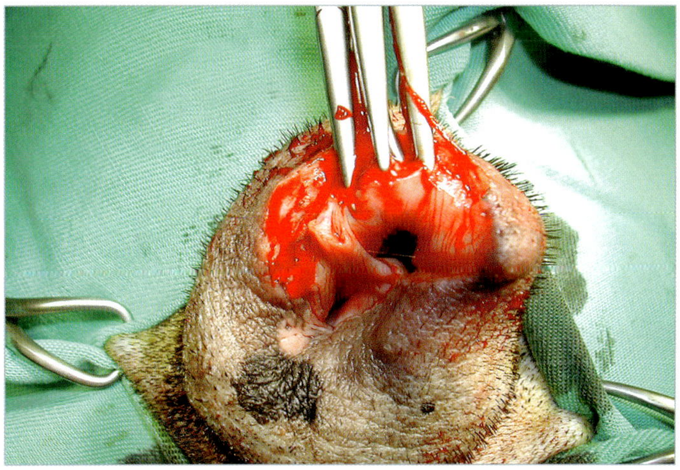

Fig. 4. Once the tumour is resected, haemostasis is achieved by diathermy or by ligating the bleeding vessels.

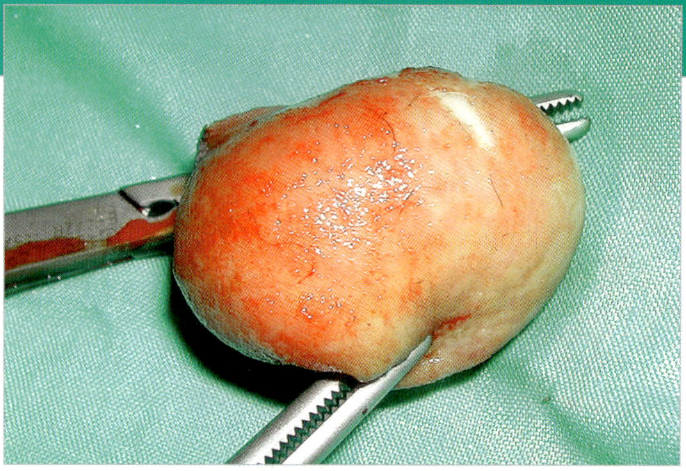

Fig. 5. After removal, the tumour was submitted for histopathology, which confirmed the diagnosis of fibroma.

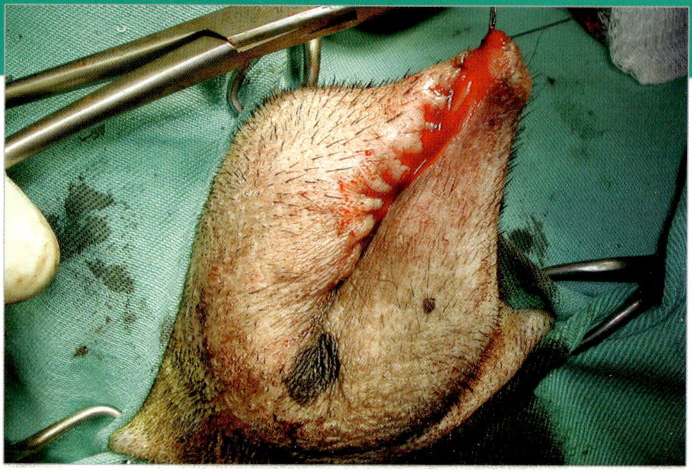

Fig. 6. The wound is closed with a continuous suture through the skin and the mucosa of the labium, using 2/0 monofilament absorbable suture material.

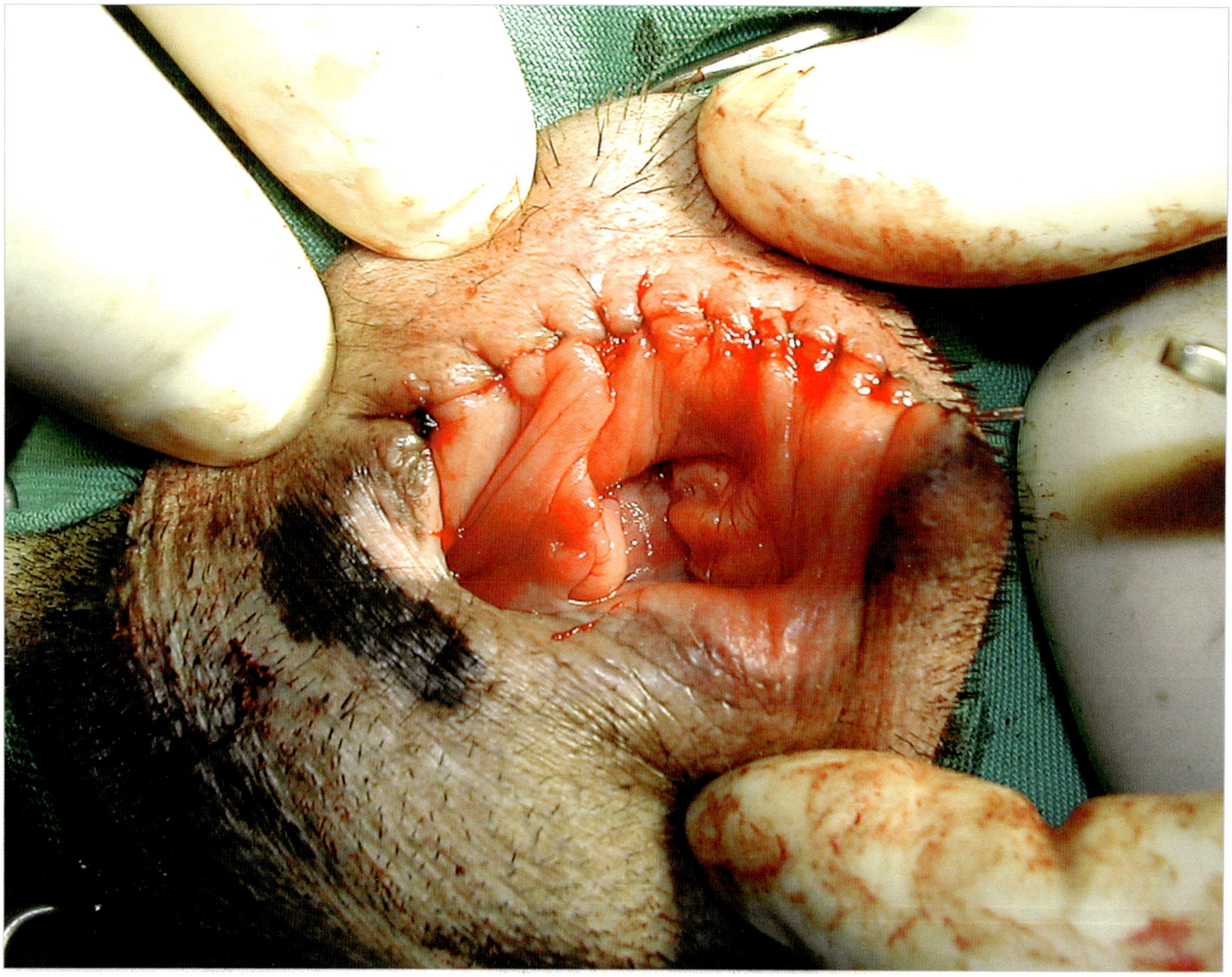

Fig. 7. Final appearance of the suture, showing the reconstruction of the edge of the vulvar labium.

Neoplasia. Case 2 / Transmissible venereal tumour

"Pitusa", a 5-year-old bitch, was presented showing signs of non-productive partus of 12 hours duration. Radiography revealed a foetus in the birth canal. The ratio between foetal head size and pelvic diameter did not explain the dystocia (figs. 1 and 2).

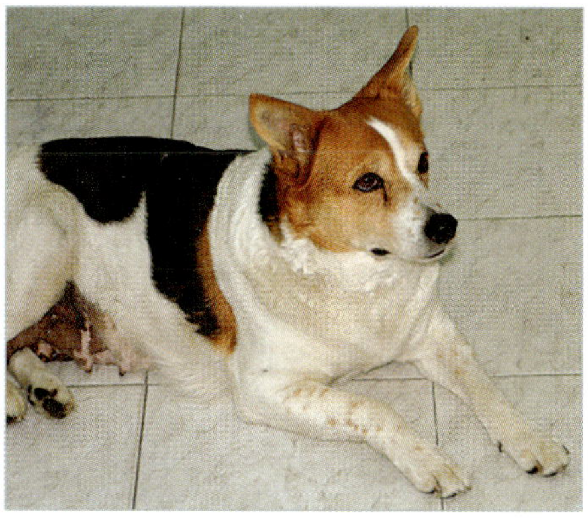

Fig. 1. The patient on the day of admission to hospital.

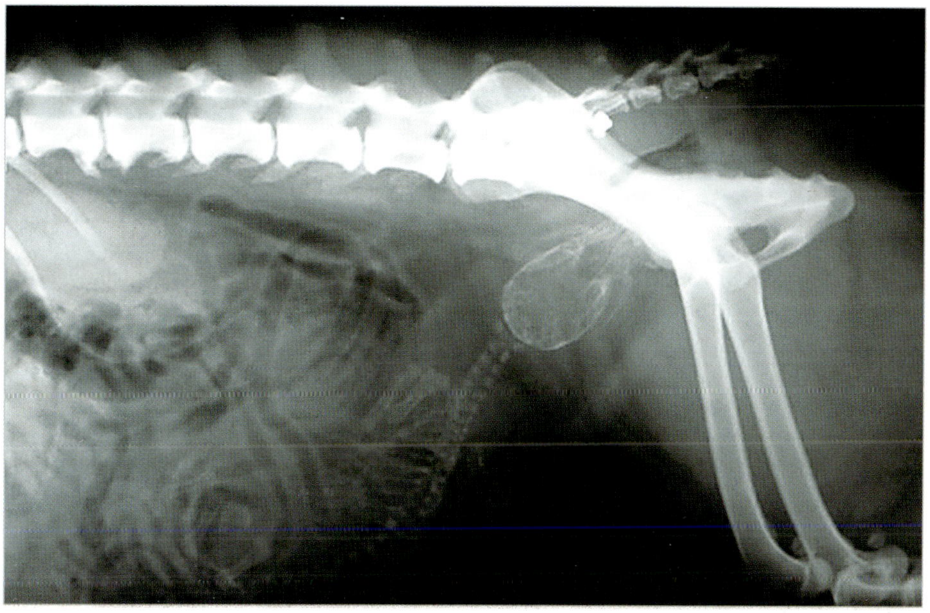

Fig. 2. Radiograph of the caudal abdomen showing the head of the solitary foetus engaged in the pelvic canal.

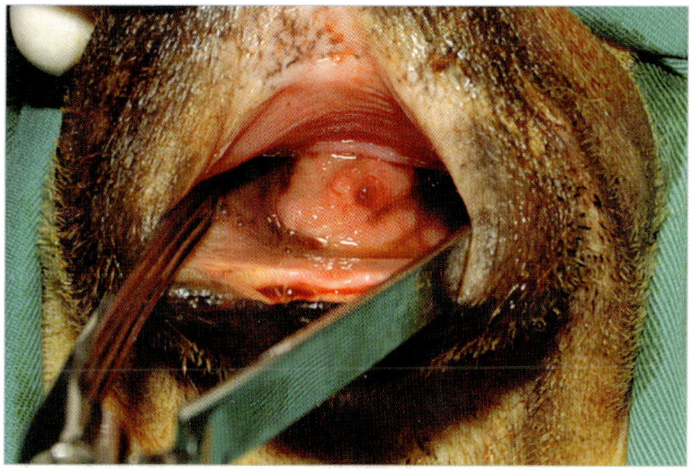

Fig. 3. Examination reveals a cauliflower-like mass, located deep in the vagina, obstructing the birth canal. This is consistent with transmissible venereal tumour (TVT). The decision is made to perform a caesarean section to resolve the dystocia, followed by an episiotomy that will allow removal of the tumour.

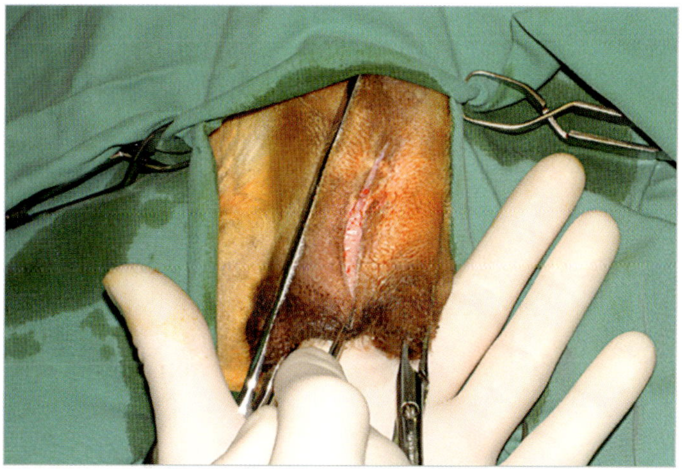

Fig. 4. The patient is prepared for episiotomy in the usual way: in sternal recumbency with the rear end elevated, placement of an anal purse string suture and the tail tied to the back. After placing the surgical drapes, two Doyen forceps are placed to minimise bleeding and to indicate the limit of the episiotomy incision line. A scalpel is used for the episiotomy skin incision.

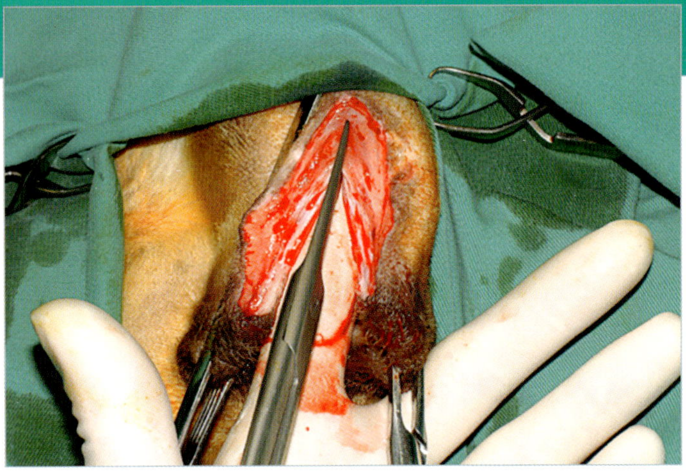

Fig. 5. The episiotomy is completed using scissors until the vaginal lumen is reached. Fingers inserted in the vaginal canal help to protect the internal canal tissues during dissection.

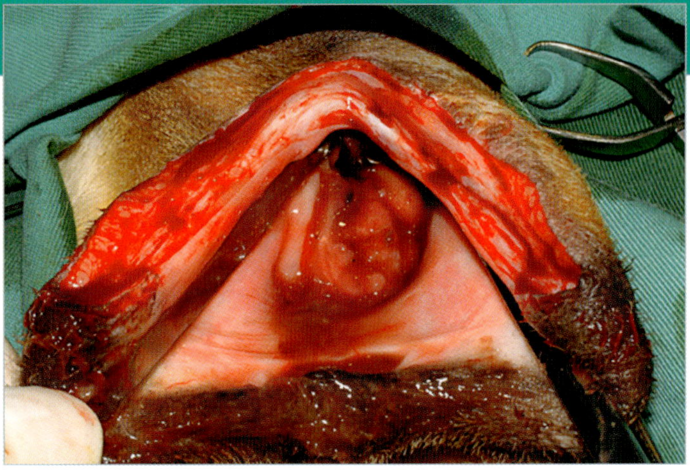

Fig. 6. Once the episiotomy is completed, the wound edges are spread widely to access the inside of the vagina and the tumour.

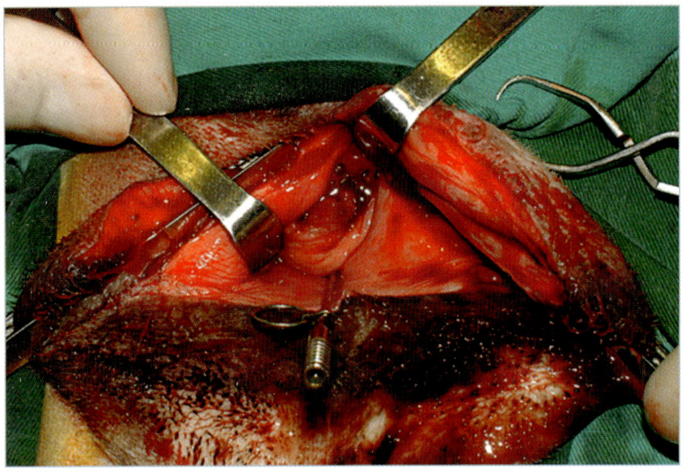

Fig. 7. Before excising the neoplastic mass, catheterisation of the urethra is recommended to locate its position and avoid accidental injury.

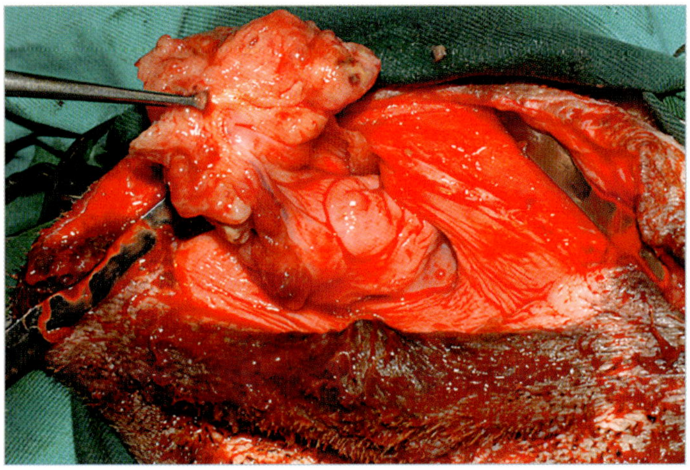

Fig. 8. The tumour mass is dissected at the pedicle. Haemostasis is achieved by ligation and/or diathermy depending on the size of the vessels.

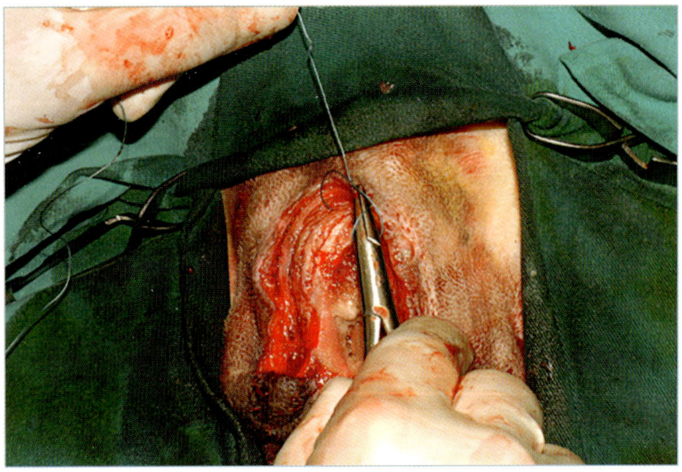

Fig. 9. The episiotomy wound is closed in different layers according to the technique described in pages 254-258.

Final comment

Histopathology confirmed the diagnosis of TVT. For this reason, a chemotherapy course with vincristine was initiated after surgery.

Chemotherapy following surgery is necessary in TVT cases. Surgery alone does not guarantee the elimination of all tumour cells.

Neoplasia. Case 3 / Tumour of the vaginal floor

"Honey", an 11-year-old bitch was presented with a purulent, haemorrhagic vulvar discharge of two months' duration. Examination revealed a soft, mandarin-sized swelling of the perineal area between the vulva and the anus. Vaginal palpation confirmed the tumour to be located in the vagina and attached, as is usual in these tumours, to the vaginal floor, cranial to the urinary orifice (figs. 1 and 2).

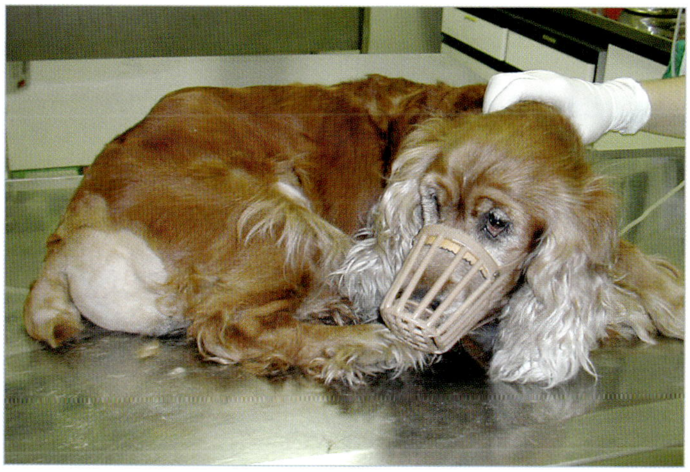

Fig. 1. The patient during surgical preparation.

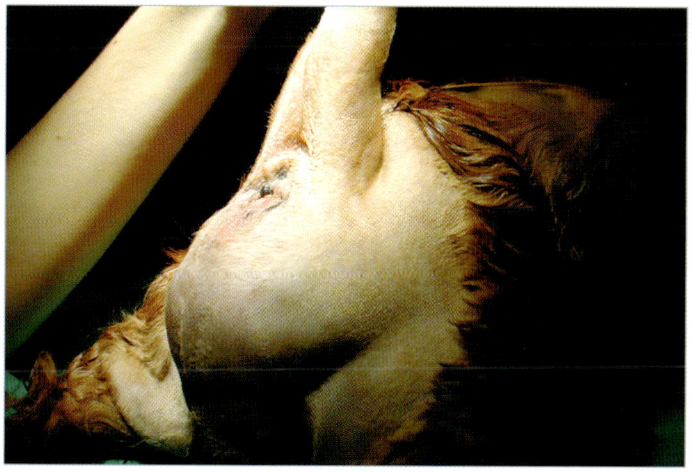

Fig. 2. A large swelling is seen between the vulva and the anus.

Faced with a mass in the perineal area in particular if, as in this case, it does not protrude through the vulva, it is essential to carry out vaginal and rectal palpation in order to determine its origin.

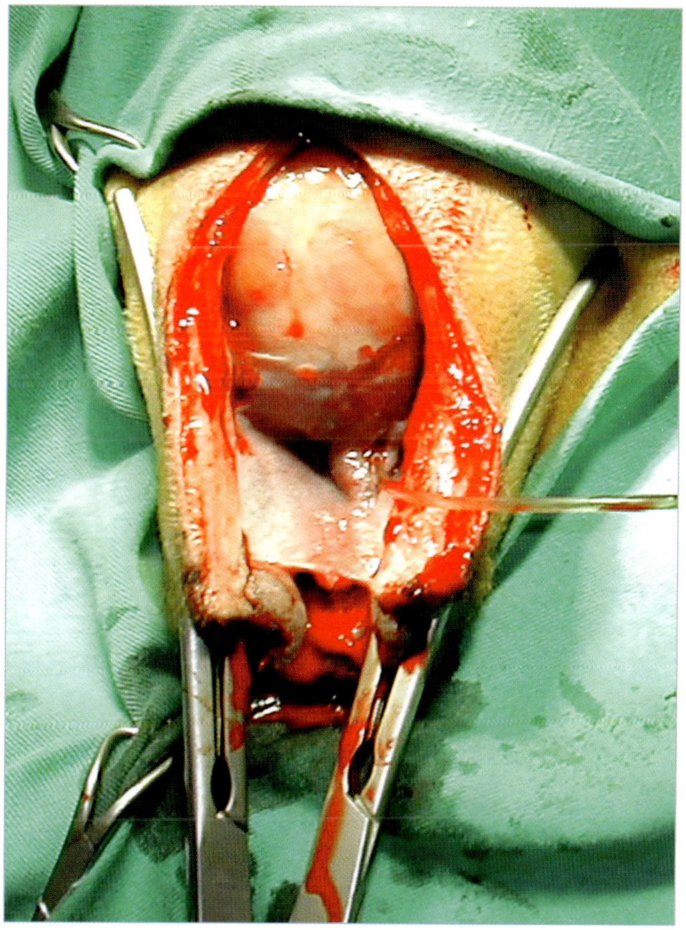

Fig. 3. After episiotomy, the neoplastic mass is visible inside the vagina. The next step will be to place a catheter in the urethra, to avoid trauma during the rest of the procedure. It is important not to mistake the urinary orifice for the fossa clitoridis.

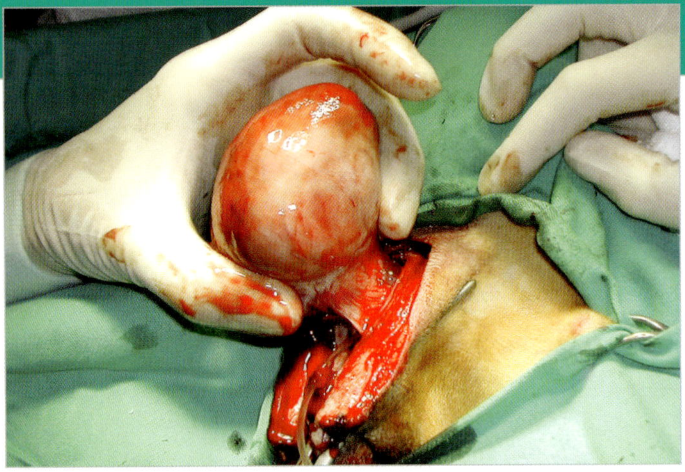

Fig. 4. These types of tumours are usually pediculated and can easily be exteriorised by simple traction. Note the characteristic implantation of the pedicle.

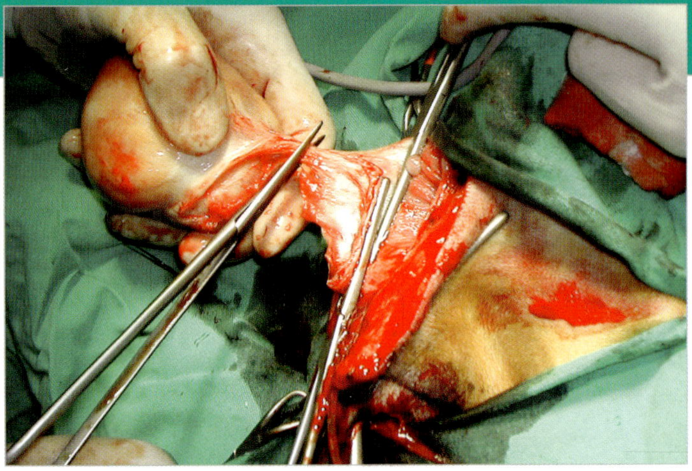

Fig. 5. At the base of the tumour pedicle, two Kocher clamps are placed in opposite directions, to prevent haemorrhage.
Distal to the clamps, the pedicle is first incised with a scalpel and then cut with scissors.

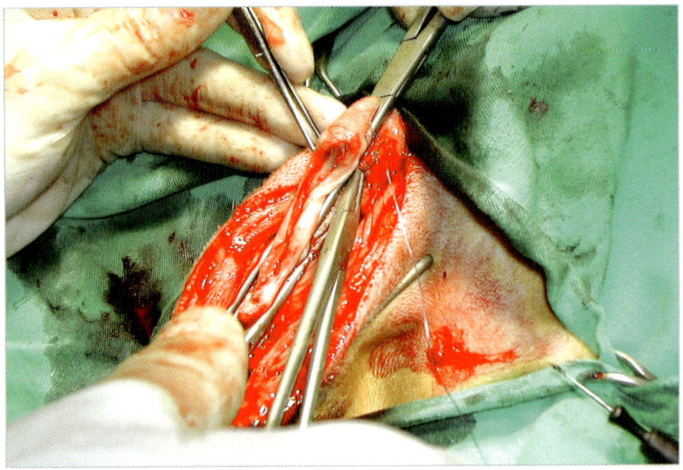

Fig. 6. The vaginal mucosa is closed with mattress sutures, below the clamps. This will contribute to haemostasis of the wound upon their withdrawal. The wound edges of the mucosa are brought together using a continuous suture over the mattress sutures. This aids the reconstruction of the vaginal floor and improves haemostasis.

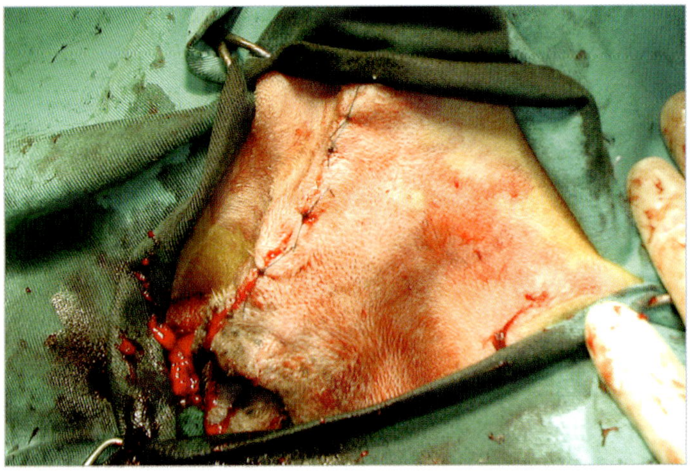

Fig. 7. The procedure is completed by closing the episiotomy as usual, in three layers.

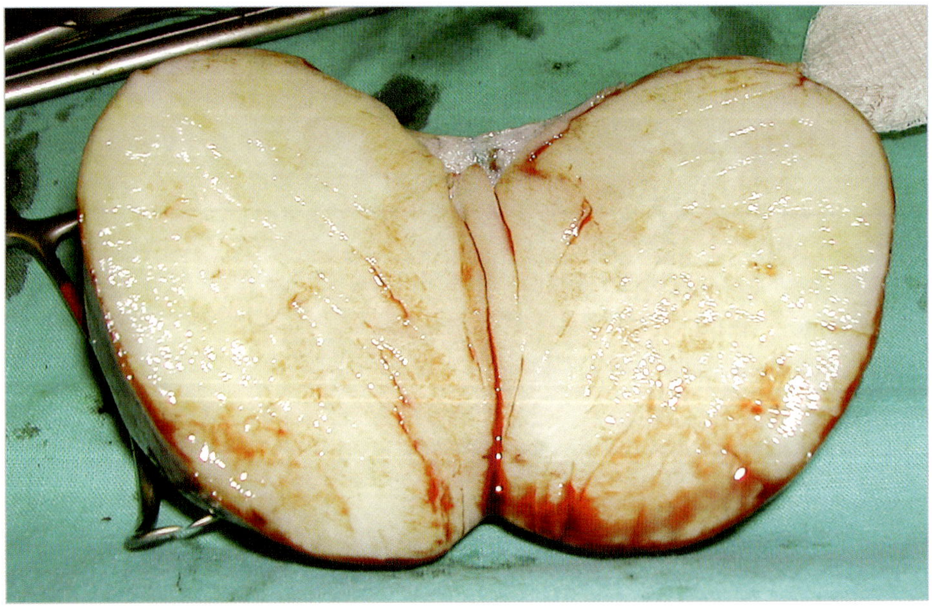

Fig. 8. The tumour after removal. Biopsy confirmed the initial suspicion of a fibroma.

Neoplasia. Case 4 / Tumour of the vaginal roof

Fig. 1. "Belle" on the day she was presented, with tenesmus.

A female, 8-year-old Giant Schnauzer is presented following continued difficulty urinating and defaecating.
Plain radiographs of the abdominal cavity reveal marked faecal retention and a severely distended bladder (figs. 1 and 2).

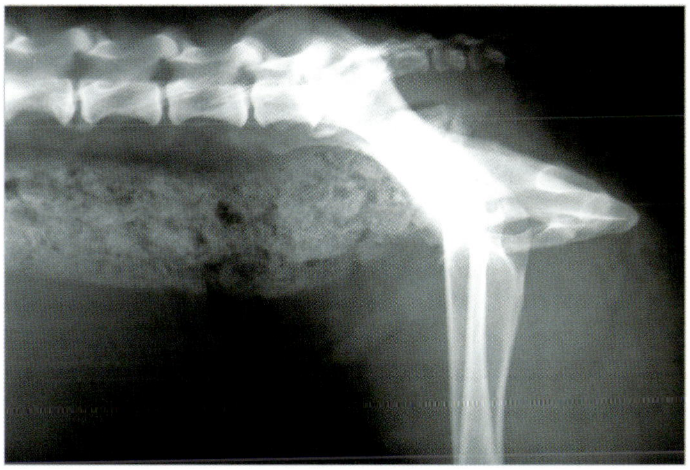

Fig. 2. Lateral radiograph of the abdomen showing faecal and urinary retention.

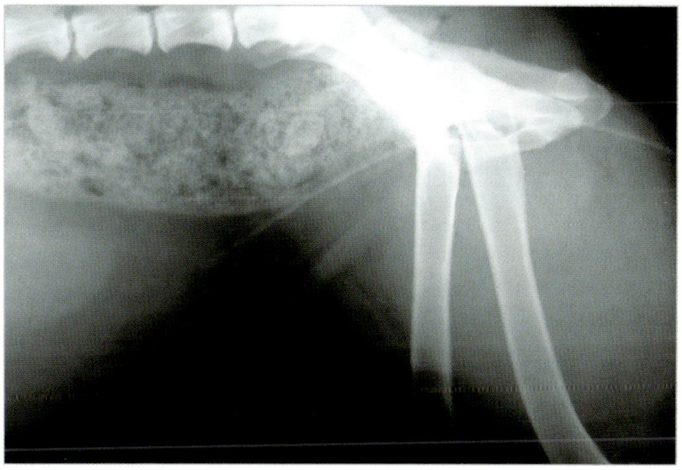

Fig. 3. When catheterising the patient to empty the bladder, a large mass is found occupying the vaginal lumen, exerting pressure on the urethra and rectum, hence the clinical signs. The deep location of this tumour means it may remain undetected.

A deep-seated vaginal tumour can be invisible and cause urethral and/or intestinal obstruction as the only clinical signs.

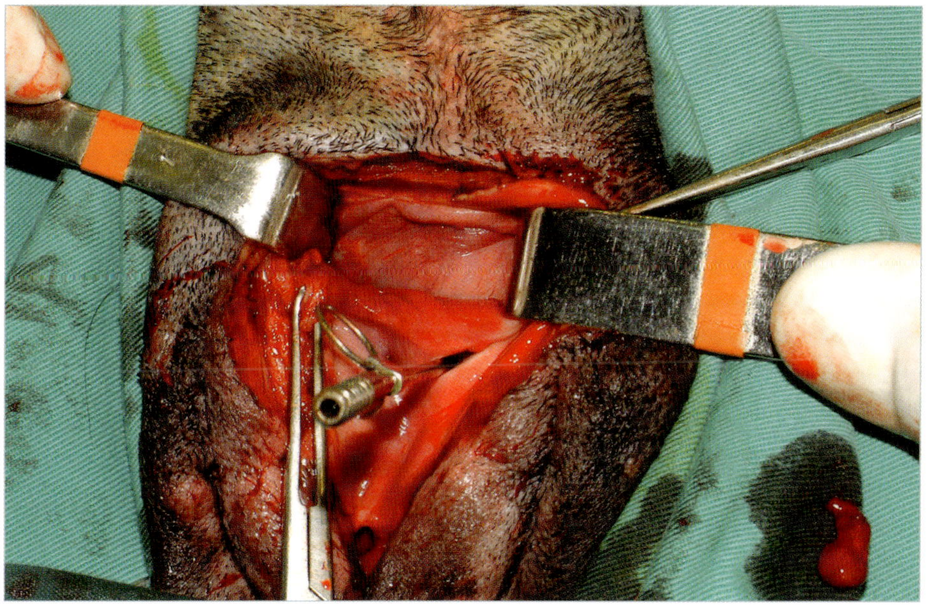

Fig. 4. The patient is prepared in the usual way, as described earlier, and an episiotomy is performed, exposing the tumour. The urethra should remain catheterised for the duration of the procedure.

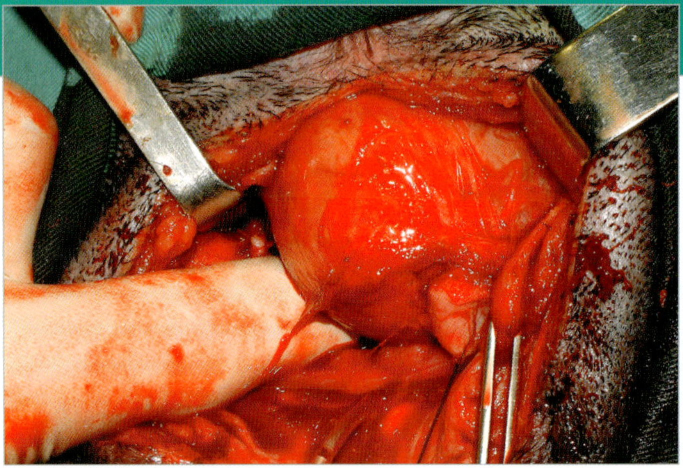

Fig. 5. In spite of the deep location of the tumour, its exteriorisation is achieved using gentle finger traction.

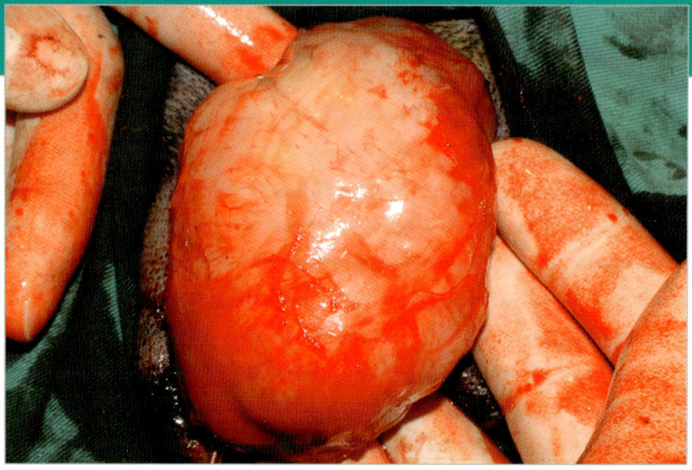

Fig. 6. Once exteriorised, the tumour is carefully pulled outwards to expose the short pedicle.

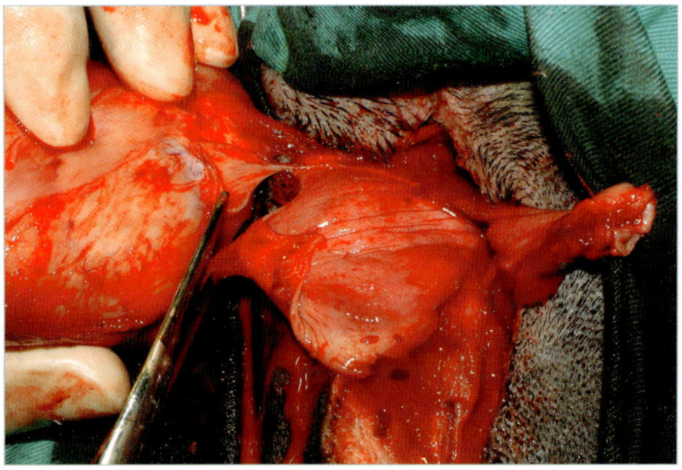

Fig. 7. Next, the pedicle is cut with scissors. Haemostasis is achieved with ligatures or electro-coagulation.

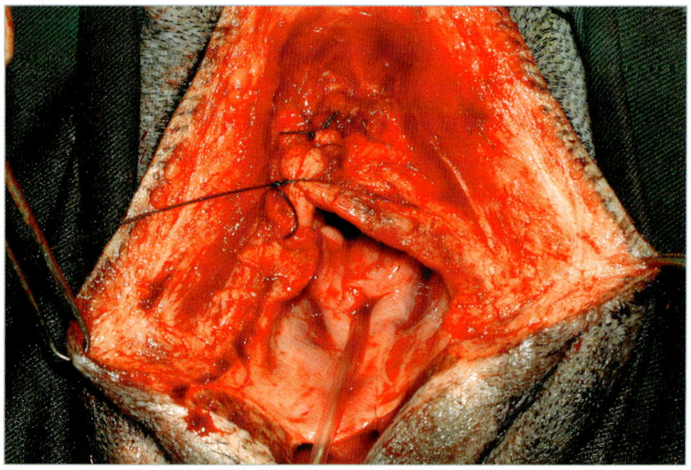

Fig. 8. The episiotomy is closed as described earlier, starting with closure of the vaginal roof, followed by the subcutaneous tissue and the skin.

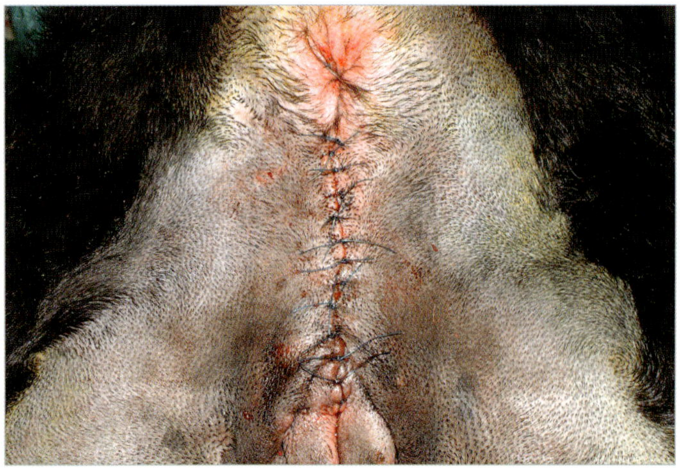

Fig. 9. Final appearance of the perineum at the end of the intervention.

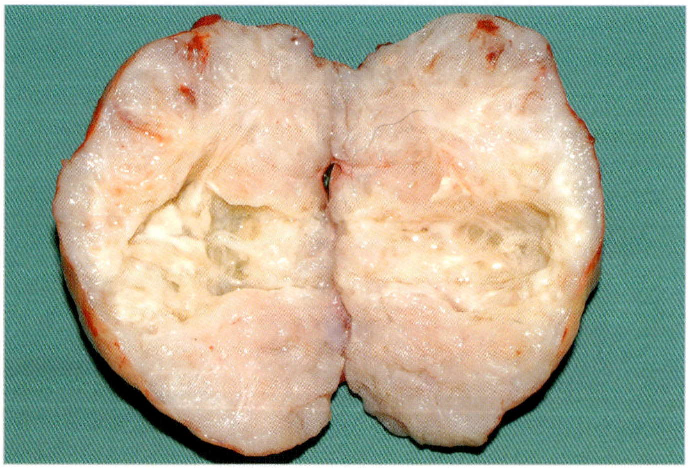

Fig. 10. Longitudinal cross-section of the tumour. Histopathology confirmed that it was a fibro-leiomyoma.

Neoplasia. Case 5 / Vulvar polyps

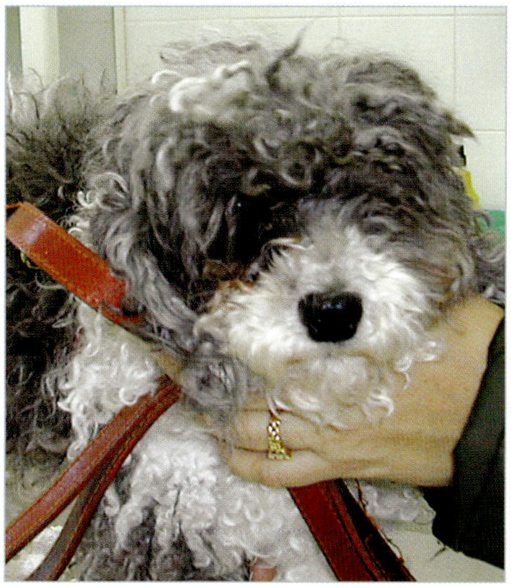

Fig. 1. "Bolita" on the day of her first visit to the hospital.

This case concerned a small 9-year-old female Poodle, whose owner had noted that "she had suddenly grown testes".
Examination revealed two pediculated masses emerging from the vulva, which did indeed resembles testes. They were found to be two vaginal polyps, one of which had a torsion accounting for the discolouration (figs. 1 and 2).

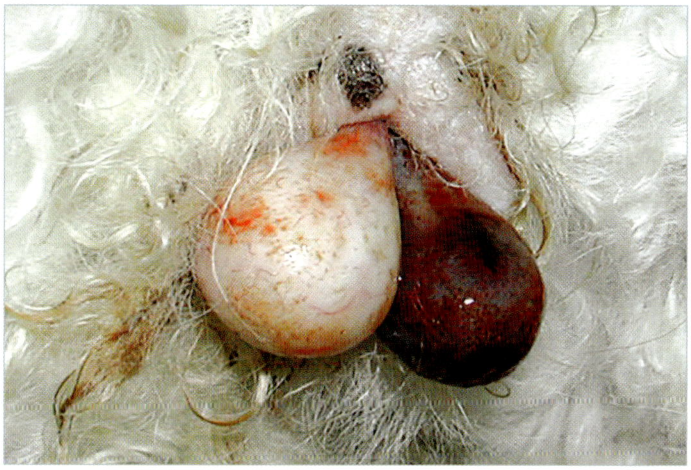

Fig. 2. The "testes" of "Bolita".

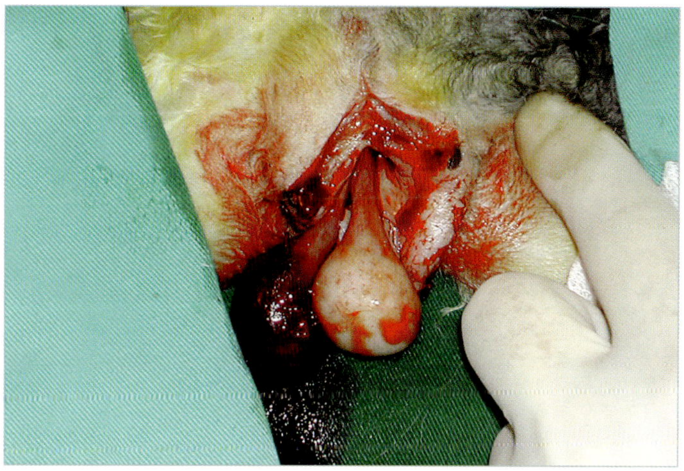

Fig. 3. It is decided to excise the polyps, requiring a small episiotomy to gain access to the point of attachment. These polyps were pediculated and originated from the vaginal floor, cranial to the urinary orifice, as is typical in these cases.

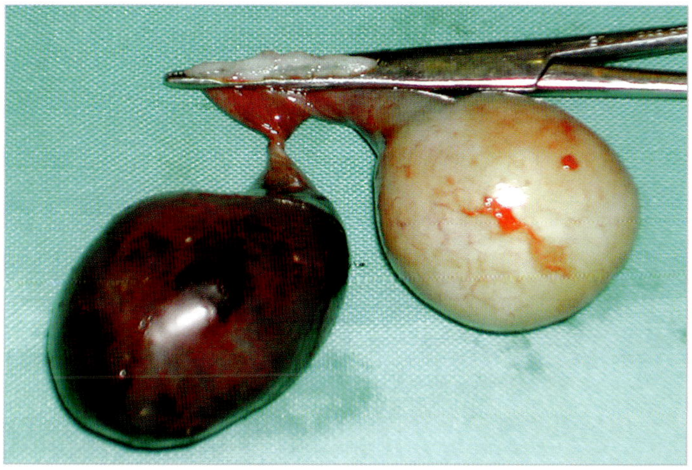

Fig. 4. Note the common origin of the two polyps, clamped by the forceps. On the left, the twisted pedicle of the congested polyp.

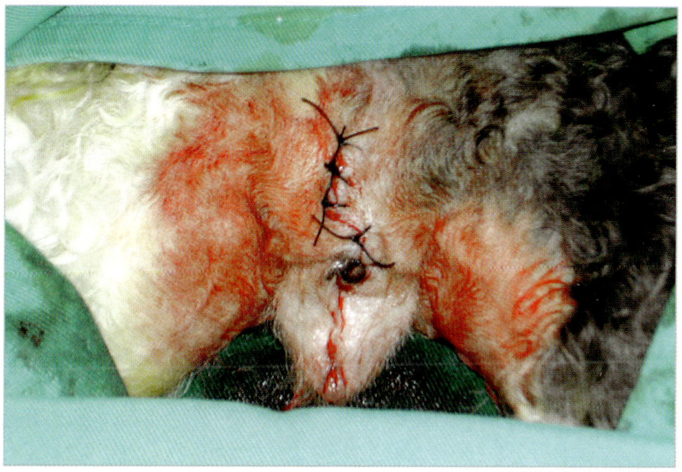

Fig. 5. Final appearance of the surgical wound following closure of the episiotomy site.

Neoplasia. Case 6 / Vaginal tumour

A small 8-year-old Schnauzer bitch was presented as an emergency following the sudden appearance of a mass in the vulvar area.
On examination, a congested, necrotic mass is found protruding through the vulva. It is assumed the tumour developed inside the vagina before protruding (fig. 1).

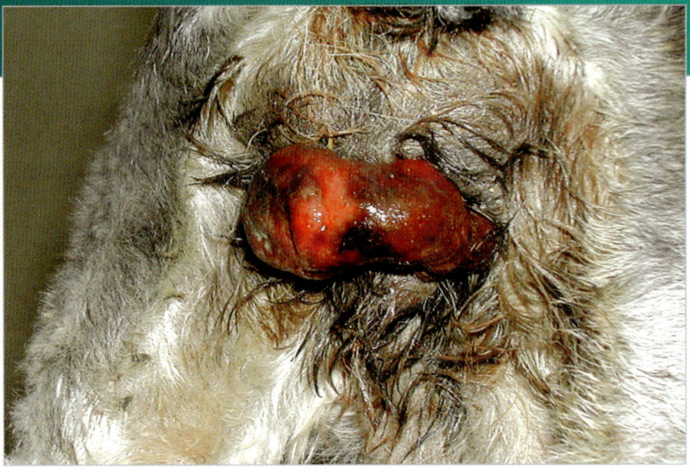

Fig. 1. Caudal view of the patient, showing the mass.

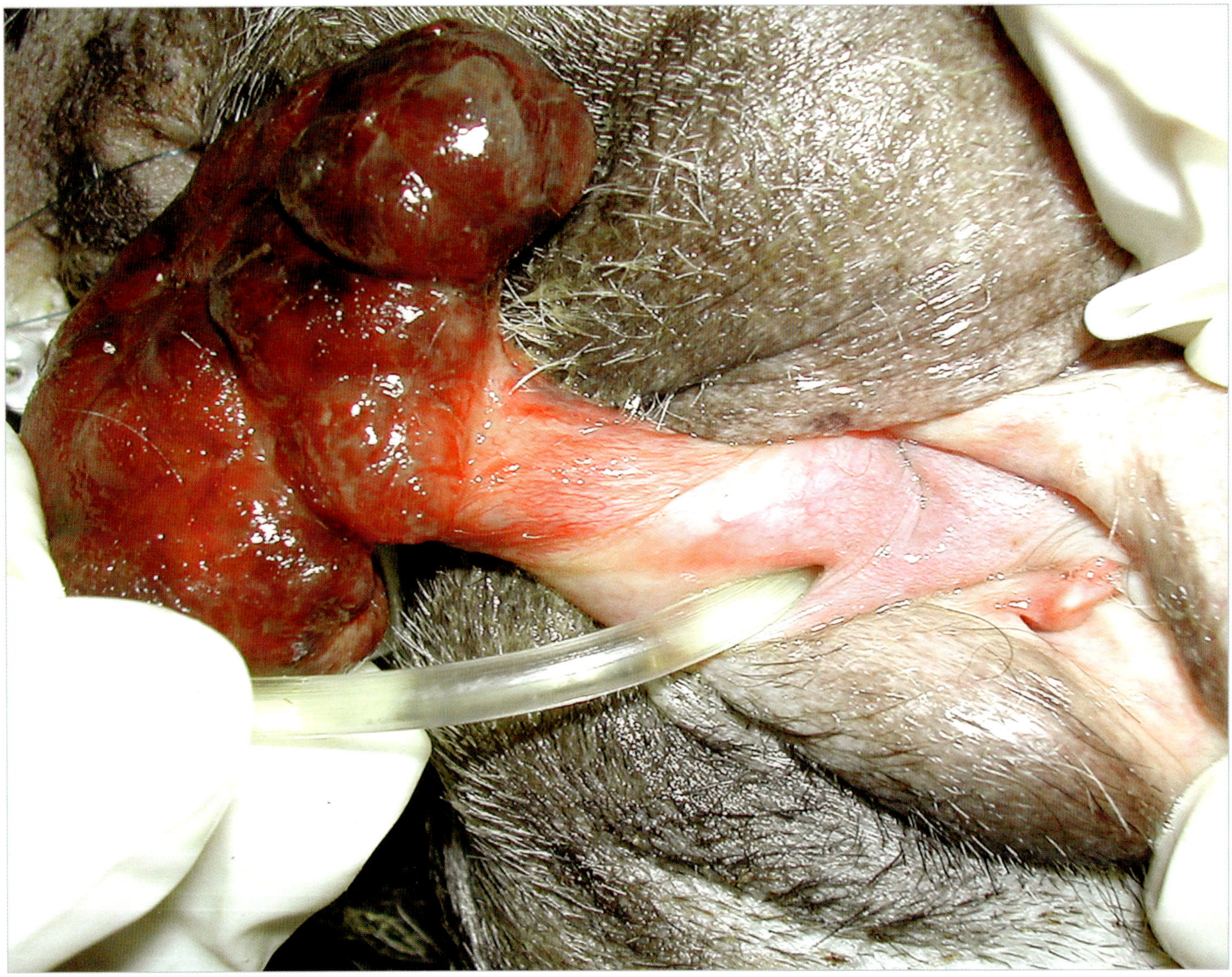

Fig. 2. Closer examination revealed that the tumour originated more caudally than is usual in these cases. Catheterisation of the urethra revealed that the urinary orifice was included in the base of the long pedicle. It was decided to resect the tumour. Due to the accessibility of the tumour, it was not necessary to perform an episiotomy.

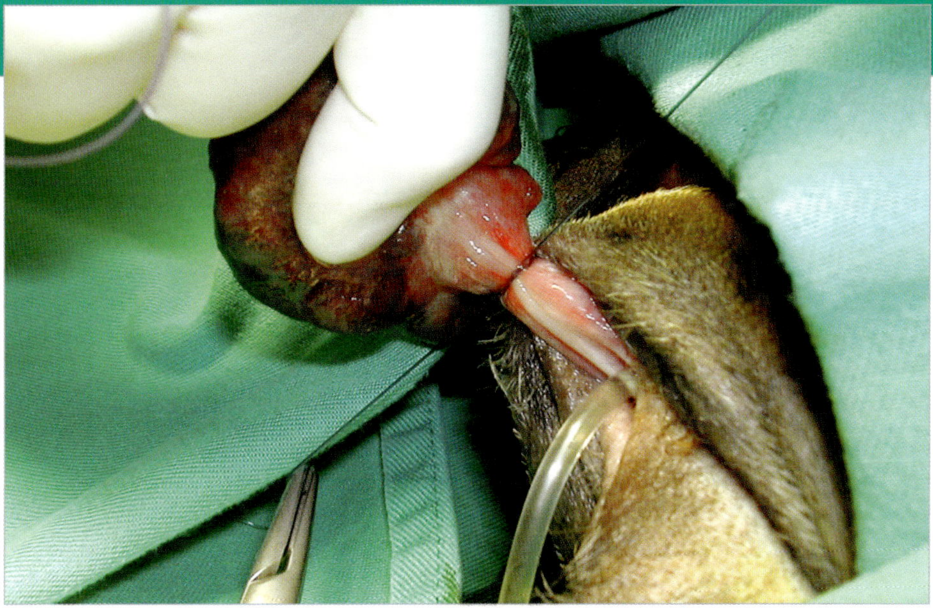

Fig. 3. During surgical procedures on the vagina, it is essential to keep the urethra catheterised at all times to confirm its location and avoid inadvertent damage. In this case, catheterisation was particularly important in view of the inclusion of the orifice in the tumour pedicle. Before resecting the mass, a transfixating ligature is placed around the base of the pedicle using absorbable 2/0 monofilament material.

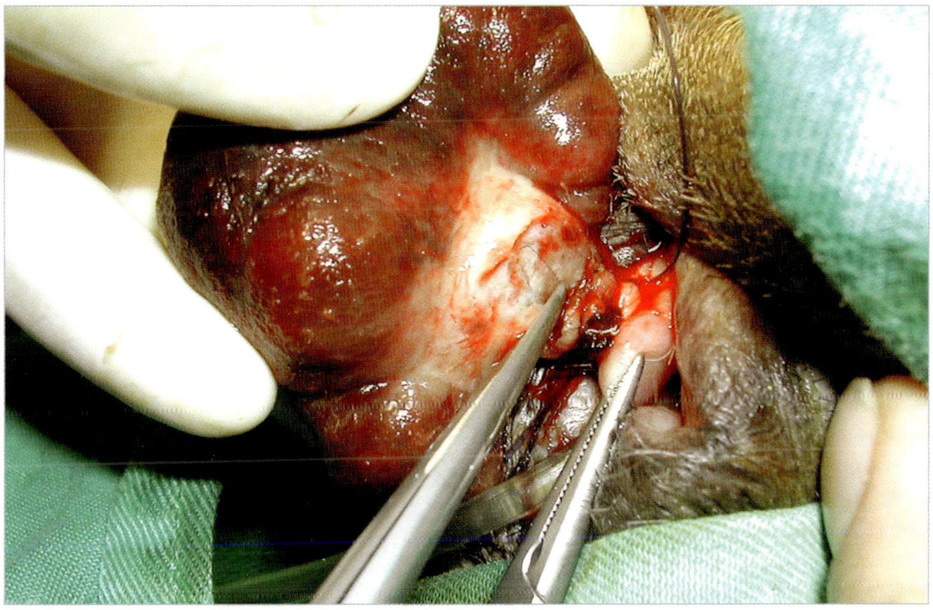

Fig. 4. The pedicle is cut distal to the ligature and the tissue is held with forceps to keep it in view. A second ligature is placed proximal to the first to ensure haemostasis.

For any vaginal procedure, it is essential to keep the urethra catheterised throughout surgery.

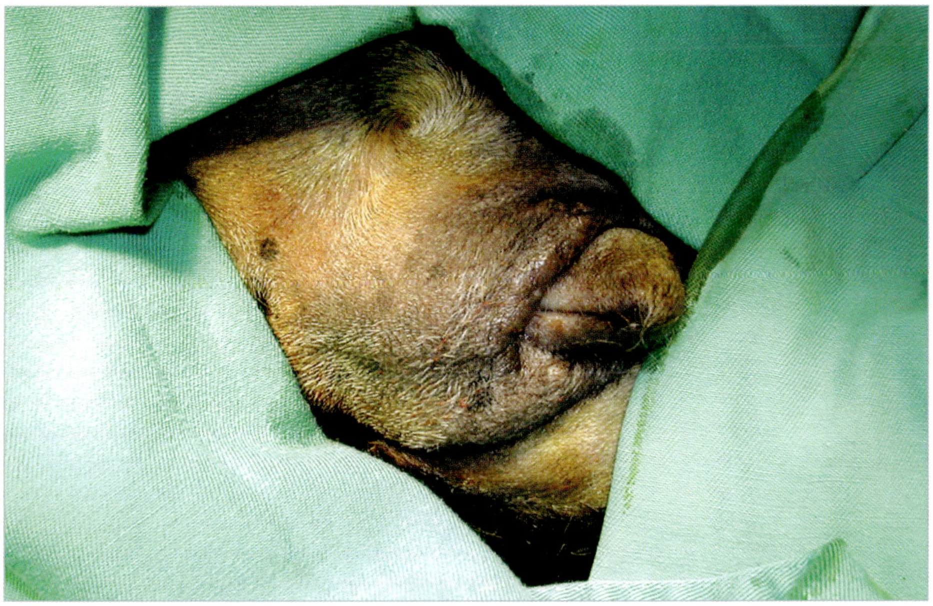

Fig. 5. Final appearance of operative site.

Neoplasia. Case 7 / Subcutaneous lipoma

A 7-year-old German Shepherd-cross bitch is presented with a large mass in the perineal area, dorsal to the vulva. The owner reports that the swelling has grown rapidly over past weeks. The patient presents no difficulty urinating or defaecating, and there is no vaginal discharge. Examination reveals a mass occupying the entire perineum, from the dorsal commissure of the vulva to the anus. Its appearance is suggestive of a vaginal tumour. Nevertheless, vaginal examination reveals the tumour is located outside the vagina, occupying the subcutaneous space between the vulva and the anus (figs. 1 and 2).

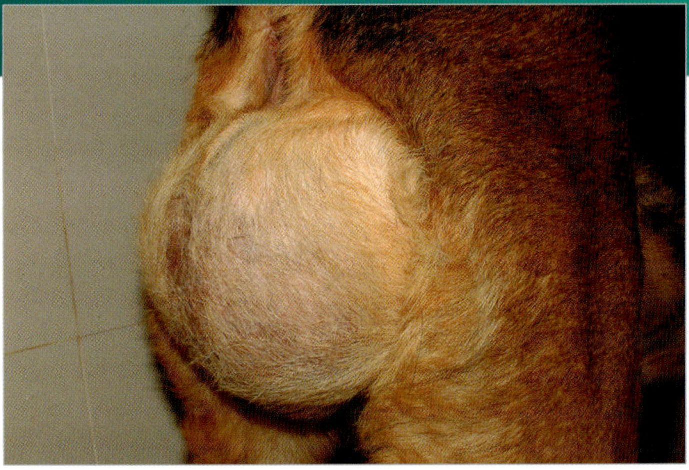

Fig. 1. The patient at the time of surgical preparation.

For accurate diagnosis of a perineal mass, its site of origin should be determined via vaginal and rectal palpation. This will influence the surgical technique used.

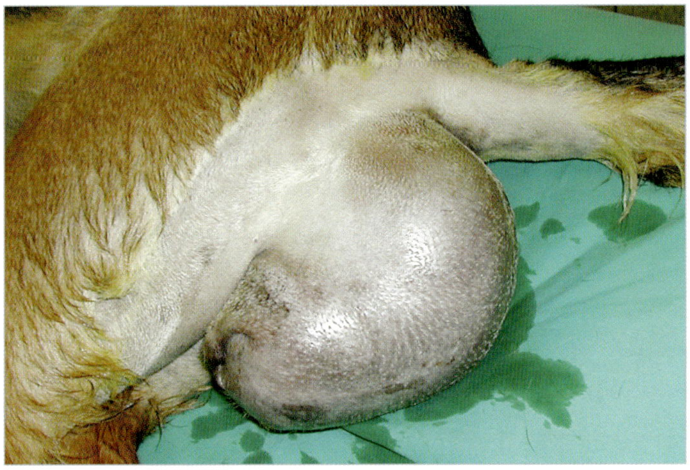

Fig. 2. Appearance of the perineum of the patient after shaving and disinfection of the area.

See patient positioning → *page 248*

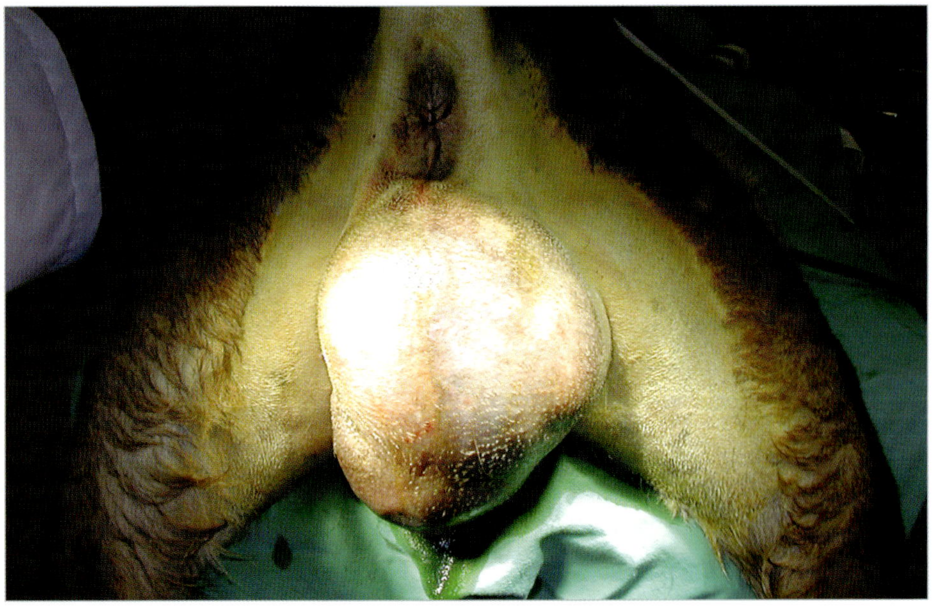

Fig. 3. It was decided to surgically remove the mass. For this, the patient is prepared in the usual way.

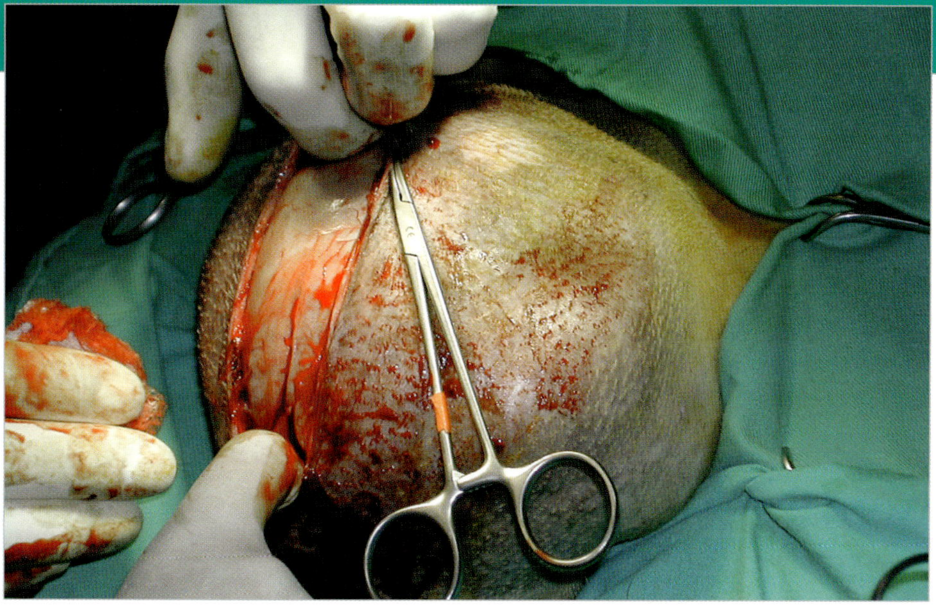

Fig. 4. First, a midline incision is made over the perineum. Blunt dissection is used to separate the skin from the tumour wall, until its base is reached.

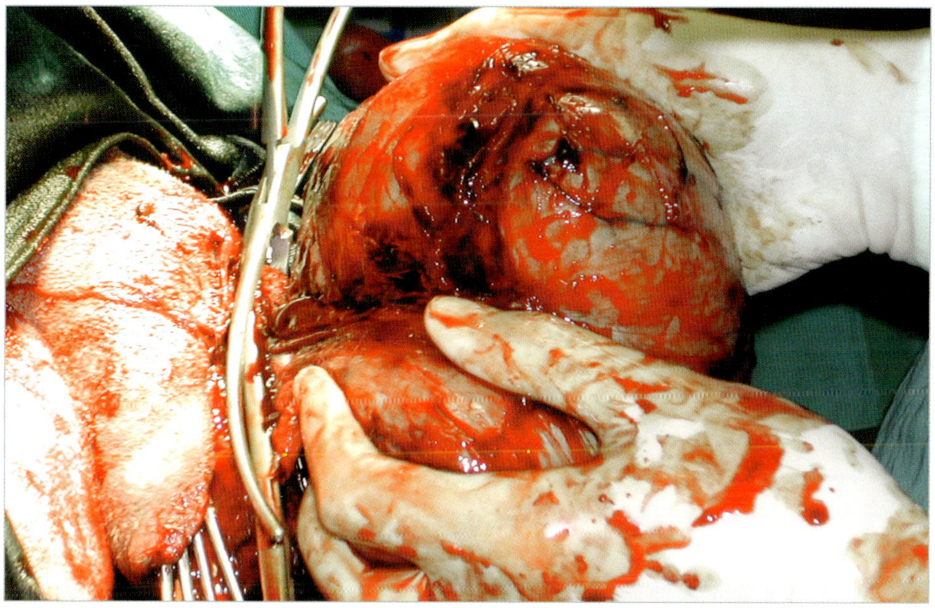

This part of the body is highly vascularised and considerable haemorrhage should be anticipated.

Fig. 5. The base of the tumour is clamped using two forceps in order to avoid haemorrhage.

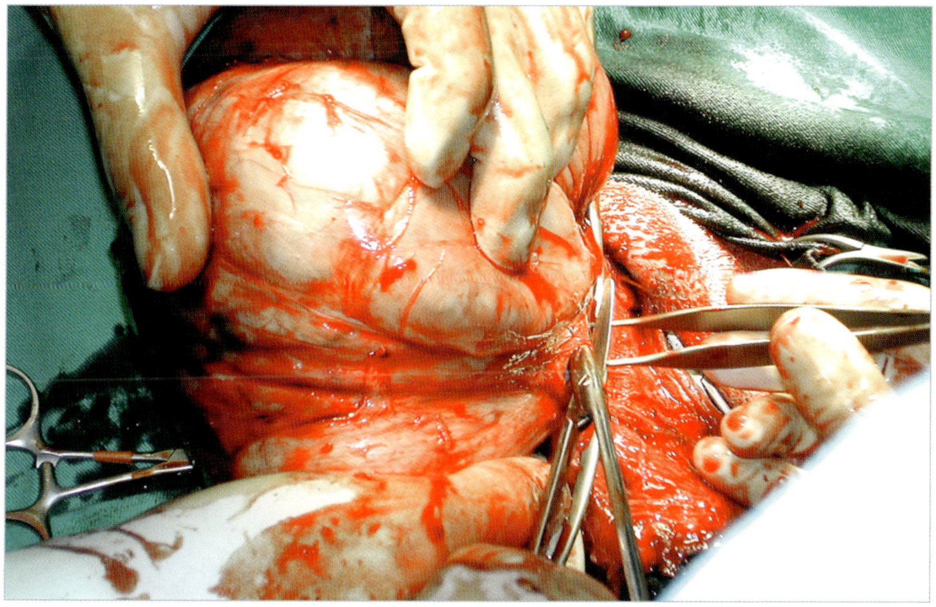

Fig. 6. Resection is completed by sectioning the pedicle.

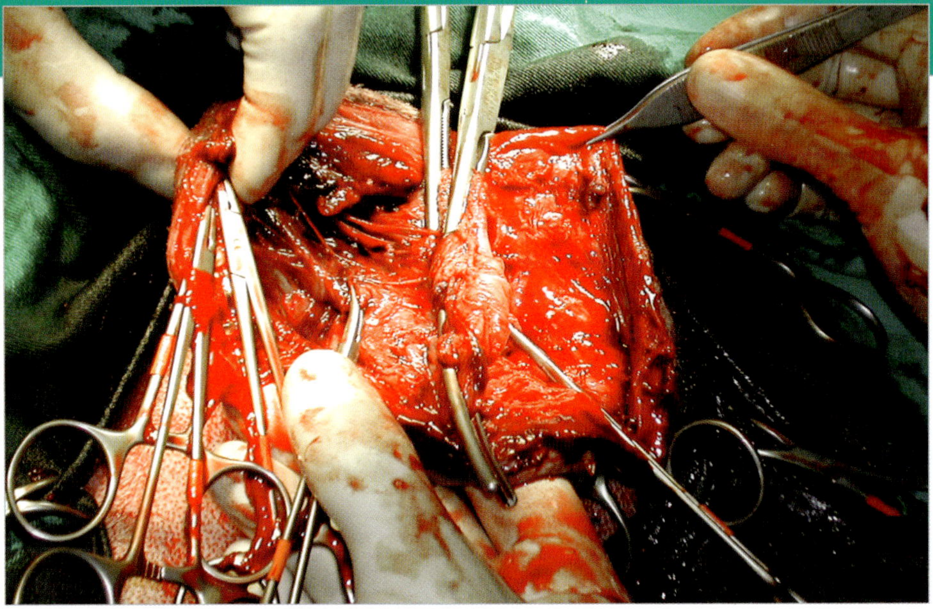

Fig. 7. Before removing the clamps, well-placed ligatures are required to achieve good haemostasis.

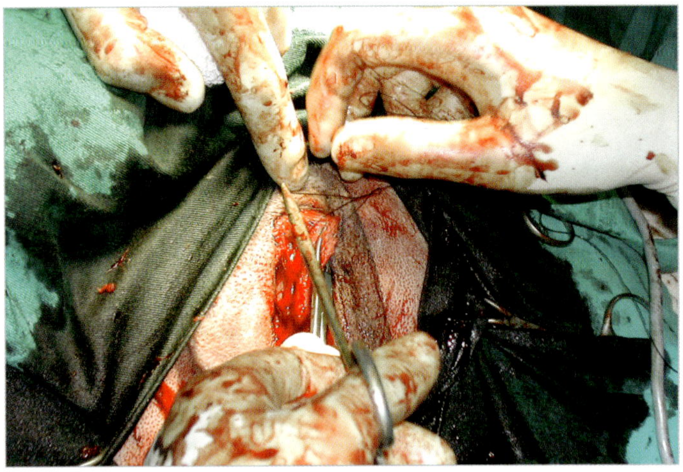

Fig. 8. Starting with the subcutaneous tissue, the wound is closed in two layers, using 2/0 monofilament absorbable material.

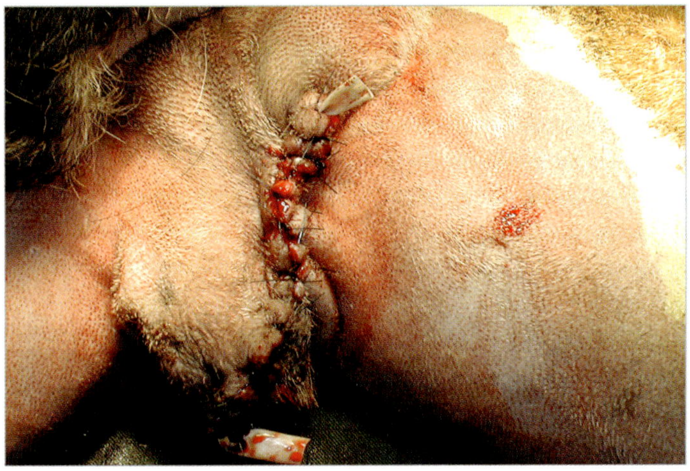

Fig. 9. After resection of the excess skin and placement of a Penrose drain, the skin is closed with mattress sutures using non-absorbable monofilament material.

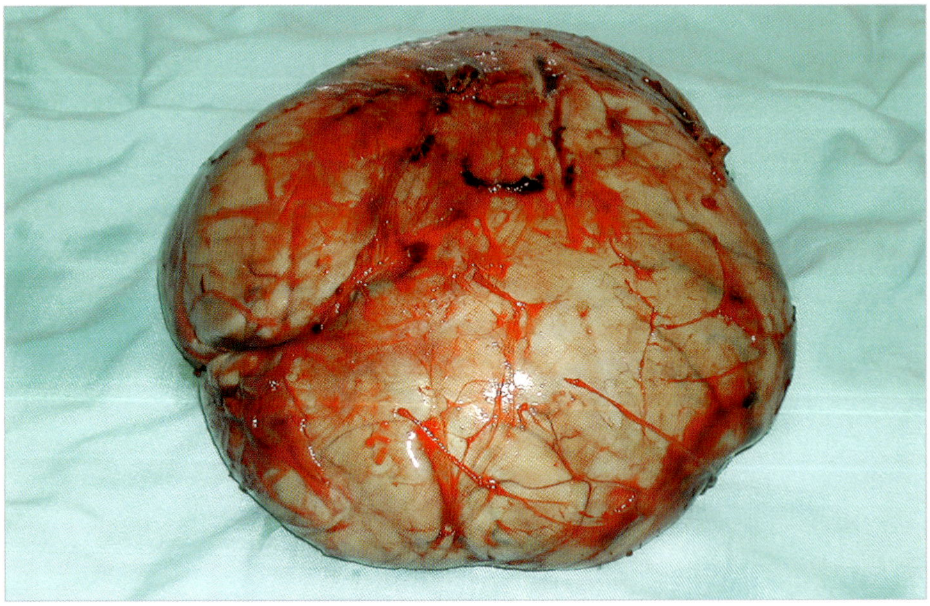

Fig. 10. The tumour was diagnosed as a subcutaneous lipoma. Its anatomical location, in the midline of the perineum, and its symmetrical form initially suggested a vaginal tumour.

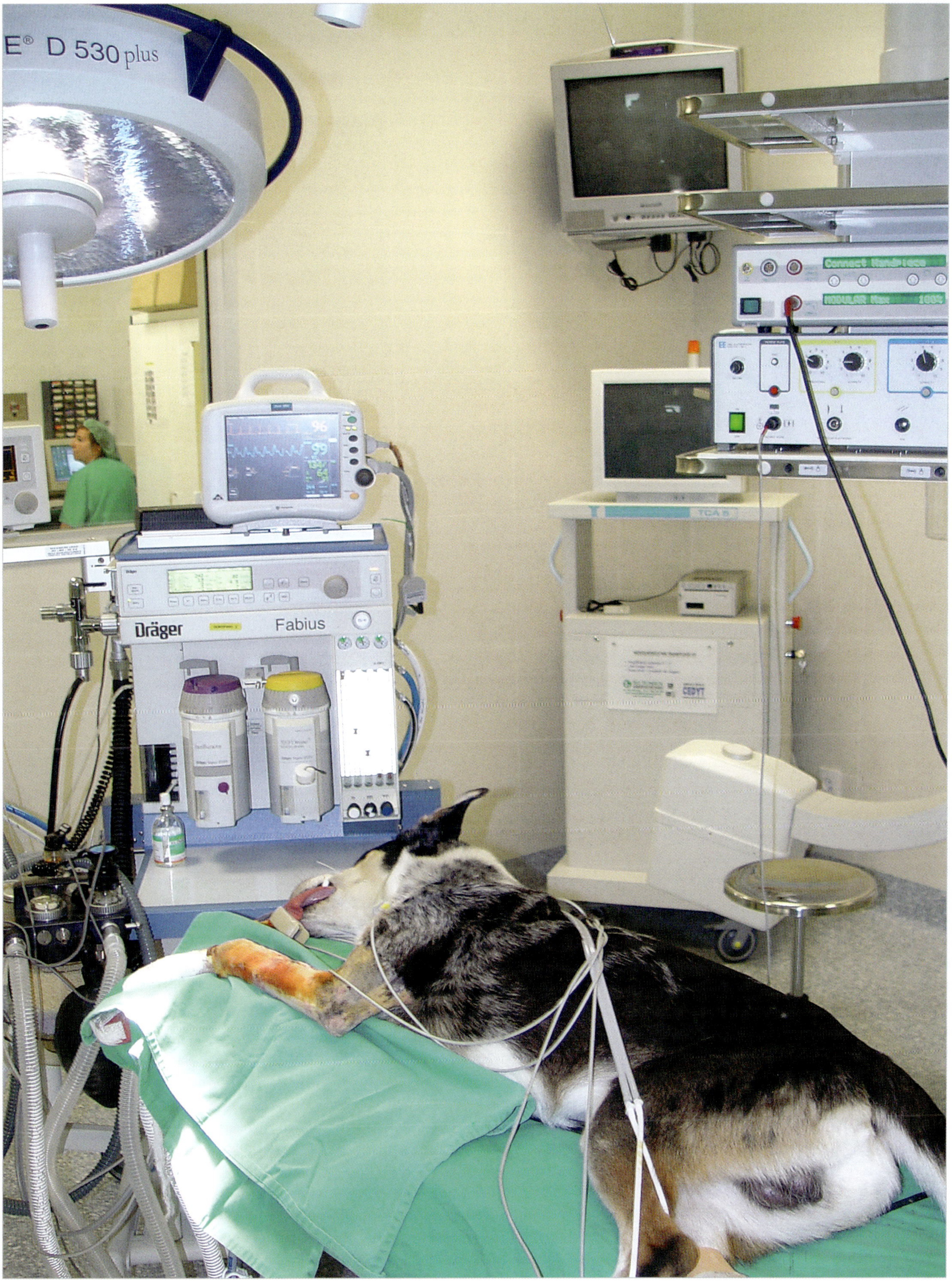
D 530 plus
Dräger
Fabius

Persistent hymen

Prevalence	■				
Technical difficulty	■	■			

Due to abnormalities in the fusion of the Müllerian ducts during embryonic development, different forms of persistent hymen exist. Both the annular form and the vertical septum will lead to stenosis at the vestibulovaginal junction.

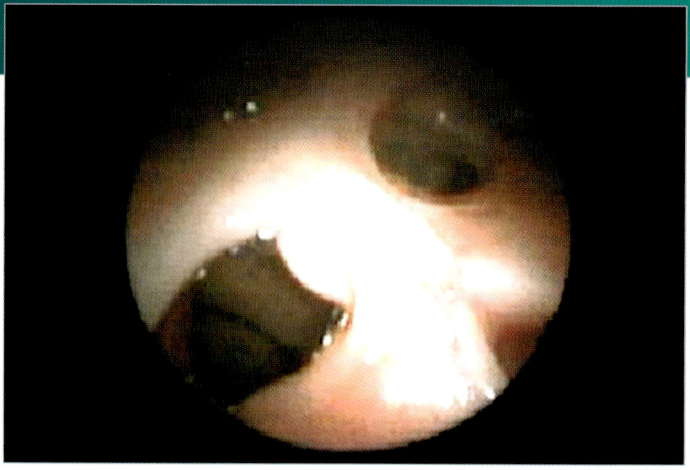

Fig. 1. Using endoscopy, the origin of the problem can be identified.
It comprises a vertical fibrous band, which is causing a division and stenosis of the vagina at the vestibulovaginal junction.
In the lower right of the picture, the urethral papilla is visible.

This dog had recurring infections of the vagina that did not respond satisfactorily to medical management. For the last treatment prior to referral, the veterinarian prescribed vaginal suppositories, which could not be inserted.
The patient was referred to the hospital for a vaginoscopy (fig. 1).

✱ ***Persistent vaginitis results from poor drainage of the uterine and vaginal fluids, which favours bacterial colonisation.***

See patient positioning ➜ *page 248*
See episiotomy ➜ *page 254*

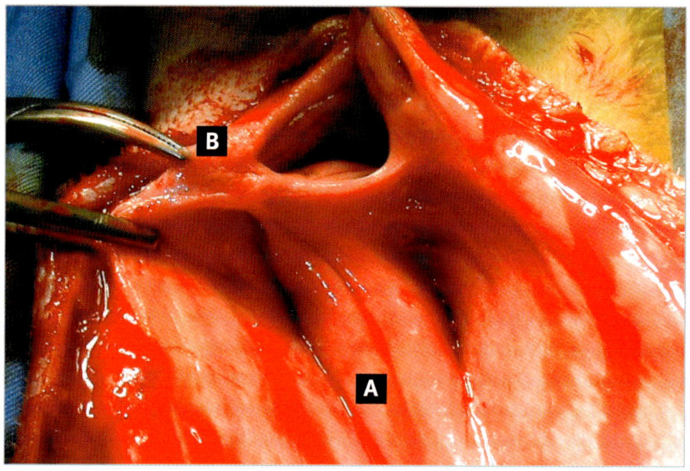

Fig. 2. An episiotomy allows visualisation of the urethral papilla (A) as well as the persistent hymen (B).

Surgical treatment

After performing an episiotomy, the edges of the incision are parted to allow a view of the vestibulovaginal junction (fig. 2).
Next, the fibrous band is cut with scissors (figs. 3 and 4).

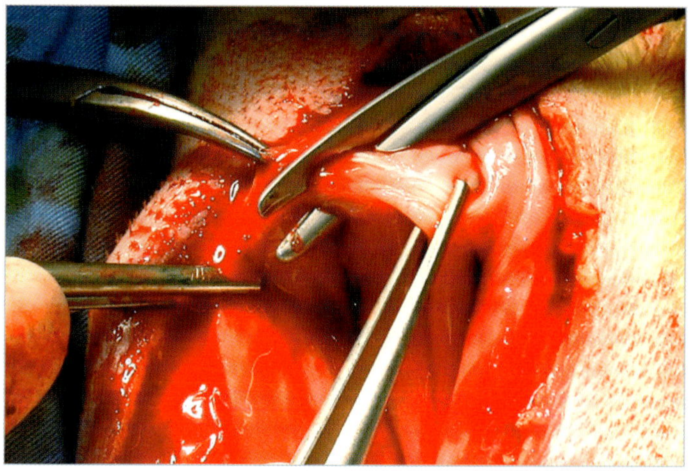

Fig. 3. After exposure of the persistent hymen, the dorsal and ventral attachments to the vagina are resected. This picture shows the incision of the dorsal part.

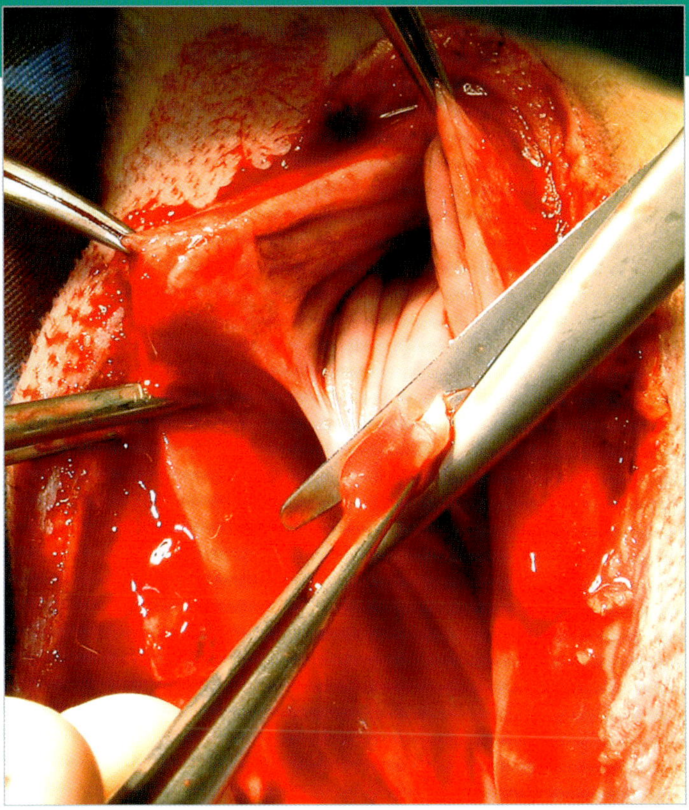

Fig. 4. Next, and always under strict monitoring of the urethral papilla to avoid damaging it, the ventral part of the hymen is sectioned.

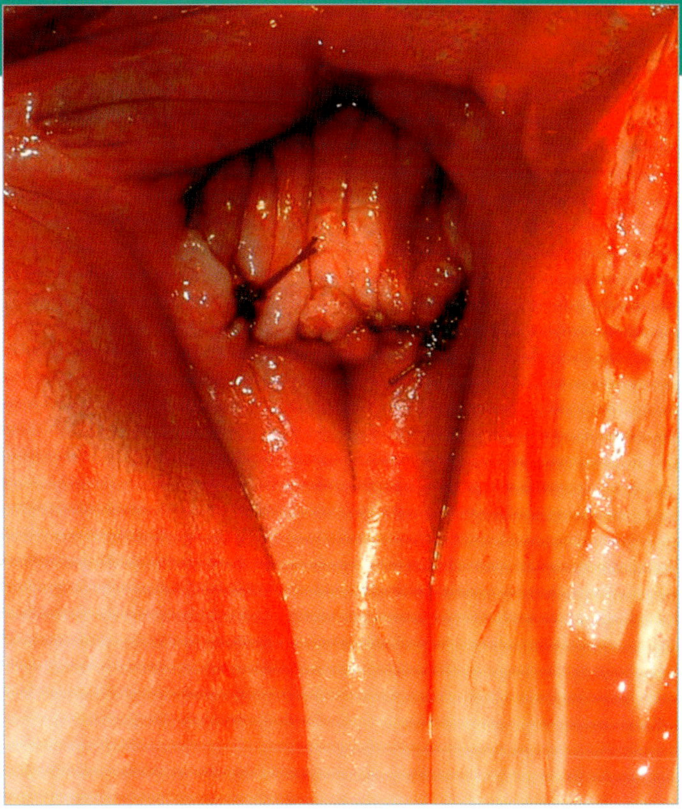

Fig. 5. To ensure haemostasis of the vaginal mucosa, it may be necessary to place a continuous interlocking suture, using absorbable 3/0 monofilament material.

To control haemorrhage of the vaginal mucosa, it is recom-mended to place a continuous suture with absorbable material (fig. 5).

> ✱ *Identify the urethral papilla to avoid trauma. If it is difficult to locate, place a urethral catheter.*

Some patients may have both types of persistent hymen (vertical band and annular stenosis). Therefore, it is important to remember to examine the vaginal diameter again. After surgical correction, the episiotomy wound should be closed (fig. 6).

After surgery

- Rinse the vagina topically with a povidone iodine solution.
- In case of vaginitis, treat medically based on bacterial culture and sensitivity testing.

The prognosis is very good following resection of the fibrous band with complete resolution of the original clinical signs.

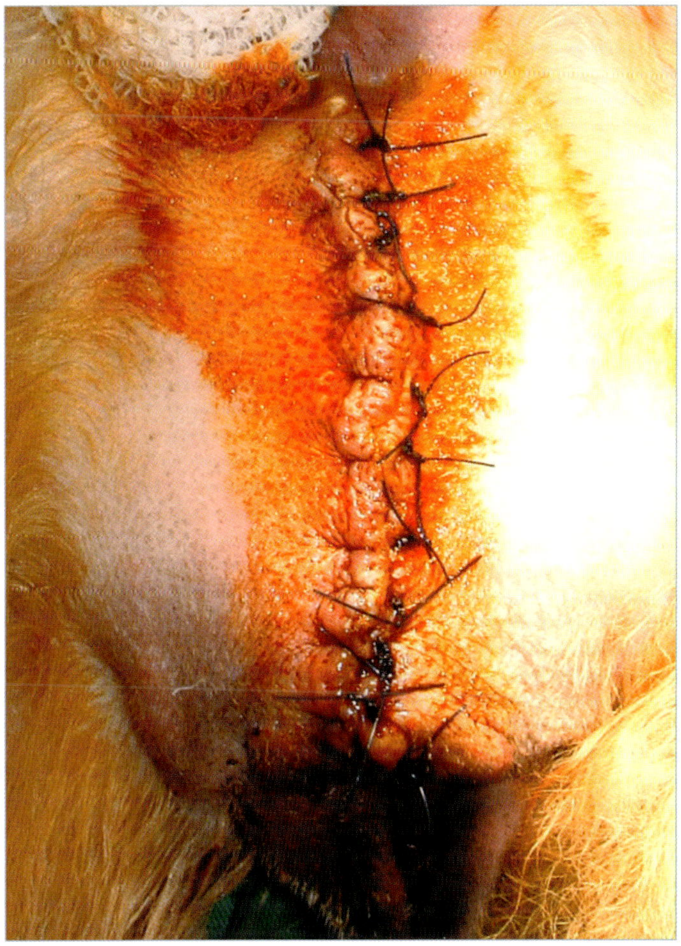

Fig. 6. The episiotomy is closed in three layers, using 2/0 absorbable material for the mucosa and muscular layer, and non-absorbable monofilament material for the skin.

Median section of the penis of the dog

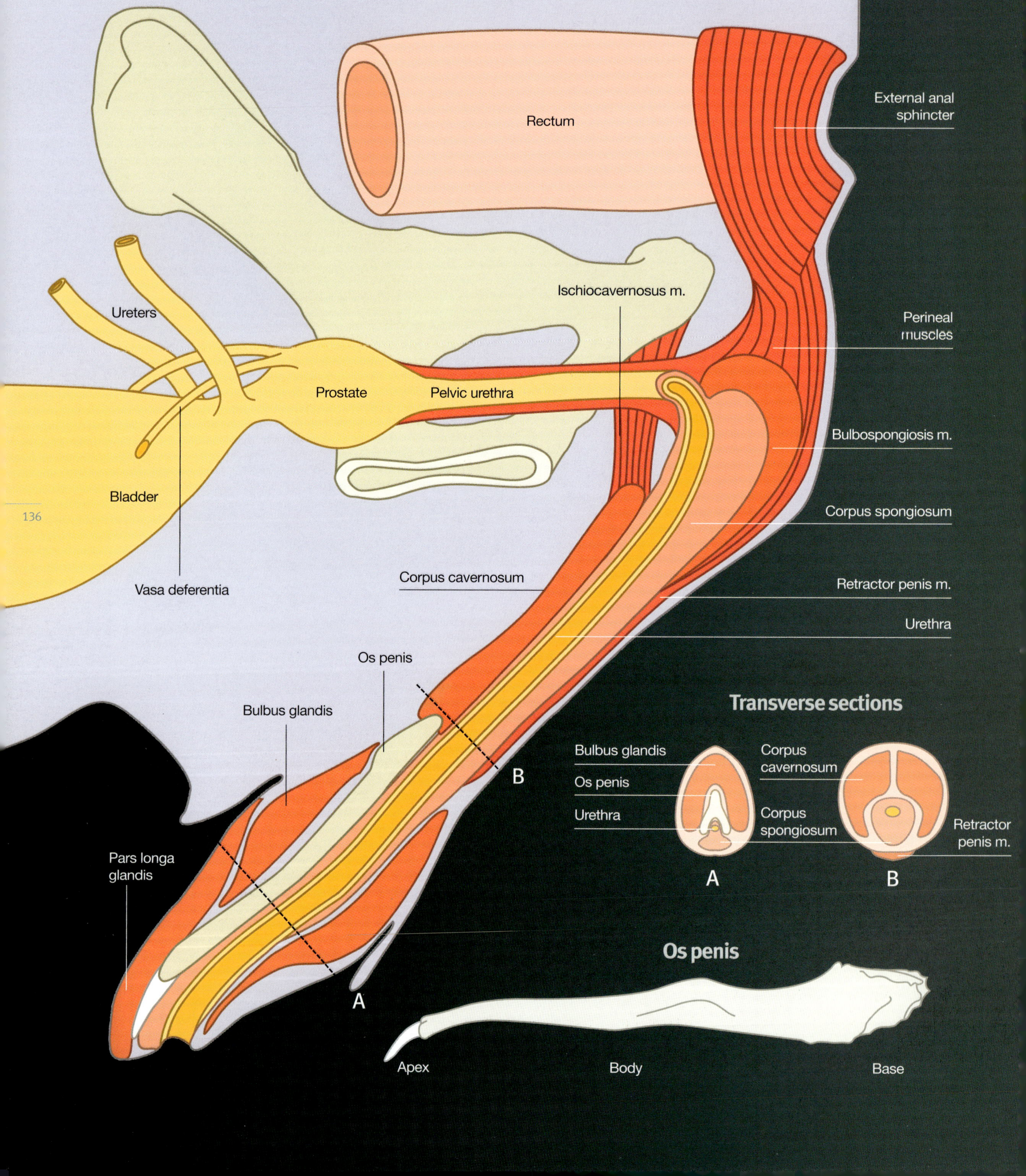

Dorsal view of the section of the penis of the cat

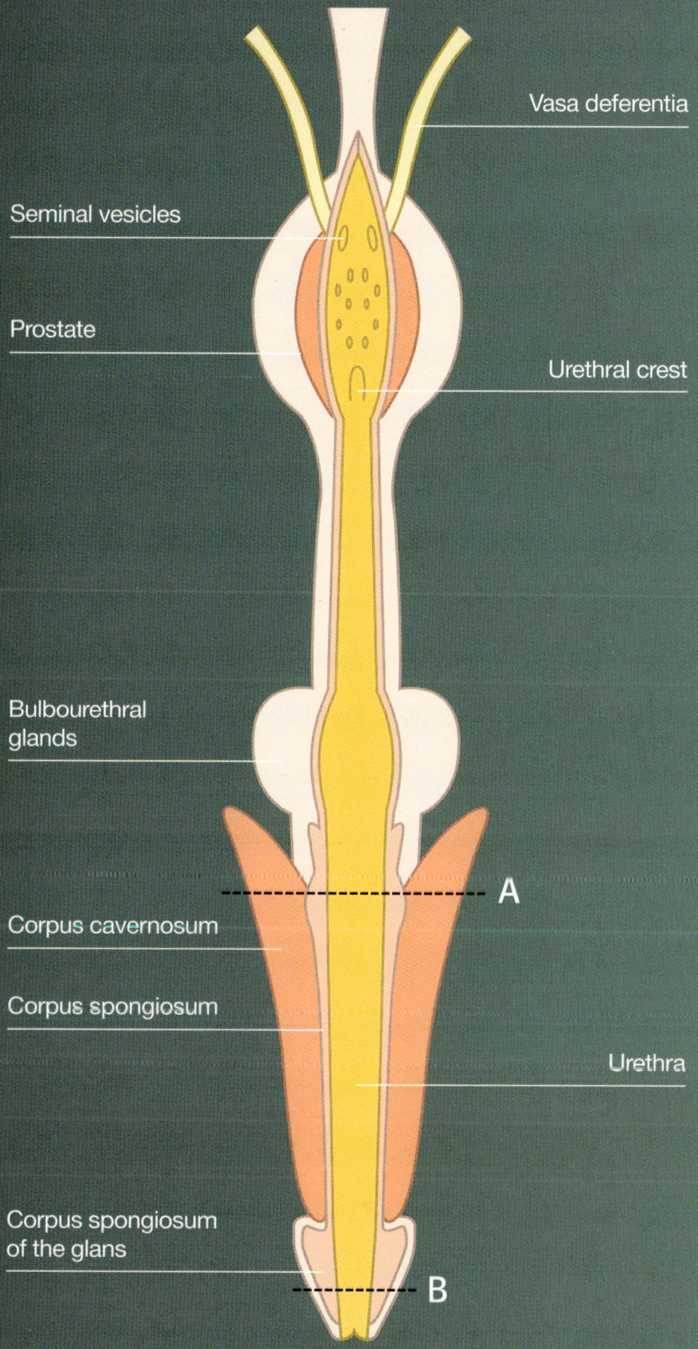

Transverse sections

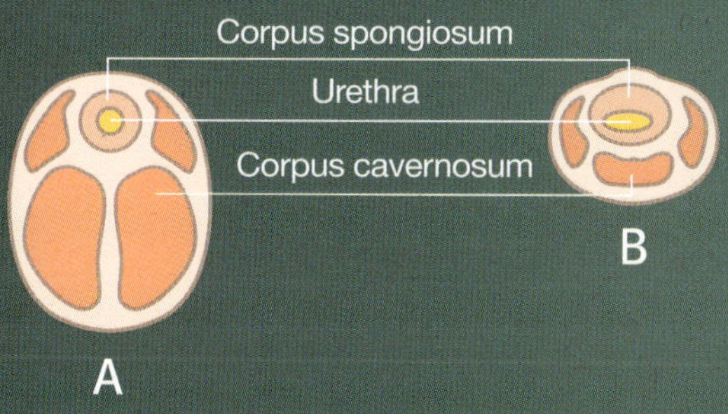

Urethra

Urethral obstruction in the dog

Urethral calculi in the dog

Case 1 / Urohydropropulsion technique

Case 2 / Prescrotal urethrotomy

Case 3 / Scrotal urethrostomy

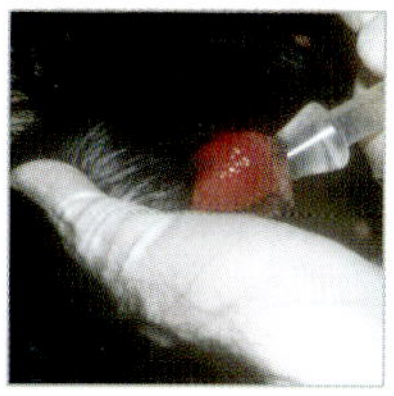
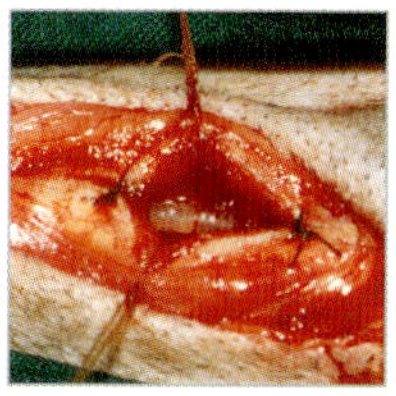
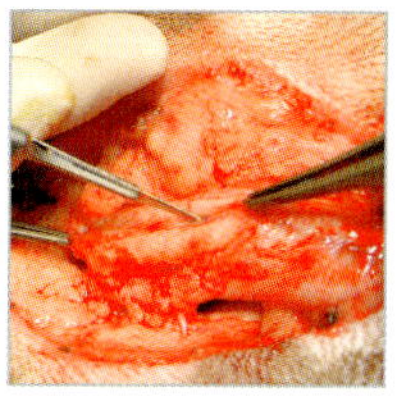

Urethral stenosis

Case 1 / Scrotal urethrostomy

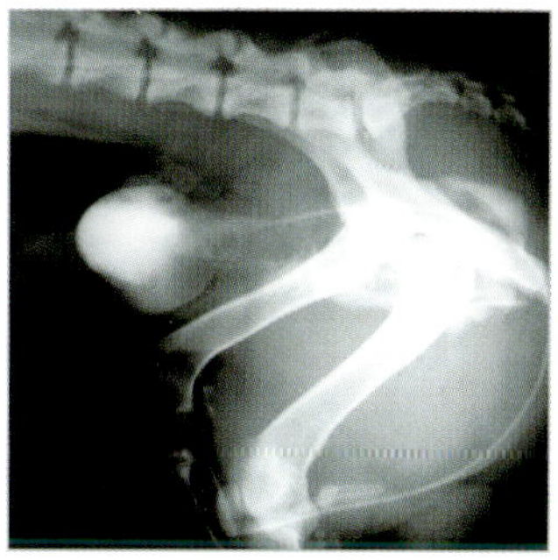
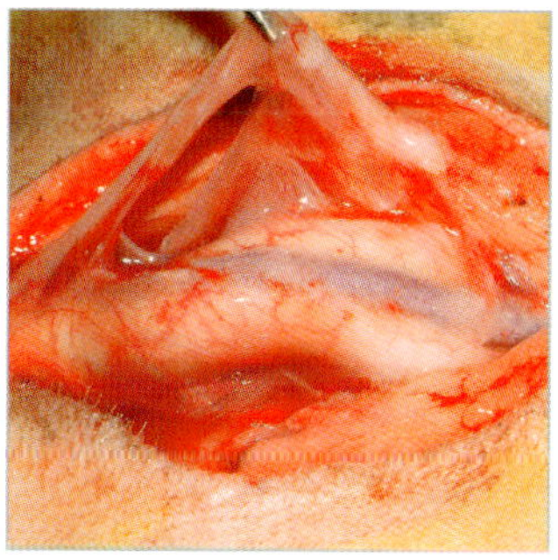

Feline lower urinary tract disease (FLUTD)

Case 1 / Perineal urethrostomy

Case 2 / Scar stenosis

Case 3 / Skin inflammation and necrosis

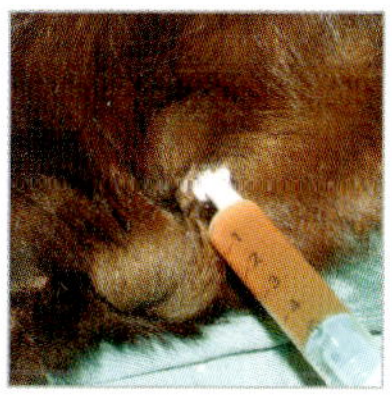
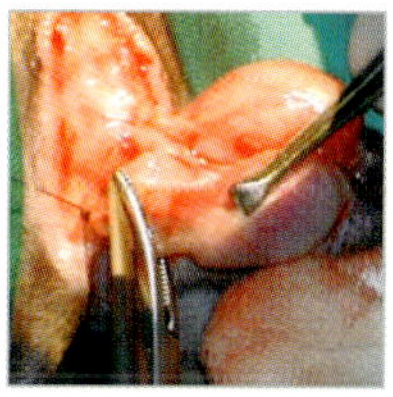
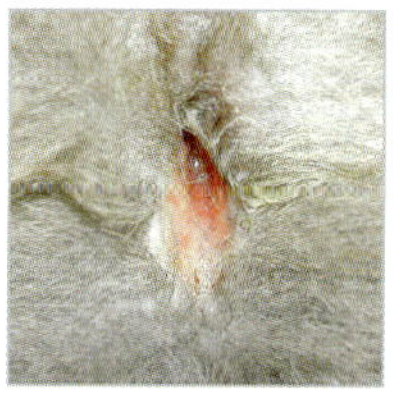
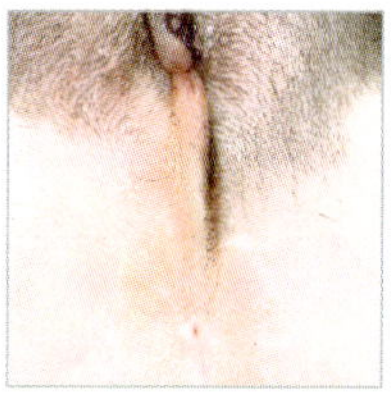
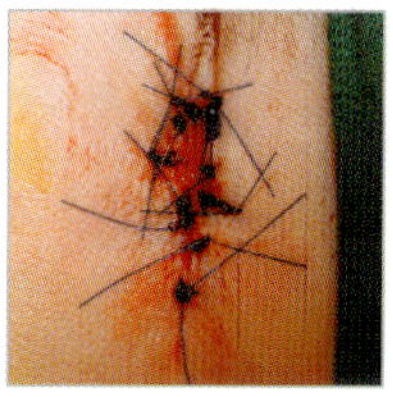
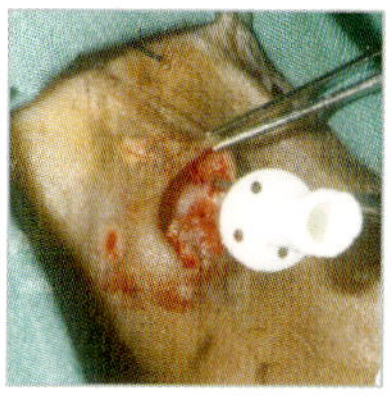

Urethral obstruction in the dog

Prevalence

Urethral obstruction can be caused by calculi obstructing the urethra, inflammation-induced stenosis secondary to voiding calculi, trauma (road traffic accidents, fights...) or following procedures on the urethra. In these cases, surgery is recommended to resolve the obstruction (figs. 1 and 2) and to retrieve calculi for compositional analysis. This aids dietary management to prevent recurrence.

Type of calculus	Frequency of occurrence
Struvite[1]	
Calcium oxalate	
Urate	
Silica	
Cystine	
Mixed	

[1] Ammonium magnesium phosphate.

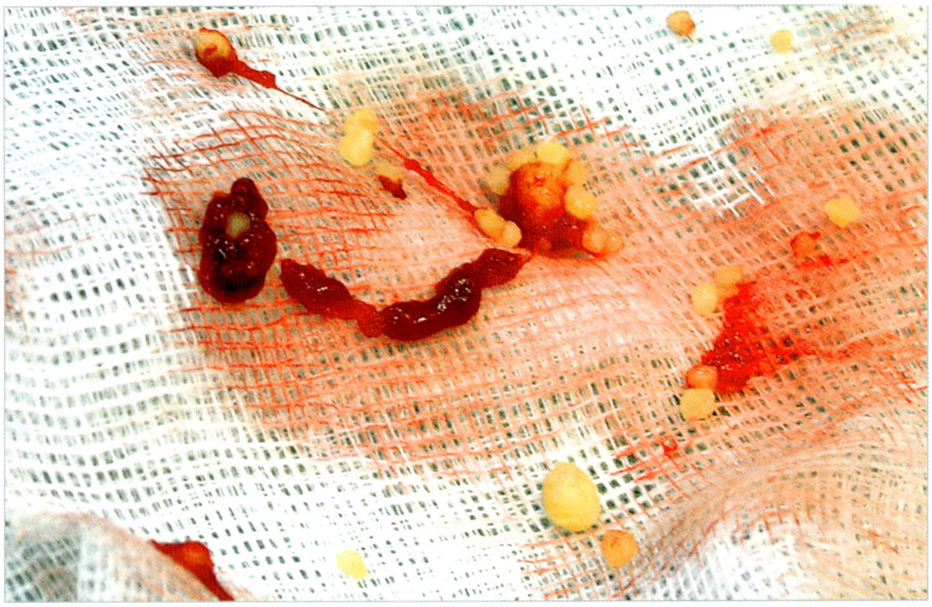

Fig. 1. Calculi extracted from the urethra of a dog.

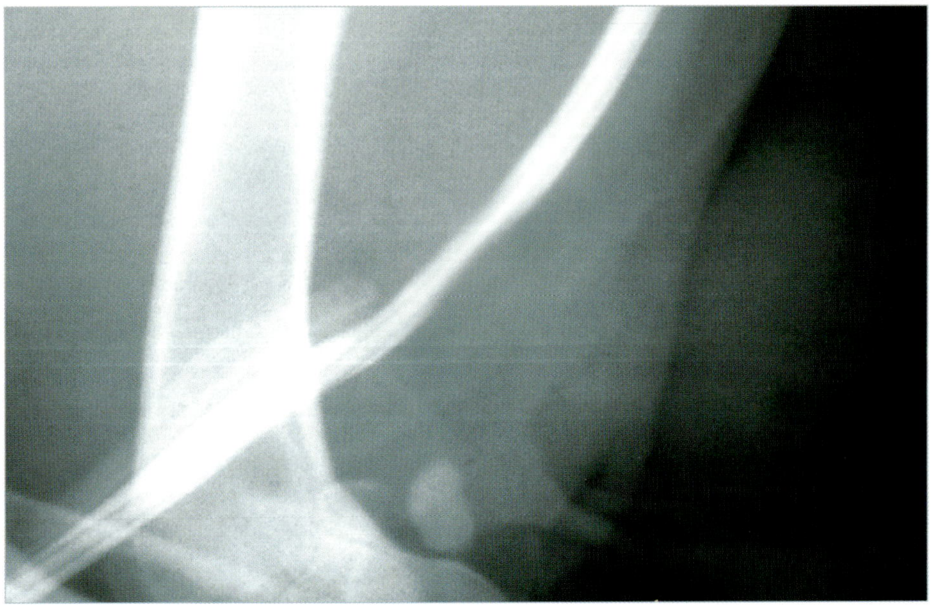

Fig. 2. Urethral stenosis, following urethrostomy, carried out to remove a stone lodged next to the os penis. In this case, the dog had hardly any difficulty urinating.

Urethral calculi in the dog

Prevalence	■■■■

Urolithiasis is the most common cause of urethral obstruction, both in the dog and cat.

Clinical signs

- Dysuria, haematuria, anuria, tenesmus, abdominal distension, pain.
- Signs of post-renal uraemia: vomiting, depression, anorexia, dehydration…
- Occasionally, the bladder can rupture, leading to a uroabdomen.

Diagnosis

Should be reached on the basis of the clinical signs, the physical examination of the patient and, in particular, radiology, which will render the calculi visible (figs. 1-5).

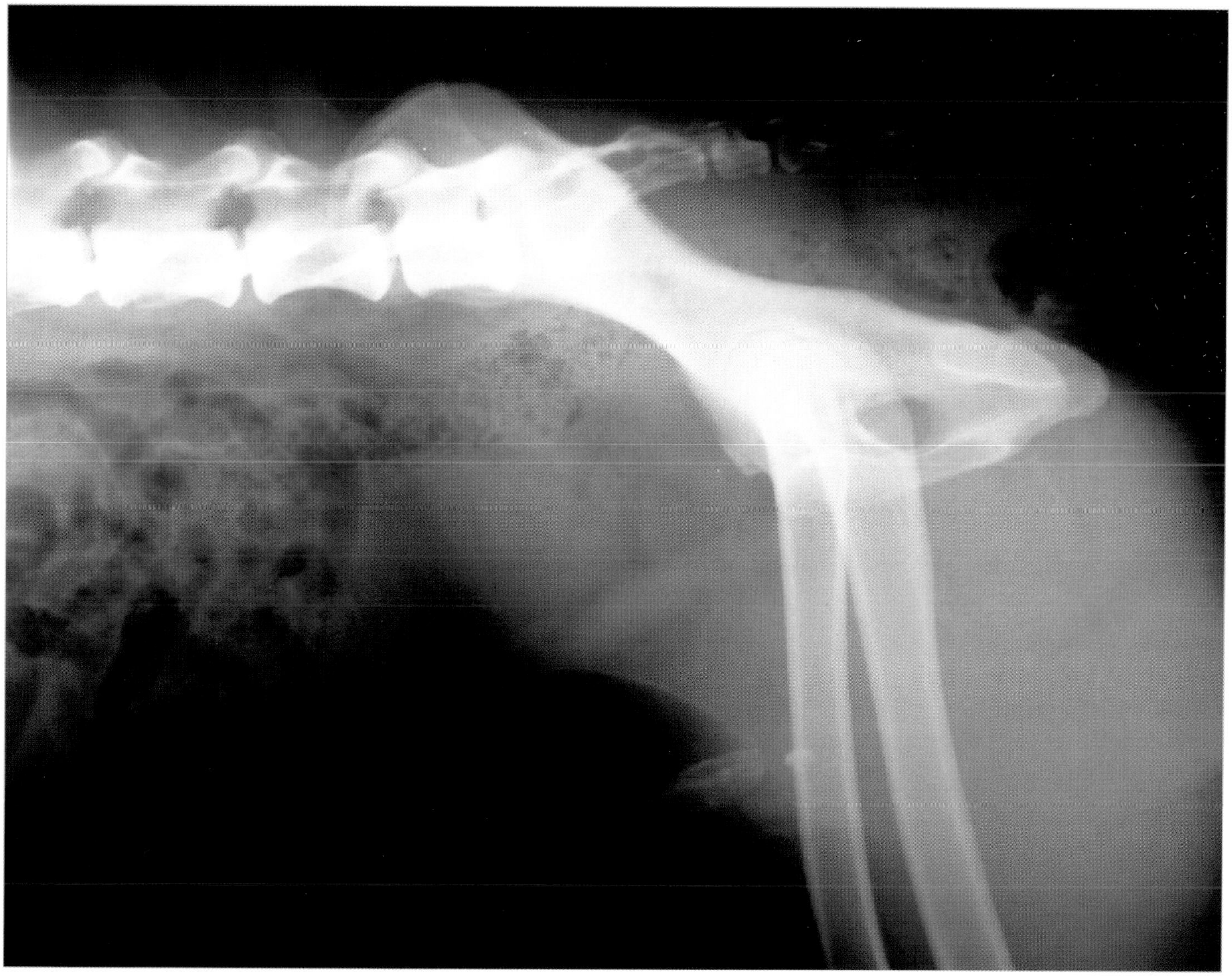

Fig. 1. Calculi lodge most commonly at the base of the penile bone.
In this case, a high-density stone was easily identified caudal to the os penis.

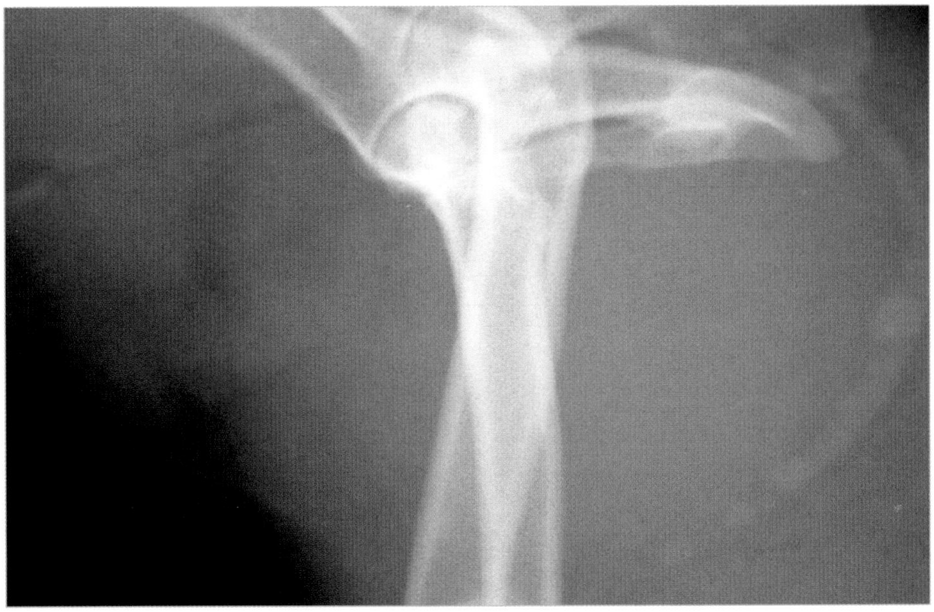

Fig. 2. Nevertheless, they may be found along the entire length of the urethra, including the sciatic arch. This radiograph shows a large number of uroliths of different diameters obstructing the urethra.

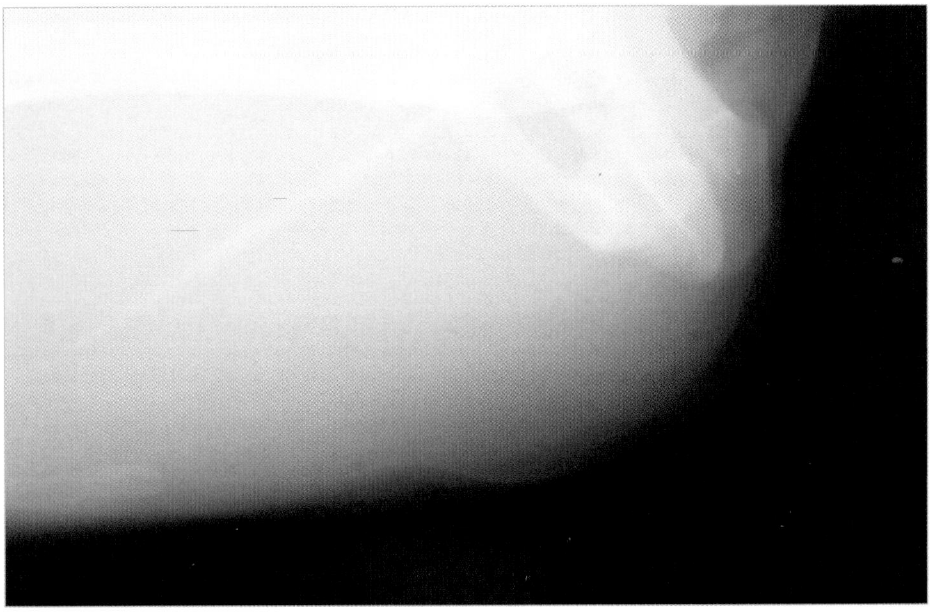

Fig. 3. To obtain the best image of the perineal area without the hind legs superimposing on the urethra, they should be pulled forward when taking the radiograph. In this dog, no uroliths were identified, even though it showed signs of obstruction.

Fig. 4. The retrograde infusion of iodine contrast medium into the urethra (urethrocystography) demonstrates radiolucent uroliths (rare) that were not visible in the previous image.

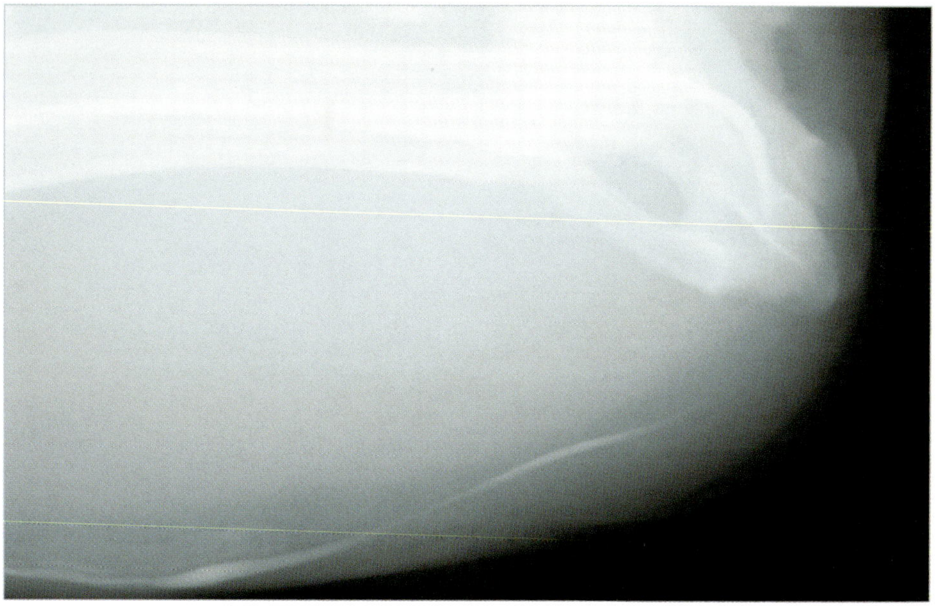

Fig. 5. Positive contrast radiographs are also useful for the identification of urethral stenosis. This patient had great difficulty urinating.

Radiodensity of based on size and composition		
Oxalate		Large - solitary
Struvite		Small - multiple
Apatite		
Silica		
Cystine		
Urate		Sand

> *Administer calcium gluconate to protect the heart against hyperkalaemia.*

Laboratory tests

- Complete blood cell count and a general chemistry profile including electrolytes (potassium, sodium and chloride).
- Urinalysis and bacterial culture, of a urine sample obtained by cystocentesis.

These patients usually have post-renal uraemia and hyperkalaemia, which should be controlled prior to surgery:

- Promote diuresis with isotonic saline, only if the patient is catheterised or not obstructed.
- Administer IV boluses of 50% dextrose.
- Administer insulin (0.5 IU/kg IV) with dextrose (2 g per unit of insulin) to reduce potassium levels.

See cystocentesis ➔ page 240

> *In all cases of urolithiasis where a urinary infection is suspected, this should be identified and treated appropriately, preferably prior to surgery.*

Treatment

The urethral obstruction can be relieved by flushing the uroliths into the bladder using urohydropropulsion. In this way, patency of the urinary tract is restored, while all uroliths are grouped in the bladder, from where they can easily be extracted.
If the uroliths cannot be flushed into the bladder, a urethrotomy should be performed (see case 2), and in recurring cases, a permanent urethrostomy (see case 3).

> *Cystotomy is easier to perform and has fewer complications, both intraoperatively and in particular postoperatively, than a urethrostomy.*

Urethral calculi in the dog. Case 1 / Urohydropropulsion technique

Technical difficulty	■	□	□	□	□

"Blacky" is a 10-year-old mixed breed dog that cannot urinate. In spite of numerous attempts to do so, only small drops are passed. Intermittent bleeding has been observed and he keeps licking his penis.

Fig. 1. "Blacky" also has a distended abdomen which is painful on palpation.

A radiograph of the pelvic area is taken to locate the urinary obstruction (fig. 2).

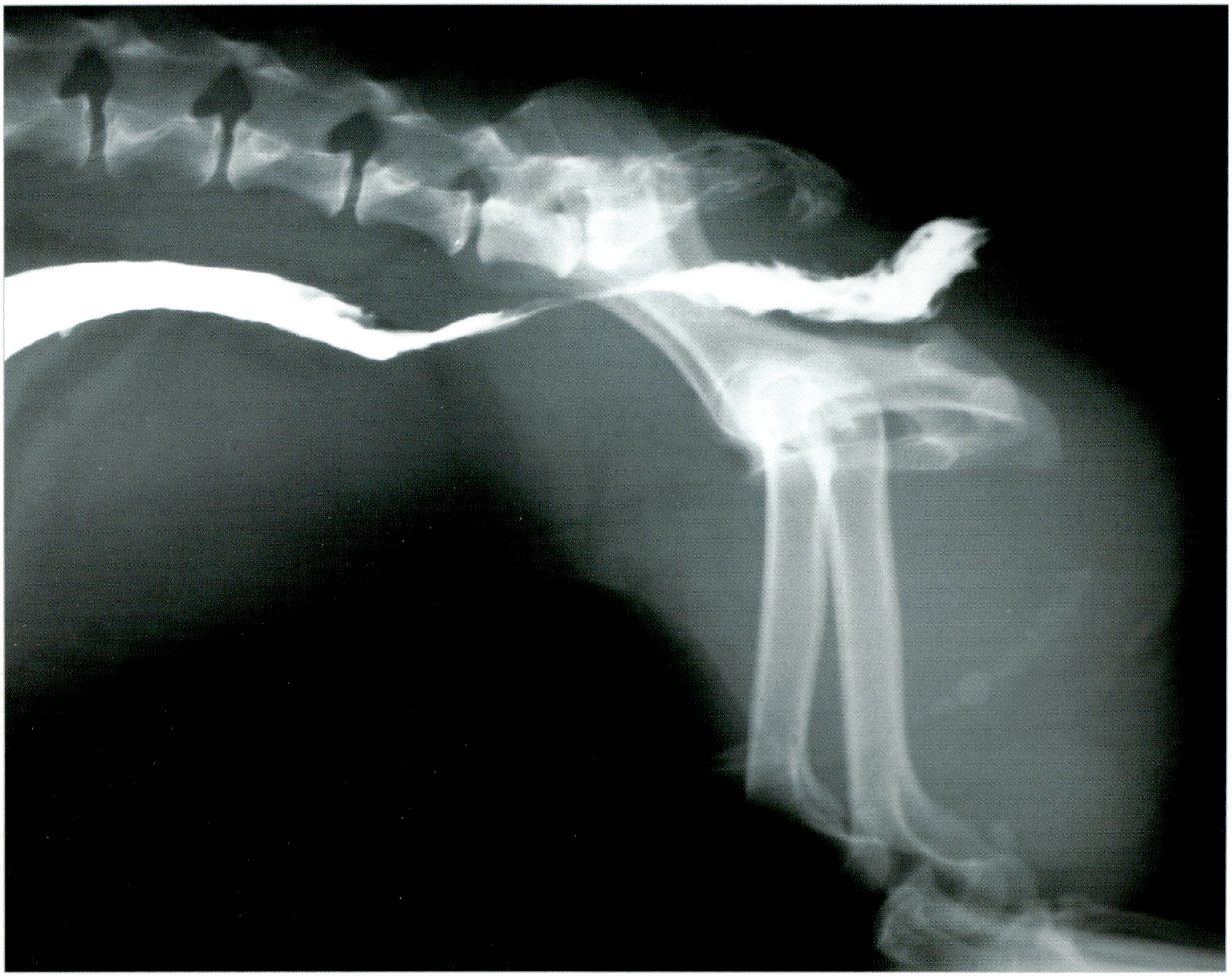

Fig. 2. In the penile urethra, a large number of uroliths are visible. Prostatic hyperplasia is also present.
In this case, a barium enema was administered for a better view of the caudal abdominal and perineal area. It is not necessary to do this routinely.

Urohydropropulsion is used to flush urethral calculi back into the bladder to relieve the urethral obstruction.

Technique

- Sedation and/or epidural anaesthesia.
- Urethral catheterisation to the point of obstruction (figs. 3-5).
- Insert a finger into the anus, palpate the urethra on the pelvic floor and compress it with sustained, even pressure (fig. 6).
- Close the glans penis over the catheter to avoid saline flowing out.
- Inject sterile saline into the urethra under moderate pressure while the upper part is blocked by the finger in the rectum.
- Through the rectum, the distension of the urethra can be clearly felt.
- After a few seconds, release the pressure on the membranous urethra so that the saline flushes the uroliths into the bladder (fig. 6).

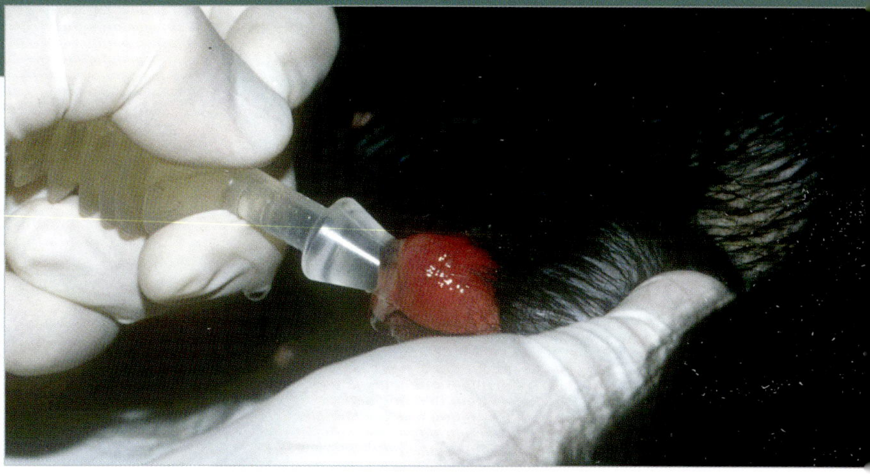

Fig. 3. Instill a urological lubricant and local anaesthetic into the urethral lumen. Let it take effect for a few minutes while preparing the rest of the materials.

See urethral catheterisation in the dog → *page 236*

> *Do not use catheters that are too rigid since these might damage the urethral mucosa. Do not attempt to push the uroliths with a rigid catheter; this will only lead to additional trauma to the area.*

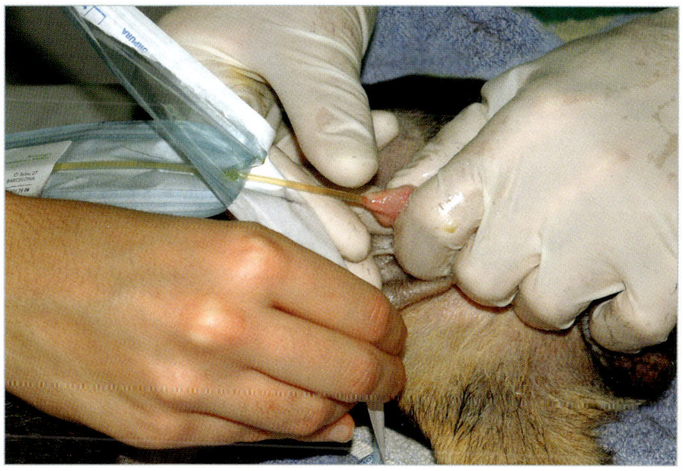

Fig. 4. Pass a sterile urinary catheter into the urethra until the obstruction is reached.

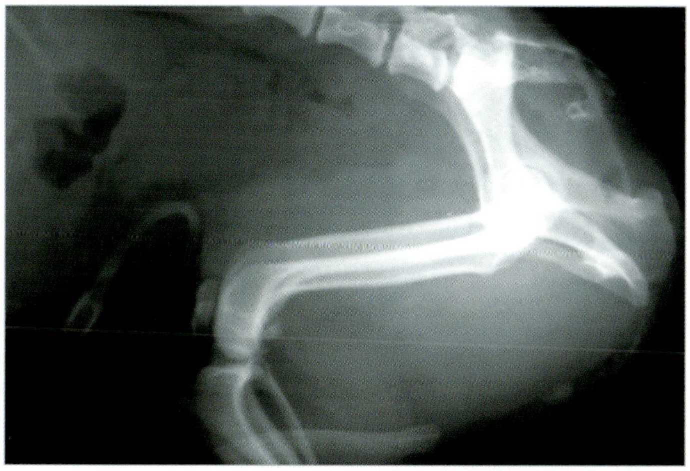

Fig. 5. A radiograph prior to the urohydropropulsion is necessary to locate the uroliths and to compare post-procedure radiographs to confirm the uroliths have been removed.

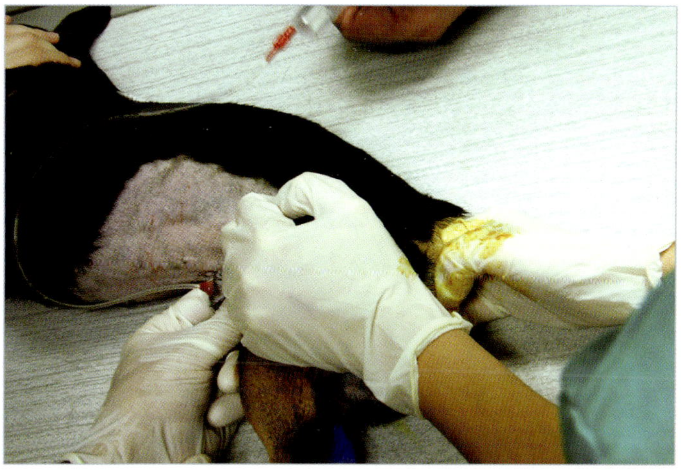

Fig. 6. The urethra is compressed against the pelvic floor by digital pressure through the rectal wall. The glans penis is closed around the urinary catheter. Saline is injected using moderate pressure.
When the urethral distension becomes palpable, the pressure is released and the uroliths are flushed into the bladder.

- The same procedure is repeated two or three times and a radiograph is taken to assess the results (figs. 7 and 8).

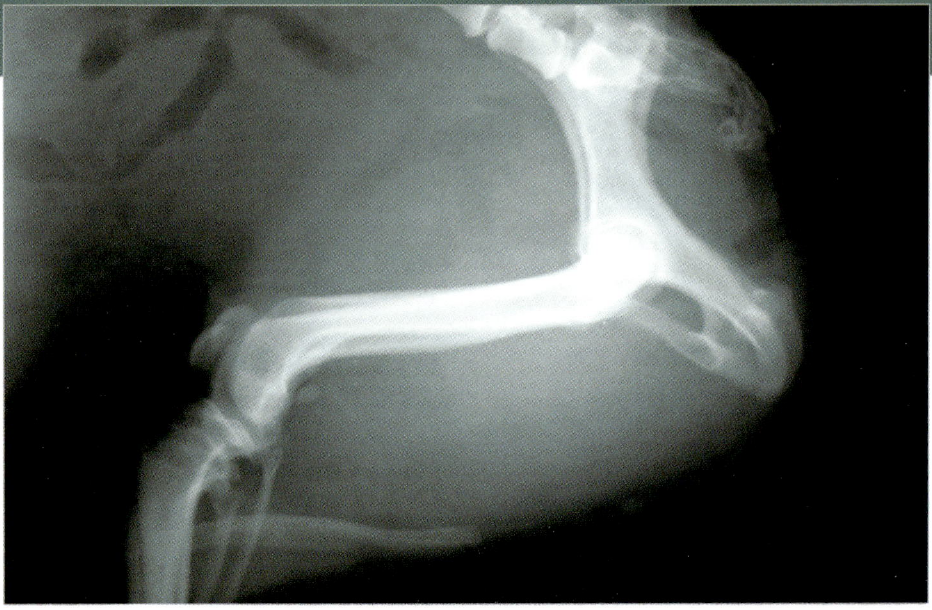

Fig. 7. After the first urohydropropulsion attempt some of the uroliths have moved, but the largest are still visible in the urethra.

> *Remember that the bladder can already be very distended due to urinary retention, and its wall can be damaged due to secondary cystitis. Take care not to overload the bladder with saline.*

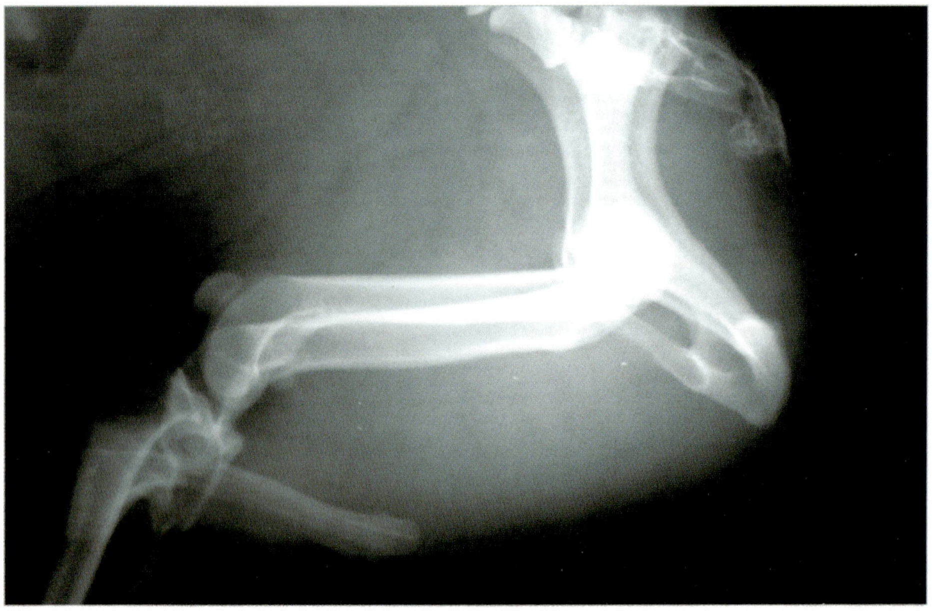

Fig. 8. By repeating the technique twice more, all uroliths are propelled back into the bladder.

> *Try to get the uroliths into the bladder, and then remove them by cystotomy. This will results in fewer complications than performing a urethrotomy.*

See cystotomy ➔ page 289

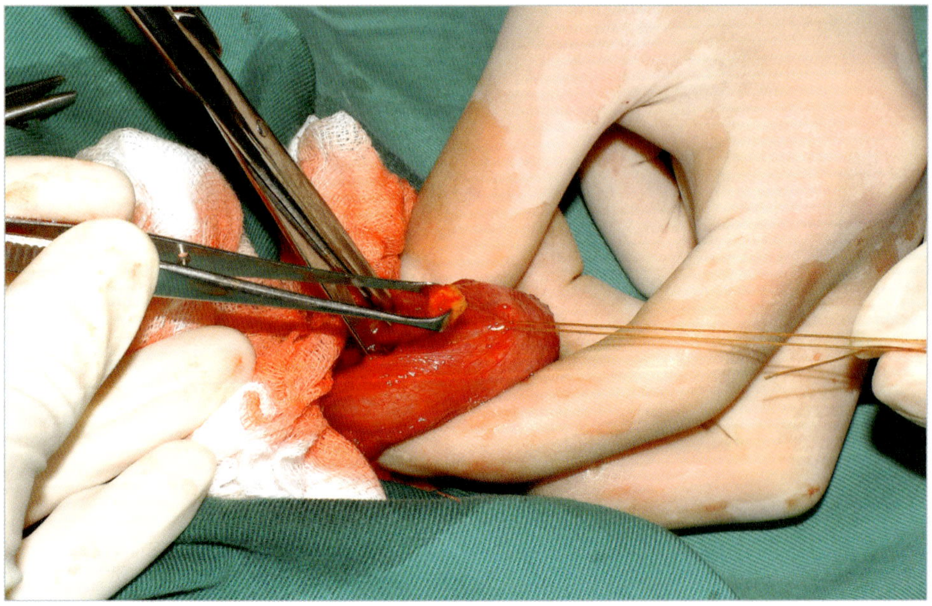

Fig. 9. Next, the uroliths are removed by cystotomy.

Urethral calculi in the dog. Case 2 / Prescrotal urethrotomy

Technical difficulty	■■■□□

Prior to surgery

Correct dehydration and any electrolyte and metabolic imbalances before surgery.
Have you tried to perform hydropropulsion (see case 1) of the uroliths into the bladder without success?

Anaesthesia

In uraemic or severely depressed patients, it is possible to perform the technique under deep sedation and local anaesthesia.

A urethrotomy is performed to eliminate the uroliths that are lodged behind the os penis if they cannot be flushed into the bladder by urohydropropulsion.

> ✱ *Cicatricial fibrosis is a complication of urethrotomy that may cause stenosis of the urethra in the medium term.*

Technique

■ Preparation of the surgical field (figs. 1 and 2).

See urethral catheterisation in the dog ➜ *page 236*

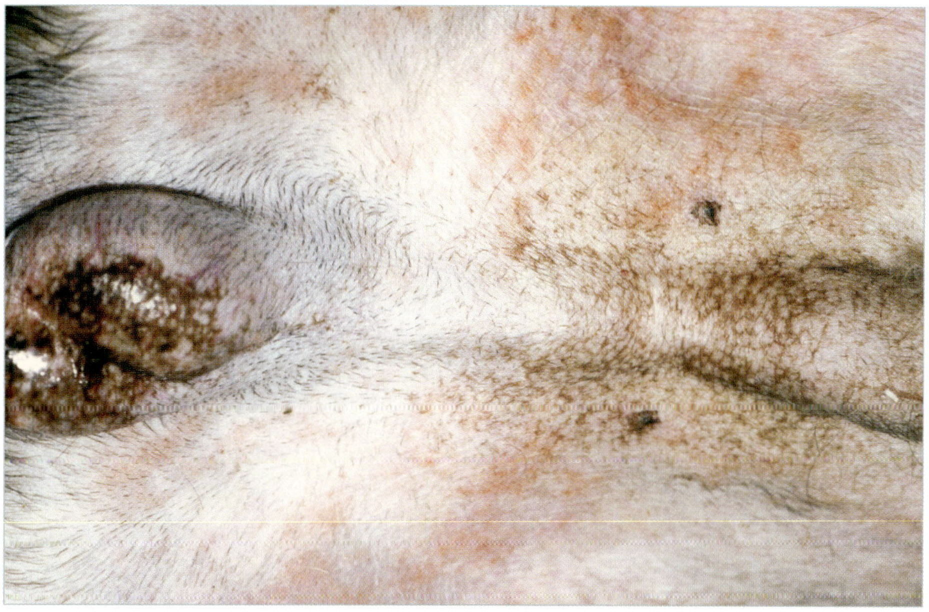

Fig. 1. Shaving and preparation of the surgical field in the usual way, centred on the area between the testes and the prepuce. The patient is placed in dorsal recumbency.

Fig. 2. After placing the surgical drapes, a sterile urinary catheter is inserted up to the site of obstruction.
▼

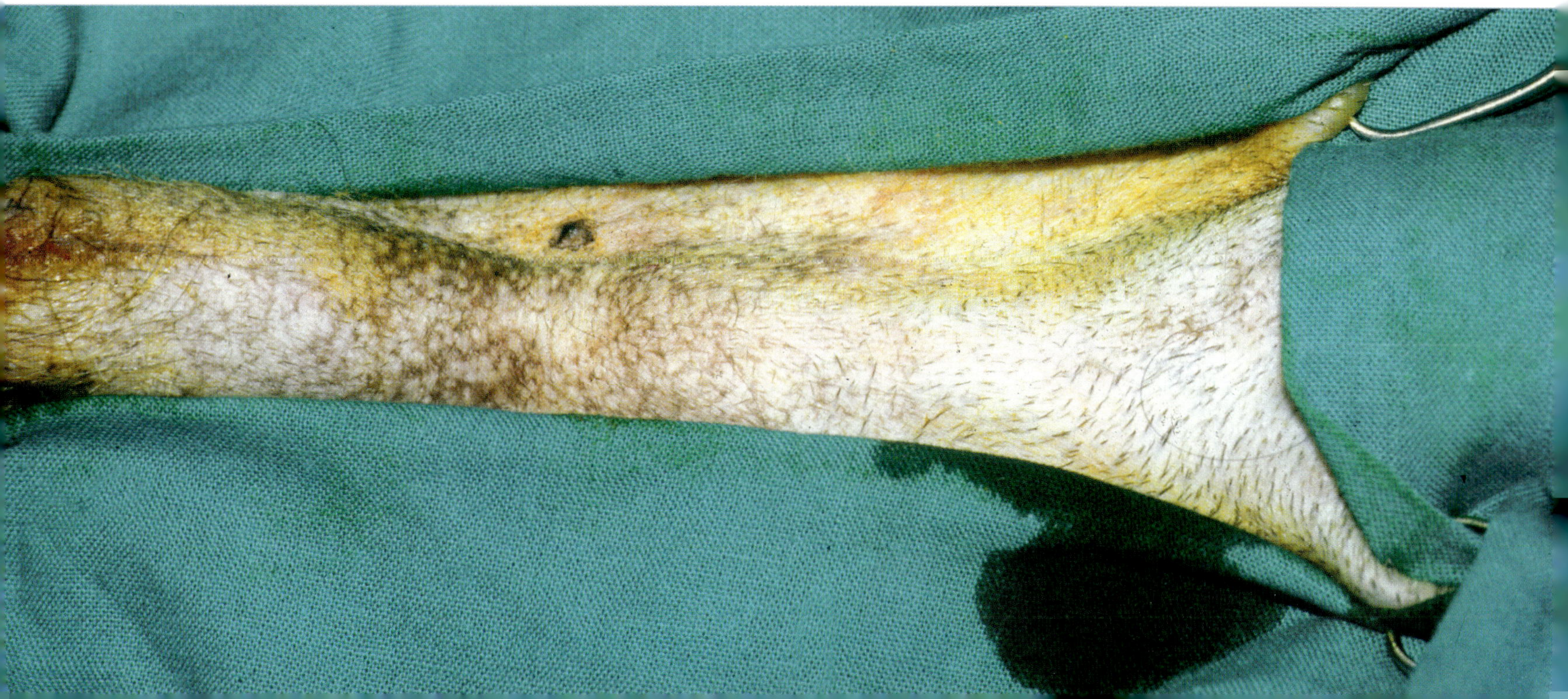

- Using a scalpel, the skin and subcutaneous tissue between the scrotum and caudal part of the os penis is incised (fig. 3).
- Using a fine blade (nº 11), an incision is made in the urethra through its midline into the lumen, taking care to avoid damage to the corpora cavernosa (fig. 4).
- If it is necessary to extend the incision, fine iris scissors should be used. Always follow the midline of the urethra.

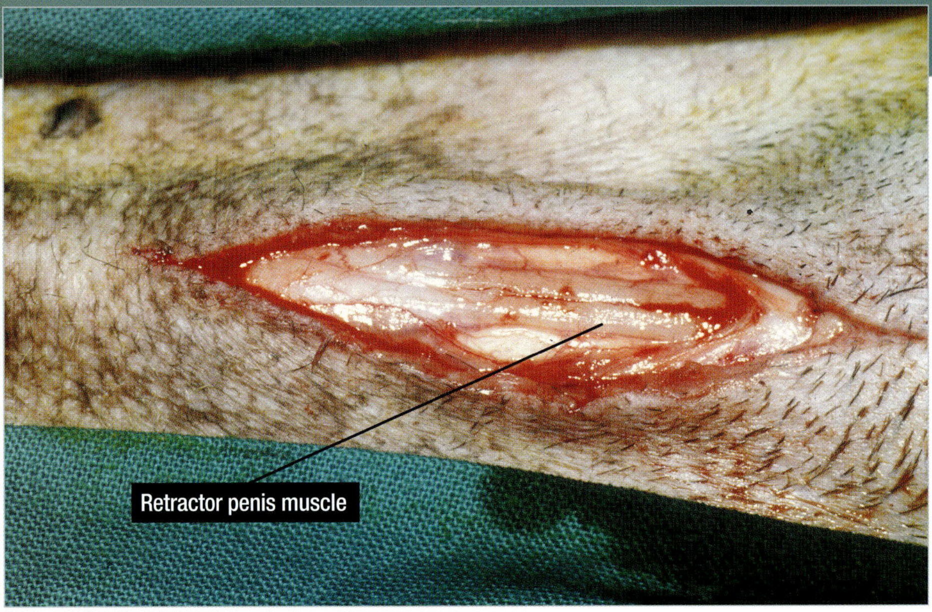

Fig. 3. The retractor penis muscle is located, dissected and moved to the side to access the urethra.

Flush the operating field regularly with lukewarm saline to prevent exposed tissues drying out.

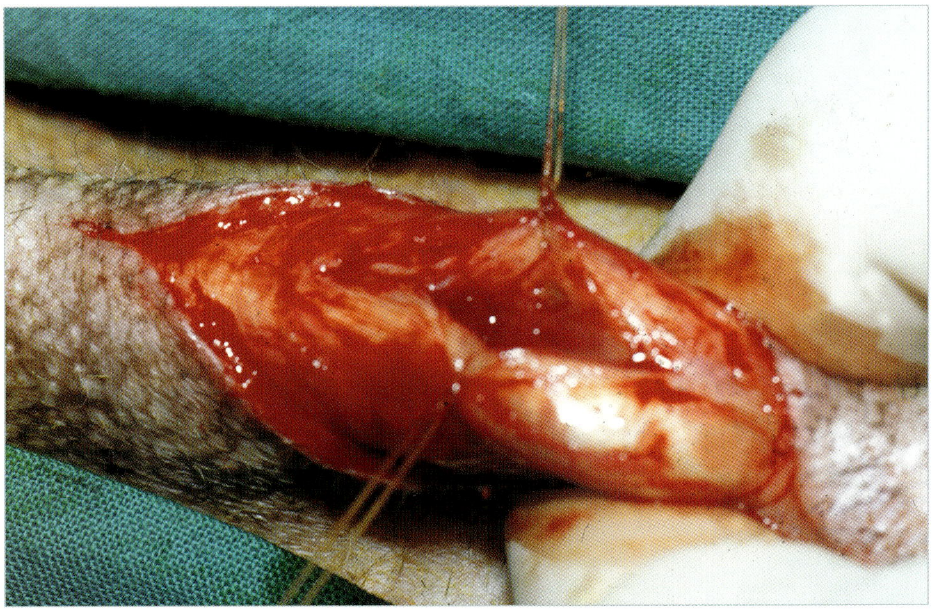

Fig. 4. Incising the urethra will cause bleeding; try to incise in the midline to avoid excessive bleeding (due to cutting into the corpora cavernosa).
The placement of stay sutures will help to visualise the urethral lumen without damaging the urethral mucosa.

- Remove the calculi with fine dissecting forceps and by flushing lukewarm saline through the urinary catheter.
- Once the obstructions have been removed, the catheter is passed into the bladder, making sure that there are no more calculi (fig. 5).

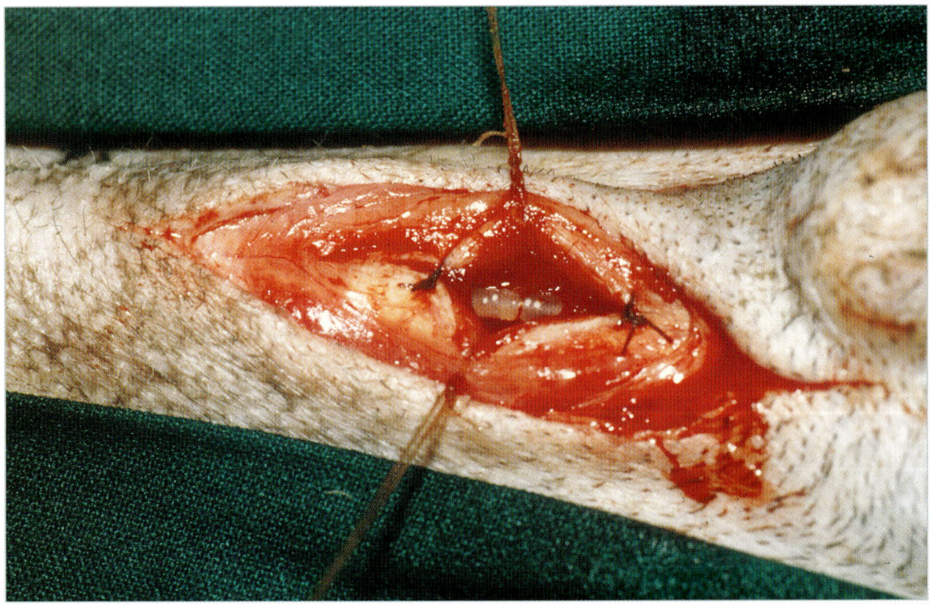

Fig. 5. The catheter is visible in the urethrotomy wound.

- If the surgeon is inexperienced or if appropriate surgical material to reconstruct the urethra is not available, it is better to leave the penile wound unsutured to avoid excessive fibrosis. In this situation, local haemorrhage is highly probable during recovery from anaesthesia. This complication will be present for 4 or 5 days post-surgery, particularly when the patient urinates.
- Ideally, the urethra and penis should be sutured to avoid postoperative bleeding and for reconstruction of infiltration of urine into the subcutaneous tissue, which can cause cellulitis and focal necrosis (fig. 6).
- Finish by suturing the skin using the surgeon's technique of choice. (fig. 7).

> ***Do not forget to have the calculi analysed to aid selection of appropriate dietary management to prevent or reduce the risk of recurrence.***

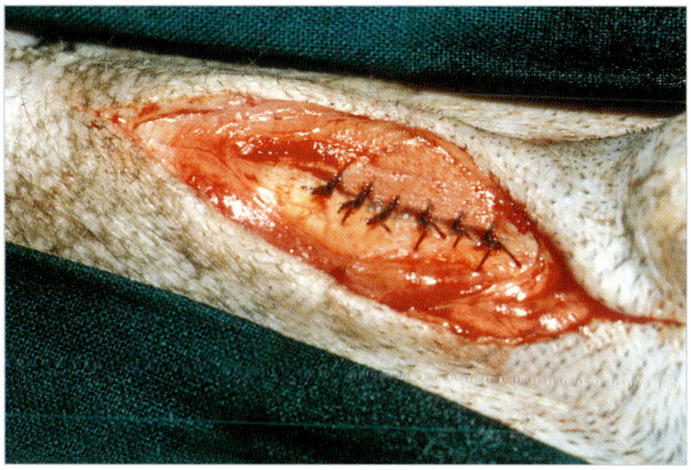

Fig. 6. Suture the urethra with absorbable 5/0 or 6/0 synthetic monofilament material using simple interrupted sutures.
Try to include as little tissue as possible, without compromising the stability of the suture.

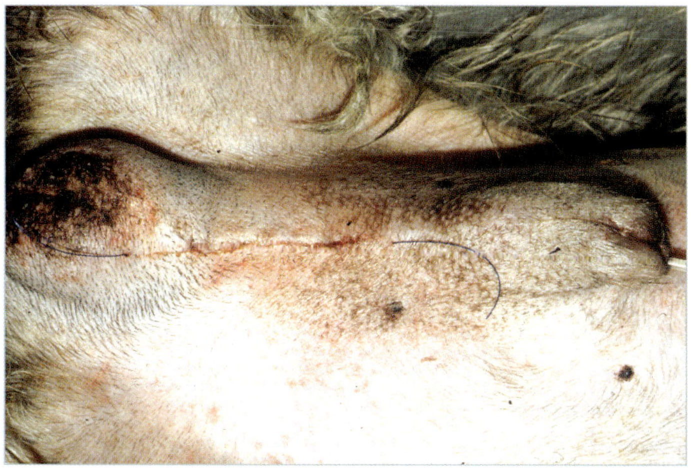

Fig. 7. In this case, an intradermal suture was placed using non-absorbable monofilament synthetic material.

After surgery

The urinary catheter is left in place for 2 days to ensure elimination of urine.

If the patient is not catheterised and urethral inflammation develops during the immediate postoperative period, or if blood clots obstruct the urethra, urinary retention may recur. Should this happen, the urinary tract will need to be catheterised again, risking damage to the operated area, rupture of sutures and exacerbating inflammation. This may result in excessive cicatricial fibrosis.

The main problem with leaving the catheter in place is the risk of ascending infection. Broad-spectrum antibiotics that undergo renal excretion (e.g. amoxicillin & clavulanic acid) are recommended while waiting for sensitivity testing results.

Possible complications

Bleeding for several days after surgery if the urethra is not sutured. In some cases, bleeding is profuse and a causes concern for the owner and veterinarian. To minimise bleeding, suture the wound using fine absorbable synthetic material. If the wound cannot be closed, warn the owner, hospitalise the patient and control urethral bleeding by applying pressure with a gauze swab, especially after urinating.

Cicatricial stenosis results from marked fibrosis in the area following excessive trauma, inflammation or urethral lesions caused by calculi or surgical intervention.

To prevent this, operate promptly, avoid repeated urethral catheterisations, do not attempt to push the uroliths with the catheter and try urohydropropulsion and if you perform an urethrotomy, do so with care (and in the most atraumatic way) and use absorbable synthetic monofilament material.

If stenosis occurs, the surgeon will have to resort to permanent urethrostomy (see case 3).

Urethral calculi in the dog. Case 3 / Scrotal urethrostomy

Technical difficulty	■■■□□

"Bulit" is a 6-year-old Bulldog brought to the hospital with recurrent urethral obstruction.

Fig. 1. "Bulit" has difficulty urinating, making frequent non-productive attempts.

Clinical history

A few months ago, the dog was treated for an obstructive urinary problem. At the time, several uroliths were identified in the bladder and penile urethra at the level of the os penis (fig. 2).

Several unsuccessful attempts at urohydropropulsion were made (see case 1). Since the uroliths could not be moved into the bladder, a urethrotomy was performed to remove the calculi trapped at the level of the os penis.

When presented, the dog had been dysuric for 3 days despite dietary treatment. He had great difficulty urinating, straining to produce a few drops, sometimes tinged with blood.

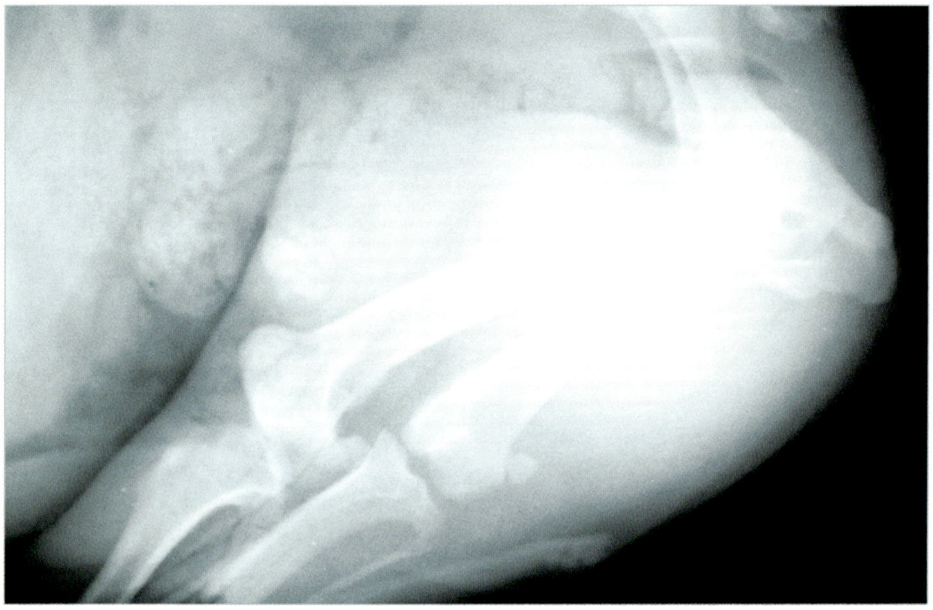

Fig. 2. The urethral calculi were trapped at the level of the os penis. In the bladder, a large number of uroliths of different sizes were found.

Radiography

A lateral radiograph of the perineal area shows several uroliths in the bladder, but none in the urethra. To identify a possible urethral stenosis secondary to the previous operation, a retrograde contrast radiograph is done (fig. 3).

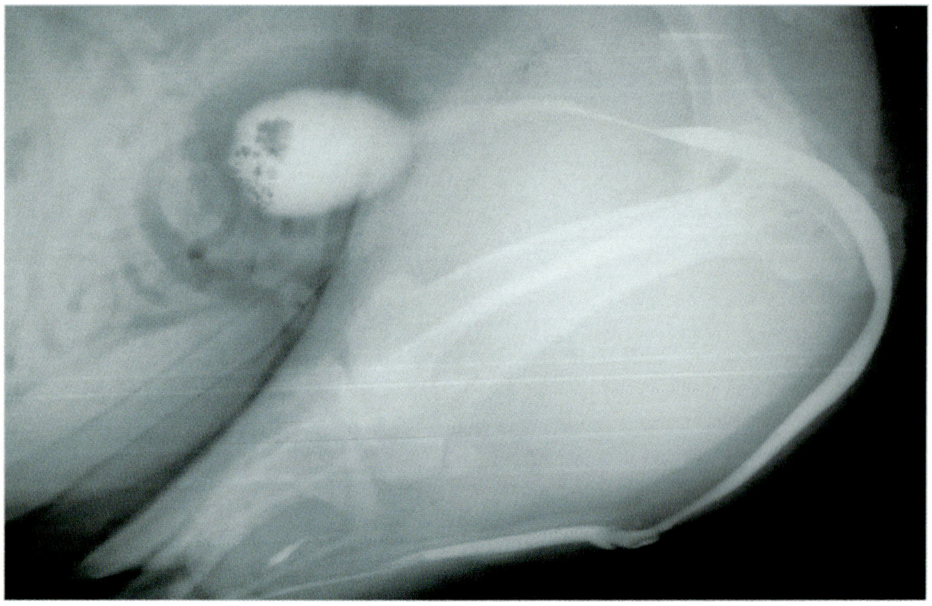

Fig. 3. An iodine contrast medium demonstrates the presence of cicatricial stenosis caudal to the os penis and the filling defects (uroliths) in the bladder.

This is the technique of choice if a permanent urethrostomy needs to be performed. At this level, the urethra is wider, runs more superficially and has a thinner layer of cavernous tissue covering it than anywhere else. Postoperative bleeding and cicatricial stenosis are therefore less severe. The disadvantage is that it requires castration of the patient.

Surgical technique

Indications for scrotal urethrostomy:

- Obstructive and recurrent urethral calculi that cannot be controlled medically.
- Uroliths that cannot be removed by urohydropropulsion (see case 1) or urethrotomy (see case 2).
- Urethral stenosis.
- Distal neoplasia of the penis or urethra.
- Distal trauma to the penis.

Before surgery

- If possible, remove the obstruction from the urethra (urohydropropulsion) and insert a catheter.
- Take a urine sample for culture and sensitivity testing.
- Correct any dehydration and electrolyte imbalances due to the urinary obstruction.

During surgery

Be patient with bleeding of the urethral incision and do not panic. Do not use aggressive haemostatic methods.
Suture the urethral mucosa to the skin with monofilament material swaged on a round-bodied needle.

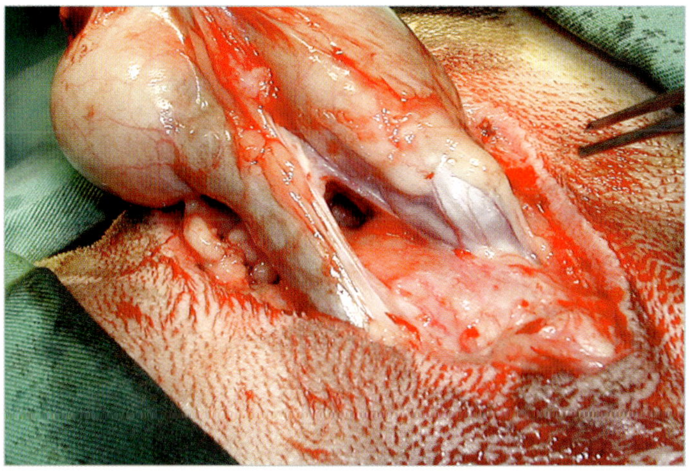

Fig. 4. In the first part of the procedure, scrotal castration is performed.

See castration → page 264
See urohydropropulsion ← page 142

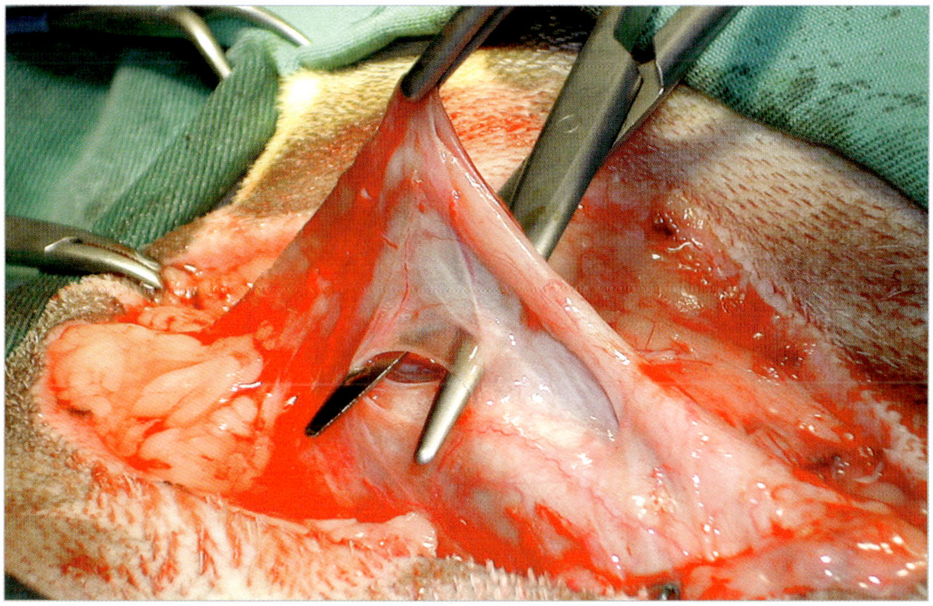

- Shaving and preparation of the surgical field in the usual manner.
- Dorsal recumbency.
- Preparation of the surgical field in the scrotal region.
- If possible, placement of a sterile urinary catheter in the urethra, to facilitate the incision and later suturing of the urethra.
- Elliptical incision of the skin at the base of the scrotum (fig. 4).
- Careful dissection of the ventral area of the penis (fig. 5).
- Identification and incision of the urethra (figs. 6-8).

Fig. 5. Next, the retractor penis muscle is identified and dissected to visualise the urethra.

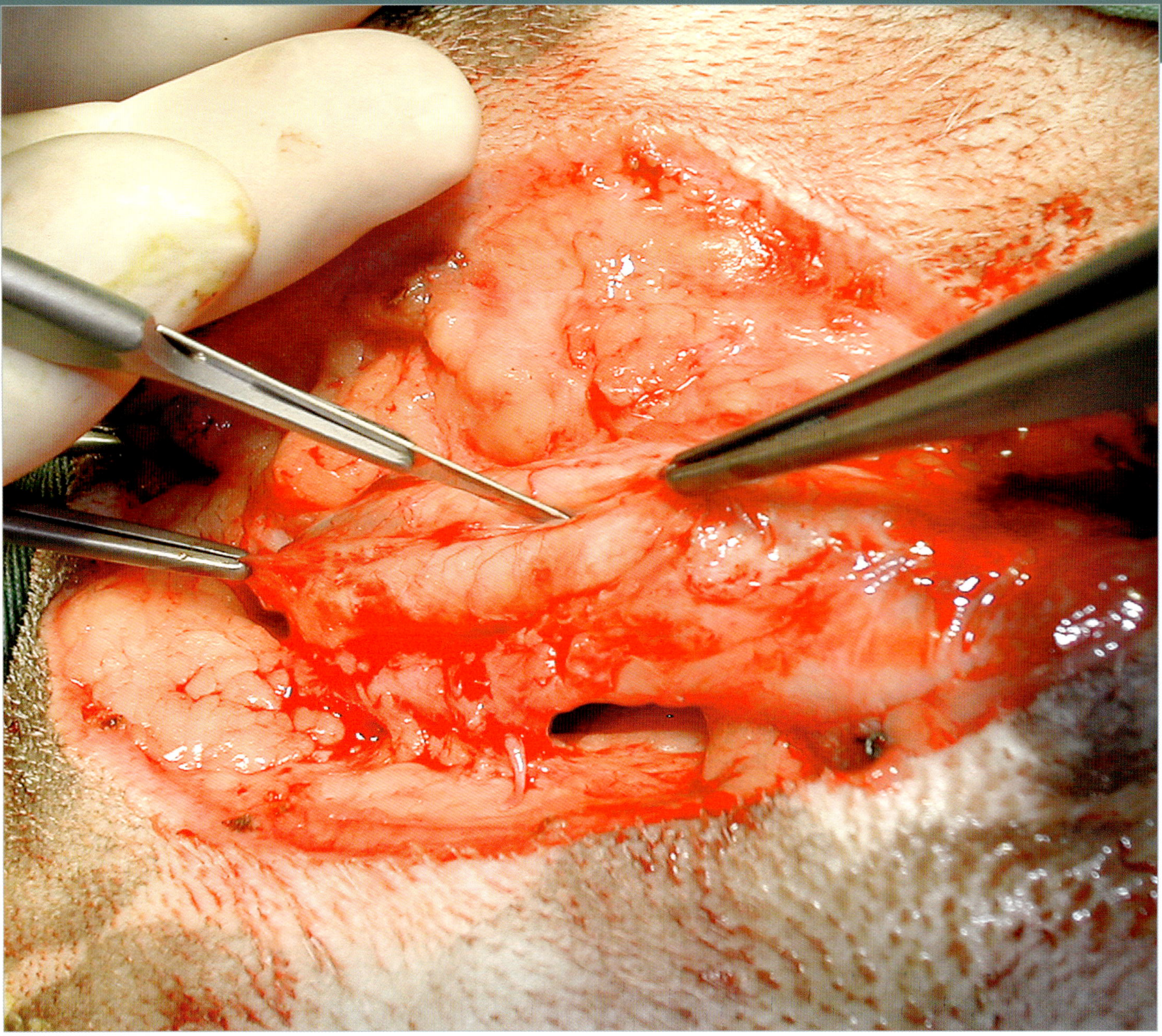

Fig. 6. After pushing the retractor penis muscle aside, the urethra is located (it has a bluish tinge), flanked by whitish structures, the corpora cavernosa of the penis. A midline incision is then made into the urethra with a n° 11 scalpel blade. Cutting through the spongy tissue surrounding the urethra will cause bleeding of variable intensity.

The urethral tissue is relatively fibrous, which means that some pressure is needed to incise into it.

Incising the urethra causes continuous and diffuse bleeding, which must be controlled by applying pressure using gauze swabs. In case of intense localised bleeding, haemostatic forceps should be used. Do not use thermal or electric coagulation methods.

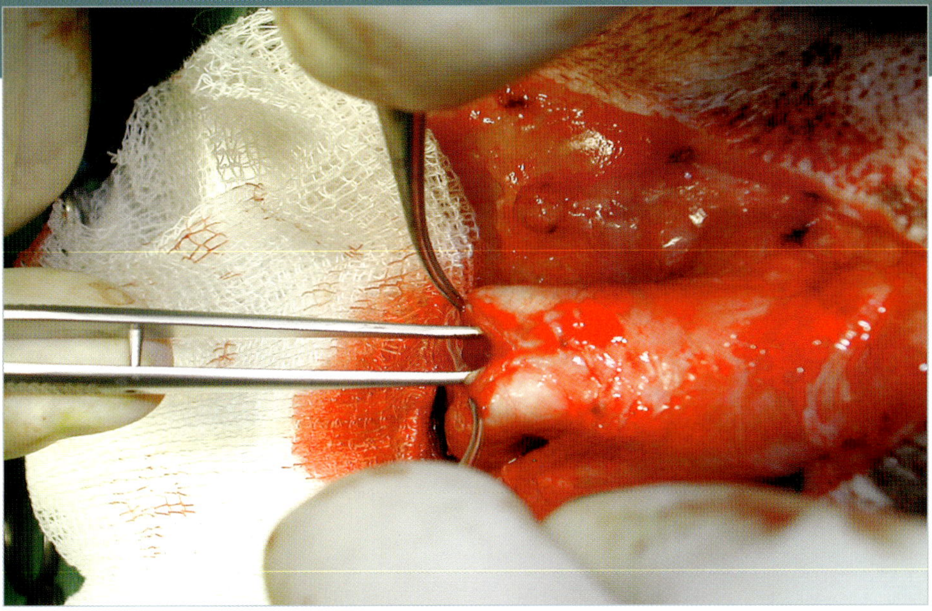

Fig. 7. It can be confirmed that the goal has been achieved by introducing a pair of forceps into the urethral lumen.

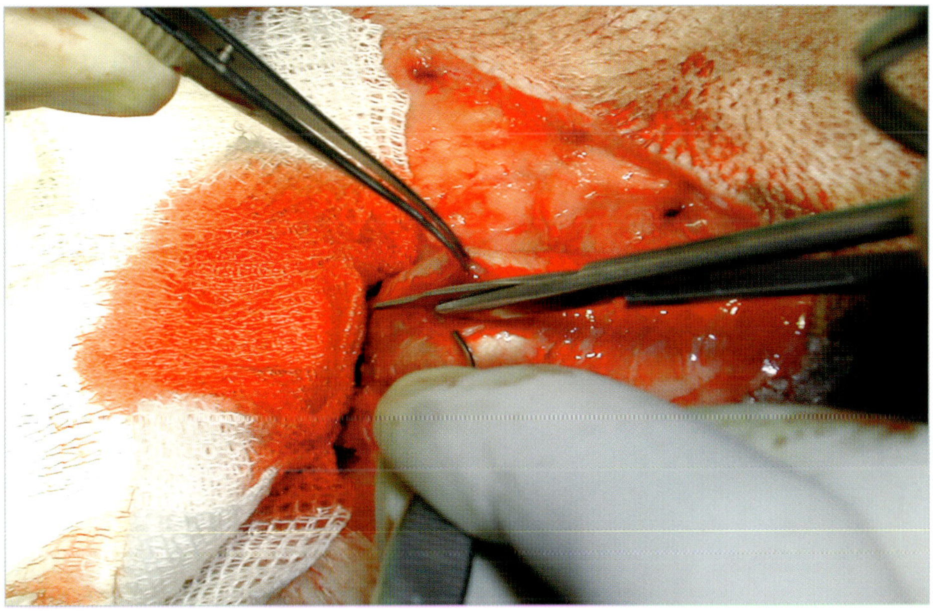

Fig. 8. The urethral incision is enlarged along its midline using iris scissors. The length of the urethrostomy should be about 4 to 5 times the diameter of the urethral lumen in this area.
Use gauze swabs to control haemorrhage of the spongy urethral tissue and haemostatic forceps in cases of focal and profuse bleeding.

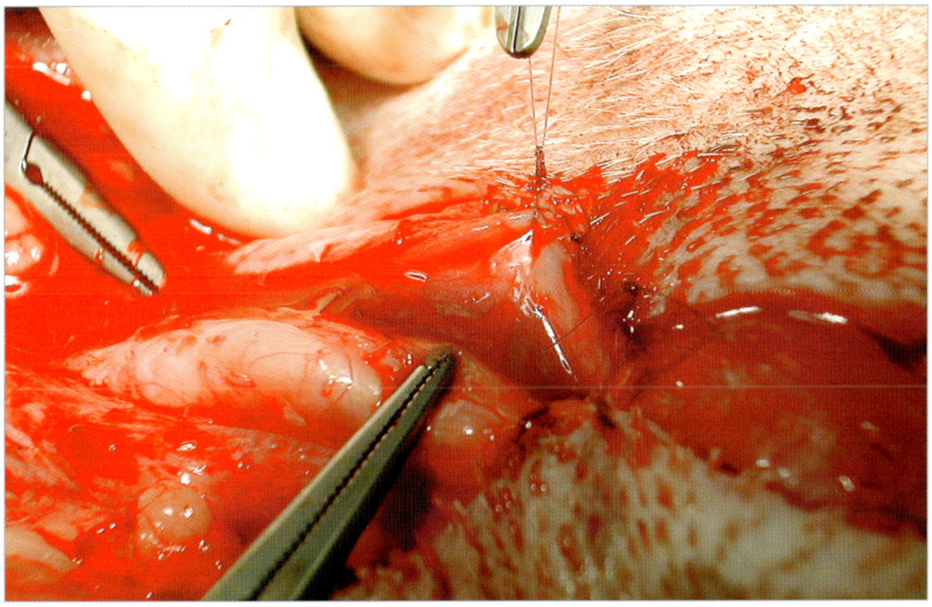

Fig. 9. Next, the urethral mucosa is sutured to the skin using fine synthetic monofilament material. The needle should be atraumatic to avoid damaging the urethral mucosa. In this case, an absorbable 5/0 suture was used.

- Suturing of the urethra to the skin (permanent urethrostomy) (figs. 9 and 10).
- The skin on both sides of the urethrostomy is closed in the usual manner (fig. 11).

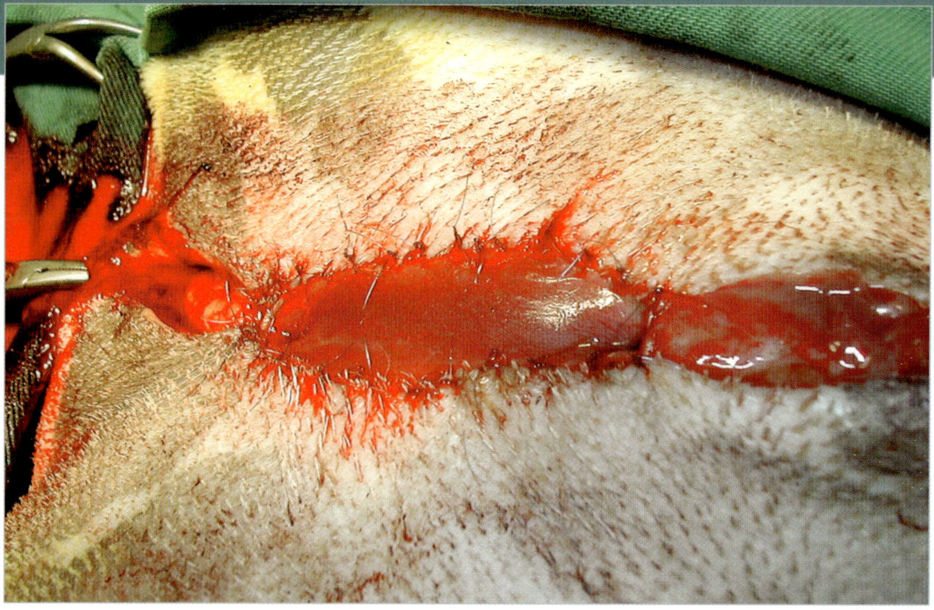

Fig. 10. It is important that each suture is restricted to the urethral mucosa and the skin. Make sure that no other adjacent tissue is included. By suturing the urethra to the skin, haemorrhage is reduced.

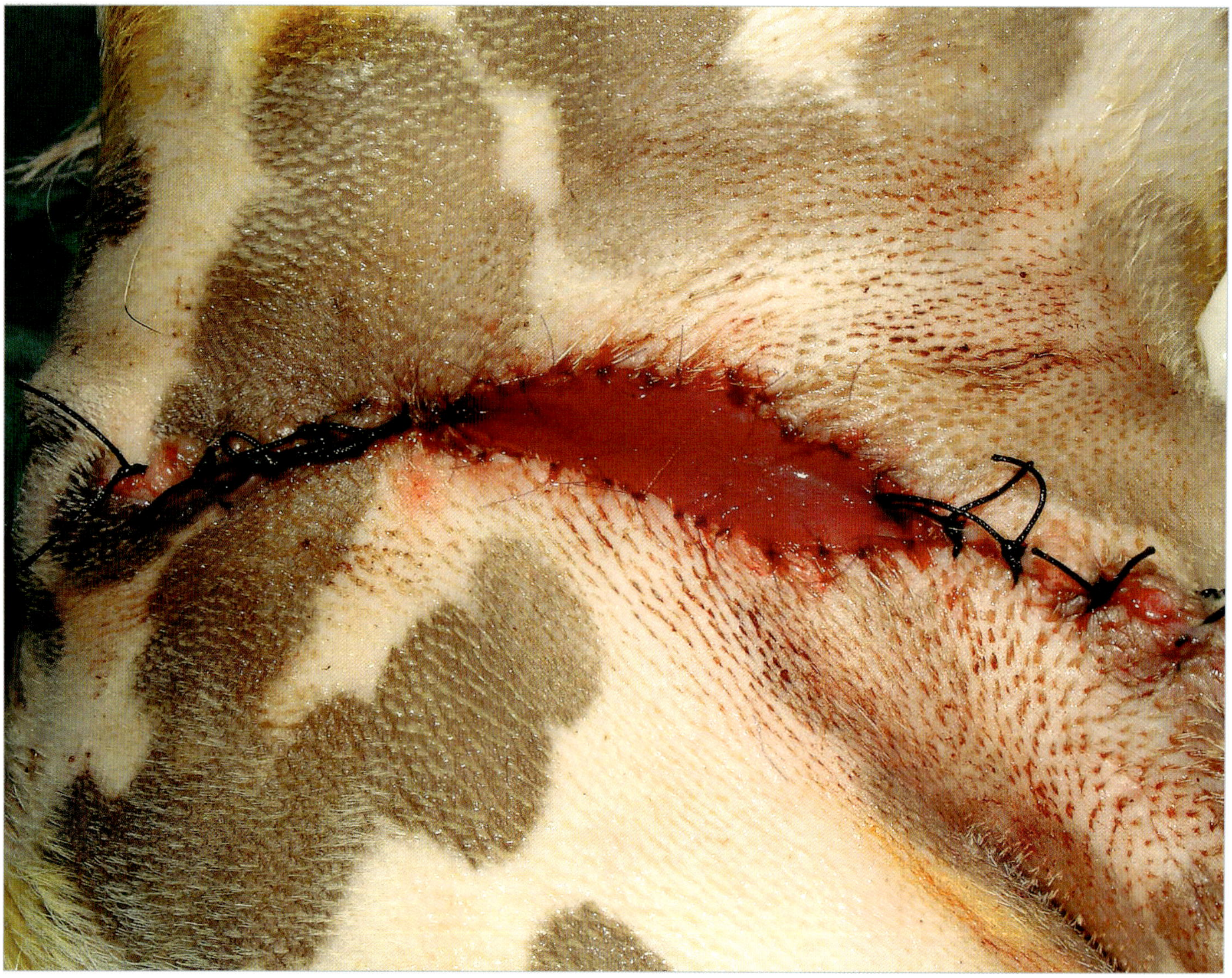

Fig. 11. The end result of the operation. After surgery, it is not necessary to leave the catheter in the urethra. From the day after surgery, the patient will urinate normally.

After surgery

- Initially, control of local and urinary tract infections with broad-spectrum antibiotics, later using those indicated by sensitivity testing of a urine sample.
- Daily cleaning of the urethrostomy wound.
- Application of topical ointment and vaseline to prevent urine scald.

Advice to the owner

- It is normal to see blood each time the patient urinates, there can even be a lot of blood.
- Teach the owner how to stop the bleeding by applying pressure with sterile gauze, moistened with hydrogen peroxide diluted 1:1 with saline.
- From now on the dog will urinate sideways, and will often soil his legs. Recommend drying of the area and local hygiene to avoid secondary dermatitis.

Postoperative care

The patient should be closely monitored during the first few postoperative days. Bleeding through the urethrostomy is usual in all patients (figs. 12-15).

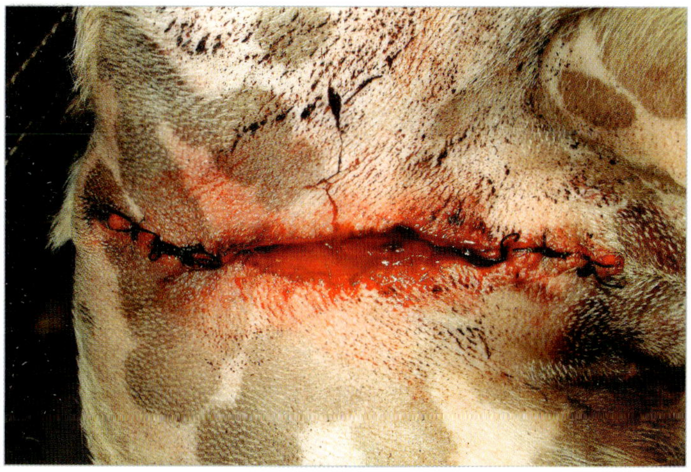

Fig. 12. 24 hours after the operation, moderate bleeding from the wound is seen, which worsens each time the patient urinates.

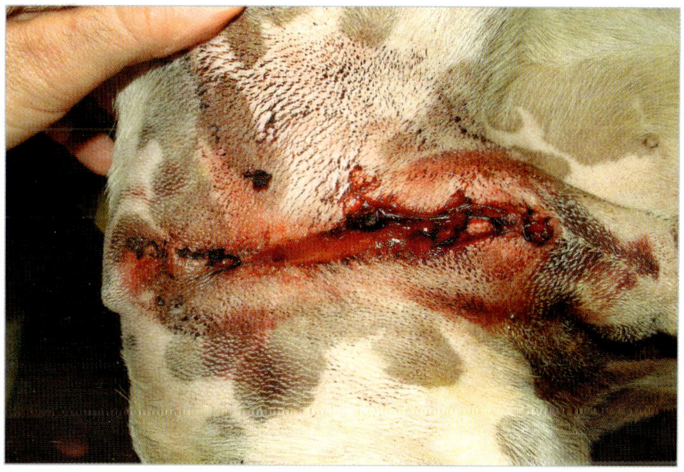

Fig. 13. 48 hours after surgery, progress is checked. The bleeding is much reduced. Strict cleaning and antisepsis of the area is required. Blood clots adhering to the sutures should be removed to avoid infection under the scab.

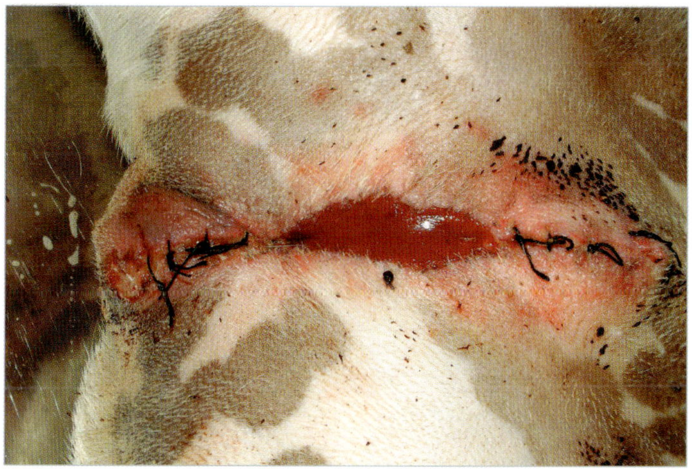

Fig. 14. 13 days after the procedure, inflammation is observed in the areas cranial and caudal to the urethrostomy due to poor postoperative care.

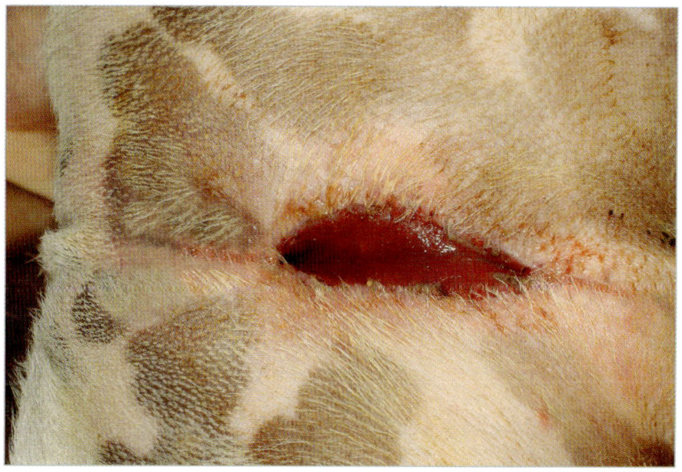

Fig. 15. 15 days after surgery, the sutures are removed and treatment is complete.

Urethral stenoses

Prevalence

Urethral stenosis can be caused by fibrosis due to urethritis following recurrent urolithiasis or prior surgery, as well as external trauma and wounds (bite wounds, cuts...) (figs. 1 and 2). Extrapelvic stenoses should be resolved by permanent urethrostomy at the site of the stenosis.

5% of dogs suffering from pelvic trauma (mainly due to road traffic accidents) have urethral lesions. A possible rupture should be considered when attending these patients.
If this is the case, a urinary catheter should remain in place for 4 or 5 days.

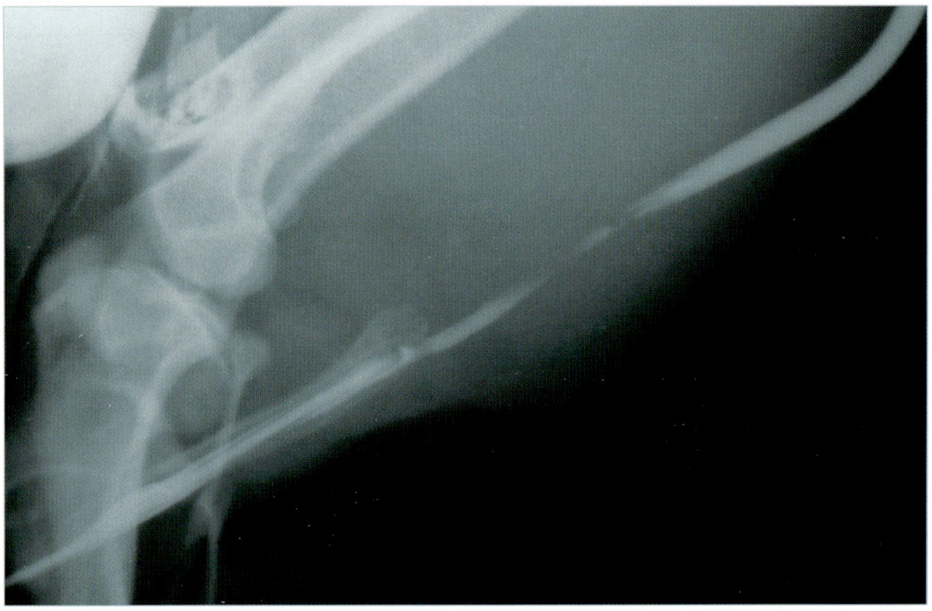

Fig. 1. In this case, marked stenosis of the urethra is observed caudal to the os penis. Cause of the stenosis was previous urethral surgery.

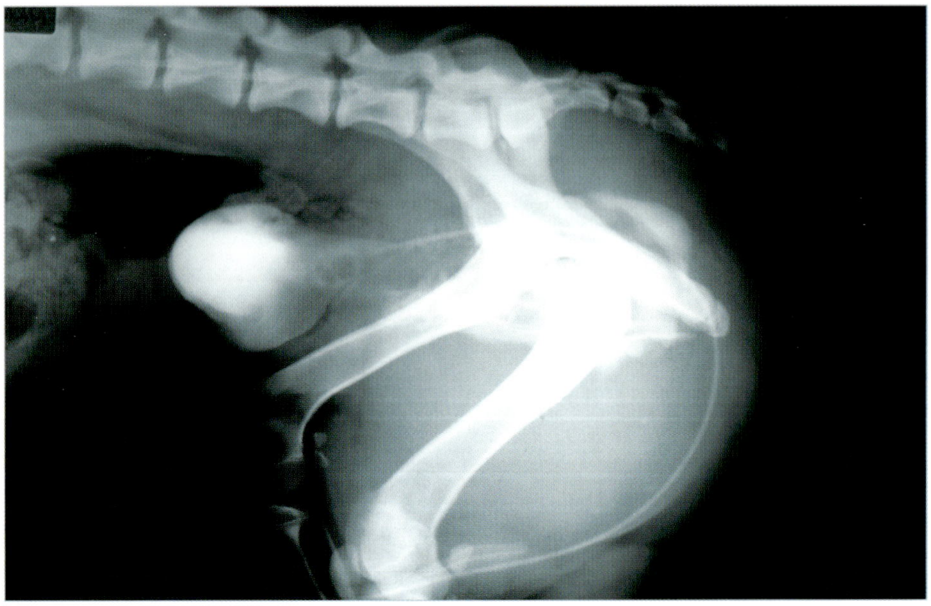

Fig. 2. Rupture of the intrapelvic urethra as a result of a pelvic fracture. The patient should be catheterised to avoid leakage of urine and thereby limit secondary scar formation.

Urethral stenoses. Case 1 / Scrotal urethrostomy

Technical difficulty	■■■□□

"Jan" is an 8-year-old mixed-breed dog that has had problems urinating for 2 weeks. At first, he could still urinate with effort, but now only a few drops are passed.

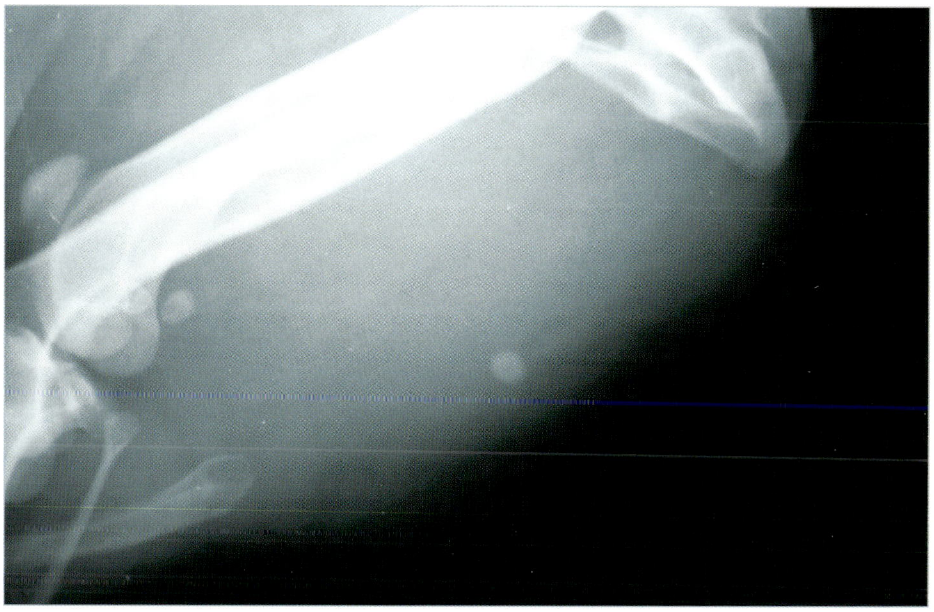

Radiography

Urohydropropulsion, the standard protocol for this type of obstruction, is performed to move the stone into the bladder from where it is extracted via cystotomy (fig. 2).

See cystotomy → page 289

See urohydropropulsion ← page 142

Fig. 1. The perineal radiograph shows a stone lodged in the middle section of the urethra.

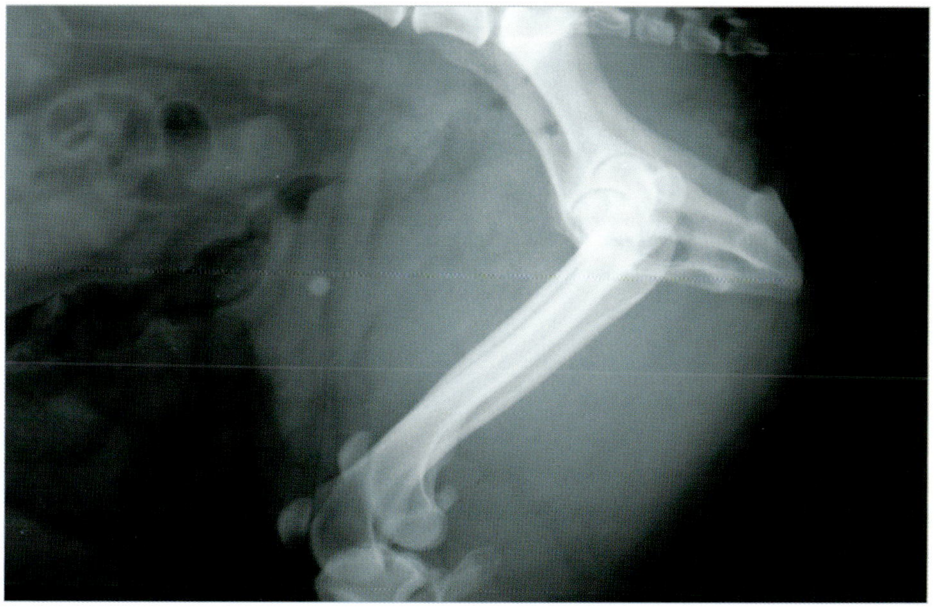

Fig. 2. This radiograph shows the stone in the bladder. No other obstruction is visible in the urinary tract.

On reflection, it does not seem logical that the urethra has become obstructed at the level of the scrotum; there must be a stenosis.
To examine the urethra, contrast radiographs are taken of the perineum (figs. 3-4).

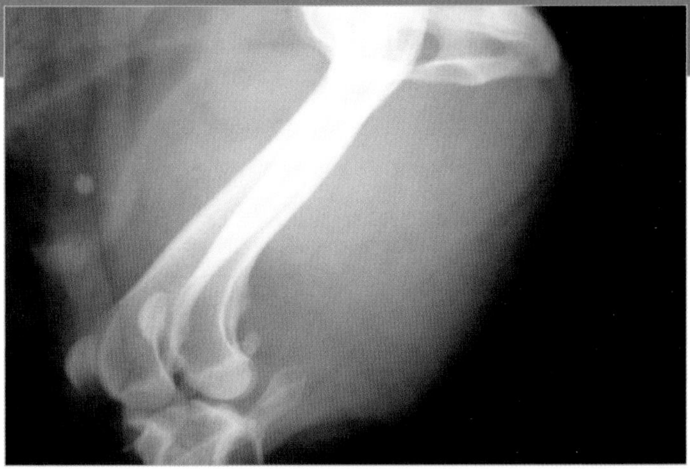

Fig. 3. By injecting air into the urethra, the dilated bladder can be seen (as well as a thickened bladder wall due to cystitis) and a dilated urethra over its entire length, with the exception of an area just behind the os penis, is visible.

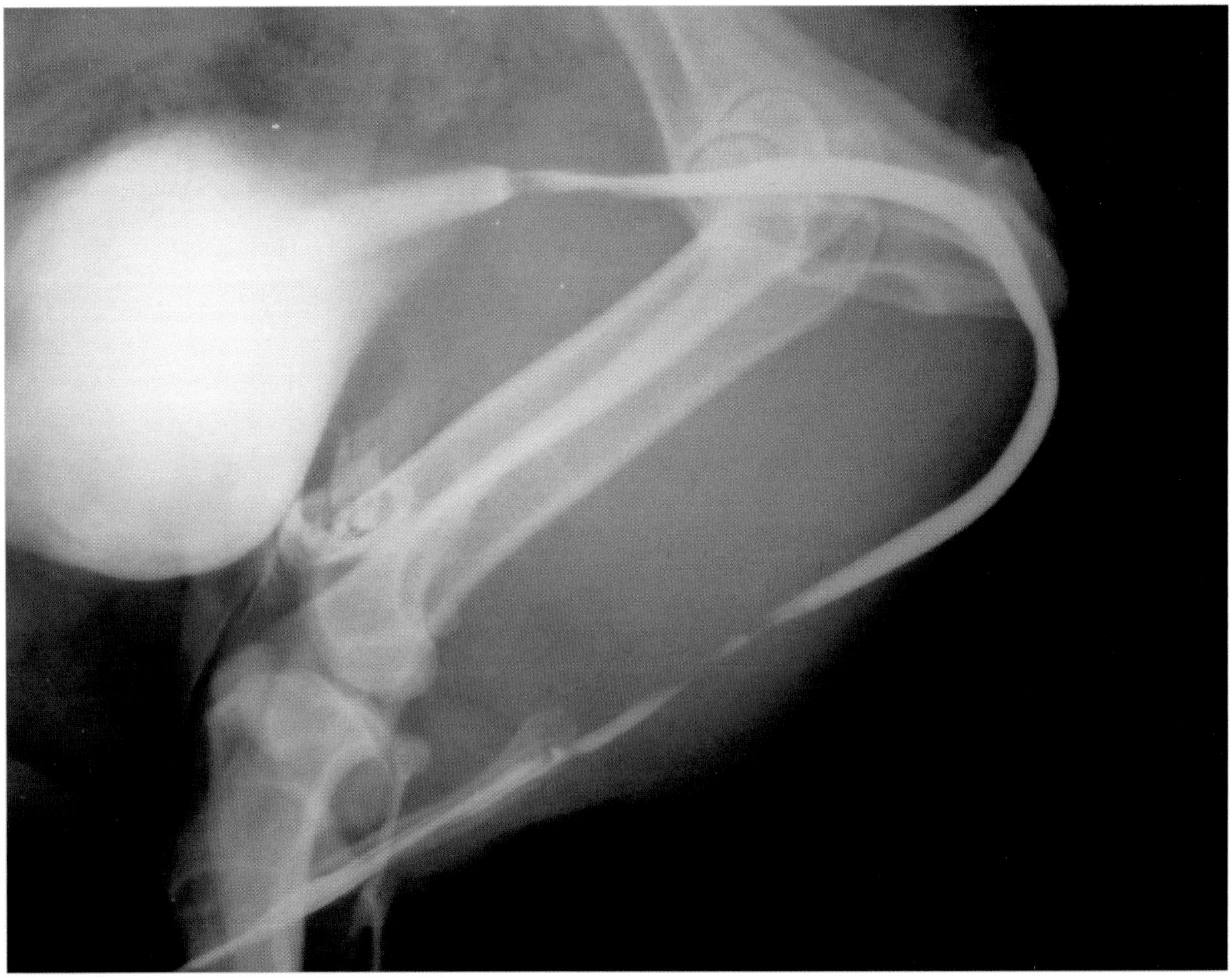

Fig. 4. Using (water soluble) contrast medium, the degree and extent of the stenosis can be accurately determined.

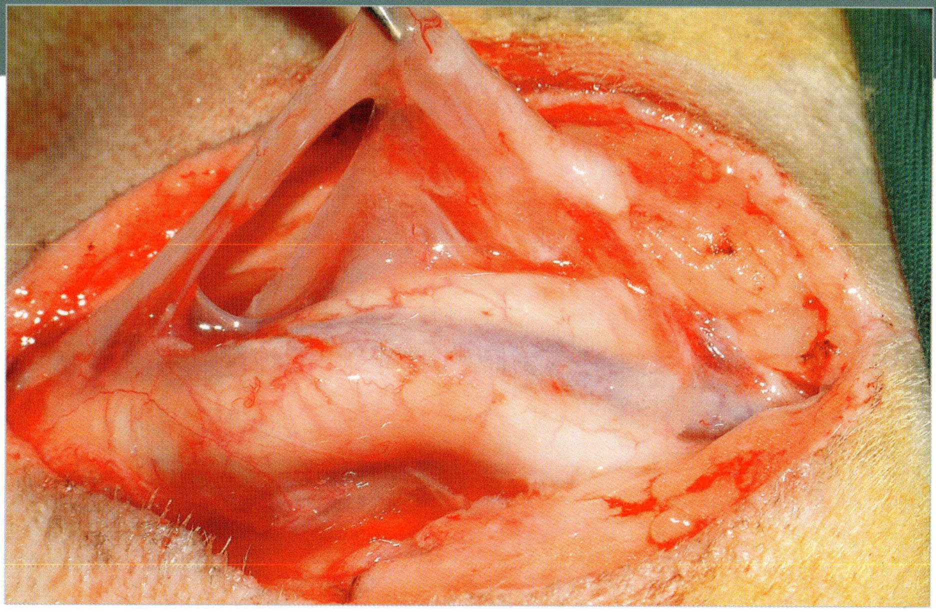

Fig. 5. As a first step in the urethrostomy, the retractor penis muscle is dissected and moved aside.

Fig. 6. The urethra is incised along its median raphe over approximately 3 or 4 cm. Next, the urethral mucosa is sutured directly to the skin using monofilament material.
In this case, a 4/0 non-absorbable suture was used.

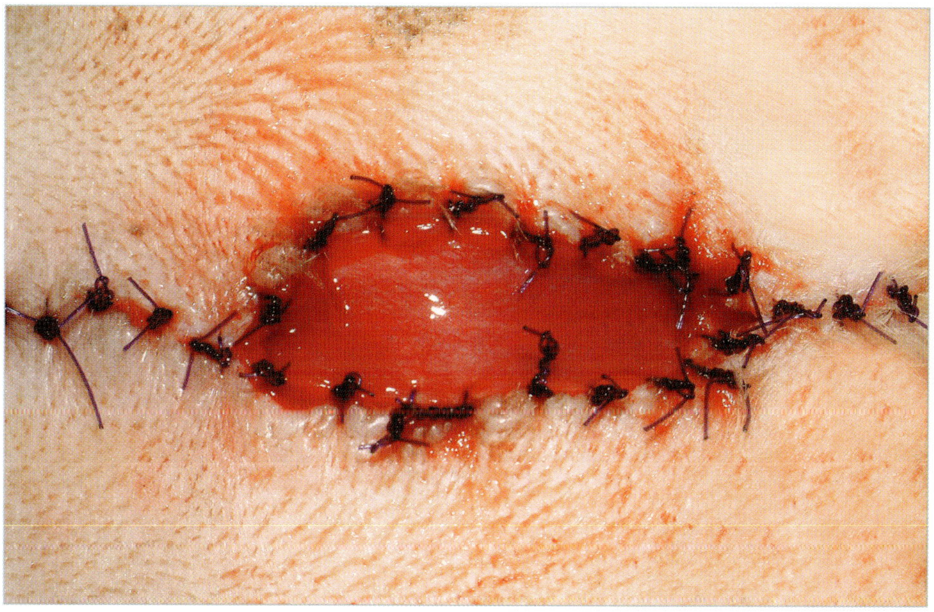

Surgical indication

Scrotal urethrostomy is performed to avoid recurrent obstruction by a small stone that could be eliminated with the urine in the absence of urethral stenosis (figs. 5 and 6).

Postoperative care

During the postoperative period antibiotic therapy should be administered based on sensitivity testing of a urine sample. The healing process should be closely monitored. The patient should be kept from licking the area and secondary contamination should be avoided as this may lead to suture dehiscence (figs. 7 and 8).

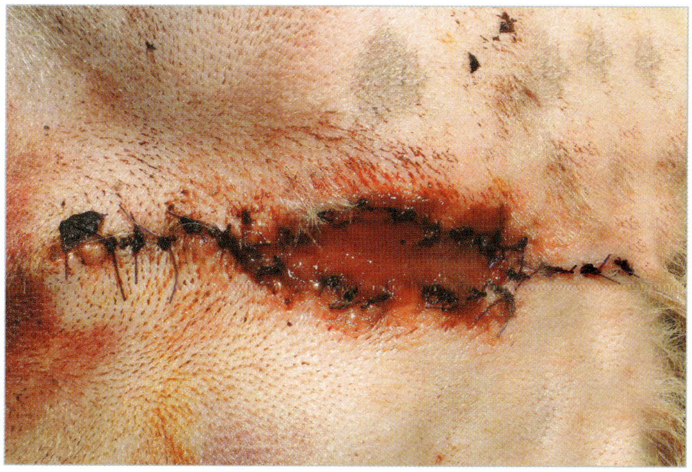

Fig. 7. 3 days after the urethrostomy. The result is satisfactory.

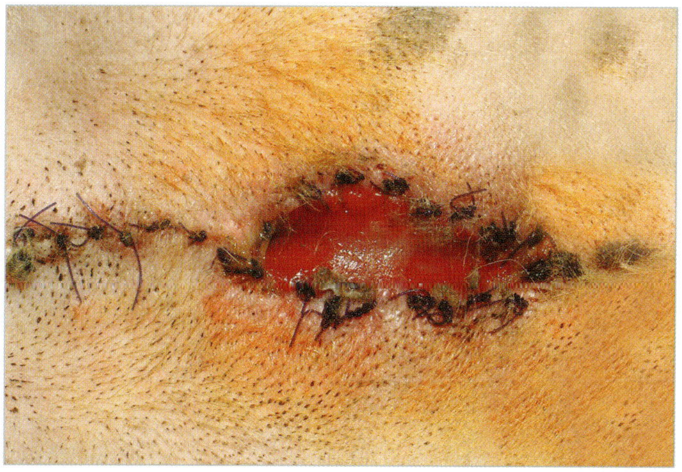

Fig. 8. 11 days after surgery, the sutures are removed and Jan's treatment is complete. In the two years since the operation, the dog has had no more obstructive problems.

Feline lower urinary tract disease (FLUTD)

Prevalence

This syndrome is characterised by idiopathic inflammation of the lower urinary tract. The cat shows difficulty urinating, with or without urethral obstruction or uroliths.

Although there are individual predisposing and triggering factors, the aetiology is not completely clear. It is a multifactorial disease.

> *This syndrome represents 10% of all feline pathologies seen by veterinarians.*
>
> *Not all cats with FLUTD have crystals or uroliths in the urethra.*

Possible factors associated with FLUTD

- Obesity.
- Diet.
- Highly concentrated urine.
- Crystals in the urine.
- Infections (bacteria, viruses, fungi…).
- Anatomical abnormalities (urethral stenosis…).
- Neoplasia (bladder, urethra…).
- Trauma.
- Neurogenic lesions.
- Iatrogenic causes.

The clinical history includes the following elements:

- Frequent visits to the litter tray with unsuccessful to urinate.
- Only passes small drops of urine.
- Haematuria.
- Frequent licking of the penis.
- Vocalisation when urinating due to pain.

Clinical signs	
Cats without obstruction (only inflammation) or recent obstruction	Blocked cats
■ Dysuria. ■ Pollakiuria. ■ Tenesmus. ■ Haematuria. ■ Urinating small amounts with much effort. ■ Constant licking of the penis. ■ Abdominal pain.	■ Depression. ■ Dehydration. ■ Anorexia. ■ Vomiting. ■ Halitosis. ■ Mouth ulcers (due to uraemia). ■ Abdominal distension (if the bladder is not ruptured). ■ Cardiac disturbances due to increased potassium levels.

Diagnosis

- Clinical history. The clinical signs are usually quite characteristic.
- During the physical examination, a distended bladder is palpated and the patient shows pain (be careful when palpating, since the bladder in blocked cats can rupture).
- Radiographs reveal the state of the bladder, its integrity and possible inciting causes (figs. 1-3).
- Perform a culture and sensitivity test on a urine sample obtained by cystocentesis prior to treatment.
- Urinalysis allows the identification of bladder cells, bacteria and crystals.
- A complete blood cell count and general chemistry profile should be performed to assess BUN, creatinine, phosphorus, potassium and, if possible, blood pH.

> *These patients may die as a result of dehydration, electrolyte and acid-base imbalances.*

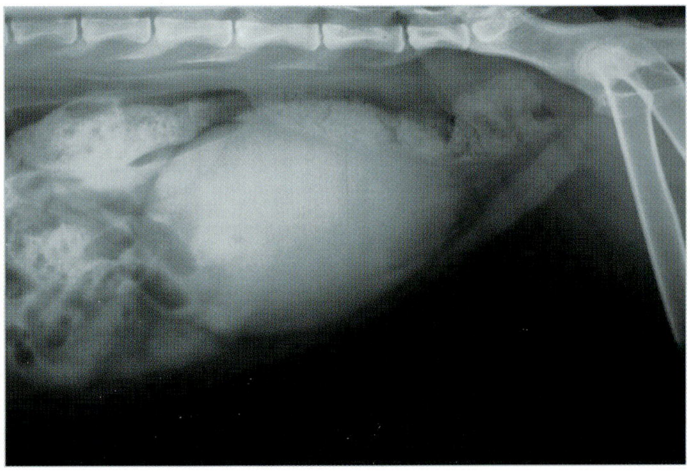

Fig. 1. Distended bladder in a cat with FLUTD due to urethral obstruction with struvite crystals.

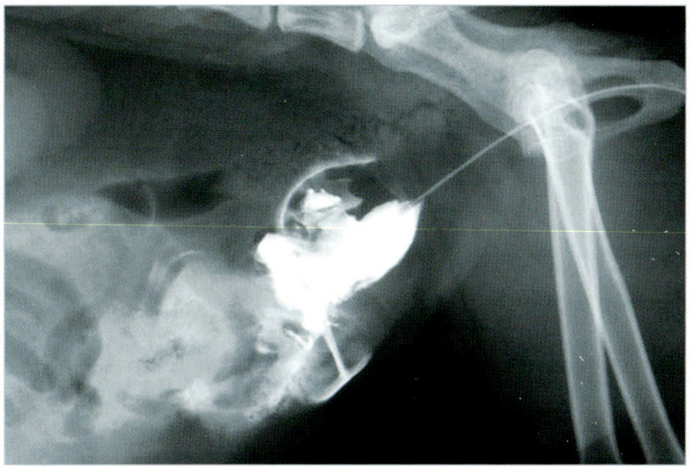

Fig. 2. Ruptured bladder in a cat with FLUTD visualised using a contrast medium introduced via the urinary catheter.

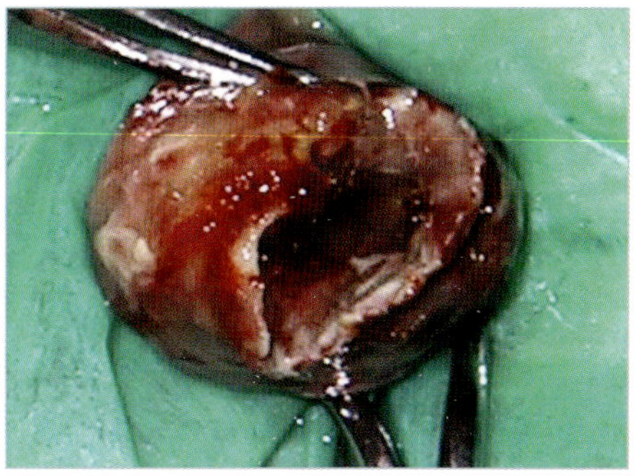

Fig. 3. Intraoperative image of a cat with FLUTD and a ruptured bladder.

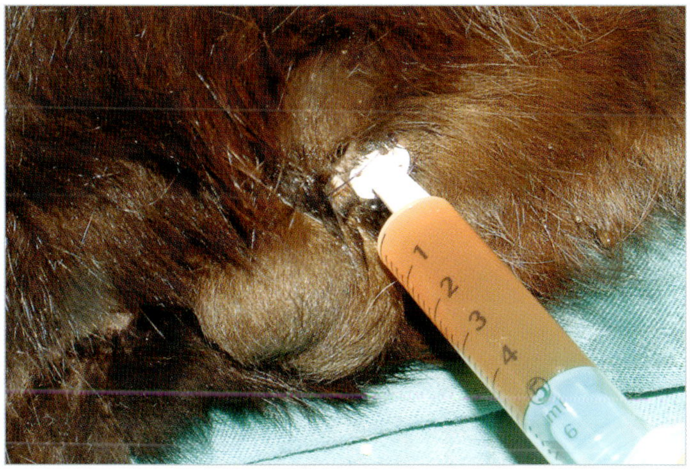

Fig. 4. Urethral catheterisation to withdraw the urine and decompress the bladder.

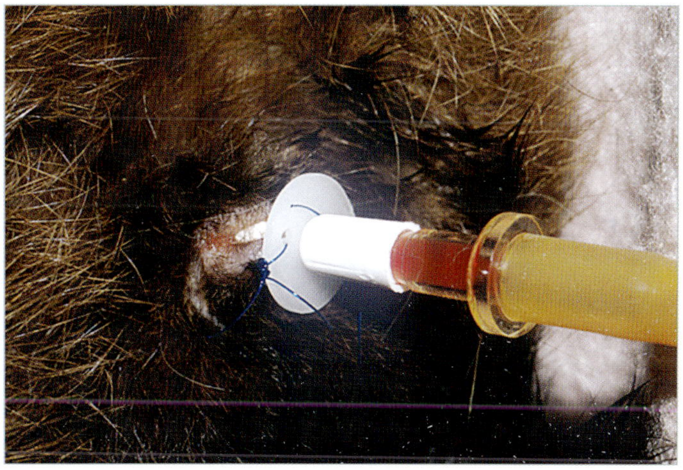

Fig. 5. The urinary catheter is fixed to the prepuce with two sutures and is connected to a urinary collection system while the cat is under sedation.

Treatment

Treatment should be adapted to each individual case, depending on the underlying cause.

Generally speaking, it is based on:

- IV fluid therapy as soon as possible to correct dehydration, uraemia and the hyperkalaemia.
- Next, catheterisation of the bladder (figs. 4 and 5). In animals that are very depressed, sedation may not be necessary, others may need to be sedated or even anaesthetised.

Urinary catheterisation is often difficult and slow due to the marked urethral inflammation or obstruction by small crystals. Most specialists recommend cystocentesis to provide rapid relief, and advise only to catheterise afterwards.

- Antibiotic therapy. The drug of choice is amoxicillin with clavulanic acid until the results of a sensitivity test are available.

Surgical treatment

Perineal urethrostomy is indicated to prevent recurrent obstruction or to treat those cats that cannot be catheterised.

See catheterisation of the cat	page 232
See perineal urethrostomy in the cat	page 160

In 39% of cats, this syndrome is a recurrent problem.

Ascending urinary tract infections are more common in patients that have undergone perineal urethrostomy.

Feline lower urinary tract disease. Case 1 / Perineal urethrostomy

Prevalence	■■■■
Technical difficulty	■■■■

"Ceniza" is a 3-year-old entire male European cat suffering from obstructive episodes every few months over the past year (fig. 1) that cannot be controlled by diet.

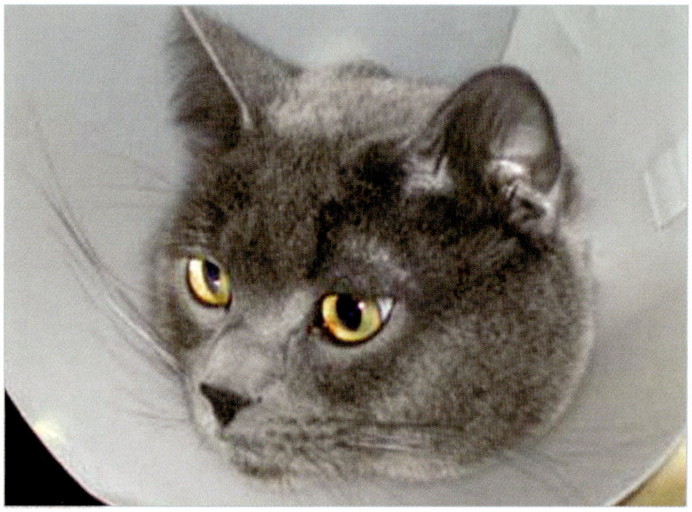

Fig. 1. During the last episode, "Ceniza" was catheterised and surgery was advised.

Perineal urethrostomy is indicated in cases of urethral obstruction if urinary catheterisation is impossible, and in recurrent cases of obstruction that cannot be controlled by medical and dietary treatment.
A thorough anatomical knowledge of the area is required to perform the operation and to minimise complications.

Before surgery

- Decompress the bladder by cystocentesis or urethral catheterisation.
- Check and correct any biochemical changes (uraemia...) and electrolytes levels (hyperkalaemia...).

See catheterisation of the cat ➔ page 232
See cystocentesis ➔ page 240

Anaesthesia

- **Premedication:** ketamine 20 mg/kg + buprenorphine 0.06 mg/kg + acepromazine maleate 0.01 mg/kg.
- **Induction:** propofol, dose depending on the effect of the premedication.
- **Maintenance:** isoflurane + fentanyl as necessary.

Surgical technique

See patient positioning ➔ pág. 248
See purse string suture ➔ pág. 252

During surgery

- Control bleeding with a bipolar coagulator.
- If possible, place a catheter in the urethra so it is easier to identify later (fig. 2).
- Flush the tissues regularly with sterile saline.
- Carefully dissect the attachments of the penis to the pelvis.
- Take care when dissecting structures deep in the operative field.

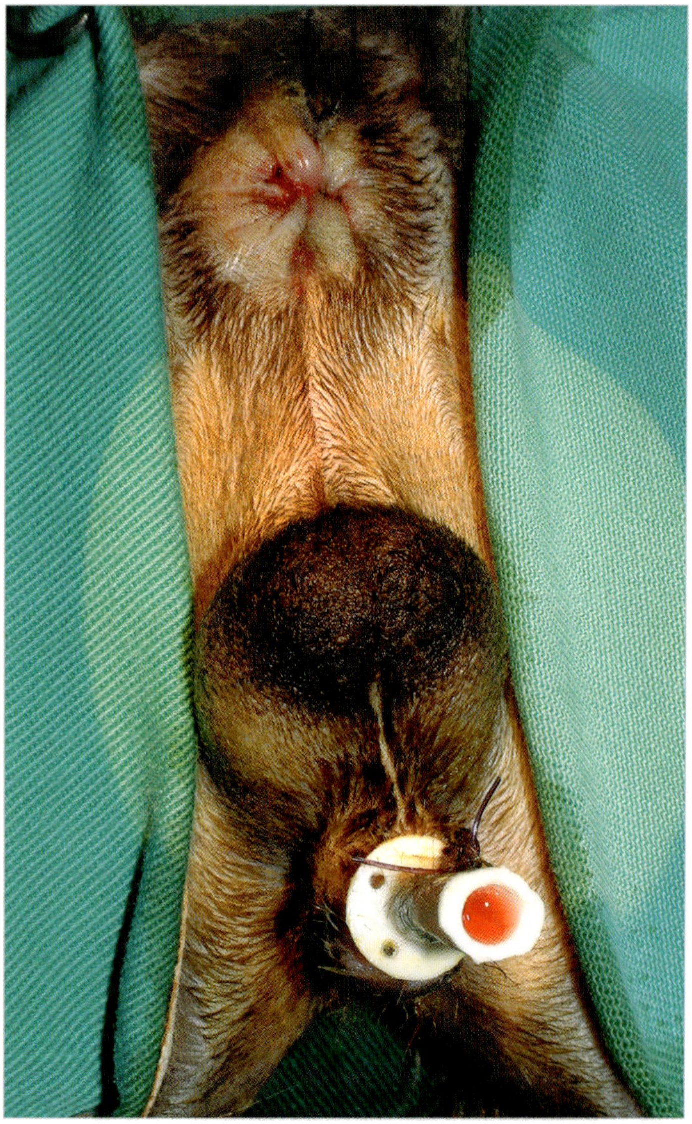

Fig. 2. Preparation of the surgical field. It is very important to place a purse string suture around the anus to avoid faecal contamination during the procedure. Catheterise the urethra if possible.

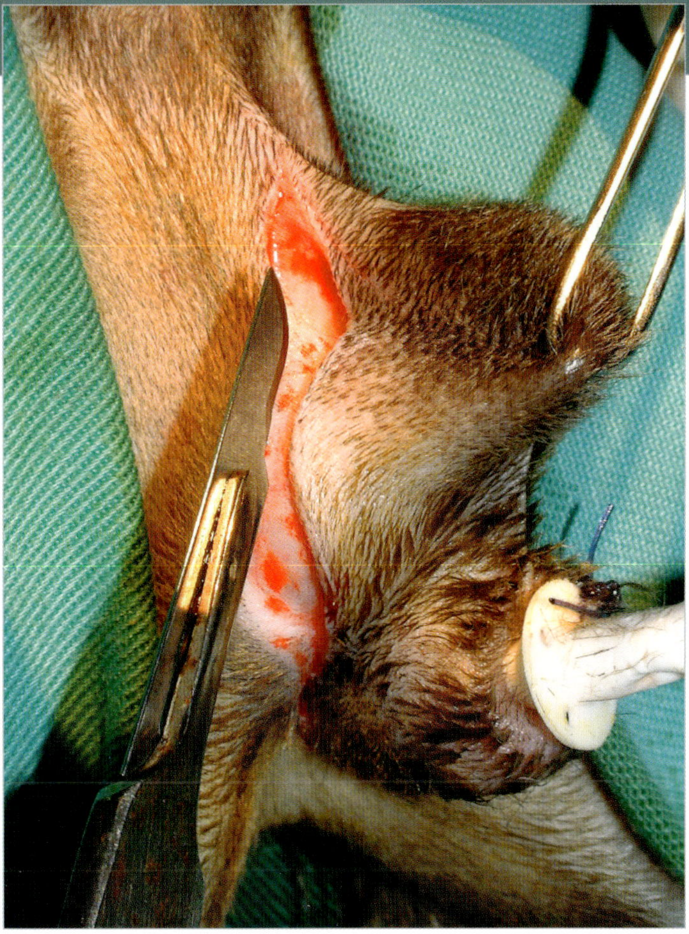

◀ Fig. 3. An elliptical skin incision is made around the scrotum and prepuce, which will be resected later. The testes are identified in entire males and fatty tissue in castrated animals.
Control the bleeding of small subcutaneous vessels.

Fig. 4. In entire animals, castration should be performed as a preliminary step prior to visualising and dissecting the urethra.
▼

See castration ➔ page 264

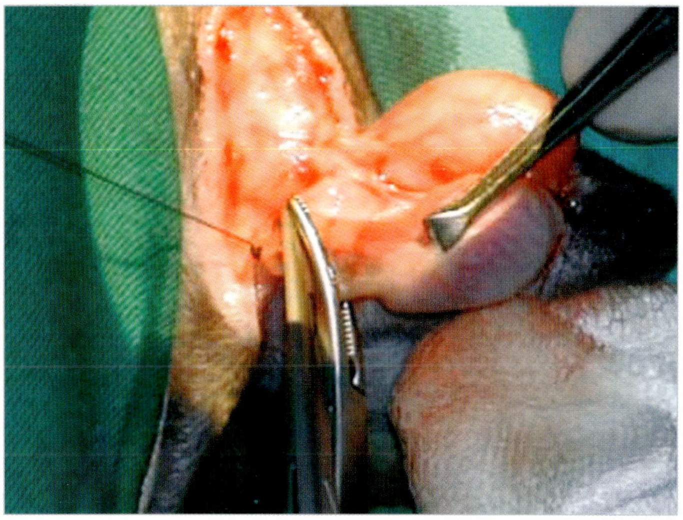

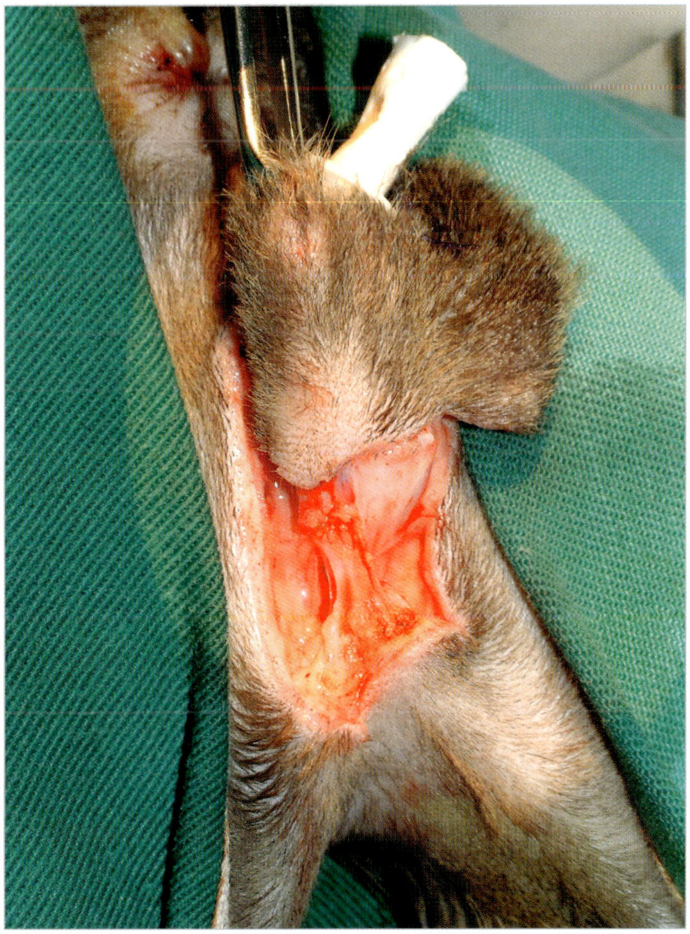

◀ Fig. 5. The penis is moved dorsally and the surrounding tissue is dissected in the direction of the pelvis.
Accurate haemostasis of the small local blood vessels is required to prevent the blood from interfering with the dissection.

Fig. 6. It is essential to free all attachments between penis and pubis. This dissection will facilitate exteriorisation of the penis.
▼

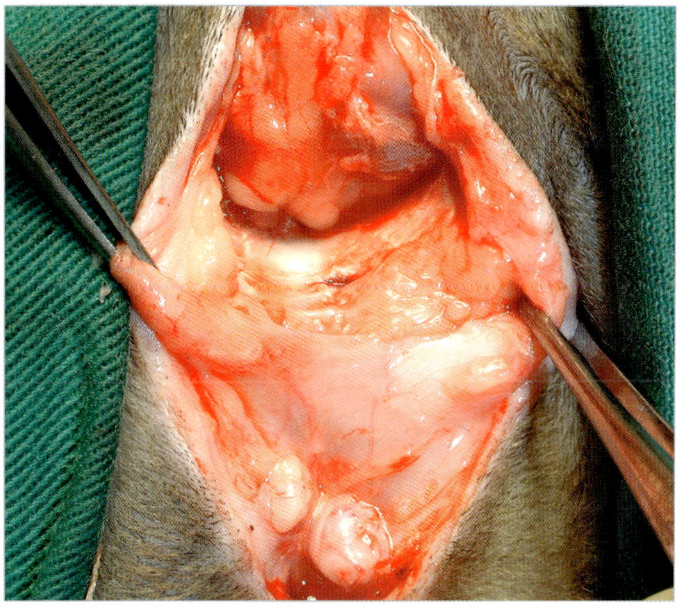

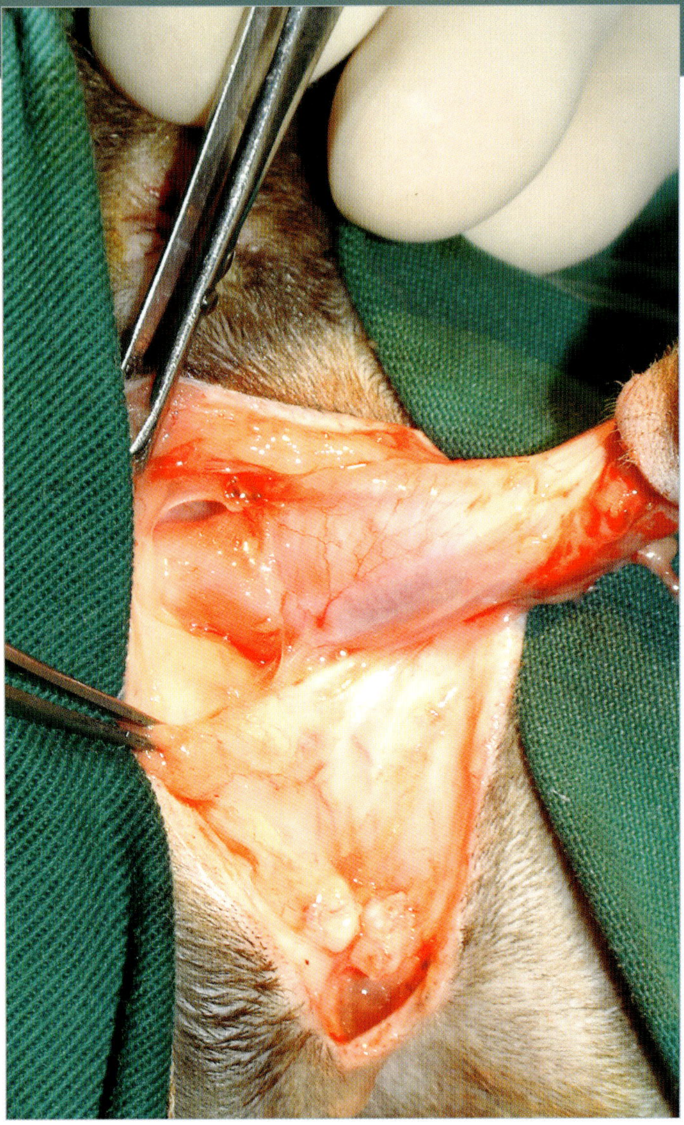

Fig. 7. The ischiocavernosus and ischiourethral muscles are found on both sides of the penis, attaching it to the pelvis.
To facilitate accurate identification and dissection of these muscles, the penis is moved to the opposite side.

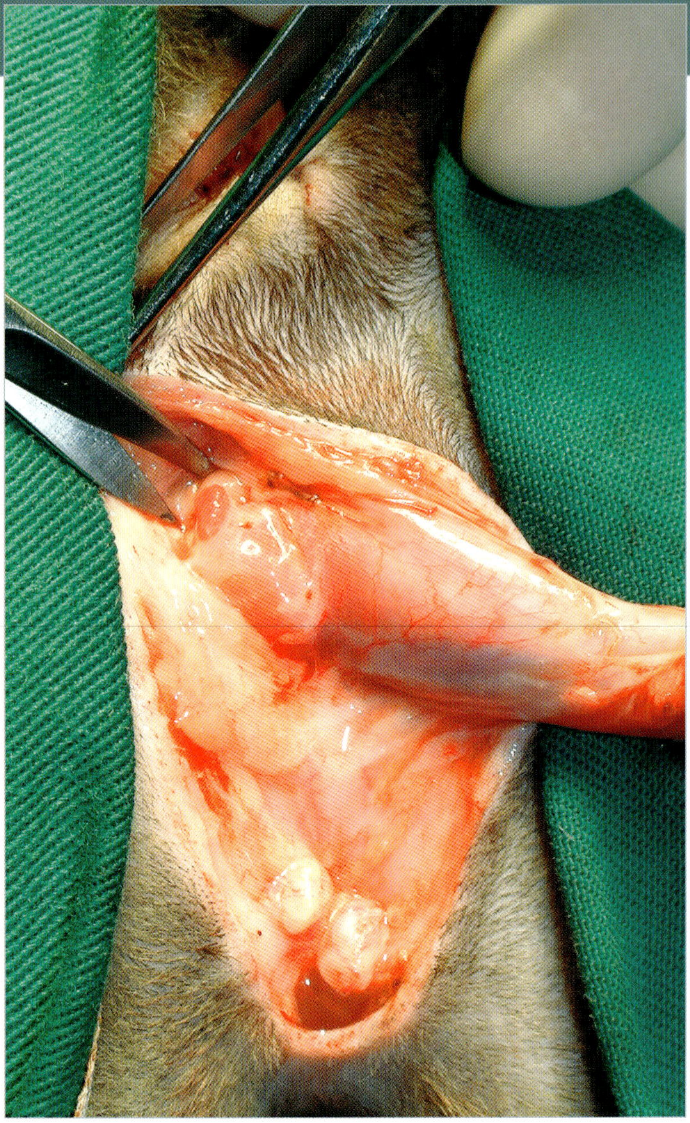

Fig. 8. To avoid haemorrhage of the ischiocavernosus and ischiourethral muscles, it is recommended to cut their insertion point at bone level.
If using scissors in this area, they should always be parallel to the bone to avoid injuring the urethra. The same procedure is performed on both sides of the penis.

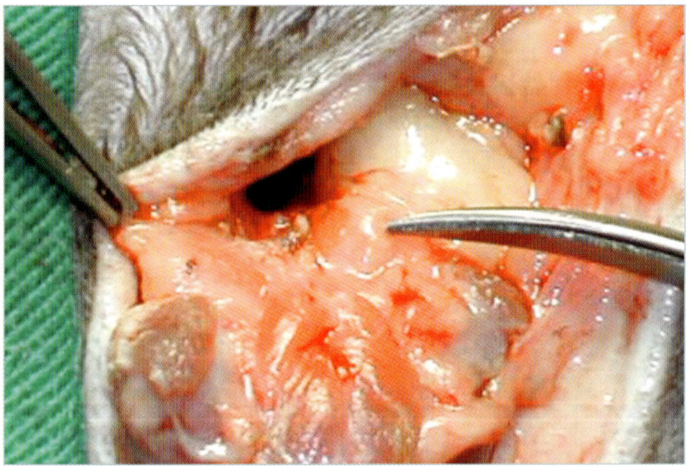

Fig. 9. This photograph shows the severed ischiocavernosus and ischiourethral muscles on both sides of the penis. The scissors indicate the site where the new urethral orifice will be created.

*

Accurate dissection of the penis and its attachments to the pelvis permit exteriorisation of the penis without tension.

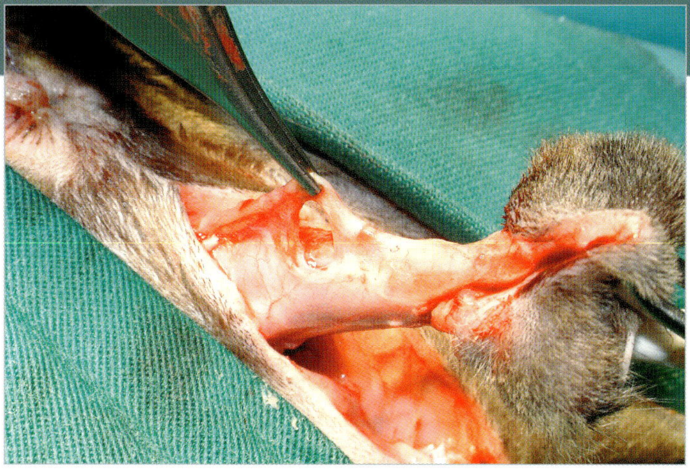

Fig. 10. Next, the retractor penis muscle is located, dissected and resected, allowing a good view of the urethra underneath.

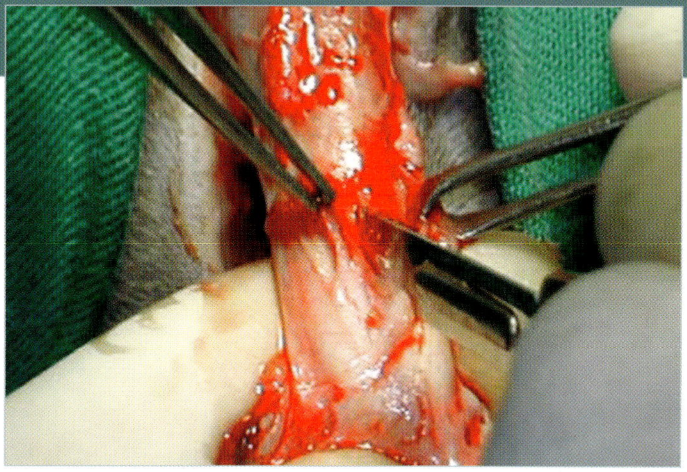

Fig. 11. Using a fine blade (nº 11), the urethra is incised along its midline to avoid excessive bleeding of the corpora cavernosa. This is easier to do if the patient is catheterised.

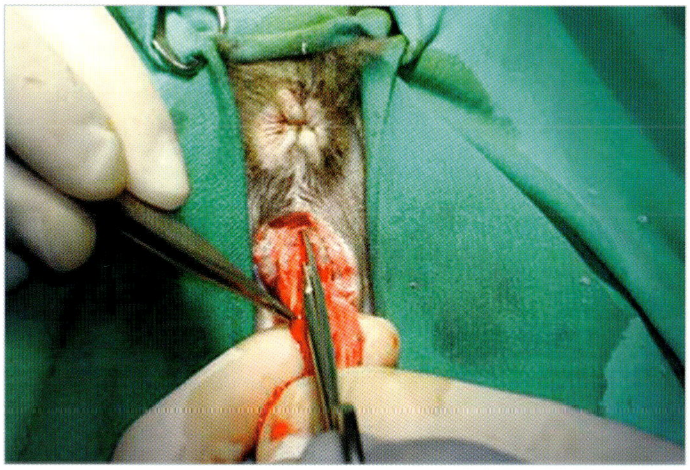

Fig. 12. Using fine dissection scissors, the incision is extended cranially up to the bulbourethral glands, which are easy to spot in entire males, but which are atrophied in castrated animals. It is not necessary to resect these glands.

If the incision is not made over the median raphe, sectioning the corpora cavernosa will lead to extensive bleeding.

Each suture should include the smallest amount of subcutaneous tissue possible, to reduce the risk of cicatricial stenosis.

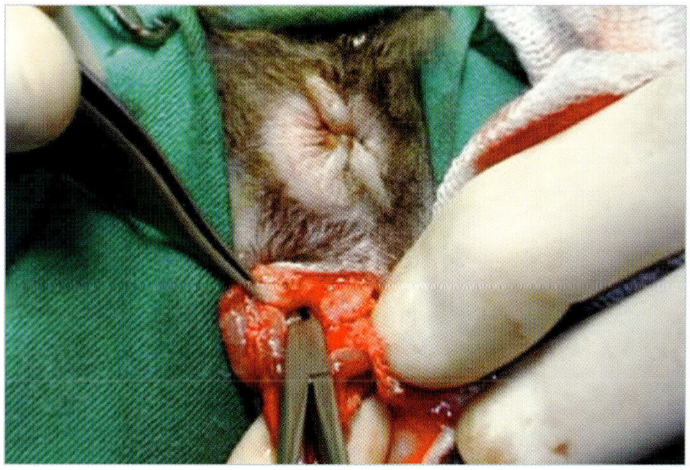

Fig. 13. At this level, the urethral diameter is wide. To confirm this, closed straight haemostatic Pean forceps can be inserted up to their hinge without any resistance.

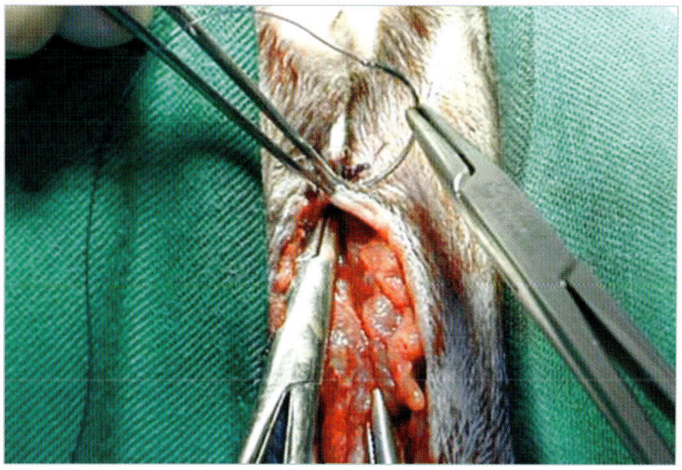

Fig. 14. The pelvic urethral mucosa is sutured to the skin with 4/0 or 5/0 absorbable monofilament material. The two dorsal sutures are placed at an angle of 45° to the midline, to ensure maximal opening of the urethra at this level.

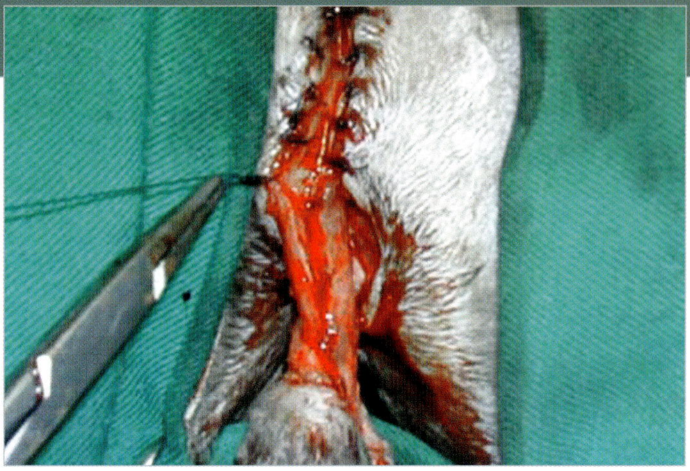

Fig. 15. Fine absorbable synthetic monofilament material is used for suturing and the sutures should be distributed uniformly along the urethra until the distal third of the penis is reached.

> ✱ *At the end of the procedure, do not forget to remove the purse string suture.*

It is not necessary to place a urinary catheter, the patient will urinate normally within a few hours of surgery.

After surgery

- Control bleeding along the suture line using gauze swabs and hydrogen peroxide diluted 1:1 with sterile saline.
- Replace the litter in the cat tray with strips of newspaper, so that the urethra is not obstructed accidentally.
- Instigate appropriate antibiotic treatment.
- Use an Elizabethan collar to prevent the patient from licking the wound, thereby avoiding contamination and suture dehiscence. The Elizabethan collar should be worn as long as possible, even weeks, if it does not cause too much stress.

Postoperatively

- Postoperative progress should be assessed regularly.
- The area should be strictly cleaned. Check regularly to make sure that there is no infection of the wound edges and no obstruction of any kind of the new urethral orifice (figs. 17-20).

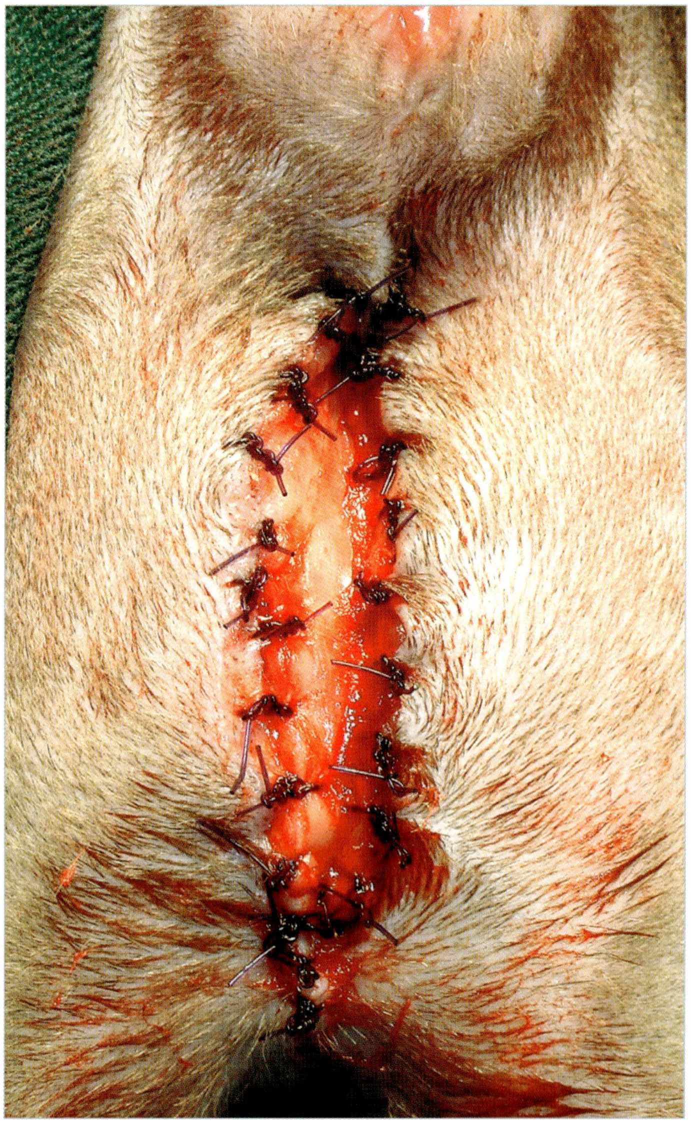

Fig. 16. The tip of the penis is sectioned. To control bleeding of the corpora cavernosa, full-thickness horizontal mattress sutures are placed through the penis. This is the appearance at the end of the procedure.

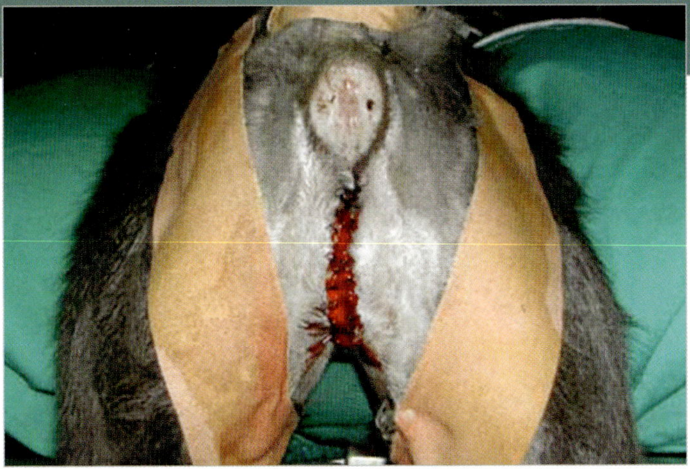

Fig. 17. After recovery from anaesthesia, urethral bleeding is often observed. It can be controlled by light external pressure for a few minutes.

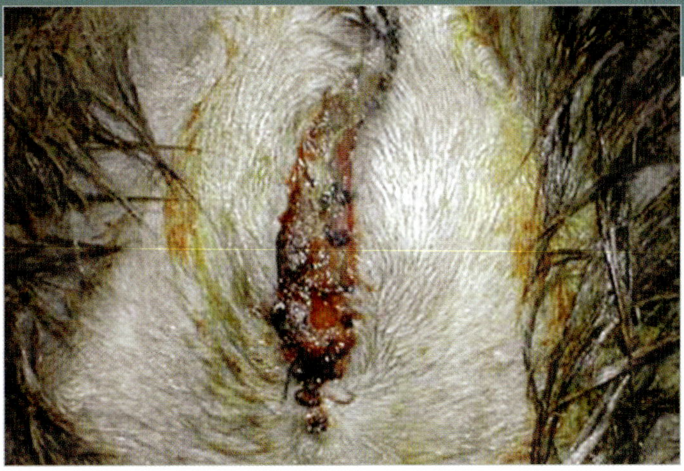

Fig. 18. Appearance 3 days after the operation.

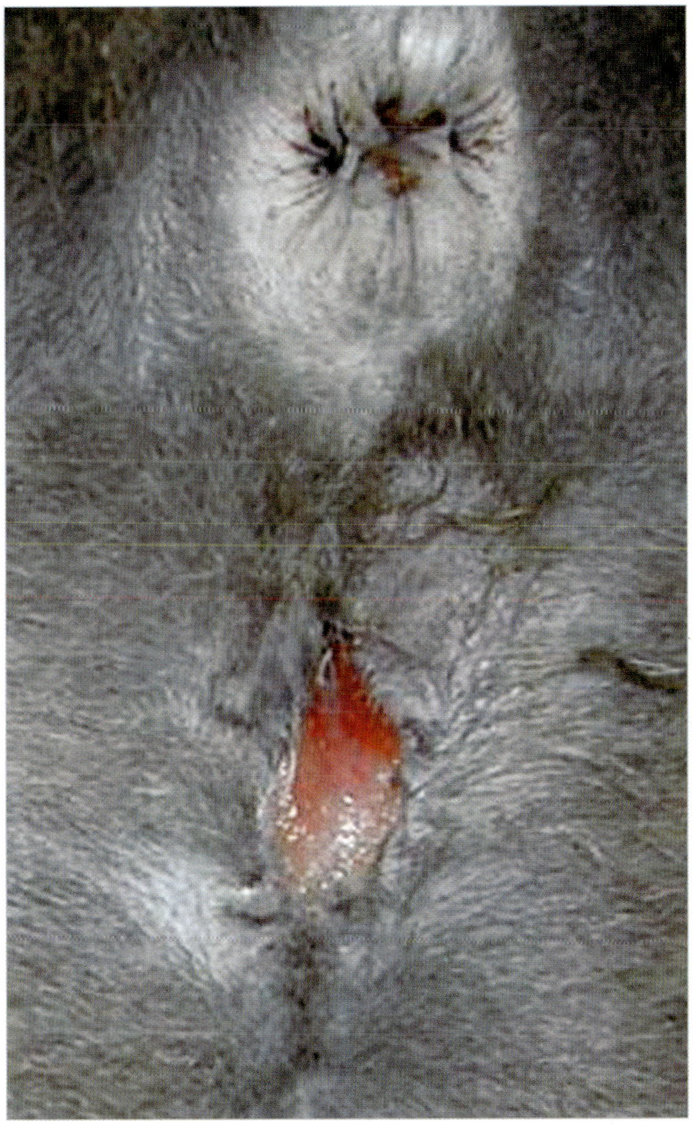

Fig. 19. Result 3 months after the operation.

Possible complications

A recurrent urinary obstruction due to cicatricial stenosis of the urethrostomy is the most common complication. This may be due to:

- Incomplete dissection of the urethra and therefore a small urethral orifice.
- Excessive fibrous reaction of the subcutaneous tissue due to the urine leakage.
- Faecal and urinary incontinence due to nerve damage when dissecting the intrapelvic urethra.
- Recurrent urinary tract infections due to the anatomical changes caused by the operation (a shorter urethra that offers less resistance to the penetration of external bacteria into the bladder).

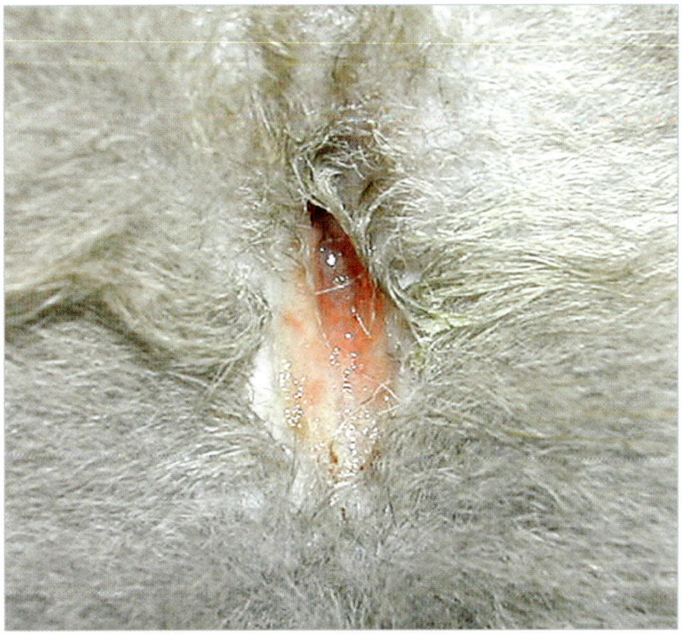

Fig. 20. Appearance of the perineal urethrostomy one year later.

Feline lower urinary tract disease. Case 2 / Cicatricial stenosis

Prevalence	■	■	□	□	□
Technical difficulty	■	■	■	■	□

One year ago, "Pituso" underwent a perineal urethrostomy following recurrent FLUTD. Since then, he has not had urinary problems until last week. Examination of the perineal area shows an almost complete closure of the urethrostomy (fig. 1).

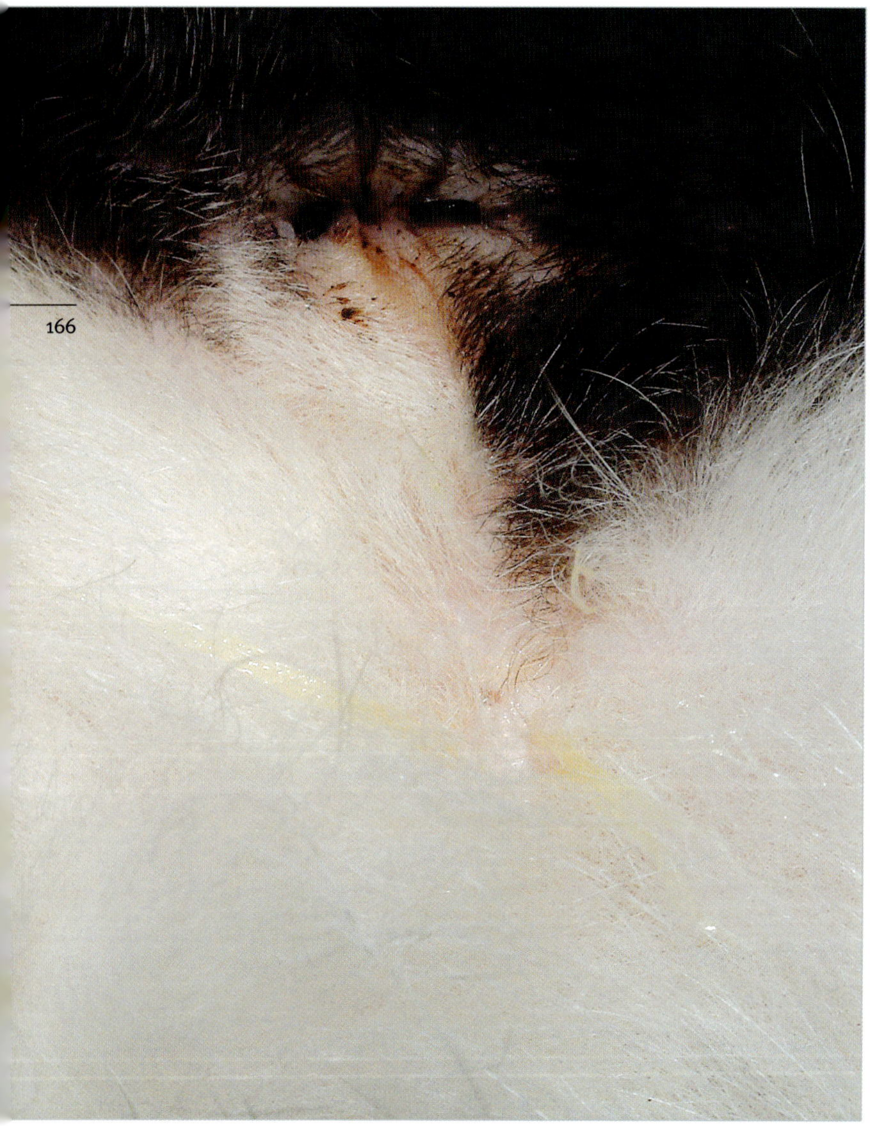

Fig. 1. The urethral orifice is difficult to identify. Only a few drops of urine are seen, wetting the hairs of the area.
The stenosis does not even allow the passing of the smallest urethral catheter.

Urethrostomy sites can develop to stenosis due to excessive fibrosis of the area.

Aspects of the surgical technique that should be considered to limit fibrosis:

- Aseptic surgical technique.
- Accurate skin resection.
- Careful dissection of the tissues.
- Regular flushing of the tissues with sterile saline.
- Complete detachment of the penile muscles from the pelvis.
- The suture type used. Avoid multifilament and non-synthetic absorbable suture material.
- Limit trauma to the corpora cavernosa.
- Include minimal amounts of skin when suturing the urethral mucosa.
- Do not include subcutaneous tissue in the suture.
- Correct placement and distribution of sutures.
- Watch out for local infection after surgery, and for a possible infection under the scab.
- Avoid excessive manipulation of the area, e.g. cleaning, checking the patency of the urethra or use of catheters.
- Use an Elizabethan collar for an extended period, at least until the wound is completely healed. If the patient can tolerate it, it is advisable to leave it on for 2-3 more days after suture removal.

> ✱ ***Correct any electrolyte and metabolic changes prior to surgery.***

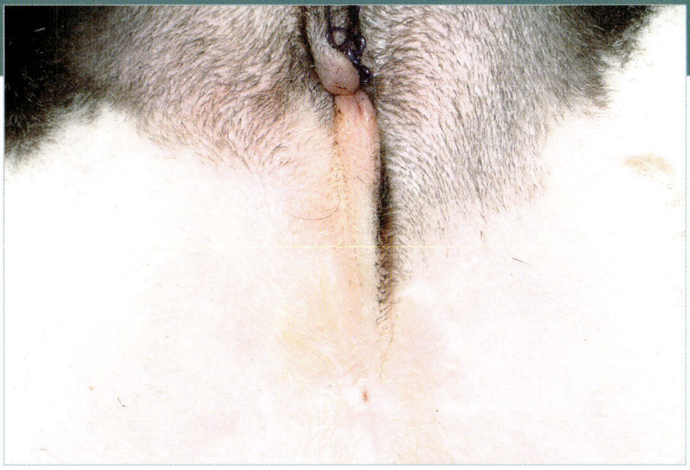

Fig. 2. After shaving the perineal area, the small urethral orifice can be appreciated. A purse string suture is placed around the anus to avoid expulsion of faeces during surgery.

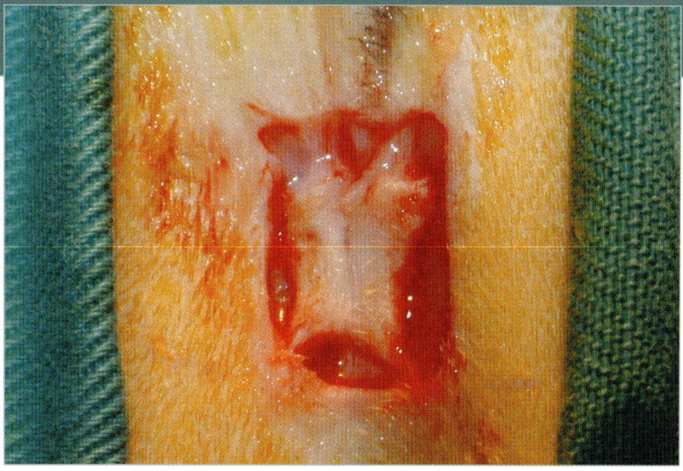

Fig. 3. A rectangular skin incision is made around the stenosis and the adhesions of the subcutaneous tissue are dissected. Careful haemostasis of the subcutaneous vessels is required.

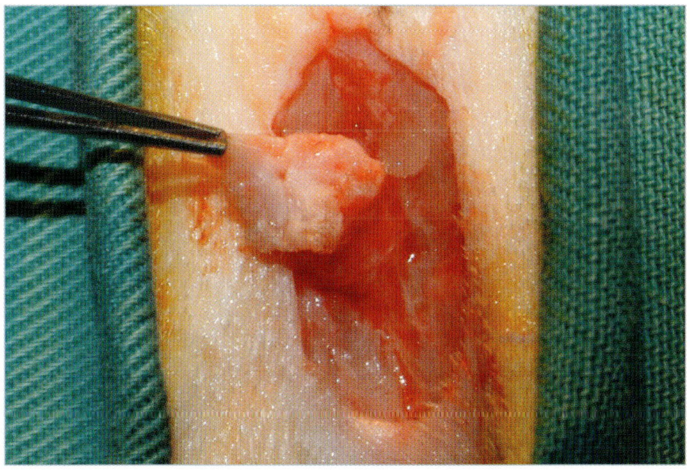

Fig. 4. Dissect the penis slightly from the surrounding fibrous tissue. Do not manipulate these tissues excessively.
It is important to be as atraumatic as possible to minimise local inflammation and subsequent fibrosis.

A deeper incision is indicated if, during the first operation, the dissection and detachment of the ischiocavernosus and ischiourethral muscles were not carried out correctly.

See purse string suture ➔ *page 252*

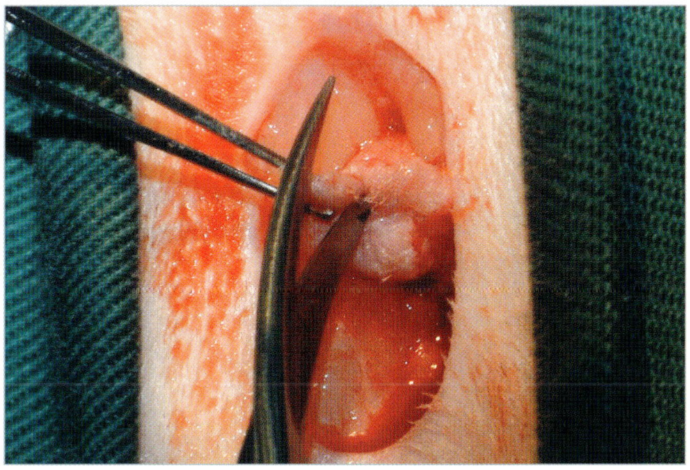

Fig. 5. Using fine, sharp scissors, the urethra is incised dorsally to widen the opening.

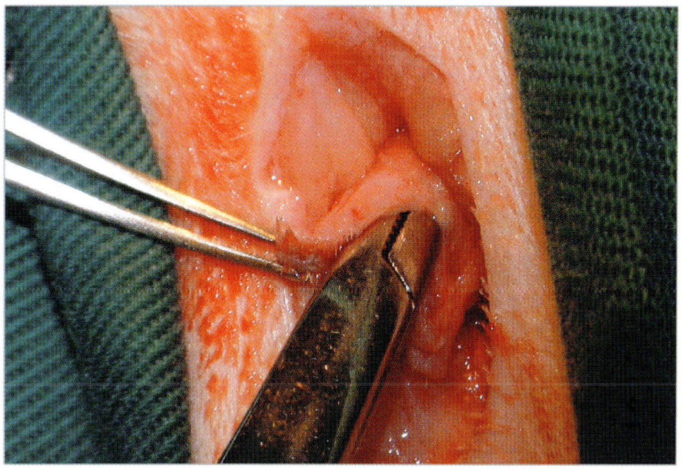

Fig. 6. The urethral incision should be sufficiently long so that haemostatic (mosquito) forceps can be introduced up to their hinge without resistance.

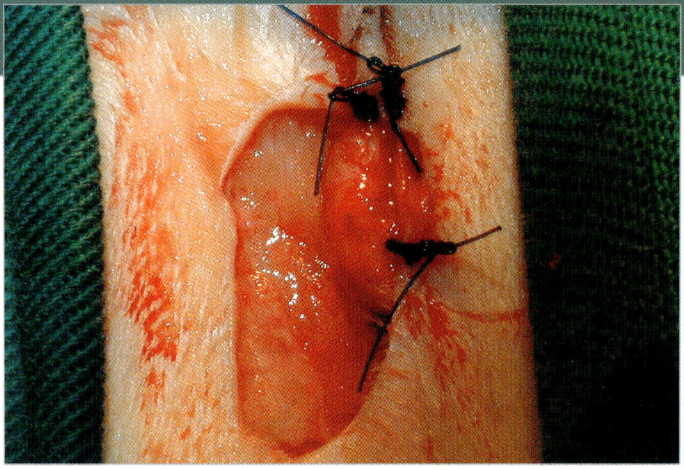

Fig. 7. Next, the skin adjacent to the stenosis is resected and the mucosa is sutured at a 45° angle to the four corners of the skin defect.

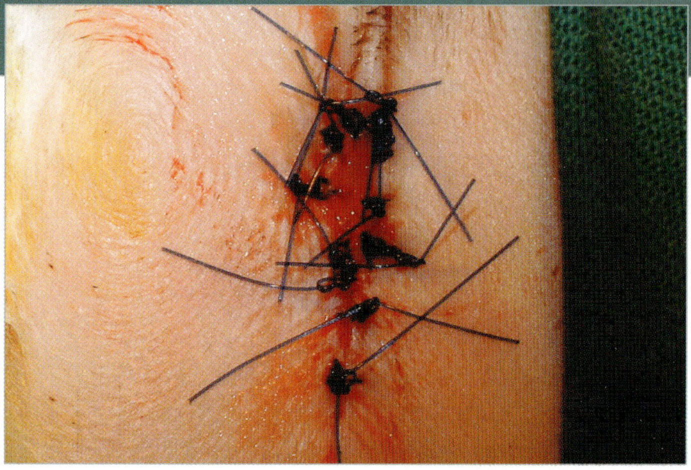

Fig. 8. In this case, non-absorbable 5/0 monofilament material was used.

Catheterisation of the urethra is not indicated in these cases since the urethra is not blocked, and to avoid unnecessary trauma and infections.

Postoperatively

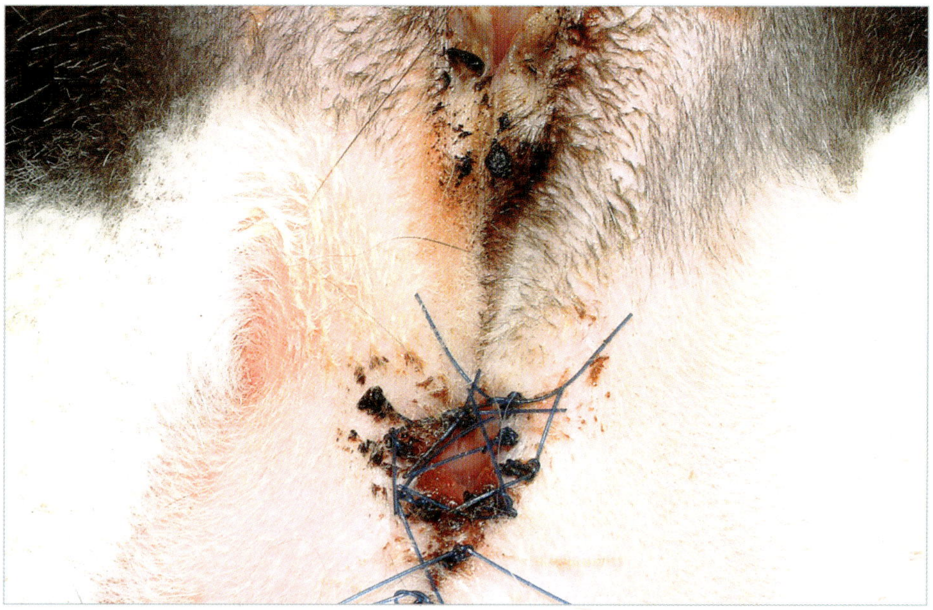

Fig. 9. The result 3 days after surgery. Progress is satisfactory. The owner should be reminded of the importance of strict hygiene measures.

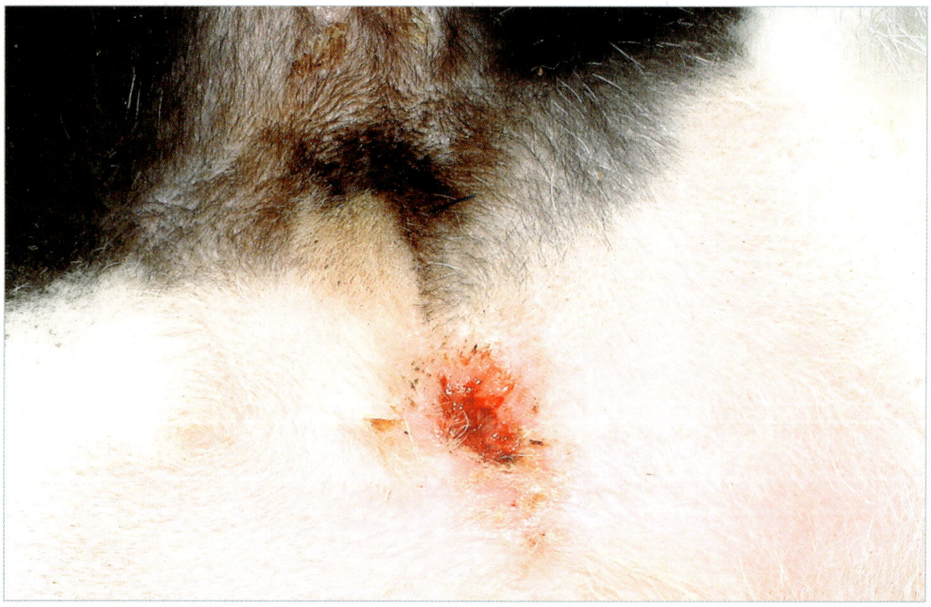

Fig. 10. Ten days after the operation, healing is satisfactory. The sutures are removed and treatment is complete.

Feline lower urinary tract disease. Case 3 / Skin inflammation and necrosis

Prevalence

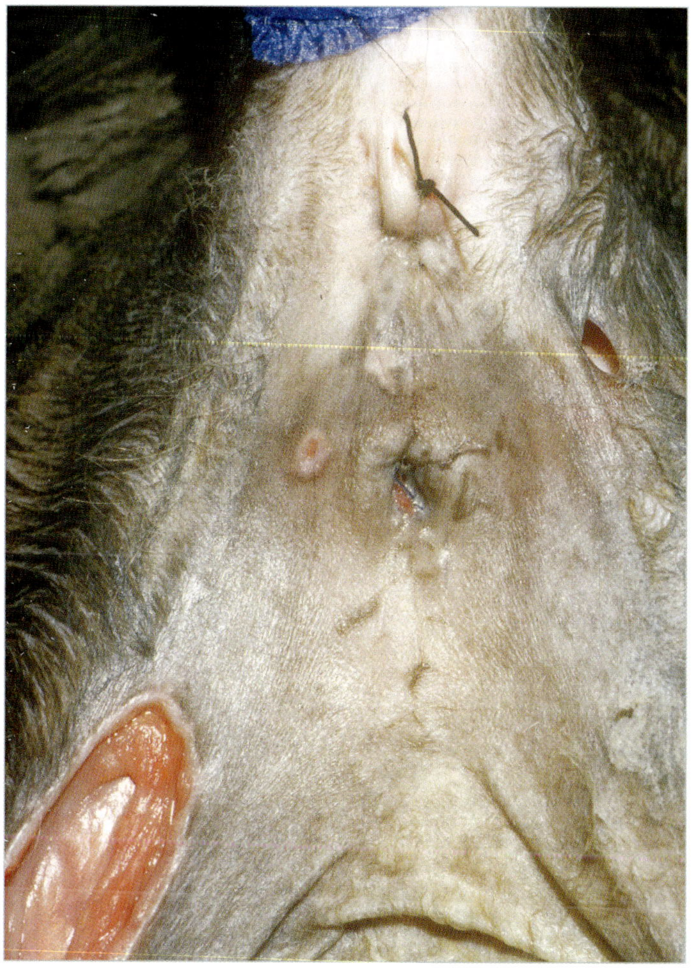

Fig. 1. Skin lesions around the urethrostomy and on the caudal side of the thigh due to urine leakage following urethrostomy performed three weeks earlier.

This cat underwent a perineal urethrostomy three weeks ago, but for seven days it has had problems urinating and various skin lesions have appeared which are leaking urine (fig. 1).

This problem is the result of urine leaking into the subcutaneous tissue due to poorly placed sutures or suture dehiscence as a result of excessive tension between the urethra and the pelvic canal.

> *The situation is more severe if the urine leaks into the abdominal cavity, which will lead to uroperitonitis.*

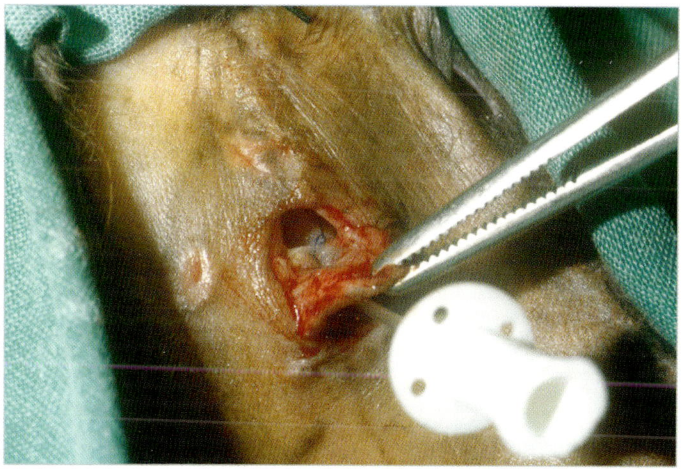

Fig. 2. To resolve the problem, the urethral mucosa should once more be sutured to the skin. Deep in the surgical field, a loosened suture from previous surgery can be seen.

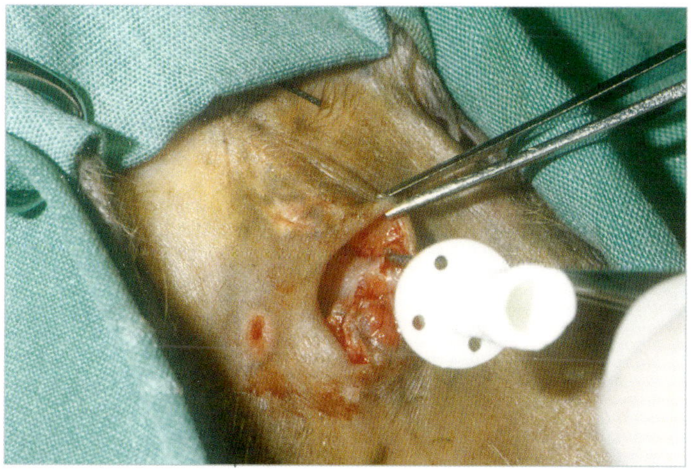

Fig. 3. This photograph provides a dorsal view of the dissected urethra before it is sutured to the skin.

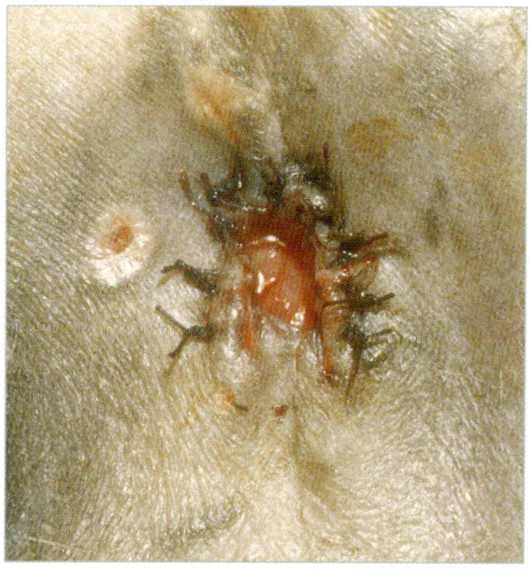

Fig. 4. The same principles described for the urethrostomy technique should be followed. The skin defects should be reconstructed with the skin suture of the surgeon's choice.

Schematic drawing of the male genitalia

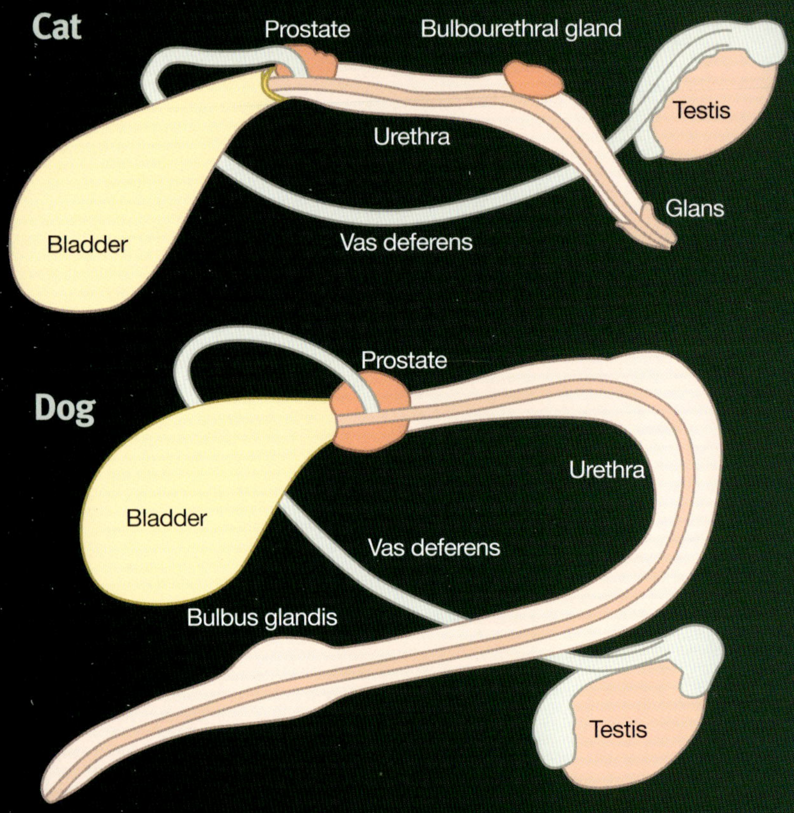

Testes

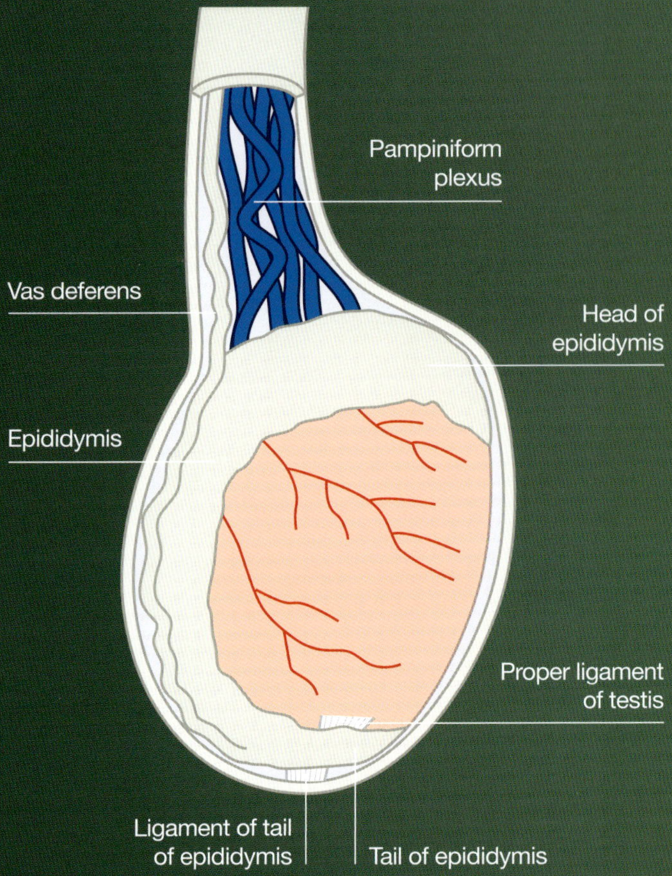

Schematic drawing of the vaginal tunic of the testis

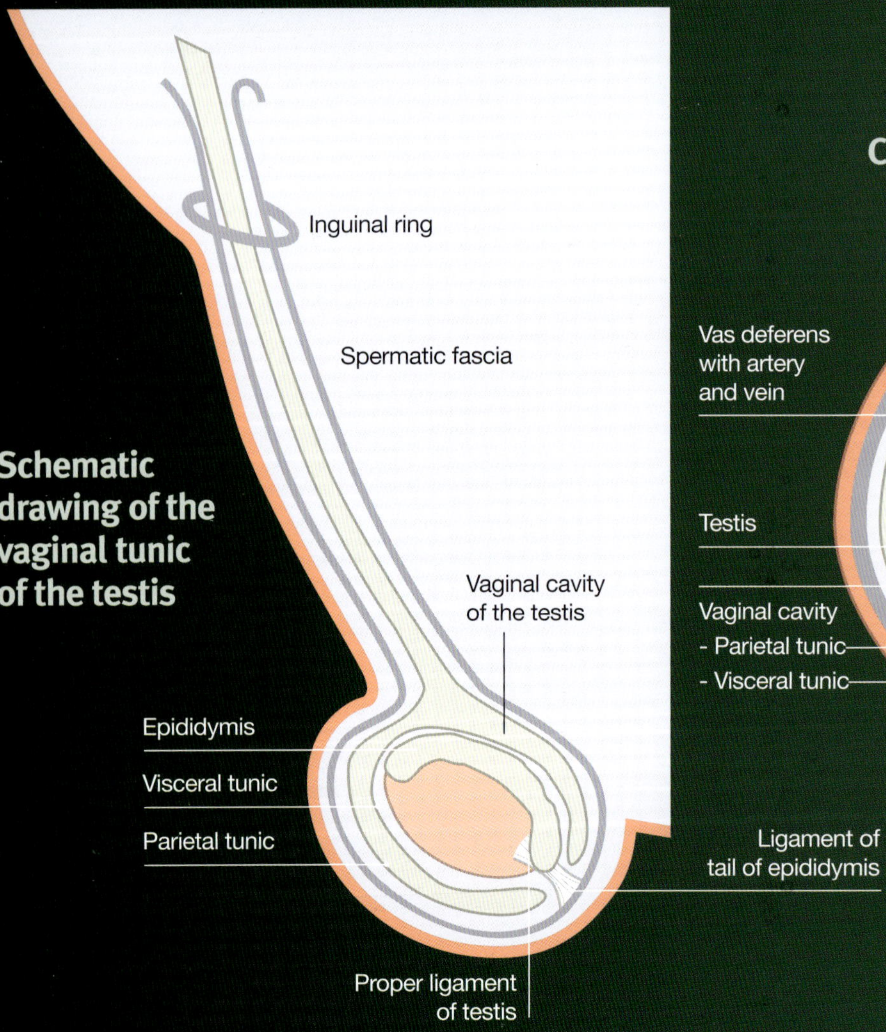

Cross section of the scrotum and testes

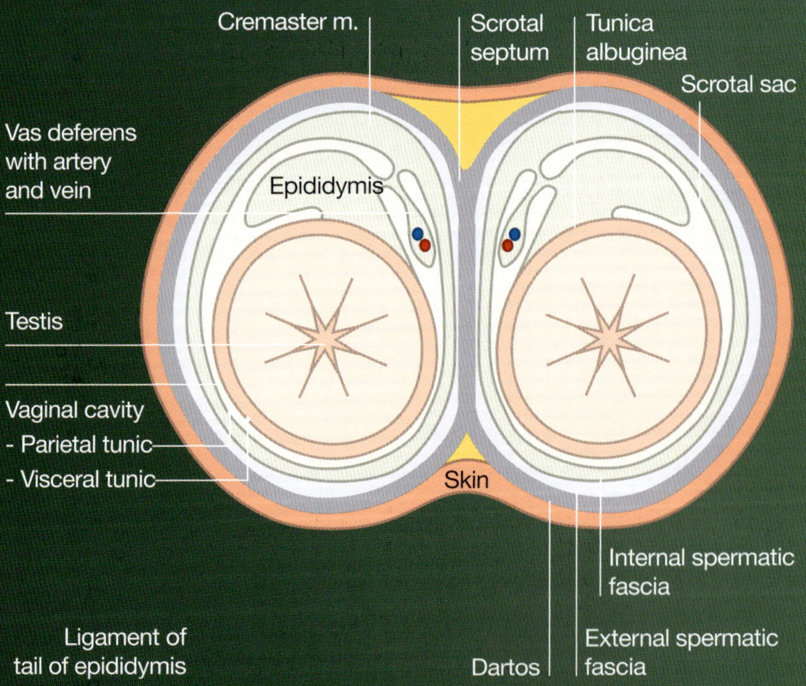

Schematic drawing of testicular descent

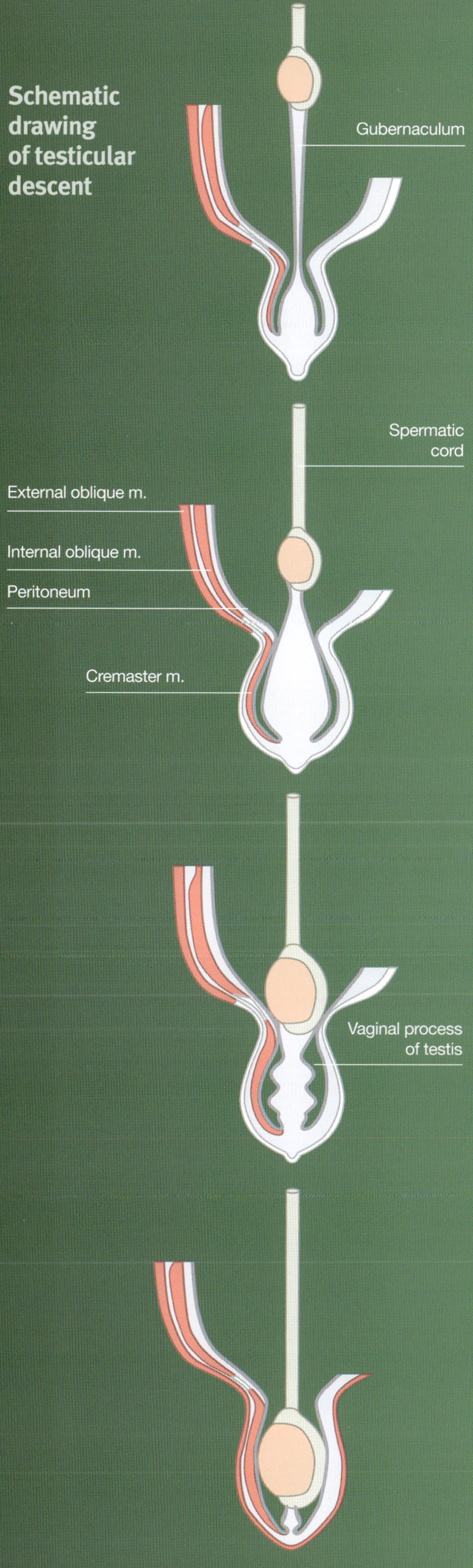

Testes

Testicular neoplasia

Case 1 / Sertoli cell tumour

Case 2 / Seminoma and perianal adenomas

Case 3 / Sertoli cell tumour and prostatic cysts

Case 4 / Leydig cell tumour

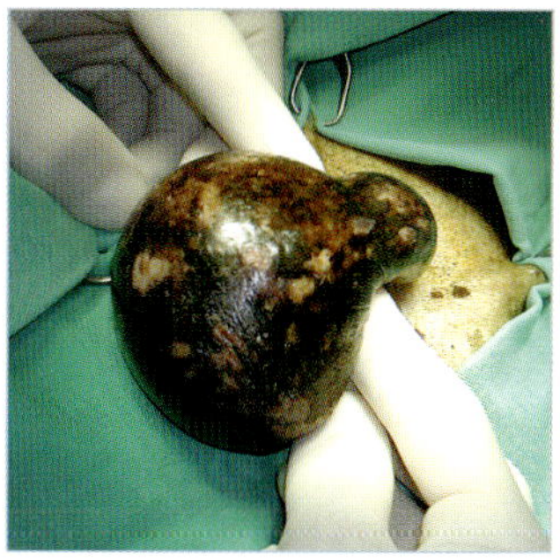

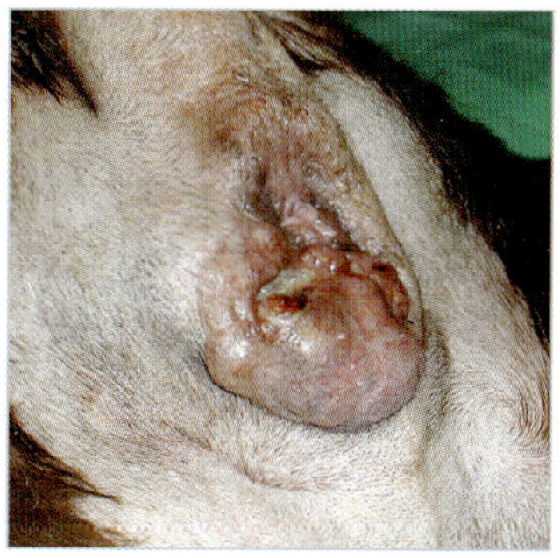

Ectopic testes

Case 1 / Abdominal monorchid

Case 2 / Inguinal monorchid

Case 3 / Inguinal cryptorchid

Case 4 / Abdominal cryptorchid

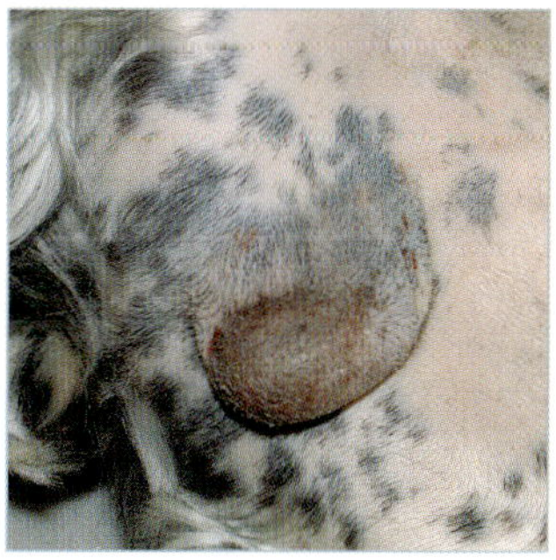

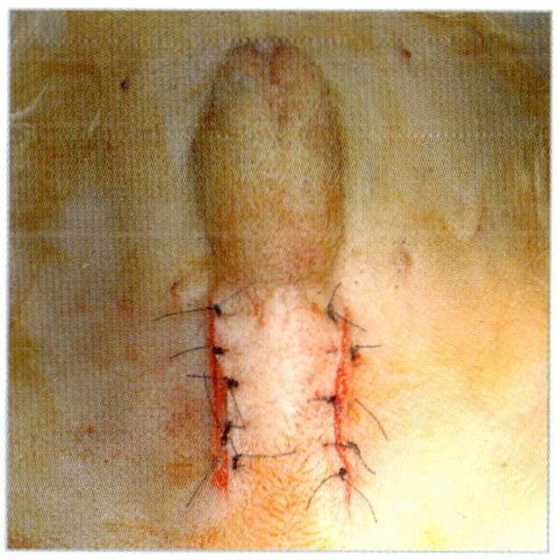

Scrotal lesions

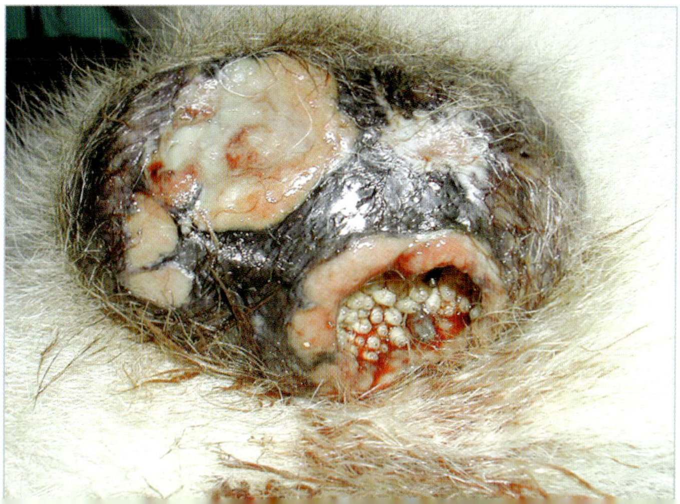

Testicular neoplasia

Prevalence

Scrotal and testicular tumours are more common in dogs than in cats. They usually occur in patients over 10 years of age, except in cryptorchid animals, in which they appear from 6 years of age. The cryptorchid testis is approximately twenty times more likely to develop a tumour than a scrotal testis.

The three most common testicular tumours are:

- Sustentacular or Sertoli cell tumours.
- Interstitial or Leydig cell tumours.
- Germinal cell tumours or seminomas.

Whether tumours are malignant or benign depends largely on whether the testis is scrotal or cryptorchid. All tumours in scrotal testes are, in principle, benign. In contrast, if the testis is cryptorchid, the tumour is more likely to be malignant. For this reason, it is important to detect a retained testicle early on, during routine puppy consultations, so that preventive castration can be recommended.

Always examine the scrotum of puppies. In case of cryptorchidism, preventive castration should be recommended to the owner.

Metastases are rare with this kind of tumour. If they occur, they do so at an advanced stage and are most commonly located in the lumbar, pelvic and inguinal lymph nodes. Metastases to the lungs and liver are rare.

Interstitial or Leydig cell tumours are benign and usually produce testosterone that may contribute to the development of perianal adenomas, perineal hernias and benign prostatic hypertrophy. They are more common in scrotal testes, but may go unnoticed during palpation due to their small size (1 to 2 cm diameter) and soft texture, similar to the testicular parenchyma. They are well-encapsulated tumours, with a yellow-orange colour, that grow inside the testis without protruding beyond the surface.

Sertoli cell tumours originate from the cells that provide structure to the testis. Their metastatic capacity is greater than that of other testicular tumours. They usually produce oestrogens, which cause squamous metaplasia of the prostate, leading to intra- and paraprostatic cysts and abscesses, feminisation syndrome and myelotoxicity.

Sertoli tumours occur more frequently in cryptorchid testes, both the inguinal and abdominal forms. The tumour is firm on palpation, lobular, often protruding beyond the testicular surface and has a grey colour.

The most malignant testicular tumours are also the ones that are more likely to go unnoticed as they are located in the abdomen.
If feminisation is observed in a cryptorchid dog, a Sertoli cell tumour should be suspected.

Seminomas originate from germinal cells. They usually do not give rise to metastases and rarely lead to clinical signs of hormonal imbalance. They occur in both scrotal and cryptorchid testes.

Depending on the type of tumour, the patient may be asymptomatic, with the owner having detected a testicular mass or the tumour may be discovered when examining a patient with signs of hormonal imbalance, e.g. coat changes, feminisation syndrome, perianal tumours or prostatic disease.

When locating cryptorchid tumours, radiography and ultrasound examination are of useful. Haematology can be altered in cases of Sertoli cell tumours. Where bone marrow aplasia as a result of tumour-induced oestrogen production, leads to anaemia, thrombocytopaenia and leucopaenia.

Signs of the feminisation syndrome

- Reduced libido.
- Male animals attractive to other males.
- Dogs no longer lift their leg to urinate.
- Pale mucous membranes due to anaemia and bone marrow suppression.
- Symmetrical bilateral alopecia, starting on the flanks and the perineum.
- Hyperpigmentation of the skin.
- Gynaecomastia.
- Pendulous prepuce.
- Enlarged prostate.
- Prostatic cysts or abscesses.

Bilateral castration is the only practical and efficient treatment of testicular tumours. Surgery is usually curative, given the delay with which metastases occur. The feminisation syndrome and bone marrow aplasia observed with Sertoli cell tumours usually resolves within 2-3 weeks.

Testicular neoplasia. Case 1 / Sertoli cell tumour

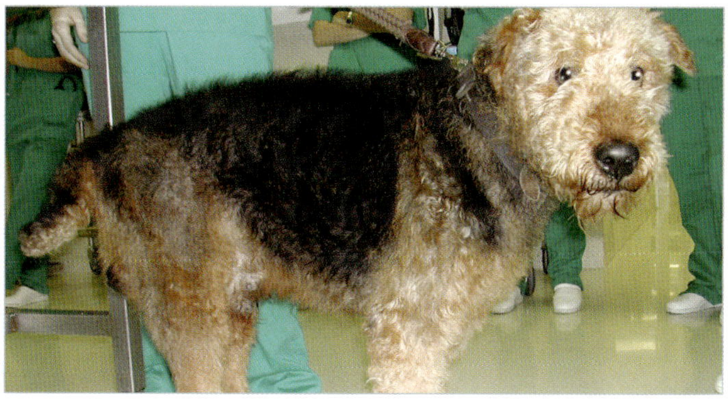

Fig. 1. "Anso" on the day of initial consultation at the hospital. The alopecia is noticeable.

Technical difficulty

A 12-year-old male Airedale Terrier is presented for examination of an enlarged testis. Loss of hair and hyperpigmentation, compatible with feminisation syndrome is observed (fig. 1).

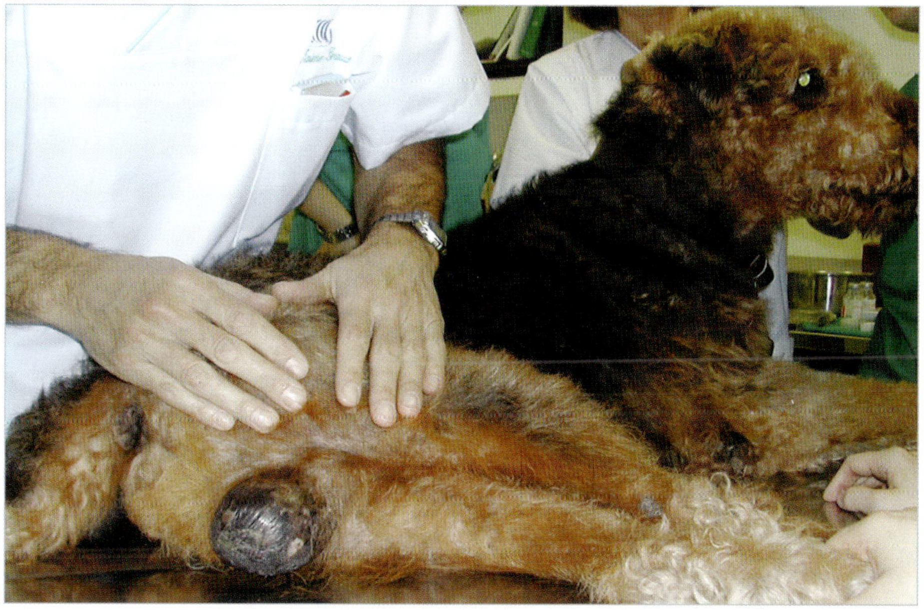

At examination, both testes are palpated in the scrotum. The right testis is hypertrophic, while the left is atrophied (fig. 2). Additionally, signs of feminisation, such as gynaecomastia and hypertrophy of the nipples are noted (fig. 3). A fine needle aspirate is taken from the mammary gland. Cytology is consistent with a mammary adenocarcinoma. In view of the clinical signs, a Sertoli cell tumour is suspected, in spite of its scrotal location, which is uncommon for this type of tumour.

Fig. 2. The owner noted an increase in testicular size. Palpation of the scrotal area revealed that this was due to enlargement of the right testis.

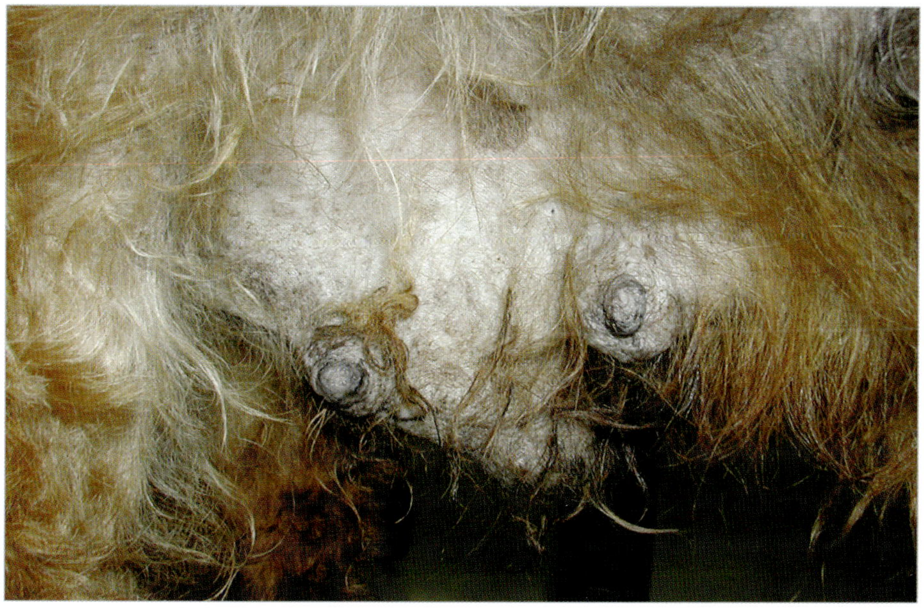

Fig. 3. Close-up of the mammary glands during the examination.

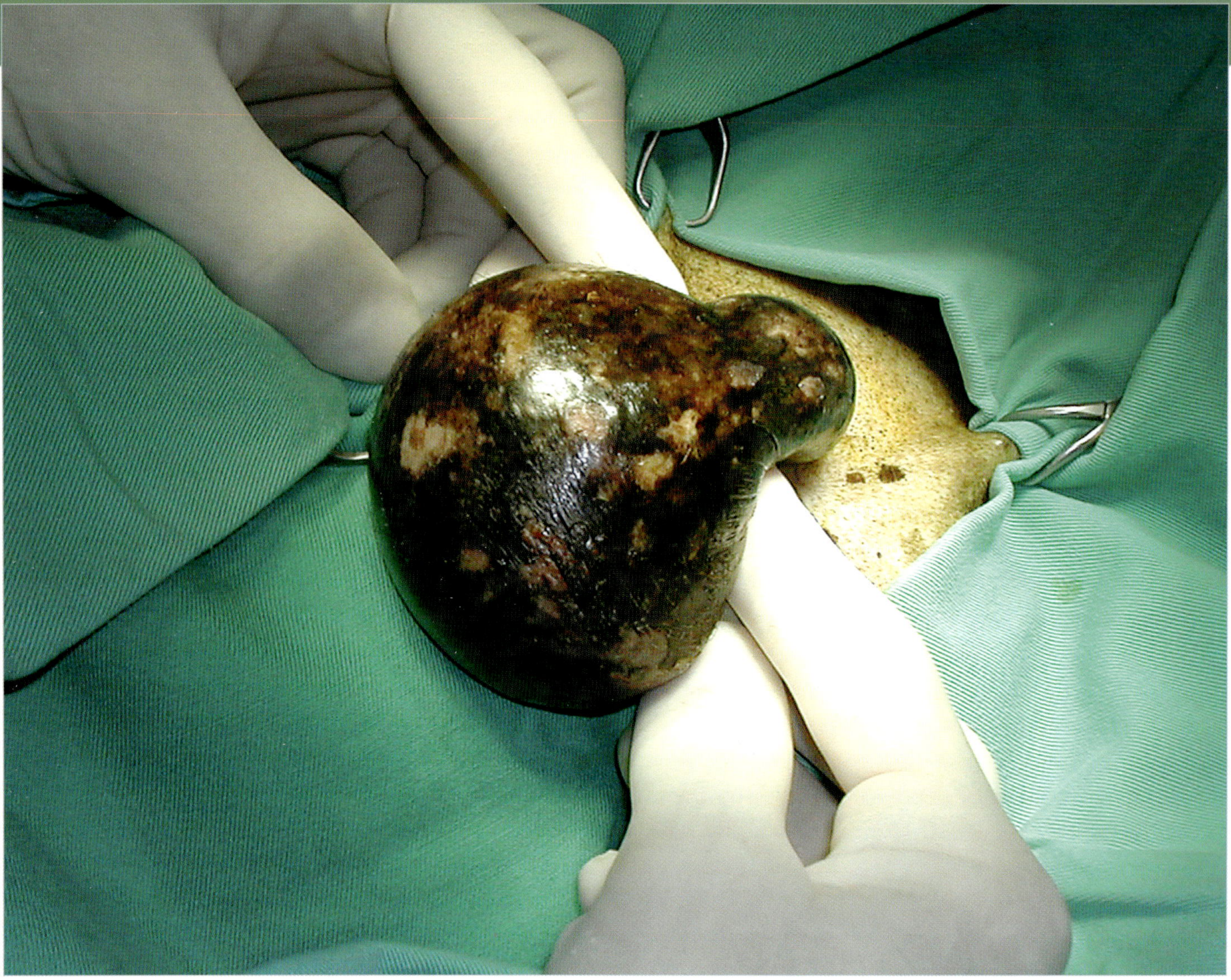

Fig. 4. In this case, the patient is prepared for scrotal castration as it is possible that there are adhesions between the neoplastic testis and the scrotum. In addition, it may be difficult to move a hypertrophic testis into the prescrotal area. Note the size difference between the neoplastic and the atrophied testis.

Whatever the cause of testicular disease, inflammatory, infectious or neoplastic, castration is always recommended.

See castration ➔ *page 264*

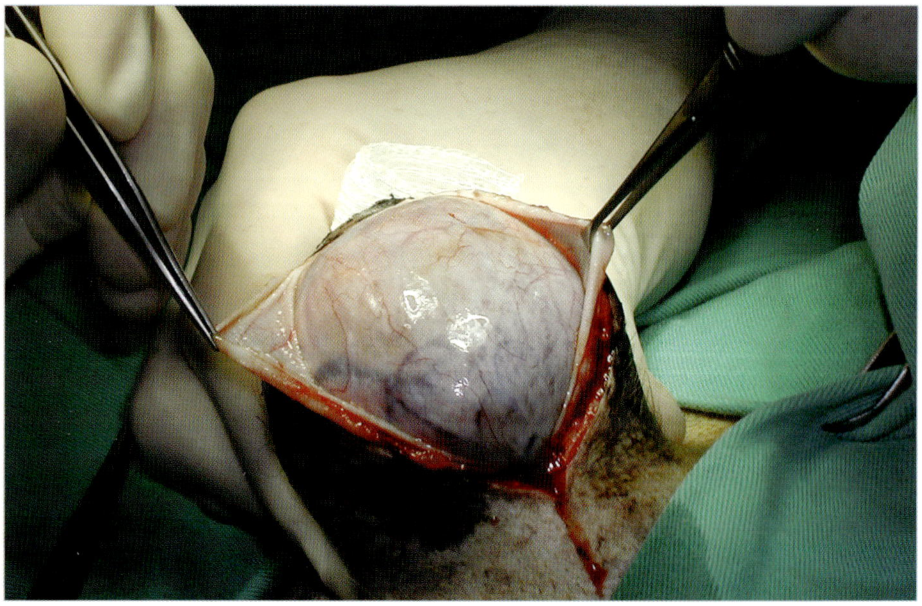

Fig. 5. The removal of both testes is achieved through a single skin incision at the base of the scrotum. For the rest, the surgical technique is identical to pre-scrotal castration as described. In the photograph, all layers of the scrotum have been incised to expose the neoplastic testis.

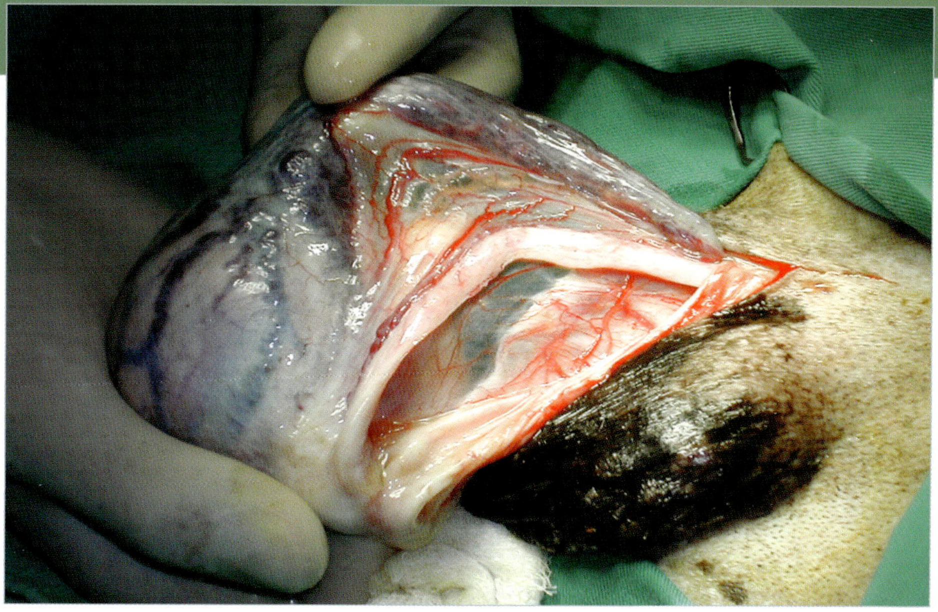

Fig. 6. View of the pampiniform plexus, vas deferens with its blood supply and the cremaster muscle.

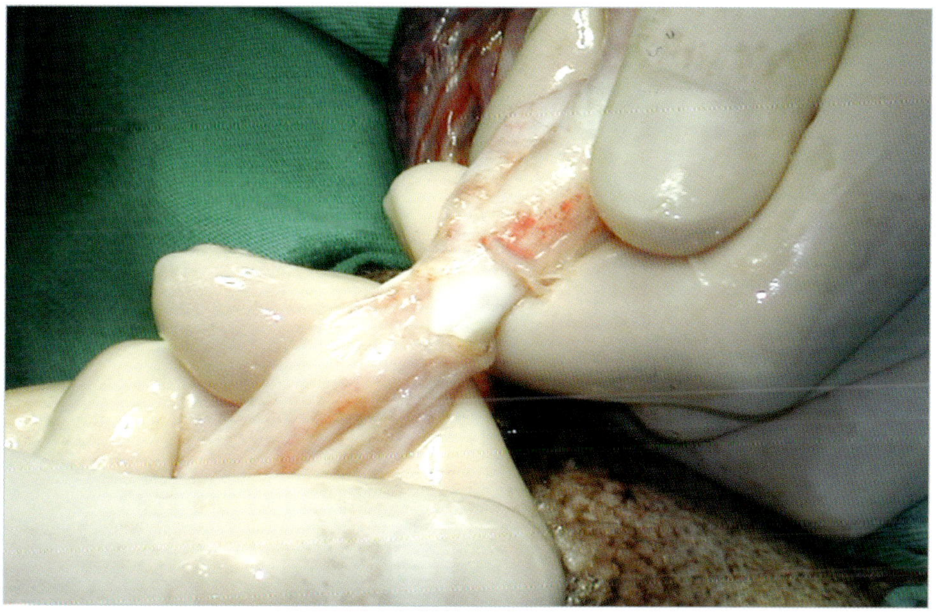

Fig. 7. Separation of the cremaster muscle and the vaginal tunic from the caudal testicular pole.

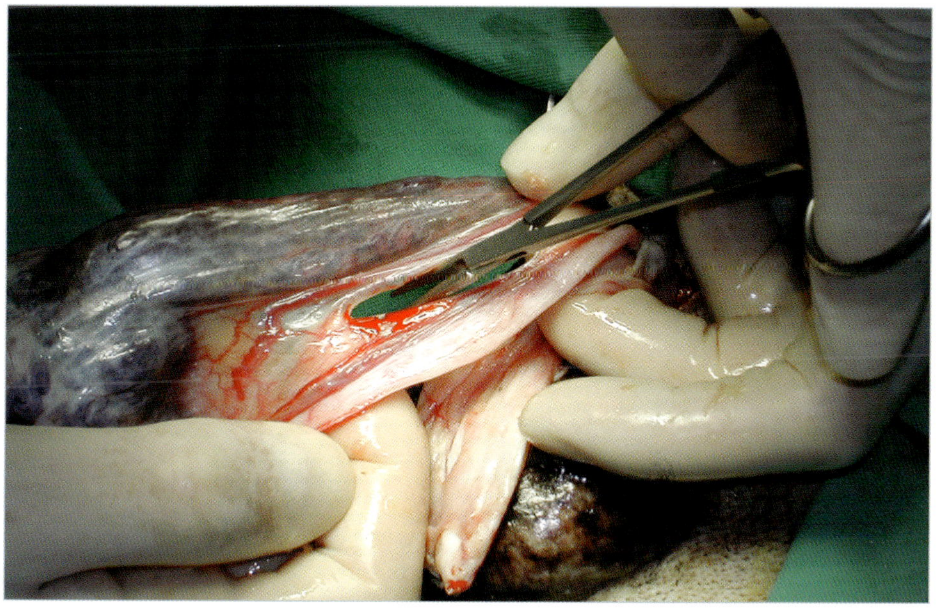

Fig. 8. Creation of an opening between the pampiniform plexus and the vas deferens, using mosquito forceps, for the placement of separate ligatures.

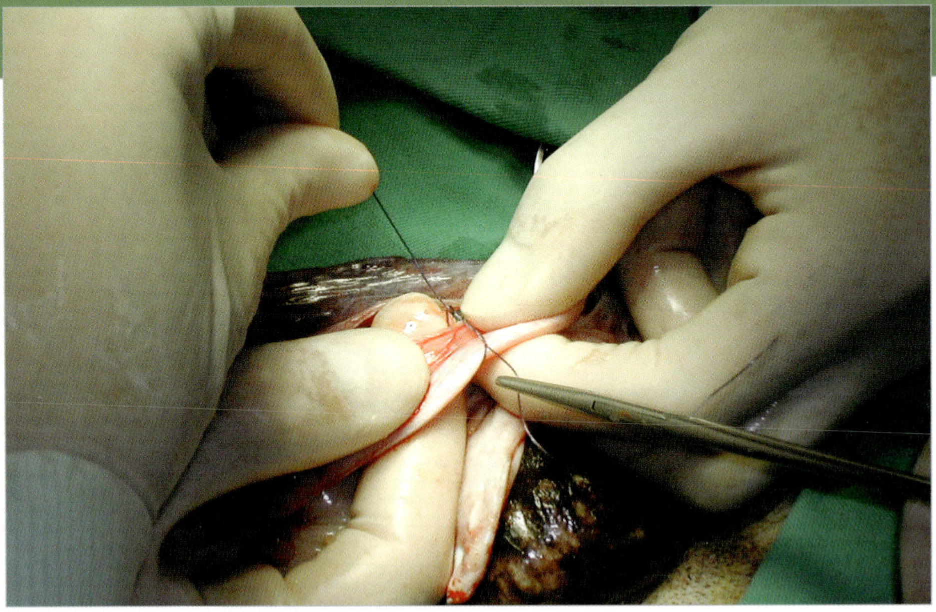

Fig. 9. Ligation of the vas deferens and its blood supply with absorbable material.

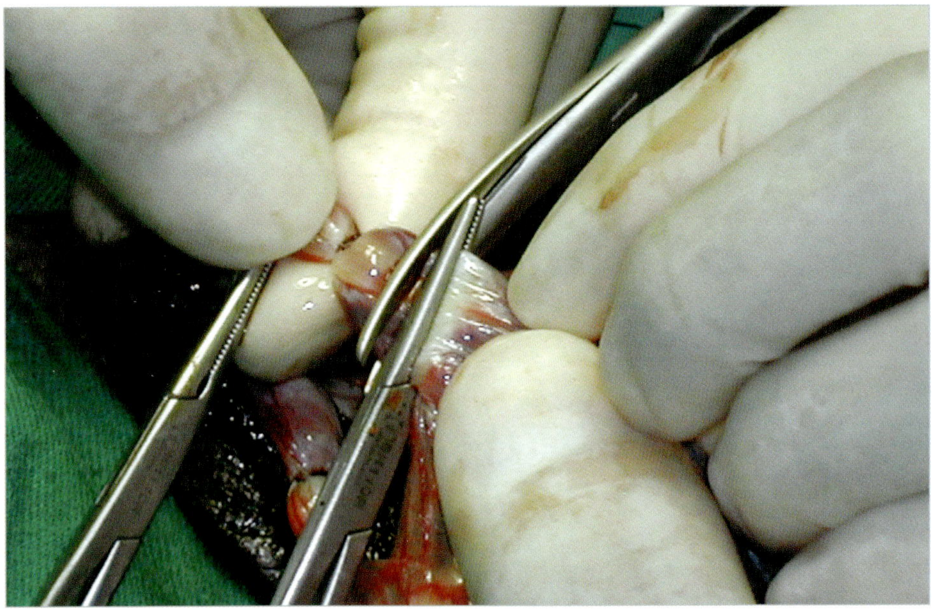

Fig. 10. Ligation of the pampiniform plexus with the same material, sectioning of the ligated structures and placement of a clamp at the proximal end of the testis to prevent bleeding when cutting.

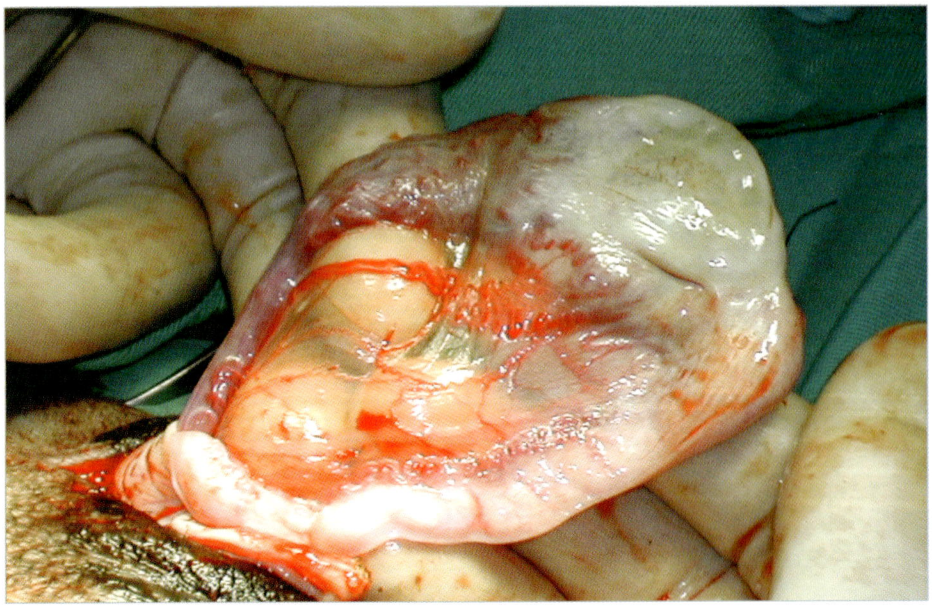

Fig. 11. Removal of the atrophied testis through the same incision as the neoplastic testis.

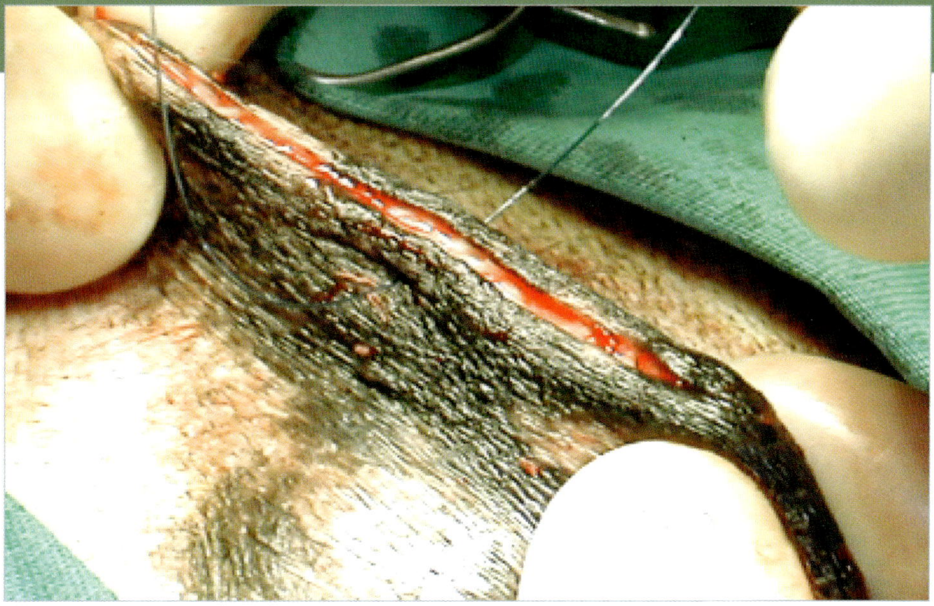

Fig. 12. Suturing the skin incision with non-absorbable material (nylon) using simple interrupted sutures.

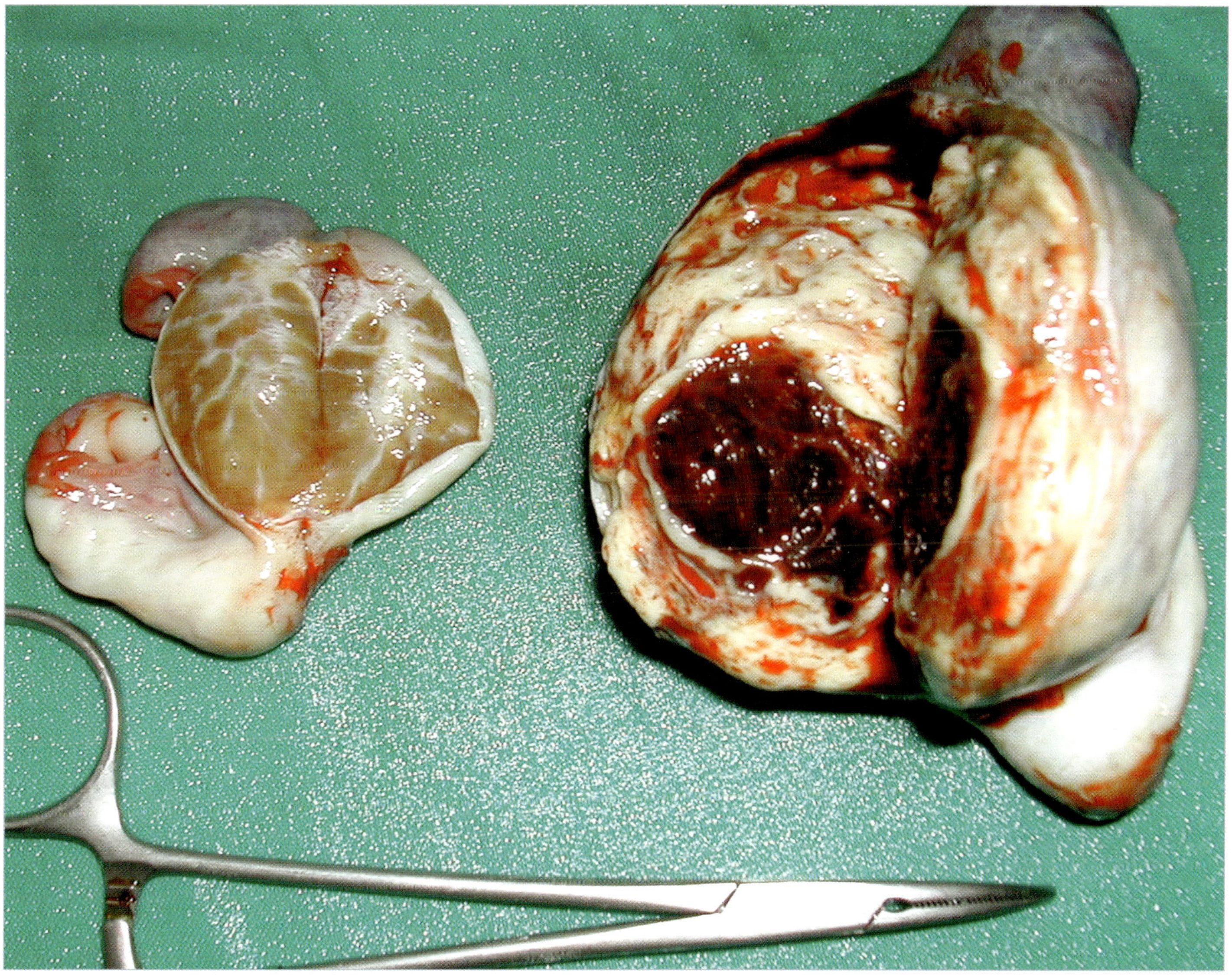

Fig. 13. The removed testes. On the right, the neoplastic testis. Histopathology confirmed the suspicion of a Sertoli cell tumour.

Testicular neoplasia. Case 2 / Seminoma and perianal adenomas

Technical difficulty

An 11-year-old male Fox Terrier is presented with a bleeding tumour in the perianal area. Results of the cytological examination of the mass are compatible with an adenoma. Considering the hormone dependency of perianal adenomas, the decision is made to remove the tumour and castrate the dog at the same time (figs. 1 and 2).

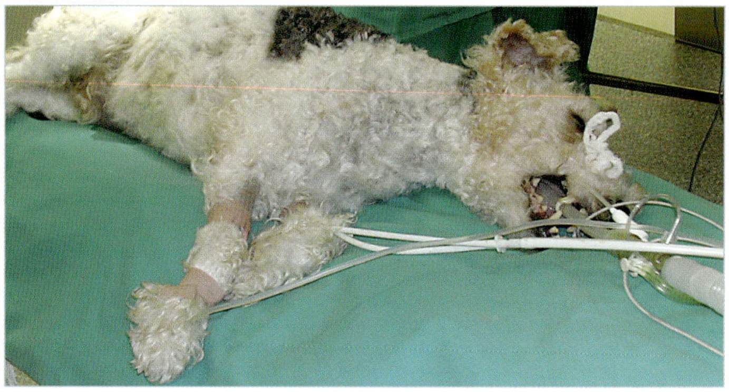

Fig. 1. "Rex" under anaesthesia for the double procedure.

Perianal adenomas appear almost exclusively in entire males, as their development testosterone dependent.
For this reason, castration is a mandatory part of treatment to reduce the risk of new tumours.

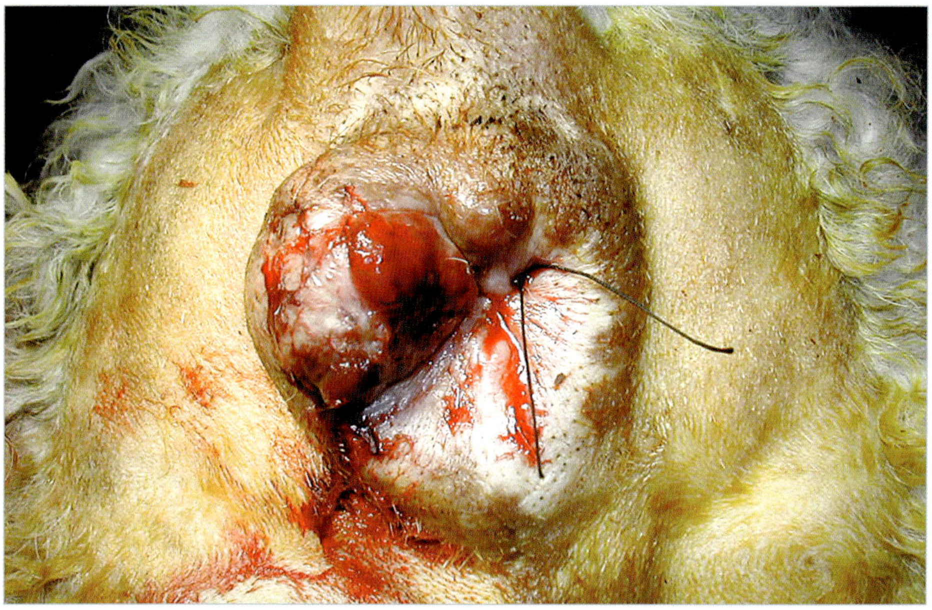

Fig. 2. View of the perianal tumour before surgery. A purse string suture has been placed around the anus.

See purse string suture → *page 252*

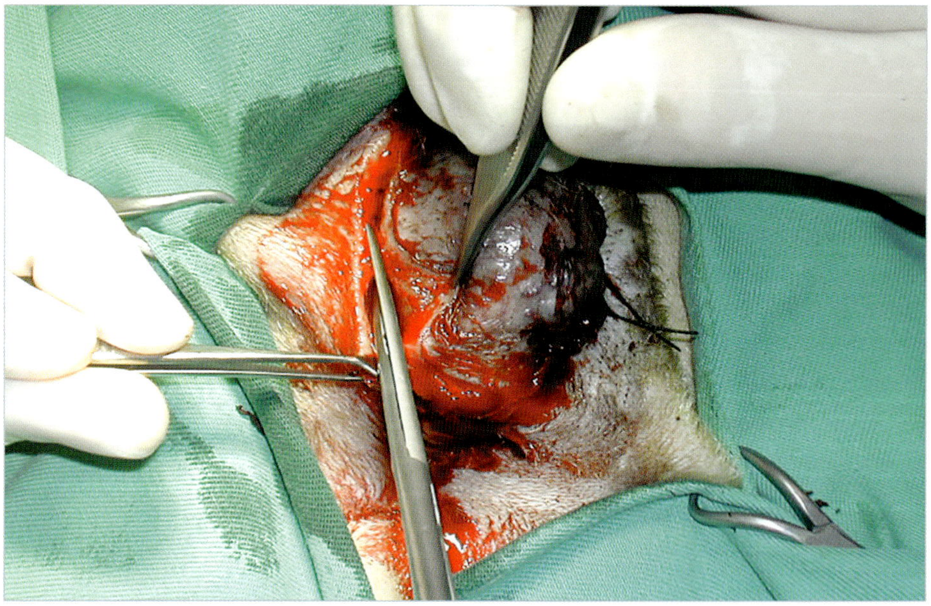

Fig. 3. The perianal tumour is removed by blunt dissection.

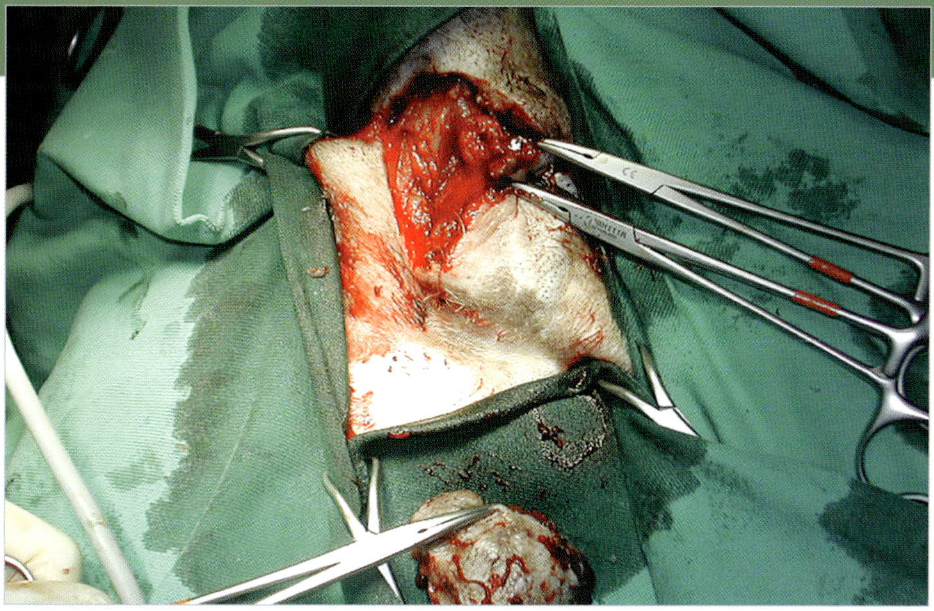

Fig. 4. Once the tumour has been removed and bleeding is under control, the surgical wound is closed.

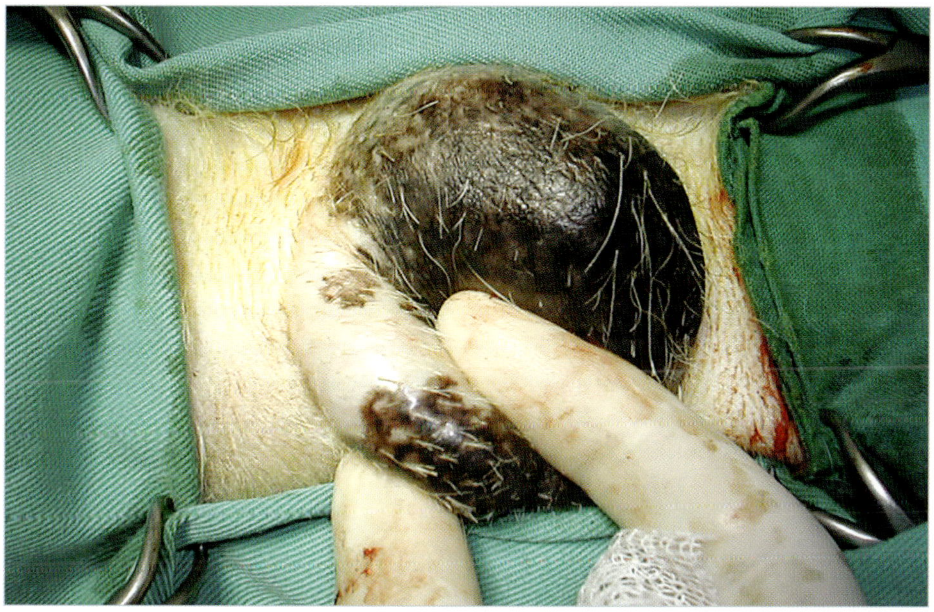

Fig. 5. View of the testes. Note the great difference in size, which suggests this is a hormone-producing testicular tumour. The atrophy of the other testis results from pituitary FSH inhibition caused by the high levels of hormones produced by the neoplastic testis.

See castration page 264

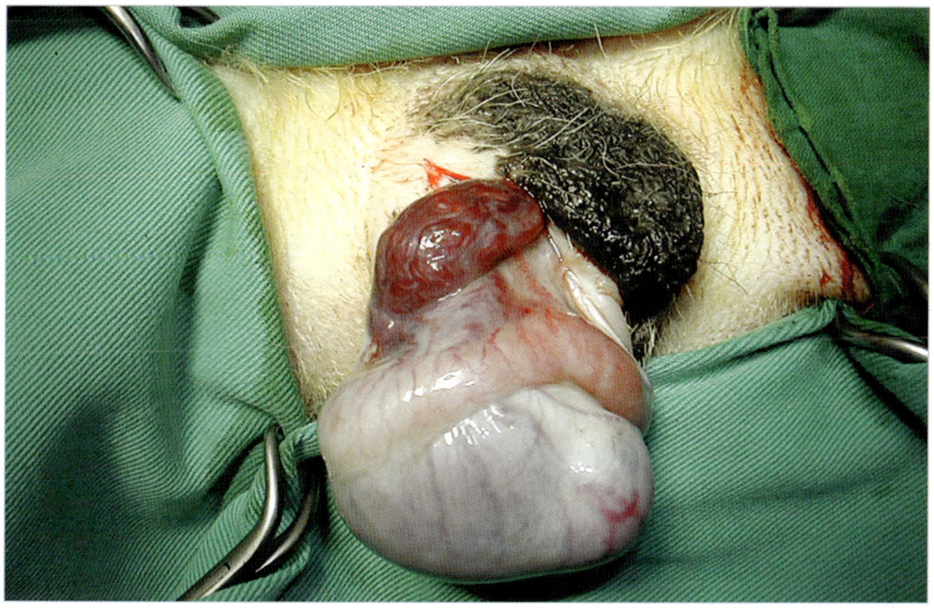

Fig. 6. Surgical detail of the removal of the hypertrophic testis.

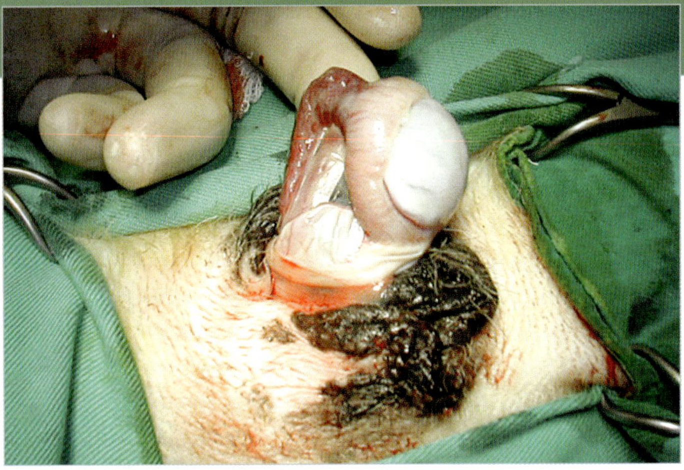

Fig. 7. Removal of the atrophied testis.

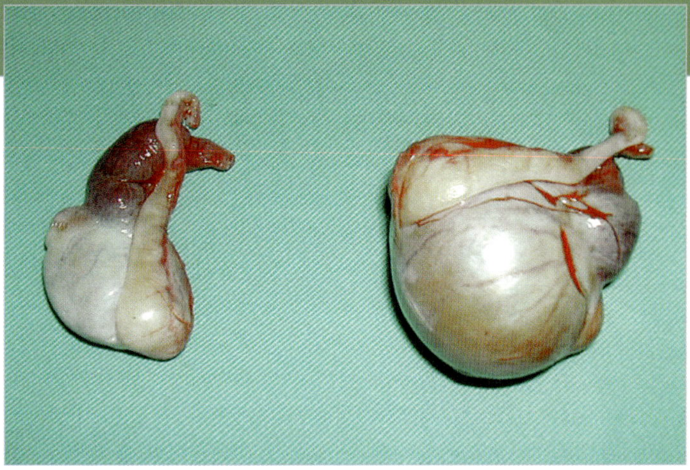

Fig. 8. Testes after removal. Note the difference in size and structure.

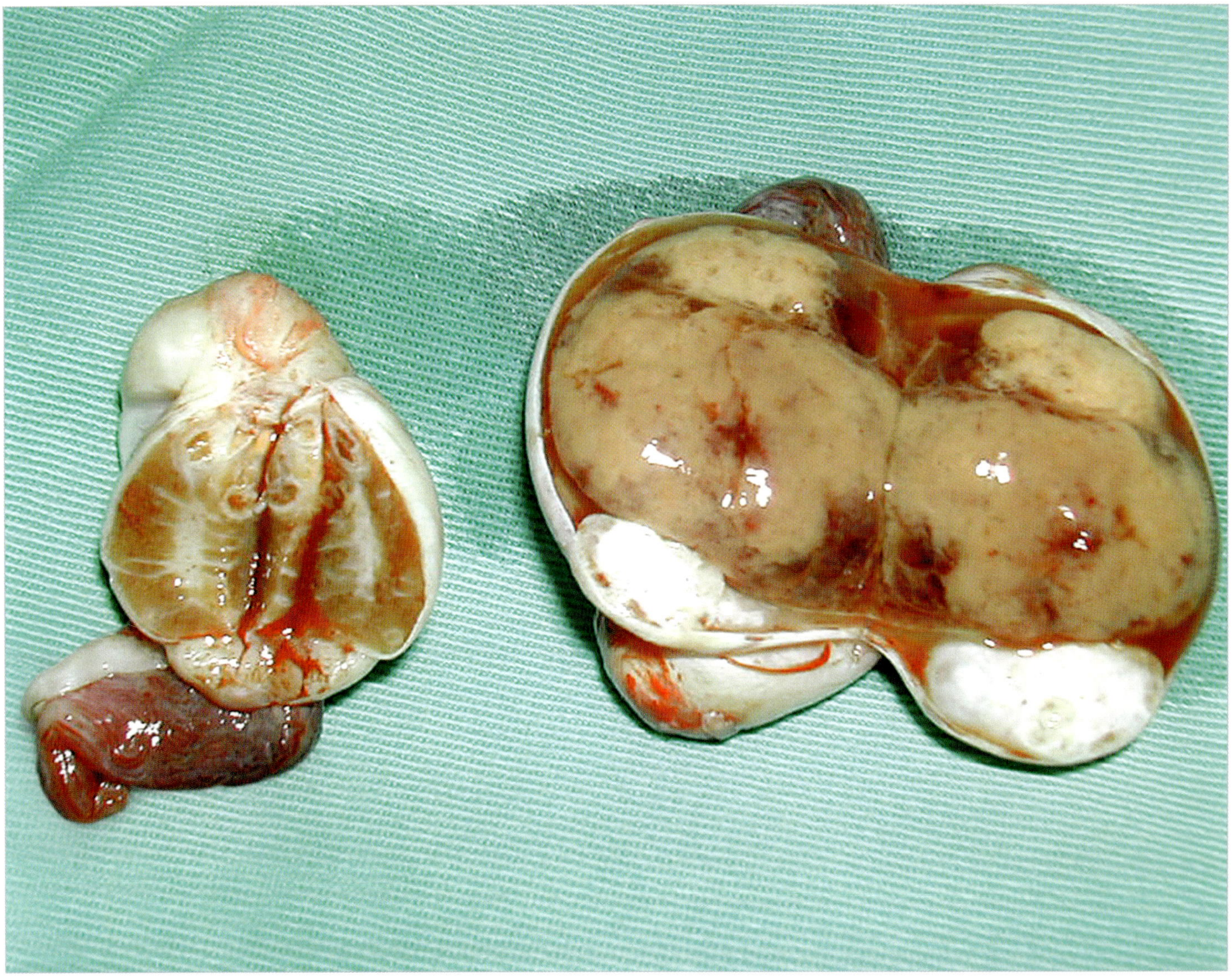

Fig. 9. Histopathology confirmed that the enlarged testis was neoplastic. It was a hormone-producing seminoma, quite rare among testicular tumours. Examination of the perianal tumour confirmed it was an adenoma.

Testicular neoplasia. Case 3 / Sertoli cell tumour and prostatic cysts

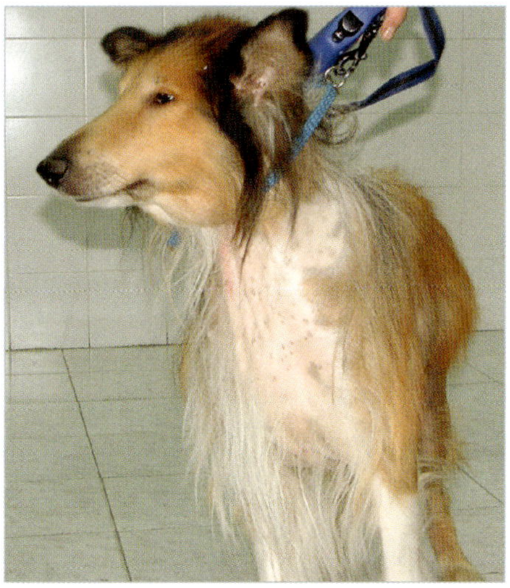

Fig. 1. "Brandy" on the first day of consultation, presenting with severe alopecia.

A 6-year-old male Collie is presented with alopecia of 6 months' duration. The owner reports that other male dogs have tried to mount it.

During examination, symmetrical alopecia of the trunk is observed. Other clinical signs include hyperpigmentation and gynaecomastia. On palpation, a large abdominal mass is found. Examination of the scrotum reveals unilateral cryptorchidism and an atrophied scrotal testis. Based on all these signs, the presence of a Sertoli cell tumour in the abdominal testis is suspected (figs. 1-4).

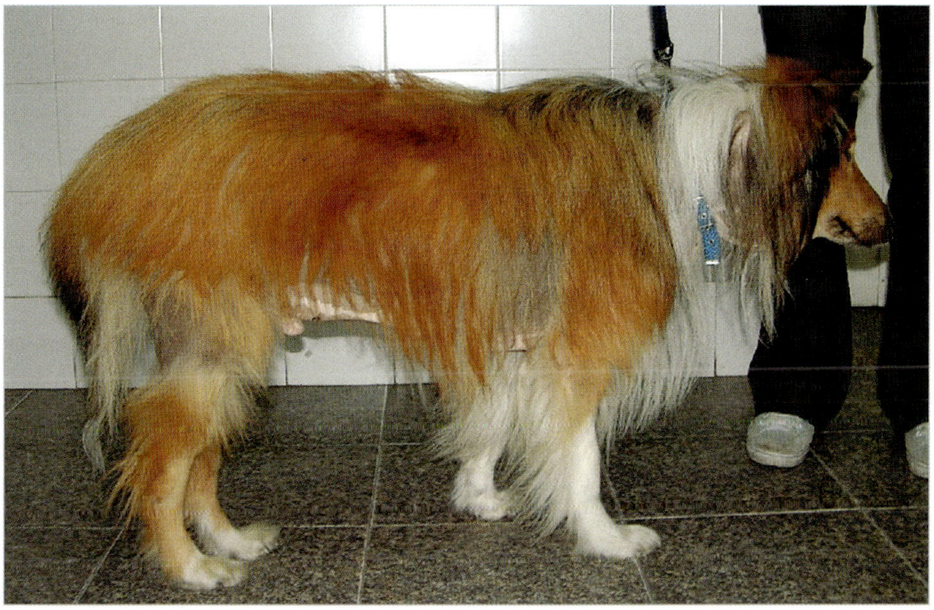

In a case of alopecia in a cryptorchid dog, a Sertoli cell tumour should be considered as the most likely diagnosis.

Fig. 2. Hyperpigmentation of the alopecic areas on the trunk is noted.

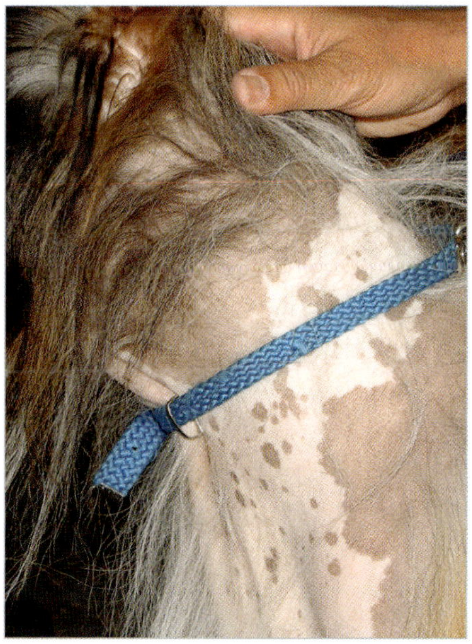

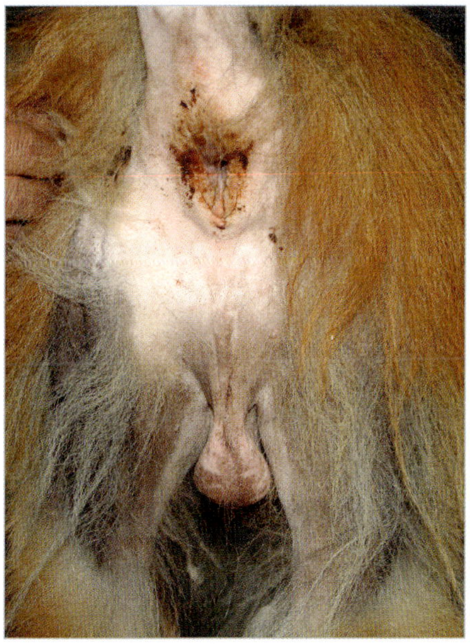

Fig. 3. Hair loss extends to the neck of the patient.

Fig. 4. Note the alopecia, hyperpigmentation in the perineal area and the presence of a single scrotal testis.

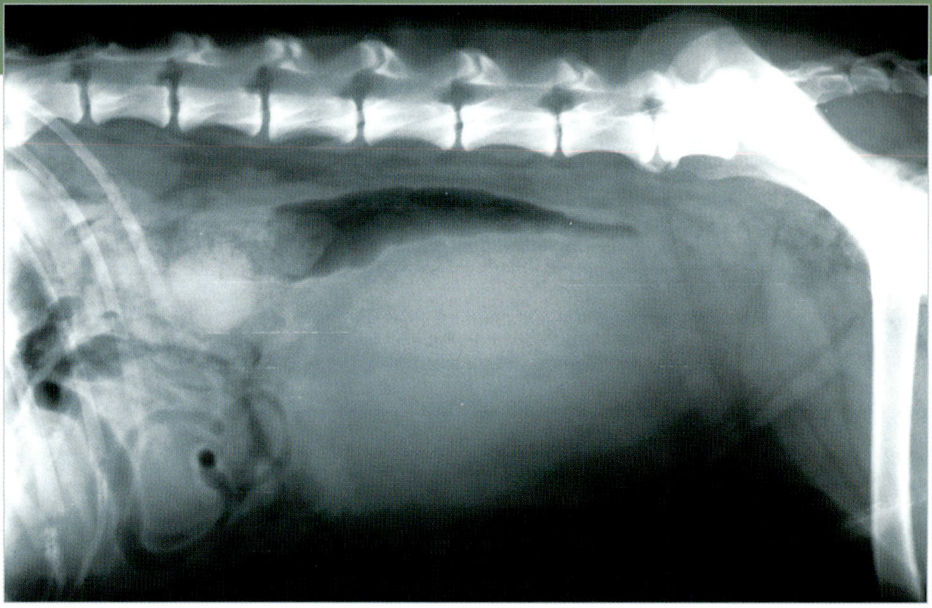

Fig. 5. To confirm the diagnosis, a plain radiograph is taken, and reveals a large abdominal mass. This suggests a testicular tumour, but differential diagnoses include the bladder, a hypertrophic prostate or a paraprostatic cyst.

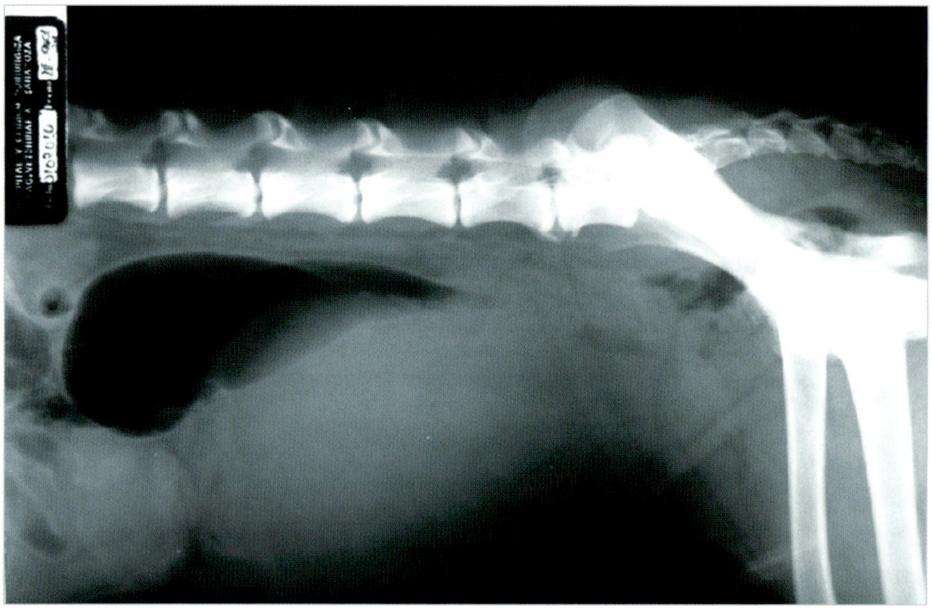

Fig. 6. To identify the bladder, a pneumocystogram is done, demonstrating a dorsally displaced bladder. Ventrally, the mass can still be seen, and cranial to this, another smaller, rounded mass is also visible. The bladder has been excluded as part of the mass.

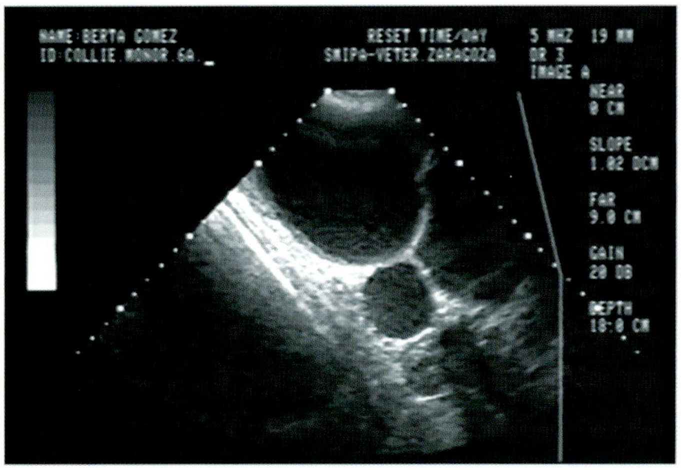

Fig. 7. Ultrasound examination identifies the large mass as a partitioned, liquid-filled cavity. This could correspond to a paraprostatic cyst.

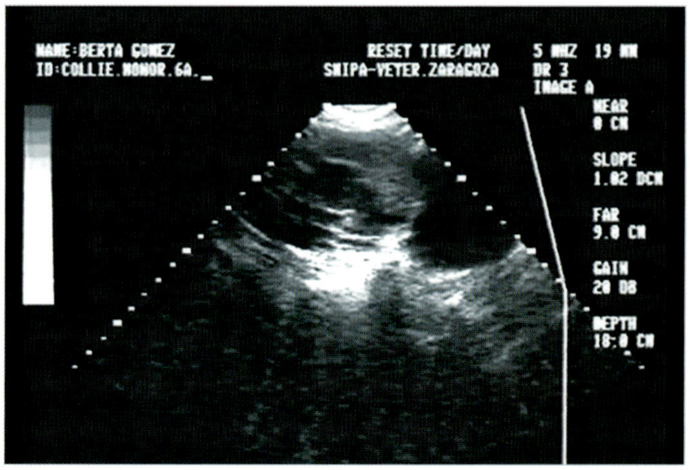

Fig. 8. The smaller, cranial mass is hyperechogenic, and is likely to be a testicular tumour. One of the consequences of oestrogen production by a Sertoli cell tumour is the development of prostatic and paraprostatic cysts.

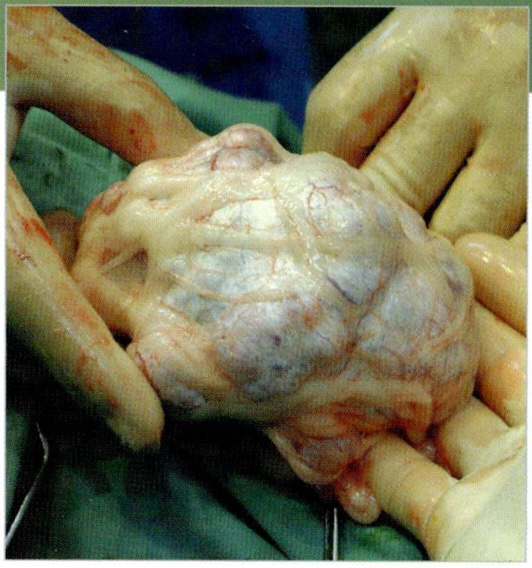

Fig. 9. An exploratory laparotomy is performed. A cryptorchid testis with the typical appearance of a Sertoli cell tumour: large, lobular and firm to the touch, is found. Its location and size correspond to the cranial mass found on the X-ray.

See infraumbilical laparotomy page 282

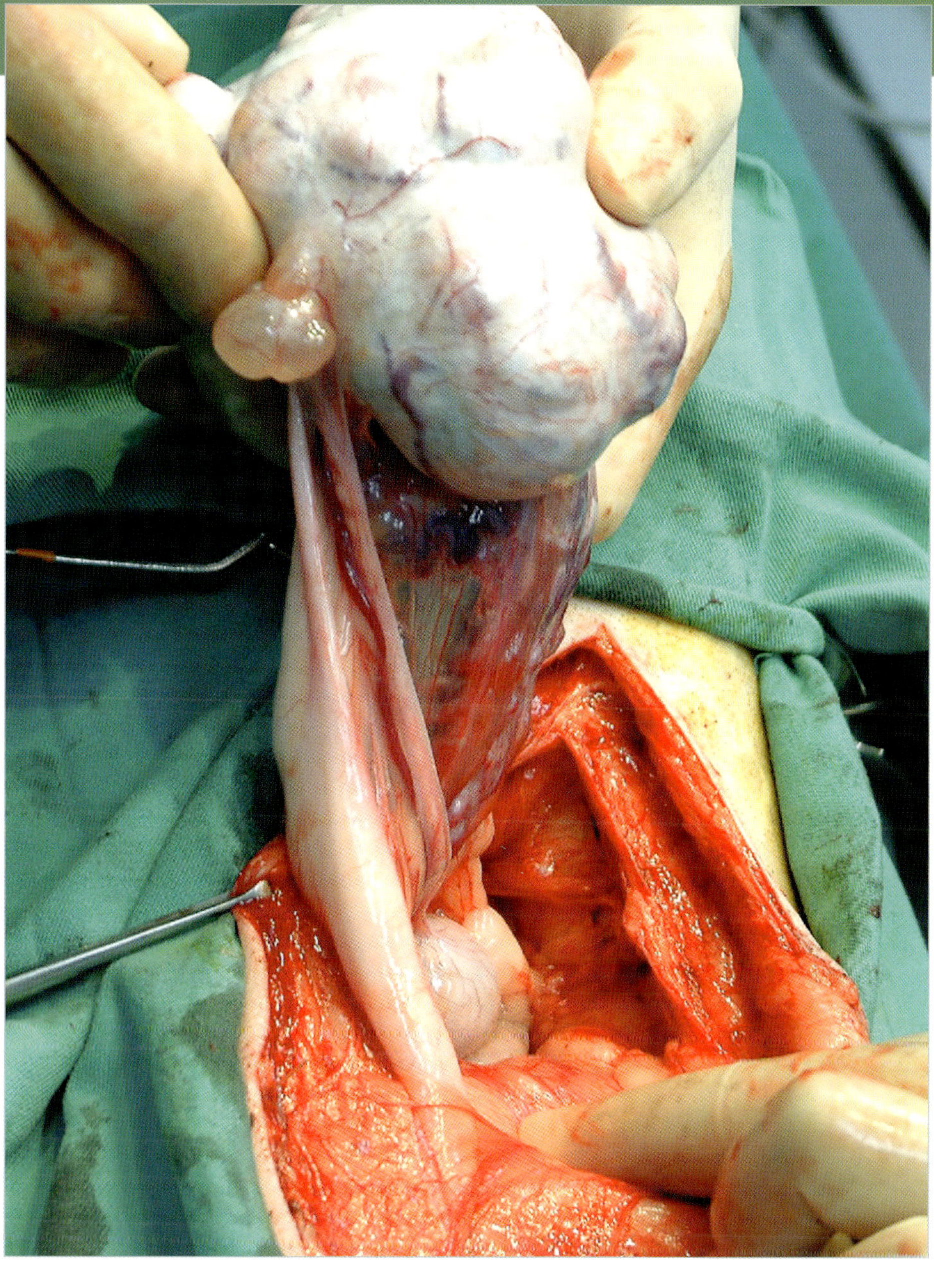

Fig. 10. The cryptorchid testis is removed along with cysts in the vas deferens.

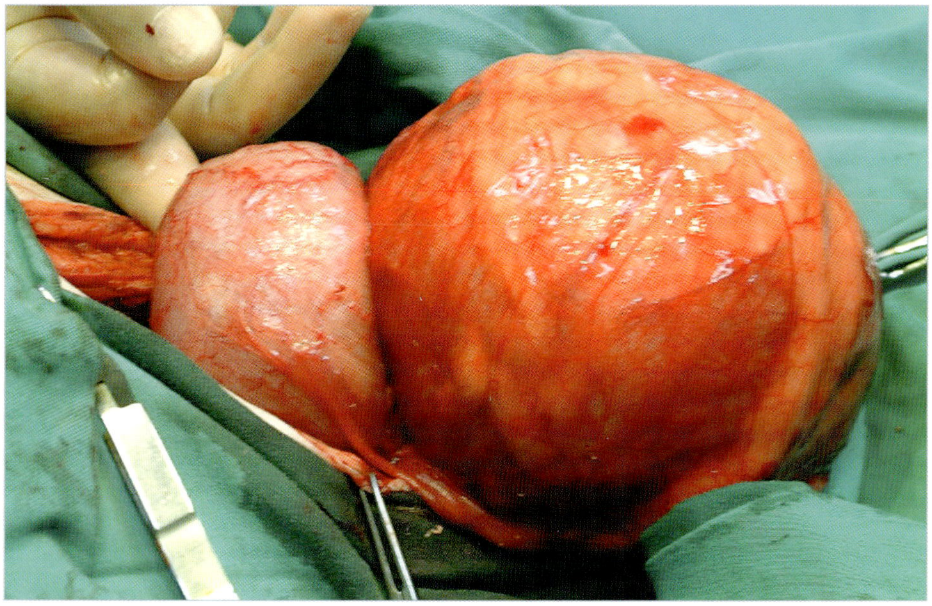

Fig. 11. The larger caudal mass identified by X-ray turned out to be a paraprostatic cyst adjacent to the bladder (right). Surgical removal is followed by marsupialisation of its attachment to the prostate.

When removing an intra-abdominal Sertoli cell tumour, always check the prostate to rule out possible cysts or abscesses.

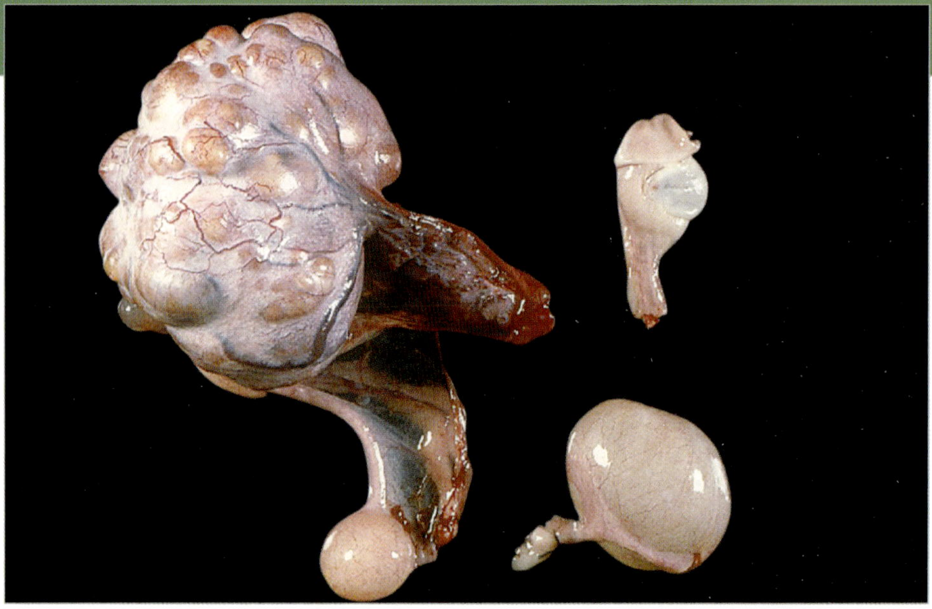

Fig. 12. The excised tissues: to the left, the neoplastic testis, to the upper right, the atrophied scrotal testis and below, the cysts in the vas deferens. Histopathology confirmed the diagnosis of a Sertoli cell tumour.

Photograph supplied by Dr. José Antonio García de Jalón Ciércoles, Professor of the Department of Animal Pathology at the Veterinary Faculty of Zaragoza.

Fig. 13. Four months after surgery. "Brandy" is looking well and has gained weight.

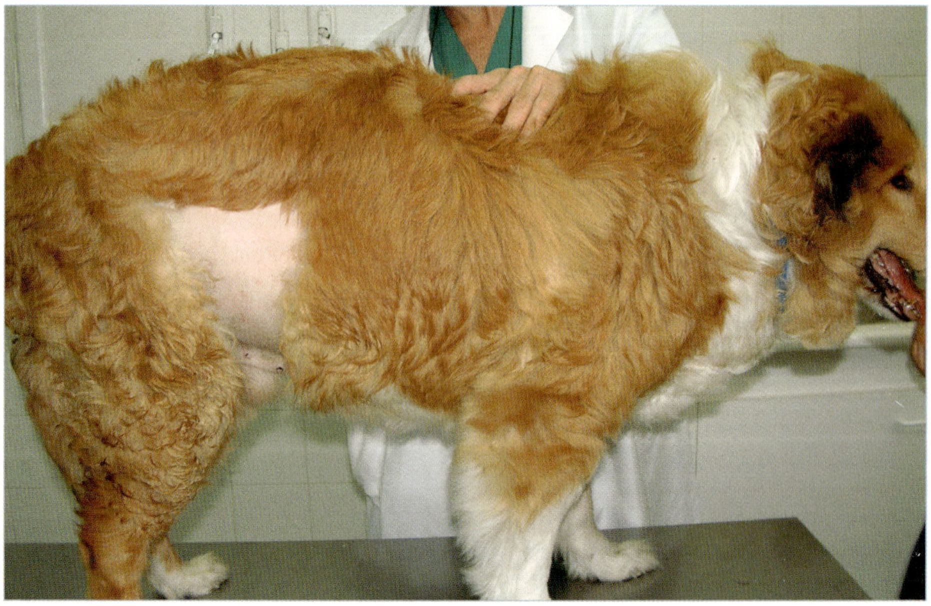

Fig. 14. Note the growth of the coat. The shaved area on the flank corresponds to the preparation of the patient for ultrasound examination of the prostate, which was normal.

Testicular neoplasia. Case 4 / Leydig cell tumour

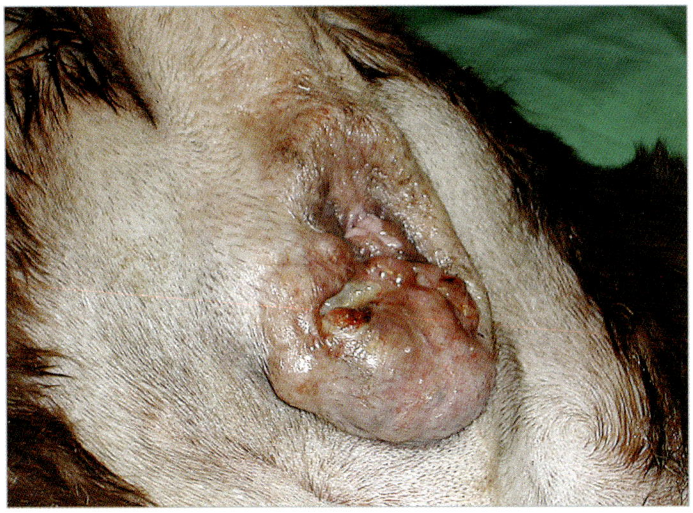

Technical difficulty	■■□□□

A 10-year-old, entire male mixed-breed dog was presented with a perianal tumour that had developed occasional bleeding over the past few months (fig.1).

Fig. 1. View of the perineum during surgical preparation, showing the perianal tumour.

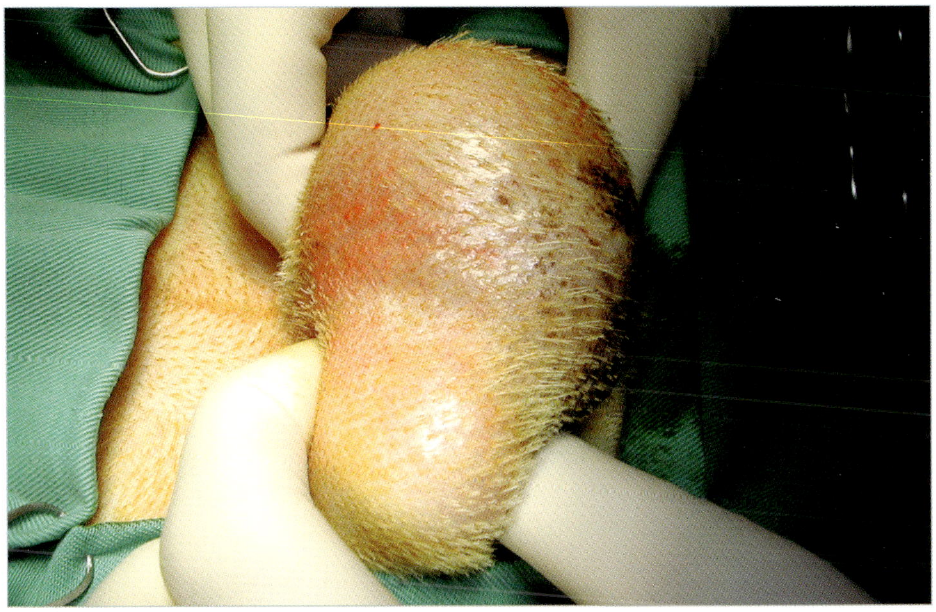

During examination, both testes are found in the scrotum, although a size difference between them is observed (fig. 2). This suggests the presence of a testicular tumour. Cytology of the perianal tumour shows that it is an adenoma. As this type of tumour depends on testicular androgens, it is decided to perform castration at the same time as the tumour removal.

Fig. 2. The presence of an enlarged testis and a perianal adenoma strongly suggests an interstitial or Leydig cell tumour. This is the most common scrotal testicular tumour and typical in older patients.

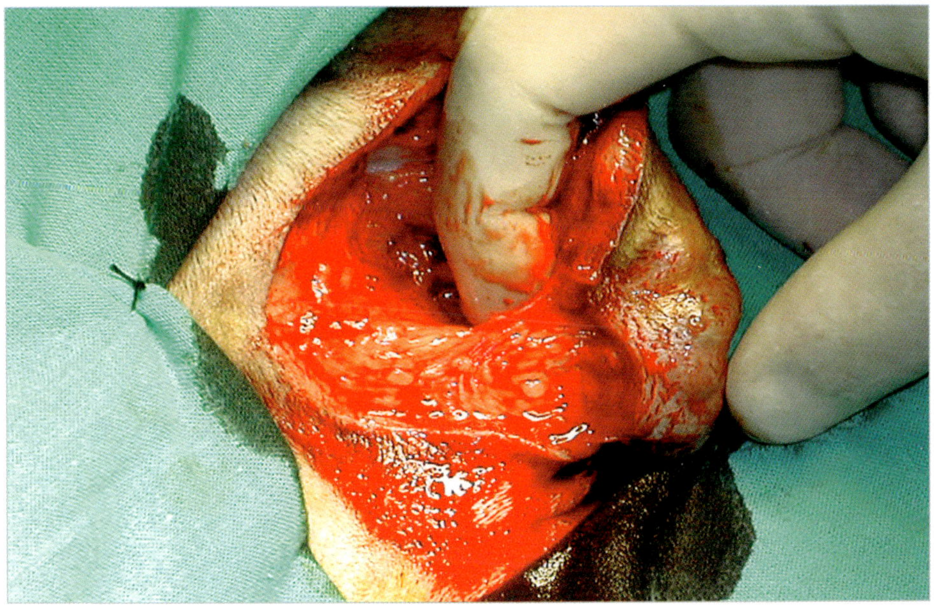

Fig. 3. The perianal tumour is bluntly dissected.

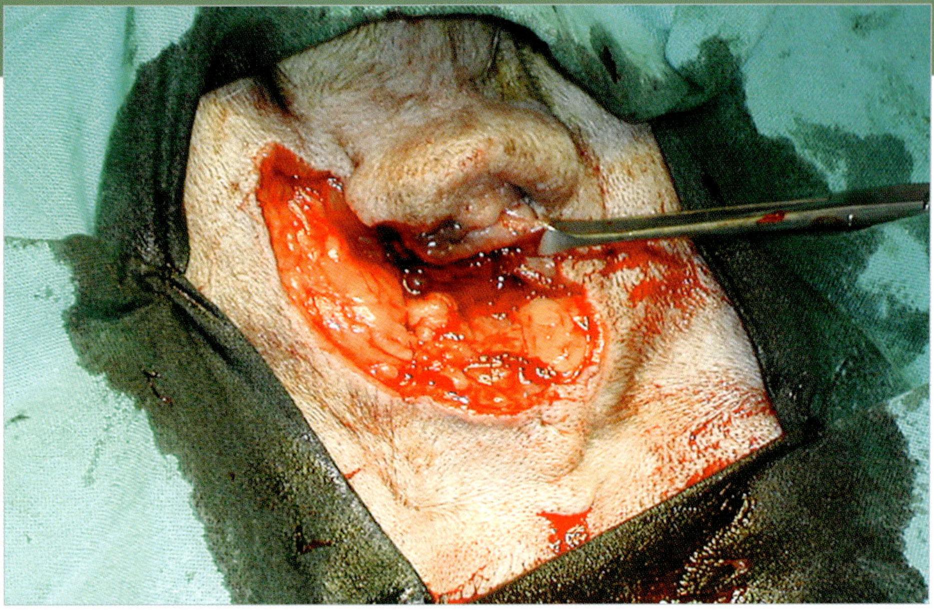

Fig. 4. View of the area after removal of the tumour, before closing the surgical wound.

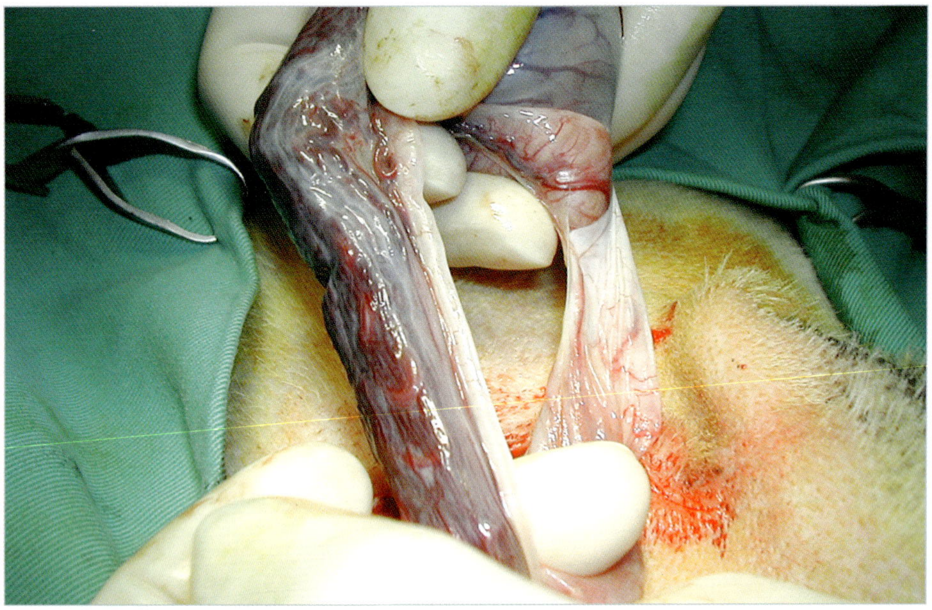

Fig. 5. Castration is performed in the usual manner, by identifying the structures of the spermatic cord and ligating them separately.

See prescrotal castration → page 265

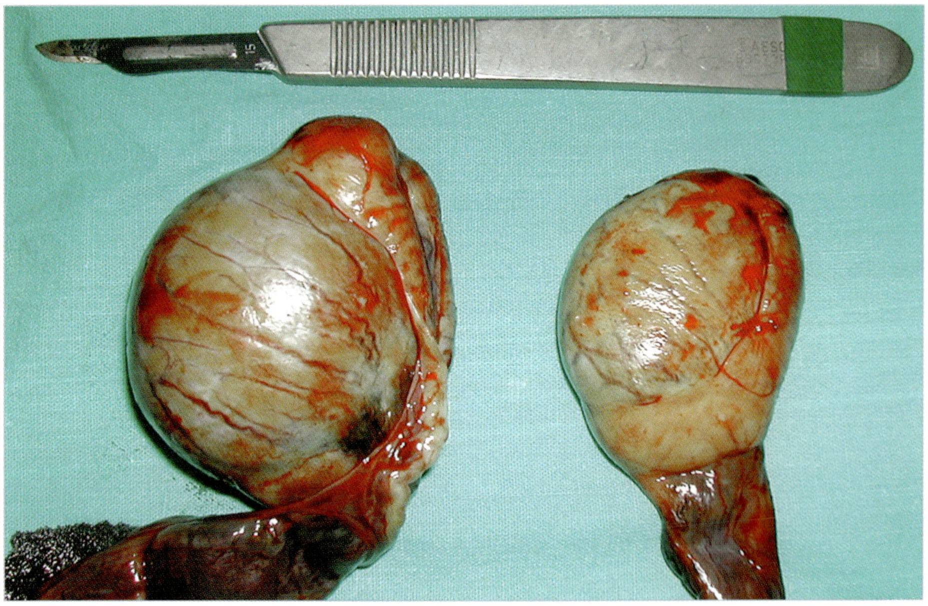

Fig. 6. View of the two testes. Note the difference in size.

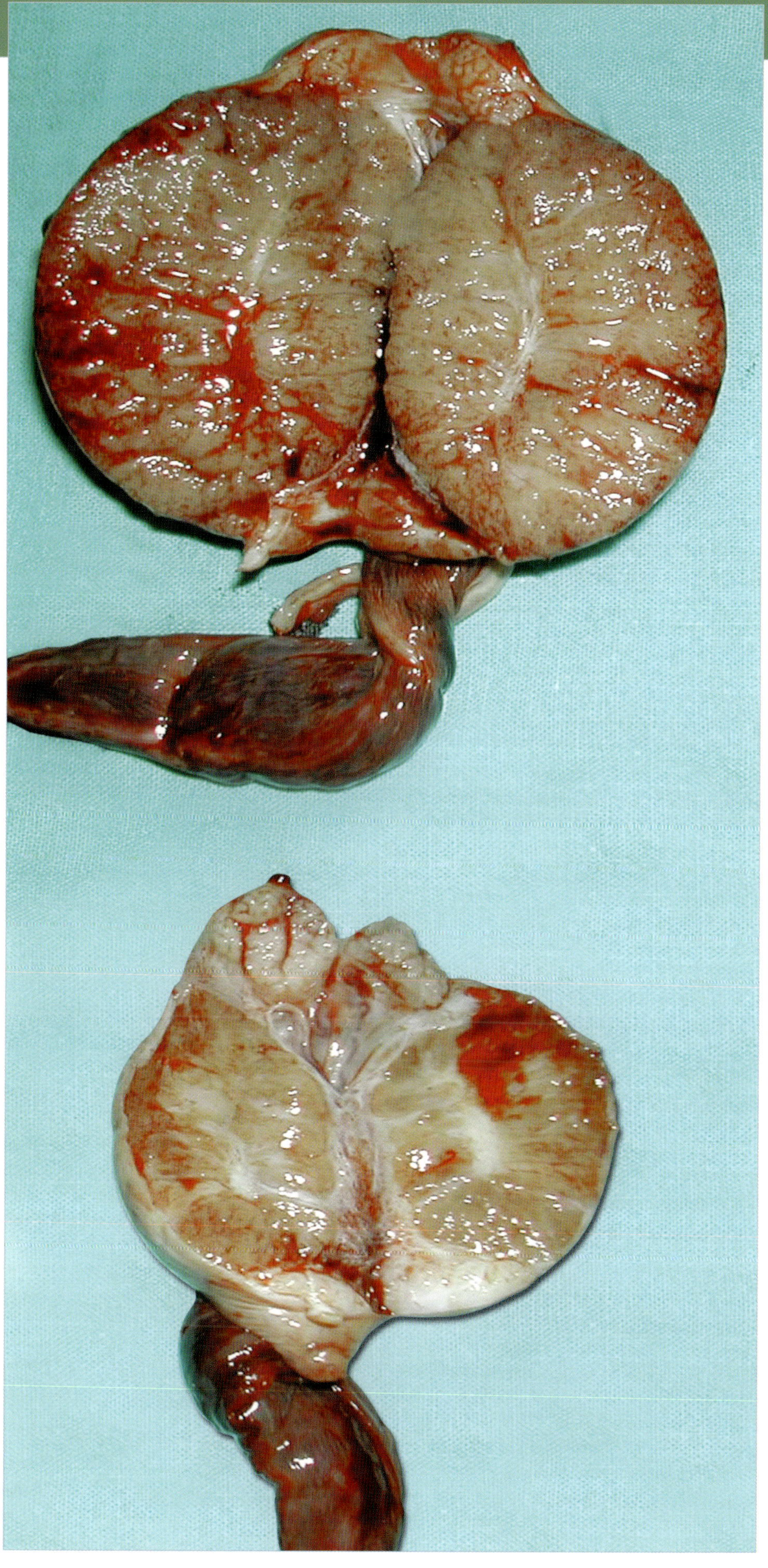

Perianal tumours are typically found in older dogs and most are hormone dependent, which is why castration should always be carried out. Leydig cell tumours often go unnoticed because their texture is similar to that of the testis itself and they do not protrude above the testicular surface.

Fig. 7. Histopathology confirmed a Leydig cell tumour.

Ectopic testes

Prevalence

The testis forms inside the abdominal cavity and descends to its definitive location in the scrotum shortly after birth, in both the dog and cat. Cryptorchidism is the consequence of a failure of the descent of one or both testes into the scrotum. Studies of incidence provide variable data, ranging from 1 to 10% in dogs, depending on the source.
Cryptorchidism is hereditary, even though its genetic basis is not very clear. The incidence varies by breed and is nearly three times more common in small breeds than medium-sized or large breeds. It is particularly common in Yorkshire Terriers and Miniature Schnauzers. Among the large breeds, the Boxer is most commonly affected.
A definitive diagnosis of cryptorchidism can be made from 3-6 months onwards, depending on the breed. In puppies, the small size of the testes makes palpation difficult, especially in obese animals or in those where the testes move freely between the scrotum and the inguinal canal. Furthermore, at this age, descent into the scrotum is still possible.
The ectopic testis can be in a prescrotal, inguinal or abdominal position. Statistically speaking, abdominal cryptorchidism is the most common, particularly unilateral cryptorchidism of the right testis. A complete diagnosis of ectopic testis should include its exact location. In cases of atrophy, this can be difficult. In general, the ectopic testis is smaller than the scrotal one, unless it is neoplastic or diseased. It is necessary to examine the scrotal area and the inguinal canal in detail. Intra-abdominal testes are rarely palpable. Abdominal ultrasound examination is helpful to confirm the presence of a testis in the abdomen.

Before deciding to carry out a laparotomy, make sure that the testis is not in the inguinal area. This requires careful examination.

The higher temperature to which the ectopic testes are exposed damages both germinal epithelial development and sperm cell production. Nevertheless, the interstitial cells are functional and androgen production nearly normal, maintaining secondary sexual characteristics, even in bilateral cryptorchidism cases.
Ectopic testes, in particular those in the abdomen, develop tumours and torsions much more often than scrotal testes. Torsion results from the increased mobility of the testis inside the abdomen. The risk of neoplasia is about twenty times higher than in scrotal testes. Also, neoplasia in cryptorchid testes appears at an earlier age. In cases of Sertoli cell tumours, feminisation signs are more common if the affected testis is ectopic.

Medical and surgical treatments that aim to move the ectopic testis into the scrotum do not give good results. This combined with a higher incidence of tumours and torsions, justifies preventive castration of the ectopic organ. Bilateral castration is also recommended to prevent genetic transmission of the defect.
Prescrotal and inguinal testes are removed by making an incision directly over their location. In case of an abdominal testis, an infraumbilical laparotomy is needed to locate it. This is not always easy. If the testis has atrophied, certain anatomical landmarks can be used to locate it. The simplest is to follow the vas deferens from the prostate to the testis. In most cases, the abdominal testis is found next to the bladder.

By lifting up the bladder, the vasa deferentia will become visible.
The one belonging to the scrotal testis leads to the internal inguinal canal, while the other leads to the cryptorchid testis.

If a tumour is suspected, histopathology of the testes is recommended. This also indicates the prognosis. Nevertheless, in view of the low malignancy of testicular tumours, the prognosis for the cryptorchid patient after surgery is good, even if the testis turns out to be neoplastic.

Ectopic testes. Case 1 / Abdominal monorchid

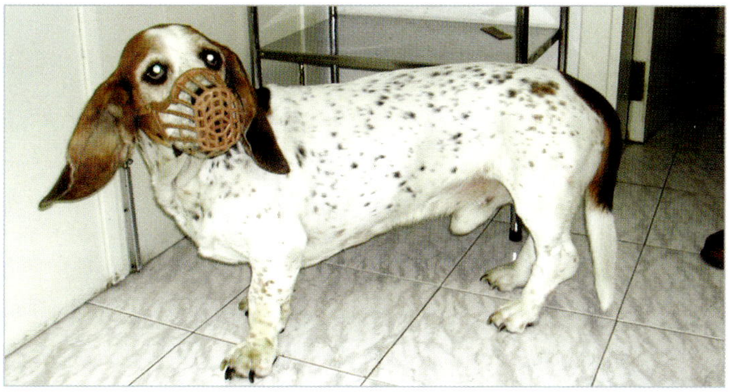

Fig. 1. "Rayo" on the day of arrival at the hospital. The abdominal pain has made him a little aggressive and it was necessary to muzzle him during examination.

A 6-year-old male Basset Hound is presented (fig. 1) with recurrent abdominal pain. Upon examination, only one testis is found in the scrotum.

A lateral abdominal radiograph is taken which shows a mandarin-sized mass in the caudal abdomen. The mass is easily palpable and could be compatible, in view of its size, with a neoplastic intra-abdominal testis. It is therefore decided to perform a laparotomy (fig. 2). Ultrasound examination of the area permits measurement of the mass, and reveals an image compatible with a testicular Sertoli cell tumour (fig. 3).

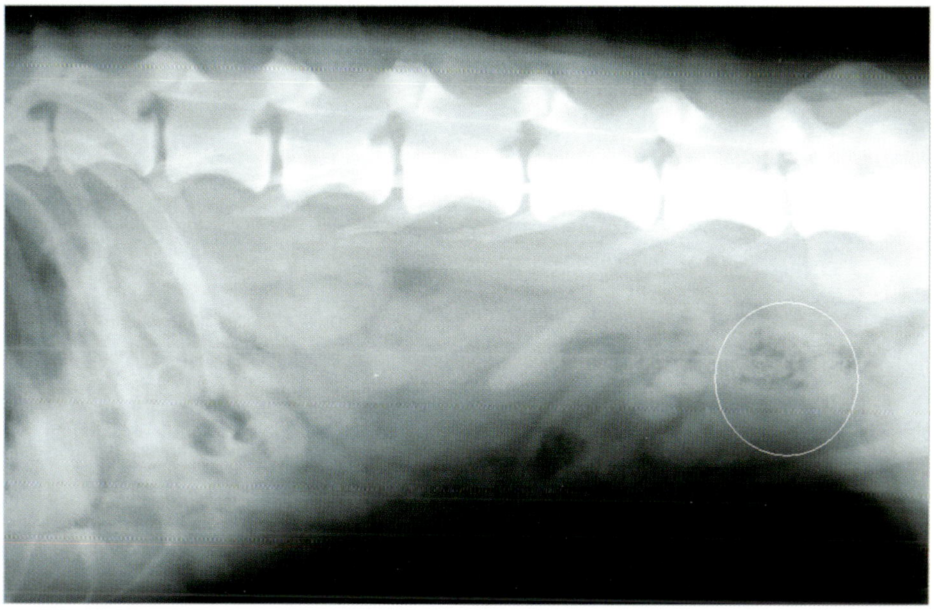

In cryptorchid patients, signs of intermittent abdominal pain can be due to reversible testicular torsions. Given the high probability that the patient will develop an acute abdomen, castration is recommended as soon as possible.

Fig. 2. Abdominal radiograph of the patient that suggests the presence of a cryptorchid, neoplastic testis.

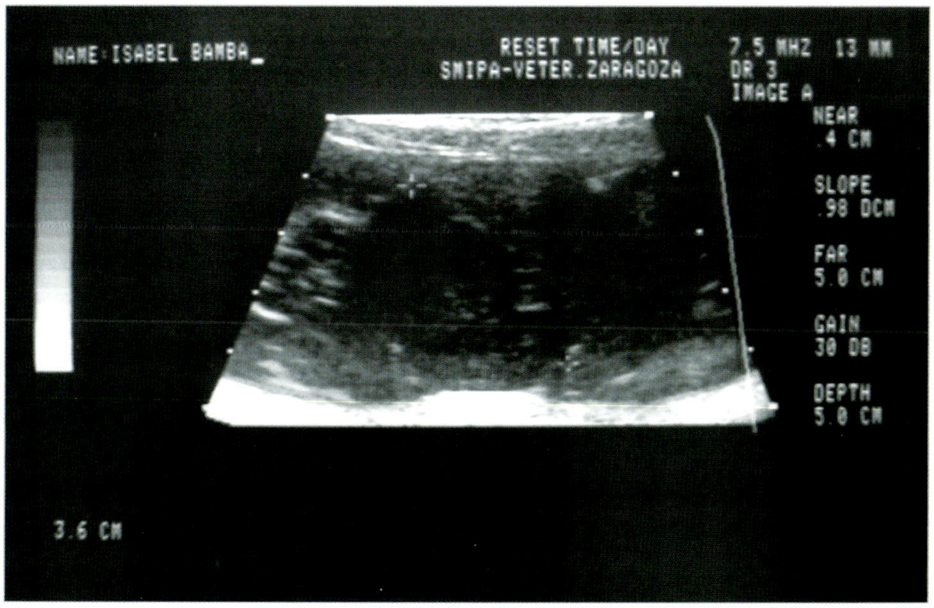

Fig. 3. The abdominal mass can be measured using ultrasonography.

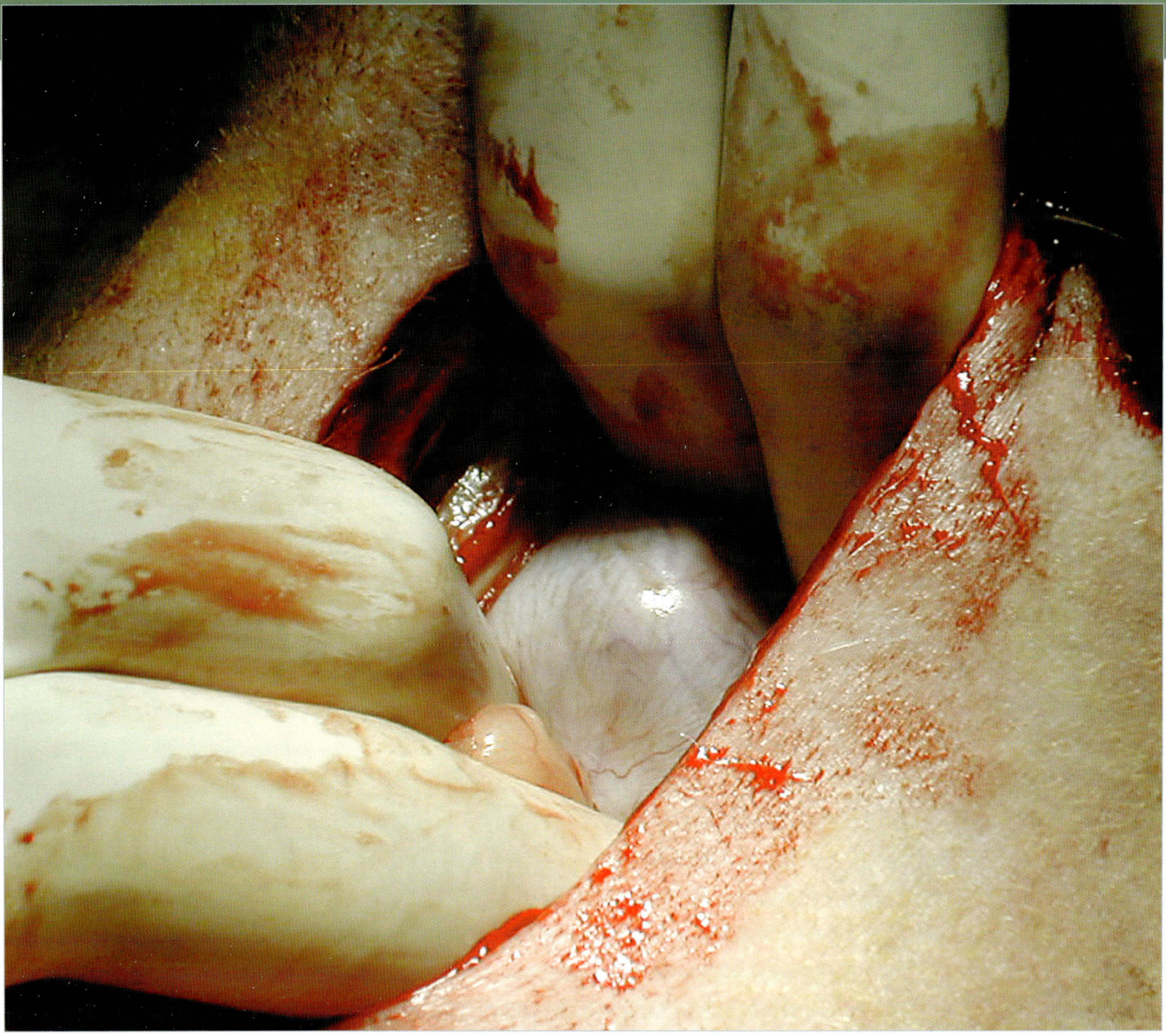

Fig. 4. Given the caudal location of the mass, an infraumbilical midline laparotomy was performed. As suspected, a large cryptorchid testis was found next to the bladder.

See infraumbilical laparotomy → *page 282*

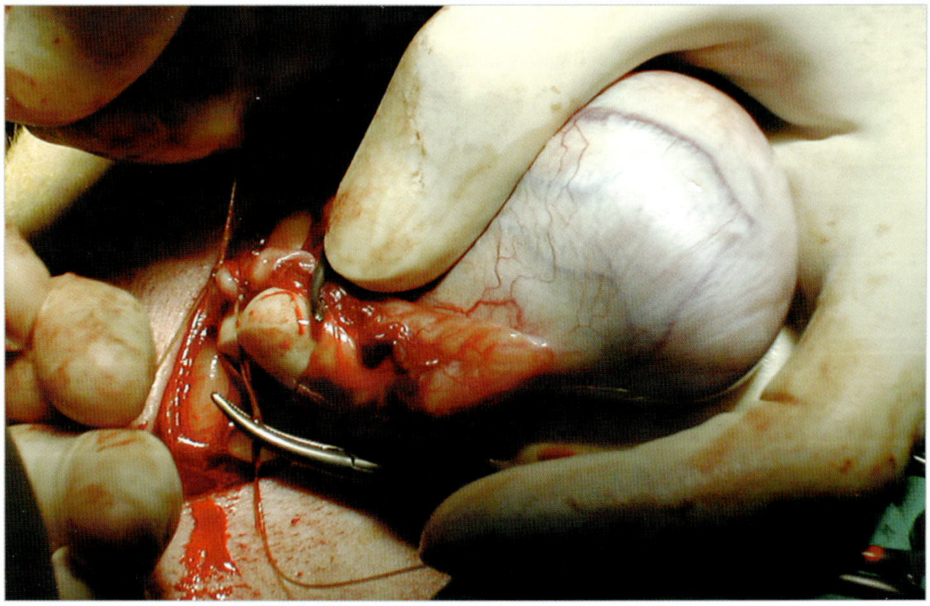

Fig. 5. The intra-abdominal testis is removed in the usual way, by ligating and cutting the structures of the spermatic cord.

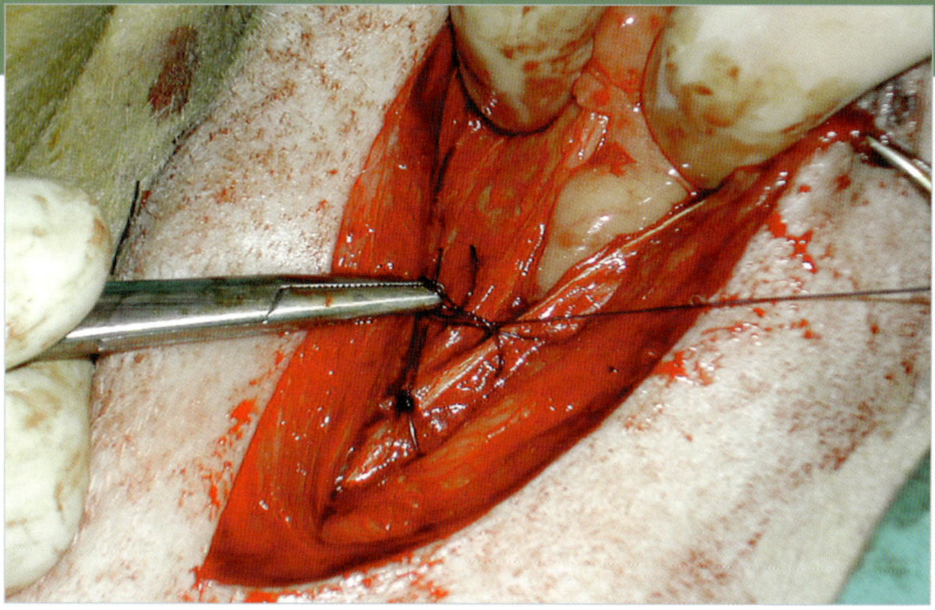

Fig. 6. The surgical wound is closed in layers.

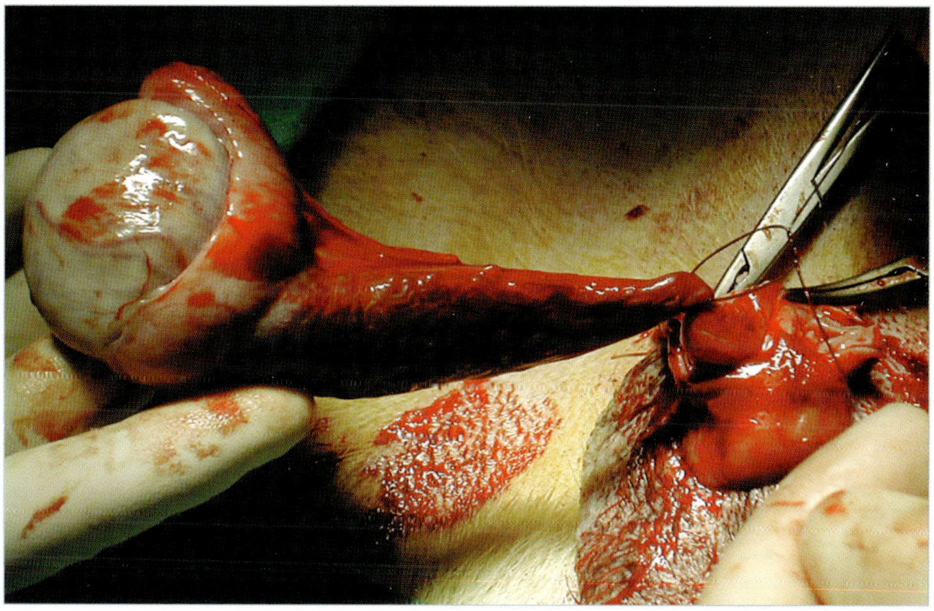

Fig. 7. The scrotal testis is removed.

See castration ➔ page 264

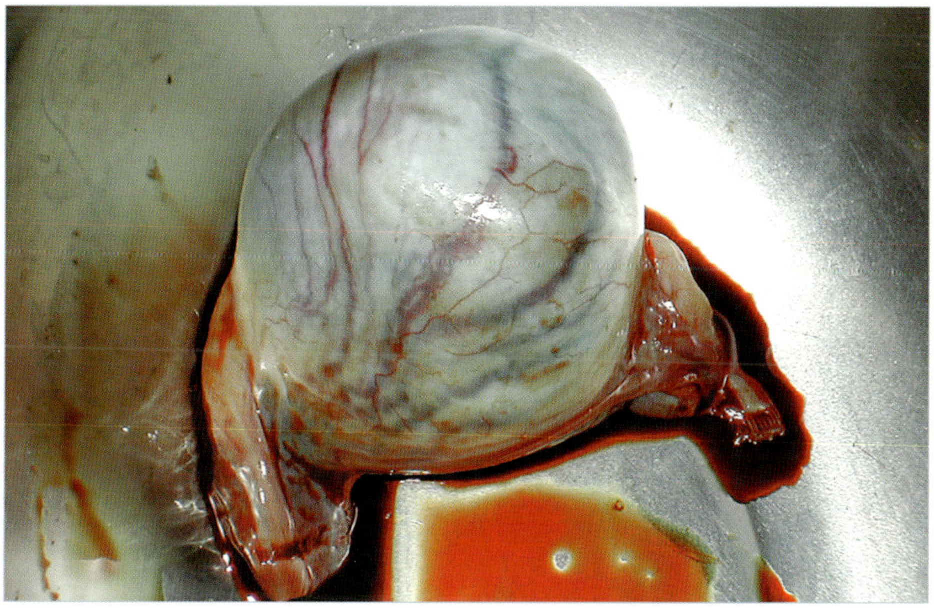

Fig. 8. View of the neoplastic testis. Histopathology confirmed the diagnosis of a Sertoli cell tumour.

Ectopic testes. Case 2 / Inguinal monorchid

Technical difficulty	■	■	□	□	□

A 7-month-old male Cocker Spaniel puppy is presented (fig. 1).

The owner reports that the animal was diagnosed as a right cryptorchid during routine examination at the time of vaccination. His veterinarian recommended castration from 6 months of age. At examination, there is indeed only one scrotal testis (fig. 2). The ectopic testis is found in the right inguinal area and is slightly smaller than the scrotal testis (fig. 3). As it is unlikely that the testis will still descend at this age, it is decided to castrate the patient.

Palpation of the testes should be part of the routine puppy examination at the time of vaccination.
If cryptorchidism is detected, this should be reassessed at every visit. If ectopy persists for more than 6 months, preventive castration is recommended.

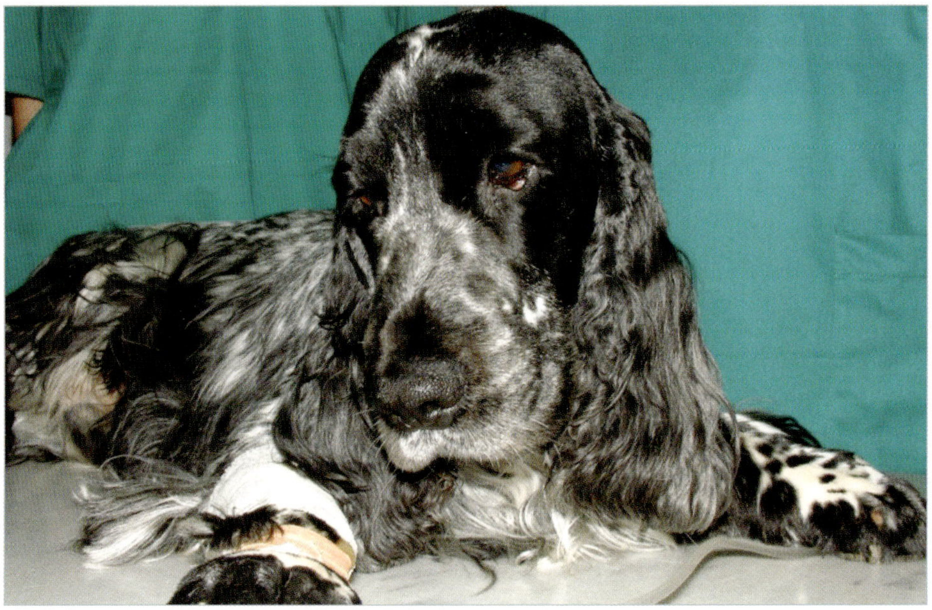

Fig. 1. The premedicated patient on the day of the operation.

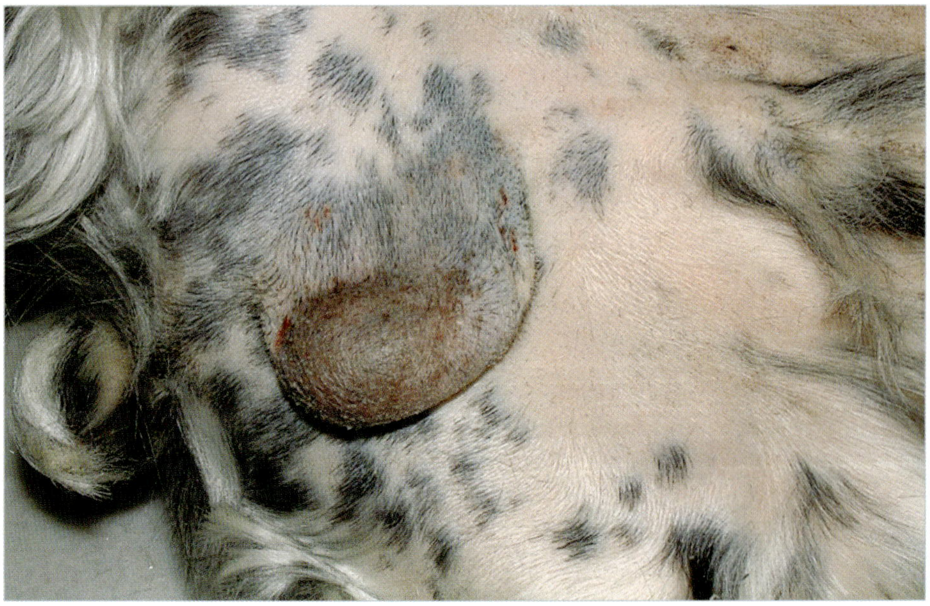

Fig. 2. Only one testis is found in the scrotum.

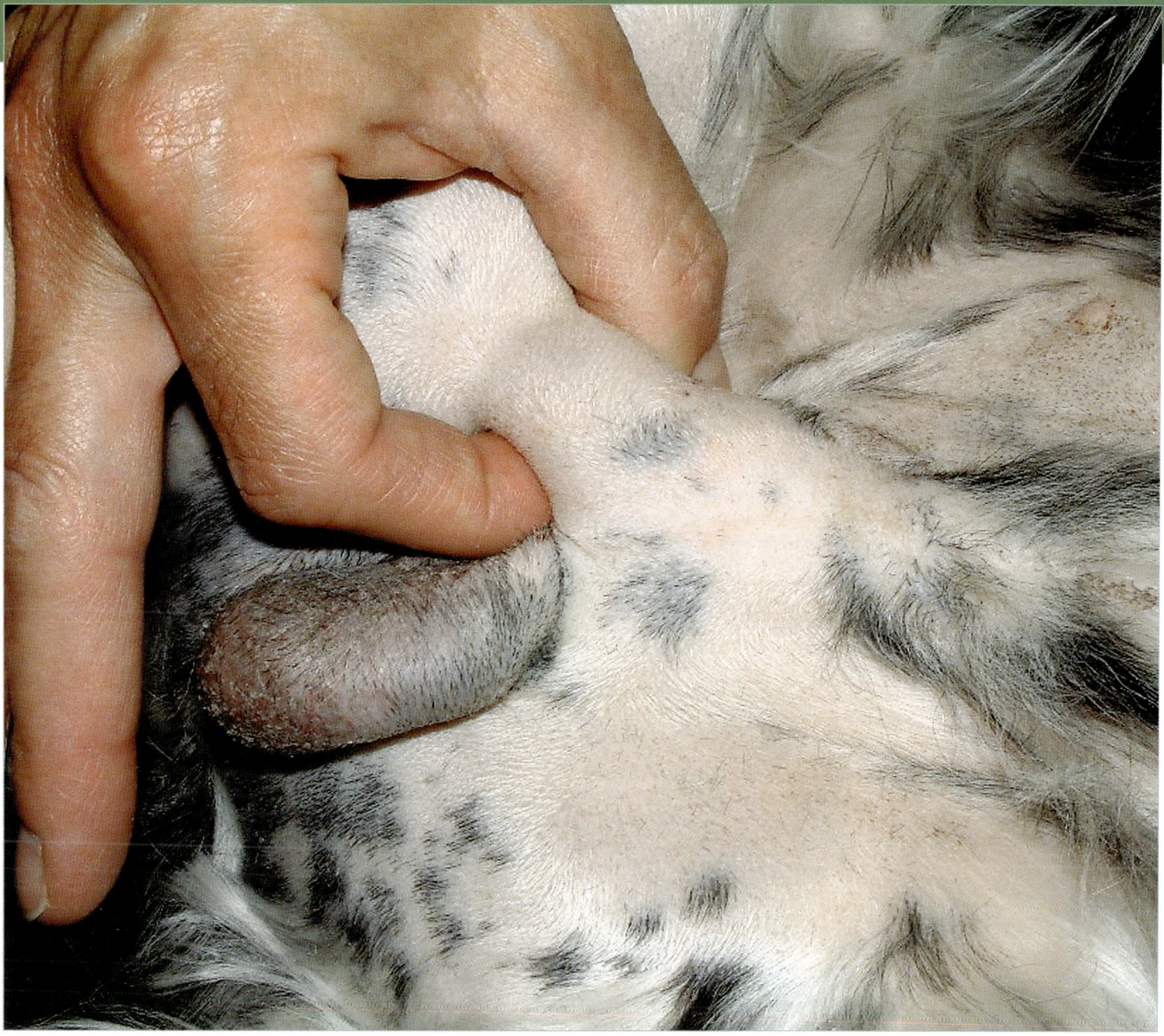

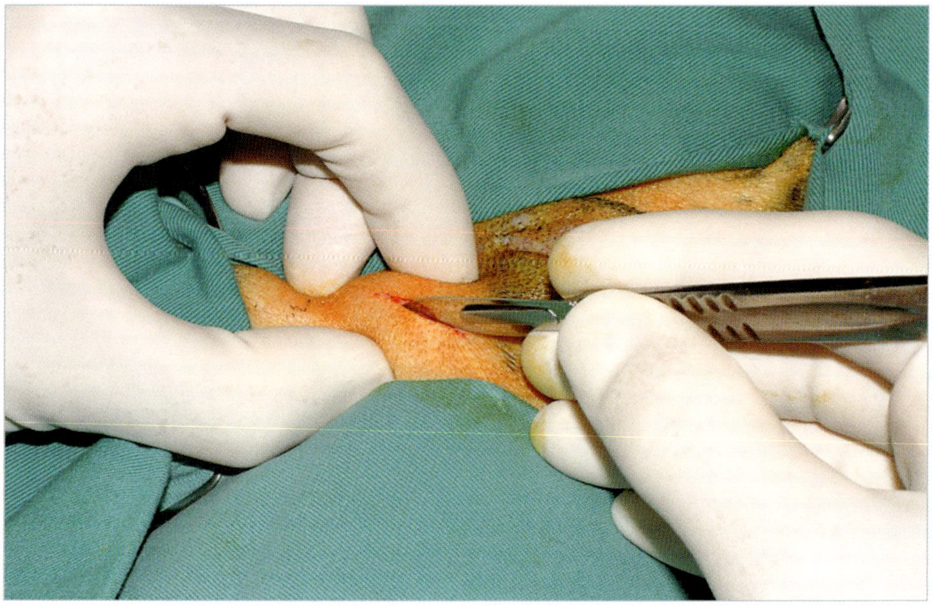

Fig. 3. Palpation reveals that the ectopic testis is located in the right inguinal area.

Fig. 4. After preparation of the surgical field, the ectopic testis is isolated between the thumb and index finger of one hand while a skin incision is made directly over it.

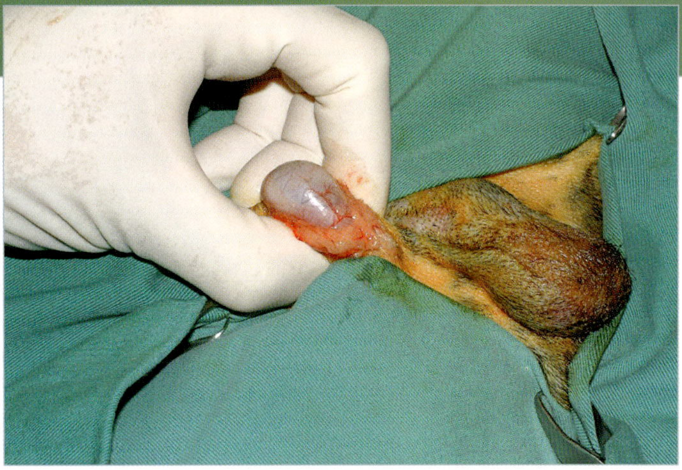

Fig. 5. The ectopic testis is exteriorised through the skin incision by applying gentle traction.

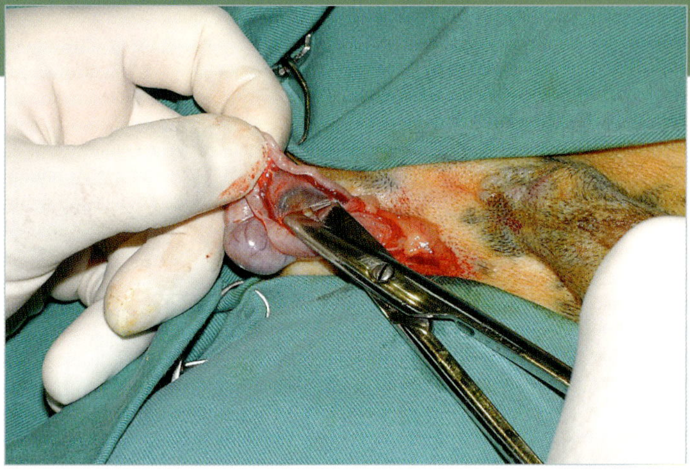

Fig. 6. The structures of the spermatic cord are isolated and ligated in the usual way.

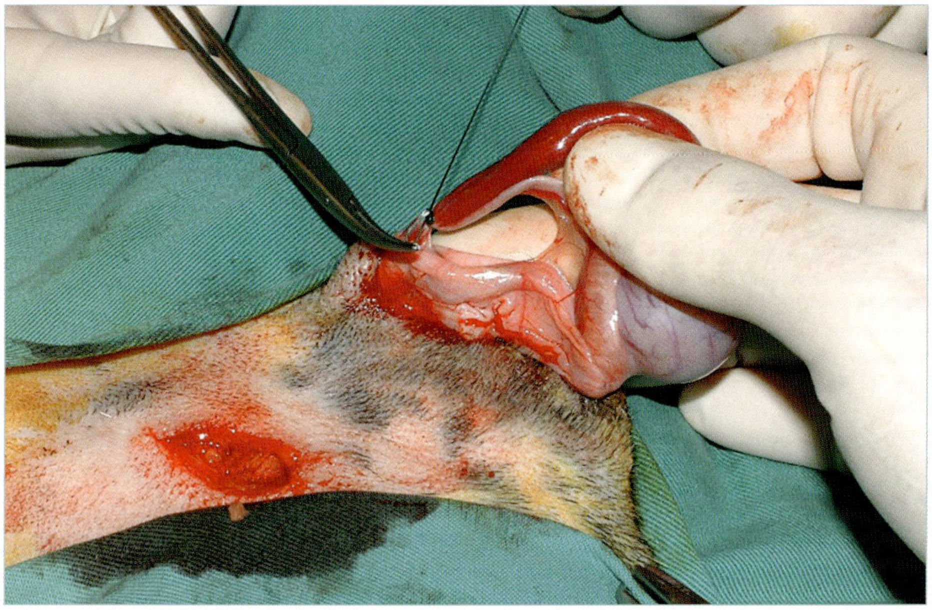

See castration page 264

Fig. 7. Next, the scrotal testis is removed.

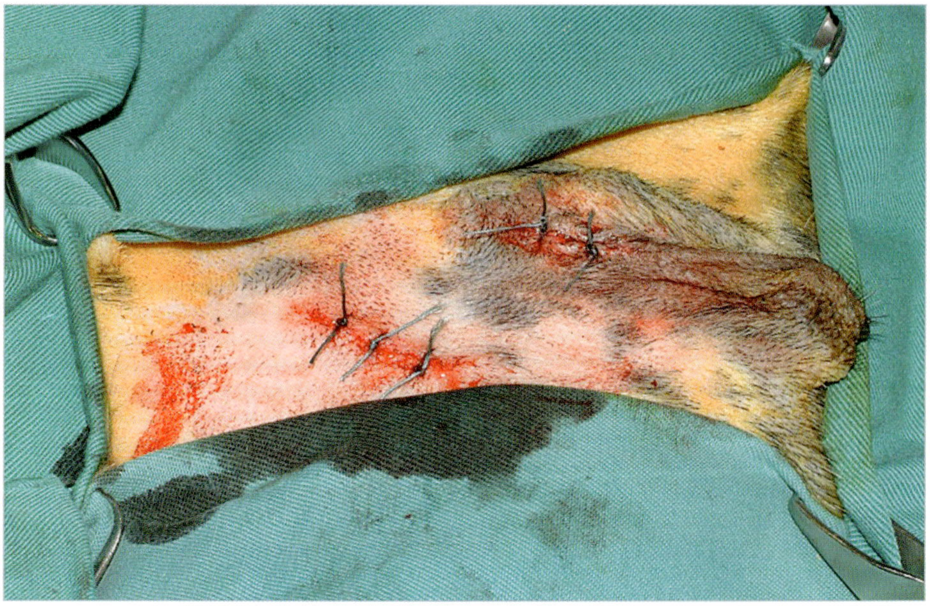

Fig. 8. Finally, the surgical wounds are closed using interrupted sutures of 2/0 or 3/0 non-absorbable material.

Ectopic testes. Case 3 / Inguinal cryptorchid

Technical difficulty

> *The probability that a cryptorchid testis becomes neoplastic is up to twenty times higher than for a scrotal testis and tumours appear in younger animals, from 6 months of age.*

A 1-year-old male Poodle is presented because its owner noted the absence of both testes. On examination, the absence of a scrotum is also noted. This is bilateral cryptorchids (fig. 1). After meticulous examination of the inguinal area, both testes are located (fig. 2). To avoid possible tumour development in the testes, the owner is advised to have the dog castrated.

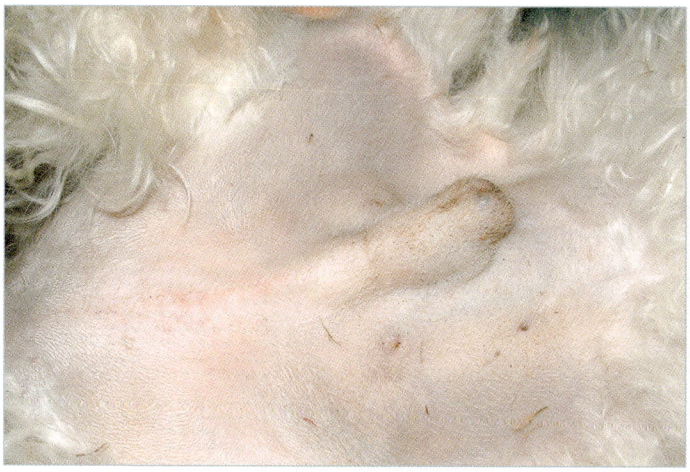

Fig. 1. The patient presents with bilateral cryptorchidism and absence of the scrotum.

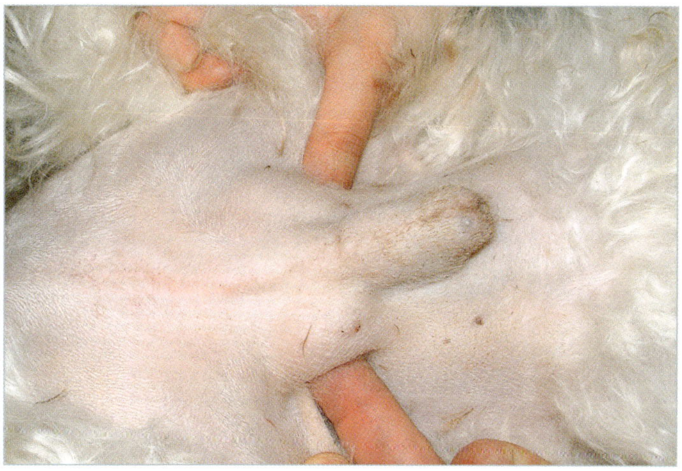

Fig.2. Both testes are found in the inguinal area.

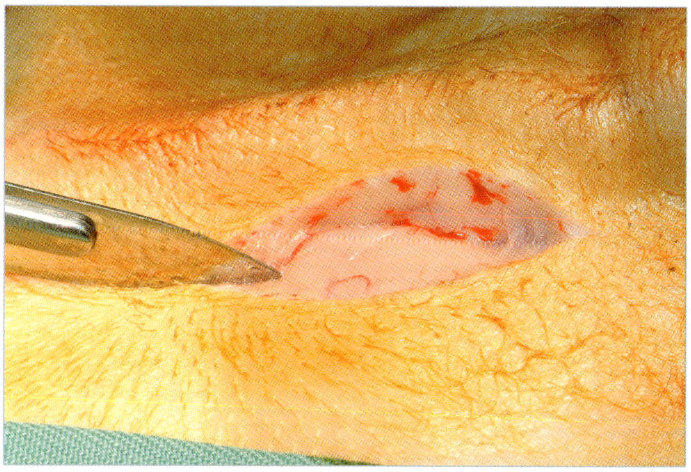

Fig. 3. A skin incision is made over the testis.

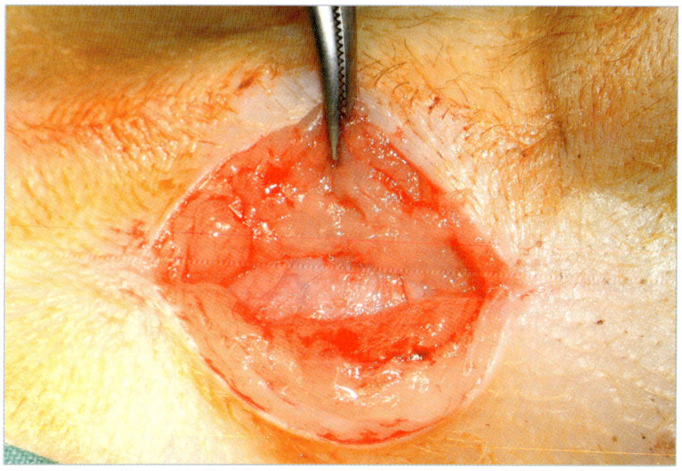

Fig. 4. In this area there is often a large amount of subcutaneous fat, which requires blunt dissection to locate the ectopic testis.

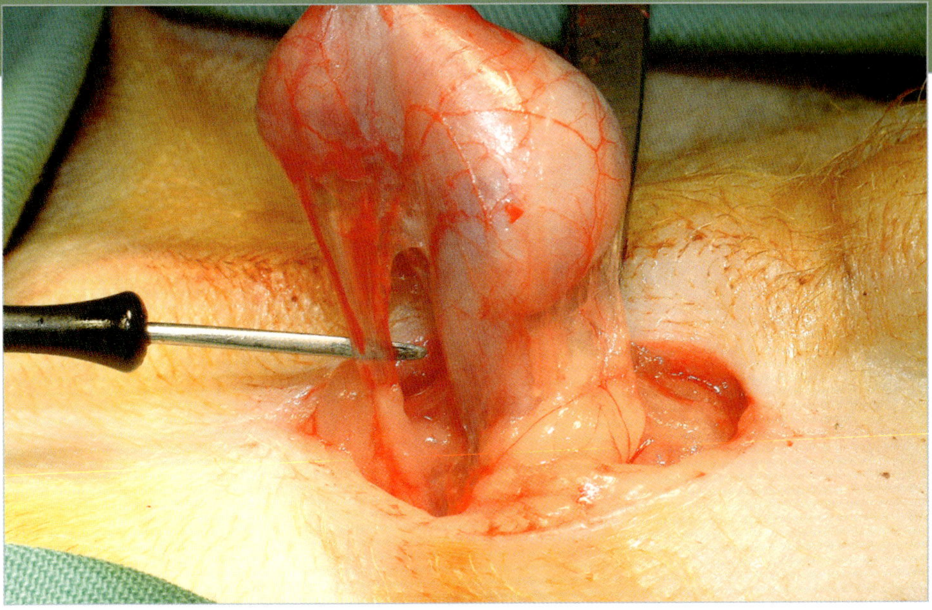

Fig. 5. The testis, still covered by the vaginal tunic, is exteriorised.

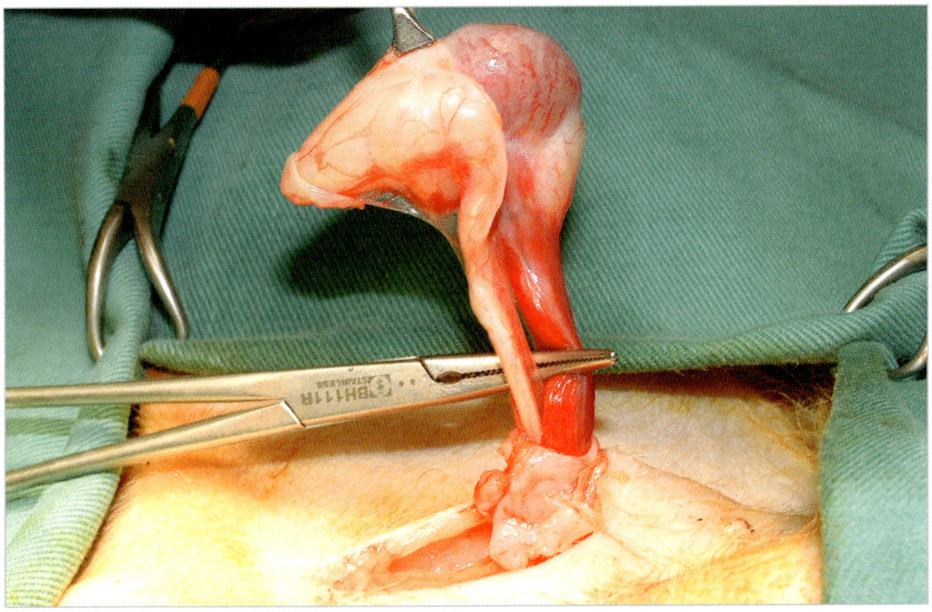

Fig. 6. Castration is performed by ligating the vascular structures and the vas deferens. This is repeated for the other testis.

See castration page 264

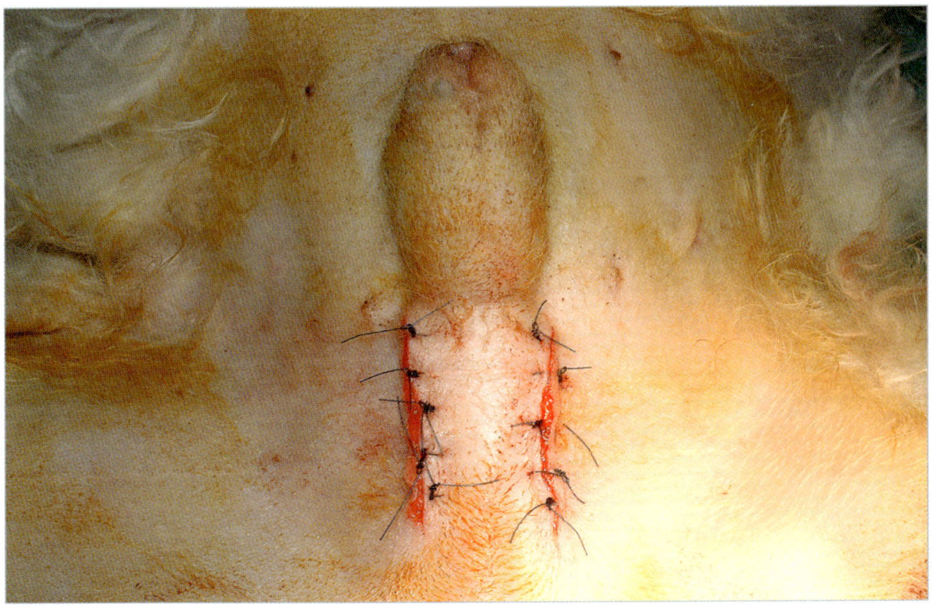

Fig. 7. View of the surgical wounds at the end of the procedure.

Ectopic testes. Case 4 / Abdominal cryptorchid

Technical difficulty

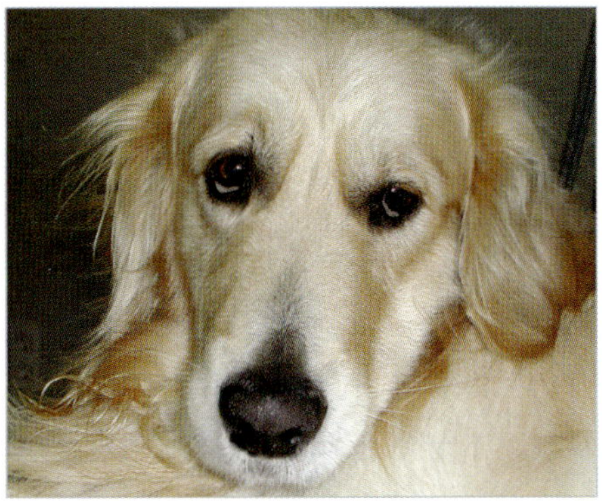

Fig. 1. "Yako" on the first day of consultation.

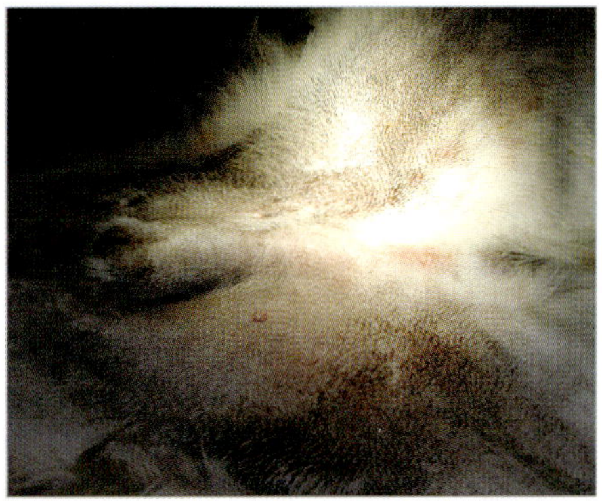

Fig. 2. The testes were not found in the scrotal or inguinal area.

A 4-year-old male Golden Retriever is presented with bilateral cryptorchidism (fig. 1). The owner was advised to have the dog castrated.

During examination of the inguinal and pre-scrotal area, the testes are not located, and it is decided to search for them in the abdomen using ultrasound (fig. 2). They are found in the caudal abdomen, on each side of and dorsal to the bladder.

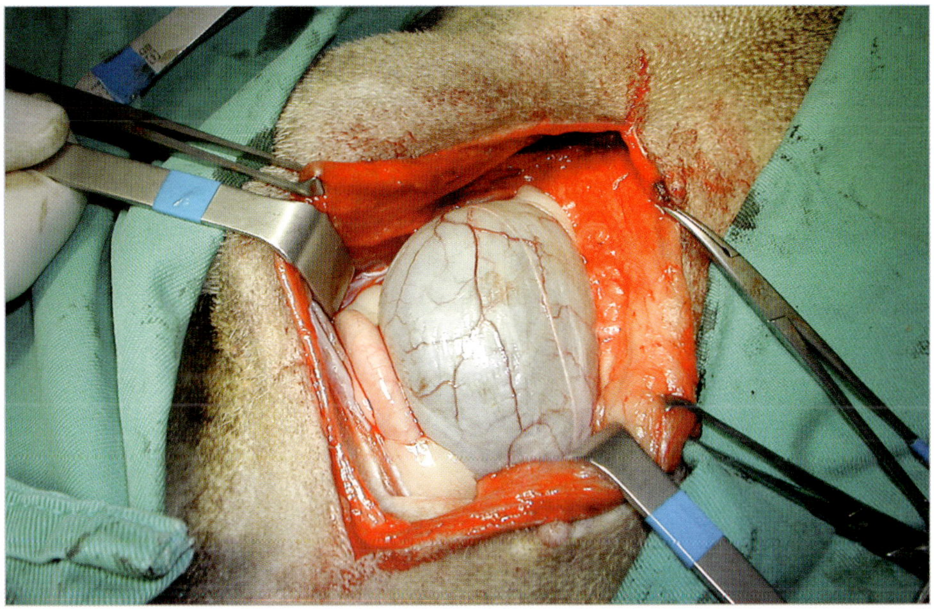

Fig. 3. Infraumbilical midline laparotomy is carried out after a para-penile skin incision. Once inside the abdomen the bladder is visualised.

See infraumbilical laparotomy → page 282

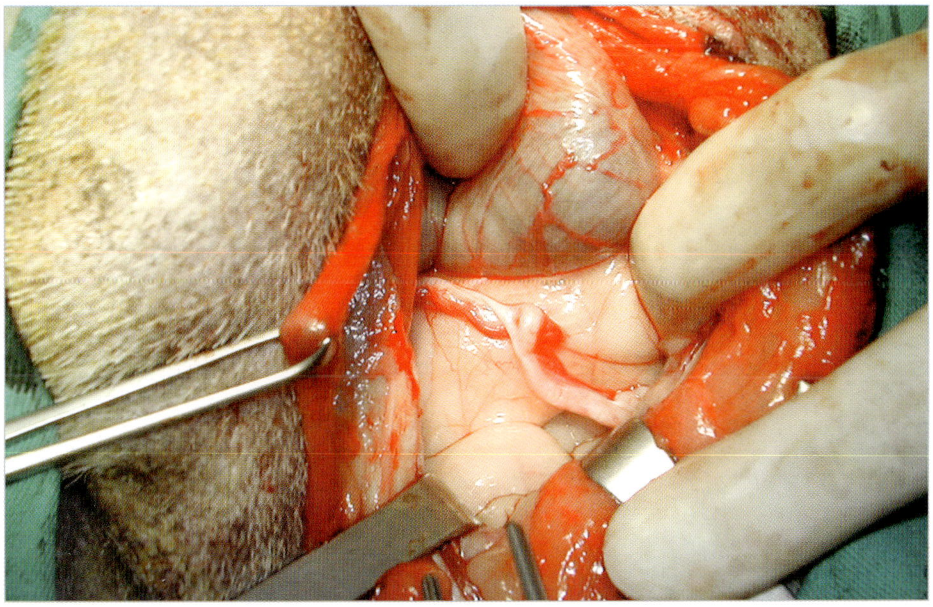

Fig. 4. By pushing the bladder caudally the right vas deferens is found leading to the prostate.

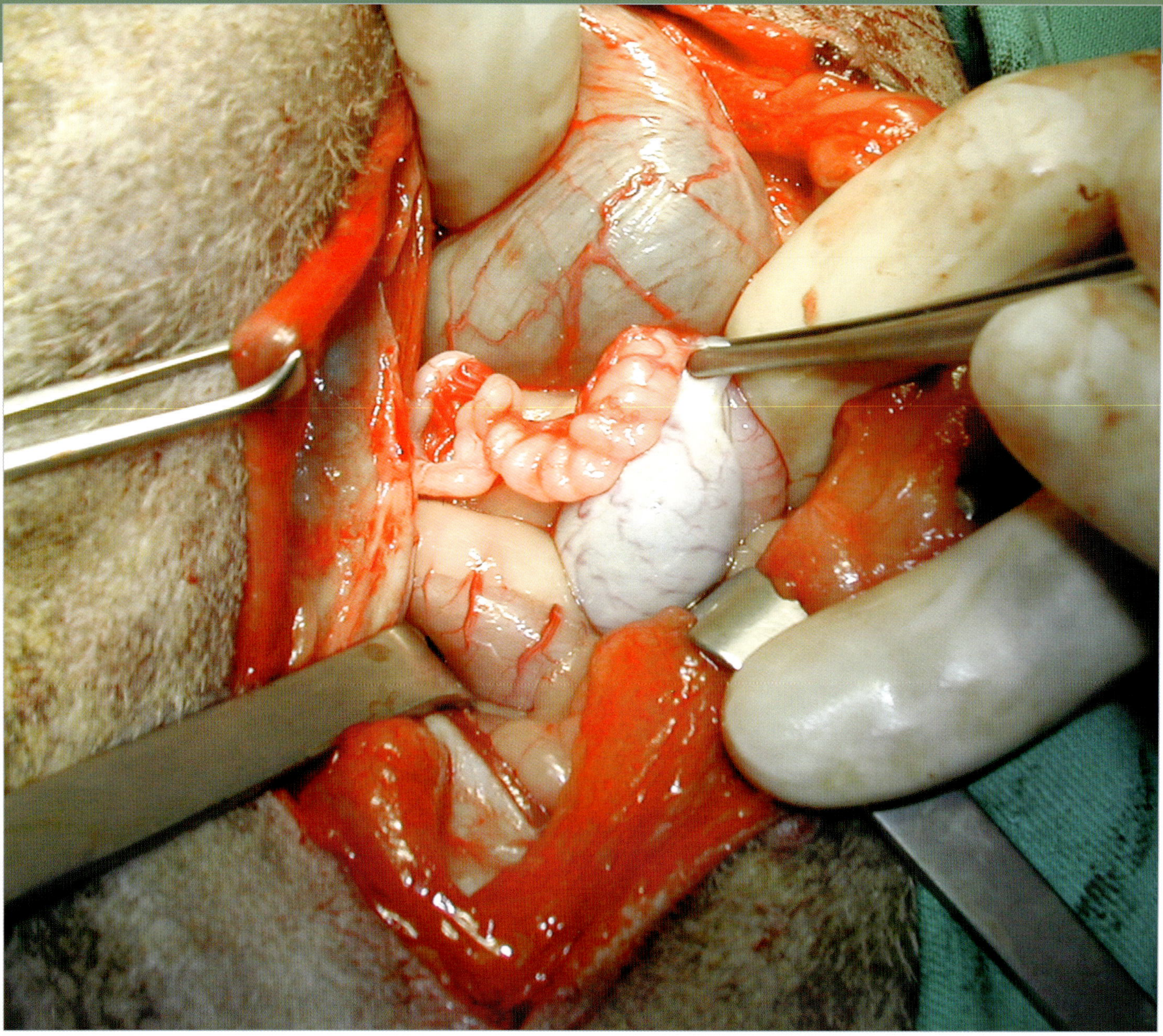

Fig. 5. Follow the vas deferens in the opposite direction to find the testis, which is exteriorised.

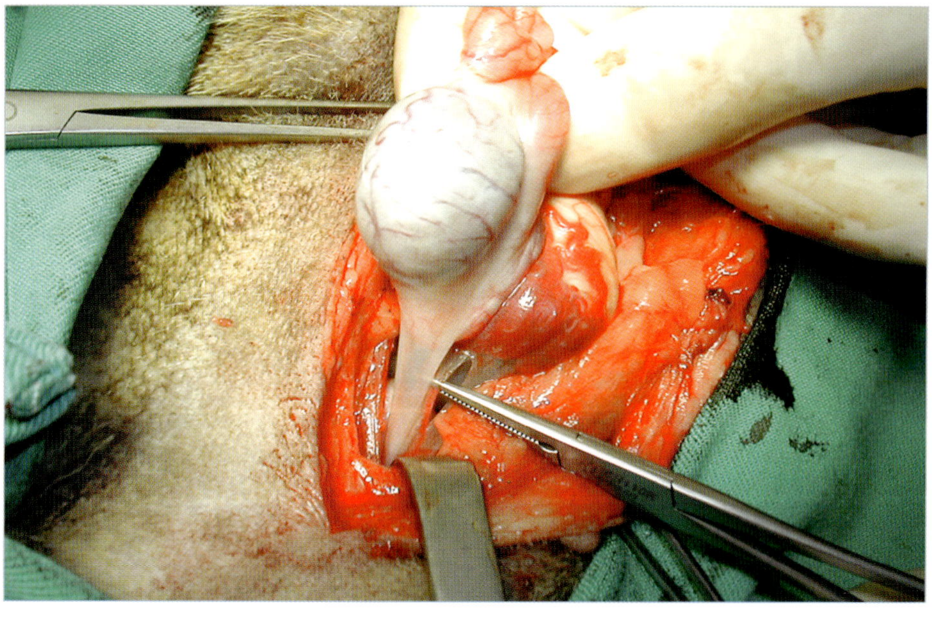

Fig. 6. The testis is attached to the spermatic cord. The spermatic fascia envelops the rest of the structures: vas deferens, pampiniform plexus, testicular artery and cremaster muscle.

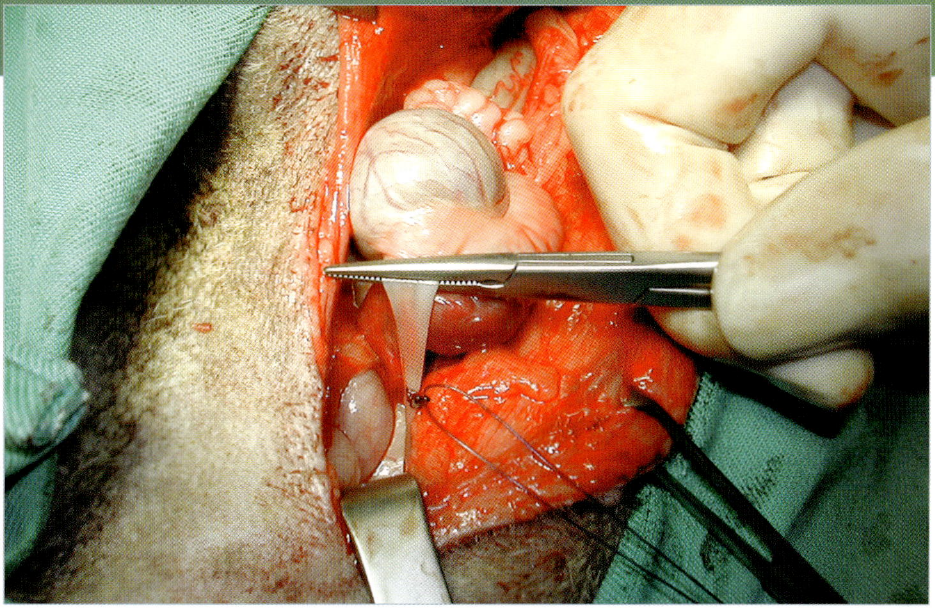

Fig. 7. The spermatic fascia hinders exteriorisation of the organ, which is why it is ligated and severed.

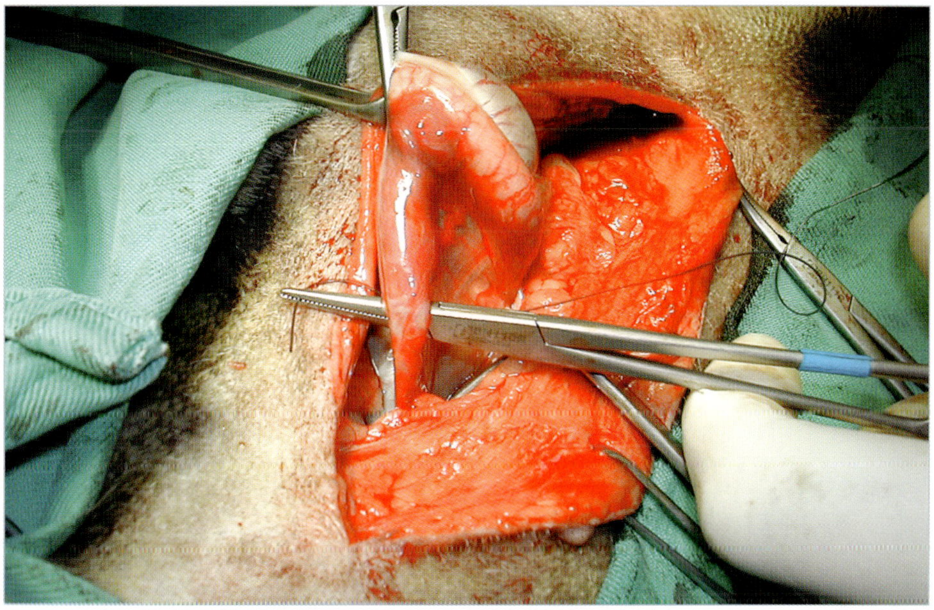

Fig. 8. The pampiniform plexus is ligated twice prior to incision.

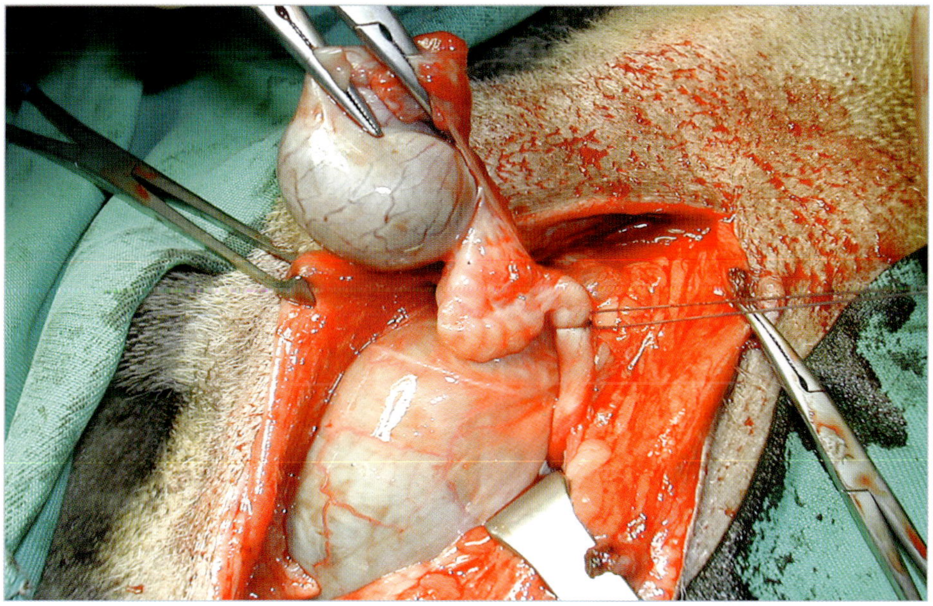

Fig. 9. The vas deferens and its blood supply are also ligated and incised.

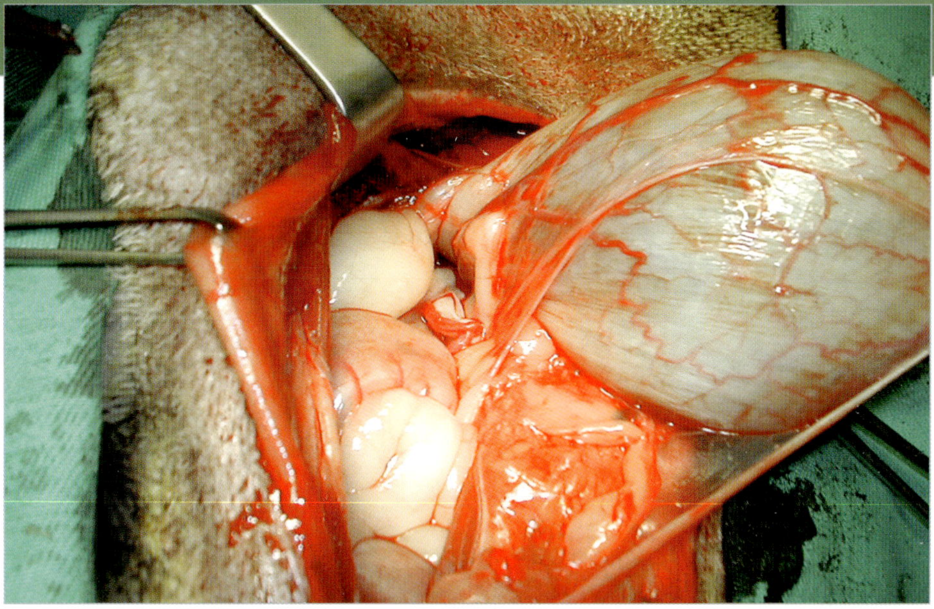

Fig. 10. To find the other testis, its vas deferens is located at the other side of the bladder.

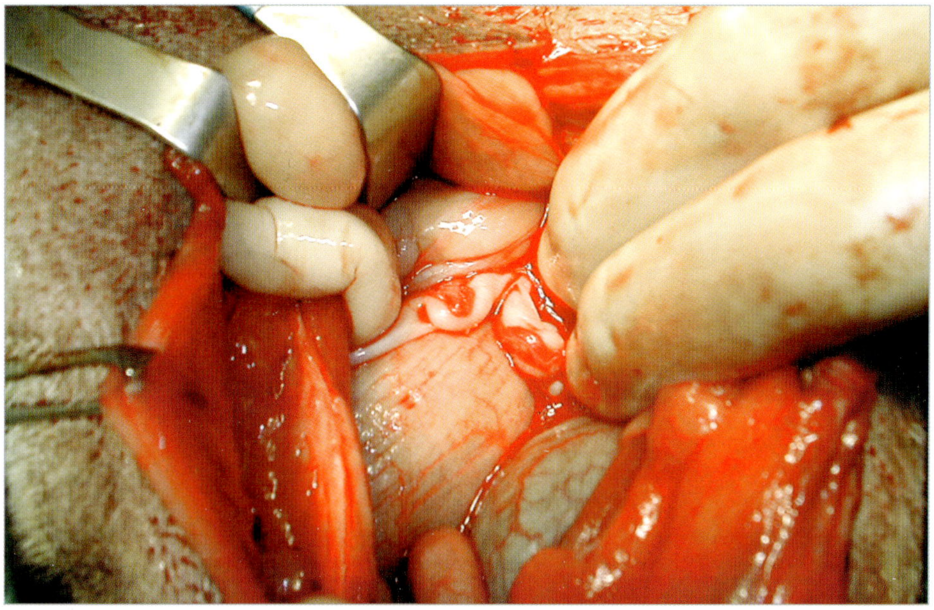

All cryptorchid dogs should be castrated as early as possible and certainly before 6 years of age.

Fig. 11. The vas deferens is visible between the bladder and the colon.

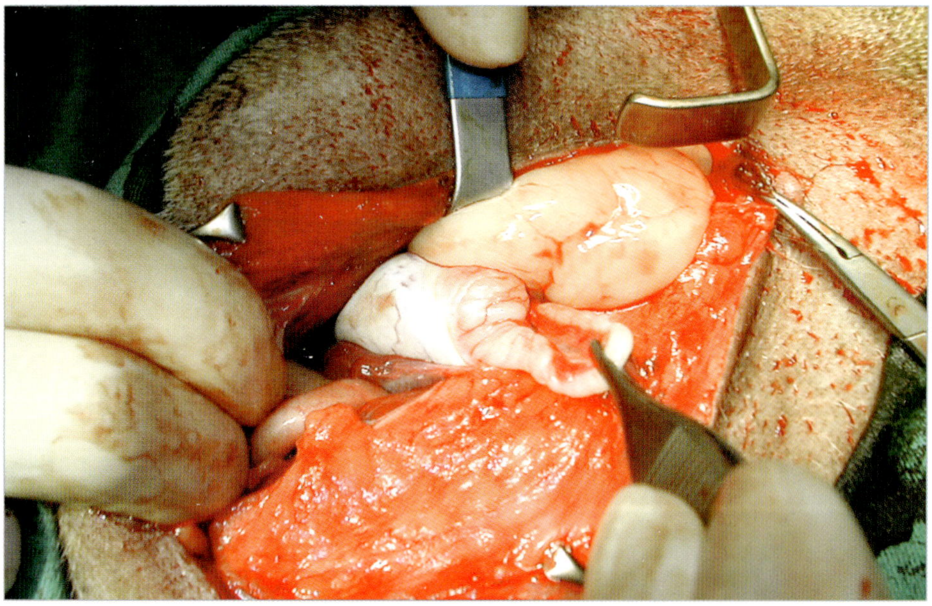

Fig. 12. By gentle traction of the vas deferens, the testis is brought to the surface. The same procedure as for the other side is repeated.

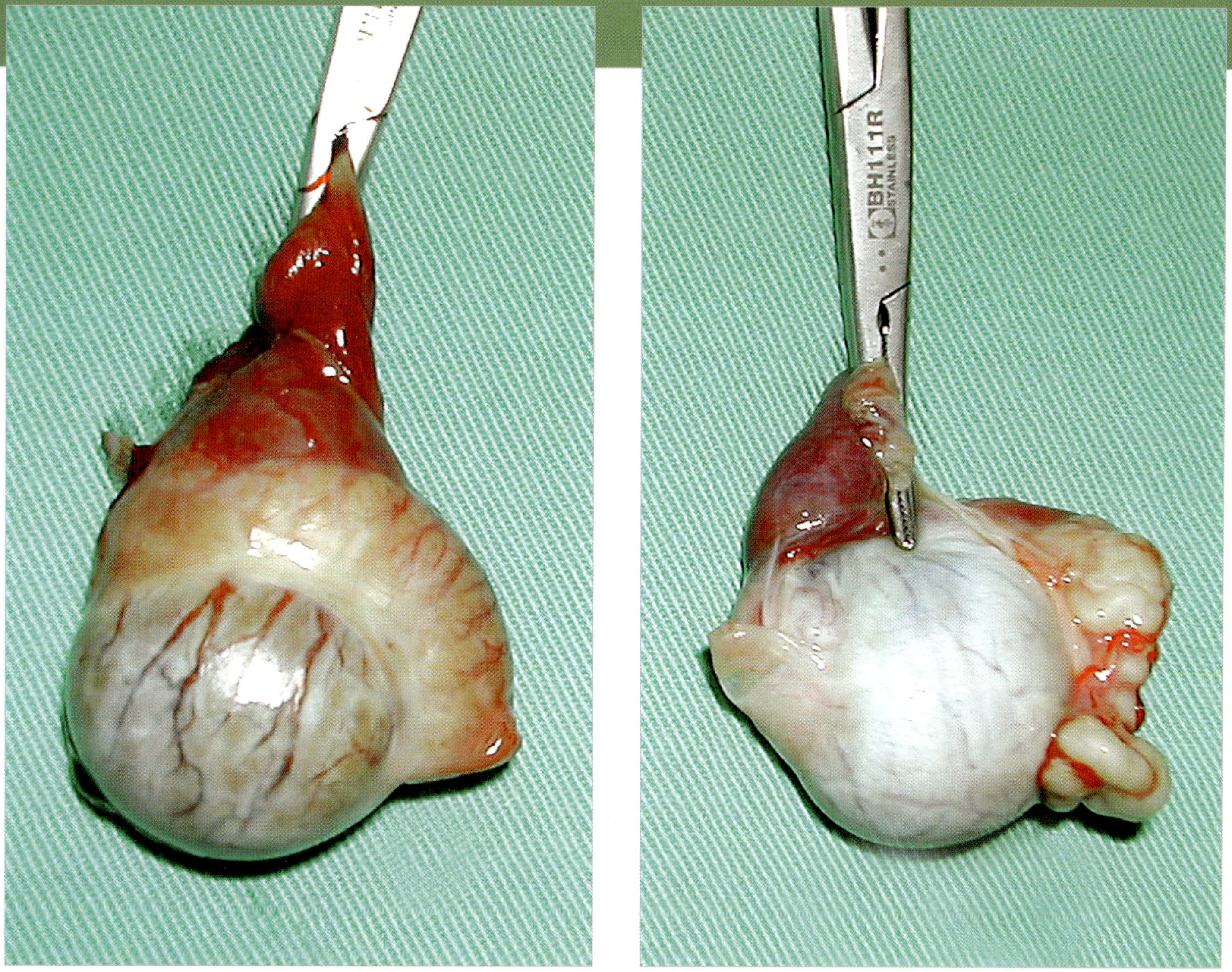

Fig. 13. The size and appearance of both testes is completely normal.

Scrotal lesions

Prevalence	■				
Technical difficulty	■	■			

A 6-year-old male German Shepherd dog is brought for examination. The owner reports that the animal was bitten on the scrotum a week ago and has now has marked inflammation of the area. Examination reveals various infected scrotal wounds. In one of them, maggots are observed. Castration with scrotal ablation is advised.

Extensive scrotal and testicular lesions require castration and ablation of the scrotum.

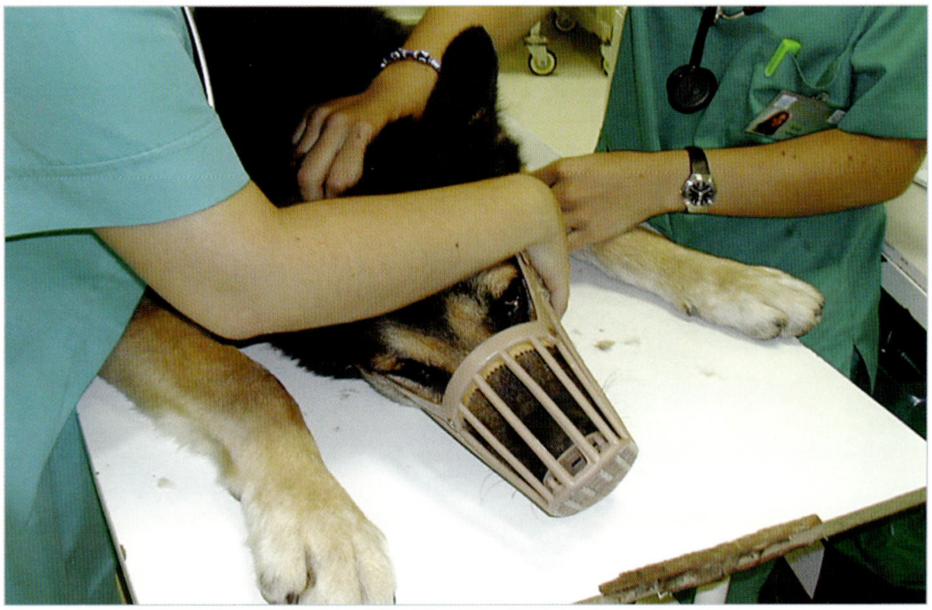

Fig. 1. The patient prior to anaesthesia.

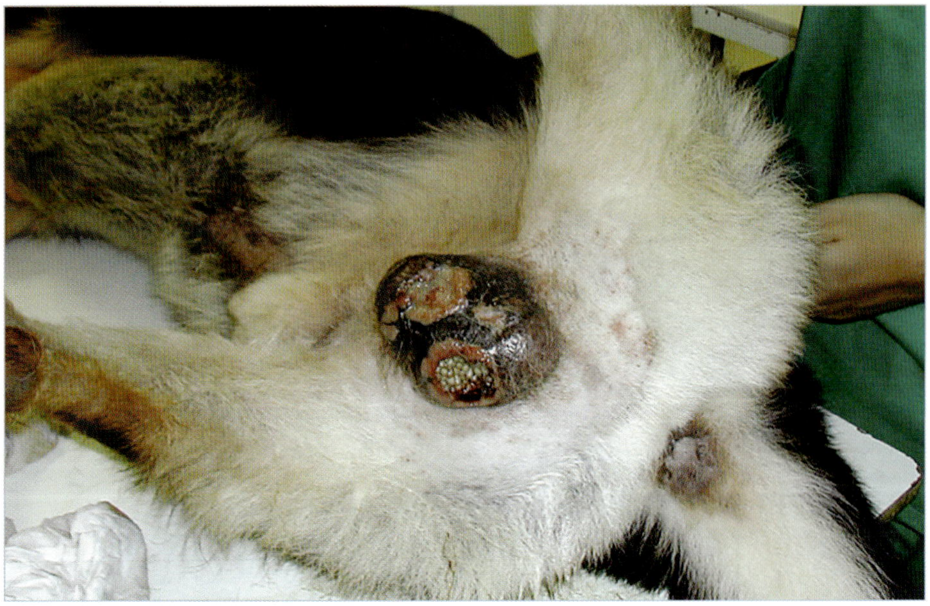

Fig. 2. The scrotum is severely inflamed with several ulcerated areas.

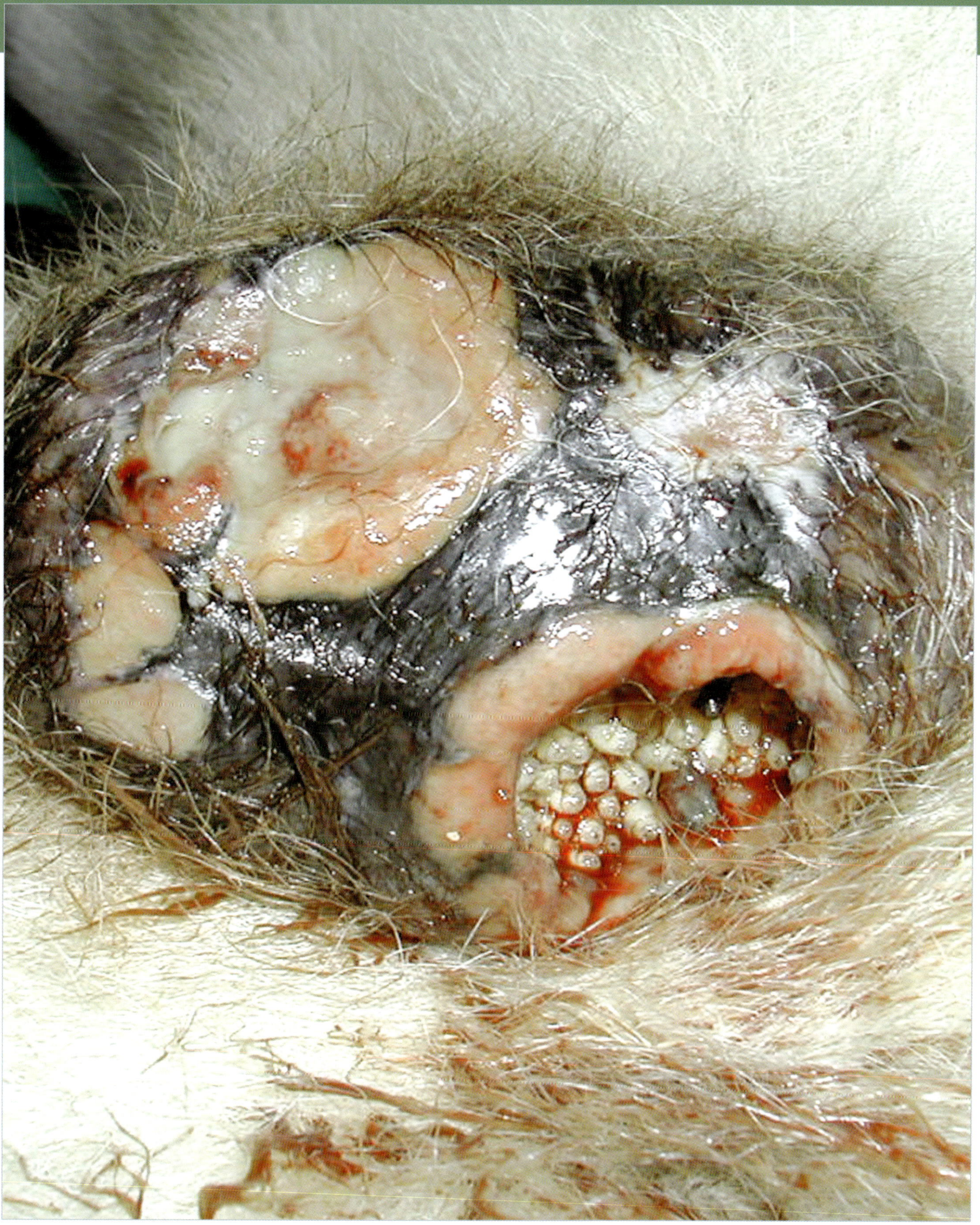

Fig. 3. Close-up view of the affected area. Several infected wounds are visible. In one of them, maggots are visible.

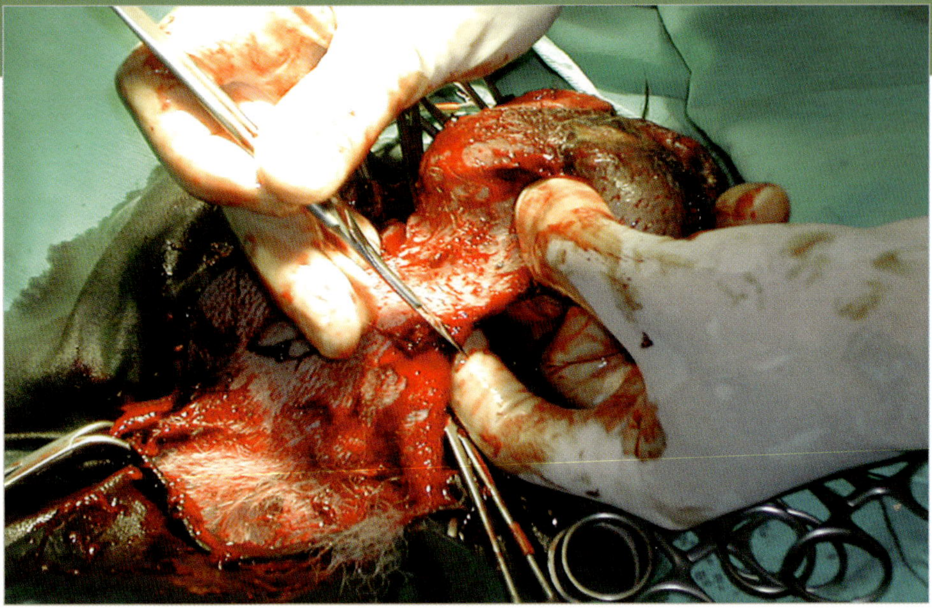

Fig. 4. To perform castration with ablation of the scrotum, an elliptical incision is made around its base.

See castration with scrotal ablation → page 277

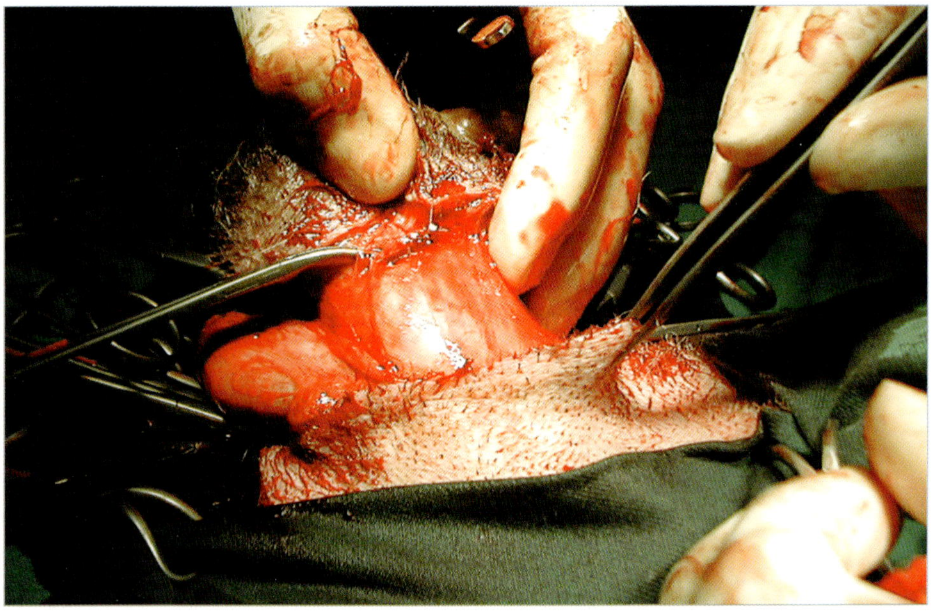

Fig. 5. The tissues are dissected to visualise both spermatic cords.

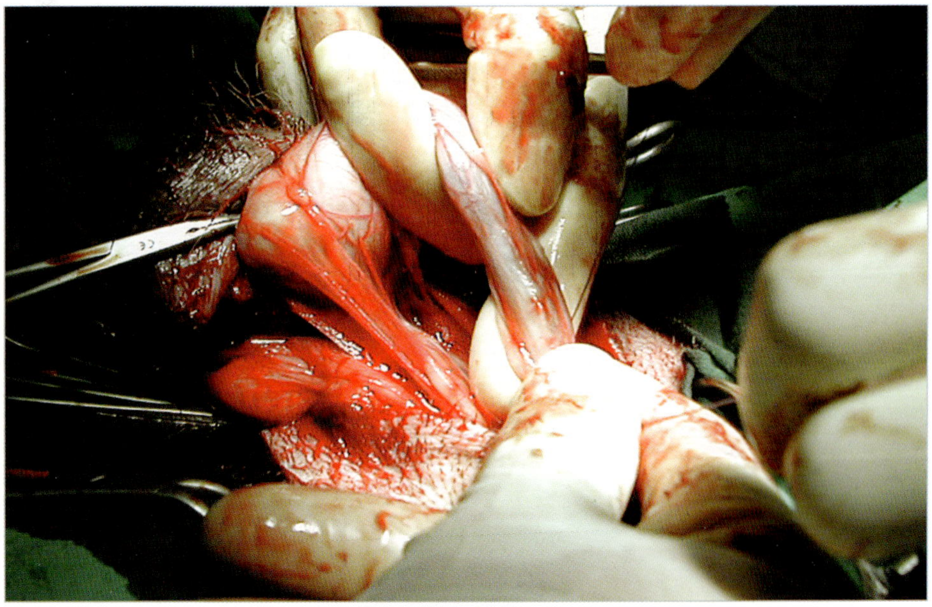

Fig. 6. After opening the vaginal tunic, the structures of the spermatic cord are ligated.

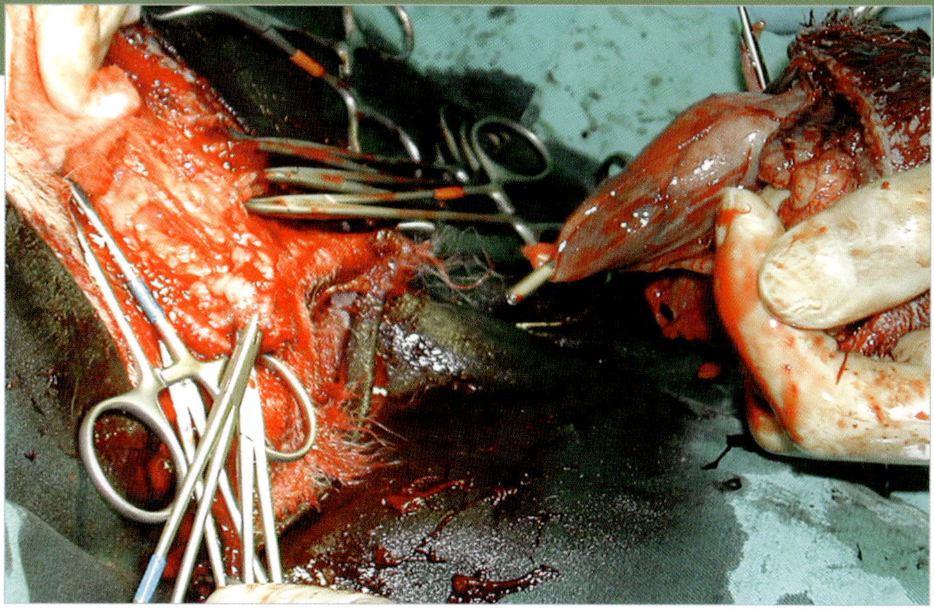

Fig. 7. After cutting the structures of the spermatic cord, the scrotum and both testes are removed.

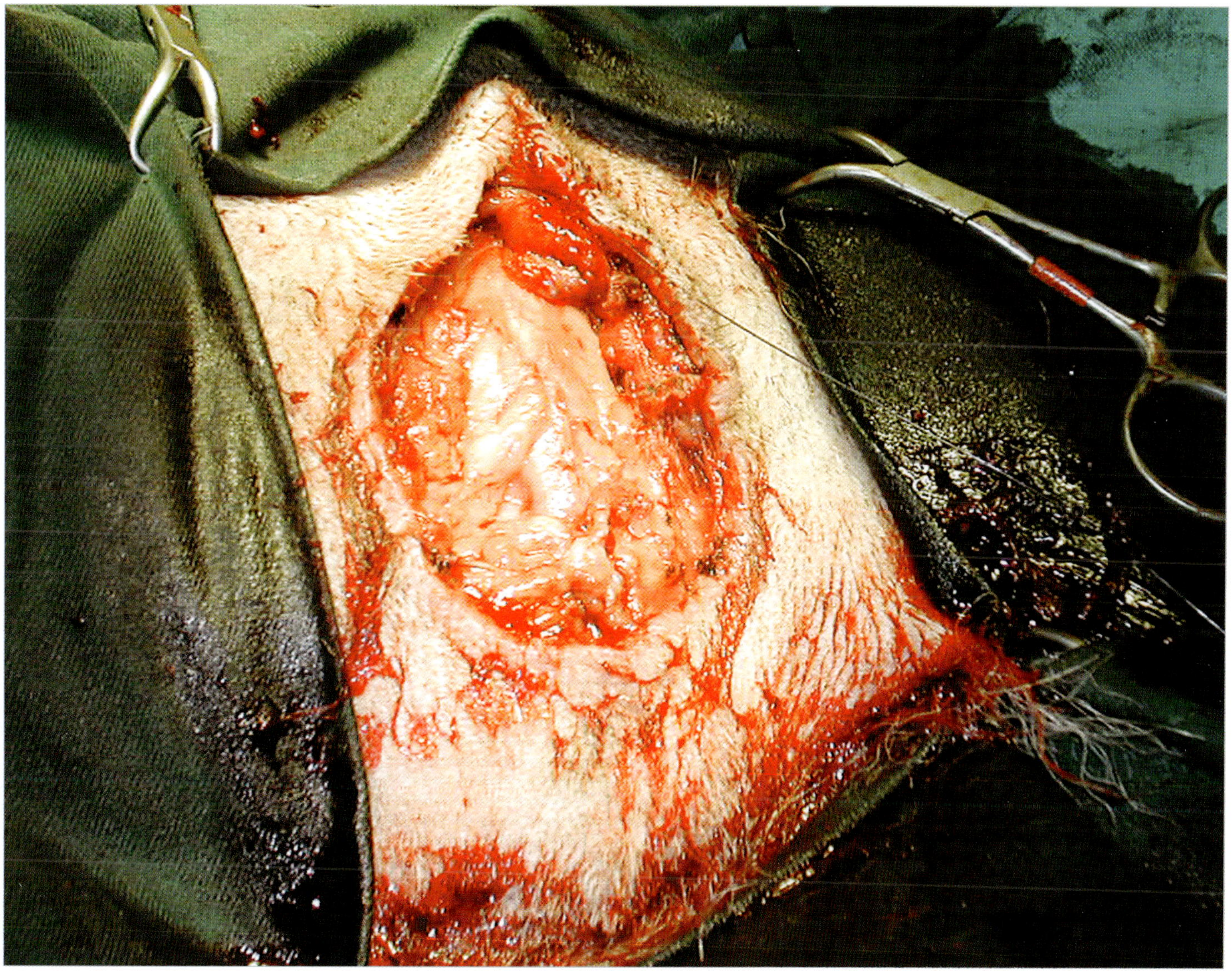

Fig. 8. To finish the procedure, the surgical wound is closed in layers.

Genitalia of the dog

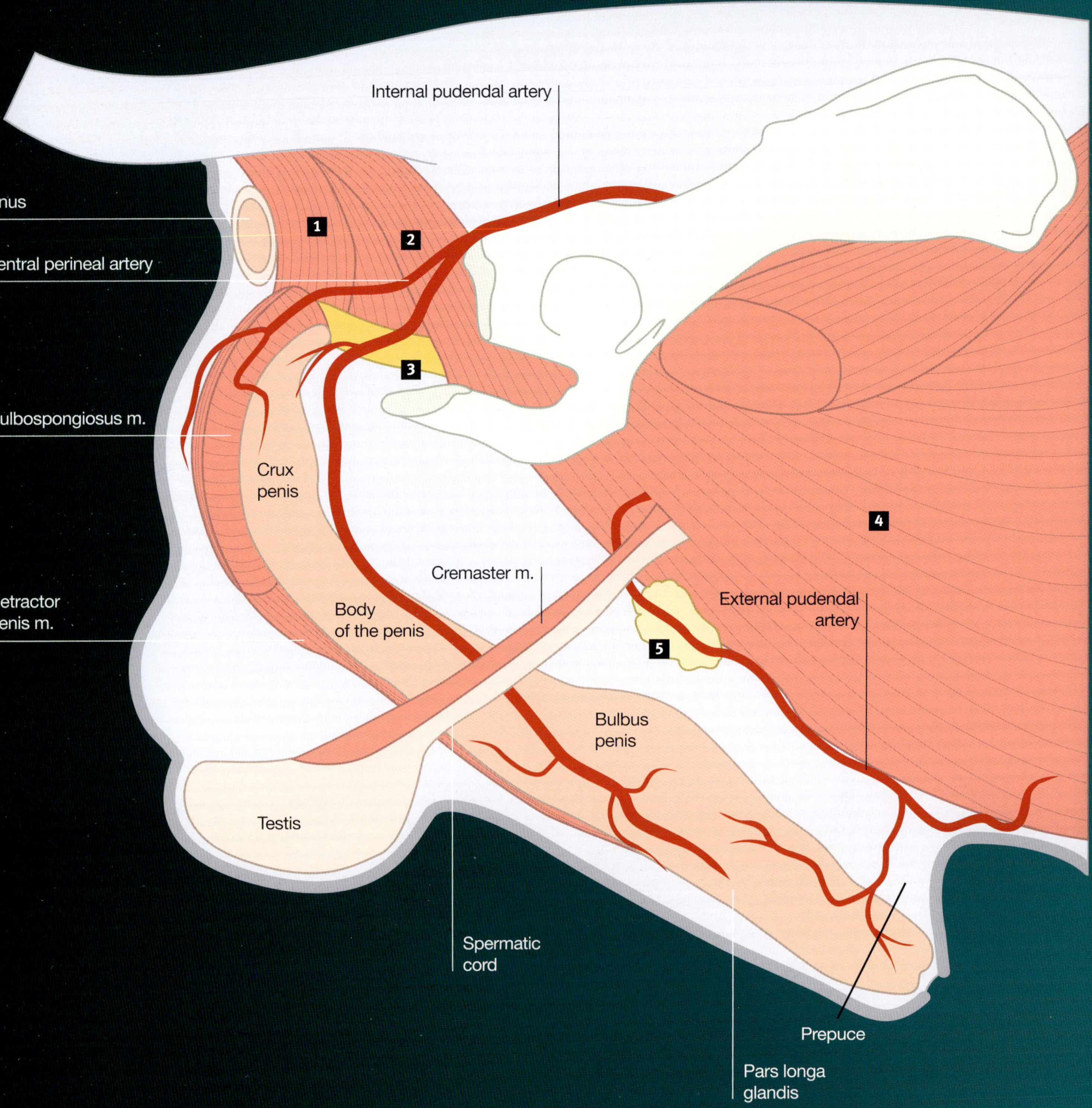

1 Levator ani m.
2 Coccygeus m.
3 Pelvic urethra
4 External oblique m.
5 Superficial inguinal lymph node
6 Sacrocaudal m.
7 Rectococcygeus m.
8 Gracilis m.

Genitalia of the cat

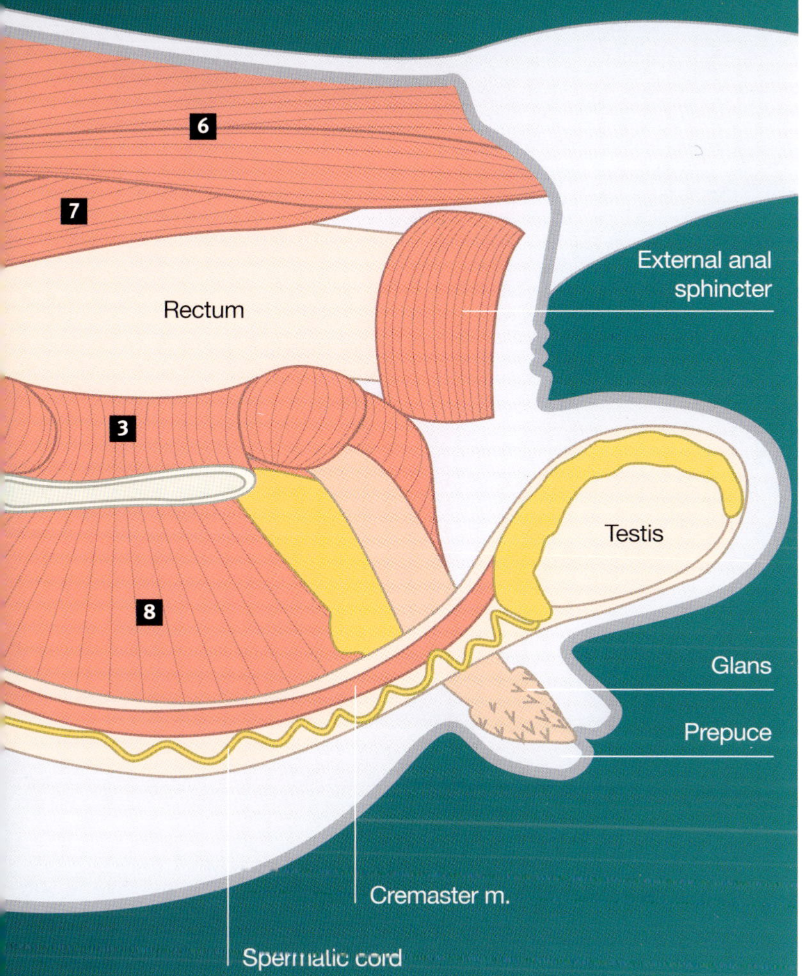

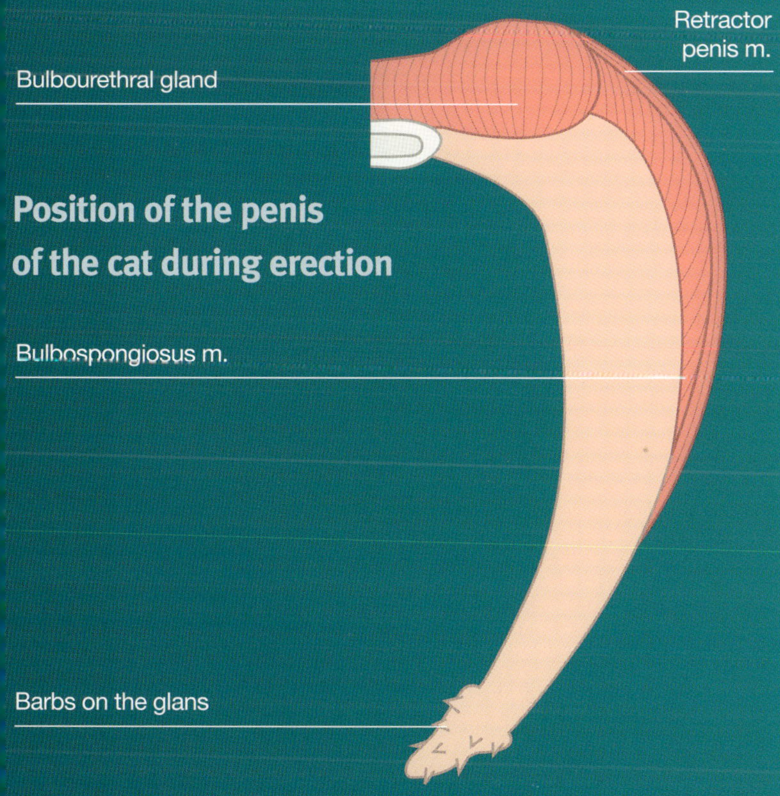

Prepuce-penis

Phimosis

Case 1 / Opening-widening of the preputial orifice

Case 2 / Reconstruction of the preputial orifice

Paraphimosis

Wounds

Case 1 / Preputial wounds

Case 2 / Wounds of the penis (distal area)

Case 3 / Wounds of the penis (perineal area)

Tumours

Case 1 / Medical treatment

Case 2 / Surgical treatment

Prolapse of the urethral mucosa

Hypospadia

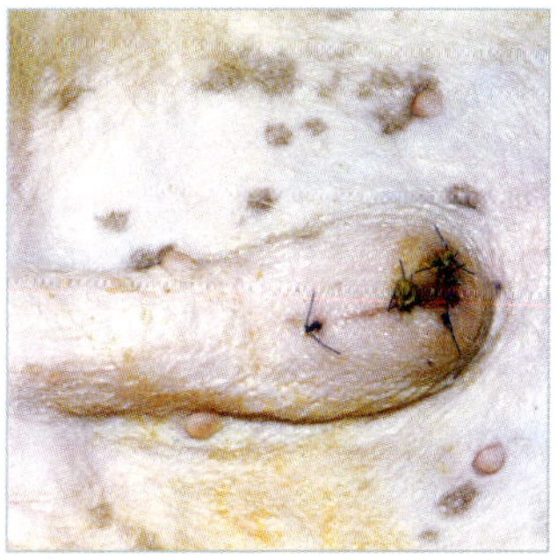

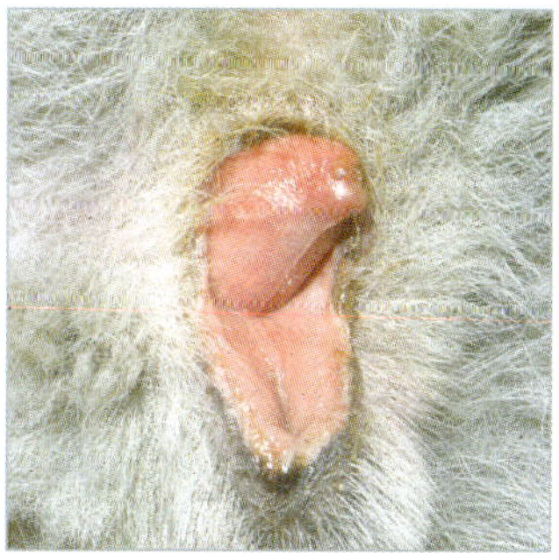

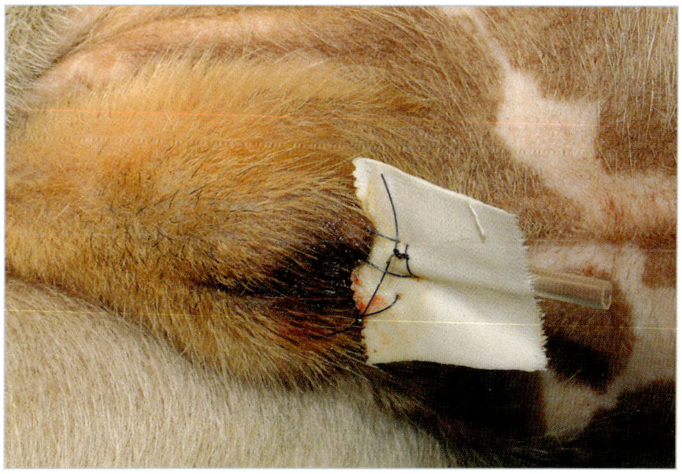

Phimosis

Prevalence

Phimosis is defined as the inability to exteriorise the penis. This can be due to a (rare) congenital absence of the preputial orifice or may be acquired following trauma or tumours.

All these cases lead to a difficulty in urinating. Urine is eliminated through one or more small openings at the end of the prepuce. Urinary retention inside the prepuce causes irritation, balanoposthitis and pain. The patient is also unable to copulate.

Surgical treatment is based on a triangular incision through the supposed preputial orifice until reaching the mucosa. The amount of skin removed should be minimal, ensuring that the penis stays covered. The mucosa is then sutured directly to the skin with monofilament material (fig. 3).

Fig. 1. "Rayas" is a male European shorthair cat with difficulty urinating. The owner reports that the cat's genitalia are very inflamed.

*

In congenital cases, castration is recommended.

To avoid difficulties when removing sutures due to their location or the behaviour of the patient, absorbable synthetic monofilament material is advised.

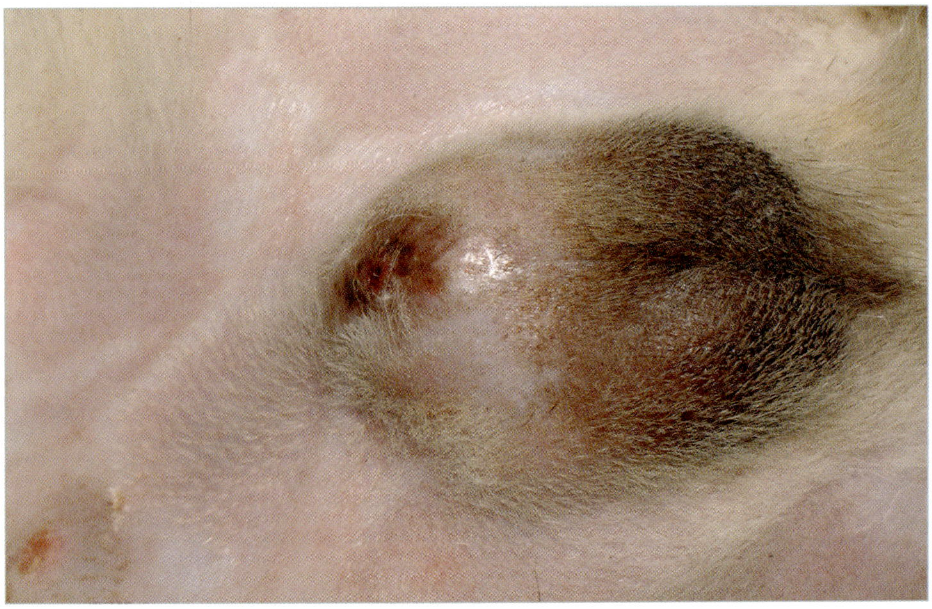

Fig. 2. Upon examination of the area, a very small preputial opening is found.
As a result of urine retention, balanoposthitis has developed, making urination even more difficult.

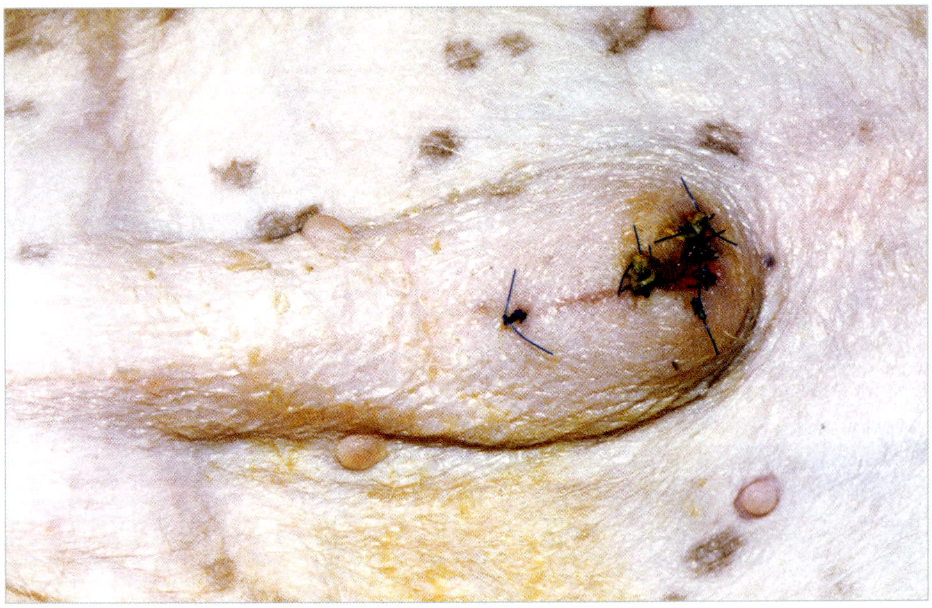

Fig. 3. Surgical result (9 days postoperatively) following reopening of the preputial orifice in a patient that had suffered post-traumatic phimosis.

Phimosis. Case 1 / Opening-widening of the preputial orifice

Technical difficulty

A 4-month old mixed-breed puppy is brought to the hospital for incomplete perforation of the prepuce. The urine exits through multiple openings in the area.

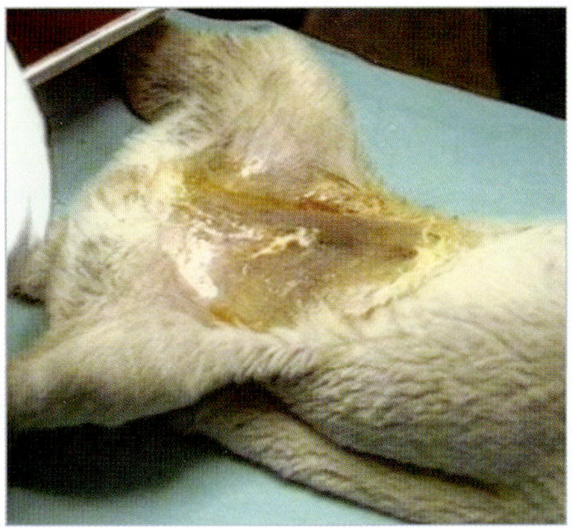

Fig. 1. The surgical field is prepared in the standard manner. The area is shaved and cleaned before surgery.

Surgical technique

The procedure will create a new preputial orifice (figs. 1-6). Afterwards, castration is performed to avoid a potential paraphimosis when the animal is adult.

See castration ➔ page 264

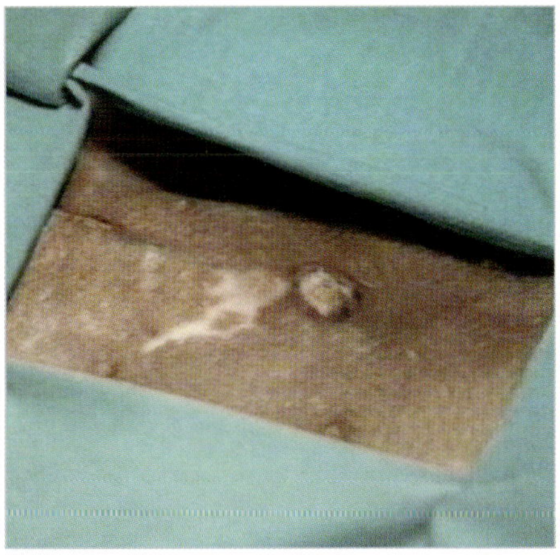

Fig. 2. In this patient, the absence of a normal preputial orifice is noted.
The skin to be resected is marked with a black felt tip pen. Fistulous tracts through which the urine drains are visible.

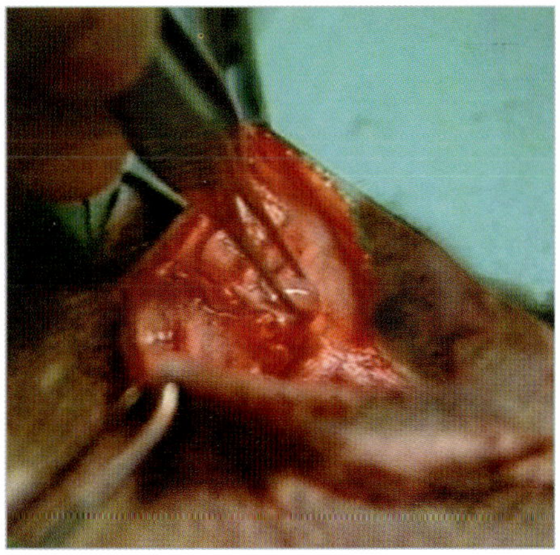

Fig. 3. This photograph shows the resected skin and mucous membranes of the prepuce and penis.

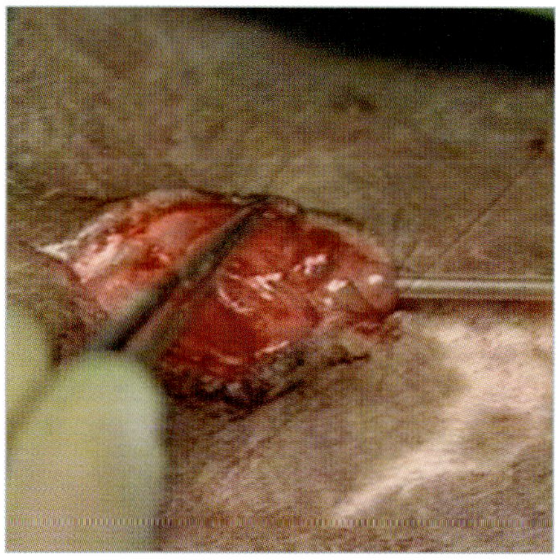

Fig. 4. Next, the mucosa of the prepuce is sutured to the skin with interrupted sutures using 6/0 monofilament material.
Catheterisation of the urethra ensures the penis is identified at all times.

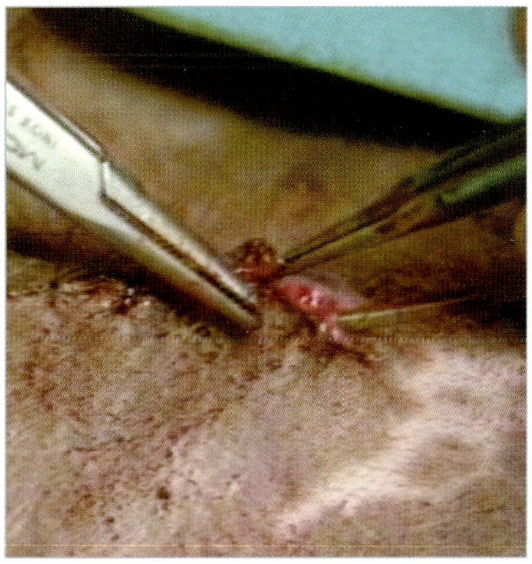

Fig. 5. Once the preputial orifice is sutured, the skin is closed with the same suture material.

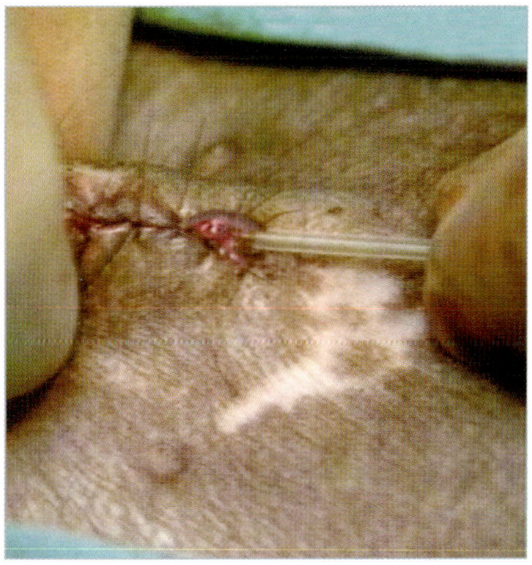

Fig. 6. After reconstructing the preputial orifice and closing the skin, the urinary catheter is withdrawn.

Possible complications

- Persistence of phimosis due to insufficient skin resection.
- Exposure of the glans due to excessive skin resection or skin resected in the ventral area.

✱ ***To avoid potential iatrogenic paraphimosis, do not remove too much skin when creating the preputial orifice.***

Phimosis. Case 2 / Reconstruction of the preputial orifice

This case concerned a 4-month-old German Shepherd puppy with difficulty urinating and an inflamed prepuce (fig. 1).

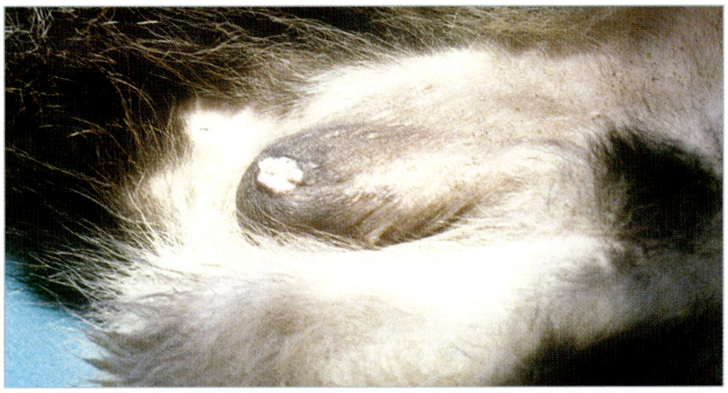

Fig.1. This photograph shows an inflamed prepuce as a consequence of the urinary retention.

During examination, the absence of a normal preputial orifice was noted. A small orifice (in the depigmented area) through which the urine drains was also visible (fig. 2).
This procedure reconstructs the preputial orifice by suturing the mucosa directly to the skin (fig. 3).

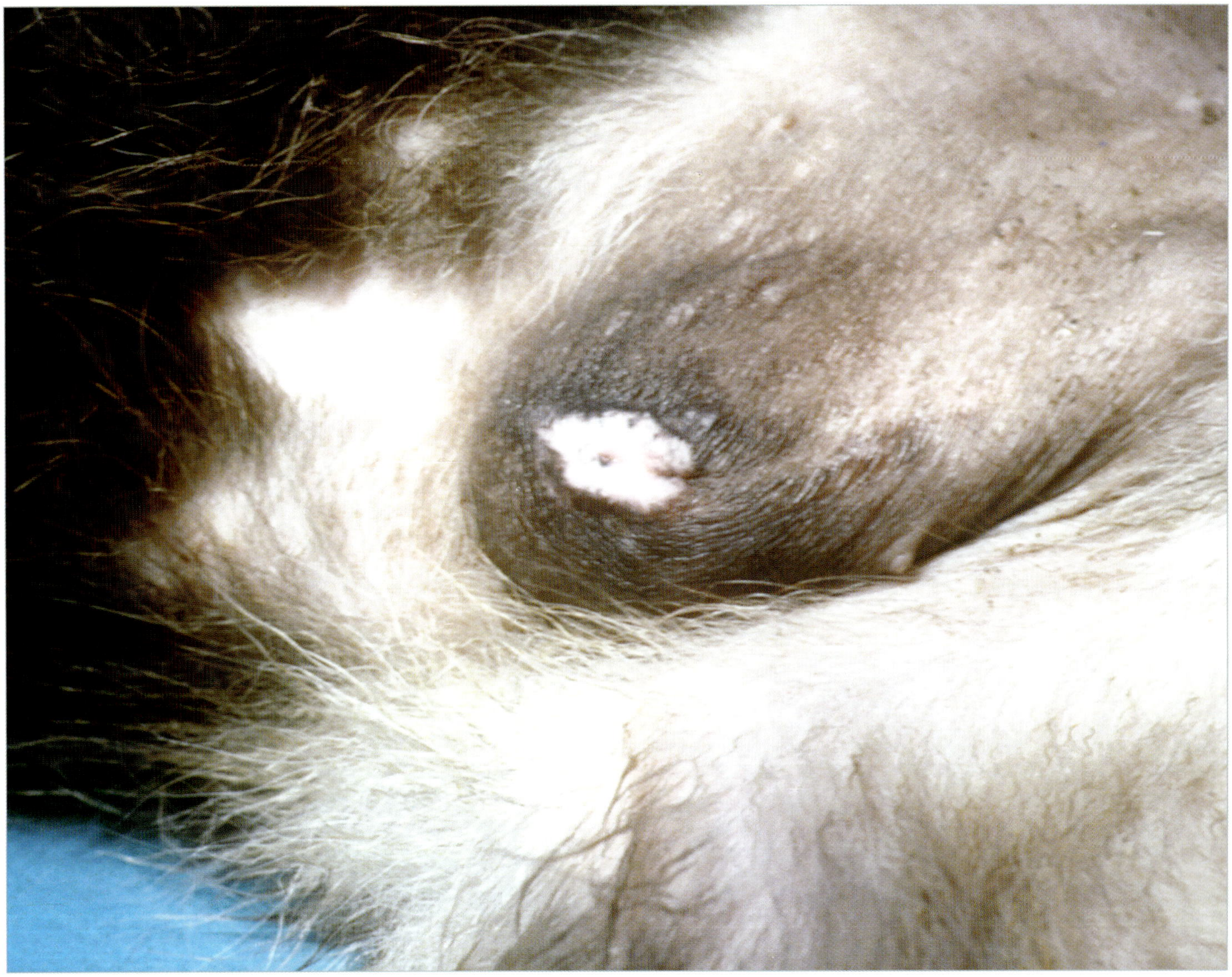

Fig. 2. Absence of a normally developed prepuce. Note the depigmented area with a small opening in its centre.

In this case, multifilament suture material was used.
Note that it is preferable to use monofilament material to avoid the capillary effect inherent to multifilament threads, thereby reducing secondary infections and irritations.

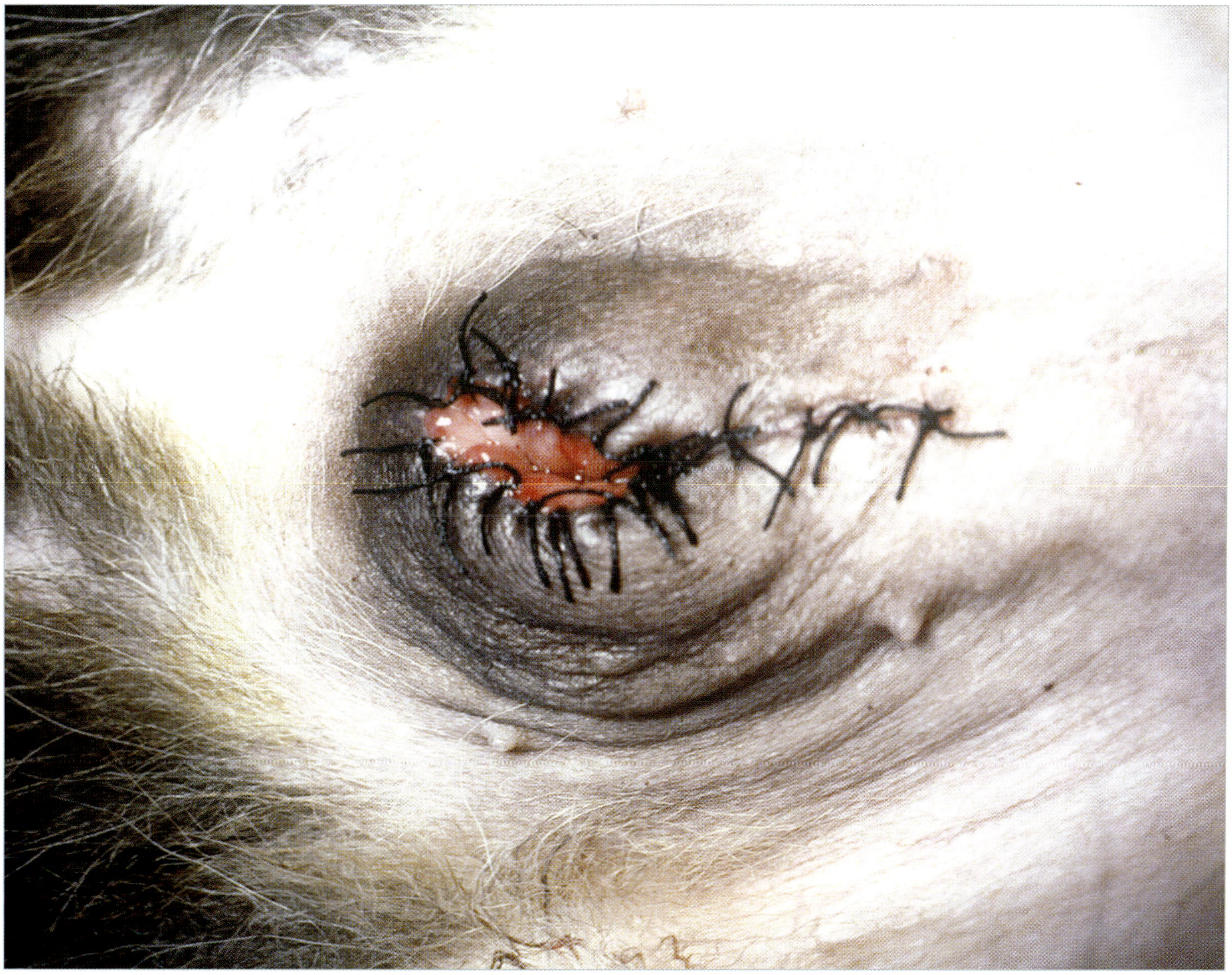

Fig. 3. Skin is resected from the area where the preputial orifice should be. The preputial mucosa is sutured directly to the skin.

Paraphimosis

Prevalence

Paraphimosis is defined as an inability to retract the penis into the prepuce.
It most commonly occurs after copulation or masturbation, particularly in young animals. It can also occur in longhaired cats when the penis is "caught" by the surrounding hair.
Paraphimosis may also result from trauma, infections or priapism (due to spinal injuries or genitourinary infections).

> ***Sexual hyperactivity is a common cause of paraphimosis in young animals.***
>
> ***Castration is recommended in cases of sexual hyperactivity to prevent recurrence.***

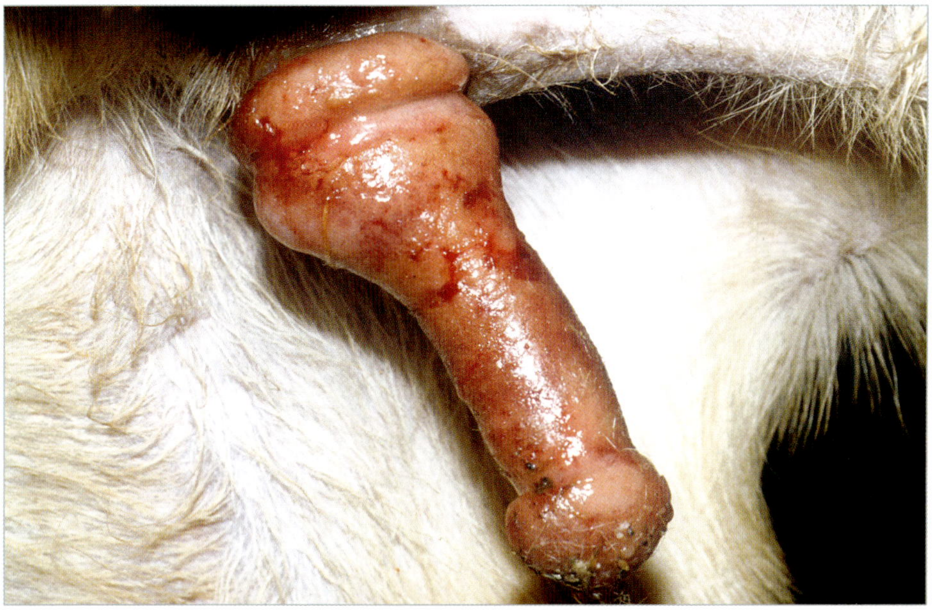

Fig. 1. The exteriorised penis becomes congested, making its retraction into the prepuce difficult. Hair around the area may also complicate withdrawal. Frequent licking of the inflamed, congested tissues exacerbates the condition.

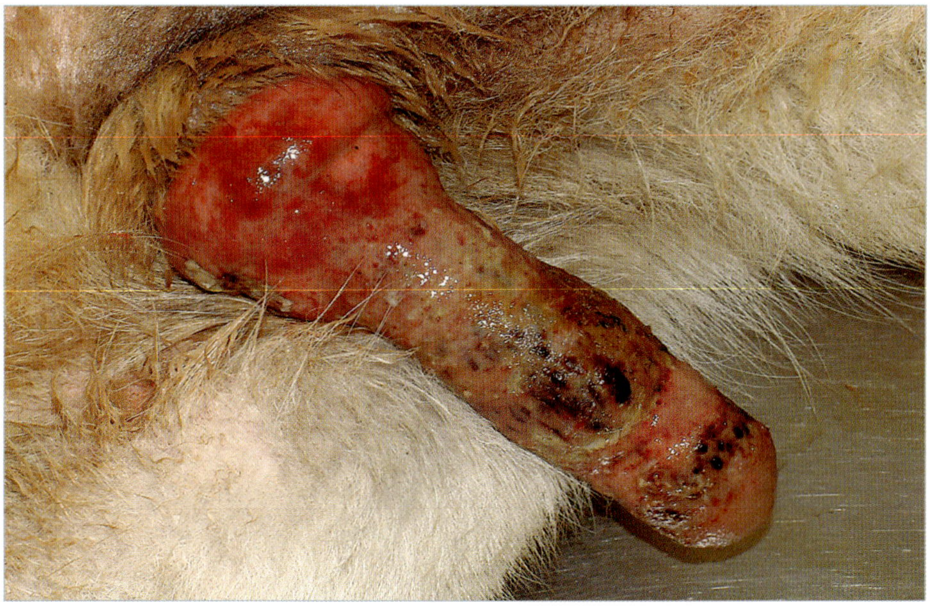

Fig. 2. Lesions of the penis worsen over time. The penis dries out, becomes inflamed, is mutilated by the patient and necrotic areas can appear rapidly.

Treatment

To reduce the swelling of the penis, sugar or hyperosmolar solutions can be applied directly to the congested, oedematous tissue.
The penis and prepuce are cleaned with a soapy antiseptic solution, then lubricant is applied to facilitate repositioning.
It may also be necessary to open the preputial orifice surgically to aid retraction of the penis.

Fracture of the os penis is another possible cause of exteriorisation of the penis (figs. 3 and 4).
If there is little displacement of the fragments, it can be resolved by catheterisation of the urethra while the fracture consolidates. If, as in this case, the fracture has caused a marked lesion of the urethra, partial amputation of the penis is indicated and a scrotal urethrostomy may also need to be performed.

The patient requires sedation or anaesthesia prior to examination.

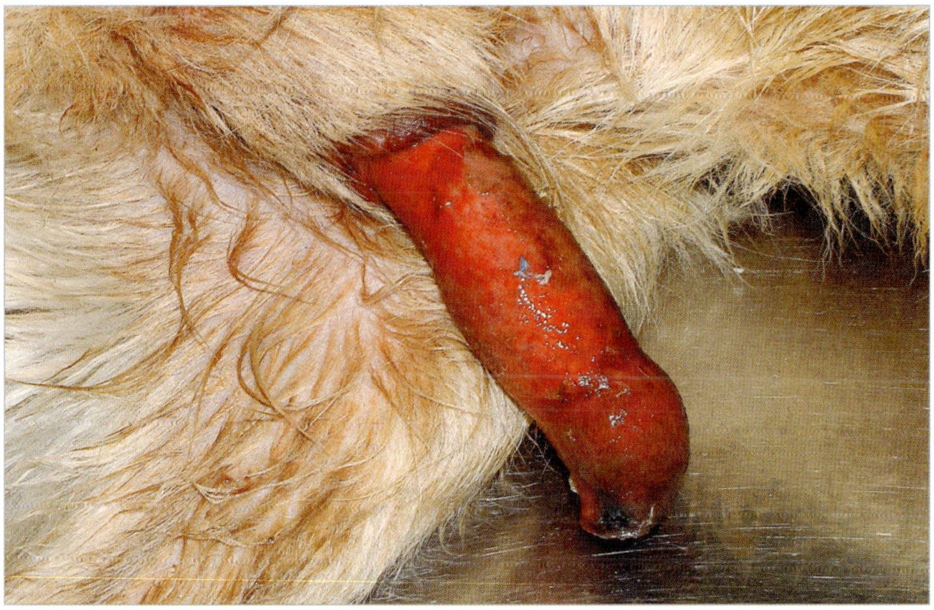

Fig. 3. This patient suffered severe abdominal trauma resulting in an acute abdomen and exteriorisation of the penis.

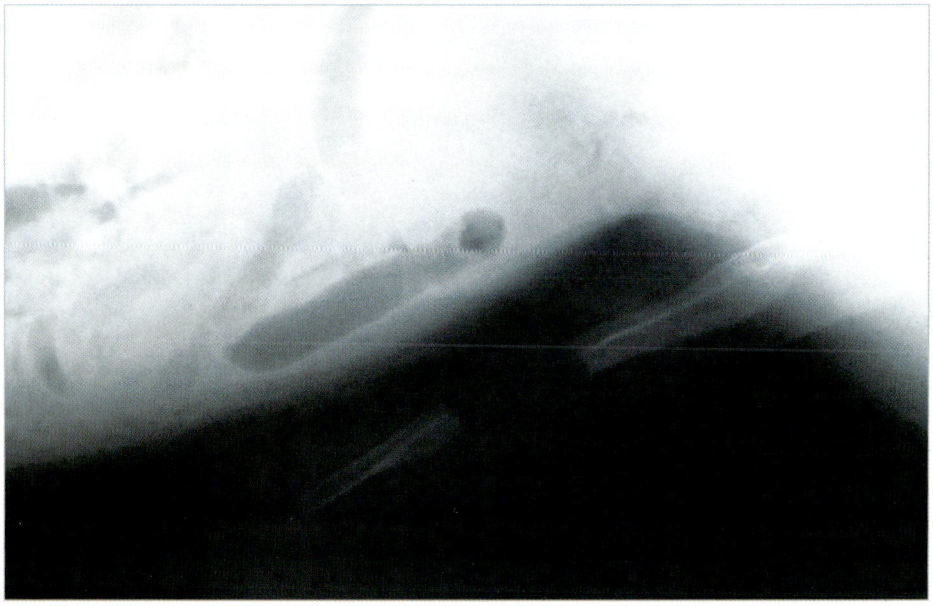

Fig. 4. The radiograph confirms a fracture of the os penis.

Wounds. Case 1 / Preputial wounds

Prevalence	■	□	□	□	□

Preputial and penile wounds occur as a result of fights, road traffic accidents, jumping fences, firearm or knife wounds and copulation.

Preputial wounds should be approached in the same manner as skin wounds (figs. 1 and 2).

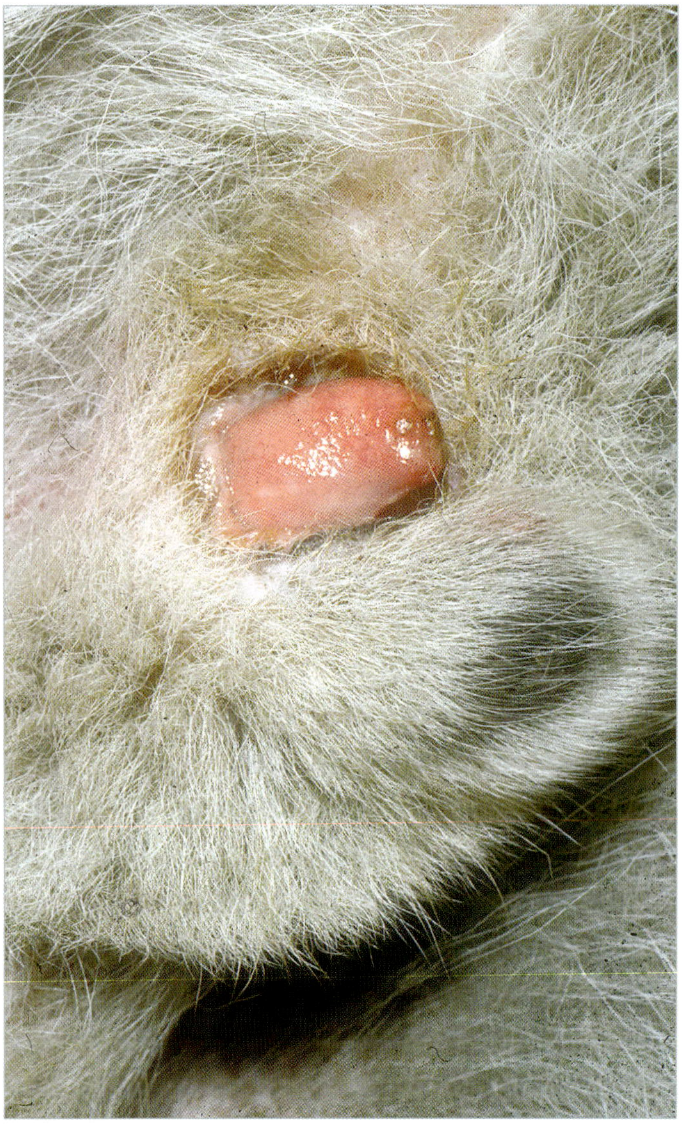

Fig. 1. Wound at the base of the prepuce after jumping over a wrought-iron gate. The glans penis is exposed and will dry out and become damaged without the protection of the skin.

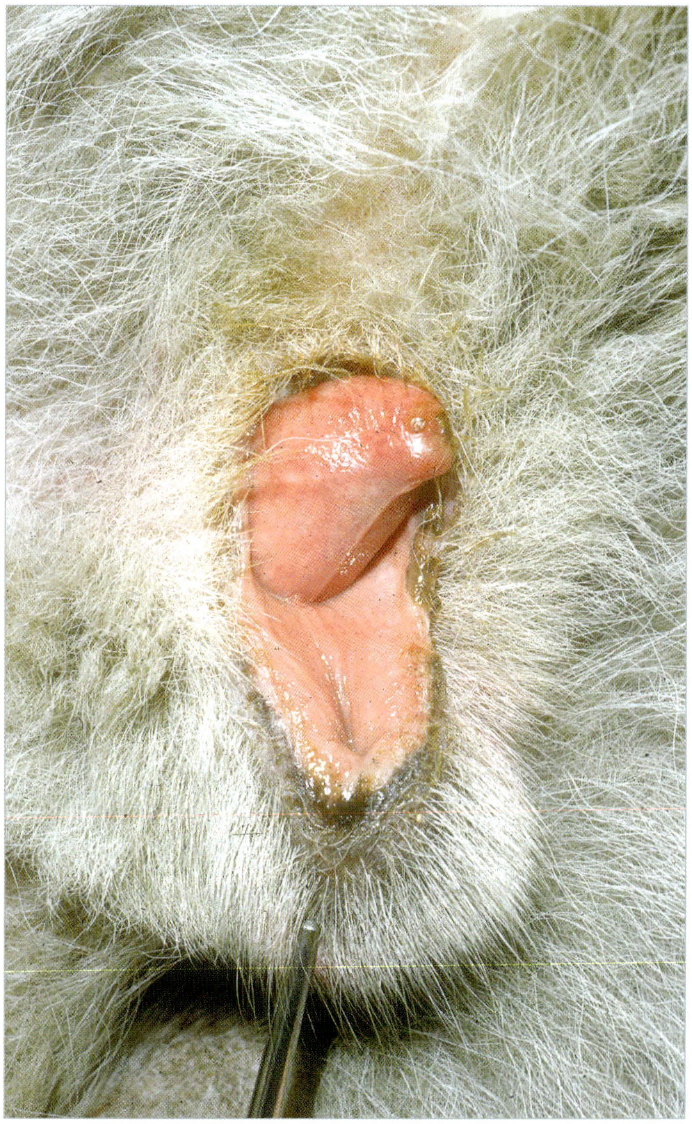

Fig. 2. This wound needs to be sutured as quickly as possible, using synthetic absorbable material for the mucosa of the prepuce and non-absorbable material for the skin. If infected, it should not be sutured until the infection is under control. Ensure the penis is adequately protected in the interim.

Case 2 / Wounds of the penis (distal area)

Prevalence	■				
Technical difficulty	■	■			

Wounds of the penis are characterised by haemorrhage, which can be quite considerable, though not always continuous. Superficial, small wounds can be managed medically by applying antibiotic ointments, and allowed to heal by secondary intention (fig. 3).
More marked wounds, and those that bleed profusely, should be sutured using absorbable material of appropriate size.

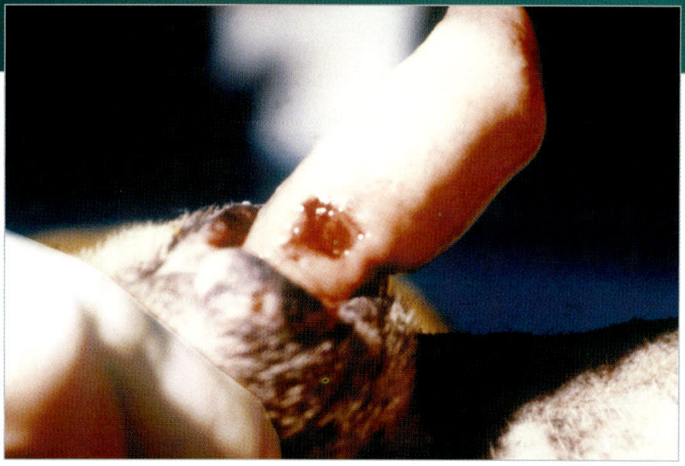

Fig. 3. Superficial wounds do not produce excessive haemorrhage and can be treated topically with local antiseptics and antibiotic ointments.

Penile erection should be avoided by administering sedatives during the healing period.

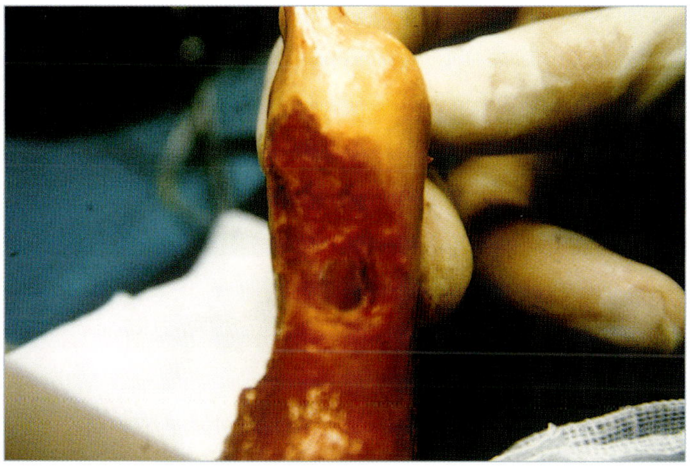

Fig. 4. Penile wounds are closed by suturing the lacerated tissue, using interrupted sutures with absorbable material.

Wounds of the glans penis are relatively common following copulation, or after compulsive masturbation behaviour (figs. 4 and 5). Some cases may require reconstruction of the urethra (figs. 6-8).

Surgical technique

After antiseptic treatment of the prepuce and penis, the latter is exteriorised by sliding back the prepuce. The penis is held in place with a gauze swab at its base.
Next, the penile wound is closed with interrupted sutures using synthetic material (figs. 4-8).

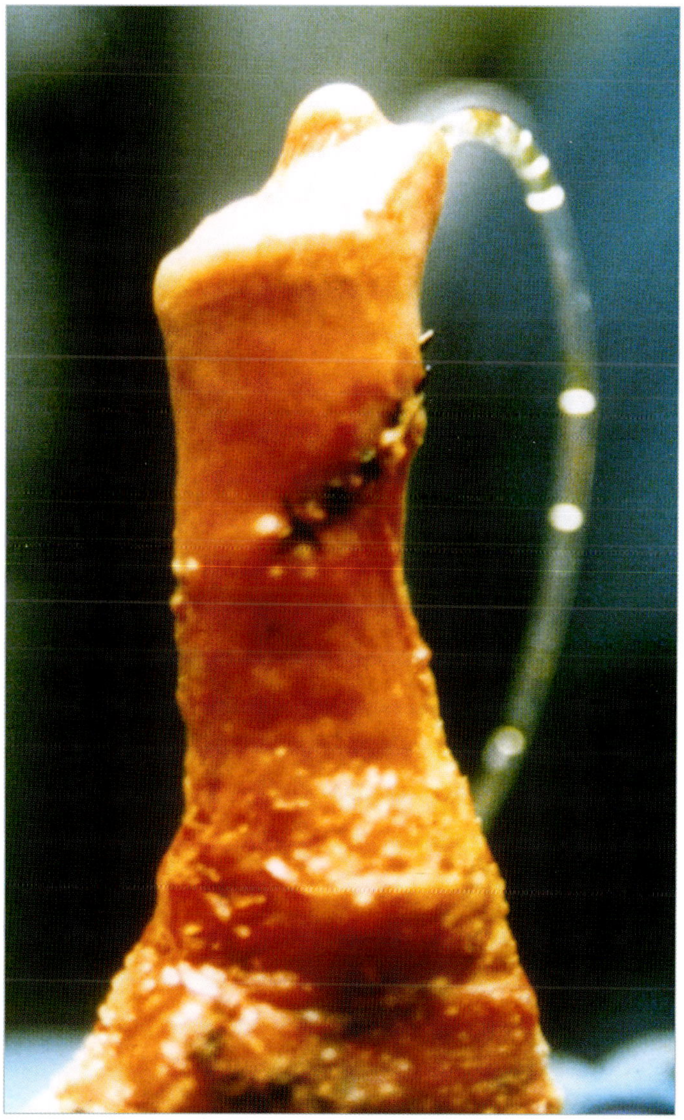

Fig. 5. When suturing these wounds, synthetic absorbable 5/0 or 6/0 monofilament material should be used.

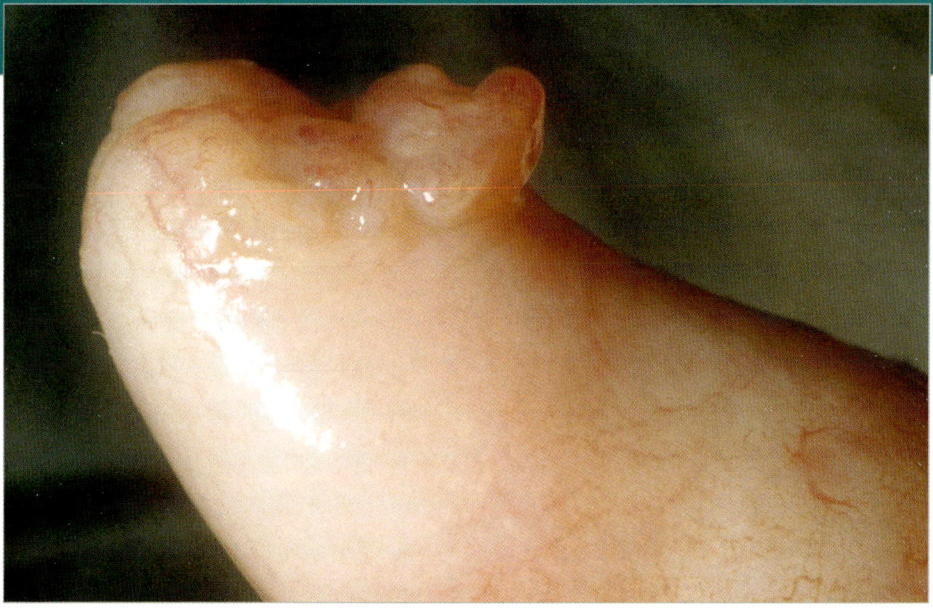

Fig. 6. Examination of the penis reveals damage near the tip, affecting the urethra.

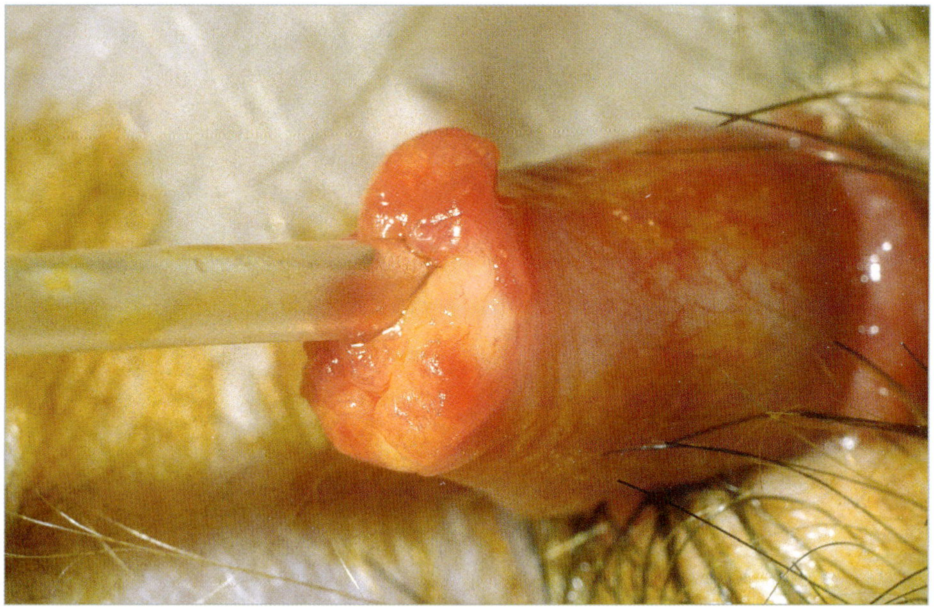

Fig. 7. The surgical field is antiseptically prepared with an iodine solution diluted 1:1 with saline. Passing a urethral catheter makes suturing easier.

Fig. 8. Simple interrupted sutures are placed, using synthetic absorbable 5/0 or 6/0 monofilament material.

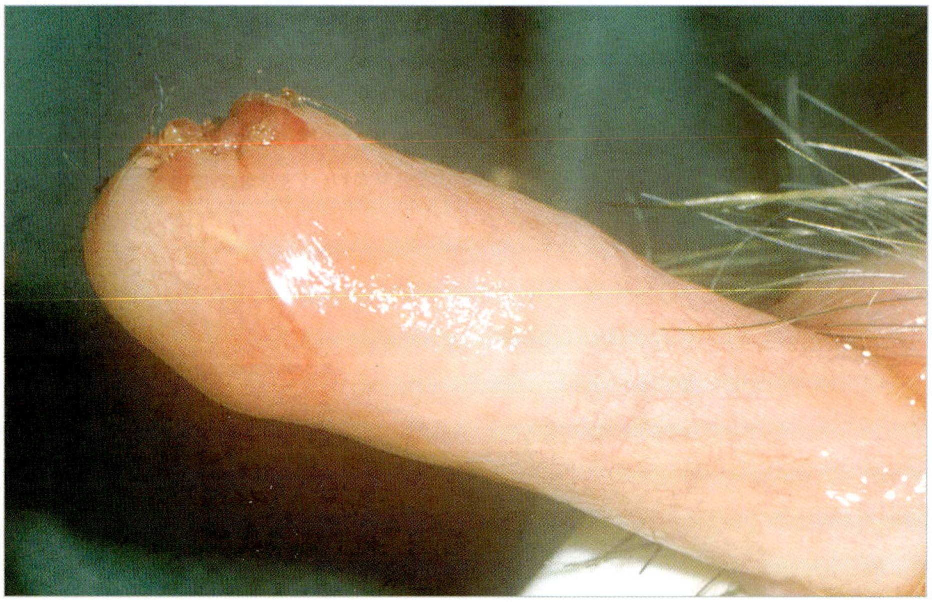

After surgery

- Maintain local hygiene, rinsing the prepuce with the iodine/saline solution or similar topical antiseptic.
- Use of an Elizabethan collar is essential.

> *Avoid sexual excitation of the patient during the healing process (7-10 days); use systemic sedatives if necessary.*

Case 3 / Wounds of the penis (perineal area)

Prevalence	■				
Technical difficulty	■	■	■	■	

Wounds to the perineal area affecting the penis and urethra cause profuse bleeding. If not treated promptly they may cause cicatricial stenosis, tissue necrosis due to urine leakage into the subcutaneous tissue and dysuria.

A mixed-breed dog was presented with perineal bite wounds following a fight 10 days earlier. The wounds were treated with topical antiseptics, systemic antibiotics and were left to heal by secondary intention.

The wounds appeared to heal satisfactorily but 5 days later, the dog presented with dysuria. Urine was visibly leaking through the perineal area (fig. 9).

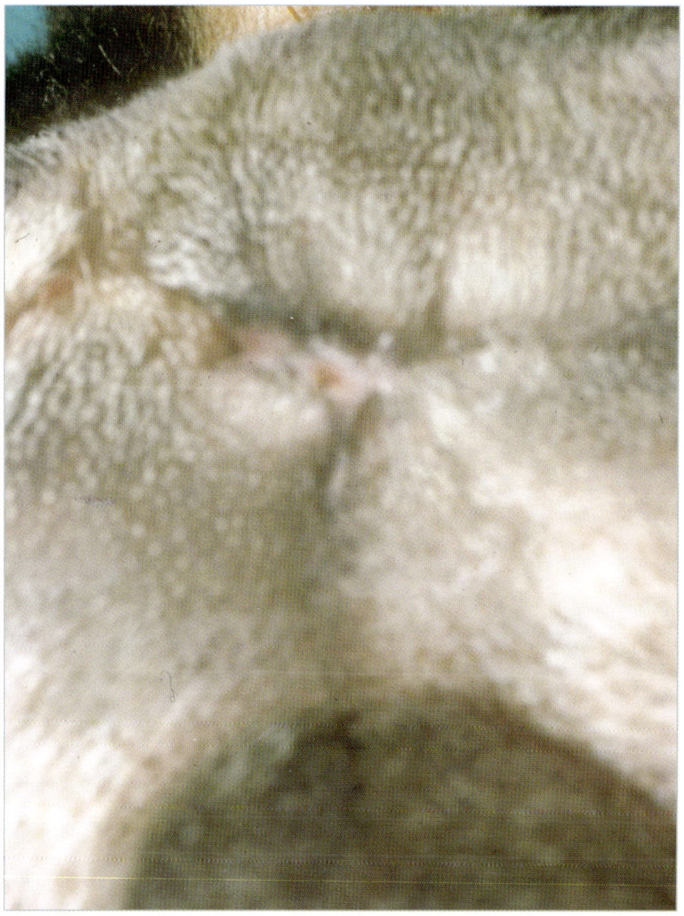

Fig. 9. In the perineal area, a large transverse scar is observed at the level of the urethra. A fistular tract leaking urine is also visible.

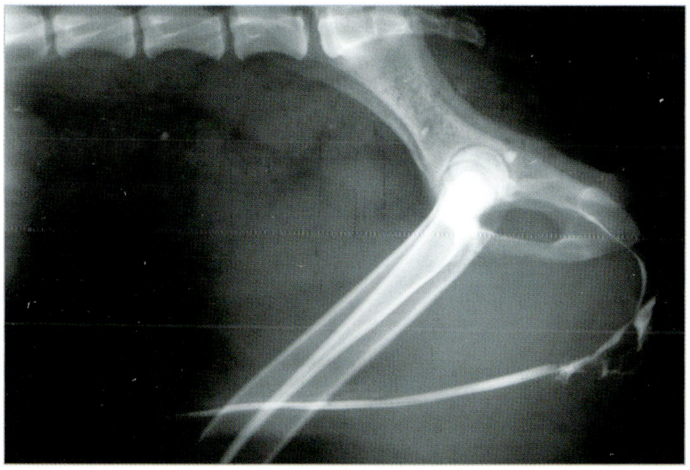

Fig. 10. A retrograde urethrogram using an iodine contrast medium demonstrates leakage of contrast medium into the perineal tissues.

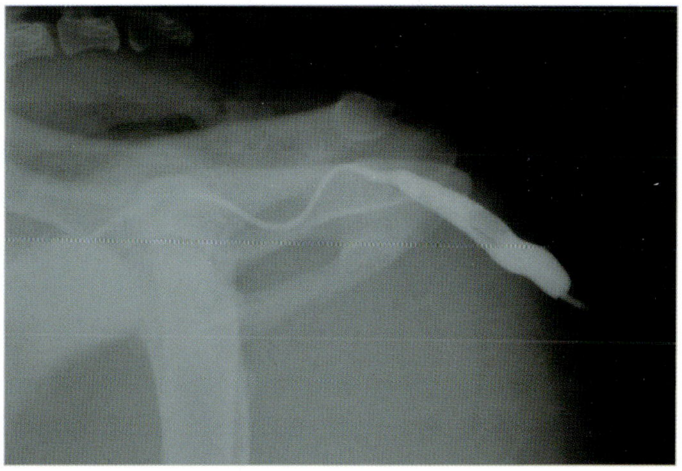

Fig. 11. Contrast medium instilled into the fistulous tract via catheter demonstrates a clear distal stenosis with marked urethral dilatation behind it.

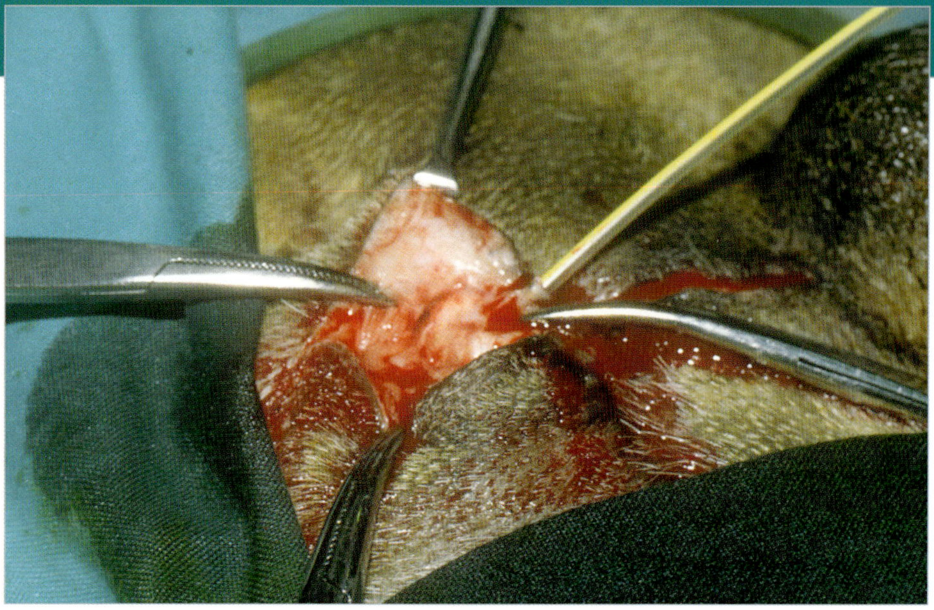

Fig. 12. The membranous urethra is approached from the perineal region via longitudinal incision over its length.
The damaged urethra and proximal fistular orifice are identified. The fistular tract is catheterised to aid identification during the procedure.

See urethral catheterisation **→** *page 236*

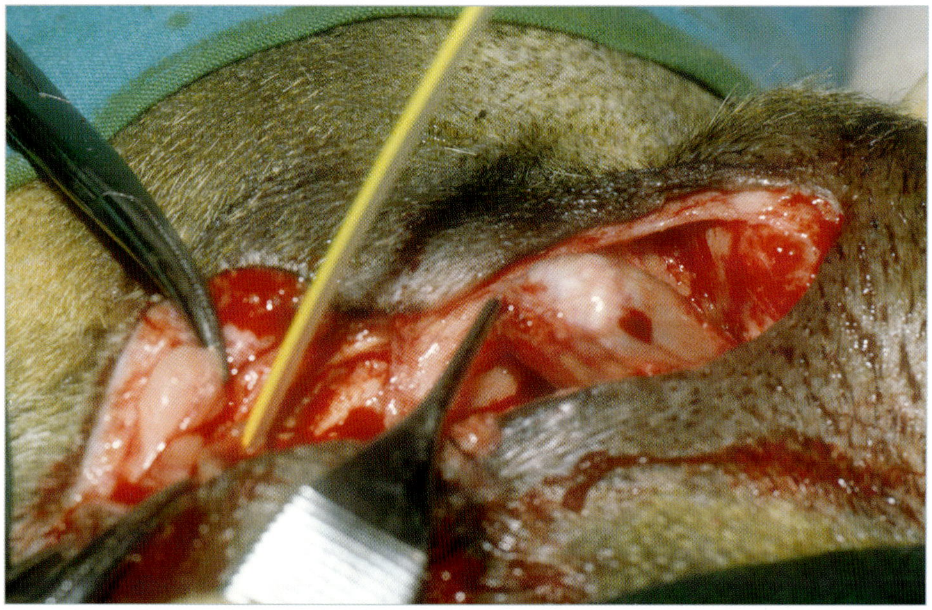

Fig. 13. The incision is extended ventrally to locate the distal end of the urethra. Another catheter is inserted up the penis to the affected area to facilitate the urethral dissection.

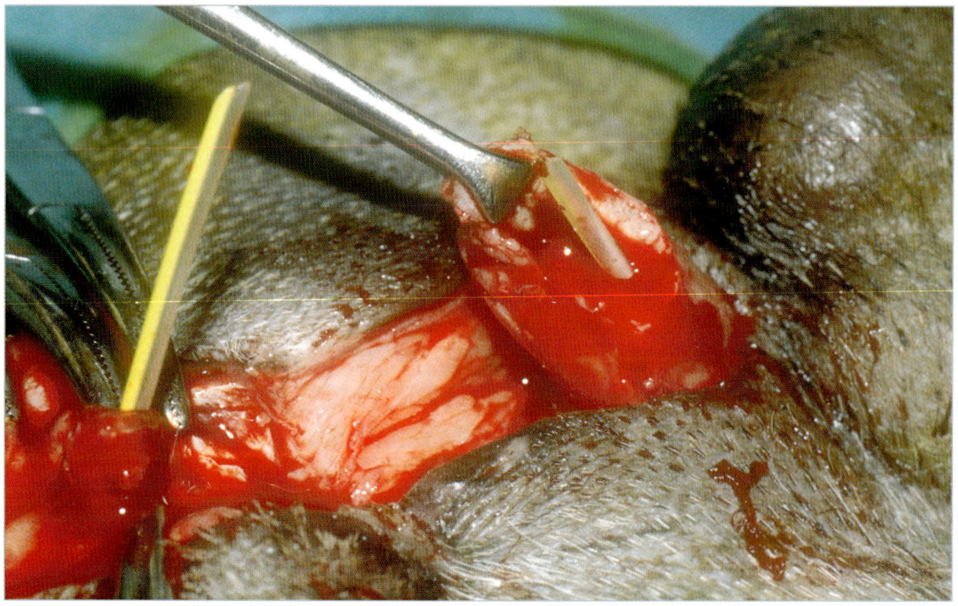

Fig. 14. The cicatricial stenoses of both segments are resected to reconstruct the urethra. Minimise the amount of tissue resected (1 to 2 mm) to prevent tension on the anastomosis which could lead to wound dehiscence.

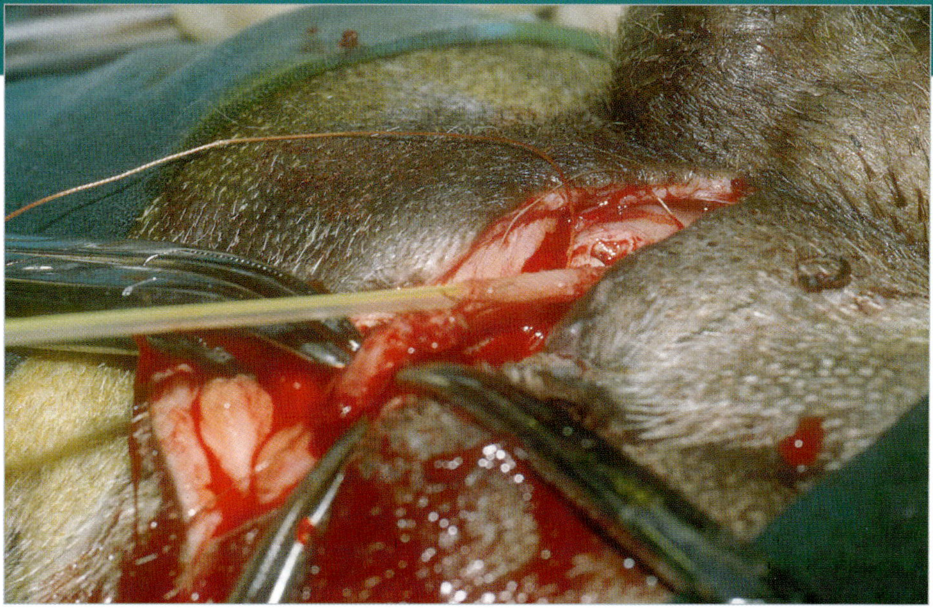

Fig. 15. Simple interrupted sutures are placed over a urinary or Foley catheter. Synthetic absorbable 5/0 or 6/0 monofilament material is used.

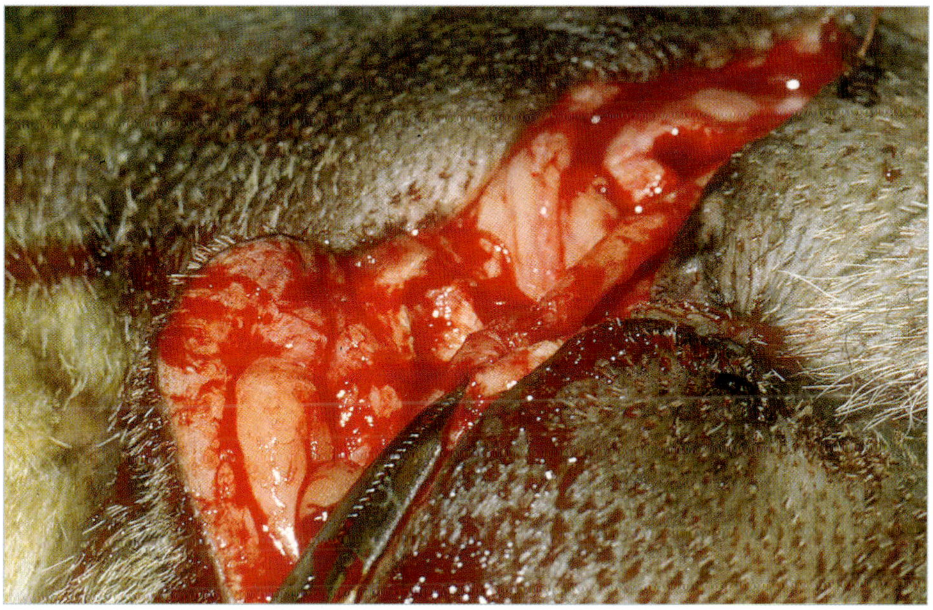

Fig. 16. After urethral anastomosis, the perineal area needs to be reconstructed. The subcutaneous tissue with absorbable material and the skin with non-absorbable monofilament material.

The urinary catheter should remain in place for at least 5 or 6 days to maintain elimination of urine while the urethra heals.

After surgery

- These patients require meticulous postoperative care. An Elizabethan collar should be worn to prevent them from pulling out the urinary catheter.
- The catheter should be protected by an abdominal bandage and should be connected to a urinary collection system to reduce the risk of ascending infections.
- The patency of the catheter should be assessed regularly by injecting saline.
- Urinalysis should be carried out frequently.
- Provide appropriate antibiotic cover.
- A postoperative recovery diet is recommended and the patient's hydration status should be monitored.

Prognosis is good, although urethral stenosis due to fibrosis may develop as a consequence of severe lesions or insufficiently meticulous surgery.

Surgical alternative

If the lesion cannot be reconstructed or if the stenosis is extensive and urethral resection is not possible, a permanent urethrostomy can be carried out proximally to permit urination.

If the patient removes the catheter, the clinician should not put it back "blindly" as this can have disastrous consequences.

Tumours. Case 1 / Medical treatment

Prevalence	■				

Penile tumours only represent 0.3% of tumours in the dog. They include transmissible venereal tumours, papillomas, squamous cell carcinomas and other tumours of the mesenchyme, such as lymphosarcoma or haemangioma/sarcoma. Venereal transmissible tumours respond well to medical treatment with vincristine (0.025 mg/kg IV, with a maximum of 1 mg, once weekly). CBC tests should be run (to monitor for leucopaenia) and treatment should be repeated until the tumours have disappeared. (figs. 1 and 2).

No tumours of the penis or prepuce have been described in the cat.

Venereal tumours are very easily transmitted.
If the patient exhibits epistaxis, examine the nasal cavity as this tumour may metastasize to this area.

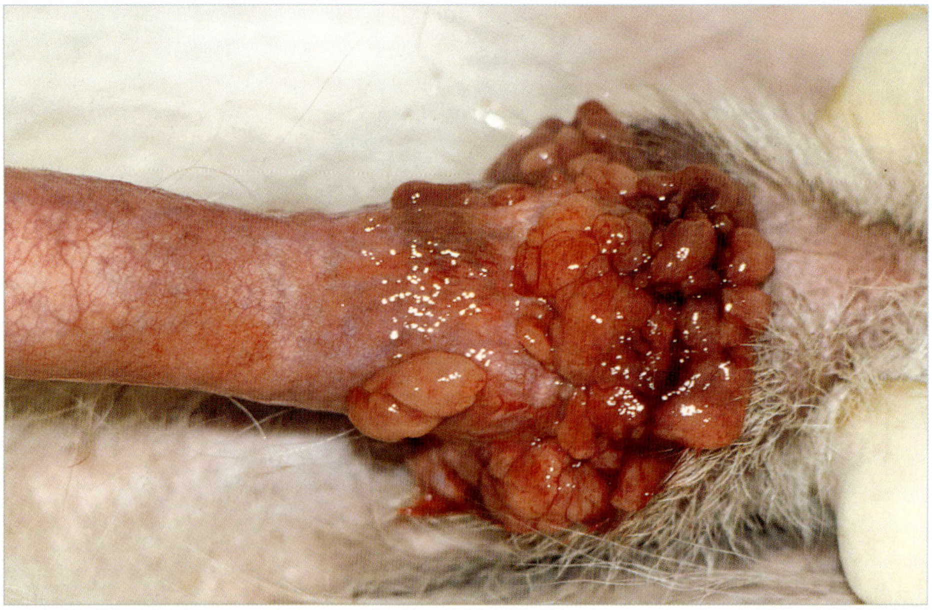

Fig. 1. Transmissible venereal tumours are the most commonly encountered. They consist of multiple pedunculated masses, are usually located at the base of the penis and normally contain ulcerated, haemorrhagic areas. Diagnosis should be confirmed by exfoliative cytology or biopsy.

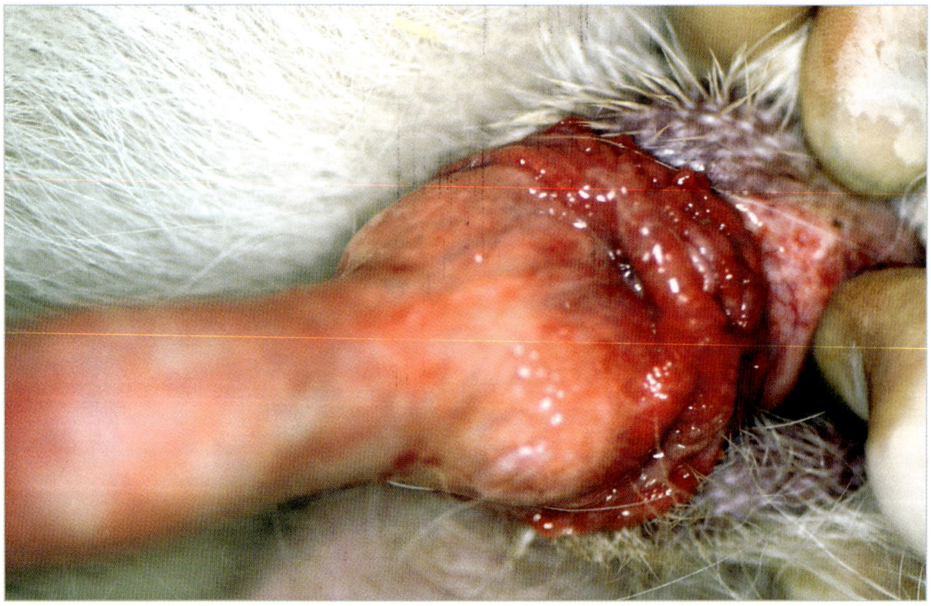

Fig. 2. Vincristine treatment is initiated; this photograph shows the result at the end of the planned sessions.

This case was treated by Dr. Díaz-Otero Medina.

Tumours. Case 2 / Surgical treatment

Prevalence	■				
Technical difficulty	■	■			

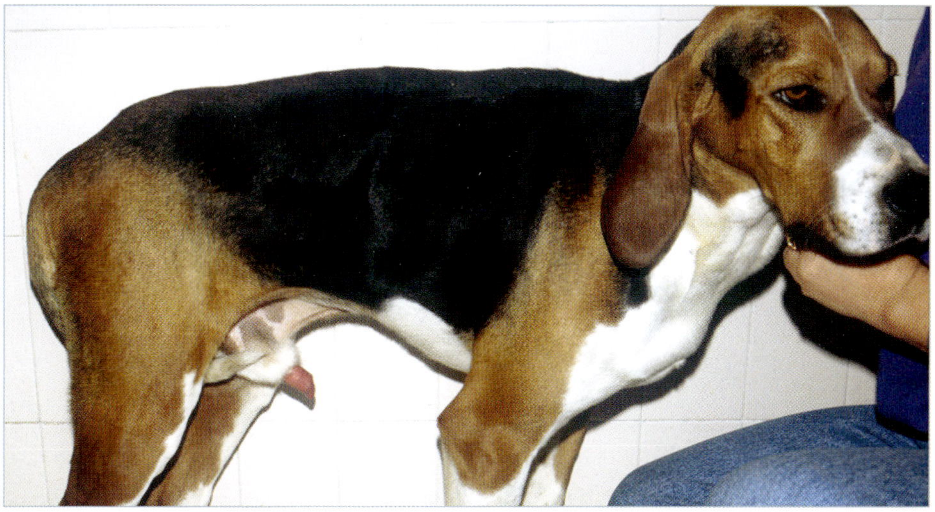

Fig. 3. "Sam" has priapism, licks his penis continuously and bleeds from the prepuce.

Other penile tumours require surgical excision using diathermy to limit bleeding and reduce the risk of local recurrence (figs. 3-5).

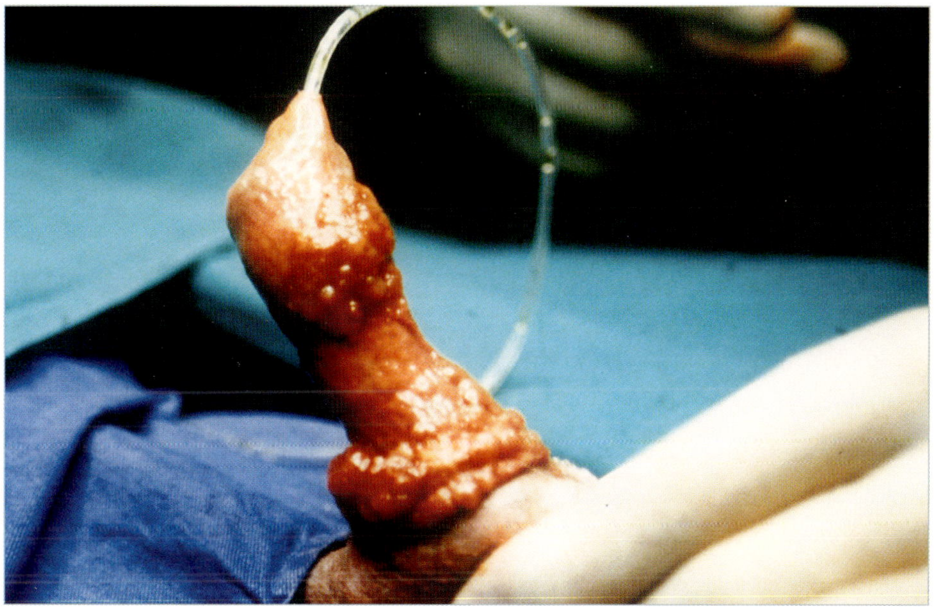

Fig. 4. When the prepuce is pulled back to expose the penis, a neoplastic mass (fibroma) located next to the glans is revealed.

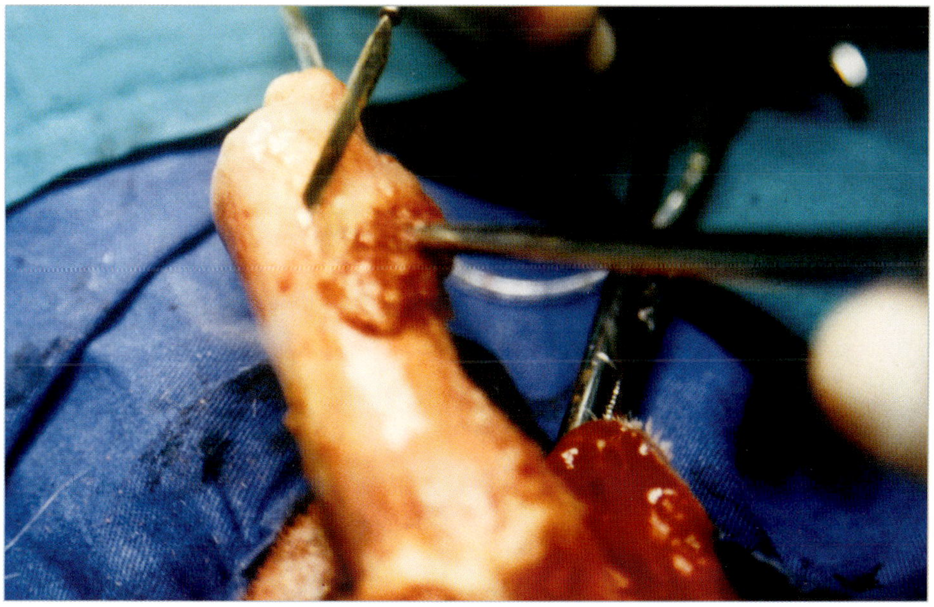

Fig. 5. Diathermy is indicated to control bleeding when resecting the neoplastic mass.

Mucosal defects are reconstructed with interrupted sutures using absorbable material, as described earlier.

See wounds of the penis (distal area) *page 215*

Prolapse of the urethral mucosa

Prevalence

Prolapse of the urethral mucosa mainly occurs in young animals following prolonged sexual arousal. The dog will be constantly licking its prepuce and glans penis.

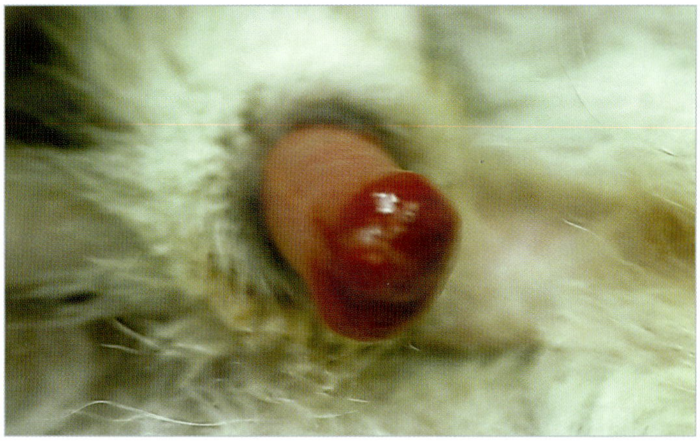

Fig. 1. Diagnosis is straightforward; by exteriorising the penis the prolapsed urethral mucosa becomes visible. The entire area is severely congested.

Conservative treatment

Technical difficulty

"Bullit" is a male, 8-month-old Bulldog referred because he is constantly bleeding from the penis (fig. 2).
The problem began two days ago when he tried unsuccessfully to mount a bitch in oestrus.

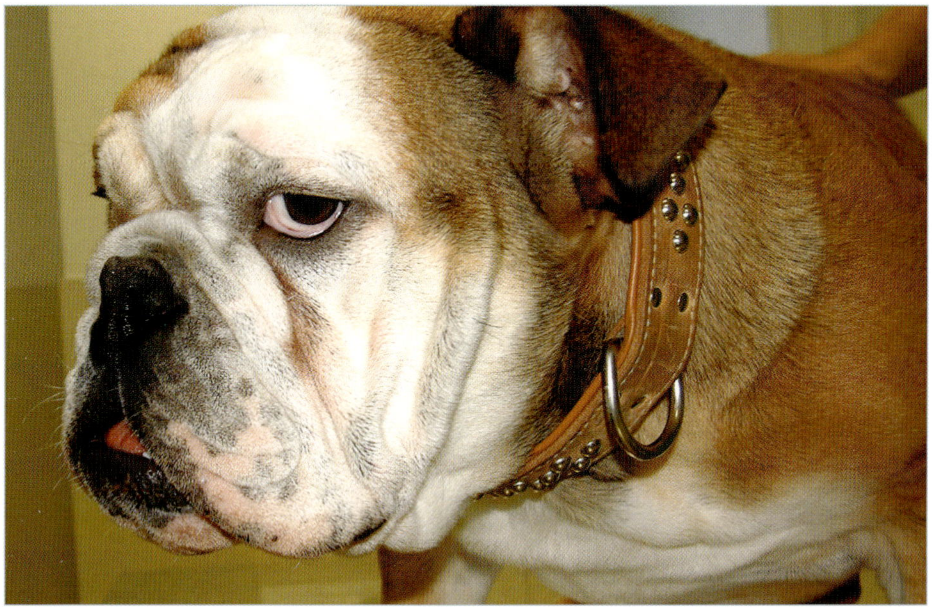

Fig. 2. "Bullit" is constantly bleeding from the penis, particularly noticeable when getting up after lying down for a while.

Examination of the penis with the prepuce retracted reveals the origin of the bleeding (fig. 3).

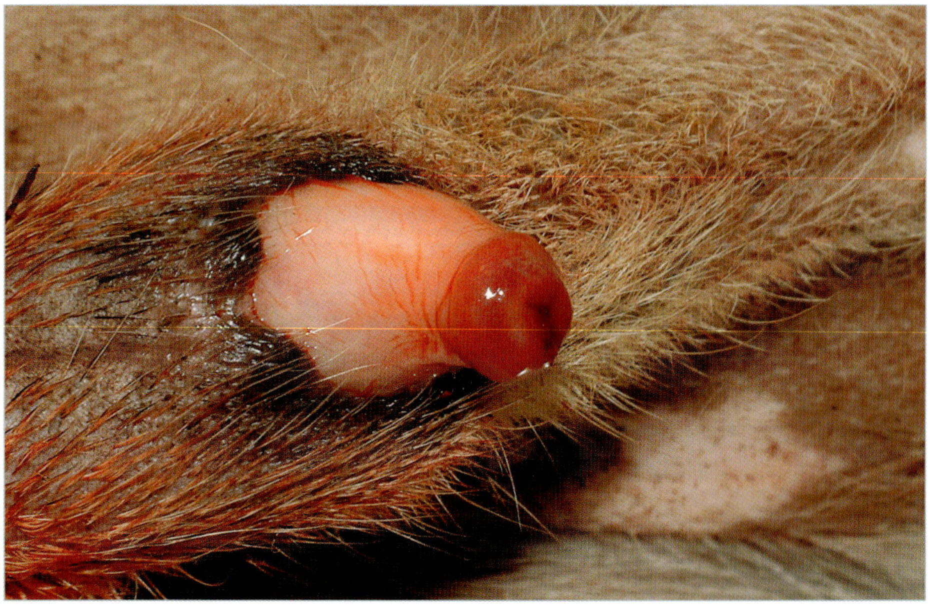

Fig. 3. Exteriorisation of the gland penis reveals urethral mucosa that has prolapsed through the penile orifice.

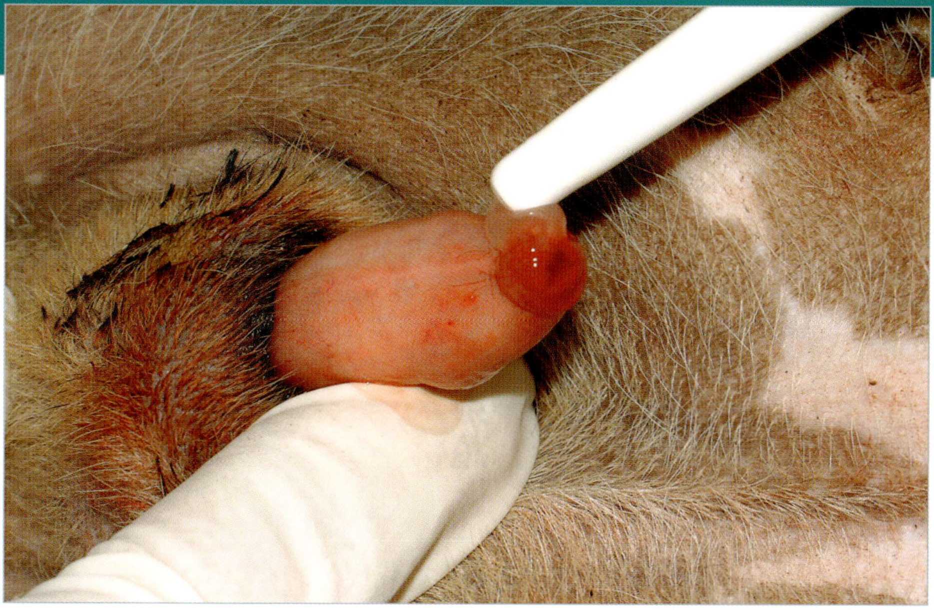

The initial treatment requires placement of a urinary catheter a short distance into the urethra (not into the bladder) and fixed with two sutures for 2 or 3 days (figs. 4-6).

See urinary catheterisation ➜ page 236

Fig. 4. A urological water-soluble gel is applied to anaesthetise the area and to facilitate urinary catheterisation.

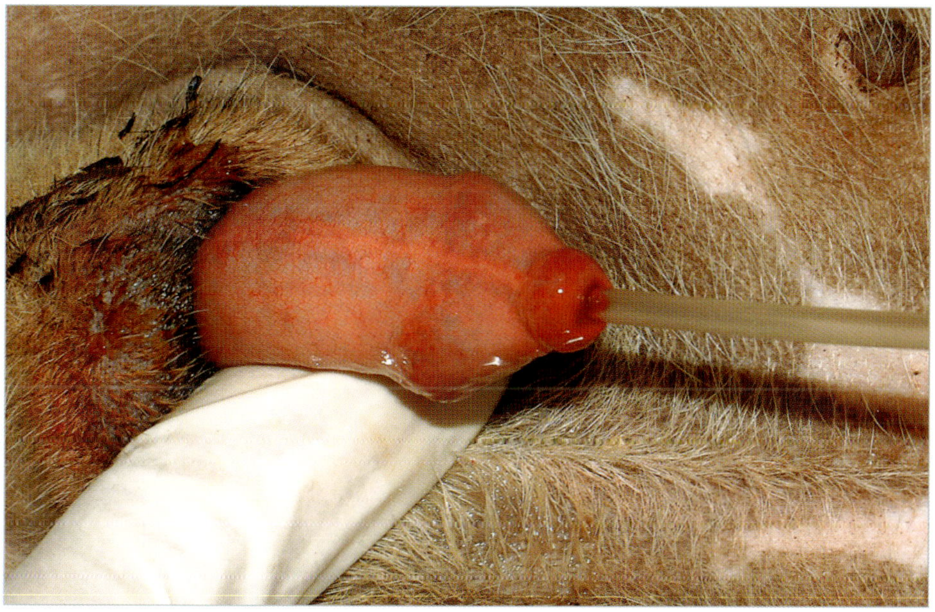

Fig. 5. The urethra is gently catheterised to ensure that the next time the patient urinates, the urine passes easily and a mucosal prolapse is avoided.

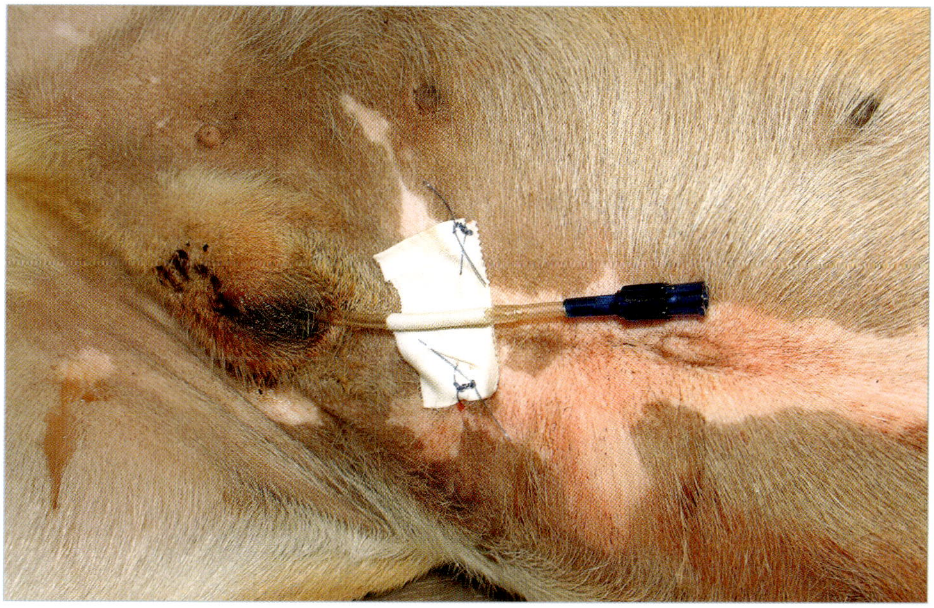

Fig. 6. The catheter is fixed to the skin with two sutures to keep it in place for the next two days.

Next steps

- Topical antibiotic and anti-inflammatory treatment for 5 or 6 days.
- Sufficiently large Elizabethan collar so the patient cannot lick the area.
- Use of sedatives if required.

Surgical treatment

Technical difficulty	■	■	□	□	□

Initially, this patient responded well to conservative treatment but a few days later the prolapse recurred and surgical treatment was recommended (figs. 7-14).

> ✱ ***Where recurrence or marked injury to the urethra has occured, resection of the prolapsed mucosa is indicated.***

Before surgery

Prior to surgery, the penis and the interior of the prepuce should be disinfected with a 50% iodine solution every ten minutes until entering the operating room.

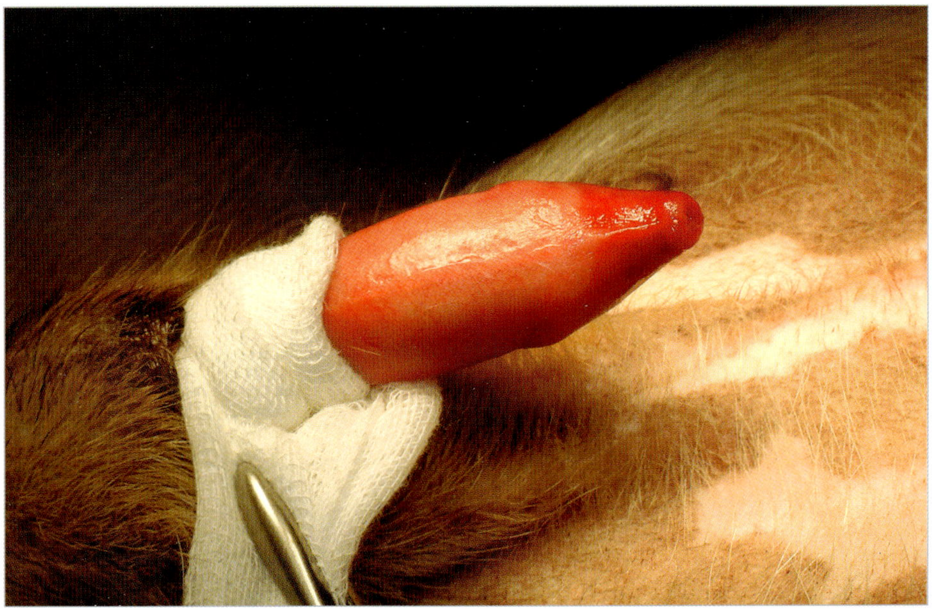

Fig. 7. To keep the penis exteriorised, a gauze swab is placed around its base like a scarf to prevent the prepuce from sliding back into its normal position.

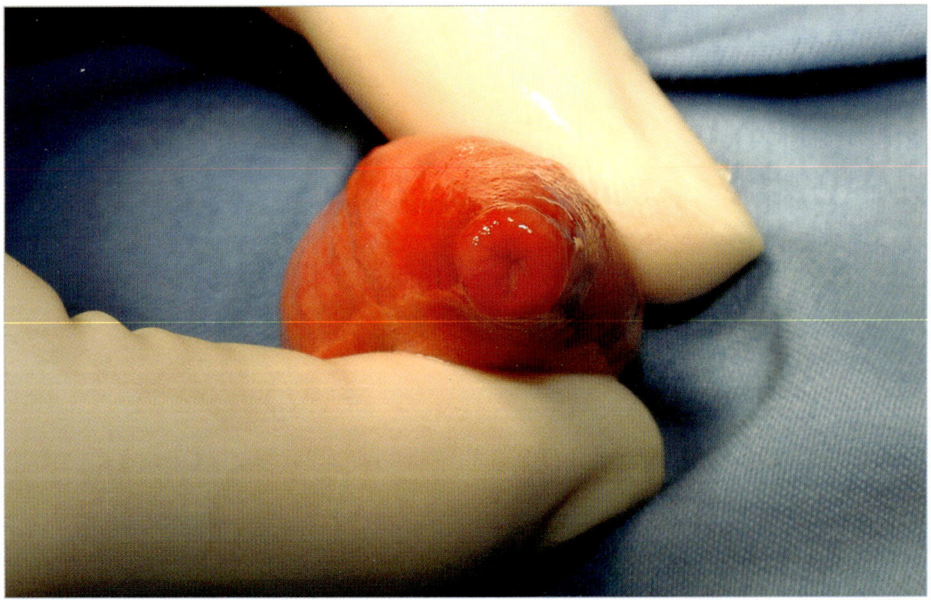

Fig. 8. This photograph shows the prolapsed urethral mucosa that will be resected.

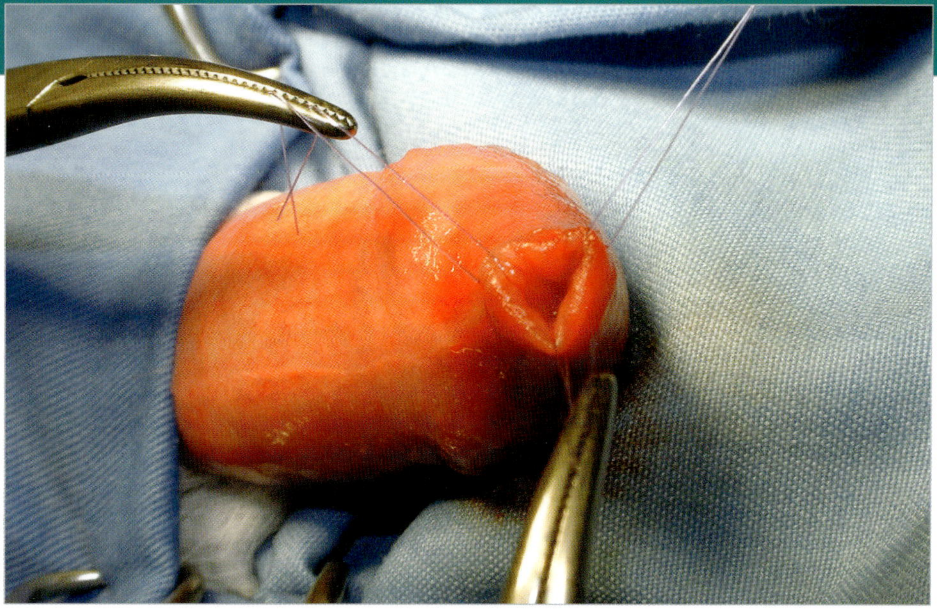

Fig. 9. To prevent retraction of the wound edges during resection, the urethra is fixed with stay sutures that keep the urethral mucosa permanently in view.

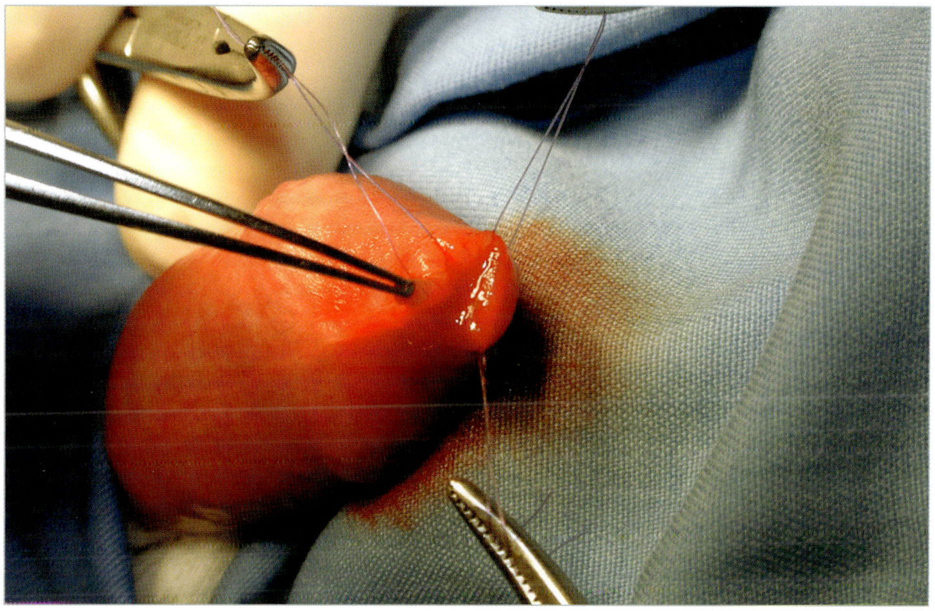

Fig. 10. The prolapsed mucosa is cut with scissors between two stay sutures. Intense haemorrhage of the wound will occur.

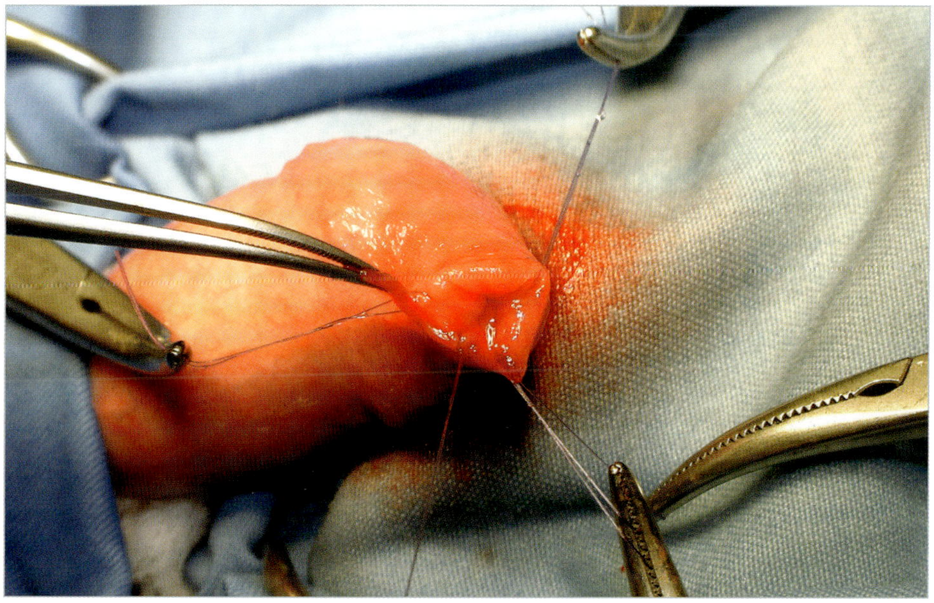

Fig. 11. To prevent excessive bleeding, the urethral mucosa is sutured to that of the penis.

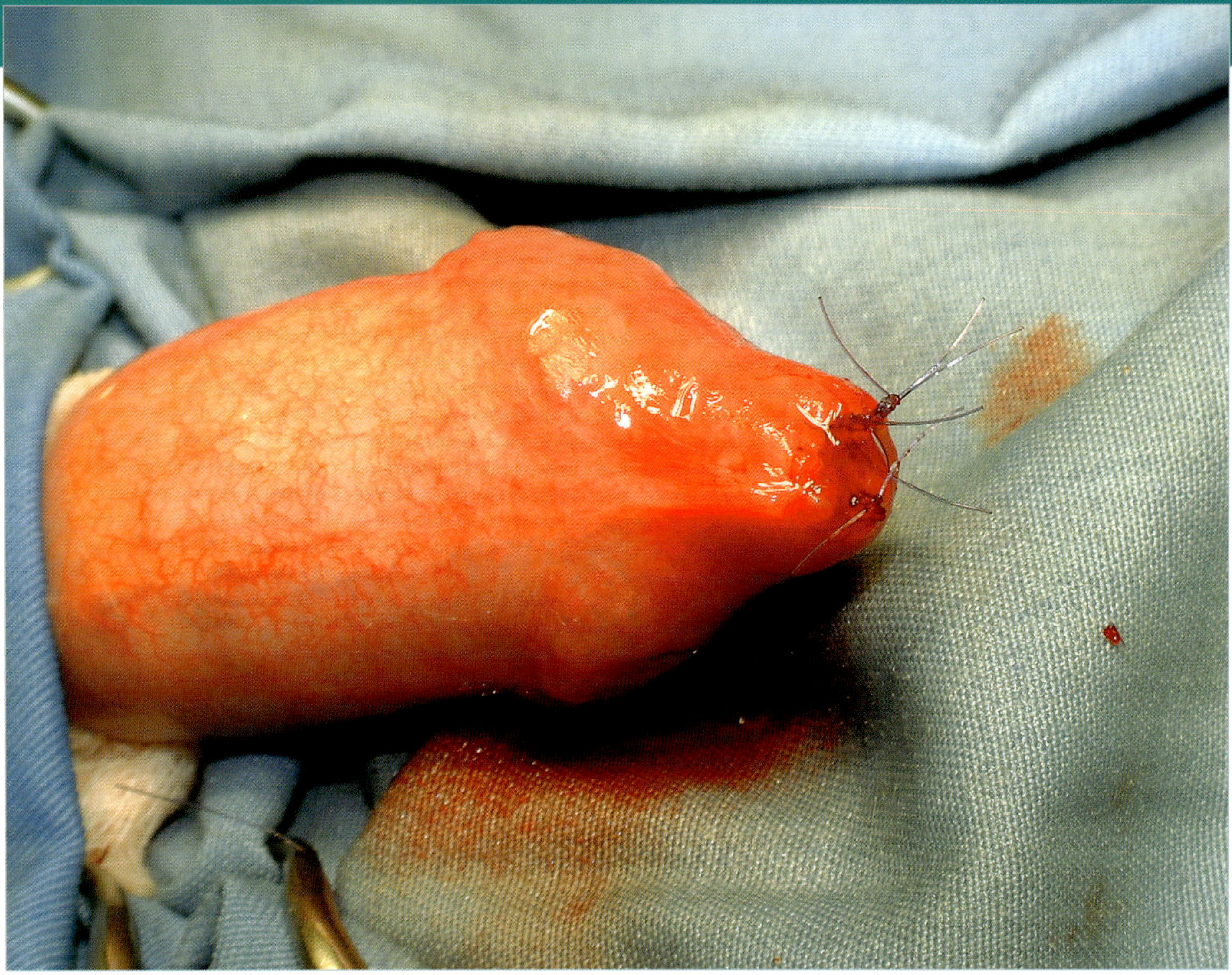

Fig. 12. Two continuous interlocking sutures are placed, using synthetic absorbable 6/0 monofilament material.

The needle used for suturing should be round-bodied and atraumatic to minimize damage to the urethral mucosa.

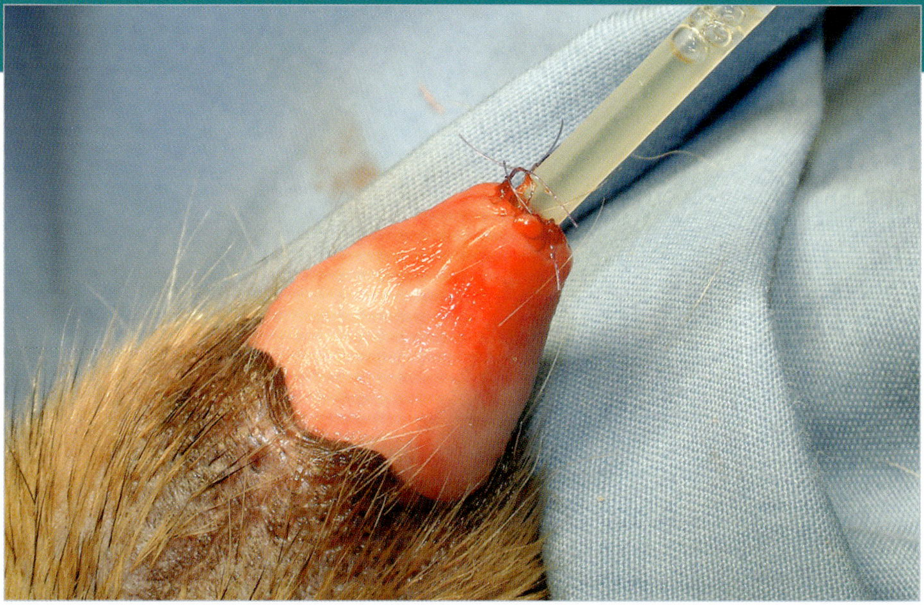

Fig. 13. If the urethra is inflamed, it is recommended to place a urinary catheter (that does not reach the bladder) for the first few postoperative days, to maintain patency and elimination of urine.

See urinary catheterisation ➜ page 236

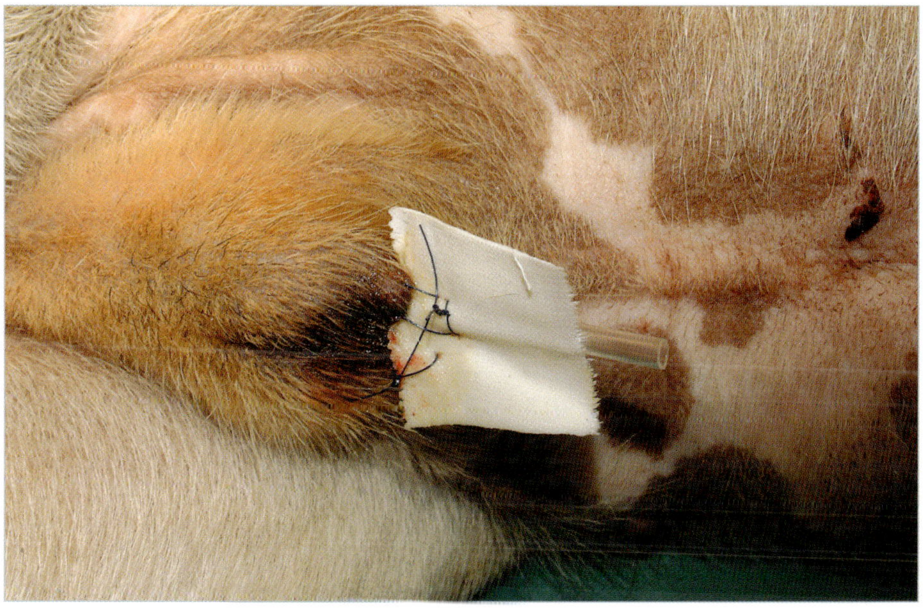

Fig. 14. The catheter is fixed to the prepuce with two sutures.

Postoperative care

- Topical antibiotic and anti-inflammatory treatment for 5 to 6 days.
- Systemic anti-inflammatory drugs (NSAID) for 6 days.
- Large Elizabethan collar to prevent licking of the area.
- Use of tranquilizers depending on the demeanour of the patient.

Slight postoperative bleeding from the penis is normal. The sparse bleeding will diminish over the next few days.

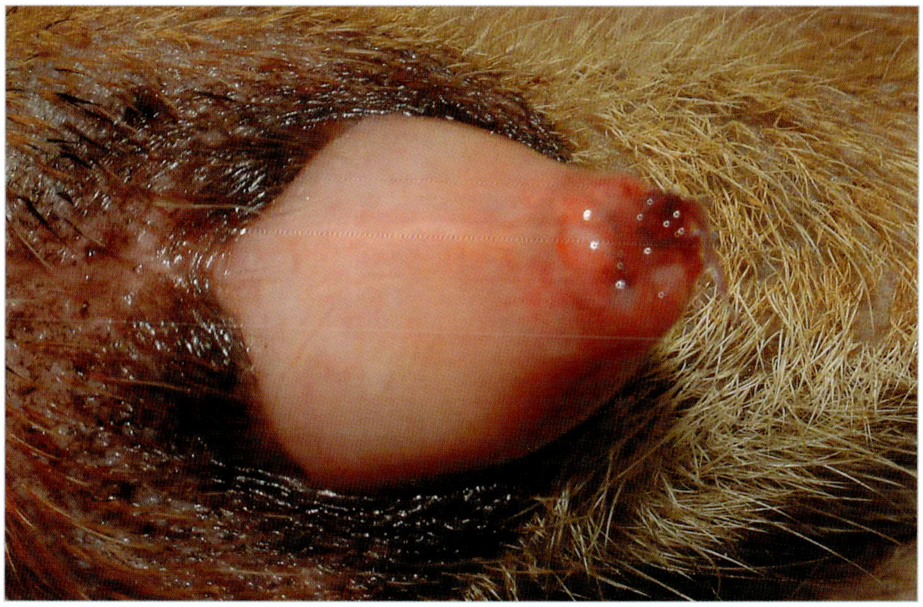

Fig. 15. Three days after the operation, the catheter is removed and the healing process is assessed.

Hypospadia

Prevalence	■	□	□	□	□

Hypospadia is the most frequently observed congenital anomaly in the external genitalia of the male dog.

It can occur to different degrees, from the least severe, where the preputial orifice is located in the ventral area (fig. 1), to severe, in which case the prepuce and penis have failed to develop.

It results from failure of the formation and union of the urogenital folds and the development of the penile urethra. The urethral orifice can be situated in any part of this area.

Hypospadia is usually accompanied by various abnormalities of the penis, including its absence (figs. 2-6).

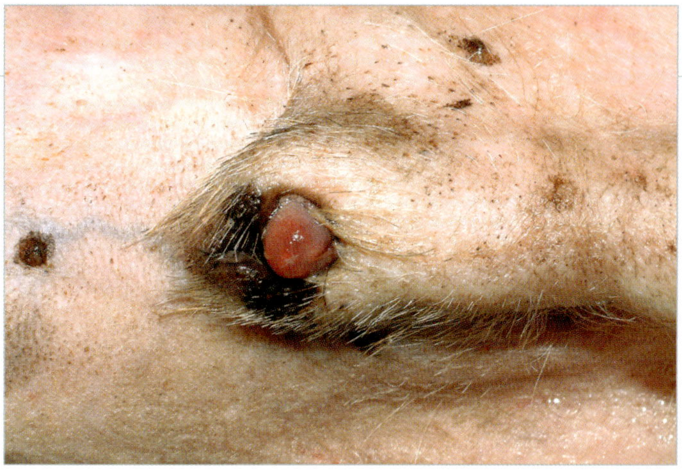

Fig.1. Hypospadia and paraphimosis in a Yorkshire Terrier. The preputial orifice is located ventrally and the glans is externalised due to a covering defect.

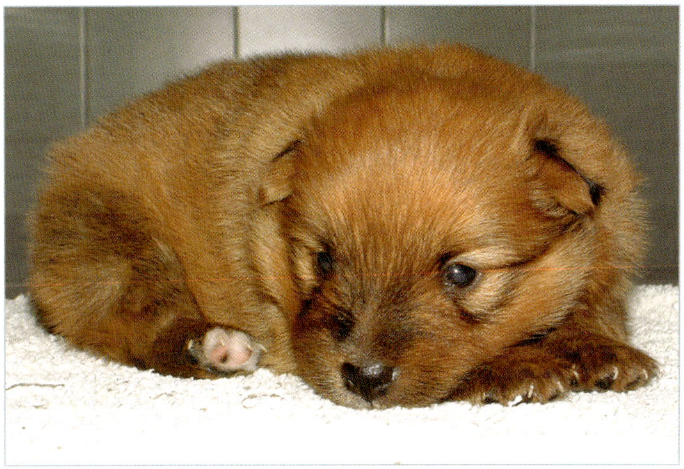

Fig. 2. A 3-week-old puppy presented for examination because "its penis is visible".

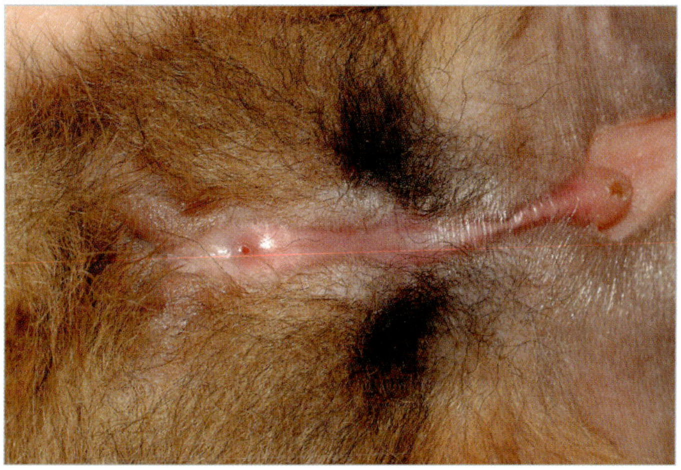

Fig. 3. The fusion defect of the prepuce and abnormal development of the penis can be seen.

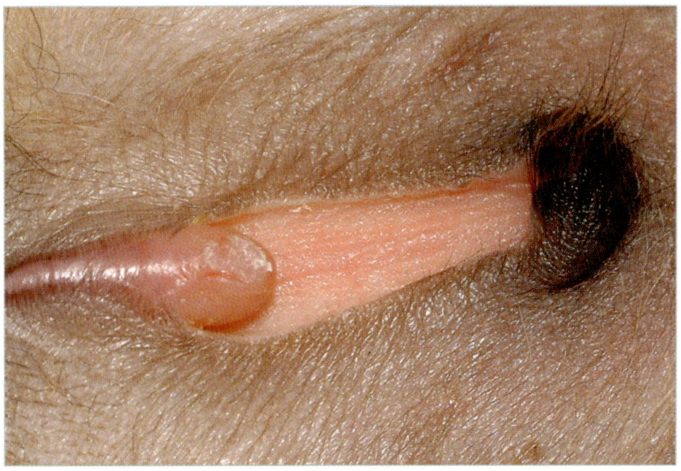

Fig. 4. The congenital abnormality of the prepuce, as well as the developmental defect of the penis are obvious. Note the absence of the urethral orifice at its tip.

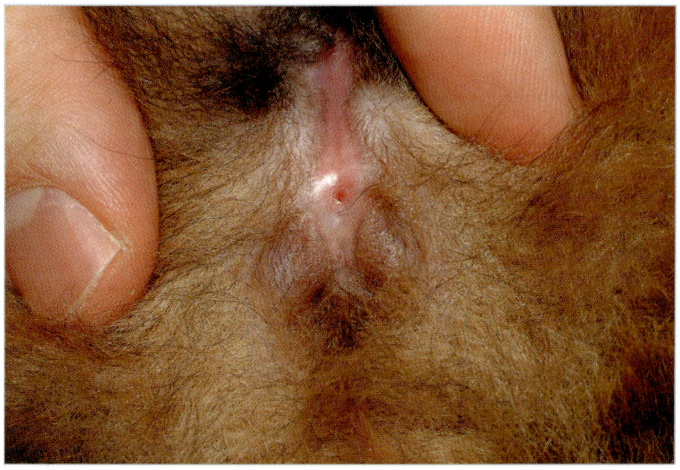

Fig. 5. The urethral opening, through which the animal urinates, is visible in the perineal region. To either side, the outline of the scrotal sacs can be seen.

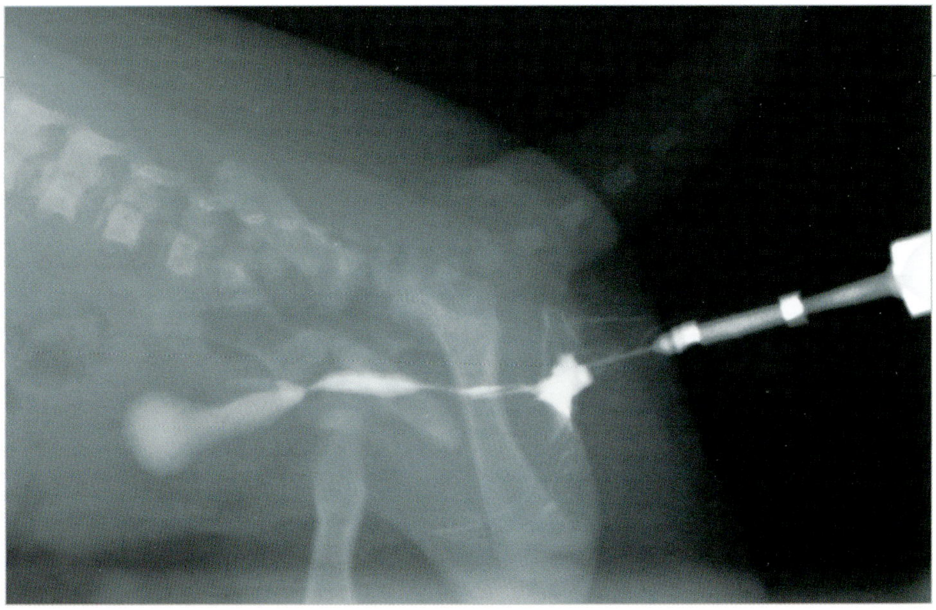

Fig. 6. When an iodated (urinary) contrast medium is introduced through the urethral orifice in the perineum, the urethra and bladder of the patient become visible.

Surgery on these patients is only indicated in very severe cases, when the poorly developed tissue remnants are repeatedly traumatised and infected. In these cases, these should be excised. However, most cases do not require surgical intervention. Assess the patient regularly and promptly treat any ascending urinary tract infections (figs. 7 and 8).

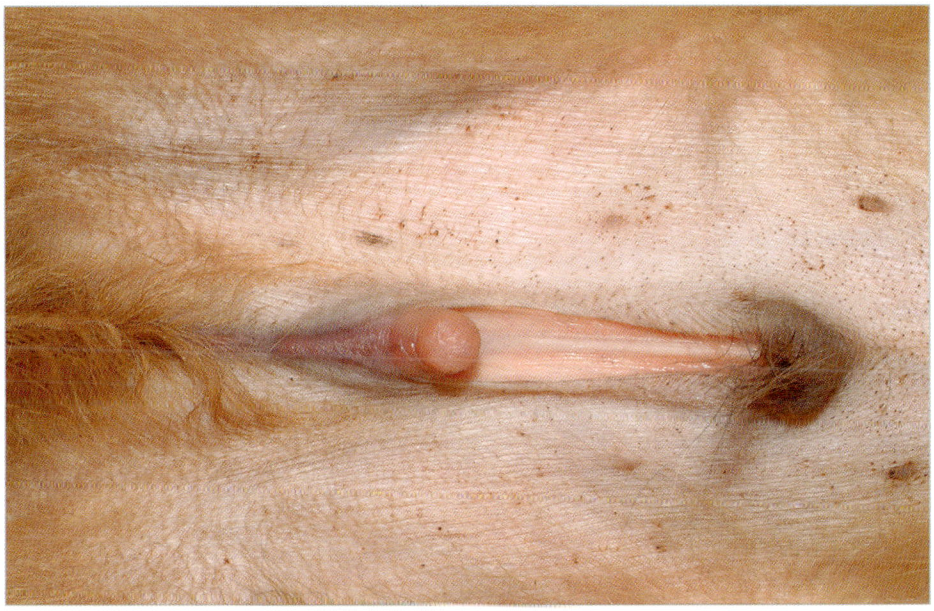

Fig. 7. Two months later, growth of the prepuce can be seen, while the penis fails to develop.

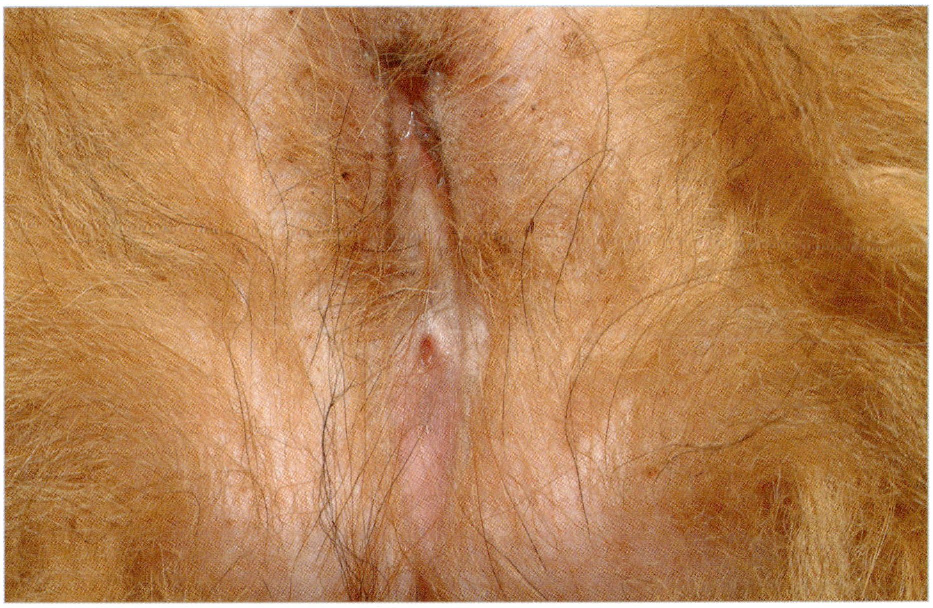

Fig. 8. The skin of the perineal area is covering the defect and the patient continues to urinate normally through the urethral opening. Regular check-ups should be carried out to monitor the patient's progress and to detect any potential ascending urinary infections.

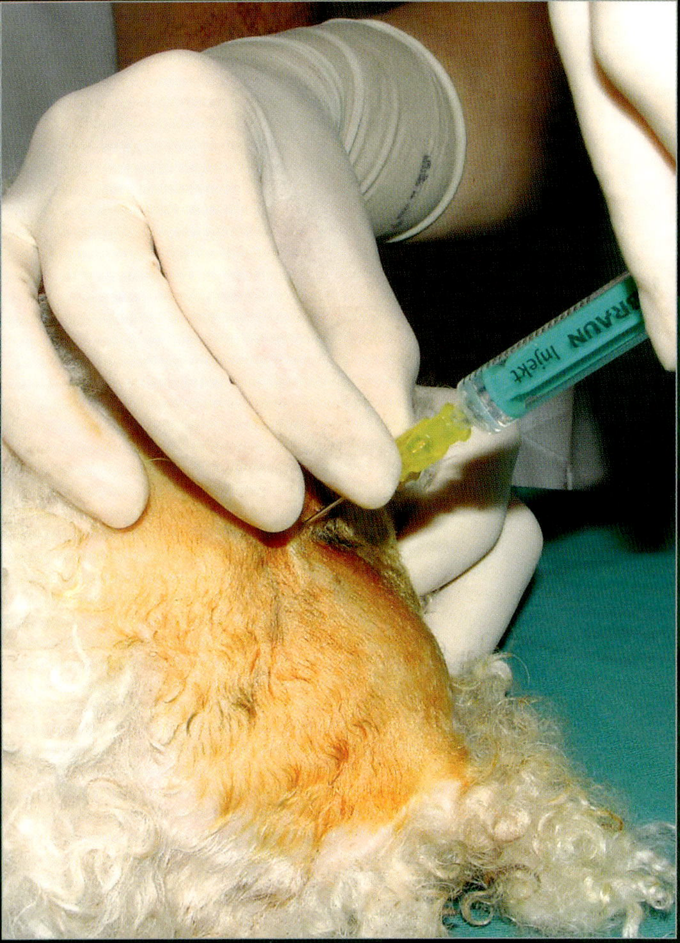
Injekt

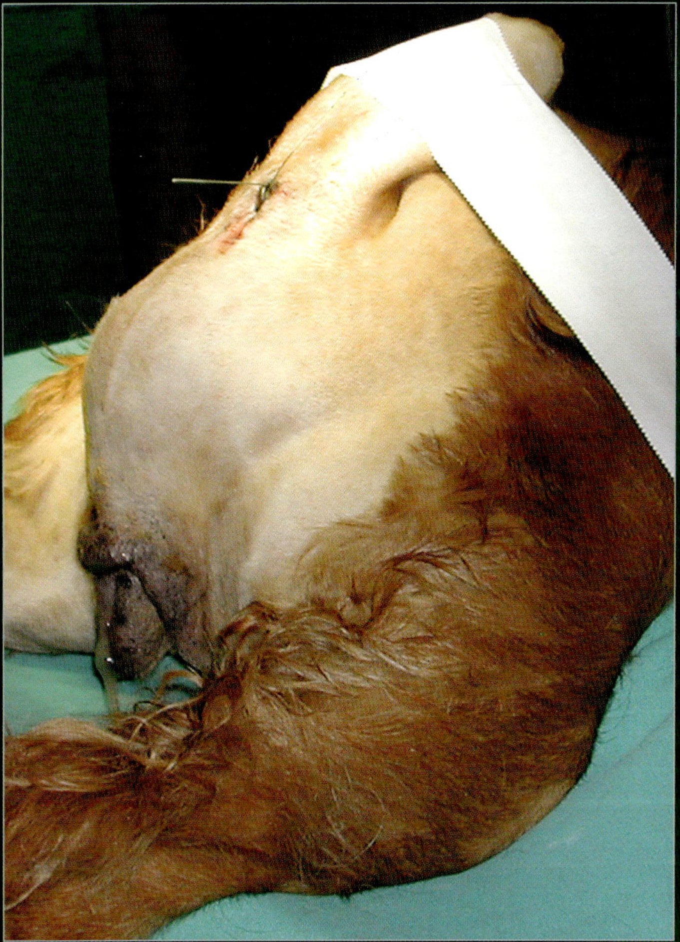

General techniques

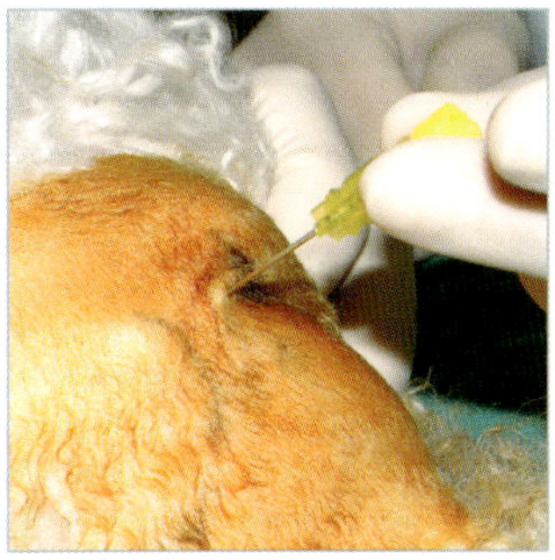 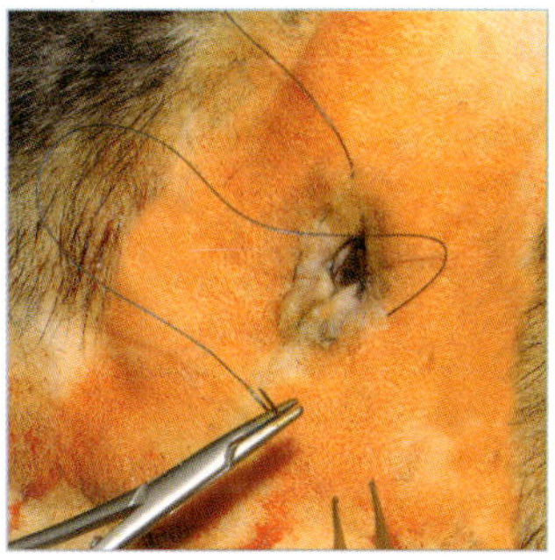

Urethral catheterisation of the cat

Frequency	■	■	■	■	■
Technical difficulty	■	■			

Urethral obstruction is a very common problem in male cats. It is a real challenge for the clinician, because the repercussions for the patient's general health are severe. The obstruction should be relieved immediately and rapidly. To achieve this, the clinician should be able to rely on a simple, effective method that removes the obstruction, requiring only light sedation in most patients.

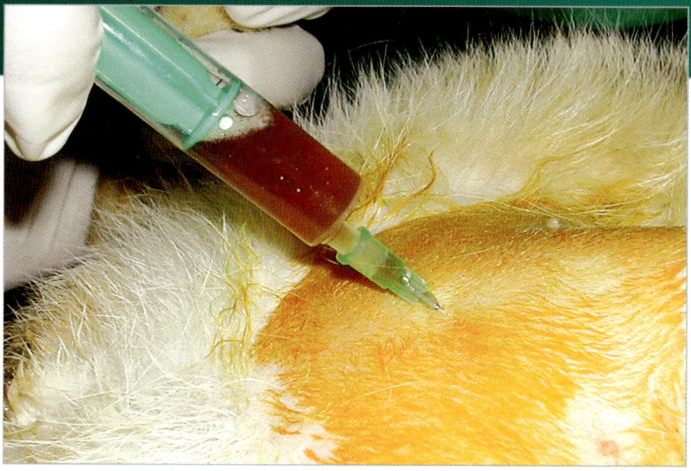

Fig. 1. Before catheterising a cat with urethral obstruction, it may be necessary to relieve the pressure in the bladder by cystocentesis. The best place to insert the needle is the midline, between the pubis and the umbilicus. The needle should be directed caudally.

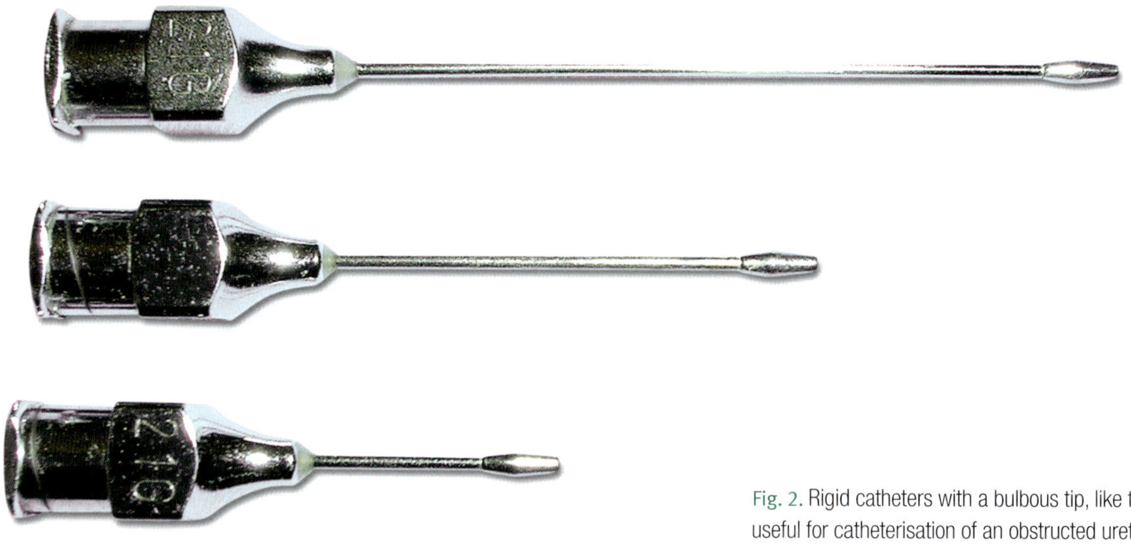

Fig. 2. Rigid catheters with a bulbous tip, like the ones in this photograph, are very useful for catheterisation of an obstructed urethra.

To assist passing the catheter into the bladder, it is essential that the penis is pointing caudally, parallel to the spinal column. This ensures the urethra is in line with the neck of the bladder.

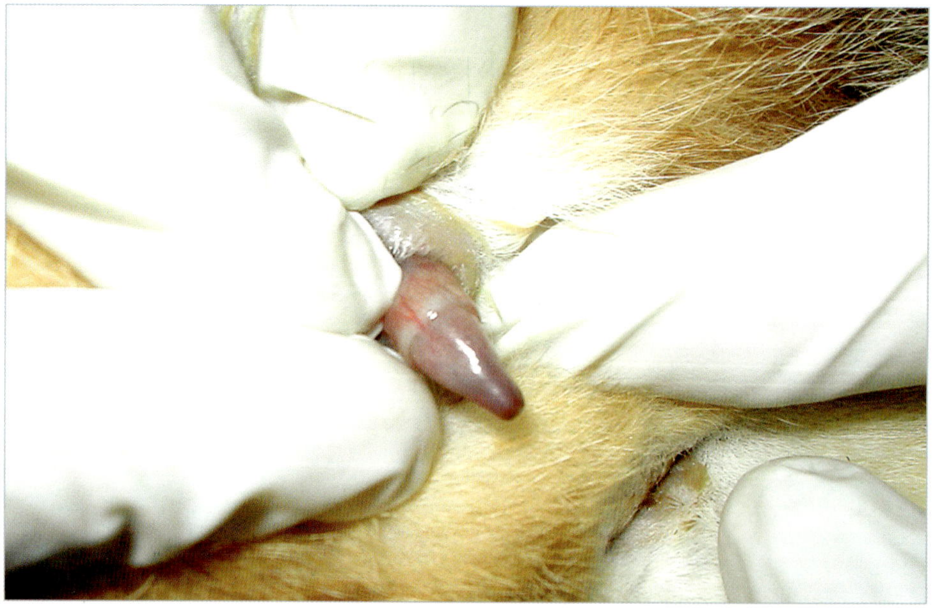

Fig. 3. The first step in catheterisation is to exteriorize the penis by drawing back the prepuce. Ensure that the penis is pointing caudally, so that the urethra is completely straight.

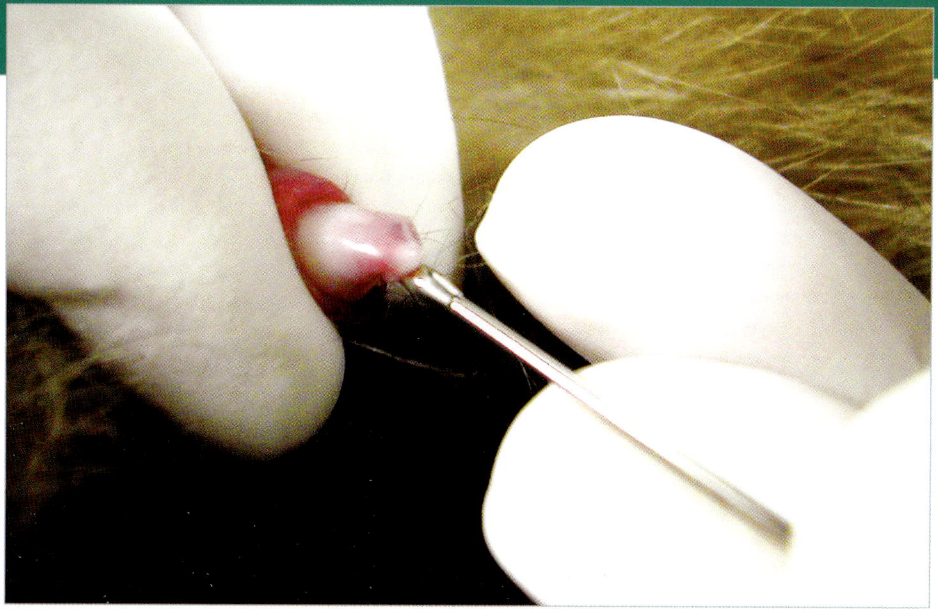

Fig. 4. Once the external orifice of the urethra has been identified, the lubricated catheter is inserted. The fingers that hold the penis should prevent its retraction into the prepuce, while maintaining its caudal direction.

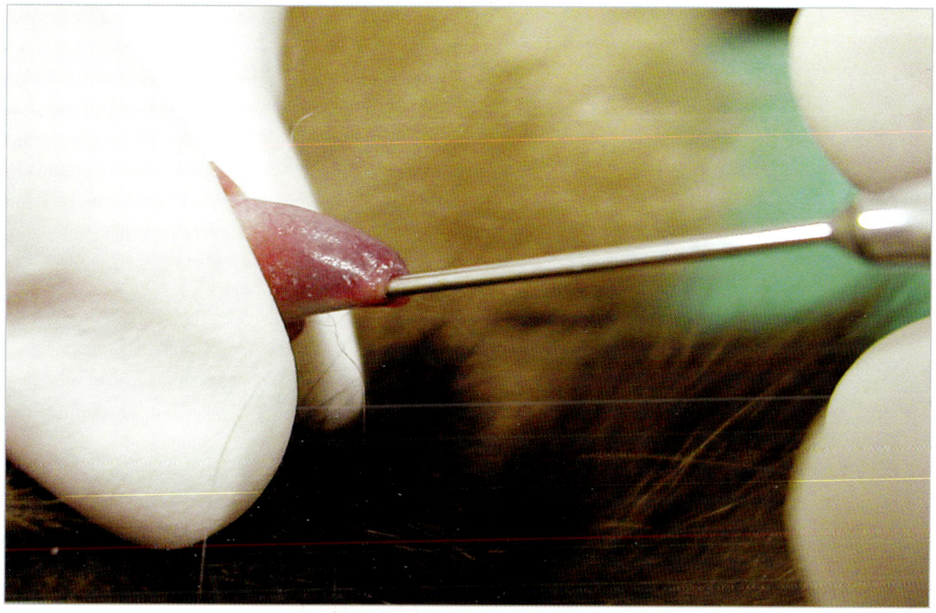

Fig. 5. The catheter is carefully inserted until it meets resistance. The obstruction is usually found in the distal third of the penis.

Once the catheter reaches the obstruction, it should not be used to push: try to dislodge it by hydropropulsion instead.

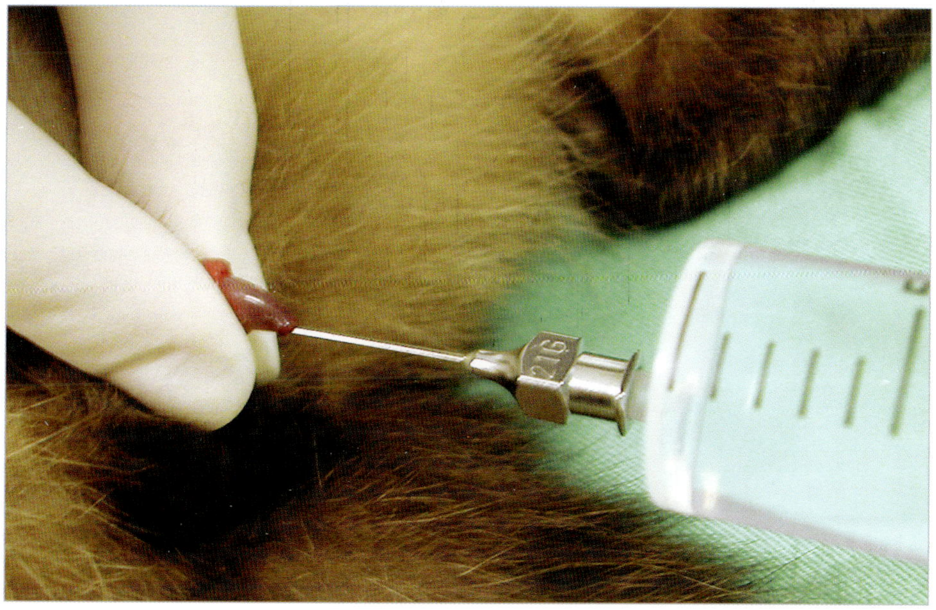

Fig. 6. Next, a 5-ml syringe with saline is connected to the catheter. By applying intermittent pressure on the plunger of the syringe, the plug is loosened and the obstruction is removed.

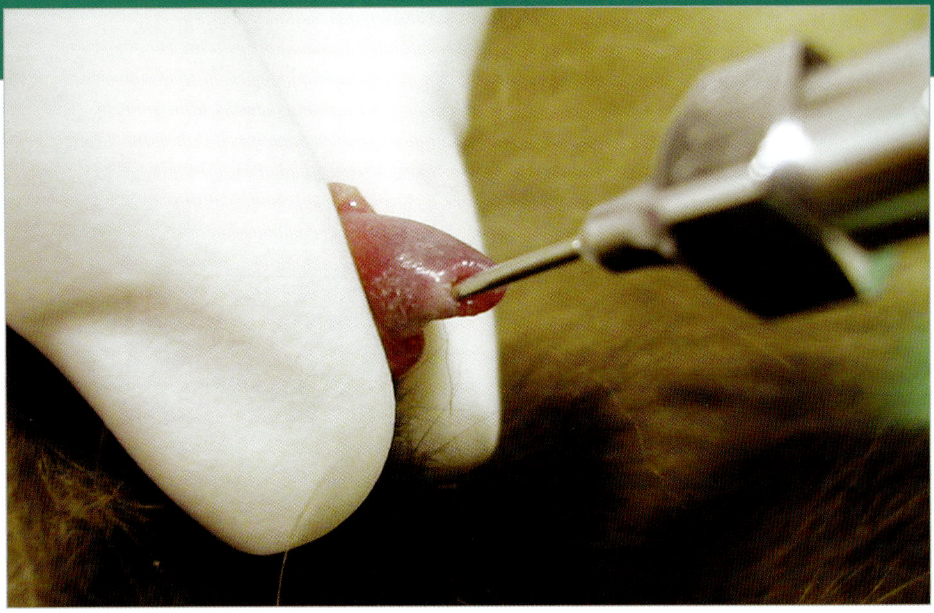

Fig. 7. Using repeated pressure pulses, the catheter is moved gently forward and the obstructing plugs are dislodged towards the bladder, thus removing the obstruction.

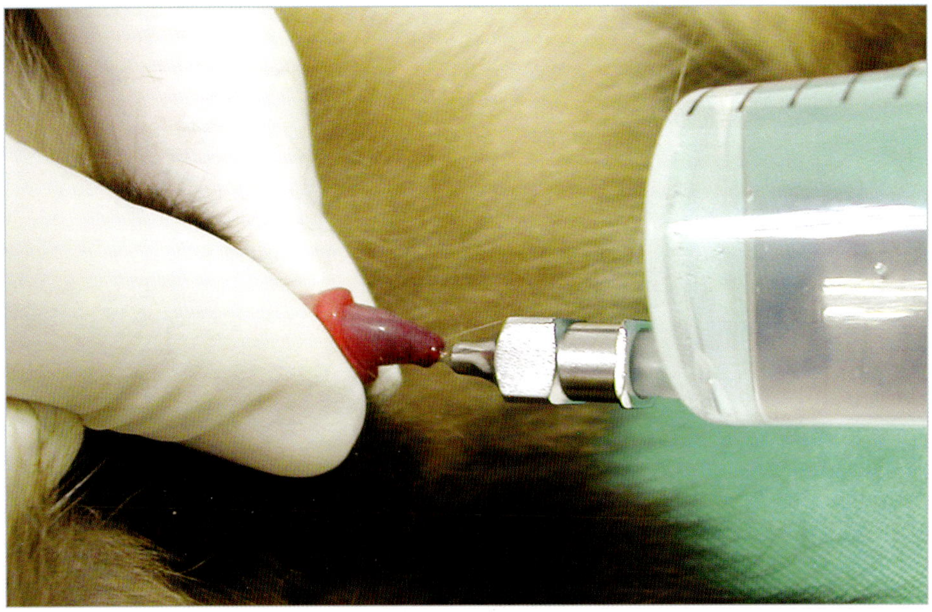

Fig. 8. Once the urethra is unblocked, the urine in the bladder can be drained and the bladder can be flushed with saline.

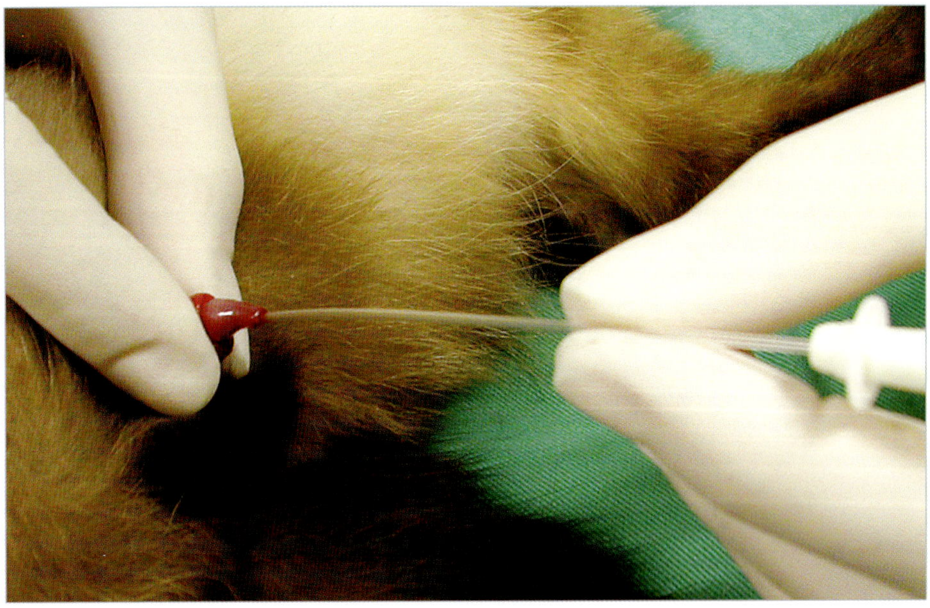

Fig. 9. The next step is to replace the catheter with a feline urinary catheter that will stay in place for two or three days.

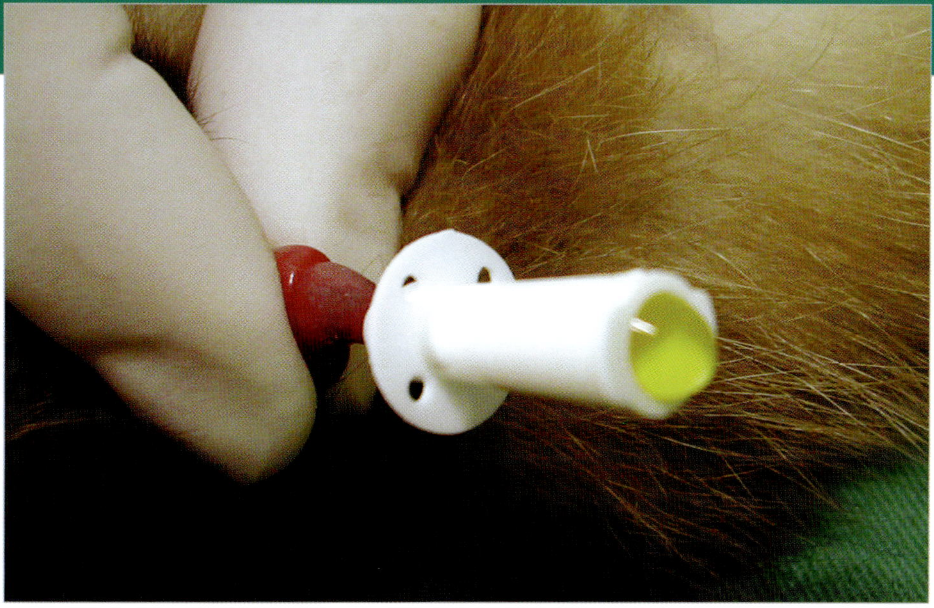

Using a rigid catheter instead of a flexible one makes removal of urinary obstructions much easier.

Fig. 10. While the catheter remains in place, the cat urinates in constant drops. This avoids distension of the bladder, and aids recovery of detrusor muscle tone.

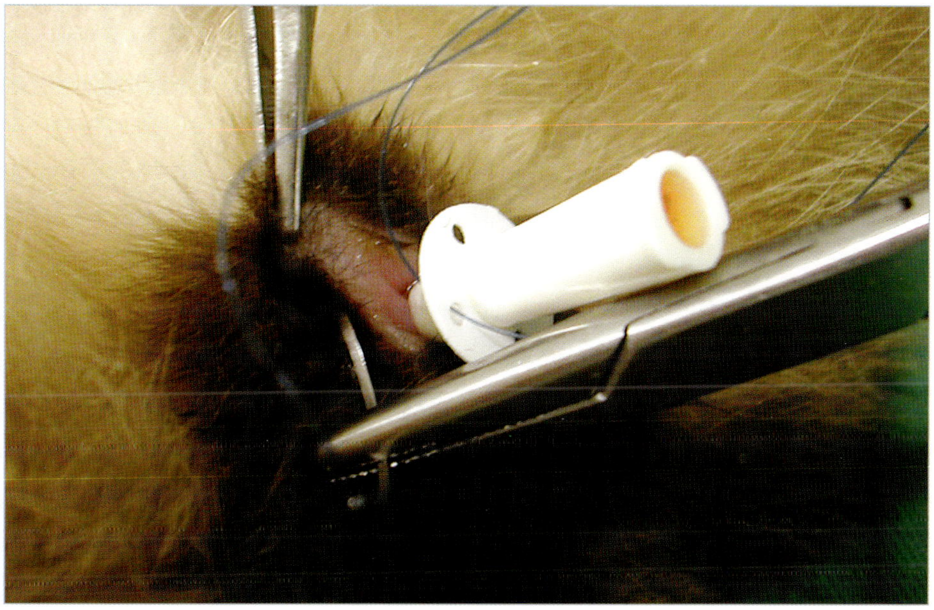

Fig 11. The catheter is secured to the prepuce by a few sutures through the holes in the rim.

Even though controversial, we are of the opinion that it is necessary to provide antibiotic cover for two or three days while the catheter remains in place. During this time, corticosteroid and spasmolytic treatment should also be administered.

Urethral catheterisation of the dog

Frequency	■	■	■	■	■
Technical difficulty	■				

Urethral catheterisation is one of the most common procedures in clinical veterinary practice. Patients that present with urine retention, for whatever reason, must be catheterised to ensure urethral patency is maintained. It may also be necessary to catheterise the bladder to obtain a urine sample for analysis.

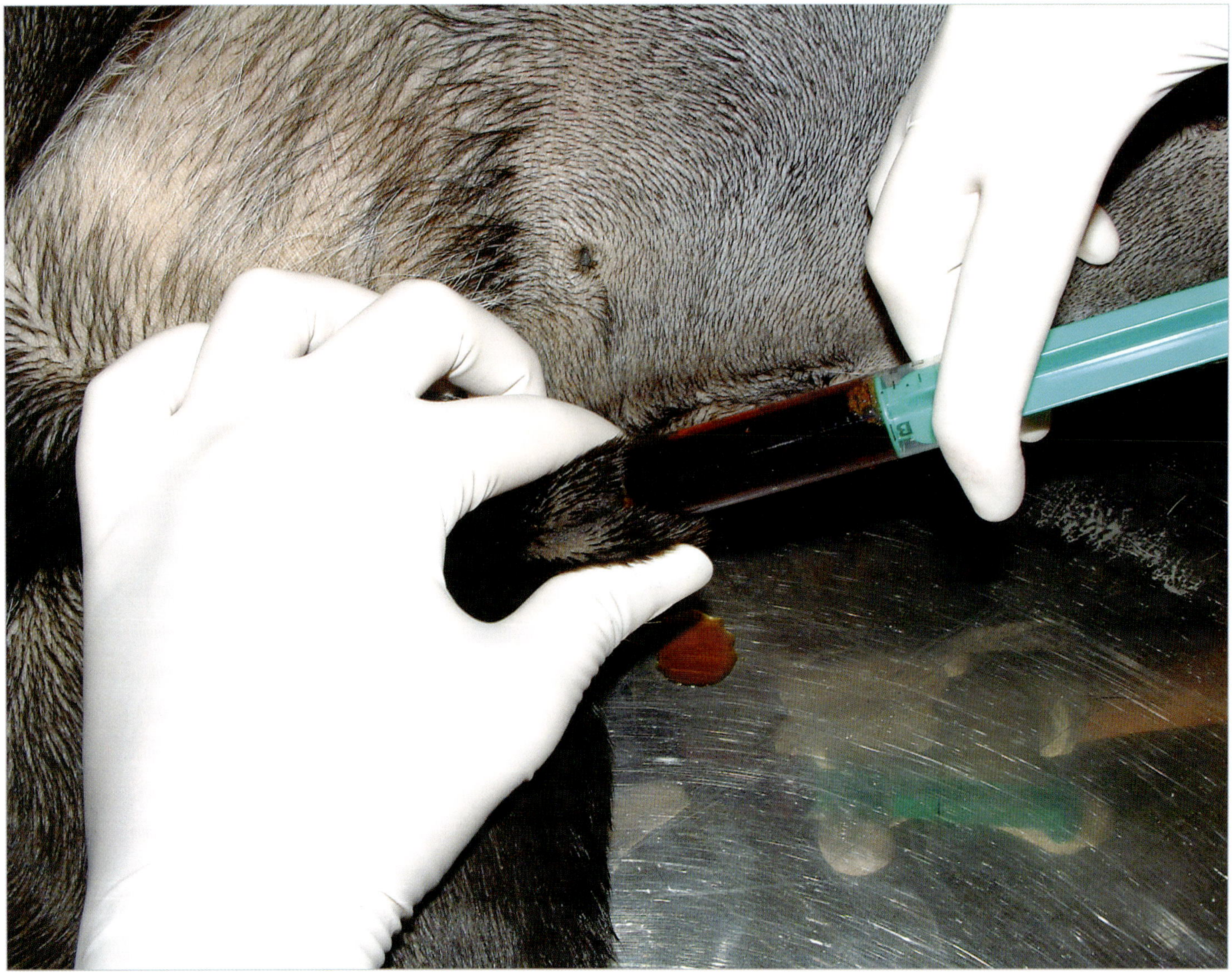

Fig. 1. Before urinary catheterisation, the area should be prepared as aseptically as possible using a diluted povidone-iodine solution, introduced into the prepuce with a syringe.

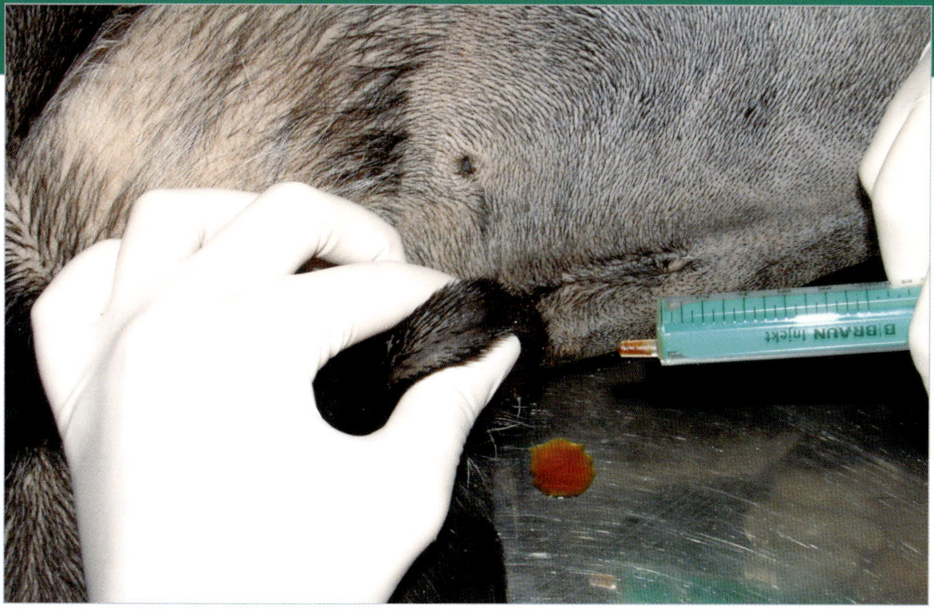

Fig. 2. After introducing the antiseptic solution into the prepuce, the syringe is removed and the preputial orifice is compressed between thumb and index finger.

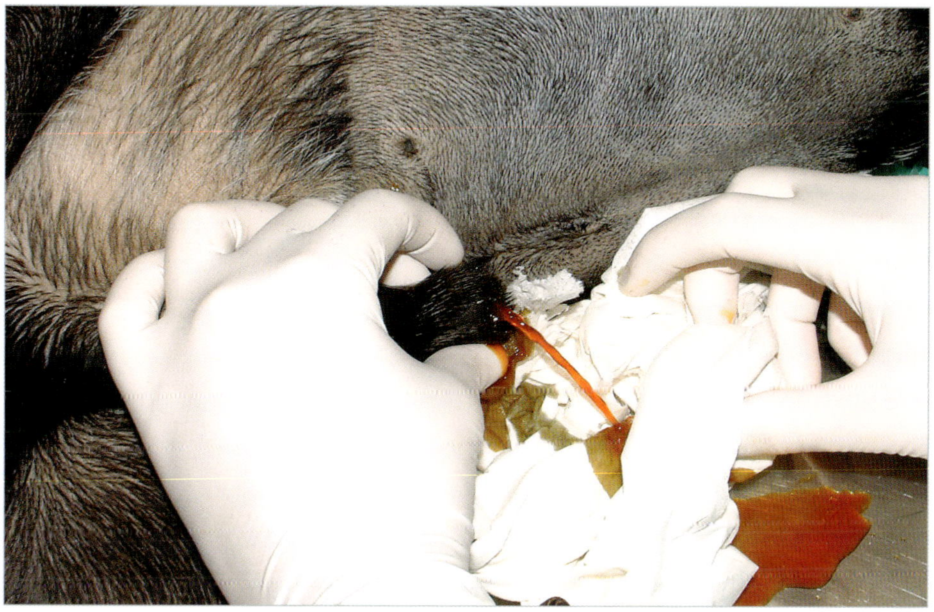

Fig 3. The antiseptic solution stays in contact with the mucosa for a short while and is then released.

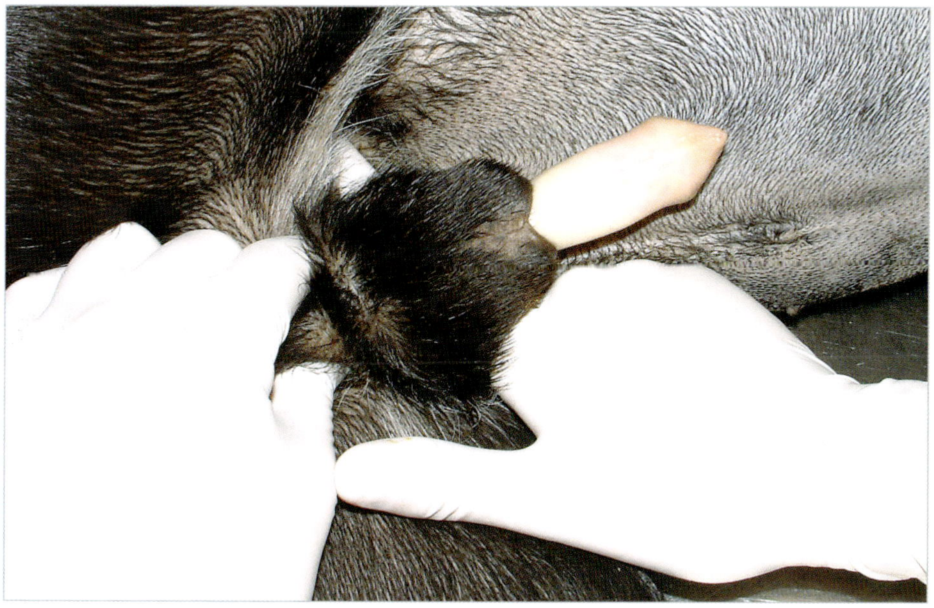

Fig. 4. Next, the penis is exteriorised. To do so, the prepuce is drawn back with one hand, while the other hand holds the base of the penis and pushes it in a cranial direction.

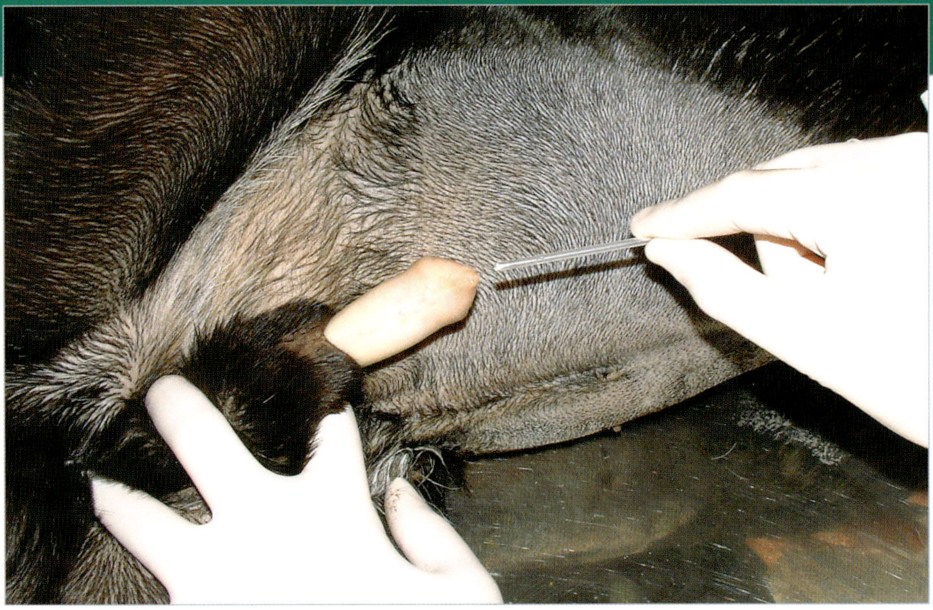

Fig. 5. The catheter has to be sterile. To avoid contamination before catheterisation, it is important that it only touches the penis.

Catheterisation may introduce infection. It is important to perform this procedure in an aseptic manner.

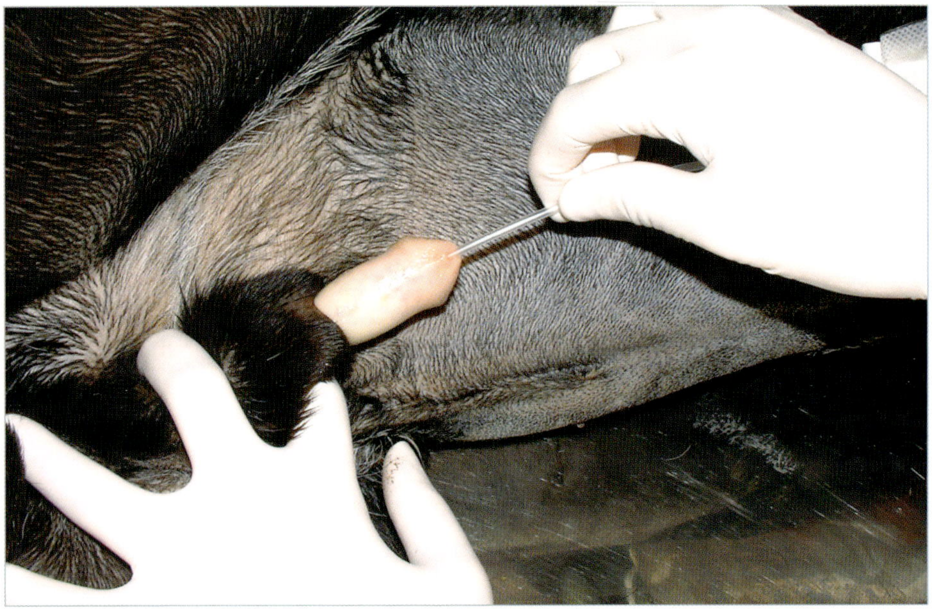

Fig. 6. While keeping the penis exteriorised with one hand, the urinary orifice is identified and the tip of the catheter is inserted.

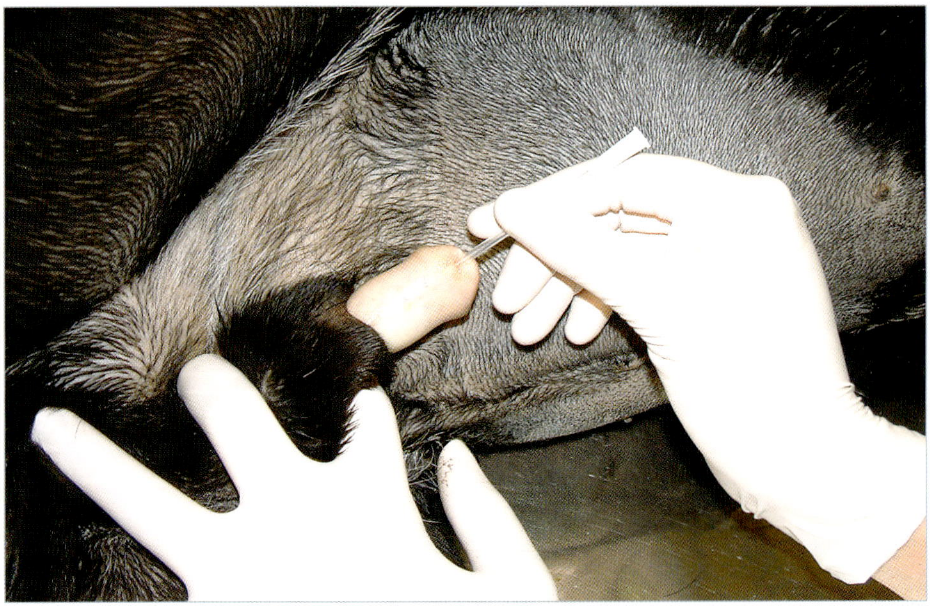

Fig. 7. The catheter is gently advanced until reaching the bladder. The use of a semi-rigid catheter facilitates this procedure, especially in cases with urethral obstruction.

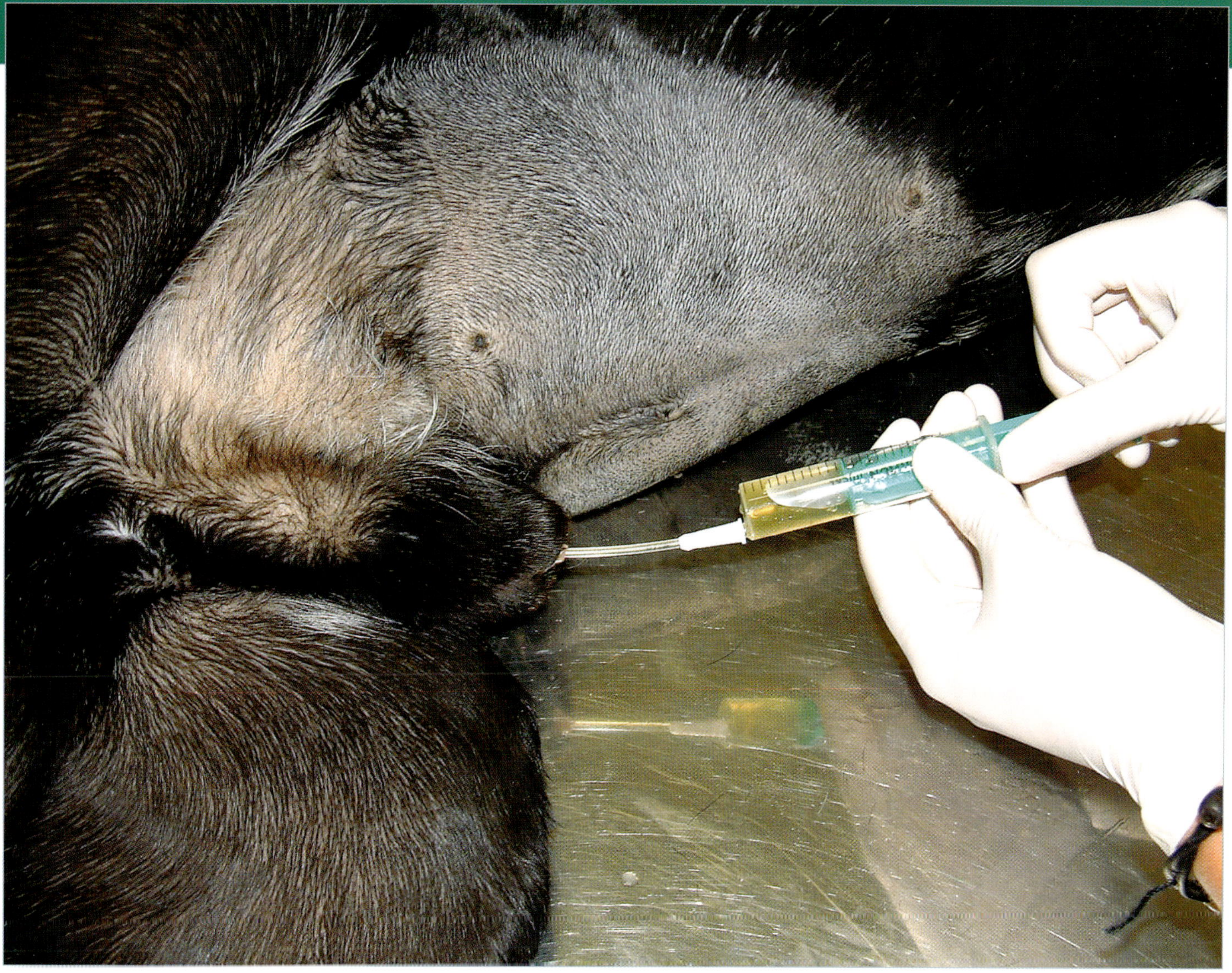

Fig. 8. The bladder is emptied by connecting a sterile syringe to the end of the catheter.

Cystocentesis

Frequency	■■■■■
Technical difficulty	■□□□□

Cystocentesis is used to obtain sterile urine samples directly from the bladder, avoiding contamination of the sample with bacteria or tissue cells from the urinary tract. It also reduces the risk of ascending urinary tract infection caused by catheterisation. Another indication is decompression of the bladder in cases of urethral obstruction that cannot be resolved by retrograde catheterisation.

> ***Cystocentesis is a rapid and simple procedure that is better tolerated by queens and bitches than catheterisation.***
>
> ***To facilitate cystocentesis it is recommended to insert the needle with the bevel facing upwards (fig. 2).***

Technique

- Shave and prepare the area aseptically.
- Locate and immobilize the bladder against the abdominal wall, taking care not to use excessive pressure (fig. 1). When the bladder is overly compressed, there is a greater risk of urine leaking around the needle into the peritoneal cavity.
- The puncture is performed with a 22-21G 40 mm needle, in the midline in females and in a paramedian position in male dogs.
- The needle is inserted at an angle (45º) in the middle of the bladder, directed towards the trigone (figs. 2 and 3).
- The syringe should be held in such a way that the plunger can be retracted without losing grip, drawing up the urine without interruption (fig. 4).

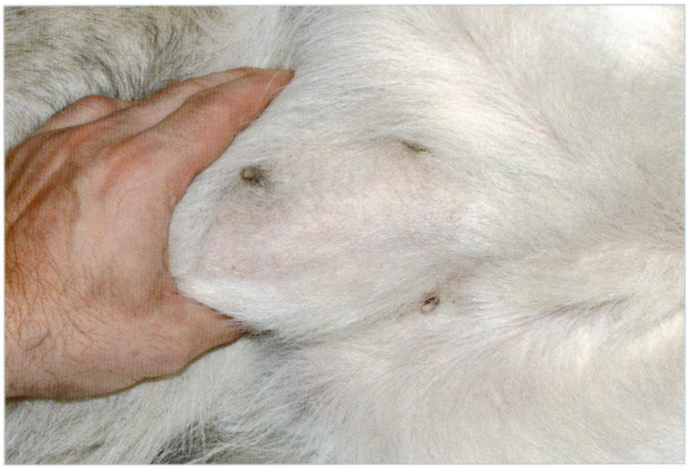

Fig. 1. Stabilise the bladder to ensure correct needle placement. If the bladder is small, and in cats, it is better to immobilise it from the pelvic end.

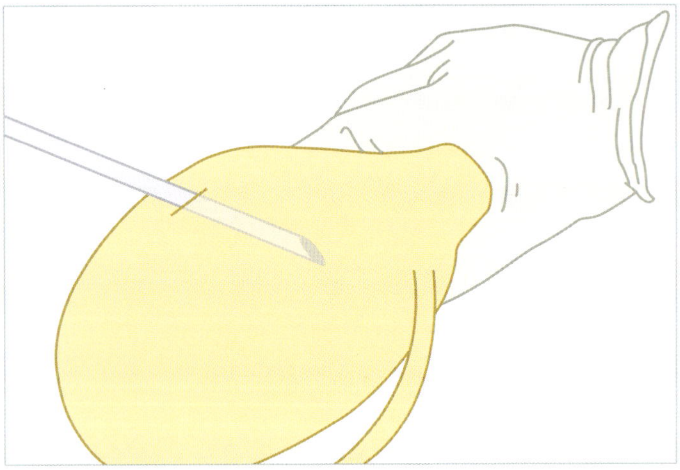

Fig. 2. Introducing the needle at an angle creates an oblique pathway in the bladder wall that helps closure of the puncture wound when the needle is withdrawn, minimising urine leaks into the abdominal cavity.

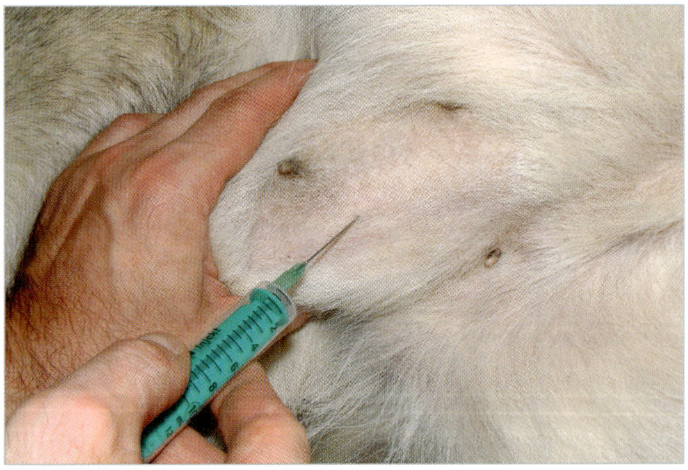

Fig. 3. The tip of the needle is directed towards the distal area of the bladder, the trigone, to ensure all urine can be completely drained, if needed, without having to insert the needle several times.

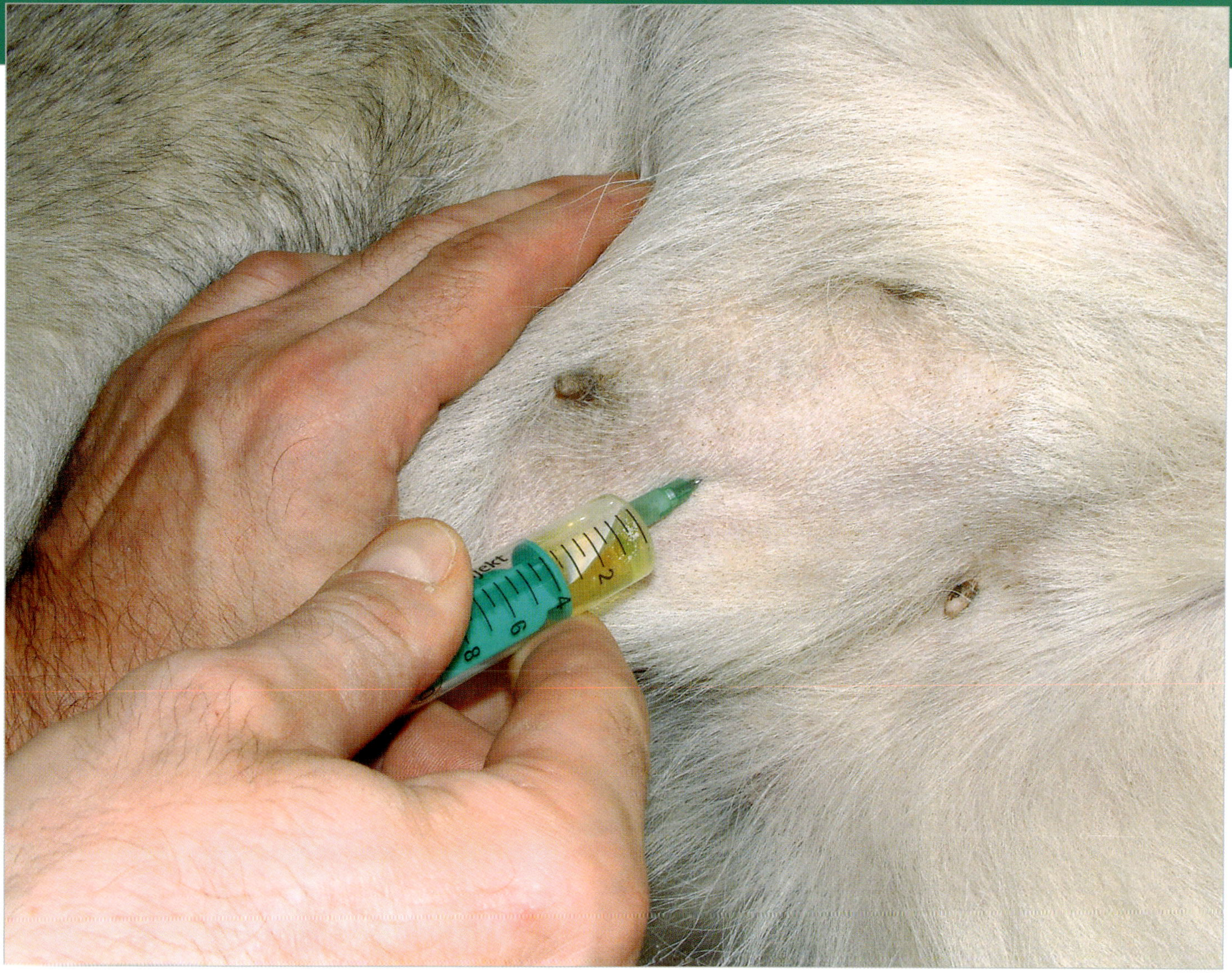

Fig. 4. Once the bladder has been punctured, urine should be extracted without sudden movements, to avoid damaging the mucosa and the bladder wall.

Cystocentesis is contraindicated if the bladder cannot be palpated, either because it is too small or because the patient is uncooperative. Do not perform a "blind" puncture.

If diuretics (furosemide) have been administered before cystocentesis, remember that this alters the specific gravity, the pH and the number of bacteria per ml.

Complications

- Generally, this technique does not lead to secondary complications.
- However, in patients that do not co-operate, or if the bladder is very small, bladder lesions, haemorrhages, peritonitis, urinary fistulas and adhesions may arise.

Lumbosacral epidural anaesthesia

Frequency	■■■□□
Technical difficulty	■■■■□

Aim

To reduce the requirement for general anaesthetics and to increase analgesia during surgical procedures on the hindquarters.
An appropriate drug is injected into the epidural space with a spinal needle inserted between the last lumbar and the first sacral vertebrae (fig. 1).

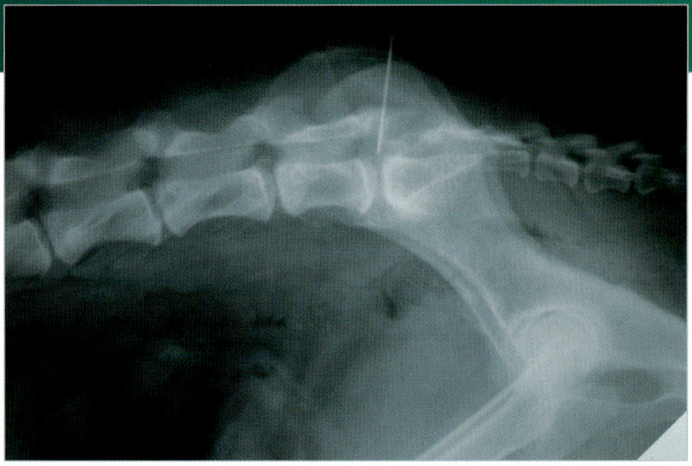

Fig. 1. Radiograph to identify the position of the spinal needle. This is done if there is uncertainty about the location of the epidural space.

Do not use epidural anaesthesia alone. If general anaesthesia is not used, the patient should be deeply sedated.

Required materials (fig. 2)

- Electric clippers.
- Local antiseptics.
- Sterile surgical gloves.
- Disposable spinal needles.
- Small syringes to check the correct position of the needle (to identify the loss of resistance).
- Syringes of different sizes to administer the drug.

Patient size	Needle type	
	Length	Gauge
Small	2.5 cm	22G
Medium	3.8 cm	20G
Large	7.5 cm	18G

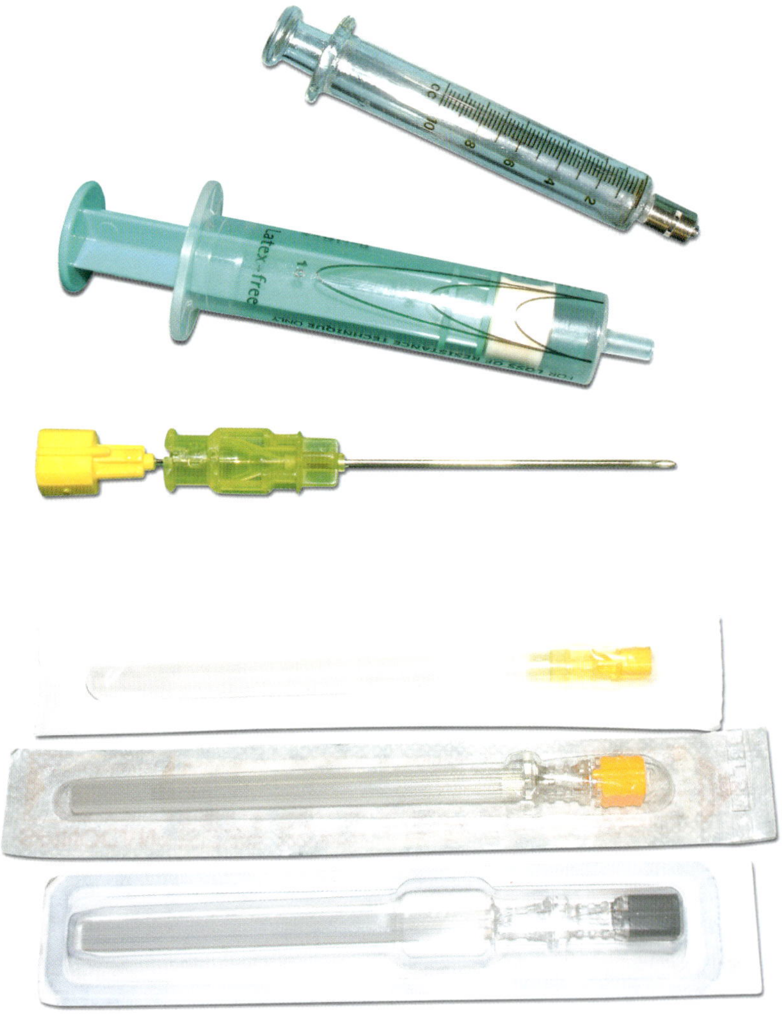

Fig. 2. Materials required for epidural anaesthesia:
- Small low-resistance syringes to locate the epidural space.
- Spinal needles of varying thickness and length.

Drugs used

Anaesthetic	Dose	Toxicity (IV)	Duration of the effect	Analgesic potency
Lidocaine 2%	1 ml/ 4.5-6 kg	>10 mg/kg	60 minutes	▲
Mepivacaine 2%		>30 mg/kg	2 hours	
Bupivacaine 0.5%		>3 mg/kg	4-6 hours	

✱ *Local anaesthetics may produce hypotension.*
Correct existing hypotension before administering epidural anaesthesia.

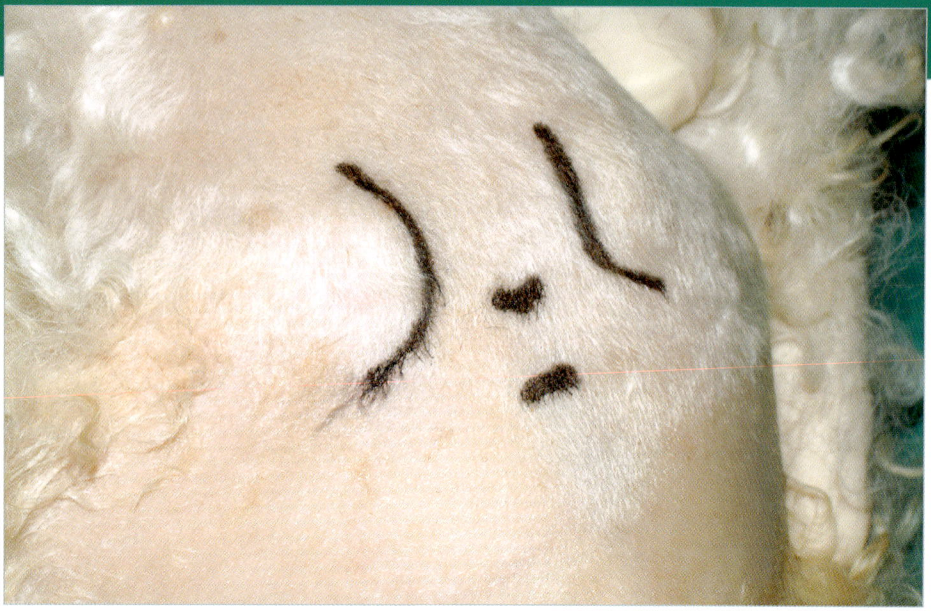

Landmarks

The iliac wings and the spinous processes of the 7th lumbar and the 1st sacral vertebrae (fig. 3).

Fig. 3. Anatomical landmarks to locate the insertion point for the spinal needle into the vertebral channel:

- Iliac wings.
- Spinous process of L7.
- Spinous process of S1.

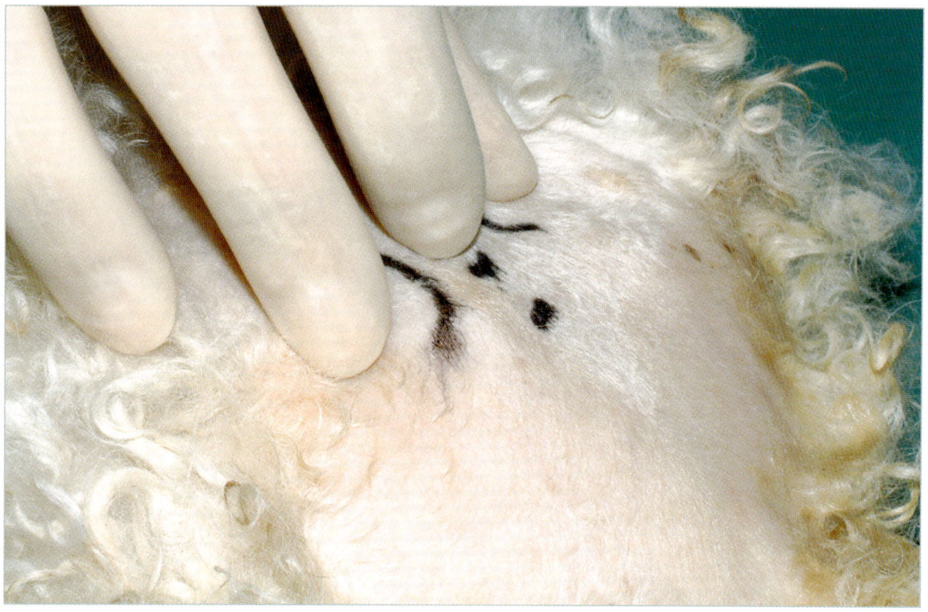

The thumb and middle finger of the non-dominant hand are used to palpate the iliac wings on both sides of the vertebral column. The spinous process of L7 is identified with the index finger of the same hand. The lumbosacral space (L7-S1), which feels like a depression, is located by caudal and cranial movement of the finger (figs. 4 and 5).

Fig. 4. The thumb and middle finger are placed over the iliac wings and the index finger palpates the spinous process of L7.

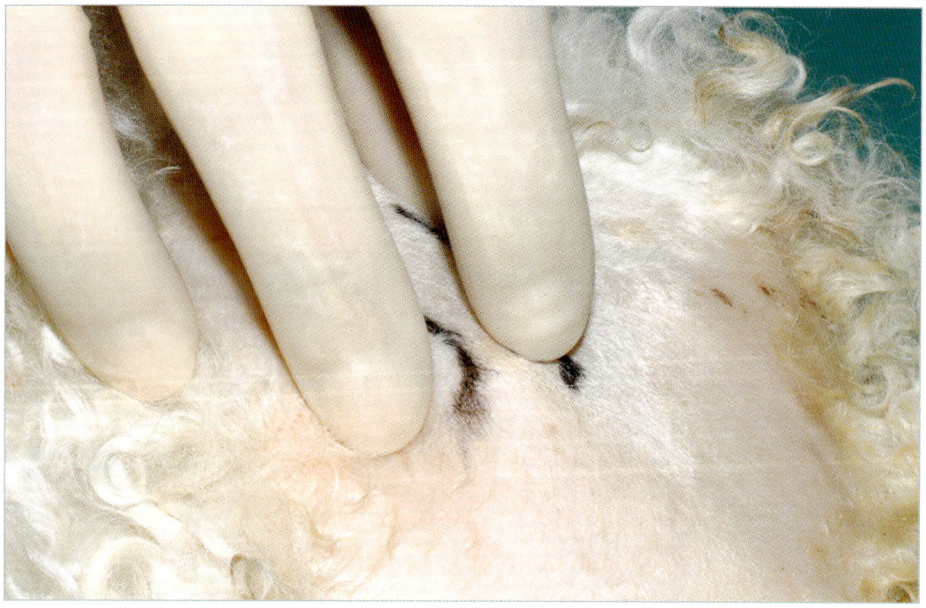

Fig. 5. Next, the spinous process of S1 is palpated to identify the space where the spinal needle will be inserted.

Technique

Patient positioning

After sedation the patient is positioned in one of the following ways, depending on the veterinarian's comfort or preference:

- On the sternum with the hind legs pulled forward (fig. 6).
- In lateral recumbency with the hind legs pulled towards the head.

In both positions, separation of the lumbosacral union will be achieved. After injecting the anaesthetic, the patient is placed in ventral or dorsal recumbency to obtain a uniform distribution of the anaesthetic on both sides of the spinal column. If the patient is placed in lateral recumbency, the anaesthesia of nerve roots on the lower side will be increased.

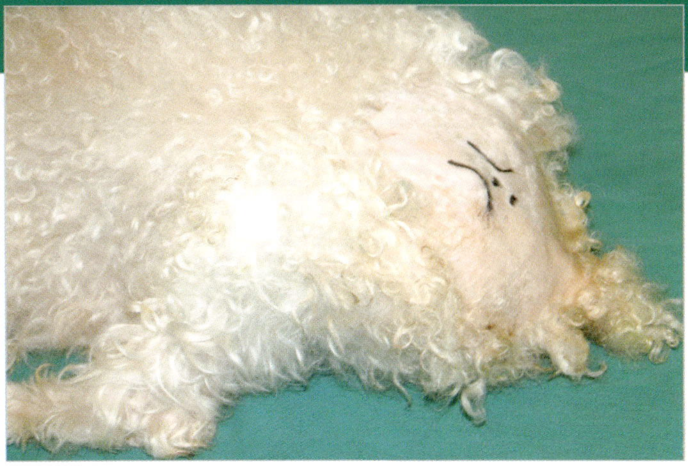

Fig. 6. The patient is positioned in sternal recumbency with the hind legs pulled forwards to widen the lumbosacral space.

Preparation of the area

- Shaving and aseptic preparation of the area.
- Use sterile gloves and meticulous aseptic technique to prevent infection.

Fig. 7. The area is prepared like any other surgical field: shaving, washing with antiseptic soap and the application of povidone-iodine.

Inserting the needle

With the dominant hand, the spinal needle is introduced perpendicularly into the space between the spinous processes of L7 and S1 (figs. 8 and 9). It is inserted slowly until perforating the ligamentum flavum, indicated by a small characteristic "pop" and a loss of resistance (fig. 10).

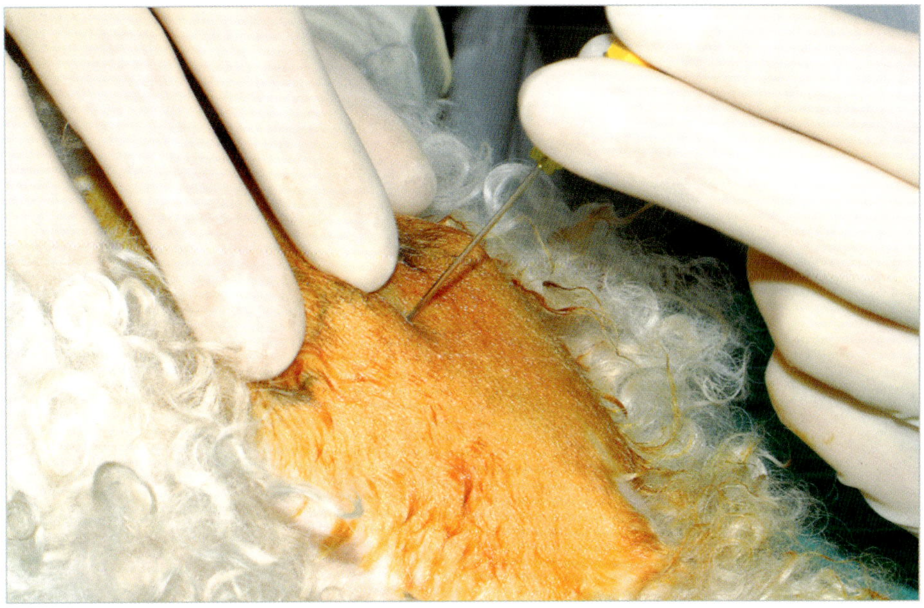

Fig. 8. The needle is inserted between the spinous processes of L7 and S1.

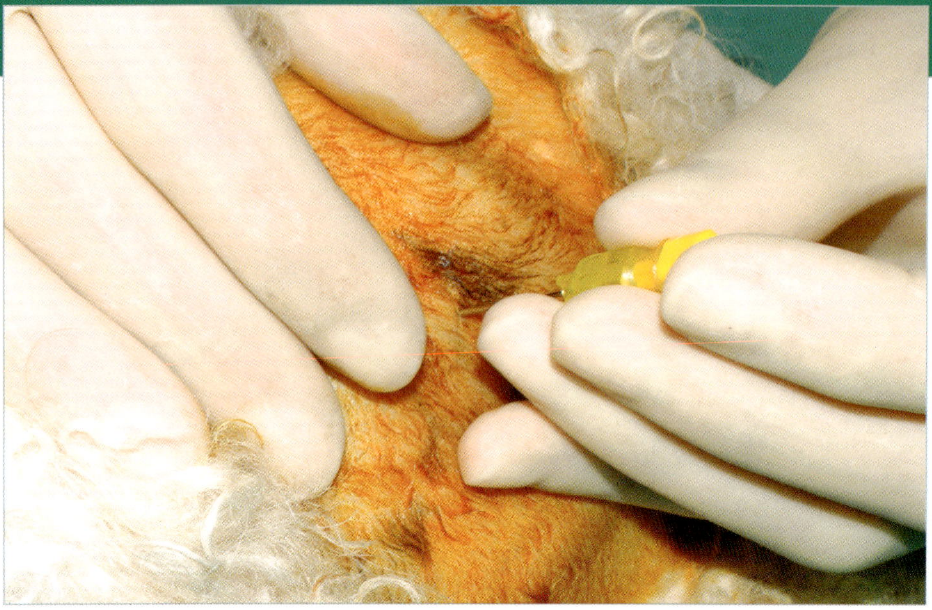

Fig. 9. The needle should be introduced perpendicular to the skin.

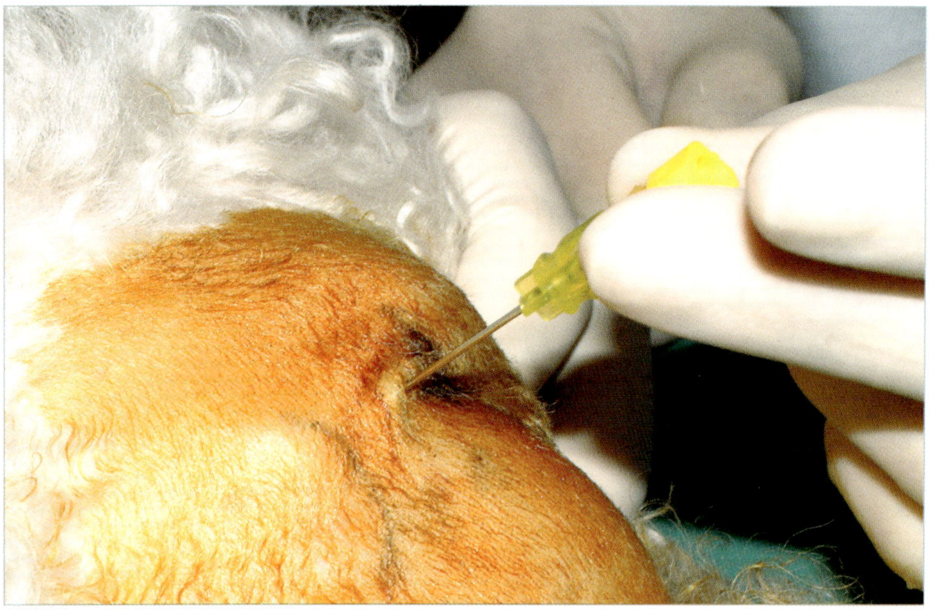

Fig. 10. When the ligamentum flavum is perforated, a metallic "pop" and a loss of resistance to passage of the needle are noted.

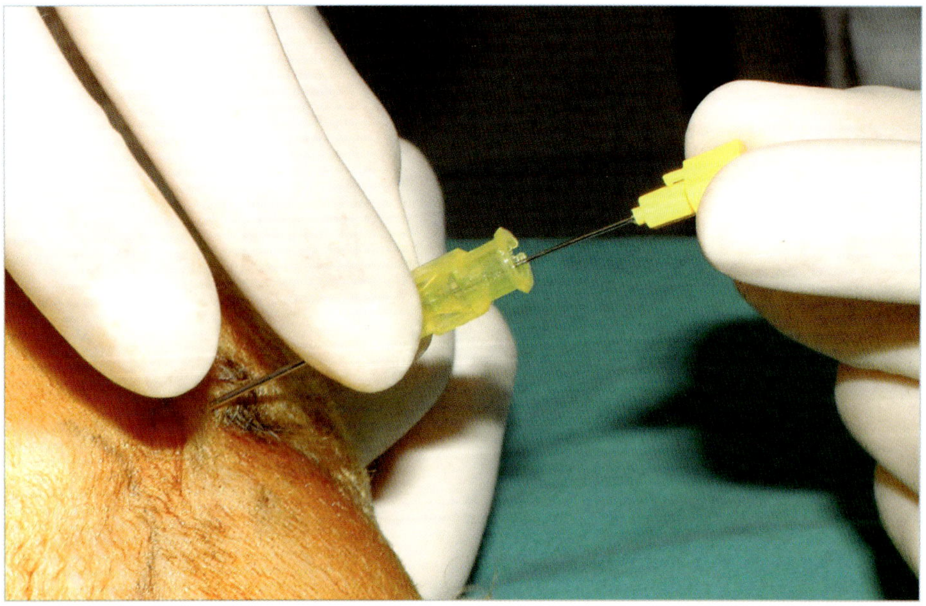

Sometimes, particularly if the veterinarian is inexperienced, the needle may hit the body of L7 and has to be redirected in a caudal direction to reach the vertebral channel. Until sufficient experience has been gained, it is advisable to take a lateral X-ray of the area to determine the length of the needle required and the depth to which it has to be inserted to reach the vertebral canal.

Fig. 11. Once the epidural space has been reached, the stylet of the spinal needle is withdrawn. If there is a need to reposition the needle, always replace the stylet to do so.

Next, the stylet is withdrawn from the spinal needle (fig. 11) and the hub inspected for the presence of cerebrospinal fluid or blood (fig. 12). The presence of cerebrospinal fluid (fig. 13) (resulting from a subarachnoid puncture) may be common in small and miniature breeds; if this happens, the needle should be redirected in a caudal direction or the dose of the anaesthetic reduced to one third of the calculated dose. If the full calculated dose is injected, complete spinal anaesthesia may ensue, with cardiovascular and respiratory depression or collapse.

If blood is observed, the ventral venous plexus that runs on the bottom of the vertebral canal has been punctured. In this case, the needle should be withdrawn and another attempt should be made to position it correctly.

If the tail moves, the nervous tissue may have been punctured. In this case, the location of the needle has to be modified slightly, but there is no need to withdraw it.

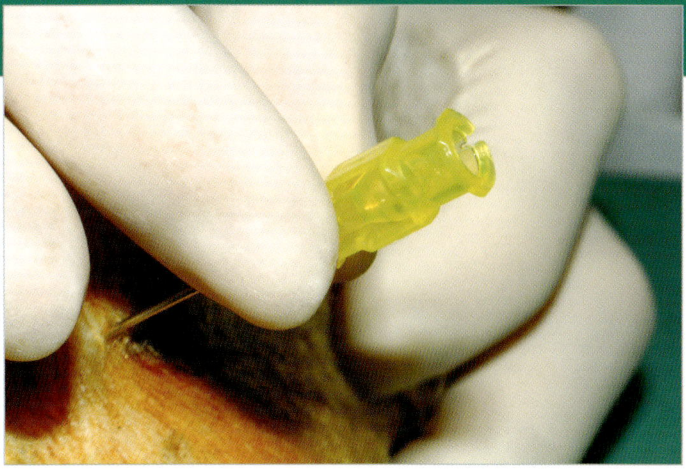

Fig. 12. Inspect the hub to ensure that no cerebrospinal fluid or blood comes out.

If the anaesthetic is injected intravascularly, convulsions, cardiorespiratory depression and the absence of regional anaesthesia may result.

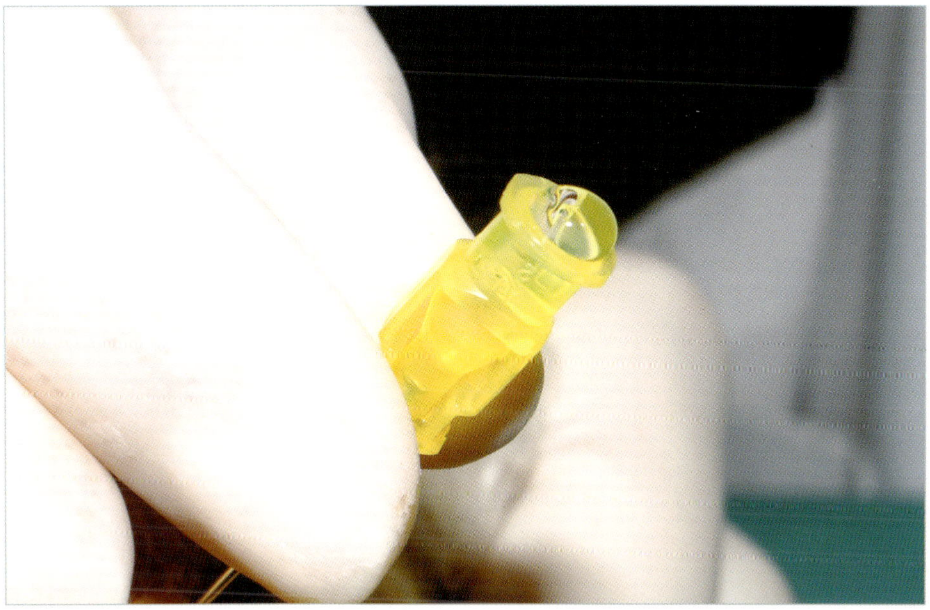

Fig. 13. If cerebrospinal fluid appears, the needle should be repositioned more caudally or the dose of the anaesthetic should be recalculated.

Checking the location

To check that the needle is correctly positioned in the epidural space, 0.5 ml air or sterile saline is injected and should enter without the slightest resistance. For this it is best to use special loss-of-resistance syringes (fig. 14), or, in their absence, a glass syringe.

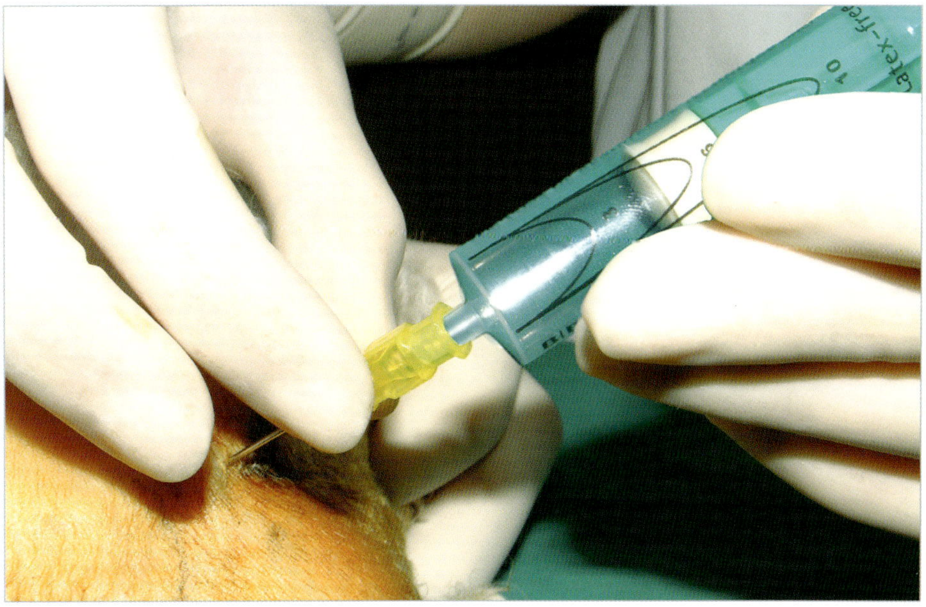

Fig. 14. To check that the needle is in the correct position, inject a small amount of air, which should enter easily without any resistance.

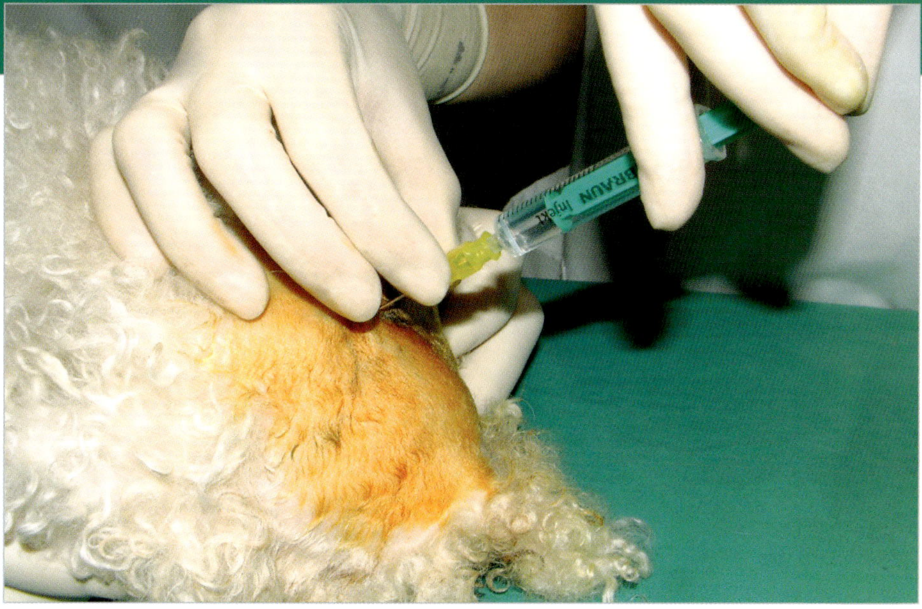

Administering the anaesthetic

The anaesthetic should be warmed to body temperature and injected slowly over 30-60 seconds. As in the previous test, this should not meet any resistance (figs. 15 and 16).
A test dose of 0.5-1 ml lidocaine hydrochloride 2% produces rapid dilatation of the external anal sphincter, which is further proof that the technique has been performed correctly.

Fig. 15. The anaesthetic is introduced into the epidural space.

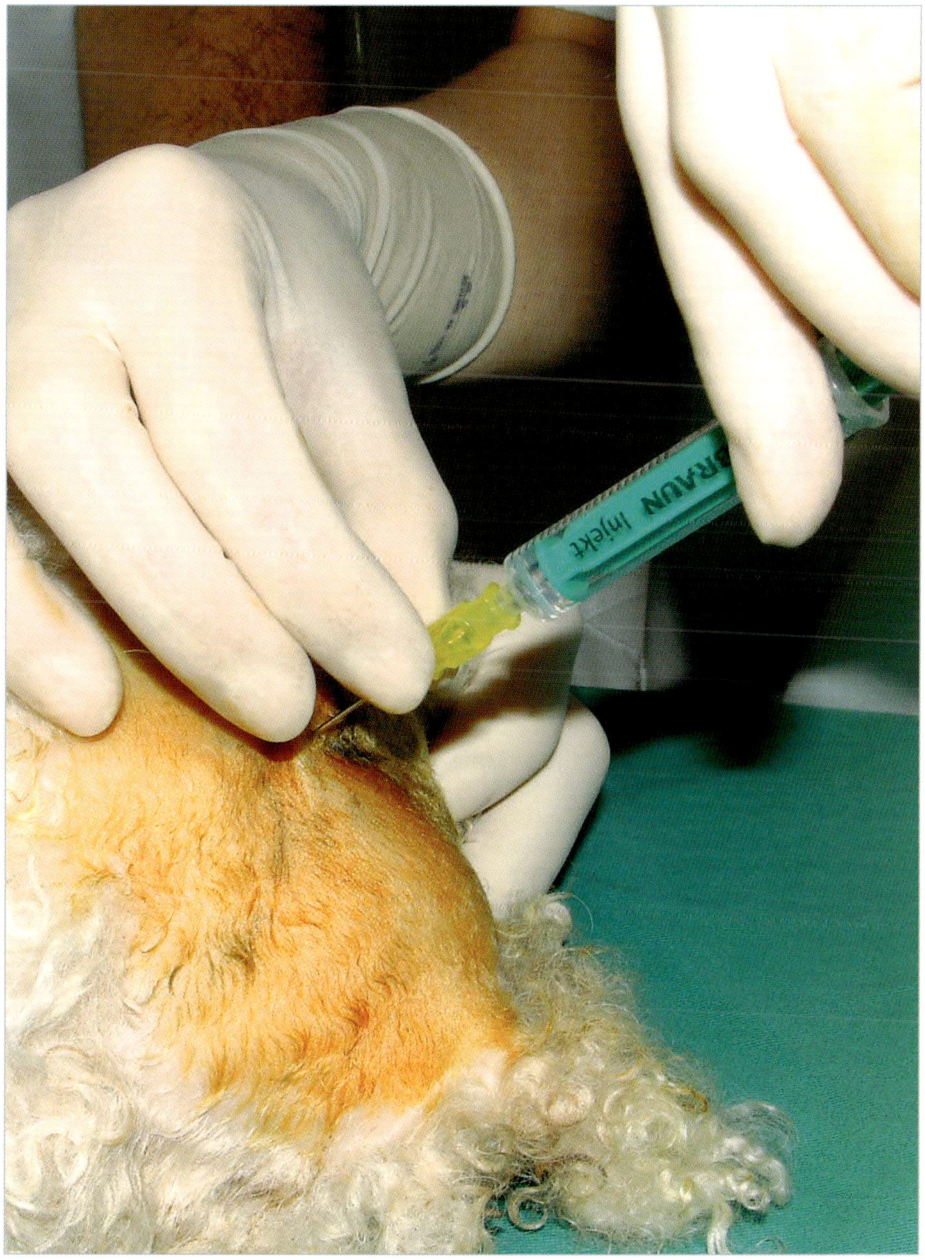

Fig.16. The liquid should enter without meeting any resistance.

Adverse effects

- Subarachnoid or intravascular injection may produce paralysis of the respiratory muscles, hypotension, Horner's syndrome, and hypoglycaemia due to sympathetic block, muscular contractions, convulsions and coma.
- If the injection technique is incorrect, anaesthesia may be delayed or absent; paresis and/or sepsis may also ensue.

Use the correct technique. Choose an ap propriate anaesthetic and calculate the dose accurately. Ensure the correct positioning of the spinal needle. Use a test injection.

Contraindications

- Local anatomical anomalies.
- Local dermatitis (lumbar).
- Sepsis.
- Clotting disorders and haemorrhages.
- Uncorrected hypovolaemia.
- Central or peripheral nerve disorders.
- Increased intracranial pressure.

The advantages of epidural anaesthesia outweigh the possible risks.

Patient positioning

Frequency

Preparation of the operative field and the positioning of the patient on the table are very important for all procedures in the pelvic area.

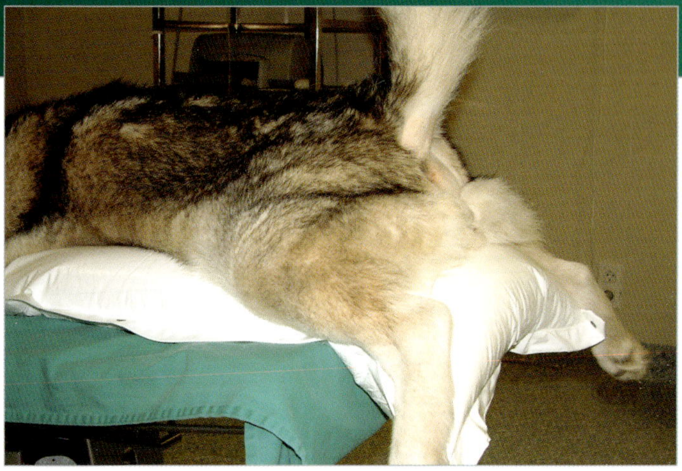

Fig. 1. This position allows the surgeon easy access to the perineal area. The cushion under the ventrocaudal area of the patient reduces damage to the femoral nerves.

Before surgery

- Low-residue diet for 3 or 4 days prior to surgery.
- Do not administer enemas during the 24 hours prior to surgery.
- Manually empty the rectum.
- Empty the anal glands.

Technique

- The perineal area is shaved, including the base of the tail, and prepared aseptically.
- The patient is placed in sternal recumbency on the edge of the table. To avoid nerve damage (femoral nerve) the animal should lie on a cushion or some towels (fig. 1). The legs are not tied to the table to minimise tension in the area.
- The anal sacs are flushed with a 50% povidone-iodine solution (fig. 2) and the operative field is disinfected once more.
- A purse string suture is placed around the anus to retain the faeces, avoiding contamination of the operative field.

See purse string suture of the anus → *page 252*

When the purse string cannot be placed, e.g. because the anus will be operated on, the rectum can be plugged with a wad of cotton wool or gauze swabs, or with a commercial tampon (figs. 3 and 4).

- Next, the tail of the animal is fixed to its back using adhesive tape (fig. 5), or, even better, a bandage, as this facilitates better control of the tension on the tail (figs. 6-9).

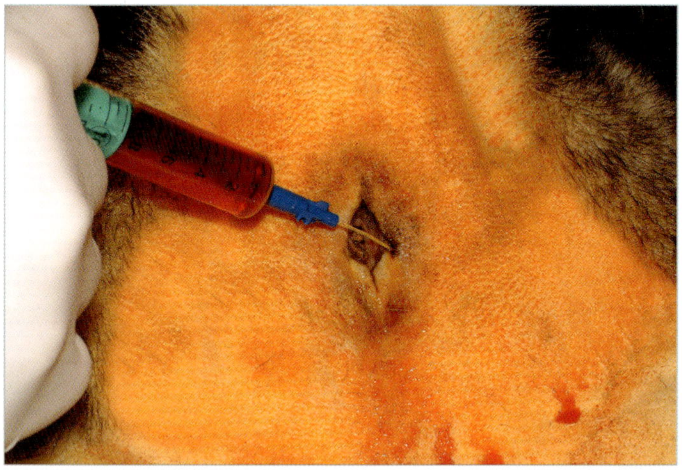

Fig. 2. The anal sacs are emptied, catheterised and flushed with an antiseptic solution.

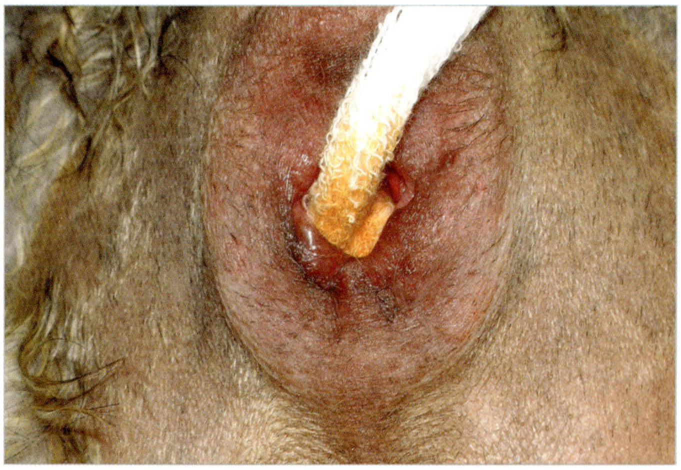

Fig. 3. A wad of gauze bandage is inserted into the rectum, leaving one end sticking out to facilitate its positioning during surgery and for removal after surgery.

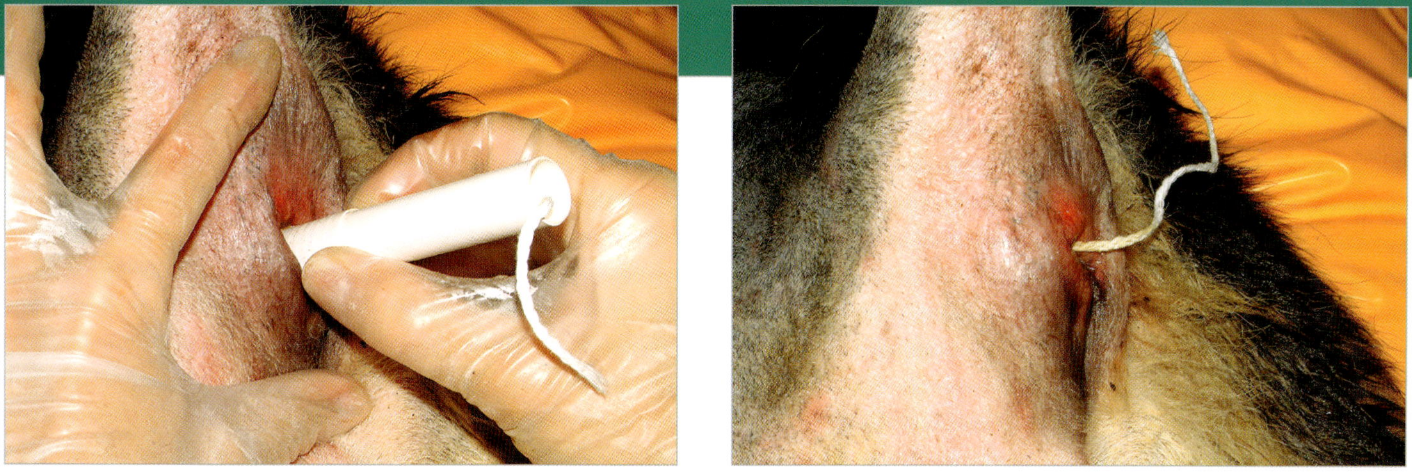

Fig. 4. An alternative to this technique is the use of a tampon, which serves the same purpose.

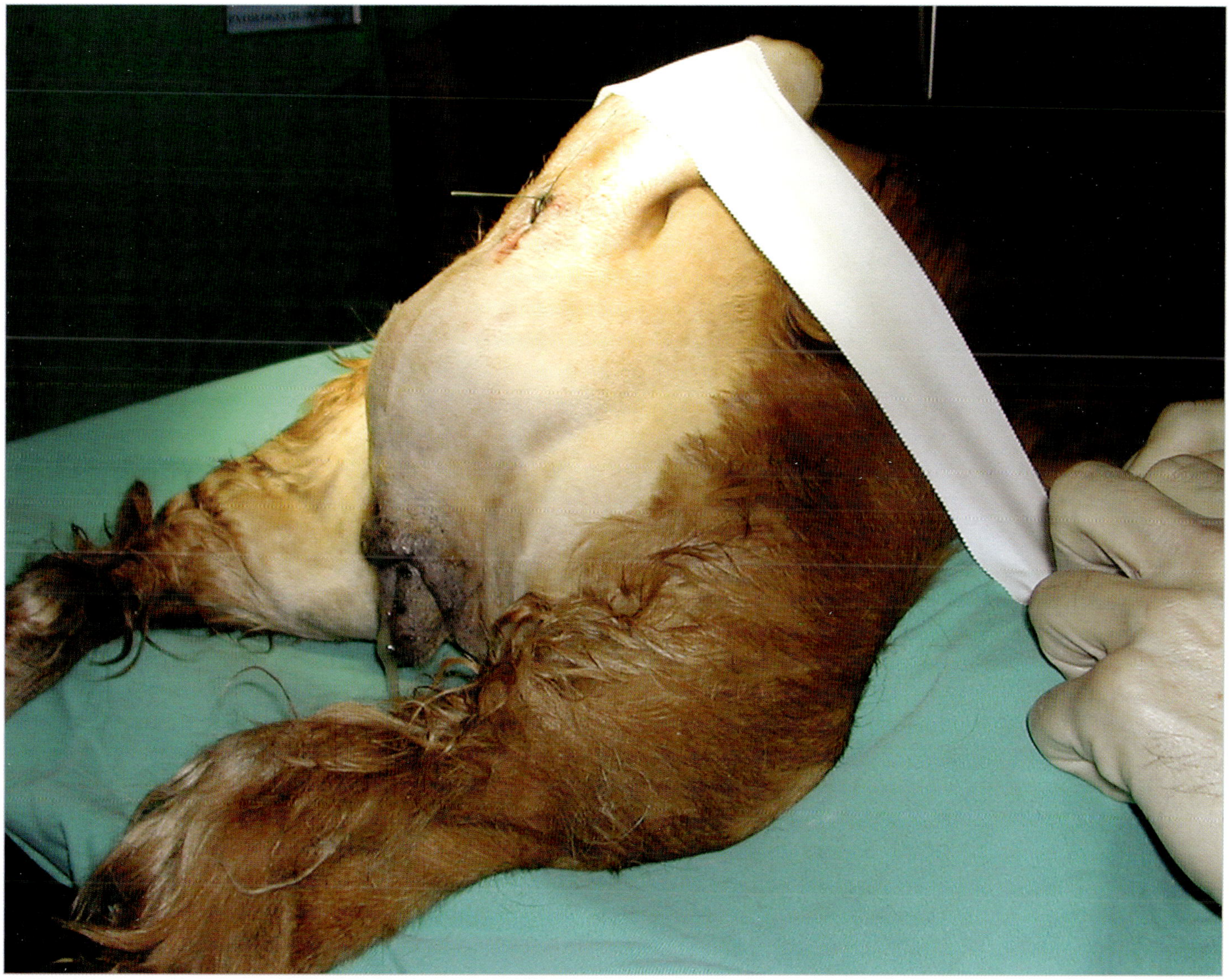

Fig. 5. Immobilisation and fixation of the tail to the table to obtain adequate exposure of the perineal area.

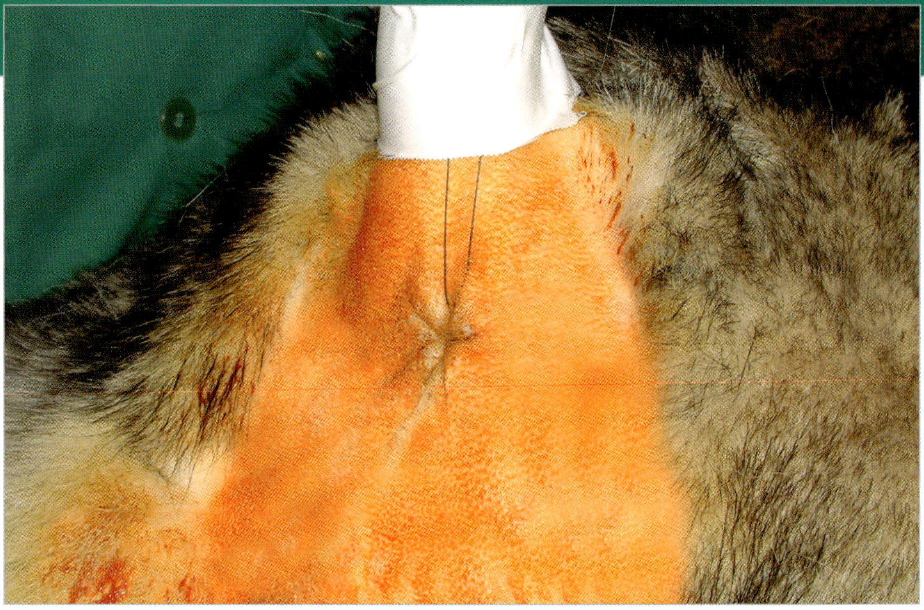

Fig. 6. The tail is bandaged starting from the base. The ends of the purse string suture and the bandage are fixed to the skin with adhesive tape to impede their movement.

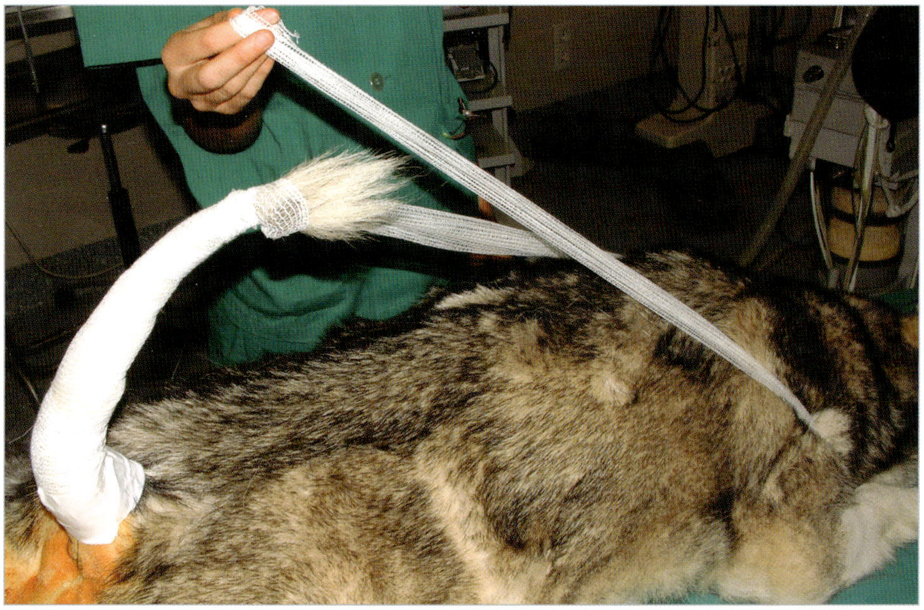

Fig. 7. The bandage is passed around the neck or the forelegs of the patient to immobilise the tail over the animal's back.

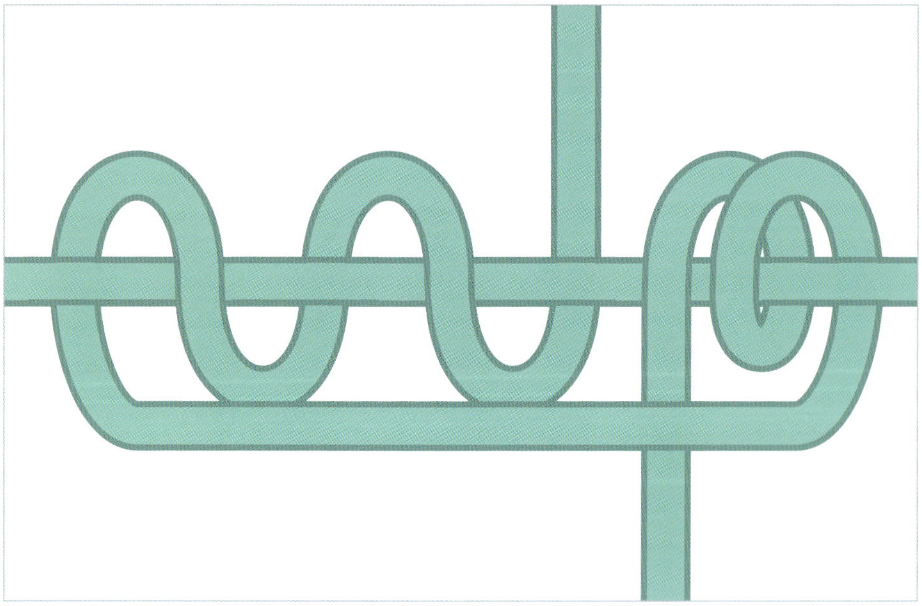

Fig. 8. A special knot is used. This is a sliding knot that supports the tension on the tail well.

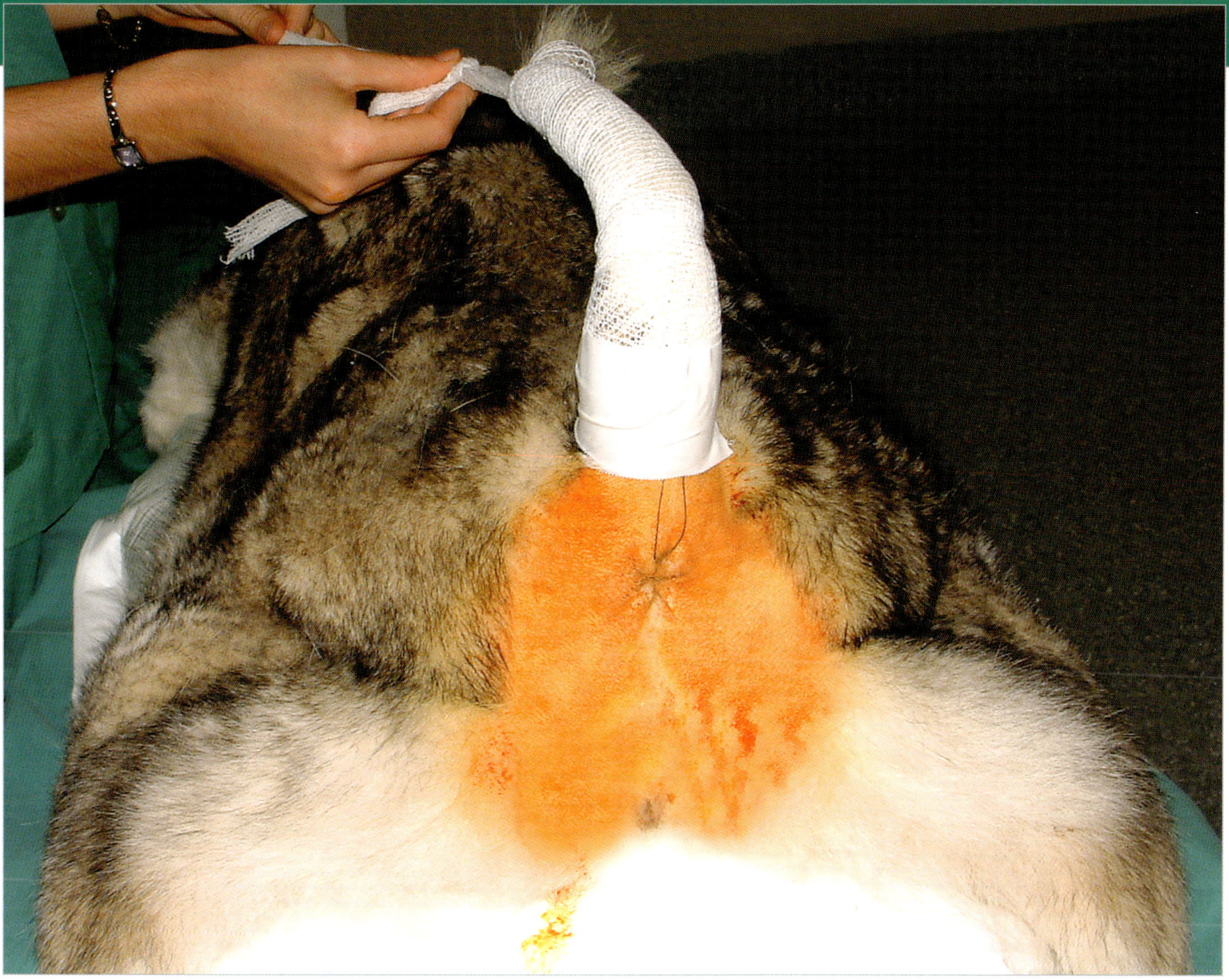

Fig. 9. To get the tail into the desired position, simply hold the knot and slide it up. Once you let go, it stays in place and does not move back.

- The operative field has been prepared and the surgical procedure of choice can begin.

> *It is recommended to fix the tail over the back with a gauze bandage as described, to minimise potential damage to the coccygeal nerves.*

Purse string suture of the anus

Frequency	■■■■■
Technical difficulty	■□□□□

The purse string suture is a continuous suture placed around the anus to prevent faecal leakage during perineal surgery and thus reduce bacterial contamination of the operative field.

Before surgery

- Low-residue diet for 3 or 4 days prior to surgery.
- Do not administer enemas in the 24 hours prior to surgery.
- Manually empty the rectum.
- Manually empty the anal glands.
- Catheterise, flush and apply an aseptic solution to the anal sacs.

Technique

- The perineal area is shaved, including the base of the tail, and prepared aseptically.
- A continuous suture is placed around the anus in multiple bites, each bite enclosing approximately 6 or 7 mm of skin (figs. 1-4). The bites should include sufficient tissue to support the tension on the suture.

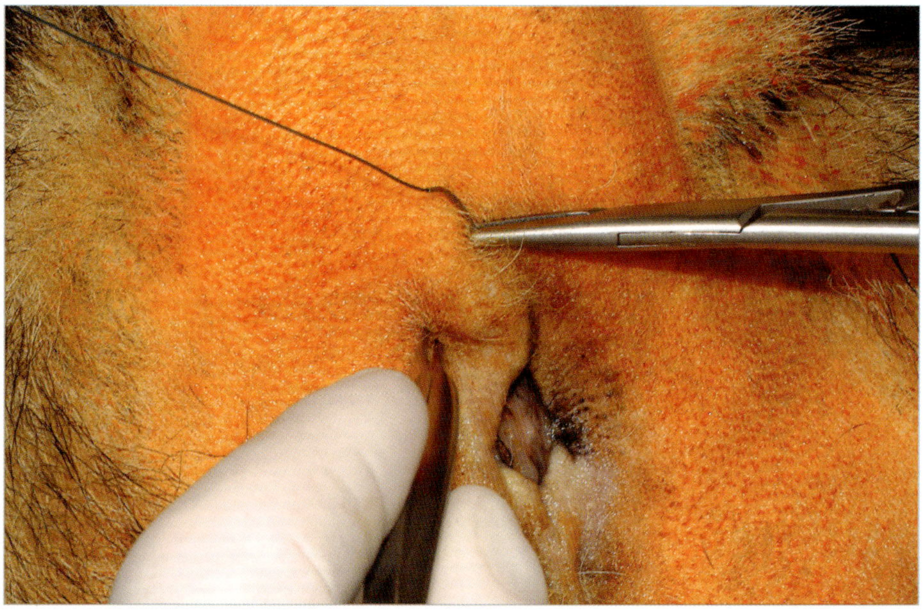

Fig. 1. The suture starts on the upper side of the anus, using 2/0 or 3/0 monofilament suture material.

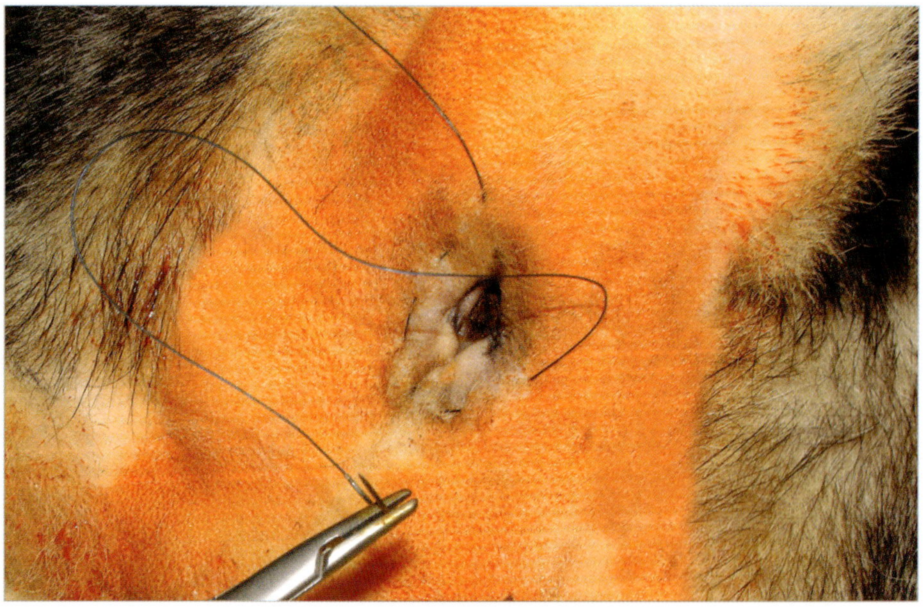

Fig. 2. When the bites are made on the lateral and ventral side of the anus, care should be taken not to damage the anal sacs.

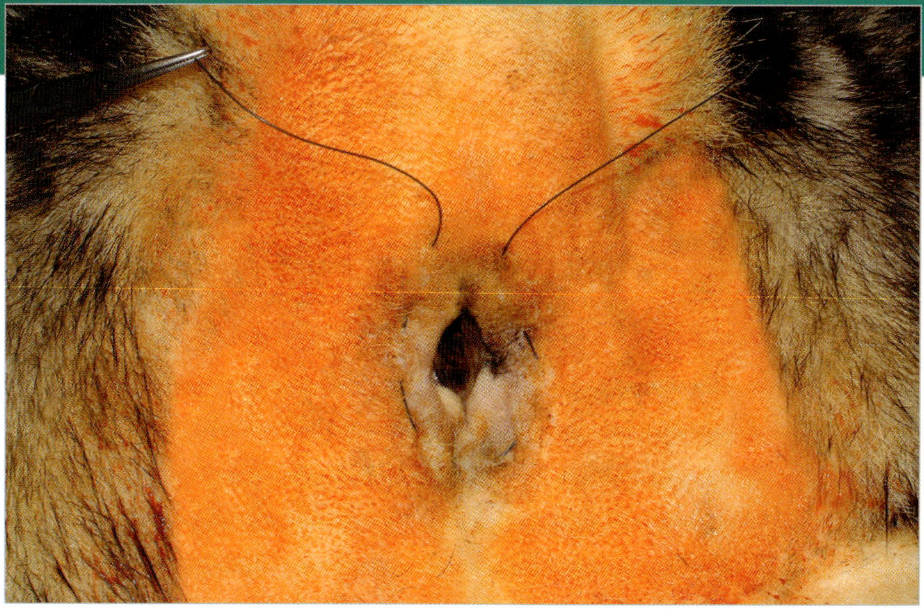

> ✱ *Remember that there are anal sacs on both sides of the anus. To avoid secondary contamination, do not perforate them.*

- After surgery do not forget to remove the suture so the patient may defaecate normally.

Fig. 3. Placement of the suture after taking between 5 and 6 bites around the anus.

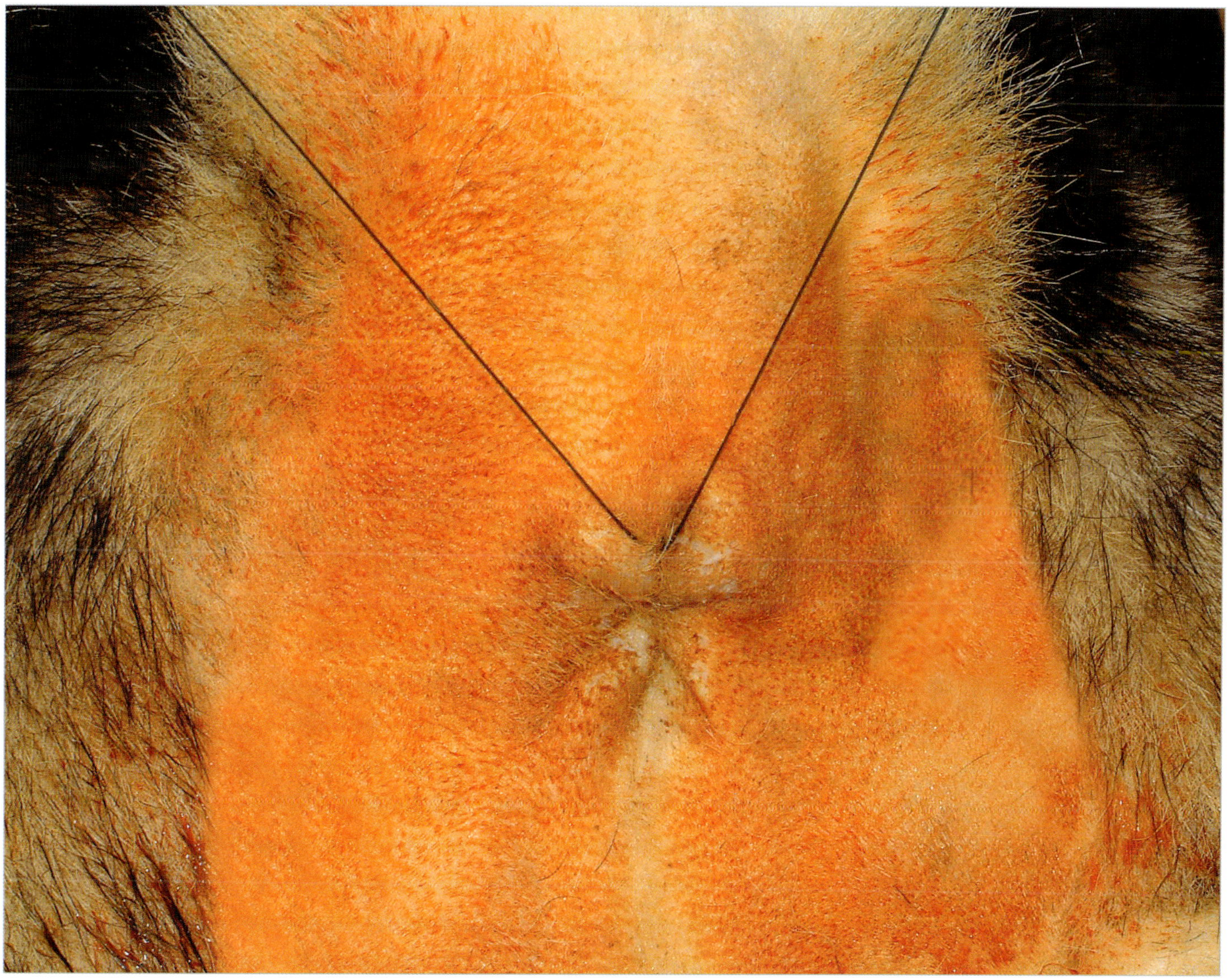

Fig. 4. When the suture is tied, the anal orifice is closed and no faeces can pass.

Episiotomy

Technical difficulty

This technique is used to create surgical access to the interior of the vestibule and vagina to: excise polyps or tumours, repair tears, aid foetal expulsion during parturition, etc.

The patient should be placed in sternal recumbency with the hindquarters elevated. The tail should be securely tied away from the operative field and a purse string suture should be placed around the anus (fig. 1).

See patient positioning **page 248**

See purse string suture of the anus **page 252**

To avoid bleeding, it is very useful to place two intestinal Doyen forceps on both sides of the dorsal midline where the incision will be made; one blade of the forceps is in the vagina, the other on the outside (fig. 2). The incision is made from the dorsal commissure of the labia of the vulva, along the midline, to just below the anal sphincter (figs. 3 and 4).

The muscles and vaginal wall can be cut with scissors (figs. 5 and 6). The bleeding, which is usually fairly light, can be easily controlled with diathermy, haemostatic forceps or a ligature if necessary.

Whatever the surgical procedure, it is very important to catheterise the urethra to identify it at all times and avoid damage (fig. 7).

The episiotomy can be closed in three layers (figs. 8-12). The first layer, the vaginal mucosa, is closed with a continuous suture using absorbable 2/0 or 3/0 suture material; the second layer, the muscle and subcutaneous tissue, in the same way and finally the skin is closed with simple interrupted sutures or with an intradermal suture. It is important to ensure perfect approximation of the wound edges at the vulvar commissure, avoiding unevenness of the wound edges. Finally, the use of an Elizabethan collar will prevent licking of the wound and subsequent inflammation.

The most common complications of procedures requiring an episiotomy are bleeding and accidental damage to the urethra. These can be avoided by making the incision exactly in the perineal midline and identifying the urethra with a catheter.

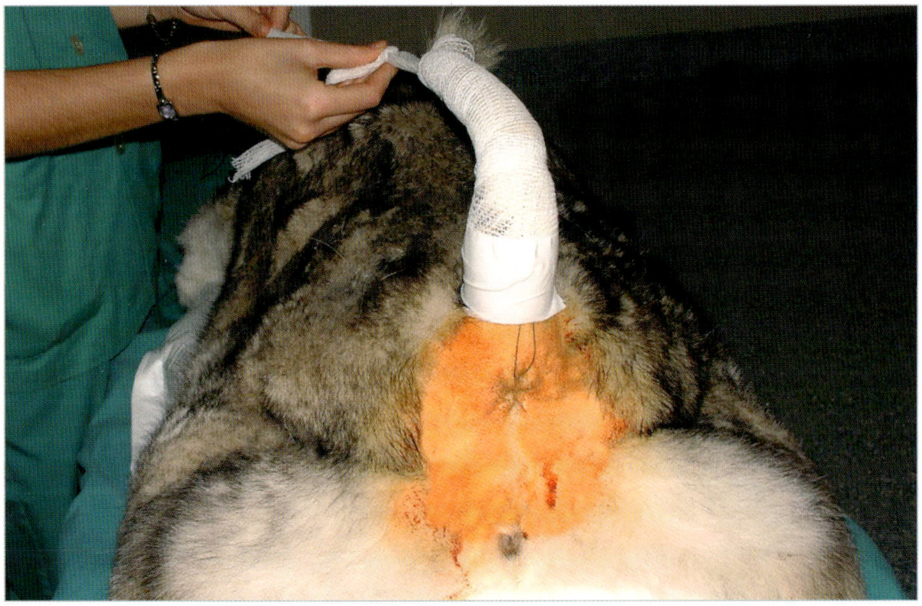

Fig. 1. The patient is placed in sternal recumbency, with the hindquarters on the edge of the table and the tail carefully tied back.

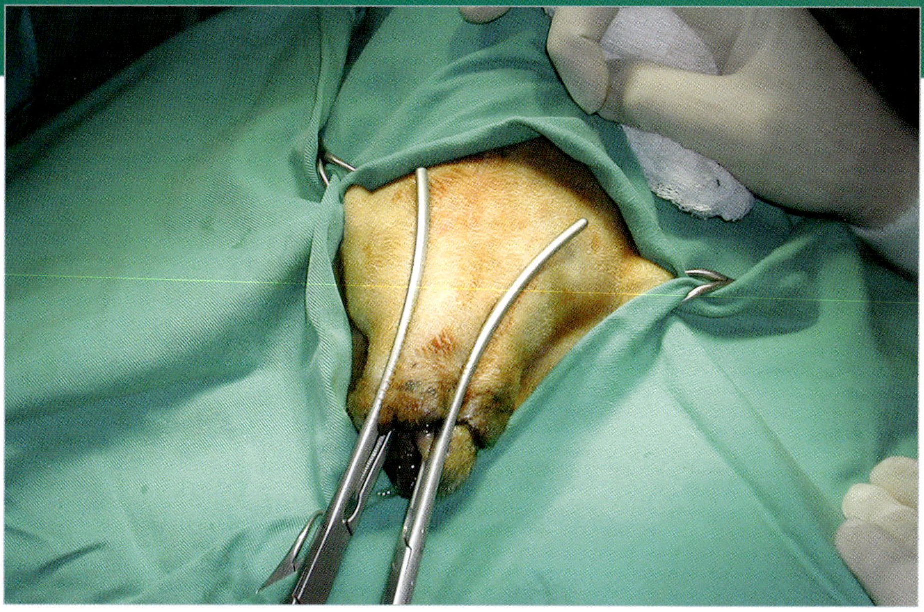

Fig. 2. The first step of an episiotomy is the placement of two Doyen forceps on each side of the incision line to reduce bleeding.

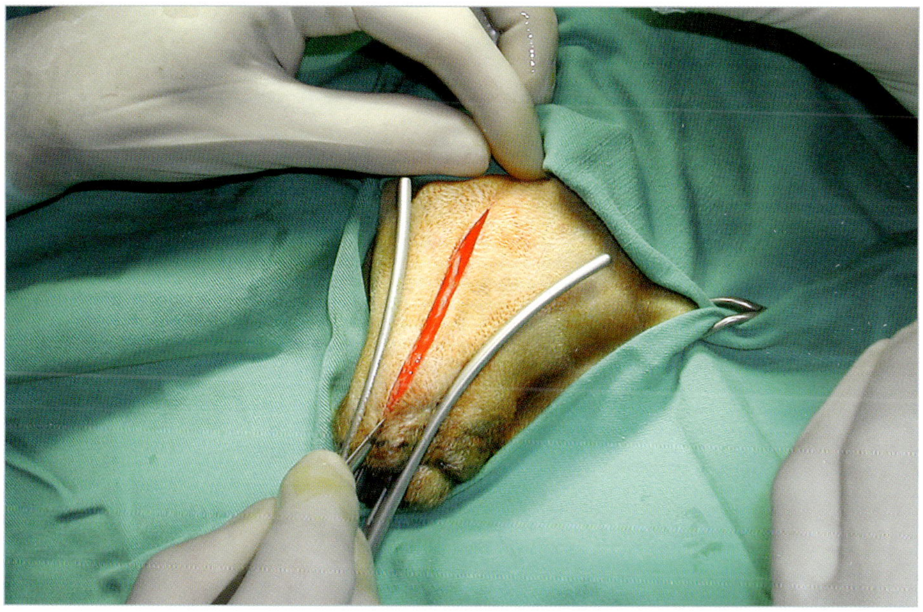

Fig. 3. Next, a skin incision is made in the perineal midline. The incision extends from the dorsal commissure of the vulva towards the anus, as far as is necessary to obtain comfortable access to the inside of the vagina. It is important to conserve the anal sphincter.

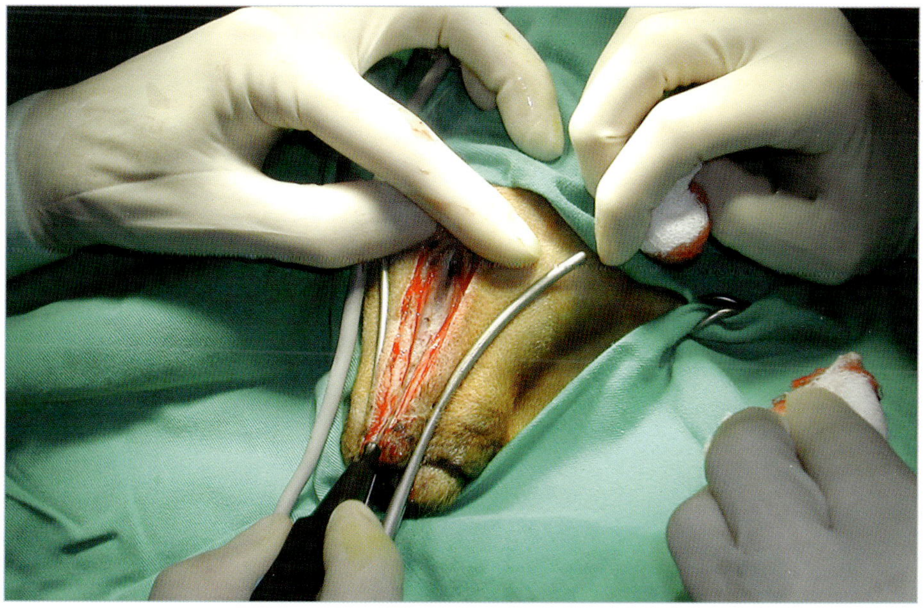

Fig. 4. The incision is deepened through the subcutaneous tissue and the muscular layer of the vaginal wall. Keep to the midline and use diathermy to reduce bleeding.

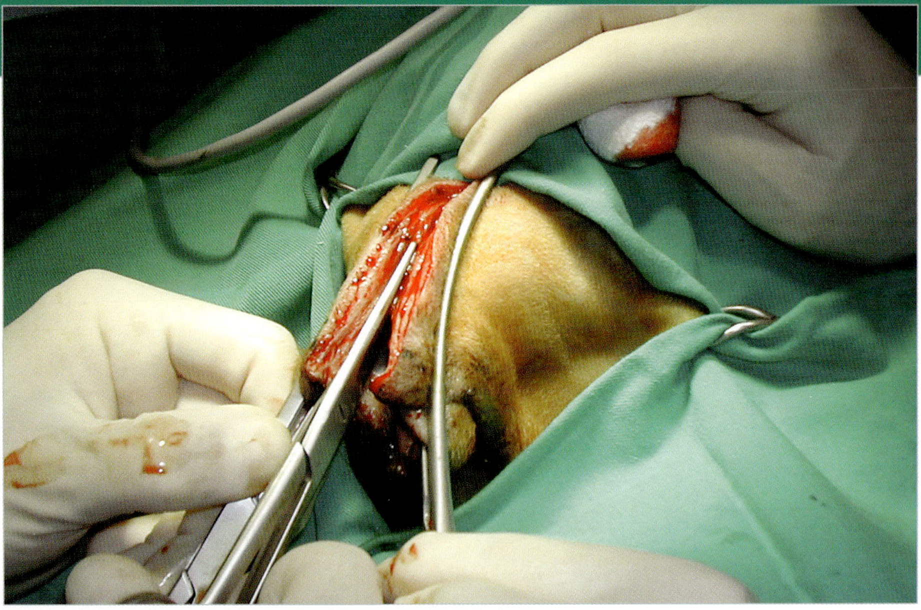

Fig. 5. When the mucosa of the vaginal wall is reached, the incision is extended with scissors into the vaginal lumen.

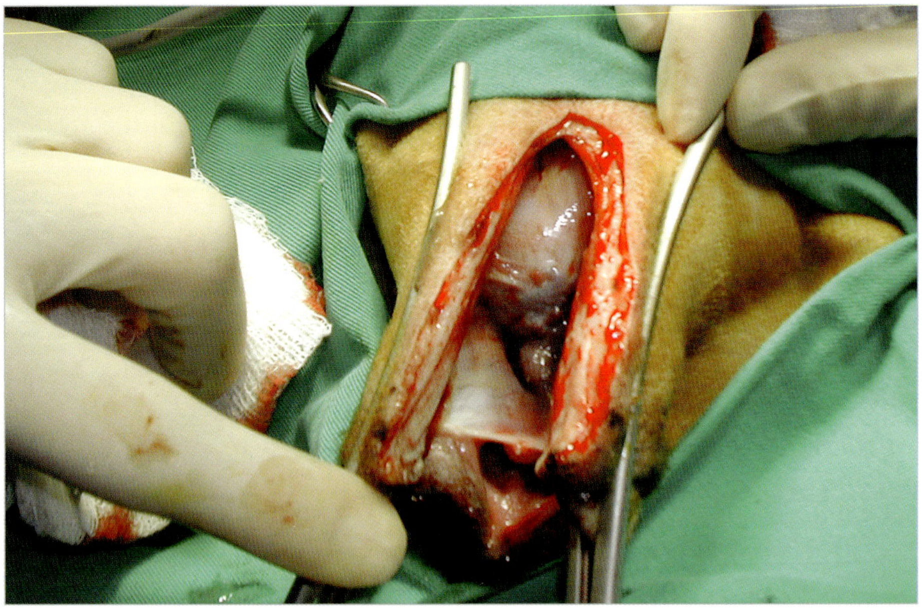

Fig. 6. Once in the vaginal lumen, the surgical procedure for which the episiotomy was performed is carried out.

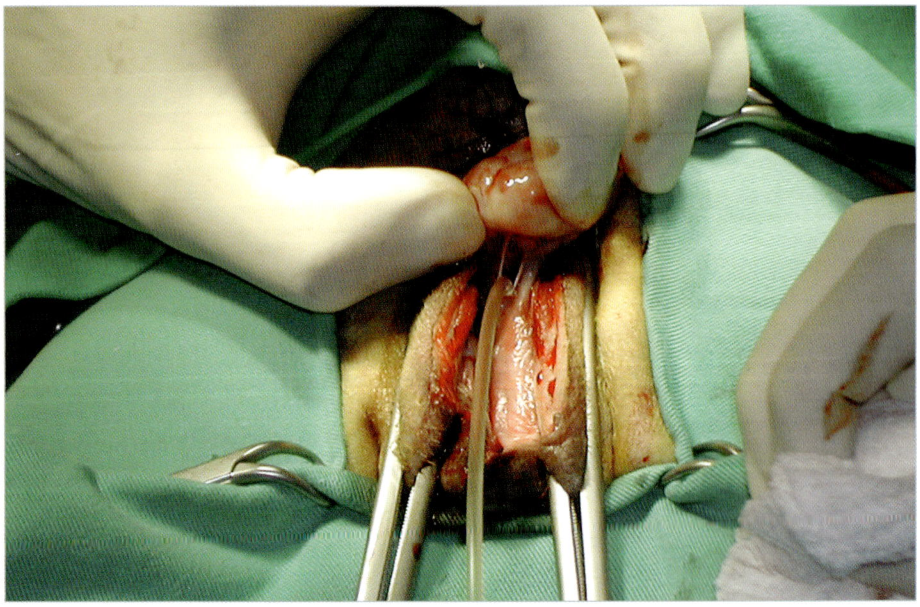

Fig. 7. It is highly advisable to catheterise the urethra to keep it identified and avoid damage during any procedure performed in the vaginal lumen.

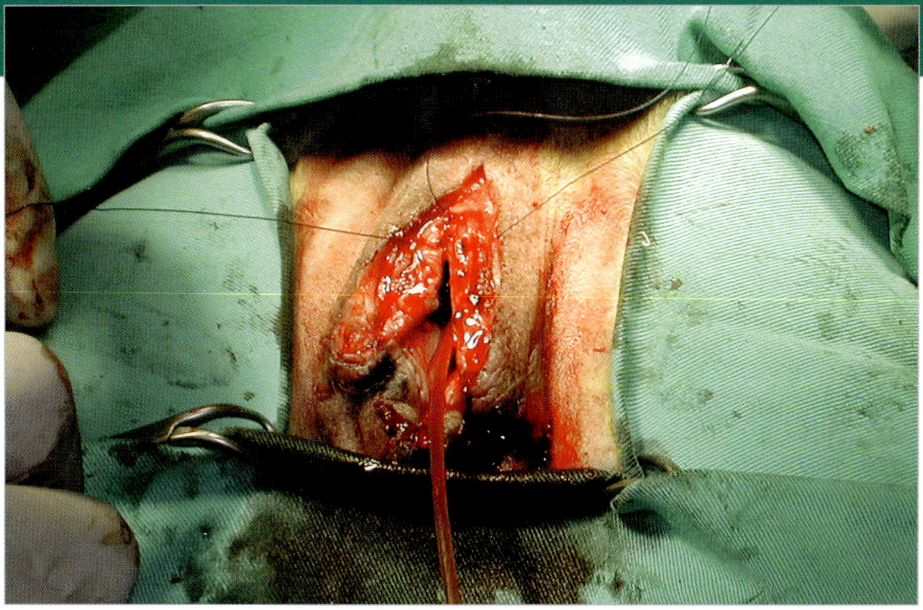

Fig. 8. The episiotomy is closed in layers, starting with a continuous suture in the roof of the vaginal wall using absorbable suture material.

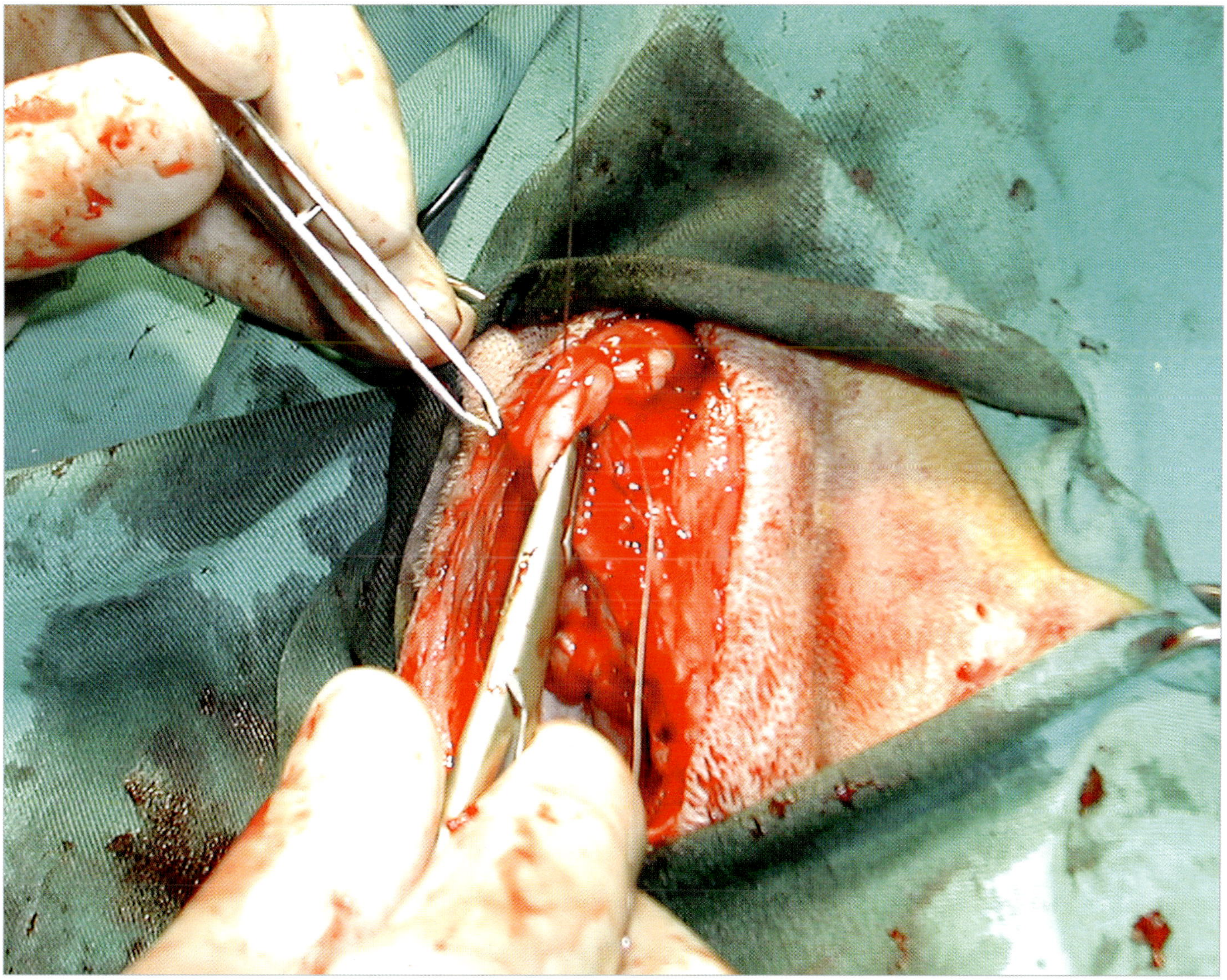

Fig. 9. The suture advances towards the vulva. Accurate reconstruction of the vaginal lumen, apposition of tissues should be ensured.

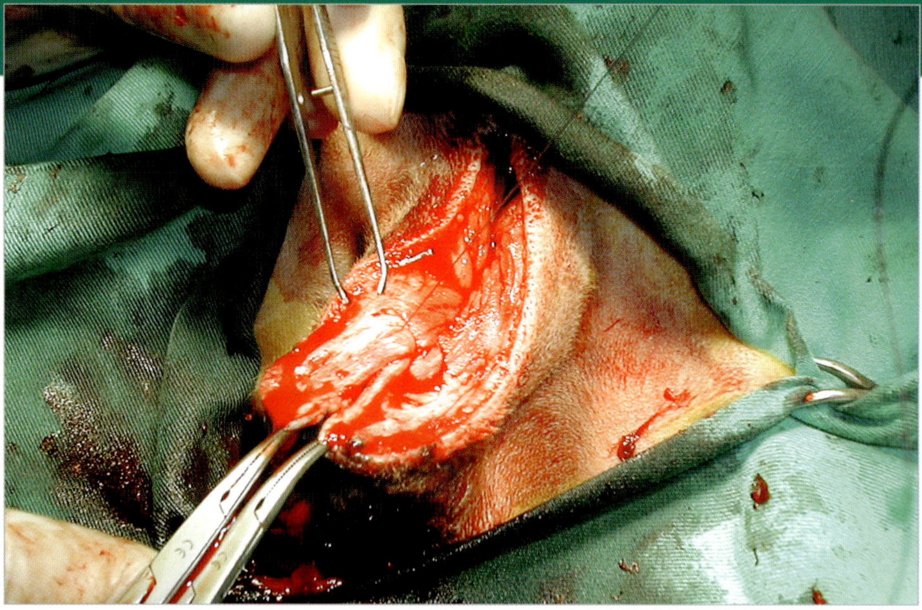

Fig. 10. To ensure correct apposition of the vulvar wound edges at the dorsal commissure, two mosquito forceps are placed as a guide.

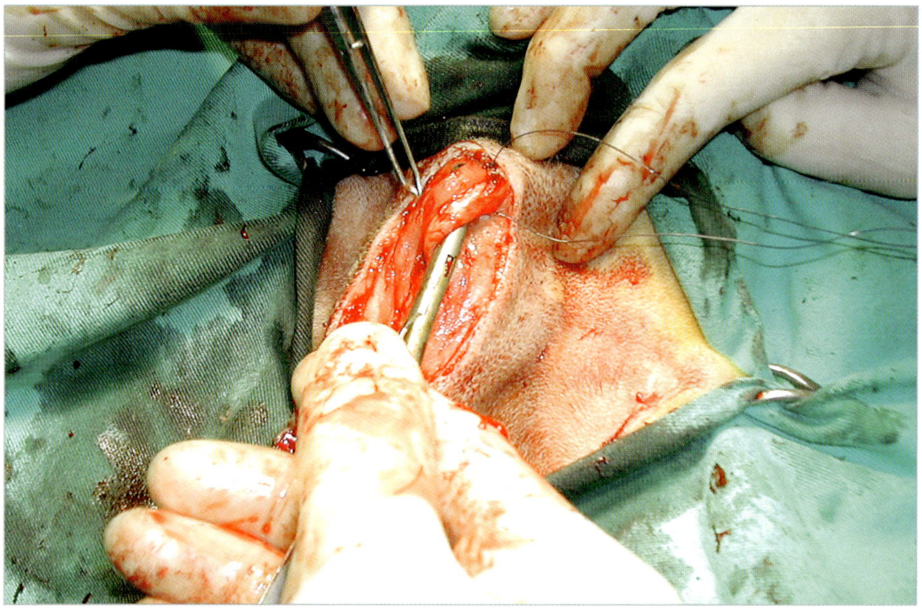

Fig. 11. Next, the subcutaneous layer is closed with a continuous suture in the same material.

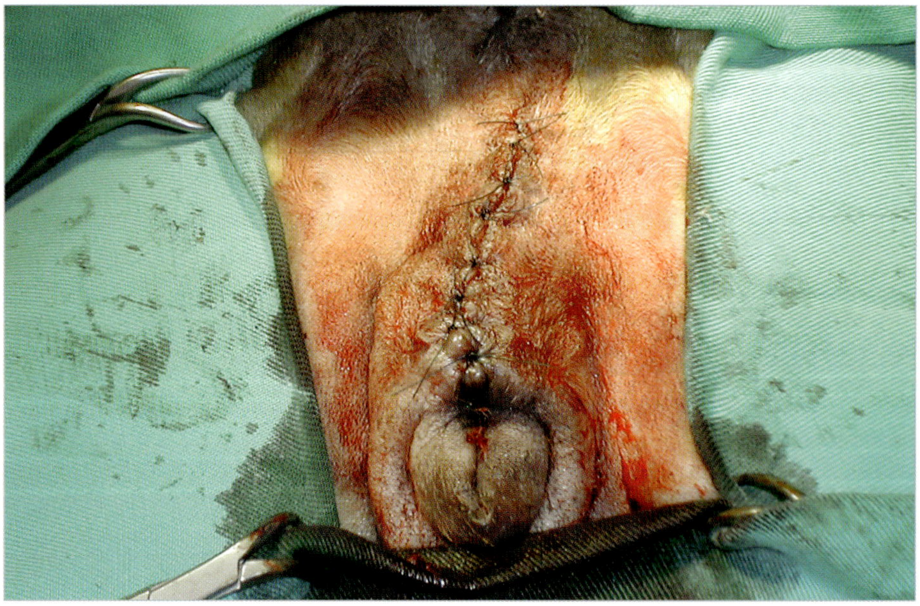

Fig. 12. Finally, the skin is sutured with simple interrupted sutures using a non-absorbable monofilament suture material.

Vasectomy

Technical difficulty	■	■	□	□	□

Vasectomy is a surgical technique that makes it possible to neuter a male animal without affecting his sexual physiology. Mechanical occlusion and/or transverse sectioning of the vas deference disrupts the passage of sperm; with this procedure the rest of the seminal fluids are still eliminated with the ejaculate.

This technique should be presented to the owner as an irreversible option. Even though vasectomy may be reversed under experimental conditions, the chances that flow in the duct will be completely restored and that the male will be fertile again are slight.
Provided that the sexual behaviour of the male is not a cause of inconvenience to the owner, this alternative method of neutering is less bloody and more physiological than castration. In the cat, the primary reason for neutering is territorial marking which will not be altered after vasectomy; for this reason it is rarely performed in the cat. This neutering technique is more commonly used in the dog.

Advantages	Disadvantages
■ Less aggressive technique ■ Does not affect the animal's instincts ■ Does not cause weight gain	■ Territorial marking and libido persist ■ Does not reduce aggressiveness nor the tendency to wander

Palpation is used to locate the spermatic cords in their prescrotal position on both sides of the penis. One cord is immobilised between thumb and index finger and approached via a small skin incision over its position (2-3 cm is enough) and blunt dissection until the cord is reached. After opening the tunica vaginalis with scissors, the components of the spermatic cord can be visualised; the firm, opalescent structure is the vas deferens.

A small membrane is attached to the cord with its blood supply. This membrane has to be incised to separate it from the vas deferens and to allow the insertion of haemostatic forceps with a ligature of absorbable suture material through the hole. Only the vas deferens is included in the ligature, the blood supply is left untouched. Next, the duct is sectioned below the ligature in two places and a 1 or 2 cm segment of the cord is resected. The end nearest to the testicle remains open, the end that is furthest away is ligated. Using this 'open-ended' technique avoids pressure-induced testicular atrophy that occurs when both ends are ligated.
The tunica vaginalis may be closed with a cruciate suture pattern or may be left open.
To finish, the incision wound is closed in two layers: subcutaneous tissue and skin.
The most common complication of this simple surgical procedure is haematoma formation as a result of inappropriate handling of the vascular structures that, together with the vas deferens, make up the spermatic cord.
As this technique does not modify libido, the dog should be kept separated from bitches in oestrus for a month after surgery. This is the time required for all remaining spermatozoa to be cleared from the vas deferens.

To confirm that the vasectomy has been effective, the semen may be analysed a month after the intervention. Until that time, the patient should be kept separated from bitches that could be in oestrus.

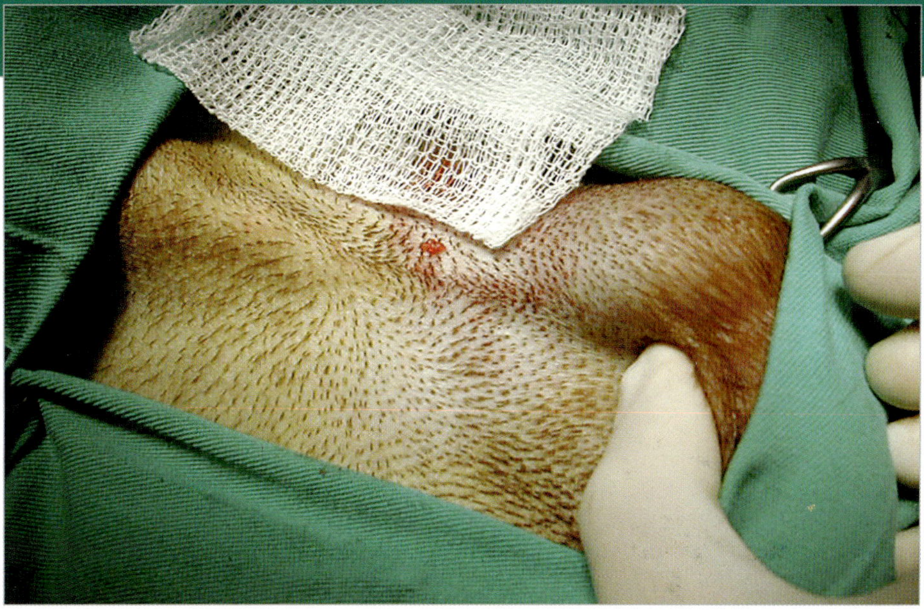

Fig. 1. The spermatic cord is located by palpation between the testis and the inguinal canal.

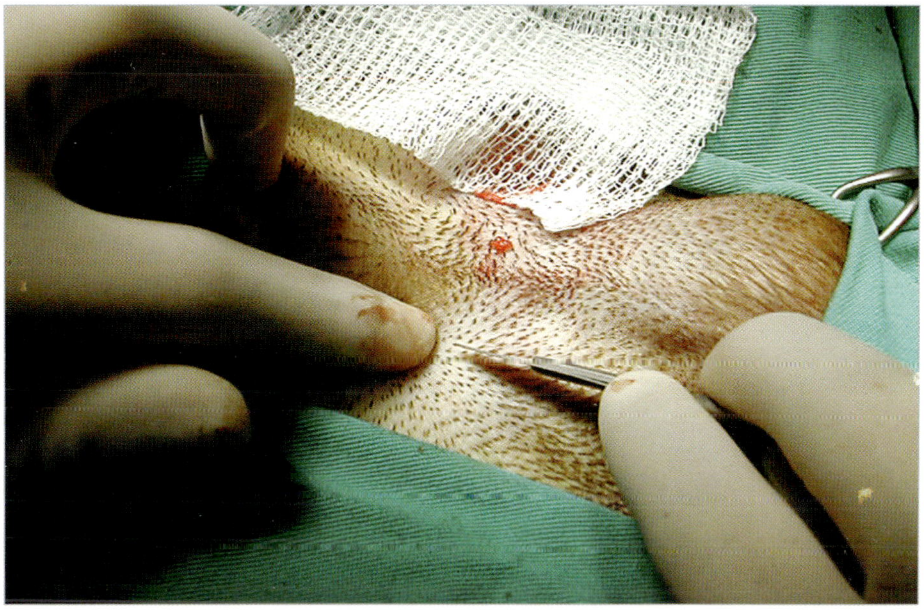

Fig. 2. The skin over the spermatic cord is incised.

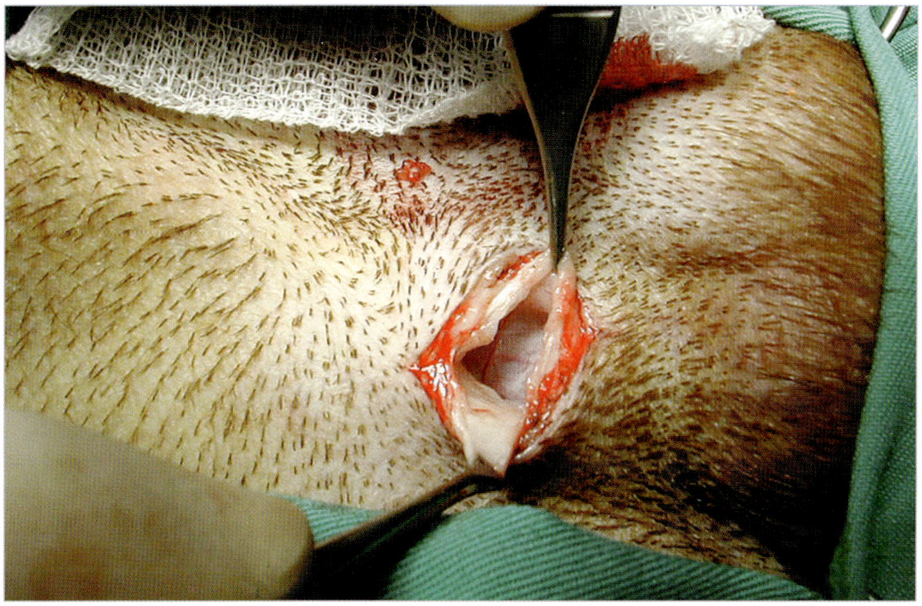

Fig. 3. The subcutaneous tissue is dissected until the spermatic cord is visualized. It is easily differentiated from the surrounding tissue by its colour.

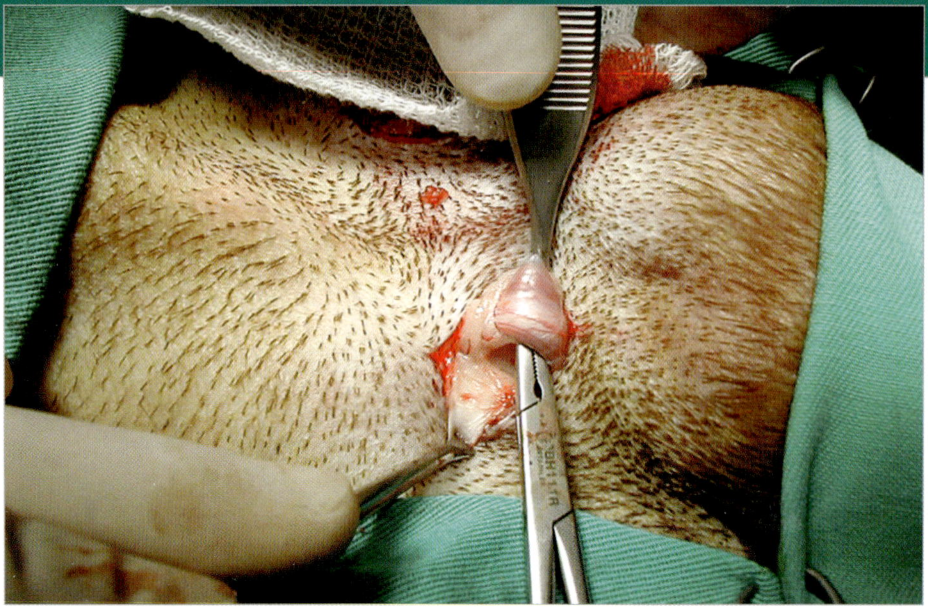

Fig. 4. Using blunt forceps, the cord covered by the tunica vaginalis is exteriorised.

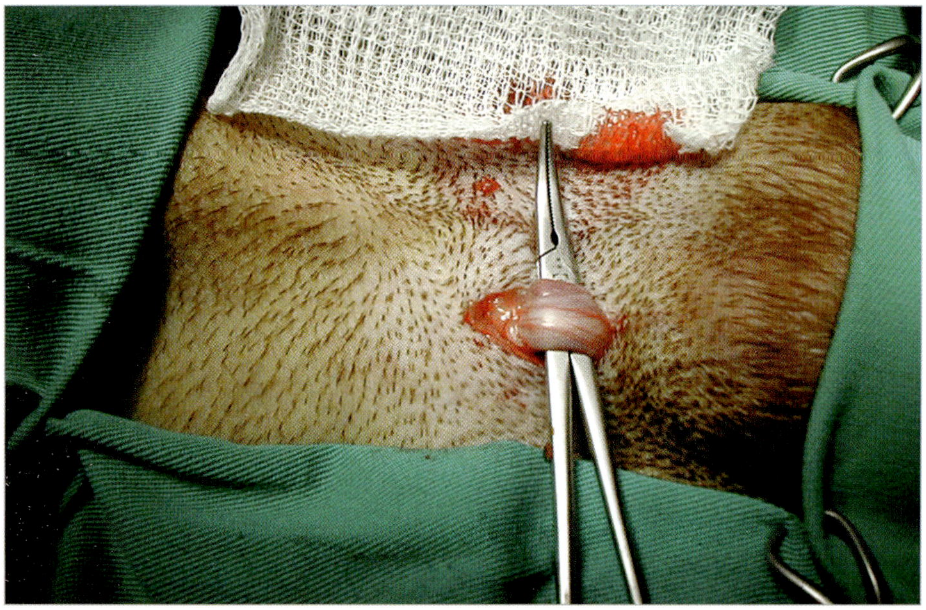

Fig. 5. The forceps are passed under the cord and are left in place for the duration of the procedure.

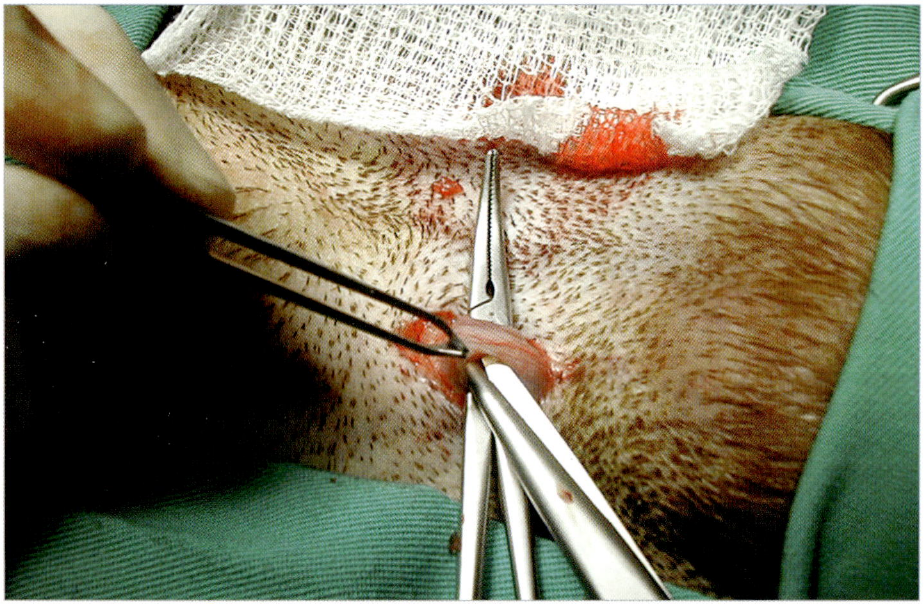

Fig. 6. Using scissors, the tunica vaginalis is incised directly over the vas deferens. In this way, damage to the pampiniform plexus is avoided.

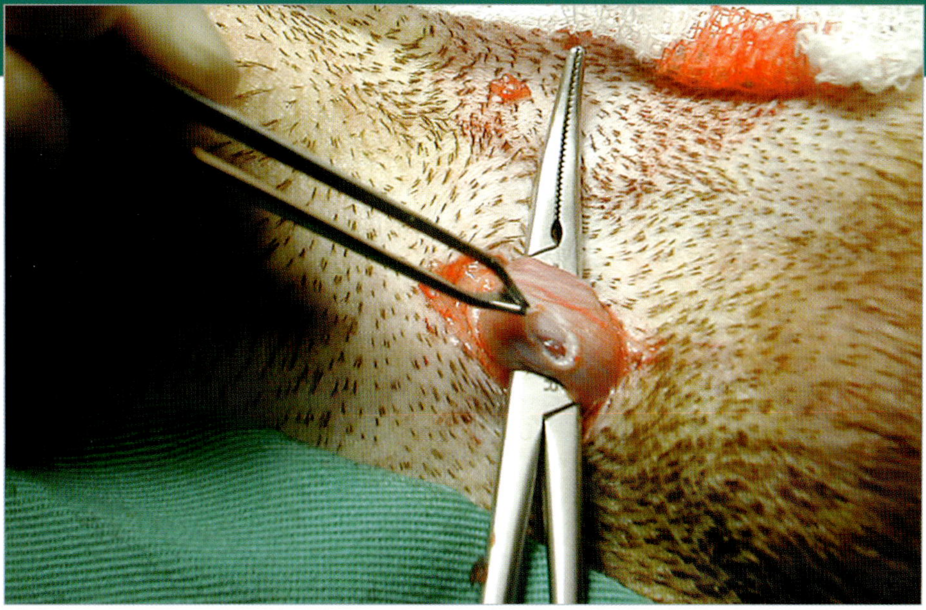

Fig. 7. After opening the tunica vaginalis, the structures of the spermatic cord are visible.

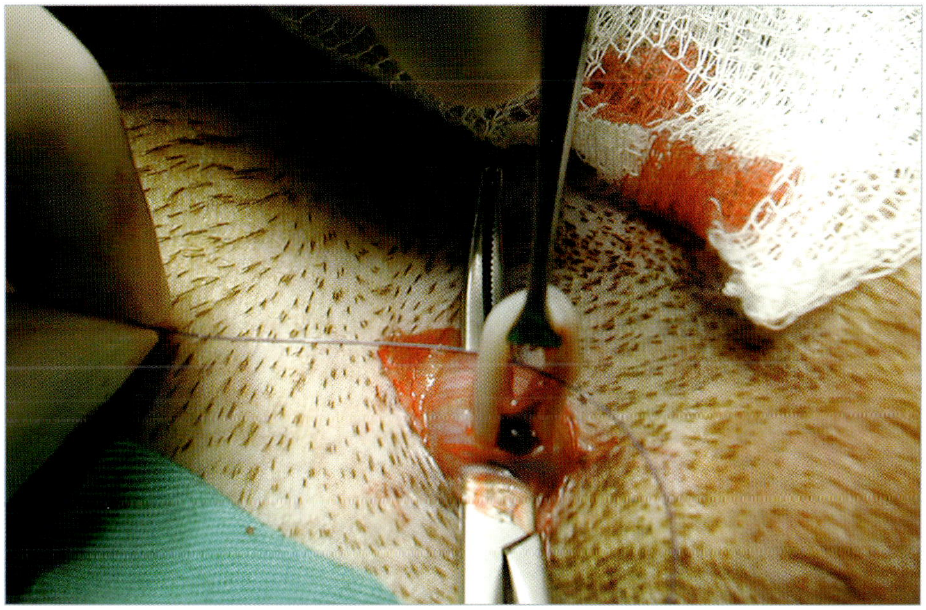

Fig. 8. The vas deferens is exteriorised through the opening in the tunica vaginalis and a hole is made between the duct and its blood supply.

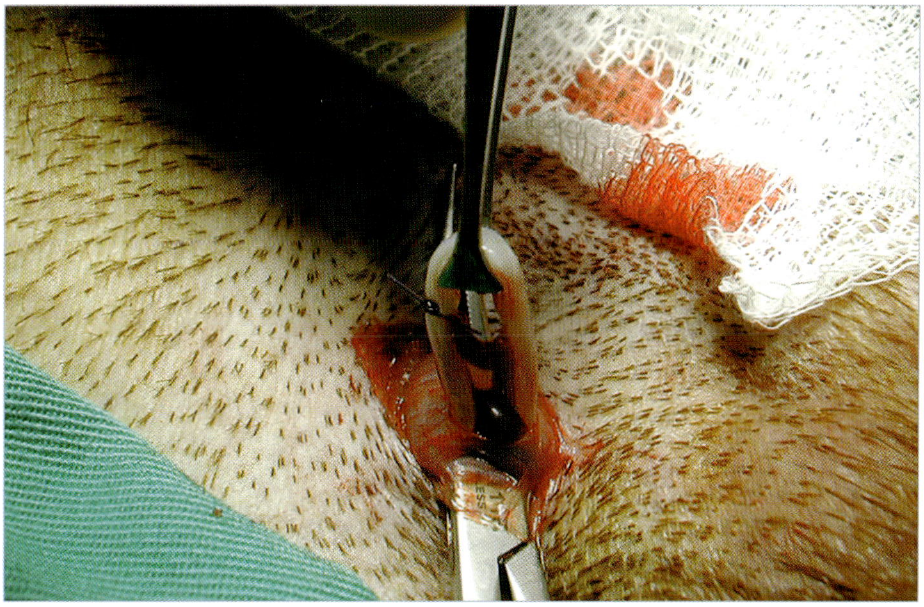

Fig. 9. A ligature of a 2/0 absorbable suture material is placed around the duct, avoiding its blood supply.

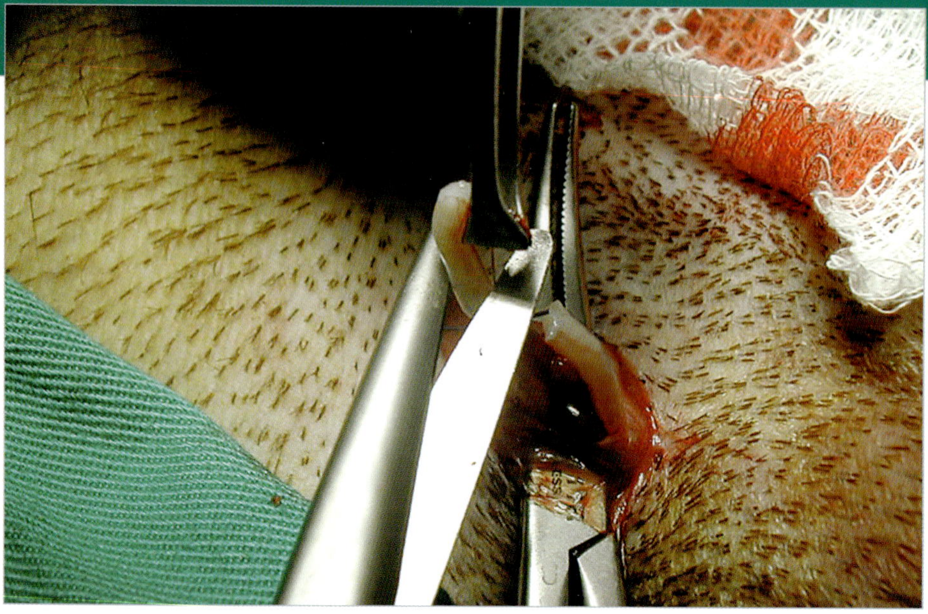

Fig. 10. Distally to the ligature, a small segment of the duct is resected, and the lumen of the duct end nearest to the testis is left open.

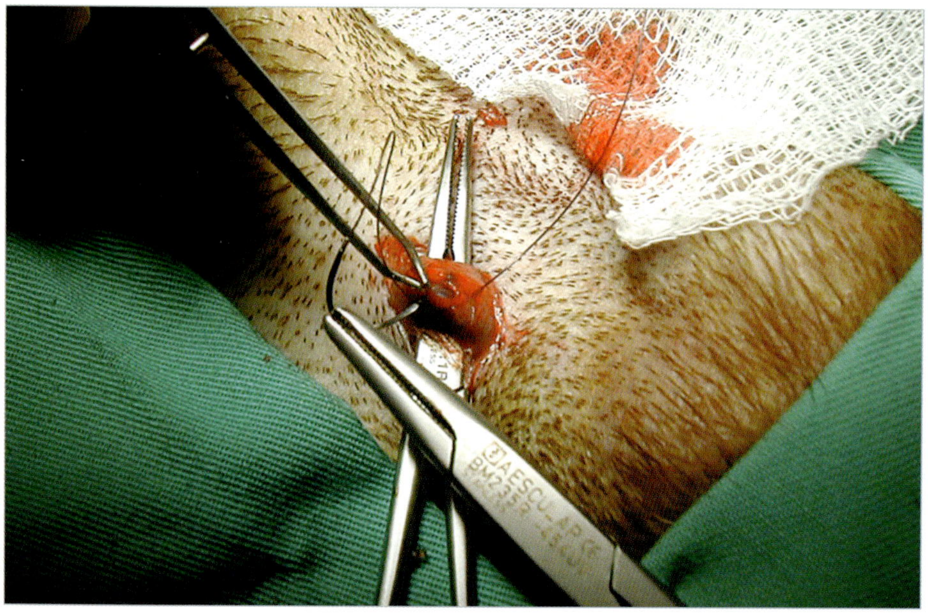

Fig. 11. The tunica vaginalis may be closed with a cruciate suture using the same material as the ligature.

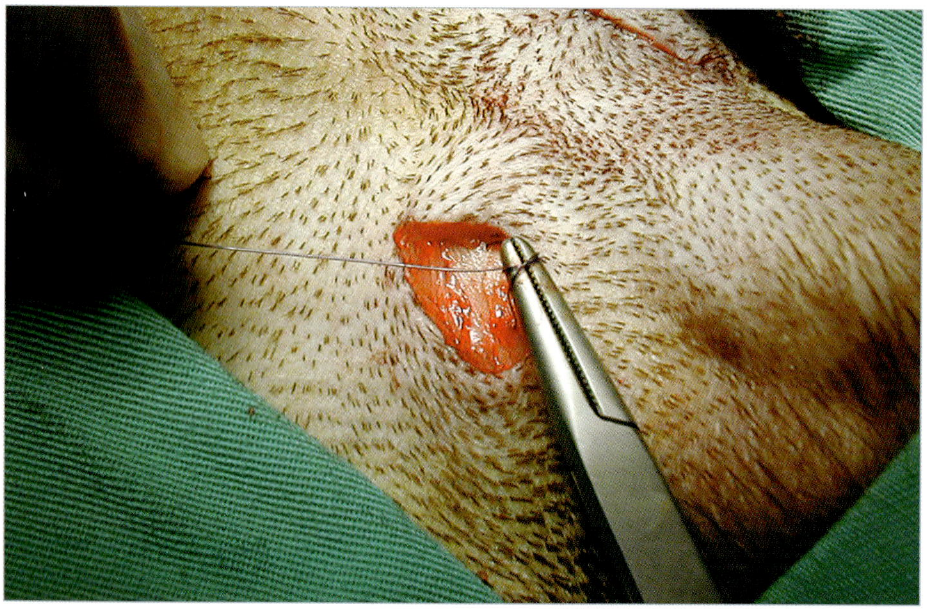

Fig. 12. After repeating the same procedure on the other side, both skin incisions are closed in one layer. An intradermal suture using absorbable monofilament suture material is used, so that there is no need to remove the stitches.

Castration of the dog and cat

Technical difficulty	■	■	□	□	□

Removal of the testes is probably the most common surgical intervention for a veterinarian. It has multiple indications ranging from population control to treatment of endocrinological, prostatic, neoplastic and behavioural disorders.

When castrating aggressive or difficult patients, it is advisable to close the incision with continuous sutures using absorbable suture material. This way there is no need to sedate the patient again to remove the stitches.

✱ ***To prevent testicular stump haemorrhages in the abdomen, the stump should be held by forceps when sectioned until it can be confirmed that there is no bleeding.***

Castration may be prescrotal, scrotal or combined with scrotal ablation. In the dog, prescrotal castration is most commonly performed and the testes are pushed cranially from the scrotum towards the prescrotal incision.

Castration with scrotal ablation is less common and is indicated in cases of scrotal trauma or when a perineal urethrostomy is necessary. In the cat, scrotal castration is the technique of choice, either via a single incision in the scrotal midline or one in each scrotal sac.

Regardless of the chosen method, the procedure always includes an incision of the skin and the parietal tunica vaginalis. The testis is exteriorised through the incision and the tunica is separated from the tail of the epididymis by digital traction. Next, the structures of the spermatic cord are identified and the blood vessels and vas deferens are ligated separately using absorbable suture material.

Closure of the scrotal incision is optional. In the cat, it is usually left open. With prescrotal castration the skin is sutured using simple interrupted sutures. Alternatively, absorbable monofilament intradermal sutures can be used to avoid the need for suture removal.

The most common perioperative complications of castration are seromas, inflammation of the scrotal sac and haemorrhage. If the ligatures on the pampiniform plexus are not placed securely enough or loosen, the risk of an undetected abdominal haemorrhage increases.

Castration. Case 1 / Prescrotal castration in the dog

Technical difficulty

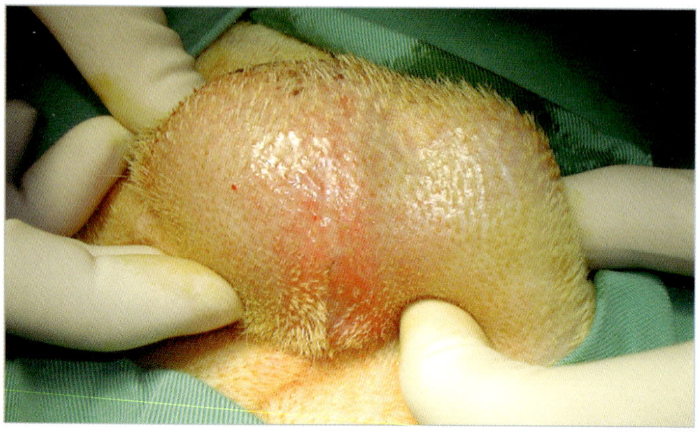

Fig. 1. For prescrotal castration, an extensive area around the scrotum is shaved and prepared aseptically.

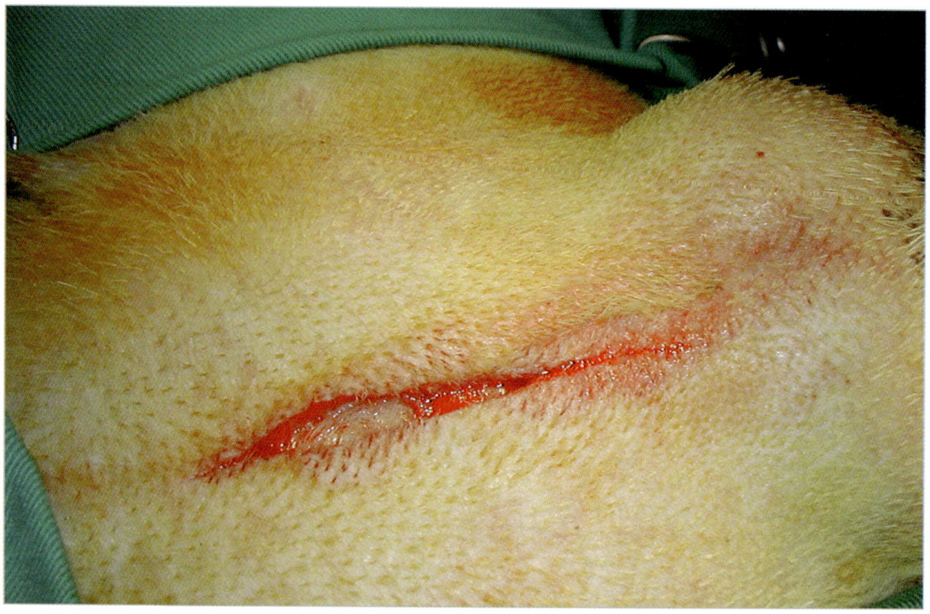

Fig. 2. A single skin incision is made in the midline immediately cranial to the scrotal sac.

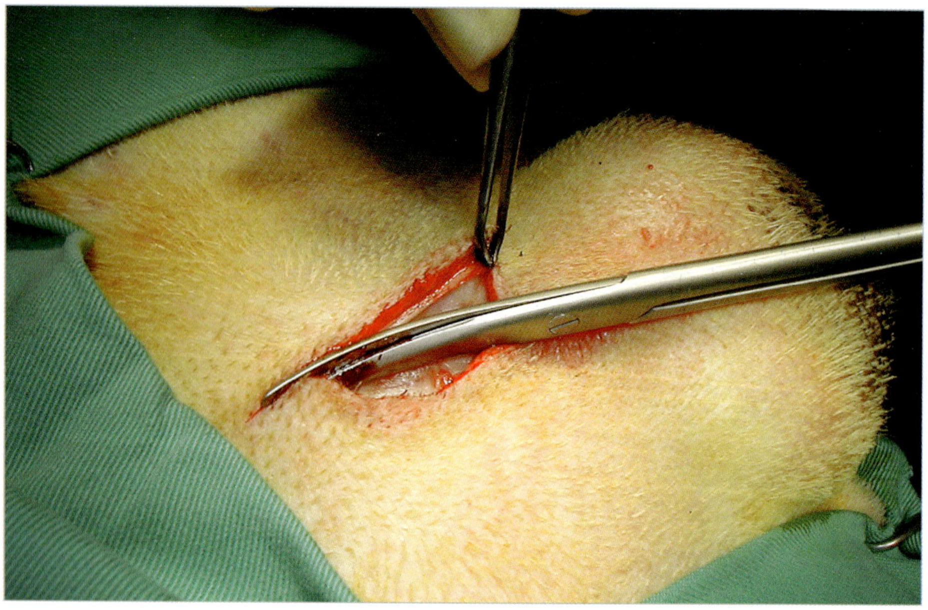

Fig. 3. The incision is extended by dissecting the subcutaneous tissue with scissors.

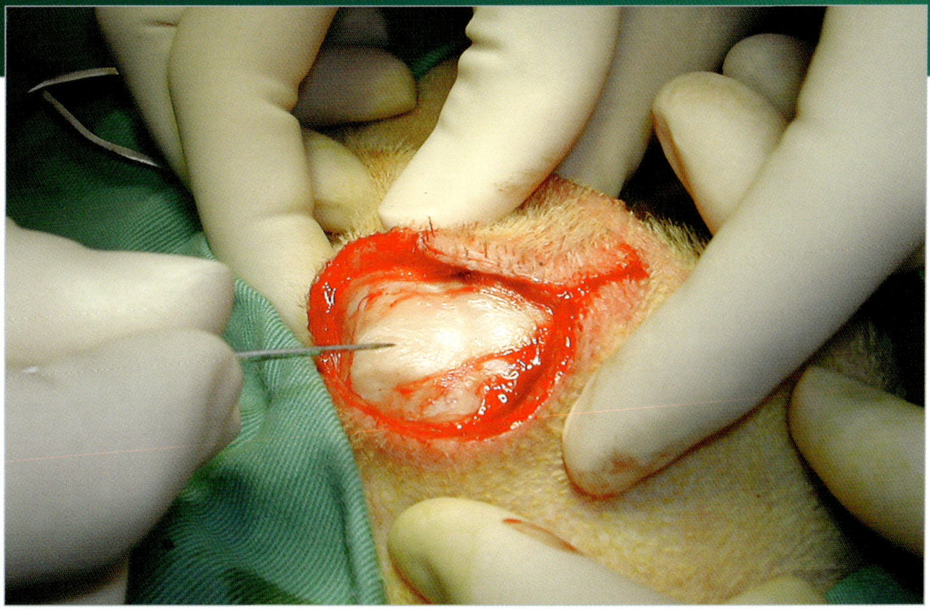

Fig. 4. The first testis is pushed towards the incision using gentle pressure until it can be visualised covered by the tunica vaginalis.

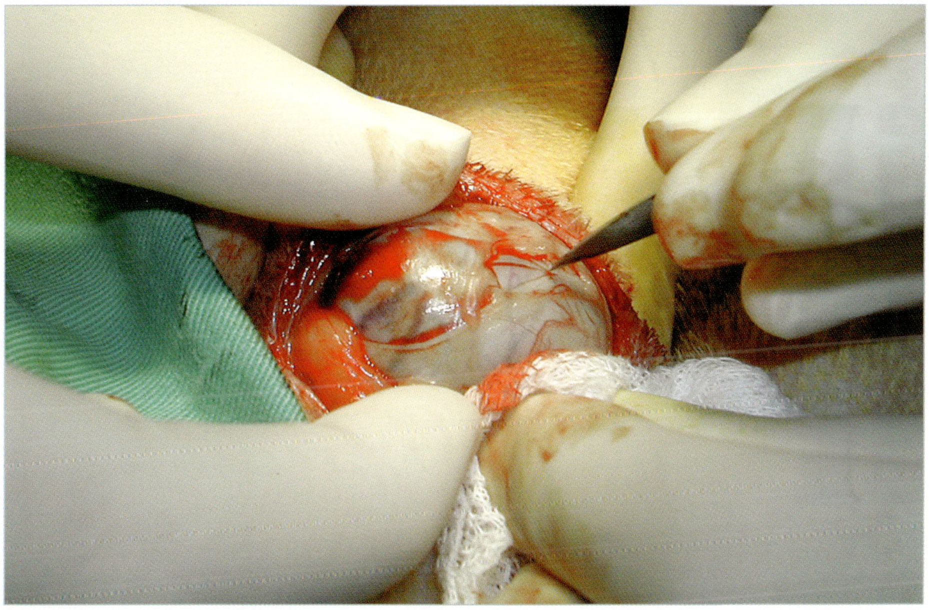

Fig. 5. Using a scalpel, the tunica vaginalis is incised, taking care not to damage the testicular parenchyma, as this results in haemorrhage.

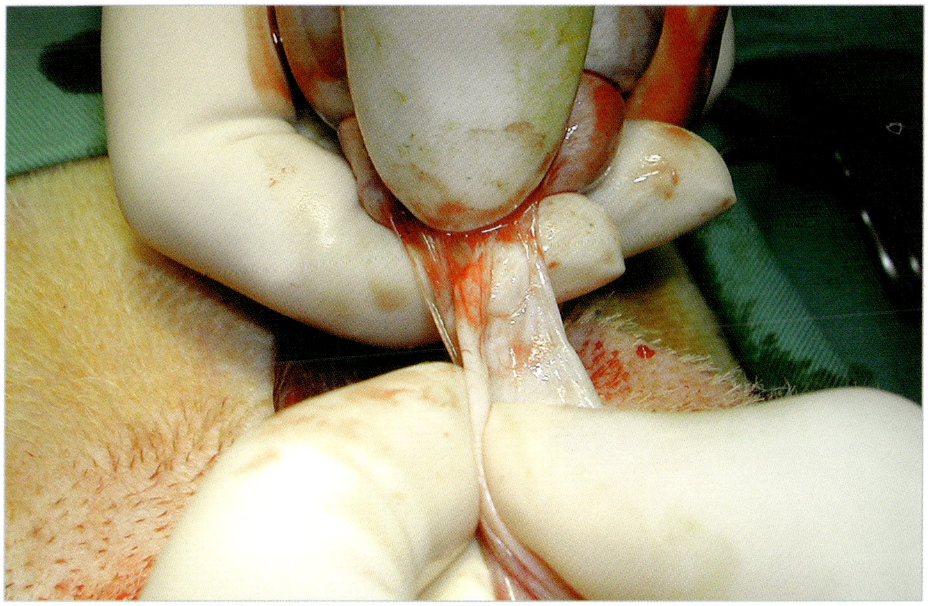

Fig. 6. Once incised, the tunica vaginalis is still attached to the caudal pole of the testis, together with the insertion of the cremaster muscle. This attachment is broken by blunt dissection with the thumb and index finger of both hands. Using the fingers rather than cutting, minimises bleeding.

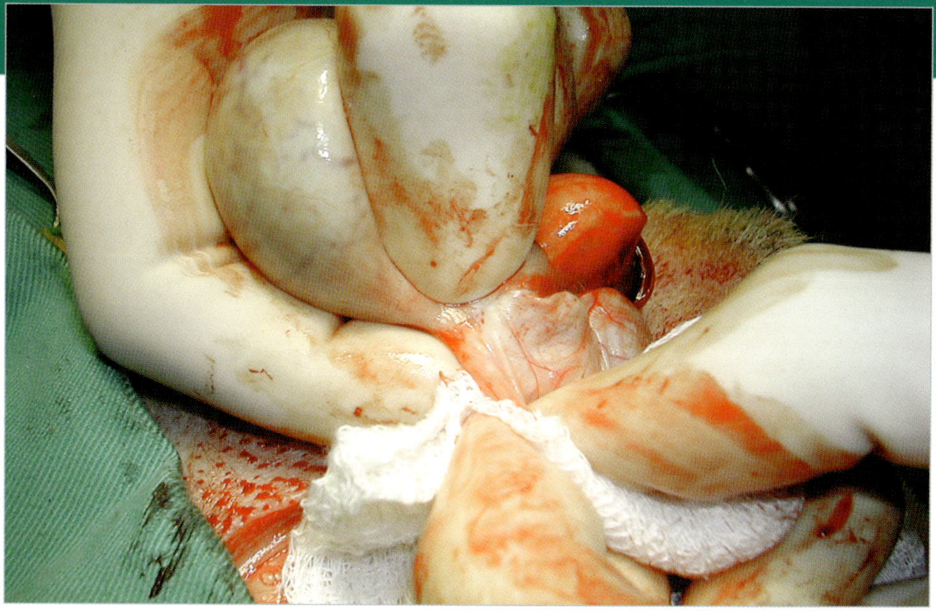

Fig. 7. A swab may be useful to detach the testis from the tunica vaginalis and insertion of the cremaster muscle.

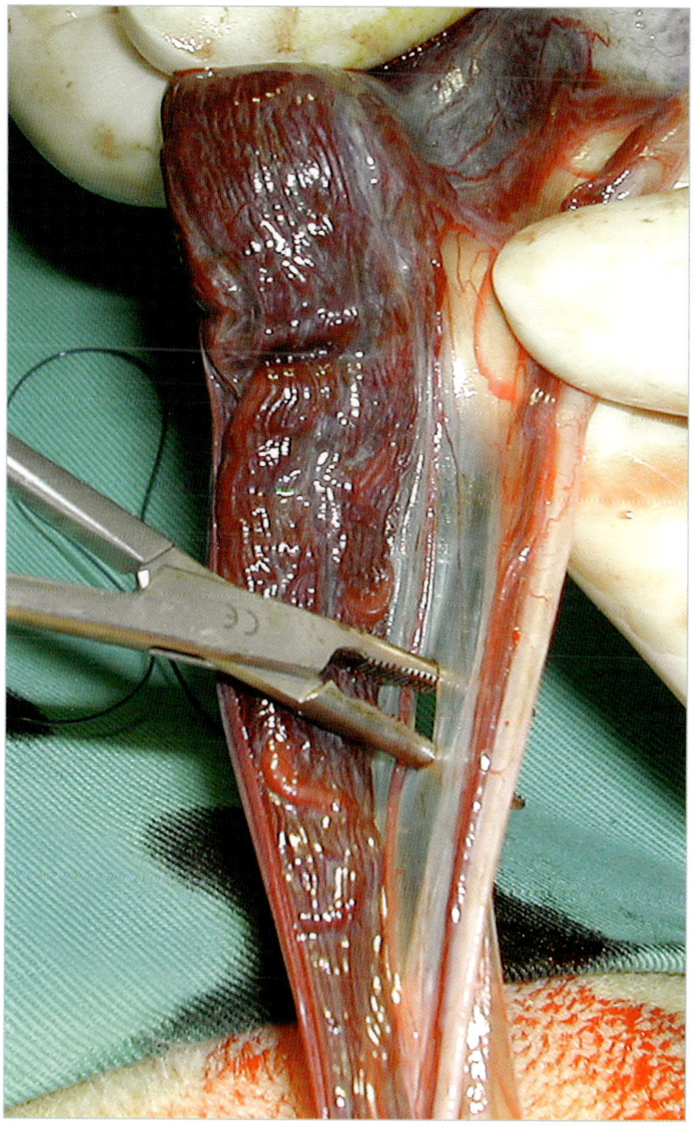

Fig. 8. In the spermatic cord, the pampiniform plexus and the vas deferens, with its own blood supply, can be identified individually. Both structures can be separated by blunt dissection of the membrane that joins them, using forceps.

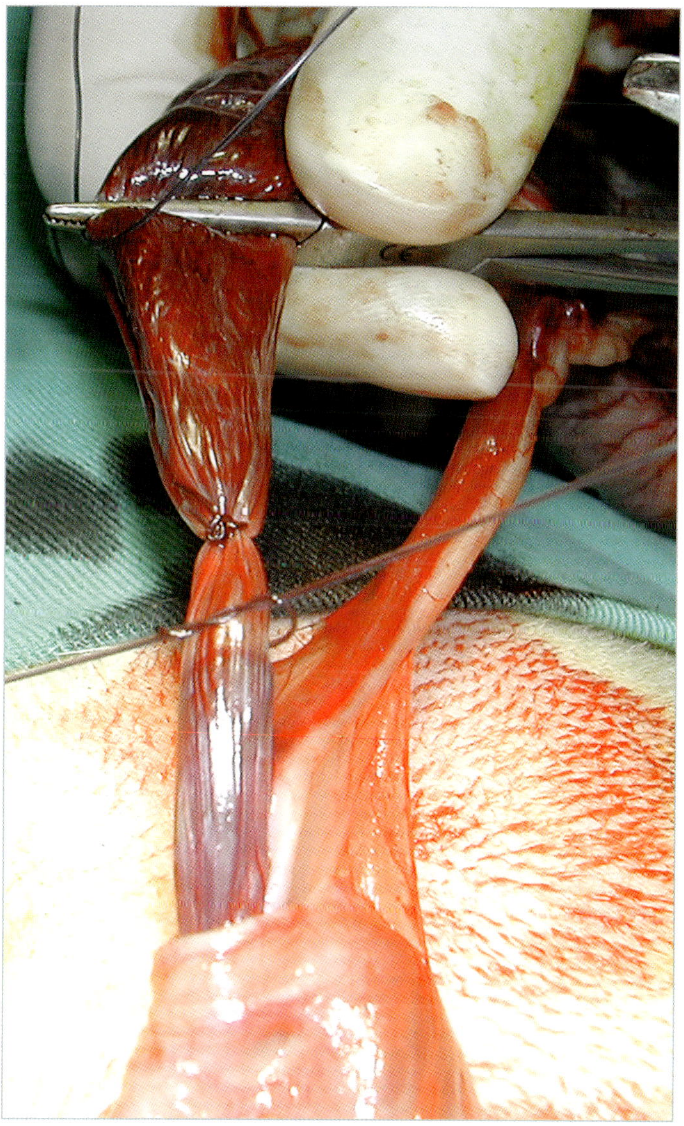

Fig. 9. Next, a double ligature is placed on the vascular structures of the spermatic cord, comprising the pampiniform plexus and the testicular artery which cannot be seen because it runs inside the plexus. An absorbable 2/0 or 0 monofilament suture material is used.

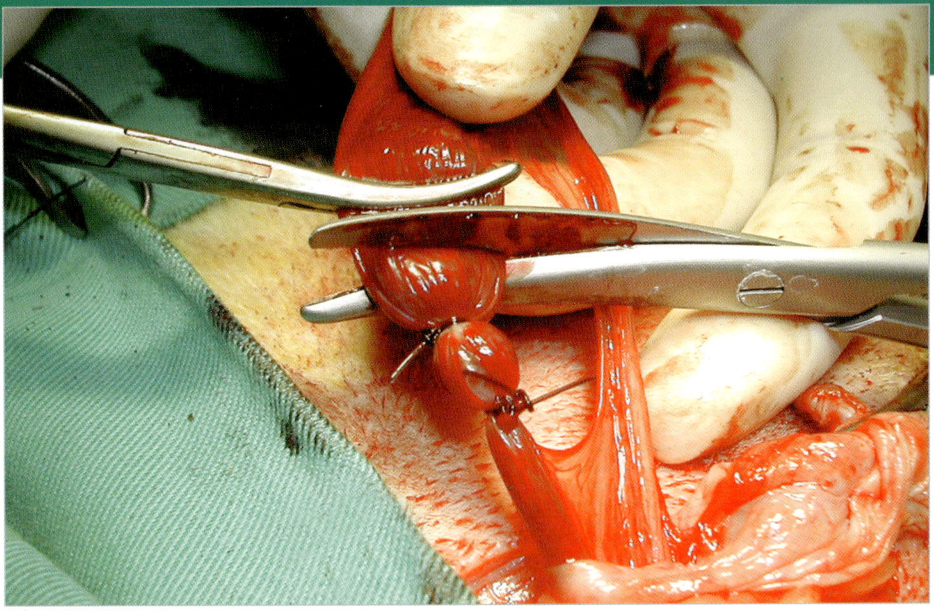

Fig. 10. The blood vessels are sectioned above the ligatures.

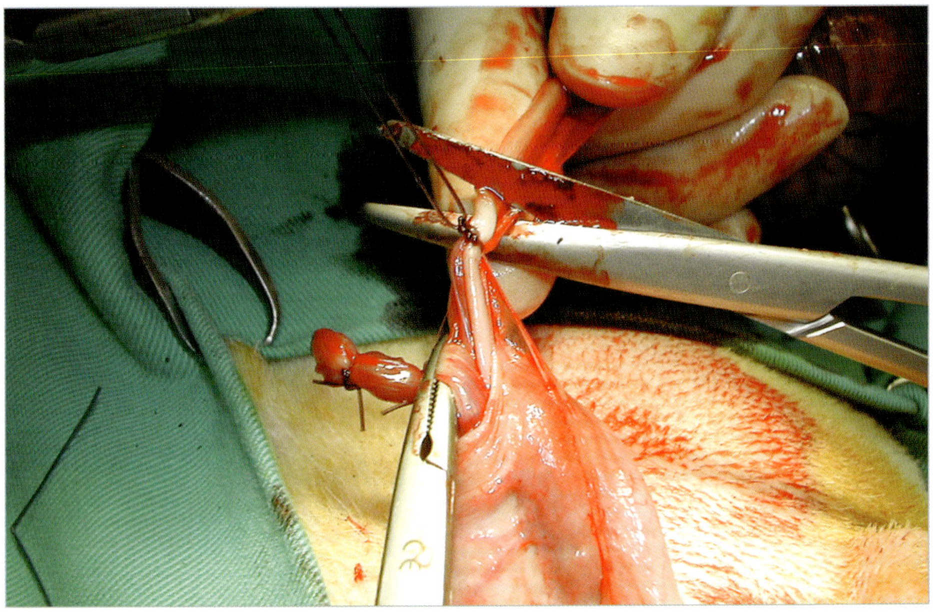

Fig. 11. The vas deferens and its blood supply are ligated together using the same material and are similarly sectioned.

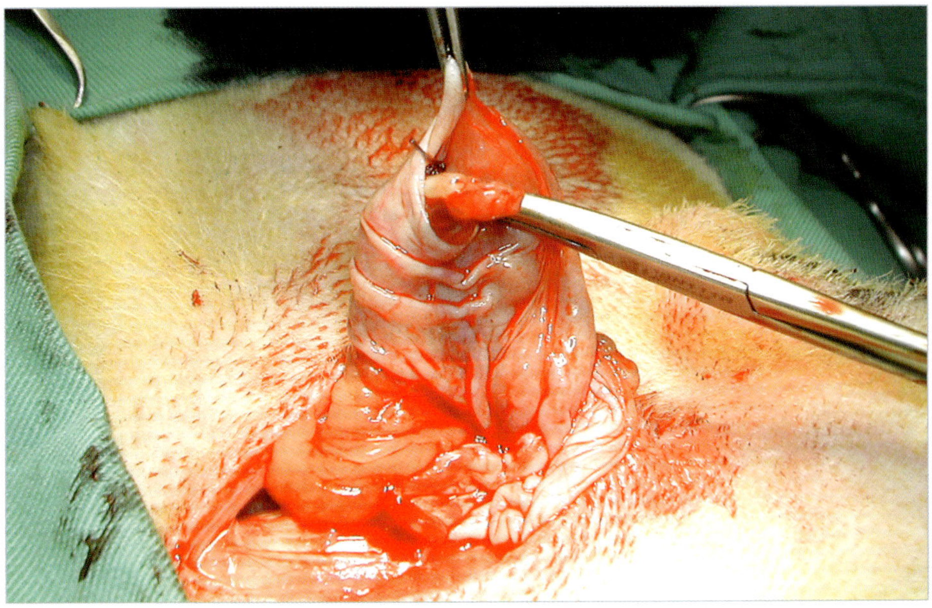

Fig. 12. Once it has been confirmed that there is no bleeding, the pedicles are pushed back into the tunica vaginalis towards the inguinal ring, using forceps.

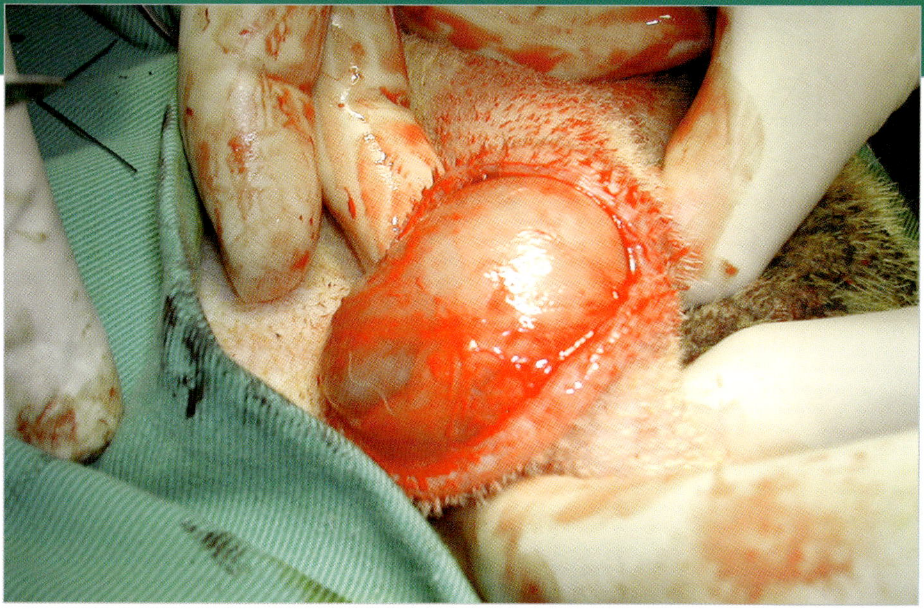

Fig. 13. The other testis is pushed towards the same incision and exteriorised, still covered by the tunica vaginalis; it is incised the same way as the first testis. Similarly the components of the spermatic cord are separated, ligated and sectioned.

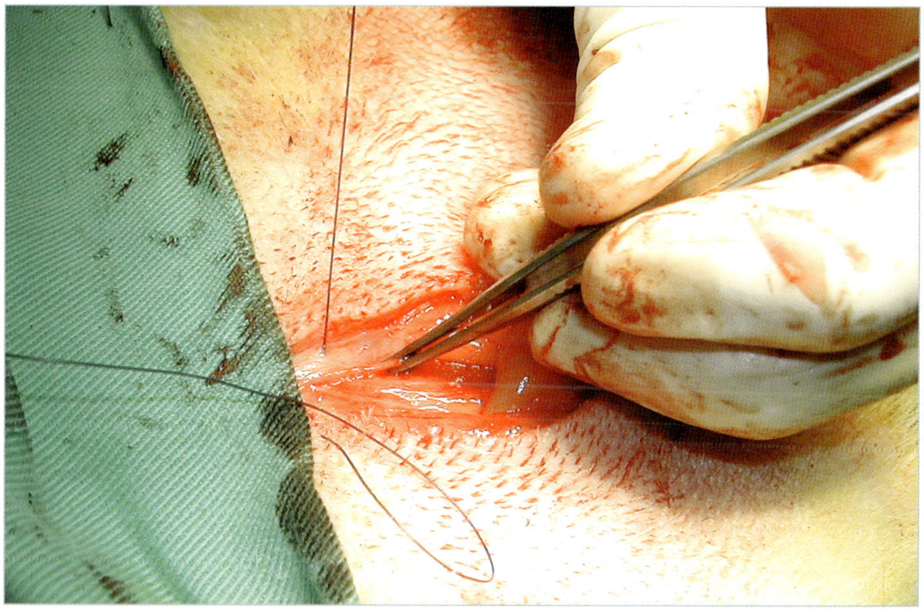

Fig. 14. The incision is closed in two layers, starting with the subcutaneous layer. A continuous suture in a 2/0 or 3/0 absorbable monofilament material is used.

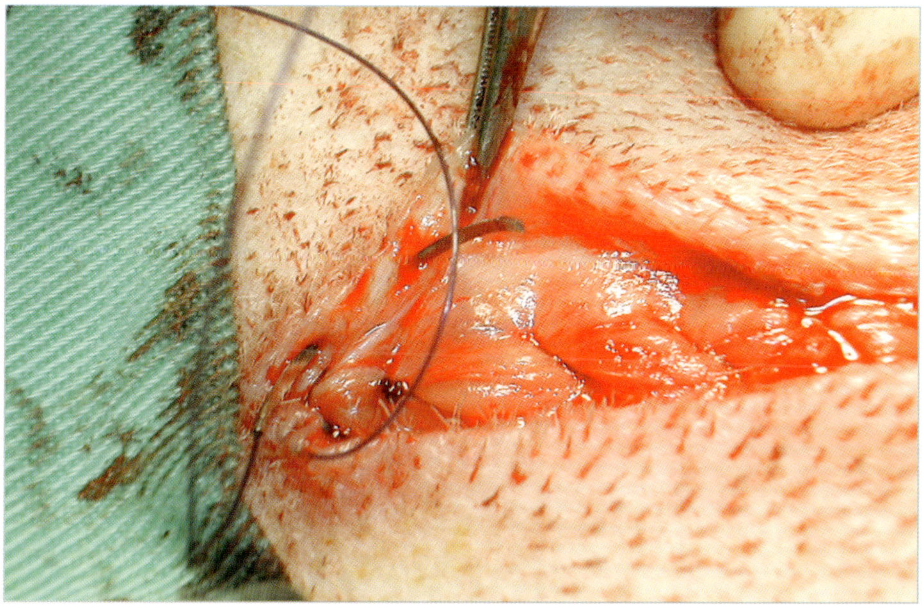

Fig. 15. Wound closure is finished with an intradermal suture in the same material.

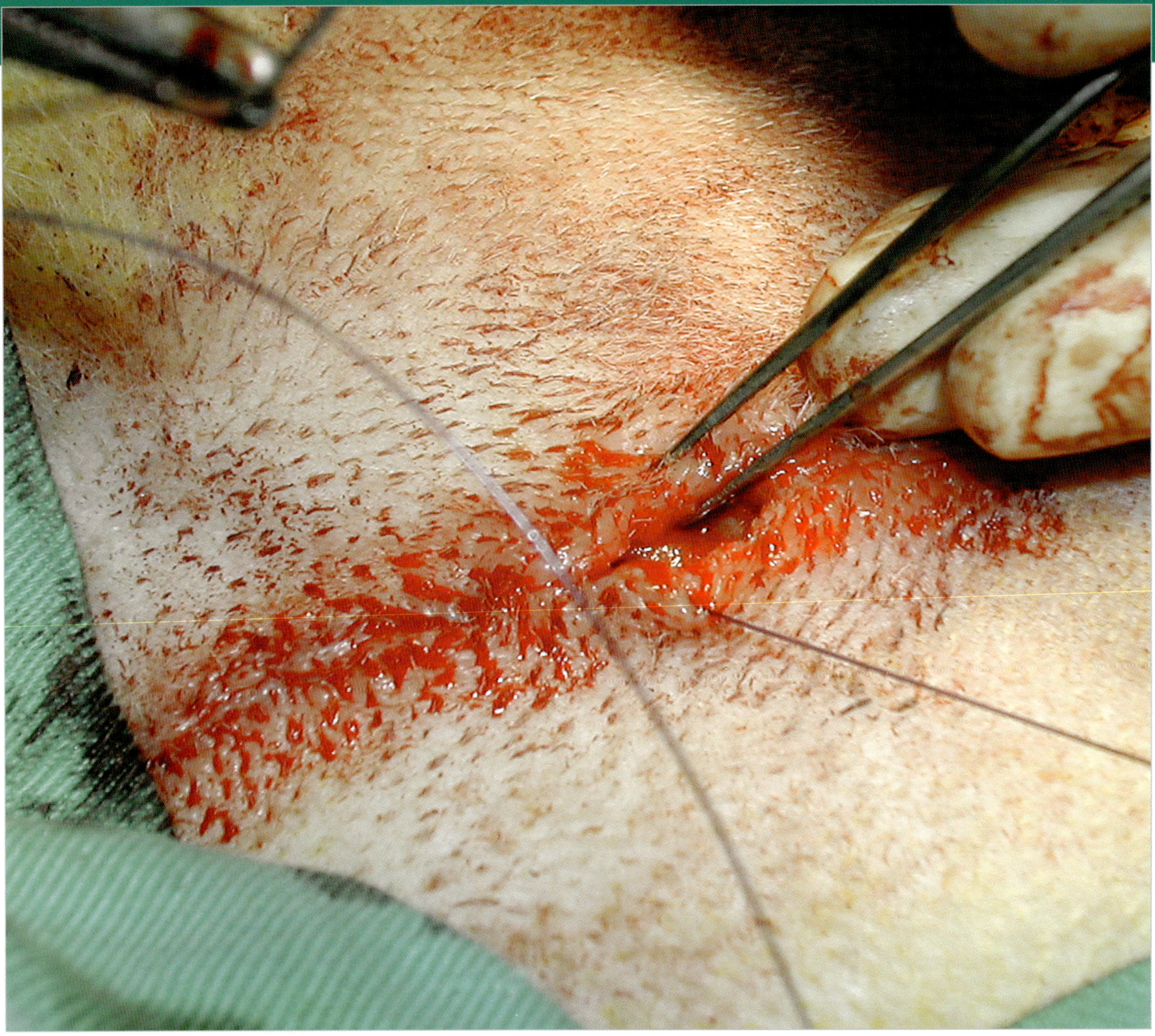

Fig. 16. The use of an intradermal suture avoids handling the patient again for suture removal.

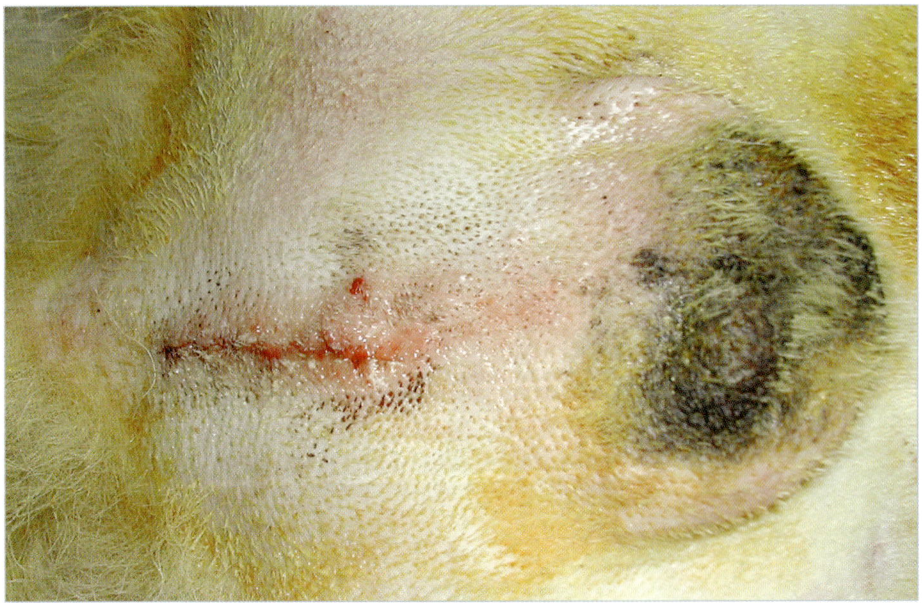

Fig. 17. Final appearance of the surgical area. The empty scrotal sac and the scar of the surgical incision can be observed.

Castration. Case 2 / Scrotal castration in the cat

Technical difficulty	■	■	□	□	□

Fig. 1. The patient.

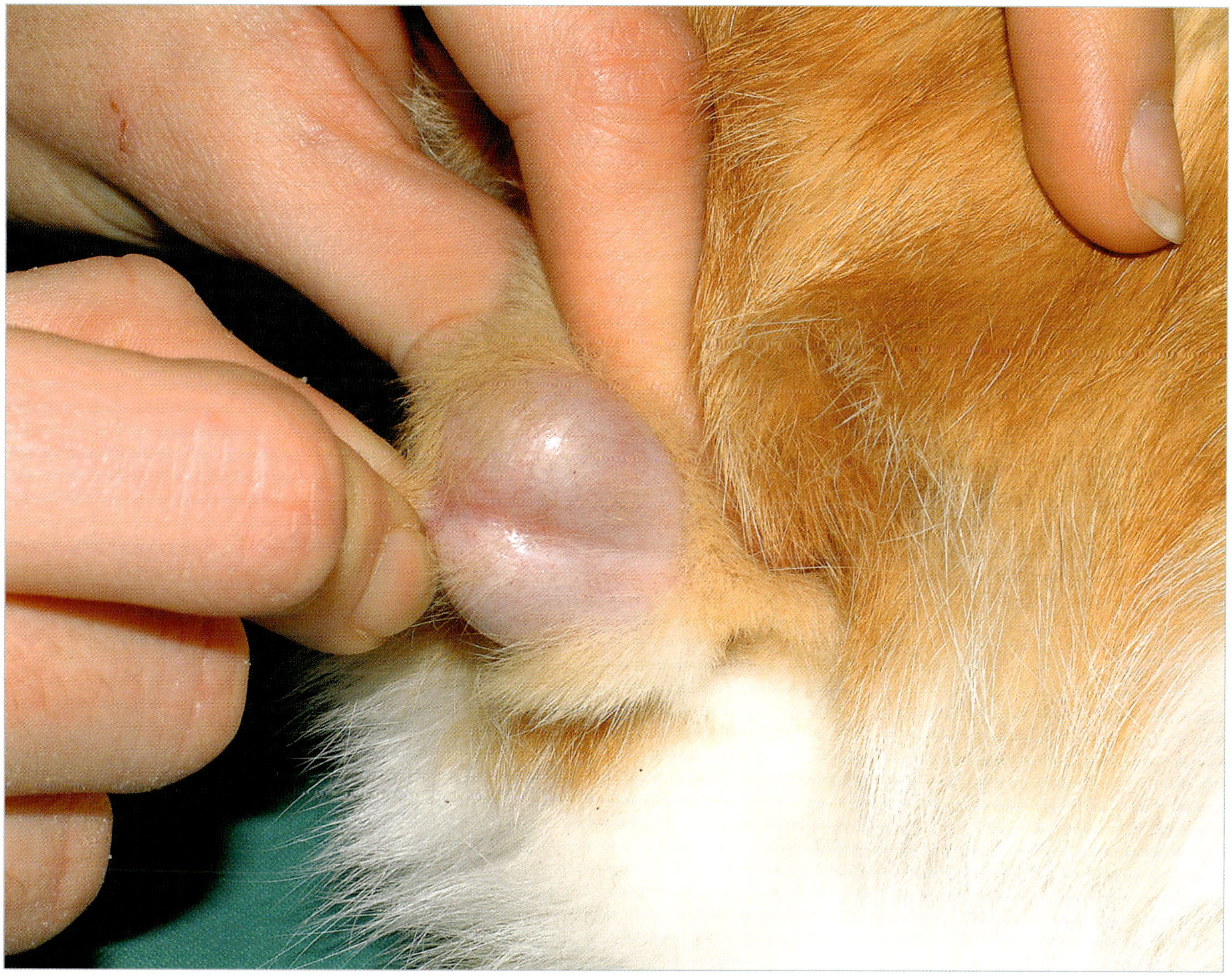

Fig. 2. First, the hair on the scrotum is plucked manually.

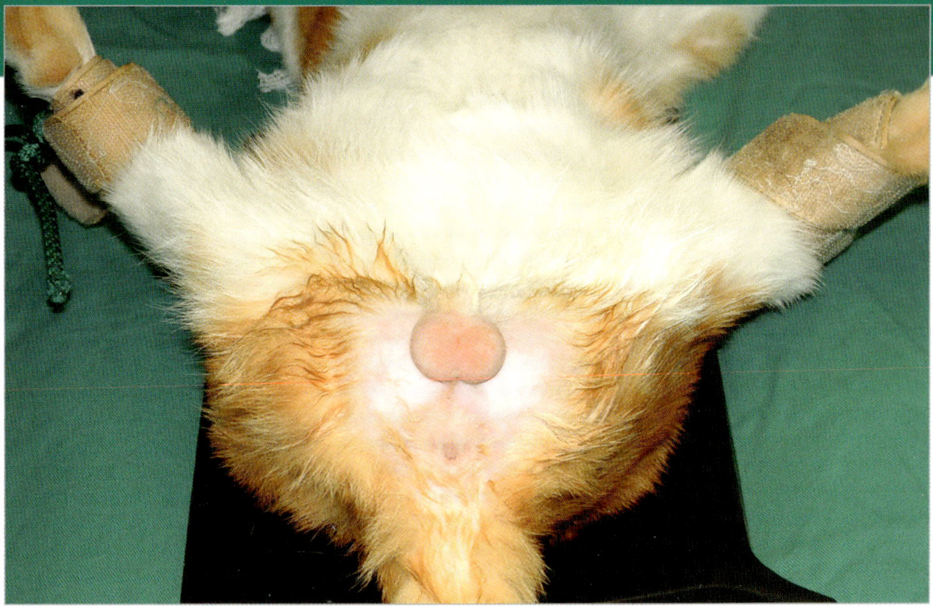

Fig. 3. To facilitate good exposure of the surgical field, the patient is placed in dorsal recumbency with the hind legs pulled cranially.

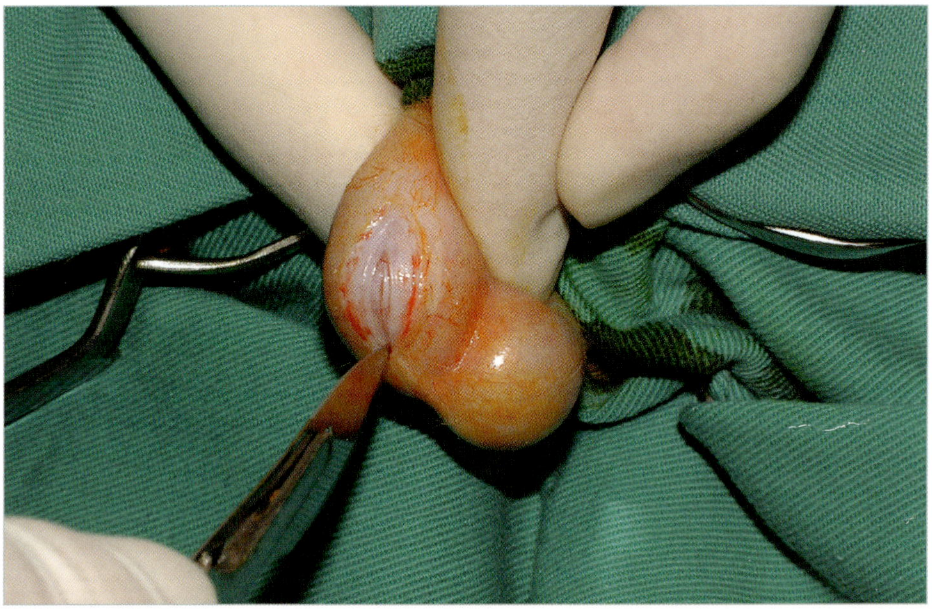

Fig. 4. The scrotum is incised directly over the first testis until the tunica vaginalis can be seen. The tunic is also incised.

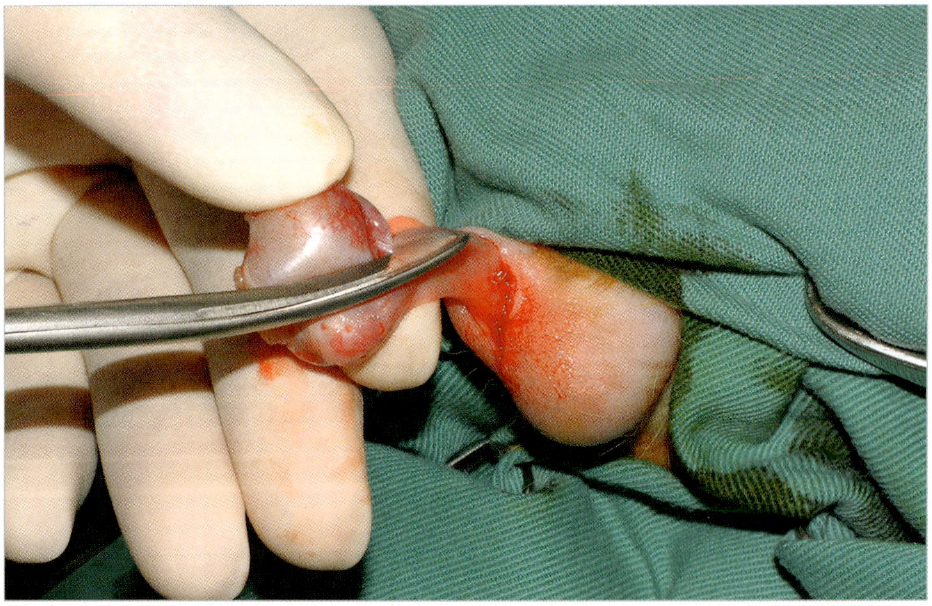

Fig. 5. The incision of the tunica vaginalis is extended longitudinally to visualise the structures of the spermatic cord.

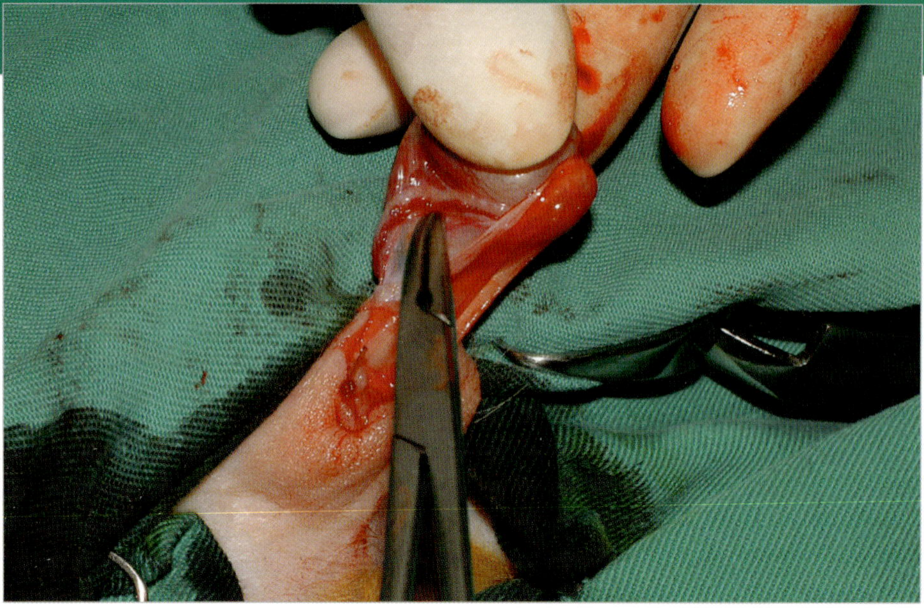

Fig. 6. The testicular membrane is perforated and the vascular structures of the cord and vas deferens are separated from the fold of the tunica vaginalis and the cremaster muscle.

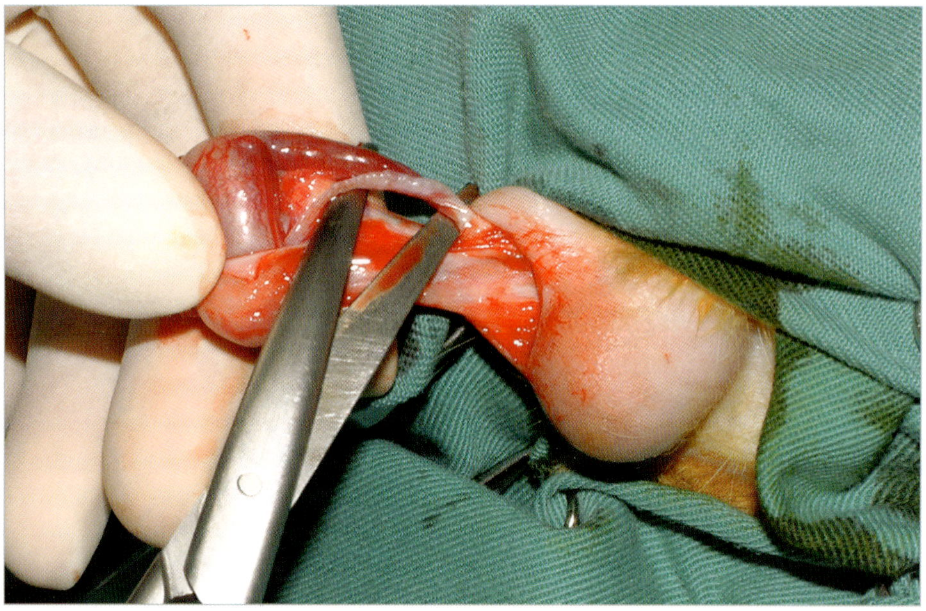

Fig. 7. The hole is enlarged to a sufficient size to comfortably pass the ligatures.

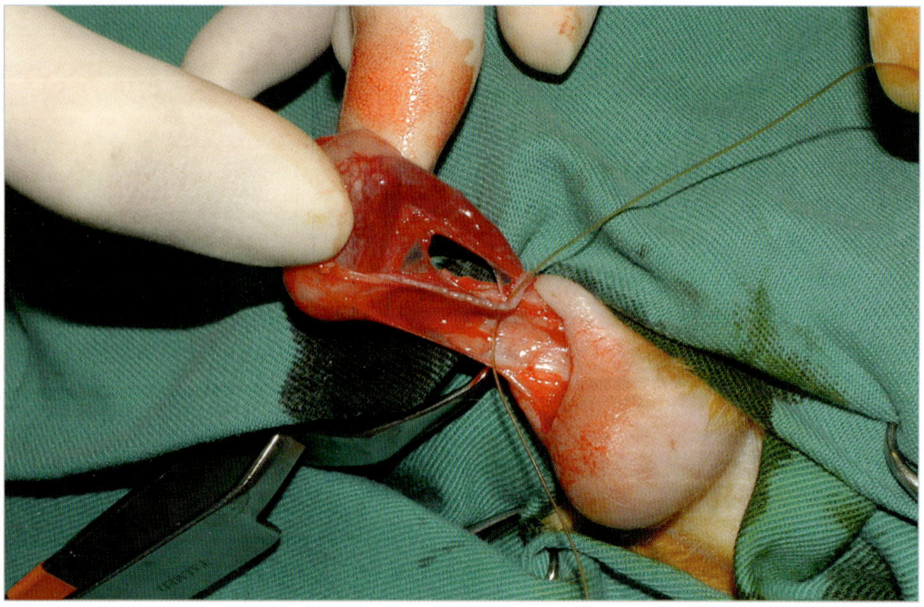

Fig. 8. After separating the vas deferens from the testicular blood supply, a ligature is placed around the vas deferens.

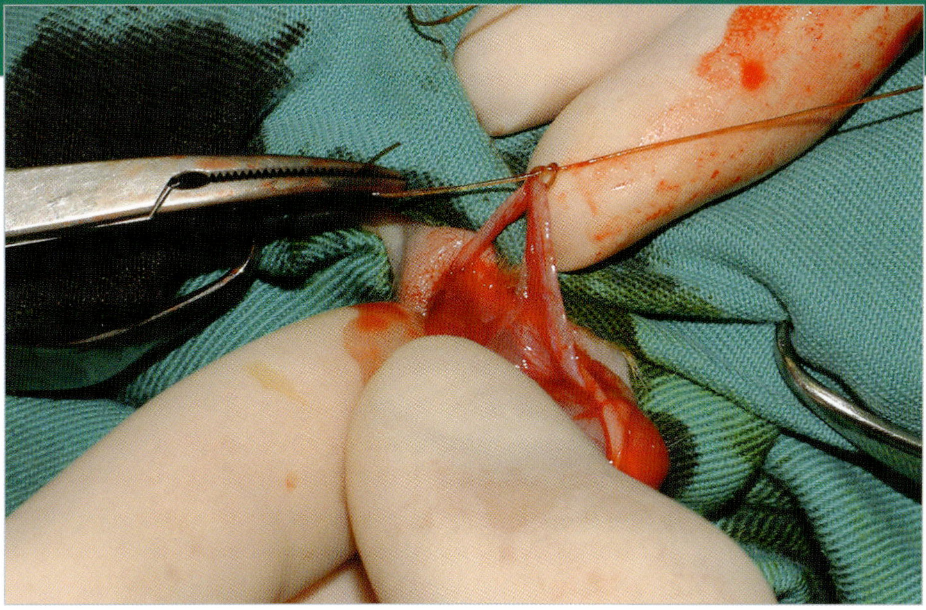

Fig. 9. The ligature is tied around the vas deferens and its blood vessel.

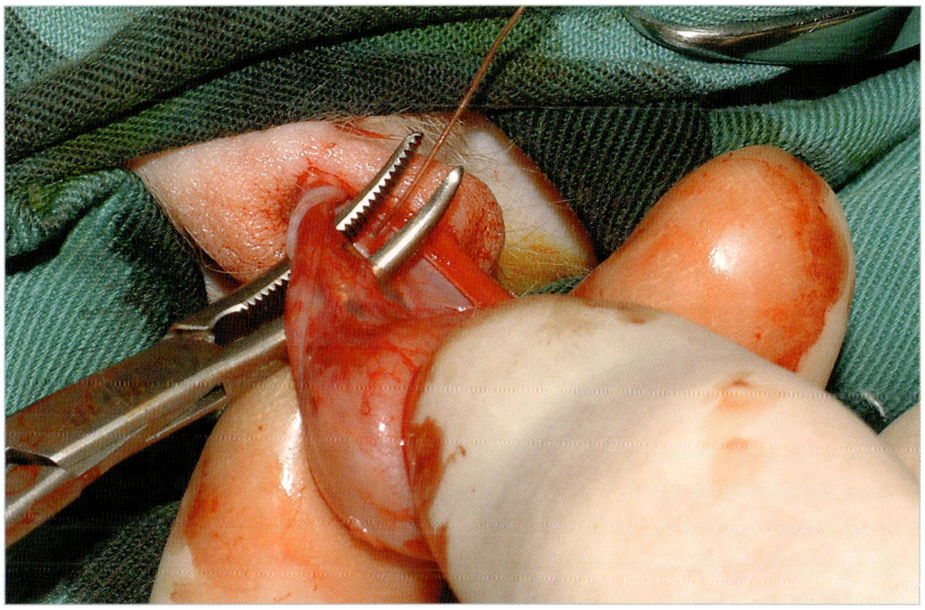

Fig. 10. Using the same hole in the membrane, a separate ligature is placed around the blood supply.

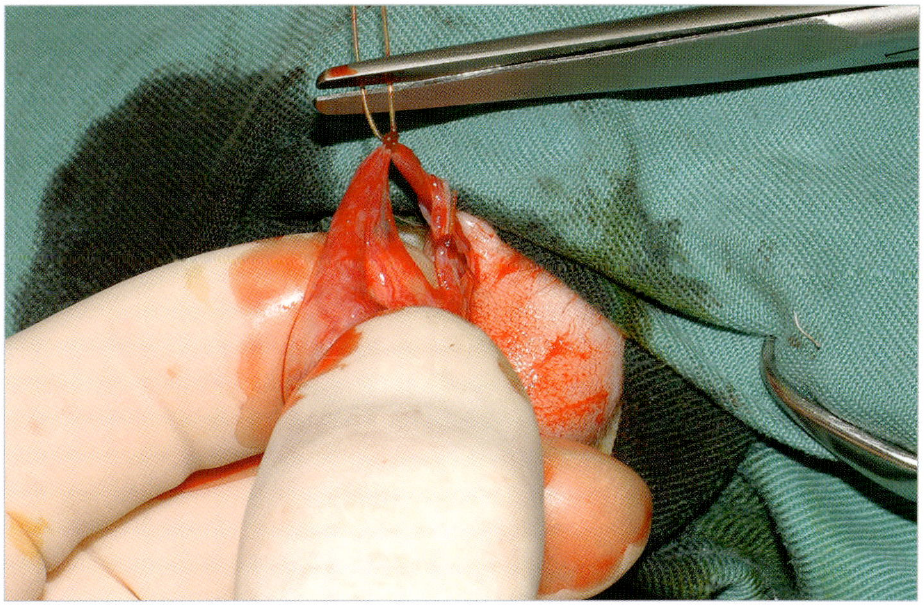

Fig. 11. The ligatures must be of an absorbable suture material.

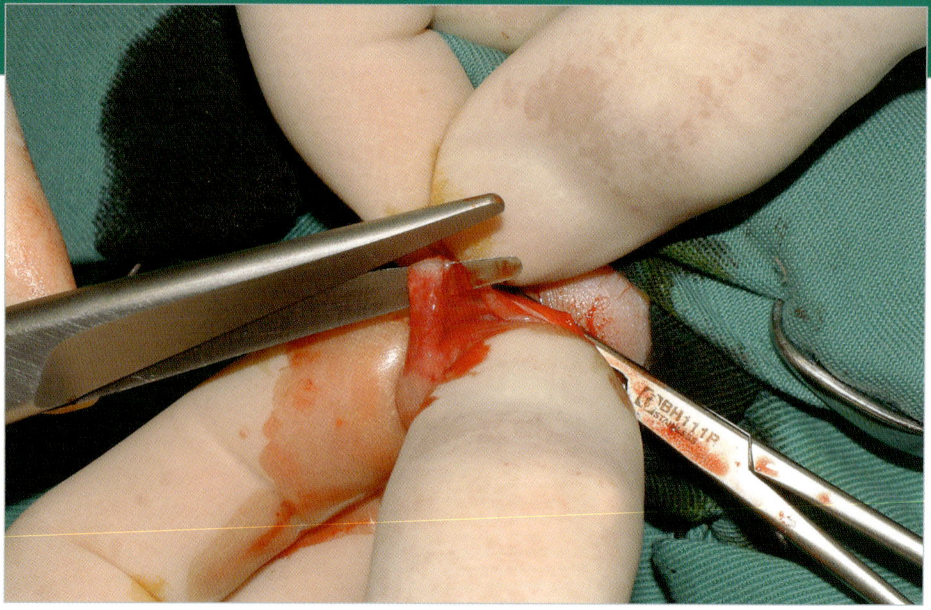

Fig. 12. Next, both structures are sectioned, but are still held by forceps until the end of the procedure.

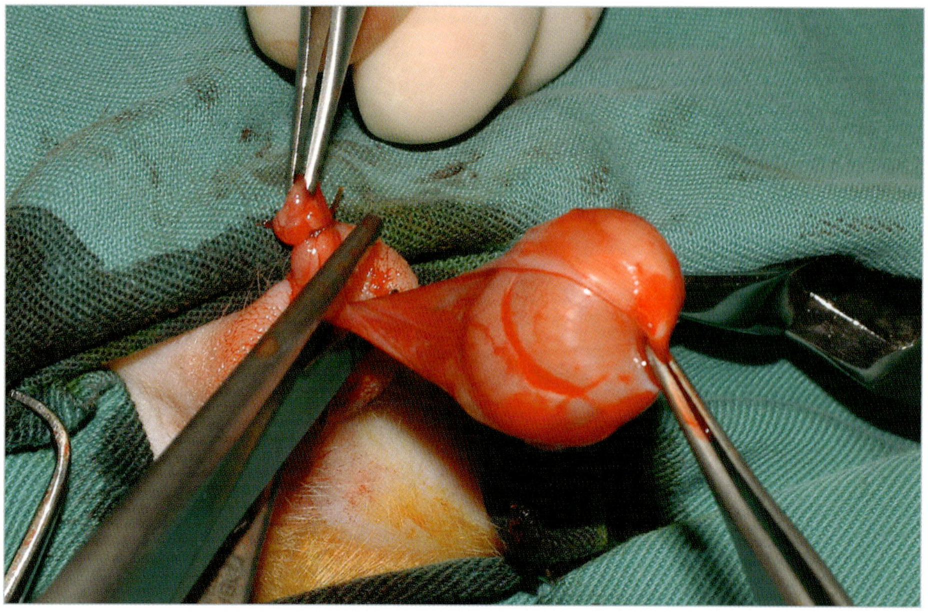

Fig. 13. The fold of the tunica vaginalis and the cremaster muscle are selectioned.

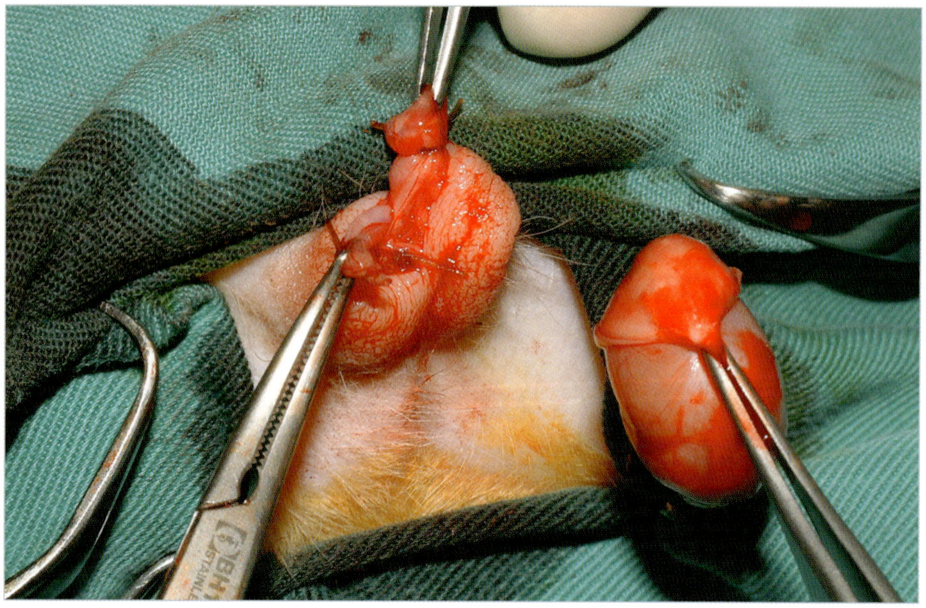

Fig. 14. Using the same incision, the procedure is repeated on the other testis.

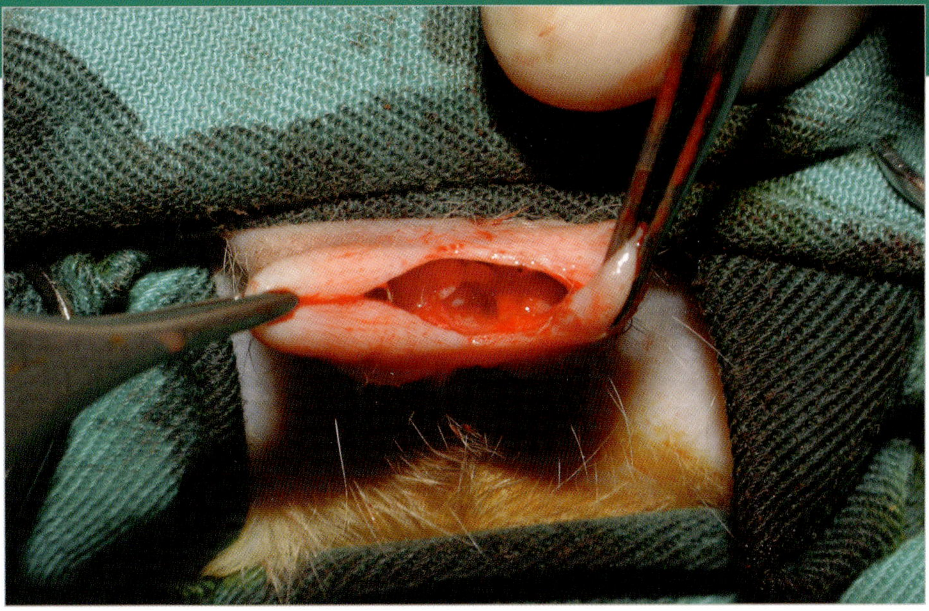

Fig. 15. After ensuring that neither of the pedicles is bleeding, they are replaced in the inguinal canal.

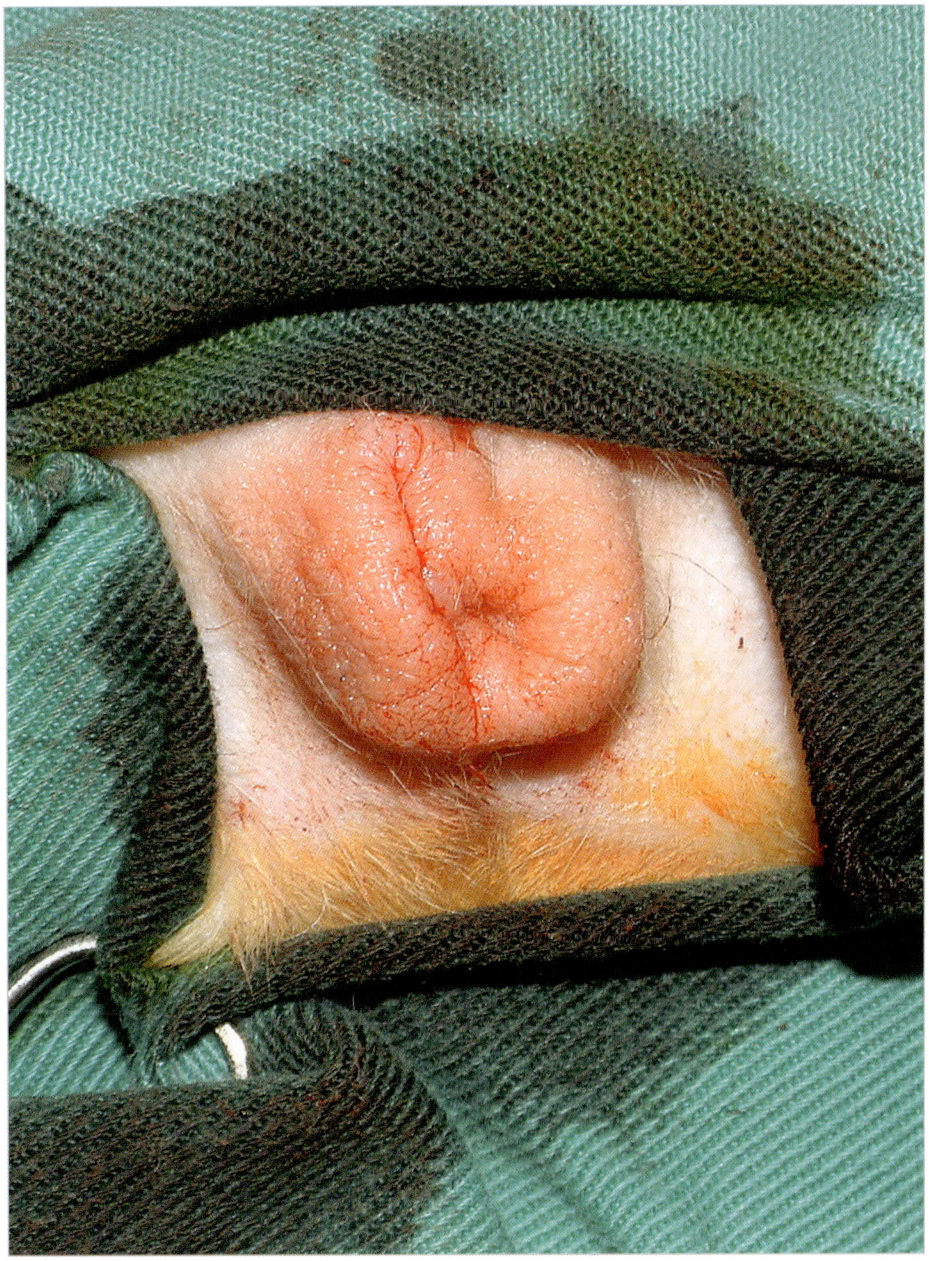

Fig. 16. Appearance of the scrotum after castration. In the cat, the scrotum is usually left open.

Castration. Case 3 / Castration with scrotal ablation in the dog

Technical difficulty	■	■	□	□	□

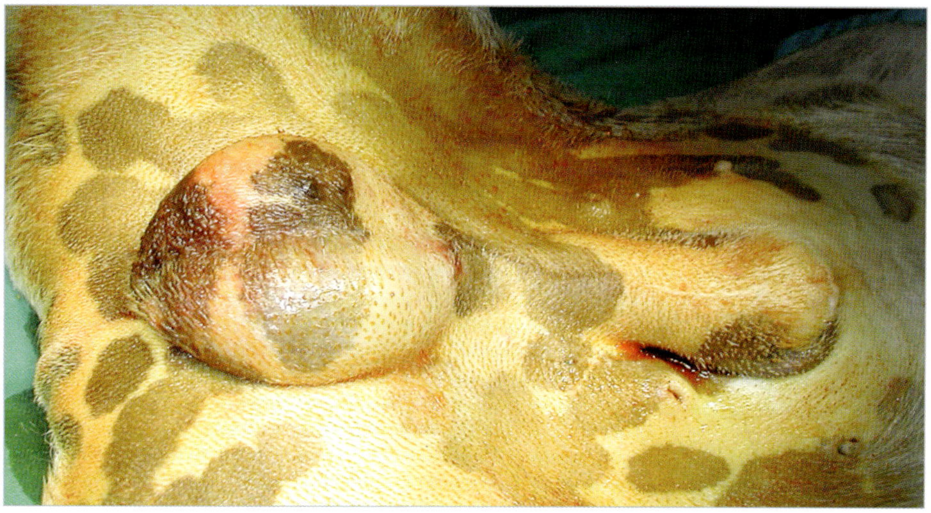

Fig. 1. For castration with scrotal ablation, the patient is placed in dorsal recumbency and an extensive surgical field is prepared around the scrotum, in the usual way.

The main indications for castration with scrotal ablation are traumatic or neoplastic lesions of the scrotum and scrotal urethrostomy.

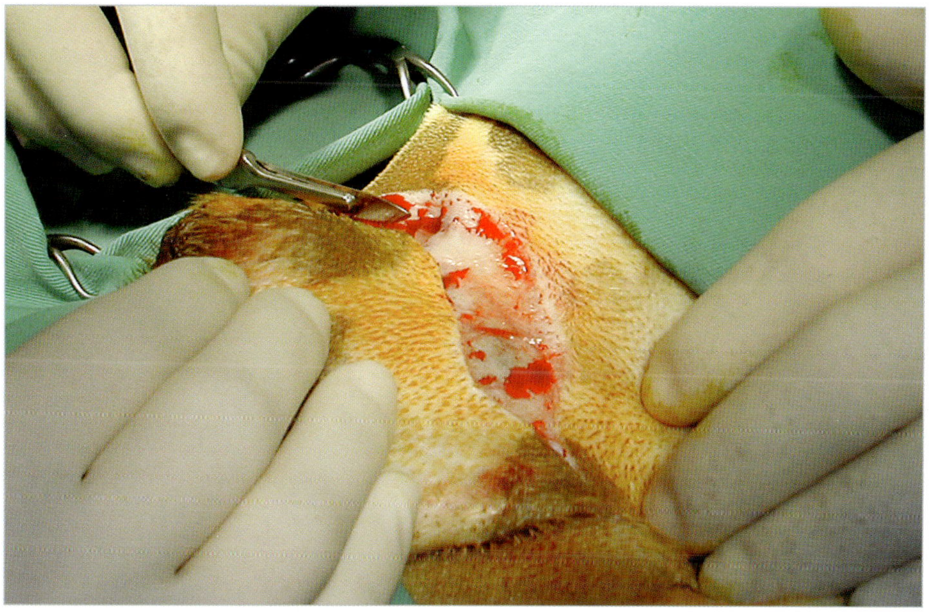

Fig. 2. An elliptical skin incision is made around the base of the scrotal sac.

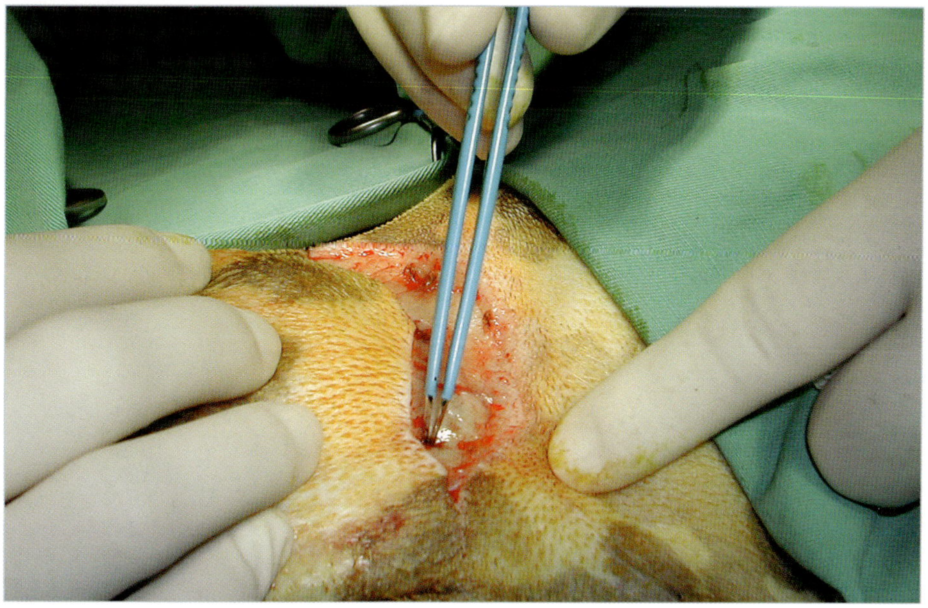

Fig. 3. As this is a well-vascularised area, meticulous haemostasis should be employed. Bipolar coagulation may be used.

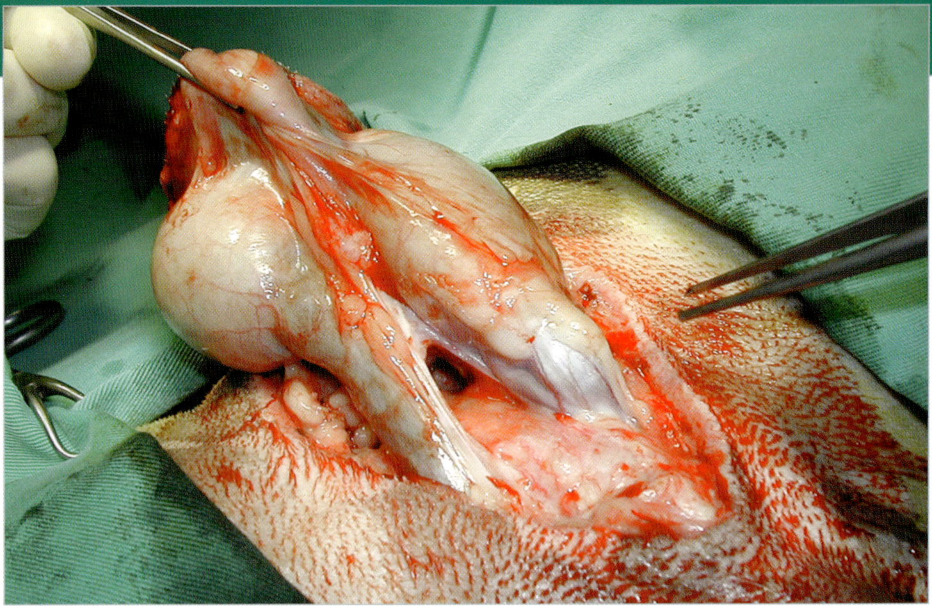

Fig. 4. After completing the skin incision around the scrotum, the scrotum and testes are raised together and the subcutaneous tissue is dissected until the spermatic cord is visualised.

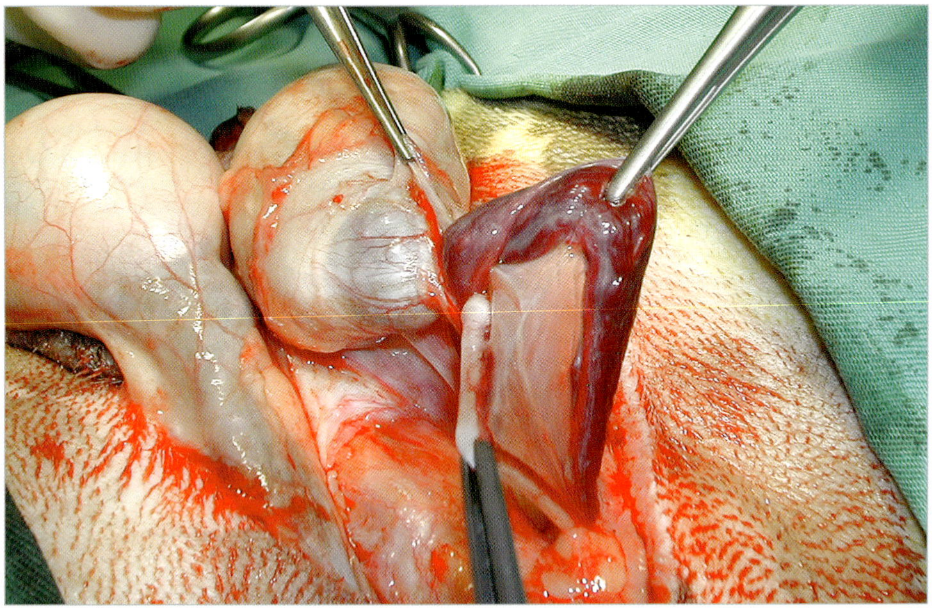

Fig. 5. The tunica vaginalis is incised over the testis and the incision is extended longitudinally over the spermatic cord to expose the vas deferens and the pampiniform plexus.

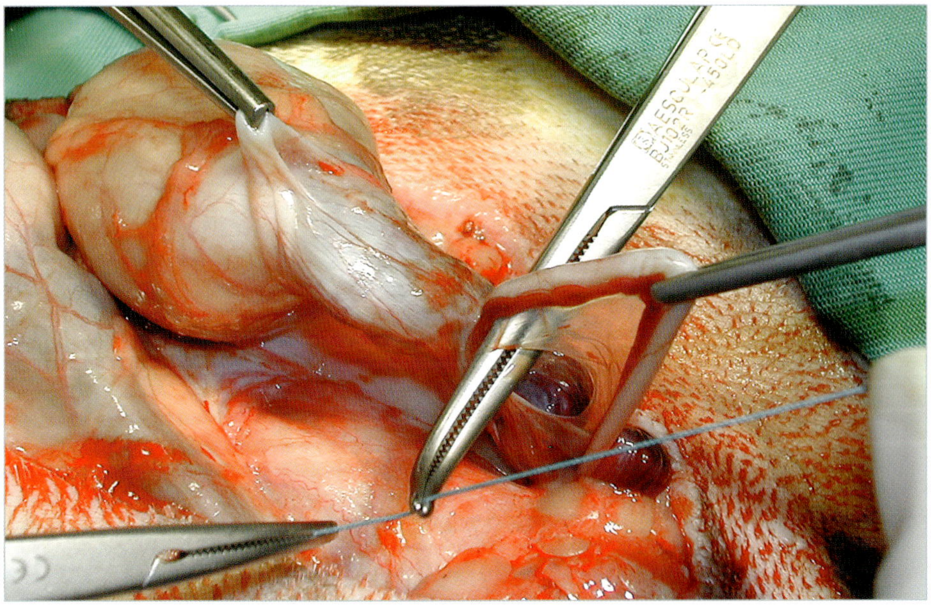

Fig. 6. A hole is made between the pampiniform plexus and the vas deferens, separating the two structures. The first ligature for the vas deferens is passed through the hole.

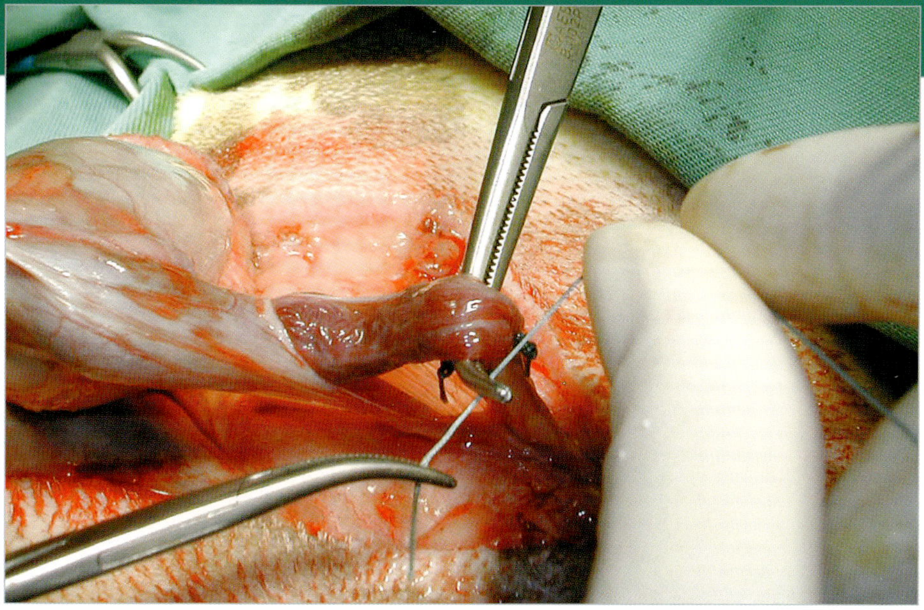

Fig. 7. Using the same hole, two ligatures are placed on the pampiniform plexus.

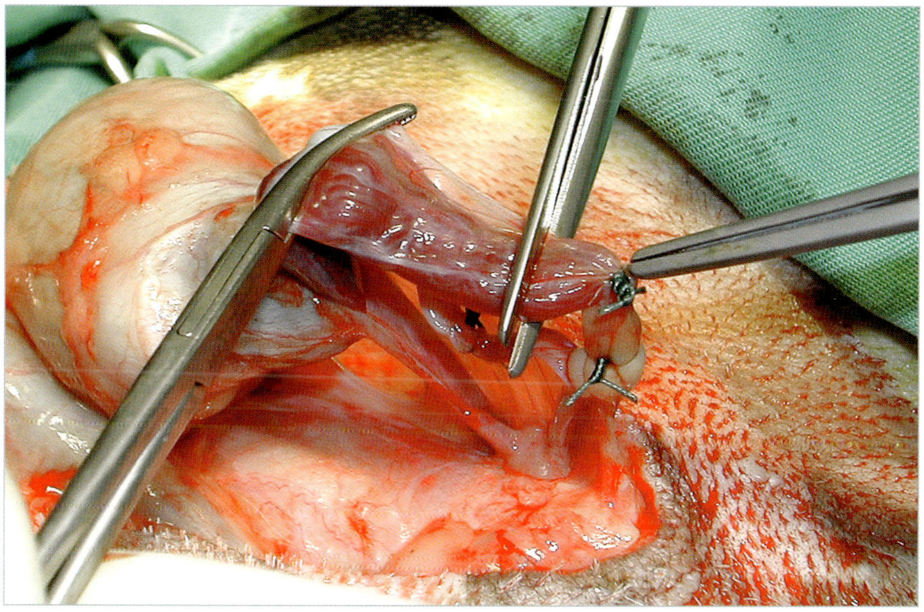

Fig. 8. The pampiniform plexus is cut distal to the ligatures. It is advisable to leave forceps in a more proximal position until successful haemostasis can be confirmed.

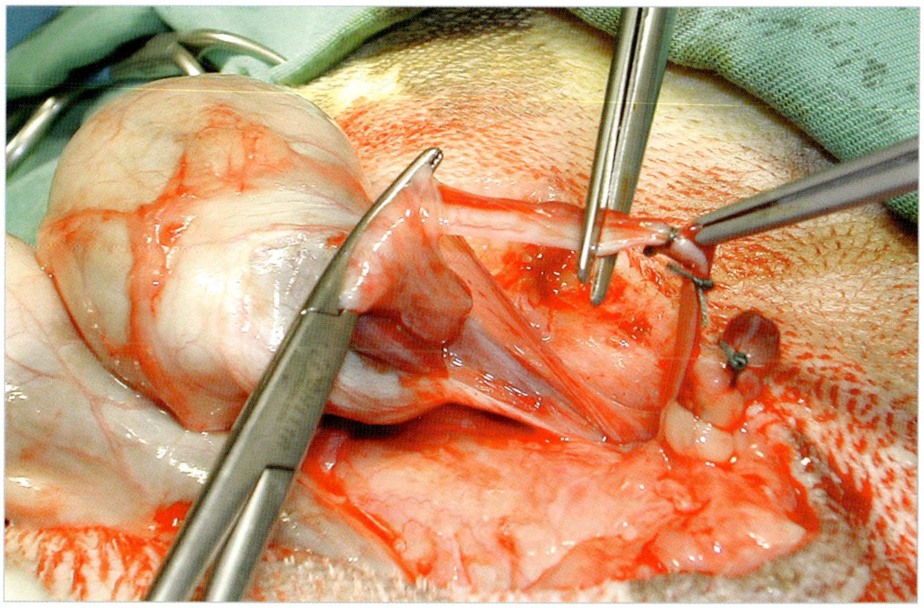

Fig. 9. The procedure for the vas deferens is the same.

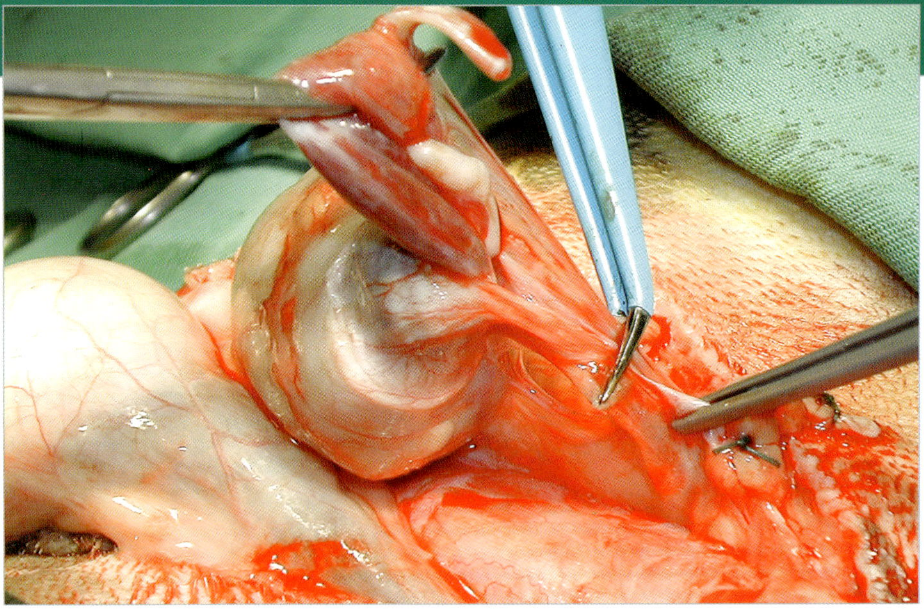

Fig. 10. Before sectioning the fold of the tunica vaginalis and the cremaster muscle, the muscle is cauterised with bipolar forceps.

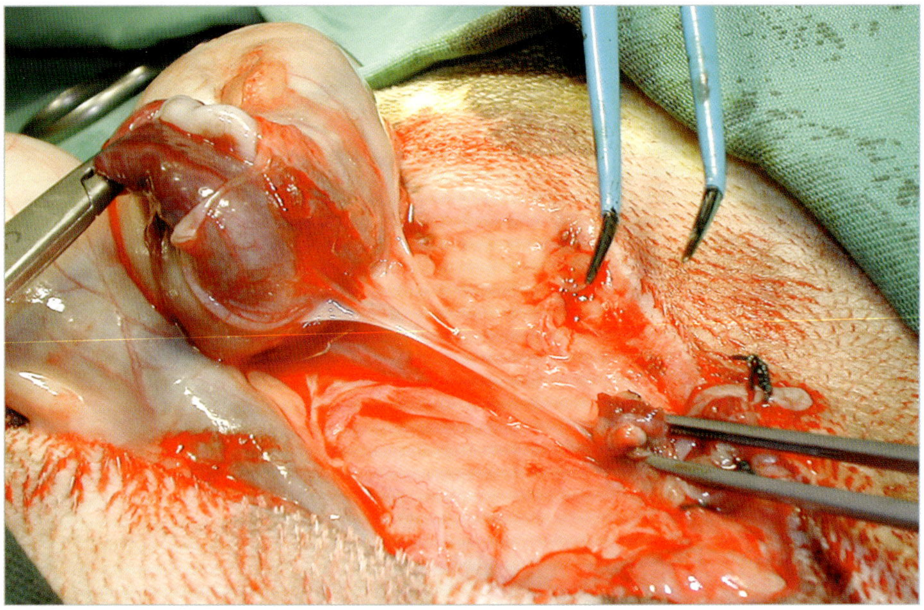

Fig. 11. After sectioning the cremaster, the testis is finally loosened by blunt dissection and gentle traction.

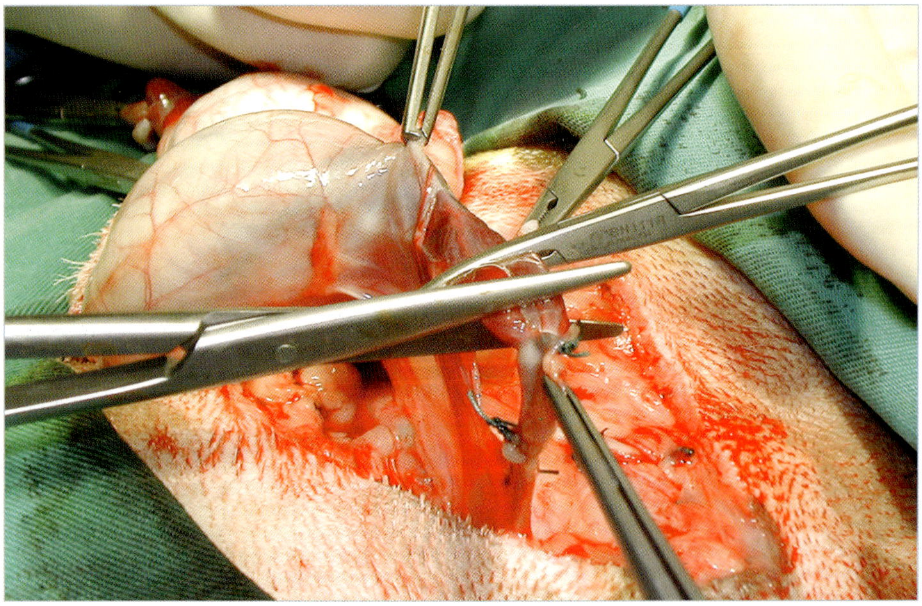

Fig. 12. The same procedure is repeated on the other testis.

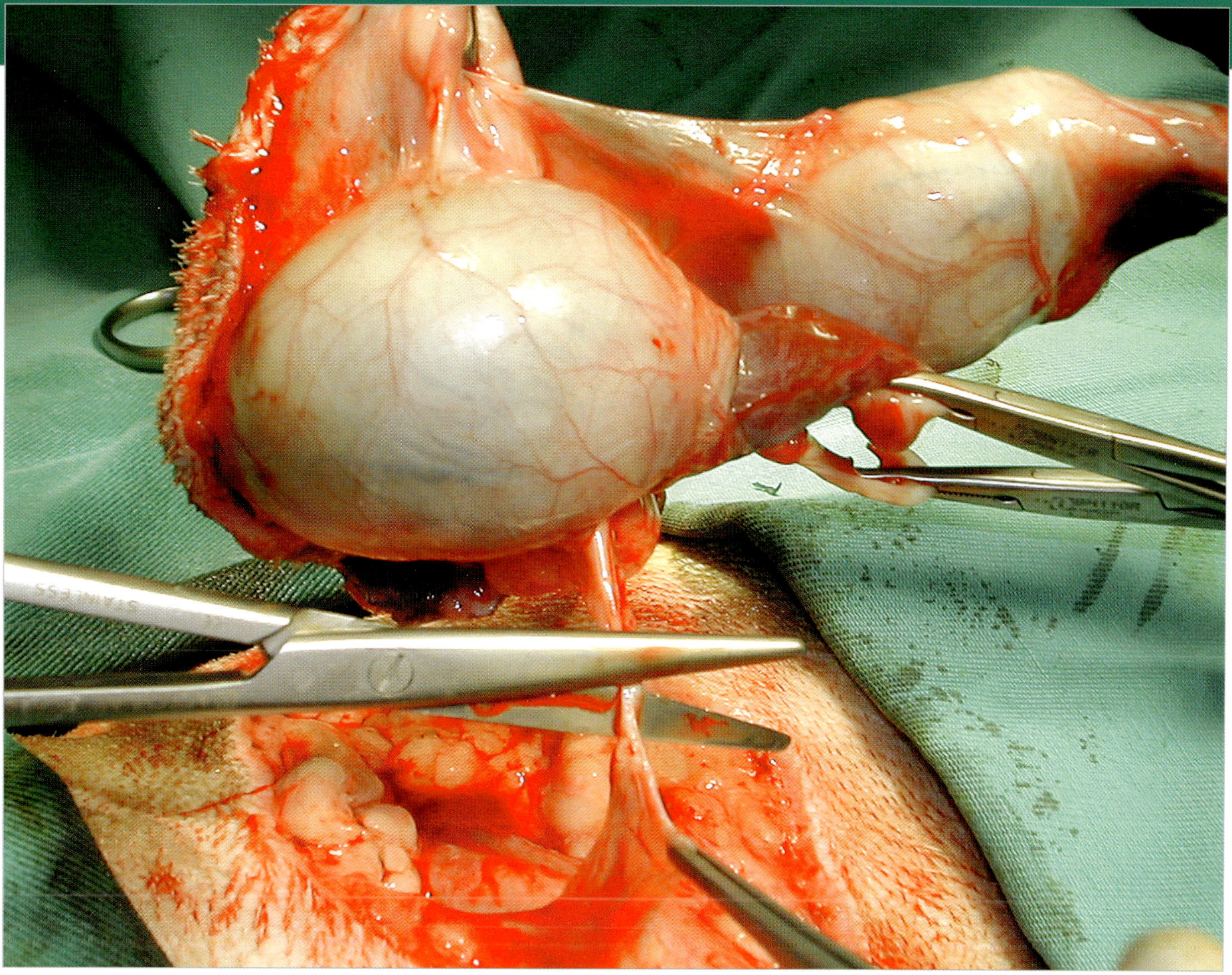

Fig. 13. After both testes have been removed, the scrotal sac attached to the testes is dissected away.

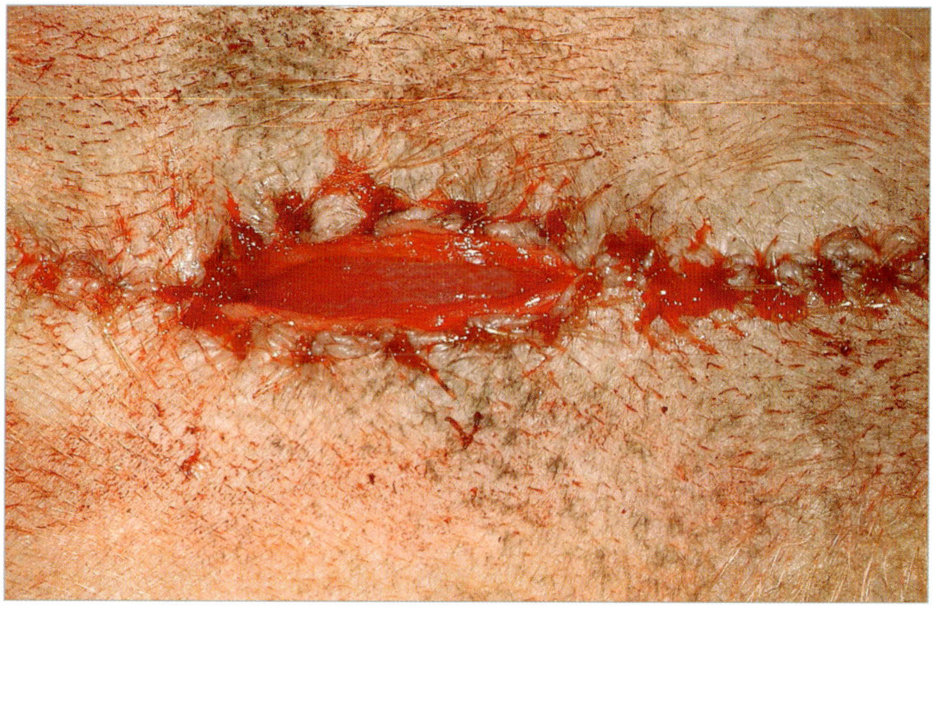

Fig. 14. Finally, the wound is closed in two layers: subcutaneous tissue and skin. In this case, castration with scrotal ablation was indicated for a scrotal urethrostomy. This image shows the urethral mucosa sutured to the skin.

Infraumbilical laparotomy

Technical difficulty

Infraumbilical laparotomy is the surgical approach of choice for the caudal abdomen. In male animals this is a common procedure to remove cryptorchid testes, perform a cystotomy or gain access to the prostate.

Meticulous cleaning of the surgical field prior to any kind of laparotomy is essential. In this case, special care must be taken with disinfection of the penis and the prepuce. This will prevent many infections.

* *To avoid eventration after laparotomy, it is essential that the external fascia of the abdominal rectus muscles is included in the suture of the linea alba. This is the layer that will anchor the suture.*

In the male, as opposed to the female, the skin cannot be incised directly over the linea alba. It is necessary to make a parapenile skin incision and push the penis to one side to access the linea alba.

The patient is placed in dorsal recumbency. Using a clamp, the prepuce is fixed to one side of the midline. The skin incision starts caudal to the umbilicus in the midline and on reaching the prepuce, deviates laterally to either side; it continues parallel to the penis in a caudal direction to end just in front of the pubis. If a long incision is not necessary, a straight skin incision parallel to the penis is sufficient. In both cases, the skin incision is extended by dissecting the subcutaneous tissue until reaching the linea alba. When dissecting the area parallel to the most cranial part of the prepuce, the preputial branch of the caudal superficial epigastric artery will be encountered. This branch should be clamped and cauterised, or ligated, before sectioning.

After careful dissection of the area to visualise the full length of the linea alba, it is incised using a scalpel or scissors; the incision is extended while taking continuous care not to damage the internal organs.

After carrying out the planned surgical procedure, the linea alba is closed either by using simple interrupted sutures or a continuous suture, which must be reinforced with three or four cruciate or X-sutures. If the continuous suture is placed correctly, there is no increased risk of dehiscence and closure of the abdominal cavity will be quicker. It has been shown that it is better not to include the parietal peritoneum when suturing the linea alba to avoid adhesions caused by an inflammatory response to the suture material. It has been found that the peritoneum rapidly covers the internal scar by cellular migration. Material selection for closure of the abdominal cavity is very important. The authors have very good experience with absorbable synthetic mono- or multifilament suture material (polyglyconate or polyglycolic acid). The diameter of the material for continuous or cruciate sutures varies from 2/0 to 1/0 depending on the size of the patient.

The subcutaneous tissue is closed with a continuous suture using the same material, in 2/0 or 3/0. The skin is sutured using either a polyglyconate intradermal suture or simple interrupted or horizontal mattress sutures in a non-absorbable synthetic monofilament suture material.

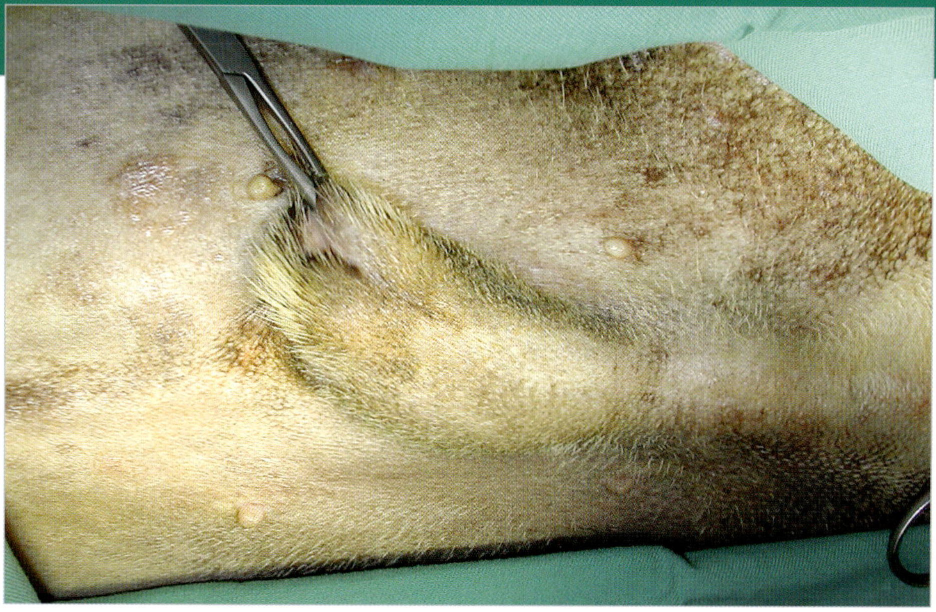

Fig. 1. The surgical field for infraumbilical laparotomy is prepared. Using atraumatic forceps, the prepuce is fixed to the opposite side to where the incision will be made.

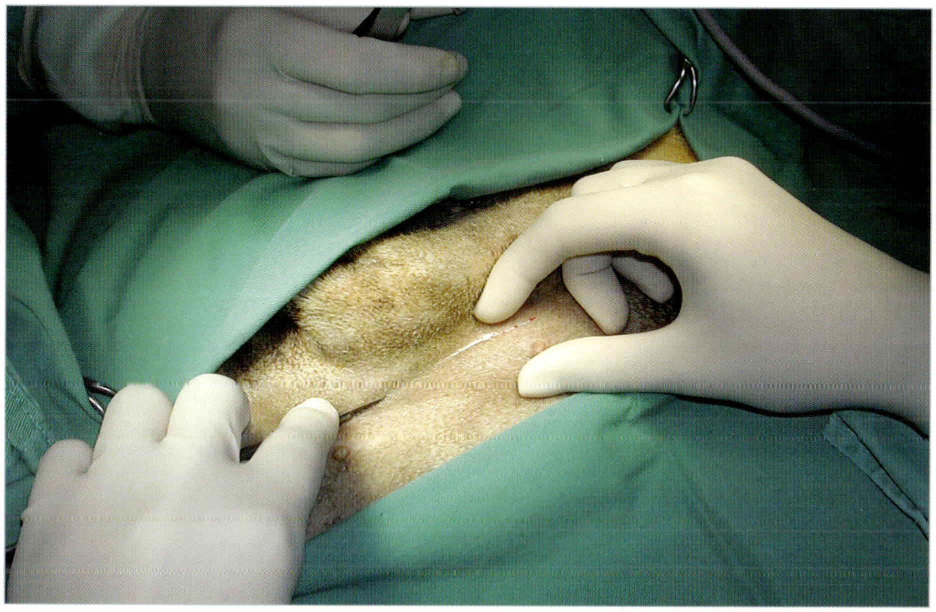

Fig. 2. A skin incision is made parallel to the penis; the length of the incision corresponds to the procedure that will be carried out. The skin is incised with a scalpel.

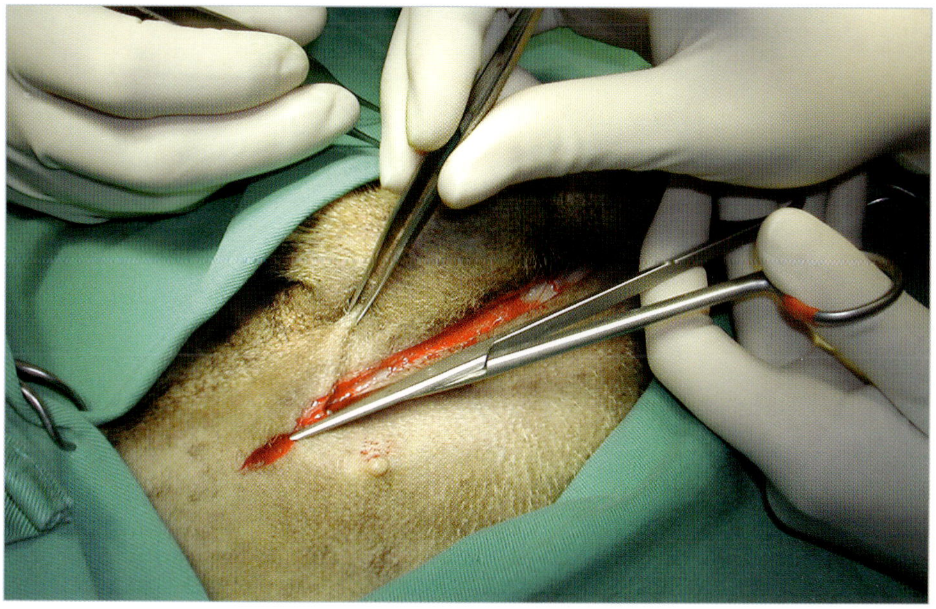

Fig. 3. The incision is extended through the subcutaneous tissue using scissors.

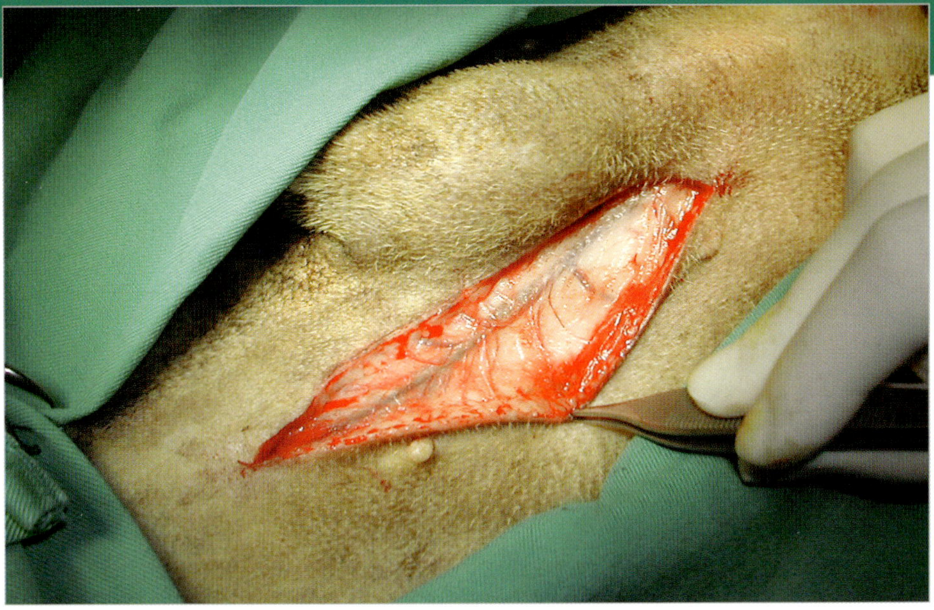

Fig. 4. When dissecting the subcutaneous tissue, the caudal superficial epigastric artery is encountered. It runs parallel to the penis and should be preserved. This artery feeds the preputial branch.

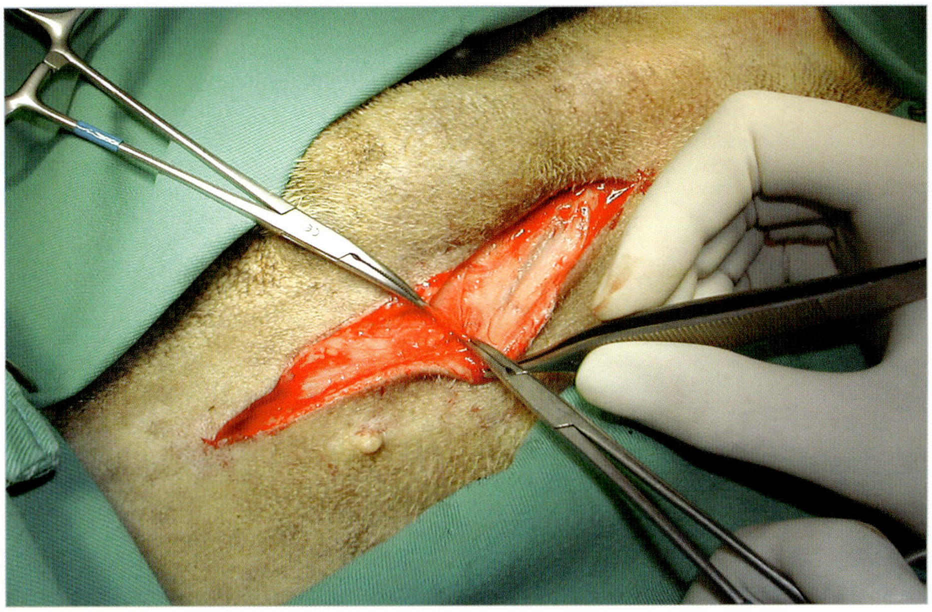

Fig. 5. Two clamps are placed on the preputial branch.

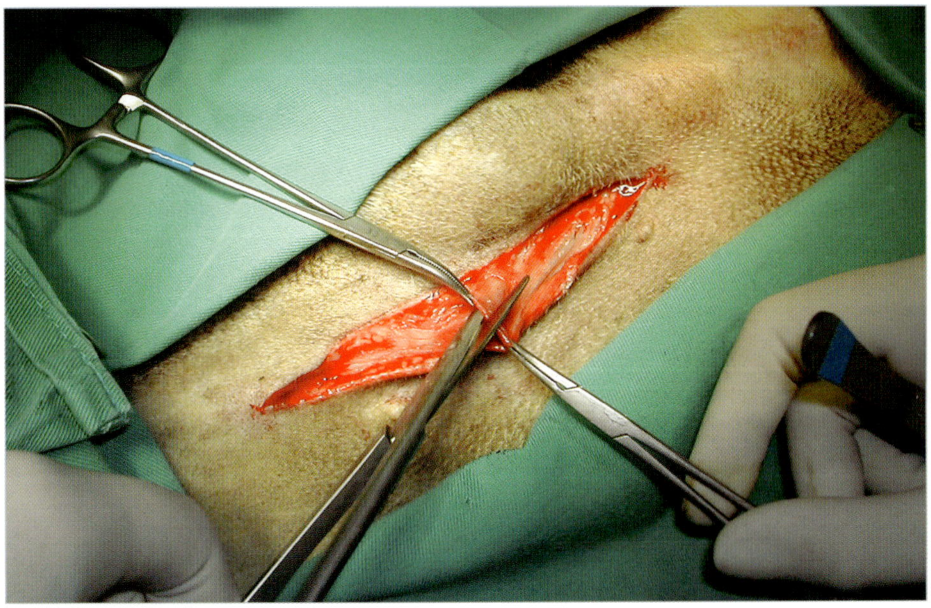

Fig. 6. The artery is sectioned between the two clamps using scissors.

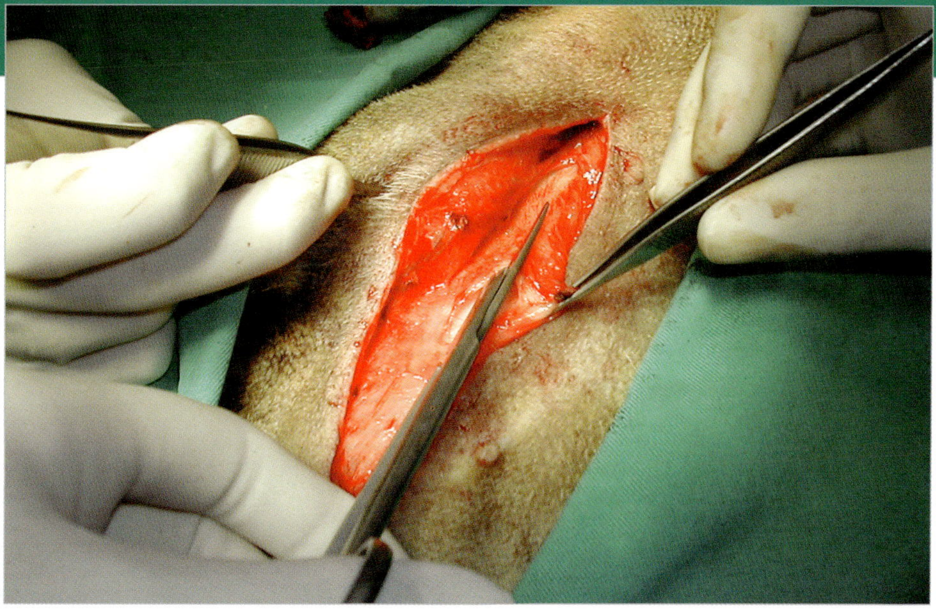

Fig. 7. After ligating the two ends of the preputial artery, dissection of the subcutaneous tissue is continued.

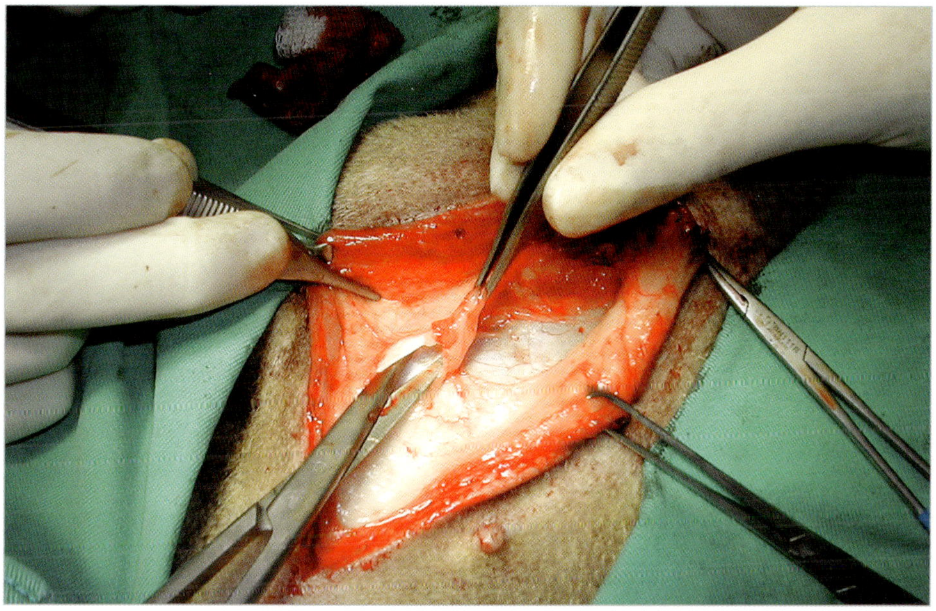

Fig. 8. The incision is extended towards the midline until the linea alba is visualised.

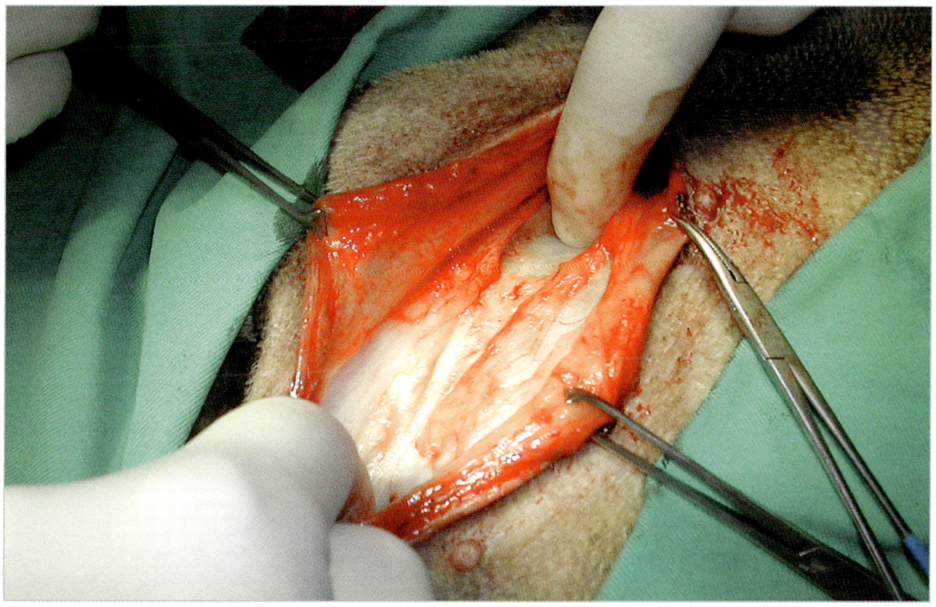

Fig. 9. Using blunt dissection the length of the linea alba that is to be incised is exposed by removing the fat covering. Adipose tissue tends to be abundant in the caudal area of the abdomen.

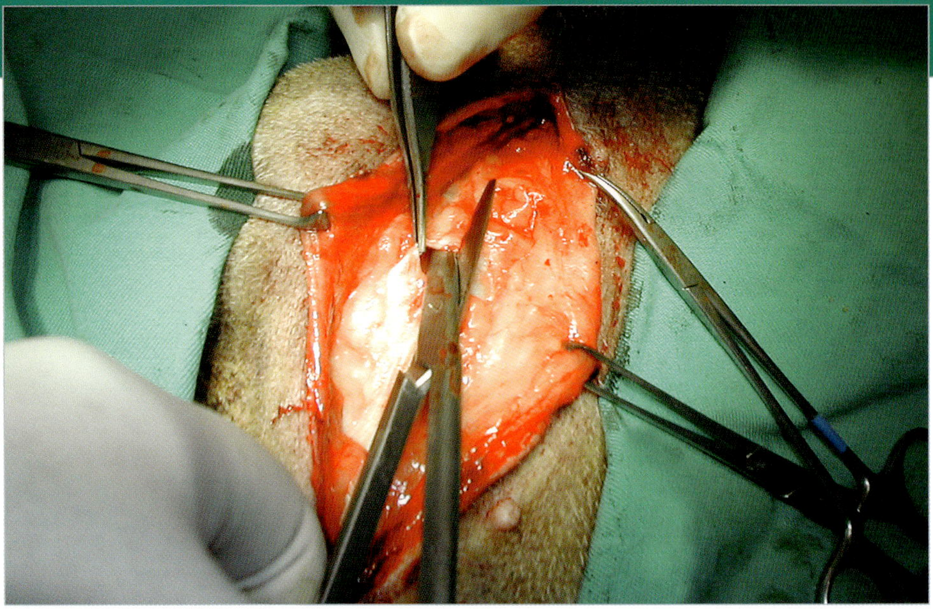

Fig. 10. A hole is made in the linea alba, using scissors or a scalpel, depending on the surgeon's preference.

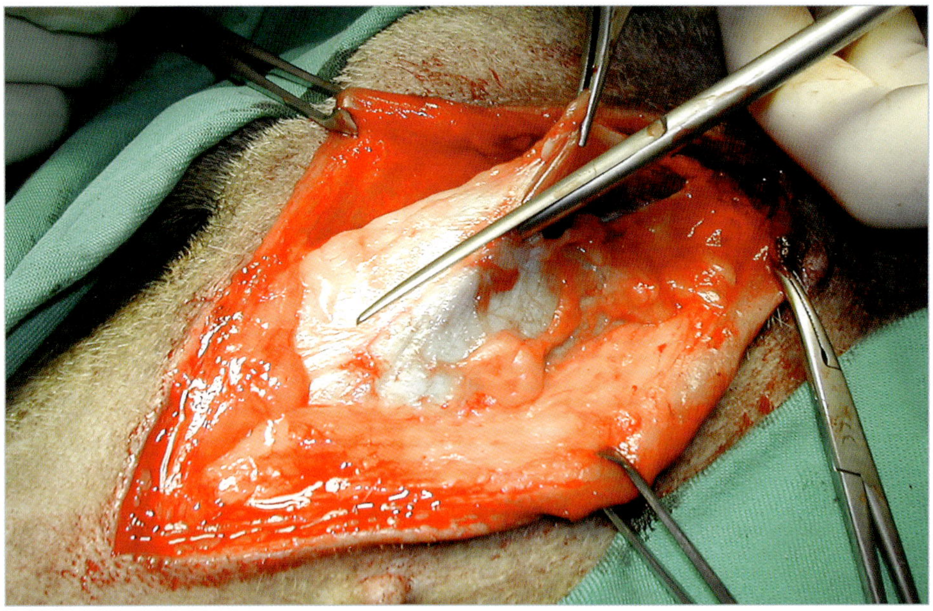

Fig. 11. The incision is extended along the entire length, using scissors and protecting the abdominal viscera at all times.

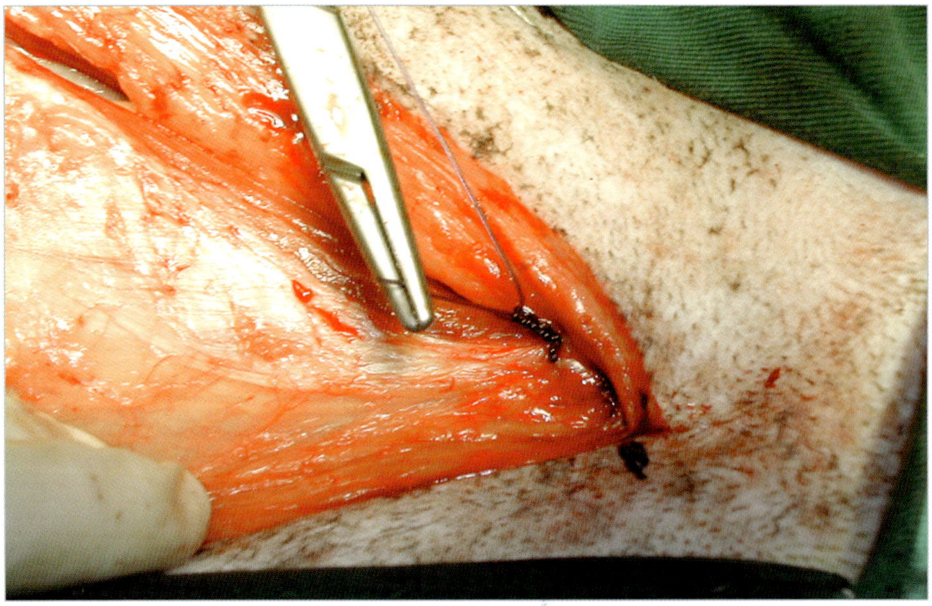

Fig. 12. After carrying out the planned surgical procedure, the abdomen is closed. To do so, a continuous suture with an absorbable 2/0, 1/0 or 0 multifilament suture material is used, depending on the size of the patient. The first knot should be anchored in non-incised tissue, just in front of or behind the starting point of the incision. The integrity of the suture depends to a large extent on the knot, so it should be tied with care.

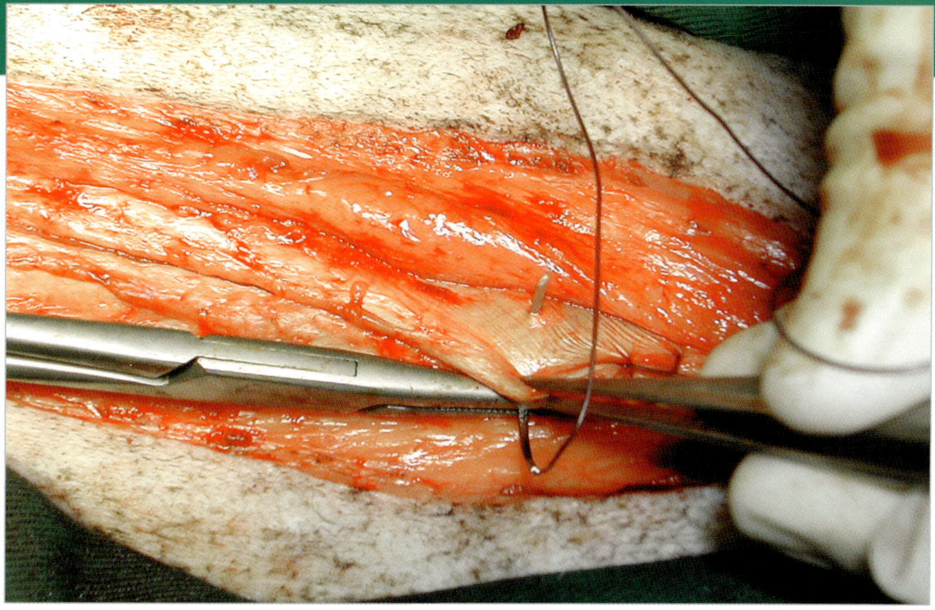

Fig. 13. For a reliable continuous suture, it is sufficient to include the fascia of the abdominal rectus muscles in each bite. It is not necessary to include the parietal peritoneum in the suture, as it has been demonstrated that non-inclusion causes fewer adhesions.

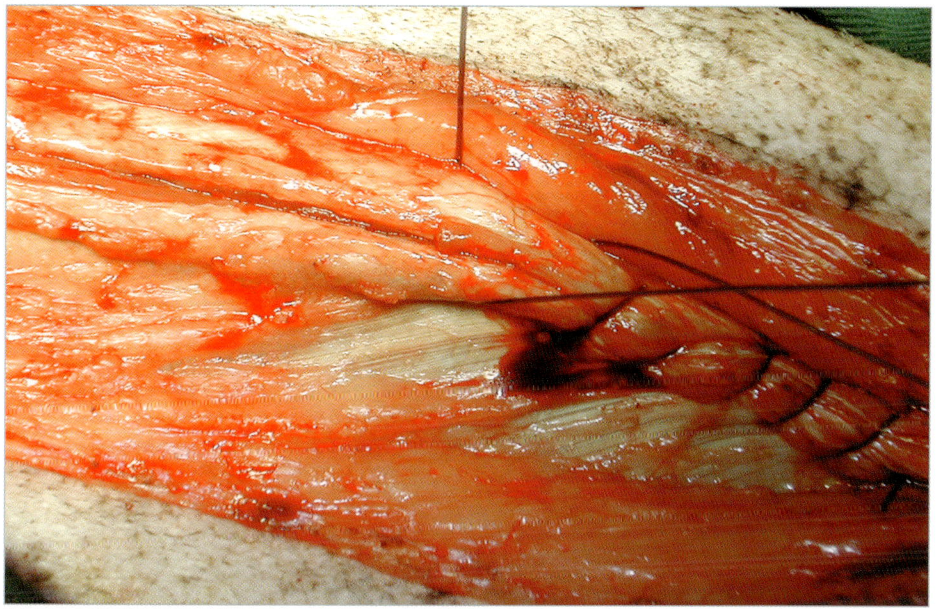

Fig. 14. The linea alba is sutured as described.

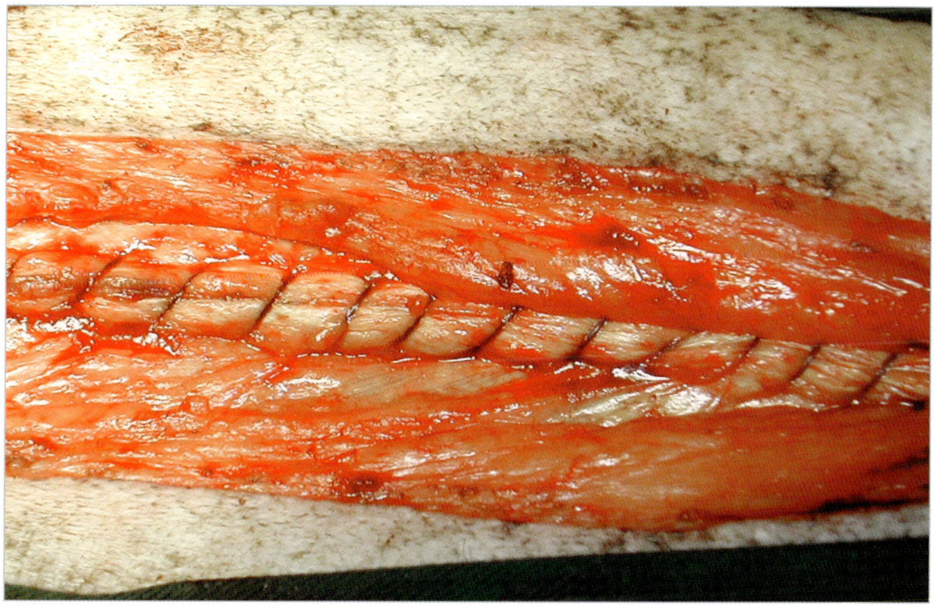

Fig. 15. When the wound commissure at the other end has been passed, the final knot is anchored. This is as important as the first knot for the suture's integrity.

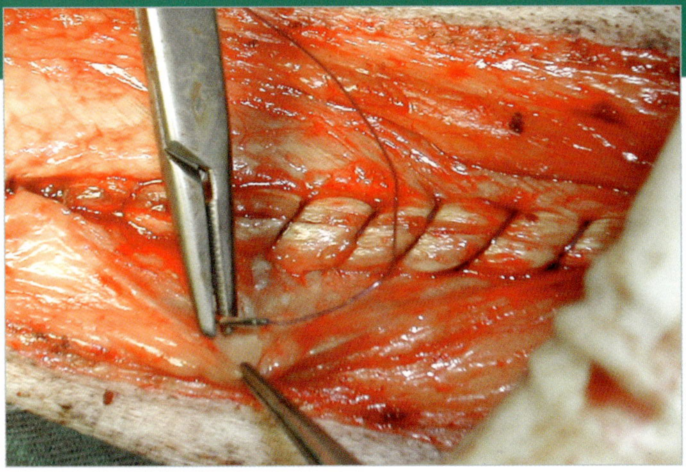

Fig. 16. The suture is reinforced with interrupted cruciate sutures. Usually, 4 or 5 are enough for this type of incision.

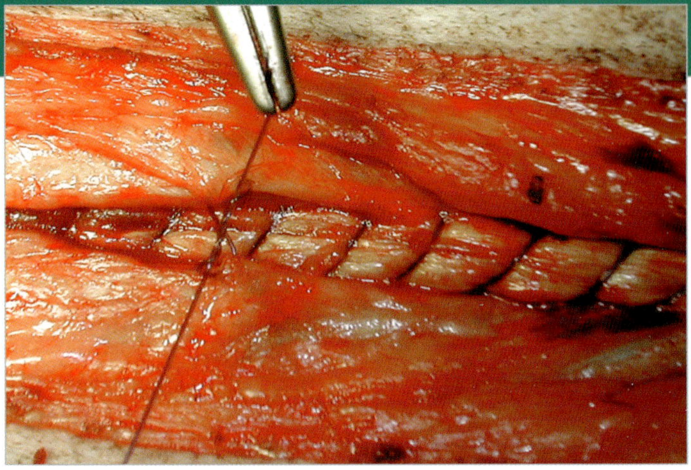

Fig. 17. An attempt should be made to only include the external fascia of the rectus muscles on each side of the incision in the suture. When taking a bite, it is important to keep the needle away from the continuous suture, to avoid cutting it.

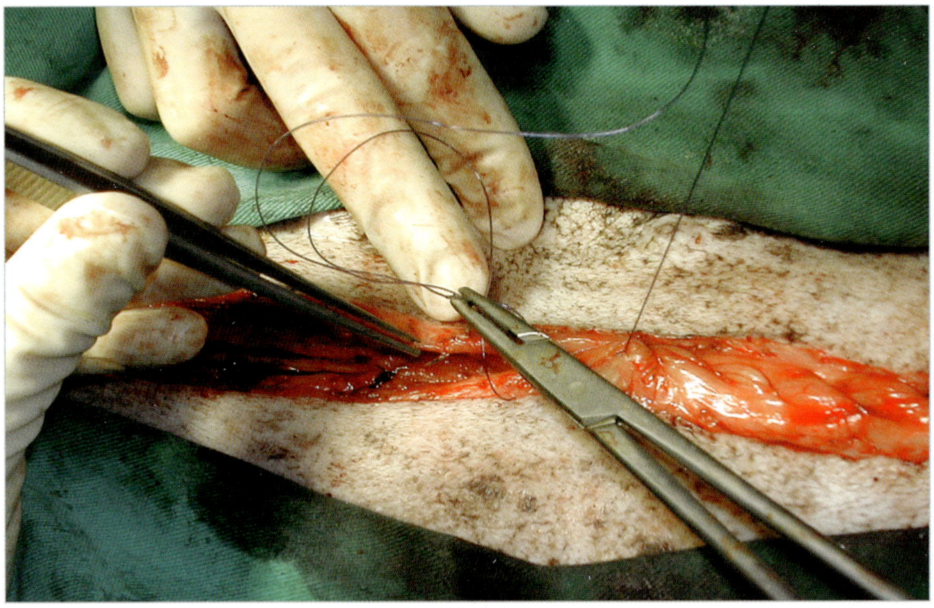

Fig. 18. Next, the subcutaneous layer is closed with a continuous suture using an absorbable 2/0 or 3/0 monofilament suture material.

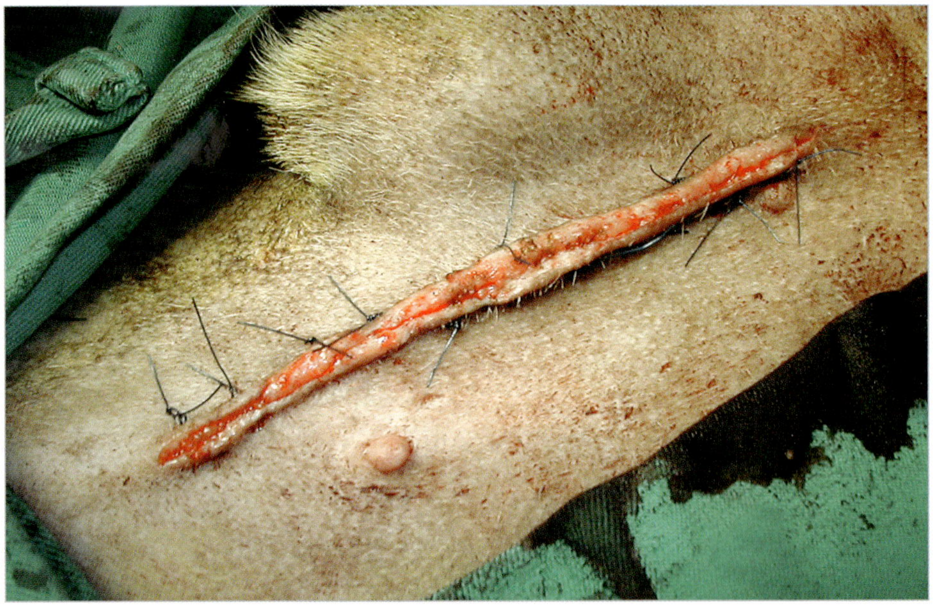

Fig. 19. To finish, the skin is closed with horizontal mattress sutures, for which a non-absorbable 2/0 or 3/0 monofilament suture material is used.

Cystotomy

Frequency	■■■□□
Technical difficulty	■■□□□

Cystotomy is the surgical incision of the bladder and is indicated to remove bladder stones (fig. 1), remove tumours, take biopsies and repair lesions.

Urinary obstruction may cause hyperkalemia resulting in secondary cardiac problems. Correct this before anaesthetising the patient.

In all animals presented with bladder stones, infection of the lower urinary tract should be suspected. Use antibiotics that are excreted by the kidneys and avoid nephrotoxic antibiotics such as aminoglycosides or tetracyclines.

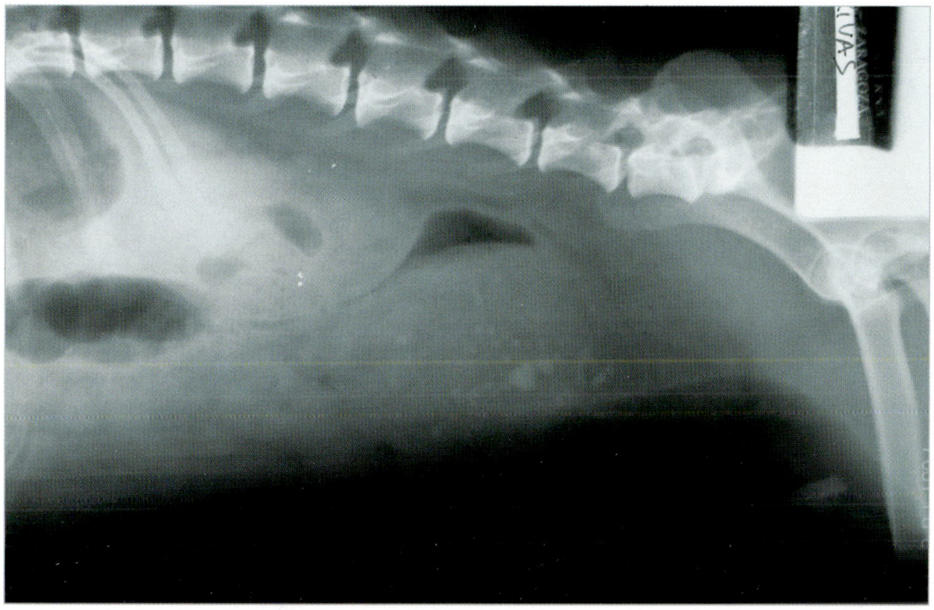

Fig. 1. This patient suffered a urinary obstruction due to calculi that had lodged in the urethra. As the first step of treatment, the calculi were flushed back into the bladder by urohydropropulsion. A cystotomy will then be performed to remove them from the bladder.

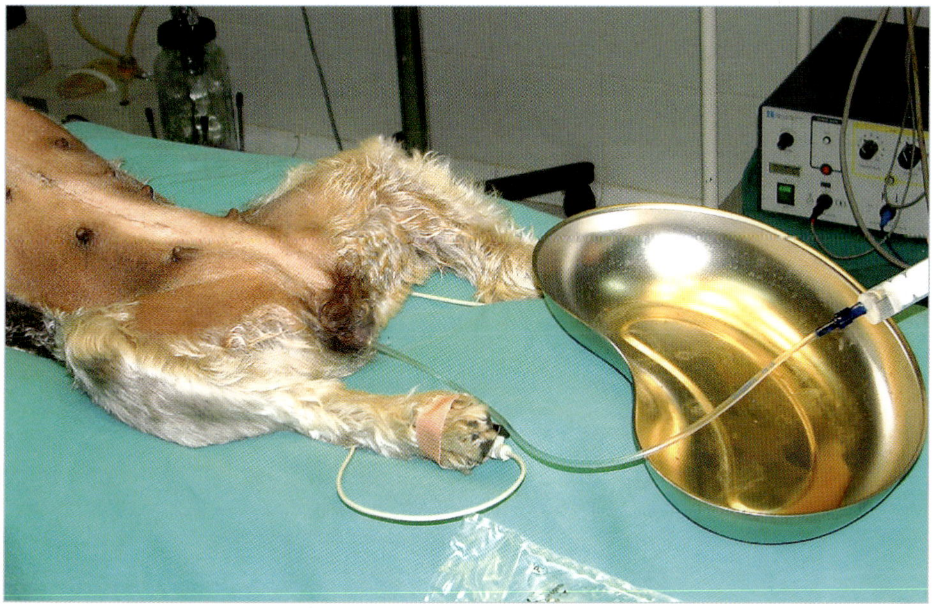

- To access the bladder, a midline laparotomy should be performed between the umbilicus and the pubis.

See infraumbilical laparotomy → page 282

- Catheterise the bladder and flush it with sterile saline to remove the urine and as many bacteria as possible (fig. 2).

Fig. 2. Repeated flushing of the bladder with saline reduces the chance of peritonitis in case the bladder contents leak into the peritoneum.

Technique 1

- Isolate the bladder from the rest of the abdominal cavity (fig. 3).
- Place two stay sutures to immobilise and handle the bladder (fig. 4).
- The bladder should be incised through its ventral side, well away from the ureters and urethra (fig. 5).
- Extract the calculi and take a biopsy of the mucosa for sensitivity testing (fig. 6).

Identify, locate and do not damage the ureters or urethra.

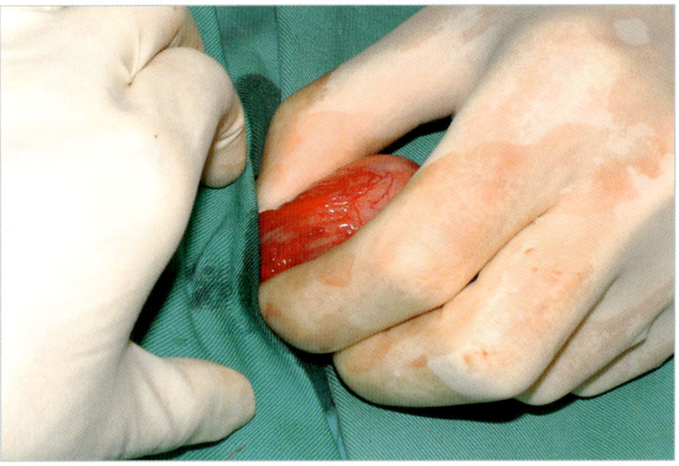

Fig. 3. Several sterile surgical drapes are placed under and around the bladder to prevent urine from leaking into the abdominal cavity.

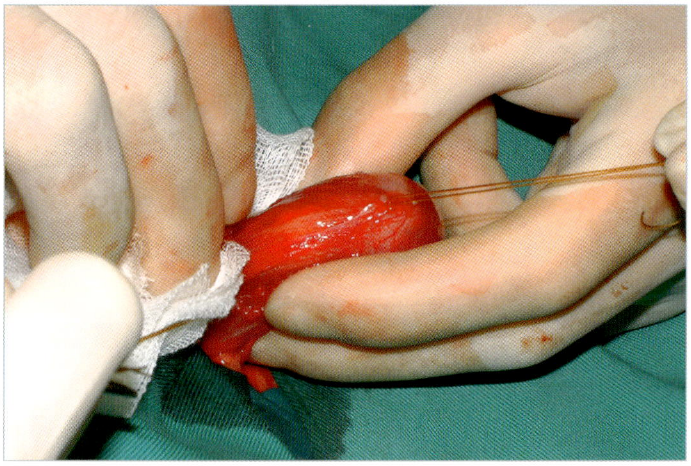

Fig. 4. Two or three stay sutures at the apex and near the neck of the bladder facilitate handling of the bladder.

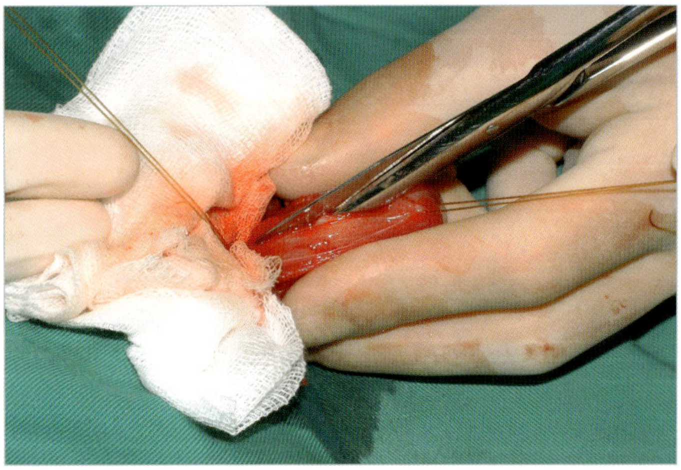

Fig. 5. The bladder incision is made with a scalpel in an area that is near to the apex and well away from the major blood vessels. It is then extended distally using scissors.

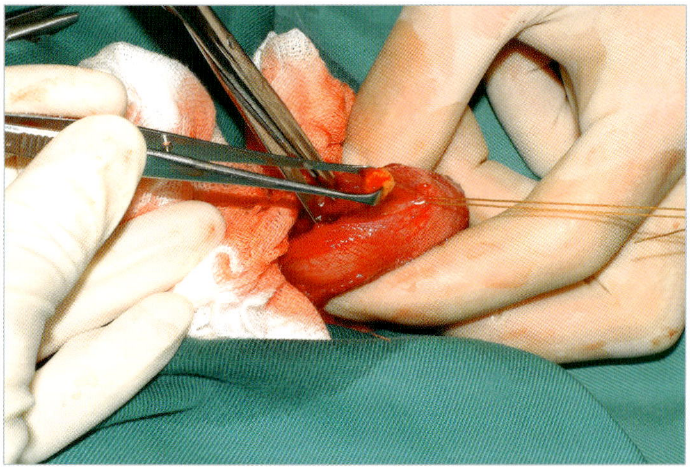

Fig. 6. Extraction of several uroliths.

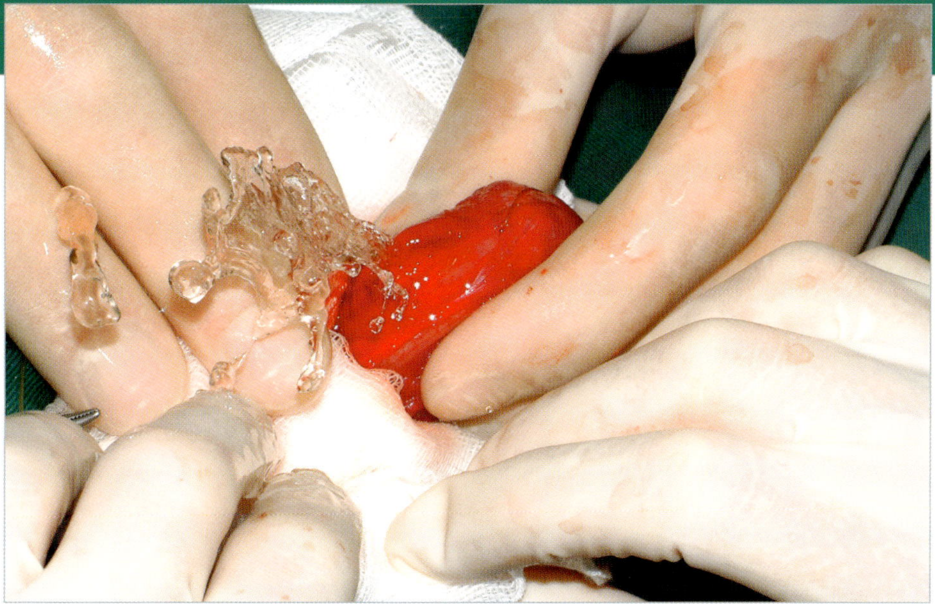

- Catheterise the urethra and flush the bladder to remove small calculi and grit that may have remained at the bottom of the bladder (fig. 7).

Fig. 7. Before suturing the bladder, it should be flushed with lukewarm sterile saline to flush out small stones and grit that are difficult to remove manually. To leave uroliths in the bladder would be a major mistake.

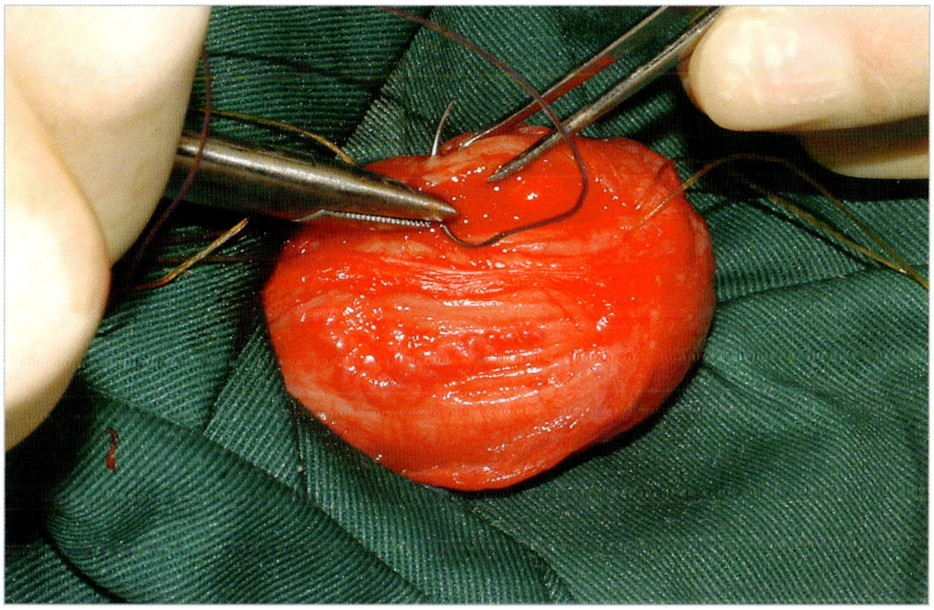

- Close the bladder in two layers with absorbable synthetic monofilament suture material (fig. 8).
- After finishing the sutures, it is advisable to check that the incision does not leak (fig. 9).
- To avoid adhesions between the bladder and other abdominal structures, it is recommended to surround it with omentum before closing the laparotomy wound.

Fig. 8. The bladder is closed with two continuous sutures; the second one should invert the wound edges. The choice of suture type is left to the surgeon (Cushing, Lembert…).

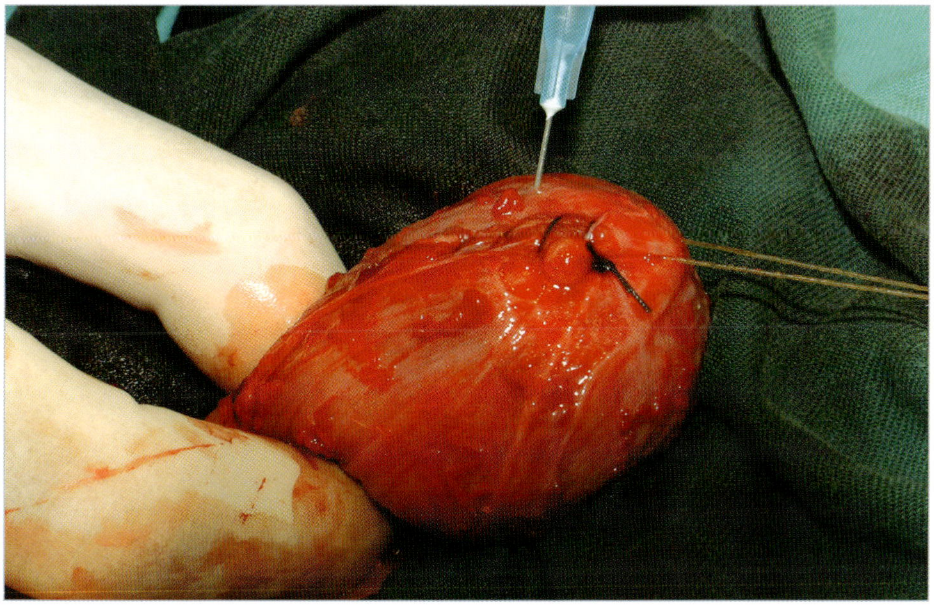

> ***For the urinary tract, absorbable monofilament suture material should be used to avoid calculus formation around the material.***

Fig. 9. To ensure that no urine leaks through the surgical site, saline is injected into the bladder lumen and the suture line is observed carefully.

Technique 2

Instead of isolating the bladder with sterile drapes, it may be sutured to the abdominal wall (figs. 10 and 11).

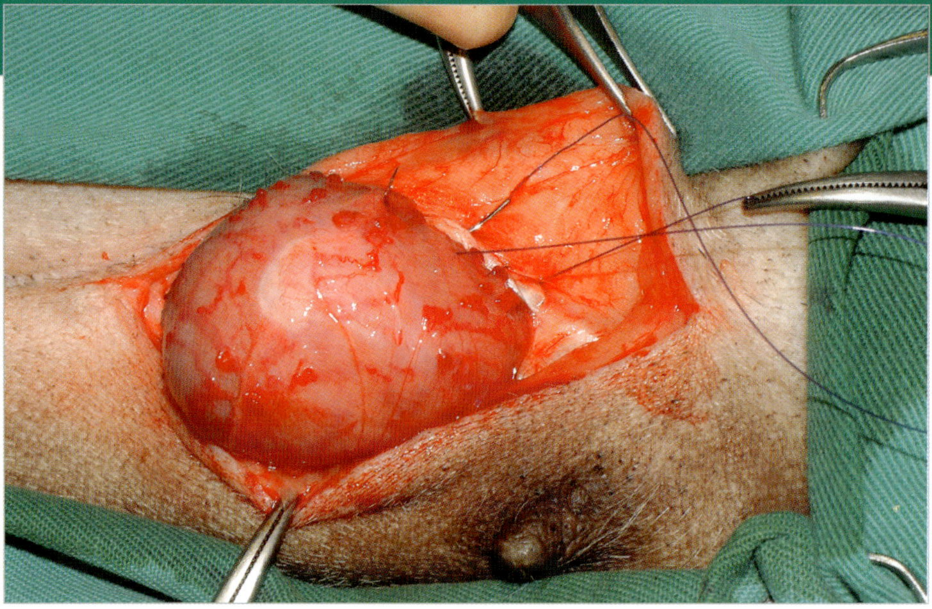

Fig. 10. After performing a micro-laparotomy in the suprapubic area, the bladder is located and exteriorised. With a 3/0 monofilament continuous suture, the outside of the bladder is fixed to the anterior aponeurosis of the abdominal wall.

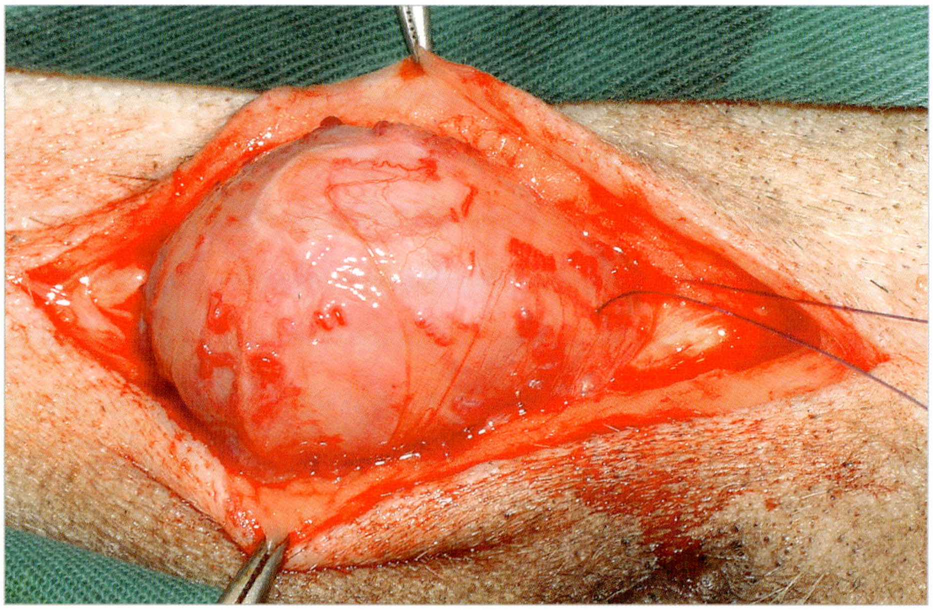

Fig. 11. When the suture is finished and tightened, the bladder wall is closely attached to the abdomen, making peritoneal contamination with urine almost impossible.

The next steps in this procedure are the same as those already described (figs. 12-15).

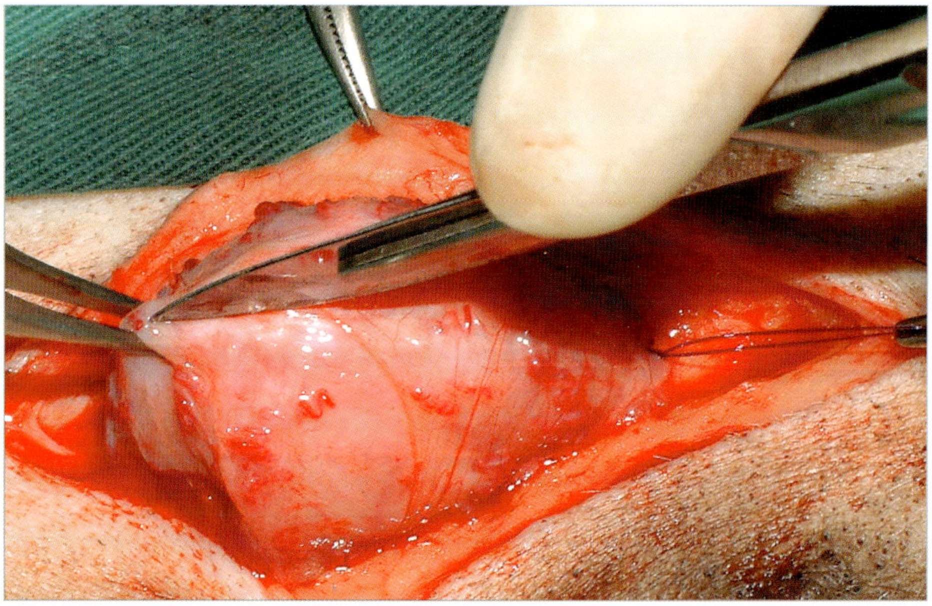

Fig. 12. Incision of the bladder with a scalpel, starting at the apex.

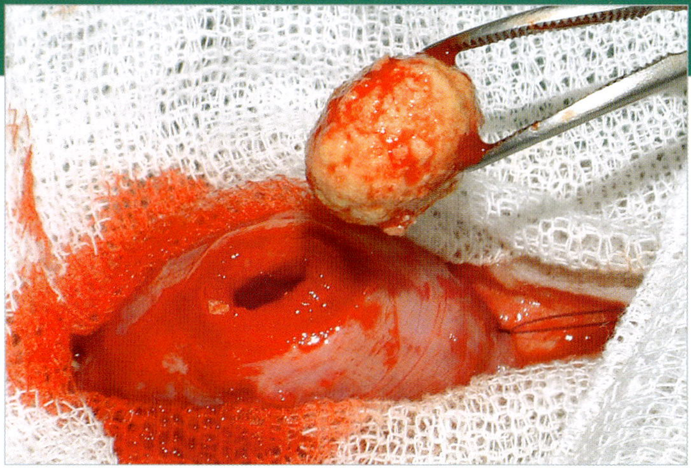

Fig. 13. Extraction of the calculi.

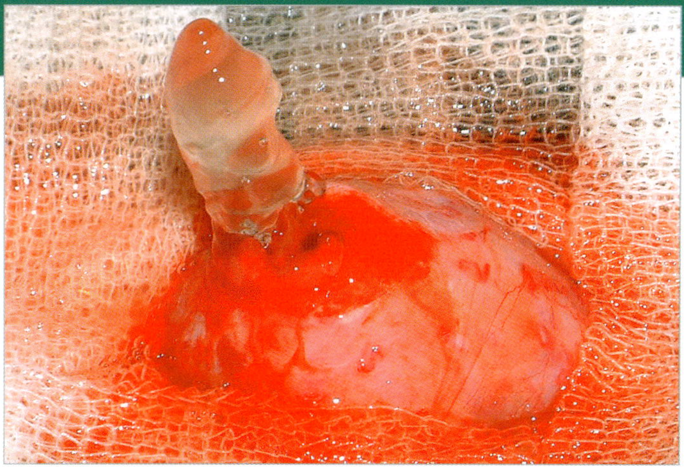

Fig. 14. Removal of small uroliths and grit by urethral catheterisation and retrograde flushing of the bladder.

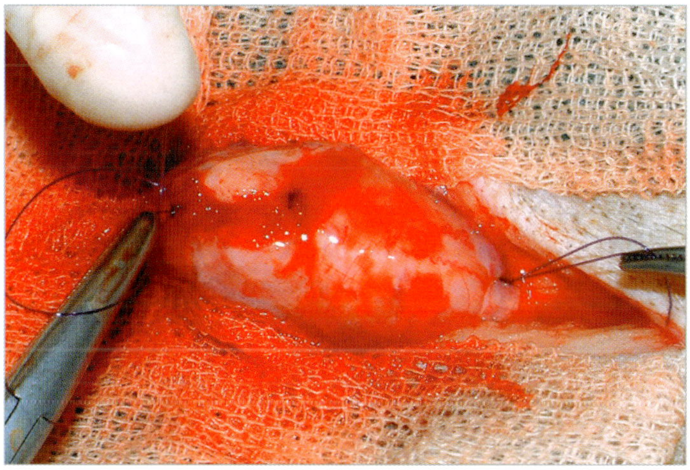

Fig. 15. Closure of the bladder with a continuous suture using absorbable synthetic 3/0 monofilament suture material.

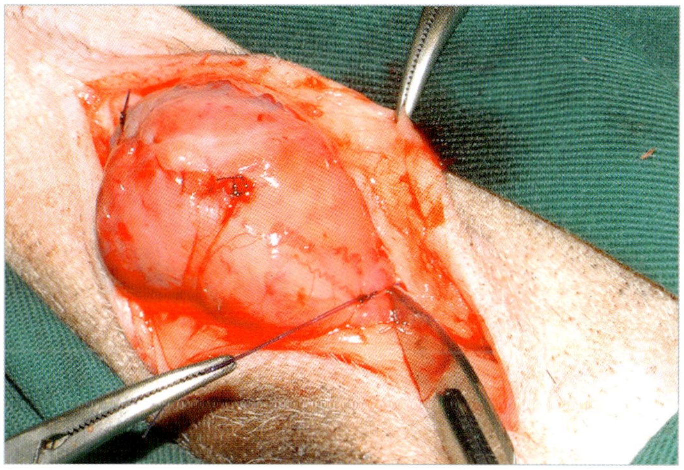

Fig. 16. The use of monofilament material enables the suture to be removed easily without damage to the bladder wall.

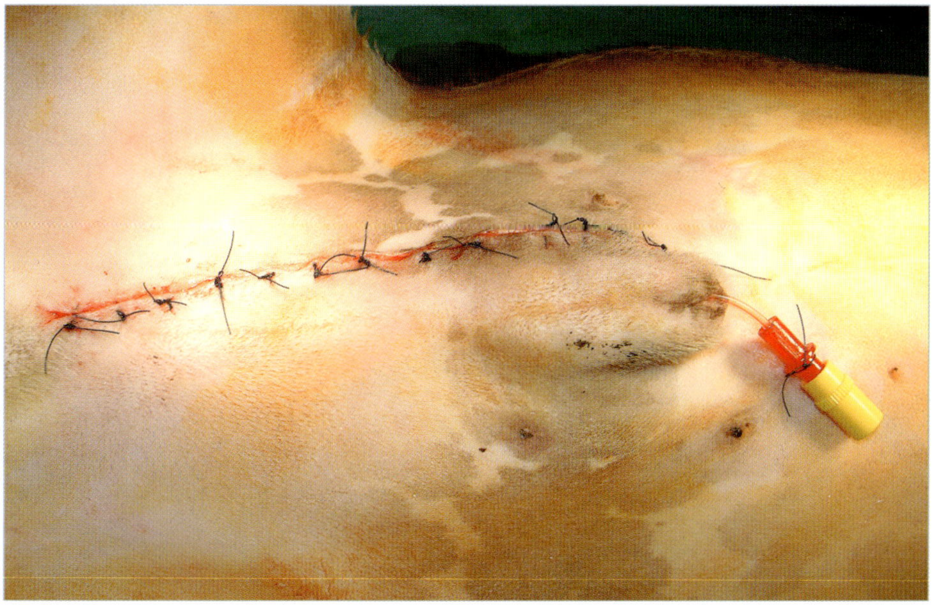

- With this technique, it is necessary to remove the continuous suture between the bladder and the abdomen (fig. 16); as with the first technique, the bladder should be "wrapped" in omentum.
- With both techniques, it is advisable to maintain the urinary catheter in place for 24-36 hours (fig. 17).

Fig. 17. For the first few hours post-surgery the urinary catheter is left in place and the bladder is emptied frequently (every 3-4 hours). This ensures the suture line does not come under too much tension from urine accumulation or because the patient strains to urinate.

MERCHANT FAMILIES of SAUDI ARABIA

MERCHANT FAMILIES of SAUDI ARABIA

2nd Edition
Revised and Updated

J.R.L. Carter

SCORPION BOOKS, LONDON

Other books by J.R.L.Carter
Tribes in Oman
Investors in Saudi Arabia
The Arabian Desert
Merchant Families of Kuwait

Merchant Families of Saudi Arabia

First published in December 1984 by
Scorpion Communications and Publications Ltd, London

ISBN 0 905906 39 X

Designed and Produced by
Scorpion Pica, London

Editor Leonard Harrow
Design and Art Direction Colin Larkin
Design and Production team
Dale Dawson, John Orley and Roger Kemlo
Typesetting ITC Garamond Light and Bold
Paper Cream Bookwove 90gsm
Printing and Binding Hazell Watson and Viney Ltd, England

Contents

Note on Spelling

As usual in books discussing aspects of the modern Arab world some confusion may arise due to spelling of Arabic names in the Latin alphabet. There is, of course, no equivocation as regards the spelling in the Arabic script. In particular, the value of Arabic vowels has led to a variety of possible spellings. For this reason it is not uncommon to find variations within an individual family as to how names are spelt in Western usage. Where possible we have attempted to render the spelling in the Latin alphabet known to be favoured by individuals or companies. Where there have been no such guidelines the spelling of names has been kept as simple and as consistent as possible.

Acknowledgements

The author acknowledges a deep debt of gratitude to his many friends in the Kingdom whose enthusiasm and kindness have made this much expanded work possible. However, many of them would not like to be mentioned by name because of their innate Arabian sensitivities, where this is just not done. So, rather than acknowledge individuals the author wishes to dedicate his work to the whole business community of the Kingdom and hope very much that it will lead to better mutual understanding and so to continued commercial success.

Introduction

In presenting this extension of a previous body of work the author wishes to maintain the same aims, namely to assist those engaged in the Saudi Arabian market. The material can be described as commercial anthropology and represents basic market research. It thus, at times, makes exposures of matters usually considered as private in Saudi Arabia, or indeed anywhere in the Arab world. The author wishes to apologise for this whilst at the same time taking responsibility for any errors that may have been made.

The book is a description of business in the Kingdom of Saudi Arabia and includes examples chosen for their variety and interest. Whilst the choice has, of necessity, been rather arbitrary, the intention has been to provide a picture of the business world and not a directory. Some famous names are still missing due to personal reluctance to provide information; some are, however, included despite this, in order to paint a more complete picture.

It is also important for the reader to understand the collection of material of this nature can rarely result in the production of uniformly up-to-date information. It has not always been possible to verify material at the time of publication.

Spelling of Arabic names is the subject of endless academic wrangling and the arguments are of little interest to the businessman. However, a basic and simplified system has been adopted which will enable him to read names easily. Where these names form part of a company name the way the Arab himself spells it has been retained as far as possible. The spelling of the names of non-Saudi companies may also be inaccurate at times. This is due to the fact that they are largely derived from Saudi sources and so the same position is reached in reverse.

A further explanation of Arab names would be useful. Very simply an Arab has his own name, followed by that of his father and grandfather. The name is then completed, as it were, by the addition of a tribal or family name. So Ali Muhammad Salih al Ghamdi is Ali son of Muhammad son of Salih of the tribe of Ghamid. However, Muhammad Salih can be one name, in which case the example would be incomplete; that is, the grandfather's name is missing. A further complication can arise over the 'al'. In the examples it simply means 'the'. But sons often wish to aggrandise their father and frequently do so by putting 'al' in front of his name too. So, Ali above might well wish to be called Ali al Muhammad; in this case the rest of the name would probably not be used. As generation succeeds generation the al Muhammad would probably become a complete new clan of the Ghamid tribe. In actual fact this practice only really has a vogue when an individual family is concerned and sometimes, human nature being what it is, it is quite deliberately used to confer an appearance of tribal origin when there is none – the Arabs being very possibly even worse snobs than the English.

The commercial world of the Kingdom has developed with immense rapidity and though Jiddah is regarded as the commercial capital, its position is no longer one of striking pre-eminence. Rather she resembles a partner.

Jiddah

Jiddah's place as the main port for the Pilgrimage to Mecca led to the foundation of the the city as the Kingdom's main business centre and it was here that the first financial and mercantile concerns were established. The commercial attraction of Jiddah forming a focus for the establishment of a thriving business community is a good point from which to consider the characteristics of the merchant community as a whole. At first sight it may seem to be at variance with the social structures found in other towns and cities in the Arab world. However, the difference is really only one of provenance. Whereas elsewhere distinctly tribal associations have formed the social basis of the community, in Jiddah a flood of disparate groups and families has come together to achieve the same result and have welded themselves into a very similar form of social organisation. It is this fact that makes Jiddah so very interesting to those who study social change in the Arab world. Jiddah is a solidly Arabian town where successive immigrants from all over the world have settled and acquired a purely Jiddawi identity. Naturally, this process takes a generation or two and so at any one time there are people who are more Jiddawi than others depending on how long they have been in the city.

The population thus resembles somewhat an onion: the most recent arrivals forming the outer layers, successive peelings revealing older settlements. What is of interest is that these layers are reasonably discreet and there is greater social cohesion within each layer than between people from different layers, even though their origins are the same. Thus a man settling from Hadramawt will have more contact with his contemporaries from Egypt, Syria and India than he will with subsequent Hadrami arrivals. This discreetness is naturally reinforced by marriage and commercial relationships.

The consequence of this process is to produce a society indistinguishable from other Arabian urban societies.

In practical terms this means that an Iranian business foundation will use an Afghan accountant, marry into an Egyptian or a Hadrami family and have a Moroccan lawyer. But they will all be a part of one layer of the onion and thus eschew relationships with later arrivals from Afghanistan, Syria, Egypt or Hadramawt.

This Jiddawi identity is also further reinforced in some cases by the acquisition of a claim to Arabness through recourse to genealogy.

In Jiddah the centre of the onion is really composed of the people who have been associated with the Hijaz for centuries and who participate in the *waqf*, that is the system of religious endowment, and who by their inheritances from this source have grown from the very roots of the local society. In Jiddah many of these are migrants from the Holy City of Mecca itself and are families who have held employment associated with the Holy Places. Such are the family of Abdalmajid, who still furnish guides for the pilgrims, Shalhub who deliver water from the well of Zamzam, and Abu Zinada who descend from the traditional auctioneers in the vegetable market of Jiddah. In addition to these there are old families who have always been associated with Jiddah, at least since the last half of the nineteenth century, and often as a part of the commercial life of the city. Perhaps some of the more famous of these are the Alireza, Nashar, Ba'eshan, Bin Himd, Naji and Shinkar, Sania and Binzagr, the last two having streets named after them. It was members of these families who were closely associated with the early developments which took place between the two World Wars, when the city still retained its wall. The opening of the Falah schools is an event remembered with great gratitude and was the responsibility of the far-sightedness of the Alireza, Jamjoom and Ba'eshan families. It was also in these years that the foundations of the business houses of Zahid and Tawil were laid, and that there was an influx of commercial people from the Nejd and Riyadh. Hitherto the main commercial outlet from the capital area had been towards the East and the Gulf. This wave brought to Jiddah famous names such as Zamil, Sulayman, Khereiji and Qusaybi as well as the most famous of all, the Saud and their relatives, the Sudayri. This amounted to royal participation rather than patronage and despite stories of questionable activities gave great encouragement to the commercial life of the city, an encouragement which created the environment in which the Juffalis and the Rajhis from Qasim, and the Kaakis of Mecca, began to build their commercial and financial institutions. The latter ably exploited the need for banking facilities, in which activity the Bin Mahfouz have been closely associated with the Kaakis in the National Commercial Bank.

At this point it is interesting to note how the families of some of the advisors to the late King Abdalaziz have become an integral part of the commercial life of the city too. In particular the families of his personal physicians have been able to carve out for themselves very considerable niches in the business life of the city and have been leaders in internationalising the trade links of Jiddah. These families are those of Pharaon and Khashoggi, in which connection the Yasin should not be forgotten.

The foregoing paragraphs have given a very short account of the people who make up the typical merchant community and it is now time to consider the ways that they like to do business. To many observers they appear almost furtive at times and Westerners often experience problems of communication which they ascribe to this factor. However, the only real difficulty is the difference over what each side considers private. The Arab merchant is usually most reticent with regard to financial figures and this feeling extends to sales statistics. These are thought of as strictly private matters and the foreigner has no business in making what the Arab considers brash and even inquisitive enquiries into such areas. Naturally this puts the Westerner into a difficult position, but there are ways of making discreet assessments which is what such figures would be wanted for in any case.

Local Characteristics

One of the most important aspects of commercial life to the Western observer is the 'open door' policy adopted by the senior management of Saudi companies. This means that the senior executive is not only immediately accessible to all his staff but that he is also involved in all the detail of what is going on in the company. As a consequence his office is invariably full of people who will vary in status from senior executives to junior clerks with a sprinkling of foreign salesmen. One motivation behind this way of doing things is a desire to be as open and honest as possible whilst at the same time ensuring the honesty of the employees.

In the modern business world this way of doing things has the disadvantage that it precludes a satisfactory system of delegation which itself leads to the demoralisation of staff where the employer is so concerned that he will even have to approve the wording of a simple telex. This quickly leads to a strong tendency for all employees to avoid any responsibilities whatsoever. Therefore the owner of the business finds himself having to make all the decisions and never having an opportunity to have discussions with his managers.

These factors lead to the position where the commercial world of Saudi Arabia is largely run on an ad hoc basis with very little planning at all. The business is conducted entirely in relation to the prevailing opportunities and the current cash position. With regard to this last, company financing is usually very simple and even some of the biggest Saudi companies with enormous turnovers only operate one bank account. Monies are drawn from the single central fund which is directly controlled by the owner of the company himself or by the partners. In practice for instance, the controlling management of the company feels happier if it can simply give a manager a single cheque to cover all the requirements of that manager's department. This will cover such items as salaries and the acquisition of materials, as well as rents and so on. Whilst this is indeed delegation of a sort, the manager is rarely if ever trusted with a bank account of his own. This system means that on occasions the cash runs out and all expenses, including salaries, have to remain delayed until new funds are available. In the normal course of events overdraft facilities could be arranged to get round the problem. However, many of the more traditional companies regard the borrowing of money as being a cause of shame and they are therefore extremely cautious about doing so. Because of this, a lot of companies have developed solely by utilising profits, even though borrowing would have increased the pace of that development.

All these factors create the common attitude to new business opportunities which is such a marked characteristic of Saudi Arabian business, namely that the merchants tend to grasp every opportunity they come across regardless of whether it has any relationship to either their existing business or their experience. It is important to remember too that once having embarked on a new enterprise the merchant will be very loathe to relinquish it even if it becomes unprofitable. He regards such relinquishment as a public admission of failure.

This seeming simplicity of view in Saudi commerce does, however, lead to most companies being run on a profitable basis; despite the hampering effect of lack of delegation and caution over borrowing the cost of much planning and research is avoided.

The profits of a Saudi business may either be divided between two partners or between as many as fifty or sixty relations. It is in the light of this, that the figures for investment by investors should be viewed. Further whilst the merchant families are considered to be family businesses they are not necessarily owned by all the members of a family. Frequently members of a family obtain their income from several different and entirely separate companies, which is usually an expression of the effects of the laws of inheritance enshrined in the Sharia religious law.

The businessman entering the Saudi market place for the first time should be aware of the existence of these laws. The Qur'an improved the pre-Islamic situation and increased the number of possible heirs to include a larger number of men, and also women and children. But there is almost no freedom for the owner to distribute property according to his personal wishes. The hierarchy of heirs is strictly defined, as is the proportion of the property due to each one. Only if no member of this hierarchy is living can the testator bequeath his whole estate to any other person, known as the "universal legatee". Failing the nomination of such a legatee the property reverts to the state as Bayt al-Mal. Some heirs can be excluded from inheritance by others, but there are six classes of heirs, the so-called primary heirs, who are bound to receive a portion of the property. These classes are: son(s), daughter(s), father, mother, husband, wife (wives). The amount these heirs receive may be affected by their number; for instance, in the absence of a son, one daughter receives half the property but two or more daughters share two-thirds of the property; or by the fact that one or more classes of the heirs has no representative, for instance the husband or wife's share is doubled where there are no children and no son's children. However, where there is no living member of a class of heirs he/she may be substituted by a specified secondary heir, all of whom are close blood relatives, that is the maternal grandmother can substitute for the mother. Where there is no son, the fractions of the property, divided among the primary and secondary heirs, may total more or less than unity. If more, the fractions are adjusted proportionally until unity is reached, though this is not accepted by the Shi'a. If less, the remainder is shared amongst the normal sharers with the exception of the husband or wife.

According to the law, the property is divided amongst the primary heirs in the following proportions, in the case where there are daughter(s) but no sons: husband, one quarter; wife, one eighth, and two or more wives share this fraction; father, one sixth; mother, one sixth; daughter, one half, and two or more daughters share this fraction. If there are sons as well as daughters, the husband/wife, father and mother, or the secondary heirs who represent them if they are dead, receive as above. But the sons and daughter(s)then divide the remainder so that each son receives an equal amount and each daughter receives half a son(s) share. If no other primary heirs, nor the secondary heirs who stand in for them, are living, then the sons and daughters share the whole property in the above manner. Although under Islamic law the women normally receive half as much as the men, they enjoy exactly the same legal rights over their property.

Where there are no children or children's children, the husband or wife receives a half and a quarter instead of a quarter and an eighth respectively. Finally, where most of the property goes to secondary heirs, because there are a few living primary heirs, the fractional division of the property can become even more complicated than the example given above.

Inheritance implies ownership, and the right of full ownership is accepted in Islamic law. Undisputed possession is accepted as evidence of title; anyone may acquire title to an ownerless thing that is capable of ownership by taking possession of it. On waste land enclosure is not sufficient, the squatter must break up the land and cultivate it. Buildings upon and crops of trees on land are separate from it and may be held by a separate title. In marriage a woman enters into no disabilities in respect of her property.

Property may be sold or given away by the owner. Alternatively he may declare it to be a *waqf*, which is a form of trust in which the property is considered to belong to God while its usufruct may be used to support either the family of the man who supported the *waqf* – a man's principal and most laudable duty is to provide for his family, no matter how wealthy it may be – or the maintenance of God's worship according to the tenets of Islam, or charities which support the poor, such as almshouses, or the rich and poor equally, such as schools and hospitals. Because the property is considered to belong to God the *waqf* can only be a permanent endowment and cannot be alienated. Any Muslim may create a *waqf* from a part of the whole of his uncontested property. He names the beneficiaries, and if these are his family he normally names the ultimate object of the *waqf*, those who obtain the usufruct if and when the line of beneficiaries dies out, and he may name himself as the first *mutawli*, or guardian, and obtain an appropriate remuneration. He may, in some law schools, claim the right to withdraw the property from the *waqf* in exchange for another property of at least equal value.

Apart from the benefit of creating a *waqf* of gaining favour in the sight of God, the owner obtains religious protection of his land, he may also assure the permanence of his family from generation to generation and he may evade the strict letter of the law of inheritance, and in particular escape from successive sub-divisions of the estate.

In actual practice the majority of merchant enterprises are begun by an individual or perhaps two brothers. It is customary for a younger brother to be brought into the business when he leaves school or university. This is particularly noticeable if the brothers concerned have the same mother. In general, too, older brothers and first cousins are noticeable by their absence from the business. The owners of the company will, however, assist other members of the family on an irregular basis.

When the founders of a company die, and here is the relevance of the preceding paragraphs, their assets are shared by all their relatives in accordance with Sharia law. As mentioned, it is not allowed that a man may leave his property, i.e. the company, to his more able sons for instance. Equally, he cannot disinherit a spendthrift or stupid son. Because of this a Saudi business venture can, after a couple of generations, have as many as thirty or forty partners, although only a very few may be sufficiently interested to work full time in the business. This leads to a situation where, although many members of a family may work at their own interests they will still derive income from the 'family business' whether they are actively involved in the management or not. It is only in the most modern businesses that the family members actually running it are paid a management fee separate and in addition to their rights as family participants. In any case incomes as such are taken by the individuals in an extraordinarily casual way during the business year. There are rarely auditors reports, dividends are not declared and annual general meetings are an unusual event.

Some families are efficiently organised and their owners, their wives and children draw monies from a special company account to cover their living expenses. In other family concerns monies are taken for personal spending as well as living expenses; personal spending of this kind can be used for almost anything, such as investment in real estate or foreign stock markets. Indeed, it is not unknown that one brother will finance a project in this way despite the fact that the project has been rejected by the other partners in the company. On occasions all the partners will take the same amount of money out of the company each year; in others the year's accounts show not only the business profits gained but also such sums as each member of the family has taken. This enables everyone to know how much has been taken out and by whom, but there is surprisingly little concern over the, at times, considerable disparities, there being a belief in the old adage of each unto his needs. Problems, however, do occur if the company is not doing very well.

Often in the case where there has been an argument, new companies are created. Despite the exigencies of Sharia law, disgruntled partners can quite simply sell their share in the family company to other members of the family and utilise this cash as capital to found a new business. However, this is a much more difficult operation where the business is a partnership, and has also lead to difficulties where there has been a requirement to diversify from purely trading activities into industrial operations, purely because the assets in the last event are much harder to divide.

The great difficulties consequent upon splitting a family business are matters of which any Saudi family is aware and they avoid this whenever possible. However, there are times, such as on the death of a partner, when there is no way round the problem and the result is often a split which may not be reconciled for a generation or more.

During the decade of the seventies the all too common stage of development was reached when fortunes were made in land speculation which flourished in the shadow of government plans. The small Saudi businessman understood well the value of property, having frequently been in the position of owner of a small area of land outside the commercial area of the town or city. Uncharacteristically, they borrowed heavily from the banks whilst spending as little as possible on construction costs and at the same time being extremely parsimonious in expenditure on maintenance. In the middle of the decade it was thought that a landlord spending more than one percent on this last was most unusual. At this time rents increased ferociously, multiplying six times between the years 1974 and 1976. It was a decade when the return on money was in harmony with the rocket age, if not commercial sense. At the height of this boom outlay on construction was recoverable in two or three years, and foreign companies were paying rent up to two years in advance. The helter-skelter state of affairs could not last and did not. The use of cheap materials led to the actual collapse of many buildings; in any case they were erected in such numbers that they frequently outstripped the provision of services. However, the picture was not completely doom laden and it is only fair to mention that many private developers put up first-rate buildings at this time. But, in general the investment philosophy still remains the same. This philosophy has been summarised as follows: the Arabian investor sees a building as something which will pay for itself in five years and will collapse in ten, but land is of permanent value. Note should be taken that both the construction of private homes and other buildings such as hotels has been greatly encouraged by the Saudi government; in the former case the Saudi Real Estate Development Fund provides up to fifty percent of the cost of an interest free loan, and likewise for hotels.

The availability of cheap government resources combined with the massive rise in oil prices in the seventies and with a market gap led to enormous investment in the hotel industry in particular. This situation is now reversed and there can be few more embarrassing activities than hotel ownership in Saudi Arabia at present. There is now a huge surplus of capacity and serious questions can be put as to the future of both hotels and their owners. By 1981 most of the newer hotels were running at fifty percent of capacity and it was quite unnecessary to make bookings. So far owners have responded to this problem by either making provision for greater luxury or increasing services and facilities. In addition to this the penal price of rooms has become frozen and some even offered considerable discounts. However, there has not been an actual reduction in room prices for fear of starting a price war which is not a part of Middle Eastern philosophy. The future of the hotel industry in the Kingdom continues to be risky in view of the high operating costs throughout the area. It is unlikely that the owners would convert their hotels to other uses and it is very possible that owners will maintain their prices and accept losses, hoping that the future will bring improvements.

Government encouragement has also been lavishly given to local Saudi contracting companies. In 1980 His Majesty King Fahd, then Crown Prince, announced that all of the simpler kinds of construction project would go exclusively to local companies. This policy has always been implicit in the development of the Kingsdom and will continue to be expanded.

Another side of the Saudi market concerns the selling of consumer durables. It is not an easy area in which to overcome customer resistance of a peculiarly Arabian kind. The customers are difficult to attract. Buying habits largely respond to word of mouth recommendations; the customer is very conservative, highly brand conscious and most undiscriminating in his technical comparisons.

The Concepts behind Islamic Banking

Recent events in the Middle East and the general re-emphasis of Islamic precepts have made it increasingly necessary to comprehend at least some of the ideas implicit in the traditional Islamic banking world. These ideas may seem rather simple to the Westerner at first, but they in fact present a very real difficulty and point the way to those problems met at the interface between East and West. They also serve to explain why Saudisation of Western banks is much more than a purely nationalistic activity. An underlying matter that is often treated with humourous cynicism by a Western observer concerns the Islamic rule forbidding the levying of interest. This is a very deeply rooted concept, entrenched in both Islamic law and its large supportive body of Tradition. Here it has always been held that value is created by labour and cannot therefore grow of itself. With this basic belief it is not difficult to appreciate the arguments that of necessity follow. In particular it immediately becomes apparent that it is right to expect that the work done by the bank itself is regarded as the source of increase in the value of a deposit. Subsequent gain to the customer is not a matter of interest being paid but rather a participation in profits derived from the joint effort of both depositor and bank.

This attitude alone has led to fundamental antagonisms between Eastern and Western systems of banking. These antagonisms are only exacerbated, for instance, by the method of payment of oil royalties and the lack, in the East, of very much in comparison with the West, for a Muslim to invest in.

Thus from a single idea one can readily understand the motivation to establish an Islamic banking system. The stated purpose of such a system is to free the Islamic world from what is seen as a consequent economic backwardness. It is genuinely felt in both socialist and traditionally monarchist countries in the area that there is a duty to use the region's resources to improve the economic and social lot of the inhabitants, rather than to feather or rather gild the nest of the unbeliever.

The Westerner should also remember that there is a more immediate local factor to be considered. This is political in the sense that most countries throughout the Middle East consider the Western banking system profoundly Zionist in both content and control. This alone stimulates a very strong desire for the establishment of an alternative system.

To these factors must be added an unbendable faith in the eternal nature of religious verities which must, by definition, remain true despite changes in the environment of an economic or social nature.

It might be apposite here to describe how an Islamic banking system might work in practice. The basis of the system would be direct co-operation between finance and labour in the funding of commercial, industrial and development projects. The bank itself could earn fees and commissions for work done in the transfer of funds, the opening of letters of credit, the collection of cheques and the provision of guarantees. Charges would also be made for the use of bank funds for investment, but these monies would be regarded as a wage and further income would be derived from the establishment of individual companies by the bank. The bank and its depositors would then participate in the profits deriving from these companies.

As far as the international sphere is concerned one is left with the difficulties mentioned above. It is here that implications unpleasant for the West emerge. A large body of Islamic opinion holds that the way to overcome the international problems is to block access to the Islamic market by Western banks. This view is given no little impetus by the belief that investment in the Islamic countries by the Western banks is itself harmful to the countries themselves; and in a more extreme way the reverse investment of Islamic funds in Western countries is seen as being worthless and merely represents a drain on resources.

This concept of an international Islamic bank gives little consideration to the huge Western investment in a country like Saudi Arabia where more than 40 percent of the private industrial and commercial investment is foreign owned.

The Family of Al Saud

In considering the commercial world of Saudi Arabia it is essential to say something about the commercial position of the royal family. It is a fact that they are heavily engaged in business and this calls down on them all sorts of accusations. In the West we have rather tended to disapprove of people in such a position engaging in commerce and this disapproval has led the Al Saud to be more secretive than perhaps they might otherwise be. Nevertheless, there is a considerable amount of information available. They are very open about most of their holdings as is seen below and all this information is openly published in such government publications as the *Official Gazette*. The following short account is given, with great respect for the achievements of the Al Saud in other fields, as an explanation of some aspects of the development of the commercial world in the Kingdom.

The Al Saud's business involvement is to be expected from an historical point of view. The family success consequent upon the conquests of HM King Abdalaziz did not mean that the family became separated in any way from their traditional background. In the war soaked days of tribal Arabia it was an important feature of a ruler's life that he would have strong contacts with the merchant community. These were for the same reasons that such contacts were maintained by any medieval monarch in Europe. They provided sources of funds and a rudimentary foreign service as well. As far as Saudi Arabia was concerned, King Abdalaziz was no different and in his early days the Al Gosaibi family helped him in the east as the Alireza family was to do after his conquest of the Hijaz in the west. The whole social structure of the Peninsula had depended on an influence system for centuries; it did not simply stop because some foreigners discovered rather a lot of oil. What the oil did was enable the Al Saud to pay off their debts.

Expression to this way of using the merchant community is given by the position of the Foreign Ministry itself in Jiddah. In the beginning the Al Saud in Riyadh used merchants in the east as stated, but the idea of a foreign service needed development. What the Al Gosaibi could report about the outside world from their contacts in the Gulf was limited. After the conquest of the Hijaz the Al Saud was faced with a much larger involvement with foreigners. Jiddah's position as the trading city made it natural that foreigners should be kept there. Native xenophobia helped the feeling that foreigners should be kept at something of a distance. Thus to this day the diplomatic community is in general still confined to the main trading city of the country rather than its capital.

Involvement with the world of commerce, the payment of debts, and a change of financial position which let the Al Saud be lenders rather than borrowers, automatically led them to participate in the business life of the country.

This process is enhanced by the way the older generations regarded the wealth of the country as theirs. The concept that wealth belongs to the country rather than its rulers is really a new idea, and not only in the Kingdom of Saudi Arabia. In this context the Al Saud have had a very considerable influence on the merchant community. However, their overt presence mainly appears as participation in individual enterprises rather than as partners in Saudi Arabia Ltd.

Almost two hundred individual princes and some princesses openly engage in commercial activity, and, despite several somewhat half-hearted regal attempts to stop it, have registered their interests quite publicly. The doyen of royal businessmen is HRH Prince Abdullah b. Faisal, the eldest son of the late king. He has always been interested in business and never participated greatly in purely government activity. Other princes who take a major role in commerce are really rather few; perhaps the following are the main ones: HRH Khalid Abdullah Abdalrahman, HRH Khalid Saud Muhammad, HRH Khalid Turki Abdalaziz Al Turki, HRH Muhammad Fahd Abdalaziz, HRH Nawwaf Adbalaziz, and HRH Salman Abdalaziz.

This overt commercial interest involves a very small proportion of the family as a whole. Two hundred is only ten percent of the estimated total number of the Al Saud. It should be remembered that the large size of the Al Saud is not exceptional. It is their fame as the royal family which has obscured the fact for most Westerners that many Saudi families are a thousand strong or more.

In the area of Saudi Arabia Ltd the workings of the traditional influence are at their most interesting. Here trade in its broadest sense is used to maintain the influence of government itself, both within the Al Saud and between them and the outside world. It is important to remember that it has been inevitable that the recent historical tribal influence system where rule was a matter of hegemony was bound to be continued. Access to enormous wealth occurred only just over thirty years ago and there has been little enough time for the evolution of what are now seen as more apposite institutions. In fact progress in this area has been very rapid. A ministerial system has been created as well as the bureaucracy to go with it; the latter's impenetrability has tended to enhance the old way of doing things as the old influence system is often effective in getting round the bureaucracy. It is possibly this that the late King Faisal meant when he said all would be well with the Kingdom when the Saudis learnt how to queue.

As far as the Al Saud in business are concerned there is no doubt that these factors have led to a large number of undercover commercial operations. Many of these will have been motivated by politics rather than purely commercial considerations and as such will have been carried out through the medium of middlemen and frontmen.

These factors must affect the European or American businessman in his judgement of the Saudi Arabian marketplace. They will certainly effect the Saudi citizen with whom he is contemplating doing business and are thus essential to comprehension of the Arabian commercial world.

This book is about the businessmen of Saudi Arabia today but it is important to remember how their fathers operated until very recent times; a matter of what business methods were like only four or five decades ago. In a country that really only exported hides, dates and specie from the west and dates, horses and donkeys from the east, the main concern of business was importation.

The selection of families and companies for inclusion in this work has been governed by the need to provide as comprehensive a picture as possible of the commercial part of Saudi life. Of necessity the choice has had to be rather arbitrary at times due to the availability of informants and the constraints of time. However, the author has tried to cover as wide a variety of businesses as he could, both in terms of type and size, whilst at the same time including examples of other families with the purpose of illustrating the structure of Arabian society and its Islamic nature. It is hoped that these factors will be helpful to the Western businessman in his comprehension of the Saudi market place. The author wishes to apologise for the omission of many families who will quite rightly feel that they should have been included. He asks that they should communicate with him so that these omissions can be rectified in future editions.

The Merchant Families and their Business Interests

The Family of Abbar

SALIH AL ABBAR

MAHMUD
under HRH Faisal b. Abdalaziz Al Saud, who later became King of Saudi Arabia, he was with HRH Abdullah b. Faisal Deputy Governor of the Kingdom before the present form of government was established

HASAN

AHMAD
Ex-Min. of the Interior began to work for his father's company in 1965 The Mahmud Salih Abbar Co.

ABDULLAH
Co-Chairman of the Abbar and Zainy Partnership

REDA
MA in Public Admin. Univ. of S. Calif. D.G. of Indust. Studies and Development Centre which in 1979 became the Saudi Consultancy Services company under chairmanship of Sh. Ghazi Algosaibi

ABDALRAHMAN
Vice Pres. Abbar and Zainy. BBA, Boston

GHAZI
Vice Pres. Abbar and Zainy. MBA, Harvard

WALID
graduate

ABDALAZIZ
MD, specialist in gynaccology. Dir. Maternity Hospital Jiddah and other positions in Min.

KHALID
UK experience as CPA B. Comm, Ayn Shams Univ. Egypt; asst. D.G. Western Region

MUHAMMAD
B.Sc. Civil Eng. Cairo

YAHYA
B.Sc. Electrical Eng. Cairo

DINA
RUSHA
AHMAD

FARIDA
IBRAHIM

MAHMUD

MAHMOUD SALIH ABBAR CO.

Head office P.O.Box 481 Jiddah
Telephone 6450143, 6450296, 6457354, 6457353
Telex 401790 ABARJO SJ
Cable address ABBAR
Subsidiary offices Mecca, Medina, Yanbo, Riyadh
Board of Directors Chairman Sh .Mahmoud Salih Al Abbar, Ch. Executive Sh. Khalid Ahmad Al Abbar, Sh. Ahmad Mahmoud Al Abbar, Sh. Abdullah Mahmoud Al Abbar, Sh. Reda Mahmoud Al Abbar.
Company History Began 22 years ago. Founded in Jiddah by M S Abbar.
Business Activities The company operates over the whole field of electrical matters. These activities cover trading, especially in household appliances and central air conditioning machinery, maintenance and installation. They represent White Westinghouse and their technical capabilities extend to turbine installation. The company, called ABBAR for short, is a leader in their area and their energetic use of management skills enhances their wide experience which has been accumulated over many years. They are particularly well known in all areas of refrigeration including refrigerated transport, cold-stores and rooms. They are shareholders in the Saudi British Bank.
Bankers Saudi Faransi, Jazira Bank, First National City, National Commercial Bank, Saudi Cairo Bank.

The Family of Zainy

An old family of the Hijaz, Wadi Fatima.

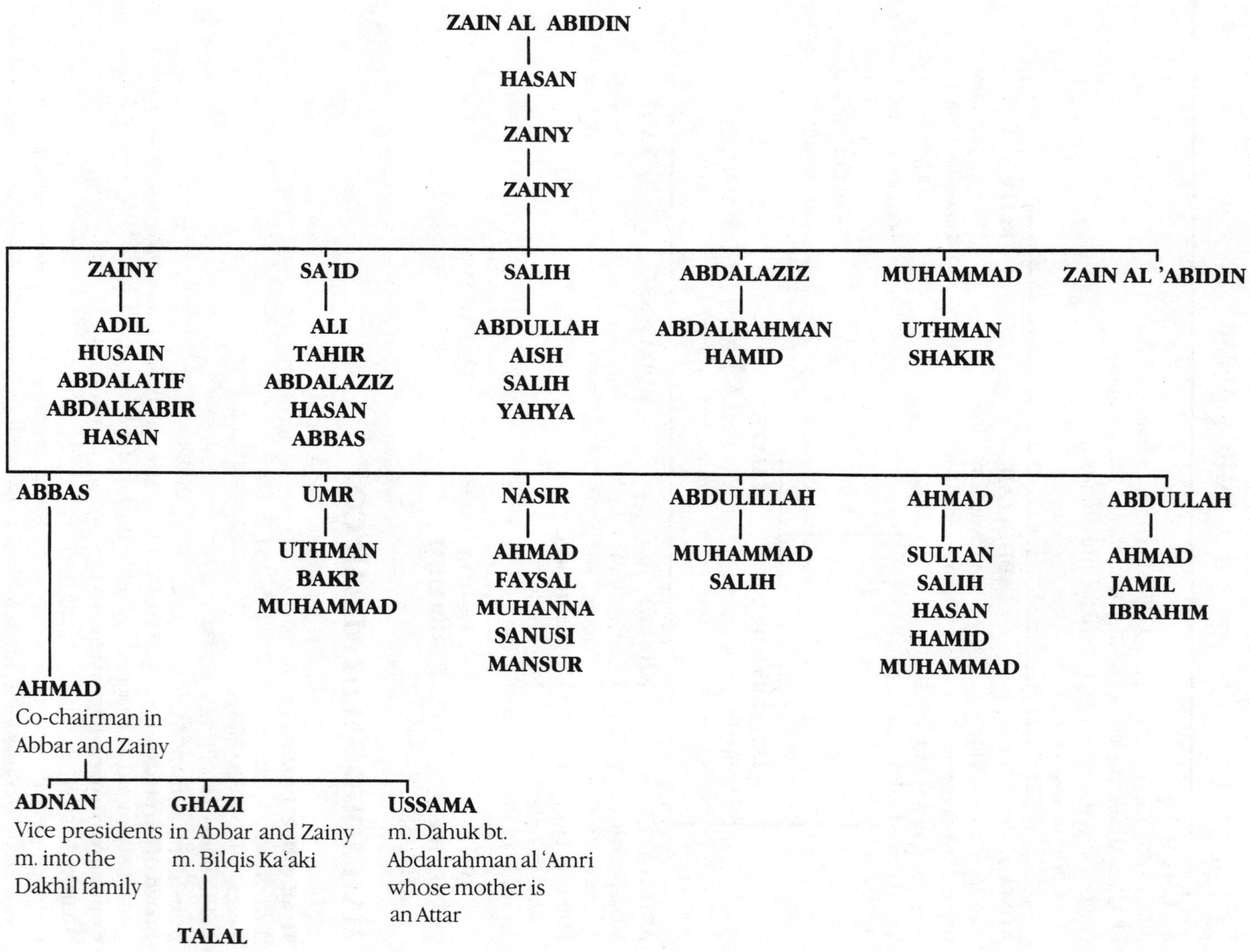

ABDULLAH ABBAR AND AHMAD ZAINY

Address PO Box 461, Jiddah
Telephone 6450143, 6450296, 6457354, 6457353
Telex 401062 MOTSIM SJ
There are offices in London (30, New Bond St, W1, tel. 4938853, tlx. 28583 MUTSIM), Riyadh, Dammam, Al Kharj, Al Qatif, Buraidah, Dhahran, Hofuf, Jizan, Jubail, Mecca, Medina, Ras al Khafji, Tabuk, Tai'if and Yanbu.
The partnership is a close one between Abdullah Abbar and Ahmad Zainy. It is one of the largest traders in the Kingdom. Founded some forty years ago it has grown enormously. Today as well as foodstuffs, household and electrical appliances, they are engaged in manufacturing, shipping, transport, construction and oil industry services.
However, at the time of writing, this concern is one of those Saudi businesses where the entrepreneurial flair and business acumen of the founding partners does not appear to have been sustained by the younger generation.
Divisions include:
Abbar and Zainy Clearing Agency
Abbar and Zainy Cold Stores
Abbar and Zainy Computer Division
Abbar and Zainy Electrical Appliances Division
Abbar and Zainy Equipment Division
Abbar and Zainy Food Division
Abbar and Zainy French Bakery Systems
Abbar and Zainy Pipes and Maintenance Division
Abbar and Zainy Ship Chandling
Abbar and Zainy Sodexco Catring Co. Ltd.
Abbar and Zainy US Beef
Arab International Gas and Transportation Co. Ltd. (London)
Azco Travel
Al Aziziah Dairy Ltd.
Bahra Hydroponics Farm
Chiyoda Petrostar Ltd.
Ecology and Environment of Saudi Arabia Ltd.
Ice Cream and Dairy Products Cortina Ltd.
Industry Services Co. of Saudi Arabia
International Technology (Saudi Arabia) Ltd.
National Tahina and Tin Co.
Ogem Saudi Arabian Construction Co. Ltd.
Petro Trade Co. Ltd.
Petro Transport Co. Ltd.
Petrostar Co. LTd.
Saudi Aviation Services Co. Ltd.
Saudi Meat Factory
Saudi Multina Gas and Transportation Co. Ltd.
Star Navigation Ltd.
Saudi Security and Technical Services Co. Ltd.
U.A.A. Decor Division
United Arab Agencies
Wadi Fatima Poultry Farm

The Family of Abdalkarim

Originate from Harma near Hawtat al Sudair of Najd.

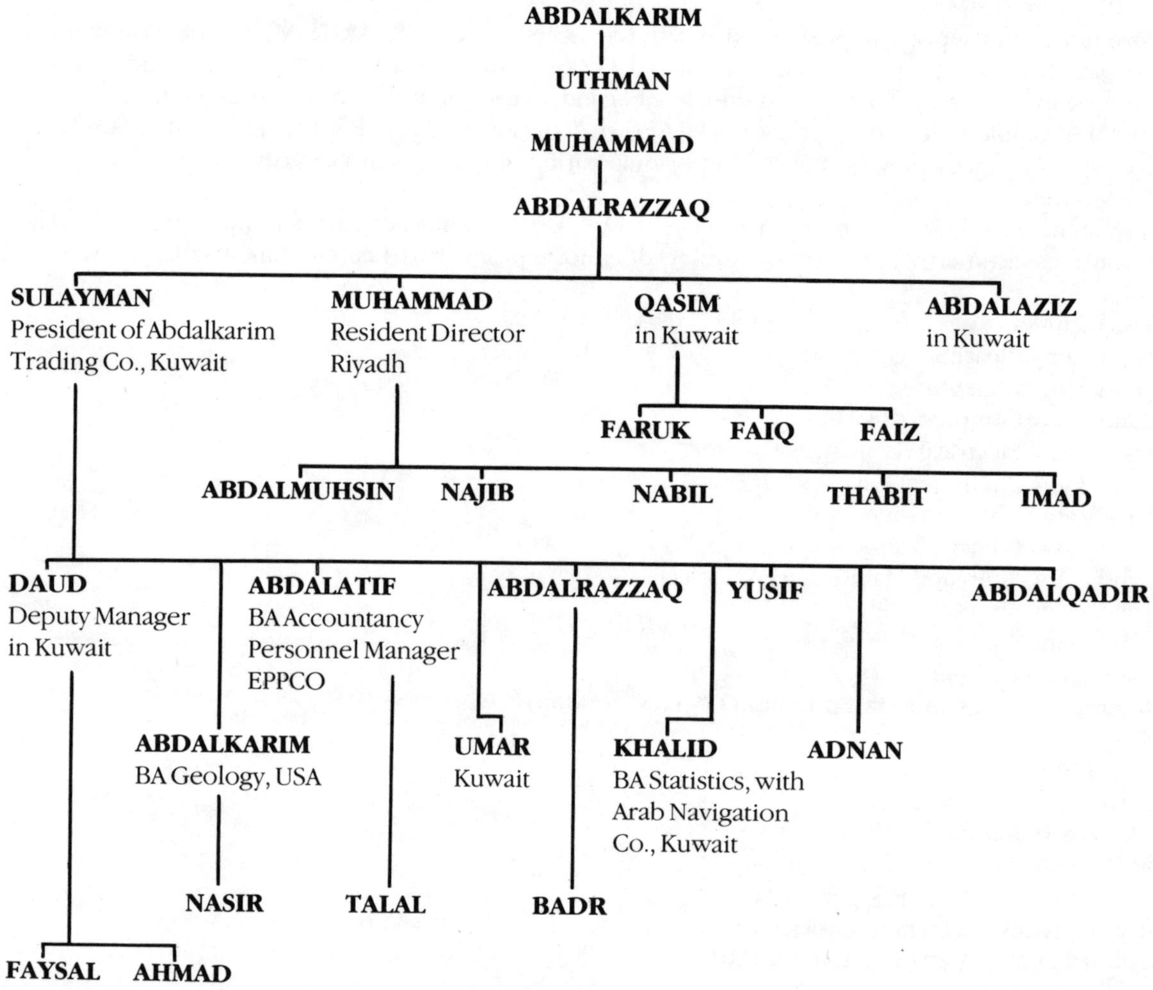

SULAIMAN A R A K AND PARTNERS CO.

Address in Saudi Arabia PO Box 4066, Riyadh
Telephone 4029454
Telex 202132 ATHLEH
Cable address ATHLEH
Head office Sulaiman Al Abdalkarim and Brothers Co., PO Box 675 Kuwait, tel. 432344, 431957, tlx 2259 OBTEH KT, cable OBTEH
Subsidiary offices Riyadh as above; Dubai: Al Abdalkarim Trading Co., PO Box 4641 Dubai, UAE, tel. 221851
Company history This company is an interesting example of the mobility of people in the Peninsula and shows a Saudi business concern that has become largely expatriate. Naturally there has been a similar flow in the other direction. The company is concerned with the importation and distribution of foodstuffs.

The Family of Abdalmajeed

The old family of Mecca who for centuries have been responsible as guides (Mutawafiyin) to pilgrims making the Hajj (Pilgrimage) to the Holy Cities. This honoured profession is maintained by them to this day through Sh. Mahmud b. Ibrahim.

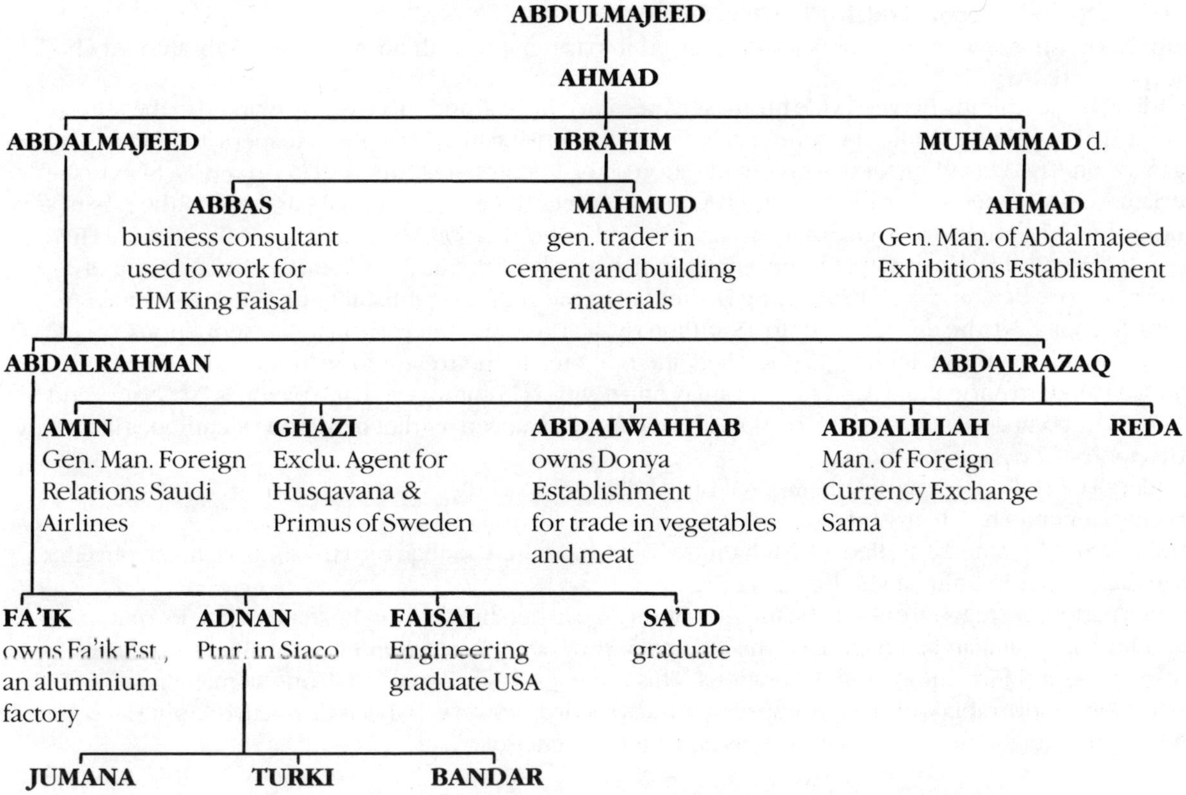

SIACO. SAUDI INTERNATIONAL CORPORATION

Address head office P.O.Box 4571 Jiddah
Telephone 6671691, 6671692
Telex 401501 SITIFO SJ, 401096 GENERY SJ, 401806 TRANSCO SJ
Cable address KAZADYOU
Subsidiary offices
SITIFO King Abdalaziz St., Jiddah, tlx. 32088 SAMESCO Riyadh
Proprietor Sh. Adnan Abdalrahman Abdalmajeed in partnership with Sh. Muhammad Ibrahim Al Hied.
Company History
Sh. Adnan began gaining his very wide business experience in 1960 and successively worked in the Ministry of Information gaining familiarity with broadcasting, advertising, marketing newspapers and fairs organisation. This last culminated in his organisation of the Jiddah Trade Fair in 1975, 76 and 77. Siaco itself specializes in all aspects of marketing and representation and the international fairs side of the business is handled by Sitifo. Sh. Adnan is Chairman of Samesco and he holds a 50% share with Sh. MuhammadAl Hied. The Saudi Medical Services Co. Ltd. specializes in the supply of medical equipment, the servicing of Government tenders, and operates a Flying Doctor Service as well as establishing specialized hospitals and clinics. Its capital is to be raised shortly to 45 million riyals. The Saudi International Transportation Co. Ltd., Siatraco, is chaired by Sh. Muhammad Al Hied and operates in the freight forwarding field. The Saudi American Modern Agricultural Co. Ltd. is a joint venture with a US company; participation is 70% Saudi and 30% US. The company is established to operate in the most advanced market-gardening techniques including hydroponics. The Saudi partners are:
President H.R.H. Prince Mansur bin Mishaal bin Abdalaziz al Sa'ud
Director General Sh. Adnan Abdalmajeed
Members: Sh. Muhammad al Hied, Sh. Muhammad bin Ghazi, Sh. Abdullah bin Ghazi, Sh. Hamdan bin Ghazi, Sh. Abdalaziz bin Ibrahim al Hied
The two partners of Siaco are also in business in Rome in partnership with Dr. Enzo Floramco in a company called Itasco, the Italian Saudi Co. Ltd. This company supplies construction materials, steel structures for turnkey jobs, and furnishings and decorations. This commercial undertaking is one of many go-ahead concerns in Saudi Arabia with a really impressive track record. However, what is distinctive about Siaco is a modern and enlightened approach to ideas and a terrific energy.

The Family of Aboubshait

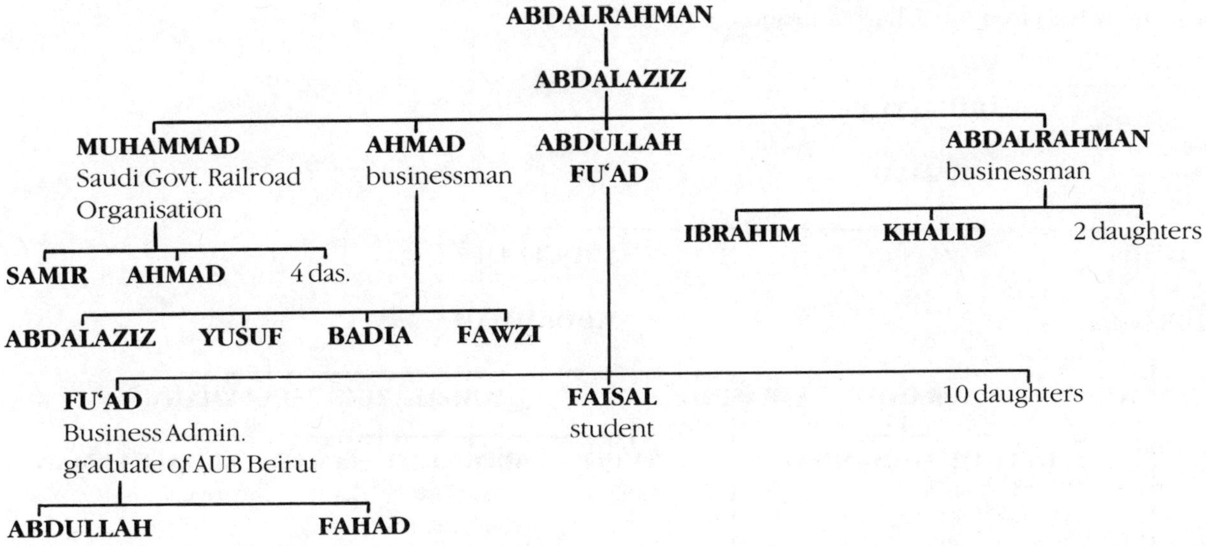

THE ABDULLA FOUAD GROUP OF COMPANIES

Address PO Box 257, Dammam
Telephone 8321360, 8324400, 8327215
Telex 601027 FOUAD SJ

Abdullah Fouad began his commercial career in the construction field at Ras Tanura in 1947. Continuing his association with ARAMCO, he entered into Tapline contracts in 1948 and confined himself to this type of work until 1963 when he began to establish the joint venture based commercial enterprise which became established as the Abdulla Fouad Corporation in 1971.

The Corporation has wide real estate interests throughout the world and is responsible for a varied and diverse investment portfolio.

The joint venture interests of the Corporation are listed under Tamimi and Fouad (q.v.).

The Corporation itself consists of the following companies and divisions: Service and Supply Division, Fouad Travel Agency, Commercial Division (heavy equipment and construction material), Abdulla Fouad Hospital, the Abdulla Fouad and Abdulla Busbate Co. Ltd. (FABCO, established 1976, suppliers of PVC pipe and paper manufacturers), Electrical and Instrumentation Division, Engineering and Contracting Division, National Industries Company (founded 1970, with Abdulla al Naimi, to manufacture uniforms), and the Aviation Division.

The Family of Abu Nayyan

The family hails from the Dhurma area to the west of Riyadh

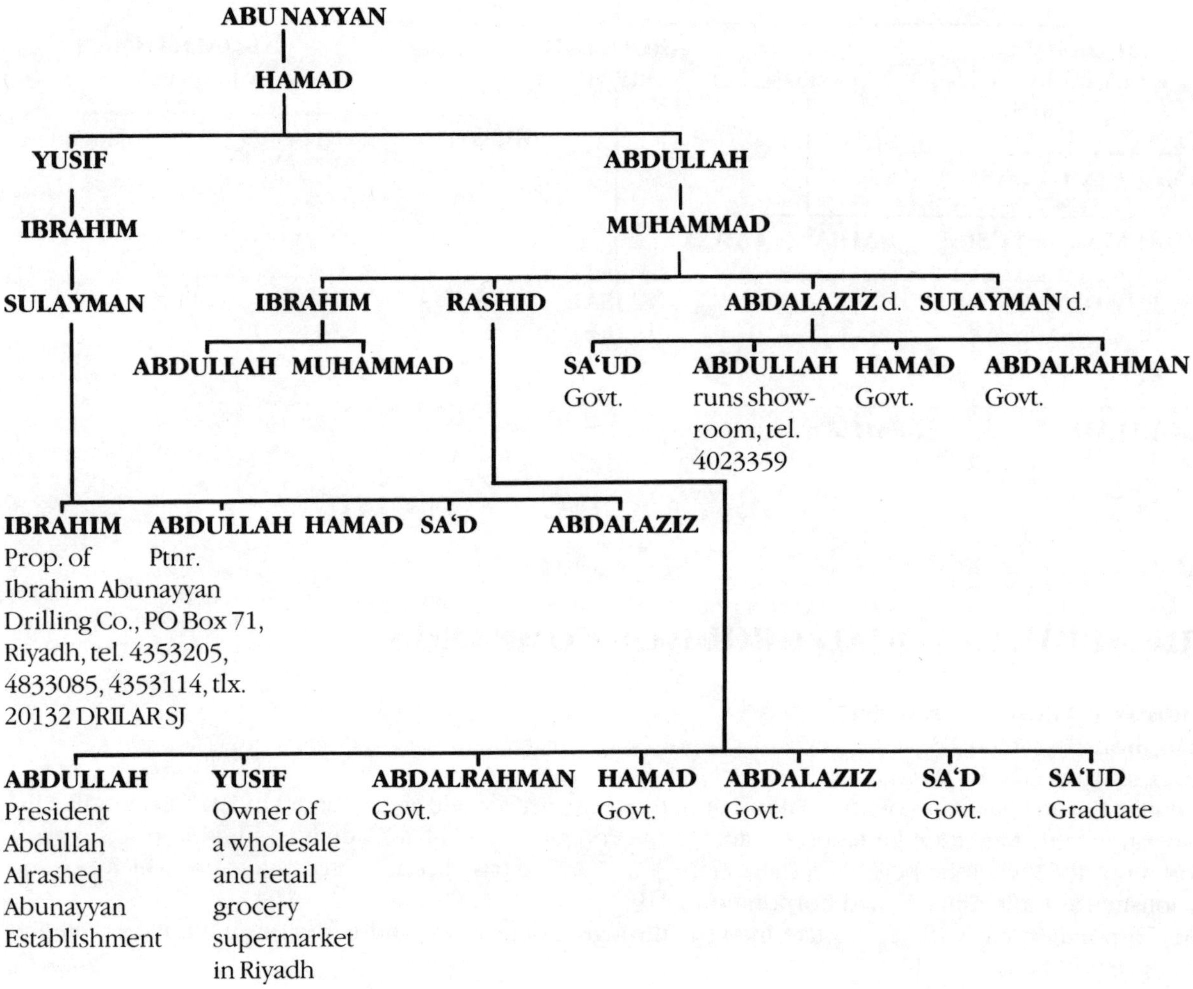

ABDULLAH AL RASHED ABUNAYYAN ESTABLISHMENT

Address head office P.O.Box 321 Riyadh
Telephone 4834769, 4023359
Telex 20201 MOON SJ
Cable address ABUNAYAN
Subsidiary offices Jiddah P.O.Box 3960, tel. 6436306
Proprietor Sh. Abdullah Al Rashed
Company History
Sh. Abdullah gained his commercial experience trading for his father in foodstuffs and travelled to Syria, Bahrain and Kuwait. The present company was started in 1954 and specializes in agricultural machinery in which field most demand is for water pumps and diesel engines.
Business activity The company operates an exclusive agency for Puma Bamford of the UK and non-exclusive agencies for Burnett Atlanta International of UK, BKB Electric Co. of UK, GFA of Brussels, Redwood of Italy and Compressor Bernard and Luchard of France. In conjunction with Pump Guinard of France they are establishing a joint venture to manufacture pumps in the Kingdom.
Bankers Saudi British Bank, National Commercial Bank, Riyadh Bank, Saudi Hollandi Bank.

ABDULLAH AL RASHID ABUNAYYAN ESTABLISHMENT

Address head office Riyadh
Activities Owned by Abdullah A Abunayyan the company was established in 1964 and has a branch in Jiddah (PO Box 4960, tel. 6436306). It deals in agricultural and horticultural machinery and equipment, industrial machinery and components

IBRAHIM ABUNAYYAN ORGANISATION (TC PIPING DIVISION)

Address head office Riyadh
Telephone 4763876
Telex 202463 AIIS SJ
Branches Jiddah, PO Box 8522, tel. 6651763, 6602668, tlx. 402076 MECCO SJ; al Khobar, PO Box 424, tel. 8642538, 8648110, tlx. 670206
Activities The company supplies carbon steel pipes and fittings, valves, pre-fabricated steel fittings, ductile iron pipes, fittings and valves.

The Family of Abu Zinada

The family has been in Jiddah for centuries and some members still carry out their traditional function as auctioneers and superintendents in the vegetable and fruit market. It is possible that the Abdullah Abu Zinada, mentioned by Hogarth as being a slave of the Dhawi Zaid Ashraf, took his eponym from this family.

- **MUHAMMAD**
  - **HUSAIN**
    - **MUHSIN**
      - **SALIH**
      - **ABBAS**
      - **ABDALRAHMAN**
      - **MUHAMMAD**
      - **HUSAIN**
      - **ABDALQADIR**
    - **HAMID**
      - **ABDALATIF** Dep. Man. in Saudi Airlines, Ex army, engineering degree, USA
        - **ZIAD**
        - **BADR**
        - **SHAHIR**
        - **SULTAN**
        - **FAYAD**
      - **ABDALAZIZ** MD, prof. at Riyadh Univ. Pres. Saudi Biological Soc., Vice Dean Faculty of Science. B. 1941
        - **NABIL**
        - **RAYID**
      - **ABDALWAHHAB** BA, Diploma in Journalism, Member of Board of Jiddah Chamber of Commerce and Asst. Dir. B. 1943
        - **BASSAM**
      - **MUHAMMAD HAMID** Engineering degree USA
    - **ABDULLAH** Market Superintendent and auctioneer
      - **TALAL**
      - **ISSAM**
      - **USSAMA**
      - **MU'TASIM**
      - **ISMAT**
- **ALI**
  - **MUHAMMAD ALI**
  - **MUHAMMAD SALIH** d. Presented the keys of Jiddah to HM King Abdalaziz
    - **ABDALRA'UF** Vice Pres. Jiddah Chamber of Commerce, prop. of Assoc. Agencies Ltd.
      - **HATIM**
    - **NURI** Clothes shop, Gen. merchant, PO Box 46, tel. 6422861, tlx. 401025 ZINADA
      - **SAMI**
  - **YUSIF**
  - **HASAN**
  - **MAHMUD**
  - **TAHIR**
  - **MUSTAFA**
    - **ALA**
    - **IMAD**

ASSOCIATED AGENCIES LTD

Associated Agencies Ltd
Address head office P.O.Box 419 Jiddah
Telephone 6422396, 6423430
Telex 401025 ZINADA SJ
Proprietor Sh. Abdalraouf Abu Zinada.
Company history Associated Agencies began as a travel agency and is still outside the IATA due to the restrictions imposed by that body on operations for more than one carrier. Today it operates as a holding company to control the various interests which have developed since its inception. Sh. Abdalraouf engages in the travel business through the Hatim Travel Agency, named after his son, and this is a wholly owned company (P.O.Box 419, tel. 6431882, 6431026, tlx.401025 ZINADA SJ). A second wholly owned company is the Arabian Establishment for Alimentary Products (P.O.Box 1450, Jiddah, tel. 6422429, tlx. 401025 JINADA SJ). In addition to these Sh. Abdalraouf has engaged in two joint ventures:

1. Al Sagr Insurance Co. of Saudi Arabia with the New Zealand Insurance Company, P.O.Box 419 Jiddah, tel. 6431820, tlx. 401025 ZINADA SJ.
2. The Jiddah Medical Center with Sh. Ibrahim Shaker, P.O.Box 419 Jiddah, tlx. 401025 ZINADA SJ, tel. 6453695, 6457324, 6690837/8/9/841/42.

Bankers Citibank, Banque du Liban et d'Outre Mer, Al Jazirah Bank, National Commercial Bank.

NURI ABUZINADA STORES

Address PO Box 46, Jiddah
Telephone 6422861
Telex 401025 ZINADA SJ
A retail concern selling readymade clothes, shoes, watches and clocks.

SAMI ABUZINADAH ELECTRONIC DIVISION

Address PO Box 5797
Telephone 6420310, 6446053, 6447309
Telex 400160 SAMI SJ
A business established in 1979 which deals in DIGICO business systems and computers.

ARABIAN FOODSTUFFS ESTABLISHMENT

Address PO Box 419, Jiddah
Telephone 6601368, 6422496
Telex 401025 ZINADA SJ
This company is owned by Abdalra'uf Abuzinada and deals in foodstuffs, canned goods, fruit juices and drinks.

ASSOCIATED AGENCIES LTD

Address PO Box 419, Jiddah
Telephone 6422429, 6423430, 6422496
Telex 401025 ZINADA SJ
This company is owned by Abdalra'uf Abuzinada and has branches in Riyadh, Dammam, Yanbu and Jizan. It deals in building materials and insurance.

AL HANA TRADING ESTABLISHMENT

Address PO Box 7126, Jiddah
Telephone 6659920
Telex 400476 HANA SJ
Owned by Muhammad Muhsin Abuzinada, this company, operating as decorating contractors, was formed in 1979.

The Family of Adham

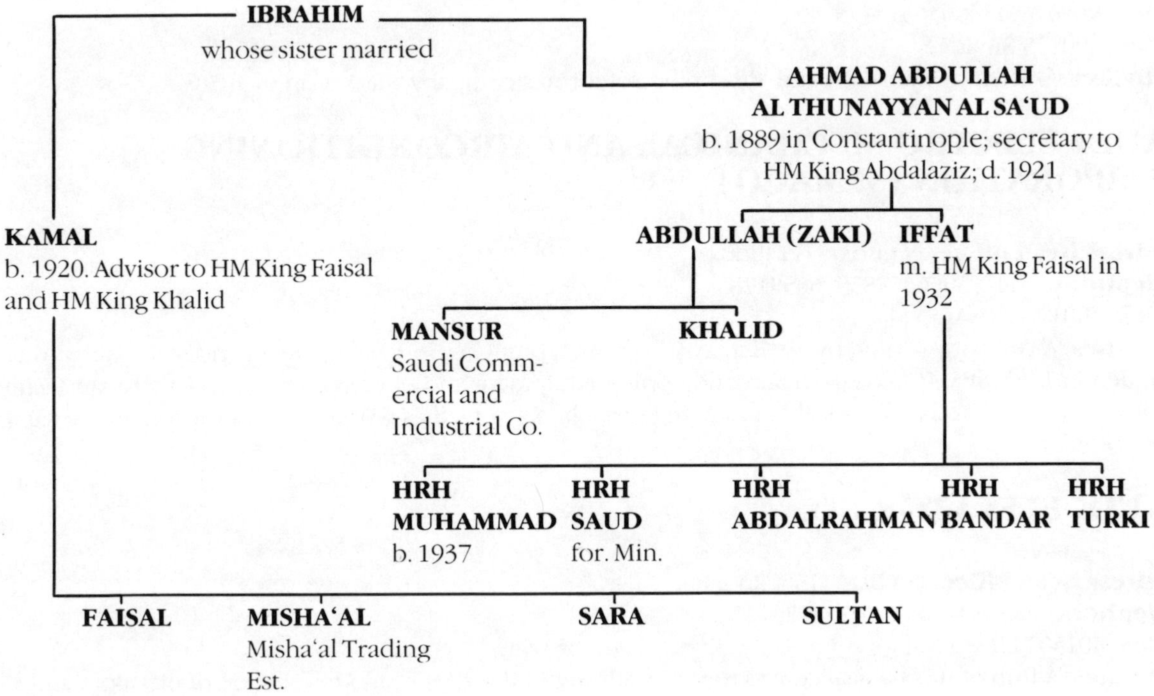

ARABIAN CONTRACTING ASSOCIATION ARCAN

Address head office PO Box 1528, Jiddah
Telephone 6424325, 6429864
Telex 401201 ARCAN SJ
Activities With a branch office in Riyadh, this company was formed in 1975. It is owned by Sh. Kamal Adham and his sons and is engaged in the contracting business, representation internationally, trading and as general agents.

SAUDI DEVELOPMENT AND COMMERCIAL CO. LTD.

Address head office PO Box 5443, Jiddah
Telephone 6421550, 6433190
Telex 401183 SDCC SJ
Activities A company formed in 1974 which is owned by Sh. Kamal Adham with Ali Abdullah Buqshan (q.v.) and Abdalaziz Abdullah Al Sulaiman (q.v.). It is in business as insurance agents and brokers, to act as real estate agents and as an investment company.

SEVEN-UP BOTTLING PLANT

Address head office PO Box 660, Jiddah
Telephone 6513400, 6514448
Telex 400125 SEVEN SJ
Activities Owned by Kamal Adham, this brand soft drinks company was set up in 1958.

SAUDI ELECTRO MECHANICAL AND AIRCONDITIONING CORPORATION (SEMACO)

Address head office PO Box 5411, Jiddah
Telephone 6427950, 6657855, 6658128
Telex 400170 SEMACO SJ
Activities A company owned by Sh. Kamal Adham with branches in Riyadh, Mecca and Medina that was founded in 1967. SEMACO deals in air conditioning equipment and operates an automobile repair facility. They are electrical and mechanical engineering consultants as well as working as contractors in the same areas of interest.

SAUDI ELEVATOR CO.

Address head office PO Box 1150, Jiddah
Telephone 6422344, 6423402, 6425935
Telex 401502 LIFTCO SJ
Activities A firm of mechanical contractors specialising in the supply and installation of elevators and escalators. The company is owned by Sh. Kamal Adham and Fu'ad Rizk.

SAUDI COMMERCIAL AND INDUSTRIAL CO. (BUILDING PRODUCTS DIVISION)

Address head office PO Box 349, Jiddah
Telephone 6823680, 6823681, 6532148
Telex 403654 SCICBP SJ
Activities A company owned by Sh. Kamal Adham and Mansur Al Thunayan with branches in Riyadh, Dammam and Yanbu
They deal in adhesives, building materials, additives for concrete, bitumen and asphalt, fibreglass, fencing, decorating materials, gypsum products, domestic paints and insulating materials, pipes and pipe fittings. They are manufacturers and suppliers of polythene and deal in pumps, pumping equipment, roofing materials, security equipment and scaffolding.

UNITED TRADING AND CONTRACTING ESTABLISHMENT

Address head office PO Box 4080, Jiddah
Telephone 8653271
Telex 401132 AREEN SJ
Activities A company owned by Mansur Abdullah (Zaki) Al Thunayan, dealing in aluminium products, building materials, sanitary ware, pipes and pipe fittings. The company also acts as commission agents and contractors.

MISHAAL TRADING ESTABLISHMENT (MATEST)

Address head office PO Box 7669, Jiddah
Telephone 6534315, 6672392, 6532676
Telex 401614 ARINCO SJ
Activities Established in 1978, the company deals in aluminium products, industrial chemicals, building materials, electronic equipment and components, educational equipment, fire fighting equipment, cassettes and tapes, confectionery, and pre-fabricated building systems. They also act as automobile distributors and dealers, as contractors for air conditioning and cleaning, sign writers and advertising, and as commission agents.

AREEN TRAVEL BUREAU

Address head office PO Box 266, Jiddah
Telephone 6433125-8
Telex 401132 AREEN SJ
Activities With branches in Dhahran and Riyadh, this travel agency business is owned by Mishaal Kamal Adham.

PHILIPPINE COMMERCIAL CENTRE

Address head office PO Box 8068, Jiddah
Telephone 6653356
Telex 400820 PCC JEDDAH SJ
Activities The company supplies products from the Philippines such as foodstuffs, manpower services, maintenance and construction. It is jointly owned by Mishaal Kamal Adham and Sh. Khalid Tahir.

The Family of Aggad

Originally from Bir Saba, Acre, Nablus and Jaffa.

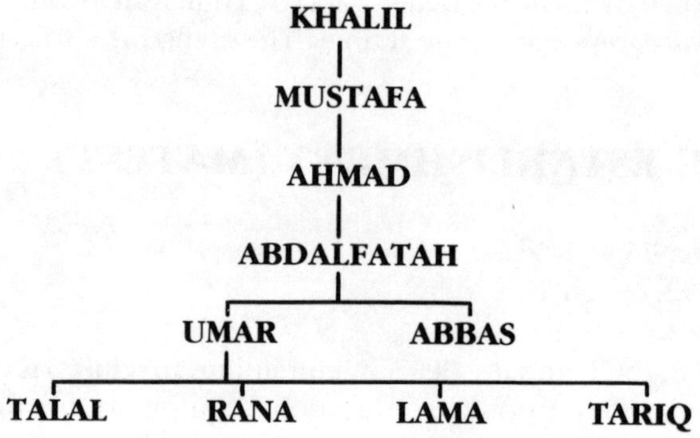

AGGAD INVESTMENT COMPANY

Address head office P.O.Box 2256 Riyadh
Telephone 24447, 22222
Telex 200276 AGGAD SJ
Cable address AGGAD
Proprietor Omar A Aggad, a founder and Board Member of the Saudi British Bank.
Bankers Arab Bank and City Bank.
The Aggad Investment Company is a limited partnership which operates the interests of Omar Aggad in the following enterprises:
1. Engineering Projects and Products Company (EPPCO)
Head office P.O.Box 987 Riyadh, tel. 22222, tlx. 201022 SJ, cables EPPCOL
Branches: Jiddah P.O.Box 1502, tel. 22222, Dammam P.O.Box 450, tel. 22222
Ownership: Sh. Ibrahim Juffali 60%
Sh. Ahmad Juffali, Chairman
Mr. Omar Aggad, Managing Director 40%
The company is the major one in the telecommunications field with a turnover of 220 million riyals annually.
2. Saudi Plastic Products Co.Ltd.(SAPPCO)
P.O.Box 2828 Riyadh, tel. 4041900, tlx. 201025 SAPPCO SJ
Sales office: Jiddh, tel. 28890
Ownership: the Partners
H.R.H. Prince Abdullah Al Faisal Al Sa'ud
Aggad Investment Company
Olayan Financing Company
Saleh and Abdalaziz Bahussain Company
Suliman Abdalmohsen Aba Nomay
Nasser Muhammad Alsaleh
Hassan Mishary Alhussein
Abbas Abdalfattah Aggad

The company, formed in 1969, manufactures PVC piping for all applications in sizes of 16mm to 400mm. SAPPCO also produces polystyrene insulation boards for industrial and domestic buildings, cold stores, air conditioned premises and refrigerated transport.

3. Arabian Plastic Manufacturing Company Ltd. (APLACO)
P.O.Box 6193 Riyadh, tel. 4013424, tlx. 201745 APLACO J, cables APLACO
Ownership: Partnership
Saudi Plastic Products Co. Ltd.
George Fischer Ltd. of Switzerland
Antone Anger of Austria
Chairman: Mr. Omar Aggad
APLACO was established in 1976 and produces and markets PVC fittings.

4. Arabian Technical Contracting Co. (ARTEC)
P.O.Box 2987 Riyadh, tel. 4780584, 4789573, tlx. 201372 ARTEC SJ
Ownership: Partners Mr. Omar Aggad, Chairman, and Mr. Fahd Hammad
The company was formed in 1973 and operates in two divisions. The Contracting Division specializes in road construction and the Industrial Division in terrazo and cement tiles, supply and laying of asphalt and the supply of cement blocks and kerb stones.

5. Aluminium Products Co. Ltd. (ALUPCO)
P.O.Box 2080 Dmmam, tel. 24934, 20789, tlx. 601148 ALUPCO SJ, 601271 ALUPCO SJ, cables ALUPCO
The company is controlled by a Board of Directors:
Mr. Omar Aggad, Chairman
Sh. Hashim S Hashim, Man. Director.
Sh. Suliman S Olayan, Member

6. Health Water Bottling Co. Ltd. (NISSAH)
P.O.Box 2948 Riyadh, tel. (office) 33300, (plant) 57512, tlx. 201102 NISSAH SJ, cable HEALTHWATER
The company produces bottled water in its own bottles in capacities of half a litre and one and a half litres. The company distributes its own product both throughout the Kingdom and in the export field, though it does act through agents on occasion. Present expansion involves the erection of a fruit juice plant to implement the licences already held by the company.
Ownership: the Partners
Abdalrahman Al Murshid
Aggad Investment Co.
Olayan Saudi Holdings Co. Ltd.
Muhammad Abdalrahman Al Fraih (q.v.)
Hiram Charl Corm
H.E. Abdalrahman Al Shaikh
H.E. Naser Hamad Al Mangour
Muhammad Abdulrahman Al Hamidi
Sulaiman Abdulrahman Al Saleh
Mazen Ibrahim Al Angari
Ossama Omar Fageh
Ramzi Habib Sanbar

7. Steel Products Co. Ltd. (STEPCO)
P.O.Box 4930 Riyadh, tel. 24447
Ownership: the Partners
Aggad Investment Co.
E.A. Juffali and Bros.
Korf Industry and Handel
Ibrahim Touq
The company was formed in 1976 and produces wiremesh for reinforcement.

8. Prefabricated Building Co. Ltd. (MABCO)
P.O.Box 1549 Riyadh, tel. 39486, 30653, tlx. 201364 MABCO SJ, cables PRECAST
MABCO was formed in 1975 and produces precast concrete elements for housing projects and other projects of a constructional or industrial nature.
Ownership: the Partners
H.R.H. Prince Fahd Ibn Salman Ibn Abdalaziz Al Sa'ud
H.R.H. Prince Abdalaziz Ibn Sattam Ibn Abdalaziz Al Sa'ud
Sh. Hassan Mishari Al Hussein
Al Aggad Investment Co.
Sh. Omar Abdulkader Faqih (q.v.)
Sh. Hamza Muhammad Boggarry
Sh. Muhammed Abdalrahman Al Fraih (q.v.)
Sh. Umran Muhammed Umran (q.v.)
Sh. Rashed Abdulrahman Al Rashed
Sh. Abdullah Abdalmuhsin Al Tuwaijri
Sh. Abdullah Ibrahim Al Hudaithi
Nefinnco B.V.
Partek B.V.
9. Saudi International Petroleum Carriers Ltd. (SIPCA)
P.O.Box 5572 Riyadh, tel. 26940, tlx. 201709 TEXACO SJ
SIPCA was established in 1977 and is engaged in the transportation of petroleum and petroleum products and tanker chartering.
Ownership: the partners
Aggad Investment Co.
Sh. Naser Al Saleh
Texaco Marine Investment Co.
10. Laminated Fabrics Manufacturing Co. Ltd. (LAMINCO)
P.O.Box 221 Riyadh, tel. 22818
This company was established in 1977 and produces thermo-plastic films, unsupported and thermoplastic coated sub-tracks.
Ownership:
Aggad Investment Co.
Sh. Muhammed Abdalrahman Al Fraih (q.v.)
Hassan Deeb Hamdan

11. Saudi Arabian Belgian Construction Co. (SABECO)
P.O.Box 4929 Riyadh, tel. 68545, tlx. 200142 SABECO SJ
Established in 1977 SABECO operates in building and civil engineering construction.
Ownership: the Partners
Compagnie d'Enterprises (CFE) 40%
Sh. Hassan Mishari 14%
Omar Aggad 14%
Abdullah Baksh 10%
Omran Muhammed Omran 10%
Mahammed Charara 4%
Abdalmuhsin Abdalaziz Tuwaijri 4%
Abdalmuhsin Abdullah Tuwaijri 4%
Brussels Office c/o CFE 7, rue Belliaro, 1040 Bruxelles.
12. Saudi SAC Contracting Co. Ltd. (SAUDI SAC)
P.O.Box 9376 Riyadh, tel. 67545
Saudi SAC was founded in 1978 and is engaged in contracting for electrical, mechanical and sanitation projects.
The company also runs and maintains electrical and mechanical machinery.
Ownership: the partners
Aggad Investment Co.,25%
Sh. Naser Al Saleh.,15%
Al-Malika Importing and Contracting Co., Liberia.,60%
13. Hygienic Paper Factory
P.O.Box 3626 Riyadh, tel. 35102, tlx. 202192 FINE SJ
The company began in 1977 and manufactures a brand of face tissues called 'FINE'. A branch in Jiddah makes diapers, sanitary towels, toilet paper and napkins.
Ownership: the Partners
Aggad Investment Co.
Abdalaziz Shiha
Elia Nuqul.

The Family of Al Ajou

The family emigrated from Jaffa in Palestine where Ahmad Sa'id Al Ajou was in the glass business. This he continued in the Kingdom on his arrival over twenty-five years ago, at first purchasing from wholesalers and cutting the glass himself. Ahmad was followed by his sons, Sa'id and Abdulghani, and the family was able to open a branch in Riyadh. The two brothers now have their own separate businesses, exhibiting the sturdy independence that led to earlier success.

SA'ID AL AJOU

AHMAD

SA'ID
owner of Sa'id Al Ajou Trading Corporation

AKRAM
runs a glass company in Jordan

ISMA'IL
business man in Cairo

KHALIL

ABDALGHANI
owner of Abdalghani El Ajou Corporation
m. Raja bint Abdalrazzaq Darwazah

TAYSEER
business man in Beirut

IBRAHIM

MARWAN **MAHIR** **MU'IN** **MAHA** **MAIY** **MUNA**

GHASSAN
educated in London and Beirut, business administration graduate, USA

KARIM
graduate

ABDULGHANI EL AJOU CORPORATION

Head office P.O.Box 78 Riyadh
Telephone 4025709, 4025710, 4025749
Telex 201088 ELAJOU SJ
Cable address ELAJOUTRADE
Subsidiary offices
Al Jeel Trading Est. P.O.Box 5012, Riyadh
El Ajou Trading Agencies P.O.Box 3202, Riyadh
National Glass Factory P.O.Box 404, Riyadh, tlx. 201869 MODOFF
Proprietor Mr. Abdulghani El Ajou
Company History Established in 1962 as a sole proprietorship
Branches overseas London, Syria, Lebanon, North Yemen, Jordan
Local branches Jiddah, Al Khobar (Dammam) and Jubail
Business Activity Agents/distributors/representatives for

1. complete photographic equipment - cameras (conventional and instant), movie projectors 8mm and 16mm, sound and silent films, processing lab equipment, VTR and tapes
2. audio visual equipment and microfilm
3. complete ranges of office equipment - furniture, typewriters, calculators, planning boards, photo copiers, Diazo material and supplies, security paper-shredders
4. indoor decorative materials - tiles, wall tiles, false ceilings, lighting
5. complete range of medical and hospital supplies, including furniture and equipment

Agencies Polaroid, Cutter, Jewett, Stryker, Dietzgen, Airshied, Cinema Prod. of USA; Eiki, Otsuka, Toitu, Stitz, Canon, Meito Shokai, Ishimitsu of Japan; Coulter, Pye Unicam, Bell and Howell, Kardex of UK; Alpia of France; Roth and Webber, Kindermann, Linhof, Arri, Ideal, Triumph and Adler of Germany; Riffe of Italy; Neustedler of Austria; Eskofot & Nordisk of Denmark.
Capital 30 million US dollars
Turnover 100 million US dollars
Bankers Arab Bank, Citibank, National Commercial Bank, Saudi Cairo Bank.

SAID AL AJOU TRADING CORPORATION

Address head office P.O.Box 435 Jiddah
Telephone 6434054, 6434641
Telex 401646 MODIRD SJ
Cable address AJOUCO
Subsidiary offices
Modern Trading Agencies, Jiddah, tel. 33775
Glass and Mirror National Factories, Jiddah, tel. 6420245
Saudi Arabian Trading & Resources, Jiddah, tel. 6455618
Nibal Trading Corporation, Riyadh, tel. 4839835
Said al Ajou Trading Corporation, Al Khobar, tel. 8641237
Proprietor Said Ahmad al Ajou, who is a shareholder in the Saudi Cairo Bank, the Arab Bank, the City Bank and the Riyadh Bank.
Company History
The Said al Ajou Corportion was established in 1975 and comprises three main divisions representing a consolidation and continuation of the original Al Ajou busines interests. These consist of Contracting (ARCON), the Electronics Division, which handles television, radios and office equipment, machinery and furniture, and thirdlythe Glass Division, which today is the largest importer and wholesaler of glass in the Kingdom.The Corporation represents Glass Export of Czechoslovakia and French and Belgian companies in the same field. They also act for Celotex false ceilings and tiles of the USA. They are agents for Graetz Televisions from West Germany, Marantz audio equipment from the USA, J.V.C. of Japan for audio and video equipment and Imperial of West Germany for photocopiers. At the moment the Corporation is investigating the contracting market and investing considerable resources in the acquisition of the best technical expertise to enable them to compete for most major Government tenders.
Bankers Arab Bank, Saudi Cairo Bank, City Bank, Riyadh Bank, Jazirah Bank.

ABDALGHANI AL AJOU CORPORATION

Office PO Box 6243, Jiddah
Telephone 6423321, 6422764, 6517760
Telex 400306 AJOU SJ
Activities The head office is in Riyadh and there is another branch in al Khobar. The company was formed in 1962 and deals in refrigeration and air conditioning equipment, office, hospital ad medical equipment, photographic equipment, computers and business systems, furniture and construction equipment. It is owned by Abdalghani Al Ajou.

SAID AL AJOU TRADING CORPORATION

Address head office PO Box 435, Jiddah
Telephone 6471911, 6475412
Telex 401694 SAJOU SJ
Activities The company was formed in 1976 and is owned by Said and Ghassan Al Ajou. It carries in prticular the following brands: JUC, Graetz, Shure Co., Koss and Wisi. The company is engaged as suppliers of electronic equipment and components, radios, televisions and video systems. There are branches in Riyadh, al Khobar, Dammam, Yanbu and Mecca.

The Family of Alireza

Followers of Ibn Al As who were forced off the Iranian plateau during the time of Shi'a supremacy under the Safavids. Alireza returned to Hijaz some two hundred years ago.

- **AHMAD**
  - **MUHAMMAD**
    - **ZAINAL**
      - **ALIREZA**
        - by his first wife
          - **ALI AKBAR** stayed in Iran. Descendants mainly in Bahrein and Kuwait → *1*
          - **ZAINAL** c. 1833-1929. Moved to Jiddah c. 1845 Co-founder of Haji Abdullah Alireza Co. Descendants in Jiddah → *2*
          - **ZAYNAB**
        - by his second wife
          - **ABDULLAH** c. 1853-1932. Governor of Jiddah 1919-32. Co-founder of Haji Abdullah Alireza Co. Descendants in Jiddah → *3*
          - **HUSAYN** c. 1858-1928. of Haji Husayn Alireza Co. c. 1910 Descendants in Jiddah
            - **ALI** d. 1948
              - **HUSAYN** b. 1931 Ch. Exec. Haji Husayn Alireza Co.
                - **ALI** at Charterhouse
                - **KHALID**
              - **HASAN** architect in Eastern Province
              - **QASIM** in Saudi Airlines
                - **HUSAYN**
            - da. who married Abdullah Abu al Hasan, whose mother was Mapari
          - **MAPARI**

1

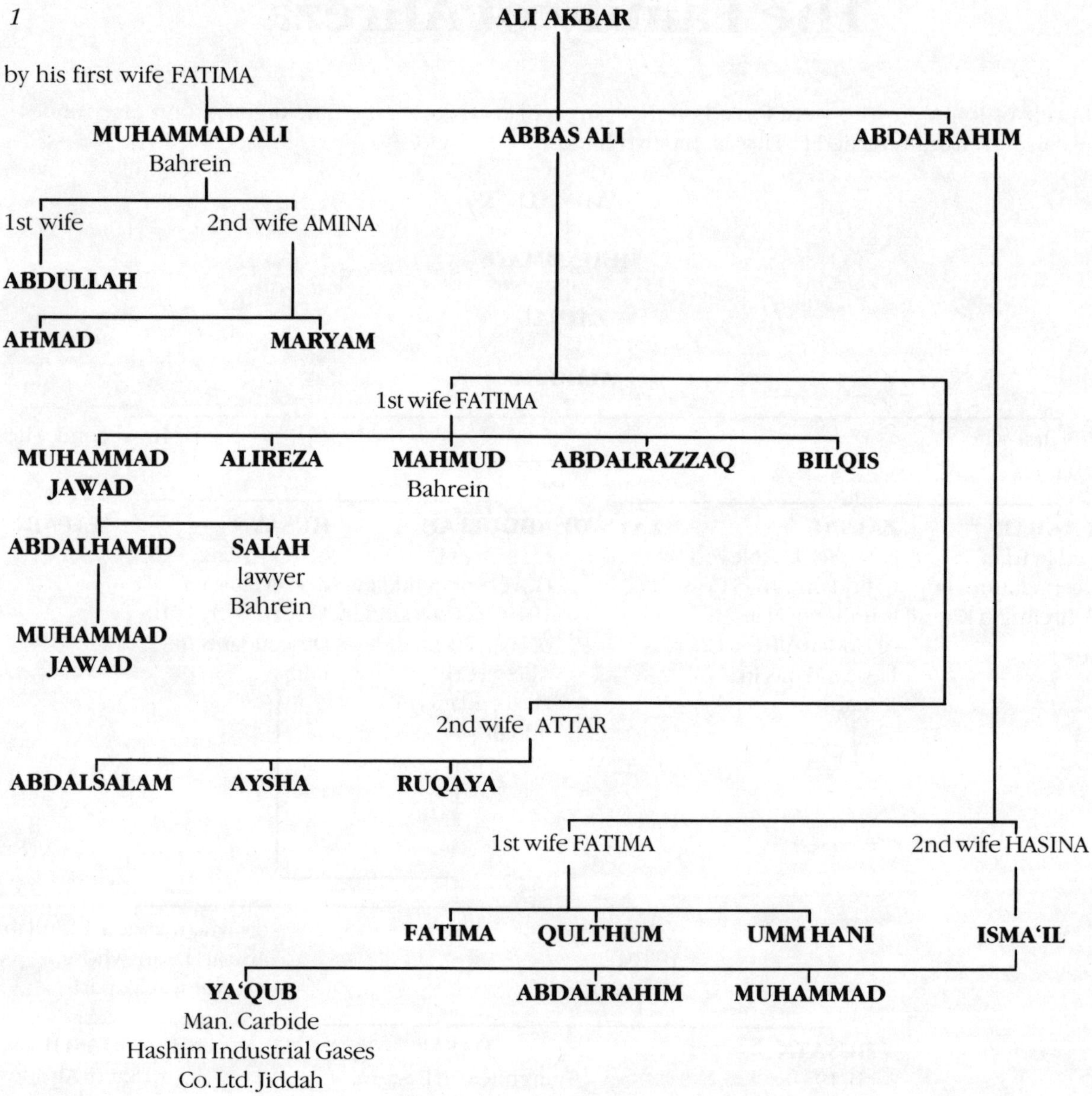
ALI AKBAR
by his first wife FATIMA
MUHAMMAD ALI
Bahrein
ABBAS ALI
ABDALRAHIM
1st wife
2nd wife AMINA
ABDULLAH
AHMAD
MARYAM
1st wife FATIMA
MUHAMMAD JAWAD
ALIREZA
MAHMUD
Bahrein
ABDALRAZZAQ
BILQIS
ABDALHAMID
SALAH
lawyer
Bahrein
MUHAMMAD JAWAD
2nd wife ATTAR
ABDALSALAM
AYSHA
RUQAYA
1st wife FATIMA
2nd wife HASINA
FATIMA
QULTHUM
UMM HANI
ISMA'IL
YA'QUB
Man. Carbide
Hashim Industrial Gases
Co. Ltd. Jiddah
ABDALRAHIM
MUHAMMAD

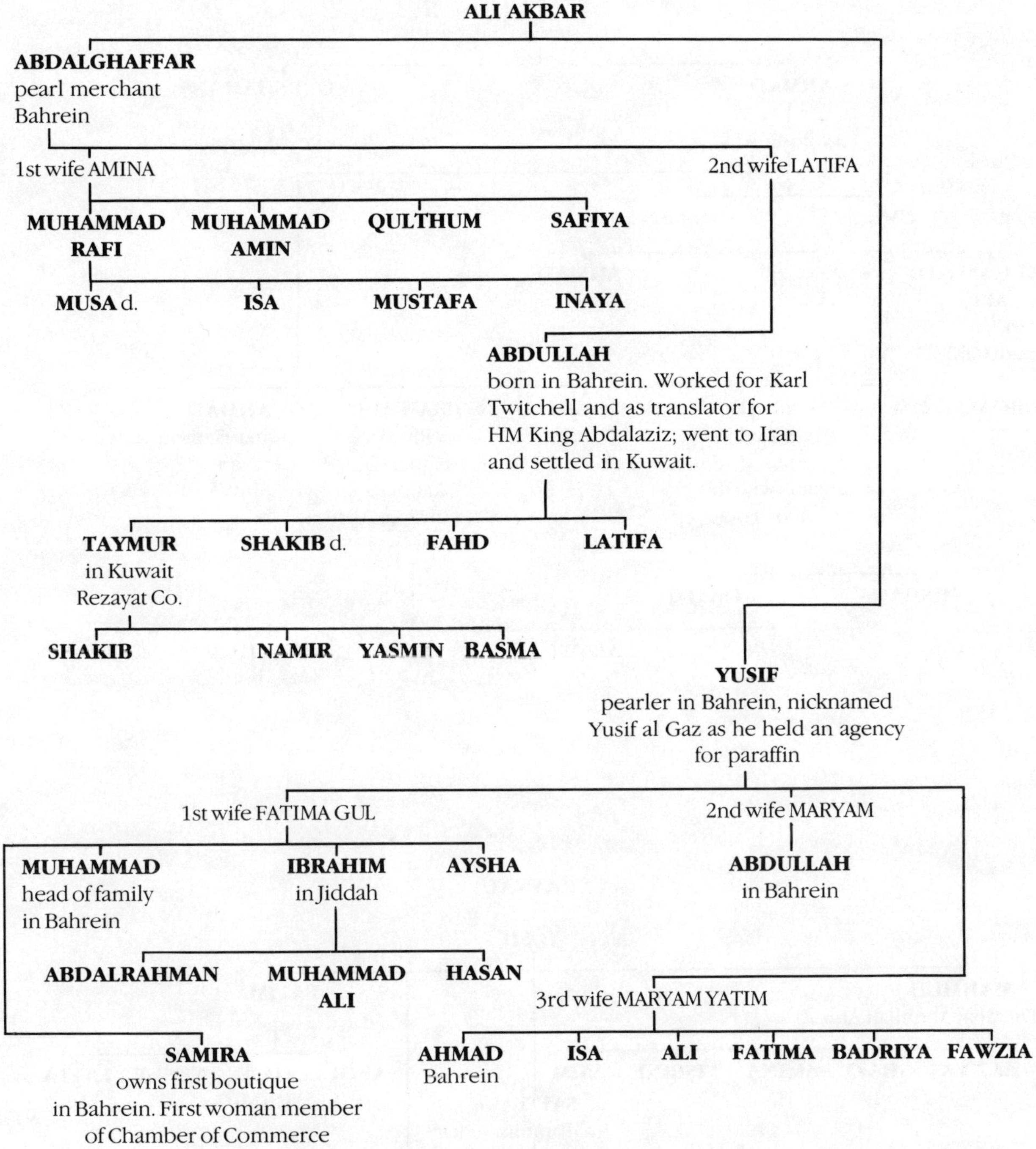

ALI AKBAR
ABDALGHAFFAR
pearl merchant
Bahrein
1st wife AMINA
2nd wife LATIFA
MUHAMMAD RAFI
MUHAMMAD AMIN
QULTHUM
SAFIYA
MUSA d.
ISA
MUSTAFA
INAYA
ABDULLAH
born in Bahrein. Worked for Karl Twitchell and as translator for HM King Abdalaziz; went to Iran and settled in Kuwait.
TAYMUR
in Kuwait
Rezayat Co.
SHAKIB d.
FAHD
LATIFA
SHAKIB
NAMIR
YASMIN
BASMA
YUSIF
pearler in Bahrein, nicknamed Yusif al Gaz as he held an agency for paraffin
1st wife FATIMA GUL
2nd wife MARYAM
MUHAMMAD
head of family
in Bahrein
IBRAHIM
in Jiddah
AYSHA
ABDULLAH
in Bahrein
ABDALRAHMAN
MUHAMMAD ALI
HASAN
3rd wife MARYAM YATIM
SAMIRA
owns first boutique in Bahrein. First woman member of Chamber of Commerce
AHMAD
Bahrein
ISA
ALI
FATIMA
BADRIYA
FAWZIA

- **ALI AKBAR**
  - by second wife
    - **AHMAD**
      - 1st wife AYSHA
        - **UMR**
        - **HASAN**
          - **MUHAMMAD ALI** — Man. in Saudi Cable Co.
          - **AHMAD**
      - 2nd wife, an Egyptian
        - **ABDALMUHSIN**
        - **NABIL** — m. a Zaidan; Lummus Alireza; works with the Buqshans
          - **HISHAM**
          - **HATIM**
        - **MUHAMMAD** — Jiddah
        - **MAHMUD** — Riyadh; m. Salma Ahmad Askar of Egypt; Ch. Lummus Alireza; b. 1932
          - **ASIM** — b. 1957
          - **ALAWI** — b. 1968
          - **LU'AY** — b. 1971
          - **YUSIF** — b. 1972
        - **AHMAD** — married an American
        - **ALI REZA**
    - **GUL SHAH**

2

- **ZAYNAL**
  - **YUSIF**
    - **MAHMUD** — Dir. Haji Abdullah Alireza
      - **GHAZWA**
      - **GHAZI**
      - **AMINA**
      - **NISRINE**
      - **ASIM**
    - **SAFIYA** — m. Ibrahim Akkar
      - **AYMAN**
      - **ABDALRAHMAN**
      - **MUHAMMAD ALI**
      - **HASAN**
    - **SALIHA** — m. Mahmud Ali Zahid (q.v)
      - **ABDALAZIZ**
      - **KHADIJA**
    - **FATIMA** d.
      - **ABDULLAH**
      - **HAMID**
      - **YUSUF**
      - **LAYLA**

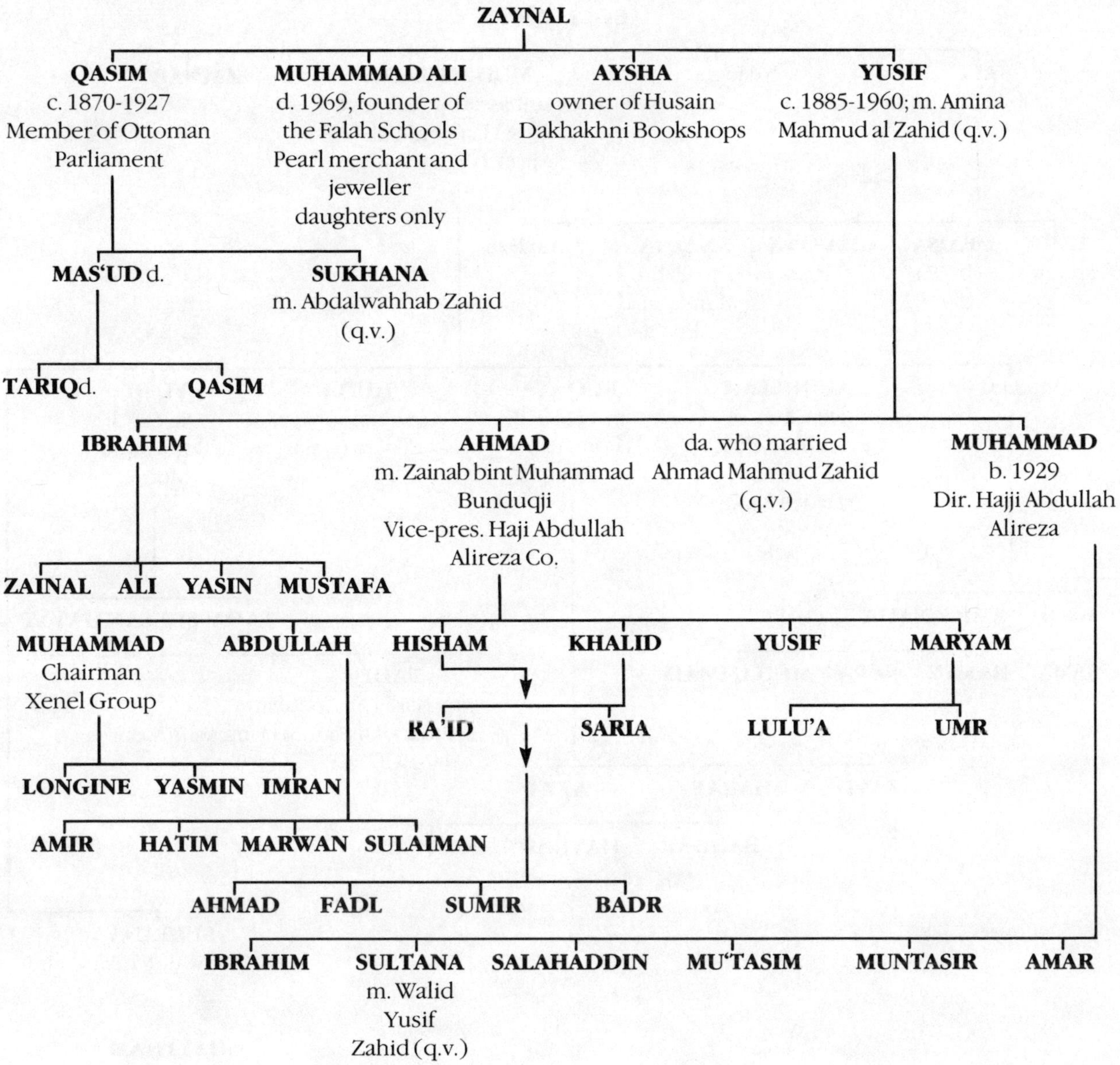
ZAYNAL
QASIM
c. 1870-1927
Member of Ottoman Parliament
MUHAMMAD ALI
d. 1969, founder of the Falah Schools
Pearl merchant and jeweller
daughters only
AYSHA
owner of Husain Dakhakhni Bookshops
YUSIF
c. 1885-1960; m. Amina Mahmud al Zahid (q.v.)
MAS'UD d.
SUKHANA
m. Abdalwahhab Zahid (q.v.)
TARIQd.
QASIM
IBRAHIM
AHMAD
m. Zainab bint Muhammad Bunduqji
Vice-pres. Haji Abdullah Alireza Co.
da. who married Ahmad Mahmud Zahid (q.v.)
MUHAMMAD
b. 1929
Dir. Hajji Abdullah Alireza
ZAINAL
ALI
YASIN
MUSTAFA
MUHAMMAD
Chairman
Xenel Group
ABDULLAH
HISHAM
KHALID
YUSIF
MARYAM
RA'ID
SARIA
LULU'A
UMR
LONGINE
YASMIN
IMRAN
AMIR
HATIM
MARWAN
SULAIMAN
AHMAD
FADL
SUMIR
BADR
IBRAHIM
SULTANA
m. Walid Yusif Zahid (q.v.)
SALAHADDIN
MU'TASIM
MUNTASIR
AMAR

3

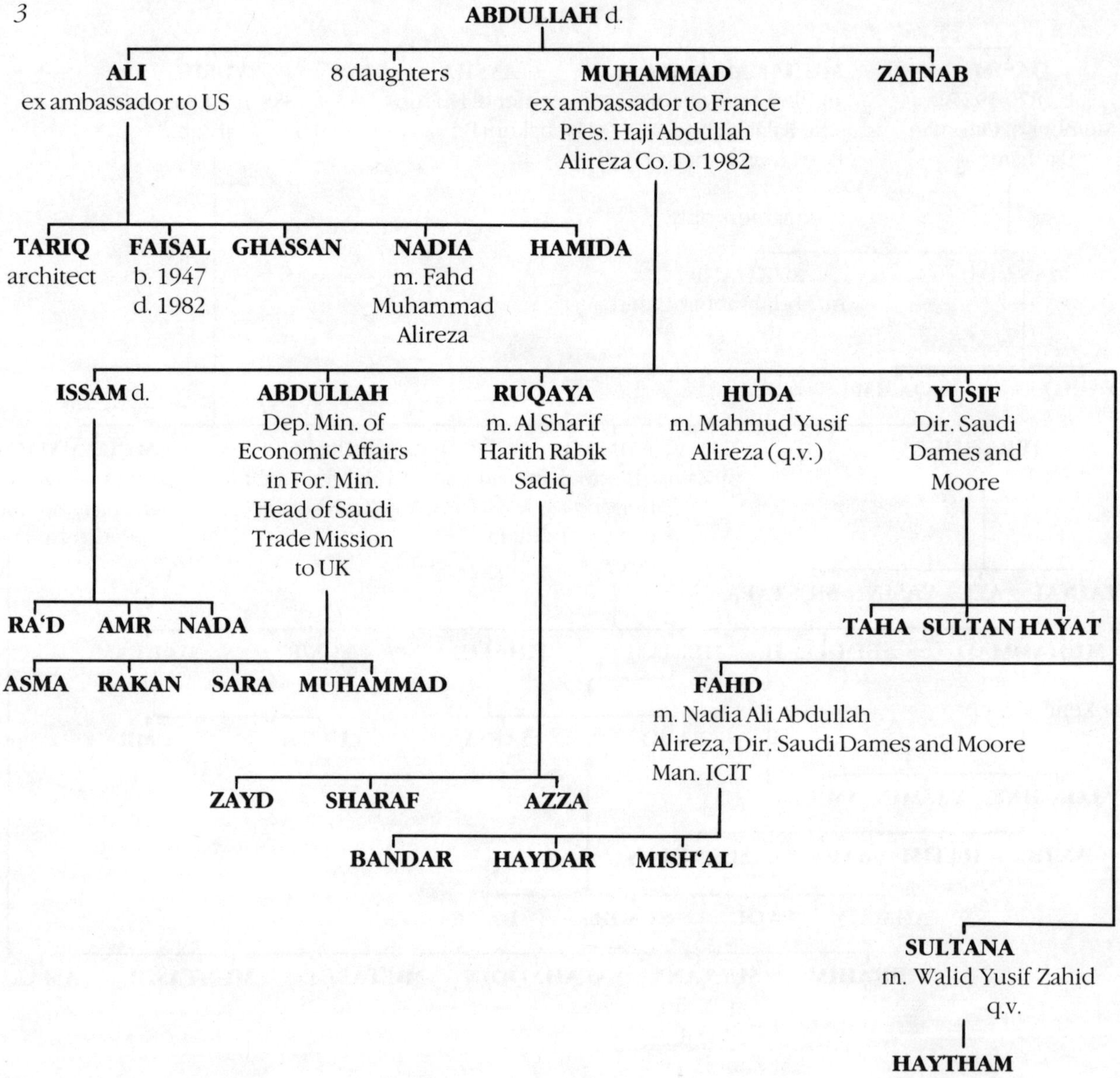
ABDULLAH d.
ALI
ex ambassador to US
8 daughters
MUHAMMAD
ex ambassador to France
Pres. Haji Abdullah
Alireza Co. D. 1982
ZAINAB
TARIQ
architect
FAISAL
b. 1947
d. 1982
GHASSAN
NADIA
m. Fahd
Muhammad
Alireza
HAMIDA
ISSAM d.
ABDULLAH
Dep. Min. of
Economic Affairs
in For. Min.
Head of Saudi
Trade Mission
to UK
RUQAYA
m. Al Sharif
Harith Rabik
Sadiq
HUDA
m. Mahmud Yusif
Alireza (q.v.)
YUSIF
Dir. Saudi
Dames and
Moore
RA'D
AMR
NADA
ASMA
RAKAN
SARA
MUHAMMAD
TAHA
SULTAN
HAYAT
FAHD
m. Nadia Ali Abdullah
Alireza, Dir. Saudi Dames and Moore
Man. ICIT
ZAYD
SHARAF
AZZA
BANDAR
HAYDAR
MISH'AL
SULTANA
m. Walid Yusif Zahid
q.v.
HAYTHAM

HAJI ABDULLAH ALIREZA COMPANY LIMITED

Address PO Box 8 Jiddah
Telephone 642233
Telex 401037 REZA SJ
Board
Muhammad Abdullah Alireza, Ahmad Yusif Zainal Alireza, Ali Abdullah Alireza, Muhammad Yusif Zainal Alireza, Mahmud Yusif Zainal Alireza, where the Executive Vice President is Ahmad Yusif Zainal Alireza. Branches in Dammam and Riyadh. The company's activities are concerned with the following; Airline and aircraft support services, jewellery, watches and clocks, insurance, travel agency and commununications equipment. They have shipping interests and are contractors in telecommunications equipment. The company, probably the oldest in Jiddah, having been formed in 1845, handles the following brand names: Vacheron, and Constantin, Jaeger, Royal Worcester, Jean Lassaille, Roger Chatelain S.A. and Heiwado. It is proud to have the prestigious commercial registration number 1.

The Alirezas dominated Jiddah commerce in the 1940s and the family was well educated and widely travelled. Ali Abdullah, a former ambassador to the US, was the first Saudi educated in the West. They maintained their connections with India and English was commonly spoken throughout the company.
With the original member of the family, Kassim, coming from Iran, the family had a long history of public service in Jiddah going back to before the First World War. This service was maintained by support for Ibn Saud during the integration of the Hijaz into Saudi Arabia in the 1920s. The Alirezas also helped in developing the 'Fallah' school system.
During the 1940s the family had all the major agencies especially in shipping. It came to represent Ford, Westinghouse, ITT, Pepsi Cola, Allis Chalmers, Goodyear and Dunlop. It also referred to other companies agencies such as General Motors, Mercedes and Siemens.
The company experienced a lull in the 1950s but the establishment of a J/V with Laing and Wimpey of the UK for air base construction revived the company's fortunes, which were followed by other major contracts.
Amongst the most enterprising of the Alirezas who initiated the family fortunes was Haji Husayn Alireza, brought from Iran to Jiddah by his brother Zainal. After working in India, he left his brother about 1910 and set up on his own. His son Ali ran the family business after Husayn's foray into the currency market led him to hoard Imperial roubles.
The family under Ali's son Husayn steadily gained a lot of hard experience in various fields, especially the motor car, with a string of different agencies. The major current agency is that for Mazda cars.

Haji Abdullah Alireza Co. partnership holdings in the sixties:

	SR	%
1. Muhammad Abdullah Alireza (President)	1,006,000	2.9
2. Ali Abdullah Alireza	4,716,250	13.5
3. Ibrahim Yusif Zainal Alireza	2,343,250	6.7
4. Ahmad Yusif Zainal Alireza (Board Member)	2,098,250	6.0
5. Muhammad Yusif Zainal Alireza	2,973,250	8.5
6. Mahmud Yusif Zainal Alireza (Board Member)	2,973,250	8.5
7. Fahad Muhammad Abdullah Alireza	782,250	2.2
8. Abdullah Muhammad Abdullah Alireza	782,250	2.2
9. Yusif Muhammad Abdullah Alireza	782,250	2.2
10. Zainab Abdullah Alireza	3,059,000	8.7
11. Ruqaya (Shareen) Muhammad Riza	392,000	1.1
12. Huda Muhammad Riza	392,000	1.1
13. Sultana Muhammad Riza	392,000	1.1
14. Amina Mahmud Ali Zahid (mother		
15. Safiya Yusif Zainal Alireza	1,485,750	4.2
16. Saliha Yusif Zainal Alireza	1,485,750	4.2
17. Hamida Alireza	273,000	0.8
18. Zulaina Qasim Zainal	1,877,750	5.4

19. Muhammad Ra'ad Issam Muhammad Riza	273,000	0.8
20. Amr Issam Muhammad Riza	273,000	0.8
21. Nada Issam Muhammad Riza	138,250	0.4
22. Muhammad Ahmad Yusif Zainal	175,000	0.5
23. Muhammad Ahmad Yusif Zainal	175,000	0.5
24. Hisham Ahmad Yusif Zainal Alireza	175,000	0.5
25. Khalid Ahmad Yusif Zainal Alireza	175,000	0.5
26. Yusif Ahmad Yusif Zainal Alireza	175,000	0.5
27. Faisal Ali Abdullah Alireza	350,000	1.0
28. Tariq Ali Abdullah Alireza	350,000	1.0
29. Ghassan Ali Abdullah Alireza	350,000	1.0
30. Nadia Ali Abdullah Alireza	175,000	0.5
31. Zainal Ibrahim Yusif Zainal Alireza	210,000	0.6
32. Yasin Ibrahim Yusif Zainal Alireza	140,000	0.4
33. Mustafa Ibrahim Zainal Alireza	140,000	0.4
34. Ali Ibrahim Yusif Zainal Alireza	140,000	0.4
And the following heirs of the late Fatima Alireza		
35. Omar Abdullah Aqil	371,400	1.1
36. Abdullah Omar Aqil	309,500	0.9
37. Yusif Omar Aqil	309,500	0.9
38. Hamad Omar Aqil	309,500	0.9
39. Layla Omar Aqil	185,850	0.5

GENTEC (General Technical Division of Alireza)

Address PO Box 1531, Jiddah
Telephone 6365279, 6367525
Telex 402332 GENTEC SJ
With branches in Dammam and Riyadh, this company is engaged as general and communications contractors and is managed by Mahmud Yusif Zainal Alireza. It shares the prestigious commercial registration number of the parent company.

INTERNATIONAL MECHANICAL AND ELECTRICAL CONTRACTING

Address PO Box 7155, Jiddah
Telephone 6422233
Telex 401037 ZEREZA SJ
A joint venture between the Haji Abdullah Alireza Co. and Fishbach and Moore Industrial Corporation operating as contractors for plumbing, sewage and water, airconditioning, and electrical and mechanical engineering. Founded in 1979 the company has a branch in Dammam (PO Box 8, tlx. 601008 ZAINAL SJ).

TKK ALIREZA LTD

Address PO Box 7065, Jiddah
Telephone 63422233
Telex 401037 REZA SJ
Owned jointly by Haji Abdullah Alireza Co. and Toyo Kanetsu KK. This concern operates as contractors for steel fabrication and the manufacture of storage tanks.

ZWAANS

Address PO Box 40, Jiddah
Telephone 6655827
Telex 401221 HUSREZ SJ
Owned by Haji Abdullah Alireza Co. This firm deals in heavy machinery and construction equipment.

LAING WIMPEY ALIREZA LTD

Address PO Box 2059, Jiddah
Telephone 6827153, 6827154
Telex 400091 LWAJED SJ
A joint venture between John Laing and Son BV and Haji Abdullah Alireza and Co. They are civil and building contractors and the association was formed in 1976.

ARABIAN PETROLEUM SUPPLY CO. S.A. (APSCO)

Address PO Box 1408, Jiddah
Telephone 6367164, 6367291, 6366842
Telex 402613 APSCO SJ
A joint venture formed in 1960 between Haji Abdullah Alireza Co. and Mobil Ltd., with branches in Riyadh (PO Box 361, tel. 4785562) Dammam (PO Box 8) and Yanbu (PO Box 113). They deal in bunkering oil, lubricants and aviation fuel.

DDG HANSA

Address PO Box 8 Jiddah
Telephone 6422233, 6422242, 6659203
Telex 401037 ZEREZA SJ
A shipping company with the Haji Abdullah Alireza orbit.

KLM (ROYAL DUTCH AIRLINES)

Address PO Box 1081
Telephone 6670888, 6673744, 6672503
The Haji Abdullah Alireza company act as agents for KLM and own the Saudi company which is concerned with air cargo services and airlines.

HAJI HUSEIN ALIREZA AND COMPANY LTD

Address PO Box 40 Jiddah
Telephone 6423509, 6423802
Telex 401221 HUSREZ SJ

Owned by Haji Husein Alireza this company was formed in 1906 and has branches in Riyadh, Al Khobar and Yanbu. Haji Husein Alireza Co. deals in diesel engines and distributes and deals in commercial vehicles and automobiles. They have a repair-shop facility and stock spare parts and accessories; and supply generators, cranes, power plant, scaffolding and tyres, as well as construction equipment.
The brand names handled by this company are: Mazda, Leiber, Same, Nardi, Goodyear, Hawker Siddley, Gerber, Lister, Montecristo, Bristol, John Rusling, Pan Aqua, ITX Ice, Sysco, Cheviot,Bellotti and Chloride Dagenits

IBRAHIM YUSUF AKBAR ALIREZA

Address PO Box 243 Jiddah
Telephone 6422968, 6363005
Telex 400756 AKBAR SJ
Founded in 1945 this company is owned by Ibrahim Yusuf and deals in building materials, foodstuffs, meat vegetables, spices and sports goods. They also act as commission agent and have a branch in Jubail.

GEORGE DEW IBRAHIM AKBAR ALIREZA CO, LTD

Address PO Box 243 Jiddah
Telephone 6690851
Telex 401562 ISLAM SJ

A company with the joint ownership of Ibrahim Alireza and George Dew International Ltd which was founded in 1977. They are landscaping contractors.

PHILIPPINE AIRLINES

Address PO Box 7101 Jiddah
Telephone 6519516, 6516192
Telex 401221 HUSREZ SJ

Owned by Ali Ibrahim Alireza this company is a travel agency and deals with airlines.

KITCHEN WORLD

Address PO Box 7101, Jiddah
Telephone 6533011, 6534960
Telex 401221 HUSREZ SJ
A company owned by Ali Ibrahim Alireza that began operations in 1970. It is concerned with the supply of decorating materials, furniture, houseware and kitchen equipment.

AIR TRADES (ABDURAHIM ISMAIL ALIREZA FOR TRADES)

Address PO Box 4545, Jiddah
Telephone 6534633, 6710356
Telex 401001 PBLTXA SJ
Formed in 1979 this company is owned by Abdalrahim Isma'il Alireza who deals in decorating and building materials, sanitaryware, wallpapers and wall coverings, as well as lifting equipment, electronic and electronic equipment.

TRANSCONTINENTAL CORPORATION

Address PO Box 7101, Jiddah
Telephone 6513859, 6519516, 6516192
Telex 401221 HUSREZ SJ, 401037 REZA SJ
Formed in 1976 the company is owned by Ali Ibrahim Alireza and managed by Yusif Ibrahim Alireza. It is concerned with general trading and contracting, building and decorating materials, commercial and domestic kitchen equipment, and acts as commission agents.

CRESCENT TRANSPORTATION CO. LTD.

Address PO Box 6670, Jiddah
Telephone 6657863, 6604103
Telex 400272 REZYAT SJ
This company's headquarters is in Dammam and there is another branch in Riyadh. It is owned by the Alireza Group and Sealand Services of the USA. It is engaged in the provision of local transport services.

REZA INVESTMENT CO. LTD.

Address PO Box 1555, Jiddah
Telephone 6442993, 6442994
Telex 401777ALREZA SJ
A company managed by Faisal A Alireza until his untimely death in 1982 and owned by the Alireza Group which specialises in swimming pool construction.

REZATRADE MARKETING AND DEVELOPMENT

Address PO Box 1555, Jiddah
Telephone 6442993-95
Telex 401777 ALREZA SJ
With a branch in Riyadh this company is a firm of marketing and management consultants which sponsors foreign firms. It is owned by the Alireza Group and managed by Fahad Muhammad Alireza.

SEA LAND SERVICES

Address PO Box 6670
Telephone 6657863, 6604103, 6691293
Telex 403258 SELAND SJ
A joint venture between the Alireza Group and Sealand Services Inc. They have a branch in Riyadh with their head office in Al Khobar. The company is concerned with shipping worldwide.

BROWN DALTAS AND ASSOCIATES SAUDI ARABIA LTD.

Address PO Box 4954, Jiddah
Telephone 6514611, 6514858, 6515082
Telex 402557 BRODAL SJ
This association with Benjamin Brown and Muhammad Alireza was formed in 1978. It acts as consultants for civil engineering and management projects.

CARBIDE HASHIM INDUSTRIAL GASES CO. LTD.

Address PO Box 4984, Jiddah
Telephone 6360338, 6360534
Telex 400704 CHINCO SJ
A company owned by Abdullah Hashim and managed by Ya'qub I Alireza.

HUSAIN JAMIL DAKHAKHNI BOOKSHOPS

Address PO Box 1035, Jiddah
Owned by Aysha bint Zainal Alireza, this company is involved in hairdressing and bookshops.

SAUDI ELECTRONICS AND TRADING CO (SETCO)

Address PO Box 8122, Jiddah
Telephone 6533184, 6533188, 6534216, 6517316
Telex 402952 SETCO SJ
In this company Muhammad Ali Ibrahim Alireza is in partnership with Ghassan Ahmad A Al Sulaiman and Usama Fadil Kabbani. The company trades in a wide range of goods including aviation and airport equipment, adding and calculating machines, hospital and medical equipment, marine communications and navigation equipment, telephones, video systems, security and paging equipment. They also operate a contracting facility relevant to their areas of interest.

BALLAST NEDAM GROEP NV

Address PO Box 7498, Jiddah
Telephone 6716642
Telex 400272 REZYAT SJ
With a branch in Riyadh (PO Box 5898, tel.4010070, 4010021) this company is engaged in the building and road construction business.

REZAYAT TRADING CO.

Address PO Box 6670, Jiddah
Telephone 6657863, 6691293, 6604581
Telex 400272 REZYAT SJ
The Jiddah office of a company owned by Taimur Alireza with a wide spread of activities in the trading field. Established in 1977 they operate air cargo services, manufacture aluminium products, and act as caterers, and clearing agents; and deal in fibreglass, explosives, diesel engines, desalination equipment, motors and generators, fire-fighting equipment, hoses, pipes, roofing products and scaffolding. The company is also concerned with local transport, sewage treatment plants, pipe wrapping tapes and filter membranes.

LAMNALCO SAUDI ARABIA LIMITED

Address PO Box 2010 Jiddah
Telephone 6652348, 6601235
Telex 400414 TALAL SJ
A joint venture between the Rezayat Trading Company and Royal Boskalis Westminster with a branch in Al Khobar,(PO Box 98, Tel, 8640435, Tlx 670502) Jizan (PO Box 120) Yanbu (PO Box 203 Tel. 3225277). The company is engaged in the opration and maintenance of tug and supply boats and barges, the provision of marine services, chartering, surveys and diving.

TARIK ALIREZA

Address PO Box 7503, Jiddah
Telephone 6433007
Telex 401777 ALREZA SJ
A firm of architects, engineers and planners dealing with consulting in these fields of activity and specialising in management and townplanning.

ICI TRADING AND REZATRADE

Address PO Box 1555, Jiddah
Telephone 6442993, 6442995, 6442994
Telex 401777 ALREZA SJ
Owned by Fahad Muhammad Alireza and Yusuf Muhammad Alireza, the organisational relationship between these two commercial entities is that Rezatrade is not a subsidiary of ICIT but it is administered by ICIT subsidiaries as a charged service to Rezatrade.
The ICIT subsidiaries of wholly owned companies includes ICIT Pools, Arby's and a speciality in dairy products. Associated companies and joint ventures comprise MTI, Saudi Chem and Saudi Hammard.

XENEL GROUP OF COMPANIES

The Group has its roots in Xenel Industries formed in 1973. It undertakes major projects with major foreign companies where required. Associate and subsidiary companies are supported through six departments through the Jiddah headquarters and various offices. The Xenel Group is an entirely Saudi concern.
The Xenel Group began with associations with Litton Industries of the US and Ret-Ser Engineering of Taiwan. The Group now has over thirty joint ventures and sustained growth. Turnover exceeds SR 5 billion and the Group employs over 15,000 people. Company policy is directed towards contributing to the lasting benefit of the community and the Kingdom.

XENEL INDUSTRIES LTD

Address PO Box 2824, Jiddah
Telephone 6437619
Telex 401166 XENEL SJ
Riyadh office: PO Box 3886, tel. 4782186, tlx. 201175 XENEL SJ

XENEL CONTRACTING LTD

Address PO Box 2824, Jiddah
Telephone 6437619
Telex 401166 XENEL SJ

XENEL MAINTENANCE LTD.

Address PO Box 2824
Telephone 6437619
Telex 401166 XENEL SJ

XENEL MARKETING LTD

Address PO Box 2824, Jiddah
Telephone 6437619
Telex 401166 XENEL SJ
Riyadh office: PO Box 3886, tel. 4782186, tlx. 201175 XENEL SJ

AMI SAUDI ARABIA LTD

Address PO Box 2824, Jiddah
Telephone 6431134, 6448480
Telex 403843 AMISAL SJ
Riyadh office: PO Box 7191, tel. 4821234, tlx. 204340 KKESH SJ
With American Medical International Inc. of USA, Xenel holding 60 percent.

ARABIAN BULK TRADE LTD

Address PO Box 2824, Jiddah
Telephone 6437619
Telex 401166 XENEL SJ
Offices in Riyadh (PO Box 16896, tel. 4789323, 4786168, tlx. 203106 BNEXRD SJ), and Al Khobar (PO Box 2194, tel. 8944880, 8640461, 8640665, 8645351, 8648302, 8649774, tlx. 670354 SABUT SJ, 670427 SAYARI SJ, 671096 ARBUT SJ

ARABIAN ELMEC LTD

Address PO Box 1783, Al Khobar
Telephone 8647439, 8948572
Telex 671019 GHELMC SJ
With Elmec Overseas SA, Xenel's equity is 30 percent.

ARABIAN SOIL CONTRACTORS LTD

Address PO Box 2824, Jiddah
Telephone 6601757, 6602229
Telex 400832 ASOLCO SJ
With Soil and Foundation Contracting Ltd, Lebanon, Xenel's equity is 51 percent.

ARABIAN SOLETANCHE SOIL CONTRACTORS LTD

Address PO Box 2824, Jiddah
Telephone 6601757, 6602229
Telex 400832 ASOLCO SJ
With Soletanche Entreprise SA, France.

BROWN DALTAS AND ASSOCIATES SAUDI ARABIA LTD

Address PO Box 4954, Jiddah
Telephone 6514611, 6514858, 6515082
Telex 402557 BRODAL SJ
Brown Daltas and Associates Ltd., UK Xenel's equity is 25 percent.

CORRINTEC ARABIA LTD

Address PO Box 2824, Jiddah
Telephone 6437619
Telex 401166 XENEL SJ
With Norcem, Norway Xenel's equity is 60 percent.

CTCI ARABIA LTD

Address PO Box 2824, Jiddah
Telephone 6717265
Telex 401166 XENEL SJ
With CTCI Corporation, Taiwan Xenel's equity is 50 percent.

DAR AL AMANA LTD

Address PO Box 2824, Jiddah
Telephone 6431107, 6447447, 6447787
Telex 403851 DRAMAN SJ

DRAVO ARABIA LTD

Address PO Box 2824, Jiddah
Telephone 6437619
Telex 401166 XENEL SJ
Office in Al Khobar (PO Box 1702, tel. 8645107, 8648094, tlx. 670202 DRAVO SJ).
With Dravo Corporation, USA Xenel's equity is 60 percent.

FURUKAWA SAUDI ARABIA LTD

Address PO Box 2824, Jiddah
Telephone 6437619
Telex 401166 Xenel SJ
With Chevron Maritime Transport Corporation, where Xenel holds 51 percent.

HIDADA LTD

Address PO Box 2824, Jiddah
Telephone 6431193, 6447191
Telex 404167 HIDADA SJ

INTERNATIONAL COMPANY FOR BUILDING MATERIALS LTD (BINEX)

Address PO Box 2824, Jiddah
Telephone 6519524, 6519764, 6532428
Telex 402393 BINEX SJ
Offices in Riyadh PO Box 16896, tel. 4786168, 4789323, tlx. 203106 BNEXRD SJ and Al Khobar PO Box 2194, tel. 8944880, 8640461, 8640665, 8645351, 8648302, 8649774, tlx. 670354 SABUT SJ, 670427 SAYARI SJ, 671096 ARBUT SJ
A subsidiary of Arabian Bulk Trade Ltd.

LITTON SAUDI ARABIA LTD

Address PO Box 7949, Jiddah
Telephone 6822102
Telex 402604 LSAL SJ
Office in Riyadh (PO Box 7529, tel. 4645696, 4762171, tlx. 202073 LITDSD SJ)
With Litton Industries, USA. Xenel holds 40 percent.

NEC SAUDI ARABIA LTD

Address PO Box 2824, Jiddah
Telephone 6437619
Telex 40116 XENEL SJ
Riyadh office PO Box 15534, tel. 4650273, 4653381, tlx. 204123 NECS SJ
With Nippon Electric Co. Ltd. where Xenel hold 40 percent.

RESOURCE SCIENCES ARABIA LTD

Address PO Box 2824, Jiddah
Telephone 6437619
Telex 40116 XENEL SJ
Office in Al Khobar (PO Box 1272m tel. 8645289, 8646449, 8646787, 8648116, 8649531, tlx. 670531 RSAL SJ
Xenel holds 50 percent in venture with Resource Sciences Corp. of USA.

RET-SER SAUDI ARABIA LTD

Address PO Box 3984, Jiddah
Telephone 6510979, 6530702
Telex 401343 RETSER SJ
With Ret-Ser Engineering Agency, Taiwan; Xenel holds 50 percent.

SAUDI ARABIAN INTERNATIONAL TRANSPORT CO. LTD

Address PO Box 2824, Jiddah
Telephone 6437619
Telex 401166 XENEL SJ
With Chevron Maritime Transport Corporation, where Xenel holds 51 percent.

SAUDI ARABIAN NOUHRA LTD

Address PO Box 2824, Jiddah
Telephone 6437619
Telex 401166 XENEL SJ
Xenel holds 51 percent in venture with Raymond N Nouhra and Co, Lebanon.

SAUDI BULK TRANSPORT CO

Address PO Box 2824, Jiddah
Telephone 6437619
Telex 401166 XENEL SJ
Office in Al Khobar (PO Box 2194, tel. 8944880, 8640461, 8640665, 8645351, 8648302, 8649774, tlx. 670354 SABUT SJ, 670427 SAYARI SJ, 671096 ARBUT SJ)
Xenel holds 53.5 percent in venture with Norcem of Norway.

SAUDI CABLE COMPANY

Address PO Box 4403, Jiddah
Telephone 6600156, 6600164, 6691377
Telex 402567 SABLE SJ
Office in Riyadh (PO Box 6793, tel. 4763568, 4767204, 4771633, tlx. 201686 BETTER SJ) and Al Khobar (PO Box 2194, and 272, Thuqba, Al Khobar, tel. 8648939, tlx. 671027 CABLES).
In venture with Standard Oil of California, NKF Groep of Holland, with Xenel holding 30 percent.

SAUDI SERVICES AND OPERATING CO. LTD.

Address PO Box 2824, Jiddah
Telephone 6437619
Telex 40116 XENEL SJ

SOLTRAVO GENERAL CONTRACTORS LTD

Address PO Box 2824, Jiddah
Telephone 6602229
Telex 400832 ASOLCO SJ
With Soil and Foundation Contracting Co., Lebanon and another. Xenel's equity is 51 percent.

STANLEY MILLER ARABIA LTD

Address PO Box 2824, Jiddah
Telephone 6720015
Telex 401166 XENEL SJ
Partnership with Stanley Miller Holdings Ltd., UK. Xenel hold 50 percent.

WEXICO SYSTEMS AND SERVICES

Address PO Box 2824, Jiddah
Telephone 6437619, 6448678
Telex 401166 XENEL SJ
With Westinghouse Electric Corporation, USA. Xenel hold 60 percent.

The Family of Anani

A family from Mecca.

- **KHALIL**
  - **MUHAMMAD**
    with Islamic World League
    ex D.G. of Public Works and
    ex Dir. of Min. of Finance under
    Kings Abdalaziz and Saud
    - **HASAN**
      b. 1942
      Pres. Enco Trade
      - **FAHAD**
      - **AMRU**
      - **ISSAM**
      - **HANAN**
    - **FU'AD**
      b. 1945. Owner
      Hadar Trading Est.
      Riyadh
      - **HAZIM**
      - **HAYA**
    - **FAISAL**
      ex advisor
      Min. of Planning
      Saudi Computer
      and Information
      Centre
      - **TARIQ**
      - **YASMIN**
    - **MANSUR**
      - **SALMAN**
    - **FARID**
      Ch. of Enco
      - **KHALIL**
        - **AHMAD**
      - **KHALID**
        ex interpreter to
        King Khalid
        - **FAISAL**
        - **HANA**

ANANI CONSTRUCTION AND TRADING EST.

Address PO Box 5865, Riyadh
Telephone 4766988
Telex 200454 ENANI SJ
With an office in Jiddah (tel. 4780038, 4776287, tlx. 201351 ENAN SJ) the company is a partnership between Hasan Anani and his brother Farid. It was incorporated in 1975 and is involved in wholesaling, distribution, imports and orders on commission. The company will finance stock and share in promotional expenses. It is a young and aggressive company with great influence in Saudi business.
The company has a construction division, a general trading division, electronic , navigation and transport divisions, and a subsidiary, First Arabian Management which specialises in general maintenance management.

ANANI NAVIGATION AND TRANSPORTATION CO.

Address head office PO Box 3801, Jiddah
Telephone 6531267, 6533916
Telex 401843
Activities Owned and managed by Fu'ad Anani, the company deals in building materials, local transportation services and contracting, as well as shipping.

The Family of Ansari

Originated in Medina and descend from Abdullah b. Abbas who is buried in Ta'if. The Ansari are so called because they assisted the Prophet Muhammad in his early conquests. This branch of the family migrated to Bahrein about 150 years ago, others having also settled in Iraq and Iran.

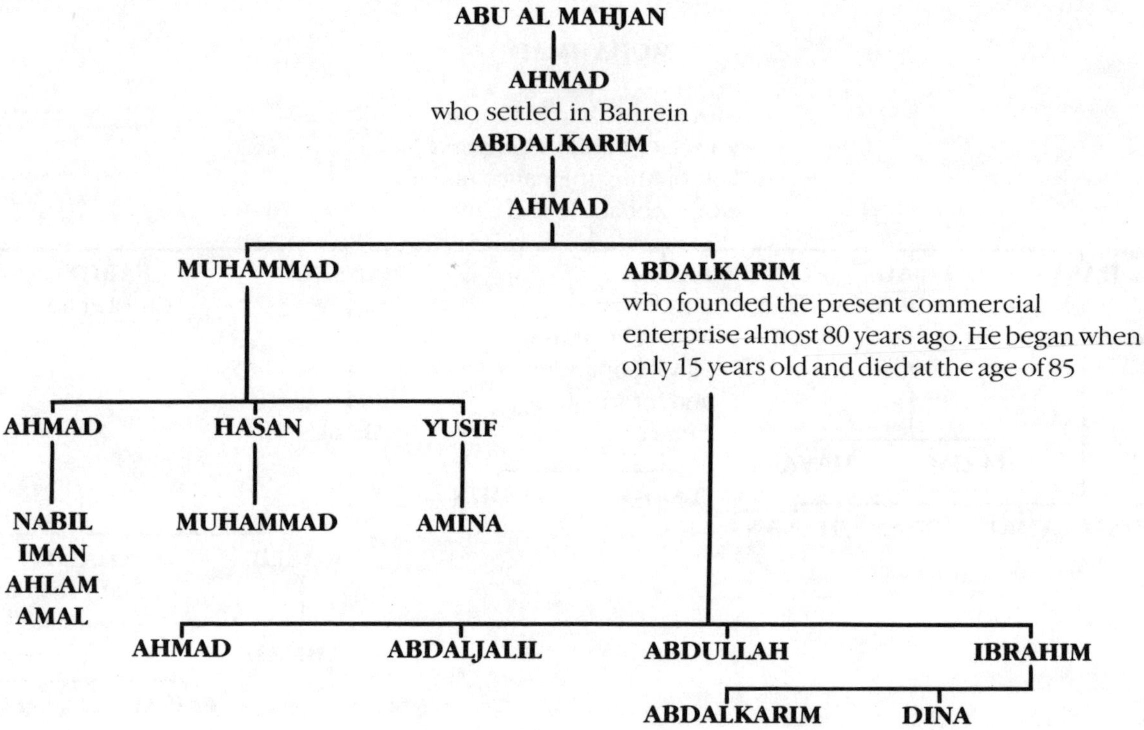

AL ANSARI ESTABLISHMENT

Address head office PO Box 137, Al Khobar
Telephone 86 42849, 86 41218
Telex 620122 JALEEL SJ
Cable address JALEEL
Proprietor Sh. Abdaljaleel b. Abdalkarim Al Ansari
Activities The company in Al Khobar is involved in construction and retails furniture from a large showroom in Amir Nasir St. In Bahrain the family holdings are controlled as a collective company between the four brothers, Ahmad, Abdaljaleel, Abdullah and Ibrahim. The following list is a partnership of 50 percent each between Sh. Abdaljaleel Al Ansari and Sh. Ali Hasan Mahmud.

1 Al Ansari Lighting Co., Manama, PO Box 5182, tel, 714780, tlx. 8848 ANSACO BN
2 Al Ansari Lights Co., Muharraq, PO box 22395, tel. 325495, tlx. 8848 ANSACO BN
3 Crystal Palace, Bahrein, tel. 254129
4 Bahrein Mattress Factory, PO Box 5648, Manama, tel. 243409, tlx. 8472

The Family of Ashmawi

Descending from early Arabian emigrants to Egypt, the family originates in the Abu Sa'id of Hama'il.

AHMAD ASHMAWI

- **MUHAMMAD**
  Chairman of Saudi Arabian Markets
  - **AHMAD**
  - **ISMA'IL**
- **HISAM**

MUHAMMAD A ASHMAWI AND SONS LTD.

Address P.O.Box 786 Jiddah
Telephone 6514868, 6515376
Telex 401469 ASHMWI SJ
Company History and Activities Formed in 1977 this company is owned by Muhammad Ahmad Ashmawi and has a wide sphere of activity including aircraft charter and sales, dealing with airlines and the sale of automobiles. The company acts as a commission agent and pipeline building contractor, and sells canned drinks, furniture, insecticides and jewellery, whilst operating a travel agency as well.

JIHAN DECORATION SERVICES

Address P.O.Box 5527 Jiddah
Telephone 6420232
Telex 401119 YATREB SJ
Company History and Activities Owned by Muhammad Ashmawi, this company deals in contracting for interior decoration and design and supplies decorating materials. It was established in 1975.

MODERN KARMA ESTABLISHMENT FOR TRADING AND CONTRACTING

Address P.O.Box 4268 Jiddah
Telephone 6601727
Activities A firm of building contractors dealing in building materials and electrical equipment.

SAUDI ARABIAN MARKETS

Head office P.O.Box 65 Jiddah
Telephone 6423140, 6423603, 6364312
Cable MARKETS
Telex 401067 MARKET SJ
Branches
Riyadh P.O.Box 48, tel. 4027860, 4027820, tlx. 201271 MARKET SJ
Al Khobar P.O.Box 246, tel.8641913, 8642257, tlx. 670065 MARKET SJ
Proprietor Sh. Muhammad Ashmawi and family
Company History and Activities Established in 1947 this company is owned by Muhammad and Hisam Ahmad Ashmawi and Mrs. Sabah Abdullah, their mother. The company deals in lubricants and greases, shelving, racking, materials handling equipment, fork lift trucks, gas-turbine generators, business systems, construction chemicals, travel agency and catering services, airlines and aircraft support, air cargo services, aviation and airport equipment, furniture, insurance and container building systems.
Brand names represented include: Shell, Rolls-Royce, Aston Martin, Lagonda, Alfa Romeo, Dexion, Lansing Bagnall, Geest, MOS, Shinko, Kalamazoo and Fosroc.
Sh. Muhammad Ashmawi is also chairman and proprietor of the National Investment and Marketing Company which specializes in real estate, real estate development and project investment.

PENINSULAR AVIATION SERVICES COMPANY LTD.

Address head office P.O.Box 6369 Jiddah
Telephone 6601539
Telex 402372 PASCO SJ
Company History and Activities Established in 1977 as a venture between Saudi Arabian Markets and Shell International Petroleum and British Petroleum Co. Ltd., this company has branches in Medina, Tabuk, Jizan, Hail, Qassim and Najran. They are concerned with airline and aircraft services, aviation and airport equipment.

SHELL LUBRICANTS DIVISION

Address P.O.Box 65 Jiddah
Telephone 6870834, 6872863
Telex 400867 SAMLUB SJ
Activities Owned by Saudi Arabian Markets this company is involved with cleaning products, detergents, lubricants and lubricating equipment and drilling equipment.

The Family of Ashoor

A family of Mecca

ASHOOR

- **AHMAD**
  a merchant who dealt in household utensils
  - **SAIF AL DIN**
    Publisher and proprietor of Saudi Economic Survey
    - **WALID**
      architect
    - **KHALID**
      English graduate of King Abdalaziz University
  - **BADR AL DIN**
    business man in Riyadh
  - **HASAN**
    in Saudia Airlines
  - **HUSAYN**
    in Min. of Information Press Dept.

S A ASHOOR

Address head office P.O.Box 1989 Jiddah
Telephone 6428245
Cable address RELSERVE
The publishing house of S A Ashoor is famous as the birthplace of the Saudi Economic Survey which is an indispensable adjunct to the business world of the Kingdom. The magazine was founded in February 1967 and has been produced weekly ever since. It is a reliable source of business statistics and reflects important economic views, containing marketing surveys and reproducing Government legislation when this is relevant to commerce. The Survey is distributed throughout Europe, the USA, Canada, Japan and Korea.

The Family of Attar

There is a tradition that they are descendants of the Caliph Abu Bakr, who was the first successor to the Prophet Muhammad.

- **MAHMUD**
  - **MUHAMMAD**
    - **MAHMUD**
      - **MUHAMMAD**
        - **MAHMUD**
          - **MUHAMMAD**
            - **MAHMUD**
              - **SADDIQ** founders and later controllers of Saddik and Mohamed Attar Co.
                - **UMR** b. 1929 Chairman of Saddik Mohamed Attar Co.
                  - **SADDIQ**
                    - **UMR**
                  - **HASAN**
                  - **MARWAN**
                  - **GHASSAN**
                  - (Saddik Omar and Bros.)
                - **SA'ID** * owns S&M
                  - **MANSUR**
              - **MUHAMMAD**
              - **ABDALRAHIM** died at Ta'if
                - **MAHMUD** D. 1971. Member Board of Dirs. of Riyadh Bank. Turned down appointment as Dep. Gov. of SAMA
                  - **ABDALRAHIM** * Dir. S & M Attar, works in Saudi Airlines
                  - **SAMI** * Dir. S & M Attar owner
                    - **MAHMUD**
                  - **MUHAMMAD** * Dir. S & M Attar and owner Mohd. Mahmud Est.
                - **HUSAYN**
                  - **HASAN** Dr of medicine
                  - **KHALID** in Riyadh
                - **JAMIL** MD of Mahmoud Abdalrahim Attar Bros. who are very important textile merchants and manufacture best head cloths or ghutras in the Arab world, exporting throughout the region
                  - **ISSAM** Civil engineer Issam Attar Est. Contracting Civil Engineering
                  - **ADNAN** business man
                  - **SAFWAN**
                  - **GHASSAN**
                  - **JAMIL**
                - **MUHAMMAD NUR** d. leaving 2 daughters

* Owners of Saddih and Muhammad Attar Co.

ESSAM ATTAR ESTABLISHMENT

Address head office PO Box 7144, Jiddah
Telephone 6511266, 6510502
Telex 401433 FAKEH SJ
Activities A contracting company formed in 1979 and ownd by Issam Jamil Attar, being managed by him and his cousin Marwan Umr.

HUSSAIN A ATTAR

Address head office PO Box 1466, Jiddah
Telephone 6424096, 6442214
Activities Dealing in foodstuffs, confectionery, biscuits and tinned goods, the company was established in 1969.

MUHAMMAD MAHMUD ATTAR ESTABLISHMENT

Address head office PO Box 9484, Jiddah
Telephone 6517627, 6517927
Telex 400470 MAFCO SJ
The company is owned by Muhammad Mahmud Attar and his brother, Sami, is manager and a board member as is their other brother, Abdalrahim. They deal in bedroom and bathroom accessories and gifts.

SADDIK AND MOHAMED ATTAR CO.

Address PO Box 439, Jiddah
Telephone 6447229, 6423244, 6423437
Telex 401075
Chairman Sh. Umr Attar with Sh. Said Saddik own 50 percent of the company, the other 50 percent being held between the other board members: Sh. Abdalrahim Mahmud Attar, Sh. Muhammad Mahmud Attar, Sh. Said Saddik Attar (Executive Director), Sh. Saddik Umr (M.D. in Riyadh), Sh. Sami Mahmud (Executive Director).
The company is general service and handling agents for British Airways, SAS, Rock Airways, Kuwait Airways, Quantas and Cyprus Air, and handling agents for Lufthansa, Korean Airlines, Olympic and Air India; they are thus the largest travel agents in the Kingdom.
They also operate a shipping department and their commecial department holds the Rolex agency. The company has invested extensively in real estate and is developing industrial interests.
Sh. Saddik Umr Attar and Sh. Hasan Umr Attar are 50-50 partners in a limited liability partnership called Al Attar Trading and Contracting Customs Clearing Public Services and Public Transport co. which presently operates in jewellery, watches and gifts. The company is situated in Khalid bin Walid Street, Jiddah and was formed in 1951. They have branches in Riyadh, Mecca, Dammam, Yanbu and Tabuk.
Bankers Saudi Faransi Bank.

SADDIK OMAR ATTAR AND BROS.

Address head office PO Box 7811, Jiddah
Telephone 6510502
Telex 400379 SOAB SJ
Activities A company owned by Saddik Umar and Hasan Umar Attar which was formed in 1978. They represent Learjet and Diebold and undertake aircraft sales.

MANSUR ATTAR FAKHRI CO. (MAFCO)

Address head office P.O.Box 2486 Jiddah
Telephone 6445512
Telex 401593 FAKHRY SJ
Cable address COMMERCIAL
Chairman H.R.H. Prince Talal bin Mansur bin Abdalaziz al Sauwd
Board Members
Said Fakhri
Sami Mahmoud Attar
Abdalrahim Mahmoud Attar
Muhammad Mahmoud Attar
The company was founded to enter the construction field but also has a joint venture subsidiary called MAFCO, Gulf United Freight Systems, with an American company based in San Francisco. This subsidiary specializes in door to door delivery of goods, freight forwarding and packing. In addition to these activities MAFCO Trade deals in cement, wood, sugar and other commodities in conjunction with Tennants Bank in London.
Bankers Citibank, National Commercial Bank.

The Family of Al Attas

A very large family of Sada (Sayid sing.). Descending from Ali, the son-in-law of the Prophet Muhammad, their immediate origins are from Huraidha in the Hadramawt. The Al Attas have for many years been one of the most important groups in the Jiddah merchant community, as is witnessed by the low number of their post office box numbers. There is great competition for these numbers when they become vacant, but, in general, the lower the number, the older the business house. The following trees are by no means complete and there have been several waves of Al Attas Sada arriving in the Kingdom over the years; in particular the family was responsible for much business activity in Indonesia at one time and some came to Jiddah from there whilst others came directly from Hadramawt.

- **SAYYID ABDALRAHMAN AL ATTAS**
  - **ALI**
    - **ABDALRAHMAN**
      - **MUHAMMAD** *see table 2*
      - **ALI**
        - **MUHAMMAD** merchant
          - **ZAIN**
            - **ZAHIR**
            - **MUHAMMAD**
            - **HANI**
            - 6 das.
          - **ABDALRAHMAN**
            - **ALI**
              - **WA'IL**
              - 3 das.
              - **SAMI**
        - **HASAN** religious teacher
          - **MUHAMMAD**
            - **ALI**
            - 3 das.
          - **ABDULLAH**
            - **ABDALRAHMAN**
            - **ABU BAKR**
          - **AHMAD** religious teacher
            - **ALI** Al Attas Refrigeration
              - **KHALID**
              - **HASAN**
              - **HUSAYN**
              - **MAJID**
              - **SAFIYA**
            - **MUHAMMAD**
              - **MAJDI**
              - **MUNA**
              - **MANAL**
            - **UMR**
              - **RAMI**
              - **HANYA**
            - **SALIM**
            - **ABDULLAH**
            - 3 das.
          - **SALIM**
            - **MUHAMMAD** and 2 das.
        - **ABDALRAHMAN**
          - **MUHAMMAD**
            - **MUHSIN**
            - **HASAN**
            - **ALI**
            - 5 das.

2

MUHAMMAD B. ABDALRAHMAN

- **ABDULLAH**
  - **SALIM**
    - **MUHAMMAD**
      - **UMR**
      - **ANWAR**
      - **KHALID**
      - **MARYAM**
    - **HASAN**
      - **ALI**
      - 3 das.
    - **ALI**
      - **HUSAIN**
      - 3 das.
- **SALIM**
  - **UMAR**
    The Al Attas Centre
    Real Estate
  - **ABDALRAHMAN**
    - **HUSAIN**
      - **ALAWI**
      - **ABDALRAHMAN**
      - **MUHAMMAD**
      - **ABU BAKR**
      - **MUHSIN**
      - **UMAR**
      - **SALIM**
      - **BANDAR**
      - **FAISAL**
      - **SAFIYA**
      - **NURA**
    - **MUHAMMAD**
      - **SAMIYA**
      - **NAJDA**
    - **UMR**
      merchant
      Real Estate
      - **FAHAD**
      - **KHALID**
      - **ALI**
      - **HUSAIN**
      - **FAISAL**
      - **ABDALRAHMAN**
      - **MUHAMMAD**
      - **MUHSIN**
      - **SALIM**
      - **AHMAD**
      - **ABDULLAH**
      - **SAFIYA**
      - **JAWHARA**
      - **FAWZIYA**
      - **BADRIYA**
      - **ASMA**
      - **LATIFA**
    - **SALIM**
      Al Attas
      Refrigeration
      - **UMR**
      - **MUHAMMAD**
      - **HUSAIN**
      - **ABU BAKR**
      - **ABDALRAHMAN**
      - **MUHSIN**
      - **BADRIYA**
      - **ZAKIYA**
      - **KARIMA**
    - **MUHSIN**
      Jewellery
      and perfume
      business
      - **HANI**
      - **HASHIM**
      - **HUSAIN**
      - **ABDALRAHMAN**
    - **NURA**
    - **SHAIKHA**
    - **MARYAM**
    - **ALWIYA**
  - **HUSAIN**
    - 1 da.
- **HUSAIN**
  - **MUHSIN**
    - **ALI**
      - **ABDALRAHMAN**
      - **MUHAMMAD**
      - **MUHSIN**
      - **UMR**
      - 2 das.
  - **HUSAIN**
    - **UMR**
      - **MUHAMMAD**
      - 4 das.
    - **ALI** ↓

A part of the family arriving in Jiddah, having first emigrated from Hadramawt to Indonesia.

- **MUHAMMAD**
  - **HUSAIN**
    d. 1981
    Chairman Saudi Hollandi Bank;
    came to Jiddah from Indonesia
    - **MUHAMMAD**
      Board member of Saudi
      Hollandi Bank
      Al Attas Commercial Agencies
      - **NI'MAT**
      - **HUSAIN**
      - **NADA**
      - **TARIQ**
    - **ABDULILLAH**
      - **MISHA'AL**
  - **ABU BAKR**

- **ABDALMUTALLIB**
  - **HASHIM**
    - **HUSAIN**
      b. 1922. Owner Al Attas Hotels
      Founder member Arab National Bank
      - **HANI**
        B.A. Bus. Admin.
        Univ. N Carolina
        Man. Al Attas
        Hotel
      - **WALID**
        b.1959, High
        School Grad. La
        Rose of Switzerland
      - **MUHAMMAD**
        b. 1972
      - **KHALID**
        b. 1973
      - **AMIRA**
        b.1976
    - **AHMAD**
      National Transport
      and Trading Est.
      - **MUHAMMAD**
      - **ABDULLAH**
      - **HASHIM**
      - 8 other children

AL ATTAS AGENCIES

Address head office PO Box 4, Jiddah
Telephone 6443350, 6428333, 6428529
Telex 401009 ALSHIPS SJ
Activities Al Attas Agencies deals with pre-fabricated building systems, bakeries, shipping and forwarding and clearing

AL ATTAS OCEAN TRANSPORT CO.

Address head office PO Box 6822, Jiddah
Telephone 6428333, 6428529, 6428779
Telex 401009 SHIP SJ
Activities Shipping agents and the provision of local transport services through a joint venture with the Ocean Transport and Trading Company of UK where they hold 60 percent.

AL ATTAS BIG LIFT CO. LTD.

Address head office PO Box 4, Jiddah
Telephone 6428333, 6443350, 6449644
Telex 401009 ALSHIP SJ
Activities Established in 1979 Syd. Husain al Attas Co. owns 51 percent of this joint venture with Big Lift Transport of the Netherlands. The company deals with the transport and erection of heavy lifts as well as rigging and crane services.

AL ATTAS

Address head office PO Box 1299, Jiddah
Telephone 6420400, 6420211, 6420418
Telex 401158 ATASEL SJ
Activities To the ownership of the Al Attas Hotel, one of the largest established hotels in Jiddah, is to be added the Haramain Palace Hotel, Haramain Hotel and the Al Attas Holiday Beach Hotel (Obhur). Other companies controlled by Syd. Husain Hashim are the Al Attas Tourist and Travel Agency, Al Attas Trading and Contracting, Al Attas Oasis Decoration and Furniture Centre, Montana Pastries, Al Attas Operations and Maintenance. Syd. Husain is also chairman of the board of Saudi Limousine.

NATIONAL TRANSPORT AND TRADING ESTABLISHMENT

Address head office PO Box 3688, Jiddah
Telephone 6874596, 6870357, 6875261
Telex 401364 NATRAN SJ
Activities The company is owned and managed by Syd. Ahmad Hashim al Attas and is engaged in providing air cargo services, representing airlines, acting as commission agents and for shipping companies, as well as acting as travel agents.

AL HARAMAIN MODERN HOTEL

Address head office PO Box 86, Jiddah
Telephone 6426655, 6426823, 6445340
Telex 401619 HARMEN SJ
This hotel business was started in 1949 and is owned by Syd. Husain Hashim al Attas

AL HARAMAIN PALACE HOTEL

Address head office PO Box 85, Jiddah
Telephone 6421894, 6448044
Telex 403122 AMIRAH SJ
The hotel is owned by Syd. Husain Hashim al Attas.

AL ATTAS REFRIGERATION ESTABLISHMENT

Address head office PO Box 3523, Riyadh
Telephone 4025884, 4035942, 4036986
Telex 201418 ALATTAS SJJiddah branch: PO Box 3577, tel. 6310648, 6312007, tlx. 402136 ARABI SJ
Al Khobar: PO Box 1467, tel. 8649009, tlx. 671295 ARE SJ
Jubail: tel. 3612112
Dammam: tel. 8264962
Activities The company was formed in 1973 to distribute and service refrigerators, air conditioners, compressors, electric motors and condensers. In 1974 household appliances were added and the acquisition of the franchise for Frigidaire GM in the same year gave them a firm coverage of both the domestic and the industrial markets for this kind of equipment. In 1975 they took up the franchise of Tecumseh Products from the USA.
Bankers
National Commercial Bank, Cairo Saudi Bank, Arab National Bank, Al Bank Al Saudi Al Faransi

AL ATTAS COMMERCIAL AGENCIES

Address head office PO Box 4908, Jiddah
Telephone 6655878
Telex 400486 ACA SJ
Activities The company is engaged in the provision of facilities for exhibitions, as commission agents, as packers and as contractors for building painting and plumbing
The company owns Crown Pacific (Saudi Arabia) Co. Ltd. (PO Box 4908, Jiddah, tel. 6653732, 6602677, tlx. 400486 ACA SJ) which is a clearing and forwarding concern and also deals in packaging services.

The Family of Babtain

They descend from the Ubaydah of Qahtan who originally migrated from the Yemen. The immediate origins of the family are, however, in Rawdat al Sudayr of Najd. The family comprises some six hundred males and the trees shown here only show individuals relevant to the commercial information. A further section is given in the Kuwait volume where they have huge interests.

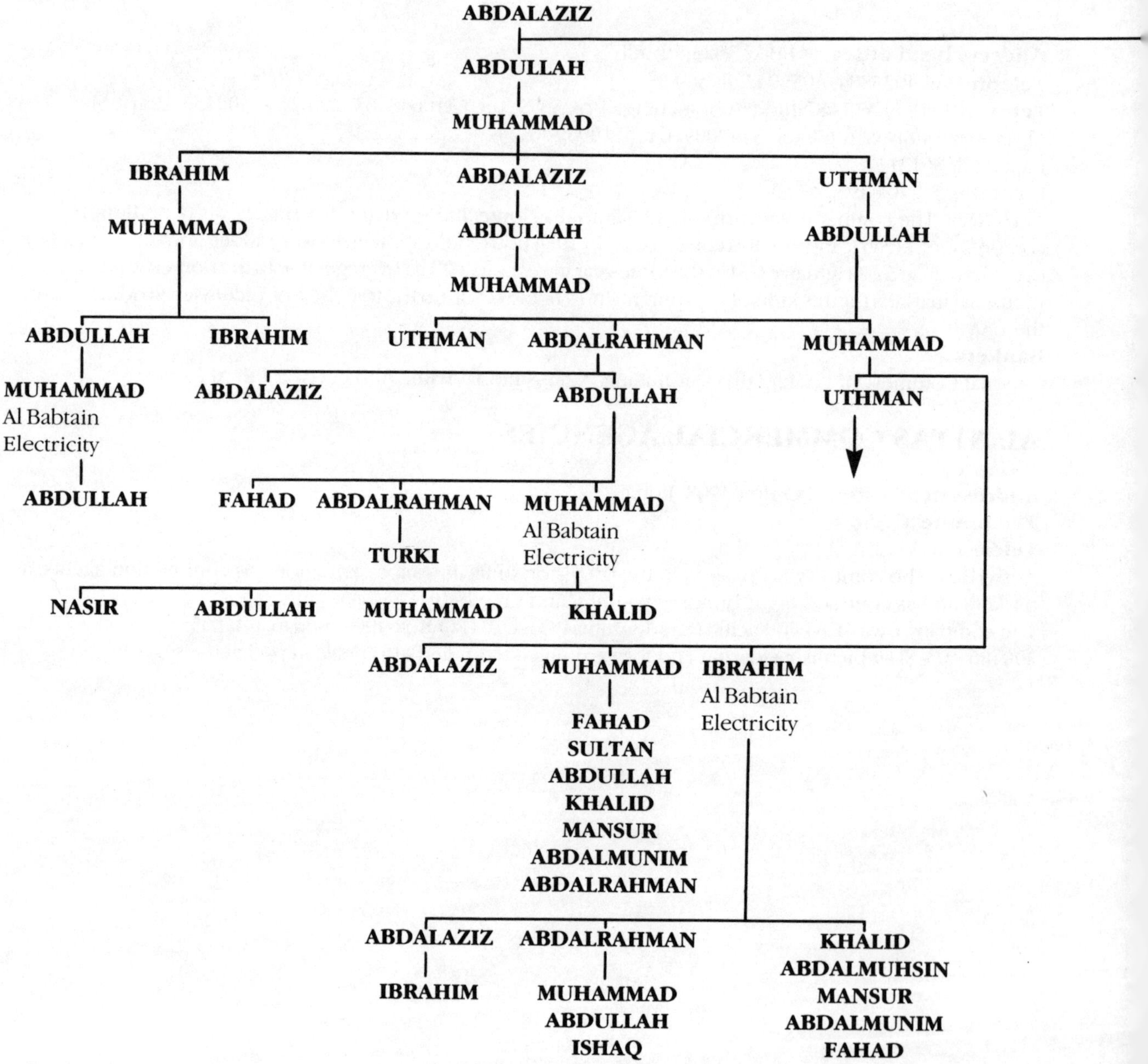

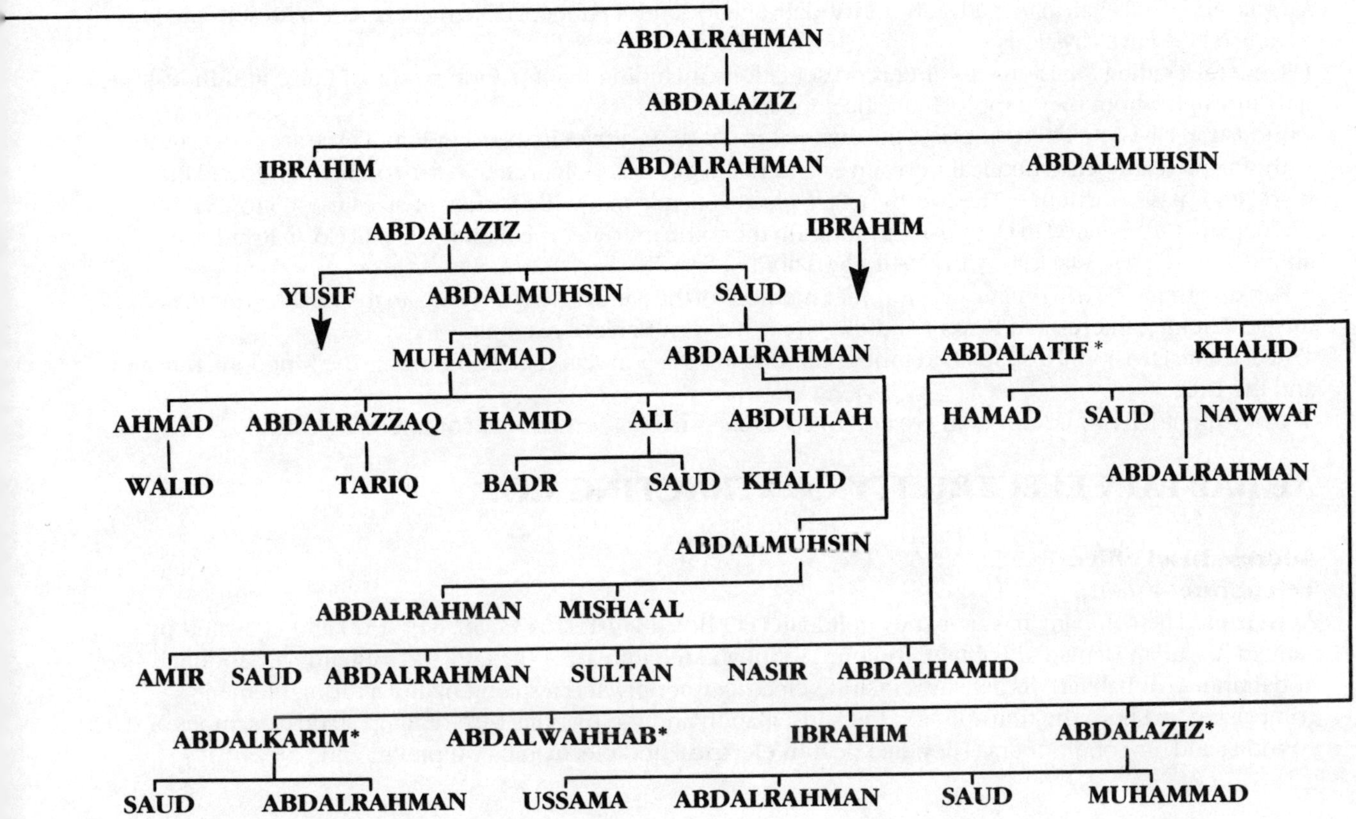

* In Abdalatif Saud al Babtain and Bros.

ABDALATIF SAUD AL BABTAIN AND BROTHERS CO.

Address head office PO Box 494, al Khobar
Telephone 8642761
Telex 780178 SHUROOK SJ
Activities The company is a commercial entity of considerable power and possessed of both high integrity and a modern dynamic approach to business. Within the Kingdom they have branches in Riyadh (PO Box 2711, tel. 4025024, 4027122, cable SHUROOK), Jiddah (PO Box 2103, tel. 6443081, 6440237), Qasim, Ha'il, Turaif and Najran. The company is owned by Abdalkarim, deputy chairman in Kuwait, Abdalaziz, chairman in Kuwait, Abdalatif, chairman in Riyadh, and Abdalwahhab Saud al Babtain, deputy chairman in Riyadh, and is organised into five divisions.
1. General Trading Division. Holding representations including that for Eastern Co. of Cairo and Indesit of Italy through whom they supply domestic appliances.
2. Industrial Division. This comprises the ownership of four factories in the Kingdom. Three are concerned with downstream petrochemical derivatives and make plastics, polyurethane for roofing and foundation work, and plastic furniture. The fourth makes plastic barrels in a wide variety of sizes from 5 to 255 litres. These plants are situated in Dammam. In addition the company owns the Babtain Biscuit Co. in Riyadh and an interest in a paint factory with Yusuf Algosaibi.
3. Banking Branch. The company is a founder member of the Saudi American Bank in the Kingdom and has further banking interests in Kuwait and the Great Western Bank of Arizona.
4. Real Estate Division. This looks after the company's interests in real estate holdings in the Kingdom, Kuwait and the USA.
5. Investment Division. A division created to control a varied international commercial portfolio.

AL BABTAIN ELECTRICITY CONTRACTING CO.

Address head office Riyadh
Telephone 4028012
Activities The company has branches in Jiddah (PO Box 4849, tel. 6433758, 6433132) and is owned by Hamad Abdullah Hamad al Babtain, Ibrahim Abdullah Muhammad al Babtain and Muhammad Abdullah Abdalrahman al Babtain. Its activities include electricity supply and a strong manufacturing element comprising, in short, the transmission lines installation and the manufacture of lamp standards, pipes and conduits and air conditioners. They also deal in electrical and electronic equipment and parts.

The Family of Baeshan

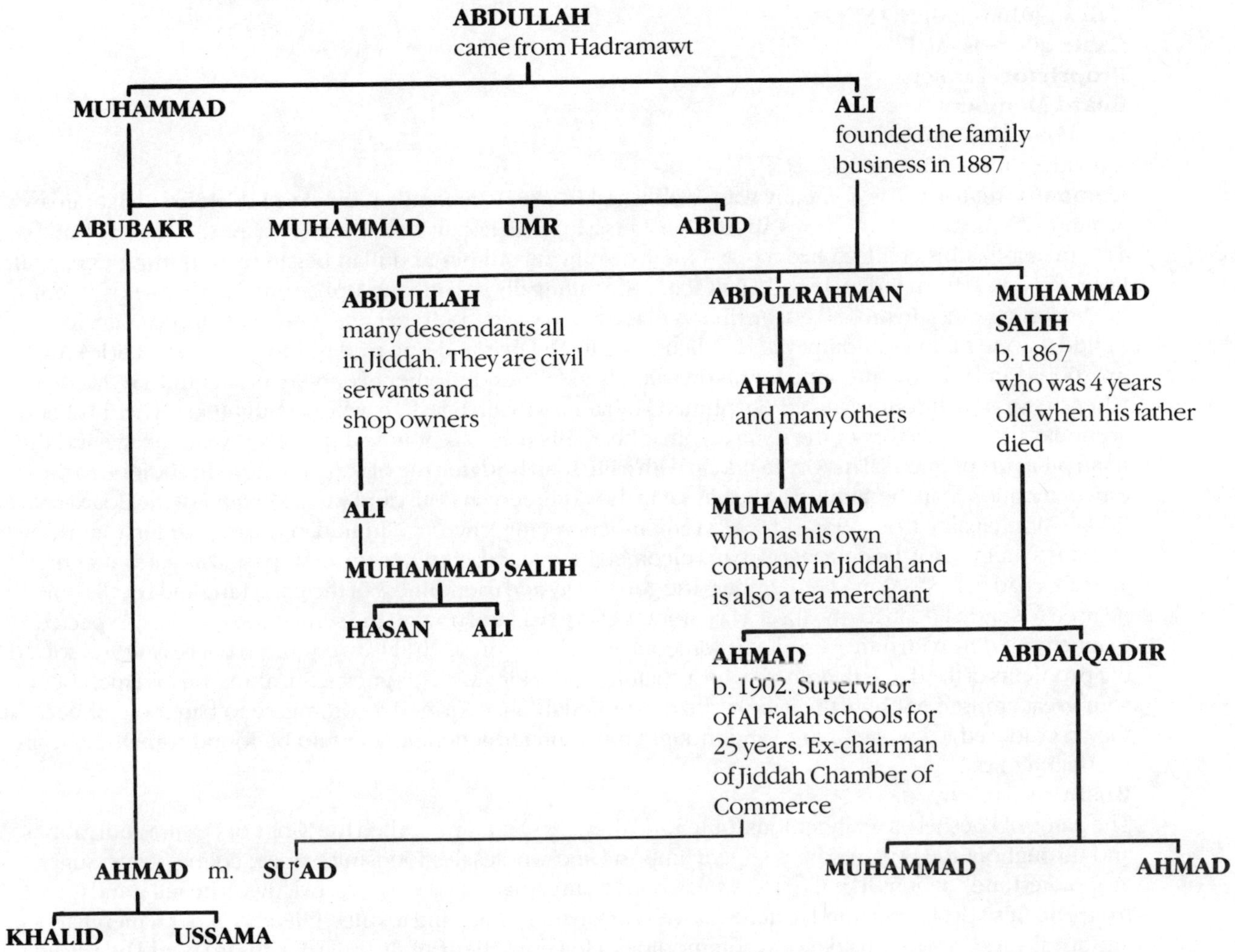

AHMAD MOHAMED SALEH BAESHEN AND COMPANY

Address head office P.O.Box 18 Jiddah
Telephone 6432964, 6431471
Telex 401664 FRIEND SJ
Cable address AMEEN
Proprietor Partnership
Board Members
Su'ad Bint Ahmad Baeshen
Ahmad Abubaker Baeshen
Company history The company was established in 1887.The family moved to Jiddah from Hadramawt around 1790 because the father of Abdullah left his garden in Robat, Wadi Du'an, to a mosque he had built. This meant that his children had to earn their own living. Ali bin Abdullah began by importing rice, white flour and goods from India. He had a half share in a sailing dhow with one Muhammad Jawhar whose family has become extinct. In those days the dhows made two voyages each year and there were three main fleets in Jiddah, one sailing to Bombay and Calicut, one to Malabar and one to Basra for dates and barley.Ali prospered and built a compound for his own family in 1849 and another twenty years later in 1869. He died when he was ninety four years old. Sh. Ahmad Muhammad Salih Baeshen, whose daughter and her husband are today the proprietors of the company that bears his name, is now seventy seven years of age and the main pillar of commercial history in Jiddah with a life span bridging the old and the new. In addition to the offices mentioned in the family tree he has sat in the Commercial Court and was a Member of the Board of Jiddah Municipality from 1933-1969. He remembers seeing Lawrence in Jiddah during the First World War and was a member of the delegation that welcomed King Abdalaziz when the city opened its gates after the Sharif Ali had fled. Sh. Ahmad remembers the generosity and friendliness of the great king and recalls how he used to stay in Jiddah for the three Hajj months every year and how all the senior citizens were expected to lunch and dine with him every day. If someone was absent the King always enquired the reason and solved the problems of the day as they arose whilst chatting and joking with his guests. Sh. Ahmad also remembers with great amusement how the senior citizens of Jiddah once formed a committee to ban football because they considered it a waste of time and thought the younger generation should be found something more profitable to do.
Business Activity
The name of Baeshen is really famous for tea and they are sometimes called the Kings of Tea in Saudi Arabia and throughout the region. The company imports and wholesales foodstuffs, ghee, coffee beans, sugar, evaporated and condensed milk, rice, wheat, butter, jams, marmalade, sweets, biscuits, fruit juice and tinned fruit. They also deal in soap and matches as well as polythene bags and textiles, gifts and general merchandise and are always keen to consider new commodities. However, they rightly insist that these should be priced CIF Jiddah and any offer must be accompanied by samples.
Bankers Saudi Faransi Bank.

AHMAD ABDALRAHMAN BAESHAN AND SONS

Address head office PO Box 24, Jiddah
Telephone 6433183, 6433184, 6433185
Activities Established in 1910, this company is owned by Ahmad Abdalrahman and deals in grain, tea, tobacco and similar commodities.

The Family of Baroom

A family of Sayyids, descendants of the Prophet Muhammad, who, though originating in the Holy City of Mecca, more recently immigrated to Jiddah from the Wadi Du'an in Hadramawt.

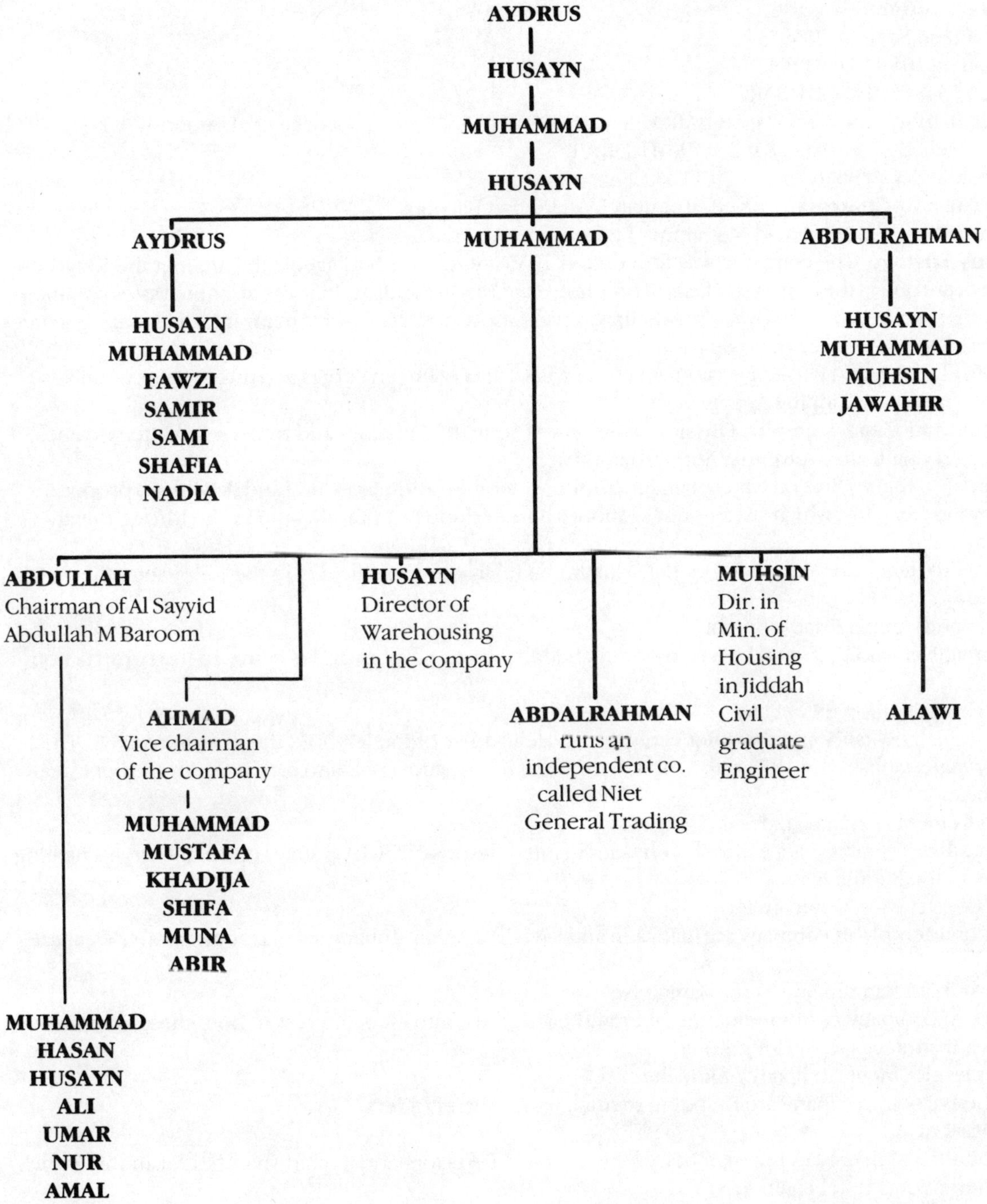

AL SAYED ABDULLAH MUHAMMAD BAROOM COMPANY

Address head office P.O.Box 1346 Jiddah
Telephone 6422366
Telex 401165 BAROOM SJ
Cable address PORTLAND JIDDAH
Subsidiary offices
Riyadh, Sitteen St., tel. 4763873
Bahrain, tlx. 9106 TRARAB BN
Cairo, tel. 934845, tlx. 2421 BAROOM
London, tel. 01 486 2466 tlx. 24458 BAROOM LDN (6 Portman Towers, George St., London W.1.)
New York, tel. 212 751 0566, tlx. 236496 TUDR UR
Houston, tel. 713 795 5102-3, tlx. 79 1125 USA
Proprietor and Chairman Sayed Abdullah Muhammad Baroom
Vice Chairman Sayed Ahmad Muhammad Baroom
Company History The company was founded in 1955 and established agents throughout the Kingdom. Today they are one of the largest stockists of building materials in Saudi Arabia with an annual sales volume of nearly five hundred million riyals. The main company above now represents many international companies and is organised into three main divisions.
1. Baroom Shipping and Barges Division which controls a fleet of fifteen barges and three motor vessels as well as operating as Shipping Agents.
2. Baroom Cranes and Transport Division which owns some fifty tractors and trailers and fifteen cranes of capacities varying from twelve to a hundred and twenty tons.
3. Baroom Real Estate Division which manages the considerable holdings in land and developed properties owned by the company, which last amount to about a hundred and fifty buildings and villas throughout the Kingdom.
In addition to the above Al Sayed Abdullah Muhammad Baroom has interests in the following other companies
1. Bilmat Saudi Arabia Establishment
This company is wholly owned by Sayed Abdullah Muhammad Baroom and is active in the construction business.
2. Saudi Steel Re-inforcement Ltd
Sayed Abdullah owns 75% of this joint venture and Helical Bar of the UK hold the remaining 25%. The company was established in 1978 with a capital of three million Saudi riyals and produces cut and bent steel to specification.
3. Jiddah Cement Company Ltd
Sayed Abdullah's company is a major shareholder in this enterprise which operates one of the largest floating terminals in the Middle East.
4. Saudi Construction Company
The headquarters of this company are in Riyadh and Sayed Abdullah Muhammad Baroom owns a 25% share of it.
5. Trans Arabian Bahrain and Trans Capital New York
The Baroom company is a founding member and holds the controlling interest in both these companies.
6. Red Sea Insurance Ltd of Hong Kong
Red Sea Development Company of Jiddah
Where the Baroom company are founding members and shareholders.
7. Nova Park AGAL
Sayed Abdullah Muhammad is a member of the Board of Directors and a main shareholder in this Zurich based international hotel chain group.

8. The Saudi National Maritime Transportation Company
Baroom is a founding member and holds 5515 shares.
9. Saudi Swiss Outworker Services
A majority shareholder and founding member, Al Sayed Abdullah Muhammad Baroom operates general maintenance services through this company throughout Saudi Arabia.
Bankers Saudi British Bank, National Commercial Bank, Bank Melli of Iran, Saudi Cairo Bank.

BAROOM ESTABLISHMENT FOR TRADE AND CONTRACTING

Address head office PO Box 6976, Jiddah
Telephone 6364835
Telex 401165 BAROOM SJ
Activities This company is owned by Husain Aydrus Baroom and deals in industrial and domestic paints, the supply of building materials and sanitary ware.

BLUE CIRCLE INDUSTRIES LTD.

Address head office PO Box 1346, Jiddah
Telephone 6422388, 6422377, 6422366
Telex 401165 BAROOM SJ
Activities The company was formed in 1929 and is owned by Blue Circle and managed by Syd. Abdullah Muhammad Baroom. It handles the brand names Blue Circle and Sandgex and is concerned with domestic and industrial paints, roofing products, concrete additives and decorating materials.

AL DABAL CO. (SGB SCAFFOLDING AND FRAMEWORK DIVISION)

Address head office PO Box 1346, Jiddah
Telephone 6674674
Telex 401165 BAROOM SJ
Activities The company supplies scaffolding and is owned by Syd. Abdullah Muhammad Baroom. It has branches in Riyadh and Dammam.

ELITE ESTABLISHMENT FOR TRADING AND CONTRACTING

Address head office PO Box 2870, Jiddah
Telephone 6510147, 6519847, 6530924, 6517812
Telex 401165 BAROOM SJ
Activities Formed in 1977, this company acts as commission agents and deals in foodstuffs, consumer products and electronic equipment and components. Among the agencies held are Panda Chocolate, Finn Crisp, XF Toothpaste, and in the western area, Kirsch dietary and regular drinks. The company is owned by Syd. Abdalrahman Baroom.

JIDDAH STEEL TRADING AND SERVICE CENTRE

Address head office PO Box 1705, Jiddah
Telephone 6880416
Telex 403395 JSTS SJ
Activities A company owned by Syd. Abdullah Muhammad Baroom which deals in structural beams, steel sheet, profiles and pipes.

The Family of Batterjee

A family who established themselves in Jiddah during the last decade of the last century when they settled from India.

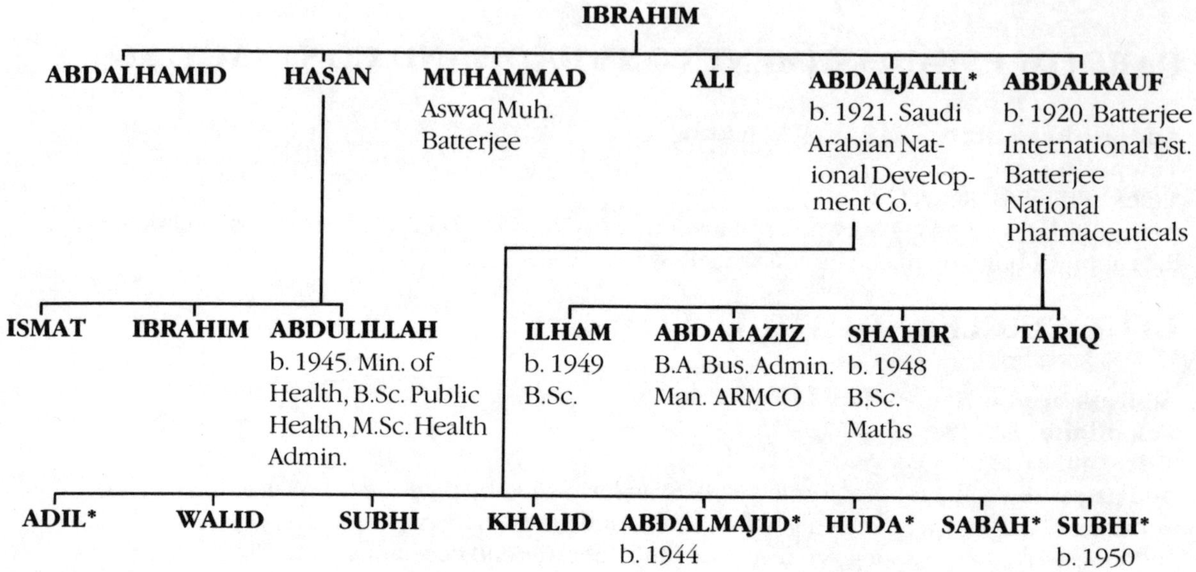

* Shareholders in Batterjee Export Import Co.

BATTERJEE NATIONAL PHARMACEUTICALS STORES AND PHARMACY

Address head office PO Box 2, Jiddah
Telephone 6432550, 6423326, 6424668
Telex 401451 IBRAHM SJ
Activities This, the co-foundation of the Batterjee commercial holdings, is one of the oldest businesses in Jiddah. It was founded in 1908 and today is owned by Abdalrauf Ibrahim Batterjee and his brothers. The company deals in drugs and pharmaceuticals, cosmetics, perfumes, scientific and laboratory equipment, medical and surgical equipment. The company also owns the Jiddah National Pharmacy, PO Box 3175, Jiddah, tel. 6431681.

ALLKEM CHEMICAL INDUSTRIES CO. LTD.

Address head office PO Box 3270, Jiddah
Telephone 6654326, 6693697
Activities The company deals in aggregates, ready-mix concrete and building materials and is managed by Ismat Batterjee and owned by Muhammad Wahida Mahmud.

ABDALRAUF IBRAHIM BATTERJEE AND BROS CO.

Address head office PO Box 2, Jiddah
Telephone 6432550, 6423326
Telex 401541 IBRIHM SJ
Activities Under the same ownership as the above, this company was also originally founded in 1908. It is concerned with the supply of hospital and medical equipment, cosmetics and perfume, pharmaceuticals and drugs.

BATTERJEE INTERNATIONAL ESTABLISHMENT

Address head office PO Box 5853, Jiddah
Telephone 6432566, 6445079, 6511234
Telex 400172 BATRJE SJ
Activities This business was begun in 1975 and is owned by Abdalrauf Ibrahim Batterjee and managed by him and three of his sons, Abdalaziz, Shahir and Tariq; other members of the family participate in the partnership. It represents a departure from the family pharmaceutical interests and deals in aggregates, are suppliers and manufacturers of aluminium products, architects , suppliers of sanitary ware and building materials such as concrete blocks and bricks, building systems and pre-fabricated buildings. They also act as building contractors and supply doors and windows, furniture, domestic and industrial paints, tiles, marble, perfumes and cosmetics.
The company owns Armco Pre-engineering Buildings, PO Box 5853, Jiddah, tel. 6690412, 6651393, 6632566, tlx. 400172 BATRJE SJ. The company was founded in 1978 and is active as building contractors in the pre-fabricated building systems field.

BATTERJEE EXHIBITION

Address head office PO Box 161, Jiddah
Telephone 6444414
Activities This company is owned by Ali Ibrahim Batterjee and deals in rugs and carpets as well as clocks and watches, cosmetics and perfumes. The business started in 1970.

ELHAM ABDALRAUF BATTERJEE ESTABLISHMENT

Address head office PO Box 5853, Jiddah
Telephone 6432566, 6651393
Telex 400172 BATRJE SJ
Activities The enterprising daughter of Abdalrauf founded in 1977 and now manages this her own interior design business. The company not only supplies design but also decorating materials on a contract basis.

ASWAQ MUHAMMAD BATTERJEE

Address head office PO Box 2694, Jiddah
Telephone 6519427
Telex 402512 MBM SJ
Activities The company was established in 1975 and supplies tinned foodstuffs, drinks, fruit juices, fruit and vegetables.

SAUDI ARABIAN DEVELOPMENT CO (SAND)

Address head office PO Box 6033, 2550, Jiddah
Telephone 6693423, 6693428, 6672054
Telex 401253 SAND SJ;402154 SAUPER SJ
Activities With a branch in Riyadh, this company was founded in 1973 and is owned by Abdaljalil Batterjee and his sons, Subhi and Abdalmajid.
The company operates as general and electro-mechanical contractors in the following areas: business systems amd computer software, operation and maintenance of security systems, hospital management, real estate developers, food supermarkets, furniture and petroleum industry and shopping centres. They also own and operate private hospitals.
Abdaljalil Ibrahim Batterjee is also part of a limited partnership which is confined to his family. This is the Saudi Arabian Company for Trade and Development Ltd, where he and his five sons hold 14 percent, two daughters hold 7 percent and his wife 3 percent. As the Abdaljalil Batterjee Establishment he holds 56 percent of Saudi Cap Co. Ltd., which is a joint venture with Cap Co. Ltd. (Middle East) of the UK (which withdrew in 1980 assigning 40 percent of the shares to the Batterjee company), 75 percent of Fiberean Saudi Arabia Ltd and a large investment in the Batterjee International Establishment Plastics Factory and the Batterjee International Establishment (q.v.)

AL MAHMODIAH ESTABLISHMENT

Address head office PO Box 3270, Jiddah
Telephone 6654326, 6693697
Activities Founded in 1975 this business is owned by Wahida Muhammad Salih Mahmud and managed by Ismat Batterjee. It deals in aggregates, building materials, water tanks, marble, fibreglass and ready-mix concrete.

The Family of Bohaimid

Originate in Manfuha Riyadh

BOHAIMID

IBRAHIM

SULAIMAN

ABDALAZIZ
contracting in Riyadh

ABDALRAHMAN
owner of Bohaimid antique shop in al Khobar

NASIR
contracting in Riyadh

BOHAIMID ANTIQUE SHOP

Address head office PO Box 252 Al Khobar
Telephone 86 44189
Cable address BOHAIMID
Proprietor Abdalrahman b, Sulaiman Bohaimid
Company history This successful small business was established in 1968 and moved to its present larger premises in 1975. Abdalrahman Bohaimid started because a bedouin asked him to sell a chest for him. Abdalrahman was able to do this quickly and easily, and the consequence was that he was inundated with antiques. Sadly this source of supply is now exhausted. However, Abdalrahman takes a real interest in his wares and guarantees their authenticity. In any case his shop is the best place in the Eastern Province to see traditional Arabian artefacts.
Bankers Riyadh Bank, Saudi British Bank

The Family of Binladen

A family with origins in Hadramawt, claiming Kinda descent from Imr al Qays.

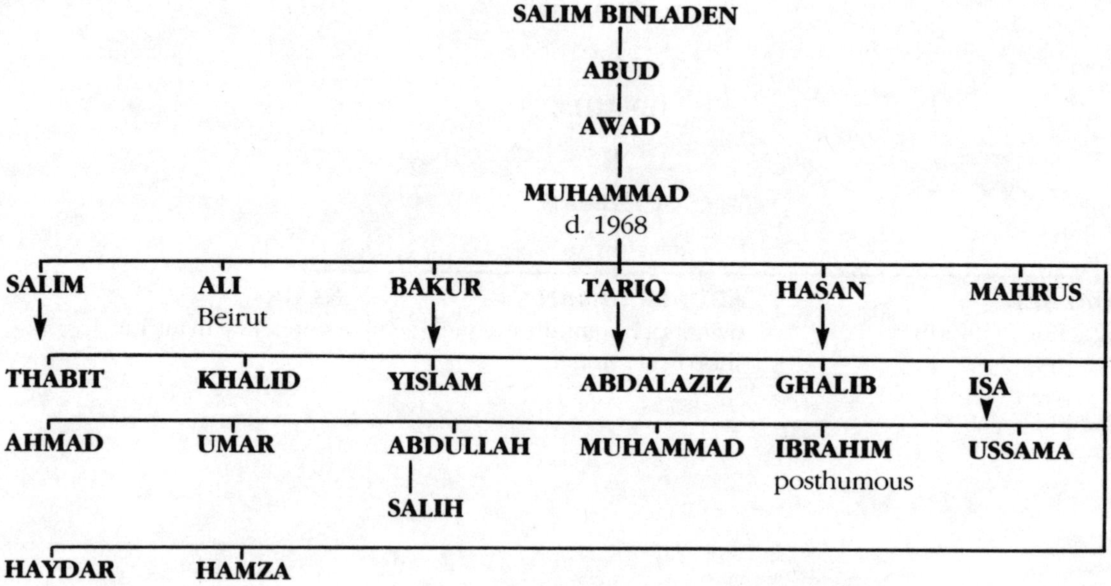

BINLADEN BROTHERS FOR CONTRACTING AND INDUSTRY

Address head office P.O.Box 2734 Jiddah
Telephone 29088, 29333, 28487
Telex 401044 BINLDN SJ, 401071 BINBRS SJ
Cable address LADENCO
Subsidiary offices
Riyadh P.O.Box 105, tel. 61427, 61428, tlx. 201104 BINRIAD SJ
Dammam P.O.Box 58, tel. 24070
Amman P.O.Box 5181, tel. 41620, tlx. 1207 JURHTL JO, 1267 JURHTL JO
Dubai P.O.Box 1555, tel. 21516, 27726, 27632, tlx. BINLADEN DB
Cairo 19 Arab League Building, tel. 708634, 707252
Beirut P.O.Box 113-5013, tel. 346662, tlx. 21692 RAYCO LE
London Suite 2, 140 Park Lane, W1, tel. 01 493 0522/3, tlx. 299971 BINLON G, 269885 SALLAN G
Houston Texas Suite 1109, Fannin Bank Building, tel. (713) 795 0004, tlx. 774552 BINBROS HOUS, 775858 EXECJET HOUS

The company acts as the main holder of joint family interests in the famous commercial empire founded by Sh. Muhammad. The company is administered by a Board of Directors under the Chairmanship of Sh. Salem Mohammad Binladen and was founded in 1972.

Board Members
Sh. Hassan Muhammad Binladen
Sh. Bakr Muhammad Binladen
Sh. Ghalib Muhammad Binladen
Sh. Thabit Muhammad Binladen
Sh. Omar Muhammad Binladen
Sh. Mahrous Muhammad Binladen

Company History

In all Sh. Muhammad had some fifty four sons and many work in the family business whilst others have formed their own companies either as well or independently. The story of Sh. Muhammad's journey from Hadramawt and his rebuilding of Mecca, which job he obtained having built a ramp to enable King Abdalaziz to get his car into his palace, is one of the most romantic success stories in the history of Saudi Arabian business. However, the romance of the company and its present controllers should not be confused with the sturdy business acumen which holds the group so successfully together and which has led them to develop and diversify into the very self-sufficient organisation we see today.

In addition to the above, Binladen Brothers have a substantial stake in Al Fadl Binladen J & P for pre-fabrication and a joint venture with Hunting Surveys Ltd. of the UK. These enormous resources demonstrate clearly the capabilities of the Binladen Brothers Group and they are rounded off by a Trading Division which imports structural steel elements and acts as exclusive agents for Heras Hekwerk of Holland for fencing materials, Alphacoustic of France for quality suspended ceilings and Pander Projects of Holland for standard and luxury contract furniture.

Addresses of Subsidiaries, Joint Ventures and Partnerships
Binladen Kaiser, P.O.Box 2734 Jiddah, tel. 51512, tlx. 401071 BINBRS, 401044 BINLDN
Al Mihdar Binladen, P.O.Box 4445 Jiddah, tel. 74791, 73403
Binladen Saxons Co., P.O.Box 3143 Jiddah, tel. 36873, 35705, tlx. 401071, 401044; P.O.Box 54 Al Khobar, tel. 41933
Binladen TelecommunicationsCo., P.O.Box 6045 Jiddah, tel. 52041, 55186, tlx. 401071 BINBRS
Binladen Trading, P.O.Box 2742 Jiddah, tel. 34543, tlx. 401071, 401044
Ready Mix Saudi, P.O.Box 5948 Jiddah, tel. 55161/2/3, tlx. c/o Binladen Brothers
Saudi Traffic Safety, P.O.Box 105 Riyadh, tel. 33676, tlx. 201104 BINRIAD

The Family of Bin Mahfouz

Originating in Kharaikhar near the Wadi Du'an in Hadramawt, the Saudi branch descend from Salim Ahmad Bin Mahfouz who first worked in the Kaki household until he was able to establish his own business which developed into the banking colossus seen today. They come from Al Mahfouz, a separate section of the Sai'ar (see Binzagr).

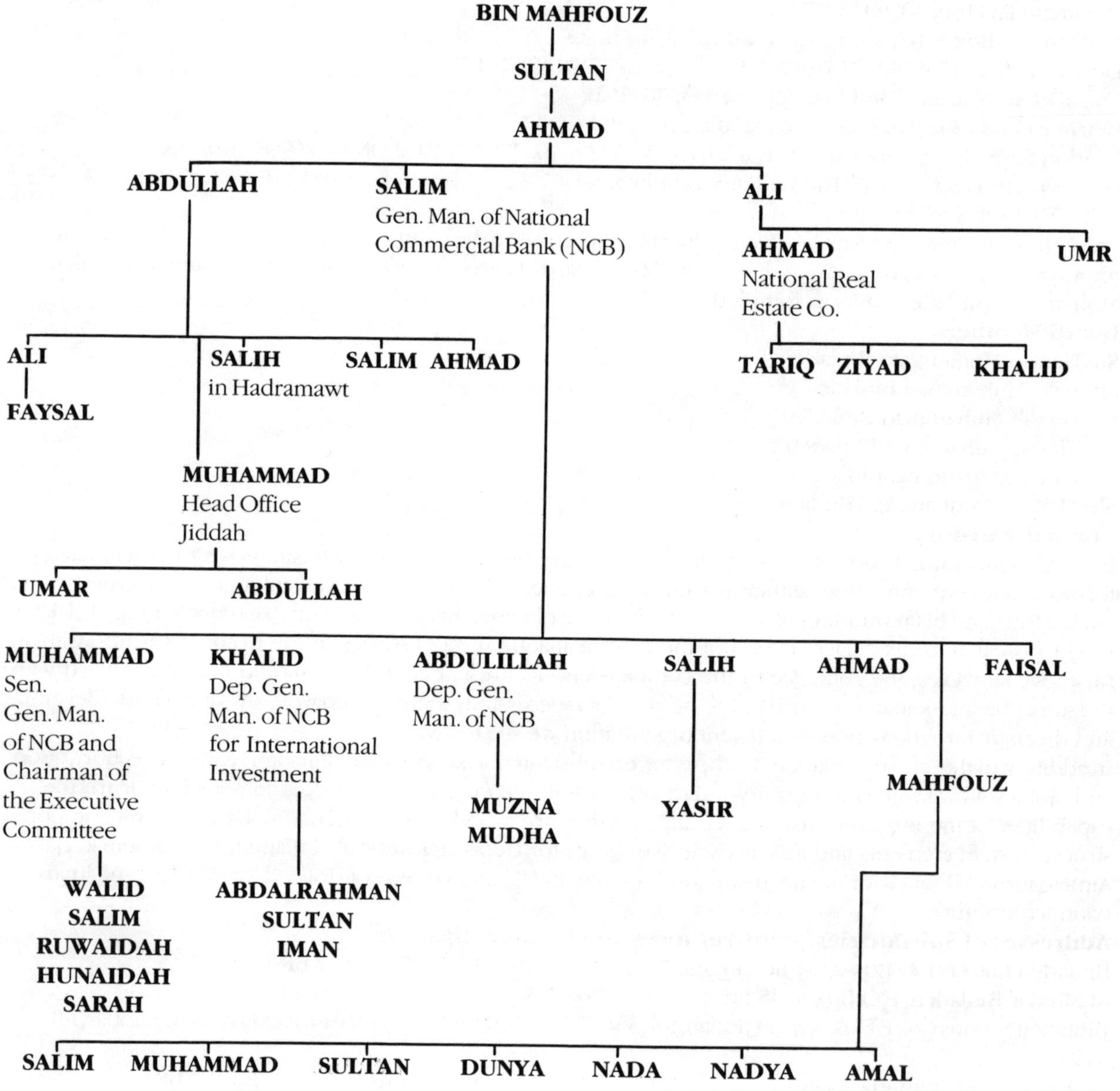

THE NATIONAL COMMERCIAL BANK

Address head office PO Box 3555, Jiddah
Telephone 6423794, 6443404, 6448393
Telex 403060
Cable Bank Saudi
Major branches
General Management, PO Box 3555, Jiddah; tel. 6423794, 6443404, 6448393; tlx. 403060.
Management International Division, PO Box 3555, Jiddah; tel. 6825935, 6825883/4; tlx. 403249, 403250
Management Central Region, PO Box 34, Riyadh, tel. 4776058; tlx. 201296
Management Western Region, PO Box 5171, Jiddah; tel. 6603485/6; tlx. 403548
Management Eastern Region, PO Box 5558, Dammam; tel. 8645138, 8645916, 8645039; tlx. 670548, 670549
Computer Centre, PO Box 3555, Jiddah; tel. 6879491, 6886694; tlx. 401102
Jiddah Main, PO Box 104; tel. 6473780, 6478132; tlx. 401086
Madinah, PO Box 26; tel. 8224248, 8229355, 8235346; tlx. 470010
Abha, PO Box 12; tel. 2246583, 2246545, 2240712; tlx. 901009
Riyadh Main, PO Box 34; Tel. 4034100, 4013200; tlx. 201009
Dammam Main, PO Box 13; tel. 8320760, 8321717, 8321566; tlx. 601116
Al Khobar Main, PO Box 1; tel. 8949665, 8949669, 8949657; tlx. 670023, 671340
The bank has overseas branches and representative offices in Beirut, Bahrein, London, Frankfurt, Singapore, Seoul, Tokyo and New York. The total of branches nationally and internationally exceeds 150.
Salim Ahmad Bin Mahfouz began his career as a foreign exchange dealer in Mecca where he worked for the Kaki family. He is seventy-five today and whilst he is still Chairman of the NCB, his son Khalid is the most active member of the family in the Bank's affairs. He owns a large holding in the Mercantile Texas Corp. as well as real estate in Texas and Florida, in addition to his share of the family's 51 percent stake in the NCB. It has been estimated that all this would make him worth about one billion dollars.
The Bank has shares in the following local companies: Badana Electric and Water Company, the National Gas and Manufacturing Co., Electric Company of Riyadh, Yamama Cement Company, Saudi Provisions Company, National Gypsum Company, Medwa Electric Company, Saudi Islamic Preaching Society, Jiddah Electric Company, Saudi Arabian Cement Company, Arabic Fertilizer Co. (SAFCO), Electric Company of Makkah, Tabuk Electric Company, Baljurashi Electric Company, Red Sea Insurance Services Company, Saudi Hotel Services Company, Saudi Investment Banking Corporation, Saudi Real Estate Company, Yanbu Cement Company, Southern Cement Company, Saudi National Marine Transport Company, Saudi Consolidated Electric Company, Tihama for Advertising, Public Relations and Marketing Research.
The Bank participates in the following banks: Saudi International Bank Ltd., Compagnie Arabe et Internationale d'Investissements, Arab Jordan Investment Bank, Saudi Investment Banking Corporation, Arab Malaysian Development Bank, Arab Latin American Bank, Saudi Spanish Bank, Banco Bozano Simonsen, Arab Tunis Investment Bank, Arab Tunis International Bank, Arab European Holding Company.

The Family of Binzagr

The family has been an important part of Jiddah's commercial life for over a century and a street behind the National Commercial Bank is named after them. Originally they came from the north of the Wadi Hadramawt, from Ajlaniya village in the Sa'yar country, and are of Kinda stock. Sh. Wahib is probably the only Saudi citizen who assists the game of cricket and both he and his brother Abdullah presented the Binzagr Cup for the Saudi Cricket League Tournament in Jiddah in honour of the One Flame Match Co. The Binzagr Company has its own team too, and has played matches in the Sudan as well as all over the Kingdom.

UBAYD

- **MUHAMMAD** began trading in Jiddah. He had been brought up by his stepfather Nasir al Harbi and sailed with him on trading voyages to Bahrein. On Nasir's death Muhammad took over the ship.
  - **ABDULLAH** d.
  - **SA'ID** Chairman of the Binzagr Group
    - **WAHIB** Chief Exec. of Binzagr Group, ex Vice Pres. of Jiddah Chamber of Commerce. Dir. of SIBC. BSc (Econ.) UK; other appointments held: Dir. of Saudi Airlines, Mayor of Jiddah, Founder Member King Abdulaziz University, Board Member Riyadh Bank, Board Member UBAM, Member of Saudi German and Saudi British Economic Commissions, Chairman of Al Alamiya Insurance Co., Board Member of Swiss Arab and Arab British Chambers of Commerce.
    - **SORAYA**
    - **FAISAL** Dir. Binzagr Group m. sister of Husayn Linjawi
      - **GHAZI**
      - **NADIM**
      - **HIBAR**
    - **MUHAMMAD UBAYD** Dir. Binzagr Group m. into Attar
      - **SA'ID**
      - **LUJAYN**
      - **AHMAD**
    - **IMJA**

SAFIYA artist of great reputation and talent, much of whose work has been published	**ABDULLAH** Dir. Binzagr Gr.	**SU'AD**	**OFFAT** a graduate of Wellesley. MA Columbia, D.Phil Oxford

Both the Binzagr and the Bin Mahfouz (q.v.) emanate from the Sa'yar of Hadramawt and both are very successful. In the old days this tribe had a fearsome reputation for raiding and were feared throughout the Empty Quarter; Philby called them the wolves of the desert. However, today they are even more successful at a more peaceful form of commerce.

SAID M O BINZAGR AND PARTNERS CO.

Address head office P.O.Box 54 Jiddah
Telephone 23529, 23769, 23188
Telex 401131 IKBAL SJ
Cable address IKBAL
Subsidiary offices
Riyadh P.O.Box 392, tel. 20802, 20803, tlx. 201702 IKBAL SJ
Al Khobar P.O.Box 96, tel. 8641430, 8641431, tlx. 670021 IKBAL SJ
Proprietor The Partnership
Board Members
Chairman, Said M O Binzagr
Chief Executive, Wahib Said Binzagr
Director Faisal Said Binzagr
Director Muhammad Obaid Said Binzagr
Director Abdullah Said Binzagr
Company History
Historically what is nowadays known as the Binzagr Group began over a hundred years ago when Sh. Mohamed Obaid Binzagr started trading in Jiddah. It is thus one of the oldest companies in the Kingdom. In 1825 a partnership was formed called Shinkar and Binzagr Co. It is this company which is the direct ancestor of the present enterprise in which sound modern management is combined with a desire for innovation to provide one of the most successful and skilled selling organisations in the Saudi market. The company's activities in the marketing field include the following services: importation, modern central and regional warehousing, selling, direct distribution, advertising and merchandising. The company is organised into three regional offices and ten local branches. The range of products is arranged in divisions as follows:
Household and Toiletries Division
Food and Drinks Division
Tobacco Products Division
Agriculture and Chemical Products Division
Industrial and Automotive Products Division
Consumer Durables Division
The Binzagr Group holds the following other commercial interests:
1. Wholly owned companies
Binzagr Match Factory in partnership with A.H. Herring of Germany.
Binzagr Saudi Shipping Ltd. with Barber International of Norway.
Saudi Express Services with Palm Line of UK for customs clearance and freight forwarding.
Advance Services with Advance Linen Services Ltd. of the UK for cleaning services.
2. Foreign Joint Ventures
Binzagr Lever Ltd. with Unilever Commonwealth Holding Ltd. of the UK for soaps and toiletries manufacture.
Binzagr Coro Group with Coro A S of Denmark for soft drink manufacture.
Trans Arabia Ltd. with S.J. Investments CI Ltd. of the Channel Islands for trucking.
Binzagr Pauling Ltd. with Pauling Middle East Ltd. of the UK for contracting.
Cicatrade Ltd. with the Cica Group of Brazil for export from Brazil.
Saudi Danish Technical Installation Ltd. with Monberg and Thorsen of Denmark for mechanical and electrical contracting.
3. Minority Interests in the following:
Al Alamiya Insurance Co. Ltd. UK with Sun Alliance Ltd. UK for insurance.
Saudi Ghee Industry Ltd. with Saudi partners for oil and fat refining.
Wilkinson Sword Middle East Ltd. with Wilkinson Sword UK and the Egyptian Government for the manufacture of razor blades.

The Souqs Co. Ltd. with Southland of USA and Saudi partners for supermarkets and convenience stores.
Utility companies with Saudi partners for electricity.
Saudi British Bank with the British Bank of the Middle East.
Saudi Investment Banking Corporation (q.v.) with Chase Manhattan.
4. Other Binzagr Companies
Wahib Saudi Arabia Binzagr and Brothers for property investment, representation of foreign companies and the assisting of them in Saudi Arabia.
International Agencies Ltd. Saudi Arabia for office equipment, furniture and security equipment. Managed by East Asiatic Co. Ltd. of Denmark.
ARMSA Arabian Resource Management SA Switzerland for new business development, consulting services and marketing (address: 29 Boulevard Helvetique, 1207 Geneva, tel. (022) 358121, 368787, tlx. 23584 ARMSA CH).
ARMSA Arabian Resource Management Saudi Arabia, as above.
PLYMS NV for international investment, managed by ARMSA.
Saudibras Investimentos for investment property.
Agropecuaria E Representacoes Ltda, Brazil, for investment.
Binzagr International Trading Co., managed by ARMSA for specialized trading in Saudi Arabia, USA and Europe.
Binzagr Services Ltd. UK commercial and marketing services.
Bankers (Saudi Arabia) Al Bank al Saudi al Hollandi, The Saudi British Bank, Al Bank al Saudi al Faransi, Citibank, National Commercial Bank, Riyadh Bank, Saudi Investment Banking Corporation, BBME, Saudi International Bank.

INSTITUTIONAL AND CATERING DIVISION

Food and drink, disposables, industrial cleaning products for hostels, camps and hospitals.

WAHIB SAID BINZAGR AND BROTHERS

Address head office PO Box 209, Jiddah
Telephone 6423769, 6423188
Activities This is the holding company for the Binzagr Group and is owned as follows: Abdullah b. Said, Faisal b. Said, Muhammad Ubaid b. Said and Wahib b. Said 15.4 percent each and Uffat bint Said, Su'ad bint Said, Safiya bint Said, Imja bint Said and Soraya bint Said 7.7 percent each.

BINZAGR BARBER SAUDI SHIPPING CO. LTD.

Address head office PO Box 208, Jiddah
Telephone 6519136, 6519132, 6519308
Telex 401818 BINZGR SJ
Activities Formed in 1976 this company is owned by Wahib Said Binzagr and Bros. It has branches in Riyadh and Yanbu and its activities cover liners, tankers, tramp representation, clearing and forwarding, inland trucking, container and cargo storage.

BINZAGR CORO LTD.

Address head office PO Box 7004, Jiddah
Telephone 6370233
Telex 4011131 IKBAL SJ, 401830 ZGRBRO SJ
Activities This company is owned by the Abdullah and Said M O Bonzagr Co. and Co-Ro Food AS of Denmark. It is managed by Faisal Said Binzagr and operates as a soft drink manufacturer making the brand names Suntop, Sunquick, Sunlolly, and Paf.

ARABIAN DANISH BUILDING AND ENGINEERING CO. LTD.

Address head office PO Box 6877, Jiddah
Telephone 6714534
Telex 400796 ARDAN SJ
Activities The company is jointly ownd by Abdullah and Said M O Binzagr and Hoejgaard and Schultz of Denmark. They are civil engineering consultants and building contractors.

BINZAGR LEVER LTD.

Address head office PO Box 5694, Jiddah
Telephone 6447006
Telex 401131 IKBAL SJ
Activities A company owned by Abdullah Said M O Binzagr and Co. which was established in 1975 in joint venture with Unilever Commonwealth Holdings Ltd. It deals with detergents and cosmetics.

BINZAGR MATCH FACTORY

Address head office PO Box 6994, Jiddah
Telephone 6362997
Activities The company, set up in 1976, manufactures matches with the brand names Flame and Clock.

CHUBB SAFES AND LOCKS (INTERNATIONAL AGENCIES) LTD

Address head office PO Box 5018, Jiddah
Telephone 6513940, 6516740, 6516492
Telex 401131 IKBAL SJ
Activities Dealing in security equipment this company was established in 1950. It is owned by the Binzagr Group.

INTERNATIONAL AGENCIES LTD

Address head office PO Box 5018, Jiddah
Telephone 6513940, 6516492, 6516740
Telex 401131 IKBAL SJ
Activities A company formed in 1974 and owned by Wahib, Faisal, Muhammad and Abdullah Said Binzagr. The company supplies adding and calculating machines, office furniture and equipment, computer and business equipment, materials handling equipment, building materials, shelving and racking systems, security equipment, bookbinding, photo composers and graphic cameras. Brand names represented include Chubb, Compugraphic, Facit, ISS, Olivetti, Sweda, Muller Martini, Eskofot, CPT and Electrolux. There are branches in Riyadh (PO Box 9468, tel. 4774195, 4774085, 4774196) and al Khobar (PO Box 1840, tel. 8647608, 8649396).

AL RUBAIYAT COMPANY FOR INDUSTRY AND TRADE LTD

Address head office PO Box 209, Jiddah
Telephone 6422449
Telex 400795 ASMOB SJ
Activities The company is owned by the Binzagr Group and managed by Faisal Said Binzagr. There are branches in Riyadh (tel. 4641353) and al Khobar (tel. 8641430). This company is concerned with trading, investment, company representation and sponsorship, as well as joint ventures.

The Family of Buqshan

This very important family of Jiddah businessmen has ancient roots in the Hadramawt which probably stretch back to the time of the Himyarites and one of the two great ancestors of the Arab race, Qahtan. They come from the area around Subaikh in the Wadi Du'an and are attached tribally to the Banakhr Halqi of Saiban. In Jiddah they descend as below, as far as the main part of the family is concerned; others of the same name will have a different grandfather.

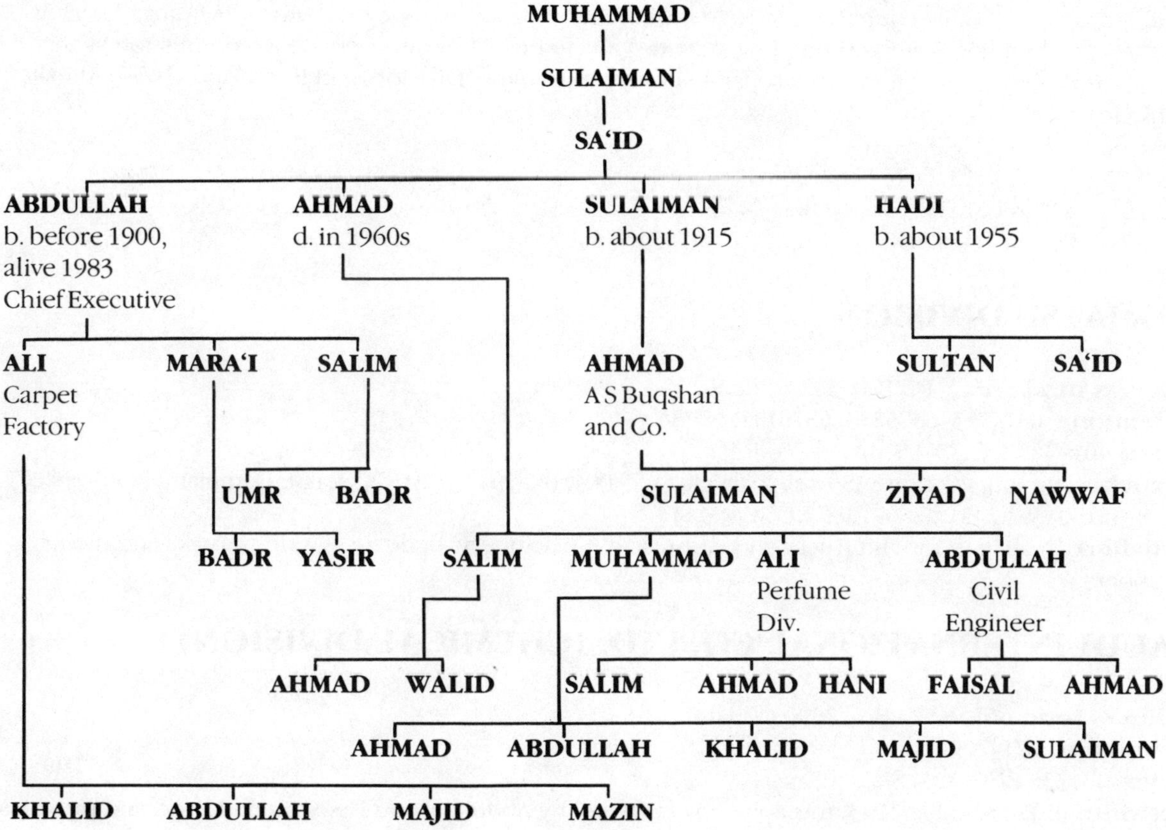

ABDULLAH SAID BUQSHAN AND BROTHERS

Address head office PO Box 378, Jiddah
Telephone 6429211, 6429434
Telex 402677, A ASBROS SJ, 402677 B ASBROS
Branches Riyadh, PO Box 80, tel.4028438, tlx. 201144 BGSHAN, Dammam, PO Box 103, tel. 8332188, tlx. 601065 BGSHAN
Activities This commercial entity is one of the largest companies in Saudi Arabia and is really a holding company for the family's business interests. The company is managed by Ali Abdullah Buqshan. Its activities cover a broad spectrum of general trading and contracting, but despite their eminence the family like to keep a very low profile.
Abdullah Said Buqshan and Bros. is owned by Ali Abdullah, Salim Ahmad and Mara'i Abdullah. The brand names carried by the company include Komatsu, Norge, Admiral, Bridgestone, Fedders, KHD, SKF, and Rockwell International.
The company deals in many areas of business: communications and navigation equipment, craft sales, paints, repair services, domestic and industrial and marine paints, poultry farms, power transmission equipment, printers and bookbinders, refrigeration equipment, estate agents, security equipment, restaurants,sanitary ware, boots and shoes, soft drinks, tailoring , textiles, water heaters, tyres and tube fittings, supply of ice making equipment, jewellery, construction equipment, household and kitchen equipment, engines and generators, agricultural and horticultural equipment, they deal in and distribute automotive parts, operate repair facilities, airconditioning equipment and parts, aviation and airport equipment, bathroom fittings, bearings, blankets and building materials, building systems and clothes. They also operate as commission agents.
The Perfume Department is run as a separate entity rather like a Division, and is managed by Ali Ahmad Buqshan:
Address: PO Box 5218, Jiddah
Tel. 6474533, 6475572, 6473970
Tlx. 402774 PERFUM SJ
Branches: Riyadh, tel. 4043818, Dammam, tel. 8332188.

KOMATSU DIVISION

Address head office PO Box 3329, Jiddah
Telephone 6874793, 6875253, 6870141, 6873404
Telex 401336 BUGCOM SJ
Branches Riyadh, PO Box 3586, tel. 4768530, 4774004, tlx. 202337 BUGCOM SJ, Dammam, PO Box 2277, tel. 8946180, 8946186, tlx. 671389 BUGCOM SJ
Activities Dealing in fork lift trucks and construction machinery, bulldozers, dump trucks and motor scrappers.

SAUDI INTERNATIONAL CO. LTD. (CHEMICAL DIVISION)

Address head office PO Box 2899, Jiddah
Telephone 6714209
Telex 401336 BUGCOM SJ
Activities Established in 1973, this company is owned by Abdullah Said Buqshan and Bros. and provides pest control services

SAUDI RAS STEEL CONSTRUCTION CO. LTD

Address head office PO Box 6902, Jiddah
Telephone 6718433, 6718416, 6716319
Telex 402677 ASBROS SJ
Activities A joint venture formed in 1981 between A S Buqshan and Bros. and Ras Co. of the USA. They trade in prefabricated building systems, steel buildings and structural steel.

WATTS GRIFFIS AND MCOUAT LTD.

Address head office PO Box 5219, Jiddah
Telephone 6693971, 6653045
Telex 401179 BOGSHN SJ
Activities The company is owned by Abdullah Said Buqshan and was established in 1979. They are geological and mining engineering consultants.

AL AFAK AVIATION AND TRANSPORT SERVICES CO. LTD

Address head office PO Box 2195, Jiddah
Telephone 6651404, 6652366, 6602961, 6692331, 6602953
Telex 400137
Activities Established in 1979, this company has branches in Riyadh and Dammam. It is owned by Ali Abdullah Buqshan in partnership with Umar Said Bafaqih and is concerned with air cargo services, chartering aircraft, aviation support services, aviation and airport equipment. They are clearing and forwarding agents and have interests in local and international transport services, travel agents and packers.

SAUDI ARABIAN PROJECT DEVELOPMENT CO.

Address head office PO Box 3330, Jiddah
Telephone 6659671, 6657816, 6534592
Telex 400258 SARDCO SJ, 400637 PREDC SJ
Activities Concerned with general contracting this company also operates in the spheres of marine work and electro-mechanical engineering. It is owned by Salim Abdullah Buqshan.

BUQSHAN TRADING CO.

Address head office PO Box 2372, Jiddah
Telephone 6432190, 6426992, 6449080, 6825450, 6820648
Telex 401179 BTRDCO SJ, 400271 MSB SJ
Activities Ahmad Sulaiman Buqshan is the owner of this company, set up in 1979. There are branches in Riyadh and Dammam. The company operates as commission agents and deals in cleaning equipment, medical equipment, jewellery and sports equipment. They are also building, maintenance and cleaning contractors.

BUQSHAN TRADING CO. (ENGINEERING CONTRACTING DIVISION)

Address head office PO Box 2372, Jiddah
Telephone 6820648, 6825450, 6827188
Telex 400271 MSB SJ
Activities With the same ownership as the preceding company, this concern is involved in civil engineering, marketing and public relations consultancy, in addition to operating as building contractors.

RED SEA COMPANY FOR INSURANCE AND DEVELOPMENT

Address head office PO Box 5761, Jiddah
Telephone 6422898, 6442631, 6442632
Telex 401228 RESIN SJ
Activities A company dealing in real estate and insurance which is owned by Ali Abdullah Buqshan and managed by Muhammad Salim Bin Mahfouz (q.v.). There are branches in Riyadh (PO Box 5908, tel. 4163642) and Dammam (PO Box 1939, tel. 8324256).

SAUDI ARABIAN CARPET FACTORY

Address head office PO Box 2371, Jiddah
Telephone 6432310, 6426928
Telex 400503 SUJAD SJ
Activities This company is a partnership between Ali Abdullah Buqshan, Ali Abdullah al Esayi (q.v.) and Siraj Umar Buqary. The company manufactures rugs and carpets and also operates as a decorating contractor.

SAUDI ARABIA PROJECTS DEVELOPMENT CO.

Address head office PO Box 3330, Jiddah
Telephone 6517460, 6517464, 6534593, 6531538, 6531546
Telex 400258 SAPDCO SJ, 400637 PREDCO SJ
Activities A partnership headed by Salim Abdullah Buqshan which was formed in 1978. The company deals in a very comprehensive list of products covering aviation, agriculture, communications, landscaping, building, foodstuffs, manufacture of polythene products and household goods.

SAUDI BAZAAR

Address head office PO Box 3948, Jiddah
Telephone 6534443
Telex 400295 SALEM SJ
Activities Founded in 1979 this company is owned by Salim Ahmad Buqshan. It covers industrial chemicals, china and glassware, cosmetic, perfumes, electrical equipment, cleaning products, household and kitchen equipment and they are also suppliers of hotel and restaurant equipment. They have the following branches throughout the city: Al Hamra Gift Store (tel. 6654056), Houseware Showroom (tel. 6604406), Saudi Bazaar Drugstore (tel. 6534443), Saudi Bazaar Tools Showroom (tel. 6445676) and Al Shouhada Pharmacy (tel. 6673435).

BUQSHAN HOSPITAL FOR WOMEN AND CHILDREN CO.

Address head office PO Box 5860, Jiddah
Telephone 6690356, 6690244, 6690876, 6691292, 6691222
Telex 402519 HELTHY SJ
Activities The company is owned by Ali and Salim Abdullah Buqshan in partnership with Dr Hasan S Badrek Amoudi. It is concerned with hospitals, hospital and medical equipment, medical staff, medical and surgical equipment, drugs, pharmaceuticals, paper and paper products, scientific and laboratory equipment.

AHMAD SULAIMAN BUQSHAN AND CO.

Address head office PO Box 1768, Jiddah
Telephone 6426992
Activities Owned by Ahmad Sulaiman, this company deals in readymade clothes, jewellery and building contracting.

ALI ABDULLAH BUQSHAN SHOWROOM

Address head office PO Box 699, Jiddah
Telephone 6423560
Activities Founded in 1960, this company is owned by Ali Abdullah Buqshan and deals in automobiles, parts and accessories.

BUQSHAN PRINTING PRESS

Address head office PO Box 1768, Jiddah
Telephone 6422991
Telex 400295 SALIM SJ
Activities A company established as printers and bookbinders in 1979. It is owned by Ahmad Sulaiman Buqshan.

SALIM AHMAD BUQSHAN

Address head office PO Box 428, Jiddah
Telephone 6422991
Telex 400295 SALIM SJ
Activities Owned by Salim Ahmad Buqshan and managed by his brother Muhammad, the company was formed in 1925 and deals in auto parts and accessories, tyres and tube fittings. There are branches in Riyadh and Ta'if.

The Family of Al Esayi

The family originates in Upper Yafa from the Bani Malik, though the present members have been citizens of the Kingdom for over a quarter of a century, and first began business in Jiddah 35 years ago. The two branches of the family represented by the partners in the Al Esayi Trading Corporation are related as cousins.

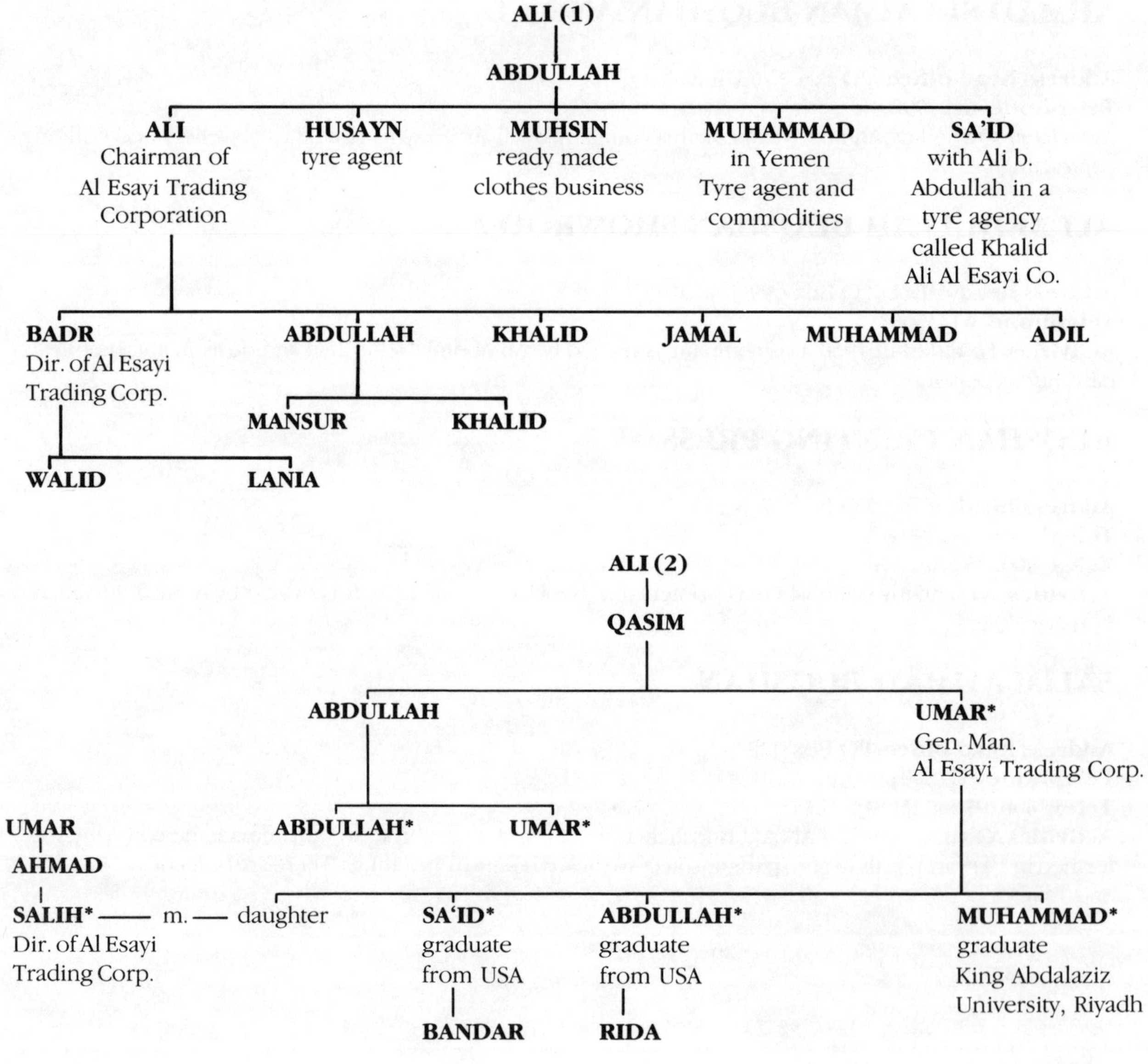

* Shareholders in Omar Qasim Al Esayi Trading Corporation

AL ESAYI TRADING CORPORATION

Address P.O.Box 1342 Jiddah
Telephone 6878444, 6878662, 6872201
Telex 401063 ESAYCO SJ
Cable address AL ESAYCO
Proprietors The company is an equal partnership between Sh. Ali Abdullah Al Esayiand Sh. Omar Qasim Al Esayi.
Activities The company was founded in 1961 and is engaged in operating the following agencies:
Chrysler cars and trucks.
Mitsubishicars, trucks and excavators.
Tokyu, cranes.
Newplan of West Germany, buses. Arrangements have been made to supply SATCO, the partly Government owned Saudi Arabian Transport Company.
Bankers National Commercial Bank, Al Jazira Bank, Citibank.
The partners have other commercial interests apart from this company.
Sh. Ali Abdullah Al Esayi
Canada Dry Factory, Nitto Tyres, textiles, Concord tyres, Armstrong Tyres, Tongshin of Korea (tyres), Ureidestin of Holland (tyres), CEAT of Italy (tyres), General (air conditioners).
Sh. Omar Qasim Al Esayi industrial interests
A founder of Saudi Arabian Carpets Factory, Saudi Ceramic in Riyadh, the Yanbo Cement Co., the Saudi Vegetable Oil and Ghee Co., MARWA advertising (q.v.), The Canada Dry Factory in Riyadh and Dammam which is a joint venture with Bugshan Bros. called the Arabian Beverage Corporation.
Investments
1. The Yemen
The Yemen Marketing and Trading Co. which is a partnership. He is a shareholder in the Yemen Ghee and Soap Co., The National Company for Plastic and Sponge Ltd., ARWA for Mineral Water and ARWA for Aluminium.
2. Lebanon
Broadway Centre, Omar Al Esayi and Partners, Beirut, The Astral Centre, Beirut.
3. France
A building at 65 Avenue Dlena, Paris.
4. United Kingdom
Jiddah International Trading Services, 49 Park Lane, London W.1., tel. 01 499 7546, tlx. 266038 JIT G.
Other interests include partnership in the Maternity and Children's Hospital, Jiddah, and as a founder of the Red Sea Insurance Company. Both partners also have very valuable Real Estate Holdings.
Other Companies
1. Omaco, Omar Al Esayi Trading and General Contracting which is wholly owned.
2. Omar Saudi Trading Corporation which is owned 50/50 with Muhammad bin Shayhoon and is engaged in tyres and batteries.
3. Omar Al Esayi for clothes and textiles which is wholesale.
4. Omar Al Esayi for engineering and architectural contracting (q.v.).
5. Al Esayi Saif Noman (q.v.).
6. The Saudi French Company which is a joint venture with Jean Lefebure and Bugshan Bros. and H.R.H. Prince Sa'ud bin Na'if bin Abdalaziz Al Sa'ud.This company is engaged in road construction in Yemen.
7. National Trading Construction and Development Company which is engaged in general construction and the operation of commercial agencies. P.O.Box 2926 Jiddah, tel. 6652304, Riyadh branch 36304. Apart from Sh. Omar Al Esayi the other membersof the Board of Directors are: Chairman Sh. Salim Ahmad Buqshan, Sh. Sulaiman Abdalaziz Rajhi, Sh. Khalid bin Salim bin Mahfouz, Sh. Ali Abdullah Buqshan, Sh. Salih Abdalaziz Al Rajhi, Sh. Mohammed Salim bin Mahfouz.

UMAR K AL ESAYI AND CO. LTD.

Address head office PO Box 8361, Jiddah
Telephone 6441914, 6434550
Telex 400895 OKACO SJ
Activities A company owned by Umar Qasim al Esayi and Salih Ahmad and Aydrus Ahmad al Esayi and managed by the two latter and Said Umar Qasim. The company is involved in an enormous range of trade goods which include building materials and systems, rugs, carpets, china and glassware, textiles and clothes, foodstuffs, furnishings and household equipment, computer and business systems, communictions equipment, curtains, decorating materials, petrol and diesel engines, fire fighting equipment, pumps, laboratory and hospital equipment, paper, and many more. The company are commission, real estate and travel agents.

UMAR K AL ESAYI AND CO. LTD. (FOODSTUFF DIVISION)

Address head office PO Box 8680, Jiddah
Telephone 6441580
Telex 400895 OKACO SJ
Activities Owned by the owners of the preceding company, this concern is run as a separate entity. It operates cold stores and deals in foodstuffs and fertilizers. It was set up in 1980.

AL ESAYI FOR COSMETICS AND PERFUMES

Address head office PO Box 436, Jiddah
Telephone 6442980, 6420623
Telex 401677
Activities This is a partnership between Umar Qasim al Esayi and Muhsin al Huraibi, which deals in cosmetics, textiles and perfumes.

CARPETS AND DECORATION CENTRE

Address head office PO Box 8361, Jiddah
Telephone 6693169, 6671253
Telex 400895 OKACO SJ
Activities This company is really a division of Umar K al Esayi and Co. Ltd. It was formed in 1980 and is managed by Abdullah Umar al Esayi and deals in carpets, rugs, adhesives, furniture, partitions, and room dividers, upholstery, venetian blinds, wallpaper and coverings, interior decorating contractors, shelving and storage.

UMAR K AL ESAYI AND CO. LTD. (HEAVY EQUIPMENT DIVISION)

Address head office PO Box 8361, Jiddah
Telephone 6879433, 6879455
Telex 400895 OKACO SJ
Activities Run as a separate commercial entity, this division was established in 1981. It deals with grinding materials and abrasives, batteries compressors, hydraulic plant and equipment, diesel engines, industrial tools, welding equipment and services.

UMAR K AL ESAYI FOR TEXTILES

Address head office PO Box 436, Jiddah
Telephone 6422723, 6420623
Telex 401148 OMACO SJ, 401677 ESAYI SJ
Activities Founded in 1947, the company is owned by Umar Qasim al Esayi. It has branches in Riyadh and Dammam and deals in textiles.

UMAR AL ESAYI TRADING AND GENERAL CONTRACTING CORPORATION

Address head office PO Box 5537, Jiddah
Telephone 6440781, 6432162
Telex 401572 OMACO SJ
Activities This company, owned by Umar Qasim al Esayi, has a branch in Riyadh and deals with air conditioning equipment and parts, building materials, foodstuffs, furniture and household equipment. They operate an engineering consultancy and are also electrical and civil contractors.

The Family of Saif Noman Said

The family originates from Hujariya near Ta'iz in the Yemen.

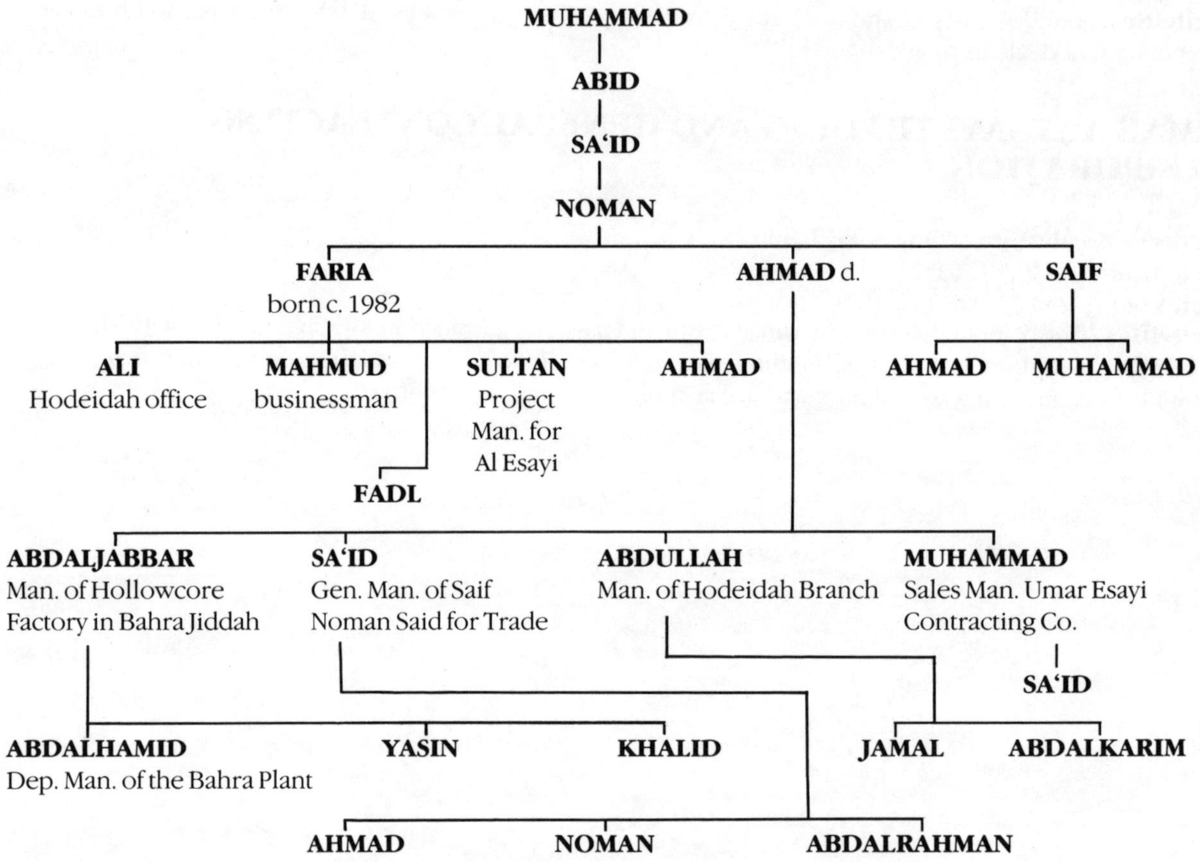

OMAR K AL ESAYI OFFICE FOR ENGINEERING AND ARCHITECTURALCONTRACTING

Address head office P.O.Box 2837 Jiddah
Telephone 6422698, 6425408
Telex 401547 SAIF SJ
Cable address OMAR AL ESAYI
Proprietor Sh. Omar K Al Esayi
General Manager Sh. Saif Noman Said
Asst. General Manager Said Ahmad Noman
Company History The company is an old and well established business in the contracting field. In 1976 a company was formed called Saif Noman Said and Partners which operates two plants producing Hollowcore as a commercial association with Holloware and J.R.C. of the UK. The plants are in Jiddah and Riyadh. This company is a partnership between Sh. Omar Esayi, Sh. Saif Noman Said, Sh. Mohammad Salim Mahfouz and Sh. Khalid Salim Mahfouz. A third part of this group is called the Saif Noman Said For Trade Establishment (P.O.Box 4544, tel. 22698, 25408, tlx. 401547 SAIF SJ). This company specializes in the provision of building materials. The fourth member of the group is Al Esayi Saif Noman Douglas Ltd. which is a joint venture with R.M. Douglas Construction Ltd. of Birmingham UK and is a building contracting and civil engineering concern.
Bankers National Commercial Bank.

The Family of Faqih

An old family of Mecca descending from religious teachers as their name implies.

MUHAMMAD AL FAQIH

ABDULQADIR d.
started a business which is carried on today by his son Mustafa

MUHAMMAD
Poet. Ex. Dir. of Mecca Information Office

ADIL
electrical engineer

SANA'A m.
WAFA m.
ADNAN
ASIA
HAYMAN

ABDALRAHMAN
b. Mecca, 1923. Major business man. Member Mecca Chamber of Commerce, Municipal Council of Mecca, Ports Directorate, Water Supply and Drainage Directorate, tel. 5422289, 5422297. Kingdom's major poultry supplier.

FAWZIA
SU'AD
KHAYRIA
TALAL
TARIQ
ABDALQADIR
MAHMUD

UMR
Dir. Gen. of Audit Bureau, of ministerial status

USSAMA
ISSAM
GHADA
NAHA
HANAN

SULAIMAN
Prop. of the Solaiman Faqih Hospital, MD Cairo University

SALAH
Prop. of Faqih Plastics Factory

YASIR
YUMNAH

MUSTAFA
Man. of Abdalqadir Faqih Co. dealing in dyes, silver thread and silk textiles in Mecca

LUTFIYAH
FU'AD
NA'ILA
HANIYA
YUSUF
TAHANI

ABDULLAH d.

DR SOLAIMAN FAQIH HOSPITAL

Address head office P.O.Box 2537 Jiddah
Telephone 6671451, 6671452/3/4
Telex 401433 FAQIH SJ
Cable address FAQIH
Proprietor Dr Solaiman Faqih
Board members Dr Abdalmajid Hajar, DrJabir
Activities The hospital was founded in 1976 and has a prominent position amongst the private hospitals in Jiddah. Dr Solaiman used to be in the Government Health Service and held positions as Director of the Giad and Maternity Hospitals in Mecca, and later he was transferred to Jiddah as General Director of the Western Region. He held this post for four years and then when a regulation appeared making it impossible to work both for the Government and in private practice he resigned from administrative medicine and in conjunction with Goldfinch of the UK designed the present hospital. To begin with there was an enormous financial problem but a personal appeal by Dr Solaiman to H.M. King Faisal led to the Government arranging loans of up to half the cost for private hospitals. Building took three years and installation had to be done three times to achieve the perfection seen today. Dr Solaiman recruits all the staff himself and has travelled the world in search of people. The present hospital is luxurious but in fact cheaper than many hotels. The combination of high standards of medical care, beautiful wards and cheap treatment leads to the hospital's 125 beds being full most of the time. The eight storeys contain three classes of room having their own washing facilities and television as well as comfortable facilities for visitors; all parts of the hospital are reached by lifts and gleaming marble corridors. The medical facilities can hardly be equalled anywhere and combine kitchens in the basement and a central sterile supply department. Facilities for out patients and internal medicine, paediatricians, obstetrics, gynaecology, ear nose and throat, cardiology and a dental clinic, physiotherapy, pathology, laboratory and a comprehensive pharmacy are all placed on the ground floor. The hospital operates its own X-ray department and a range of the most up-to-date operating theatres.The future of private medicine seems assured in the Kingdom though the Government has recently put a ban on the erection of private hospitals of this sort as there are now enough of them to serve the present community.

The Family of Fatany

This is a typical professional and learned family with recent origins in the Holy City of Mecca. However, they relate that in Abbasid times an ancestor who was of the Thaqif tribe in the Ta'if region and named Isma'il became a soldier and fought in the East. He married a local girl and his son Muhammad stayed in his mother's country as did his descendants until Da'ud returned to Mecca some 175 years ago. The family thus has many relatives in Malaysia and Thailand where there is today a district called Fatany after them.

- **DA'UD FATANY**
  - **ISMA'IL**
    - **MUHAMMAD** author of religious works
      - **MUHAMMAD NUR** d. graduated from Al Azhar as an Alim; author of works on religion and astronomy; Qadi of the Hijaz Supreme Court
        - **AHMAD** d.
          - **MAHMUD** Inspector at Min. of Educ. Mecca
        - **ZAYN** d. returned to Malaysia
        - **ABDALGHAFFAR**
          - **ABDALAZIZ** Justice Sec. Mecca
        - **YASIN** retired as Head of Admin in old Dept. of Justice
          - **JAMIL** Advanced Computer Systems Co.; M.A. Columbia
          - **KHALID**
            - **WALID**
          - **MUHAMMAD NUR** Ph.D.; ex Head of Lab. Dep. Min. Communications
          - **AMIN** doctor
        - **HASAN** ex teacher
        - **MUHAMMAD** General retired
          - **RIAD**
          - **ADNAN**
          - **BANDAR**
        - **HAMID** Justice Sec. Mecca
          - **HISHAM**
        - **ABDULLAH** in Min. of Commerce

SH. KHALID FATANY

Address Apartment 311 Azizia Building, King Faisal St. Riyadh, PO Box 376
Telephone 25459, 4780459
Telex 200175 FATANI SJ
Cable Address MORAGUIN
Subsidiary Offices Khalid Fatany Accountants and Auditors
Jiddah PO Box 445, tel. 6426446
Dammam PO Box 1122, tel. 25137
Proprietor Sh. Khalid Fatany
Accountant and Auditor
The first partnership was established in 1965 between Sh. Abdalwahab Abdalwasi who is now the Minister of Hajj and Sh. Abdalaziz Daghestani presently Deputy Minister of the Audit Bureau. Sh. Khalid joined the partnership in 1970 and took over in 1972 when the other partners relinquished their work to take up government appointments. The assisting partner in Riyadh is Abdalatif Othman.
Bankers National Commercial Bank

The Family of Al Firaih

Originally from Ushayqar in Najd.

FIRAIH

IBRAHIM

ABDALMUHSIN

AHMAD
born only three months before his father died. Owner of Ahmad al Firaih Co.

ABDALKARIM
businessman in Kuwait

Sons of Ahmad:

ABDALMUHSIN
deals in real estate

RI'AD
PR Manager for VBB of Sweden

MUHAMMAD
Appointment's Office, King Faisal Hospital

NABIL
in Ulaya Electricity Company

MUSTAFA
Assistant to his father

AHMAD AL FIRAIH CO.

Address of head office PO Box 128 Riyadh
Telephone 4024317
Cable address RADWAN
Proprietor Sh. Ahmad b. Abdalmuhsin Al Firaih
Company history
The family was established in 1949 and the office occupies a central position in the capital between Batha and Wazir St. opposite the Arab Bank.
Activities
Their activities concern the import and supply of spare parts for air conditioners as well as general trading.
Agencies
Ranio Controls of Plymouth, UK
Pleuger Unterwasser Pumpen GmbH, West Germany
Imperial, USA
J.B. Industries, Illinois, USA
Turnover 1.5 million Saudi riyals

The Family of Fitaihi

A family settled in Jiddah for many generations and one which still maintains its place in the small goldsmith's area of the old suq where they have two shops.

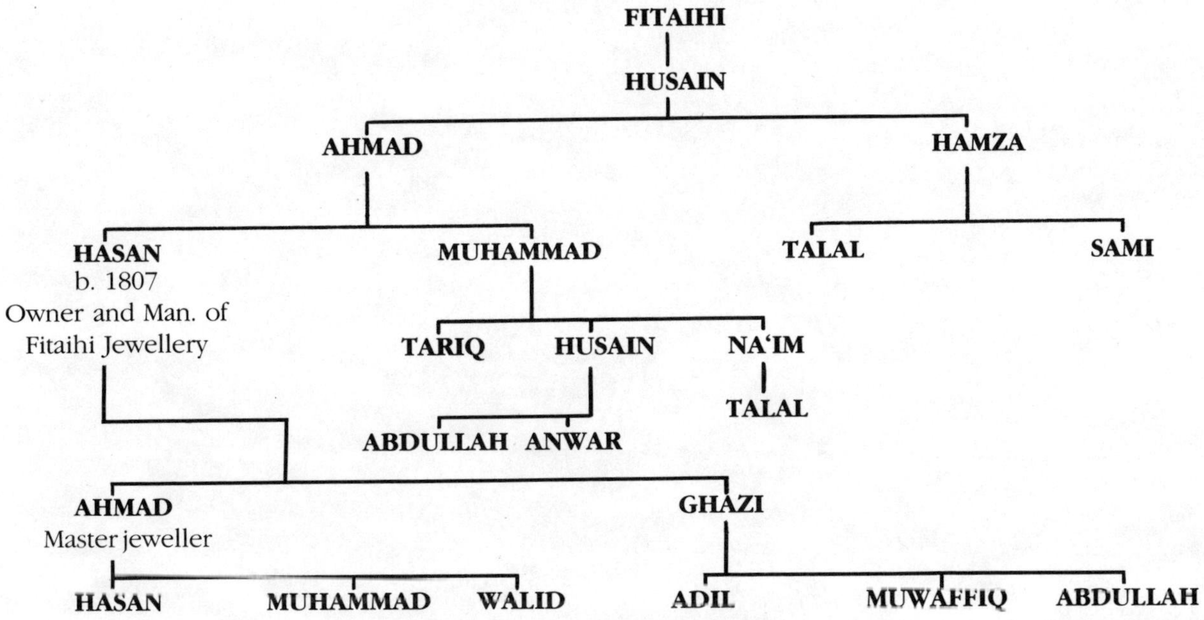

AHMED HASAN FITAIHI

Address head office PO Box 2606, Jiddah
Telephone 6421014, 6442734
Telex 401084 FTAIHI SJ
Cable address AHMAD FITAIHI JIDDAH
Branches
Main showroom, King Abdalaziz St., tel. 6434649, 6442114
Queen's Building shop, tel. 6442734
Gold St. shop, tel. 6421864
Al Zubair St. shop, tel. 6421864
Company history Sh. Ahmed Fitaihi is the proprietor of one of the oldest jewellery businesses in Jiddah; the family business began in 1931. Whilst still retaining their interests in the traditional trade in gold in the old suq, they have been able to build a flourishing modern business on this foundation. Sh. Ahmed is particularly enthusiastic about Arabian and Islamic design and always selects pieces that reflect the highest standards in this respect. He himself set up an independent business ten years ago and the faithfulness of his many customers demonstrates the quality and honesty with which he conducts his affairs. He represents leading manufacturers around the world and Sh. Ahmed's great personal knowledge of precious metals and stones enhances his company's reputation for integrity and quality.
Bankers Riyadh Bank, National Commercial Bank.

NA'IM MUHAMMAD FITAIHI

Address head office PO Box 1618, Jiddah
Telephone 6426083, 6443173
Activities Another family jewellery business which was established in 1940. They also deal in watches and clocks. The company is owned by Na'im Muhammad Fitaihi.

The Family of Al Fraih

Originate by descent from Tamim and came to Riyadh some forty years ago from Anaiza.

- **IBRAHIM AL FRAIH**
  - **UTHMAN**
    - **IBRAHIM** d.
      - **UTHMAN** doctor
    - **SALIH** Ptner, Ibrahim Uthman al Fraih & Bros.
      - **UTHMAN** Prof. of Arabic Lang., Riyadh Univ.
      - **MUHAMMAD** Government
        - **ADIL**
        - **ADNAN**
      - **ABDALAZIZ**
      - **AHMAD**
    - **ABDALRAHMAN**
      - **MUHAMMAD** M.D. of Eastern Corporation
    - **ALI** partners in Ibrahim Uthman al Fraih & Bros.
      - **UTHMAN** architect, dir. of City Planning Dept. Riyadh
    - **SULAYMAN** partners in Ibrahim Uthman al Fraih & Bros.
      - **UTHMAN** manages the contracting company

EASTERN CORPORATION FOR TRADING CONTRACTING AND INDUSTRY

Address head office P.O.Box 792 Riyadh
Telephone 4023473, 4023475
Telex 201089 ETCORP SJ
Cable address ETCORPE
Subsidiary office Dammam P.O.Box 375, tel. 8326441, tlx. 601565 ECHSSA SJ
Proprietors Sh. Muhammad bin Abdalrahman Al Fraih 50%
Sh. Muhammad bin Abdalaziz Al Dughaithar Al Hasan 50%
Sh. Muhammad Al Fraih is the President of the Chamber of Commerce in Riyadh and a partner in the Saudi Ceramic Company. He is also a member of the board of the Saudi Hollandi Bank, the Saudi Banque of Paris, MABCO, the Nissah Co., al Alamiya Insurance Company and the Lightweight Concrete Company.
The Eastern Corporation of which Sh. Muhammad Al Fraih is Managing Director was started in 1966 and is divided into two main divisions: a construction division and a commercial division. This last contains a considerable travel section. The company represents the following interests: Hawker Siddeley Power Engineering, Hawker Siddeley Electric Export Ltd., Brush Switchgear Ltd., Brush Electrical Machines, Brush Power Equipment, Brush Transformers Ltd., Brush Fusegear Ltd., Hawker Siddeley Power Transformers Ltd., South Wales Switchgear, Yorkshire Electric Transformers Co. Ltd., Crow Hamilton and Co. Ltd., all in the UK. Also Cremar of Italy and Waste Management of the USA.
Turnover 30 million Saudi riyals.
Bankers National Commercial Bank, Riyadh Bank, Saudi Hollandi Bank, Saudi Faransi Bank, First National City Bank.

The Family of Al Ghunaim

The family are Al Saif of Shamar and this family tree illustrates in a structural way the method by which Arabian society is constructed. The eponymous ancestor of the Al Saif has been underlined to illustrate this, as has the eponymous ancestor of the al Ghunaim. The tree also illustrates what happens when a child is born after the death of his father. In this case it is usual for the baby to be given his father's name.

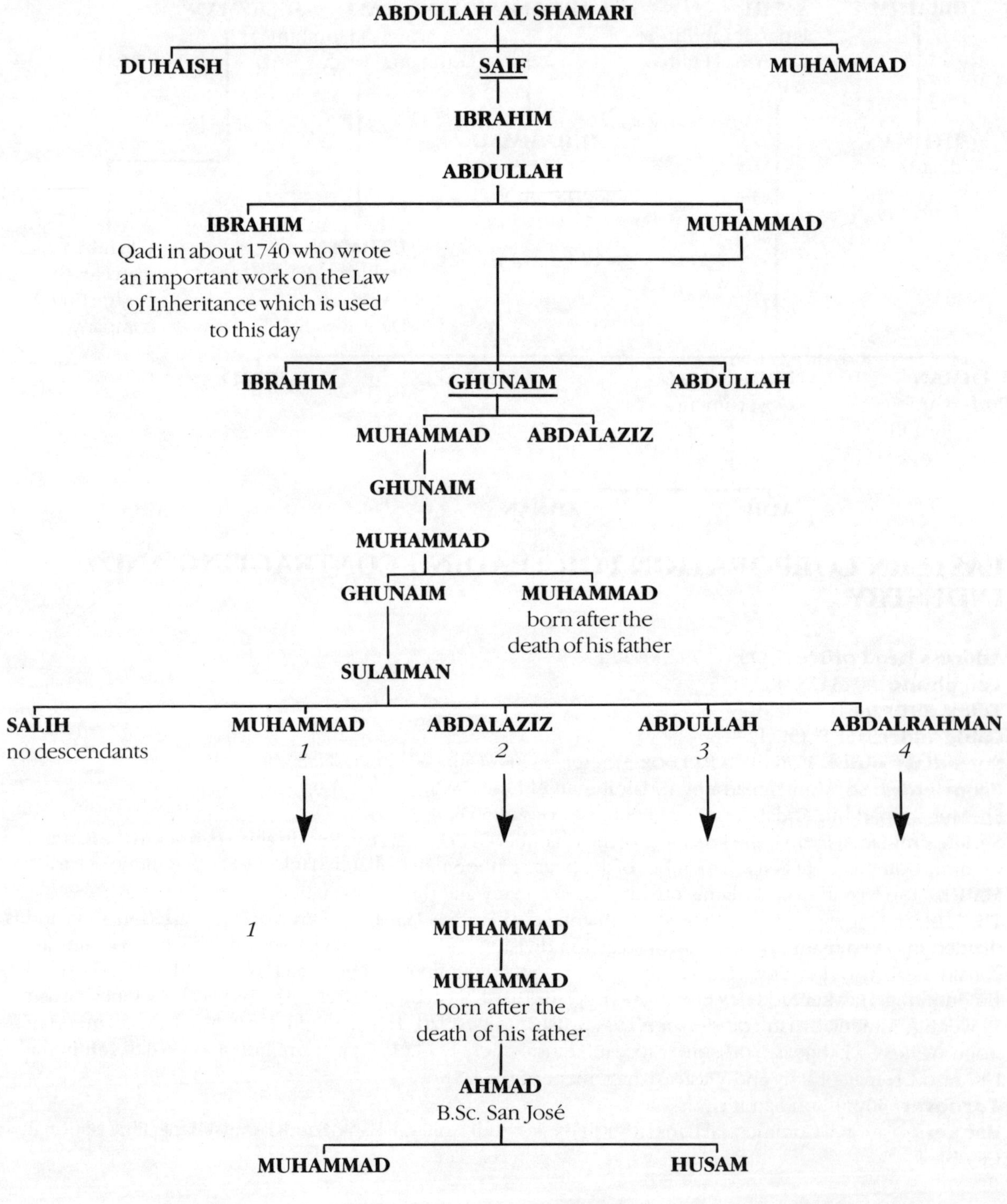

2

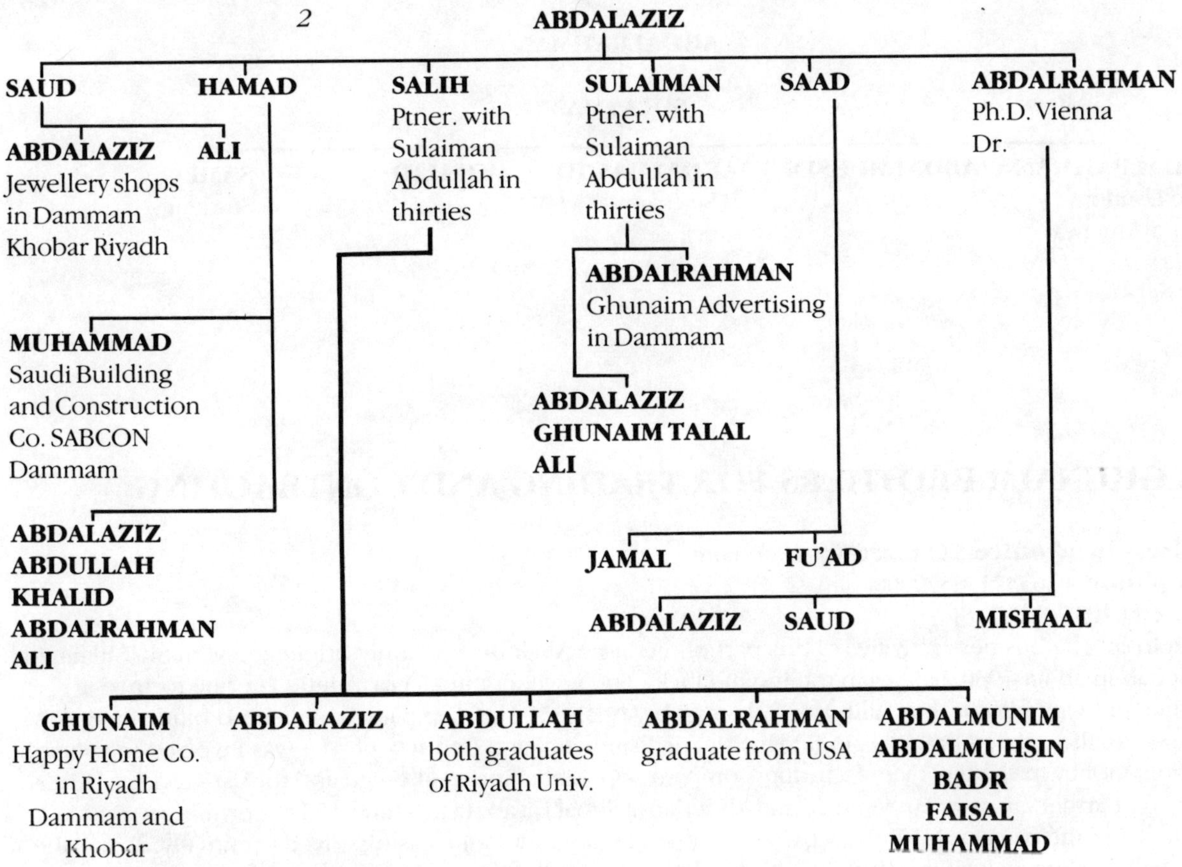
ABDALAZIZ
SAUD
HAMAD
SALIH
Ptner. with Sulaiman Abdullah in thirties
SULAIMAN
Ptner. with Sulaiman Abdullah in thirties
SAAD
ABDALRAHMAN
Ph.D. Vienna Dr.
ABDALAZIZ
Jewellery shops in Dammam Khobar Riyadh
ALI
ABDALRAHMAN
Ghunaim Advertising in Dammam
MUHAMMAD
Saudi Building and Construction Co. SABCON Dammam
ABDALAZIZ GHUNAIM TALAL ALI
ABDALAZIZ ABDULLAH KHALID ABDALRAHMAN ALI
JAMAL
FU'AD
ABDALAZIZ
SAUD
MISHAAL
GHUNAIM
Happy Home Co. in Riyadh Dammam and Khobar
ABDALAZIZ
ABDULLAH
both graduates of Riyadh Univ.
ABDALRAHMAN
graduate from USA
ABDALMUNIM ABDALMUHSIN BADR FAISAL MUHAMMAD

3

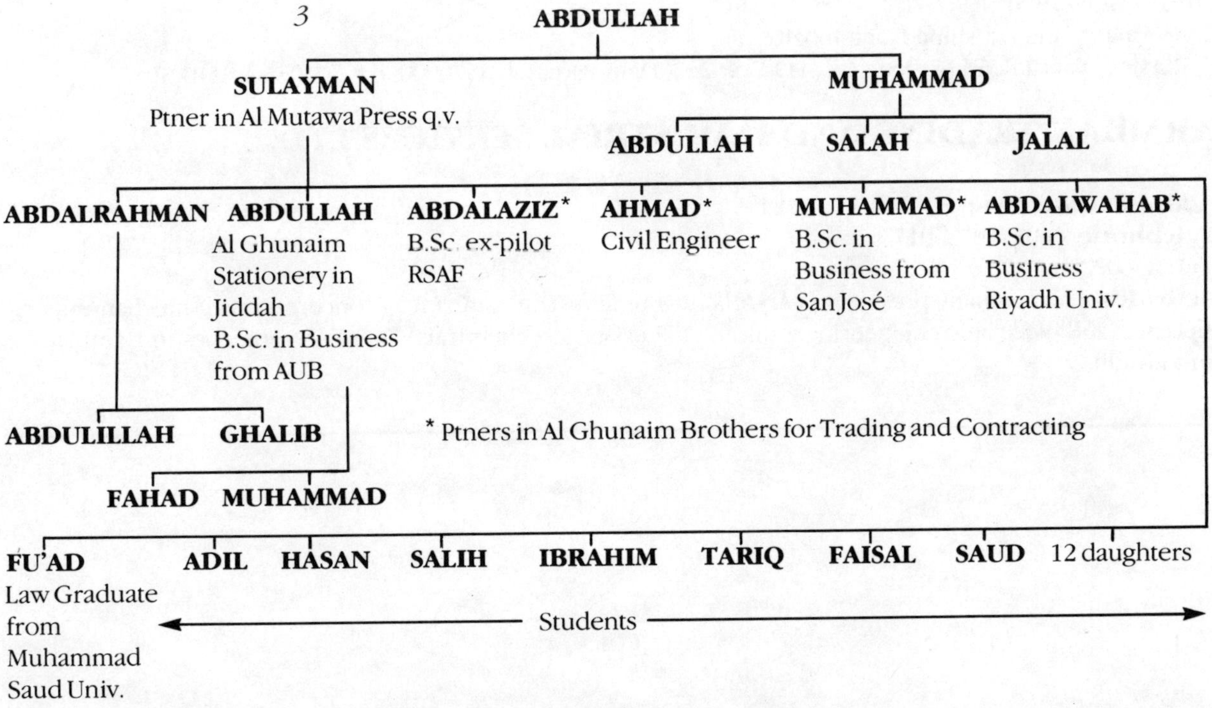
ABDULLAH
SULAYMAN
Ptner in Al Mutawa Press q.v.
MUHAMMAD
ABDULLAH
SALAH
JALAL
ABDALRAHMAN
ABDULLAH
Al Ghunaim Stationery in Jiddah B.Sc. in Business from AUB
ABDALAZIZ*
B.Sc. ex-pilot RSAF
AHMAD*
Civil Engineer
MUHAMMAD*
B.Sc. in Business from San José
ABDALWAHAB*
B.Sc. in Business Riyadh Univ.
ABDULILLAH
GHALIB
* Ptners in Al Ghunaim Brothers for Trading and Contracting
FAHAD
MUHAMMAD
FU'AD
Law Graduate from Muhammad Saud Univ.
ADIL
HASAN
SALIH
IBRAHIM
TARIQ
FAISAL
SAUD
12 daughters
Students

4

ABDALRAHMAN

SULAYMAN

ABDALRAHMAN	**ABDALMUHSIN**	**ABDALHAMID**	**KHALID**	**SAMI**
B.Sc. London Man. al Mutawa Press	Dr in Egypt	B.Sc. from San José	Student	Student

AL GHUNAIM BROTHERS FOR TRADING AND CONTRACTING

Address head office PO Box 6800, Dammam
Telephone 8263321, 8570000
Telex 601035 GSAIB SJ
Activities The business activities of this part of the large Al Ghunaim family originated with Sh. Sulaiman Abdullah in about 1930. He began trading in fabrics and jewellery in Mecca. A little later he formed a partnership with his cousins, Salih and Sulaiman b. Abdalaziz. This company had its head office in Riyadh and eventually opened branches in Jiddah, Mecca, Dammam, and Beirut, where it was involved in general trading, money exchange, manufacturing, company representation, real estate and tourist services. He also formed a partnership with Muhammad and Abdullah al Subai'i at about this time. In 1962 printing was added to the list of the cousins' business activities. This original partnership was dissolved eventually, as was the one with the Subai'i brothers, but Sh. Sulaiman Abdullah still retains a 50 percent interest in the printing business, al Mutawa Press (q.v.).
In 1980 Al Ghunaim Brothers for Trading and Contracting was established and the four board members are Abdalaziz, Muhammad, Abdalwahhab and Ahmad b. Sulaiman Abdullah Al Ghunaim.
The business has taken shareholdings in the following enterprises; their partners are the Khalifa Algosaibi Group.

1. Delmon Co. Ld. Al Ghunaim and Algosaibi. PO Box 6800, Dammam, tel. 8570000; Jubail, tel. 3610889, tlx. 601035 GOSAIB SJ.
2. A1 Quarry and Crushing Plant, Jubail.
3. ROMAC, Saudi Road Marking Co., PO Box 222, Dammam, tel. 8570000, tlx. 601035 GSAIB SJ.

ARABIAN TRADING AND INDUSTRIAL SERVICES LTD.

Address head office PO Box 15, Jiddah
Telephone 6601708, 6601736
Telex 402276
Activities The company president is Abdullah Ghunaim. The company is concerned with mechanical, electrical and electronic engineering, building materials and chemicals. There are branches in Dammam and Riyadh.

ALGOSAIBI BUSINESS INTERESTS

KHALIFA ALGOSAIBI GROUP

Address P.O. Box 222 Dammam 31411
Telephone 8570000
Telex 601035 GSIB S.J.
Cable Address CONTRACTS
Board Members
Khalifa Abdalrahman Algosaibi, Vice Chairman, Muhammad Khalifa Algosaibi, Vice Chairman, Saud Khalifa Algosaibi, Director, Badr Khalifa Algosaibi, Director, Sami Khalifa Algosaibi, Director, Salah Khalifa Algosaibi, Director, R. A. Simcoe-Gerson, Finance Director.
Activities Khalifa Algosaibi early became independent from his father and went into business with his younger brother, Adil, and also entered the food business in the Hijaz where he supplied food to the Saudi Armed Forces. The partnership with Adil did not last and Khalifa left him in about 1971, with the Westinghouse account. Following a decline during the later part of that decade, Khalifa's business acumen and determination led him to re-establish his fortunes with great success by the early eighties. It is an interesting facet of his business career that even during times of reversal Khalifa has always remained loyal to all employees. Today there are several people who have worked for him for over twenty years. In a country where commercial and industrial growth has taken place with such speed this is not a characteristic frequently met with.
Khalifa Algosaibi's business concerns are rooted in Khalifa Algosaibi Contracting (KAC) and founded on the Food Business. The cold-store in Damman is the largest and most superbly equipped of its kind in the Middle East.
The Group is composed of the following divisions:
Food Division, Services Division, Manufacturing and Industrial Division, Construction Division, International Division, KAC, apart from its own contracting activities, provides the anchor by acting as a Corporate Division. The expansion of this enterprise has been very remarkable in the last few years, particularly when measured against declining oil revenues and the concomitant depression in many parts of the Saudi Arabian market. This is itself a tribute to the Group's management skills and flexible attitudes. The following companies are wholly owned by the Group:
Khalifa Algosaibi Cold Stores KACS, Construction Materials Co. Ltd. CMC, Construction Materials Chemical Industries CMCI, Diving Service Khalifa Algosaibi DSKA, Khalifa Algosaibi Fishing Co. KAFC, Algosaibi International Travel Agency AITA, Khalifa Algosaibi Real Estate Development, Khalifa Algosaibi Trading KAT.
The following companies are joint venture or partnership enterprises:
Algosaibi Grandmet Services Ltd. AGML with Grand Metropolitan Ltd. of the UK, Saudi Electrification and Development Co. SEDCO with Global Electrification Systems Inc. of the Philippines, Saudi Japan Development Company SAJA with Mitsui of Japan, Saudi Toyo Engineering Company SATEC with Toyo Engineering of Japan, Algosaibi Thermal Aire ATA, Algosaibi Thermal Aire Industries ATAI, Sigma Paints Saudi Arabia Ltd. with Sigma of Holland, Algosaibi Geo – Oilfield Services – with Geo International of the USA, Delmon for Trading Contracting and Transportation with Al Ghunaim family q.v., De Groot Arabia Ltd. with Grootint BV of Holland, National Fruit Juice Co. with the Al Moaibid Family q.v.

The Family of Algosaibi

The family originates in Hofuf where they were involved in agriculture and traded through Bahrein to India with dates. There are family connections with Huraymlat and possibly Qasab.
The part of the family shown, which is the most important part, descends from two brothers (the second of whom married his brother's wife on his death). Agriculture produce led to diversification into trade in pearls and gold and the establishment of the wide range of family businesses seen today.

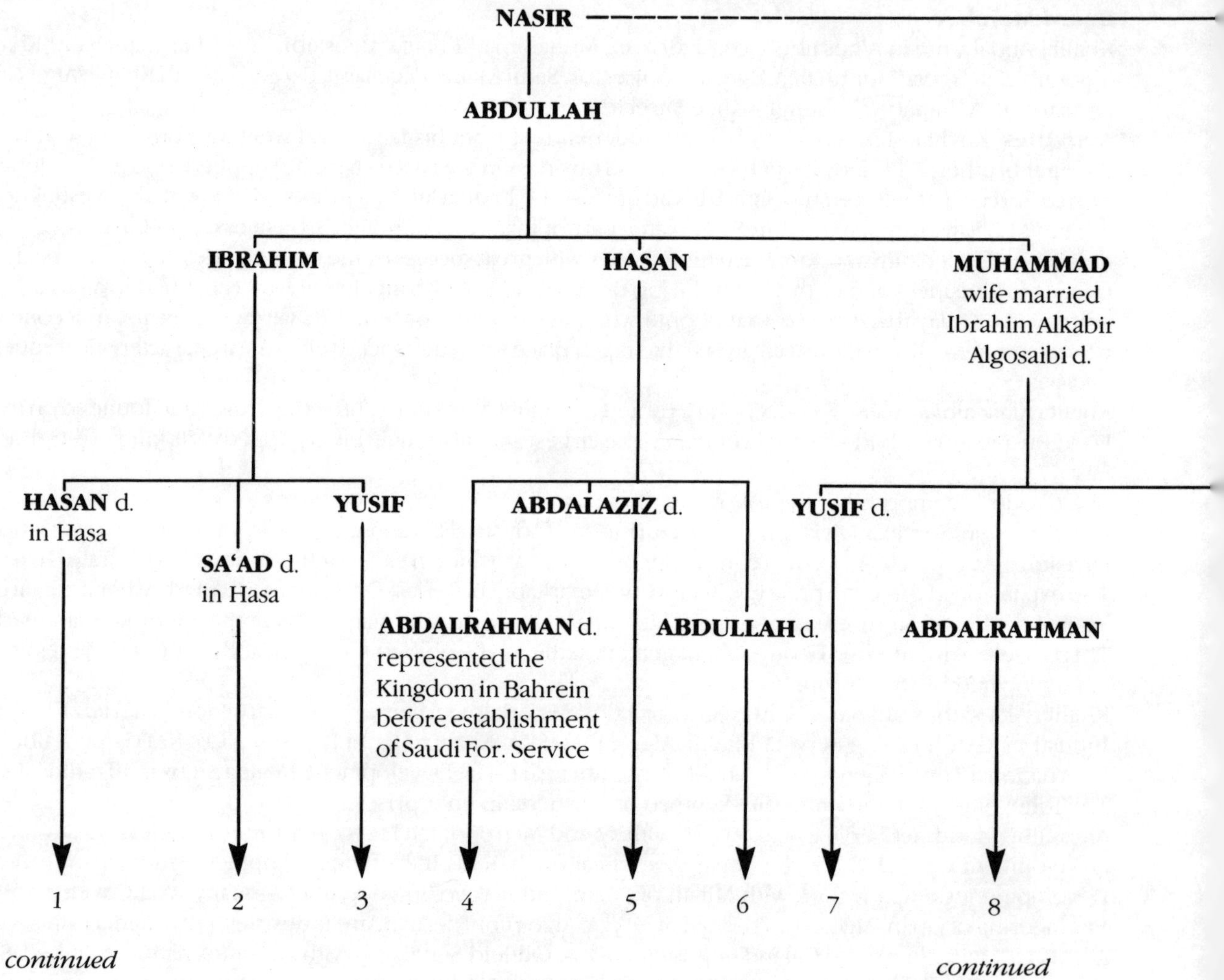

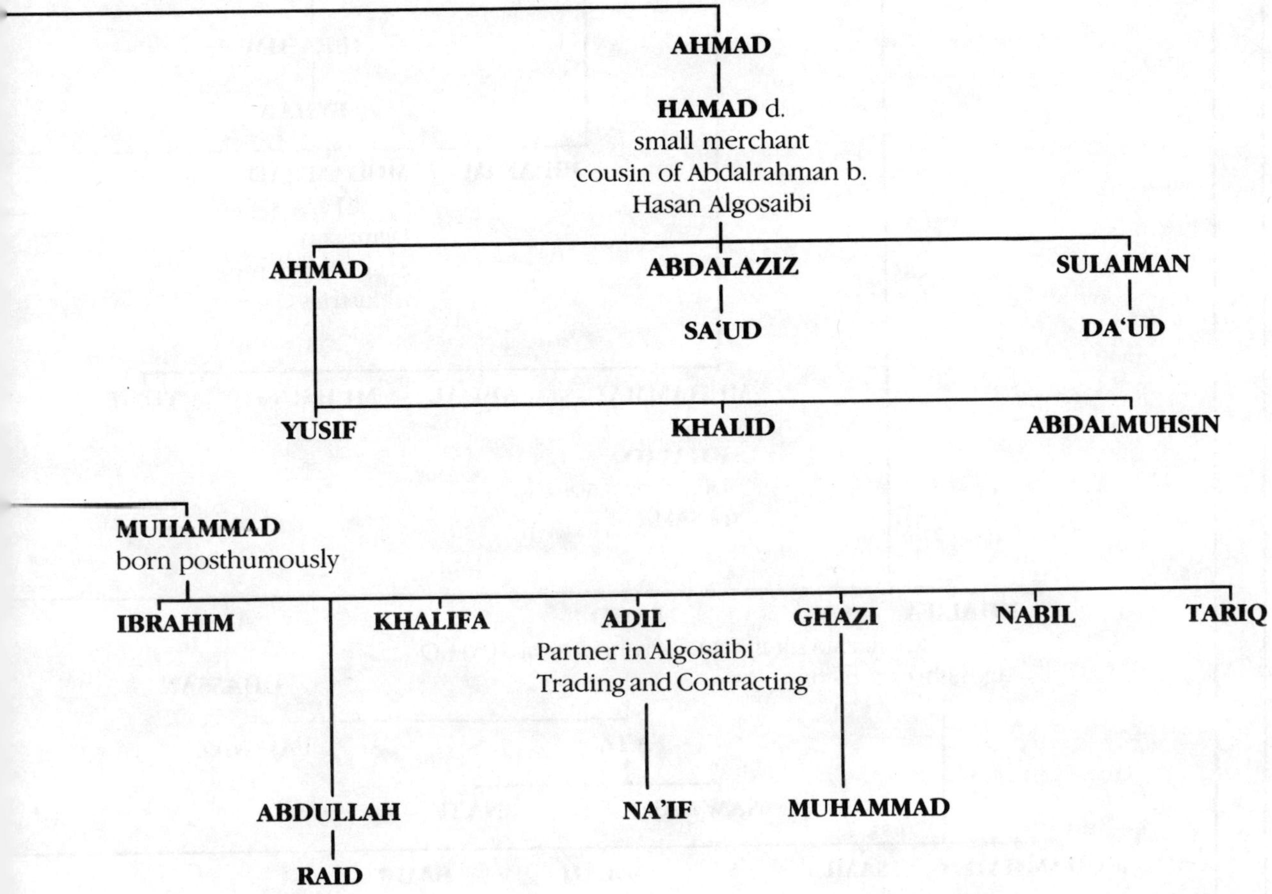
AHMAD
HAMAD d.
small merchant
cousin of Abdalrahman b.
Hasan Algosaibi
AHMAD
ABDALAZIZ
SULAIMAN
SA'UD
DA'UD
YUSIF
KHALID
ABDALMUHSIN
MUHAMMAD
born posthumously
IBRAHIM
KHALIFA
ADIL
Partner in Algosaibi
Trading and Contracting
GHAZI
NABIL
TARIQ
ABDULLAH
NA'IF
MUHAMMAD
RAID

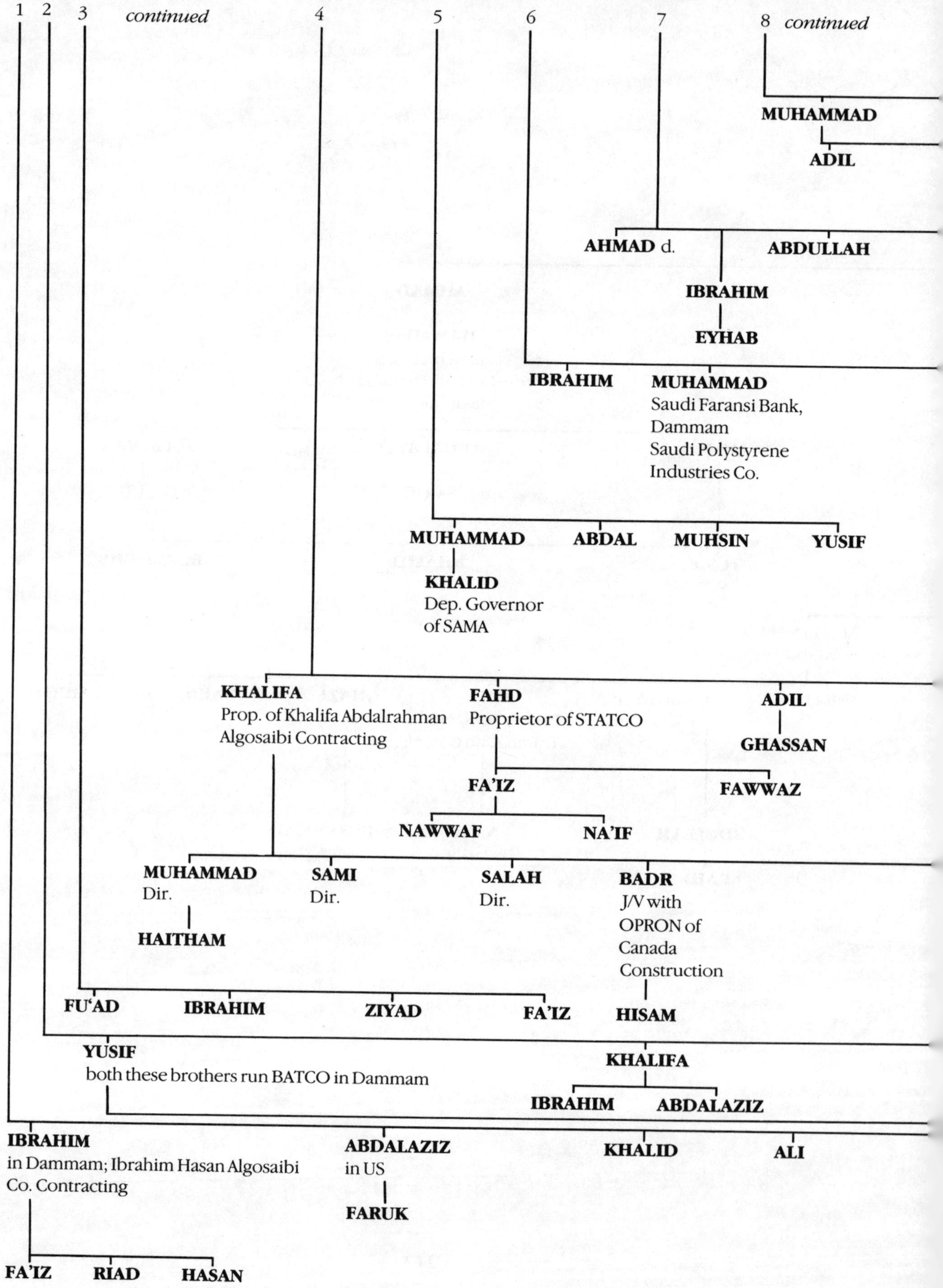
1 2 3 continued
4
5
6
7
8 continued
MUHAMMAD
ADIL
AHMAD d.
ABDULLAH
IBRAHIM
EYHAB
IBRAHIM
MUHAMMAD
Saudi Faransi Bank, Dammam
Saudi Polystyrene Industries Co.
MUHAMMAD
ABDAL
MUHSIN
YUSIF
KHALID
Dep. Governor of SAMA
KHALIFA
Prop. of Khalifa Abdalrahman Algosaibi Contracting
FAHD
Proprietor of STATCO
ADIL
GHASSAN
FA'IZ
FAWWAZ
NAWWAF
NA'IF
MUHAMMAD
Dir.
SAMI
Dir.
SALAH
Dir.
BADR
J/V with OPRON of Canada Construction
HAITHAM
FU'AD
IBRAHIM
ZIYAD
FA'IZ
HISAM
YUSIF
both these brothers run BATCO in Dammam
KHALIFA
IBRAHIM
ABDALAZIZ
IBRAHIM
in Dammam; Ibrahim Hasan Algosaibi Co. Contracting
ABDALAZIZ
in US
FARUK
KHALID
ALI
FA'IZ
RIAD
HASAN

FAISAL **FU'AD**

GHAZI **ADNAN**

MUHAMMAD **MAHMUD** **FAWZI** **UMAR** **SA'UD** **KHALID** **USSAMA**

ABDALAZIZ **KHALID**

GHAZI
b. 1940. Poet. Ph.D. London
Minister of Industry and Electricity

FARIS **SUHAIL**

MUSTAFA

SAMIR

KHALID

WALID **MAZIN**

IBRAHIM
Ibrahim Algosaibi
Co. Qatar
General Trading

ABDALAZIZ **FARID** **HISHAM**

NABIL d.

RASHID
Partner in Algosaibi Trading
and Contracting Co.

KHALID **ABDALAZIZ** **ABDALWAHHAB** **MUHAMMAD**

ADIL **WALID** **SA'D**

SA'D

SA'D

BADR

HASAN

FU'AD **FA'IZ** **ADIL**

The Group's trading activities have been rationalised and all their agency agreements are now dealt with using the recently created Khalifa Algosaibi Trading, KAT. Agencies presently held are as representing Hyundai Corporation, Pirelli General, Fox Industries, Mitsui and Co., Life Construction, Jos Hansen and Sochure, Linvar Ltd., Mitchell Systems, Facet Enterprises, Aurora Pumps and Cardox.
Bankers Al Bank al Saudi al Hollandi, Lloyds bank International, Saudi International bank, Chase Manhattan bank, Bahrain Middle East Bank, Saudi American bank, Al Jazira bank, Bank of America, Gulf Riyad bank, American Express Banking Corporation

ABDALREHMAN ALGOSAIBI GENERAL TRADING BUREAU

Address PO Box 215, Riyadh
Telephone 21213, 20816, 20811
Telex 201125
Established in 1942 the company has offices in Jiddah and Al Khobar. Main activities include tenders, government supplies, wholesale and retail. It owns National Milk Factory, Riyadh, Saudi Travel and Tourist Agency, Al Khobar, the Algosaibi Travel Agency, Bahrein and 50 percent in Riyadh Beverage Co. It handles a large number of Western agencies.

AL AMAR TRADING AND CONSTRUCTION ESTABLISHMENT

Address head office P.O.Box 274 Dhahran Airport
Telephone 8324157 Dammam
Telex 601044 ARNDASS SJ
Cable address AMARCO
Proprietor Sh. Ibrahim bin Hasan Al Gosaibi
Company History Sh. Ibrahim founded his company in 1969. Specialising in construction, it has been responsible for the successful completion of many contracts. At the present time his company is anxious to expand its activities and is showing considerable interest in entering into a joint venture with a UK concern willing to start negotiations. It is in partnership with a French company, Girard Dot Co., for electrical contracting, fittings and maintenance.
Bankers Saudi Cairo Bank, Riyadh Bank, Arab Bank.

AL GOSAIBI TRADING AND CONTRACTING COMPANY

Address head office P.O.Box 2784 Dammam
Telephone 27221
Telex 601382 GTCC SJ
Cable address HIACO
Subsidiary offices
Riyadh, tel. 66284, 69899
Hasa, tel. 25255, 24744, P.O.Box 367, cable GOSABCO
Jiddah agent - Nasir Al Adwan
A Collective Partnership Ghazi Muhammad Muhammad Al Gosaibi (Riyadh Director)
Rashid Khalifa Abdalrahman Al Gosaibi (Dammam Director)
Adil Muhammad Muhammad Al Gosaibi
Company History This young company which continues the family predilection for forming new and independent businesses was founded in 1974. It is a go-ahead concern concentrating on a narrow range of commodities and agency relationships. They import foodstuffs and tinned goods from Korea, Japan, Singapore and Thailand and market California rice for Tewfiq the importer.

Agencies Their agencies are thus a marketing relationship with Pacific International Rice Mills and directly with the Shin Heung Flourmills Co. Ltd. of Korea.
Bankers Saudi British Bank, Bank al Jazira, and the National Commercial Bank in Hasa.

BATCO

Address head office P.O.Box 613 Dammam
Telephone 44408
Telex 670185 BATCO SJ
Proprietor Sh. Khalifa bin Sa'ad Al Gosaibi
Company History The foundation of Sh. Khalifa's company dates from 1968 when he entered the building and contracting field and also conducted business as a general trader. His activities are typical of his independently minded family. His company is extremely successful and one that is most attractive to the business man from Europe.
Partnership
A partnership has been formed, called BATCO Kent with an Irish company and they operate in the field of electrical contracting and maintenance.
Turnover 2 million Saudi riyals(partnership)
Bankers Saudi Faransi Bank.

AHMAD HAMAD AL GOSAIBI BROTHERS

Address head office P.O.Box 106 Al Khobar
Telephone 42666, 42862
Telex 670123 ALGOSO SJ; 601069 GACSHIP SJ; 671335 SUICO SJ (insurance)
Cable address AHMAD AL GOSAIBI
Subsidiary offices Branches in Dammam, Ras Tanura, Al Khafji, Al Hasa, Riyadh and Jiddah.
Proprietor Collective Company in which the following are the partners:
Sh. Ahmad bin Hamad Al Gosaibi
Sh. Abdulaziz bin Hamad Al Gosaibi
Sh. Sulaiman bin Hamad Al Gosaibi
Company History
The business was founded by Sh. Hamad bin Ahmad in 1937 as a general trading concern which has developed into a modern business with wide and diversified interests. It owns the following companies:
Ahmad Hamad Al Gosaibi & Bros (Commission Agents), tel. 42666, 42862
Al Gosaibi Trading Company, tel. 42666, 42862
Al Gosaibi Real Estate
Al Gosaibi Service Station
In the manufacturing field they also own the National Bottling Co. (Pepsi Cola), tel. 43222, 43366; A H Al Gosaibi & Bros Co. Plant, tel. 43222, 43366; A H Al Gosaibi & Bros Ice Plant, tel. 42666. The company owns the Al Gosaibi Hotel in Al Khobar, tel. 42466, 46466, tlx. 670008 GOSTEL SJ, P.O.Box 51 Dhahran Airport, and has a founding shareholding in the Saudi Hotel Services Co. Ltd. in Riyadh (Riyadh Palace Hotel) and the Egyptian Saudi Hotel Co. (Ramada). Their wholly owned shipping interests are in Al Gosaibi Shipping Co., Dammam, tel. 23813, 23426, 23427; the Gulf Agency Co. (Saudi Arabia) Ltd., Dammam, tel. 23813, 23426; and International Offshore Services Corporation, Dammam, tel. 23818, 23426. In the transportation field they have two wholly owned companies, International Associated Cargo Carriers, Dammam, tel 23813, 23426, and Yousuf Al Gosaibi Travel Agency, Al Khobar, tel. 41916, 41922.
Ahmad Hamad Al Gosaibi and Brothers are also founders and shareholders in the following companies:

Saudi Cement Company
Dhahran Electric Supply Co.
Hofuf Electric Supply Co.
El Khat Co. (Printing Press), tel. 42666, 22343
Saudi Glass Manufacturing Company, Dammam
Saudi Company for Vegetable Oil and Ghee, Jiddah
Saudi Crowncaps Manufacturing Co. Ltd., Riyadh, tel. 36310
Al Gosaibi Maritime Services Co., Dammam, tel. 23813, 21095
Gulf Ro-Ro Services, Dammam, tel. 23813, 23426, 23427
International Air Cargo Corporation, tel. 23813, 23426, 23427
Gulf Marine Transport Co. KSC, Kuwait, tel. 449981
The Saudi British Bank
Al Jazira Contracting Company, Bahrain
Saudi United Insurance Co. Ltd., Al Khobar, tel. 42863, 45866, 45716, in which they have 60%
Their joint venture enterprises are in the Oilfield Chemical Company (Saudi Arabia) Ltd., Dammam, with Essochem of Belgium, tel. 42666; the Continental Can of Saudi Arabia Ltd., Dammam, with the Continental Group Inc. of USA, tel. 42666; the Saudi National Pipe Co., Dammam, the Saudi Korean Stevedoring Co., tel. 23813, 28762; the International Trucking Express Co., Dammam, tel. 23813, 23426, 23427. These interests are rounded off with partnerships in the Swiss Reinsurance Co. of Switzerland, the Commercial Union Assurance Company of Great Britain and Baloise Insurance Company Ltd. of Switzerland.
Bankers Arab Bank, Riyadh Bank, Saudi British Bank.

INTERNATIONAL ASSOCIATED CARGO CARRIER

Address head office Dammam
Activities A company of clearing and forwarding agents, dealing also with both international and local transport services. Set up in 1975, the company is owned by Abdalaziz Hamad Algosaibi and has a branch in Jiddah (PO Box 7697, tel. 6514740, 6514508, tlx. 402771 IACCJ SJ), as well as one in Riyadh.

SAUDI UNITED INSURANCE CO. LTD.

Address head office PO Box 933, al Khobar
Telephone 8642863
Telex 671335 SULCO SJ
Activities The company is a joint venture between Ahmad Hamad Algosaibi, Commercial Union Assurance of the UK, the Swiss Reinsurance Co. and the Baloise Insurance Co. Ltd. of Switzerland. There are branches in Jiddah (PO Box 6971, tel. 6534272, 6534768, tlx. 402258 SUICO SJ), Riyadh (PO Box 74, tel. 4022589 and tlx. 201309 GOSRYAD SJ). The company is a general insurance company, non-life, covering fire, hull, liability, accident, cargo contract work, car aviation and engineering risks.

SOUTH EAST ASIA SHIPPING AGENCIES

Address head office PO Box 477, Dammam
Activities The company was founded in 1975 and is owned by Abdalaziz Algosaibi. It has a branch in Jiddah (PO Box 6706, tel. 6534264, 6532968, tlx. 401779 SOASIA SJ) and is a shipping and forwarding agent.

The Family of Al Hammad

The family originates in Shaqra of Najd, though many have also settled in Zubair. Despite the fact that Najdis like to stick together, Abdullah represents their independent qualities and migrated to Al Khobar to set up on his own.

ALI AL HAMMAD

AL ABDALRAHMAN

ABDULLAH

KHALID
student at Univ. of Imam Muhammad Saud in Hasa

MUHAMMAD

ABDALRAHMAN

HAMMAD HOTEL

Address head office PO Box 1454, 1455, Al Khobar
Telephone 8646245, 8646557, 8648686, 8646155
Telex 670183 HAOTEL SJ
The hotel opened in 1983 and is situated right in the busy suq area of Al Khobar. It is thus very handily placed for business purposes. The hotel has a hundred rooms and a friendly and helpful staff. The cuisine is Indian, European, Chinese and Korean. It is perhaps Al Khobar's answer to one of the small better hotels in London and a much needed facility. The Kingdom has really too many of the larger luxurious international hotels. The Al Hammad is scrupulously clean and its rates are very reasonable.
Abdullah Hammad has other business interests which are of an educational nature. He runs two junior and elementary schools in Dammam, and two business schools, one in Dammam and one in Al Khobar. They are staffed by teachers from Jordan, Syria and Egypt, and offer courses in English translation, accounting, typing - both English and Arabic - as well as secretarial work.

The Family of Hafiz

The Hafiz family is the oldest publishing family in the Kingdom and commenced operations in Medina some fifty years ago. At this time they founded the National Daily Al Medina which was wholly owned by them. Today the family retains two shares in the paper having relinquished its total ownership twenty years in response to the government's wish to spread ownership in this field. The family are of Bani Hisham descent and thus descendants of the Prophet Muhammad.

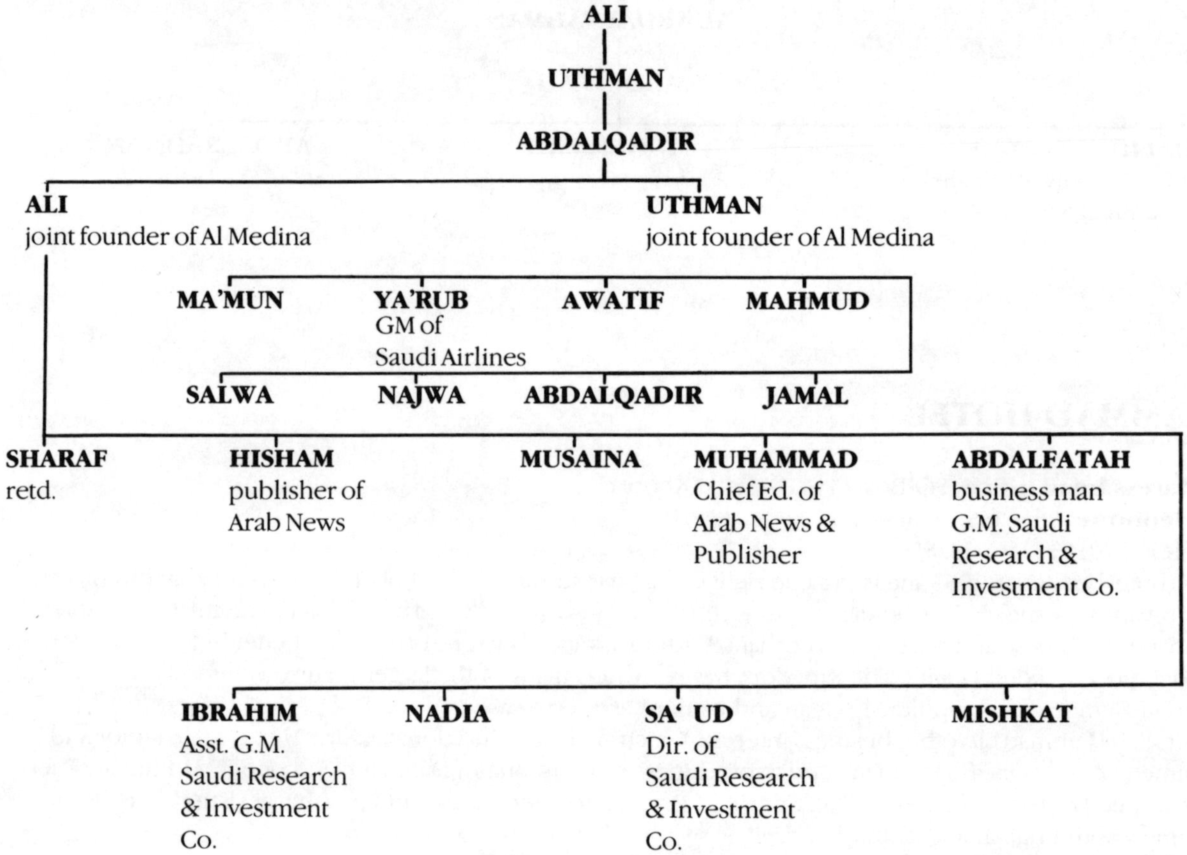

SAUDI RESEARCH AND INVESTMENT CO. LTD.

Address head office PO Box 4556, Jiddah
Telephone 6653908
Telex 400509 SARANI SJ
Activities This company is owned by Sayyid Hisham and Sayyid Muhammad Ali Hafiz and was formed in 1978. It acts as a finance broker and deals with investment companies.

SAUDI RESEARCH AND MARKETING CO.

Address head office P.O.Box 4556 Jiddah
Telephone 6534743, 6534239, 6533723, 6532911
Subsidiary offices
Riyadh, PO Box 478, tel. 4776068, 4774176, tlx. 201660 MARAD SJ
al Khobar, tel. 864678, 8642991
Bahrein, PO Box 20534, tel. 232328, tlx. 9496 ARNEWS BN
Cairo, 31 Jazirat al Arab St, Madinat al Mohan Diseen, Adokki, tel. 815121, 650121
Khartoum, PO Box 2944, tel. 71707, 71782
London, 6-7 Gough Sq, Fleet St, EC4A 3OJ, tel. 3534413-6, tlx. 889272 ARABNEWS G
USA, Houston, 2100 West Loop Sth, Suite 1650, Houston, Texas 77027, tel. (713) 961 0245, tlx. 440568 ARABNEWS HOU
Washington, 359 National Press Building, DC 20045, tel. (202) 638 7183, tlx. 440568 SAUDI U
Tunis, tel. 256611
San'a', PO Box 1298, tel. 207636, 207639, tlx. 2342 LAHOM YE
This company owns the *Arab News* newspaper which is the leading English language paper of the Kingdom.

FOOD AND INDUSTRIAL SUPPLY CO. LTD. (FISCO)

Address head office PO Box 9411, Jiddah
Telephone 6531336, 6531332, 6531324, 6531240, 6531328
Telex 402857 SAWAN SJ
Activities This company deals in industrial equipment and foodstuffs, having a branch in al Khobar (tel. 8646383). It is owned by Sayyid Abdalqadir Uthman Hafiz.

HEAVEN EXPRESS

Address head office PO Box 92, Jiddah
Telephone 6514236, 6422105
Telex 402049 OSAKOK SJ
Activities With the head office in London, this company is a partnership managed by Sayyid Ali Hafiz. They are marketing consultants, general contractors, and travel agents; they also deal with shipping companies and manpower recruitment.
The company is run as a partnership in which the executive partners are Syd. Hisham Ali Hafiz and Syd. Muhammad Ali Hafiz. The remaining are sleeping partners. The business is operated in two divisions:
1. The Publishing Division
This produces three papers, two daily and one weekly. Arab News, 50,000 per day. Sharqal Awsat, 64,000 per day in Saudi Arabia and 20,000 per day in London. This paper is published in London and printed in Jiddah, London and Riyadh. Saudi Business Weekly, 12,000 per week.
2. The Circulation Division
Which is responsible for the distribution of the company's own publications as well as others. Advertising is handled by Tihama (q.v.). The company owns Central Press Photos of London.
Bankers Saudi British Bank.

The Family of Howaish

From Anaiza in Najd.

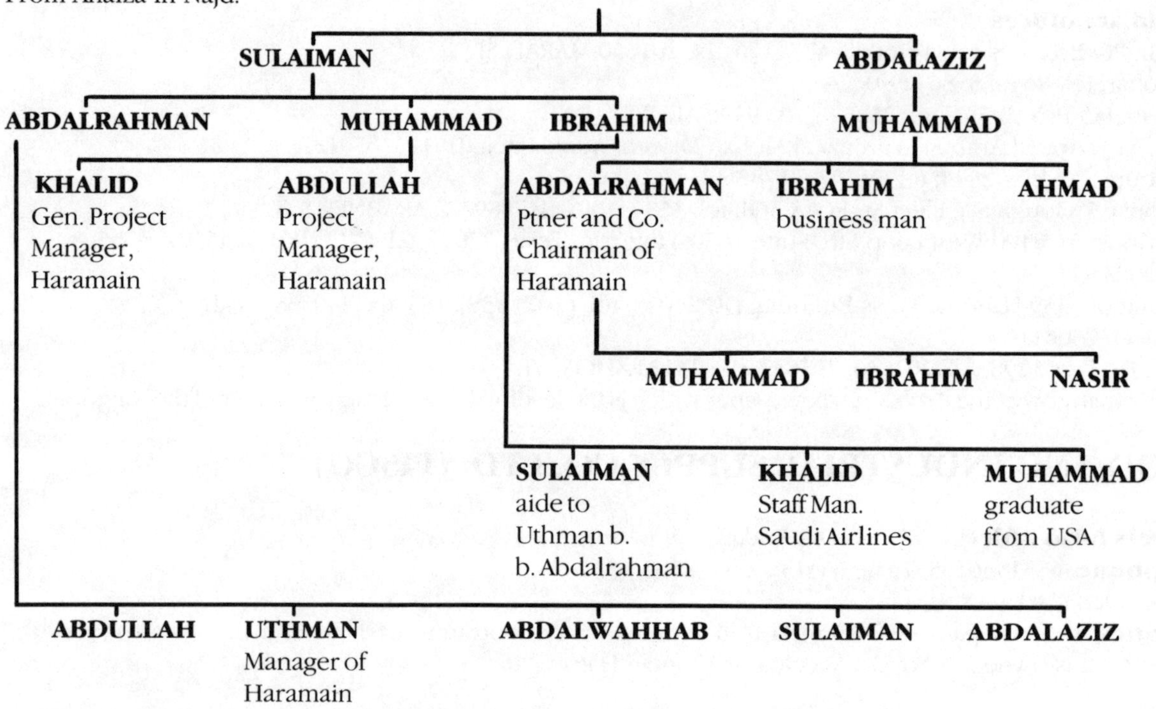

AL HARAMAIN COMPANY

Address head office P.O.Box 2233 Jiddah
Telephone 54415, 58896, 51169, 53147, 50196
Telex 401404 ZIRWAH SJ
Cable address AL ZARWA
Subsidiary offices Riyadh, tel. 47664737, Ta'if P.O.Box 940, tel. 7325610
Proprietor The Company is a partnership between Sh. Abdalrahman Muhammad Al Howaish and Sh. Salih Ibrahim Zamil.

Company History

The company was founded in 1958 and registered in 1962 and is a leader in the contracting and construction field. Their main activity is the building and maintenance of roads in which area they operate several contracts in Turbah, Dalam, Aqiq and Afif. However their main importance is their participation as main contractors with Sh. Muhammad Aboud Al Amoudi and Letco in the major project of 'New Jiddah'. At the present time they are involved in the first phase which is the construction of 870 villas. Haramain also operates a Technical Trading Division, tel. 51192, telex as above, which holds an agency for Friedrich air conditioners which the company imports from the USA and sells and maintains in the Western Province. They are also agents for Diakin air conditioners from Japan. This division replaces YINC. Haramain also operate a real estate office, tel. 51169.

Partnerships

1. Insulation Factory making polystyrene in partnership with Sh. Abdalrahman Sayyigh.
2. Metal Work Factory making metal water tanks, trailers and tippers in partnership with Sh. Ali Thunayan.
3. The Jiddah Shopping Centre in partnership with Sh. Hasan Mahmud Arif.
4. Saudi Metalco, where Sh. Salih Zamil and Sh. Abdalrahman Al Howaish are in partnership with Sh. Abdullah Ibrahim Al Miman. Each partner has participated in one third of the six million riyal capital. The company import and market steel products, iron ore, spare parts and aluminium sheet.

The Family of Huseini

A very old and respected family descending from the son of the fourth Caliph, Ali, who was himself the son-in-law of the Prophet Muhammad. Sayyids (Sada).

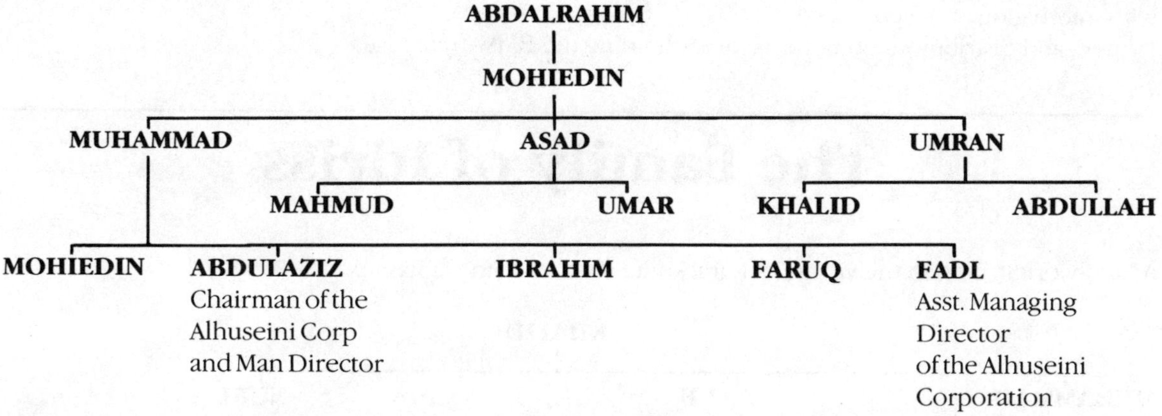

ALHUSEINI CORPORATION

Address head office P.O.Box 851 Jiddah
Telephone 6444877, 6445133, 6427429, 6438008
Telex 401163 HUSENI SJ
Company History
The business was founded by the late Syd. Muhammad Alhuseini who was a native of Medina. To begin with he operated in the commodity and textile fields starting in the early thirties. In 1947 an office was established in Karachi as most of the trading was with Pakistan at that date. In 1954 the head office was established in Jiddah and the import of building materials was developed. A Travel Office was set up in 1963 and in 1972 the Construction Division was founded to work in both the public and the private sectors. In 1977 expansion resulted in the establishment of an Automobile and Heavy Machinery Division.
Business Activities Under the Chairmanship and direction of Syd. Abdulaziz the Corporation now operates in six divisions:
1. Trading Division
2. Travel Agency Division
3. Construction Division
4. Automobile and Heavy Machinery Division
5. Solar Energy Division
6. Freight Transportation and Handling Division

Agencies Travel: Sales Agents for SDI, Saudi Arabian Airlines. General Sales Agents for Pakistan International Airlines, VARIG Brazilian Airlines, KM Air Malta Limited.
Automobile: The Corporation is the BMW concessionaire for the whole of the Kingdom of Saudi Arabia.
Partnerships/Joint Ventures
The Alhuseini Corporation holds 51% in the following enterprises:
Alhuseini-ADA Saudi Arabia Company Ltd.
The National Construction Saudi Arabia Co. Ltd.
Alhuseini Macdonald Layton Company Ltd.
Boremaster Saudi Arabia Company Ltd.

AL HUSSEINI CORPORATION

Address head office PO Box 851, Jiddah
Telephone 6310771, 6310772
Telex 402150 AHCORP SJ, 401163 HUSEINI SJ
Sponsor Fracht AG of Switzerland, PO Box 851, Jiddah, tel. 6658085, tlx. 401163 HUSEINI SJ. Concerned with internationa transport services.
Dealers and distributors of motor vehicles holding the BMW franchise.

The Family of Idriss

A family originating in the village of Kara, some 90 kms from Damascus.

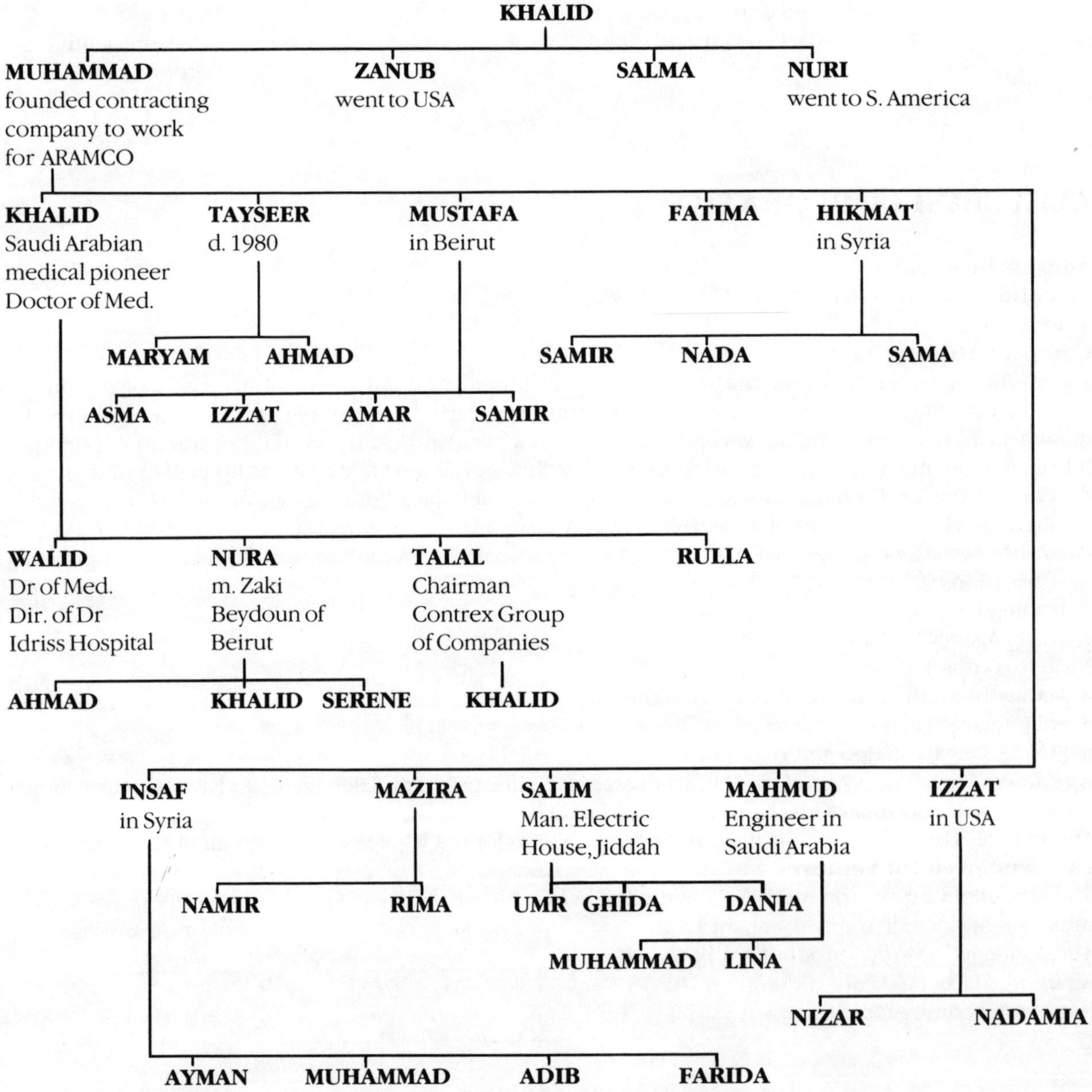

CONTREX GROUP OF COMPANIES

Address PO Box 75, Jiddah
Telephone 6659870, 6655234
Telex 400077 CONTRX SJ

The Chairman and proprietor of the Group is Talal Khalid Idriss. Member companies are:

1. MIDCO, engineering and contracting, and geotechnical engineering.
2. Contrex International, a holding company for some of the Group's Saudi investments. It also holds agencies and representations.
3. Contrex Trading, wholesale and retail of electro-mechanical equipment (showroom Southern Market Center, Bab Makkah, tel. 6447420).
4. Contrex Transport, project transport, heavy lifts and general cargo. Dammam branch tel. 21727, tlx. 601488 CONDAM SJ.
5. ITRACO (Idriss Trading and Contracting Co. Ltd.), wholesale and retail of building materials.
6. Electric House, wholesale and retail of electrical goods (showroom Southern Market Center).
7. Electro-mechanical Projects Establishment, wholesale and retail of electro-mechanical material (PO Box 5823, Jiddah, tel. 6445948).
8. Saudi Hospitals Co., turnkey design, construction, equipment supply and management of medical facilities.
9. United Transport Co., projects and inland transport.
10. Al Aman Co. Ltd., wholesale and retail and foodstuffs.
11. Dr Khalid Idriss and Sons Co. Ltd., health facilities investment.
12. Consolidated Engineering Co. (CI) Ltd. (CEC), wholesale of electrical and electro-mechanical materials, project management and procurement; address Contrex Building, 104 Park Street, London W1, tel. 491 2890, tlx. 298808 CONTRX G.
13. Contrex Research and Development (CI) Ltd., holding company for European investments (address, etc. as for CEC).
14. Hospital Supply International, medical equipment and turnkey projects covering Arabia, Africa, North and South America; address 870 Twisted Oak Lane, Buffalo Grove, Ill. 60090, tel. (312) 5413518.

The Family of Jamil

A family whose origins go to the Sa'di of Palestine in the early part of the nineteenth century.

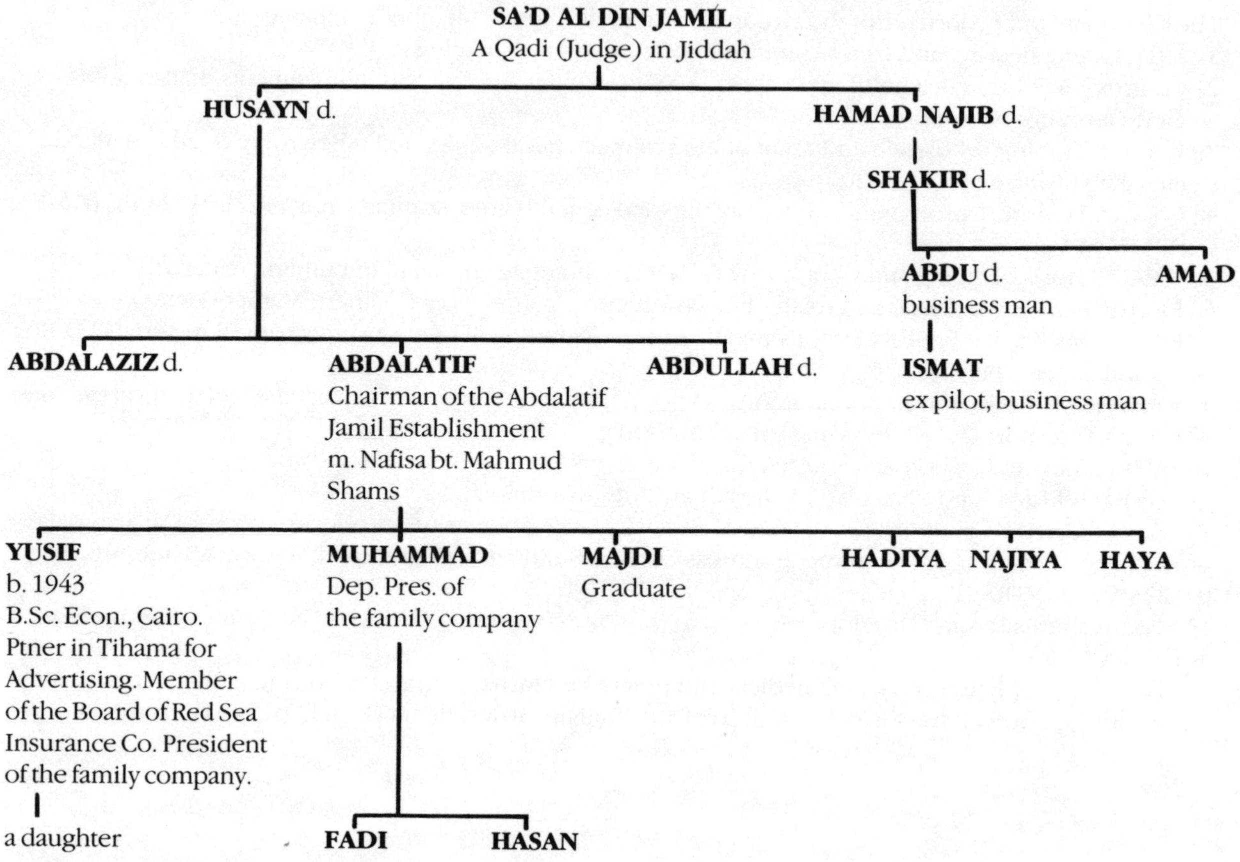

ABDALATIF JAMIL ESTABLISHMENT

Address head office P.O.Box 248 Jiddah
Telephone 6456119, 6456151, 6456154
Telex 401139 YOUSEF SJ
Cable address YOUSEF
Subsidiary offices
Jiddah Branch Office, tel. 72025, 72026, 73301,tlx. 401139 YOUSEF SJ
Riyadh, tel. 4765234, 4764896/7, 4761999, 4764898, tlx. 201237 YOUSEF SJ
Ta'if, tel. 7320682, tlx. 451021
Dammam, tel. 8326657, 8326920, 8331318, 8331658, 8321004, tlx. 601076Al Khobar, tel. 8647645, 8647392
Mecca, tel. 5420664
Hofuf, tel. 25160, tlx. 661008
Jiddah Central Parts Dept, tel. 645785
London office: Jamil Organisation Ltd., 99 Bishopsgate, London EC2M 3XD, tel. 01 588 4239/4230

Proprietor Sh. Abdalatif Jamil
Board Chairman Sh. Abdalatif Jamil
President Sh. Yusif Jamil
Deputy President Sh. Mohamed Jamil
Administration Director Khalid Habash
Marketing Director Shakir Nabulsi
Finance Director Colin Parker
Parts and Services Director Dennis Richmond
Company History Sh. Abdalatif Jamil, who though over seventy is still energetically overseeing his company's activities, began as a clerk in Jiddah Customs. However, in about 1938 he resigned and with a joint capital of 8,000 riyals he and his friend Ali Dafa went into business as partners. With the advent of the Second World War importing became almost impossible and apart from the distribution of aid from the USA and UK, Jiddah merchants were reduced to getting what goods they could from passing ships. Eventually this trade, long winked at by the Saudi Government, became legal. After the war the partnership concentrated on spare parts for American cars and developed into an association between Sh. Abdulatif and his brothers. This lasted until 1952 by which time they had established the first petrol station and the largest mechanical workshops in the Kingdom and were agents for Pirelli Tyres, Oldham Batteries, spare parts and Plutolite of the USA. In 1952 Sh. Abdalatif went into business by himself and acquired the Vittiwinkle paints agency from Holland and dealt in various goods from the UK and serviced Government tenders. At this time he was to build the largest petrol station in the Kingdom. In 1954 he held the Borgward Isabella agency but relinquished it after a year; he then acquired a sub-dealership from Chrysler. It was in 1955 that he imported the first Toyota. This was a Landcruiser and his first customer was H.R.H. Prince Khalid ibn Abdalaziz al Sa'ud who was to become the King of Saudi Arabia.
Agencies Toyota of Japan, represented throughout their range including fork lift trucks.
Kubota of Japan, agricultural equipment, generators and tractors.
MAN of Munich, West Germany, trucks.
Other interests include ownership of Jamil Housing Projects in Jiddah and Riyadh, each comprising 150 villas, shipowning and shipping agency.
Bankers National Commercial Bank, Citibank, Arab Bank, Saudi Cairo Bank, Saudi British Bank, Riyadh Bank, Leitz Bank, First National City Bank of Chicago, BBME London and Geneva, Chase Manhattan, American Express, Bank of America, and Manufacturers Hanover Trust Company.

JAMIL AND CO. LTD.

Address head office PO Box 248, Jiddah
Telephone 6672772
Telex 401453, 401139 YUSEF SJ
Activities A company established in 1979 and owned by Yusif Abdalatif Jamil and his brother Muhammad. They are concerned with contracting in building, civil engineering, electrical, plumbing and general fields.

ABDALATIF JAMIL UNITED CO. LTD.

Address head office PO Box 248, Jiddah
Telephone 6604488
Telex 401453 USEF SJ
Activities The company was set up in 1955 with branches in Jubail, Hofuf, Riyadh, Dammam, Mecca, Ta'if and al Khobar. They are active as car dealers and distributors, carrying the following agencies: Toyota, MAN, Toshiba, and Kubota. They operate repair and service facilities and also deal in motors and generators, electric and electronic appliances, foodstuffs and advertising services.

UNITED FOODS LTD.

Address head office PO Box 8914, Jiddah
Telephone 6656855, 6657454, 6657080
Telex 401453 USEF SJ
Activities The company is owned by the Abdalatif Jamil Group and has branches in Riyadh and Dammam. It supplies foodstuffs, including canned goods, fruit, meat, vegetables, fruit juices and drinks, baby foods, oil and butter.

UNITED TECHNOLOGY PRODUCTS CO. LTD.

Address head office PO Box 248, Jiddah
Telephone 6604488, 6656657
Telex 401453 YUSEF SJ
Activities A company established in 1981 and owned by Abdalatif Jamil, having branches in al Khobar (tel. 8578452), Yanbu (tel. 3226207), Riyadh (tel. 4656358), and Tabuk (tel.34930, tlx. 881193). The company represents Toshiba radio and television equipment and deals in home appliances, kitchen wares, office equipment, video games, medical and surgical equipment and electronic goods.

JAMJOOM BUSINESS INTERESTS

ABDALATIF MUHAMMED SALAH JAMJOOM AND BROS.

Address PO Box 2127, Jiddah
Telephone 6423190, 6423195
Telex 401169 JAMJOOM SJ
Board
Chairman Dr. Abdalatif Salah Jamjoom
Sh. Husayn Salah Jamjoom
Sh. Ahmad Salah Jamjoom (ex Minister of Commerce)
Sh. Hamza Salah Jamjoom
Sh. Yusuf Salah Jamjoom
Company History
The Jamjoom family settled in Jiddah about a hundred and fifty years ago when Salah came for the Hajj and stayed, founding his business on the pilgrimage trade. Early misfortune was overcome when Abdalraouf and Muhammad Salah took over and a prospering business allowed the family to take an interest in charitable foundations and education. At this time the family business centred around foodstuffs, timber and kerosene. The family's first business was Muhammad Nur Salah Jamjoom and Bros., and then Muhammad Nur became independent and handles finance, administration, shipping and real estate. He is also director of the Badwa Trading Company. The parent company then operated under the name of Abdalatif Muhammad Salah Jamjoom and Bros. with the following divisions:
Jamjoom Construction Co.
A partnership with Babich, the Jamjooms holding 70%. This company deals in partitions, aluminium doors and windows, building materials and steel products.
Jamjoom Medicine Stores
Run by Sh. Yusuf Salah Jamjoom and represents the Pfizer Pharmaceutical Agency, Continental of Belgium, Hausmann of Switzerland, Allergan EUE Products of the USA.
Depot Pharmaceutical Du Moyen Orient
Controlled by Dr. Abdalatif Salah Jamjoom and representing CIBA GEIGY and Merek Darmstadt.
Jamjoom Vehicles and Equipment
Headed by Sh. Ahmad Salah, agents for Peugeot, Hino trucks, Kleber tyres and motoring accessories.
Jamjoom General Agencies
Run by Sh. Hamza Salah Jamjoom.
The Jamjoom commercial interests have now become more widely diffuse, as per the following.

CHEMTEC INDUSTRY

Address PO Box 4376, Jiddah
Telephone 6711156, 6711283, 6714962
Telex 401812 KEMTEC SJ
Established in 1976 this company deals in building materials and operates as building contractors. It is owned by Muhammad Salah Jamjoom.

The Family of Jamjoom

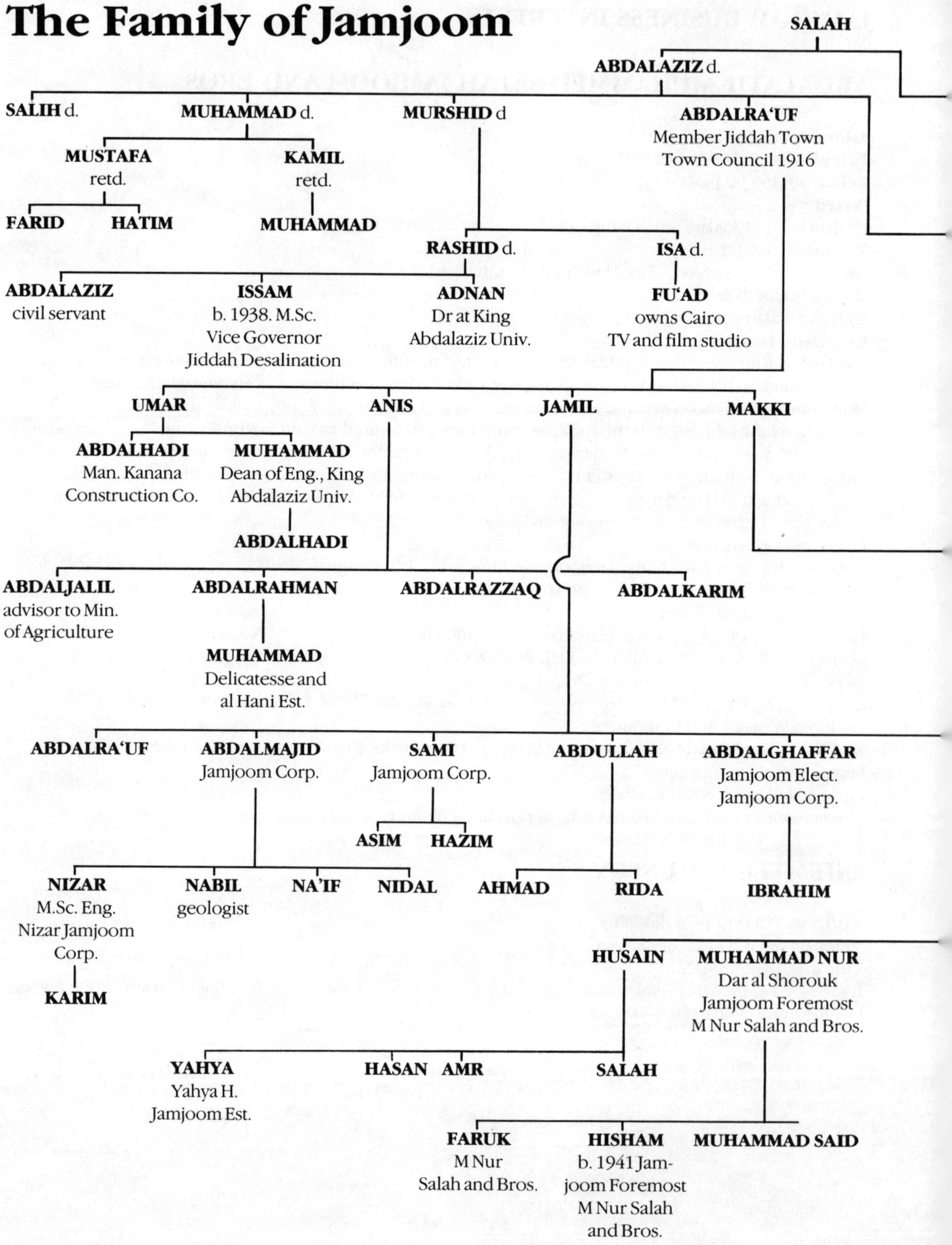

A notable Jiddah family originating immediately in Egypt, where they were early immigrants from the Hijaz.

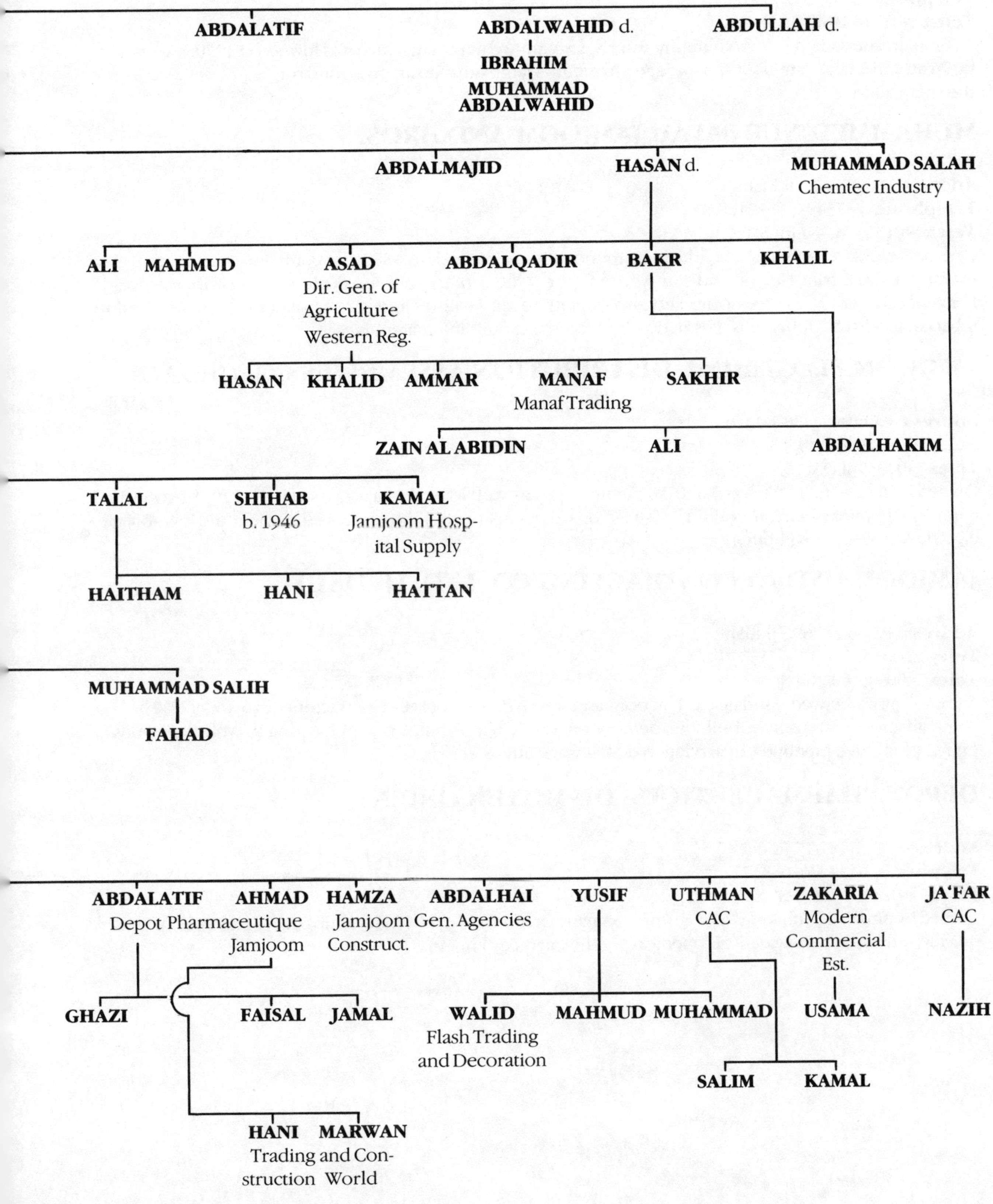

JAMJOOM LABS AND STUDIOS

Address P.O.Box 1580 Jiddah
Telephone 6447723, 6656178
Telex 401718 JAMUID SJ
A company specializing in photography and photographic equipment which was formed in 1970. It is owned by Fu'ad and Shihab Jamjoom and managed by Samir A Jamjoom who also own and run Jamjoom Video from the same address.

MUHAMMED NUR SALAH JAMJOOM AND BROS.

Address P.O.Box 12 Jiddah
Telephone 6875497, 6872168
Telex 401365 MONEER SJ
One of the oldest companies in Jiddah, its foundation dating back to 1850, the company is managed today by Faruk and Hisham Muhammad Nur whose father is the owner. They are dealers and distributors for Peugeot cars, parts and accessories and also operate repair facilities and service stations. They also deal in tobacco, foodstuffs, lubricants, cosmetics, perfumes and building materials.

JAMJOOM ELECTRICAL DISTRIBUTION ASSEMBLIES CO. (JEDAC) .

Address P.O.Box 6838 Jiddah
Telephone 6364340, 6364339
Telex 402039 JEDAC SJ
Owned by Ghassan Shabir (q.v.) and Ali Tamini (q.v.) as well as Abdalgafar Jamjoom, this 1971 established company supplies electrical equipment, switchboards, panel-boards and control equipment and low voltage electric distribution equipment.

JAMJOOM HYDRO CONTRACTING CO. LTD. (JEDAC)

Address P.O.Box 7696 Jiddah
Telephone 6715251, 6715379
Telex 400449 JADRO SJ
A joint venture between Abdalgafar Jamjoom and the Hydro Resources Contractors Corp. in 1977. The company are contractors for building, demolition, dredging, drilling and landscaping as well as painting, piling, plumbing, pipelines, quarrying, roads, sewage and water.

DEPOT PHARMACEUTIQUE DU MOYEN ORIENT

Address P.O.Box 415 Jiddah
Telephone 6429986, 6431711
Telex 401689 DEPOT SJ
Owned by Abdalatif Muhammad Salah, this company was formed in 1954. It is a supplier of paper and paper products, drugs, pharmaceuticals, medical and hospital equipment.

JAMJOOM MEDICINE STORE

Address P.O.Box 935 Jiddah
Telephone 6422563, 6422463
Telex 400349 MAMOON SJ
The company is owned by Abdalatif Muhammad Salah Jamjoom and Bros. and managed by Yusuf Salah. It was founded in 1956 and deals in cosmetics, perfumes, medical and surgical equipment, optical goods, drugs and pharmaceuticals. The brands carried include: Pfizer, Allercan, Continental Pharma, Rodenstockoptik, Swarovski Optik, Sans Souci. There are branches in Riyadh (Middle East Drug Store, P.O.Box 479, tel. 6519989) and Al Khobar (Middle East Drug Store, P.O.Box 205, tel. 41612).

JAMJOOM CONSTRUCTION LTD

Address P.O.Box 8624 Jiddah
Telephone 6885159, 6897369, 6877196
Telex 400953 TAWAKI SJ
A firm of contractors in the areas of building, pipelines, plumbing, electrical work, sewage and water. Formed in 1980 and owned by Ahmad Salah Jamjoom.

JAMJOOM GENERAL AGENCIES

Address P.O. Box 2127 Jiddah
Telephone 6423190, 6423195, 6433319
Telex 401169 JAMJOM SJ
The company is owned by Jamjoom Bros. and has branches in Riyadh (tel. 4027242) and Al Khobar (tel. 8642775). It deals in perfumes and cosmetics, foodstuffs and camel goods, grains, oil, butter and ghee and also stationery. The manager is Hamza Muhammad Salah Jamjoom.

JAMJOOM HOSPITAL SUPPLY

Address P.O.Box 214, P.O.Box 9158
Telephone 6427790
Telex 400706 JMHOSP SJ
Formed in 1977 this company has a branch in Riyadh (P.O.Box 1230, tel. 4650984, 4650988, tlx. 203043 JAMSUP SJ). They supply hospital and medical equipment, chemicals, pharmaceuticals, laboratory and surgical equipment. The company is owned by Muhammad Kamal Makki Jamjoom.

JAMJOOM VEHICLES AND EQUIPMENT

Address P.O.Box 1247 Jiddah
Telephone 6872710, 6871876, 6871708
Telex 401324 SALAH SJ
The company has branches in Riyadh and Dammam and deals in commercial vehicles, compressors and construction equipment. Brand names carried include: Benati, Davey, Dyna, Hino, Sakai, Salma and Whiteman. The company is owned by Ahmad Salah, Hamza Salah and Yusuf Jamjoom.

DAR AL SHOROUQ PUBLICATION DISTRIBUTION AND PRINTING

Address P.O.Box 4146 Jiddah
Telephone 6426610
Telex401209 SHORCO SJ
This company is concerned with book-binding, printing and publishing. Established some thirty years ago, the company is a partnership between Muhammad Nur Jamjoom and Muhsin A Baroom.

YAHYA H JAMJOOM ESTABLISHMENT

Address P.O. Box 7123 Jiddah
Telephone 6421391
Telex 401324 YAHIA SJ
Founded in 1978 and owned by Yahya Husain Jamjoom, this company deals in foodstuffs, houseware, kitchen equipment and gifts.

DELICATESSE-HANAA

Address P.O.Box 7107 Jiddah
Telephone 6675318
Telex 00244 ALHANI SJ
Muhammad Abdalrahman Jamjoom formed this company in 1979. It specializes in candies, cookies and confectionery.

AL HANI ESTABLISHMENT FOR ENGINEERING AND TRADE

Address P.O.Box 7107 Jiddah
Telephone 6310177
Telex 400244 ALHANI SJ
A company operating as commission agents, architects and as general traders and building contractors.

NIZAR JAMJOON CORPORATION

Address P.O.Box 2207 Jiddah
Telephone 6877097, 6874288
Owned by Nizar Abdalmajid Jamjoom, this company was formed in 1977 and is a contracting concern for building, electricals, fencing, plumbing, roads, pipes and domestic paints.

AL MADINA

Address P.O.Box 807 Jiddah
Telephone 6880344, 6891009, 6877095, 6871929
Telex 401356 MADINA SJ
Founded in 1956, this is one of the most famous publishers of newspapers and magazines in the Kingdom. Ahmad Salah Jamjoom is a part-owner of the enterprise. There are branches in Mecca, Medina, Riyadh, Taif, Buraida, Dammam and Abha.

MANAF TRADING ESTABLISHMENT

Address P.O.Box 2548 Jiddah
Telephone 6884781
Telex 400480 KHALID SJ
Owned by Manaf Asad Hasan Jamjoom who established the company in 1971, this concern deals as a contractor in building and food.

MODERN COMMERCIAL ESTABLISHMENT

Address P.O.Box 2352 Jiddah
Telephone 6432000
Telex 401842 MODCO SJ
Owned by Zakaria Salah Jamjoom and formed in 1970, this company deals in rugs, carpets and batteries.

MODERN VEHICLES AND EQUIPMENT

Address P.O. Box 2352, Jiddah
Telephone 6719015
Telex 401842 MODCO SJ, 401946 MODEST SJ
Owned by Zakaria Salah Jamjoom, this company is an automobile dealer and distributor and also deals in accessories and spare parts. It was established in 1979.

AL KINANA FOR CONTRACTING AND PROJECTS EST.

Address P.O.Box 7828 Jiddah
Telephone 6429217, 6448178, 6423750
Telex 403275 NAZEEH SJ
A firm of general and building contractors owned by Dr. Muhammad Umar Jamjoom and managed by his son Abdalhadi.

SAUDI MARKETING ESTABLISHMENT

Address P.O.Box 5235
Telephone 6434939, 6443285, 6445688
Telex 401532 SME SJ
Owned by Abdalhadi Umar Jamjoom and with a branch in Riyadh, this company deals in electrical equipment, flour, foodstuffs, grain, sugar, barley, wheat, refrigeration, sanitaryware, video systems, tape recorders and fans.

NESR AL JAZIRA CONTRACTING COMPANY

Address P.O.Box 4110 Jiddah
Telephone 6600382, 6600390
Telex 400853 ALNESR SJ
Abdalgafar Jamjoom formed this company in 1977. It is a contracting concern involved with air-conditioning, building, decorating, painting and electrical and mechanical contracting. They also operate metal workshops and deal in diesel and petrol marine engines, and motors and generators.

RADWA TRADING COMPANY

Address P.O.Box 2489 Jiddah
Telephone 6438654, 6429393
Telex 403281 RADWA SJ
Owned by Muhammad Nur Salah Jamjoom and Bros., this company is managed by Faruk Jamjoom and deals in perfumes and cosmetics, stationery, lighters, ready-made clothes and jewellery.

SAUDI BAUER FOUNDATION CONTRACTORS LIMITED

Address P.O.Box 5812 Jiddah
Telephone 6658457, 6602881
Telex 400333 SDB SJ
Owned by Jaafar and Osman Jamjoom in partnership with Kavi Bauer, the company operates as a general contractor specializing in piling and drilling. There are branches in Al Khobar (tel. 8646760) and Dammam (tel. 8335084).

AL SHARAFIAH HOTEL

Address P.O.Box 59
Telephone 6447998
Established in 1978, this hotel is owned by Muhammad Umar Jamjoom.

TRADING AND CONSTRUCTION WORLD

Address P.O.Box 2309 Jiddah
Telephone 6876819, 6659321
Telex 401324 SALAH SJ
A company formed in 1979 which deals in ready-made clothes, electronic equipment and components and plastic products. The company is owned by Hani and Marwan Ahmad Jamjoom.

UOP MANAGEMENT SERVICES SAUDI ARABIA LTD UMSA

Address P.O. Box 7989 Jiddah
Telephone 6711540, 6717093
Telex 402627 UMSAJH SJ
A joint venture between the Jamjoom Corp. and UOP Management Services Inc. of the USA under the chairmanship of Abdalgafar Jamjoom. The company is concerned in the operation and maintenance of desalination plant, water treatment, refineries, power plants; management training and management consultancy.

WESCON JAMJOOM SA CO. LTD.

Address PO 2864 Jiddah
Telephone 6656498
Telex 400389 WESJAM SJ
The enterprise is a joint venture managed by Abdalgafar Jamil Jamjoom and is engaged in general, mechanical and electrical contracting.

CAC

Address head office P.O.Box 6285 Jiddah
Telephone 6874288, 6877098, 6873825
Telex 401365 MONEER SJ, 401169 JAMJOOM SJ
CAC is an architectural and design firm with a growing reputation and a fine record of achievement.
Partners
Sh. Osman Salah Jamjoom
Sh. Ja'afar Salah Jamjoom.

CONSULTING ARCHITECTURAL CORPORATION

Address P.O.Box 6285 Jiddah
Telephone 6874288, 6877097
Telex 400183 GMCNAL SJ
A firm of architectural consultants owned by Osman and Jaafar Salah Jamjoom.

JAMJOOM CORPORATION FOR COMMERCE AND INDUSTRY

Address P.O. Box 59 Jiddah
Telephone 6432578, 6438631
Telex 401812 KEMTEC SJ
A company owned by Abdalgafar Jamil Jamjoom and managed by his brothers Abdalmajid and Sami and formed in 1971. They supply chemicals and act as contractors for air-conditioning, electric installations, desalination plant and equipment, as well as local transport services and acting as commission agents.

JAMJOOM FOREMOST LTD.

Address P.O. Box 6905
Telephone 6364007, 6361843
Telex 400942 JAMFOR SJ
Founded in 1978 this company is owned by Jamjoom Bros. and McKesson Inc., and managed by Muhammad Nur Salah and his son Hisham Muhammad Jamjoom. It manufactures dairy products.

The Family of Jumaih

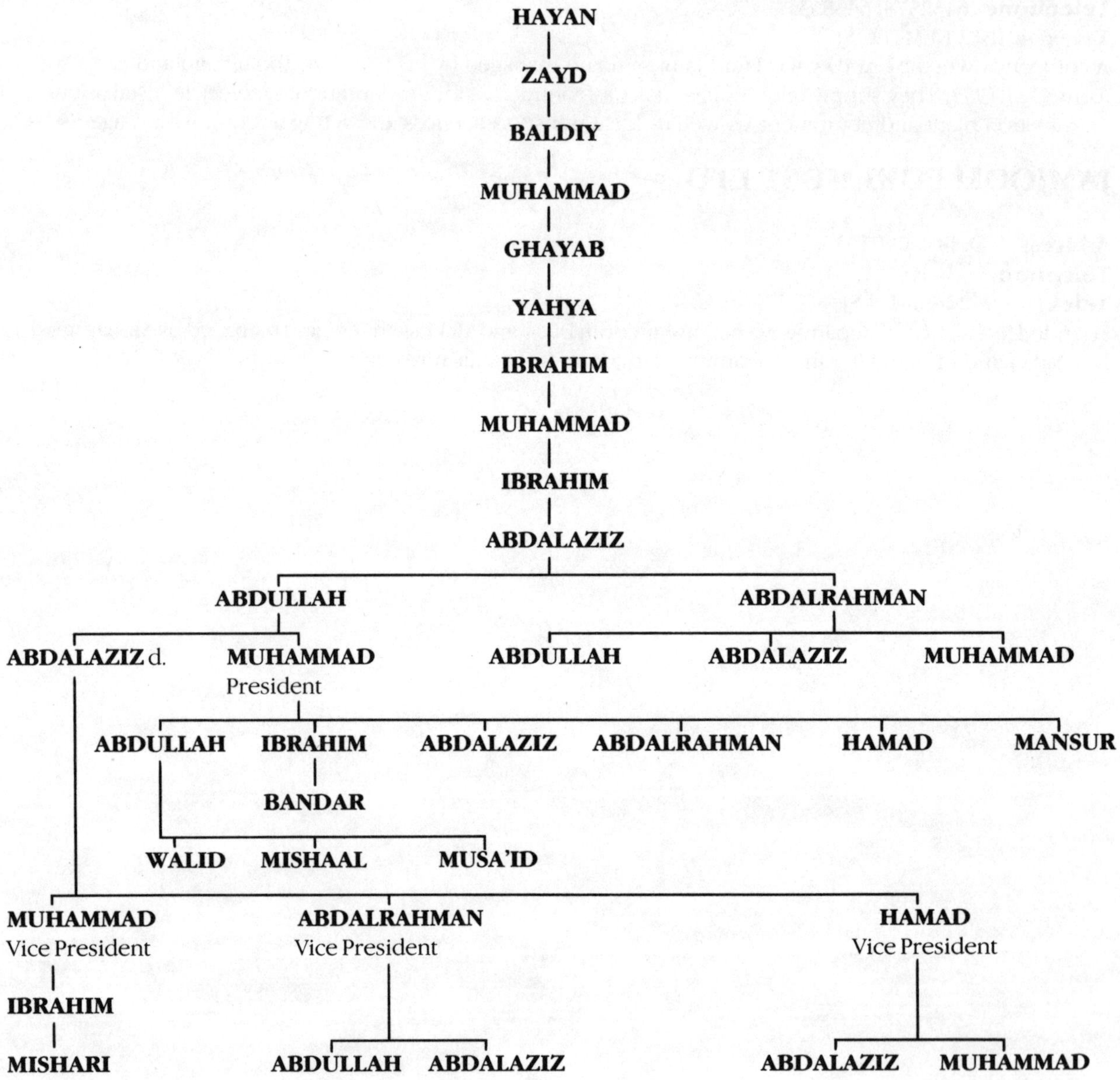

AL JOMAIH CO.

Address PO Box 132, Riyadh
Telephone 4788811
There are offices in Jiddah (PO Box 467, tel. 6605111), Dammam (PO Box 224, tel. 8343424) and New York (375 Park Ave, New York, NY 10022, tel. 7532102, tlx. 428790).
Al Jomaih became a major trading company in cars, oils, tyres and heavy construction equipment in the 1950s and has since diversified. The company is a partnership under Muhammad Abdullah Al Jomaih, an original founder, and the sons of the other founder, Abdalaziz. Each partner has his own specialised area. Many younger members of the family have had Western educations and have joined the company. It is now a major business enterprise.
1. Vehicle Division. Supply and servicing to the highest standard of General Motors vehicles for whom it is the largest dealer in the Kingdom.
2. Heavy Equipment Division - Earth Moving. Main agents for such names as Fiat/Allis, Perkins Engines, ABG, Galion, Compaction Equipment, TCM, Le Roi Air Compressors, Macmoter Skid Steer. There are wide facilities at Riyadh, Dammam and Jiddah, wih over 80 percent of spares in stock. Plans are in hand to expand and develop even further.
3. Heavy Equipment Division - Generators. Power supply in difficult terrain is a speciality with a wide range of generators from MTU container units through AIFO medium units to small Perkins power units.
4. Agricultural Division. Al Jomaih has been an innovator in supplying contract equipment. It stocks tractors, harvesters, pumps, ploughing equipment, and includes names such as Fiat-Allis, Claas, Jacuzzi, Perkins and Ransomes.
5. Lubricants, tyres and fire extinguishers. Al Jomaih holds the franchise for Shell oils and greases as well as Shell Construction Products. It carries a wide range of extinguishers by Bavaria. It is the sole agent for Yokohama Tyres.
Among foreign companies represented are M.A.N., M.T.U., Krupp Polysius, Lurgi, and Metallgesellschaft. The Aljomaih Pepsi-Cola plant distributes millions of bottles in the Riyadh area. Mirinda and Teem are also bottled in a plant capable of handling over 90,000 bottles per hour.

Another major area is the wholesale foods division which warehouses and ever-increasing range of foodstuffs from canned goods, to powdered milk, fruit juices and cereals.

The Family of Juffali

The family tradition is that they descend from the great conqueror, Khalid b. al Walid. They migrated from Anaiza in Qasim and the present commercial giant is based on an early association with GEC. The family name is said to derive from one of two beautiful horses owned by the mother of Abdullah b. Salih. These were named Fadl and Jaffal and both gave their names to famous families.

- **SALIH**
  - **ABDULLAH** who came to Mecca from Qasim
    - **IBRAHIM** Chairman of the Board
      - one daughter
    - **ALI** Board Member
      - **AMIN**
      - **SAMI**
    - **AHMAD** Man Dir of E A Juffali Bros and Board Member
      - **WALID** Co-ordinator of the activities of Arabian Metal Industries and the National Automobile Industries. Juffali interest in these being 70% respectively. Educated University of San Diego. Degree in Business Admin. m. Basma bint Abdalaziz al Sulayman (q.v.)
      - **KHALID**
      - **TARIQ**
      - **MAHA**

THE JUFFALI GROUP OF COMPANIES

Address head office P.O.Box 1049 Jiddah
Telephone 6422222
Telex 401130 JUFFALI SJ
Cable address JUFFALICENT
Subsidiary offices
London, ENPRO Business Representatives Ltd., 7 Old Park Lane, W1, tel. 01 499 6620, 499 6629, tlx. 262707 ENPRO G
Beirut, P.O.Box 113 5327, tel. 353618, tlx. 22136 EAJB LE
Zurich, ENPRO, Uraniastrasse 34, CH 8001, tel. 2113431, tlx. 52859 ENPRO CH
Jiddah, P.O.Box 297, tel. 6422222, tlx. 401530 JUFFALI SJ
Riyadh, P.O.Box 86, tel. 22322, tlx. 201049 JAFFALI SJ
Dammam, P.O.Box 24, tel. 23333, tlx. 601025 EPPCO SJ
Jubail, c/o P.O.Box 24 Dammam, tel.51300, tlx. 631280, 631281 JABEEN SJ

Offices of subsidiary and associated companies

EPPCO head office P.O.Box 987 Riyadh, tlx. 201022 EPPCO SJ; Jiddah P.O.Box 1502, tlx. 401130 JUFFALI SJ; Dammam P.O.Box 450, tlx. 601025 EPPCO SJ

SEMCO Arabia Ltd. P.O.Box 215 Dhahran Airport

Saudi Electric Co. Ltd., Ta'if P.O.Box 54; Mecca P.O.Box 386 ; Jiddah P.O.Box 1213

Saudi National Power Co., Jiddah P.O.Box 433

Medina Electric Power Co., Medina P.O.Box 128; Jiddah P.O.Box 1049

Al Hasa Electric Co., Hofuf P.O.Box 32

Saudi Cement Co., Dammam P.O.Box 306, tlx. 601068 CEMENT SJ

Fluor Arabia Ltd., Dammam P.O.Box 24

Petroserv, Dhahran Airport P.O.Box 215

Pool Arabia Ltd, Dhahran Airport P.O.Box 2568

Juffali Real Estate, Jiddah P.O.Box 1049, tlx. 401130 JUFFALI SJ

National Insurance Co., Jiddah P.O.Box 5832, tlx. 401130 JUFFALI SJ

E A Juffali & Brothers Central Parts Organisation, Jiddah P.O.Box 1049, tel. 6877687, 6877649, tlx. 400246 JUFCPO SJ

E A Juffali & Brothers, E.D.P. Centre, Jiddah P.O.Box 1049, tel. 6877687, 6877649, tlx. 400246 JUFCPO SJ

E A Juffali & Brothers, Technical Training Centre, Jiddah P.O.Box 1049, tel. 6872122, tlx. 401130 JUFFALI SJ

Diesel Electric, Jiddah P.O.Box 1049, tel. 6422222, tlx. 401130 JUFFALI SJ; branches: Jiddah P.O.Box 197, tel. 6872122, tlx. 401530 JUFFALI SJ; Riyadh P.O.Box 86, tel. 6422622, 6422125, tlx. 201049 JUFFALI SJ; Dammam P.O.Box 24, tel. 6422444, tlx. 601025 EPPCO SJ.

Company History

The activities of the Group began in 1948 and have contributed more than most to the economic development of the Kingdom, characterised as they are by great energy, efficiency and enthusiasm. The JuffaliGroup of Companies forms the largest association of industrial and commercial enterprises in Saudi Arabia today. In size it is the equal of one of the three hundred largest industrial corporations in the world. The Group operates through some two dozen subsidiaries, affiliates and fully independent branches whose activities embrace the following: General Trading, Electric Power Utilities, Cement Production, Commercial Vehicle Assembly and Body Manufacture, Engineering Construction and Management Services for the petroleum industry, Oil Well Workover Services, Real Estate Development and Insurance.

Agencies held by E A Juffali and Brothers

American Lincoln USA, Adolf Mohr Maschinen Fabrik Germany, AC-DECCO (Gen.Motors Corpn.) USA, Barber Greene Overseas USA, BICC Ltd., BICKEL K.G., E.Germany, Bunce (Ashbury) Ltd. UK, ButlerManufacturing Co. USA, Clark International Marketing SA USA, Compagnie Francaise, BLAW-KNOX France, Comp Air Construction and Mining Ltd. UK, Copperweld Steel International Co. USA, Daimler Benz AG Germany, DEMAG AG Germany, Demag Foerdertechnik Germany, Deutsch and Babcock AG Germany, the Ferrantz Engineerig Co. Ltd. UK, FMC Corporation USA, Frigor Denmark, GEC (Lamps and Lighting) Ltd. UK, Gallion Mfg. Division USA, General Motors Oveseas Distribution Corporation USA, GENT Chloride Ltd. UK, H.U. Sheldon and Co. Inc. USA, Heidelberger Druckmaschinen AG Germany, IBM World Trade Corporation USA, Kelvinator International Corp. USA, Klimsch & Co. Germany, Landis and Gyr AG Switzerland , The Liner Concrete Machinery Co. Ltd. UK, Linotype and Machinery Ltd UK, Litton Microwave Ovens USA, Massey Ferguson Ltd.UK, Michelin et Cie France, The Perolin Co.Inc.USA, The Phoenix Engineering Co. Ltd. UK, Peiner AG Germany, Triumph Adler Vertriebs GmbH Germany, Servis Domestic Appliances Ltd.UK, Siemens AG Germany, Simon Engineering Dudley Ltd.UK, Stahl 2 Co. Germany, Sunroz International Division USA, Sulzer Brothers Ltd. Switzerland, Transformation Union AG Germany, Tyler Division (Clark International Marketing) USA, Volkswagenwerk AG Germany, Wallace and Tierman Ltd.UK, Worthington Corporation USA, York International.

Agencies held by the Juffali Subsidiary Diesel Electric Company

Abacus International USA, Becker Autoradiowerk GmbH Germany, Robert Bosch GmbH Germany, Zahnradfabrik Friedrichschafen AG Germany.

Wholly Owned Subsidiaries

Engineering Projects and Products Co. Ltd. EPPCO Riyadh P.O.Box 987, tel. 22222, tlx. 201022 EPPCO SJ with branches in Jiddah and Dammam.

This company has installed all the exchange and subscriber systems in the Kingdom under Government contract and operates its own training centre as well as monitoring communications systems for development and its own research centre. The company is a partnership where Sh. Ibrahim Juffali holds 60% and Umar Aggad 40%. Sh. Ahmad Juffali is the Chairman.

Joint Ventures

Arabia Electric

Jiddah P.O.Box 4621, tel. 6659521, tlx. 401864 JUFSIE SJ

A joint venture with Siemens of Germany which designs, engineers and installs large scale electrical and electronic projects. Branches in: Riyadh P.O.Box 86, tel. 22322, tlx. 201049 JUFFALI SJ and Dammam P.O.Box 24, tel. 25364, tlx. 601025 EPPCO SJ

Arabian Chemical Co. Ltd.

Dammam P.O.Box 24, tel. 25364

Branches in: Jiddah P.O.Box 1049, tel. 6422222, tlx. 40113 O JUFFALI SJ and Riyadh P.O.Box 86, tel. 57138, tlx. 201049 JUFFALI SJ with DOW Chemicals USA.

Arabian Metal Industries Ltd.

Jiddah P.O.Box 5937, tel. 6655035, 6655243, tlx. 401130 JUFFALI SJ

With Carosserie Abillama of Lebanon the company produces special bodies for tippers, trailers and water and fuel bowsers.

Beck Arabia

Dhahran Airport P.O.Box 378, tel. 42905, tlx. 670152 BECK SJ

This company is a joint venture between E A Juffali Bros. and the Dallas based Heung C. Beck Company. They provide management services for large scale civil construction projects required by Saudi Arabia's Development Plans and the needs of the real estate development division within the Juffali Group.

Fluor Arabia Ltd.

Dhahran Airport P.O.Box 360, tlx. 601010 FLURAB SJ, with a branch in Riyadh (P.O.Box 86, tel. 61967, tlx. 200233 FLURY SJ) with the Fluor Corporation of USA and engaged in oil and gas development in the Kingdom extending to equipment leasing, construction management and training.

Juffali Sulzer Saudi Arabia Ltd.

Jiddah P.O.Box 5357, tel. 6657434, tlx. 401262 JSULZ SJ. Branches in Riyadh (P.O.Box 86, tel. 66176, tlx. 201049 JUFFALI SJ) and Dammam (P.O.Box 24, tel. 31268, tlx. 601025 EPPCO SJ). A joint venture company with Sulzer Brothers of Switzerland, the leading air conditioning contractor in Europe.

Maintenance of Airconditioning and Refrigeration Co. (MARCO)

Jiddah P.O.Box 6290, tel 6658385, tlx. 401826 MARCOL SJ. Branches in Riyadh (P.O.Box 86, tel. 63383, tlx. 201049 JUFFALI SJ) and Dammam (P.O.Box 7023, tel. 25365, tlx. 601025 EPPCO SJ). A company formed with York International which is a division of Borg-Warner, the Kingdom's leading supplier of air conditioning equipment.

National Automobile Industry Co. Ltd.

Jiddah P.O.Box 5938, tel. 6655035, 6655333, tlx. 400099 NAICAR SJ.

A joint venture with Daimler-Benz AG of Germany the company assembles commercial vehicles in Saudi Arabia. Present production is nineteen vehicles a day and takes up 87% of the Saudi Market. The company operates its own extremely well equipped training centre which supplies its needs for skilled manpower.

Saudi Bahraini Cement Company

Dammam P.O.Box 2464, tel. 25362, tlx. 601359 SBCDAM SJ.

A joint venture between the Saudi Cement Co. and the Government of Bahrain.

Saudi Building Systems

Jiddah P.O.Box 4980, tel. 6658749, tlx. 401130 JUFFALI SJ. Branches in Riyadh (P.O.Box 86, tel. 60230, tlx. 201049 JUFFALI SJ) and Dammam (P.O.Box 24, tel. 45838, tlx. 601025 EPPCO SJ).

A joint venture between E A Juffali and Batler International of the USA.

Steel Products Co. Ltd. (STEPCO)
Riyadh P.O.Box 4930, tel. 22222, tlx. 201022 EPPCO SJ.
Partners: E A Juffali Bros., Aggad Investment Co., Korf Industry and Handel, Ibrahim Touq. Produces meshes for reinforcement.

Associate Companies

Saudi Cement Company
Dammam P.O.Box 306, tel. 22480, tlx. 601068 CEMENT SJ. The branch office in Jiddah is the Technical Advisor's office (P.O.Box 1049, tel. 6422222, tlx. 401130 JUFFALI SJ). The company is one of the largest cement manufacturers in the Middle East. The plant is situated in Hofuf and produces over 4,500 tons a day using natural gas to fire the kilns. This company is a publicly owned company in which E A Juffali are the major shareholders and of which Sh. Ahmad Juffali is the Managing Director.

Medina Electric Company
Medina P.O.Box 128, tel. 21122, tlx. 470014 KAHRBA SJ.
A public company in which E A Juffali are major shareholders. The chief engineer's office is in Jiddah (P.O. Box 1049, tel. 6422222).

Aster S.P.A.
New Jiddah International Airport P.O.Box 5909, tel. 692700 ex.4015, tlx. 401130 JUFFALI SJ.
A company formed to fulfil the air conditioning and mechanical sub-contract for the new international airport in Jiddah. This project is the largest ever undertaken in the Kingdom involving 12 chillers of 1000 tons each and this is only an initial specification. It is expected that this will be increased to a total of 52,000 tons.

National Electric Products Co. Ltd. NEPCO
Jiddah P.O.Box 6619, tel. 6659404, tlx. 400297

National Insurance Co. SA
Jiddah P.O.Box 5832, tel. 6430167, 6436861, tlx. 401791 NICOM SJ. Branches in: Riyadh P.O.Box 86, tel. 67548, tlx. 201049 JUFFALI SJ and Dammam P.O.Box 2312, tel. 25237, tlx. 601025 EPPCO SJ.
This company is incorported in Luxembourg and E A Juffali Bros. are major shareholders in partnership with the Munich Reinsurance Company. The company is engaged in all classes of non-life insurance, and specialises in engineering, fire and marine risks.

Orient Transport Company
Jiddah P.O.Box 6983, tel. 6446745, tlx. 401832 OTC SJ. Branches in: Riyadh P.O.Box 86, tel. 22322, tlx. 201049 JUFFALI SJ for OTC and Dammam P.O.Box 24, tel. 31359, tlx. 601025 EPPCO SJ for OTC.

Petroserv
Dhahran Airport P.O.Box 215, tel. 44994, tlx. 670151 PETSER SJ.
Provides supply and maintenance services to the petroleum industry.

Pool Arabia
Dhahran Airport P.O.Box 2568, tel. 44407, 43280, tlx. 670154 POOLSA SJ with Pool International a subsidiary of the Lone Star Gas Company.

The Family of Kaki

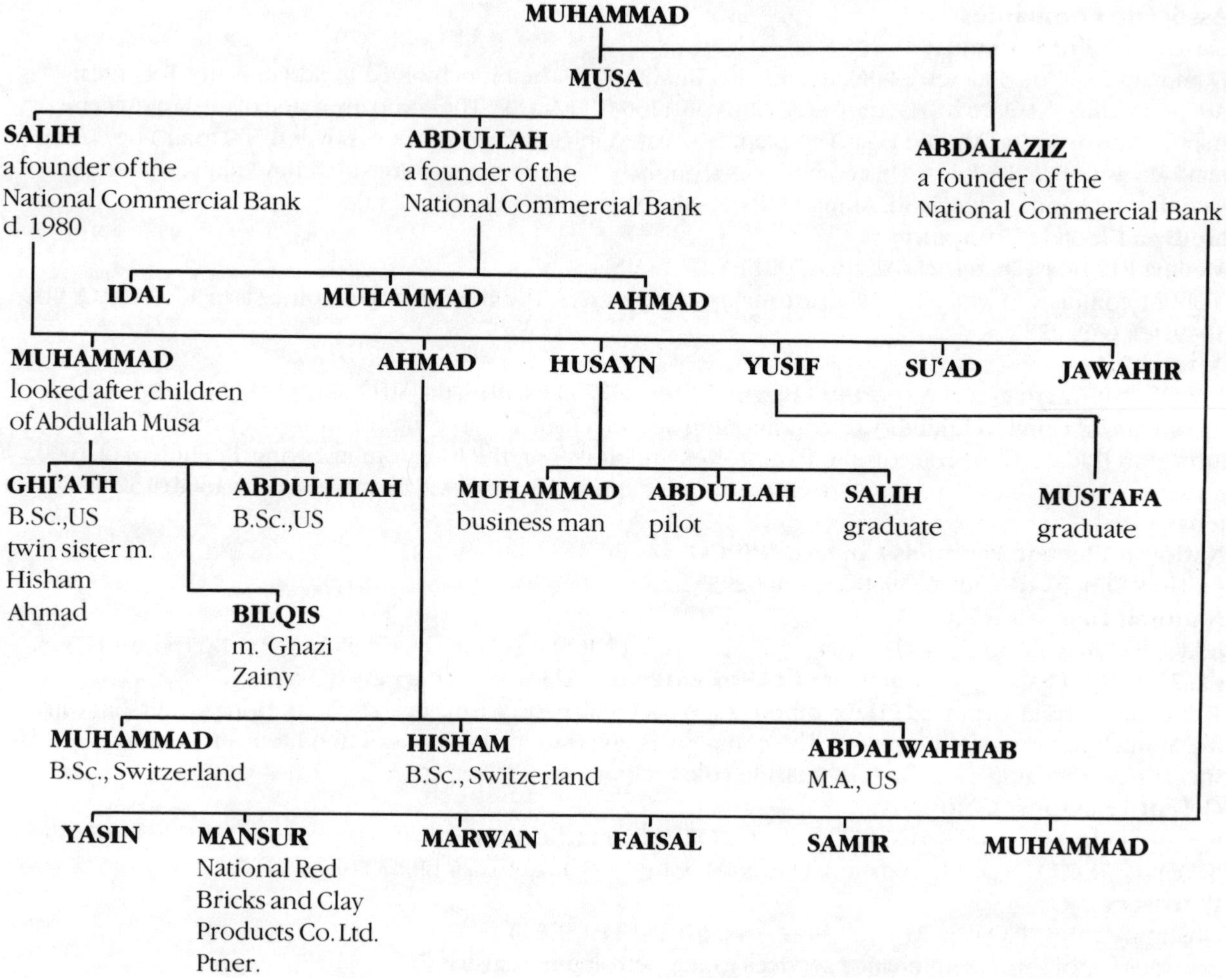

AHMAD AND MUHAMMAD SALEH KAKI

Address head office P.O.Box 208 Riyadh, tel. 28880, 37455; P.O.Box 1224 Jiddah, tel. 31555
Telex 201313 AMSKRH SJ (Riyadh); 401503 AMSKJD SJ (Jiddah)
Cable address WATANI
Subsidiary offices
P.O.Box 263 Dammam, tel. 21176
P.O.Box 234 Mecca, tel. 21697
P.O.Box 53 Medina, tel. 24448
P.O.Box 49 Ta'if, tel. 21665
Proprietor The Board

Board Members
Joint President Sh. Muhammad Saleh Kaki
Joint President Sh. Ahmad Saleh Kaki
Members of the Board of Directors of the National Commercial Bank
Vice Presidents: Sh. Ghiath Muhammad, Sh. Abdulillah Muhammad, Sh. Muhammad Ahmad, Sh. Abdalwahab Ahmad, Sh. Hisham Ahmad

Company History
The company was established in 1945 in the city of Mecca and initially specialised in finance and foreign exchange, an activity expressed by their foundation of and continued interest (10%) in the National Commercial Bank. This led to expansion into the fields of merchandising, construction and contracting, an expansion which has continued successfully into the present day. A and M Saleh Kaki are a company whose history and present policies consist of a careful mixture of the cautious and the innovative.
Today the company is divided into six divisions:
1. The Engineering and Construction Division
Established 1950 this division produces revenues annually of some seventy million riyals.
2. The Industrial Division
comprises the group activities which involve manufacturing
a) Kaki Manufacturing Company: set up in 1961 this is primarily a textile and clothing factory which specializes in uniforms for the Saudi Arabian Armed Forces.
b) Kaki Marble Factory: this was established in 1958 as a joint venture to meet rising demands in the construction field and imports high quality marbles into the Kingdom.
c) National Press Company: prints books and stationery for both the public and private market.
d) Aluminium Processing Company: a company which processes, cuts and assembles raw extruded aluminium into doors, windows and frames.
3. The Real Estate Division
This division manages the Kaki land and buildings throughout the Kingdom. These include the Kaki Hotel in Jiddah, P.O.Box 2559, tel. 48071/2/3, tlx. 401739.
4. Technical Services Division
The most recent formation in the Kaki Group, this division handles the need for high technical services. At present efforts are concentrated in the fields of electronic security and detection systems, telecommunications, aircraft maintenance and operation, and the maintenance of facilities and engineering.
Of necessity this enormous and skilfully managed spread of commercial interest has necessitated the formation of many close relationships with foreign companies. A and M Saleh Kaki represent the following companies within the Kingdom:
Dynalectron USA; Wild Heerbrugg Ltd., Switzerland; Ernst Leitz Wetzlar GmbH, West Germany; Javelin Electronics, USA; Albert Nestler KG, West Germany; Kawasaki Heavy Industries, Japan; Sheer Pride Ltd., UK; Umberto Mascagni SPA, Italy; Drevounia Foreign Trade Corporation, Czechoslovakia; John Tann Ltd., England; Homexpo Canada Ltd., Canada; Traun SRL, Italy; Leonardo D'Arienzo, Italy; Photocan Surveys Ltd., Canada; Plan Hpld, USA; Varian AG, Switzerland; Downs Surgical Ltd., England; De Havilland Aircraft, Canada.
The Abdullah Muhammad Kaki and Muhammad Ahmad Kaki Company has formed a limited liability partnership with the Todesco Giovanni establishment of Milan; the shares are 44% and 56% respectively. This new company called the United Todesco Constn. Company was formed in Spring 1979.
5. The Investment Division
Formed to manage A & M Saleh Kaki investments which comprise shareholdings in the following Saudi companies:
National Commercial Bank, Riyadh Gypsum Company, The Riyadh Bank, Riyadh Cement Company, Jeddah Cement Co., Arabian Navigation Company, Riyadh Electric Power Company, Dammam Electric Power Company, Jeddah Electric Power Company, Saudi Fertilizer Company, Jeddah Oil Refineries Company, and in the following overseas investments: Dubai Electric Power Company, Cement Company Dubai, Arab Hotels and Tourism Company Cairo, Alexandria Company for Navigation and Sea Operation Cairo, Cairo Investment and Development Company, Arabian Company for Wooden Products Cairo, Arab Company for Aluminium Industries Amman, Sheep and Chicken Co. Ltd. Amman, Jordanian Chinaware Co. Amman, Glass Manufacturing Co. Jordan, Sharjah Heavy Industries Company Sharjah.

6. The Commercial Division
This division is responsible for the supply of goods on a project retail and wholesale basis through Kaki warehouses, showrooms and stores. The areas of specialization include: office furniture, office supplies and equipment, technical and optical equipment, domestic electrical appliances.
Capital 330 million riyals
Bankers The National Commercial Bank, The Riyadh Bank.

JIDDAH KAKI HOTEL

Address head office PO Box 1224, Jiddah
Telephone 6312201
Telex 401739 KHOTEL SJ
Activities One of Jiddah's major hotels, owned by Ahmad and Muhammad Salih Kaki.

JURDI AND KAKI FACTORY

Address head office PO Box 303, Jiddah
Telephone 6872437, 6873024
Telex 401303 JURDI SJ
Activities A partnership between Muhammad Salih Kaki, Najib al Jurdi and Said Muhammad Faqih operating a factory for aluminium products and tiles, as well as supplying marble.

AHMAD AND MUHAMMAD SALIH KAKI

Address head office PO Box 1224, Jiddah
Telephone 6602160
Telex 401503 AMSKJD SJ, 400674 GTRADE SJ

AHMAD AND MUHAMMAD SALIH KAKI EST. FOR UNIFORMS AND TENTS

Address head office PO Box 1003, Jiddah
Telephone 6423121, 6602160
Telex 405103 AMSKJD SJ
Formed in 1962.

AL KAKI COMPANY

Address head office PO Box 5732, Jiddah
Telephone 6652570
Telex 400012 ALKAKI SJ
Activities A company formed in 1974 to deal in furniture, lighting, vehicle spares, computers and word processors and stationery. It is owned by Muhammad, Ahmad and Amin Abdullah Kaki.

ABDALAZIZ MUHAMMAD KAKI REAL ESTATE OFFICE

Address head office PO Box 6973, Jiddah
Telephone 6310107, 6310073
Telex 401672 NAKHEL SJ
Activities Formed in 1977, this company manages the Kaki family properties. It is owned by Abdalaziz Muhammad Kaki (of the National Commercial Bank) and is managed by his son Yasin.

AL NAKHEL ESTABLISHMENT FOR TRADING AND CONTRACTING

Address head office PO Box 6973, Jiddah
Telephone 6310107, 6310073
Telex 401672 NAKHEL SJ
Activities A company owned by Yasin Abdalaziz Kaki which is engaged as building contractors. It was formed in 1970.

NATIONAL FACTORY FOR CHROMIUM AND METAL WORKS

Address head office PO Box 1224, Jiddah
Telephone 6431164
Telex 401503 AMSKJN SJ, 400675 GTRADE SJ
Activities Formed in 1979 and owned by Ahmad and Muhammad Salih Kaki. A factory for manufacturing furniture.

NATIONAL PRINTING PRESS

Address head office PO Box 234, Jiddah
Telephone 5427853 (Mecca)
Telex 401503 AMSKJD SJ, 400674 GTRADE SJ
Activities Owned by Ahmad and Muhammad Salih Kaki and managed by Abdalwahhab Ahmad, the company supplies paper and paper products, stationery and educational supplies.

SAUDI PHOTOCAN CORPORATION LTD

Address head office PO Box 1224, Jiddah
Telephone 6602160, 6672160
Telex 400674 GTRADE SJ
Activities The company is a joint venture between Hisham Kaki and Roland Hunter. There is a branch in Dammam and one in Riyadh (PO Box 208, tel. 4037455). The companies activities are aerial mapping and photography, topographical and cadastral surveying.

WORLD PROJECTS AND TRADING CORPORATION LTD.

Address head office PO Box 1224, Jiddah
Telephone 6602160
Telex 400674 GTRADE SJ
Activities The company is a joint venture managed by Abdulillah Muhammad Kaki. There is a branch office in Riyadh (PO Box 420, tel. 4037455, tlx. 201313 AMSKRH SJ). The company is a building and mechanical contractor and is involved in aircraft sales.

GENERAL ESTABLISHMENT FOR TRADE AND CONTRACTS

Address head office PO Box 1224, Jiddah
Telephone 6602160, 6602168, 6602176, 6602184, 6431749
Telex 401503 AMSKJD SJ
Activities A company formed in 1969 and owned by Muhammad Ahmad and Abdulillah Muhammad Kaki. There is a branch in Riyadh (PO Box 208). The company deals as engineering consultants and general building contractors. They supply electronic equipment, air conditioners, building materials, furniture, office equipment, medical and surgical equipment and act as commission agents and money changers, providing management for hotels and restaurants and operating a real estate business.

The Family of Kamel

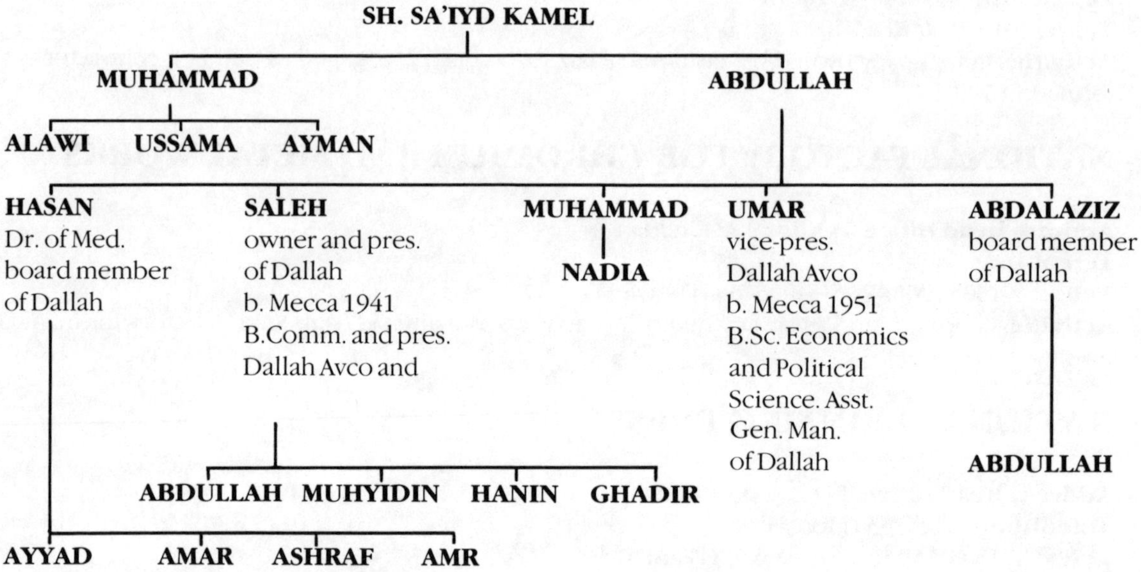

DALLAH ESTABLISHMENT

Address head office P.O.Box 1438 Riyadh
Telephone 4641131
Telex 201036 DALLAH SJ
Cable address DALLAH
Branch office Jiddah P.O.Box 2618, tel. 55422, tlx. 401482 AVCO SJ
Proprietor Sh. Saleh Abdullah Kamel
Activities The activities of this fast growing giant reflect an almost wholesale consumption of technology which justifies the great success of the company. Dallah is engaged in four main groups of activity and employs over four thousand people:
1. Contracting: road and civil construction and the erection and operation of driver training schools.
2. Maintenance and operation of air defence facilities, Government administration complexes, Government boarder centres and training facilities, pilgrimage air terminal facilities, traffic lights and control systems throughout the Kingdom.
3. Electronic, mechanical and electrical activities, which embrace weather surveillance, radar, runway visual range systems, transmitters, automatic stations as well as power generation and installation of power networks.
4. The commercial activities of the company cover the representation of leading international companies and procurement and commissioning for complete turnkey projects.These involve traffic and instrumentation, meteorology and electronics, radar, navigational aids, avionics, satellite systems and weather stations, air traffic control equipment, landing systems, telecommunications covering both public and private systems as well as microwave systems. They supply and market TV and videotapes. Dallah represent Doron of the USA for the production of simulator equipment and electronic teaching aids. They also represent Kongsberg of Norway for gas turbine generators and leading TV organisations in the Arab world producing and distributing programmes. Dallah also supply both light and heavy mobile workshops.

Affiliated Companies

1. Dallah Avco Trans Arabia

Head office Jiddah, tel. 55422, tlx. 401158 ATTAS SJ; branches in Riyadh, Najran, Weijh, Qasim, Hail, Jouf, Medina, Talif, Tabuk, Bisha and Khamis Mushayt.

Board of Directors: Chairman Sh. Salem Kamel, Sh. Omar Kamel, Sen.Vice President General Muhammad Tayyeb Al Tounisi, Mr. G. Newman, General F. Higgins, Mr. L. Bogan, Mr. D.F. Walter.

Dallah Avco undertakes major maintenance of civil, mechanical and electrical facilities in the Kingdom of Saudi Arabia and throughout the Middle East.

2. The Medical Centre Company Ltd.

Engaged in the installation of electro-medical equipment in co-operation with Philips and Siemens. They also cover hospital furnishings, turnkey hospital projects and mobile hospitals.

3. The Arab Media Company

Representation of Arab TV organisations, production and distribution of programmes.

4. The Saudi Prefab and Precast Housing Co. Ltd.

5. Dallah Industries Co. Ltd.

Undertakes study, survey and implementation of medium and small scale industrial projects.

6. The Concrete Works Company

7. The Saudi Air Conditioning Company

8. Amartec Company Ltd.

Specializes in environmental research.

9. Saudi Marketing and Trading Company

Engaged in the supply and marketing of chemicals and medicines.

10. Saudi Electro Mechanical Company

11. Trans Arabia Supply Company

12. National Employment Saudi Company

Dallah is also involved in the activities of the Tihama Advertising Corporation (q.v.), OKAZ Printing and Publishingand the Saudi Arabian Hotel and Tourism Company. Sh. Saleh Kamel also officiates as president of the Concrete Co.,the Arab Media Co., Fast Co., the Saudi Pre-Fab Co. He is a member of the Board of DAR OKAZ Co. for Printing and Publishing, OKAZ Organisation for Press and Publication, OKAZ for Distribution, Tihama Advertising Corporation, the Services and Maintenance Co., Saudi Hotels and Resort Areas Co., the Saudi Overseas Marketing Co., the Saudi Construction Co., the Amartech Co., the Shobel Co. for Tourism (Egypt) and Shobel Switzerland and UK, the Arabian Investment Co. and the National Video Company in Egypt as well as Misr Investment and Development Co., the Faisal Islamic Egyptian Bank, the Faisal Islamic Sudanese Bank, the Red Sea Cement Co., Sudan Halad International, the Islamic Investment Co., Video Simen of the Bahamas, Simen Co. of Greece, the International Investment Group of the USA and the Oriental Production and Distribution Co. of Sharjah.

The Family of Kanoo

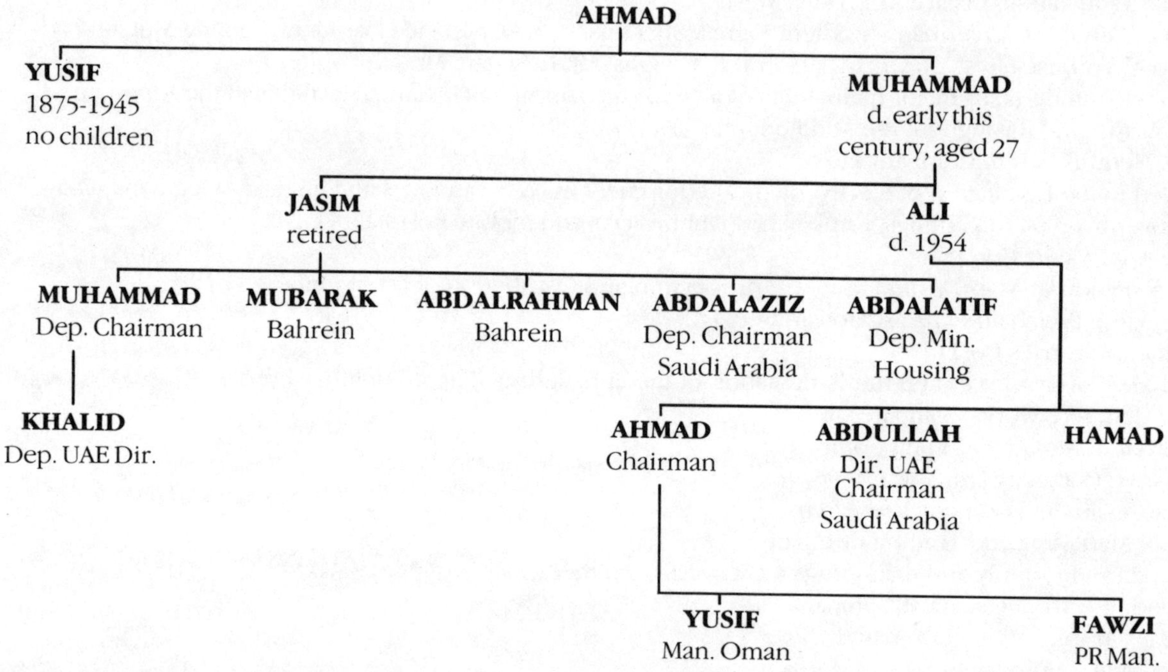

CABLE AND WIRELESS SAUDI ARABIA

Address head office PO Box 6196, Riyadh
Telephone 4657092
Branches Jiddah, PO Box 812 , tel. 6823759, tlx. 402051 KNSHP SJ and 401039, and Dammam
Activities A joint venture between Yusuf b. Ahmad Kanoo and Cable and Wireless Ltd of the UK. Operating as communications contractors and supplying communications equipment.

YUSUF B. AHMAD KANOO

Address head office PO Box 812, Jiddah
Telephone 6823759
Telex 401039 YBAK SJ
Activities Carrying the brand names Esso and Exxon the company has branches in Riyadh, al Khobar, Dammam, Yanbu and Jubail. They deal with industrial chemicals, concrete additives, marine paints, electronic equipment, insulation materials, laboratory and hospital equipment, lubricants, drilling products and welding equipment.
The machinery trading division supplies compressors, construction equipment, generators, hoisting, material handling, electrical and hydraulic equipment, automotive tools and pumps.

NORWICH WINTERTHUR INSURANCE (ARABIA) LTD.

Address head office Al Khobar
Activities The company is sponsored by Yusuf Ahmad Kanoo and has branches in Jiddah (PO Box 812, tel. 6820140, tlx. 401039 KANOO SJ), Riyadh and Yanbu.

SAUDI ARABIAN TRANSPORT ORGANISATION LTD.

Address head office PO Box 812, Jiddah
Telephone 6659905
Telex 401497 SATOL SJ
Activities This joint venture between Yusuf Ahmad Kanoo and the World Transport Organisation of San Francisco was formed in 1975 and is involved in heavy trucking, cranes, fork lifts, equipment rental, customs clearance and marine transport, barges and tugs.

The Family of Karshi

The Karshi family is of Somali origin and is an interesting example of absorption. They are a referral group for the Saudi community but do not have responsibility for them. This function illustrates in a diluted way the method in Arabian society whereby individual families answer for the group they represent. Thus there are some Hadrami families which represent, as it were, the whole Hadrami community in an informal way to the Saudi community as well as government. This really only occurs today where a foreign community has no diplomatic representation. The Karshi family tree is given here in shortened form.

MUHAMMAD AL KARSHI

- **ABDULLAHI** businessman (building materials and transport)
- **ABDU** was cook to HM King Abdalaziz Al Saud in 1940s. Finance Dir. of Saudi Cover Co.
  - **MUHAMMAD**
  - **AHMAD** b. Jiddah c. 1955
  - **KHALID** student
  - **WALID** naval cadet
  - 1 da.

ABDU MUHAMMAD KARSHI

Abdu Muhammad Karshi went into business in 1950 when he relinquished his employment with HM King Abdalaziz. He established a commercial bakery which was the first in the Kingdom to employ modern machinery and methods. This was a great success and the Karshi family extended their business interests into representation, construction and associated service industries.

KARSHI AND SONS

Address head office PO Box 4922, Jiddah
Telephone 6439050, 6653971
Activities At present the company deals in contracting and livestock, having in the past represented such companies as Tretum, York, Stillitron, Heil and L M van Moppes and Sons Ltd. This company is owned by Abdu Karshi and managed by his son Ahmad.

SAUDI COVER FACTORY

Address head office PO Box 4922, Jiddah
Telephone 6374050, 6376870
Telex 404251 SCF SJ
Activities This concern is managed by Ahmad Karshi and his father is the finance director. At is establishment at the end of the seventies it was the first manufacturer of profiled steel in the Kingdom; in 1983 they produced 10 million sq. m. at the factory in Jiddah Industrial Estate. The product is used for cladding, wall covering and roofing; there is a purchasing office in Riyadh (tel. 4784764, 4768961;tlx. 205275 SCFRYD SJ).

Activities This concern is managed by Ahmad Karshi and his father is the finance director. At its establishment at the end of the seventies it was the first manufacturer of profiled steel in the Kingdom; in 1983 they produced 10 million sq. m. at the factory in Jiddah Industrial Estate. The product is used for cladding, wall covering and roofing; there is a purchasing office in Riyadh (tel. 4784764, 4768961; tlx. 205275 SCFRYD SJ).

The Family of Al Khamis

IBRAHIM

ABDALRAHMAN — **MUHAMMAD**

IBRAHIM AL KHAMIS & SONS COMPANY

Address head office Riyadh; subsidiary offices in Jiddah, Qasim, Ta'if, Beirut and Cairo
Telephone 4026256
Telex 201532
Cable address AL TASSHELE
Proprietors Partnership between Abdalrahman b. Ibrahim and Muhammad b. Ibrahim
Company history The company was established by Ibrahim al Khamis who was a confidant of H.M. King Abdalaziz al Saud. He was the first person to import goods to Riyadh from Syria, which he did by camel in the twenties and thirties. It is said he was also the first person to build a stone house outside the walls of Riyadh which he did with the aid of Syrian masons he also brought back to Riyadh. The story goes that hearing the masons at work the citizens were at first fearful that Ibrahim was making idols and they reported him to the king. Today the company has a license to import goods from the USSR and holds the agency for the Lada, Moskavitch and Volga trademarks in cars, heavy agricultural equipment and tractors.

KHASHOGGI BUSINESS INTERESTS

TRIAD INTERNATIONAL MARKETING SA

Address PO Box 6, Riyadh
Telephone 4784607
Telex 201112 TRICOR SJ
Branches Jiddah, PO Box 398, tel. 63107611, tlx. 401208 TRICOR SJ
Proprietors Adnan and Issam Muhammad Khashoggi
Activities The company engages in investment and financing activities, marketing, real estate, and a wide range of commercial activities including the petroleum industry.
Adnan and Issam Khashoggi. Formed in 1971, its activities are concerned with furnishings and household acumen developed at an early age when a student at Stanford University. The Triad Organisation manages the interests of Adnan and the family. The holding company based in Luxembourg has worldwide interests including real estate, banking, insurance, agriculture, films and hospitals. This complex organisation has offices in Paris, Geneva, New York, London and Texas, as well as in Riyadh. Overseas investments have included holdings in a number of US banks as well as substantial land acquisitions, for example in Arizona and Colorado. Adnan Khashoggi is also involved in multi-million dollar developments in Utah and Houston. Far Eastern interests are held in Hong Kong and Seoul. As well as holdings in European companies there are interests in South America and the South Seas.

The Family of Khashoggi

The family name derives from a Turkish term indicating the guardian of the treasury, and probably dates from the Turkish administration of the Hijaz or the Sherifian administration which continued the use of Turkish nomenclature in official designations.

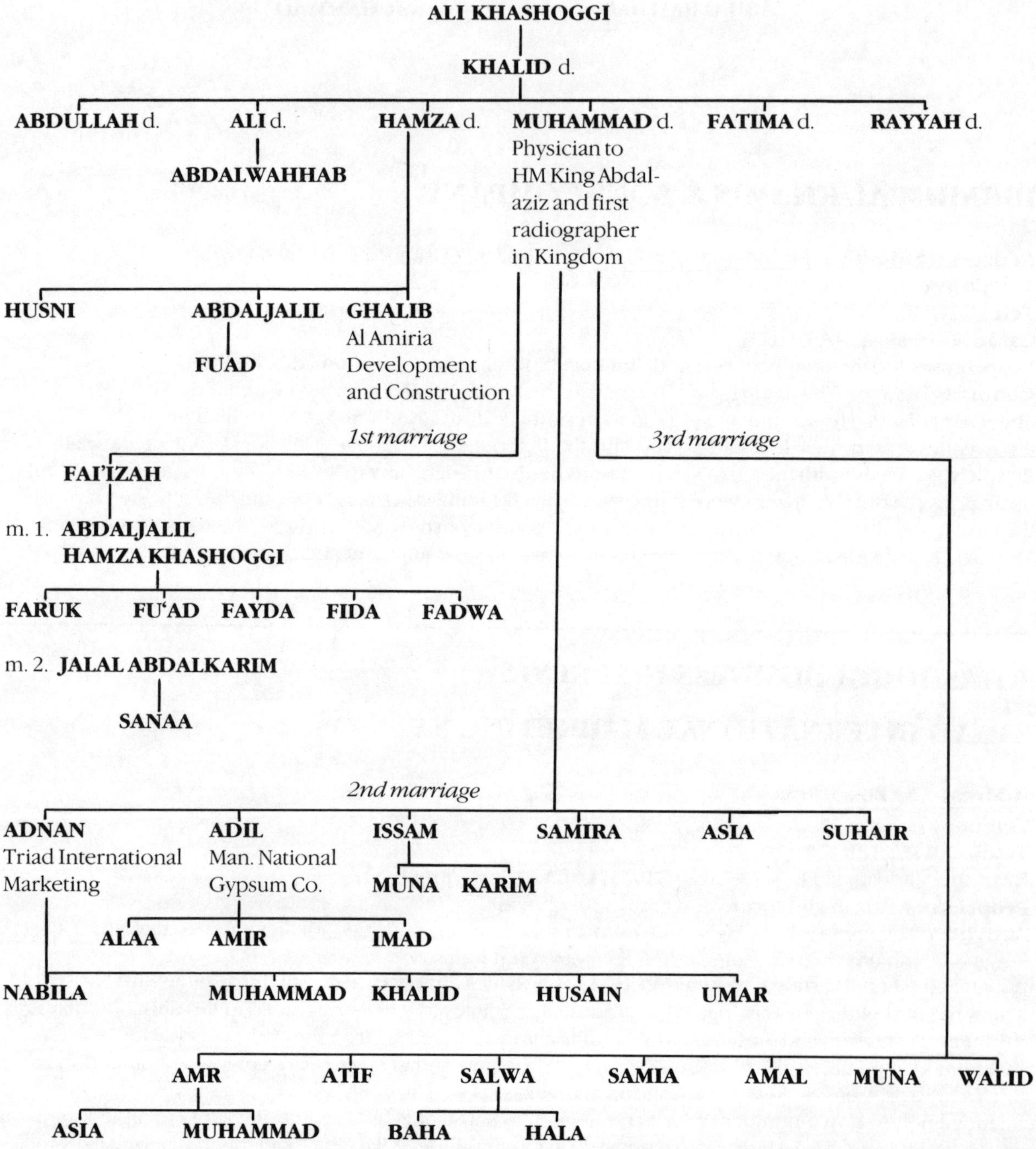

TRIAD CONDAS INTERNATIONAL LTD

Address head office PO Box 6175 Jiddah
Telephone 6673988, 6673972
Telex 400331 CONDAS SJ
Activities The company is owned by Triad Holdings International which is under the proprietorship of Adnan and Issam Khashoggi. Formed in 1971, its activities are concerned with furnishings and household equipment, decorating material, furniture and furniture manufacture. The company also provides an architectural service and acts as commission agents.

AL AMIRIA DEVELOPMENT AND CONSTRUCTION EST.

Address head office PO Box 6462, Jiddah
Telephone 6679418, 6657551, 6667548
Telex 401755 AMIRIA SJ
Proprietor Ghalib Hamza Khashoggi
Activities A company of architects engaged in consultancy for civil and engineering projects and also the supply of building materials

ARABIAN CONSTRUCTION AND DEVELOPMENT CO.

Address head office PO Box 2385, Jiddah
Telephone 6311086
Telex 401208 TRICOP SJ
Activities Founded in 1970, this company is owned by Issam b. Muhammad Khashoggi and his sister Asia. It is a building contracting business

KHASHOGGI ESTABLISHMENT (METROPOLE STUDIO)

Telephone 6435326
Activities This business is owned by Abdaljalil Hamza Khashoggi and managed by his son Fu'ad. It is concerned with the supply of photographic equipment and they are photographers too.

CONSULTANCY CONVENTION (CONCENTRE)

Address head office PO Box 7914, Jiddah
Telephone 6658352, 6659450, 6671843
Telex 401876 MASJED SJ
Activities Founded in 1979, this company of architects also operates a consultancy in the electrical, agricultural, civil, electrical communications and hydraulic engineering fields. It is owned by Abdalwahhab Ali Khashoggi.

The Family of Khazindar

Originating in Saudi Arabia, the family name derives from a Turkish term indicating the guardian of the treasury, and probably dates from the Turkish administration of the Hijaz or the Sherifian administration which continued the use of Turkish nomenclature in official designations.

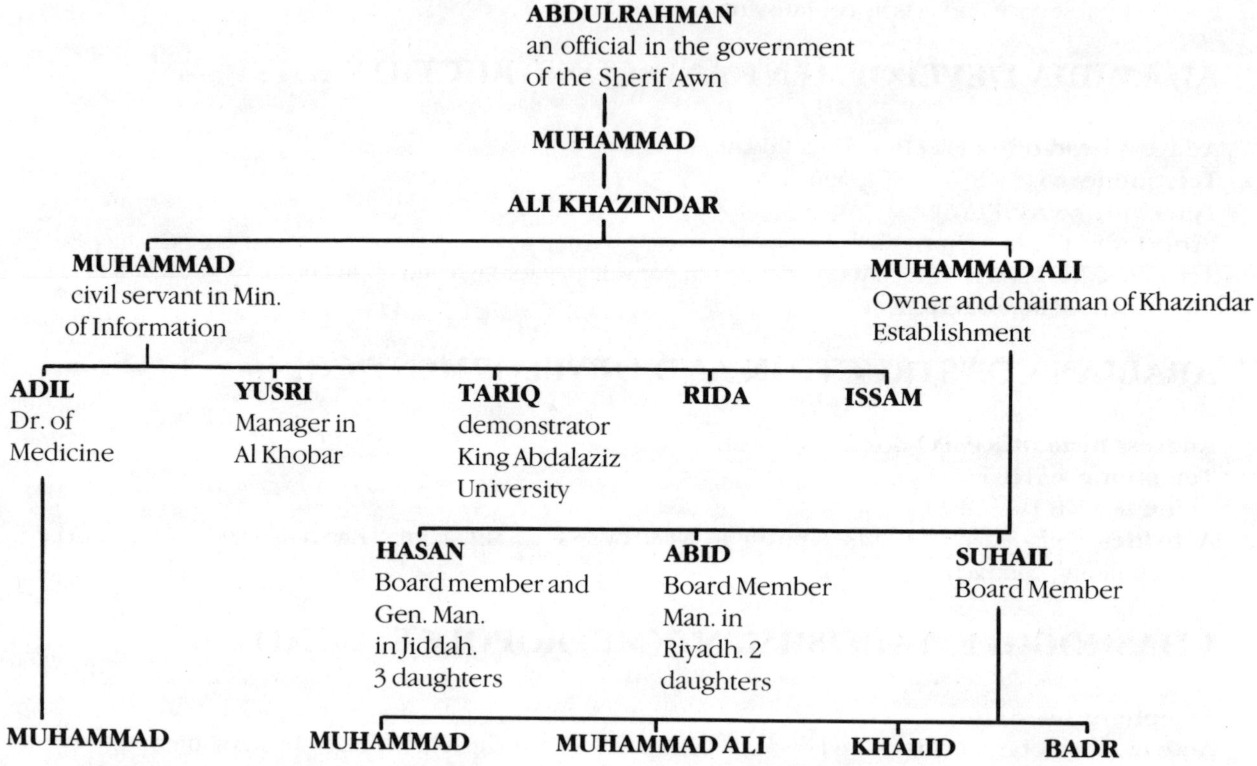

KHAZINDAR DISTRIBUTING ESTABLISHMENT

Address head office P.O.Box 157 Jiddah
Telephone 6871869, 6874893, 6423303
Subsidiary offices
Riyadh, tel. 4653674, 4659364, tlx. 201319 SJ
Also branches in Mecca, Ta'if, Khamis Mushait, Yanbo, Medina, Tabuk, Buraidah and Al Khobar.
Company History
The present company was formed in 1958 but grew out of the now defunct Dabbus Stores which owned the company from 1952. Khazindar are the most comprehensive distributors of books, newspapers and periodicals in the Kingdom. This they accomplish both directly through their modern and attractive shops in the main cities and through a very wide net of sub-agents who cover the whole of the Kingdom. They act as sole agents for a wide range of materials from English, Arab, French, American, German and Italian sources acting as distributors for the following:
Hatchette Gotch, Comag, Hatchette International, World Wide Media, Luchelle, International Herald Tribune, Time, OUP, Newsweek, International Communications, Burda, Bush Hansa, Agencie Internazionale Italiana, Rizzoli Editori, Rasconi Editori, Correra della Sera, Transworld, C.B.S., Feffer Symonds, Dell.
Bankers National Commercial Bank, Saudi Cairo Bank, Saudi Faransi Bank, Al Jazira Bank.

SAUDI OPERATION MAINTENANCE AND ADMINISTRATION CO. (SOMAC)

Address P.O.Box 3931 Jiddah
Telephone 6654418
Telex 402526 SOMAC SJ
Company History
Owned by Suhail Muhammad Ali Khazindar in partnership with Abdalaziz Bughdadi. The company came into existence in 1979 and is engaged in providing maintenance for air conditioners, plumbing and electric installations, carpentry, fire-fighting systems, cleaning and insecticide sprays, and the marketing of disinfectants and detergents.

EL KHEREIJI BUSINESS INTERESTS

When Abdullah b. Abdalkarim moved from Medina to Jiddah he formed a company with Sulaiman b. Abdalaziz called Sulaiman El Khereiji Company. Acquaintance with the West led to them importing new products to the Saudi market. Abdalkarim b. Abdalaziz was sent to study in England and Yusif b. Abdullah to the US. On their return they went into the family business. Abdalkarim took over in Dammam and Yusif in Riyadh. Later Yusif left and founded DITCO and Abdullah b. Abdalaziz took over in Riyadh. After three years he too became independent and Abdalmuhsin took his place in Riyadh.
The move to independence is a strong one in the family as later generations show. Sulaiman b. Abdalaziz formed a company for his sons called The United Brothers Co., Yusif b. Abdullah formed DITCO and TPCC, Yusif, Ibrahim and the other sons of Abdullah b. Abdalkarim formed the International Centre, Abdalkarim b. Abdalaziz formed El Khereiji Trading and Electricity, Abdullah b. Abdalaziz formed the El Khereiji Corporation, Ibrahim Abdullah formed Al Gazira Corporation and Sulaiman b. Abdullah established an architect's practice. The original partnership of Abdullah and Sulaiman has become absorbed and developed by the Khalid Abdalrahman Trading Corporation.

THE EL KHEREIJI CORPORATION

Address PO Box 3971, Riyadh
Telephone 4780925
Telex 201747 KHEREIJI SJ
The proprietor is Sh. Abdullah b. Abdalaziz El Khereiji who is a member of Lloyd's. Ali b. Abdalaziz is Chairman and other members of the Board are Abdullah b. Abdalaziz, Syd. Khalil M Saraf and Syd. Michel Karam. Business activities include the El Khereiji Hotel, Riyadh, Lana Printing Press, Nada Laundry Airport Services, Riyadh and Dhahran and Medina and Jiddah Insurance representing General Accident of the UK and INA.

EL KHEREIJI TRADING AND ELECTRONICS

Address PO Box 25, Dammam
Telephone 8322985, 8322555, 8324442
Telex 601022 KHEREIJI SJ
There are subsidiary offices in Jiddah, Riyadh and Qatif. The proprietor is Abdalkarim b. Abdalaziz El Khereiji who is also Chairman. He was a founder partner of Al Jazira Bank and subscriber to Saudi Faransi Bank, Saudi Hollandi Bank, Saudi Cairo Bank, Member of Lloyd's, the Municipal Council of Dammam and Dammam Chamber of Commerce and a founding member of Al Yowm newspaper. This company has some common interests with El Khereiji Corporation; it is concerned with insurance, electronic and electrical equipment, general trading, household appliances and real estate investment. In addition it holds a number of agencies.

The Family of El Khereiji

An old family of Najd directly related to Zamil.

EL KHEREIJI

ABDULLAH

ABDALAZIZ
at age 11, his father died and left him nothing. He went to live with his sister and later formed a partnership with Abdalkarim in a house in Medina, still owned by the family. To help his protector he formed a company with Muhammad b. Abdalkarim; this was the first El Khereiji company and represented HM King Abdalaziz Al Sa'ud as food distributors, taking over from Ibrahim Hamid al Sani'e (q.v.). Later they turned their attention to real estate and traded with India and Syria

RUQAYA

RUQAYA m. Abdalrahman Salih

ABDALKARIM
Chairman of El Khereiji Co. for Trade and Electronics, Dammam
m. daughter of Abdullah b. Abdalkarim

ABDULLAH
Chairman of El Khereiji Corporation, Riyadh

ALI
lawyer who runs El Khereiji for Legal Advice

SULAYMAN
Chairman of United Brothers Co. Jiddah

ABDALAZIZ

KHALID
Pilot, RSAF

ABDALQADIR
Dir. United Brothers

MUHAMMAD
Dir. United Brothers

ABDALAZIZ
Dr of Medicine, Cairo
Dir. United Brothers

BADRIYA

ABDALRAHMAN
business man in Medina

NURA
m. Abdullah Sulayman al Hamdan who signed first oil agreement between Kingdom and USA

ABDULLAH
Ph.D, Dean Sociology King Abdalaziz Univ.

AHMAD
Dir. Gen. Petromin

FATIMA

YUSUF
DITCO President

SULAYMAN
US qualified as an architect

IBRAHIM
TPCC Chairman
US business degree

ABDALGHANI
International trade degree from Cairo

RA'D
FAISAL
MUHAMMAD
FATIMA

ABDULLAH

AL UMR

ALI MUHAMMAD

ABDALKARIM
moved from Najd to Medina, m. Ruqaya, sister of Abdalaziz b. Abdullah, a religious and adventurous man.

MUHAMMAD
Senior member of the family still living in original house in Medina

ABDULLAH

UMR
Umr El Khereiji Co. for Architectural Planning

FAHD
graduate USA

MUHAMMAD

ABDALAZIZ

TARIQ

ABDALHADI
graduate

ABDALRAZZAQ
US graduate

ABDALHAMID
graduate

ABDALMAJID
US graduate

ABDULILLAH

HISHAM

ABDALAZIZ

MANSUR

MUHAMMAD
Legal advisor Petromin Cairo graduate

ABDALWAHHAB
US business law graduate

ABDALRAHMAN
US industrial engineering graduate

USSAMA
US architecture graduate

The Family of El Khereiji (Branch)

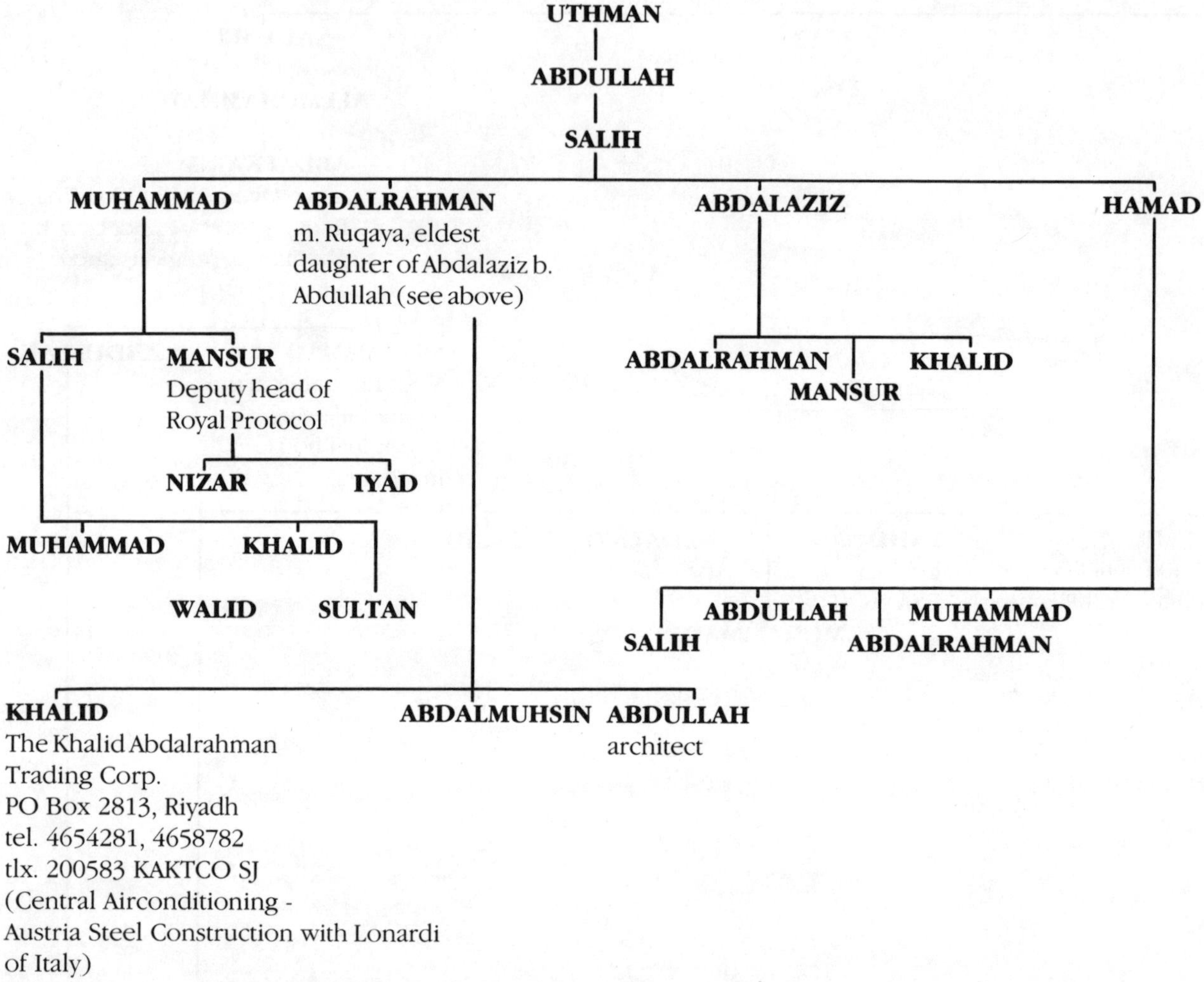

TECHNICAL PRODUCTS CONTRACTING CO. LTD.

Address head office PO Box 5467, Jiddah
Telephone 6655458, 6650741, 6673064
Telex 401112 DITCO SL
Activities Owned by Yusif Abdullah el Khereiji and managed by his brother Ibrahim, the company was formed in 1975 and is a firm of building contractors, specialising in building systems and the supply of building materials

AUTOMATION COMPUTER STUDIES OFFICE (ASCO)

Address head office PO Box 2388, Jiddah
Telephone 6670108, 6655670, 6825961, 6825832
Telex 400534 INCENT SJ
Activities Founded in 1979 this company is owned by Sulaiman and Abdullah Sulaiman el Khereiji. They have branches in Jiddah and Dammam, dealing in computer and business systems for which they establish centres for computer studies which they maintain and operate.

DEVELOPMENT INTERNATIONAL TRADE CO. LTD. DITCO

Address head office PO Box 9057, Jiddah
Telephone 6601606, 6655458
Telex 403136 KSC SJ
Activities The company is owned by Yusif Abdullah el Khereiji and deals in aviation and airport equipment, as well as operating in the contracting field for building, air conditioning, acoustics, decorating, demolition, drilling and dredging, electrics, mechanics, landscaping and plumbing, pipelines, piling, quarrying, road construction, escalators and elevators, hotels, motels, marine constrction and pre-cast concrete.

ELF-UNION C/O UNITED BROTHERS

Address head office PO Box 6093, Jiddah
Telephone 6441128, 6441129
Telex 401177 UBC SJ
Activities Owned by Abdalqadir Sulaiman el Khereiji, this company was formed in 1976 and is an automobile dealer and distributor for Renault cars, parts and accessories, lubricants and lubricating equipment.

INSURANCE COMPANY OF NORTH AMERICA

Address head office Dammam
Telephone 6424441
Activities Owned by Abdalkarim Adbalaziz el Khereiji, this insurance business was established in 1972. There is a branch in Jiddah (PO Box 3414, tel. 6432442, 6447756, tlx. 401544 TAMIN SJ).

INTERNATIONAL CORPORATION FOR TRADE AND CONTRACT SERVICE

Address head office PO Box 3414, Jiddah
Telephone 6432442, 6447756
Telex 401544 TAMIN SJ
Activities This company is owned by Abdalkarim el Khereiji and was established in 1972. It has branches in Dammam and Riyadh, and deals in insurance.

INTERNATIONAL CENTRE FOR COMMERCE AND CONTRACTING

Address head office PO Box 2388, Jiddah
Telephone 6825961, 6825832, 6829487
Telex 400534 INCENT SJ
Activities Formed in 1977, this company is owned by Yusif, Ibrahim Sulaiman and Abdalghani Abdullah el Khereiji. It has branches in Riyadh, Dammam and Yanbu. Its activities include dealing in aluminium products, catering, commission agency, furniture and household equipment and building materials. It also acts as a contractor for air conditioning, building, demolition, cleaning, drilling, dredging, landscaping, mechanics, pumping, electrics, road construction and drainage. The company is also a publisher and a furniture manufacturer.

INTERNATIONAL MARKETING CO.

Address head office PO Box 7112, Jiddah
Telephone 6449689
Telex 401898 UNITED SJ
Activities The company was established in 1978. It is owned by Abdalqadir, Abdalaziz and Muhammad Sulaiman el Khereiji. It deals with trade centres, radio and television equipment, office equipment, housewares and domestic equipment, watches and clocks. They are also electrical contractors.

KHEREIJI SHOWROOM CO.

Address head office PO Box 8589, Jiddah
Telephone 6825822, 6825420
Telex 403136 KSC SJ
Activities With a branch in Yanbu, this company was formed in 1981 and is owned by Yusif el Khereiji. It deals with pumps, electric and electronic equipment, plastic products, pipes, power transmission equipment, switchgear cables and generators.

SULAIMAN ABDULLAH EL KHEREIJI

Address head office PO Box 2388, Jiddah
Telephone 6825832, 6825961
Telex 400534 INCENT SJ
Activities An architectural practice established in 1978 and owned by Sulaiman Abdullah el Khereiji. The practice acts as civil, engineering and town planning consultants.

PROJECT DEVELOPMENT CORPORATION

Address head office PO Box 7112, Jiddah
Telephone 6423859
Telex 401177 UBL SJ, 401898 UNITED SJ
Activities Representing CEI and Universal the company was established in 1977. It is owned by Abdalqadir, Abdalaziz and Muhammad Sulaiman el Khereiji. It is engaged in electrical, landscape contracting, the supply of watches and clocks, construction equipment and the provision of maintenance services.

SAUDI ABV ASPHALT

Address head office PO Box 5387, Jiddah
Telephone 6604522, 6655218
Telex 401115 JDAPHT SJ
Activities A joint venture between Abdullah Abdalaziz el Khereiji and Armerad Betong Vagforbattringar, operating an asphalt and crusher plant. The company was formed in 1980 and has a branch in Yanbu (PO Box 498, tel. 3224686).

SAUDI METAL INDUSTRY CO.

Address head office PO Box 6137, Jiddah
Telephone 6604946, 6654053
Telex 400104 METIN SJ
Activities A company founded in 1976 and owed by Yusif and Ibrahim Abdullah el Khereiji with a branch in Dammam. The company manufactures pressure and non-pressure tanks, hangers, slips modules and fences. They are also structural engineers and have a sand blasting capability.

SAUDI PACIFIC CONSTRUCTION LTD.

Address head office PO Box 5030, Jiddah
Telephone 6655458, 6601601, 6675520
Telex 401112 DITCO SJ
Activities Yusif Abdullah el Khereiji formed this joint venture in 1981. The company is a contractor concerned with building, demolition, painting, road construction, drainage and landscaping.

TARGETS ADVERTISING

Telephone Jiddah 6712452
Telex 401177 UBC SJ
Activities The company is owned by Abdalqadir Sulaiman el Khereiji and was founded in 1980. It is an advertising agency.

UNITED BROTHERS CO.

Address head office PO Box 6093, Jiddah
Telephone 6441128, 6441129
Telex 401177 UBC SJ
Activities The company was formed in 1976 and is owned by Abdalqadir, Muhammad and Abdalaziz Sulaiman el Khereiji. With branches in Riyadh and Yanbu, the company represents Renault and Elf, is a car distributor and dealer; it supplies parts and accessories, lubricating equipment and lubricants. They are civil engineering consultants, chemical manufacturers and suppliers. They operate machine workshops and supply tools. The company also has an insurance division (PO Box 6093, Jiddah, tel. 6430512, tlx. 401177 UBC SJ). This division was actually established in 1975.

The Family of Mana'

The family originates in Jalazil of Sudayr in Najd and is a part of the Dawasir. Abdullah b. Mana' emigrated to Zubair in Iraq where Muhammad was born. When he was ten the family moved to Bombay and in 1926 Sh. Muhammad joined the court of King Abdalaziz as chief translator and interpreter. In 1935 he left royal service, and following two years in India was employed with his brother in similar duties by ARAMCO. Since 1954 he has devoted himself to his business interests and has also been able to write a compelling and important book about his years with King Abdalaziz called *Arabia Unified*.

MANA'

ABDULLAH

ABDALAZIZ
d.; worked in translation office of ARAMCO. Later in partnership with Muhammad as contractor, which business ended in 1964

- **AHMAD**
- **NASIR**
- **MAJID**
- **KHALID**
- **FARIDA**

MUHAMMAD

- **AYSHA** Ph.D., Univ. of Colorado, Dr. of Sociology, Chief of Social Affairs in Eastern Province
- **FATIMA** M.Sc. Geology A.U.B.
  - **LULU'A**
- **MUNIRA** Sociology Masters Denver, Colo.
  - **KARIMA**
- **IBRAHIM** M.Sc., Chem Eng., Mellon Inst.of Technol., Pittsburgh
  - **NURA**
- **MANSUR** Bus. Admin. M.A., Idaho
- **NAJIB** Civil Eng. graduate
  - **ABDULLAH**
- **ABDALMUHSIN** Univ. of Riyadh B.A., teacher
- **JAMAL** hospital clerk
- **SALWA** Riyadh B.A. teacher
- **SANA** Medical student King Faisal Medical College

ABDALMUHSIN
no issue ; d.

ALMANA GENERAL HOSPITAL

Address head office PO Box 311, al Khobar
Telephone 8642330, 8980772
Telex 670069 ALMANA SJ
Activities As a small boy Sh. Muhammad al Mana' was in Bombay and met many people coming from the Arabian Peninsula seeking medical treatment. He was concerned to learn they had no facilities in their homeland. Throughout his early career he maintained his ambition to put that situation to rights. It was an ambition that he was not able to fulfil until 1957 when he brought medical equipment and staff from Germany to establish the Almana Eye and Dental Specialty Hospital. Twenty-four years later the present hospital was created on that firm foundation.
Reaching to six storeys the Almana General Hospital has facilities for gynaecology, obstetrics, paediatrics, surgery, orthopaedics, radiology, pathology, ENT, dermatology and physical therapy. It provides the best available medical skills and equipment for its patients as well as invaluable training opportunities for the Kingdom.

The Family of Mentakh

The Mentakh family is of great interest as it demonstrates how fluid and absorptive tribal life used to be. The family genealogy shows how important this was for survival during the desert wars which in this case led to the consolidation of the Kingdom by King Abdalaziz. The immediate origins of the family are in Hofuf, though they have relatives in Kuwait and Baghdad as a consequence of migration during the Ajman wars of the 1920s.

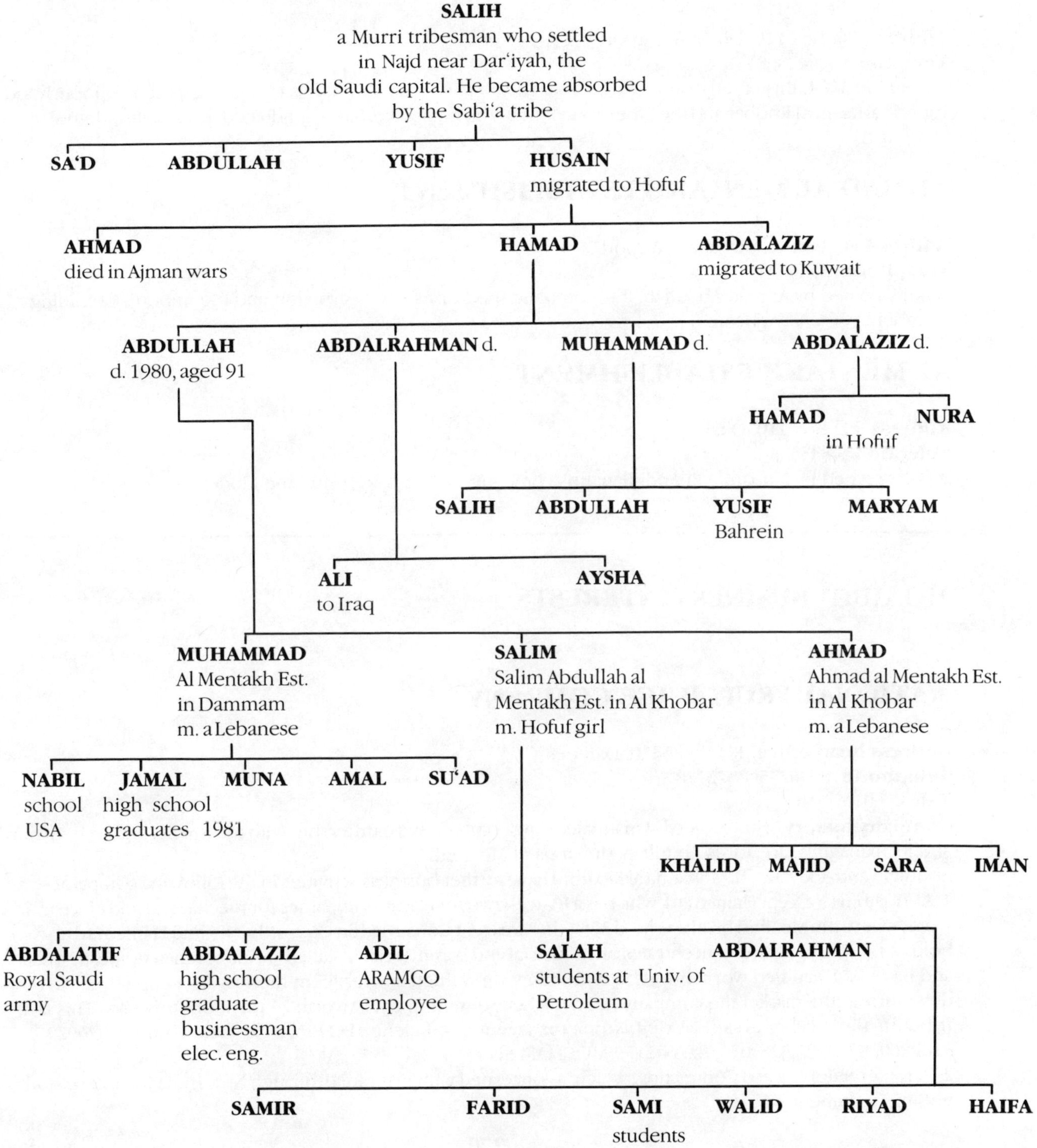

AL MENTAKH TRADING COMPANY

Address PO Box 111, Dhahran Airport
Telephone 8328419
Concentrating on construction, importing and marketing this company forms a base which serves as a holding company for the three brothers, Muhammad, Salim and Ahmad, who are equal partners. In addition each has his own company.

SALIM ABDULLAH AL MENTAKH ESTABLISHMENT

Address PO Box 110, Dhahran Airport
Telephone 8647898
Formed in 1971, this enterprise is wholly owned by Salim Abdullah. It has two interests: a neighbourhood supermarket in Al Khobar and the other concentrates on real estate. Salim graduated in agricultural studies from AUB.

AHMAD AL MENTAKH ESTABLISHMENT

Address PO Box 110, Dhahran Airport
Telephone 8643094
Wholly owned by Ahmad Abdullah, this company specialises in construction and the import of building materials, cement and iron.

AL MENTAKH ESTABLISHMENT

Address PO Box 110, Dhahran Airport
Telephone 8336730
Wholly owned by Muhammad Abdullah, this company owns a bakery and the Modern Printing Shop.

MOAIBID BUSINESS INTERESTS

NATIONAL FRUIT JUICE COMPANY

Address head office PO Box 5310, Dammam
Telephone 8578275, 8572728
Telex 601651 NFJ SJ
Company history This successful manufacturing company is a partnership with the Khalifa Algosaibi Group and its managing director is Abdullah Muhanna al Moaibid.
Abdullah and Abdalaziz b. Muhanna al Moaibid have further business activities in the following companies:
1. Al Moaibid Crescent Hamco Ltd, which is a J/V with two American companies for mechanical and electrical work, where the Moaibid brothers hold 52%, the Crescent Construction Co. holds 24% and Hamco Ltd also holds 24%. The company concentrates on industrial and commercial installations rather than domestic ones and has so far handled work throughout the Kingdom valued at over 55 million riyals. Despite the current downturn in the market the company has a further 30 million riyals worth of work on its books. This is a tribute to their technical skills as well as their management efficiency. PO Box 2431, Dammam, tel. 8269287, 8269860, 8269977,8269056; tlx. 602179 MOCHAM SJ.
2. Summer Shipping and Contracting, which is concerned with insurance through New India Insurance, and trading in timber.

The Family of Moaibid

The family originates in Dar'iyah, the old capital of the Saudi Amirs of Najd. Their ancestor was forced to flee during the early part of the nineteenth century as a consequence of the invasion by Egyptian troops under the command of the Turkish ruler of that country, Ibrahim Pasha. Abdullah b. Hamid was nicknamed Moaibid and this soubriquet stuck as a family name after he had settled in Hofuf. His descendant Muhammad b. Abdalaziz was a historian who obtained his education in Bahrein and Kuwait during the 1920s, and subsequently in India, where he was employed by the Qusaibi family in their pearling business. Later, in 1928, he was part of an educational delegation sent by King Abdalaziz Al Saud, then Sultan of Najd, to Cairo. On his return he worked in the nascent oil industry from 1932 for the government. In 1945 he was part of the Saudi delegation to the United Nations. In 1947 he returned to the Kingdom and developed his interest in agriculture. This led to the growth of an idea born in 1968 which grew with the founding of Basic Chemical Industries. Since his death the family interest is carried on by his sons.

- **HAMID**
  - **ABDULLAH** called Moaibid who moved from Dar'iyah to Hofuf
    - **SALIH**
      - **MUHANNA**
        - **YUSIF**
          - **ABDALAZIZ**
            - **MUHANNA**
              - **ABDALAZIZ**
                - **YUSIF** d.
                  - **SALIH**
                    - **YUSIF**
                  - **FA'IZ**
                  - **ABDALAZIZ**
                - **MUHANNA** b. 1913, d. 1980
                  - **ABDALAZIZ** Ptner with brother
                  - **ABDULLAH** B.Sc. Civil Eng, Seattle, 1974; M.D. Basic Chemical Industries; M.D. National Fruit Juice Co.
                    - **NASIR**
                - **ABDALRAHMAN** National Paper Products Co. Carlton Al Moaibid Hotel
                  - **ABDALAZIZ** Petroleum Services and Contracting Al Moaibid Dental Clinic. Real Estate
                    - **SAUD**
                  - **SAMI**
                  - **JAMAL**

NATIONAL PAPER PRODUCTS COMPANY

Address head office Dammam
Telephone 8571222
Telex 601049 NAPCO SJ
Activities The company, owned by Abdalrahman Abdalaziz al Moaibid and Georges Freme Bros. was formed in 1956. It has branches in Jiddah (PO Box 7319, tel. 6671449, 6603329, 6674358) and Riyadh (tel. 4039931, 4053176) and Hasa (tel. 5821559). The company is concerned with packaging material, paper and paper products. They are polythene suppliers and manufacturers and also supply tissue paper and cement bags.

BASIC CHEMICAL INDUSTRIES

Address head office PO Box 1053, Dammam
Telephone 8572466
Telex 601568 UCI SJ
Cable address CHEMICALS
Company history The company is a partnership, the major partners being Ali Tamimi (q.v.), Abdullah Fu'ad (q.v.), Abdullah Abdalaziz al Uthman, Abdullah Ibrahim al Mu'amar and Abdalaziz and Abdullah al Moaibid. It was formed in 1972 and started production three years later in 1975. The chairman is Abdullah Fu'ad Bubshait and the managing director his cousin, Abdullah Muhanna al Moaibid. In association with other companies such as ICI, Basic Chemical Industries manufactures concrete chemicals and imports chemicals as a trading activity. Its main concern is, however, the production of hydrochloric acid, chlorine, caustic soda in liquid and flake form, and sodium hypochlorite.

The Family of Mo'ajil

This family originates in Hawtat Sudair in Saudi Arabia.

See also Kuwait volume.

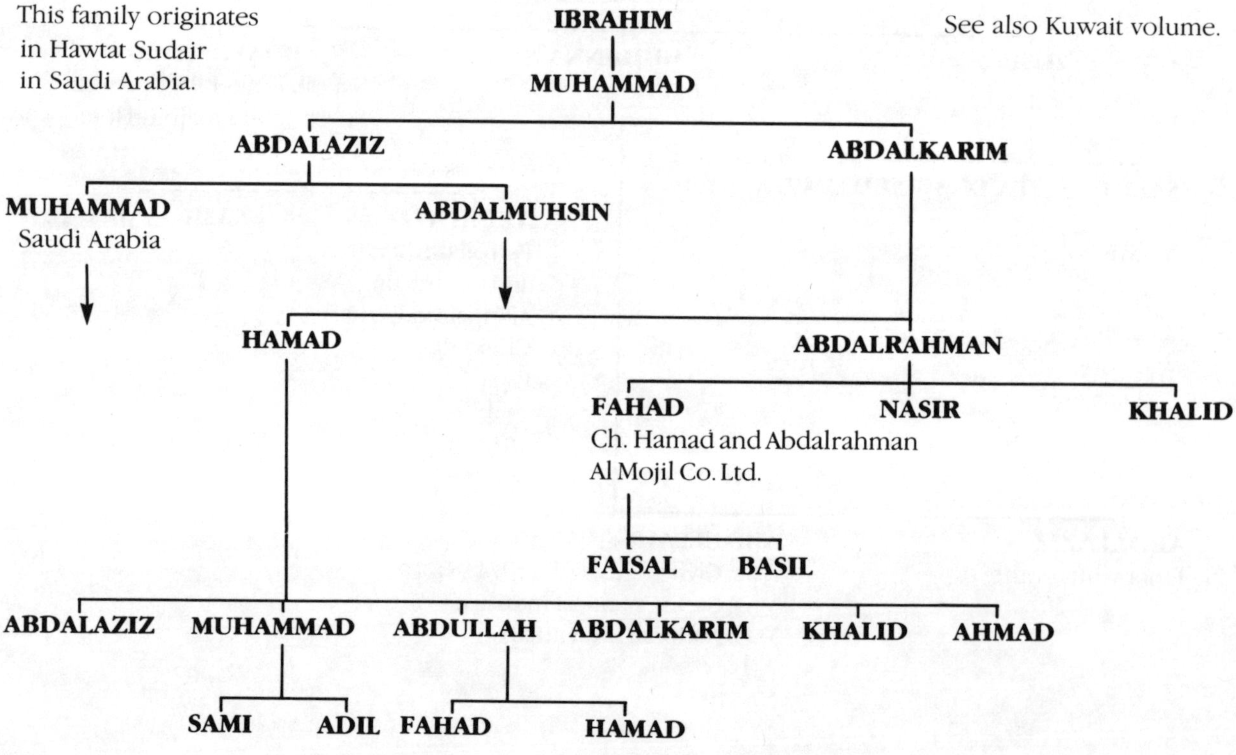

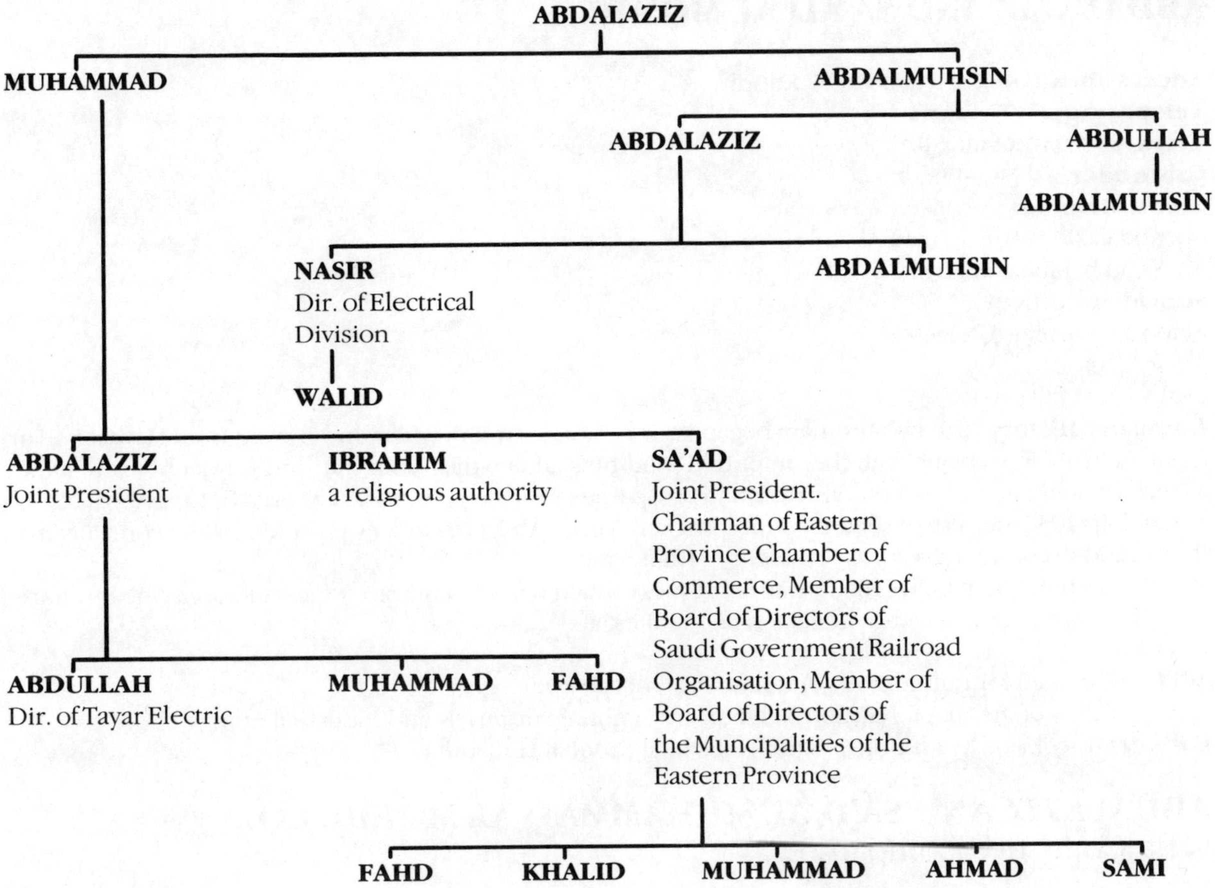
ABDALAZIZ
MUHAMMAD
ABDALMUHSIN
ABDALAZIZ
ABDULLAH
ABDALMUHSIN
NASIR
Dir. of Electrical Division
ABDALMUHSIN
WALID
ABDALAZIZ
Joint President
IBRAHIM
a religious authority
SA'AD
Joint President. Chairman of Eastern Province Chamber of Commerce, Member of Board of Directors of Saudi Government Railroad Organisation, Member of Board of Directors of the Muncipalities of the Eastern Province
ABDULLAH
Dir. of Tayar Electric
MUHAMMAD
FAHD
FAHD
KHALID
MUHAMMAD
AHMAD
SAMI

ABDALAZIZ AND SA'AD AL MO'AJIL

Address head office P.O.Box 207 Riyadh
Telephone 27357, 28053
Telex 201203 MOAJIL SJ
Cable address MOAJILCO
Board Members A collective company
Sh. Abdalaziz b. Muhammad Al Mo'ajil 50%
Sh. Sa'ad b. Muhammad Al Mo'ajil 50%
Subsidiary offices
Al Mo'ajil Furniture, tel. 20687
Tayar Electric, tel. 39271
Real Estate Office, tel. 27357
Company History The two brothers began their business careers when they moved from Hawtat Sudair to Jubail in 1935. To begin with they imported foodstuffs and textiles from Iraq and Kuwait but at first they suffered many losses due to bedouin raids and prospered only when peace was restored by King Abdalaziz al Sawd. In 1950 they established the office in Qatif. Today Abdalaziz acts as President of the company in Riyadh and his brother, Sa'ad, as President in Dammam.
The Riyadh business handles the furniture business which deals in contract, office and domestic furniture as well as carpeting, electrical installation and real estate.
Agencies
ACEC of Belgium for transformers and high/low voltage switch gear.
Crowse Hinds of the USA for airport lighting, area lighting, materials and industrial fittings.
Bankers City Bank, Saudi British Bank, Al Bank al Saudi al Hollandi.

ABDALAZIZ AND SA'D AL MUHAMMAD AL MOAJIL CO.
(The Collective Company)

Address head office PO Box 53, Dammam
Telephone 8321256, 8322307
Telex 601055 MOAJIL SJ

SAUDI POLYPROPYLENE SACK FACTORY

Address head office PO Box 254, Dammam
Telephone 8574098, 8574099, 8579124, 8579245
Telex 602797 SPSF SJ
Activities Manufactures sacks for foodstuffs and chemicals to their customers' specifications.

AL MOAJIL CEMENT PRODUCTS PLANT

Address head office PO Box 1758, Dammam
Telephone 8576452, 8578638
Telex 602798 MCPP SJ
Activities Manufactures blocks, tiles and cement products.

AL MOAJIL PALLET PLANT

Address head office PO Box 254, Dammam
Telephone 8574098, 8574099, 8579237
Telex 602797 SPSF SJ
Activities Manufactures wooden pallets

The Family of Mohandis

Family tradition relates that the ancestor of the family came to Jiddah on the Hajj some two hundred years ago; they still possess a deed dated 1841 AD giving them title to one of the coral block houses of old Jiddah. The same house is still standing today. The family originally came from the Sulaimaniya of Afghanistan.

- **MUHAMMAD**
  - **ABU BAKR** house builder
    - **SALIM** house builder and purchaser of the building mentioned above
      - **BAKRI**
        - **SALIM**
          - **ABDULLAH**
            - **AHMAD**
              - **ABDALMAJID**
                - **AHMAD** accountant
                - **ASHRAF**
                - **MUHAMMAD**
            - **SALIM** studied at the Al Falah schools founded by Zainal Alireza and sent by them to India for further education and work
              - **WAHIB** d.
              - **HASAN** d.
              - **MUHAMMAD** Saudia
              - three daughters, two of whom are M.A.s from Pakistani universities
              - **ABDULLAH** Lockheed
              - **AHMAD** Min. of Health
              - **ADIL** Commerce graduate, Cairo
            - **MUSTAFA**
              - **MUHAMMAD** owns a restaurant in Jiddah
              - **ABDULLAH** civil servant in Desalination Plant
              - **REDA**
              - **WAHIB**
              - **USSAMA**
            - **ABID** d.

ABDALMAJID AHMAD MOHANDIS

Address PO Box 524, Jiddah
Telephone 6432805, 6434665
Telex 400329 MANDIS SJ
Also an office in Riyadh.
Abdalmajid Mohandis is an extremely professional public accountant and auditor whose two hundred or so clients testify to his success and quality. He obtained his academic qualifications at Cairo University and polished this achievement by working in a professional concern, SABA, for eight years to gain experience. During this time he refined his skills by taking Arthur Anderson Training Courses. He founded the present firm in 1970. The firm corresponds with Klynveld Main Goerdeler International. Abbdalmajid is Vice-president and Treasurer of the Arab Society of Certified Accountants which is affiliated to the Association of Certified Accountants in the UK. He is also a Member of the Board of the Saudi Association of Accounting.

The Family of Mouminah

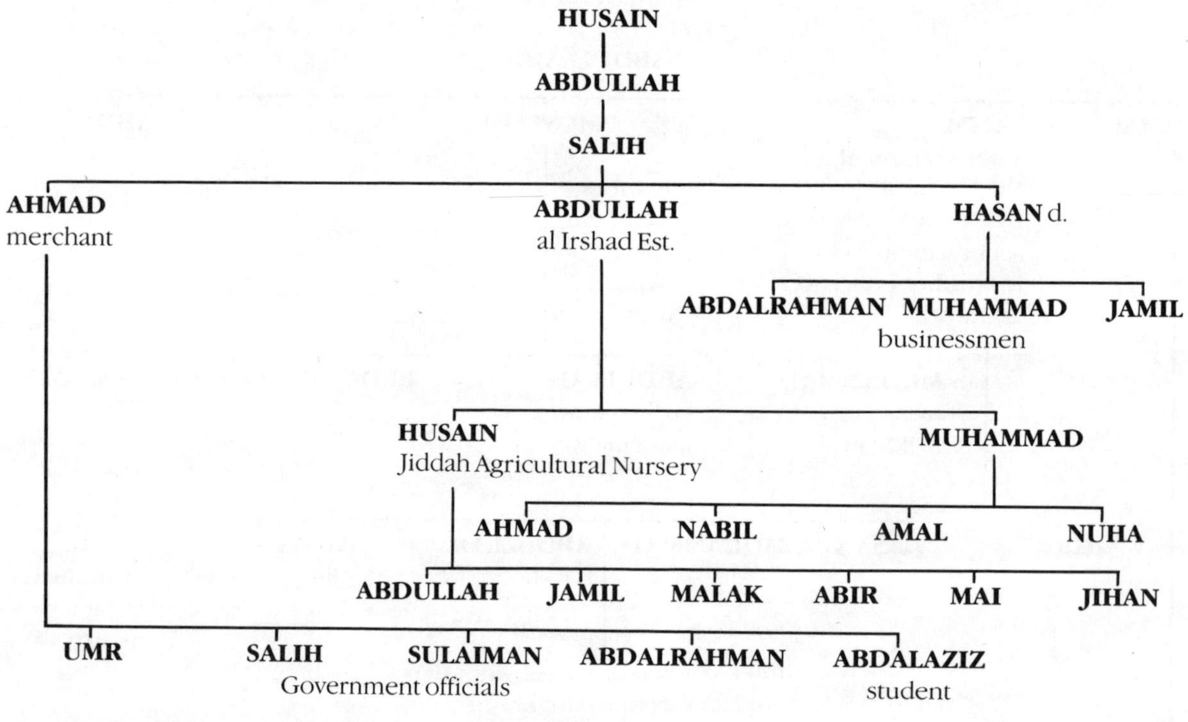

JIDDAH AGRICULTURAL NURSERY

Address PO Box 6555, Jiddah
Telephone 6310928, Nursery 6600069
Telex 403700 ROS
Situated on the Madina Road by Palestine Square, this nursery supplies garden ornaments, fertilizers, tools and over two hundred varieties of plant.
With branches in Riyadh and Jubail, they also operate a contracting business and have successfully completed projects for both central government and municipalities in all regions of the Kingdom. Their specialities include landscaping and irrigation and expansion into other areas is being planned.

NATIONAL TECHNICAL SERVICES COMPANY LTD

Address head office PO Box 8110, Jiddah
Telephone 6692642, 6670944, 6674078
Telex 400993 NTSC SJ
Activities Founded in 1979 this company is owned by Abdalrahman Mouminah. There is a Riyadh branch (tel. 4659787) and they are engaged in telecommunications contracting and the supply of electronic equipment and components.

MOUMINAH EXHIBITION

Address head office Jiddah
Telephone 6653709
Activities Owned by Hamid Abdalwahhab Mouminah, this concern deals in ready made clothes.

MUFARRIJ BUSINESS INTERESTS

ABDALRAHIM ABDULLAH MUFARRIJ

Address head office Jizan; there is no formal address as the establishment is well known
Telephone 1312, 1313, 1611
Subsidiary offices Jiddah main office: PO Box 1337, cables MOFARRIJ,
tel. 6433115, tlx. 401423 MUFRIJ SJ
There are two other branches in Jiddah
Proprietor Abdalrahim Abdullah Mofarrij
Company history The business was founded in 1946 and based on the importation of sorghum and grain from Jizan to Jiddah. Abdalrahim Abdullah had his own dhows and also carried money on behalf of clients to make purchases in the Jiddah entrepot market, as in the early days there were no banks.
Today the company acts as a general importer, specialising in foodstuffs and building materials. Developments have included the addition of an ice factory at Rabigh, which is equipped from the UK, and the establishment of improved farming interests in Jizan. The company possesses considerable real estate assets in Jiddah and elsewhere, and is represented by agents in Yanbu, Wejh and Tabuk.

MIDDLE EAST MARKETING CORPORATION

Address head office PO Box 4347, Jiddah
Telephone 6603756, 6602564
Telex 401423 MUFRIJ SJ, 402668 SAREE SJ
Activities The company was formed in 1973 and is owned by Abdalghani Abdalrahman al Mufarrij. It deals with cold stores, ice factories and air conditioning equipment, and supplies computer and business systems as well as engaging in market consultancy activities.

The Family of Mufarrij

A family of Rabigh on the Red Sea Coast, originating from the tribe of Harb.

- **AWADH**
  - **MUFARRIJ**
    - **ABDULLAH**
      - **MUHAMMAD ID** owns fishing boats
        - **ABID**
        - **MUFARRIJ**
        - **HAMAD**
        - **ZAKI**
        - **WAHIB**
        - **ABDALKARIM**
      - **ABDULLAH** works in the Jizan Office
        - **MUHAMMAD**
        - **AHMAD**
      - **ABDALRAHMAN** owner of the family company, which he runs from the Jizan office
        - **ABDALGHANI** Man. of foreign relations in company. UK educated
          - **ABDULLAH** at school
        - **ABDALHAMID** Man. of the Jiddah office
          - daughters
        - **ALI** Asst. man. Jizan
          - **SULTAN**
        - **MUHAMMAD**
        - **KHALID**
      - **MUHAMMAD** independent of the family business. Medina POB 1219, Rabigh POB 11
        - **ABDULLAH**
        - **ABDALRAHMAN**
        - **FAHAD**
        - **MAJID**
        - **RIFAT**
      - **ABDALAZIZ** runs the ice plant owned by the family in Rabigh
      - **SABRI**

The Family of Al Mutawa

The family originates in Najd. Mutawa describes a religious person.

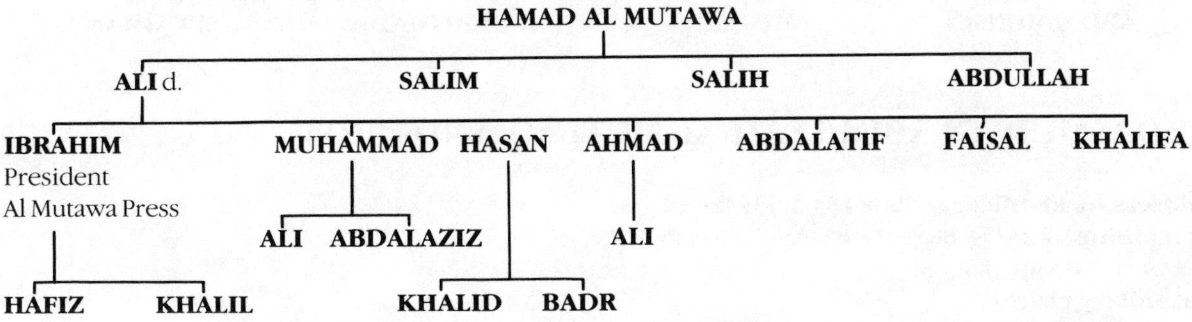

AL MUTAWA PRESS CO.

Address head office PO Box 343, Dammam
Telephone 8263321, 8266080
Telex 601486 SJ
Activitics This was a partnership between Sulaiman Abdullah al Ghunaim (q.v.) and Ali Hamad al Mutawa; on the latter's death the al Mutawa interest was shared between all his sons.
The company is a publishing and printing business, mainly occupied with the production of periodicals, annual reports, brochures and books. They produce 2,000 copies of *Al Qafilah* each week for Aramco as well as 7,500 copies of *Al Iqtisad* for the Dammam Chamber of Commerce. Books have been produced for the University of Petroleum, King Saud University and the Ministry of Information

The Family of Al Mutlaq

ABDULLAH

ABDALMUHSIN — MUTLAQ — MUHAMMAD — SULAIMAN

ABDALMUHSIN ABDULLAH AL MUTLAQ AND BROS.

Address head office P.O.Box 153 Al Khobar
Telephone 8643254, 8641077, 8644360, 8644253
Telex 670015 MUTLAQ SJ
Subsidiary offices
Riyadh P.O.Box 1321, tel. 4028800, tlx. 201179 MUTLAQ SJ
Jiddah P.O.Box 4645, tel. 6455236
The operation is controlled by the holding company, Al Mutlaq Brothers.
Board of Directors
President Sh. Abdalmuhsin A Al Mutlaq
Vice President Sh. Mutlaq A Al Mutlaq
Sh. Muhammad A Al Mutlaq
Sh. Sulaiman A Al Mutlaq
Na'aman A Hantouli
The company was formed some thirty years ago in Al Khobar by the two men who are now President and Vice President of what has become the holding company. Sh. Abdalmuhsin is a member of the Board of the Dammam Chamber of Commerce and Sh. Mutlaq a member of the Board of Riyadh Chamber of Commerce.
Business Activities The various companies in the Group cover a wide field of interests which include the manufacture of and trading in furniture, building construction, furnishing and contracting. The supply of steel buildings, industrial engineering services, the manufacture of automobile radiators, electrical engineering, real estate and the representation of foreign companies.
The Al Mutlaq Group of Companies
1. Al Mutlaq Furniture Company, which trades in furniture, Riyadh P.O.Box 1321, tel. 4028800, tlx. 201179 MUTLAQ SJ. Man. Dir. Sh. Mutlaq A Al Mutlaq.
2. Al Mutlaq Furniture Manufacturing Company, Industrial Zone, Dammam P.O. Box 710, tel. 8327808, 8328640, tlx. 601492 MUTLAQ SJ. Man. Dir. Sh. Abdalmuhsin A Al Mutlaq.
3. Al Mutlaq Bossert Construction Company Ltd., Riyadh P.O.Box 1321, tel. 4764127, tlx. 201179 MUTLAQ SJ. Man. Dir. Sh. Mutlaq A Al Mutlaq.
4. Al Mutlaq Real Estate, Al Khobar P.O. Box 153, tel. 8641226, tlx. 670015 MUTLAQ SJ. Man. Dir. Sh. Muhammad A Al Mutlaq.
5. SISCO (Saudi Industrial Service Company), Dhahran Airport P.O.Box 319, tel. 8344252, tlx. 671311 MUTLAQ SJ. Man. Dir. Sh. Muhammad A Al Mutlaq. Supply of warehouses and oil industry servicing.
6. SAPAT (Saudi Pan-Arab Technologists), Dhahran Airport P.O.Box 429, tel. 8343075, tlx. 671265 MUTLAQ SJ. Man. Dir. Mr. Ray Landen. Engineering and power station supply.
7. Al Mutlaq Design Decorating and Furnishing Company, Riyadh P.O. Box 1321, tel. 4028192, tlx. 201179 MUTLAQ SJ. Man. Dir. Sh. Mutlaq A Al Mutlaq.
8. Lugano Office(Giovi SA), Riva A Caccia 1, 6900 Lugano, Switzerland, tel. 091 546341/2, tlx. 73992 GIOVICH. Swiss liaison office.
9. Al Mutlaq Brothers (UK) Ltd., 82 Mount Street, London W.1., tel. 01 499 5894/5, tlx. 299123 MUTLAQ G. British liaison office.

The offices in Switzerland and the UK service the Saudi companies and also offer the services of the Group to business men visiting Saudi Arabia.

The Family of Al Nassar

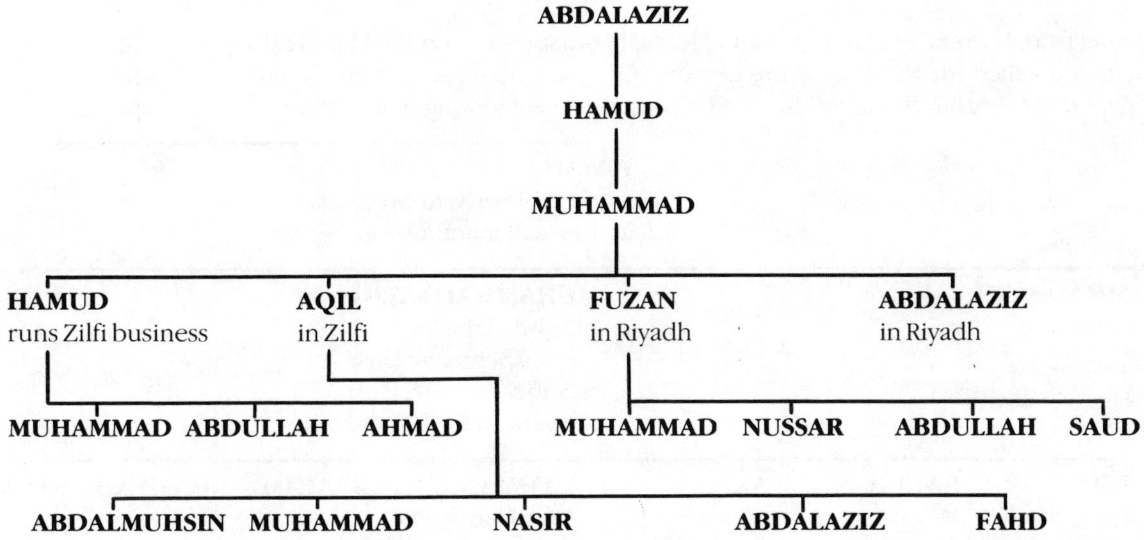

THE FUZAN MUHAMMAD AL NASSAR ESTABLISHMENT

Address head office PO Box 2254 Riyadh; subsidiary office in Zilfi, 300kms south-west of Riyadh, tel. (from Riyadh) 06422-1343
Telephone 4833124
Telex 2001435 FUZAN SJ
Cable address NASSARCO
Proprietor Sh. Fuzan b. Muhammad al Nassar
Company history Sh. Fuzan returned from employment in Kuwait some thirty five years ago and settled in Riyadh with his family to start the business. At present his company operates as commission purchasing agents and specialises in crockery and building materials. However, he aims to expand into domestic appliances and is acquiring agencies for refrigerators, television sets and washing machines.
Turnover 2 million Saudi riyals
Bankers Riyadh Bank

The Family of Nassif

Originating from Harb, between Jiddah and Mecca, the first station on the Hijaz Railway from Medina to Damascus was called Bir Nassif after the nearby well. Some sources give the family a more recent origin from Egypt due to earlier immigration, a quite common event among many families of the Hijaz.

- **HASAN** — worked his private property and owned a grain shop
  - **MUHAMMAD SA'ID** — inherited the grain business
    - **ABDULILLAH** — retired
      - **MUHAMMAD SA'ID** — Saudi Air Lines
        - **USSAMA**
      - **NABIL** — Member of Binayti Board Lines and working in Nat. Commercial Bank
        - **GHASSAN**
        - **TAMIR**
        - **HATAN**
      - **USSAMA** — Saudi Air
        - **IHAB**
      - **IMAD**
      - **ZAHIR**
      - **BASSEM**
      - **NIHAD**
    - **ABDULLAH** — Saudi Air Lines
      - **ATIF**
      - **ALA'A**
      - **AZI**
    - **MUHAMMAD HASAN** — retired
      - **SAMIR**
      - **YUSIF**
      - **ADIL**
      - **AHMAD**
    - **ABDALMAJID** — Saudi Air Lines
      - **NAJI**
  - **MUHAMMAD SALIH** — published the first newspaper in the Hijaz; Member of Council of Advisors to King Abdulaziz
    - **UMR** — Director General of Binayti Public Relations
      - **MUHAMMAD SALIH**
    - **BAKUR** — Min. of Agriculture Jiddah
      - **AYMAN**
      - **AHMAD**
    - **ALI** — Chairman of Binayti. Architect
      - **ANIS**
    - **UTHMAN** — Gen. Man. Binayti
      - **MA'AN**
    - **IBRAHIM**
    - **SA'DIYAH**
    - **SALWAH**

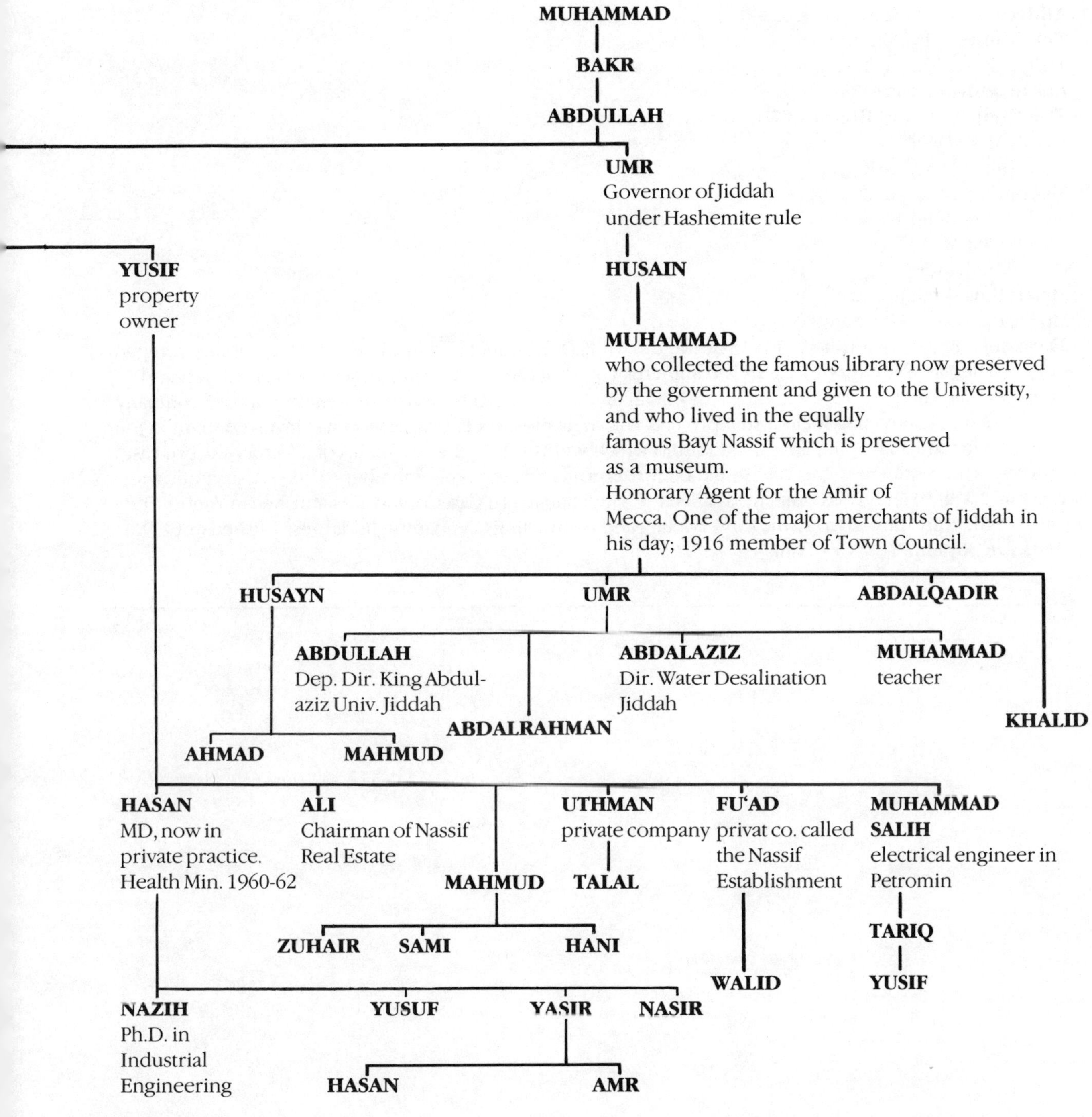
MUHAMMAD
BAKR
ABDULLAH
UMR
Governor of Jiddah
under Hashemite rule
HUSAIN
MUHAMMAD
who collected the famous library now preserved
by the government and given to the University,
and who lived in the equally
famous Bayt Nassif which is preserved
as a museum.
Honorary Agent for the Amir of
Mecca. One of the major merchants of Jiddah in
his day; 1916 member of Town Council.
YUSIF
property
owner
HUSAYN
UMR
ABDALQADIR
ABDULLAH
Dep. Dir. King Abdul-
aziz Univ. Jiddah
ABDALRAHMAN
ABDALAZIZ
Dir. Water Desalination
Jiddah
MUHAMMAD
teacher
KHALID
AHMAD
MAHMUD
HASAN
MD, now in
private practice.
Health Min. 1960-62
ALI
Chairman of Nassif
Real Estate
MAHMUD
UTHMAN
private company
TALAL
FU'AD
privat co. called
the Nassif
Establishment
WALID
MUHAMMAD
SALIH
electrical engineer in
Petromin
TARIQ
YUSIF
ZUHAIR
SAMI
HANI
NAZIH
Ph.D. in
Industrial
Engineering
YUSUF
YASIR
NASIR
HASAN
AMR

BINAYTI DEVELOPMENT COMPANY

Address head office P.O. Box 3305 Jiddah
Telephone 6454240, 6674406, 6674410
Telex 400412 BINAYT SJ
Cable address BINAYTI
The Chairman and Board of Directors Chairman: Sh. Umr M.S. Nassif
Sh. Ali M.S. Nassif
Sh. Uthman M.S. Nassif
Sh. Ibrahim M.S. Nassif
Sh. Nabil Abdulillah Nassif
Sh. Ussama Abdulillah Nassif
Dr. Bakhashwin
Mrs. Fatima Ibrahim Nassif
Mrs. Sadia Nassif, Mrs. Salwa Nassif
The company was established in 1975 as the Binayti Establishment and became a limited liability company in 1978. The Nassif family is not a purely commercial one but represents many generations of scholars and public servants and is one of the oldest in Jiddah. At the present time Binayti is a multi purpose company specialising in contracting for housing projects and their most recent expansion has involved them in joint venture with an Italian company called Premo which will result in the setting up of a factory for pre-cast concrete. This venture involves Premo and Binayti as principals and other members of the Nassif family with Talaat and Wahib Lami. This company is called the Saudi Italian Pre-Cast Co. and is established in Yanbo. The Lami brothers are the owners of the Lami Trading and Contracting Company in Jiddah, established in 1979.
Bankers Riyadh Bank, City Bank

NOWAILATY BUSINESS INTERESTS

ECONOMIC INTEGRATION COMPANY LIMITED

Address head office P.O.Box 6540 Riyadh
Telephone 60127
Telex 201505 SELECT SJ
Subsidiary offices Jiddah P.O.Box 5096, tel. 6422157
Ownership The company is a partnership between H.R.H. Prince Saud ibn Na'if ibn Abdalaziz al Sa'ud, Sh. Mazhar Musallim Al Nowailaty and Sh. Muhammad Salahuddin Hussain Omar.
The company was formed in 1979 and is an example of the assimilation of modern management techniques in that its purpose is to provide management for a consortium of small companies who will be invited to join and benefit from the latest information and management methods. The company will specialise at first in the shipping, road construction and foodstuffs fields but is open to suggestions including the establishment of joint ventures.
Bankers Saudi British Bank, Riyadh Bank

AL NOWAILATY

Address head office P.O.Box 583 Jiddah
Telephone 6420718, 6693512
Telex 400489 ADDAS SJ
A company owned by Ali Musallam Al Nowailaty which supplies embroidery work.

AL NOWAILATY STORES

Address head office P.O.Box 582 Jiddah
Telephone 6420718
Also owned by Ali Musallam, this company provides tailoring supplies.

SAUDI FACILITIES ENTERPRISES ESTABLISHMENT

Address head office P.O.Box 5096 Jiddah
Telephone 6891367, 6422157
A company of general contractors formed in 1974 and owned by Ghassan Mazhar Nowailaty and managed by his father.

The Family of Nowailaty

The family comes from the Holy City of Mecca and descends from clothmakers, as their name suggests (*nuwayl* means a loom). They branched out from manufacture, finally marketing their own product and latterly importing textiles.

all born in Mecca

ALI
radio operator for HRH Prince Faisal later King of Saudi Arabia, during conquest of Yemen in 1920s. Now owns the Nowailaty Stores (Textiles) in Jiddah

FU'AD
civil servant and diplomat, served in Indonesia and Consul Gen. in Benghazi

ANWAR
civil servant, Dir. of Airport Affairs Dept. in Civil Aviation Authority

RASHAD
b. 1929. Political Science graduate, Cairo 1953 diplomatic attaché Foreign Min. 1953, Amb. to Hague and Senegal

HANI
physicist

MUSALLIM
Chem. Eng. graduate Petromin rep. in Texas

MARWAN
lawyer in Jiddah

AYMAN
lawyer

HAITHAM
Business admin. E A Juffali Bros.

SAMIR
Admin. for British Steel and Min. of Petroleum

HASAN
Civil Eng. graduate US

GHAZI
manages companies of Gen. Hashim Saiyd Hashim, ex commander of RSAAF

ABDALHADI
RSAAF pilot

FAWZI
Saudia pilot

- **RAGHAB**
  - **SALIM** textile trade
    - **MAHMUD** textile trade
      - **MUSALLIM** d. 1943 textile trade
        - **MAZHAR** Man. Dir. of Economic Integration Co., 25 years in Min. of Defence and Aviation, ex-head of Eng. Dept. Jiddah Int. Airport; retd. 1976. Electronics engineer
          - **GHASSAN** student
        - **MAHMUD** Dir. of Meteorological Dept., Aviation Affairs
          - **WALID** Electrical Eng. US
          - **NIZAR**
        - **ABDALBADIA** Consul Gen. Cairo graduate of Whittier US; Min. of Foreign Affairs, Jiddah
          - daughter
        - **MUHAMMAD** d. of German measles aged 3
      - **RAGHAB**
        - **MAHMUD** textile trade
        - **ADIL**

- **MUHAMMAD** Pol. Sci. graduate Cairo; journalist on Al Madina newspaper
- **MAYSAR**

The Family of Omran

Probably the oldest family in the capital, Riyadh.

- **ABDALRAHMAN**
  - **MUHAMMAD**
    - **ABDULLAH**
      - **MUHAMMAD**
        - **ABDALRAHMAN AL OMRAN**
          - **HAMAD**
            - **ABDALRAHMAN**
              - **ABDALAZIZ**
              - **SALIH**
              - **ABDALMUHSIN**
              - **MUHAMMAD**
          - **MUHAMMAD** moved from Riyadh to Hofuf
            - **ABDULLAH** PhD in law, Univ of Dijon; Ex Min of State, now in private practice as a consultant
              - **HISHAM**
              - **FAHD**
            - **OMRAN** Business Degree University of Texas
              - **MUHAMMAD**
              - **ABDALMUHSIN**
              - **ABDALRAHMAN**
              - **MUSA**
            - **ABDALAZIZ** Deg in Business Admin Cairo
              - **MUHAMMAD**

HASAN

- **ABDALRAHMAN** Ambassador to Tunis
  - **MUHAMMAD**
  - **ZIYAD**
  - **KHALID**
- **ABDALAZIZ**
  - **ABDALMUHSIN**
  - **HASAN**
- **ABDULLAH**
  - **HASAN**
  - **ABDALRAHMAN**
- **SALIH**
  - **ABDULLAH**
  - **ABDALAZIZ**
  - **ABDALRAHMAN**
  - **MUHAMMAD**
  - **OMRAN**
  - **KHALID**
  - **HASAN**

ABDALAZIZ

- **ABDALRAHMAN**
  - **ABDULLAH**
  - **FAHD**
  - **ABDALRAHMAN**
  - **KHALID**

ABDALRAHMAN d. 1980
Deg in Engineering
USA; Man of
Dammam Office

- **KHALID**
- **ABDALAZIZ**

UMRAN AND UMRAN AND BROTHERS

Address head office P.O.Box 550 Riyadh
Telephone 30059, 22758
Telex 201935 SASCOM SJ
Cable address VENSCO
Subsidiary offices
Jiddah P.O.Box 4319, tel. 6651696; Dammam P.O.Box 1238; Riyadh, Khazzan St., tel. 85017
Proprietor Sh. Umran b. Muhammad and his brothers Abdalaziz and Abdalrahman.
The Company acts as a holding company for the family interests. Sh. Umran has a wide personal involvement in commercial affairs. He is the Managing Director of the Rashid and Al Umran Co., whose partners are his uncle (by marriage) Rashid Al Rashid (40%) and Sh. Umran and his brothers hold 20% each. Sh. Umran is also Managing Director of the Civil Works Co. in which the holdings are The Rashid and Al Umran Co. 60% and Tamimi and Fouad 40%, and Managing Director of the Arabian Industries Co. which is shared 70% by the Civil Works Co. and 30% by others. This company is concerned with silica sand, bricks and a hydrated lime factory and will shortly manufacture white cement; it was established in 1977. Sh. Umran is a partner in Dirab Co. for quarrying and ready mixed asphalt, has 50% of Al Umran and Toug Co. with Sh. Ibrahim al Toug holding the other 50%. Sh. Ibrahim is second Chairman of the Riyadh Chamber of Commerce and General Manager of Messrs. Juffali. Sh. Umran is a member of the board of the Saudi Faransi Bank, MABCO for pre-cast concrete, and SABICO the Saudi Belgian Company, the Saudi Public Transport Company and his interest in the Saudi Arabian Service Company is through the Rashid and Al Umran Co. which owns 70%, the remaining 30% being owned by Salih Mosaad.
The Al Rashid and Al Umran Company, the Civil Works Company and Arabian Industries share the offices and telephones of Umran and Umran and Brothers. Sh. Abdalaziz b. Muhammad uses the Riyadh subsidiary office and acts as deputy for Sh. Umran. The Al Umran and Al Toug Company is in King Faisal St., P.O.Box 2743, tel. 37356. SABICO is at Riyadh P.O.Box 987, tel. 68545, tlx. 20022.
Bankers American Express Bahrain, al Saudi al Faransi Bank, the National Commercial Bank.

The Family of Olayan

The Shammar have four divisions Sinjarah, Tuwman, Aslam and Abdu. The Abdu comprise five clans and the Dughiyrat are made up of eight sub-clans, one of which is further divided into four sub sub-clans.

SHAMMAR-ABDU DIVISION, AL DUGHIYRAT CLAN

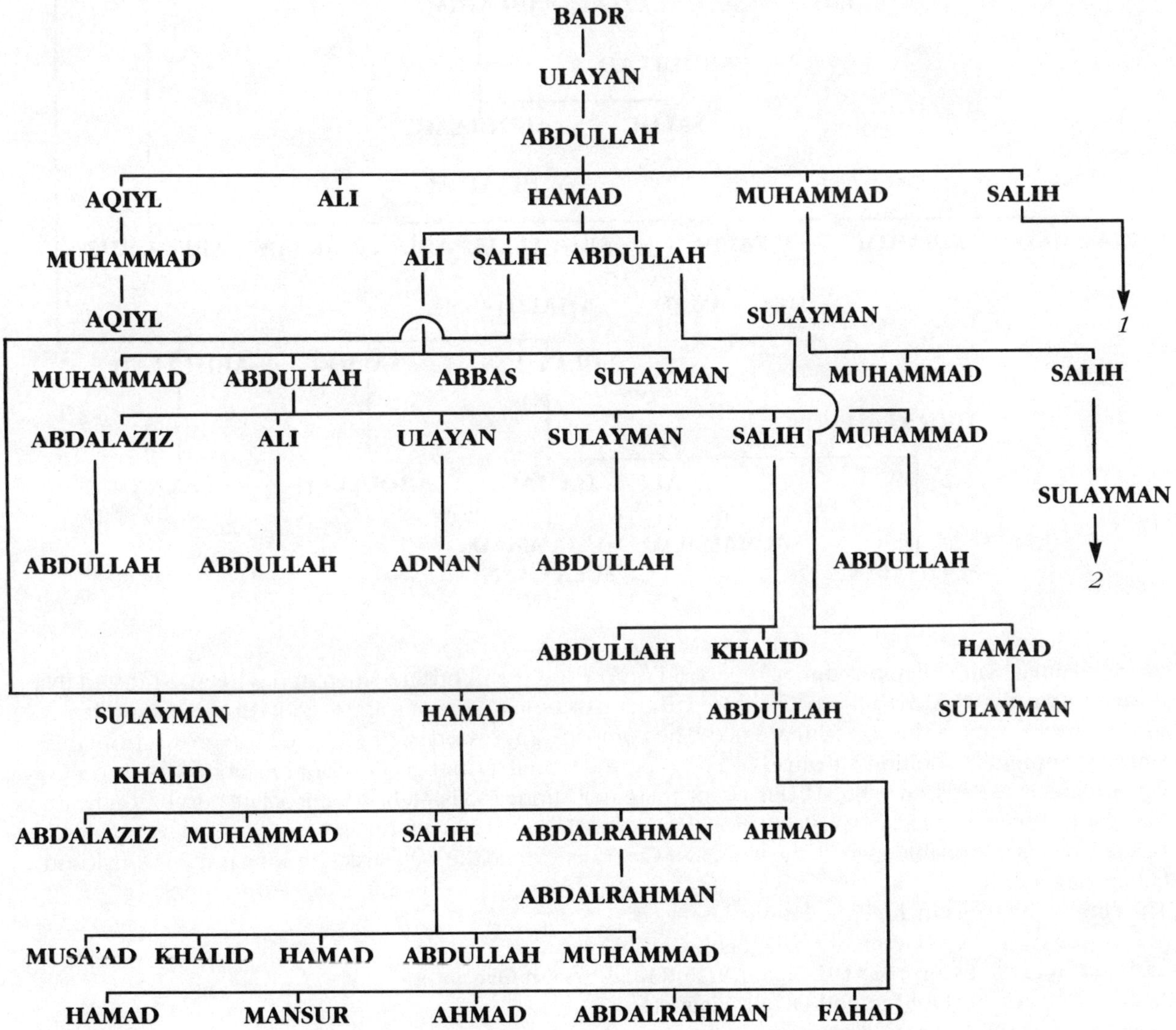

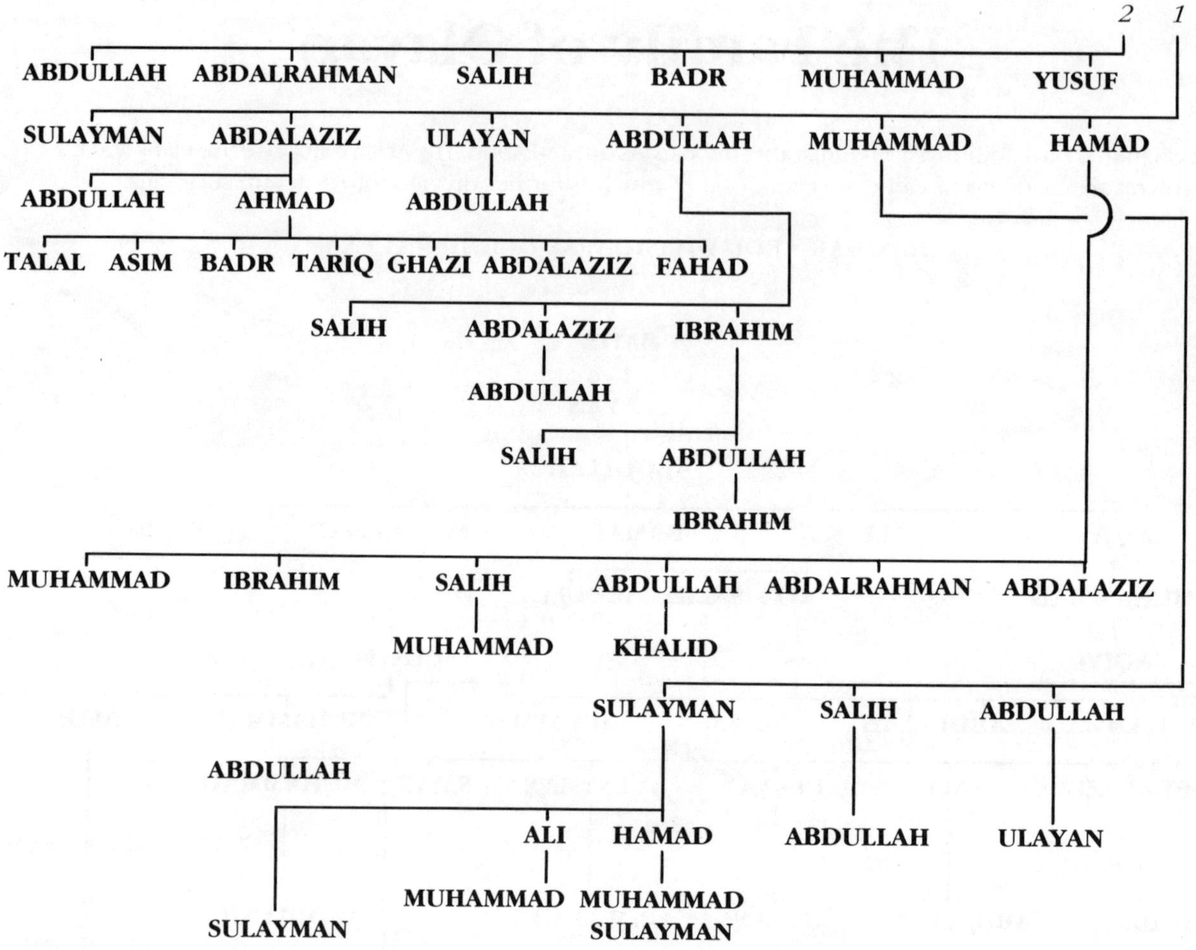

At 65 Sulaiman Salih Olayan is one of the world's most successful businessmen. It has been estimated that he may be worth some two billion dollars. He is the son of a spice merchant and founded a contracting firm in 1947 after giving up his job with Aramco. The company interests described here have grown from this small beginning. In addition Sulaiman owns 7.6 percent of First Chicago Corporation, about 10 percent of Chase Manhattan Bank, an interest in First Bank System of Minneapolis, Mellon Bank of Pittsburgh, Southeast Banking Corporation of Miami, Valley National Bank of Arizona and First Interstate Bancorp. of Los Angeles. He also owns a reasonable share in the Whittaker Corporation and the Wall Street broking firm of Donaldson, Lufkin and Leurette.

The family's interests include the following:

Ace Travel, owned by Hayat and Khalid Salih Olayan
Arab Commercial Enterprises Ltd, Sulaiman and Khalid Salih Olayan
Arabian Bechtel, Bechtel Inc. and Olayan Financing
Conam Services SA, Olayan Financing Co.
General Contracting Co., Sulaiman Olayan
General Trading Co., Sulaiman Salih and Khalid Sulaiman Olayan
Olayan Financing Co., Sulaiman Olayan
Olayan Saudi Holding Co., Olayan family
Owens Corning Saudi Co., J/V with Olayan Saudi Holding Co. and Owens Corning Fiberglass of the USA
Saudi Chemical Co., Olayan Financing Co. with Mawarid Investment Co., Nitro Nobel AB
Saudi Forwarding and Transportation Co. (SaudiTrans), Olayan Saudi Holding Co.
Saudi Polyester Products Co., Al Mawarid and Olayan Financing and Nobel Nitro
United Technologies Saudi Arabia Ltd, Olayan Financing, Al Mawarid and United Technologies Corporation

PHARAON BUSINESS INTERESTS

SAUDI RESEARCH AND DEVELOPMENT CORPORATION (REDEC)

Address head office P.O. Box 1935 Jiddah
Telephone 52940
Telex 401122 REDEC SJ
Cable address REDEC
Subsidiary offices
P.O.Box 611 Riyadh, tel. 61357/8/9, cable REDEC RIYADH, tlx. 201133
P.O.Box 998 Dammam, tel. 22011, 25421, cable REDEC DAMMAM, tlx. 601019
P.O.Box 2514 Beirut, 408 Starco North, tel. 296703, 290424, cable INTEREDEC BEIRUT, tlx. 20984 REDEC
61 Rue de la Boetie, 75008 Paris, France, cable REDEC PARIS, tel. 256 3860, tlx. 640997 REDEC
Via Della Camilluccia 697, 00135 Rome, cable ITEREDEC ROME, tel. 3279341-5, tlx 63067 REDEC
c/o Epirotiki Lines, Epirotiki Lines Building, 87 Andrea Mialuli, Piraeus, Greece, tel. 420648, tlx. EPIR 212302
28 Al Jalaa Street (Al Yazigi), PO.Box 3598, Damascus, Syria, tel. 332 588, tlx. 11358 REDEC
60 Park Lane, Flat 29, London W1, cable INTEREDEC LONDON, tel. 493 6595, 493 3580, tlx. 21253 INTEREDEC
100 Rue du Rhine, Geneva, Switzerland, tel. 289811/2/3, tlx. 28764 REDEC
Suite 2410, Penzoil Place, 700 Milam Street, Houston, Texas 77002, tel. 713 237 9216, tlx. 775022 ARAB CORP HOU
Proprietor The company is owned as follows:
Dr. Ghaith R Pharaon 61%; Sh. Wabel R Pharaon 25%; Mrs. Nada R Pharaon 7%; Sh. Hattan R Pharaon 7%.
Company History

The family arrived comparatively recently in the Kingdom and are said to descend from a lordly Kurd who was given the nickname of Pharaoh. Rashad, Ghaith's father, has advised all the kings of Saudi Arabia.

The family owns all of REDEC with Ghaith holding 61 percent. The widespread interests of the company cover banks, insurance, sewage treatment, hotels, shipping, real estate, finance, food, cement, refineries and buses.

The company's borrowing policy means it put one dollar to every four borrowed and thus loans to it are heavily oversubscribed.

REDEC favours operating in the USA. It owns International Systems of Mobile, a major interest in Hyatt International, Sam P. Wallace and the CRS Group. The expertise acquired has been put to use in major hotel, construction and engineering projects in Saudi Arabia. REDEC also has large real estate interests in the US. Ghaith Pharaon once controlled Detroit's Bank of the Commonwealth and twenty percent of Main Bank, Houston. He also holds almost all of the National Bank of Georgia.

Dr Pharaon has also been busy in Europe. He has acquired interests in France and Italy which support REDEC's food supply and supermarket operations. These have included BSN Gervaise Danone, Industrie Buitoni Perugina, Montedison, Société Nouvelle de Constructions Industrielles and Compagnie Internationale de Dessalement.

REDEC has bought a cement plant in Canada, owns hotels in Macao and the Gambia, palmoil processing in Malaysia and an interest in a Brasilian investment company.

The Family of Pharaon

It was Tawfiq Pharaon and his half brother Sabri Al Taba'a who created the opportunity for the family to come to Saudi Arabia from Syria. Tawfiq sold camels to the Turks. When he bought some from King Abdalaziz in 1916 the British objected and these two were imprisoned by the King in somewhat luxurious circumstances. Salim was also liked by the oldest son of the King, the Emir Turki, who died of Asian 'flu in 1919. Dr Rashad came to the Kingdom in 1936 and worked with Dr Midhat Shaykh Al Ardh as the King's physician. Sagri finally settled with King Abdullah in Jordan.
The ancestor of the family, Talib, is said to have been a Kurd and his lordly behaviour, dressed in trousers and carrying a whip, gained him the nickname of Pharaoh which has stuck with the family ever since.

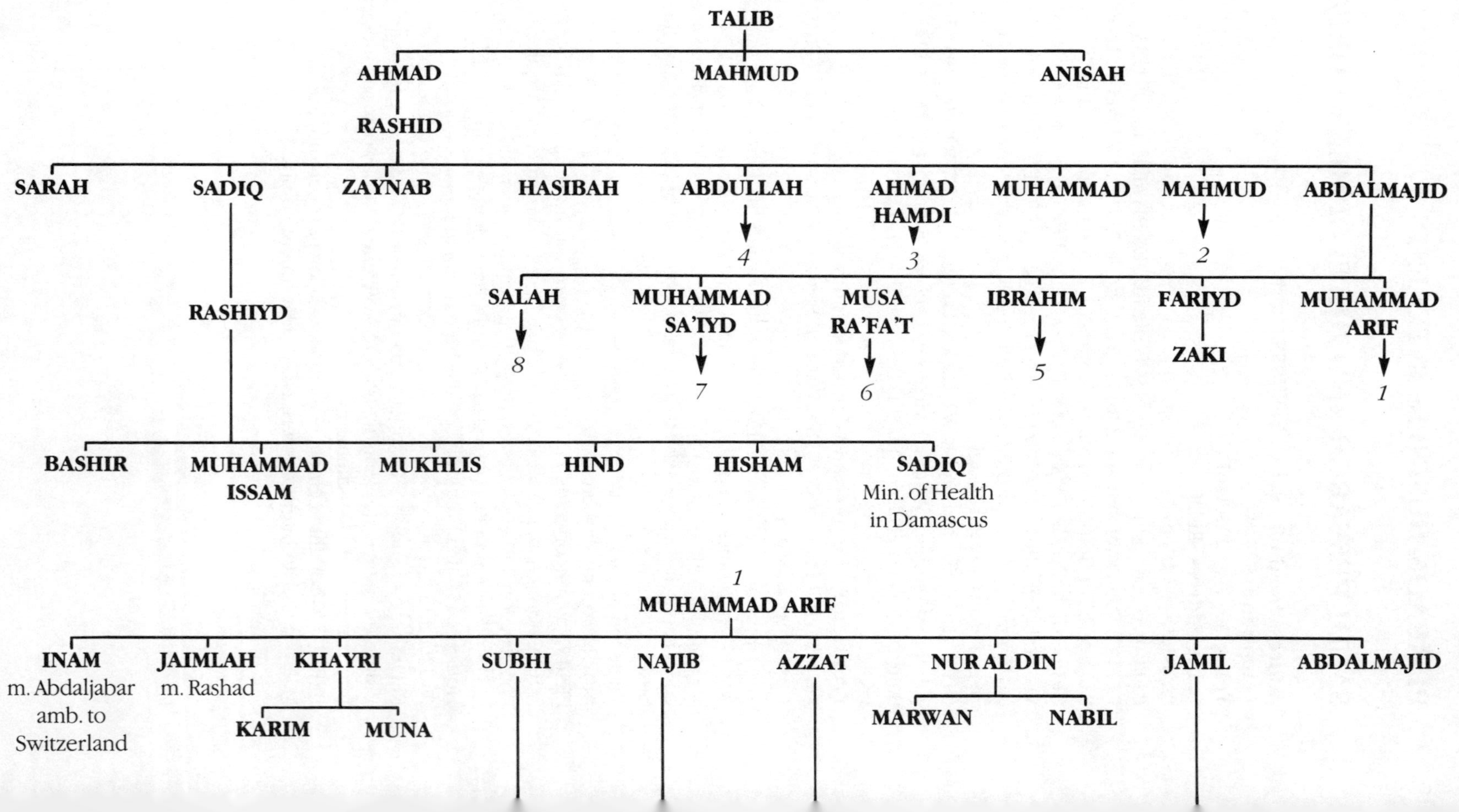

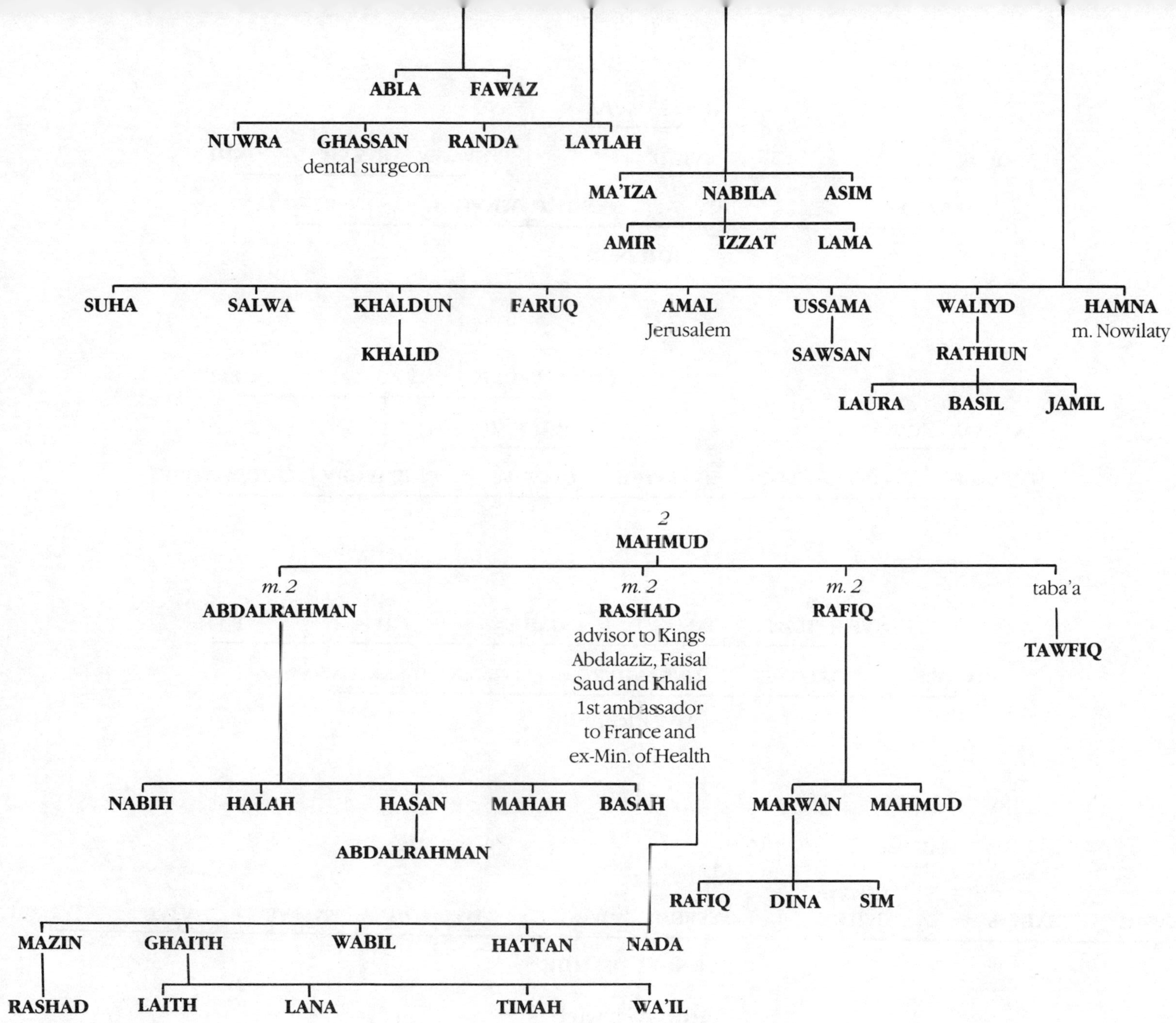
ABLA
FAWAZ
NUWRA
GHASSAN
dental surgeon
RANDA
LAYLAH
MA'IZA
NABILA
ASIM
AMIR
IZZAT
LAMA
SUHA
SALWA
KHALDUN
KHALID
FARUQ
AMAL
Jerusalem
USSAMA
SAWSAN
WALIYD
RATHIUN
LAURA
BASIL
JAMIL
HAMNA
m. Nowilaty
2
MAHMUD
m. 2
ABDALRAHMAN
m. 2
RASHAD
advisor to Kings
Abdalaziz, Faisal
Saud and Khalid
1st ambassador
to France and
ex-Min. of Health
m. 2
RAFIQ
taba'a
TAWFIQ
NABIH
HALAH
HASAN
ABDALRAHMAN
MAHAH
BASAH
MARWAN
MAHMUD
RAFIQ
DINA
SIM
MAZIN
RASHAD
GHAITH
LAITH
LANA
WABIL
HATTAN
TIMAH
NADA
WA'IL

3

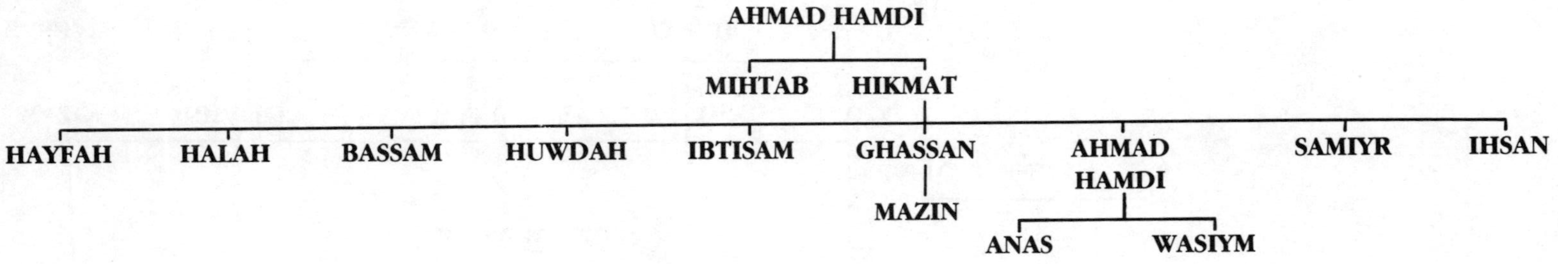
AHMAD HAMDI
MIHTAB
HIKMAT
HAYFAH
HALAH
BASSAM
HUWDAH
IBTISAM
GHASSAN
AHMAD HAMDI
SAMIYR
IHSAN
MAZIN
ANAS
WASIYM

4

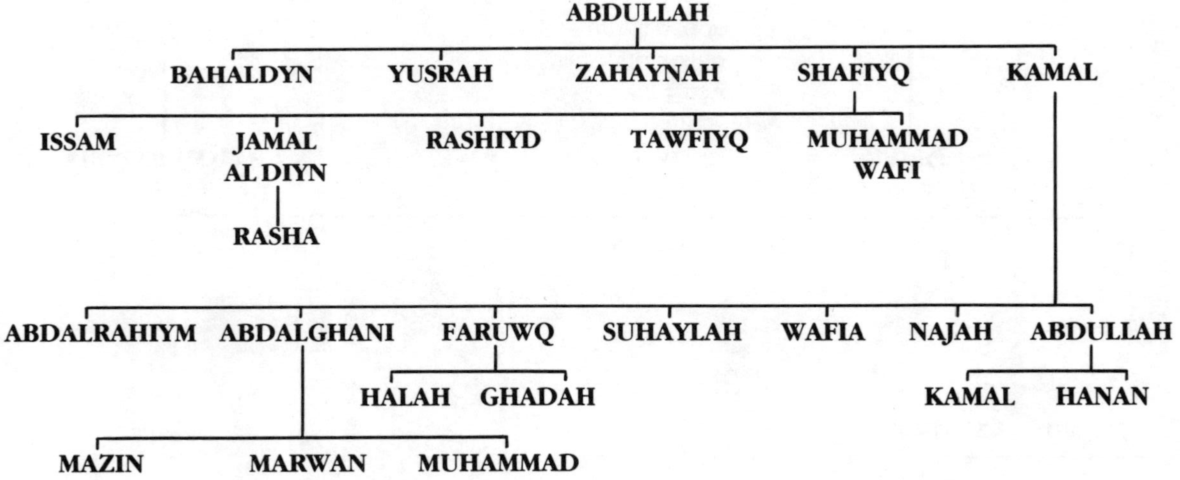
ABDULLAH
BAHALDYN
YUSRAH
ZAHAYNAH
SHAFIYQ
KAMAL
ISSAM
JAMAL AL DIYN
RASHIYD
TAWFIYQ
MUHAMMAD WAFI
RASHA
ABDALRAHIYM
ABDALGHANI
FARUWQ
SUHAYLAH
WAFIA
NAJAH
ABDULLAH
HALAH
GHADAH
KAMAL
HANAN
MAZIN
MARWAN
MUHAMMAD

5

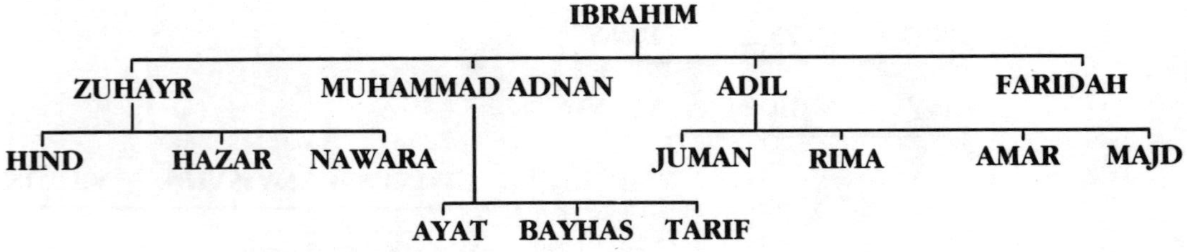
IBRAHIM
ZUHAYR
MUHAMMAD ADNAN
ADIL
FARIDAH
HIND
HAZAR
NAWARA
JUMAN
RIMA
AMAR
MAJD
AYAT
BAYHAS
TARIF

6

MUSA

- **SUHAYL**
  - HANI
  - DHAYALA
  - AMIR
- **HISHAM**
  - MUNA
  - ALIYA
  - RANIA
  - MUSA
- **ADNAN**
  - HANI
- **SAMI**
  - RANDA
  - BASMAH
  - RIMAH
  - BASSAM
- **BILQIS**
- **HASAN**
  - ALI
  - UMAR
  - TARIQ
- **SULAYMAN**
  - AMAD
  - UMRAN
  - YAMAN
  - LINA

7

SAIYD

- **GHAZI**
  - KHALDUN
  - KHALID
- **TAHSIN**
  - BASHAR
  - HANAN
  - HASNA
  - HASAN
  - WAFA
- **NASRAT**
  - MUHAMMAD SAIYD
  - LUTFIYAH
  - FAYSAL
- **RIFAT**
  - MA'MUN
  - HATUWN
  - WA'IL
  - MUHAMMAD RIYADH

8

SALAH

- **IMAN**
- **MUHAMMAD HAYTHAN**
  - SALAH
- **HALA**
- **NADIA**
- **LAYLA**

Redec was incorporated with limited liability in January 1966 and since that date has developed into a highly diversified holding company whose pre-eminent position in Saudi commercial affairs has been due to imaginative and positive management. The company is one of the largest employers in the Kingdom and has made a tremendous contribution to the development of the country.

Business Activities

The Company operates through nine major divisions:

1. The Engineering and Contracting Division

This division has developed special capabilities in the following fields: airport construction, high quality buildings, irrigation and drainage projects, industrial construction, water distribution systems, sewage systems and treatment plants, highway construction, and city beautification projects.

This division is involved in joint ventures with a number of firms with related capabilities: Incas Bona Saudi, 99% Redec owned, is involved with urban beautification and road construction.

Saudi Arabian Vianini, 60% Redec owned, designs and constructs ports, offshore facilities and irrigation projects.

Redec-Dailem, 50% Redec owned, and Saudi Arabian Parsons also 50% Redec owned, both design and construct heavy industrial and petrochemical complexes.

The activities of this division are supported by a very comprehensive training capacity operated in association with leading American and European firms. Its field operations are backed up by one of the world's largest and most up to date heavy equipment repair and parts supply facilities.

Lastly this division is fully integrated with International Systems Inc.of Mobile, Alabama. This company is 90% owned by Redec and specialises in the production of modular housing and solid concrete walled shipping containers.

2. The Industrial Division

This division, more than any of the others is responsible for Redec's contribution to the Saudi Arabian economy. This has been achieved by collaboration with leading international industrial companies, and this division manages Redec investment in enterprises that Redec itself has helped to create or that have especial promise. The division also works outside the Kingdom where Redec's investment programme can benefit research and development. Within the Kingdom the following areas of investment are managed by this division.

a. Water Bottling Plant producing under the brand name Safa with technical assistance from Evian.
b. Bus Assembly in Jiddah with Ward Industries of Conway, Arkansas.
c. Two steel fabrication workshops for the production of steel structures, pressure vessels and metal panels for housing.
d. An offroad tyre re-treading plant in Jiddah with Brad Ragan Inc. of North Carolina.
e. Pharmaceutical manufacturing with Sterling Drug International.
f. An industrial complex for manufacturing, construction and residential areas with full supporting services.

Among the heavy industry investments, where Redec's participation varies between 50% and 25%, made in collaboration with foreign companies within the Kingdom as well as abroad are the following:

a. A granular super phosphate plant.
b. A petrochemical plant at Jubail.
c. A reinforcing steel bar plant in Dammam.
d. A lube oil plant in Riyadh.
e. A salt extraction plant in Jubail.
f. A magnesite plant in the EasternProvince
g. A white sugar syrup plant in Hofuf.
h. An industrial gas plant in Jubail.
i. Sulphur slating in the Eastern Province.
j. A graphite and carbon industrial complex.

3. The Commercial Division

This division serves as Middle East representative for foreign firms interested in turnkey projects or equipment supply to the Saudi Government. Major representations include those for Finmecannica and Montedison of Italy, Balfour Beatty of the UK, VACRS and Bes Engineering Corporation of Taiwan, Mitsui of Japan and Mowlem Construction Co. of the UK.

The division supports its principals with a sophisticated information bank and very superior liaison facilities. It also assists with customs clearance, bid preparation and immigration.
4. The Catering Division
Possessing a versatile inventory of specialist equipment this division has provided the very best in catering services to some of the world's largest companies in the most remote areas of the Kingdom.
5. Desalination Division
Operating Redec's Saudi Desalination Company this division plays a prominent part in the development of the vital resource, fresh water, in the Kingdom.
6. Electro-Mechanical Division
This division provides design, consultancy, supervision, installation, operation and maintenance services to the Group as well as to outside clients.
In addition to this primary function the division is involved in a 50% joint venture operation with Foley Electric and Sam P Wallace of Dallas and in other ventures with the following:Balfour Kilpatrick International, China Technical Consultants, DRD Montagebau, Air et Chaleur.
7. Maritime Shipping Division
This division was established to undertake general sea-transport through two Saudi based shipping companies and a wholly owned Panamanian subsidiary. The division transports crude oil and dry cargo in its own ships, as well as passengers. The operation is managed by International Shipping Inc.
8. Trading Division
Managed by Redec's Intertrade subsidiary this division supplies the Saudi building industry with timber, cement, steel, pre-fabricated buildings, construction machinery, furniture and appliances.
9. Computer Services Division
Operating one of the two largest systems in the Kingdom this division is operated by a joint venture with Demographics Inc. of the USA called Saudi Computer Services (Demographics). They use an IBM 370/135 with a 384,000 character memory and four 3330 type disc drives with a capacity of 400 million characters. Initially oriented towards the needs of the construction industry this division has readily accommodated itself to the fields of banking, distribution and manufacturing as well as offering financial and accounting services.
Bankers National Commercial Bank, First National City Bank.

NABIL ESTABLISHMENT FOR TRADING AND IMPORT

Address P.O. 3558 Jiddah
Telephone 6654785
Owned by Nabil Nuri Pharaon the company is a building contracting business that also supplies electronic components and equipment.

AL RASHAD CLINIC

Address P.O. 7286 Jiddah
Telephone 6519748, 6519752
Telex 401122 REDEC SJ
The clinic is owned by Dr Rashad Pharaon.

ROSENTHAL STUDIO LINIE

Address P.O. 7378 Jiddah
Telephone 6892338, 6652037
Established in 1979 this company is owned by Nabih Pharaon and managed by Inge Pharaon. They supply decorating materials, china and glassware.

ARABIAN INVESTMENTS COMPANY LIMITED

Address P.O. 6471 Jiddah
Telephone 6692203, 6692206
Telex 400043 HOFNA SJ
The company has a wide range of activities including acting as architects and contractors. They also deal in sanitary ware, cleaning, clothing , textiles, building materials, food, furniture and household goods, as well as hotels, investment, restaurants and manpower. The company is owned by Mazin Rashad Pharaon and co-managed by him and Hattan Rashad Pharaon.

ARABIAN PETROLEUM COMPANY

Address P.O. 6471 Jiddah
Telephone 6692203, 6692206
Telex 400042 AIDA SJ, 400043 HOFNA SJ
Owned by Mazin and Hattan Rashad Pharaon this company, formed in 1980, deals with oil companies for drilling and prospecting, oil, tankers, and oil refining machinery and maintenance.

AL DAMMAM NAVIGATION COMPANY LIMITED

Address P.O. 6471 Jiddah
Telephone 6674628, 6675792, 6659672
Telex 400042 AIDA SJ, 400043 HOFNA SJ
Owned by Mazin Rashad and his son Rashad the company is managed by Hattan Rashad Pharaon. It was formed in 1976 and deals in marine charter and transport services.

AL FADHIL NAVIGATION CO. LTD

Address P.O. 6471 Jiddah
Telephone 6674628, 6692206, 6691707, 6691699
Telex 400042 AIDA SJ, 400043 HOFNA SJ
Set up in 1978 this company deals in transport services and marine charter. It is owned by Hattan and Mazin Rashad Pharaon and Rashad Mazin.

JIDDAH DENTAL CLINIC

Address P.O. 4553 Jiddah
Telephone 6692904, 6658784, 6658516
Telex 402476 PHARO SJ
Owned by Dr Ghassan Najib Pharaon this concern operates both medical and dental clinics.

ARABIAN HOMES

Address P.O. 4553 Jiddah
Telephone 6828381, 6824210
Telex 403229, ARAHOM SJ
Building Contractors, Development Projects, Turnkey, Rental and Real Estate.

INTRASS INTERNATIONAL FORWARDING

Address P.O. 7378 Jiddah
Telephone 6671830
Telex 400655 BINKAI SJ
The company has a branch in Dammam and is owned by Nabih Pharaon and is concerned with international forwarding and trading.

JUBAIL NAVIGATION CO. LTD.

Address PO Box 6471, Jiddah
Telephone 6692203, 6692206
Telex 400042 AIDA SJ, 400043 HOFNA SJ
A marine charter and transport company formed in 1979 and owned by Mazin and Hattan Rashad Pharaon and Rashad Mazin.

KHAFJI NAVIGATION CO. LTD.

Address PO Box 6471, Jiddah
Telephone 6692203, 6692206
Telex 400042 AIDA SJ, 400043 HOFNA SJ
A marine charter and transport services company formed in 1977 and owned by Mazin and Hattan Rashad Pharaon and Rashad Mazin.

KHURAIS NAVIGATION CO. LTD

Address PO Box 6471 Jiddah
Telephone 6674628, 6675792, 6659672
Telex 400042 AIDA SJ, 400043 HOFNA SJ
A marine charter and transport service company formed in 1979 and owned by Mazin Rashad Pharaon and his son Rashad.

AL MABANI-ICORI ESTERO SA

Address PO Box 2141, Jiddah
Telephone 6604625
Telex 450090 MICESA SJ
Set up with their head office in Taif, in 1972, this company of building, road and drainage contractors is owned by Mazin Rashad Pharaon, Raja Salim Saab and Arcan.

NATIONAL BUNKERING CO.LTD

Address PO Box 6471, Jiddah
Telephone 6692206, 6692203, 6691706, 6691699
Telex 400042 AIDA SJ, 400043 HOFNA SJ
Formed in 1977 this company is owned by Mazin and Hattan Rashad Pharaon, Rashad Mazin and Khalid Aswad. The company supplies marine equipment, deals in marine charter and ship bunkering, and acts as a commission agent.

NATIONAL MAINTENANCE CO. LTD.

Address PO Box 6471, Jiddah
Telephone 6718579, 6715223
Telex 400043 HOFNA SJ
A company dealing in air-conditioning equipment and acting as an air-conditioning contractor. Owned by Mazin Pharaon.

SAFFANIA NAVIGATION CO. LTD

Address PO Box 6471, Jiddah
Telephone 6674628, 6675792, 6659672
Telex 400042 AIDA SJ, 400043 HOFNA SJ
A transport services company formed in 1979 and owned by Mazin and Hattan Rashad Pharaon and Rashad Mazin.

SAUDI TRADERS CO. LTD

Address PO Box 5413, Jiddah
Telephone 6657195, 6654162
Telex 402079 YAZAN SJ
Founded in 1976 this company is owned by Wabil Rashad Pharaon and Asim H Pharaon.

WABIL CONTRACTING CO. (WABELCO)

Address PO Box 7882, Jiddah
Telephone 6601720, 6670029, 6674083
The company was formed in 1979 and is owned by Wabil Rashad Pharaon. It is a building, electrical and mechanical contractor.

WABIL TRAVEL CO. LTD

Address PO Box 1935, Jiddah
Telephone 6448724
Telex 401122 SROC SJ
Owned by Wabil Rashad Pharaon and established in 1977 the company has a Dammam branch and is in a travel agency.

GENERAL NAVIGATION CO. LTD

Address PO Box 6471, Jiddah
Telephone 6692203, 6692206
Telex 400042 AIDA SJ, 400043 HOFNA SJ
Owned by Mazin Rashad and his son Rashad, this marine charter and transport services company was formed in 1979.

GHAWAR NAVIGATION CO. LTD

Address PO Box 6471, Jiddah
Telephone 6674628, 6692203, 6692206, 6691707, 6691699
Telex 400042 AIDA SJ, 400043 HOFNA SJ, 402080 AICO SJ, 400540 HRP SJ
A company trading as ship chandlers and charterers, with bunker and transport services. It was formed in 1977 and is owned by Mazin Rashad Pharaon.

HAQL NAVIGATION CO. LTD

Address PO Box 6471, Jiddah
Telephone 6692203, 6692206
Telex 400042 AIDA SJ, 400043 HOFNA SJ
A marine charter and transport services company owned by Mazin Rashad and his son Rashid. Established in 1979.

AL HOFUF NAVIGATION CO. LTD

Address PO Box 6471, Jiddah
Telephone 6692203, 6692206
Telex 4000AIDA SJ, 400043 HOFNA SJ
A marine charter and transport services company owned by Mazin Rashad, his brother Hattan, and his son Rashad.

PHARAON (GHAITH)
FALCON CEMENT

Address P.O. 1935 Jiddah
Telephone 6439210
Telex 400709 SAFA SJ
Owned by Dr Ghaith Rashad Pharaon the company deals in cement and has branches in Riyadh, Dammam, Yanbu and Jizan.

IN CAS BONNA SAUDI ARABIA

Address P.O. 4360 Jiddah
Telephone 6691306, 6600696
Telex 402474 INBO SJ
A joint venture between Dr Ghaith Pharaon and Montedison of Switzerland which was formed in 1976 and is engaged in quarrying and the supply of aggregates; the manufacture and supply of bitumen and asphalt and in building contracting and road construction.

INTERDEC ASWAD CONTRACTING AND ENGINEERING CO LTD

Address P.O. 1935 Jiddah
Telephone 6435312, 6435298, 6448498
Telex 401122 REDEC SJ
A company of contractors for civil, mechanical, electrical, roads, drainage, and pipeline work which also supplies building materials. It was formed in 1978 and is owned by Dr Ghaith Pharaon and Hazem F. Aswad.

INTERNATIONAL BUSINESS FORMS (IBF)

Address P.O. 1935 Jiddah
Telephone 6824864
Telex 401122 REDEC SJ
Owned by Dr Ghaith Pharaon this is a company of printers.

MECCA WATER COMPANY

Address P.O. 1935 Jiddah
Telephone 6448880, 6448498
Telex 401122 REDEC SJ
Established in 1976 to supply drinking water, desalination plant and equipment, this company is owned by REDEC and Dr Ghaith Pharaon.

RED SEA CEMENT JIDDAH CO.

Address P.O. 1935
Telephone 6448880, 6445413
Telex 401122 SRDC SJ
The company was formed in 1979 and is owned by Dr Ghaith Pharaon in partnership with Salih b. Mahfouz (q.v.) and Abdullah Baroom (q.v.).

AL SABAH MARITIME SERVICES CO. LTD.

Address P.O. 5650 Jiddah
Telephone 6445369, 6445139, 6441887, 6424286, 6365352
Telex 400363 SMSCO SJ, 401695 SABAH SJ
The company is a partnership between Dr Ghaith Pharaon and Ali Muhammad Al Ghamdi. There are branches in Dammam, Jizan and Yanbu and the company is involved with local transport services, shipping companies and as clearing and forwarding agents.

SAUDI COMPUTER SERVICES LTD.

Address P.O. 1935
Telephone 6448880, 6448331
Telex 401112 SRDC SJ
Owned by Dr Ghaith Pharaon and REDEC the company was established in 1976. There are branches in Riyadh (P.O. 611, Tel. 4764088) and Dammam (P.O. 998, Tel. 8322011). The company is concerned with computer and business systems, and management consultancy. It represents Texas Instruments, CICOM, MEMOREX, Software International and MICOR.

SAUDI FOOD CO. LTD.

Address P.O. 1935 Jiddah
Telephone 6448383, 6448880
Telex 400709 SAFA SJ
The company was established in 1977 and is owned by Dr Ghaith Rashad Pharaon and his son Laith. It is engaged in trading in foodstuffs, fruit, vegetables and frozen meat.

The Family of Al Quraishi

The family has its origins in Bani Khalid of Ha'il.

ALI

ZAID

ALI
Ptnr.

ABDALAZIZ
Governor of SAMA

KHALID
Ptnr. in Jiddah

SALIH
Ptnr.

ABDALKARIM
Ptnr. in Dammam

ABDALRAZZAQ
Ptnr.

2 daughters
1 m. Saudi ambassador to Dubai
2 m. in Kuwait

ALI ZAID AL QURAISHI AND BROTHERS

Address head office P.O.Box 339 Dammam
Telephone 21596, 21790
Telex 601058 AZAQ SJ
Proprietor The company is a partnership between the brothers who controlAZAQ, the holding company, which is responsible for group planning financial control and development. In this way they direct the operations of the following members of the group:
1. AQOS which operates agencies for cigarettes.
2. AQ Leisure Services operating further agencies for Dunhill and also Shaeffer, Ronson and Canon.
3. WESCOSA which handles the distribution of electical supply equipment as well as manufacture.
4. AQ Furniture Corporation. Responsible for retail and contract furnishing, office planning and design, and the distribution of Westinghouse Architectural Systems and Design.
5. Bowater Arabia which handles contract furnishing for hotels and domestic housing and operates a complete design and installation system.
6. Teamwork. This is a 50/50 partnership with Taylor Woodrow.
7. AQ Shipping Agencies which operates a complete service for shipping, clearing and forwarding.
8. AQ Investments. This company deals in financial investment property and new venture investment.

The Family of Silsilah

A family of Mecca

- **ABDULRAHIM SILSILAH**
  - **IBRAHIM**
    ex-Director General of Posts and Telecommunications before this organisation became a Ministry, whose sister married Abdullah Rajab
    - **ABDULLAH**
      Partner in Rajab and Silsilah
      - **USSAMA**
      - **AYMAN**

The Family of Rajab

A family of Jiddah

- **RAJAB**
  - **ABDULLAH**
    - **ABDALQADIR**
      Electrical Marketing Establishment Jiddah
      - **SAMIR**
      - **TALAL**
      - **WALID**
      - **BASSAM**
      - **NABIL**
    - **UMAR**
      Engineering and Electrical Establishment, Jiddah
      - **IHAB**
      - **NIHAD**
      - **RA'ID**
    - **ABDALAZIZ**
      Partner in Rajab and Silsilah
      - **KHALID**
      - **JAMAL**

A RAJAB AND A SILSILAH COMMERCIAL DIVISION

Address head office PO Box 203, Jiddah
Telephone 6424417, 6425188, 6425382, 6438571
Telex 401180 ARNDAS SJ
Activities The company is owned equally by Abdalaziz Abdullah Rajab and Abdullah Ibrahim Silsilah, and has branches in Mecca, Riyadh, Dammam and al Khobar.

Company History

The company was started in 1945 as an import company supplying electrical and electronic equipment, consumer goods and household appliances. With foresight a projects department was established twenty-two years ago and presaged the company's present development. Today the company represents considerable overseas interests and operates on a broadfront with particular specialisation in generating installations, street lighting, fittings, scientific and industrial equipment, cables, fire alarms, power stations and telecommunications.

Brand names represented are Philips, Leonard, Union Carbide, Tecnogas, H D Sheldon, Horst G F von Valtier, Antiference, Nippon Gakki.

Project Division

This part of the company was established in 1962 in Riyadh (PO Box 2815, tel. 4788070, 4781320, 4764056, 4761092, tlx. 201331 ARNDAS SJ). It is really a separate commercial entity and has its own branches in Mecca, Dammam and al Khobar. It deals with the maufacture of aluminium products, aviation and airport construction supplies, computer and business systems. The company acts as electrical, mechanical and communications consultants as well as being contractors for electrical and mechanical engineering and communications. They supply glass, mirrors and frames, power transmission, security and traffic signal equipment. This division represents the following brand names: Philips, Motoren Werke Mannheim (MWM), ICL, E Erni, E G Kistenmacher, Cable Export, Pye Dynamic, Pye Unicam, American Export Group, Le Grand and Aluminium Wire and Cable.

Associated Companies

1. Saudi Trading Co. for consumer products and contracting. This company is wholly owned by the partnership and trades in fertilizers and chemicals operating in Jiddah.
2. Rajab and Tayeb Co. in Riyadh. A partnership between Rajab and Silsilah and Ahmed Tayeb working as electrical and mechanical contractors.
3. Saudi Air Conditioning Co. in Jiddah and Riyadh specialising in installation and maintenance; this company is a partnership between Rajab and Silsilah and various other partners.
4. Arabian Mechanical and Electrical Contracting Co. (AMECCO) in Riyadh.
5. Sagr Insurance Co. Saudi Arabi Ltd. This is a joint venture company with Hong Kong Middle East Holdings Ltd. The partners in Saudi Arabia are:

Sh. Abdullah Ibrahim Silsilah
Sh. Abdalaziz Abdullah Rajab
Sh. Abdalra'ouf Abu Zinada (q.v.)
Sh. Zaid Muhammad Al Sudairi
Sh. Saad Muhammad Al Mo'ajil (q.v.)
Sh. Abdalatif Banajah
Sh. Abdalrahman Turki

Bankers Arab Bank, National Commercial Bank, Riyadh Bank, Saudi Hollandi Bank, Saudi Britani Bank, First National City Bank.

RAJAB TRADING, IMPORT AND ELECTRICAL CONTRACTING

Address head office PO Box 356, Jiddah
Telephone 6651513
Telex 400873 HAMIDCO SJ
Activities Owned by Ibrahim Abdalwahhab Rajab and formed in 1974, this company is active as electrical and building contractors, suppliers of sanitary ware, household equipment, foodstuffs and electrical equipment.

SAUDI TRADING AND DISTRIBUTION CO.

Address head office PO Box 6533, Jiddah
Telephone 6654137, 6693093
Telex 401810 ULMEL SJ
Activities A partnership between Abdalaziz Abdullah Rajab and Abdullah Silsilah which was formed in 1977. Here they are concerned as commission agents for consumer products, dealing also in agricultural and industrial chemicals and fertilisers. They are also polythene maufacturers and suppliers.

SAMIR SHAIKH ALI TRADING ESTABLISHMENT

Address head office PO Box 7676, Jiddah
Telephone 6511608
Telex 402129 RANDAM SJ
Activities The company dates from 1976 and is a partnership between Umar Abdullah Rajab and Jamal Muhammad Malki. There is a branch in Ta'if. They are engaged in the supply of furnishings, household equipment and building materials as well as air conditioners. They are contractors for air conditioning, building, decorating and electrical equipment.

ELECTRICAL ENGINEERING CORPORATION

Address head office PO Box 1082, Jiddah
Telephone 6535031, 6534787
Telex 401607 EECRJB SJ
Activities Established in 1946, this company is owned by Umar Abdullah Rajab and has branches in Riyadh, Dammam, Ta'if and Mecca. They distribute adding machines, cassettes and tapes, air conditioners, cleaning machinery and cleaning products, compressors, electrical equipment, furniture, generators, motors, water coolers and heaters, office equipment, housewares and kitchen equipment.

AL RAJHI BUSINESS INTERESTS

AL RAJHI COMPANY FOR EXCHANGE AND COMMERCE

Address PO Box 28, Riyadh
Telephone 4836922, 4836606, 4836606, 4835644, 4836977
Telex 201073 RAJHI SJ, 201630 RAJH SJ
Branches Jiddah, PO Box 605, tel. 6447674, 6447675, tlx. 401058 RAJHI SJ, and some eighty other branches throughout the Kingdom.
Board Members
Sh. Salih Abdalaziz Al Rajhi
Abdullah Abdalaziz Al Rajhi
Sulaiman Abdalaziz Al Rajhi
Muhammad Abdalaziz Al Rajhi
Company History
Salih Abdalaziz Al Rajhi, who is 62, is the Chairman of this company. He began in partnership with his brother Sulaiman in Qasim as a foreign exchange dealer in the 1930s. Following the lure of the potential of the pilgrim trade, they later moved and established offices in Jiddah, Makkah and Madinah. Later they became advisors to King Faisal in the days before the oil boom. Salih is probably worth a billion dollars today and has disclaimed any direct or indirect relationship with his sons' unfortunate speculations in 1982.
The company was formed in 1978 by merging the banking interests of Sh. Salih, Sh. Abdullah and Sh. Sulaiman with the contracting business of Sh. Muhammad. The resulting company is the giant of the family concerns and controls enormous real estate holdings and huge interests in national industries and factories.
The company is engaged in currency exchange, dealing in currency throughout the world as well as bullion. There is hardly a country in the world with which the company does not correspond.

AL RAJHI AND AL SEDAIS COMPANY

Address PO Box 1597, Jiddah
Telephone 6880509, 6880868
Telex 401311 THENCO SJ
With branches in Riyadh, Dammam and Buraidah and Abha, this company is owned by Sulaiman Abdalaziz Al Rajhi and Abdalaziz Ali Sedais. They act as commission agents and contractors for building, decorating, dredging, demolition, drilling, electrical engineering, plumbing and pipeline installation and drilling. They are associated with shipping companies and operate poultry farms and coldstores.
The company owns as a subsidiary to the partnership Al Rajhi and Al Sedais Jewellery (PO Box 7940 Jiddah, tel. 6423815, 6424097, 6420934; tlx. 401058 RAJHI SJ). As their name implies this firm is concerned with the jewellery trade and was formed in 1979.

AL RAJHI AUTOPARTS

Address PO Box 3844 Jiddah
Telephone 6317592, 6317609
Telex 401321 SPARME SJ
A company dealing in car accessories and spare parts which is owned by Salih Abdullah Abdalaziz Al Rajhi.

The Family of Al Rajhi

There are over seven hundred male members of this family, which originates from the Al Bukhariya in Qasim and is Bani Zayd of Qahtan.

NASIR AL RAJHI
(Al Kabir)

HAMAD
ALI
MANSUR
MUHAMMAD
ALI
ABDALAZIZ
ABDULLAH

ABDULLAH
settled in Burayda and his 2 sons migrated to Syria. Their descendants returned to Saudi Arabia, but only 2 left of this branch by 1979

SULAIMAN

MUHAMMAD **MANSUR**

MUHAMMAD
MUHAMMAD
ALI
ABDALAZIZ
ABDULLAH

ABDULLAH **SULAIMAN**
SALIH

MUHAMMAD d. **ABDALAZIZ**

SALIH

SALIH
has some 43 children, eldest are:
ABDALRAHMAN[1]
ABDULLAH[2]
SULAIMAN[3]
ABDALMUHSIN
NASIR
MUHAMMAD
KHALID
BANDAR
ABDULILLAH

ABDULLAH
has some 28 children, eldest are:
MUHAMMAD
SALIH
ABDALRAHMAN
SULAIMAN
AHMAD
YUSIF

SULAYMAN
has 26, children, the eldest are:
SALIH[4]
ABDULLAH
MUHAMMAD
FAHD
ABDALRAHMAN
KHALID

MUHAMMAD
has 16, children, the eldest are:
MANSUR
SALIH
KHALID
ABDALKARIM
BADR

SALIH **HAMAD** **ALI** **MUHAMMAD** **SULAIMAN**

SALIH
MUHAMMAD
ABDULLAH
SALIH
ABDALAZIZ
ALI
ABDALRAHMAN

MUHAMMAD
ALI
Head of Jiddah office of Al Rajhi Co. Exchange and Trade
sister m. Sulayman b. Abdalaziz

ABDULLAH **MUHAMMAD** **YASIR**

SULAIMAN
ABDULLAH
MUHAMMAD

[1]owner of Al Rajhi Trading Establishment
[2]owner of Abdullah Salih al Rajhi Est.
[3]Foreign Exchange Dept. of Al Rajhi Co. in Riyadh for Exchange and Trade.
[4]in Riyadh.

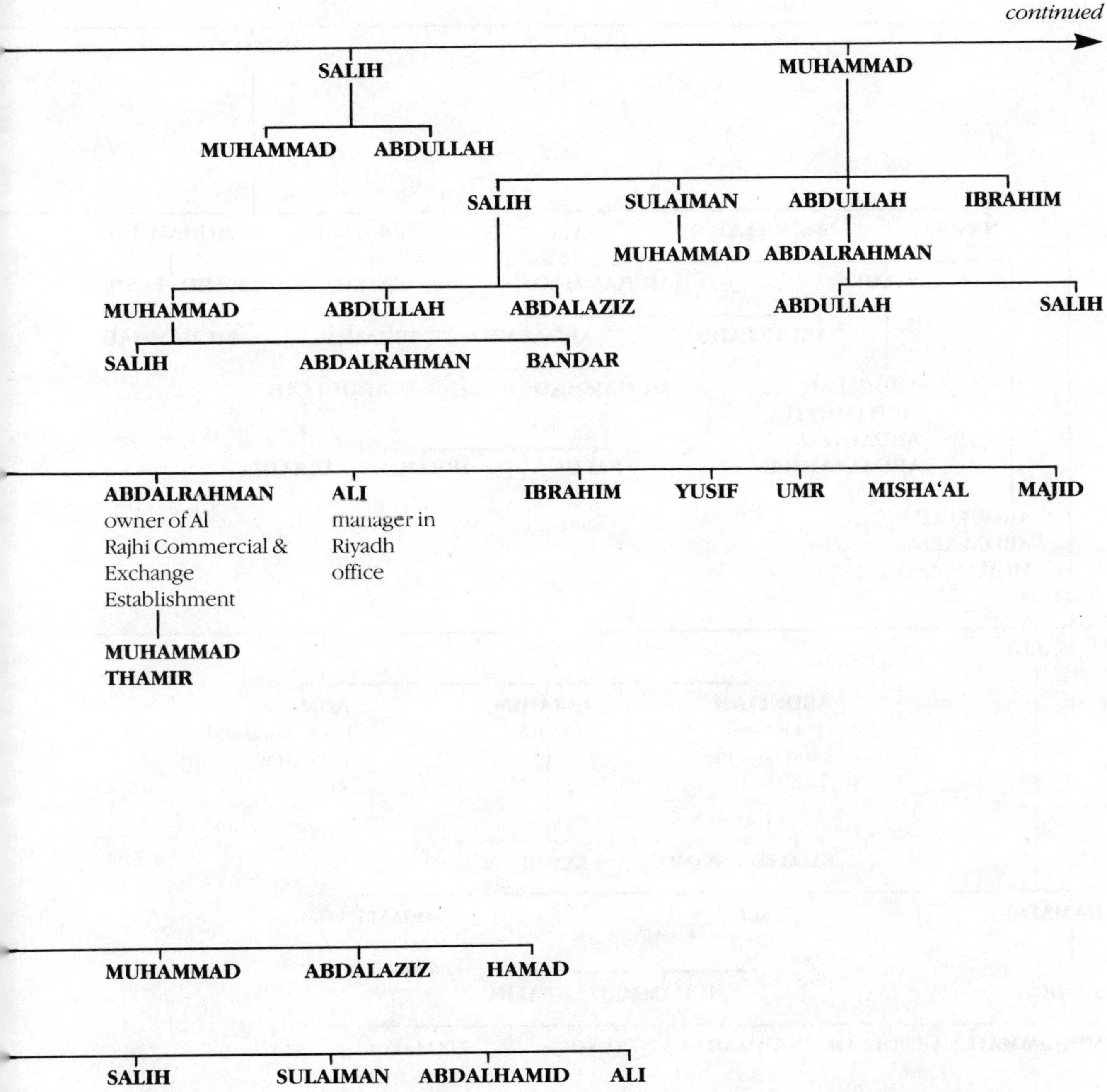

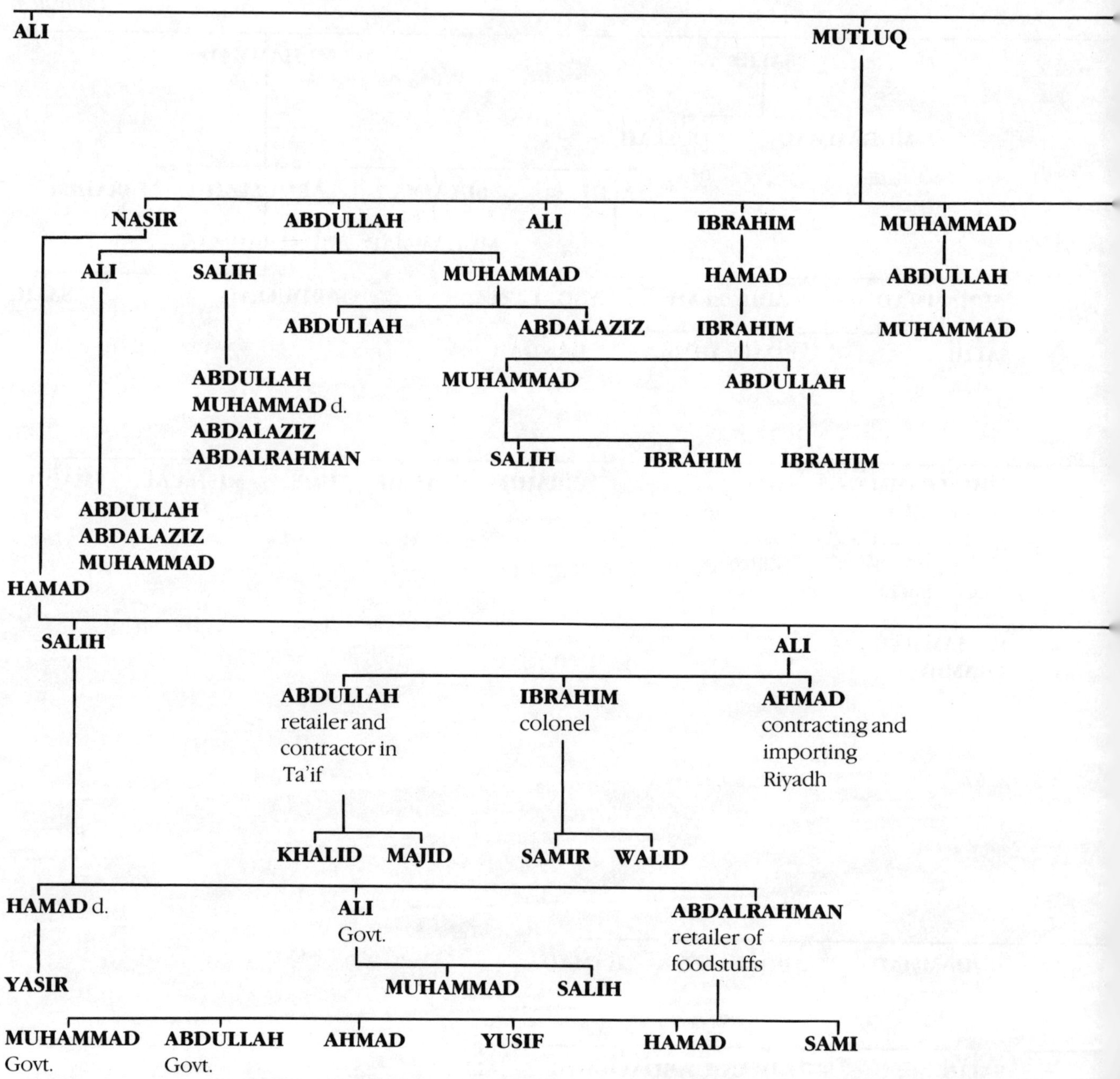
ALI
MUTLUQ
NASIR
ABDULLAH
ALI
IBRAHIM
MUHAMMAD
ALI
SALIH
MUHAMMAD
HAMAD
ABDULLAH
ABDULLAH
ABDALAZIZ
IBRAHIM
MUHAMMAD
MUHAMMAD
ABDULLAH
ABDULLAH
MUHAMMAD d.
ABDALAZIZ
ABDALRAHMAN
SALIH
IBRAHIM
IBRAHIM
ABDULLAH
ABDALAZIZ
MUHAMMAD
HAMAD
SALIH
ALI
ABDULLAH
retailer and
contractor in
Ta'if
IBRAHIM
colonel
AHMAD
contracting and
importing
Riyadh
KHALID
MAJID
SAMIR
WALID
HAMAD d.
ALI
Govt.
ABDALRAHMAN
retailer of
foodstuffs
YASIR
MUHAMMAD
SALIH
MUHAMMAD
Govt.
ABDULLAH
Govt.
AHMAD
YUSIF
HAMAD
SAMI

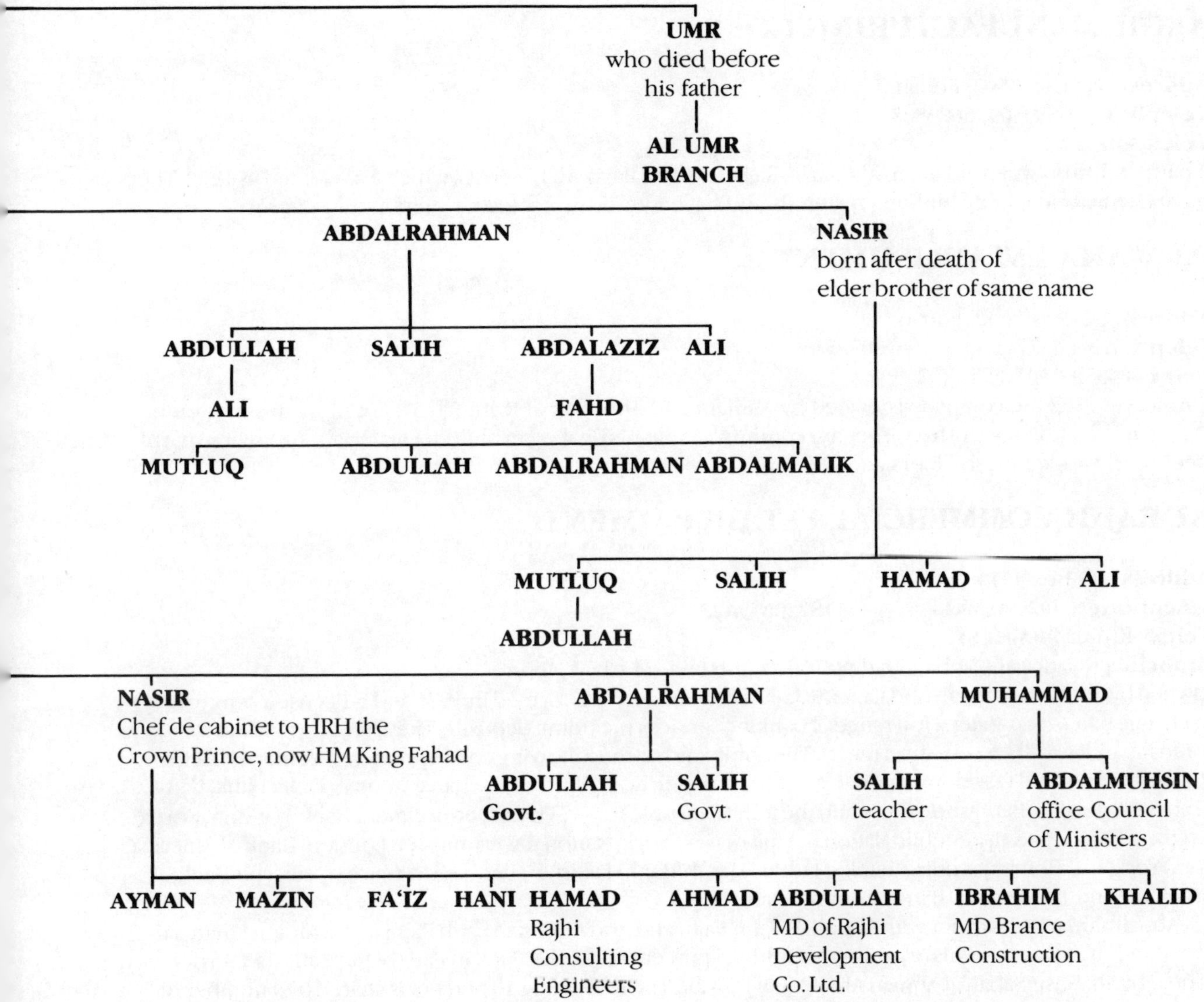

All these brothers are members of the Board of the Rajhi Development Co. Ltd.

ARABIAN GULF MANUFACTURING LTD

Address PO Box Jiddah
Telephone 6871808, 6870781, 6424493, 6797916
Telex 400229 PLASTIC SJ
Owned by Sulaiman A Al Rajhi, Abdalaziz Tayar and the heirs of Hashim Sadiq Hashim, this company manufactures plastic products and supplies pipes and fittings.

ARGIL MANUFACTURING CO.

Address PO Box 1597, Jiddah
Telephone 6880509, 6880868
Telex 401311
A partnership between Sulaiman Abdalaziz Rajhi and Abdalaziz Ali El Sedais, which was formed in 1978. They manufacture and supply building materials and have interests in coldstores and poultry farms.

AL WAHA ESTABLISHMENT

Address PO Box 2632, Jiddah
Telephone 6447741, 6431298, 6872513
Telex 401740 WAHEST SJ
Formed in 1972 the company is owned by Muhammad Abdullah al Rajhi. There are branches in Riyadh, Dammam and Khamis Mushayt. They are commission agents dealing in building materials, supplying marble, steel, steel welded mesh, doors and windows.

AL RAJHI COMMERCIAL ESTABLISHMENT

Address PO Box 4514, Jiddah
Telephone 6442590, 6444465, 6431182, 6659422
Telex 401602 ARAJHI SJ
Branches Riyadh, Al Khobar, Madina, Yanbu, Khamis, Mushayt, Jizan
Owned by Sh. Abdalrahman Abdalaziz Al Rajhi, the company was formed in 1975 and is licensed as a currency exchange bank; it operates a full range of banking services including deposits. They rarely operate as a source for loans and if at all on very short terms. The company has the following correspondents: Yemen Bank for Reconstruction and Development, San'a', Arab Bank Beirut, Halim Sulfiete Bank Amman, Delta Bank, Cairo, Arab Bank, Jordan, Banque du Caire and the National Bank, Egypt, Trade Development Bank, London, Korea Exchange Bank, Seoul, Republic National Bank of New York, National Westminster, London, Bank of America, New York and Bombay, Indian Bank, Madras, Habib Bank, Pakistan, Bank Misr, Cairo, Deutsche Bank, Frankfurt and Düsseldorf, Banca Commerciale, Milan.
Sh. Abdalrahman is a partner with Abdullah Salih Rajhi and Abdalrahman Salih Rajhi in the Alrajhi Financial Corporation in Geneva. This organisation holds 45 percent of the IFA Bank in Paris, where another 45 percent is held by Sh. Nasir Sabah al Ahmad Al Sabah of Kuwait. The remaining 10 percent is shared by a number of other Arabian companies.

ALRAJHI GEM JEWELS

Address PO Box 6904, Jiddah
Telephone 6440687, 6438434
Telex 401602 ARAJHI SJ
Owned by Abdalrahman Abdalaziz Al Rajhi, this company deals in clocks and watches as well as jewellery. It was established in 1978 and has its own workshops, representing the brand name Glycine.

RAJHI TRADING ESTABLISHMENT

Address PO Box 4514
Telephone 6431182, 6444465, 6442590
Telex 401602 ARAJHI SJ
Established in 1976, this company is also owned by Abdalrahman Abdalaziz Al Rajhi. It operates as an informal bank and money exchange.

MUHAMMAD ABDULLAH AL RAJHI CORPORATION

Address PO Box 2632, Jiddah
Telephone 6447741, 6431298, 6314577, 6314977
Telex 401720 WAHET SJ, 402546 MARJCO SJ
Acting as commission agents this company was formed in 1970. They also act as building contractors supplying building materials such as concrete, marble, roofing material, paint, steel and sanitary ware. The company is owned by Muhammad Abdullah Abdalaziz Al Rajhi.

ABDULLAH SALIH AL RAJHI ESTABLISHMENT

Address Jizan, admin. office PO Box 968, Dammam
Telephone 4020331, 8528765
Telex 601158 AL RAJHI SJ
Branches Jiddah (PO Box 6727, tel. 6427451, 6425606, tlx. JMSRAF SJ), Riyadh, Makkah, Al Khobar, Buraydah, Khamis Mushait, Al Thuqba, Al Qatif, Dhahran Airport, Jubail and Hafi al Batin.
Owned by Sh. Abdullah Salih Al Rajhi, the company was formed in 1972 and engages in currency exchange and dealing. They have correspondents worldwide. They have joint ventures with Al Jassar and Al Rajhi, Kuwait, and Al Hariri and Al Rajhi Co., San'a', YAR.

AL RAJHI TRADING ESTABLISHMENT

Address Al Khobar
Telephone 8641704
Subsidiary offices
Jiddah, PO Box 5822, tel. 6425158, 6434716, 6437124; tlx. 401709 RAJEST SJ
Dammam, tel. 8323336
Owned by Abdalrahman Salih Abdalaziz Al Rajhi, the company is engaged in currency exchange.

RAJHI CONSULTING ENGINEERS

Address PO Box 7669, Riyadh
Telephone 4768853
Telex 201249 NASIR SJ
The owner Sh. Hamad b. Nasir Al Rajhi was born in 1948 in Mecca, and holds engineering degrees from the University of California. He has contributed to professional journals and represents the younger generation of highly qualified professionals emerging in the Kingdom. The consultancy specialises in water supply projects for the Government but also handles a certain amount of architectural work. The consultancy has links with TCB Morris International of Houston and the JE Sirrien Company of Greenville, South Carolina.

RAJHI DEVELOPMENT CO. LTD

Address PO Box 4301, Riyadh
Telephone 4765116, 4760567
Telex 201249 NASIR SJ
The company has associates and representatives in Jiddah, Dammam, Khamis Mushait, Ta'if, Yanbu, Madinah, Makkah and Tabuk. The board, which owns the company, consists of the sons of Sh. Nasir b. Hamad Al Rajhi. The managing director is US educated Sh. Abdullah b. Nasir. The company comprises a building materials import and supply division, a transport division, contracting division and a bio-medical division. Reflecting the developing needs of the Kingdom, they also operate a landscape gardening division. A joint venture is operated with Hydrosoil BV of the Netherlands called Al Rajhi Hydrosoil.

AL RAJHI FOR BUILDING MATERIALS

Address PO Box 1087, Jiddah
Telephone 6432149, 6433615, 6438034
Telex 401373 RAJHI SJ
This company is owned by Salih Abdalaziz Al Rajhi and managed by his nephew Muhammad Abdullah. It supplies building materials such as cement and timber and has branches in Riyadh (PO Box 242, tel. 4485633), Dammam (PO Box 176, tel. 4021845) and Khamis Mushayt (PO Box 438, tel. 687417).

AL RAJHI FURNITURES-LUSTRES

Address PO Box 4827, Jiddah
Telephone 6655932
A company owned by Salih Abdullah which deals in lustre electrical equipment and also furniture.

RAYAC TRADING AND CONTRACTING

Address PO Box 6904, Jiddah
Telephone 6518512
Telex 401602 ARAJHI SJ
Abdalrahman Abdalaziz established this company in 1977. It deals in general merchandise, building materials, cleaning and maintenance, as well as acting as commission agents and business consultants in the creation of joint ventures and the provision of manpower.

The Family of Rashid

Originally from the environs of Riyadh, they spread throughout Najd and are Al Dughaithar of Anaiza. Rashid b. Ibrahim, his son and his grandson Yusif were traders in horses to India.

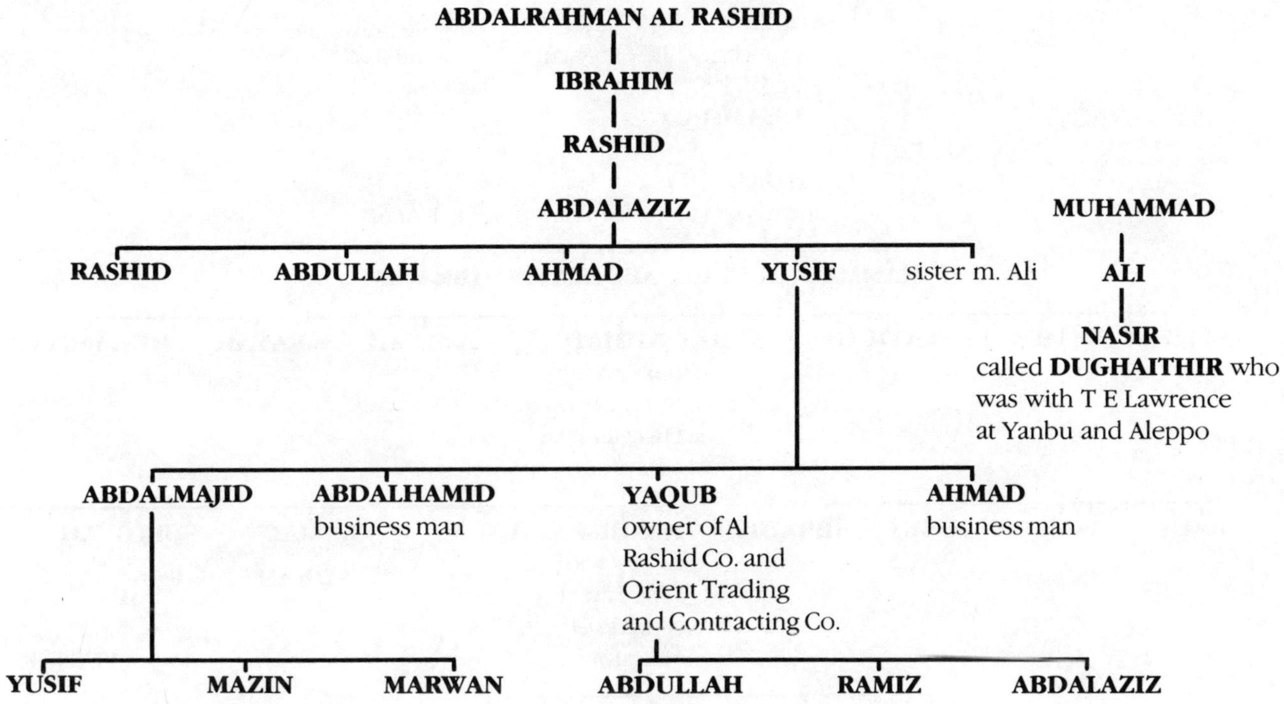

AL RASHID COMPANY

Address head office P.O.Box 610 Riyadh
Telephone 4022261, 4020109
Telex 201260 RAMEZ SJ
Cable address RAMEZ
Subsidiary offices Jiddah, Dhahran, Jubail and Tabuk
Proprietor Sh. Yacoub Yusif Al Rashid
Activities Sh. Yacoub began business in 1966 and specializes in the area of mechanical, electrical and industrial engineering. He represents many Western companies and is extremely alert to commercial possibilities whilst being a little reticent as to the details of his precise interests. He acts for Hawker Siddeley, Trans America and John Brown Turbines. He has a partnership with MOCOL for fibre glass pipe, where his company owns 65%, and another with Felton of West Germany.
Turnover 600 million US dollars
Bankers Arab Bank, First National City

The Family of Al Salah

Originating in the Palestine Sanjac of the Ottoman Empire.

- **SA'ID BEY AL SALAH** a landowner in Lebanon, Syria and Palestine honoured by the Ottoman sultan of the day
  - **MUHAMMAD**
    - **AHMAD** and his son Mustafa met Napoleon at Acre
      - **MUHAMMAD**
      - **MUSTAFA**
        - **IZZAT**
        - **MAHMUD**
        - **LATIFAH**
        - **ASMA**
        - **AHMAD** Supervising Engineer on the Hijaz Railway at Medina, Ghaza and Damascus
          - **RADI**
          - **JAMAL**
          - **SUBHI**
          - **IBRAHIM**
          - **HASHIM** fought with King Faysal at battle of Maisaloun
            - **AIDAH**
            - **NAJUA**
            - **SA'ID**
              - **NAHDAH** authoress of cookery and women's books. Educated in Florence.
              - **BASEM** graduate of Univ. of Petroleum
              - **HASHEM**
            - **JAMAL**
          - **UMAR**
          - **KAMAL**
            - **ADNAN**
          - **SUBHIYAH**
          - **MUSTAFA**
          - **YUSSUR**
          - **NAJI**
        - **AMINAH**
        - **RAYAH**
        - **MUHAMMAD**
      - **ABDALATIF**
      - **IBRAHIM**

INTERNATIONAL PUBLICATIONS AGENCIES

Address head office Said Salah Building, 28th Street Al Khobar; for airmail, P.O. Box 70 Dhahran Airport.
Telephone 86-41784, 86-46767
Telex 671229 SALAH SJ
Cable address SALAH AL KHOBAR
Subsidiary offices Jiddah, Beirut, Al Khobar, Singapore, Dubai
Proprietor Said H. Salah
Company History
Said Salah commenced operations in Jiddah in 1957 and in the following year established his business in the Eastern Province in Al Khobar. Initially he represented almost all newspapers and magazines of note and supplied the whole of Aramco. However he has relinquished most of this huge number of agencies and the business has developed into a noted publishing house in its own right and has invested in real estate.Today the I.P.A. publishes books and brochures in its own name and concentrates on the distribution of books and art work. A recent venture is the construction of a new bookshop to be called Supreme Bookshop which will occupy a space of 1500 squaremetres and will thus almost certainly be one of the largest bookshops in the world. The Supreme Bookshop will display technical and social works in Arabic, English and French as well as children's books. I.P.A. also owns a large warehouse from which they re-export to Kuwait, Bahrain, the U.A.E. and Beirut and they are happy to extend credit facilities for the right projects. I.P.A. is on top of an expanding market and a most go-ahead and modern concern.
Turnover 15 million Saudi riyals
Bankers Arab Bank

The Family of Al Saidi

Originate in Najd at al Shara, west of Riyadh.

RASHAID
|
HASAN
|
ABDULRAHMAN
|
HASAN
|
MUHAMMAD
about 75 and used to
trade in foodstuffs as did his father

HASAN
owner of Al Saidi Trading Store

ABDULLAH
graduate

Children of HASAN:

MUHAMMAD
attended Petroleum
University, Dhahran

ABDULLAH

ABDULRAHMAN

KHALID

ABDALAZIZ

AL SAIDI TRADING STORE

Address head office PO Box 1501, Dammam
Telephone 83 22085
Cable address HASAN AL SAIDI
Proprietor Sh. Hasan Muhammad Al Saidi
Company history Having left Aramco, Sh. Hasan began operations in 1965 running a poultry farm. This enterprise was sold in 1971 and Saidi Trading founded. This business specialised in the import of foodstuffs and provided the basis of the current main activity which is real estate; holdings include some six buildings for domestic accommodation. There have been moves to expand into manufacturing.
Bankers Riyadh Bank, Saudi Faransi Bank

The Family of Samman

Descending from the Abdulsamad of the Wadi Muhrim between Ta'if and al Hada mountains, they are Al Numur of the Thaqif tribe. They acquired their present name because Abdullah and Da'ud traded in the export of dates from the Hijaz to Syria. On the return journey they brought back foodstuffs and in particular ghee (Arabic *samn*). Some of the family settled in Syria and relations are to be found in Damascus to this day.

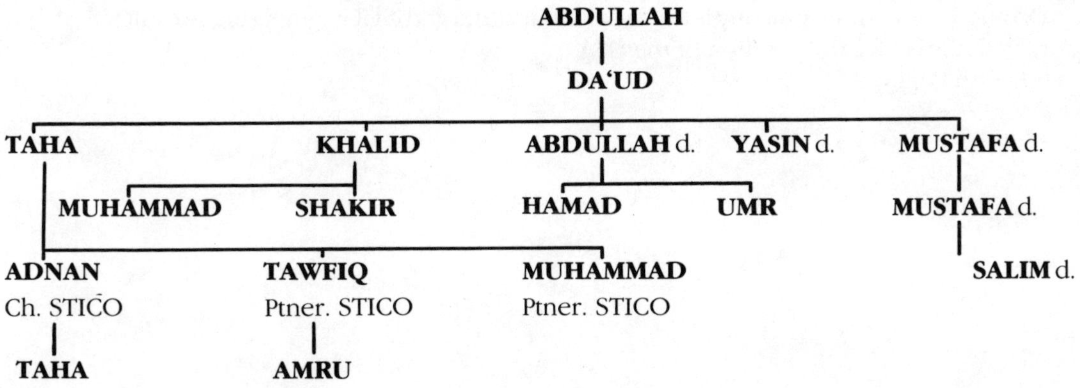

SAMMAM TRADING & IMPORTING CO.

Address head office P.O.Box 4180 Jiddah
Telephone 6515251, 6515392
Telex 401907 SAMMAN SJ
Cable address NESYAN
Board Members
Sh. Adnan Taha Samman 40% Chairman
Sh. Tewfiq Taha Samman 30% Member
Sh. Muhammad Taha Samman 30% Dir. General
Activities
The company was established in 1976 as a corporation, becoming a limited company in 1977. Sh. Adnan completed his period of public service in 1976 having finally held office as Executive Vice Governor of the Saline Water Conversion Corporation before entering private business. This company specializes in the import and marketing of the finest decorating materials, project installation in this field, and furniture and decor studies to the highest and most luxurious standards.The company acts as agent for the following: Sommer of France, carpets and wall coverings; Labiche of Canada and the US, carpets and wall coverings; Boisseliers Durif Furniture; Roman Deco and Decovea; Laque d'Argent Marlin for lighting and wall coverings; Vorwerk; British Carpets and Forfar for carpets.
Bankers Saudi British Bank, Saudi Cairo Bank, Banque Liban Francaise, Paris.
Subsidiary Companies
1. Saudi Arabian Electronic Equipment Company, P.O.Box 1874 Jiddah, tel. 6692207, 6446607, tlx. 400167 SAEECO SJ.
Owned by Adnan Taha Samman this company was formed in 1977. It deals in radio and television equipment, electronic equipment and components, security equipment and video systems.
Bankers Saudi British Bank.

2. Samman Trade and Industrial Investment Corp., P.O. Box 1874 Jiddah, tel. 6515251, 6515392, tlx. 401907 SAMMAN SJ.

Owned by Adnan Samman and founded in 1976, this company's activities are concerned with dealing in carpets and rugs, supply of aluminium products, decorating materials, electrical equipment, lighting and lumber. They also act as building contractors specializing in hotel and hospital projects.

Bankers Saudi British Bank.

3. Samman Construction and Contracting Corp., P.O.Box 5268 Jiddah, tel. 6655029, 6652338, tlx. 401907 SAMMAN SJ.

Owned by Adnan Taha Samman this company is a firm of architectural and civil engineering consultants. It is a joint venture with the Antler Corporation of the USA.

Bankers Saudi British Bank.

The Family of Sania

Originate in Majma'a of Najd, some 225 km north of Riyadh. Salih and Muhammad, the sons of Sh. Ahmad b. Nasir, were the first to come to the capital.This family is a branch of the same group mentioned in the Kuwait volume (q.v.).

- **AL SANIA**
  - **AL SALIH**
    - **IBRAHIM**
      - **SALIH**
        - **AHMAD** mediated on behalf of King Abdalaziz Al Saud between the Sa'dun of Najd and the Ruler of Kuwait
        - **NASIR** Governor of Majma'a
          - **AHMAD** a teacher of religion
            - **SALIH** owns Maha Contracting Co., tel. 6354458
            - **MUHAMMAD** owns the Asima Hotel
              - **ABDALRAHMAN** manages the Asia and Asima Hotels. Ptnr. in Umaya Co.
              - **FAHD**
              - **YAHYA**
              - **KHALID**
              - **YASIR**
              - **WALID**
              - **GHANIM**

SH. MUHAMMAD B. AHMAD AL SANIA

Address head office Asia Hotel, Riyadh
Telephone 4026461, 4835127, 4835736
Proprietor The Asima Hotel, Riyadh, is fully owned by Sh. Muhammad
Company history Sh. Muhammad b. Ahmad acquired the Asima hotel in 1968 and began to rent the Asia Hotel from the Minister of Finance, Sh. Muhammad Al Ali Aba Al Khail, in 1972. Since then he has not wished to expand his business except to rebuild and redecorate his hotels, which cater mainly for middle class Saudi nationals. Sh. Muhammad b. Ahmad is religious and his learning and humility are widely respected.
Partnerships Sh. Abdalrahman b. Muhammad, besides managing his father's hotels, is a partner in the Umaya Company for building, construction and the transport of heavy machinery (PO Box 8133, Riyadh, tel. 4835736, tlx. 200222 AMUDI SJ.

The Family of Sanie

The family originated in Anaiza of Qasim some centuries ago, and is an old Jiddah family more landowning and professional in character than commercial. Sanie St. in the old city is named after them and its current value is estimated at three hundred million riyals. The streets of Jiddah can be confusing to the visitor, for instance some, like King Faisal Street, have more than one name. This thoroughfare is also called New Street and Gold Street as well. When it was built it was obvious to call it New Street; but the third name was given to it due to the habit of the old merchants of burying their gold. Much was found in forgotten hiding places when houses had to be pulled down to build New Street. The more cynical say that the epithet derives from the compensation paid by the government to the owners of the destroyed properties!

- **ABDULLAH**
  - **HAMID**
    - **IBRAHIM** d. 1962. Head of Police in the Kingdom for 3 yrs. Founder member Jiddah Chamber of Commerce. A big merchant trading in foodstuffs and textiles. The business was closed at his death. Traded with India and Japan. He distributed food for King Abdalaziz and handed over this work to the Khereiji family, q.v.
      - **HAMID** assisted his father, now manages family property
        - **SALIH** in Saudia
        - **SULAYMAN** in Ambar Trading
      - **MUHAMMAD** ex Foreign Service. Now lives in London; real estate.
        - **KHALID**
        - **ISSAM**
      - **ALI** educated in Manchester, now in W Germany
        - **KHALID**
      - **UMR** educated UK and Switzerland
      - **ABDALAZIZ** owner of Al Hizam Al Akhdar Contracting Co.
      - **ABDALRAHMAN** MA business behaviour Asst. Man. Design Centre
      - **YUSIF** graduate
    - **MUHAMMAD**
    - **ABDULLAH**
      - **HAMIDA** d.
      - **KHADIJA**
    - **UMR** a farmer
    - **SALIH**

AL HIZAM AL AKHDAR CO.

Address head office PO Box 1527 Jiddah
Telephone 6455741
Proprietor Sh. Abdalaziz Ibrahim Al Sanie
Company history The company was formed in 1973 and its first contracting job was acting as a subcontractor on a road project in Jizan. Today the company specialises in villa construction and house extensions. Whilst it is small it is noted for meticulous and closely calculated work.

The Family of Shaker

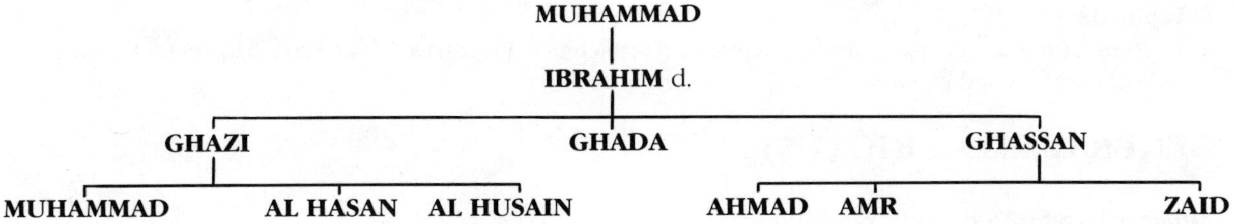

IBRAHIM SHAKER CO.

Address head office PO Box 78, Jiddah
Telephone 6446233, 6435211, 6427911
Telex 401535 SHAKER SJ
Branches in Riyadh, al Khobar and Dammam
Activities The business founded by Sh. Ibrahim Muhammad Shaker holds the important agencies of General Electric and Electrolux products for whom they operate a full maintenance service facility. The company supplies cleaning machinery equipment and products, and also operates as a cleaning contractor. They sell air conditioning equipment, electrical and electronic equipment, laundry equipment, radio and television sets, power transmission equipment and spare parts, as well as water coolers, sewing machines, refrigeration equipment, water treatment and water heating equipment.
The business has passed to the direction of Sh. Ibrahim's children and a family holding company called Ghazi Ibrahim Shaker and Bros. Co. has been created. Ghassan and Ghazi hold 40 percent each and their sister Ghada 20 percent. Important investments and business relationships of their father's original company were Saudi Aluminium Metal Industrial Co. Ltd. 25 percent, Ibrahim Mahmud Shaker and Ptner 50 percent, this latter being an investment with Abu Zinada, q.v., in the Jiddah Medical Centre, and a joint venture with General Electric of the USA called General Electric Technical Services Co.
However, the business interests of the sons have grown considerably since 1970 and include the following:
Sh. Ghazi Shaker: Saudi Communications Co. 50 percent, Saudi Presio Ltd. 60 percent, and Saudi Trading and Distribution Co. Ltd. 20 percent.
Sh. Ghassan Shaker, owner of the Baraka Est. and Ghassan Shaker Saudi Communications Co. 20 percent, Cementation Saudi Arabia 50 percent, Bilad Vinell Co. Ltd. 25 percent, Saudi Electrical Materials Ltd 50 percent, Cedra Trading , Industrial and Contracting Ltd. 50 percent, Concrete Construction Co. Ltd. 15 percent, Jamjoum Electrical Distribution Assembly Co. Ltd. 4 percent, Sadelini Shaker Tamimi Construction Co. Ltd. 20 percent, BBC Brown Boveri Saudi Arabia Ltd 10 percent, Saudi Specialist Construction Co. Ltd. 51 percent.

SAUDI ESTABLISHMENT FOR TRADING AND DISTRIBUTION

Address head office PO Box 7909, Jiddah
Telephone 6657149
Telex 400845 GIS SJ
Activities A company owned by Ghassan Shaker and founded in 1979. It has branches in Riyadh and Dammam and deals with cleaning products, detergents and cosmetics, as well as a range of tinned foodstuffs and fruit juices.

SAUDI TRADING AND DISTRIBUTION CO.

Address head office PO Box 50, Jiddah
Telephone 6428257
Activities This is a cigarette trading concern with branches in Riyadh (tel. 4020520, 4020545) and Dammam (tel. 83224403) owned by Ghassan Shaker

GENERAL ELECTRIC (US)

Address head office PO Box 1634, Jiddah
Telephone 6427911, 6420300
Telex 401535 SHAKER SJ
Activities A company formerly under the sponsorship of Ibrahim Shaker working as electrical contractors.

GENERAL ELECTRIC TECHNICAL SERVICES CO. INC. (GETSCO)

Address head office PO Box 1634, Jiddah
Telephone 6427911, 6420300, 6421673
Telex 401535 SHAKER SJ
Activities As with the previous entry, sponsorship of this concern will have passed to the heirs of Ibrahim Shaker. This company specialises as contractors for the installation of power generation systems.

SAUDI AMERICAN GENERAL ELECTRIC CO.

Address head office PO Box 50, Jiddah
Telephone 6445043, 6447005, 6446891
Telex 402439 GEJED SJ
Activities Originally sponsored by the Ibrahim Shaker Co., the company has a branch in al Khobar, PO Box 230, tel. 8570250, 8576525, tlx. 601582. The company are electrical contractors and deal in electrical equipment.

JIDDAH MEDICAL CENTRE HOSPITAL

Address head office PO Box 419 and 7360, Jiddah
Telephone 6515935, 6515939, 6515943, 6515947
Telex 401025 ZINADA SJ
The medical centre was founded in 1978 and is owned by the heirs of Ibrahim Shaker and Abdalrauf Abu Zinada (q.v.) who manages it

SAUDI ELECTRIC SUPPLY CO. (SESCO)

Address head office PO Box 6838, Jiddah
Telephone 6820339, 6820356
Telex 403287 SESCO SJ
Activities A partnership between Ghassan Shaker and Ali Tamimi (q.v.), which has branches in Riyadh and al Khobar and supplies electricity.

The Family of Shalhoub

The family originates in Yanbu Al Nakhl in the Hijaz and are hereditary Zamzamis. These are a group of people in charge of the delivery of water from the holy well of Zamzam in Mecca. The other two occupations of a similar hereditary nature are those of the Mutawafin (see Abdalmajid) with whom the Zamzami almost exclusively deals and the Wukala Mutawafin or agents who operate from Jiddah.

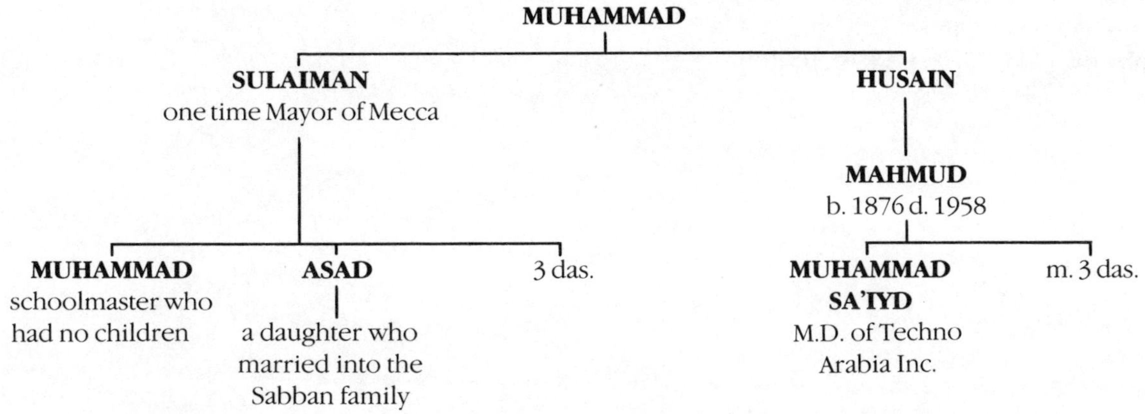

SHALHOUB

TECHNO ARABIA INC.

Muhammad Sa'iyd was brought up under the guardianship of Sh. Ahamad b. Abbas Zainy due to the death of his father. It was this which led him to take a position with Abbar and Zainy where he was employed in the then Port Division during 1971 and 1972. However, in 1972 he travelled to the USA where he acquired a Masters Degree in history. On his return he considered a career in teaching but finally decided to be the first member of his family to enter commerce.

Thus Techno Arabia Inc. was formed and registered in 1975. The new company was started with RS 450,000 capital from Muhammad Sa'iyd's own resources and began specialising in photographics, meteorological equipment and other kinds of sophisticated electronic equipments and instruments.

In 1977 it was decided to concentrate on the photographics as the other aspects of the company were not doing very much business. It was in this year that the 'Lens' shop was opened in the Caravan Shopping Centre in Jiddah. This side of the business took three years to establish and the addition of a small RS 600,000 Photo Lab was achieved with an overdraft facility guaranteed by Sh. Ahmad Zainy. The success of the enterprise by 1979 had led to such confidence in the Banks that no guarantor was required for drawing facilities up to RS 500,000 in 1980 and 1,900,000 in 1981.

Consequently it was planned to double the number of retail outlets and add a lab to each one. The first additions have been made at Al Khobar and in Jiddah itself, whilst further branches are planned for Riyadh and Yanbo.

The company looks for further development too in the 'media' field and the provision of the very best television equipment. To this end the company is organised into two Divisions, the Photographic Division and the Technical Division.

Today Techno Arabia Inc. act as agents for IKEGAMI of Japan who manufacture very advanced television equipment for use in TV stations and professional news coverage and have done so since 1981.
The company has not neglected to take a keen and enthusiastic look at the future and in its representation of the Copper Mining Co. of Finland (Outokumph Engineering Division) is preparing to participate in the development of mineral resources other than oil. MET is a highly sophisticated machine for ore analysis in the field which will greatly facilitate this aim.
The company also represents Leitz, Outokumph and Colenta and now deals in a wide range of aviation and airport equipment, communications equipment, computer and business systems, laboratory and hospital equipment, and equipment for marine communications and navigation, radio, water treatment, security, professional television and closed circuit applications.

Address PO Box 5258
Telephone 6532372, 653728, 6530826
Telex 403037 TECHNO SJ

The Family of Sharbatly

A family of Sada, and very influential in the commercial sector of Jiddah. They are dignified individually by the epithet *sayyid*.

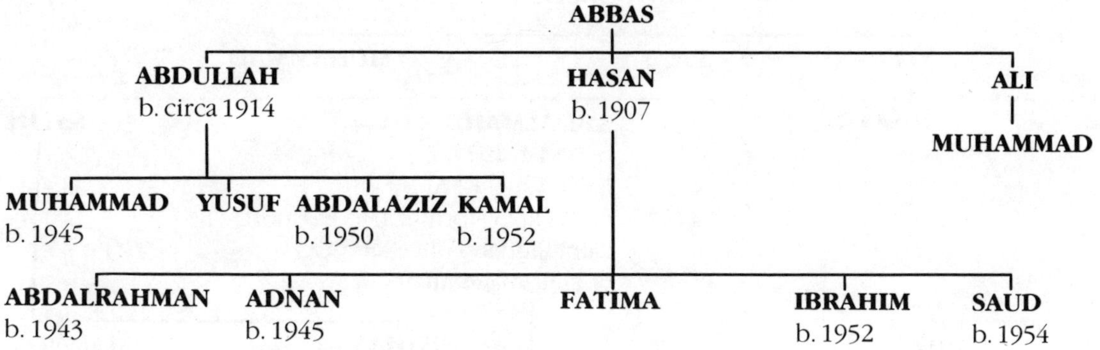

SAUDI ARABIAN MARKETING CORPORATION

Address head office PO Box 5968, Jiddah
Telephone 6672951, 6655568, 6672440
Telex 402069 SAMCO SJ
Activities A company owned by Ibrahim Hasan Sharbatly which was formed in 1978. It deals in boats, marine craft servicing, camping equipment, caravans and trailers, marine diesel engines, education equipment, garden furniture, paints and toys.

The Family of Shobokshi

The family have been resident in Jiddah for many years and tradition states that they are originally from Egypt.

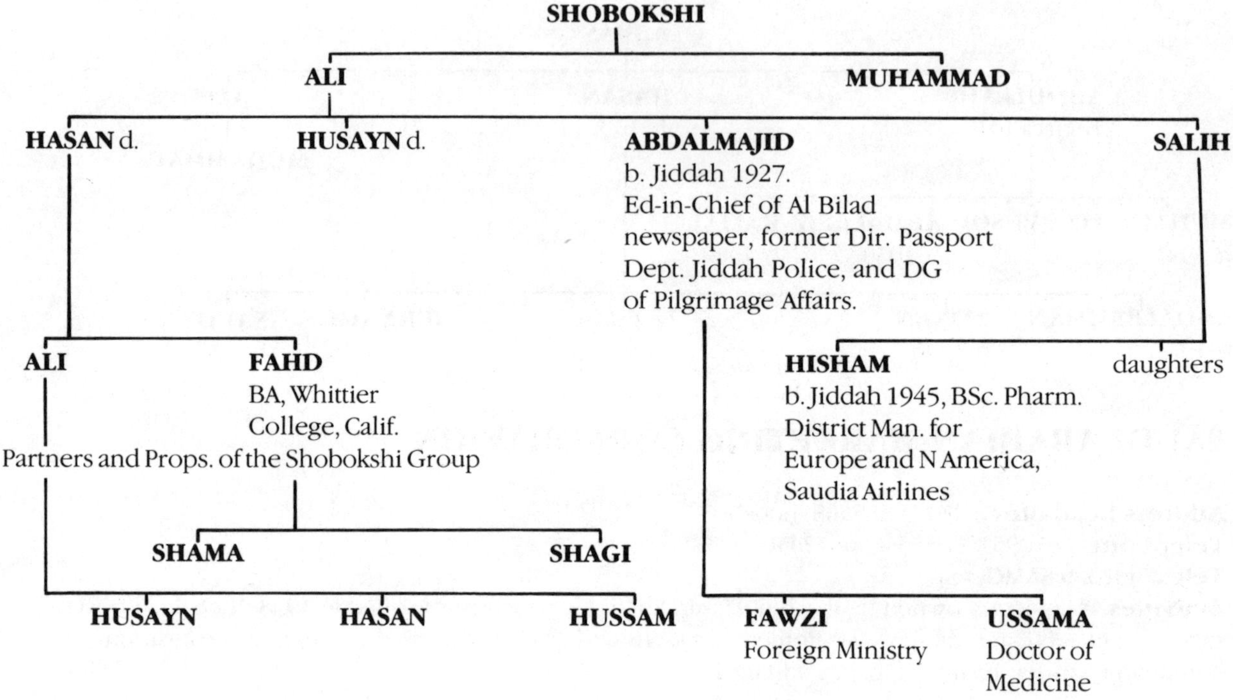

ALI AND FAHD SHOBOKSHI GROUP

AL AROUSA FOR INDUSTRY AND TRADE

Address head office PO Box 4515, Jiddah
Telephone 6433621, 6423061
Telex 401523 OIA SJ
Activities A company owned by Ali and Fahad Husain Shobokshi, dealing in furniture and decorative goods and school supplies

AL AROUSA FOR FURNITURE

Address head office PO Box 292, Jiddah
Telephone 6433840, 6425203
Telex 401523 OIA SJ
Activities This company deals in wallpapers, carpets, etc.

SHOBOKSHI COMMERCIAL ENTERPRISES

This Athens based company is a subsidiary of the Shobokshi group and its activity is mainly in the tours field. The company operates Government agency franchises in Greece and undertakes guided tours in the Aegean as well as a chartered yacht service.

SHOBOKSHI INDUSTRIAL COMPLEX

Produces aggregate, asphalt, concrete kerbstones and hollow blocks. Most of the output is used in the group's own projects.

DAR OKAZ PRINTING AND PUBLISHING

Address head office PO Box 5941, Jiddah
Telephone 6600789, 6600765, 6600905
Telex 402645 OKBOK SJ
Activities The company publishes the *Okaz* daily paper as well as the *Saudi Gazette*. They are also printers. Owned by Ali Husain Shobokshi.

OKAZ NEWSPAPER

Address head office PO Box 1508, Jiddah
Telephone 6432166
Telex 401360 OKAZ SJ
Activities Founded in 1959 and owned by Ali Husain Shobokshi, the company is a newspaper and magazine publisher.

ELECTRICAL WORK AND MAINTENANCE

Address head office PO Box 7240, Jiddah
Telephone 6604761
Telex 401523 OJA SL, 401008 SJ
Activities Operating as contractors in the general, electrical and communications fields, the company also deals in power transmission equipment. It was formed in 1973 and is owned by Ali ad Fahad Husain Shobokshi.

GENERAL AGENCIES CORPORATION (GAC)

Address head office PO Box 1988, Jiddah
Telephone 6658208, 6658209, 6601659, 6601799, 6654826
Telex 401008 GAC SJ
Activities Operating as road and building contractors, as well as printers and bookbinders, the company deals in office equipment, newsprint and paper products. It was formed in 1963 and is owned by Ali and Fahad Husain Shobokshi. Shaima, a contracting company (PO Box 9271 Jiddah, tel. 6601320, 6601328, tlx. 402274 SHAIMA SJ) is a branch of GAC.

KURBAN TRAVEL SERVICES

Address head office PO Box 5039, Jiddah
Telephone 6531135, 6532159, 6532391, 6511376
Telex 401808 KURBAN SJ
Activities A travel agency recognised by IATA, which was set up in 1977. It is owned by Fahad Husain Shobokshi, Salih Kamel (q.v.) and the General Agencies Corporation (q.v.). The agency has the following branches: Riyadh (PO Box 17971, tel. 4770672, 4770673, tlx. 203079 KURBAN SJ), al Khobar (PO Box 2256, tel. 8649835, 8649824, tlx. 670576 KURBAN SJ), Yanbu (PO Box 19, tel. 3222616, 3221759, tlx. 461021 KURBAN SJ), Jubail (PO Box 209, tel. 3611900, 3611904).

ORIENT MARKETING AND TRADING CO. (OMATRA)

Address head office PO Box 5039, Jiddah
Telephone 6533683, 6511672, 6511172
Telex 401809 OMATRA SJ
Activities This company is a partnership between Ali and Fahad Shobokshi with Salih Kamel (q.v.). It was set up in 1977 and deals with crushing plants, mixers, pumps, trailers, screening and batching plants, rollers, cranes, dozers, loaders, elevators, trucks, buses and tractors.

ALPHATRANS

Address head office PO Box 32, Jiddah
Telephone 6516968, 6516964
Telex 401237 HADEEL SJ
Activities Established in 1970 and owned by Salim Ali Shobokshi, this company acts as clearing and forwarding agents, and deals in both international and national transport services. The company has branches in London, Germany, USA, France, Switzerland and the Far East.

AUTOMOTIVE DIVISION

A branch of the Shobokshi group which acts as the sole distributor within the Kingdom for the Hyundai Company of the popular Pony range of Korean cars and trucks. The company provides a complete after-sales service from its own workshops.
The Group has further diversified into the area of management services, an operation carried out by the Saudi International Consulting Centre (SICC); into catering through the medium of Shobak which carries out a full range of catering services to hospitals, schools, labour camps and airlines. A specialisation from this activity has developed into the comprehensive Shobokshi Aviation Division which provides maintenance services to private aircraft operators as well as Shobal which is a partnership with Sh. Salih Kamel (q.v.) and Brothers for hotels based in London.
Sh. Ali Shobokshi holds the following commercial posts:
President of Orient International Agencies
Chairman of the OKAZ for Printing and Publishing Company (shareholders: Sh. Muhammad Ibrahim Al-Haid, Sh. Ghaith Rashad Pharoun, Sh. Abdullah Taha Baksh, Sh. Muhammad Ibrahim Al-Issa, Sh. Dakhil Muhsen Al-Harthi, Sh. Abdullah Baroom, Sh. Saleh Abdullah Kamel, Sh. Ali Hussein Shobokshi, Sh. Fahd Hussein Shobokshi, Sh. Ibrahim Al-Ghamdi, Sh. Hisham Muhieddin Nazer)
Chairman of OKAZ Organisation for Press and Publication
Founder of the Saudi International Consulting Centre
Chairman of the MISR Group for Investment and Development
Founder and Managing Director of Tihama for Advertising, Public Relations and Marketing Studies (q.v.)
Sh. Fahd Shobokshi holds the following commercial posts:
Member of the Board of the Red Sea Insurance Company
Co-Founder of Tihama
President of the General Agencies Corporation
President of the Electrical Work and Maintenance Company
Managing Director of OKAZ for Distribution
Managing Director of Saudi EXPO
Managing Director of Saudi AD
Member of the Board of the Egyptian Islamic Faisal Bank
Member of the Board of the Saudi Corporation for Catering and Tourism

ORIENTAL INTERNATIONAL AGENCIES

Address head office PO Box 292, Jiddah
Telephone 6425203, 6433840
Telex 401523 OIA SJ
Activities A company dealing in carpets and rugs, wallpapers and coverings and operating as contract decorators. The company is owned by Ali and Fahad Shobokshi.

ALI AND FAHAD SHOBOKSHI GROUP

Address head office PO Box 5470, Jiddah
Telephone 6658208, 6658209, 6601659
Telex 401008 GAC SJ
Activities The company has branches in Riyadh and Dammam and is owned as its name implies. It is a car dealer and distributor, supplying spare parts and accessories. It represents the brand name of Pony. It also supplies aircraft support services, building materials such as aggregate and ready mix concrete. It also acts as a contractor for road construction, drainage and building.

SHOBOKSHI MARITIME CO.

Address head office PO Box 6560, Jiddah
Telephone 6670086, 6675954, 6690568
Telex 402654 SHOM SJ, 400506 WARNE SJ
Activities The company is owned by Ali Husain Shobokshi. It has branches in Yanbu, Jizan and Dammam. It acts as a clearing and forwarding agent, operating shipping companies and local transport services.

SAUDI ADVERTISING

Address head office PO Box 6557, Jiddah
Telephone 6650380, 6602286, 6658208
Telex 402229 ADVERT SJ
Activities This company with branches in Riyadh and Dammam is owned by the Okaz Organisation. It is an advertising agency and, on a contract basis, erects outdoor signs and posters. They are also the publishers of a very comprehensive commercial directory and act as marketing and public relations consultants.

The Family of Al Solaiman

A family of Najd

- **SOLAIMAN HAMDAN**
  - **MUHAMMAD** Secretary to HM King Abdulaziz
    - **ALI**
    - **HAMAD** ATCO Saudi Arabia
  - **ABDULLAH AL SOLAIMAN AL HAMDAN** d. Min. of Finance to HM King Abdalaziz b. Abdalrahman Al Sa'ud in 1929 which post he held for a quarter of a century. Signed the oil concesson with Lloyd Hamilton, 3 May 1933.
    - **MUHAMMAD** Partner with his brothers
      - **MAJID**
      - **SALAH**
    - **ABDULAZIZ** Proprietor of Rolaco. B. Mecca 1934. Studied at La Fayette Univ. USA, financial training with Chase Manhattan
      - **SA'UD**
    - **KHALID*** used to run his father's office. Prop. Al Walid Co.
      - **WALID**
      - **YAZID**
      - **TARIQ**
    - **BASMA** m. Walid Juffali
    - **AHMAD*** b. Mecca 1938, B. Comm. Prop. of Al Sawary (Onan & Datsun) Gen. Man. of Siraj Hamid Zahran. Member of Board of Al Bilad, Tihama, and investor in the Arab Cement Co., Saudi Arabian Bandag
      - **GHASSAN**
    - **ASMA*** m. Gen Hashim Snack Foods Co. Ltd.
    - **FAHD** b. 1939, BA (Econ) in charge of hotels for Abdulaziz Solaiman & Brothers, Jiddah Palace Hotel and Kandara Hotel, Inter-Continental in Mecca and Cairo
      - **ZAID**
      - **ABDULLAH**

* children of Nura El Khereiji (q.v.)

THE AL SOLAIMAN GROUP

Abdulaziz Al Abdullah Al Sulaiman and Company
Address head office P.O.Box 222 Jiddah
Telephone 51067, 54109
Telex 401029 ROLACO SJ
Cable address ROLACO
Subsidiary offices Riyadh, Dammam, Paris and New York
Proprietor Sh. Abdulaziz Al Abdullah Al Sulaiman
Company History
Leaving the government service in 1954 Sh. Abdulaziz founded a company called Abdulaziz Al Abdullah Al Sulaiman Business Office which represented various Swedish and West German companies. Rolaco was formed shortly after this and soon became the largest importer of building materials in the Kingdom. Today the company deals in both bagged and bulk cement (Rolaco has its own silos in Jiddah Port with a capacity of 6,000 tons), steel re-inforcement, heavy equipment including Nissan Diesel and Skania trucks, Kato cranes, Furukawa Drills, Champion motor graders and has in addition a contrasting department for carrying out the many and diverse interests of the family.
The family are the oldest hoteliers in the Kingdom owning the Kandara (P.O.Box 473 Jiddah, tel. 23155, tlx. 401095 SJ), the Jiddah Palace Hotel (P.O.Box 473 Jiddah, tel. 32387, 32255, tlx. 401095 SJ). A third hotel in Jiddah is under construction and the family also owns Intercontinental Hotels in Dammam, Cairo and Mecca. The Abdulaziz Al Abdullah Al Sulaiman and Brothers Company is also part of the Arab Hotel Company in which the only other participants from the private sector are the Gosaibi family (q.v.), the remaining shareholders being the Arab Investment Company (a Saudi Kuwait group), the National Commercial Bank, and the Riyadh Bank.
Sh. Abdulaziz founded the Arabian Cement Company and today he is its Chairman. Present capacity is 2,000 tons daily but when the Rabigh extension is fully operational this figure will be more than doubled.
Sh. Abdulaziz is a Member of the Board of the Saudi Arabian Refining Company (SARCO) of which 75% is owned by the Government, the Saudi National Electric Company (SNEC), FRAB Bank Paris and FRAB Holdings of Luxembourg. He is the Chairmanof the Al Jazira Bank, the Zahran Contracting Company, Siraj Zahran and Co. which holds the Datsun agency selling 90,000 cars a year and La Fonciere Jiddah Insurancefor which the brokers are Stewart Wrightson of the UK. He is also Chairman of the Saudi Light Industry Corporation (SLIC) which runs two flexible foam factories, Saudi Arabian Barclay which operates a tyre re-tread factory producing 13,600 re-treads a year, and the Cement Products Industry Company as well as Al Sulaimaniyah Real Estate.
A further company within the family group is Saudicorp which functions as a screen for feasibility studies identifying and initiating industrial projects. The Saudi Capital Corporation is wholly owned by the group also and handles financial investment.
Sh. Abdulaziz represents the following as agent in the insurance field: Nasco Karaoglan and Company, La Fonciere, La Camat, Groupement Francais d'Assurances and Bankers Insurances.

The Family of Al Sultan

A family of importance in the business community of Riyadh. They originate from the Badran of Dawasir.

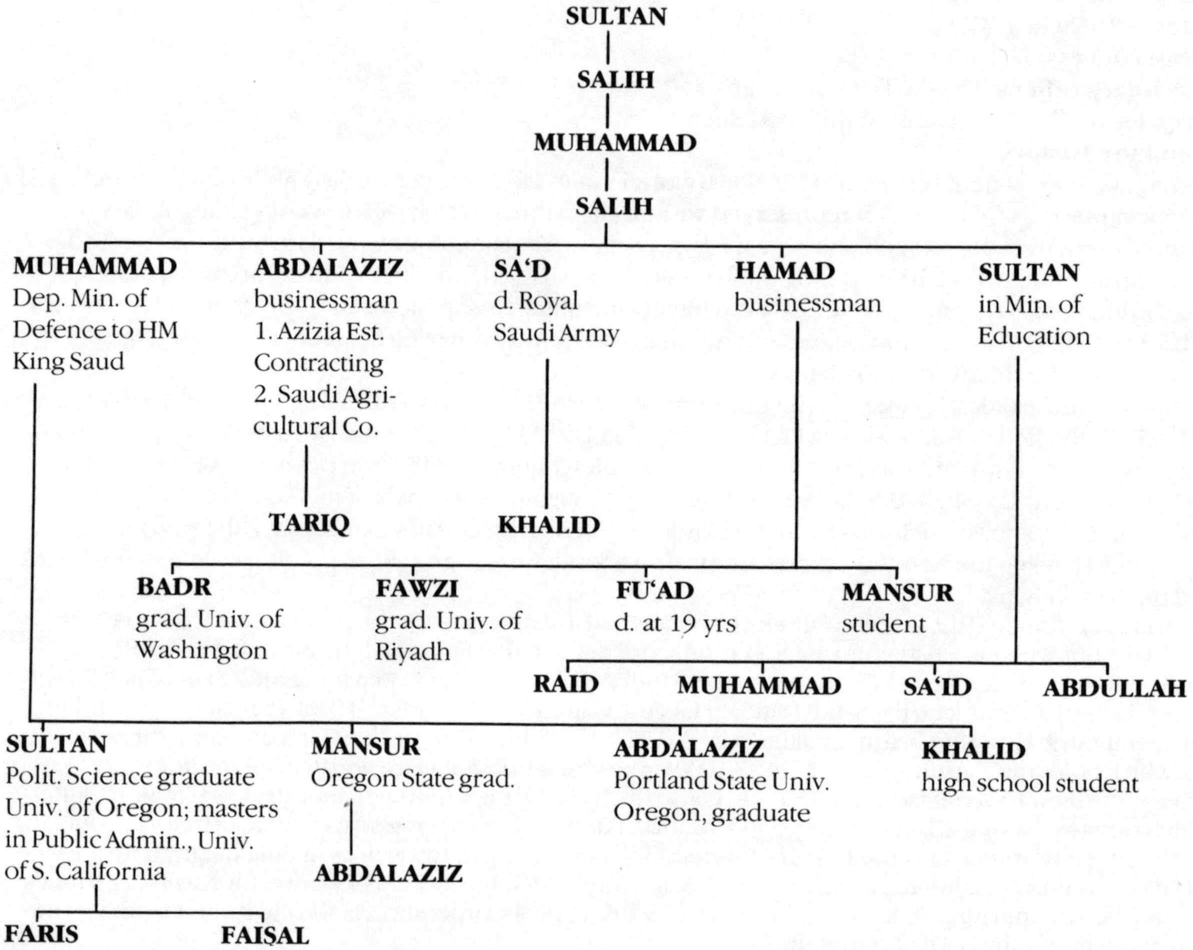

SAUDI AGRICULTURAL COMPANY

Address PO Box 6158, Riyadh
Telephone 4050421
The company is owned by Abdalaziz b. Salih. It deals with agricultural contracting and development.

The Family of Tamimi

The Bani Tamim were a powerful and famous tribe of northern Arabia in classical times. Amongst their descendants today are the Al Thani rulers of Qatar.
The family of Al Tamimi used to supply horses to India.

- **MUHAMMAD**
  - **ALI**
    - **ABDULLAH**
      - **ALI** businessman
        - **TALAL**
        - **TARIQ**
        - **HISHAM**
        - **AHMAD**
      - **MUHAMMAD** ptner. in business with his brother
        - **FAHAD**
        - **AYAD**
        - **ABDULLAH**

TAMIMI

Address head office P O Box 230, Al Khobar
Telephone 8641128, 8642912, 8642049
Telex 670030 TAMIMI SJ, 670206 TAMIMI SJ
Sh. Ali Abdullah Tamimi is a graduate of the American University if Beirut and like so many successful businessmen in the Eastern Province he was employed by ARAMCO. When he left the oil company in 1948 he formed an association with Bahsain and Laheg which was a pipeline construction business. Experience accumulated and his business interests expanded so that in 1956 the Tamimi Commercial Division was formed. This had the purpose of acting as a general agent and distributor for foreign representation. Today the following formidable list of companies is represented: GEC, Firestone International, Johns-Manville, Gardner-Denver Co., Dresser Industry, Crouse-Hinds Co., Harris Corporation, OTIS Engineering Corporation, Seamless Industries, Red Wing International, Pittsburgh Corning Corporation, Unichem International, Petroleum and Mining Equipment, T A Short and Associates, Howard Smith Screen Co., T R Oil Services Ltd., Newman Hattersley, Sterling Cable Co., William Hare Ltd., National Supply Co., Sim-Chem Ltd., Thetford Moulded Products Ltd., Powermaker International Ltd., CFPI (Foster), Insulco, Gates (Europe), Hermann Ludwig, McProducts Ltd., Telectron Ltd.
During the sixties the Tamimi Estates Division was added and the Tamimi Sevices Division followed. These companies amply demonstrate the huge breadth of Sh. Ali's business interests today.
1. Auto Marketing Co., PO Box 108, Al Khobar; vehicle sales and services.
2. Tamimi and Saihati (TASECO),PO Box 230, Al Khobar; vehicle and equipment leasing.
3. Tamimi-Hermann Ludwig, PO Box 230, Al Khobar; freight forwarding.
4. Saudi Electric Supply Co., PO Box 230, Al Khobar; with GE and Shaker, electrical equipment supplies.
5. Arab International Tire Re-Treaders, Dammam.
6. Anaiza Electric Powers Co., Anaiza; major expanding utility.
7. Dammam Laundry Co.
8. Saudi Plastic Factory, PO Box 230, Al Khobar.
9. Middle East Engineering Saudi Arabia, PO Box 1446, Dammam; with GE.

10. Saudi Mcinerney Construction Co., PO Box 230, Al Khobar; with ABMS-Mcinerney, all aspects of precast and prefabricated buildings.
11. TROS Saudi Arabia Ltd., PO Box 230, Al Khobar; with UCC of USA and TROS of UK, special chemicals for petro-chemical industry.
12. Sadelmi-Shaker-Tamimi Construction Co. Ltd., PO Box 230, Al Khobar; electrical and mechanical projects.

The above list shows how successful Sh. Ali Tamimi is in the formation of partnerships, but perhaps the most flourishing partner he has is Sh. Abdulla Fu'ad Boubshait. The Tamimi and Fouad combination is one of the most powerful and well known commercial in Saudi Arabia.

Tamimi and Fouad is a general partnership formed in 1963 and operates in pipeline construction, civil and building construction, materials supply, water treatment, real estate, catering, wholesale and retail food distribution, transportation and industrial chemicals.

The pipeline division has expanded rapidly over the years and contributed the construction of some 60 percent of the Kingdom's pipelines.

The Mechanical Division specialises in equipment for the petro-chemical and related industries. In 1978 a J/V was formed with Pyung Wha Construction of Korea to build refineries, water and power plants of all sizes.

Equipment Lease and Rental Division operates throughout the Eastern Province transporting asphalt and fuel.

The Construction Division supports the group's other divisions and has been active in construction and maintenance of factories, office buildings and residential compounds with capacity for block making and kerbstone production.

The Housing Division leases villas and housing compounds in the Eastern Province.

The Insulation Division covers all aspects of thermal and acoustic insulation systems. The Division's factory is in Dammam.

The Civil Works Company, a partnership with Tamimi and Fouad, Rashid A AL Rashid and Omran and Abdulaziz Al Omran, maintains and operates water and sewage systems, treatment plants and general construction. The partners also own a motel in Dammam.

Tamimi and Fouad Foods Ltd. has opened with Safeway Stores of the USA a major shopping supermarket of somc 35,000 sq. m. in Al Khobar.

The Family of Al Turki

A family from the numerous Bani Khalid of the north east coastal region of Saudi Arabia.

- **ABDALRAHMAN**
  - **ALI**
  - **MANSUR** had a reputation as a negotiator in local political affairs 'a mandub'
    - **AYSHA** d. 1982
    - **ABDALRAHMAN** d. 1982
    - **ABDALAZIZ** Cultural attaché Royal Saudi Embassy, London
      - **AMAL** m. Abdalaziz b. Zaid al Quraishi, q.v.
      - **KHALID** Pres. Al Turki Trading and Contracting B.Sc. Civil Eng., St Martin's Olympia, USA m. Lulu'a Abdalrahman Zamil of the Al Mansur, q.v.
        - **MANSUR**
        - **ABLAH**
        - **ABDALAZIZ**
      - **SA'D** Vice chairman and M.D. of Arab Investors Group, tel. Riyadh 4767006 tlx. 203522
      - **NOHA**
      - **SIHAM**
      - **NOHAD**
      - **MARWAN** attorney, read law at Magdalene Coll. Oxford
    - **ABDULLAH** a mutawa, religious teacher
    - **MUHAMMAD** accountant in Govt. service Real Estate interests
    - **NURA**

AL TURKI TRADING AND CONTRACTING

Address head office PO Box 440, Dammam
Telephone 843266, 8431640
Telex 602650 TURKI SJ, 601613 TTCE SJ
Activities This medium sized contracting company has specialised successfully in the procurement of government work and since its inception in 1975 has completed projects involving the erection of schools, warehouses, law courts, mosques and government buildings. They have also handled contracts for irrigation, fencing and asphalting. On the civil side they have put up a number of villas and at the time of writing have thirty-eight contracts in process.
The company also operates as a trading concern dealing in construction materials and tools where their inventory is worth over six million riyals.
In joint venture with Koffral of Belgium they deal in scaffolding and form work.
Bankers Riyad Bank, Cairo Bank, Saudi French Bank, Arab National Bank, National Commercial Bank, Saudi American Bank.

ZAHID BUSINESS INTERESTS

THE ZAHID COMPANIES

The commercial enterprise created by Mahmud Ali in the earlier years of this century has become diversified into one of the most powerful business groups in the Kingdom. The growth this has entailed has been enhanced by individual independence and skill as well as participation in the original corpus of wealth created by the founder of the business in Jiddah.

ZAHID INDUSTRIES AND INVESTMENT CO. LTD.

Address head office PO Box 1588, Jiddah
Telephone 6876366, 6877010, 6871004
Telex 401042 ZATRAC SJ
Activities A company owned by the family of Yusif Zahid and acting as a kind of holding company. Known shares are as follows, apportioned on the death of Sh. Yusif:
Sharifa Arina Sharaf Adnan 8.3 percent, Dina bint Yusif Zahid 8.3 percent, and 16.6 percent to each of the following: Fahad Yusif Zahid, Muhammad Yusif Zahid, Nabil Yusif Zahid, Talal Yusif Zahid and Walid Yusif Zahid.
In a J/V with Heanor Haulage Co. Ltd. this company owns Zahid Heanor Heavy Transport Co. Ltd. (PO Box 8223, Jiddah, tel. 6874598, tlx. 401042 ZATRAC SJ). It is engaged in local and international transport services. They also own NCR Corporation (Zahid Industries and Investments Co. Ltd.), PO Box 2740, tel. 6512727, 6512723, tlx. 400020 NCRJED SJ, which deals in complete computer systems.

ZAHID TRACTOR AND HEAVY MACHINERY CO. LTD.

Address head office PO Box 8928, Jiddah
Telephone 6671156
Telex 402851 ZATRAC SJ, 402852 ZAHGRP SJ
Branches Jiddah, PO Box 1588, tel. 6876366, tlx. 401042 ZATRAC SJ, and in Riyadh, Jubail, Abha, Qasim, Tabuk and Madina.
Board members
Talal Yusif Zahid, chairman with 13.7 percent
Walid Yusif Zahid, president with 13.7 percent
Fahad Yusif Zahid, executive vice president with 13.7 percent
Remaining shares are held by Nabil Yusif 13.7 percent, Sharifa Arina Sharaf 8.4 percent, Dina Yusif 6.25 percent, Lamia Yusif 2.3 percent, Mahmud Ahmad 4.7 percent, Muhammad Ali Ahmad 4.7 percent and Muna Ahmad 2.4 percent.
Activities The company is involved on a large scale with construction equipment, buses, trucks, lifts and generators. They hold a very comprehensive number of agencies amongst which the most important are Caterpillar machines, engines and lift trucks, Ingersoll Rand, Lorain Cranes, Uniroyal Tyres, Armco-Lincoln Welding, DJB, British Ropes, Peerless Pumps, Bearcat Tyres, Volvo Trucks and Buses, JLG Lifts, Kelly Tyres, Kismet Ynaflex.

The Family of Zahid

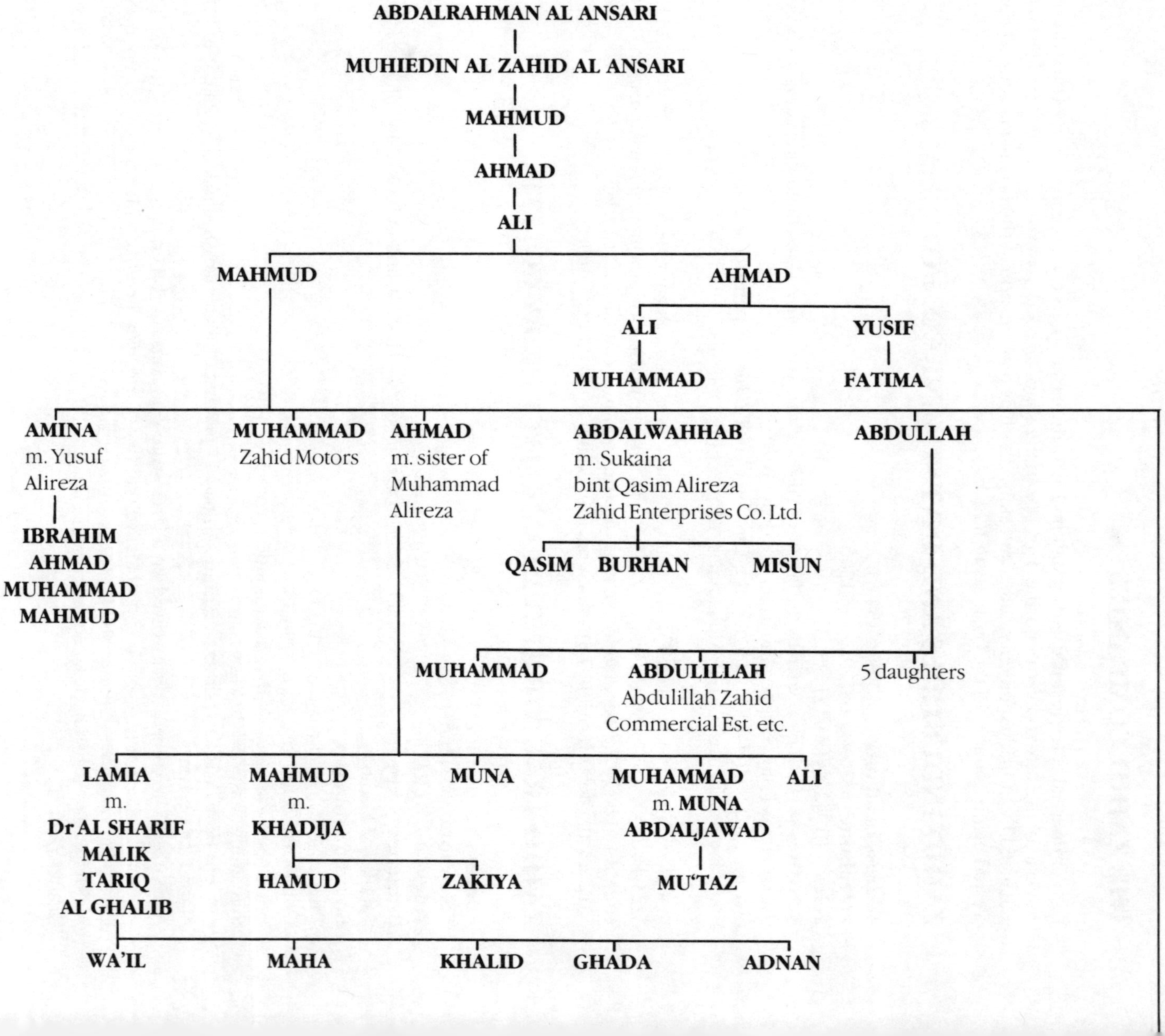

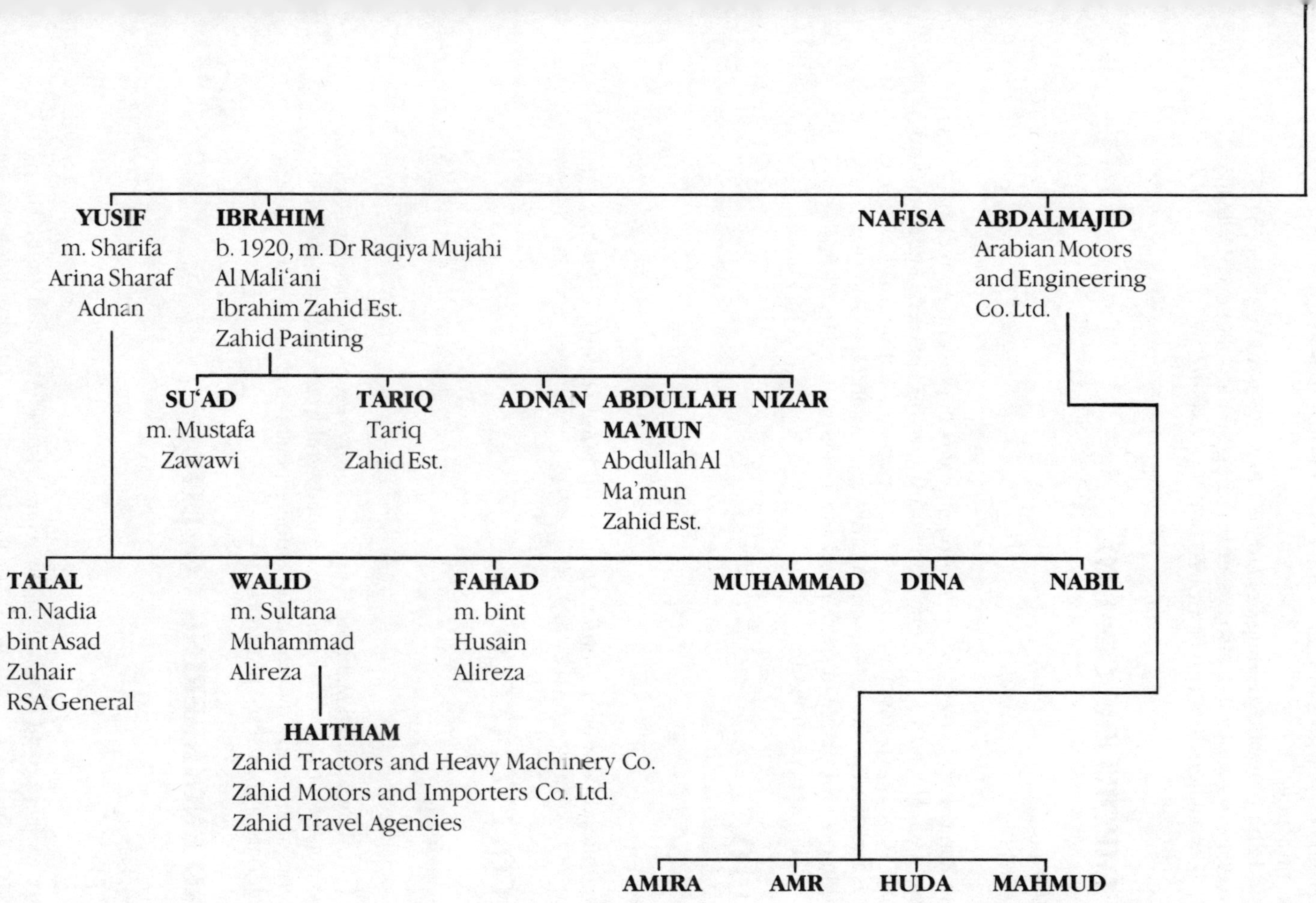
YUSIF
m. Sharifa
Arina Sharaf
Adnan
IBRAHIM
b. 1920, m. Dr Raqiya Mujahi
Al Mali'ani
Ibrahim Zahid Est.
Zahid Painting
NAFISA
ABDALMAJID
Arabian Motors
and Engineering
Co. Ltd.
SU'AD
m. Mustafa
Zawawi
TARIQ
Tariq
Zahid Est.
ADNAN
ABDULLAH
MA'MUN
Abdullah Al
Ma'mun
Zahid Est.
NIZAR
TALAL
m. Nadia
bint Asad
Zuhair
RSA General
WALID
m. Sultana
Muhammad
Alireza
FAHAD
m. bint
Husain
Alireza
MUHAMMAD
DINA
NABIL
HAITHAM
Zahid Tractors and Heavy Machinery Co.
Zahid Motors and Importers Co. Ltd.
Zahid Travel Agencies
AMIRA
AMR
HUDA
MAHMUD

Zahid Tractor owns Zahid International Communications Ltd. (PO Box 1588, tel. 6871004, tlx. 401042 ZATRAC SJ). The head office is in Riyadh, tel. 4654350, with a further branch in al Khobar. It is engaged in communications equipment and contracting.
The company also owns Caltex Zahid Shipping and Trading Co. Ltd., PO Box 3054, Jiddah, tel. 6531092, 6530856, tlx. 403051, (this concern deals in lubricants), also Lesser Building Systems, PO Box 1588, Jiddah, tel. 6876366, 6876420, tlx. ZATRAC SJ, which deals in pre-fabricated building systems.

ZAHID MOTORS AND IMPORTERS CO. LTD.

Address head office PO Box 4690, Jiddah
Telephone 6877586, 6876366, 6876420
Telex 401042 ZATRAC SJ
Proprietors Owned by Talal Yusif Zahid 12.5 percent, Sharifa Arina Sharaf 6.25 percent, Ahmad Mahmud 25 percent, Fahad Yusif 12.5 percent, Lamia Ahmad 4.15 percent, Mahmud Ahmad 8.33 percent, Muhammad Ali Ahmad 8.33 percent, Muhammad Yusif 12.5 percent, Muna Yusif 4.15 percent, Walid Yusif 12.5 percent.
Activities The company are dealers and distributors for General Motors, Pignon, and GMODC (Isuzu) and operate repair shops., selling in addition a full range of spare parts and accessories, batteries and servicing facilities for commercial vehicles and hoisting equipment.

ARAB BUILDERS CO. LTD.

Address PO Box 6552, Jiddah
Telephone 6873082
Telex 401042 ZATREC SJ
Established in 1978 this business is confined to general contracting and road-building and is owned by Talal Yusif Zahid.

ZAHID ENTERPRISES CO. LTD. (ZECO)

Address head office PO Box 352, Jiddah
Telephone 6312502, 6310969
Telex 400952 DIHAZ SJ
Activities The company is owned by Abdalwahhab Mahmud Zahid and his two sons, Burhan and Qasim. The company is engaged in a wide variety of activities, including: readymade children's and women's clothes, contracting as painters and decorators, dairies and dairy products, domestic and industrial paints, plastic products, building and roofing materials and car care products.

ARABIAN MOTORS AND ENGINEERING CO. LTD.

Address head office PO Box 166, Dammam
Telephone 8262411, 8273363, 8273508
Telex 601033 AMEACO SJ
Activities The president and owner of 60 percent of the company is Abdalmajid Mahmud Zahid. His two sons, Amr and Mahmud own 20 percent each. The company holds the General Motors dealership for the Eastern Province. They act as general sales agents for TWA and operate vehicle rental and maintenance facilities for Chevrolet, Oldsmobile and Cadillac.
Abdalmajid Zahid is a considerable investor in other enterprises, having interests in the following portfolios: Trans Arabian Services Co (48 percent), Gulf Company for Trade, Contracting and Industry Ltd (33.3 percent), Saudi Foods and Refreshment Co. Ltd. (50 percent), J A Jones Saudi Arabia Ltd. (12 percent), Saudi Bulk Transport Ltd. (4 percent), Delta Electronic and Mechanical Installations Ltd. (55 percent), National Pipes Co. Ltd. (1 percent), Saudi Cairo Bank (0.5 percent).

ABDULLAH ZAHID COMMERCIAL ESTABLISHMENT

Address head office PO Box 3842, Jiddah
Telephone 6446438
Activities This concern operates on a largely consultancy basis over a broad spectrum of engineering skills, covering agro engineering, civil, electrical and mechanical engineering and communications and hydraulic engineering. The consultancy activities extend to management, marketing and town planning. The company also acts as suppliers of electrical equipment, engines and industrial gas and diesel.

BAKARABIA LTD.

Address head office PO Box 3842, Jiddah
Telephone 6446438
Company history The company is a consultancy in the field of civil, electrical, hydraulic and mechanical engineering, as well as management and marketing. They are also suppliers of engines and industrial gas and diesel.

The Family of Zaidan

Originating in Mecca, this family shows the capacity for absorbing technology of the most advanced kind which is a feature of much of the Kingdom's industry.

- **ZAIDAN**
  - **HASAN**
    - **MUHAMMAD**
      - **HASAN** Bureau de Change in Mecca
        - **MUHAMMAD** civil servant in Min. of Civil Aviation
        - **RASHAD** Ph.D. geology UK
      - **AHMAD** President of the Beta Co. Ltd., leader in systems engineering; Kingdom's first radio ham; born Mecca 1915; Radio Technical Centre graduate 1932; Diploma of Meteorology, RAF Iraq, 1944, Diploma UK GPO telecommunications 1951, Dir. Jiddah radio station 1936, PTT Director Hasa 1938, 35 years in this Ministry of which he was Deputy Minister in 1973 Ptner also in EECC
        - **FAISAL** b. Mecca 1938, B.Sc. Chairman of Board of Governors of Arab Satellite Communications Organisation, Deputy Min. PTT
          - **AHMAD**
        - **MUHAMMAD** b. Mecca 1942, M.Sc. Electronics, ex civil servant Min. of Information as Gen. Supervisor of maintenance of broadcasting stations, studios and transmitters; Dir. of Telecomms. Dept. and Technical Dir. of Western Region. Ptner in EECC.
          - **YASIR**
          - **AMAR**
          - **AHMAD**
        - **ABDALAZIZ** Gen. Man. of Beta Co. Ltd.
          - **AHMAD**
        - **ZIYAD** Gen. Man. of Idea Centre M.A. Detroit Architect
      - **SAMI** Prof. at Univ. of Petroleum
      - **AFAF**
      - **FAISAL**

INTERNATIONAL DESIGN ENGINEERING AND ARCHITECTURE IDEA CENTRE

Address head office P.O.Box 1999 Jiddah
Telephone 40015, 46026
Telex 400220 IDEAMC
Cable address MOHANDISZAIDAN
Branch office Riyadh P.O.Box 2824, tel. 62732, tlx. 202093
Proprietor Sh. Ziyad Ahmad Zaidan
Activities This is probably the most go-ahead and exciting architectural firm in the Kingdom and it was founded in October 1974. Sh. Ziyad specializes in adapting Islamic and Arabian architectural themes to modern materials. He himself has had wide experience in the USA; having taken his degree at Detroit he gained practical experience by working with Wakely Kushner from 1968 to 1975, and Eggers and Higgins from 1967 to 1968. He is a member of the Board of the Prince Fawwaz Project for co-operative housing and the Idea Centre has already won two awards from the Ministry of Municipal Affairs.
Few architectural firms can see the whole job through but the Idea Centre has a Construction Supervision Department which ensures that both architect and client obtain satisfaction that work is executed in accordance with design. The following list of some of the projects awarded to this firm is not exhaustive but gives an accurate picture of the scope and versatility of its work.
The housing complex for the Yanbo Cement Company comprising 315 units; the Commercial Centre, Jiddah; the Fish Market Jiddah; the Foreign and Information Ministries complexes in Riyadh; a computerized information system for the Ministry of Municipal and Rural Affairs; the Headquarters of the BETA company in Riyadh; the Riyadh Hotel in Jiddah and the Mecca Hotel in Mecca. Residences for H.R.H. Prince Misha'al b. Abdalaziz and H.R.H. Prince Hamoud b. Abdalaziz and Sh. Wabel Pharaon, the Okaz printing and Publishing Centre, offices for the King Faisal Charitable Foundation in Dammam, complete designs for Royal Saudi Missions abroad, the Safwa Anik road in the Eastern Province, an interim building for the Ministry of Foreign Affairs in Jiddah, the Yanbu Master Plan and Design Study.

ELECTRICAL AND ELECTRONIC CONTRACTING CO. LTD

Address head office P.O.Box 1999 Jiddah
Telephone 690221, 690223
Telex 400477 EECCGO SJ
Cable address MOHANDISZAIDAN
Branch office Riyadh P.O.Box 2824, tel. 62732, tlx. 20293 IDEACN SJ, cable MOHANDISZAIDAN
Proprietorship
Sh. Ahmad Muhammad Zaidan 50%
Sh. Muhammad Ahmad Zaidan 50%
The company was begun in 1978. The Managing Director, Sh. Muhammad Ahmad Zaidan, obtained his M.Sc. at Berlin in 1971 and gained experience with training courses at the Mechanical Institute Berlin, Ambig, Fritz Hanaman, Siemens, Institute of Computer Science Berlin, ITV Geneva and the Research Institute of Telefunken Germany. In addition he speaks three languages fluently, Arabic, English and German.
EECC are consultant contractors for electrical and electronic projects and the importation of teleprinter, telex and facsimile equipment. They effect sales to both the Government and the private sector of the market and cover installation operation and maintenance.
The company holds agencies for Datotek communications security equipment and Digital Facsimile Machines, for Data Source Office Computer Systems and Radio Stampa of Italy.
Bankers National Commercial Bank, Al Jazira Bank.

The Family of Zamil

A family originating from the Bani Thawr of Sbiya' and from the Qasim area and Anaiza.

- **ZAMIL**
  - **MUHAMMAD**
    - **IBRAHIM**
      - **MUHAMMAD**
        - **HAMAD**
          - **MUHAMMAD**
            - **HAMAD**
              - **ABDULLAH**
                - **MUHAMMAD** — Chairman in Bahrain
                  - **ABDULLAH**
                  - **NAWWAF**
                  - **AMAL**
                  - **MAHA**
                - **ABDALRAHMAN** — Dep. Governor Riyadh Electrical Corporation. Ph.D. in Political Science and International Relations
                  - **BANDAR**
                  - **ASIYL**
                - **HAMAD** — President of the Group. In the Al Khobar office. M.A. in Business and Hospital Admin.
                  - **ABDULLAH**
                  - **YASIR**
                  - **GHASSAN**
                  - **RIYM**
                  - **HAYFA**
                - **ABDALAZIZ** — Vice-Chairman and M.D. of SABIC in Riyadh. M.A. in Industrial Eng.
                  - **USSAMA**
                  - **SATTAM**
                  - **MADAWI**
                - **ZAMIL** — President of Zamil Marine. M.A. in Petroleum Eng.
                  - **SUFIAN**
                  - **MANAL**

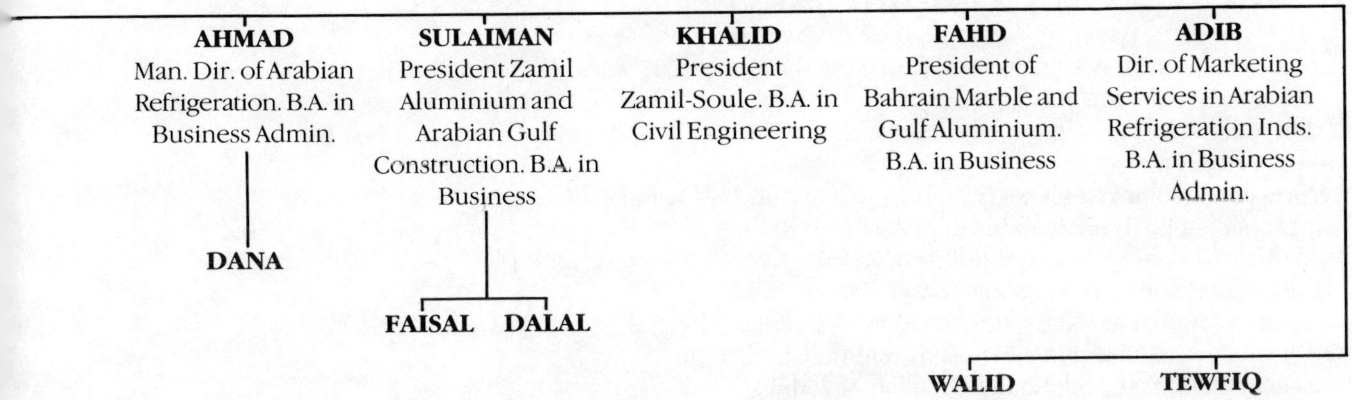
AHMAD
Man. Dir. of Arabian Refrigeration. B.A. in Business Admin.
DANA
SULAIMAN
President Zamil Aluminium and Arabian Gulf Construction. B.A. in Business
FAISAL
DALAL
KHALID
President Zamil-Soule. B.A. in Civil Engineering
FAHD
President of Bahrain Marble and Gulf Aluminium. B.A. in Business
ADIB
Dir. of Marketing Services in Arabian Refrigeration Inds. B.A. in Business Admin.
WALID
TEWFIQ

The Family of Al Mansur Al Zamil

This branch of the Zamil family is called the Al Mansur and emanates from Anaiza. For another branch see p. 248.

- **MUHAMMAD AL MANSUR AL ZAMIL**
  - **IBRAHIM**
    - **SALIH** — Ptner and Co-Chairman of Haramain
      - **IBRAHIM**
      - **MANSUR**
      - **MUHAMMAD**
      - **SULAIMAN**
    - **ABDULLAH** — Civil Eng. graduate, USA

ABDULLAH H AL ZAMIL AND SONS

Address head office P.O. Box 9 Al Khobar and P.O. Box 285 Manama, Bahrain.
Telephone 42567, 42784; Bahrain 53445
Telex 601114 ARI SJ; Bahrain 8381 ZAMIL GJ
Board of Directors
Chairman and Joint President Sh. Muhammed Abdullah Al Zamil (Bahrain)
Joint President Sh. Hamad Abdullah Al Zamil (Al Khobar)
Vice Chairman Sh. Abdalaziz Abdullah Al Zamil
President of Zamil Marine Sh. Zamil Abdullah Al Zamil
Man. Dir. of Arabian Refrigeration Sh. Ahmad Abdullah Al Zamil
President Zamil Aluminium Sh. Sulaiman Abdullah Al Zamil
President Zamil Soule Sh. Khalid Abdullah Al Zamil
President Bahrain Marble and Gulf Aluminium Sh. Fahd Abdullah Al Zamil
Director of Marketing Services, Arabian Refrigeration, Sh. Adib Abdullah Zamil.
Company History
Sh. Abdullah b. Hamad left Anaiza and after a short stay in Jubail settled in Bahrain where he became a well known merchant. He died in 1961 and his children returned to the Kingdom building on the commercial foundations laid by their father. This most remarkable and energetic family expresses the hopes and policies of the Royal Saudi Government and puts them into action with amazing vigour. To begin with they developed the commercial and real estate aspects of the family business finally founding the Industrial Division in 1972 with the establishment of Zamil Aluminium; in 1974 they began work on the first air conditioner factory in the Kingdom which began production in the following year and today this production is measured as giving a seven times growth rate. In 1976 the Soule joint venture for the manufacture of structural steel buildings was added to the list and this went into production in 1978 with an annual capacity of 30,000 tons. They operate the first and only factory in Jubail for meat processing and dairy products, they produce aluminium, marble and nails in Bahrain and their investments involve them in many other companies. On the service side Zamil Marine deals with Aramco serving offshore rigs with their supply boats and they own the only floating dry dock in the Kingdom which is used permanently by Aramco. They also operate a Commercial Division which handles their representation business, a travel agency and the Arab Gulf Construction Company.

The Commercial Division

This division is responsible for the management of the company's real estate investment, land development and property leasing business, marketing all A H Al Zamil and Sons products, both represented and manufactured, and other commercial activities which include:

Agencies

Allis Chalmers Services Inc: mineral processing equipment and cement manufacturing equipment, electrical switch gear, motors and voltage regulators.

Artex Investments Ltd: camp catering.

Carl Freudenberg and Co: floor coverings, rubber needle felt and tufted carpeting.

Core Laboratories Inc: engineering and consulting services.

English Rose Kitchens Ltd: kitchen furniture.

Emerson Electric

Pacific Logistics SA: base vessels for banking services.

Teledyne Exploration, Teledyne Geotech, Teledyne Media: gas lift equipment, supervisory control systems and computer time sharing.

Texas International Company: drilling equipment and equipment for oil and gas well workover, rig manufacture.

Commercial Activities

Granada Jewellers (Orient Arts), P.O.Box 197 Al Khobar, tel. 41266

Al Zamil Opticians, P.O.Box 25 Riyadh, tel. 25265

Zamil Travel, P.O.Box 9 Al Khobar, tel. 45634, 45646, tlx. 670132 ZAMIL SJ

The Industrial Division

Zamil Petroleum Services, P.O.Box 9 Al Khobar, tel. 42567, 42784, tlx. 601115 ARI SJ. Oil well servicing and workover, water well drilling and development.

Arabian Refrigeration Industries, P.O.Box 294 Dhahran Airport, tel. 21939, 26529, tlx. 601115 ARI SJ. Manufacture of Friedrich room air conditioners, central plant both split systems and packaged units. The company covers system design, duct manufacture and installation and its nationwide after-sales service includes a complete spare parts stock, all manufactured within the Kingdom.

Yamama Factories for Red Bricks and Clay Products, P.O.Box 4572 Riyadh, tel. 61343. Manufacture of red bricks, roof tiles and clay products.

Bahrain Marble Factory, Mina Sulman Industrial Estate P.O.Box 285 Manama, Bahrain, tel. 713085, tlx. 8381 ZAMIL GJ. Produces marble fascia and marble materials for floors and stairways.

Zamil Greatways Food Industries Ltd., P.O.Box 9 Al Khobar, tel. 42567, 42784, tlx. 601115 ARI SJ. Food processing and refrigerated warehousing.

Zamil Marine Services, P.O.Box 9 Al Khobar, tel. 42567, 42784, tlx. 601115 ARI SJ. Marine Services and dry docking where they control the only manoeuvrable floating dock in the Middle East.

Zamil Soule Steel Buildings Co. Ltd., P.O.Box 9 Al Khobar, tel. 42567, 42784, tlx. 601115 ARI SJ. Manufacture and fabrication of pre-engineered metal buildings for industrial, commercial, leisure and residential purposes.

Zamil Aluminium Factory and Gulf Aluminium Factory, P.O.Box 1633 Dammam, tel. 26679, tlx. 601115 ARI SJ. Mina Sulman Industrial Estate P.O.Box 285 Manama, Bahrain, tel. 713725, tlx. 8381 ZAMIL GJ. Both these factories produce aluminium doors and door frames and window frames; building and shop fronts, office partitions, handrails, banisters and balconies.

AL ZAMIL REFRIGERATION INDUSTRIES

ZAMILE SOULE STEEL BUILDINGS CO. LTD.

Address head office PO Box 270, Dammam

Telephone 8331291, 8329452, 8331479

Telex 601414 ZSBLDG SJ

Activities Owned by the H Al Zamil and Sons Group with branches in Jiddah (PO Box 8076, tel. 6600012, 6693105, tlx. 400626 ZSBLDG SJ) and Riyadh (PO Box 251, tel. 4764602, 4764650, tlx. 200439 ZAMIL SJ). Suplliers of pre-fabricated building systems and steel fabricators.

MERCHANT FAMILIES of KUWAIT

MERCHANT FAMILIES of KUWAIT

J.R.L. Carter

SCORPION BOOKS, LONDON

Other books by J.R.L.Carter
Tribes in Oman
Investors in Saudi Arabia
The Arabian Desert
Merchant Families of Saudi Arabia

Merchant Families of Kuwait

First published in December 1984 by
Scorpion Communications and Publications Ltd, London

ISBN 0 905906 40 3

Designed and Produced by
Scorpion Pica, London

Editor Leonard Harrow
Design and Art Direction Colin Larkin
Design and Production team
Dale Dawson, John Orley and Roger Kemlo
Typesetting ITC Garamond Light and Bold
Paper Cream Bookwove 90gsm
Printing and Binding Hazell Watson and Viney Ltd, England

Contents

Note on Spelling

As usual in books discussing aspects of the modern Arab world some confusion may arise due to spelling of Arabic names in the Latin alphabet. There is, of course, no equivocation as regards the spelling in the Arabic script. In particular, the value of Arabic vowels has led to a variety of possible spellings. For this reason it is not uncommon to find variations within an individual family as to how names are spelt in Western usage. Where possible we have attempted to render the spelling in the Latin alphabet known to be favoured by individuals or companies. Where there have been no such guidelines the spelling of names has been kept as simple and as consistent as possible.

Introduction

For the visiting businessman the most startling thing about Kuwait is the almost complete lack of published commercial information. Even the Chamber of Commerce produces no directory. This is in stark contrast to the openness and charming generosity of the Kuwaitis themselves. The reason is perhaps obvious when one considers the historical development of this comparatively small town. Even the very name of Kuwait is a diminutive, meaning a small fortified place surrounded by houses. Kuwait lived entirely by its wits for over two hundred years and today the wealth of its oil has made commercial privacy an even more important characteristic than it was before. Throughout her history this small town has had to struggle for survival in an environment of immense potential hostility. Her neighbours are comparatively huge and the talents which made Kuwait created more than avaricious glances in her direction from everyone. The Turks, Iran, Iraq, Saudi Arabia, Great Britain and Holland have all brought their several influences to bear at one time or another, and only the immense skill of the Kuwaitis has prevented them from being swallowed up and permitted them to retain their independence. For an Englishman this creates an image of gallantry; for the Kuwaitis it has meant the development of the need to play one's commercial cards very close to one's chest.

This need has received historical and added emphasis from the way in which the population has been moulded into modern Kuwaiti society.

The establishment of Kuwait had its precarious beginnings two and a half centuries ago against the background of a great tribal migration from southern Saudi Arabia towards the east and north of the peninsula. Whilst this created friction with the tribes already in place it also established a series of settlements, particularly in Najd, which had familial connections. At this time too the main trading outlet of the east was towards the Gulf. The Anaiza were the tribe involved and this confederation was eventually to spread itself as far north as Damascus whilst clans settled on the way, some attaining considerable individual positions of power. Thus the Al Saud came to rule in Najd whilst the Al Khalifa succeeded in Bahrain and the Al Sabah in Kuwait.

These settlements quite naturally grasped the opportunities presented by the commercial needs of the area. In Kuwait this process led to economic prosperity which acted as a magnet to other groups, either because they themselves were further links in the commercial chains stretching into Iraq and Arabistan of Iran, or because the settlements simply provided suitable conditions in which to conduct business, which last particularly encouraged migration from commercial centres in decline at this time.

The early picture of Kuwait therefore centres around a comparatively small group of families who settled in the town as it was founded, some of them were in the area before this of course, though the main dominance in the population tended to be Anaizi and Najdi. They formed sub-groupings which became the basis for what are now regarded as the traditional geographic divisions of old Kuwait. The Sharq or eastern part was populated in the main by such families as the Sabah, Rumi, Nusuf, Mudaf, Shamlan, Jasim, Qutami, Marafi and Shahin. The Murqab area contained the Shay', Wazzan, Mu'ajil, Muzami, Wahaib and Du'aij. Whilst, thirdly, the Qiblah area contained the Sabih, Badr, Ghanim, Humaidhi, Saqr, Khalid, Marzuq, Fawzan, Hamad, Rashid, Falah, Sudairawi and Awadhi.

The above list is by no means exhaustive but it serves to highlight one important aspect of Kuwaiti society. In effect the early settlers created a typical Arabian town as one would expect. It had specific geographic sub-divisions. However, whereas elsewhere in Arabia such divisions, (called Harat) are specifically tribal, in Kuwait they are familial. The writer believes this to have been an important factor in the evolution of Kuwaiti society and one which can only have been helpful to the maintenance of the liberality and democracy to be seen today.

From a commercial point of view the early families quickly established a flourishing entrepot trade which created of itself such profitable activities as the provision of transport for the pilgrimage to Mecca. Contacts with Iraq led to the creation of an immensely powerful trading fleet and the active participation in the India trade and further afield to Africa and the Red Sea. A trade which survived surprisingly well into the era of the steam ship. Wealth was also derived from the pearling industry until the Japanese invention of the cultured pearl earlier in this century. In this century too several rather roguish fortunes were made as a consequence of the lack of gold in India, but this is regarded as being something of a sporting activity even though its practitioners prefer to be excessively tactful about their participation.

Since the end of the Second World War much money has also been obtained by individual families as a consequence of the purchase of land by the government.

The reader may wonder why mention of oil has been left to this late point in a resume of the sources of Kuwaiti wealth. It is because the businessman aspiring to trade with Kuwait may be dazzled by its sheer quantity to the extent that he doesn't see the wealth of commercial talent to which the oil revenues are merely an adjunct. In Kuwait wealth from both oil and more historical activities such as the entrepot trade, pearling, gold smuggling, and land sales, has become a commodity in its own right. It can be said that the sons of the men who bartered Iraqi dates in Bombay now trade in money. It is for this reason that the sophisticated financial institutions of Kuwait are of such importance, and why they have received more attention in this commercial picture of the city than comparable institutions in the Saudi volume.

In this connection mention of the Manakh scandal must be made. It is not a matter of which Kuwait is very proud and in many Kuwaiti circles the very mention of this disastrous unofficial stock exchange causes profound embarrassment. In brief what happened was that the shares of rather a few private Arabian companies were traded in, payment being largely made in post-dated cheques which were themselves used for trade. The consequence was financial mayhem. In the long run the matter will be seen to have been a useful if expensive lesson; those from the Western World who are prepared to sneer should remember the Wall Street collapse or the South Sea Bubble. Oddly enough the method of transaction was perhaps only an expression of the proud traditionalism which is such a feature of Kuwait. In the old days a bedouin would see some sheep and the owner would let him have them against a promise to return them with an agreed addition at a later date. This was a perfectly normal way of doing business, but it did not work with cheques. The Government is still involved with sorting out the consequences and is treating the matter with close attention to the justice of individual cases.

The visitor to Kuwait will be struck by the survival of Arabian traditions and institutions alongside wholesale modernity and very sophisticated appreciation of what he may like to call Western progress. There is an air of confident maturity in the city and a quiet pride in just being Kuwaiti.

This is enhanced by the continuation of the majlis system. Each family meets together regularly either at the house of the head of the family or in a building specially used for this purpose. At these gatherings, where strangers are made most welcome, all family decisions are made. Sons are set up in business, education of the young is settled, family money is allocated for special projects, the old and the sick are taken care of, and last but not least, the way the family would like to vote in elections is discussed. Hence the saying that in Kuwait they do not have political parties they have families instead.

One of the charming aspects of this majlis system is that each family tends to arrange the timing of its majlis so that it does not clash with anyone else's. In a week a visitor can thus meet practically everyone if he knows his way around.

In presenting this small picture of a great and generous people the author would like to say that it is only a picture and can in no way be a directory. Any errors are his and whilst he owes a deep debt of thanks to all his many informants he is aware that too public an acknowledgement is not the Arabian way. However, he would ask the following to accept his thanks on their own account as well as that of their colleagues.

Saud al Fawzan, Khalid al Hamad, Muhammad Yusif al Badr and Abdalatif al Thuwaini.

Finally, he wishes to dedicate this small volume to the merchant community of Kuwait in the hope that in its own way it will be a help.

The Family of Al Abdalhadi

The family originates in Anaiza of Saudi Arabia. Like so many of the older Kuwaiti families was involved in the pearl trade and took to new activities when this business died.

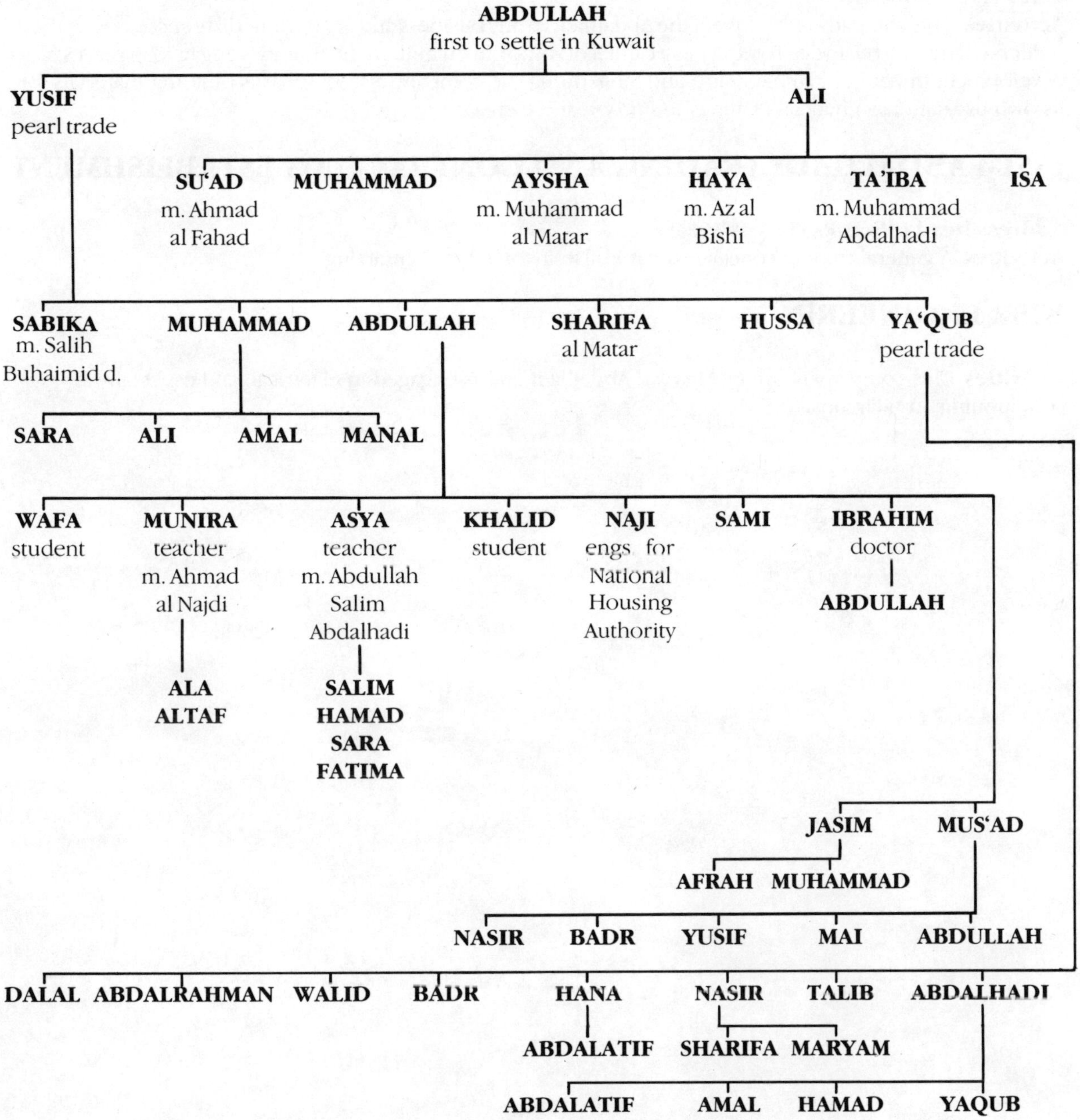

ABDULLAH YUSIF ABDALHADI TRADING AND CONTRACTING ESTABLISHMENT

Address head office P.O.Box 1973 Safat
Telephone 421790, 421797
Telex 44615 GRANCO KT
Activities This company is the core of the Abdalhadi family business and is the immediate successor of the older pearl trading business. Today it has a capital of some fifteen million dinars and is engaged in real estate development in Bahrain, Dubai, Cairo and Singapore. The company also purchases building materials for its own use, and has financial dealings in Europe and Geneva.

JASIM ABDALHADI TRADING AND CONTRACTING ESTABLISHMENT

Address head office P.O.Box 1973 Safat
Activities A general trading concern which is also involved in contracting.

KISR ENGINEERING

Activities This company is run by Musa'ad Abdalhadi and is engaged in electrical, and especially air-conditioning, installations.

The Family of Al Abdali

The family has roots returning to the Bani Zayd of Qahtan through Quda'at. In the Kingdom of Saudi Arabia they have relatives in Shuqara and Qasim.

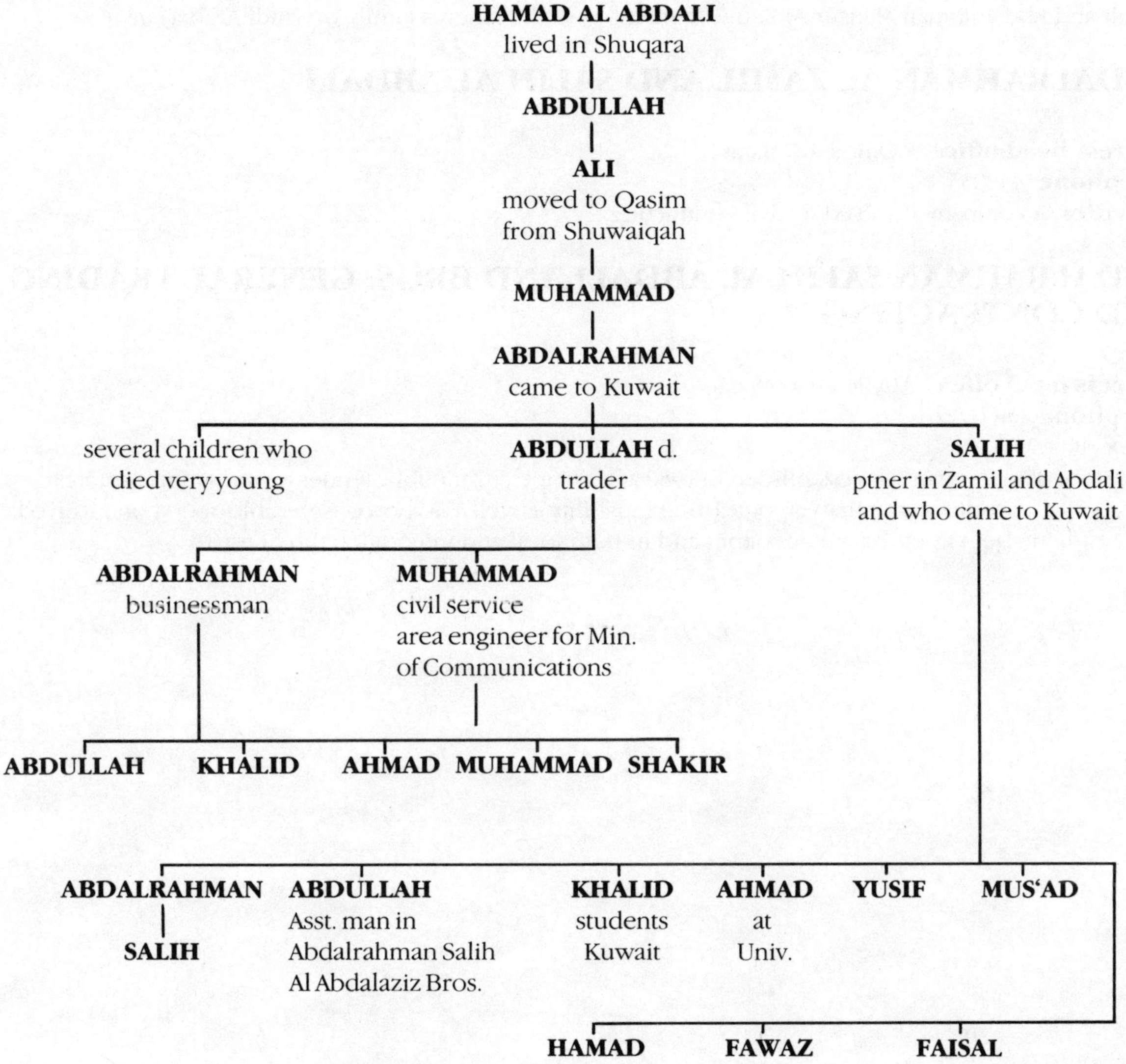

AL MANSUR AND AL ABDALI TRADING AND CONTRACTING CO.

Address head office P.O.Box 1207 Safat
Telephone 844300
Telex 22199 MAC KT
Activities The company is a general trading company which is also engaged as a contractor specialising in road construction, drainage, and multi-storey buildings. It is a partnership between Salih Abdalrahman Al Abdali and Abdalrahman Mansur Al Zamil (a member of the famous family of Saudi Arabia)[q.v.]

ABDALRAHMAN AL ZAMIL AND SALIH AL ABDALI

Address head office P.O.Box 427 Safat
Telephone 432935
Activities A company involved in civil contracting.

ABDALRAHMAN SALIH AL ABDALI AND BROS. GENERAL TRADING AND CONTRACTING

Address head office P.O.Box 4560 Safat
Telephone 2460022
Telex 46669 KT
Activities The company was established in 1982 and competes for public tender business and operates as an importer. In addition, they have a contracting capability as well as a very considerable operation involved in investment, both as exchange operators and in both local and international real estate.

The Family of Abdalkarim

Originate from Harma near Hawtat al Sudair of Najd in Saudi Arabia.

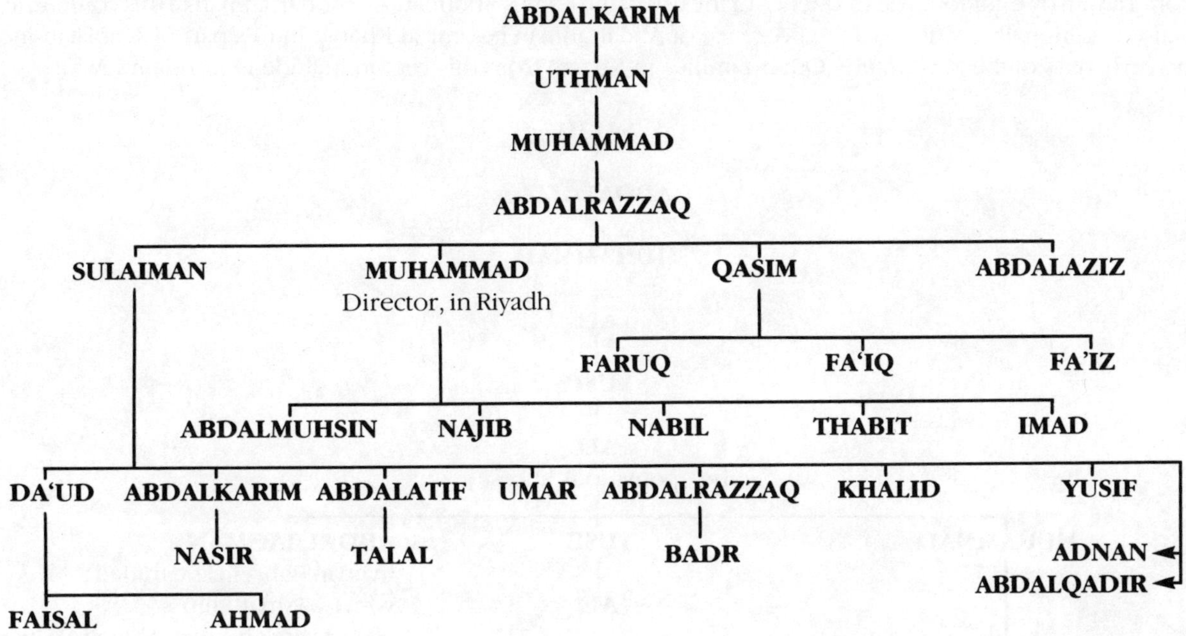

SULAIMAN AL ABDALKARIM AND BROS. CO.

Address head office P.O.Box 20204 Safat
Telephone 422119, 440817
Telex 23881 WAZAH KT
Activities Owned by Sulaiman and his brothers, the company deals in paper products, paper, stationery, general goods and ready-made garments.

SULAIMAN AL ABDALKARIM AND BROS. CO.

Address head office P.O.Box 675 Safat
Telephone 425866, 432344
Telex 22297 OTBEH KT
Activities The General Manager of this company is Abdalaziz Abdalrazaq Al Abdalkarim and it is engaged in trading in fruit juices and foodstuffs which they wholesale and distribute. The company has a branch in Riyadh (P.O.Box 4066, telex 202132 ATHLEH SJ) which is managed by Muhammad Abdalrazaq.

The Family of Al Ali

In old Kuwait the water carriers came from Kandar in Iran and were called Kandaris. This name came to be applied to people from the same area of the Gulf littoral. The Al Ali have been given this name but descend from Tamim by tradition. The frequency of the use of the names Abdullah and Abdalrahman in this community is also traditionally ascribed to the presence of Abdalrahman b. Umr al Khatab in this part of Arabistan in the early days of the Muslim era. Other families in Kuwait from this region include Qaband and Asfur.

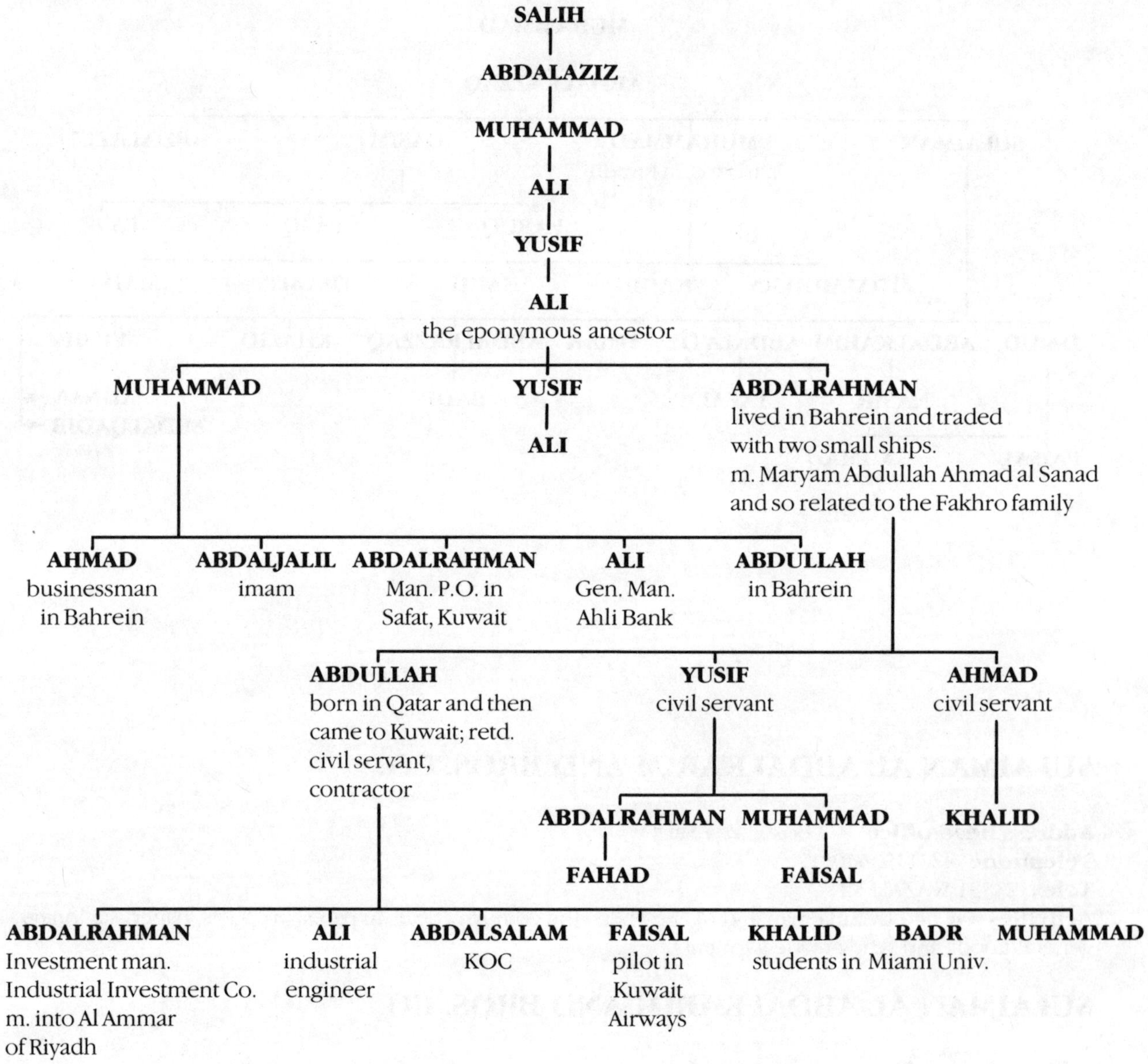

A family showing clearly how diversification and growth of the economy has created opportunity for ways of earning one's livelihood without going into business on one's own account. The original commercial activities of this family have not survived and the younger generation is, without exception, engaged in employed professional capacities. The family also shows the close familial links which exist between one country and another in the Gulf region.

The Family of Alireza

The complete tree for this most distinguished family is laid out in the Saudi volume.

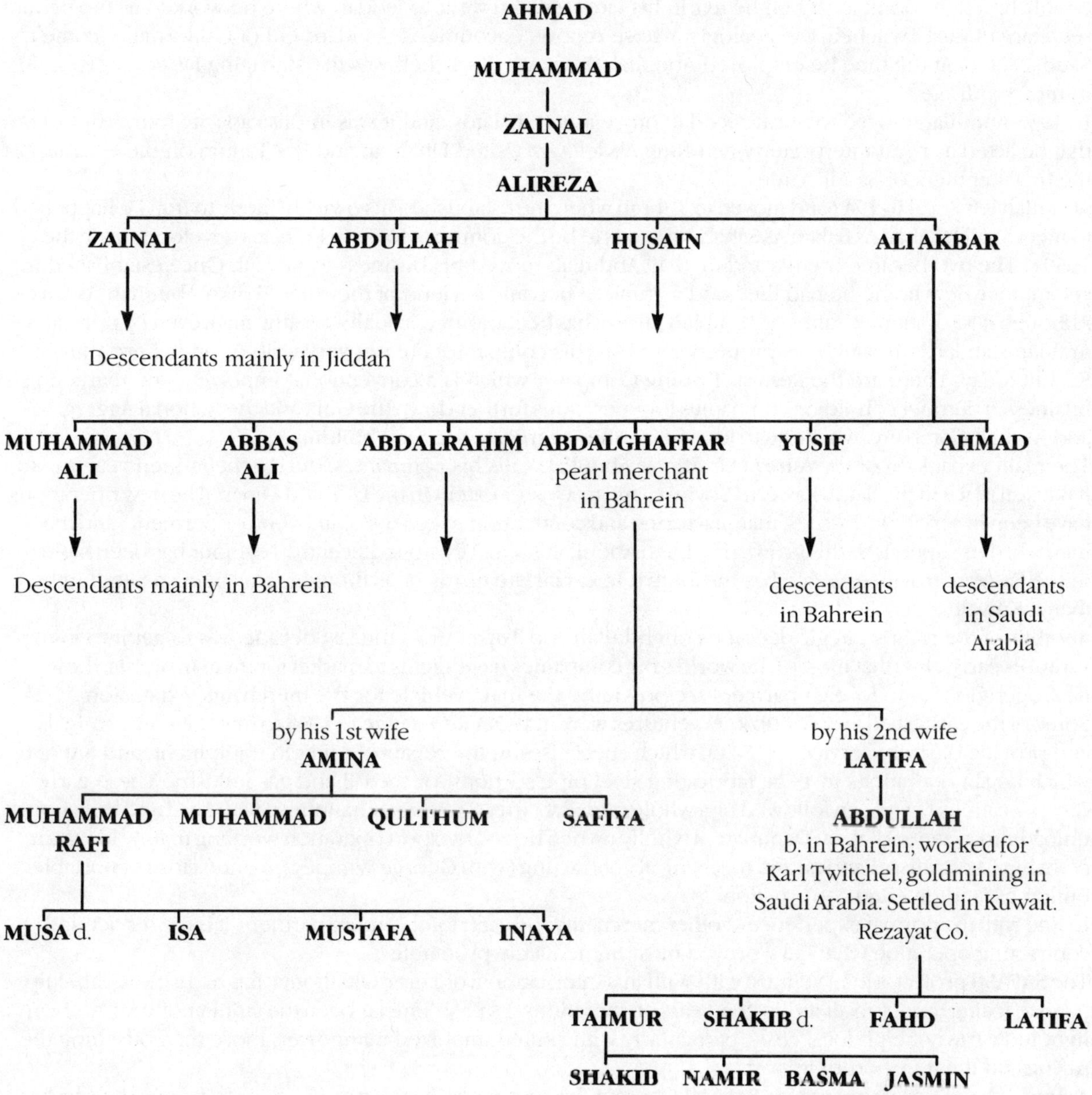

During the thirties Abdalghafar was in the pearl business having moved from Iran to Bahrain, the centre of the Gulf pearling industry, at the beginning of the century. He did much of his selling through 62 rue Lafayette, the Paris offices of Muhammad Ali Alireza, his cousin from the Jeddah branch of the family, who used his income from pearls to finance the charitable schools he established in the Hijaz and the Gulf.

Travel, together with a good education, has been the secret of success for all branches of the Alireza family. And true to this pattern the son of Abdalghafar, Abdullah, was sent to St. Xavier's School, the Jesuit establishment in Bombay. When he left in his late teens he went to Jeddah where he worked as the private secretary of Carl Twitchell, the geologist whose reports encouraged Standard Oil of California to come to Saudi Arabia. At the time he employed Abdullah, however, Twitchell was the Managing Director of a gold mining syndicate.

In 1935 Abdullah moved to Socal's Jeddah office as a translator, and it was in this capacity four years later that he acted as royal interpreter when King Abdel-Aziz visited Dhahran and Ras Tanura on the occasion of the first shipment of Saudi crude.

Abdullah left Socal in 1942 and moved to Tehran where he established his own business. In Iran he happened to meet Shaikh Fahad As Salam As Sabah, who was to be the dominant force in Kuwait's development in the 1950's. The two became friends and in 1949 Abdullah moved his business to Kuwait. Once established in yet another new home he had the good fortune to become a friend of the ruler Shaikh Abdullah As Salam.

Although it is sometimes said that Abdullah Alireza has become an unusually wealthy man, even by normal Arabian standards, through his property interests, his companies are not very visible "on the ground" in Kuwait today. There are the Rezayat Trading Company, which is a conventional importing and marketing business, a number of holding companies for operations further down the Gulf, and the National Aggregate and Asphalt Company, which quarries and crushes aggregate for road building.

The main expansion of the Alireza Group, as Abdullah calls his companies, during the last ten years or so has taken place in the Saudi Eastern Province, and to a lesser extent in the UAE and Oman. The new operations have been in service industries, manufacturing and contracting - often with joint-venture partners - and the man who has supervised this growth has been Abdullah's son, Teymour. Recently, Teymour has been based in the Eastern Province, which has meant that in expatriate terms he is thought of as being a Saudi rather than a Kuwaiti.

Another of the right strategic decisions of Abdullah and Teymour in the last decade was to get into joint ventures early. Now that most of the world's big companies have agents to market for them in Arabia, these new operations with foreign partners are providing the main vehicle for the merchants' expansion.

Some of the earliest Alireza Group joint ventures were: LAMNALCO, set up in 1963 to maintain oil terminals and provide offshore services; SAECO, which specialises in the repair of oil field equipment; and SAFAMI, which began operations in 1974, fabricating steel pipe sections for the oil and gas industry. These early diversifications have been followed by a whole range of others: container handling (with Sea-Land), offshore unloading of cement bags at Dammam, a wholly owned heavy transport operation working mainly in Oman, plant hire, specialist electrical and mechanical contracting (with George Wimpey), manufacture of portable buildings, and pipeline construction.

In line with the normal experience of other merchants and their joint venture partners, it is the service and contracting operations that have proved most immediately profitable.

The SAFAMI project, a joint venture with Williams International of Tulsa, Oklahoma, has had a more difficult history, losing money in all its first few years of operations. Its problem has been the familiar one for Arabian light industries of high local costs, particularly with skilled imported manpower, more than offsetting the savings on the transport of imports.

Aramco, the major customer for SAFAMI's output, has not made it a matter of policy to favour the local supplier as would be likely to happen in the Gulf states. So in practice SAFAMI has lost contracts where labour has been the key factor in the bids, and won contracts where the tonnage in volume terms has been the crucial factor. As from 1977 SAFAMI has been running a much more profitable operation at Juaymah, where it has a contract to manage another pipe fabrication yard on behalf of Aramco.

At present the Alireza Group is leading other Saudi entrepreneurs, in partnership with Sumitomo, in a much bigger project involving the production of welded steel piping in the Dhahran area. The project had the backing of a Saudi Industrial Development Fund loan and was completed in 1981. It is one of the two or three biggest private industrial ventures in the Kingdom, and a major test of the economics of manufacturing in the Arabian Peninsula.

ABDULLAH ABDALGHAFAR ALIREZA

Address head office P.O.Box 106 Kuwait
Telephone 428575, 433630
Telex 22070 KT
Activities A civil contracting company.

LAMNALCO LTD.

Address head office P.O.Box 11220 Dasmah
Telephone 831030, 840161, 849072
Telex 22070 REZAYAT KT
Activities The directors of this company from the family are Abdullah Abdalghafar Alireza and his son, Taimur. It is engaged in business as a marine and oil terminal operator, involved in pilotage, ship-owning and management, marine consultancy, brokerage and maritime civil engineering.

REZAYAT TRADING CO.

Address head office P.O.Box 106 Safat
Telephone 433775
Telex 22070 KT
Activities The owner of this company is Abdullah Abdalghafar Alireza and it is engaged in the contracting business, as well as being a fuel supplier.

The Family of Al Ateeqi

A family from Majma'a in Najd, Saudi Arabia. They have two traditions as to the origin of the family name, which means old or ancient. The first is that they descend from a man who was injured in a war, and having been left in the desert was found and protected by a woman from the opposing side who called him Ateeqi, the old one. Of more consequence is the tradition that they descend from Atiq, who was the son of the brother of the first caliph, Abu Bakr.

- **SALIM**
  - **ABDALRAHMAN** ex Minister of Finance
    - **ANWAR** business
    - **AKRAM** student at Kuwait Univ.
    - **SALIM**
  - **ABDULLAH** businessman, real estate and investment
    - **NA'IF** Man. Kuwait Auto-Producers
    - **HAMAD**
    - **QAYS** civil servant Min. of Finance Investment Dept.
    - **LAYTH**
  - **MUHAMMAD** owns cattle ranch in Kuwait and furniture factory
    - **AMRU** in Petrochemical Industries Co.
    - **SALIM** pilot

- **ABDALATIF**
  - **ALI**
    - **SAIF** who came to Kuwait. Died in Jahra war c. 1927
      - **MUHAMMAD**
        - **SAIF**
          - **SALAH** Investment Man. Kuwait Finance House
            - **ABDALWAHHAB**
          - **ABDALATIF** businessman
            - **AHMAD**
          - **TARIQ** Industrial Bank of Kuwait
          - **ABDALMUHSIN**
        - **SA'UD**
          - **WALID**
          - **KHALID**
        - **SULAIMAN**
      - **JASIM**
        - **MUHAMMAD** in his father's company
      - **ABDULLAH** d.
      - **ALI** d.

THE ARAB ECONOMICAL FINANCIAL AND INDUSTRIAL CONSULTING CO.

Address head office P.O.Box 5171 Kuwait
Telephone 410357
Telex 22882 AFINCO KT
Activities The Chairman of this company is Anwar Abdalrahman Al Atiqi and they are engaged in business, industry and finance consultancy.

ATEEQI TRADING AND ENGINEERING ENTERPRISES

Address head office P.O.Box 699 Safat
Telephone 717945,6,7, 717941
Telex 23007 ATEEQ KT
Activities This company is a partnership between Abdullah Salim Al Ateeqi and two of his sons, Na'if and Hamad. The business deals with civil contracting, building materials and construction machinery.

AL DERWAZA ELECTRICAL ESTABLISHMENT

Address head office P.O.Box 3409 Safat
Telephone 447817
Cable ABUSAIF
Activities A company owned by Abdalatif Saif Al Ateeqi dealing in electrical goods and appliances.

KUWAIT INDIA INTERNATIONAL EXCHANGE CO.

Address head office P.O.Box 25965 Safat
Telephone 422699, 422733, 422678
Telex 44127 KIESB KT, 44627 KIESB KT
Activities Hamad Abdullah Al Ateeqi is the Chairman of this company which is involved with mail and telex transfers, dealing with drafts and travellers cheques in the following currencies: pounds sterling, dollars and rupees.

NEUTRAL TRADING AND CONTRACTING CO. LTD.

Address head office P.O.Box 4409 Safat
Telephone 448477, 448488
Activities A company owned by Khalid Saud Al Ateeqi occupied with general trading and contracting.

The Family of Al Awadhi

There are many families of this name which derives from an Iranian town, but such families are not necessarily related. However, despite several immigrations at various times they form an important and integral part of the population of Kuwait and have contributed much to the life and commerce of the country. It is said in some sources that they brought their wealth with them, a fact highly regarded as they brought resources with them rather than appearing in Kuwait as fortune hunters.

I

- **ALI AL AWADHI**
  - **TAQI**
    - **ALI**
      - **MUHAMMAD** had factory producing soft drink, Namlait. Possibly a kind of ginger beer, not drunk today.
        - *First marriage*
          - **YA'QUB**
          - **YUSIF**
          - **ABDALATIF**
          - **FAWZIA**
          - **AYSHA**
          - **RUKAYA**
        - *2nd marriage to a Qabandiya*
          - **ABDALSALAM**
          - **ABDALWAHID**
          - **NASIMA**
          - **NAJIBA**
        - *3rd marriage*
          - **IBRAHIM**
            - **FARUQ**
            - **FAISAL**
            - **NAJIB**
              - **FAWWAZ**
            - **BADR**
            - **TALAL**
            - **ABDULLAH**
            - **FATIMA**
          - **AMINA**
      - **ABDULLAH**
        - **ABDALAZIZ**
        - **MUHAMMAD**
        - **YUSIF**
    - **SALIH**

II

- **HADI AL AWADHI** who was a sailor and had shares in trading ships
  - **MUHAMMAD** businessman Al Awadhi Trading Co.
    - **ABDALHADI** Ph.D. Social Planning Asst. Under Sec. for Planning Affairs
      - **IDAH**
      - **RIM**
      - **ABIR**
      - **UMAR**
    - **MUSTAFA** army officer
      - **NUHA**
      - **NAWWAF**
    - **ABDULLAH** army officer
      - **FAHAD**
      - **FAISAL**
      - **KHALID**
    - **FATIMA**
    - **SHARIFA**
    - **SABRIA**
    - **FATIYA**
    - **MULUK**

III

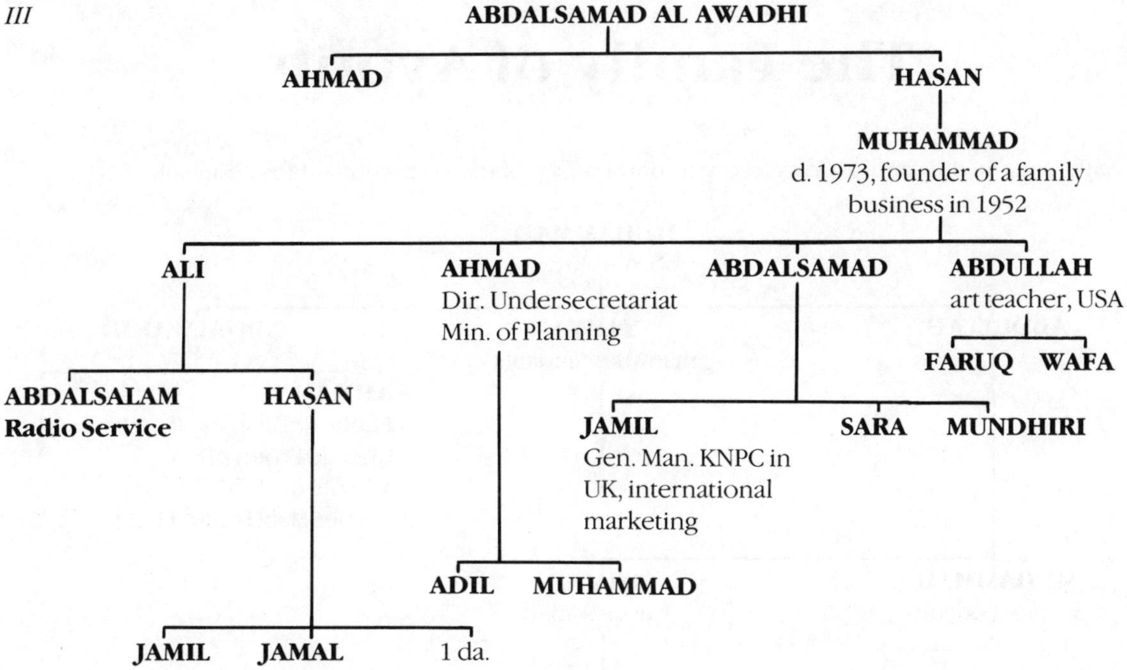

ABDALHADI AL AWADHI TRADING OFFICE

Address head office P.O.Box 3803 Safat
Telephone 423692
Activities A company owned as it is named. Acting as commission agents and general importers and exporters they deal in electronic equipment, carpets, textiles and building materials. This is the descendant of Muhammad's company but today it is run by employees rather than members of the family.

ABDULLAH MUHAMMAD HADI AL AWADHI

Address head office P.O.Box 963 Safat
Telephone 426627
Activities A firm of estate agents and building contractors.

BLOUKI TRADING ESTABLISHMENT

Address head office P.O.Box 1225 Safat
Telephone 435472, 416977
Telex 44678 AWAKJU KT
Activities This company was founded in 1952 by Muhammad Hasan Al Awadhi who imported high density timber and aluminium, pencils, carpentry tools and locks from India. Every month, in those early days, two steamers, the DAMRA and the DAWARKA, went from Kuwait to Bombay. Muhammad travelled by this means, each journey taking fifteen days, and purchased goods to wholesale to his customers at home. The business grew steadily until Muhammad extended his range to include goods from China. On his death in 1973 the control of the company passed to Ahmad Muhammad Al Awadhi and his brother Abdusamad. Today the business has both grown and developed new interests, concentrating on the supply of playing cards, games, transistor radios, torches and badges; but, above all, the company has specialised in sun-glasses. The directors have travelled widely, to Bombay, Hong Kong, Korea, Singapore and Japan. They design their own sun-glasses to the most modern and exacting specifications.

The Family of Ayoub

A part of the Jana'at, this family forms a very important part of the commercial life of Kuwait.

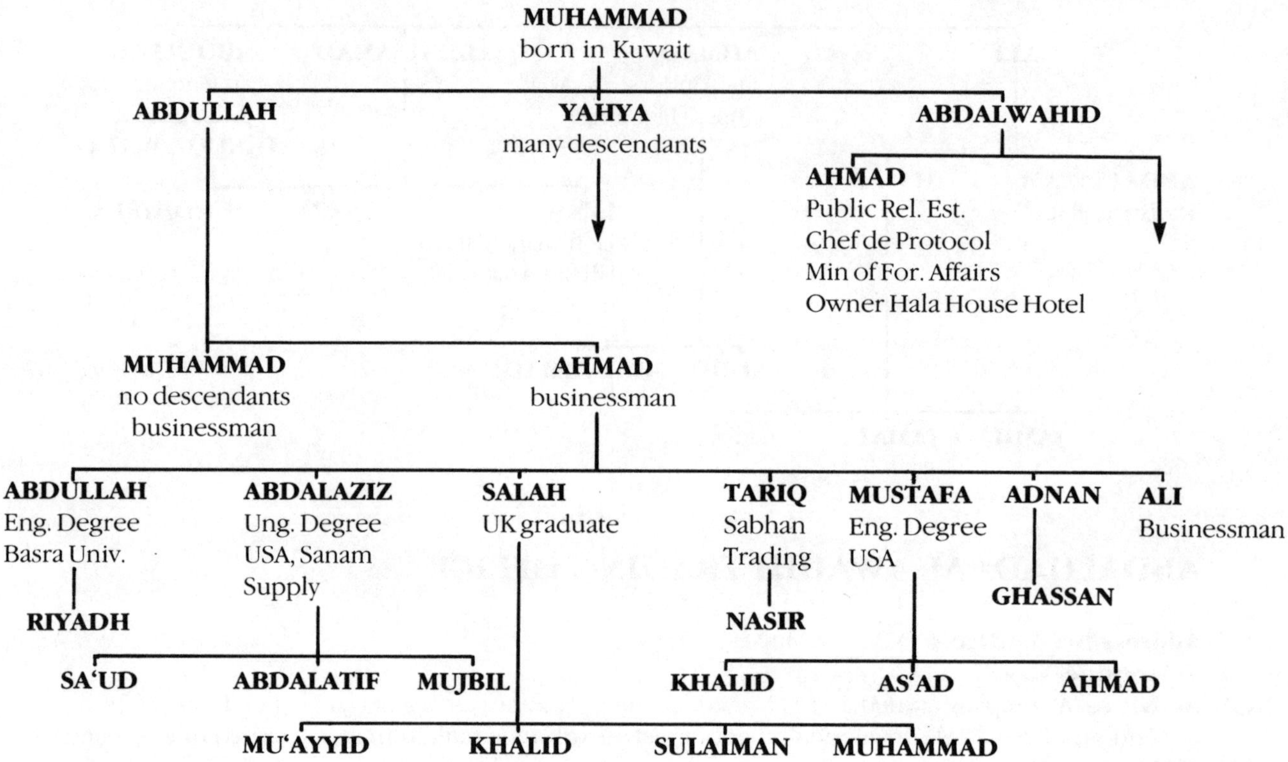

AHMAD ABDALWAHID AL AYOUB

Address head office P.O.Box 823 Kuwait
Telephone 434625
Telex 22989 HALATEL KT
Cable MODEM
Activities The company is stated to deal in souvenirs but Ahmad Abdalwahid also owns the Hala House Hotel group. Hala House 1 is a conventional hotel situated near the Hilton. It is a small comfortable hotel with very reasonable room rates and good communications. The staff are remarkably friendly and helpful and the cuisine is mainly middle eastern. Hala House 2 is a block of furnished apartments.

PUBLIC RELATIONS ESTABLISHMENT

Address head office P.O.Box 823 Safat
Telephone 433625, 415810
Telex 22087 GLOBAL KT
Activities A company owned by Ahmad Abdalwahid Al Ayoub which is engaged in professional marketing, hotels, furnished apartments and language institutes.

SABHAN TRADING BUSINESS MACHINES CO.

Address head office P.O.Box 25801 Safat
Telephone 444914
Telex 44029 SABHNCO KT
Activities A company dealing in typewriters, photocopiers, calculators, stationery and office equipment. It is owned by Tariq Ahmad Al Ayoub.

SALAH AHMAD AL AYOUB LIBRARY

Address head office P.O.Box 155 Safat
Telephone 423843
Activities A bookshop owned by Salah Ahmad Al Ayoub.

SALAH AHMAD AL AYOUB TRADING ESTABLISHMENT

Address head office P.O.Box 155 Safat
Telephone 430965, 436145
Telex 22350 ALAYOUB KT
Activities A company, owned as above, and dealing as a commission agent for general merchandise, textiles, readymade clothes and as a contractor.

SANAM SUPPLYING AND TRADING FIRM

Address head office P.O.Box 3563 Safat
Telephone 810472, 436145
Telex 22350 KT
Activities Owned by Abdalaziz Ayoub, this company deals in oil field, welding and safety equipment as well as generators.

AHMAD ABDULLAH AYOUB AND SONS

Address head office P.O.Box 155 Safat
Telephone 2462170
Telex 22350 ALAYOUB KT
Activities This company is a holding company and the participating brothers direct many other concerns. It is involved in real estate development and arranges the family investment programme in both the money market and industry on local and international levels.

The Family of Al Babtain

A large family comprising over six hundred men in both Kuwait and Saudi Arabia. They descend from Śultan b. Kitamis of Ubaydah of Qahtan and Sh. Abdalrahman Abdullah Al Babtain. The immediate origins of the family are, however, in Rawdat al Sudayr of Najd. Today the family's business activities are characterised by a progressive dynamism which has already created an international commercial edifice of very considerable size. This has been achieved by the activities of three quite distinct branches of the same family, one of which bridges between Saudi Arabia and Kuwait, one has confined itself to Kuwait, and the third has remained in Saudi Arabia. They thus represent a modification to the basic concept of a family business, though the co-operation exhibited within the family still contrasts with more 'one man' concerns like Olayan and Pharaon in the peninsula.

I

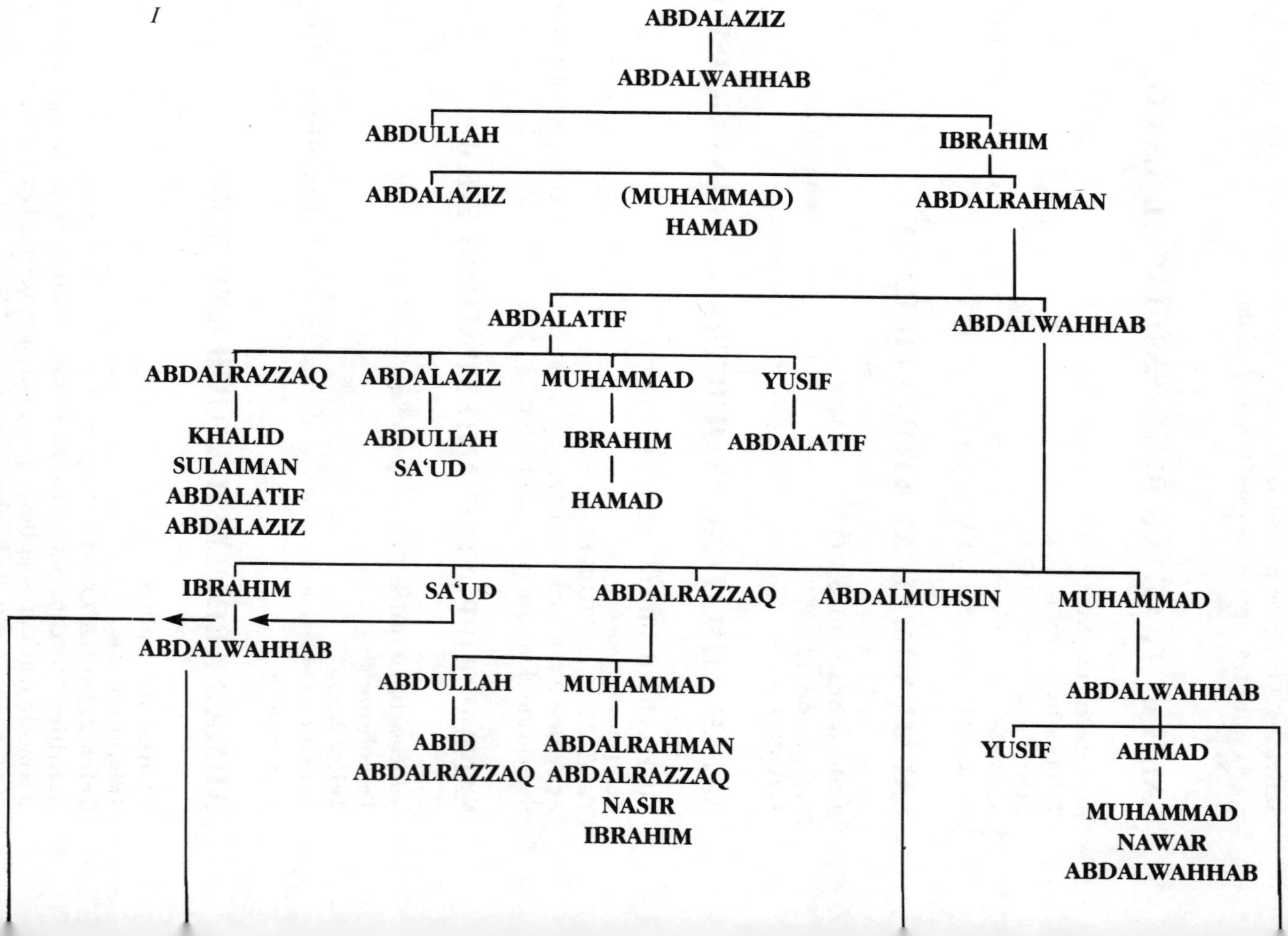

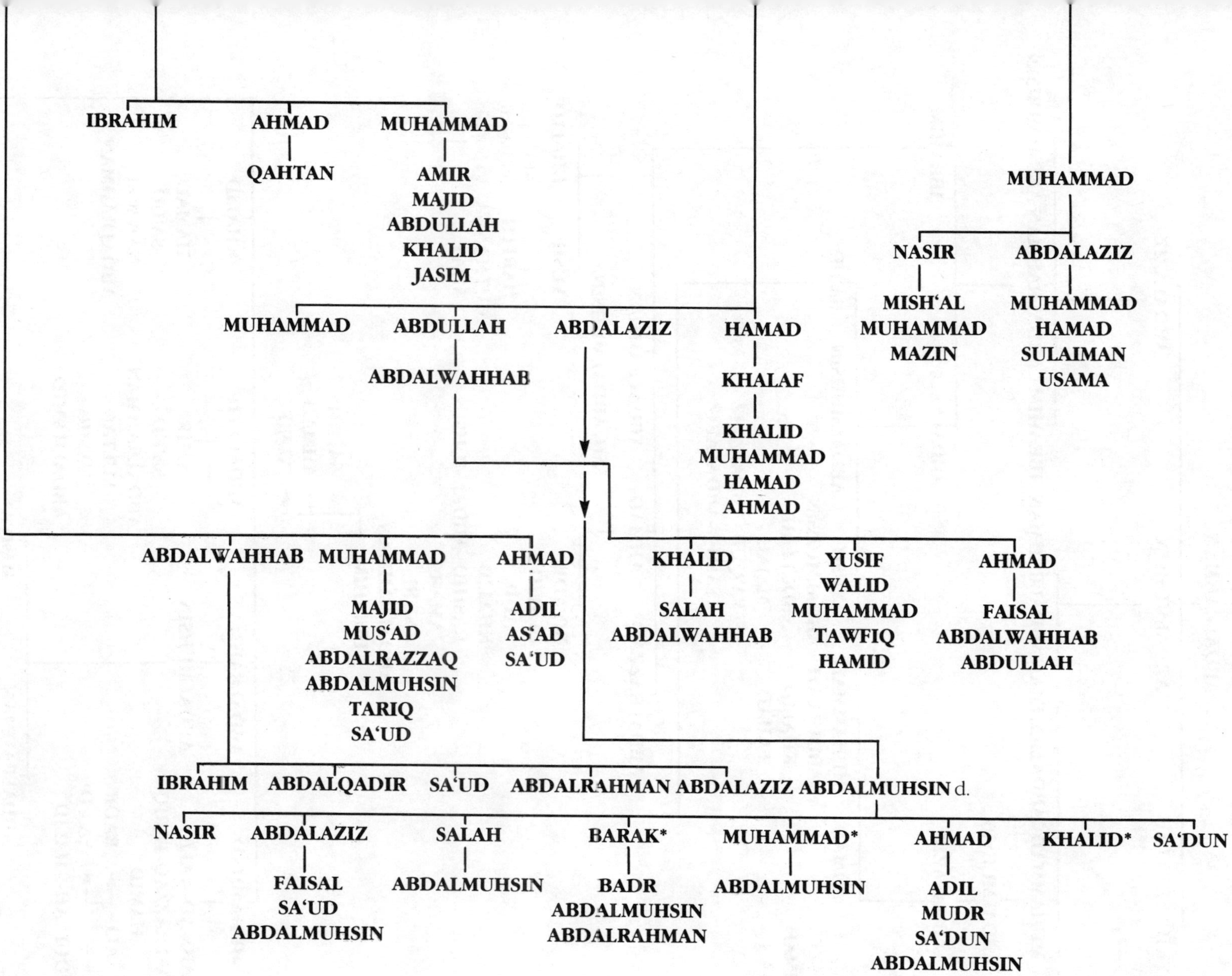

* Al Babtain Group of Companies.

* Partners in Abdalatif Saud Al Babtain and Bros.

II

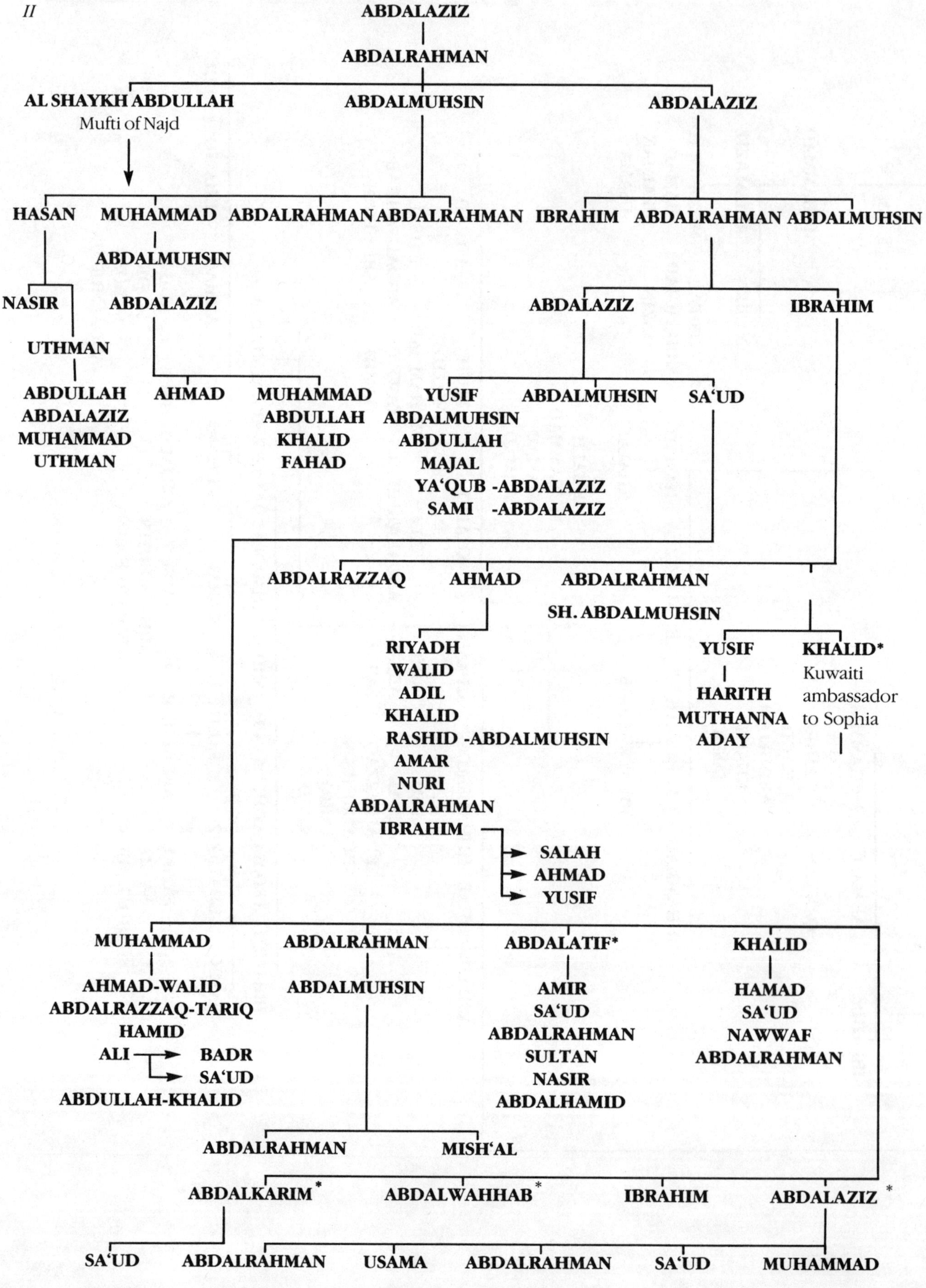

ABDALAZIZ AL BABTAIN ESTABLISHMENT

Address head office P.O.Box 599 Safat
Telephone 412730, 412736, 412738
Telex 22632 SHUROOK KT
Cable SHUROOK
Activities This company is the Kuwaiti presence of Abdalatif Saud Al Babtain and Brothers of Saudi Arabia (q.v.).Here Abdalaziz b. Saud Al Babtain is the Chairman, and in Kuwait their office is concerned with general trading and investment. The former activity includes representation for Marlborough and Phillip Morris cigarettes, whilst the latter involves participation in the ownership of the Meridien Hotel and the Saleheyah complex, which is owned by Al Saleheyah Real Estate Co. of which Abdalaziz is a member of the Board of Directors. In Kuwait the family also holds considerable investment in a number of banking interests.

AL BABTAIN GROUP OF COMPANIES

Address head office P.O.Box 766 Safat
Telephone 2448230,1,2,3,4
Telex 22272 BABTAIN KT
Cable BABTAIN
Activities The late Abdalmuhsin Abdalaziz Al Babtain began business in Kuwait in a small office in Al Salhia in 1948. He traded in car spare-parts. The company he founded now has branches in seven countries and represents fifty international manufacturers.
Today the company Chairman is Barrak Abdalmuhsin, the Vice Chairman is Abdalaziz Abdalmuhsin and the President and Managing Director is Khalid Abdalmuhsin. The group is divided into two main components.
A. The Industrial Group - which comprises the following concerns:-
1. International Farms Co. (P.O.Box 766 Safat, tel: 2448230, telex 22272 BABTAIN KT).
This company was formed in 1975 and starting with the operation of a modern automatic hatchery has now diversified to cover the following activities: a) Hatchery producing 1.5 million chicks a year. b) Vegetable growing. c) Import of foodstuffs. d) Import of agricultural implements and materials.e) Breeding and marketing of broilers. f) Import and manufacture of feedstock. g) Import of plastic housing.
2. Al Ahlia Plastic Co. (P.O.Box 766 Safat, tel: 713853, telex 22272 BABTAIN KT).
Founded in 1975 this company began production in the following year. It manufactures Polythyline rolls and bags, PVC floor tiles, gaskets and PVC conduit pipes. The company is also active as a trader in plastic products.
3. Datsun Ltd., Ireland (P.O.Box 910 Naas Road, Dublin 12, Ireland, tel: 504877 Dublin, telex 30813 DATS EI).
The Babtain interest in this concern was acquired in 1977 as a partnership with the TMG Group of Ireland. Initially holding 75%, the Babtain Group bought out the other shareholders three years later. The company assembles Datsun cars, imports manufactured cars and spare-parts, and also imports forklifts and lubricants.
4. Al Babtain Body Manufacturing Co. (P.O.Box 766 Safat, tel: 742279, telex 22272 BABTAIN KT).
The company was formed in 1976 and commercial production began in 1978. They build various types of trailer, tippers, tankers and special steel work, representing Heil of the USA. Their marketing outlets have rapidly expanded and now include Saudi Arabia, Iraq, Qatar and Oman.
5. International Paint Kuwait (P.O.Box 42255 Shuwaikh, tel: 832471, 819453, 832644, telex 23782 KPC KT).
The company is a joint venture with International Paint of the UK and manufactures International Marine and Protective Coatings, Kuwait Paint, and the KPC range of Decorative and Industrial Coatings. They also undertake Supply and Apply contracts.
B. The Commercial Group - which comprises the following companies:-
1. National Computer Services Co. (P.O.Box 766 Safat, tel: 436748, 2448230, telex 22272 BABTAIN KT).
The company was formed in 1977 and represents the Digital Equipment Corporation of the USA; VAL-3 Bilingual (English/Arabic) Terminal Systems USA; Printonix Bilingual Printers and Plotters USA; Infotron Incorporated USA; Paradyne Corp. USA; Expandor Inc. USA; Exscon Office Systems Co. USA; Vydec Word Processing Systems, Series 500 Information Processing Systems, Qyx Series 200 Electronic Typing Systems, Qwip Facsimile Systems, as well as Denco Air Ltd. of the UK. There are branches in Bahrain (P.O.Box 26766 Manama, tel: 261220, 261231, telex 8391 NCSBAH BN), and Abu Dhabi (P.O.Box 6386, tel: 725652, 725653, telex 22891 APPRES EM).

2. Barrak Al Babtain Electronic Appliances Co. (P.O.Box 766 Safat, tel: 2448230,1,2,3,4, telex ASKO 22641 KT). The company was established in 1982 and represents the following concerns: Johnson/Comco of the USA; Contacta Communications Systems UK; Grundig Electronic International UK; Static Systems Group Co. UK; James Stuart (London) and Co. Ltd. UK; Labor of Greece; Blick International UK.

3. Abdalmuhsin Abdalaziz Al Babtain Co. (P.O.Box 2198 Safat, tel: 719581, telex 22272 BABTAIN KT). This is the mother company of the Group and was formed in 1954. It holds the Nissan Motor Company agency and also represents Hyosung Corp. (National Tyres) of South Korea; GS Storage Battery Japan; NGK Spark Plug Co. Ltd. Japan, and Veedol.

4. Al Babtain Trading and Contracting (P.O.Box 766 Safat, tel: 2448230, telex 22272 BABTAIN KT). The original commercial foundation of this company, which was formed in 1965, was concerned with supplying to government tenders. Re-orientation took place in 1975 when the company specialised in heavy equipment. Today the company carries the following representations: International Harvester Trucks USA; Tadano Hydraulic Cranes Japan; Potain Tower Cranes France; Heil Refuse and Bulk Carriers USA; Rexnord Concrete Mixers and Batching Plants USA; Coventry Climax Forklifts UK; ATO Scott Cranes, ATO Huber Graders, ATO Smith Mixers UK; Arrow Dumpers UK; Medicor Hospital Equipment Hungary; JD Marshall Dumpit Concrete Pumps, Dynapower Generating Sets and White Engines.

5. International Digital Electronic Associates

A company which is American based, was formed in 1981 as a partnership where the Babtain Group owns 77% of the business and American investors the remainder. The company is engaged in the manufacture of Data Processing equipment.

6. Kuwait Travel Agency International (P.O.Box 766 Safat, tel: 428821, 428947, telex 22272 BABTAIN KT).

The Family of Al Bahar

One of the most important and distinguished families in Kuwait. Like so many of their colleagues they originally came from Najd in Saudi Arabia and are Tamim in descent.

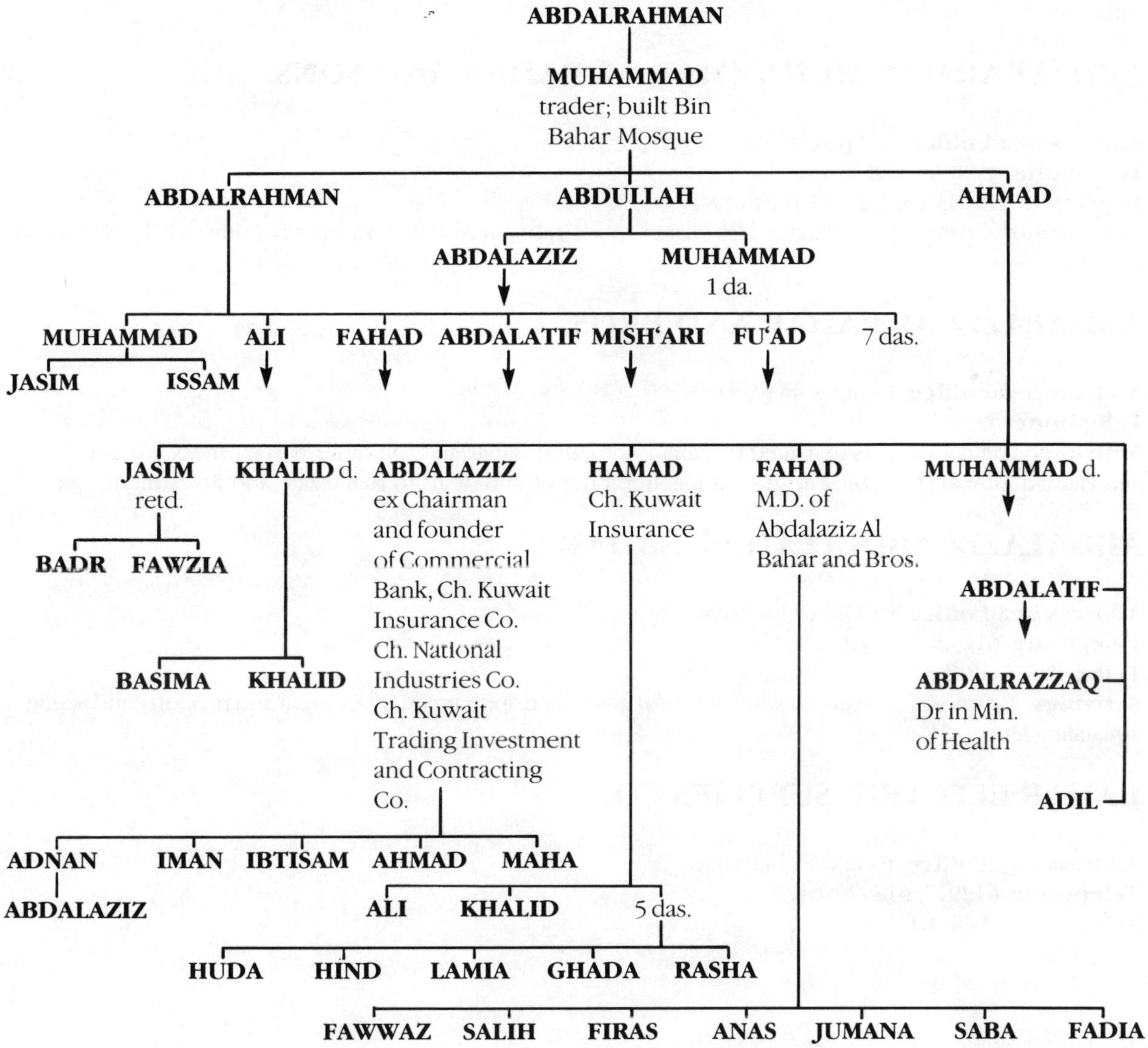

The commercial development of the family began with the trading activities of Muhammad Abdalrahman who was able to build the famous Al Bahar Mosque. He built some houses and shops at the same time and the income from these supported an Imam for the mosque as well as defraying the expenses of its upkeep. On the death of Muhammad, Abdalrahman inherited his father's business and looked after his younger brothers until they were old enough to join him. The company, at this time, was called Abdalrahman Al Bahar and Brothers. Jasim Ahmad joined them but not long afterwards the old association broke up and each of the brothers went his own way, a process which was continued by their own children, though the old entities still exist.

ABDALRAHMAN MUHAMMAD AL BAHAR AND SONS

Address head office P.O.Box 89 Safat
Telephone 459891, 460673
Telex 22014 BAHAR KT, 22951 BAHAR KT
Activities The company is managed by Mishari Abdalrahman Al Bahar and has become a firm of shipping agents.

ABDALAZIZ AL BAHAR AND BROS.

Address head office P.O.Box 463 Safat
Telephone 422477
Activities The company is managed by Fahad Ahmad Al Bahar and the other two partners are Abdalaziz and Hamad Ahmad. The company acts as a general trader and deals in real estate and investment.

ABDALAZIZ ABDULLAH AL BAHAR

Address head office P.O.Box 1140 Safat
Telephone 612927, 612929
Telex 22775 AZIZ KT
Activities A company concerned with electrical goods and appliances, investment and property and acting as estate agents.

BAHAR ELECTRIC SUPPLIES CO.

Address head office P.O.Box 1140 Safat
Telephone 612927, 612929, 612930
Telex 22775 AZIZ KT

The Family of Behbahani

There are many families of this name as, like the Al Awadhi, they are from a particular town, Behbehan in Iran. This family is a prominent representative of them and has the sobriquet Al Sharin.

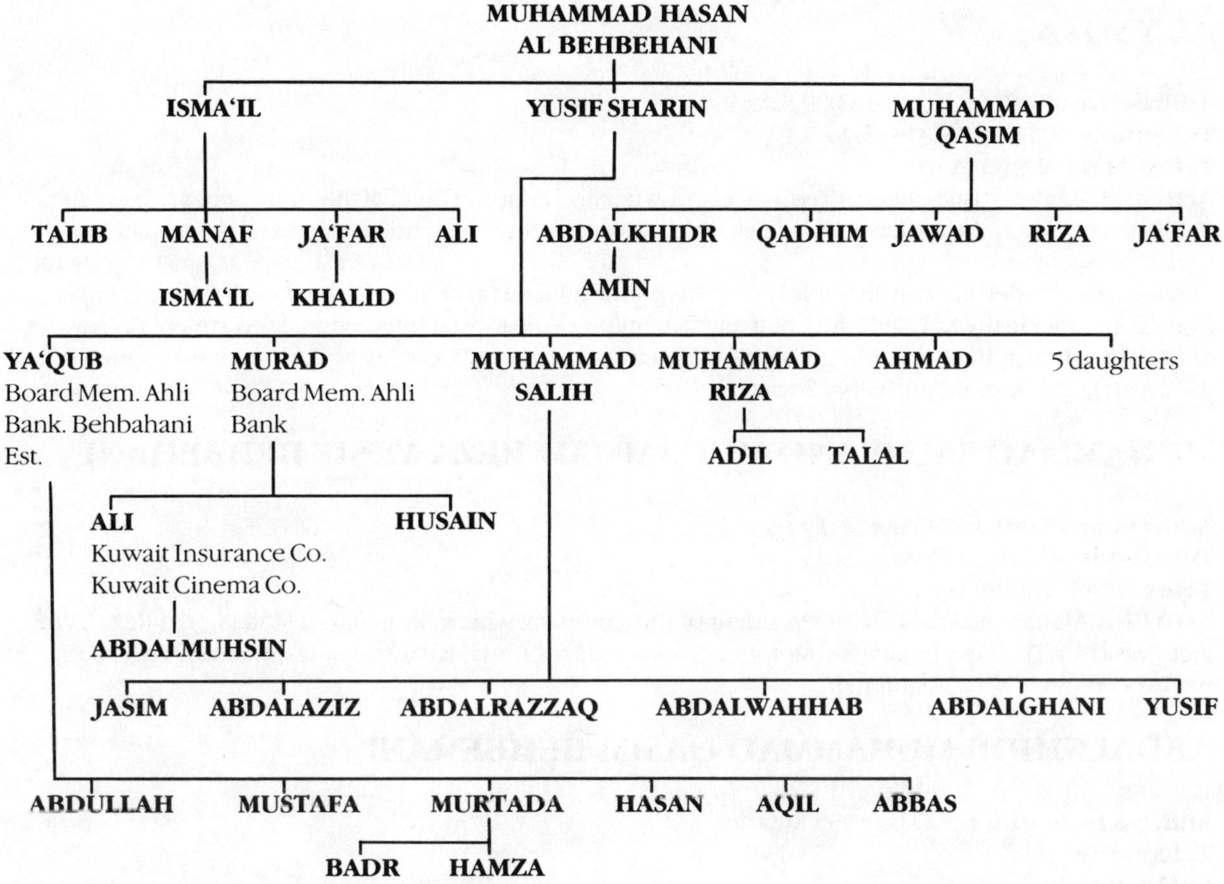

BEHBEHANI MOTORS CO.

Address head office P.O.Box 4222 Safat
Telephone 844000
Telex 23496 MOTORS KT
Activities Under the Presidency of Murad Yusif Behbehani this company represents the following manufacturers: Porsche Cars, Audi Cars, Volkswagen Cars, Mariner Outboard Engines and Becker Radio. It is a partnership within the family.

BEHBEHANI TRAVEL BUREAU

Address head office P.O.Box 3488 Safat
Telephone 439561
Telex 22048 BEHBEHANI KT
Activities A company representing, as travel agents, Swiss Air, SAS, and Thai International. The President of the company is Murad Yusif Behbehani.

AL YAQZA

Address head office P.O.Box 6000 Safat
Telephone 811171, 831318, 811971
Telex 44513 ALYAQZA KT
Activities Ahmad Yusif Behbehani is Chairman, owner and Editor in Chief of this popular news magazine. Published weekly Al Yaqza is an Arab language magazine covering local and international politics and news topics, personalities, etc.
Ahmad Yusif also devotes considerable time to his public duties as a member of the Hawali Council, and is a board member in the Kuwait Hotel Company, a member of the Kuwait International Investment Co., owner of the Ahmad Yusif Behbehani Establishment, a shareholder in Al Watan, as well as serving as a member of the board of the Kuwait Journalists Society.

MUHAMMAD SALIH AND MUHAMMAD REZA YUSIF BEHBEHANI

Address head office P.O.Box 341 Safat
Telephone 433933, 433934
Telex 22289 SHEREEN KT
Activities Muhammad Salih is the President of this company where his brother, Muhammad Reza, is the Vice President. They are the General Motors' agents and distribute GMC trucks, Buick, Skania and Uzuzu, as well as communications equipment.

ABDALKHIDR MUHAMMAD QASIM BEHBEHANI

Address head office P.O.Box 556 Kuwait
Telephone 433501
Cable ARCANI
Activities Dealer in watches, clocks, cosmetics and sanitary wares.

ARABIAN TRANSPORTATION VEHICLES INDUSTRIAL CO.

Address head office P.O.Box 5106 Safat
Telephone 875966, 875381
Telex 23042 KT
Activities Engaged in the manufacture of industrial vehicle specialities and managed by Ja'afar Ismail Behbehani.

JEANNIE BOUTIQUES CO.

Address head office P.O.Box 21712 Safat
Telephone 419883, 419886
Activities A concern dealing with ready-made clothes, cosmetics, jewellery, and baby goods. It is owned by Mustafa Yaqub Behbehani.

MURAD YUSIF BEHBEHANI

Address head office P.O.Box 146 Safat
Telephone 844000
Telex 22048 BEHBEHANI KT
Activities The General Manager of the company is Ali Murad Behbehani and they represent Carrier air-conditioning equipment, Airflow Computer AC Units, Akai and Sansui audio equipment, Barco television, TOA Public Address Systems, Ericsson telephones, Baume and Mercier watches, Omega watches, Tissot watches, Olma watches, Romer watches, Piaget watches and jewellery, Petbow generators, Wild survey instruments, and Harris communications systems.

SEVEN UP BOTTLING CO.

Address head office P.O.Box 4076 Safat
Telephone 810057, 810823, 831366
Telex 23617 SEVENUP KT
Activities A partnership between Muhammad Salih and Muhammad Riza Behbehani which operates a plant for bottling Seven-Up and crush products and their distribution.

WEST END WATCHES SHOWROOM

Address head office P.O.Box 334 Safat
Telephone 421131, 420580
Activities A company owned by Yaqub Yusif Behbehani which deals in watches and clocks.

AL LAHAB TRADING CO.

Address head office P.O.Box 23566 Kuwait
Telephone 432975
Activities The company is an importer and distributor of the following goods: foodstuffs, fashions, tools and equipment, linen towels and novelties. It is a partnership between Mansur and Masaud Hayat and Ja'afar Ismail Behbehani.

MUHAMMAD SALIH BEHBEHANI AND CO.

Address head office P.O.Box 370 Safat
Telephone 412085, 419838
Telex 22194 KT
Activities A partnership between Muhammad Salih and Muhammad Riza Behbehani which is engaged in the insurance, shipping and travel businesses.

MUHAMMAD SALIH AND RIZA YUSIF BEHBEHANI

Address head office P.O.Box 341 Safat
Telephone 433933, 433934
Telex 22289 SHEREEN KT
Activities Muhammad Salih is the President of this company and his brother, Muhammad Riza, is the Vice President. The company imports and distributes communications equipment, and also automobiles as the agent for Buick and GMC.

The Family of Bourisli

A family present in Kuwait before the arrival of the first Anaizi settlers in the eighteenth century. They operate a family cooperative arrangement to help family members in business, education and health. The system is supported by subscription.

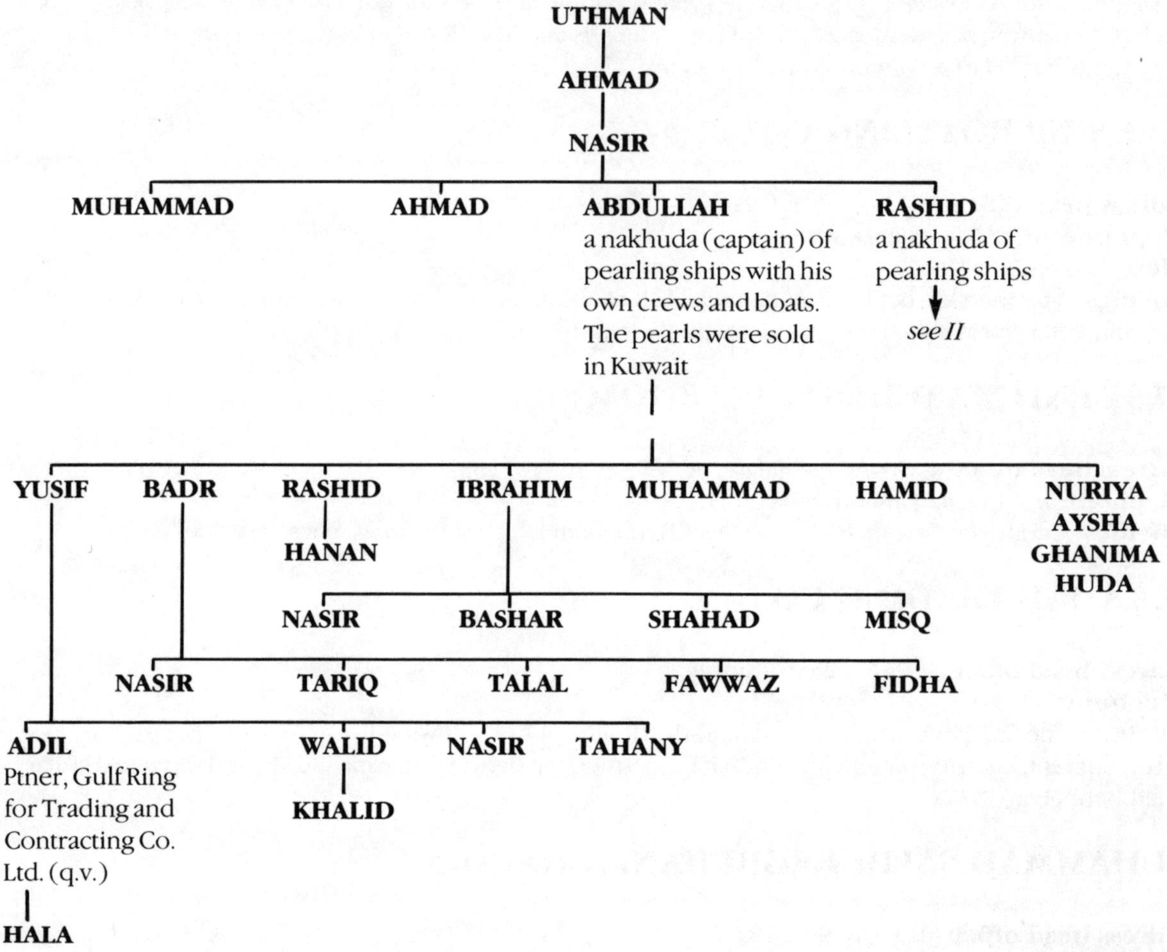

INTERNATIONAL SHIPPING AGENCY LTD.

Address head office P.O.Box 20637 Safat
Telephone 441860, 441864
Telex 22208 ISASHIP KT
Activities A company acting as marine contractors and shipping agents as well as operating a forwarding and clearing business. The director is Salih Rashid Bourisli.

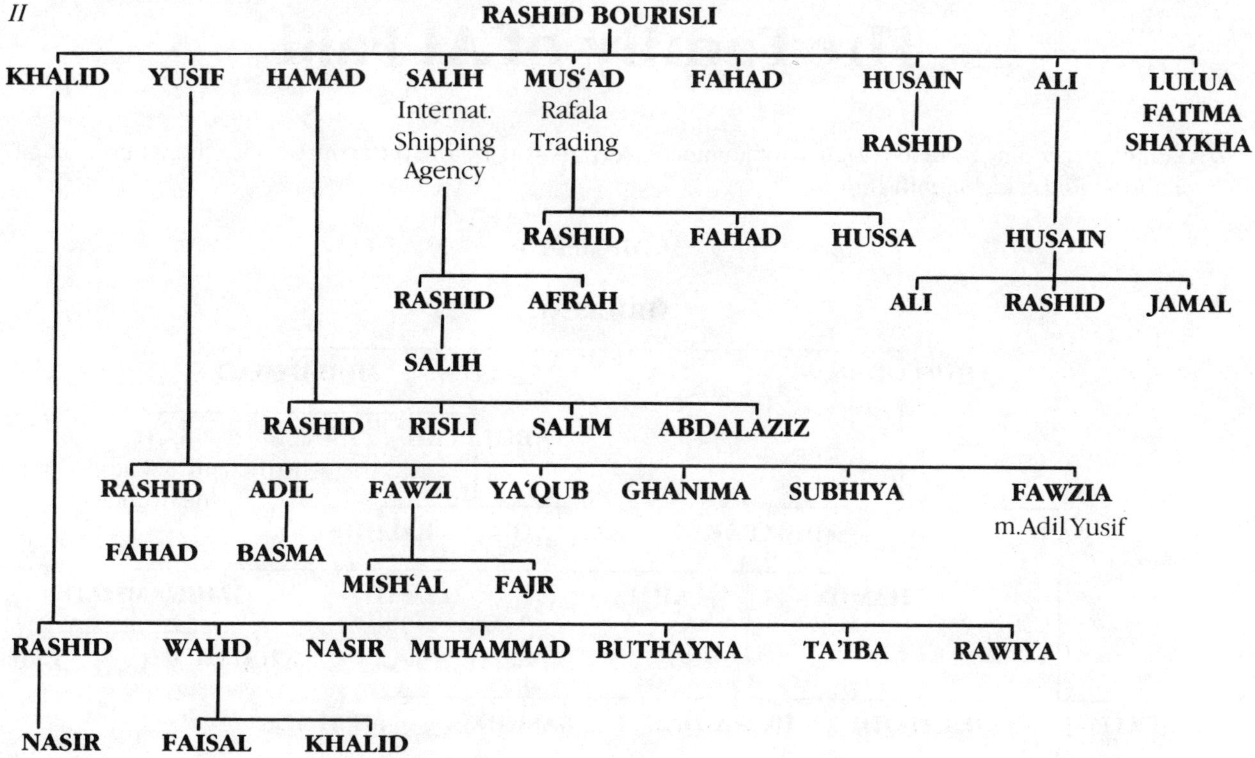

AL RABIAH LIGHTING CO.

Address head office P.O.Box 22158 Safat
Telephone 632854, 639618
Telex 23198 KT
Activities The company is a partnership between Elias I Aboudi and Salih Rashid Bourisli. It is engaged in electrical goods and contracting, the supply of furniture and false ceilings.

RAFAH TRADING BUREAU

Address head office P.O.Box 881 Safat
Telephone 410600, 412459
Telex 22034 ORAS KT
Activities A company of importers and construction contractors owned by Musa'ad Rashid Bourisli.

AL RABIAH CONSTRUCTION CO.

Address head office P.O.Box 3592 Safat
Telephone 818844
Telex 22181 ARABCO KT
Activities A company of civil contractors owned by Salih Rashid Bourisli.

The Family of Al Fajji

A family descending from the original inhabitants of Kuwait from before the arrivals consequent upon Anaizi migration in the eighteenth century.

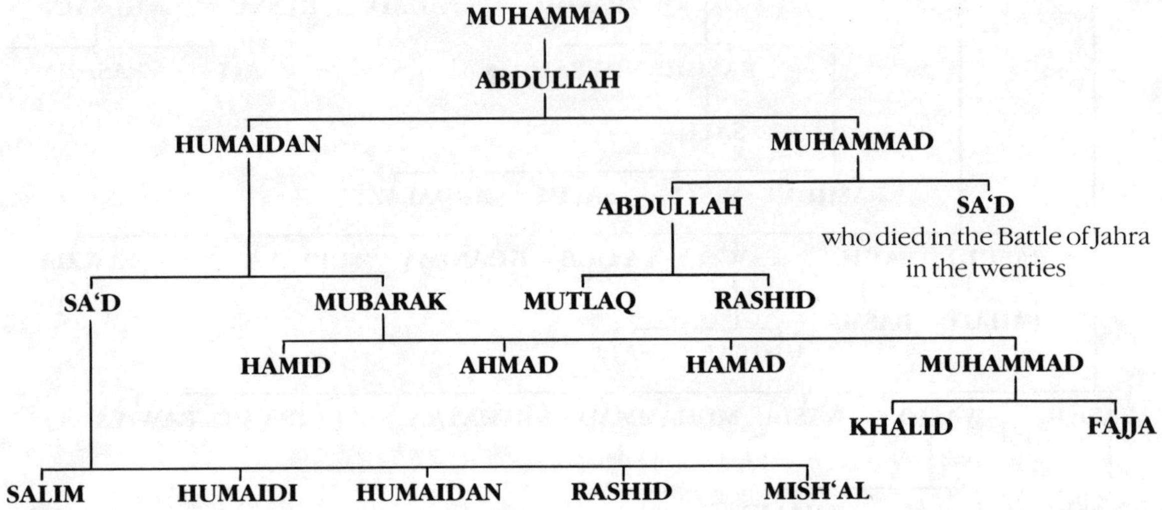

AL FAJJI TRADING AND CONTRACTING CO.

Address head office P.O.Box 24996 Safat
Telephone 451362, 451363, 451364. 451365
Telex 23895 FAJICO KT
Activities Owned by Muhammad Mubarak Al Fajji, the company is concerned with trading and contracting, the manufacture of deformed reinforcing and trading in fruit and vegetables.
The company is organised into four divisions to deal with its diverse activities
The Transport Division
A fleet of some three hundred vehicles transport trade goods to Jordan, Saudi Arabia and Iraq
The Contracting Division
The operations of this division, in the construction field, follow the multinational national interests of the transport division and are not confined to the State of Kuwait.
The Trading Division
A fully comprehensive trading operation is operated involving a variety of goods varying from foodstuffs to building materials.
The Industrial Division
The company has invested in supportive manufacturing businesses for its trading and contracting divisions. Utilising modern machinery they make doors for specialist applications and have embarked also on the establishment of a soap factory.
The Fajji Group also includes the following enterprises.

AL IQBAL TRADING ESTABLISHMENT

Address head office P.O.Box 4452 Safat
Telephone 433485
Telex 23572 RAKAN KT, 22138 RAKAN KT
Activities A parallel trading company dealing however with lubricants and cleaners. This company is agent for Slick 50 of the USA.

GULF GROUP AND ARABIAN EASTERN CO.

Address head office P.O.Box 24996 SAFAT
Telephone 2450481,2,3,4,5
Telex 22629 GULFCO KT
Activities This concern is a joint venture between the Al Fajji Group and International Business Magazine of Holland. They publish a Dutch/Kuwaiti commercial magazine which comes out monthly and carries items of mutual interest, designed to develop trade and commerce. The magazine is called Middle East Business International and its European address is P.O.Box 75106, 1117 AA Schiphol East, telephone 020-471161, tlx 12959 TRADE NL.
The company is also a dynamic and well informed business promotion concern whose activities cover business consultancy, advertising and public relations, export sales management, business promotion and marketing.

The Family of Fawzan

They are descended from Badarin of Dawasir and originate in Jalajil in the Wadi Dawasir of Najd, Saudi Arabia. An established and respected Kuwaiti family.

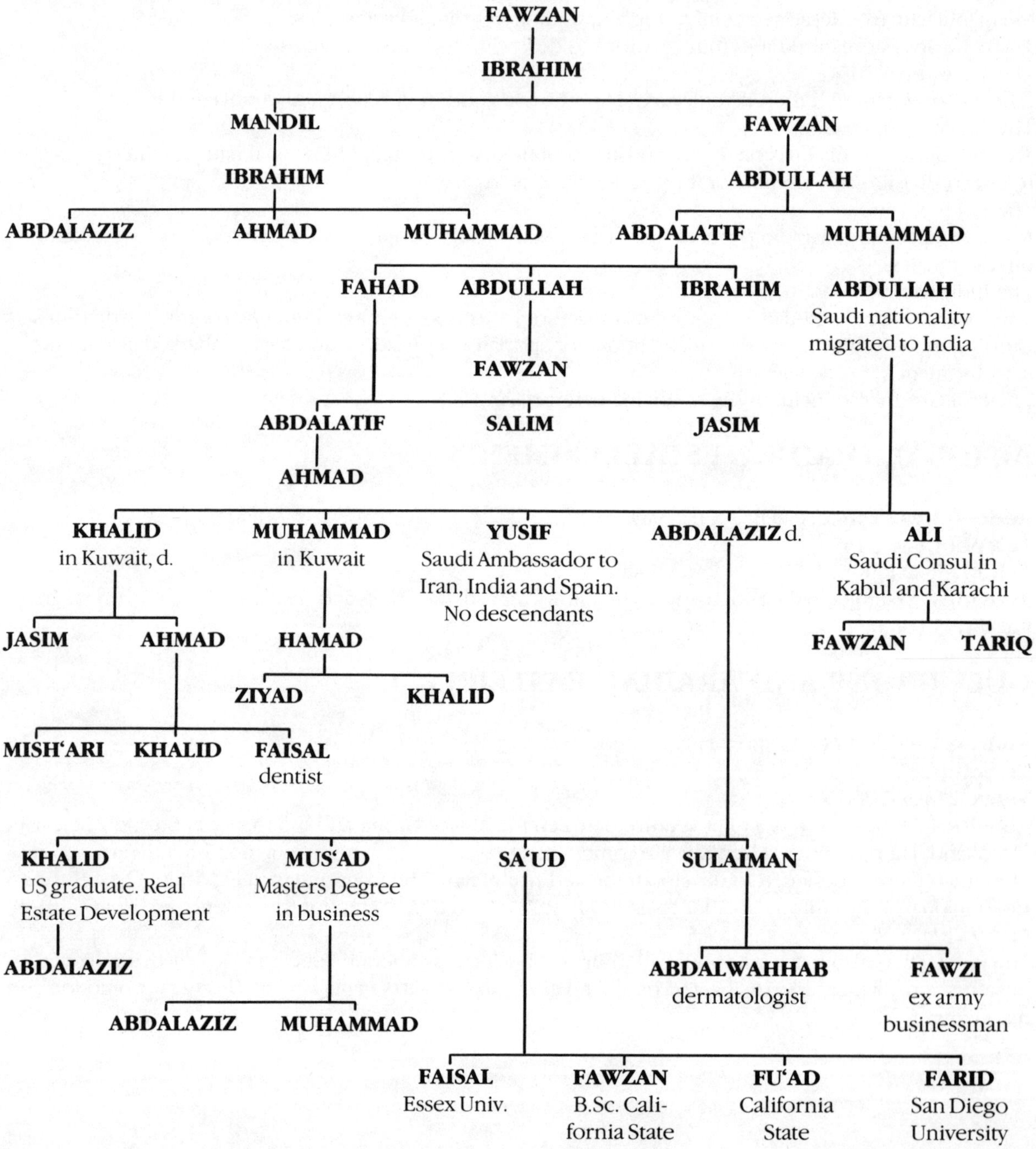

FAWZAN TRADING AND CONTRACTING ESTABLISHMENT

Address head office P.O.Box 116 Kuwait
Telephone 433605
Telex 21126 BADINE KT
Activities The company is engaged in real estate and stock market operations. They are a major shareholder in Gas and Oilfield Services Co. with whom they are associated. The company represents Krupp and Alistair Atlantic of France, and is a partnership between Saud Abdalaziz Fawzan who also controls the foodstuffs concern, The Green Cedar Co., and Sulaiman Al Fawzan.

AHMAD ABDALATIF FOZAN TRADING ESTABLISHMENT

Address head office P.O. Box 1665 Kuwait
Telephone 432858
Cable ADIL
Activities Operating as commission agents

AHMAD KHALID AL FOZAN

Address head office P.O.Box 1361 Safat
Telephone 426830
Telex MANDEEL
Activities The company is owned as its name implies and it is concerned with basic tenders, chemicals and the stock market.

DREDGING AND MARINE SERVICES CO.

Address head office P.O.Box 9014 Ahmadi
Telephone 980189, 983638
Telex 44216 VIGO KT
Activities A company managed by Sulaiman Al Fozan which is involved with marine equipment and maintenance, dredger charter, the supply of boat crews, work boats and pilot boats.

FOUZAN ABDULLAH AL FOUZAN

Address head office P.O.Box 696 Safat
Telephone 432985
Telex 22583 FOUZAN KT
Activities A company dealing in building equipment.

FOUZAN AND BADINE ENGINEERING AND CONTRACTING CO.

Address head office P.O.Box 144 Safat
Telephone 433101
Telex 22667 KT
Activities The Chairman of this firm is Sulaiman Fawzan and the Managing Director is Faisal Fawzan. They are commission agents working to government tenders and projects.

GAS AND OILFIELD SERVICES CO.

Address head office P.O.Box 9277 Ahmadi
Telephone 984681, 983681, 985261
Telex 44228 GOFSCO KT
Activities The company provides production services to the oil industry, wireline services and acts as an agent for oilfield equipment manufacturing companies. It is directed by Sulaiman Abdalaziz Al Fawzan.

KUWAIT AUTOMOBILE AND TRADING CO.

Address head office P.O.Box 41 Safat
Telephone 715314, 718960
Telex 23005 KT
Activities A partnership between Sulaiman Abdalaziz Al Fawzan and Qasim Abdalrahman Al Zayani. The company is an importer and distributor of motor vehicles, being the agents for Rolls Royce, Jaguar, Rover, Landrover, Range Rover and MAN vehicles.

MECHANICAL AND INDUSTRIAL SERVICE CO.

Address head office P.O.Box 9277 Ahmadi
Telephone 985226, 985227
Telex 44228 GOFSCO KT
Activities A company of general engineers specialising in rotating equipment and industrial maintenance. The General Manager is Fu'ad Saud Fawzan.

TECHNOLOGY AIDED SYSTEMS KUWAIT (TASK)

Address head office P.O.Box 730 Safat
Telephone 421531
Telex 44770 KT
Activities The company is owned by Faisal Saud Fawzan and is concerned with word processing equipment and computer systems.

The Family of Al Ghanim

With the Al Sagr and al Qatami, the Al Ghanim are Al Zayd of the tribe of ‘Anayza.

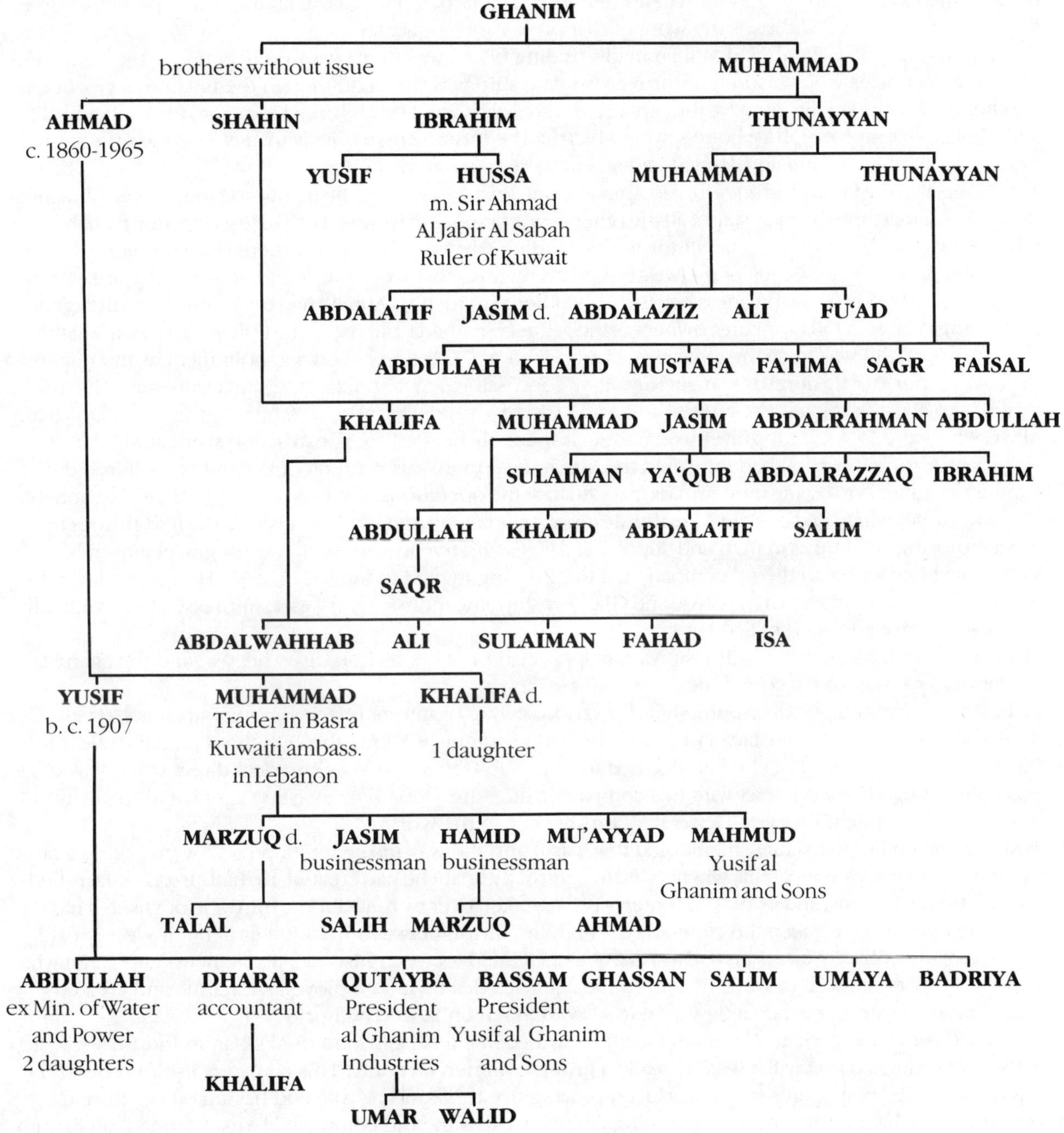

AL GHANIM INDUSTRIES

Address head office P.O.Box 24172 Safat
Telephone 842988, 843988, 436970
Telex 44900 GANIM KT, 44901 GANIM KT, 44904 GANIM KT, 44905 GANIM KT, 2793 GANIM KT

The Al Ghanim settled in Kuwait as one of the original Anaizi settlers in company with the Al Sabah who became the ruling family of Kuwait. Their commercial story begins with the family's early participation in the shipping business, and, as is the wont of that profession, a disaster too.

In the beginning of 1925 Ahmad Muhammad's trading boom was on its way to Basra under the command of one of his uncles when a sudden storm arose. The ship was sunk and though the uncle was rescued by another boom, Ahmad did not have the capital to build a new one. He was forced to go into the timber trade and take up once more a skill for bone-setting which had been one of his earlier activities. This was a traditional Arabian form of doctoring and Ahmad had a famous reputation for it.

This reversal in the family fortunes forced Ahmad's son, Yusuf, to earn his living outside the shipping business which was at that time the mainstay of all the other major families in Kuwait. He had just returned from being educated in Karachi, and had a talent for understanding what an opportunity there was commercially in being able to satisfy the needs of the western oil companies that were starting to arrive in the area. At first he developed the kerosene business began by his father as a sideline. Ahmad had been appointed the agent for the Anglo Persian Oil Company, owners of the refinery in Abada, but had done little in fact to exploit the opportunity. Yusuf was to change that. Association with APOC led to his own appointment as their agent during the course of the long drawn out Kuwait oil concession negotiations of the late twenties and thirties.

Yusuf, who always took a lot of interest in a wide variety of subjects, also accompanied survey teams from APOC who were looking for gravel which they desperately needed for construction work at Abadan. The Iraqi contractor concerned had informed them that the supply was running out. Yusuf was offered the contract and after borrowing money in Basra to finance the operation, he started to supply APOC. He bought tugs and barges which had been used in the Mesopotamian Campaign by the British. By the mid-thirties he was employing six thousand men and supplying APOC with twenty thousand tons of gravel a month.

Yusuf's involvement with the oil company led to his being invited to the UK in 1938. He spent a lot of his time in Scotland being shown the Clyde and Glasgow shipping industry and was so impressed that eventually all his sons were educated in Scotland.

The business consequence of this visit was an appreciation of the technologies he saw, and the agency agreements we was able to conclude.

To begin with he arranged distributorships for various makes of automobile, including Chrysler. However, these did not prove very satisfactory because he had problems working through the regional dealers in Baghdad and Beirut. By 1945 he had decided to switch to General Motors and deal direct with Detroit. He was able to negotiate a contract with this company which displaced GM's existing agent, and today his descendants operate the largest General Motors agency in the world.

Towards the end of the sixties, it emerged that Yusuf and the way his generation had for managing a large modern company, were not what was needed to control the giant he had created. He had already quarrelled with his two elder sons, and in 1971 the enterprise was taken over by Kutayba, the third son of Yusuf. It has been Kutayba who has taken the company through the divide between tradition and the modern world.

Yusuf Ahmad Al Ghanim and Sons had too many agencies and too centralised a management system. Kutayba was able to correct these matters; he halved the agencies dealt with, employed specialists and created autonomous departments headed by managers with much enhanced authority.

Today the company of Yusuf Ahmad Al Ghanim has become a background to Al Ghanim Industries, which is itself a holding company for what is really a group commercial entity. This company itself is one of the top five hundred companies in the world, employing five thousand people and having offices in sixteen countries. Al Ghanim Industries as a holding company owns the old company of Yusuf Ahmad Al Ghanim and is itself owned by Kutayba, Bassam, Salim and Omaya Yusuf Al Ghanim.

A hallmark of the modern company is its wholesale professionalism and, whilst it is almost certainly not as profitable as some other Kuwaiti businesses because of the high overhead of expensive management, it is a company which has taken the leap into the future and it will be far ahead of it's potential competitors when they themselves have to dispense with the traditional management style of the peninsular and follow the path down which Al Ghanim have already gone.

Activities 1. Automotive Sales and Service General Motors: Cadillac, Oldsmobile, Pontiac, Chevrolet, Opel, Vauxhall
General Motors Continental: GM and AC Delco
GMODC: Isuzu parts
2. Truck Sales and Service Paccar International:Kenworth Vauxhall Motors: Bedford GMODC Chevrolet
3. Wholesale Parts British Petroleum: Lubricating oils, greases & detergents.
Purolator Inc: Filters
4. Engineering Hitachi Ltd: Airconditioning equipment, electric motor starters, water circulating pumps, industrial pumps.
Sanso: Pumps
Blue Star Ltd: Water coolers
Foster Refrigerator: Refrigerators
5. Projects Nissei Sangyo: Hitachi power distribution stations, sub-stations and desalination plants.
Babcock & Wilcox: Steam boilers
6. Electronics Decca Radar Ltd: Radar, radio, closed circuit television, intercoms, test and measuring equipment.
Decca Navigation Co: Navigation equipment and parts.
7. Air Travel Service (Al Ghanim Travel q.v.) General Agent: British Airways, Cathay Pacific, Air India
Sales Agent: Gulf Air, Qantas, East African, Cunard
Agent: Europear
8. Kirby Building Systems: Pre-engineered steel buildings.
9. Insurance Al Amana Insurance and Re-Insurance Co.: Property, casualty and marine.
10. Gulf Trading and Refrigerating Co: Rowntree MacKintosh, Mars and Kraft Foods.
11. 999 Corporation: Private label automotive parts.
12. Serck Services: Radiators and heat exchangers.
13. Impact/Echo: Full advertising service
14. Sahara Trans: Freight forwarding, truck haulage
15. Al Ghanim Barber Shipping: Agents for Scanmel, Willine, Barber, Blue Sea and Blue Star Line.
16. Kuwait Maritime Corp: High volume shipping.

ALI AND FU'AD MUHAMMAD THUNAYAN AL GHANIM CO.

Address head office P.O.Box 1083 Safat
Telephone 814435, 439264
Telex 22142 MARATA KT
Activities The company is engaged in civil construction work and as mechanicl and electrical contractors. The company is a partnership between the two brothers.

ALI AL GHANIM ESTABLISHMENT

Address head office P.O.Box 1083 Safat
Telephone 439624,5,6,7
Telex 22142 KT
Activities A second partnership between Ali and Fu'ad which is similarly engaged in business to the foregoing company; civil contracting, electrical engineering, general and electro-mechanical contracting and merchant agents.

ABDALATIF MUHAMMAD THUNAYAN AL GHANIM

Address head office P.O.Box 203 Safat
Telephone 813704
Telex 23080 KT
Activities A contracting company which also acts as an exporter/importer of building materials.

AL DAR KUTAYBA AND MAHMUD AL GHANIM CO.

Address head office P.O.Box 20755 Safat
Telephone 632299, 616156, 639281
Telex 23344 SOHAB KT
Activities A company acting as retailers for domestic and office furniture and operating a contract furnishing facility for interior design and decoration. It is a partnership between Kutayba Yusuf Al Ghanim and Mahmud Muhammad Al Ghanim.

AL GHANIM AND ASSAD TRADING AND CONTRACTING CO.

Address head office P.O.Box 23121 Safat
Telephone 415497, 444875
Telex 23471 ASSAD
Activities A civil and electrical contracting company which participates as a partner in joint venture projects. Has interests in prefabricated buildings and trades in building materials. The company is a partnership between Hamid Muhammad Al Ghanim and Ghazi A Assad.

AL GHANIM BARBER SHIPPING CO.

Address head office P.O.Box 21708 Safat
Telephone 418845, 457990, 457994
Telex 22084 SCANREP KT
Activities A partnership between Yusuf Ahmad Al Ghanim and Sons and Wilhelm Wilhelmsen of Norway. They are ships agents dealing with liners and cargo vessels, ships surveyors and protecting agents concerned with cargo, machinery, and local and transit haulage.

AL GHANIM AND BUDEIRI TRADING AND CONTRACTING CO.

Address head office P.O.Box 5569 Safat
Telephone 425949, 425950
Telex 44378 BORAX KT
Activities An Al Ghanim company managed by Jamil A Budeiri dealing in fire-fighting equipment, chemicals, security systems and alarms.

AL GHANIM CARPETS EXHIBITION

Address head office P.O.Box 223 Safat
Telephone 419606, 418992
Telex 22069 KT
Activities A company owned by Yusuf Ahmad Al Ghanim and Sons dealing in building materials and specialising in flooring and ceiling applications. They are also concerned with carpeting and related decorating activities.

AL GHANIM FREIGHT AIR

Address head office P.O.Box 26794 Safat
Telephone 842988, 843988
Telex 46119 SATRAN KT
Activities An Al Ghanim company concerned with crating and packing, air sea and road transport, customs clearance, break bulk consolidation and a worldwide door to door service.

AL GHANIM INFORMATION MANAGEMENT SERVICES (AIMS)

Address head office P.O. Box 223 Safat
Telephone 842988, 843988
Telex 44900/1/4/5 GANIM KT
Activities A partnership between Kutayba Yusuf Al Ghanim and Garry P Diver, who is the Managing Director. This is a computer services company dealing with database software, application software, modelling software, terminals and peripherals, computer consumables and stationery. They are also involved with training courses and audio-visual training.

AL GHANIM INSURANCE OFFICE

Address head office P.O.Box 223 Safat
Telephone 830588, 831588
Telex 44440 GHAMINS KT
Activities A company owned by Bassam Yusuf Al Ghanim and active as Insurance Brokers.

AL GHANIM AND AL QUTUB GROUP OF COMPANIES

Address head office P.O.Box 25267 Safat
Telephone 737072, 737172, 737372, 737572
Telex 23447 KT, 23448 KT, 23057 KT
Activities A partnership between Faisal Thunayan Al Ghanim, Abdullah Issa Salih, Da'ud Yaqub Al Qutub and Falah Abdalhalim Falah that was established in 1978. They are international freight forwarders, liner agents, clearing and forwarding agents and project specialists. They have associated branch offices as follows:

1. Al Ghanim and Al Qutub Chartering (London) Ltd., London, England (telex 897004).
2. Brantford Alghanim Alqutub Ltd., Barking, England (telex 897256).
3. Alkunaibi Alghanim and Alqutub Shipping Agencies, Abu Dhabi (telex 22853).
4. Alghaith Alghanim and Alqutub Shipping Agencies, Dubai (telex 46579).
5. Alghanim and Alqutub (Greece) Inc., Piraeus, Greece (telex 212907).
6. Arabian Freight Services Co. Ltd., Tokyo, Japan (telex 2422944).
7. Pantransport Gmbh, Bremen, West Germany (telex 244496).
8. Transmasters Transport Services Co., Cairo, Egypt (telex 93304).
9. Maltrans Shipping Agencies Co., Aqaba, Jordan (telex 62289).
10. Yemen Express, Sanaa, North Yemen (telex 2305).

AL GHANIM SAHARA TRANS

Address head office P.O.Box 26794, 22388 Safat
Telephone 842988, 843988
Telex 46119 SATRAN KT
Activities A freight forwarding and clearance concern with the added capabilities of delivery and overland transportation which is owned by Al Ghanim Industries.

AL GHANIM TRAVEL

Address head office P.O.Box 81
Telephone 842988
Telex 44900 GANIM ATA K
Activities A travel agency which is all embracing in the range of services it offers. These include airline and sea travel reservations and ticketing, car rental, educational and holiday tours, medical appointments, business trips, facilities for travellers' cheques, travel insurance and real estate.

GULF ENGINEERING OFFICE

Address head office P.O.Box 13025 Keefan
Telephone 446204, 449671
Telex 22638 TAINC KT
Activities A partnership between Muhammad Thanayan Al Ghanim and Hamad Tawil, which is a business concerned with architecture and civil works consultants.

IMPACT AND ECHO

Address head office P.O.Box 21081 Safat
Telephone 438120,1,2,3
Telex 46443 IMPACT KT
Activities A fully comprehensive advertising agency owned by Al Ghanim Industries.

HYGIENE PRODUCTS INDUSTRIES CO.

Address head office P.O.Box 21388 Safat
Telephone 715961
Telex 22168 CLYDE KT
Activities A partnership between Yusuf Ibrahim Al Ghanim, Abdullah Yusuf Al Ghanim and Jasim Abdalaziz Al Qatami (q.v.), which is engaged in the manufacture of sanitary towels and babies' nappies.

JAWA TRADING AND INDUSTRY ESTABLISHMENT

Address head office P.O. Box 23751
Telephone 415468, 417687
Telex 23646 JAWACO KT
Activities The owner of this company is Saqr Abdullah Muhammad Shahin Al Ghanim. It is concerned with key telephone installations, domestic and gift items, cigarette lighters and other electrical appliances.

KUWAIT FIBREGLASS CO.

Address head office P.O.Box 202 Safat
Telephone 742583, 742960
Telex 23467 BATLA KT
Activities The company is a partnership between Fatma Thunayan Al Ghanim and Muhammad F Al Balhan. It is concerned with the manufacture of fibreglass for the construction of water tanks, boats, furniture and decorative items.

SAQR ABDULLAH SHAHIN AL GHANIM ESTABLISHMENT

Address head office P.O.Box 36 Safat
Telephone 432692, 426510, 441551, 413487
Telex 22695 SAGSHIP KT
Activities A company, owned as named, which is engaged as a shipping agent, clearing and forwarding, storage and transport as well as shipping services and chandling.

SHAMSAN TRADING CO.

Address head office P.O. Box 12234 Shamiya
Telephone 425821, 517275
Activities This company is a partnership between Abdullah Yusuf Thunayan Al Ghanim and Muhammad Hasan Al Sharaf and is a concern acting as commission agents and trading in domestic and electrical appliances.

SPECIALITIES COMPANY

Address head office P.O. Box 20376 Safat
Telephone 812144
Telex 22645 SPECIAL KT
Activities This firm is a partnership between Yusuf Ibrahim Al Ghanim, Jasim Qatami and Fu'ad and Labib Bardawil. They supply special building materials, joinery and concrete admixtures.

THE TECHNICAL STEEL WORKS

Address head office P.O. Box 203 Safat
Telephone 815737
Telex 23080 SHUCAFA KT
Activities A company owned by Abdalatif Muhammad Thunayan Al Ghanim which is engaged in the manufacture of prefabricated houses and PVC galvanized chainlink.

INTERNATIONAL DESIGN GROUP

Address head office P.O. Box 21326 Safat
Telephone 446793, 446795
Telex 22709 MURMUR KT
Activities Directed by Badriya Yusuf Ahmad Al Ghanim, Salwa Razouki and Michael Saad, this company is concerned with interior design, decoration and consultancy with a capacity to operate a contracting facility.

YUSUF AHMAD AL GHANIM AND SONS

Address head office P.O. Box 223 Safat
Telephone 830588
Telex 44900 GANIM KT, 44907 GANIM KT
Activities The President of this, the original company of this part of the Al Ghanim family (see Al Ghanim Industries above) is Bassam Yusuf Al Ghanim. The owner is Yusuf Ahmad Al Ghanim.

YUSUF AHMAD AL GHANIM AND SONS ENGINEERING GROUP

Address head office P.O. Box 20244 Safat
Telephone 819433, 819437, 840820
Telex 44900 GANIM KT

YUSUF IBRAHIM AL GHANIM AND CO.

Address head office P.O. Box 435 Safat
Telephone 832600/1/2/3
Telex 23607 YIACO KT
Activities This company is owned as named and deals in chemicals and pharmaceuticals, and hospital, laboratory and dental equipment.

KUWAIT OIL TANKER COMPANY

Address head office P.O. Box 810 Safat
Telephone 455455
Telex 22013 KT, 44755 KT, 44766 KT
Activities The company is chaired by Faisal Thunayan Al Ghanim who is also the Managing Director. The company is a carrier owner and tanker agent. It is concerned with crude and LPG oil products as well as filling and distribution.

MIDDLE EAST INTERNATIONAL CONTRACTING

Address head office P.O. Box 8813 Salmia
Telephone 641367, 641368
Telex 22988 MEICCO KT
Activities A company of construction contractors directed by Ali and Fu'ad Muhammad Thunayan Al Ghanim.

MUSTAFA THUNAYAN AL GHANIM AND BROS.

Address head office P.O. Box 68 Safat
Telephone 433052, 433055, 432710, 410343
Activities A company, owned as named, which supplies building equipment.

PEARL SHIPPING CO.

Address head office P.O. Box 843 Safat
Telephone 417758, 417762
Telex 22797 PRLMAR KT
Activities The company's Managing Director is Saqr Abdullah Shahin Al Ghanim and it is engaged in business as a shipping agent dealing also with clearing, forwarding, and transport and storage.

The Family of Al Hamad

A most distinguished family of Kuwait, being an old and respected pillar of the country's commercial life. Originally from Zilfi of Najd, Saudi Arabia.

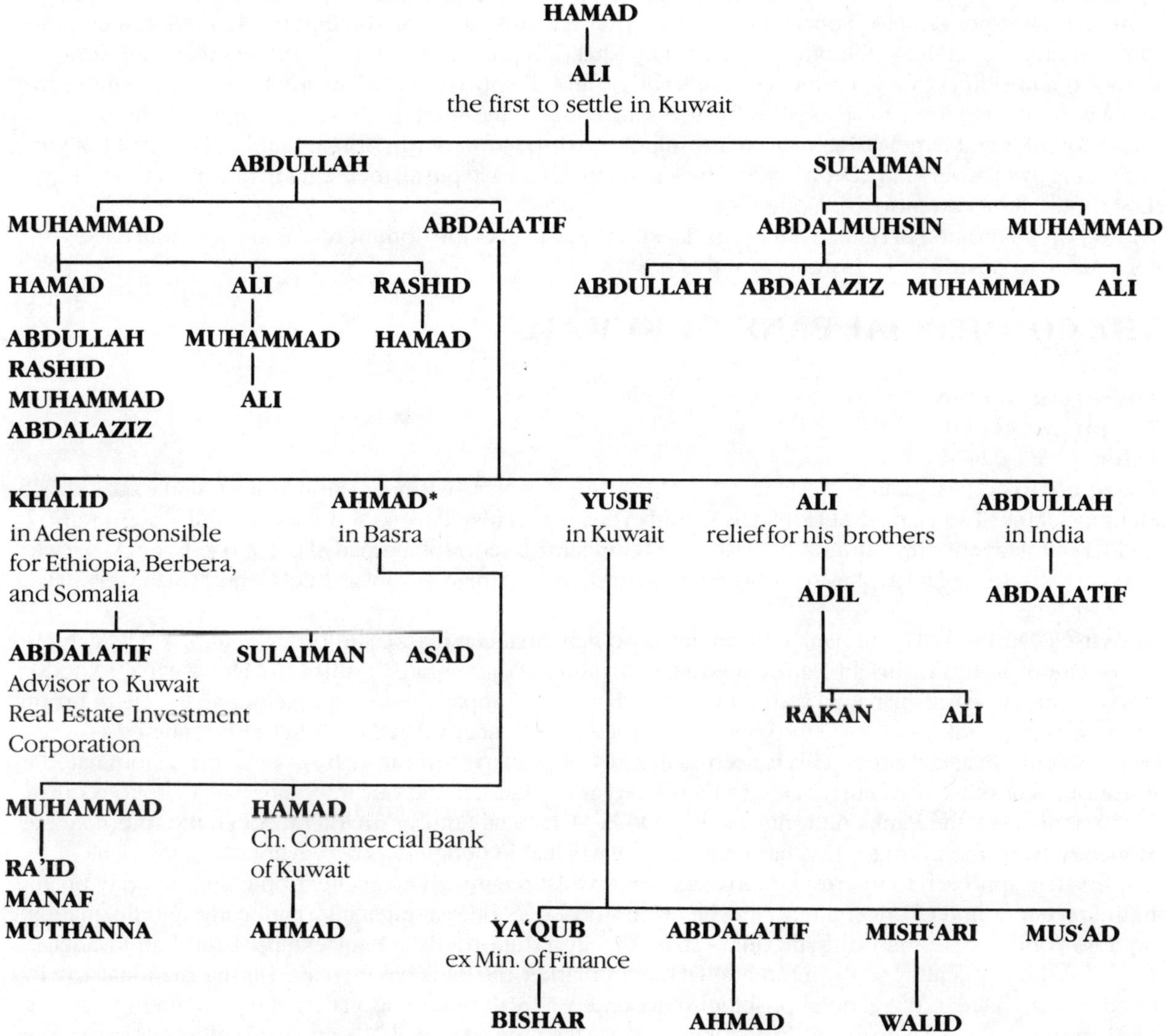

* worked for the Al Saqr family and founded the family fortune, established the National Bank of Kuwait.

THE FAMILY OF AL HAMAD

The family's immediate commercial origins start with Ali b. Hamad who transported pilgrims on the Haj by camel from Basra via Kuwait to Mecca. Eventually he settled in Kuwait and he and his sons started a business exporting Iraqi dates to Yemen, Zanzibar and India. This was a winter trade and in the summer they were involved in the pearl trade, though not to the same extent as the Roumi, Khalid, Badr and Mudaf families. His grandsons formed an empire with Ahmad in Basra, Yusif in Kuwait, Abdullah in India and Khalid based in Aden and responsible for Somalia, East Africa, Berbera and Ethiopia. The fifth brother, Ali, fulfilled the function of leave relief for the others. Today only Khalid, reputedly a hundred and five years old, remains. He holds a position of great eminence and is widely and deeply respected, in addition to maintaining an unflagging reputation as an advisor on business matters. Having seen the business empire he helped to create founder and largely disappear as a result of the dispersion of the British Empire, he is fond of wryly remarking that it would have been better if he and his brothers had put all their eggs in one basket; certainly they should have had more than one roof.

The important position of Hamad Ahmad Abdalatif as Chairman of the Commercial Bank of Kuwait makes it convenient to describe that institution at this point.

THE COMMERCIAL BANK OF KUWAIT

Address head office P.O.Box 2861 Safat
Telephone 411001
Telex 22004, 22470, 23307
Board of Directors Chairman: Hamad A A Al Hamad; Deputy Chairman: Faisal Yousuf Al Marzook q.v.; Members: Mrs. Suad Hamad Al Homaizi; Yacoub Yousuf Al Nafisi; Barrak Abdul Mohsen Al Mutair; Adnan Abdul Hamid Al Sani'a q.v.; Abdul Ghani Khalid Al Ghunaim; Jasem Mohammad Al Bahar q.v.; Jasem Marzook Boodai; Khalid Abdulatif Al Shaya q.v.; Secretary to the Board: Hamad Al Yahya; Chief General Manager: Matt Van Der Wee.
Activities During 1982, the Bank entered into two new financial markets in order to improve its liability management profile. In July the Bank issued a US$40 million floating-rate Certificate of Deposit in the London Market. This issue was managed by the European Banking Company who put together an excellent group of co-managing banks. As a result the issue was extremely well received in the market and acclaimed a success by the world's financial press. This is seen as the first of perhaps several such issues to be denominated in Eurodollars or other hard currencies, to be offered as the market and our international portfolio require.
The year also saw the Bank enter into the Eurodollar 'Financial Futures' market through the International Monetary Market in Chicago. This has proved to be a valuable hedging tool in maintaining the Bank's conservative approach to interest-risk management whilst retaining an excellent on-going liquidity profile. In the recent period of uncertain political tensions, unstable interest rates internationally, and fluctuating liquidity conditions domestically, this innovative strategy has afforded the Bank extensive funding advantages.
As well as directly dealing on the international money market, the Bank has increased its international activity in other ways. Due to the general problems encountered by the international banking community during 1982, the international loan portfolio has only grown at the modest rate of 21% and in absolute terms remains a small portion of the Bank's assets. In 1983 the Bank will pursue a cautious and prudent approach to further diversification of the portfolio through very selective participations in underwriting Eurocurrency loans. An encouraging development has been the way in which foreign contracting companies in Kuwait, having been well served by the Bank, seek the Bank's services for contracts elsewhere in the Gulf. A number of substantial projects are now being financed in this way in other Gulf countries, and it has the advantage to the Bank that they are dealing with known and proven customers. Such extensions to the Bank's activities will inevitably grow through contractors operating in the Kuwaiti market.
Among projects financed by the Bank have been:-
Industrial Relocation at Sabhan, KD10 million, and The Salmiya Sewage Project, KD6.4 million.
Construction of road and other services at Jaleeb Al-Shuyoukh, KD8.9 million.

Supply and installation of switchgear at Shuaiba North Power Station, KD6.8 million.
Warehousing and Related Works (two projects), KD29 million.
Performance Guarantees have been issued for the Kuwait National Petroleum Company regarding the modernisation of the Ahmadi Refinery and for the Kuwait Oil Company regarding the construction of a mobile drilling platform.
The Bank has also participated with other banks in financing several projects. It has been a major participant in the prestigious Al-Zour project, costing KD106 million, and has been leader or co-leader in a number of others.
Associated Banks & Affiliations Arab Co. for Trading Securities, Kuwait Arab Reinsurance Co., Lebanon Arab Trust Co., Kuwait Bank of Bahrain & Kuwait, Bahrain French-Arab Bank for International Investment, France French-Arab Holding Co., Luxembourg Industrial Bank of Kuwait, Kuwait Kuwait Asia Bank, Bahrain Kuwait Clearing Co., Kuwait Kuwait Reinsurance Co. Kuwait Pearl Holding Co., Luxembourg Pearl Investment Co., Bahrain Pearl Real Estate Co., Kuwait Rif Bank, Lebanon Salhiya Real Estate Co., Kuwait Securities Group, Kuwait United Bank of Kuwait, England

ADEL ALI AL HAMAD INC. (MARINE DIVISION)

Address head office P.O.Box 22223 Safat
Telephone 415522, 415599
Telex 22138 RAKAN KT
Activities A company operating as marine contractors specialising in transportation, diving, chartering, marine repairs and oceanography.

EASTERN DRILLING CO.

Address head office P.O.Box 22223 Safat
Telephone 415522, 415599
Telex 22138 RAKAN KT
Activities Adil Al Hamad is a Director of this company which is concerned with the drilling and the workover of oil and water wells, water resources and management, the supply of drilling bits, pipeline equipment, and specialised drilling tools.

EURO-KUWAITI INVESTMENT CO.

Address head office P.O.Box 43 Safat
Telephone 449561, 449571
Telex 44645 EKIC KT, 44649 EKIC KT
Activities Manaf Muhammad Al Hamad is the Managing Director of this company under the Chairmanship of Abdalhamid Mansur Al Mazidi. The company is an Investment Banking concern.

GAS AND NATURAL LIQUID INC.

Address head office P.O.Box 22223 Safat
Telephone 415522, 415599
Telex 22138 RAKAN KT
Activities The company is concerned with chemical and mechanical engineering, oil industry installations, repair and maintenance, chemicals, engineering inspections and they also deal in medical supplies. It is an association between Muhammad S Fadl Al Sabah and Adil Al Hamad.

GULF CONTROLLED

Address head office P.O.Box 1850 Safat
Telephone 436320
Activities Involved in general trade and contracting, this company is owned by Abdalatif Al Hamad.

AL HAMAD SUB-SEA SERVICE

Address head office P.O.Box 22223 Safat
Telephone 415522, 415599
Telex 22138 RAKAN KT
Activities In partnership with Capt. Y De Pimodan, this company is owned by Adil A Al Hamad and is engaged in offshore and diving services.

KUWAIT JAPANESE TRADING CO.

Address head office P.O.Box 3326 Safat
Telephone 431002, 427853
Telex 22135 KUJAPAN KT
Activities The company is a partnership between Yaqub Y Al Hamad and Minoru Umeda. It is active as a general trading concern and shipping agent.

MUHAMMAD AL HAMAD AND SONS CO. LTD.

Address head office P.O.Box 25741 Safat
Telephone 462634,5,6,7
Telex 23747 MARHABA KT
Activities A partnership between Muhammad Ahmad Al Hamad, Riad Muhammad, Manaf Muhammad and Muthana Muhammad Al Hamad. The company is engaged in general trading, real estate and investment.

RAITH INTERNATIONAL

Address head office P.O.Box 24635 Safat
Telephone 313393
Telex 22138 KT
Activities A company owned by Adil Ali Al Hamad which is a designing and silk screen printing concern.

WHITE STORES COMPANY

Address head office P.O.Box 3502 Safat
Telephone 812228, 814436,7
Telex 22763 WHITE KT
Activities This enterprise is owned by Yaqub Yusif Al Hamad and is concerned with the supply of cigarettes, cigars and tobacco, dry batteries, foodstuffs, lamps and general goods.

The Family of Al Issa

Genealogically a Tamimi family originating in Hawta of Saudi Arabia, but more recently emanating from Hasa (al Ahsa) on the eastern coast of the Kingdom. They should not be confused with Jana'at. The family has a small commercial presence in Kuwait but showing the development of professional interests.

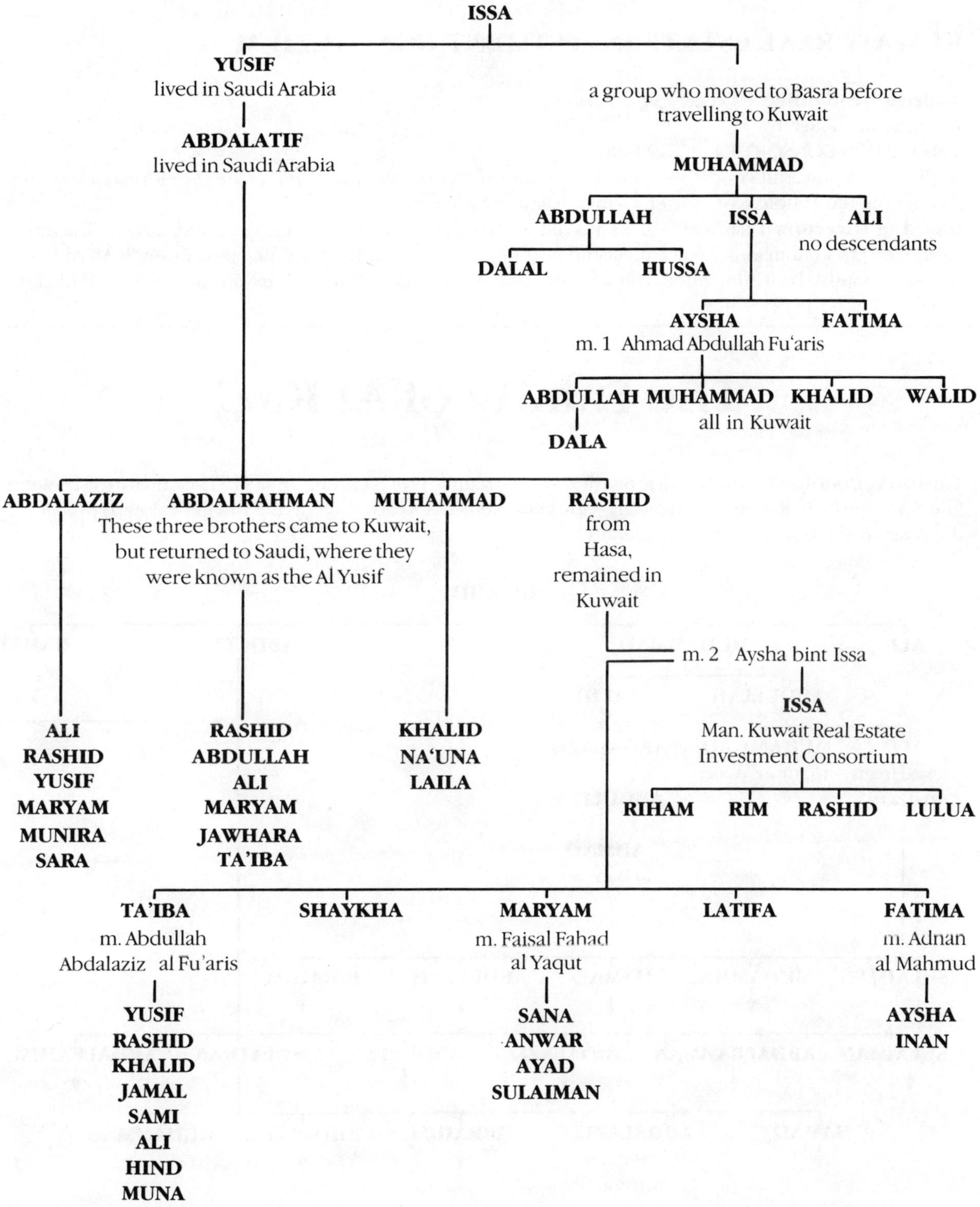

ABDALRAHMAN YUSIF AL ISSA

Address head office P.O.Box 1513 Kuwait
Telephone 810530
Cable DAHMANI
Activities A company dealing in batteries.

KUWAIT REAL ESTATE INVESTMENT CONSORTIUM

Address head office P.O.Box 23411 Safat
Telephone 448260
Telex 22620 CONSORT KT, 22849 CONSORT KT
Activities A powerful concern with widely spread and comprehensive real estate development interests throughout the Middle East, as well as manufacturing interests.
Board of Directors Chairman: Fahad Muzaid Al Raja'an; Deputy Chairman: Yusif Abdalaziz Al Wazzan; Members: Jawad Ahmad Bukhamsin, Rashid Abdullah Al Mujrin, Sha'ib Abdullah Sha'ib, Salih Ali Al Kazi, Abdalaziz Saud Al Badr, Muhammad Abdalrahim Taqi, Muhammad Mutluq Al Hisyan, Mishari Zaid Al Khalid,

---

The Family of Al Kazi

Emanating from the area of 'Anaiza in Saudi Arabia the family is of Bani Tamim stock. The much foreshortened family tree given below shows a typically wide geographical spread as well as the way genealogy is used in the Arab world to maintain family identity.

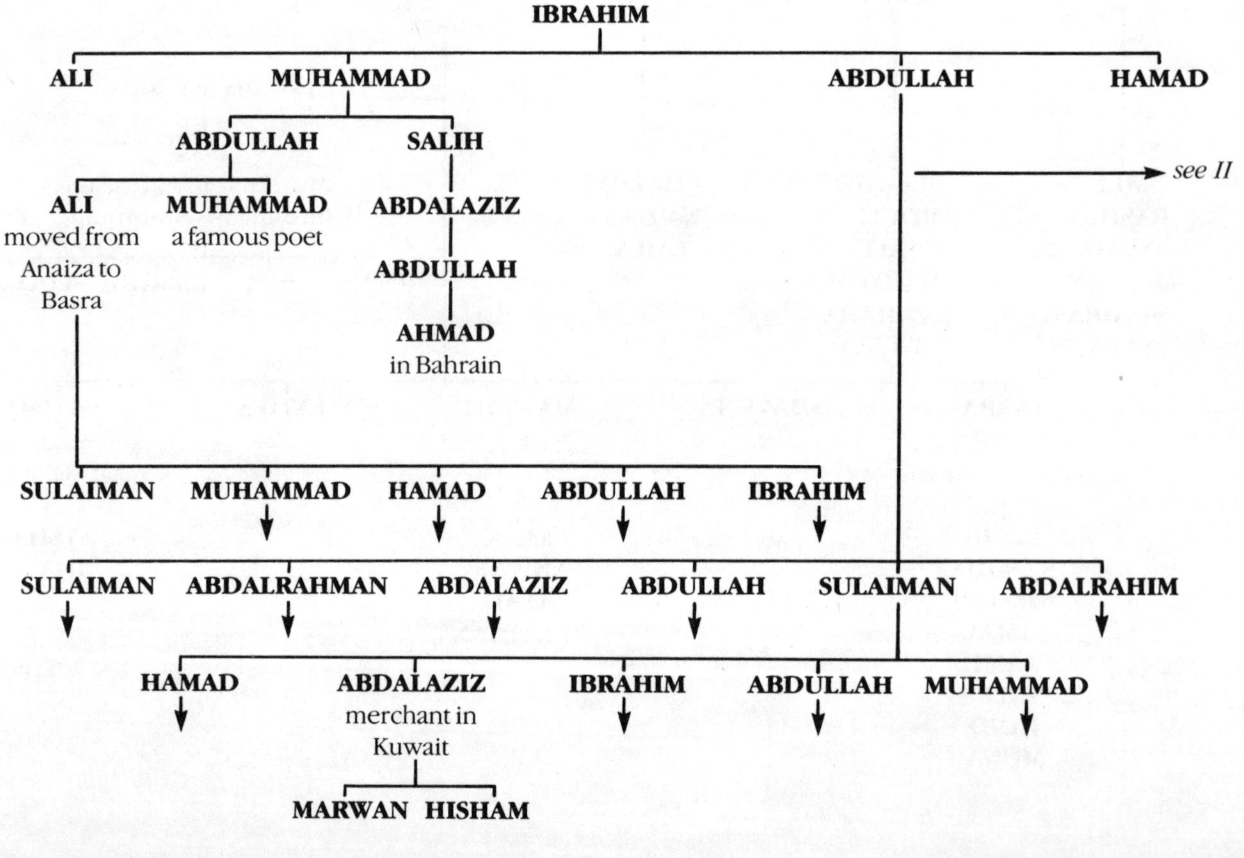

- **ALI**
  - **HAMAD** brought up as an orphan on his father's death in Basra. Emigrated to Calcutta at the turn of the century. Then, after two years, settled in Bombay where he remained until 1945. Merchant in dates, textiles and spices. D. in Beirut 1974.
    - **FATIMA** d. m. Abdalrahman Abdalaziz Al Bassam
      - **FARIDA**
      - **FAWZI**
      - **FAWZIYA**
      - **FIRDAUS**
      - **FATINA**
    - **ALI** d. in the 1940s
    - **NURA** m. Abdullah Abdalaziz Al Bassam lives in Al Khobar Saudi Arabia
      - **TARIQ**
      - **NABILA**
      - **IBTISAM**
      - **SU'AD**
      - **WIDAD**
    - **EBRAHIM** Educated at St Vincents School, Poona. Dir. Nat. School of Drama in India
      - **EBRAHIM** Al Kazi Co. Bombay with Ahmad Abdullah Al Kazi of the Bahrain branch of the family
        - **FAISAL** runs 50 camps for under-privileged children in Delhi
        - **AMAL** theatre director
    - **LULU** in Kuwait
    - **SULAIMAN** Mutawa and Kazi Co.
      - **UMR**
      - **HALA**
      - **SALWA**
      - **HAIFA**
      - **HAMAD**
    - **MUNIRA** artist in London and Kuwait
    - **FA'IZA** d. m. Muhammad Bahrani of Iraq
      - **TALAL**
      - **DINA**
    - **BASIL**

MUTAWA ALKAZI CO. LTD.

Address PO Box 626 Safat
Telephone 416193, 446942, 442752, 458713
Telex 22452 ALKAZI KT
The company is a partnership between Sulaiman Hamad Al Kazi, Abdalaziz Ali and Abdullah Ibrahim Mutawa. It is active as a general importer with emphasis on nautical equipment and general consumer products. However, the company's main activity is concerned with its sole agency for Honda. This involves the distribution of cars, motorcycles, trucks, pumps, generators, lighting equipment as well as all parts, accessories and services.

RAFIF STORE

Address PO Box 20104 Safat
Telephone 425982
A partnership between Sulaiman Al Kazi, Libo Atamian, and Abdullah Al Bassam. It deals with cosmetics, menswear and readymade clothes.

UNITED INDUSTRIES GROUP

Address PO Box 3377 Safat
Telephone 814875, 818764
A partnership between Da'ud Al Musallam, Ahmad Wahidi and Sulaiman Al Kazi.

ABDALAZIZ SULAIMAN MUHAMMAD AL QADHI

Address PO Box 1589 Safat
Telephone 416855, 417366
A company owned as named and active as a general merchant. Abdalaziz Sulaiman is one of the best known dealers in traditional perfumes. He is an expert in blending and justly famous throughout Kuwait. For the visitor, the phrases concerned with the poetic mention of the perfumes of Arabia are given added emphasis when he sees in Abdalaziz's shop special wood for burning in incense-burners which retails at 3500 Kuwaiti dinars a kilo and wood oil perfumes which fetch 17,300 dinars a kilo.

The Family of Ma'arafi

** companies independently held by family members

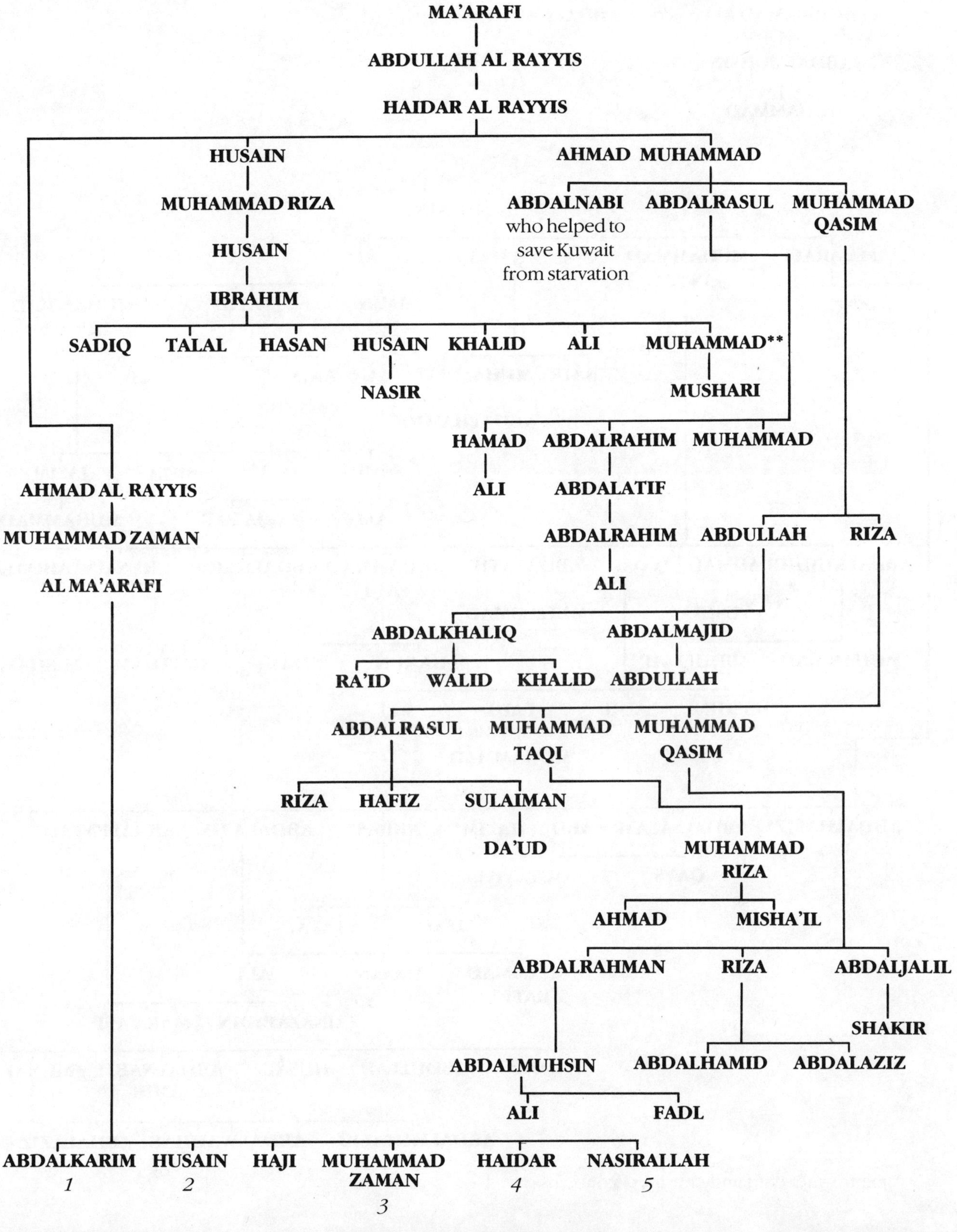

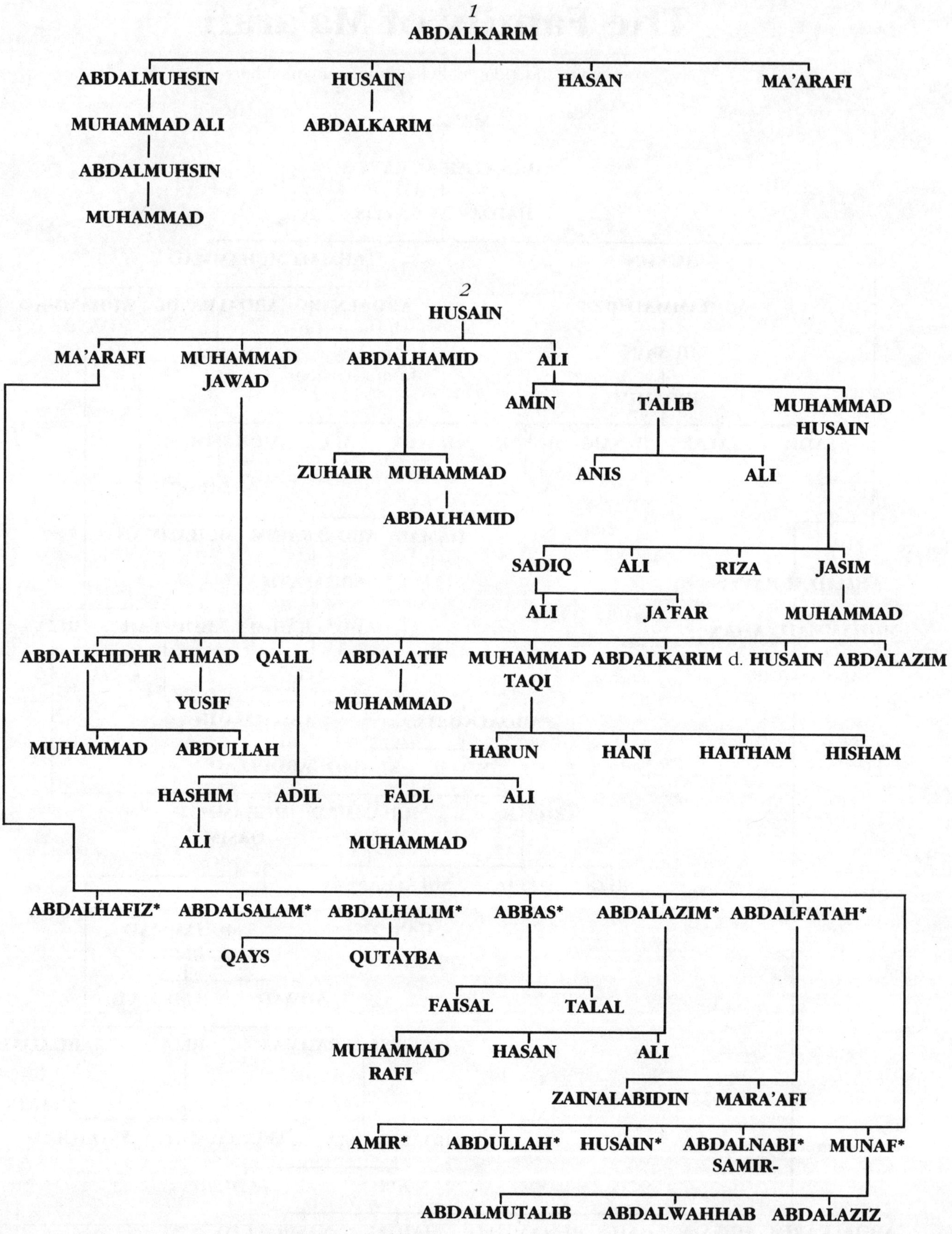

* joint owners of family business concerns

3

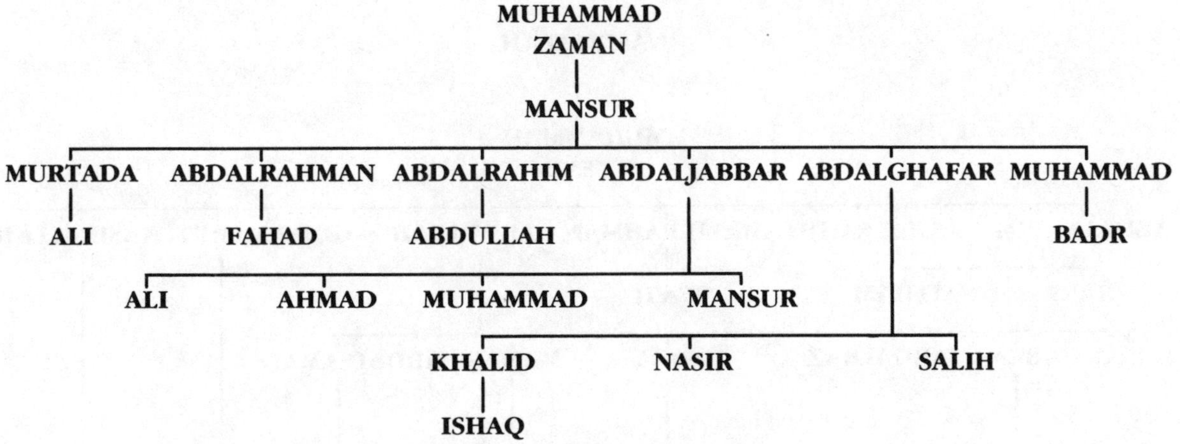

4

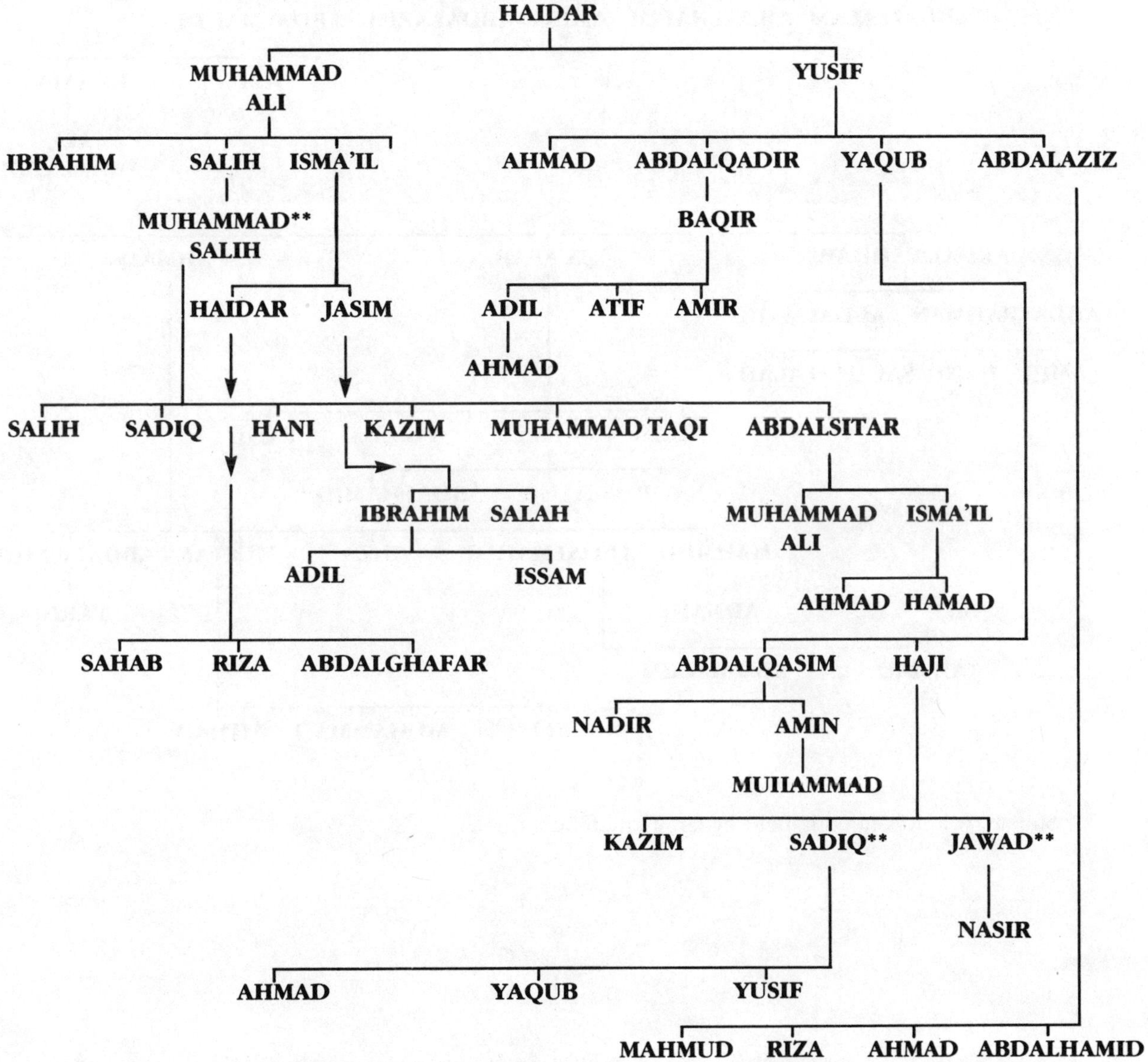

** companies independently held by family members

5

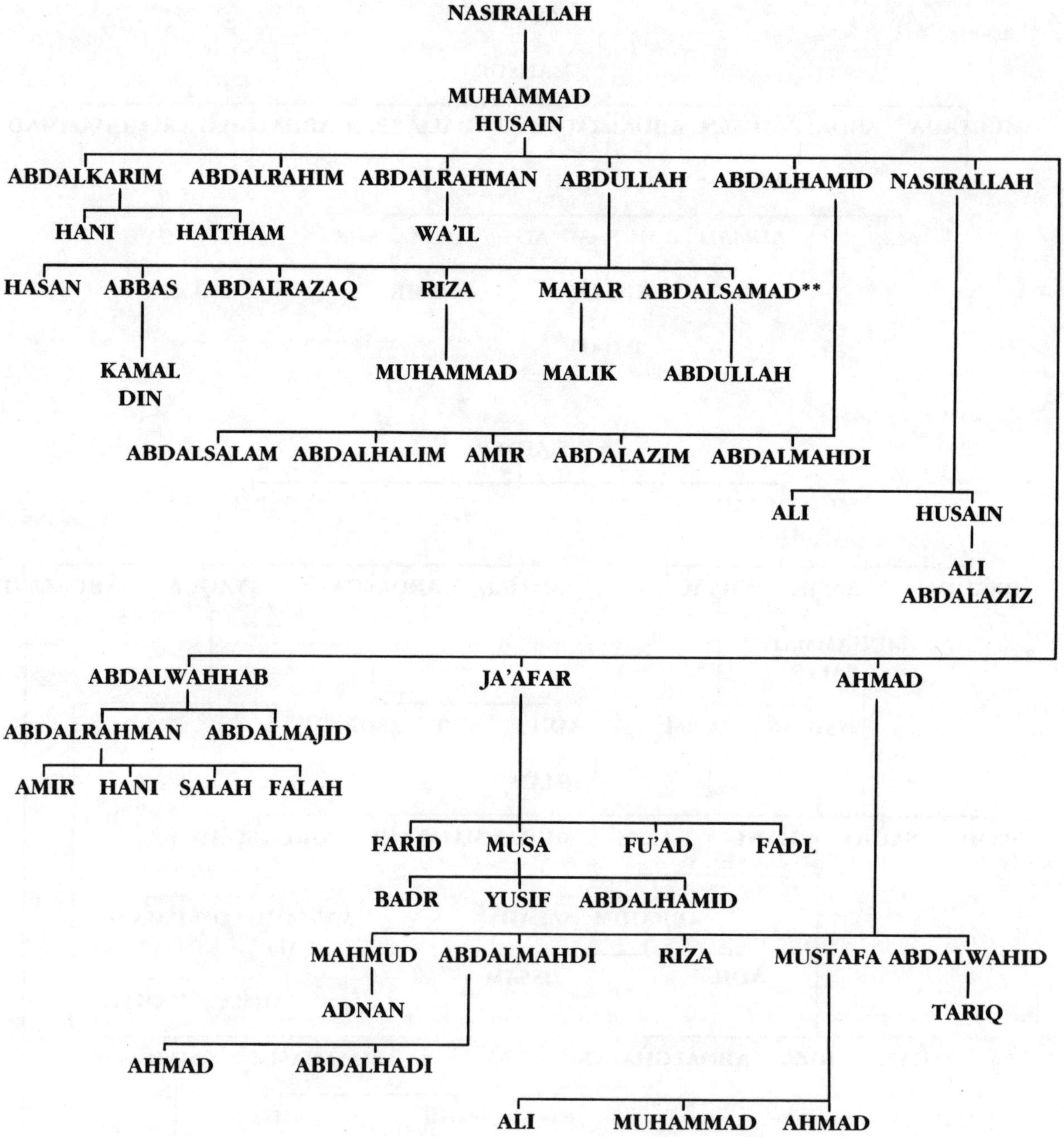

** companies independently held by family members

A family whose historical roots stretch back to the migration of the Kinda tribe of Yemen into southern Iraq during the course of the establishment of the Umayyad Caliphate. First settling near Kufa, this family of Madhaj Kinda stock moved secondly to Amara and then to Basra and then to Bandar Mashour in Arabistan. These moves took place, possibly, in the sixteenth century, and involved marriage ties with the Barri Kaab. Finally, due to a family dispute, the Ma'arafis became one of the earliest groups to move to Kuwait where they lived in the Ha'il Wasit area of the old town. Today the family numbers some three hundred and seventy males and forms an important part of the commercial life of Kuwait.

Like so many Kuwaitis their recent history is intimately connected with their country's commercial development. Initially, they began importing timber for shipbuilding from Muscat where their agent was Hajji Bakr; though Abdullah Husain Al Ma'arafi replaced him during the reign of the Sultan Taimur. When they were able to operate larger vessels, the timber was imported direct. The Ma'arafi family used their ships mainly for the date trade from southern Iraq, where they still own some 10,000 jarib of date palms (1 jarib is 1,000 trees). They would then bring back trade goods on the return journey. In their heyday they owned about forty ships, including the following, where in the old system of weights and measures 1 maund was equivalent to about 100 lbs:

The *Hasani*, *Manwar*, and the *Mansuri* which were small booms, and four more vessels of the Baghala type, all of which loaded some 3,000 maunds. Amongst the larger booms were the *Tura Awal* and *Tura Thani,* loading to 4,000 maunds, the *Alawi* loading 5,000 maunds and the pride of the Kuwaiti fleet, the *Muhammadi*, loading to 6,000 maunds. This last vessel was the largest in the whole region and is justly famous. She was built in India between 1912 and 1916 and part of the high cost of this vessel is attributed to the spendthrift ways of the family member who supervised her construction. Though now broken up long ago and her timbers used to construct smaller vessels, her memory is kept alive in *Muhammadi the Second* which, though much smaller, has been specially made as a superb restaurant moored as an integral part of the SAS Hotel.

During the course of history Kuwait has been assailed by many an enemy intent on wresting her lucrative commercial position into their own hands. The Ma'arafis have always contributed ships and arms when the need arose. They supplied both to the Kuwaiti fleet at the battle of Al Ruqa off Failaka Island in the closing years of the eighteenth century, when the Kuwaitis fought the Barri Ka'ab who had hitherto levied a tax on all shipping in the Gulf. A hundred years later Abdalnabi Al Ma'arafi was amongst a group of Kuwait citizens which included Yusif Yaqub Al Badr, Yusif Bin Sabih, the Al Ibrahim (of Dawra), Haj Abdalatif Al Atiqi and Salim Sultan, who for three years used their ships to bring food and rice, which was distributed free, to a Kuwait stricken by famine. During the war mounted by Sh. Mubarak Al Sabah on Abdalaziz Al Rashiyd of Ha'il in concert with the Sa'adun shaykhs of the Muntafiq in Iraq and Abdalaziz Al Sa'ud, the Ma'arafi and Mataqi families contributed a large quantity of arms and ammunition.

The commercial picture presented by the family today is a complex one. The old ship owning interests have become diluted and many family members have entered business on their own account. However, the sons of Ma'arafi Husain demonstrate an interesting entity as joint owners of family business concerns. They are marked with an asterisk in the family tree and have the following joint holdings in what amounts to a family holding company and that company's property.

The eleven male heirs own 51% of KDC, 49% Nilfisk, 98% Kuwait Clear Drains Co., 100% Marafie Sons Co., 100% Al Mo'eed Co., 100% Arab Consultant Co. Including female heirs, twenty eight people also own 100% Wara Real Estate (includes the SAS Hotel) and 100% Marafie Real Estate International of the USA. Other interests include real estate in Basra and Kuwait.

THE KUWAIT SAS HOTEL

Address head office P.O.Box 26199 Safat
Telephone 657000, 657700
Telex 44306 SASHOTL KT, 44307 SASHOTL KT
This modern and luxurious hotel is situated only ten kilometres from the International Airport and placed on the shores of the Gulf with its own private beach. It has all the facilities that the visiting businessman needs in terms of communications and access. The restaurants are famous for both Chinese cuisine and novel and delicious Arabian dishes. The prices of the rooms are very reasonable.

MARAFIE SONS CO.

Address head office P.O.Box 122 Safat
Telephone 2449925
Telex 22661 RAFIE KT
Where the General Manager is Amir Al Ma'arafi.

KUWAIT CLEAR DRAINS CO.

Address head office P.O.Box 56034 Al Aaqool
Telephone 2449925
Telex 46120 MEDIVON KT
Where the General Manager is Abdalfatah Al Ma'arafi who is also a member of the government body created to clear up the aftermath of the Manakh stock market collapse.

WARA REAL ESTATE CO.

Address head office P.O.Box 122 Safat
Telephone 2449925, 2449927
Telex 2875 RAFIA KT
Where the Chairman is Husain Al Ma'arafi.

KUWAIT DANISH CLEANING EQUIPMENT CO.

Address head office P.O.Box 122 Safat
Telephone 842096
Telex 23109
Where the Chairman is Abdalfatah Al Ma'arafi.

AL MO'EED TRADING CO.

Address head office P.O.Box 122 Safat
Telephone 2449925
Telex 22661 RAFIE KT
Where the Chairman is Abdullah Al Ma'arafi.

Other companies independently held by family members who are designated by two asterisks in the family tree:

MUHAMMAD SALEH MARAFI

Address head office P.O.Box 5675 Safat
Telephone 816949
Telex 23568 KT
Activities Owned by Muhammad Salih Al Ma'arafi, this company deals with electrical appliances.

MARAFIE INTERNATIONAL CO.

Address head office P.O.Box 5143 Safat
Telephone 435955, 424170
Telex 22699 RAKHSH KT
Activities An importing concern which wholesales business machines, electronic and electrical appliances and accessories, as well as tents. It is owned by Sadeq and Jawad Al Ma'arafi. The latter being a partner in Al Marafi and Al Banna Co. with Said Muhammad Al Banna (P.O.Box 894 Safat, tel: 818070), which business supplies carpentry tools, hardware and materials for interior decoration.

MARAFI UNITED CO. FOR CONSTRUCTION MATERIAL, ENGINEERING PROJECTS AND TRANSPORT

Address head office P.O.Box 4415 Safat
Telephone 410914, 410923, 426280
Telex 22467 KT
Activities Directed by Abbas Abdullah Al Ma'arafi, this company supplies construction, sanitary and decorating materials, as well as transport.

ABDALSAMAD A MA'RAFIE

Address head office P.O.Box 135 Safat
Telephone 432927, 434548
Telex 22467 MUMTZ KT.
Activities An important shipping business representing the Hansa Line, Mitsui and Mitsui OSK (Osaka Line). It also operates as a general trading business and travel agent. Abdalsamad Al Ma'arafi is a member of the Ahli Bank.

MUHAMMAD IBRAHIM MARAFIE

Address head office P.O.Box 104 Safat
Telephone 432764
Activities A general trading and contracting company.

The Family of Marzook

Originating in Najd of Saudi Arabia from Rimah. A leading Kuwait family with major financial interests belied by the small number of commercial enterprises in the family.

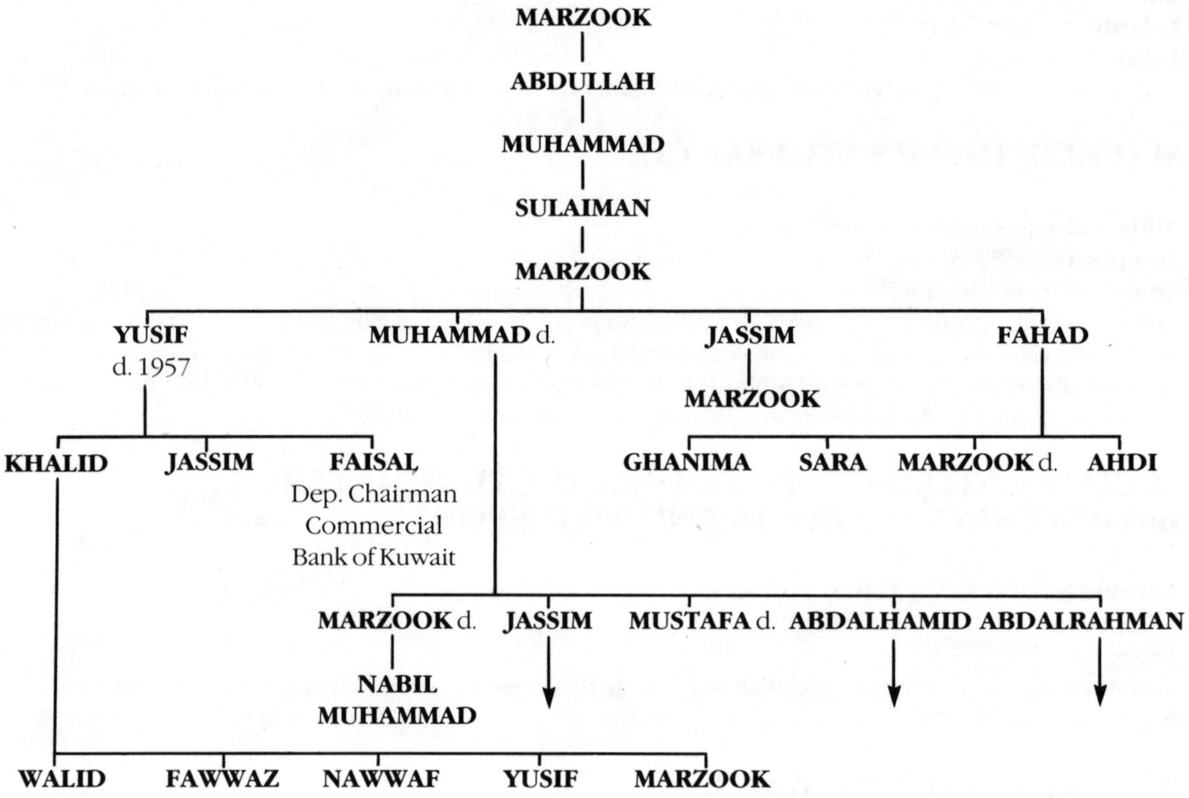

ARABIAN BUILDING AND CONTRACTING

Address head office P.O.Box 1114 Safat
Telephone 814457,8,9
Telex 22509 BYBLOS KT
Activities Marzouk Jasim Al Marzouk is a partner in this company with Omar M Bakir. They are civil contractors with building and road construction interests.

AL MARZOUK AND ABI HANNA

Address head office P.O.Box 1913 Safat
Telephone 421401, 421402
Telex 22319 ABIHANNA KT
Activities A company of consultant engineers, planners and architects where the directors are Salim Al Marzouk, Sabah Abi Hanna and Charles Bosel.

VERSAILLES

Address head office P.O. Box 5305 Safat
Telephone 615906
Telex 22509 BYBLOS KT
Activities The company is a partnership between Marzouk Jasim Al Marzouk and Omar M Bakir and is involved with the supply of high fashion for men and women as well as cosmetics and perfumes.

SARA FAHAD AL MARZOUQ ESTABLISHMENT

Address head office P.O.Box 347 Safat
Telephone 433732
Telex 22456 SARA KT
Activities A company owned as named and engaged in business as general importers and exporters as well as tendering.

THE GROUP

The families of Kuwait have progressed to the extent that the changes in trade over the years have wrought dramatic changes in family behaviour. The evolution from a single family operated business, which so often becomes the holding company for the disparate activities of succeeding generations, is no longer sufficient in Kuwait. Here the trade of today is in money rather than the entrepot dates and textiles, in investments rather than pearls. The activities of family holding companies in this process have become so vast in scope that a new commercial concept of financial operations has been built up. The description of the Group that follows is to be understood in this light rather than as a description of a single family business.
Percentage ownership in the Group:
Kuwait Real Estate Company, public company.
Kuwait Real Estate Bank, public company, 4.4 percent owned by Kuwait Real Estate Company, balance outside.*
Pearl Investment Company, public company of Bahrein; 5.15 percent owned by Kuwait Real Estate Co., 11.15 percent owned by Kuwait Real Estate Bank, 3 percent by Kuwait Projects Co., balance outside Group.*
Pearl Real Estate Company, 52 percent owned by Kuwait Real Estate Bank, balance outside Group.*
Kuwait Projects Company, 3.8 percent owned by Kuwait Real Estate Co., 5 percent owned by Kuwait Real Estate Bank, balance owned outside Group.*
Financial Group of Kuwait, 30 percent owned by Kuwait Real Estate Bank, 30 percent owned by Kuwait Projects Co., 40 percent owned by Bank of America.
Kuwait Projects Company for Contracting and Building, 36 percent owned by Kuwait Real Estate Co., 32 percent owned by Kuwait Real Estate Bank, 32 percent owned by Kuwait Projects Co.
Kuwait Projects Company for Reconstruction and Real Estate, 32 percent owned by Kuwait Real Estate Co., 36 percent owned by Kuwait Real Estate Bank, 32 percent owned by Kuwait Projects Co.
The Group started in 1972 with the Kuwait Real Estate Company and then the Kuwait Real Estate Bank. From this base a holding company was formed in 1975 to diversify the Group's interests. Thus the Kuwait Projects Company was formed which initiated three other companies, Financial Group of Kuwait, Kuwait Projects Company for Reconstruction and Real Estate and the Kuwait Projects Company for Contracting and Building. The latest development has been the Pearl Investment Company in Bahrein. The Group has considerable contacts with Kuwait's leading insurance and financial institutions. In conjunction with the Commercial and Al Ahli Bank a Pearl Holding Company was set up in Luxembourg and then the Kuwaiti French Bank was formed with the French Industrial Bank; Pearl Investment holds 32 percent. The new bank has filled a gap in the French market and has two new branches, in Paris and Nice.

* Majority of balance owned privately by individual founders of the Group.

Directors:
Khalid Y Al Marzook, Chairman
Abdul Razak Sultan Aman, Vice-Chairman
Abdalaziz A Al Rashid
Muhammad Y Al Nissif
Abdalrahman Abdul Mugni
Faisal S Al Felaij
Barrak Abdul Muhsin Al Mutair
Saad A Al Nahedh

KUWAIT REAL ESTATE COMPANY

Address PO Box 1257, Safat
Telephone 448330
Telex 22644
The company owns some of the most important buildings in Kuwait such as the Marzook Pearl, and the Souk al Kuwait.
Outside investments include holdings in the Bank of Lebanon and Kuwait, Kuwait Company for Manufacturing Building Materials, Kuwait Investments Project Co., Kuwait Shopping Centres Group, Gulf Gravel Co., the Bank of Jordan and Gulf, Spring of Country Wood Salt Lake City Project, Hong Kong Regent Hotel.

KUWAIT REAL ESTATE BANK

Address PO Box 22822, Safat
Telephone 410110
Telex 2312
In the wake of the company's original initiatives, it has invested in real estate abroad.
Investments outside the Group: Industrial Bank of Kuwait, Misr-American International Bank, Bank of Asia and Kuwait, Jordan Gulf Bank, Bank of Lebanon and Kuwait.

PEARL INVESTMENT COMPANY

Address PO Box 23859, Safat
Telephone 247493, 427494
Telex 4461 JUDI KT
The Bahrein office is at PO Box 5809, Manama, tel. 246570-5, tlx. 9353 PEARL
The company has intersts in the USA and the Far East.
Outside investments include interests in Kuwait and Gulf Financial Centre, Bahrain International Bank, United Gulf Bank, Kuwait and Gulf Financial Centre Co., Arab Coast Bank.

PEARL REAL ESTATE COMPANY

Address PO Box 23859
Telephone 427491
Telex 24461
The company specialises in real estate and portfolio investment. As well as locally it is a substantial investor in Japan. It also deals in precious metals.
Investments outside the Group: Kuwait and Gulf Financial Centre, Bahrain International Bank, Gulf International Insurance, Kuwait Markets Group Co.

KUWAIT PROJECTS COMPANY

Address PO Box 23982
Telephone 444341
Telex 2654
The company was formed to diversify the Group's interests. It is essentially a holding company, the first of its kind in Kuwait to explore activity in real estate, industrial, investment and financial markets. It has been involved in enterprises in Kuwait, Europe and the Far East.
The company has interests in the following outside the Group: Middle East International Contracting Co., Building Maintenance Co., Korea Kuwait Banking Corp., Kuwaiti Investments Projects Co., Arab International Finance Co., Arab Finance and Commercial, Marrocan Kuwait Development Co., Commercial Facilities Co., Les Terrasses de Genève Project, Bahrain International Bank.

FINANCIAL GROUP OF KUWAIT

Address PO Box 23896, Safat
Telephone 444087/91
Telex 2653 MALIA KT
The company exists to provide a wide range of investment opportunities to Kuwaitis. It is an important dealer in securities and has participated in bond issues in various currencies. It has a substantial and growing loan portfolio and is a leading spot dealer in gold and silver.

KUWAIT PROJECTS COMPANY FOR CONTRACTING AND BUILDING

Address PO Box 21281 Safat
Telephone 45180/1
Telex 2709 MURMUR
Formed in 1976, the company offers full mechanical, civil and electrical engineering services. It built the substantial Al Durrar Housing Complex and has carried many construction projects, from a single villa to the Al Murjan Complex. Its property maintenance subsidiary has won important contracts in face of fierce competition. It is the agent for glass-reinforced concrete made in Belgium and used to spectacular effect in the Late Sheikh Nasser Al Sabah Mosque which the company built on a turnkey basis. The company also represents Hepworth Plastics International Ltd of the UK and imports building material from around the world.
Investments outside the Group: Middle East International Contracting Co., Property Maintenance Co., Kuwait Industrial Marble Manufacturing Co.

KUWAIT PROJECTS COMPANY FOR RECONSTRUCTION AND REAL ESTATE

Address PO Box 4800, Safat
Telephone 446704, 443319, 443349
This company specialises in all aspects of real estate financial services. Its own investments give it a sound capital base. It is now expanding its technical and advisory services. Local conditions have enabled it to prove its ability to operate profitably and manage and assemble real estate investment portfolios in participation with others. It also has the advantage of the financial resources of the Group behind it.

The Family of Al Mojil

This is the same family as that in the Saudi volume, q.v. Mo'ajil. They originate in Hawtat Sudair in Saudi Arabia.

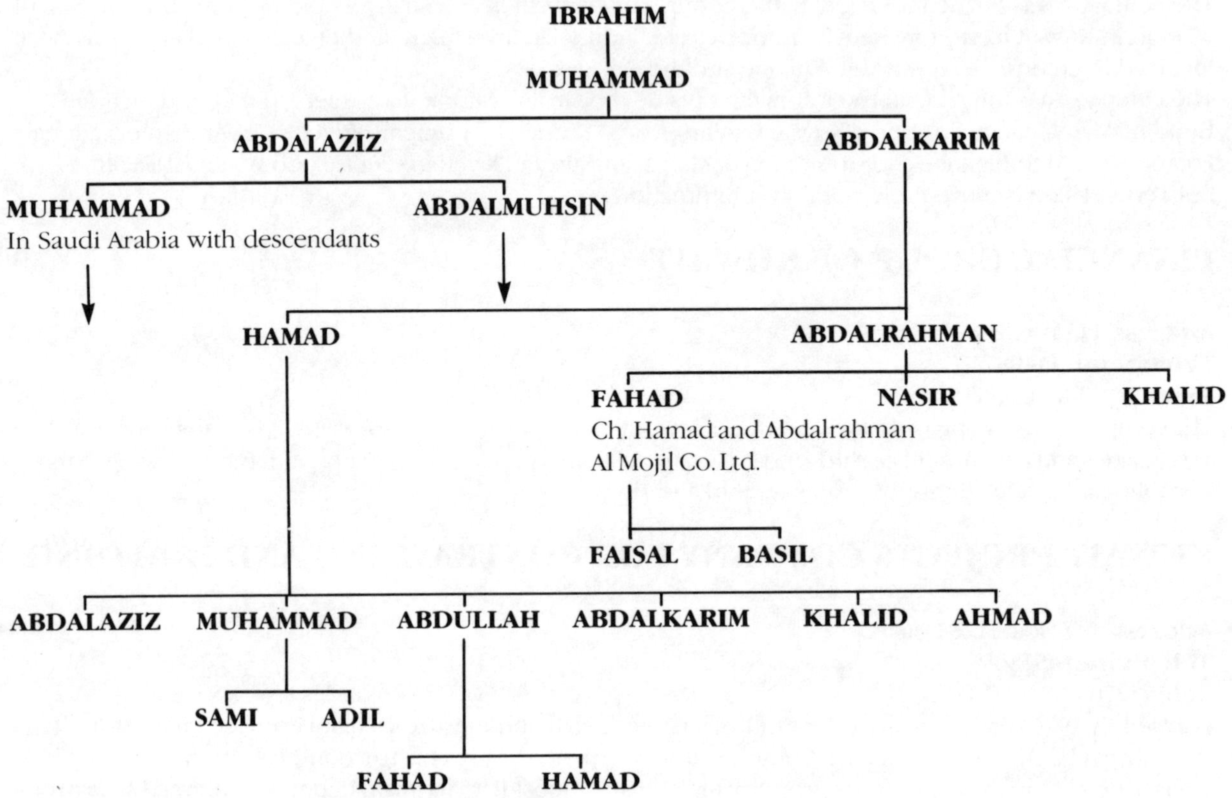

AL MOJIL TRADING GROUP

Address head office P.O.Box 1447 Safat
Telephone 2440040, 433075, 434108
Telex 23781 ALMOJIL KT
Cable MOJILGROUP

HAMAD & ABDULRAHMAN AL MOJIL

Address head office P.O.Box 1447 Safat
Telephone 422503, 433075
Cable ALMOJIL

AL MOJIL TRADING & CONTRACTING CO.

Address head office P.O.Box 1331 Safat
Telephone 422503, 433075
Cable FAHMOJIL

AL MOJIL DRUG CO.

Address head office P.O.Box 2761 Safat
Telephone 435071, 410648
Telex 22028 MOJILDRUG KT
Cable MOJILDRUG

INTERNATIONAL SUPPLY COMPANY

Address head office P.O.Box 5514 Safat
Telephone 424946, 425946
Telex 22449 ISCOL KT
Cable ISCOL

AL MOJIL TRADING & HOTELS SERVICES CO.

Address head office P.O.Box 25299 Safat
Telephone 2532100
Telex 23594, 23593 SEHO KT
Cable SECONHOME

AL MOJIL TRAVELS

Address head office P.O.Box 25376 Safat
Telephone 437305, 437385
Cable TRIDENT

AL MOJIL MACHINE SHOP EST.

Address head office P.O.Box 20462
Telephone 840391

ARAB REAL ESTATE CONSULTANTS COMPANY

Address head office P.O.Box 22281
Telephone 410241
Telex 22305 EAE KT

AL MOJIL INTERNATIONAL SA

Address head office 5 Chemin Malombre, CH-1206 Geneve, Switzerland
Telephone (022) 47 48 46/47/41
Telex 22671 SADI CH

The Family of Al Mutairi

As their name clearly indicates, the family comes from the great tribe of Mutair.

- **FAJHAN AL MUTAIRI**
  - **HILAL**
    came to Kuwait when he was 14 and began his career as an ordinary diver. He became the greatest purchaser of pearls of them all.
    m. into Al Sayer, Al Mudaf and Al Ibrahim of Zubair
    - **MISH'ARI**
      businessman
      - **ALI**
        Diplomat. Ex amb. to Madrid; m. into Al Bahar
        - **AMIR**
        - **HAZIN**
      - **GHAZI**
        Kuwait National Petroleum Co.
        - **HILAL**
      - **HILAL**
        trained at Hambros
        G.M. Kuwait Investment Co.
        Mem. Menakh Arbitration Committee
        - **KHALID**
        - **FAJHAN**
      - **FAISAL**
        engineer
      - **TALAL**
      - **BADR**
        student
    - **HAMAD**
      m. into Al Marzuq
      businessman
      - **HILAL**
      - **MUHAMMAD**
    - **BANDAR**
      m. into Al Sayer
      looks after family property
      - **ISSAM**
        In the Finance House which is run on medieval Islamic principles
    - **FAJHAN**
      d. early 70s
      m. Ghanima Al Marzuq (q.v.)
      Cairo Univ. graduate
      - **HILAL**
      - **MARZUQ**
  - daughter

This, the family of one of the most famous citizens of Kuwait, Hilal Fajhan Al Mutairi, has become, as far as business is concerned, a purely professional group with no corporate entity as such.
The story goes that at the start of the last season of pearl fishing before the crash in the market, which came as a consequence of the growth in the cultured pearl production from Japan, Hilal was warned not to go out by Saud Al Mudaf (alive in 1984 aged 92). So that year he kept his money and bought no pearls; instead he invested his funds in real estate in India, Bahrain and Kuwait. This is looked after by his son, Bandar, at the present time.
Hilal was what was called a Tawash, that is to say he was the merchant who bought pearls from the boats.

HAMAD HILAL AL MUTAIRI

Address head office P.O.Box 364 Kuwait
Telephone 434238
Cable FAJHAN
Activities A company engaged in building contractors.

MISHARI HILAL AL MUTAIRI

Address head office P.O.Box 1078 Safat
Telephone 819781, 434558
Activities A company dealing in radio and television spare parts.

The Family of Al Nouri

A family of Shammar (Qahtan) emanating from Mosul in Iraq.

- **YA'QUB**
  - **YUSIF**
    - **SALMAN**
      - **MUHAMMAD**
        - **ZAKARIA**
          - **AHMAD**
            - **MUHAMMAD JARJAS**
              - **AHMAD**
                - **SH. MUHAMMAD AL NOURI**, b. 15 Ramadan 1868, follower of Sh. Abdalwahhab al Jawadi from whom he qualified as a teacher in 1900. An imam.
                  - **SH. ABDULLAH**, imam, author, lawyer, d.
                    - *1st wife*
                      - **ABDALKHALIQ**
                      - **ABDALBAQI**
                      - **FATIMA**
                    - *2nd wife*
                      - **NURI**
                      - **AHMAD**
                      - **HAMID**
                      - **MUHAMMAD**
                      - **ANWAR**
                      - **KHAWLA**
                      - **DAWLA**
                      - **MUNIR**
                      - **MUNAWIR**
                      - **SUHAILA**
                  - **ABDALRAHMAN**
                    - **MUHAMMAD**
                    - **KAMIL**
                  - **ABDALAZIZ**, m. from Du'aij
                    - *Cont. below*
                  - **ABDALMALIK** d.
                  - **ASMA**
                  - **AYSHA**

- **NURI** into Hamid al Hindi
  - **AHMAD**
  - **ABDALWAHHAB**
  - **MARYAM**
- **SU'AD** m. Abdullah al Nuri
  - **NAJLA**
  - **HAZIM**
  - **AHMAD**
- **FAISAL** Asst. Gen. Man. Local Purchase Dept. Kuwait Univ.
  - **MISHA'IL**
  - **AHMAD**
  - **DALAL**
  - **ANWAR**
- **SUHAM** m. Sa'ud al Abdalrahman Ahmad al Bakr
  - **WA'IL**
  - **AHMAD**
  - **LU'AY**
  - **KHALID**
- **SUHAILA** Sabti
  - **GHAIDA**
  - **MARYAM**
  - **SA'UD**
- **KHALID**
- **NADIR** m.
  - **AYSHA**
  - **ABDULLAH**
  - **MUSA**
- **SALWA** m. Suhail Muhammad al Yasin
  - **MUHAMMAD**
  - **NURA**
- **SUMAYA** m. Ahmad Khalid al Ruwaishid
  - **KHALID**
- **SANA'** Samir Abdullah al Awadhi
  - **ABDULLAH**

ABDALBAQI AL NOURI

Address head office P.O.Box 632 Kuwait
Telephone 427670
Cable SERVICE
Activities Trading concern involved with electrical goods and appliances.

MINEFAH TRADING COMPANY

Address head office P.O.Box 26158 Safat
Telephone 749320, 749321, 833204
Telex 30114 KT
Activities The General Manager is Nouri Abdalaziz Al Nouri who is also Assistant Manager of the Follow-Up Department in the Industrial Bank of Kuwait. The company is a partnership between Nouri, Faisal and Hamid and trades in brass finished and brass furniture imported from Finland, Germany and France. They also deal in real estate and act as commission agents in export/import trade.

KUWAIT CONSULTING OFFICE

Address head office P.O.Box 12035 Shamiya
Telephone 437220
Telex 22604 NJT KT
Activities A company of industrial consultants which is a partnership between Ahmad Abdullah Al Nouri and the architect, Salah Abdalhamid.

NOURI INDUSTRIAL ESTABLISHMENT

Address head office P.O.Box 2829 Safat
Telephone 840219, 840055, 814803
Telex 23887 NOURI KT
Activities Owned by Abdalkhaliq Abdullah Al Nouri, the Managing Director is Nouri Abdalaziz Al Nouri. The company is a supplier of materials and equipment to government ministries and petrochemical companies.

PETROCHEMICAL INDUSTRIES CO.

Address head office P.O.Box 1084 Safat
Telephone 422141, 448280
Telex 22024 KCFC KT, 22134 KCFC KT
Activities The Chairman and Managing Director of this company is Abdalbaqi Abdullah Al Nouri. It is engaged in manufacturing and marketing liquid ammonia, urea, ammonium sulphate, sulphuric acid, salt and chlorine.

The Industrial Bank of Kuwait is under the chairmanship of Anwar Abdullah Al Nouri and it is therefore convenient to describe this important institution at this point.

THE INDUSTRIAL BANK OF KUWAIT

Address head office P.O.Box 3146 Safat
Telephone 653000
Telex 22469 SENAEY KT, 22582 SENAEY KT, 22719 SENAFEX KT
Board of Directors Vice Chairman: Fahad M Al Rajaan, Man. Dir. Kuwait Real Estate Investment Consortium KSC. Board Members: Farid Ahmad Kalander, Director of Economic Dept. Ministry of Planning. Basel Fahad Sultan (q.v.), Board Member Burgan Bank SAK. Jassim M Boodai, Board Member The Commercial Bank of Kuwait KSC. Mufarrej I Al Mufarrej, Chairman and Man.Dir. National Industries Co. KSC. Rabee I Al Noumas, Senior Chemist Kuwait National Petroleum Co. KSC. Saleh M Al Yousuf, Deputy Manager Central Bank of Kuwait (Banking Supervision Dept.). Ahmad Saud Al Zayed, Director Dept. of Industrial Supervision (Industrial affairs) Ministry of Commerce and Industry. Abdullah E Al Saleh, Vice Chairman and Man.Dir. Kuwait Metal Pipe Industries KSC.
Objectives of the Bank The Industrial Bank of Kuwait was established in late 1973, at the initiative of the Kuwait Government, as a joint undertaking between the Ministry of Finance, the Central Bank, the commercial banks, insurance companies and some large industrial establishments.The primary goal of IBK is to promote industrial development in Kuwait by pursuing the following objectives:
To participate in developing a long-term strategy for industrial growth in Kuwait, identifying those sectors and activities which would best fit local conditions and constraints.
To initiate industrial projects and investments in promising sectors.
To provide equity and medium and long-term credits for new projects as well as for the expansion of existing ones.
To finance projects outside Kuwait with emphasis on the Gulf region, especially where Kuwaiti participation is involved.
To bring needed technology to Kuwait and identify foreign partners with the necessary expertise.
To support the development of domestic money and capital markets in co-operation with other major financial institutions. The development of these markets will facilitate the channeling of private savings into industry.
Capitalization and Ownership Originally the Bank was capitalized at a paid-up capital of KD10 million which increased twice to reach KD20 million in June 1981. The following is a list of IBK's shareholders showing the percentages of their ownership:

The Government of Kuwait 31.39015 percent, The Central Bank of Kuwait 12.55605 percent, The Public Institution for Social Security 5.15695 percent, The National Bank of Kuwait KSC 8.96860 percent, Commercial Bank of Kuwait KSC 4.48430 percent, Gulf Bank KSC 4.48430 percent, Al-Ahli Bank of Kuwait KSC 4.48430 percent, Bank of Kuwait & the Middle East KSC 4.48430 percent, Kuwait Real Estate Bank KSC 2.69060 percent, Burgan Bank SAK 4.48430 percent, Kuwait Re-Insurance Co. KSC 0.67265 percent, Kuwait Insurance Co. KSC 0.67265 percent, Gulf Insurance Co. KSC 0.67265 percent, Al-Ahleia Insurance Co. KSC 0.67265 percent, Warba Insurance Co. KSC 0.67265 percent, Kuwait Flour Mills Co. KSC 4.48430 percent, Kuwait Metal Pipes Industries Co. KSC 4.48430 percent, National Industries Co. KSC 4.48430 percent. 100.000

To complement the Bank's resources with funds on terms compatible with its objectives, the Government of Kuwait has provided two long-term loans, the first of KD100 million at 2% p.a. and the second also of KD100 million at 3% p.a. Both loans were fully drawn and KD14 million of the first loan was repaid. The total commitments to industrial projects in Kuwait reached KD202.263 million by the end of 1982.

Organisation and Management IBK's Board of Directors is composed of ten members: four represent the Government of Kuwait, one represents the Central Bank of Kuwait and the remaining five members are elected by the other shareholders in the General Assembly. The Chairman of the Board is also the Managing Director.

At the operational level, IBK is composed of seven departments:

a. Projects - Responsible for evaluating the technical, economic and financial aspects of industrial projects, assessing their viability and structuring the terms of their financing in line with the Bank's established criteria. In addition, the department includes a promotion unit which identifies and develops new industrial investment opportunities, a market research unit which conducts market studies and surveys in Kuwait and the Gulf and a unit which carries out the appraisal of small projects.

b. Follow-Up - Responsible for monitoring projects financed by the Bank during their implementation and operation. The department reviews technical, financial and management performance and provides assistance in these areas.

c. Banking and Finance - Responsible for identifying those investment and lending opportunities in the domestic, regional or international money and capital markets that fit within IBK's scope of activities. Towards that end, the department is responsible for augmenting IBK's resources through tapping other sources of funds such as bonds, CDs etc. Furthermore, the accounting and disbursement functions are undertaken by this department.

d. Foreign Industrial Investment - Responsible for equity investment in industrial projects outside Kuwait on behalf of IBK and/or other public or private institutional investors.

e. Economics - Responsible for providing background information to IBK's operating departments, preparing studies relating to strategy and direction of industrial development in Kuwait, as well as monitoring economic developments in Kuwait and the Gulf region. The department is also responsible for IBK publications.

f. Legal - Responsible for providing legal advice to IBK's management and operating departments, participating in the negotiation and drawing up of agreements entered into by the Bank, as well as following up their implementation.

g. Administration - Responsible for administrative, public relations and support functions.

Review of Economic and Financial Developments Oil is the mainstay of the Kuwaiti economy. In 1981, the last full year for which figures are available, the oil sector accounted for 63.1 percent of GDP, 87 percent of export earnings and around 60 percent of public revenues.

The economy achieved high levels of investment and growth as a result of considerable oil receipts. Gross fixed capital formation represented on average 16 percent of GDP during 1977-1981 and real growth of non-oil GDP averaged 9.8 percent during 1973-1980.

Oil GDP however dropped in 1981 by 20.3 percent inspite of an average rise of 17.6 percent in Kuwaiti crude prices over the year. The decline is due to a 36.8 percent fall in oil production from an average of 1.78 million b/d in 1980 to 1.12 million b/d in 1981. This regression reflects the prevalent oil glut in the world market. It also reflects the government strategy of preserving oil wealth by its decision to cut down the oil production ceiling to 1.25 million b/d in 1981 with effect from 1st April, 1981.

In a bid to rationalise public spending, the government, prompted by falling oil revenues, adopted a belt-tightening budget for the 1982/83 fiscal year. This budget exhibits a sharp decline in revenues and a slight increase in expenditures as compared with the preceding fiscal year. Total revenues were estimated at KD3.2 billion or about 40 percent below last year's budget while total expenditures were estimated at KD3.51 billion or about 5 percent over the previous year's level. This percentage is but marginal when compared with the 26.4 percent average rise in public spending recorded between 1970/71 and 1980/81. Yet, the budget provides for KD313 million deficit to be covered from the General Reserve. This is the first such deficit since the oil price boom in 1973-74.

The expansionary trend which characterised monetary developments in the last three years lost momentum in 1982. Over the first eight months of 1982 domestic liquidity (money and quasi-money) grew at an annualised rate of 7.7 percent as against actual rates of 17.4 percent, 24.8 percent and 35.9 percent registered in 1979, 1980 and 1981 respectively. This development is mainly attributable to a significant slowing down in government expenditure which represents the major source of domestic liquidity. Expanding bank credit, however, has partly neutralised the contractionary impact of moderately growing public spending. By August 1982 bank credit was growing at an annualised rate of 37 percent compared with 26 percent in 1980 and 31 percent in 1981.

The abating world inflation exercised a stabilising effect on price movements in Kuwait. The annual rise in wholesale prices decelerated from 10.5 percent in 1980 to 6.7 percent in 1981 while the rise in the cost of living dropped from 7.7 percent to 6.1 percent during the same period.

In 1981 Kuwait's overall balance of payments surplus stood at KD2.71 billion (US$9.72 billion) as against KD3.38 billion (US$12.50 billion) recorded in 1980. The surplus on current account fell to KD3.8 billion (US$13.63 billion) from KD4.6 billion (US$17.02 billion) in 1980. This decline resulted from the combination of two main opposing factors: a 38 percent fall in the trade balance surplus due to a 28 percent drop in the value of oil exports and a 42 percent surge in net income from investments abroad reflecting both the larger volume of investments and high yields.

The impetuous and sustained rise in income from investments abroad has become a major feature of the balance of payments development in recent years. Between 1978 and 1981 this income more than trebled. In 1981 it accounted for almost 60 percent of both the value of oil exports and the current account surplus, for an estimated 35 percent of GDP and for approximately 56 percent of oil GDP. These percentages reflect the importance of this income in the balance of payments and the major role which it can play as a source of national income.

Kuwait is OPEC's second largest aid donor to the third world. In 1980 Kuwait's net disbursements of Official Development Assistance (ODA) reached US$1.2 billion. This figure represented 17 percent of total ODA extended by OPEC and is equivalent to 4.4 percent of total ODA provided by the Development Assistance Committee of OECD countries. Furthermore, Kuwait's ODA disbursements in 1980 were equivalent to 3.88 percent of its GNP while the corresponding percentages were for the United States 0.27, the United Kingdom 0.34, Japan 0.32, Germany 0.43, OECD countries 0.36 and OPEC countries 1.35. In this respect it is worthy of note that the bulk of Kuwait's GNP is from the sale of a depleting asset rather than from recurring income.

By the end of the third quarter of 1982, the Kuwaiti dinar, which is pegged to a basket of currencies of Kwait's main trading partners, appreciated substantially vis-à-vis the French franc, the Swiss franc and the Japanese yen and significantly vis-à-vis the pound sterling and the Deutschmark but depreciated slightly against the US dollar and the Saudi riyal.

Developments in the Financial Market In 1981 the Kuwaiti stock market enjoyed an unprecedented boom reflected in a record turnover and soaring prices. The ensuing atmosphere of euphoria provoked a feverish stampede for stock. A rush to establish Gulf and Kuwaiti closed shareholding companies whose share price increased many-fold over a short period, contributed in turn to overheating the market. Attracted by the exceptional prospects for substantial capital gains prevailing in the unofficial market (Al-Manakh), waves of speculative-type investors invaded this market to make an easy fortune.

Concerned about the high risks inherent in lending to such investors and heeding the Central Bank's warning, the banks tended to restrict their exposure to the market. To overcome the financing difficulties, traders resorted almost exclusively to futures dealing struck at unrealistic premiums over spot prices and against post-dated cheques. A huge unregulated 'personal credit' system was thus created, resulting in skyrocketing premiums and an ever inflating overhang of inter-related post-dated cheques. Henceforth, the market was poised for a crisis which was eventually triggered by the default in August 1982 of some major over-geared traders.

To contain the impact of the crisis, avert further adverse repercussions and breathe new life into the market, the following measures have been taken:

- Banning temporarily all forward deals in both Kuwaiti and Gulf shares as well as the setting up of new Kuwaiti closed share-holding companies.
- Establishing a KD6.5 million new stock-trading company, Kuwait Clearing Company (KCC), the primary goal of which is to manage a central clearing of debts and claims arising from trading in securities and to extend financial and technical services relatng thereto.
- Requiring compulsory registration with the KCC of all forward deals in shares for which post-dated cheques were issued and are outstanding.

Establishing an arbitration committee empowered with wide authority and jurisdiction and legally binding decisions to settle all disputes and issues resulting from share transactions.

- Suspending of all petitions pending with any court of law relating to post-dated cheques generated by forward share trading.
- Supporting share prices through governmental selective buying of Kuwaiti shares.
- Protecting bona fide investors, particularly small investors, by honouring fully or partially their holdings of cheques drawn by bankrupt stock-traders through a governmental fund established for this purpose.

However, the position of Menakh investors had not been resolved by the end of 1983 and several bankruptcies are expected. The main consequence of these events has been a severe breakdown of mutual confidence in a society where trust has been the main pillar of business dealing.

The Family of Al Omar

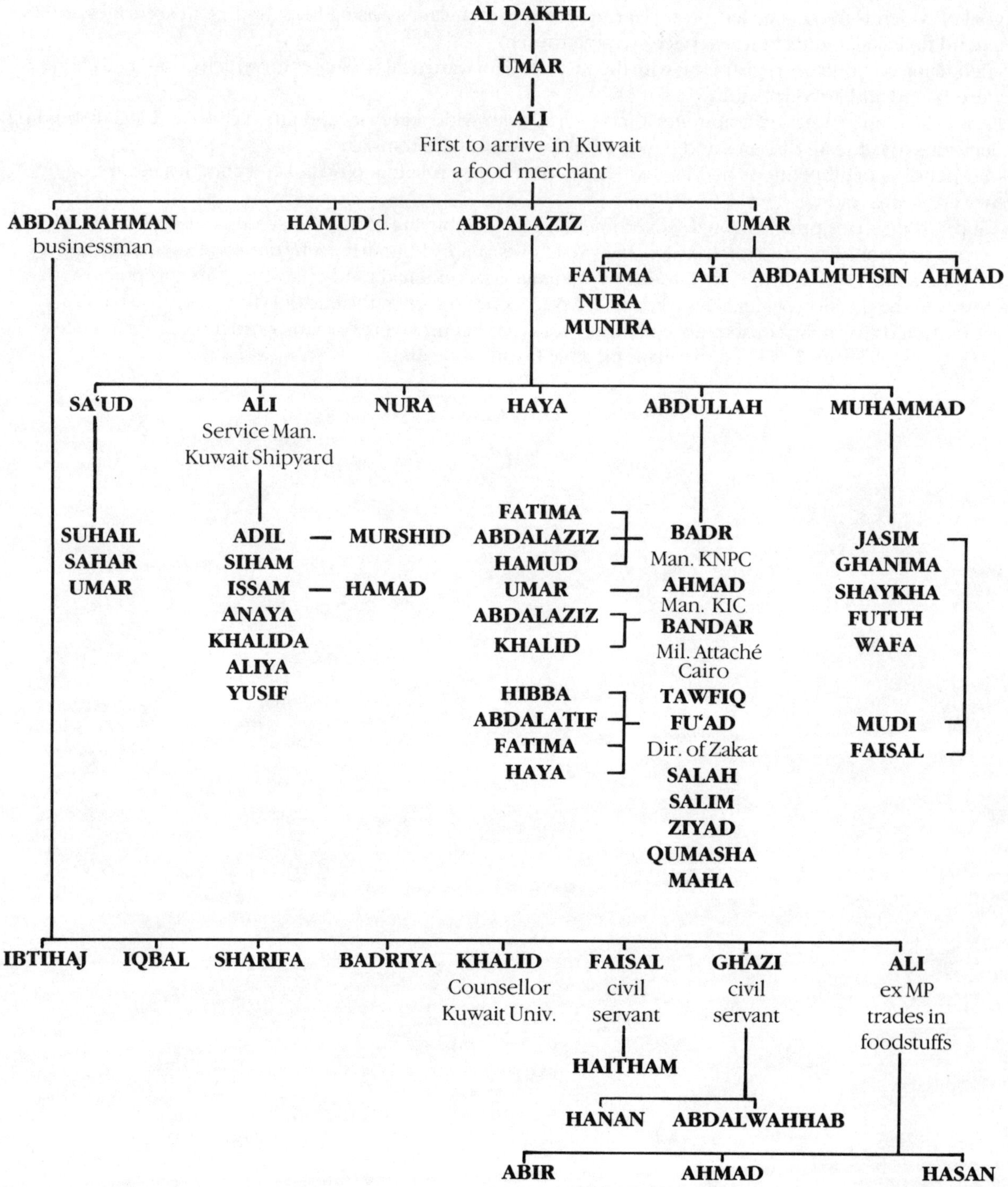

ABDALRAHMAN ALI AL OMAR

Address head office P.O.Box 4062 Safat and P.O.Box 132 Safat
Telephone 810485, 814986
Cable SALSABEEL
Activities The business deals in foodstuffs and building materials.

ABDULLAH AL OMAR GENERAL TRADING AND CONTRACTING ESTABLISHMENT

Address head office P.O.Box 1630 Safat
Telephone 434871
Cable AL OMAR
Activities The General Manager is Tawfiq Abdullah Al Omar and the company trades in bed linens and is involved with government tenders and agency representation and contracting. They have considerable real estate business and their foreign investment portfolio of bonds and securities is mainly concerned with the US and Japanese markets.

AL OMAR MECHANICAL ENGINEERING CO.

Address head office P.O.Box 293
Telephone 848842, 871811
Activities The company is owned by Muhammad Al Omar and is a firm of general, mechanical and civil contractors.

FARAH ELECTRICAL AND MECHANICAL CONTRACTING CO.

Address head office P.O.Box 23020 Safat
Telephone 425519, 443265
Activities A company owned by Abdalaziz Al Omar which supplies electrical materials and operates as an electrical installation contractor.

The Family of Al Qatami

One of the most important Kuwait families with a strong seafaring tradition. They are closely connected in descent with the Al Ghanim, being also Al Zayd in origin. A nakhuda is a ship's captain.

NASIR

ABDALWAHHAB

ABDALAZIZ

ABDALWAHHAB
nakhuda, shipowner and trader

- **ISA**
  m. Muza Shahin Al Ghanim (q.v.)
  author of books on navigation
  used today. Poet. Nakhuda.
  - **ABDALWAHHAB** d.
    a. m. da. of Abdalaziz
    Abdalwahhab
    b. a da. m. Yusif Al Ghunaim
    whose da. m. Muhammad
    Yusif Al Qatami
    c. nakhuda
    d. a da. m. Abdullah
    Thunayan Al Ghanim
    - **ABDALATIF** d.
  - **YUSIF**
    d. 1981
    m. da. of Abdalaziz
    nakhuda
    - **YAQUB**
      B. Degree
      from Cairo in
      Political Science
      - **WA'IL**
        B. in
        Business
        Tampa,
        Florida
        - **YUSIF**
      - **ADIL**
    - **FAISAL**
      B.S. Eng.
      Oklahoma
      USA
      - **KHALID**
      - **AHMAD**
      - **YUSIF**
    - **MUHAMMAD**
      - **LU'AY**
      - **YUSIF**
    - **ANWAR**
      UK accountancy
      Anwar Al
      Qatami and Co.
    - **WALID**
    - **QATAMI**
      Eng. Degree
      from Miami
      USA

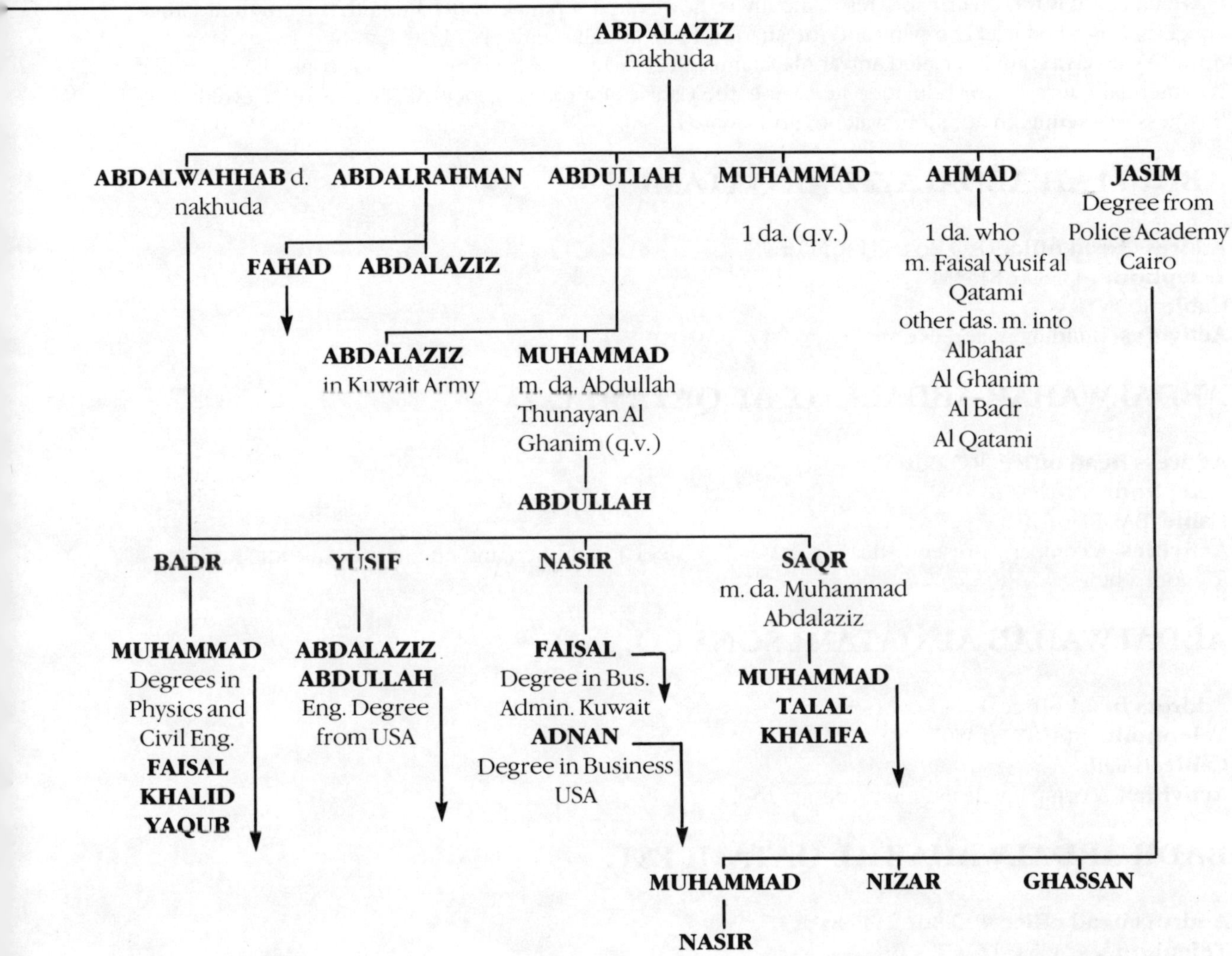
ABDALAZIZ
nakhuda
ABDALWAHHAB d.
nakhuda
ABDALRAHMAN
ABDULLAH
MUHAMMAD
AHMAD
JASIM
Degree from
Police Academy
Cairo
1 da. (q.v.)
1 da. who
m. Faisal Yusif al
Qatami
other das. m. into
Albahar
Al Ghanim
Al Badr
Al Qatami
FAHAD
ABDALAZIZ
ABDALAZIZ
in Kuwait Army
MUHAMMAD
m. da. Abdullah
Thunayan Al
Ghanim (q.v.)
ABDULLAH
BADR
YUSIF
NASIR
SAQR
m. da. Muhammad
Abdalaziz
MUHAMMAD
Degrees in
Physics and
Civil Eng.
FAISAL
KHALID
YAQUB
ABDALAZIZ
ABDULLAH
Eng. Degree
from USA
FAISAL
Degree in Bus.
Admin. Kuwait
ADNAN
Degree in Business
USA
MUHAMMAD
TALAL
KHALIFA
MUHAMMAD
NIZAR
GHASSAN
NASIR

The formal commercial history of the family began when a partnership was formed between Yusif Issa and his brother, Abdalwahab, after their cousin, Abdalwahab, left for Basra. This trading concern was itself split up when Yusif's brother retired. Yusif had a company called Al Maghanim (see below).

WORKS AND BUILDING CO. LTD.

Address head office P.O.Box 415 Safat
Telephone 814813, 813368, 816915
Telex 2316 KT
Activities The company is managed by Faisal Yusif Al Qatami and covers a diverse field of commercial interest. They manufacture prefabricated housing and run a furniture factory. They build cold stores and produce polystyrene thermal insulation material and are partners with Samir Barakat in a steel fabrication works. The Commercial Section of the company represents Hilti Tools, Festo pneumatic machinery and Watso admixtures, Febreton paints and Buildex woodwork fixtures. The partners in the company are the four brothers, Yaqub, Faisal, Wazid and Qatami. Muhammad manages another company called Al Maghanim, of which Faisal is the Chairman. This company is, however, a separate entity altogether from their father's concern. It is a financial company and the shareholders are all members of the family.
Anwar Yusif has a company called Anwar Al Qatami and Co. which is a holding company controlling various commercial interests which include Red Shoe, the Charles Jourdain agency, Al Nabras and a jewellery business marketing, in addition, watches and swords.

ABDULLAH ABDALAZIZ AL QATAMI

Address head office P.O.Box 593 Kuwait
Telephone 433806, 815351
Cable CONTRA
Activities Building materials supplier.

ABDALWAHAB ABDALAZIZ AL QATAMI CO.

Address head office P.O.Box 619 Safat
Telephone 810248, 814387
Cable BADRI
Activities A company presently dealing in cement, steel and timber, and an entity bequeathed to the founder's heirs.

ABDALWAHAB AL QATAMI SONS CO.

Address head office P.O.Box 619 Safat
Telephone 814387, 813867
Cable BADRI
Activities A company dealing in carpentry tools.

BADR ABDALWAHAB AL QATAMI EST.

Address head office P.O.Box 2145 Safat
Telephone 424654, 429352
Telex 23361 HUSSINY KT
Activities The company is owned as its name implies and is the agent for Yanmar Marine Engines and Equipment.

DECORATION CENTRE TRADING AND CONTRACTING CO.

Address head office P.O.Box 22673 Safat
Telephone 818193, 814690, 811378
Telex 22625 DECOR KT
Activities The company is managed by Adnan Nasir Al Qatami and acts as an export business dealing in building materials.

HYGIENE PRODUCTS INDUSTRIES CO.

Address head office P.O.Box 21388 Safat
Telephone 715961
Telex 22168 CLYDE KT
Activities The company is a partnership between Jasim Abdalaziz Al Qatami, Yusif Ibrahim Al Ghanim and Abdullah Yusif Al Ghanim. This business is concerned with the manufacture of sanitary towels and nappies.

THE INDUSTRIAL AND REAL ESTATE CO.

Address head office P.O.Box 23891 Safat
Telephone 874500, 874602, 874949
Telex 22145 IREC KT
Activities Abdalaziz Yusif Al Qatami is Managing Director of this company, where the Chairman is Khalid Al Issa and the Vice Chairman is Abdullah Ahmad Al Sumait. They deal with prefabricated housing, concrete, wire mesh and other building materials.

KUWAIT DAIRY COMPANY

Address head office P.O.Box 3240 Safat
Telephone 870088
Telex 23041 KUDAIRY KT
Activities A factory under the Chairmanship of Jasim Abdalaziz Al Qatami which produces fresh pasteurised milk, cheese, yoghurt and labaneh.

KUWAIT AND GULF CARS CO.

Address head office P.O.Box 23969 Safat
Telephone 429623, 812044
Telex 44097 CONFOOD KT
Activities The General Manager of this company is Nizar Jasim Al Qatami. It is concerned with the import and marketing of cars, boats and marine equipment.

KUWAIT PORTLAND CEMENT CO.

Address head office P.O.Box 42191 Shuwaikh
Telephone 835615, 835917
Telex 23487 PORCEM KT
Activities Nasir Abdalwahab Al Qatami is the Chairman of the company which imports cement in bulk and supplies the product also in bulk or bagged.

NASIR ABDALWAHAB AL QATAMI AND CO.

Address head office P.O.Box 42252 Shuwaikh
Telephone 831484, 832737, 816094
Telex 23321 NASER KT
Activities The company is engaged in export and import and deals in cement, steel, timber, construction materials, hardware and tools. It also represents manufacturers.

The Family of Al Quraishi

The family has its origins in Bani Khalid of Ha'il.

ALI
|
ZAID

ALI	**ABDALAZIZ**	**KHALID**	**SALIH**	**ABDALKARIM**	**ABDALRAZZAQ**	
Ptnr.	Governor of SAMA	Ptnr. in Jiddah	Ptnr.	Ptnr. in Dammam	Ptnr.	2 daughters 1 m. Saudi ambassador to Dubai 2 m. in Kuwait

ALI AL QURAISHI TRADING CO.

Address head office P.O.Box 2505 Safat
Telephone 434076, 454232
Activities A company owned by Ali Zaid Al Quraishi of Saudi Arabia (q.v.). This represents a branch office of his enterprise in Dammam (P.O.Box 339, telex 601058 AZAQ SJ) and likewise deals in foodstuffs, cigarettes and cigars.

The Family of Al Rajhi

The family is entirely Saudi, genealogically being Bani Zayd of Qahtan and emanating from Qasim. For a full family tree, see the Saudi volume. The extract here is only to describe the immediate relationships of Abdullah Salih Al Rajhi.

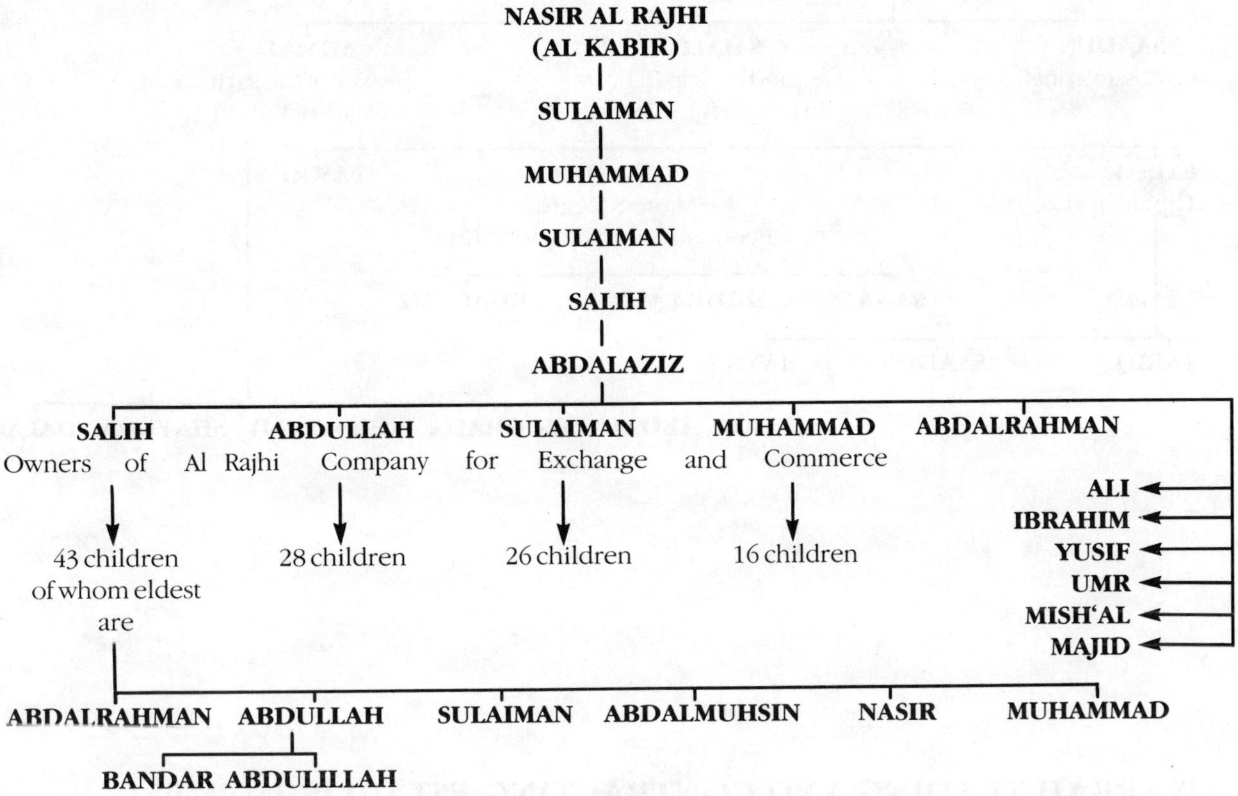

AL JASSAR AND AL RAJHI FOR MONEY EXCHANGE CO.

Address head office P.O.Box 24461 Safat
Telephone 427270, 419108
Telex 23342 JASSARCO KT
Activities This company is a joint venture between Al Jassar and a member of the famous Saudi family of Al Rajhi which is described in Merchant Families of Saudi Arabia (q.v.). The Abdullah Salih Al Rajhi Est. has its head office in Jizan but the General Administration Office is in Dammam. The Kuwaiti company deals in foreign exchange, commission and representation. The Saudi partner was involved in a scandal during 1982 which culminated in a three hundred million dollar bankruptcy.

The Family of Al Saadun

Originating from Dawasir in Saudi Arabia, there is a tradition that they came to Kuwait via the Al Ali of Qatar.

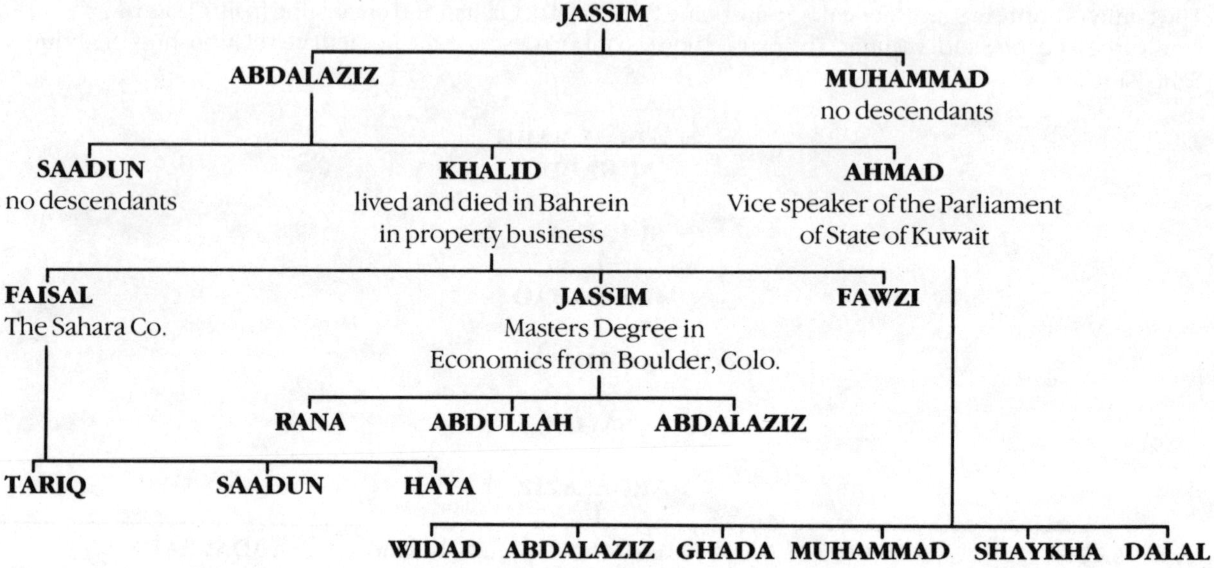

WARRAH TRADING AND CONTRACTING ESTABLISHMENT

Address head office P.O.Box 1028 Safat
Telephone 422444
Telex 22757 KT
Activities This company is a partnership between Ahmad Al Saadun and Yusuf Al Shallal. It is a general trading and contracting business.

ALSHALL ECONOMIC CONSULTANTS

Address head office P.O.Box 5935 Safat
Telephone 2451535, 2451525
Telex 46098 LASHALL KT
Activities This dynamic consultancy offers its clients services which include project feasability studies, real estate appraisal, local stock and share evaluation, analysis and evaluation of the Kuwaiti economy and recruitment services specialising in economic, financial and accountancy management.
The consultancy is owned by Jassim Khalid Al Saadun. His brother, Faisal, runs a successful business called Sahara which specialises in road drainage and civil building construction on the one hand and, on the other, deals with building materials, in particular scaffolding and shuttering on a commercial basis.

The Family of Al Sabih

Originating from Al Bir, some 40 kms from Riyadh in Saudi Arabia, where the family traded in horses. The Al Sabih are a widely respected and integral part of the community.

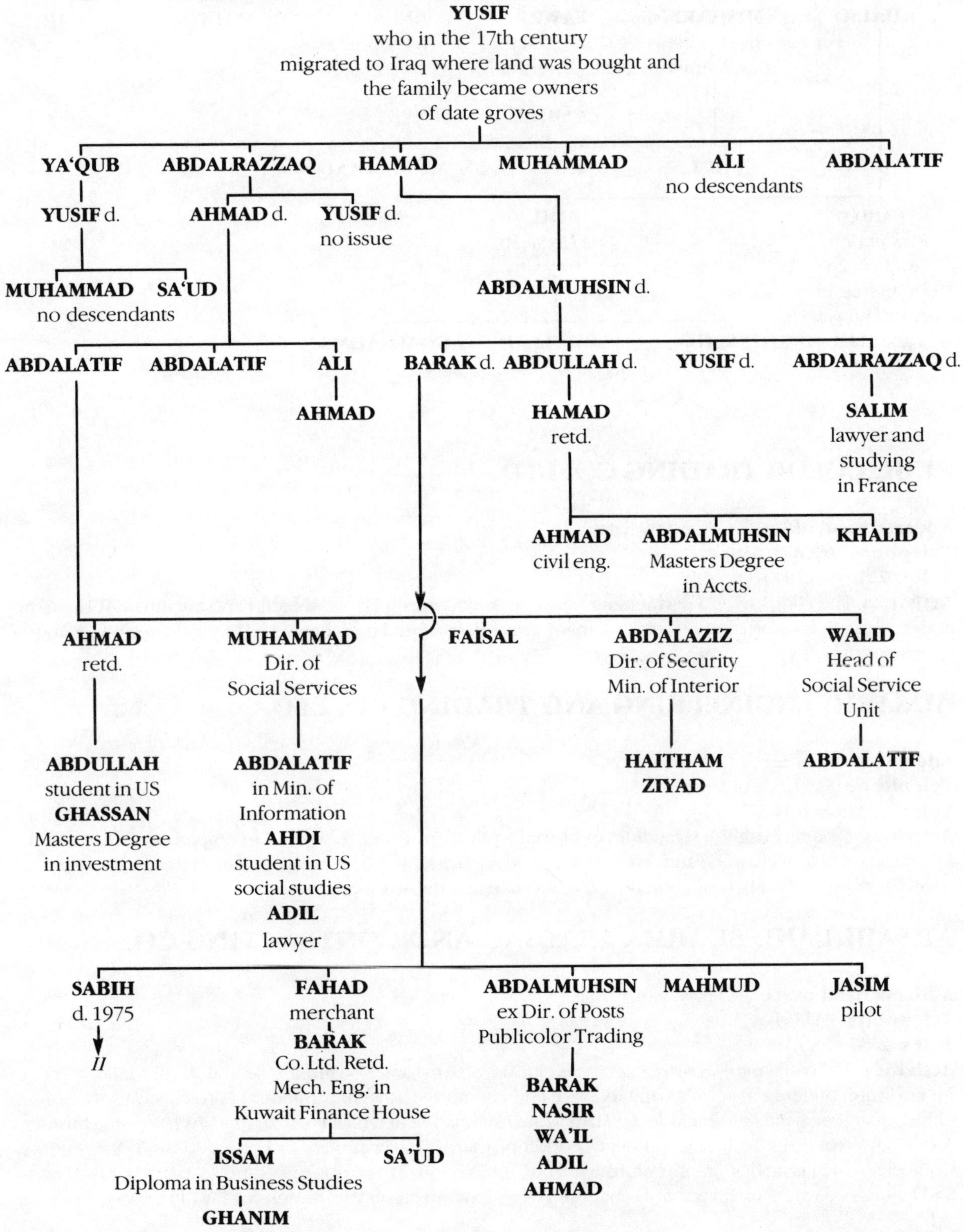

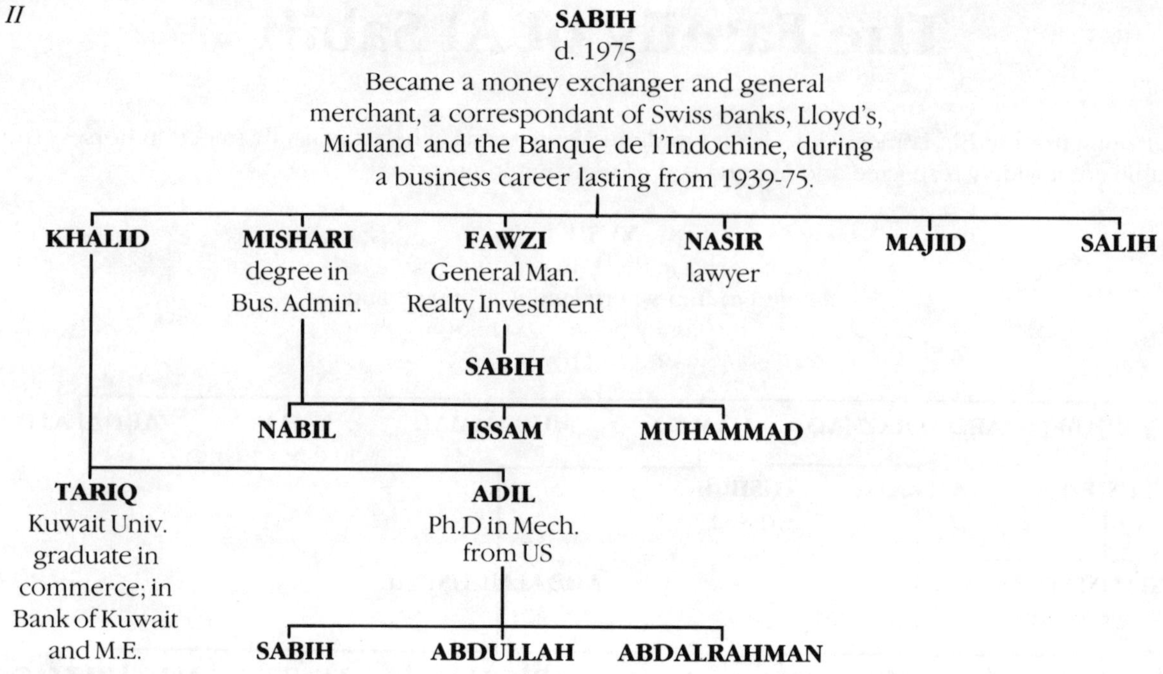

PUBLICOLOR TRADING CO. LTD.

Address head office P.O.Box 999 Safat
Telephone 636855, 638878
Telex 22184 SABIH KT
Activities The company is a partnership between Abdalmuhsin Barak Al Sabih and Sulaiman Al Haqqan, and is engaged in advertising and as a commission agent in general merchandise. They also supply toys and sports goods.

AL SABIH ENGINEERING AND TRADING CO. LTD.

Address head office P.O.Box 1366 Safat
Telephone 813915, 813916
Telex 22184 SABIH KT
Activities Dealing in light and medium industrial equipment as well as steel, this company is also a stockist for ferrous metals. It is owned and directed by Fahad Barak Al Sabih. The company represents Sulzer Bros. of Switzerland and is also concerned with real estate and the stock market.

AL SABIH AND SHARMA TRADING AND CONTRACTING CO.

Address head office P.O.Box 24004 Safat
Telephone 833814, 833815
Telex 23425 SS KT
Activities The company is a partnership between M C Sharma and Abdalmuhsin Barak Al Sabih. They deal in hardware, building materials, sanitary ware and chemicals, as well as building construction.
Other commercial interests include the Ali Al Sabih Establishment which is a general merchandising business. Ali was Director of the Traffic Department. In addition there is the important TV Production and Distribution Company which is a 50/50 joint venture with TWT of London. This company is run by Jasim Barak Al Sabih and Issam Hamawi, an ex-director of Lebanese Television represents the interests of TWT in the organisation.

The Family of Al Salim

Settled in Kuwait, originally from Iraq.

ISA
owned date gardens
in Basra

ABDALMUNIM
m. into Asfur (q.v.),
migrated to Kuwait

ISA
b. 1917, worked with first British Political Agent In Kuwait, H R P Dickson; retd. as longest serving employee of KOC where he worked for 40 years

NAJIB
Ph. D. Chemistry, lecturer in Faculty of Science, University of Kuwait

- **HANAN**
- **FAISAL**

ADIB
B.Sc. Mech. Eng., Cairo Univ. Ptner Gulf Ring for Trading and Contracting Co. Ltd.

GULF RING FOR TRADING AND CONTRACTING CO. LTD.

Address head office P.O.Box 22686 Safat
Telephone 2464091, 2464090
Telex 46972 RASSBAR KT
Activities This go-ahead young company is a partnership between Adeeb Abdalmun'im Al Salim and Adil Yusif Bourisli. The contracting part of the business has an aluminium fabrication workshop and is the agent for Dow Chemical Thermal Insulation 'Roofmate'. The other, and trading activity, specialises in medical supplies.
Gulf Ring represents the following companies:- Mennen Medical of the USA; Sakai and Sons, Japan; Nouvag, Switzerland; MLW Intermed, Mexxem, LRE, Herka, GFL, and Bernd Kraft, all of Germany; Technident, New Zealand; Megamed, Switzerland; MD Marketing AB, Sweden; Schippers Medizinteknik, Germany; AB Medett Produkter, Sweden; Rolchemie AG, Switzerland; Ultrasonics Ltd, UK; Surge, Taiwan; Kartel, Italy; G.A.S.T., Germany; P.B.I., Italy.

The Family of Al Sani'a

Originating in Majma'a of Najd, Saudi Arabia. A major family of Kuwait. Another branch is still in Saudi Arabia (q.v.)

- **NASIR**
  - **ABDALAZIZ**
    - **ABDALHAMID**
      - **ABDALAZIZ**
        - **SA'UD** d.
          - **ABDALAZIZ** no descendants
        - **HAMAD**
          - **ABDALRAHMAN**
            - **GHAZI**
            - **NAUF**
            - **AYSHA**
          - **YUSIF** exec. man. Industrial Bank of Kuwait
          - **HAMID**
          - **ADIL**
          - **WALID** student in US
        - **ALI**
          - **MAHMUD** Dir. of Planning and Control, Min. of Communs.
          - 6 das.
        - **AHMAD**
          - **SULAYMAN**
            - **MUHAMMAD**
            - 4 das.
          - **MUS'AD** d.
            - **ABDALAZIZ**
            - **KHALIFA**
          - **ABDALMUHSIN**
            - **MUS'AD**
            - 1 da.
        - **NASIR** d.
          - **KHALID**
            - **NASIR**
            - **ABDULLAH**
            - 2 das.
        - **ABDALHAMID** d. 1976. Dir. Gen. Municipality. Chairman Educ. Board. Member of Board writing history of Kuwait.
          - **ADNAN** Dir. Commercial Bank. Ptner with Al Babtain and Al Sultan in Great Western Bank and Trust of Phoenix, Arizona
          - **MUSTAFA**
            - **ABDALHAMID**
            - 2 das.
          - **FAISAL**
            - **ZIYAD**
            - 2 das.
          - **MUHAMMAD**
          - **ABDALRAZZAQ** M.P. Owner Hyatt Regency Hotel
            - **JAMIL**
            - 5 das.
          - **ABDALATIF** d. 1979
            - **KHALID**
            - **KHALDUN**
            - 2 das.
      - **MUHAMMAD**
        - 2 daughters
          - 1 m.
          - 2 m. **KHALID**

ABDALHAMID ABDALAZIZ AL SANI'A

Address head office P.O.Box 23953 Kuwait
Telephone 421024, 710765
Activities A cattle importer and supplier. The company continues in the name of its founder, now deceased, and is run by his sons.

ABDALRAZZAQ ABDALHAMID AL SANI'A

Address head office P.O.Box 700 Safat
Telephone 432363
Cable SANIE
Activities A company dealing in agricultural machinery and general trading; also a holding company.

ALI ABDALAZIZ AL ABDALHAMID AL SANI'A

Address head office P.O.Box 589 Kuwait, P.O.Box 22744 Kuwait
Telephone 817389, 817379
Activities This company is engaged as a general merchant house with an emphasis on foodstuffs and building materials.

THE ARAB CONTRACTOR

Address head office P.O.Box 26664 Safat
Telephone 730818, 730088, 730702
Telex 23058 BUILDUP KT
Activities Mustafa Al Sani'a is the Chairman of this concern which is a major contractor dealing in construction, building materials, machinery and equipment.

CASA ITALIANA

Address head office P.O.Box 4726 Safat
Telephone 412779, 412666
Telex 22671 ASHRAN KT
Activities Owned by Adnan Abdalhamid Al Sani'a and partners, this firm deals in carpets, furniture and interior decoration.

KUWAIT DEVELOPMENT COMPANY

Address head office P.O.Box 2350 Safat
Telephone 444780, 444790, 437729
Telex 22683 DEVELOP KT
Activities Adnan Abdalhamid Al Sani'a is Managing Director of this company which is concerned with investment, trading in steel and cement and acting as contractors agents.

AL SANI'A CHEMICAL PRODUCTS

Address head office P.O.Box 5629 Safat
Telephone 736740, 075509
Telex 23228 DALIL KT
Activities The Managing Director of this company is Khalid Nasir Al Sani'a and it manufactures swimming pool chemicals, detergents, disinfectants, white spirit and fire extinguisher powders. They also make chemicals for hospital laundries, hotels, cleaning companies, heavy industry, ships and the shipbuilding industry, oil field applications, domestic use and cars. The company is also a stockist for various industrial raw materials.

AL SANI'A CONSTRUCTION

Address head office P.O.Box 25901 Safat
Telephone 444721, 444731
Telex 44080 KT
Activities The company is owned by Mustafa Abdalhamid Al Sani'a and is a general trader as well as a building contractor. It is the agent for Volvo Penta marine industrial engines and Storebro leisure boats.

SANI'A TRAVEL AGENCY

Address head office P.O.Box 745 Safat
Telephone 432362
Cable SANIE Kuwait
Activities A travel agency specialising in air travel and owned by Abdalrazaq Al Sani'a, whose commercial interests include a holding company in his own name based at this address. This company handles real estate and investments such as an interest in the Hyat Regency Hotel.

The Family of Al Sanoussi

Originating from the Shammar, one of the great tribes of northern Arabia and Iraq, this family used to live in Ha'il in what is now Saudi Arabia. Muhammad b. Nasir moved to the village of Athaythi about the turn of the century and died during an epidemic, possibly the wave of Asian 'flu which swept the Peninsula after the First World War. Either Yahya or Sulaiman b. Nasir brought the young Nasir Muhammad to Kuwait.

- **MUHAMMAD**
  - **NASIR**
    - **MUHAMMAD**
      - **NASIR** came to own considerable property and real estate
        - **NURIYA** m. Sulaiman Abdaljalil
        - **MUHAMMAD** Under Sec. Min. of Information Kuwait TV
          - **TARIQ**
          - **ZIYAD**
          - **LULUA**
        - **LULUA** m. Badr al Ajil
        - **ABDULLAH** diplomat
          - **QUSAY**
          - **SULAFA**
          - **SARA**
          - **NASIR**
        - **SARA** m. Abdalatif Al Sa'iyd and **TA'IBA** m. Ali al Fahad — twins
        - **MISHARI**
          - **KHALID**
          - **NASIR**
          - **BADR**
          - **NASIR**
        - **AHMAD** businessman also runs family property holdings
        - **FAWZIA** m. Abdalaziz al Rumi
        - **BADRIYA** m. Yusif al Du'aij
        - **SU'AD** m. Khalid al Humaidi
        - **MUNTAHA** m. Salim al Rumi
        - **SALWA** m. Abdal-wahhab al Harun
      - **AFRAH** d.
      - **NURA** d.
      - **HUSSA** d.
    - **YAHYA** no issue
    - **SULAIMAN** d. in Saudi Arabia

INTERNATIONAL TRADING EXCHANGE CENTRE

Address head office P.O.Box 3226 Safat
Telephone 410888, 410999
Telex 22686 KT
Activities Active as import export agents, the representation of companies and as commission agents. Owned by Ahmad Nasir Al Sanoussi.

INTREX INSPECTION CENTRE

Address head office P.O.Box 3226 Safat
Telephone 410888, 410999
Telex 22686 INTREX KT
Activities Intrex is owned by Ahmad Nasir Al Sanoussi and is a high technology company serving the engineering inspection needs of the Middle East, and the Gulf region in particular. Whilst the company specialises in destructive and non-destructive testing it has strong capabilities in general services involving the mechanical, electrical and civil engineering requirements of their clients.
Intrex has subsidiary offices in Bahrain (P.0.Box 80 Manama, tel: 252227, 252600; telex 8553 SAKCO BN) and the United Kingdom(119 Station Road, Ellesmere Port, South Wirrall, Cheshire, tel: 051-355 6805; telex 628761 BULTEL G) and in India (REWA Chambers, 31 New Marine Lines, Bombay 400020, tel: 291228, 253498; telex 11-5214 VJAY IN). Consultancy support is provided to the company by G.R. Enck of Chase Marketing Group Ltd. (P.O.Box 12266 Lexington, Kentucky 40582, USA, tel: 502-863-3684; telex 790150 LIASON).
The services offered by this company comprise the following: welding inspection, ultrasonic inspection, magnetic particle inspection, and dye penetrant inspection; radiography, thermography and spectography, as well as coat and wrap inspection, quality control and assurance. They also provide offshore N.D.T. inspection, a variety of supervisory services, pressure and vacuum testing and cathodic protection.
Intrex has completed work for a diverse list of clients including: Aramco Jaket Construction, Kirby Building Systems, Kuwait Airways, Mitsubishi Heavy Industries, Hyundai Construction, Deutsche Babcock, McDermott International, the Ministry of Electricity and Water, Al Hani Contracting, Pan Arab Consult, Mariot Hotel, Kuwait National Petroleum Company, Sumitomo Heavy Industries and CONCO.
Bankers National Bank of Kuwait, Al Ahli Bank of Kuwait.

The Family of Sharekh

Coming originally from al Rawdah in Sudair of Najd in Saudi Arabia, this family has had trading connections with both India and Iraq.

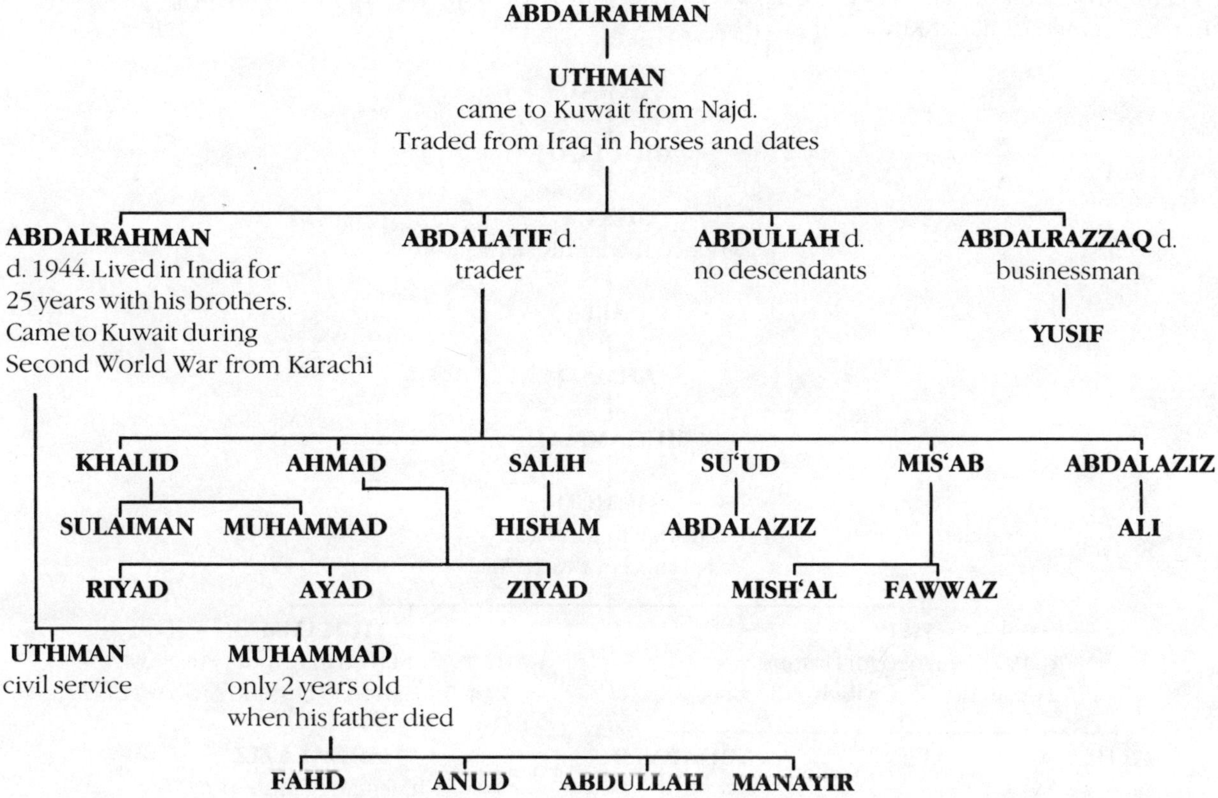

AL ALAMIAH ELECTRONICS

Address head office P.O.Box 23781 Safat
Telephone 414140, 414141, 414142
Telex 22694 EIL KT
Activities A trading, import and distribution business and one of the most go-ahead of its kind. Muhammad Sharekh deals through this company in electronic appliances representing Ricoh, JVC, Siemens, Binatone and Texas Instruments. The company also handles real estate development nationally and internationally.

AL ALAMIAH FOODSTUFF LTD.

Address head office P.O.Box 23781 Safat
Telephone 414140, 414141, 414142
Telex 22964 EIL KT
Activities A company dealing in a broad spectrum of household goods and foodstuffs. Owned by Muhammad Sharekh who also operates the Al Sharekh Trading Co. which has a car dealership and an insurance bureau (telephone 419105).

The Family of Al Shaya

A family from Zilfi of Najd, Saudi Arabia, a very distinguished group who are one of the major components of the commercial life of Kuwait.

- **AHMAD**
  - **ABDULLAH**
    - **SHAYA** whence the family name
      - **ALI**
        - **AHMAD**
          - **MUHAMMAD**
            - **HUMUD** a trader in foodstuffs who died in the 1870s
              - **ALI** d. 1966. Formed Ali Humud Shaya Co. in Bombay which still exists
                - **SALIH** Chairman retd.
                  - **AHMAD*** Board mem. Kuwait Chamber of Commerce
                    - **MUNDHIR**
                  - **SULAIMAN**
                    - **SALIH**
                  - **ABDALWAHHAB***
                    - **UMR**
                    - **SUFIAN**
                    - **ALI**
                    - **NASIR**
                  - **ABDALRAHMAN*** businessman
                    - **YUSIF**
                    - **KHALID**
                    - **NASIM**
                  - **FAHAD**
                  - **SUHAIL**
                - **ABDALATIF**
                  - **KHALID*** board member of Commercial Bank of Kuwait
                    - **WALID**
                  - **ABDULLAH***
                  - **SHAYA***
                  - **MUHAMMAD*** m. da. of Ahmad Salih
                    - **ALI**
                    - **ABDALATIF**
                  - **AYMAN**
                  - **YUSIF**
              - **MUHAMMAD** d. 1956. Stayed in Kuwait. Ptner with Ali in Muhammad Humud Al Shaya Co.
                - **ABDALAZIZ*** Chairman of Muhammad Humud Al Shaya Co.
                  - **HAMAD***
                    - **HAITHAM**
                  - **SA'UD**
                  - **KHALID**
                  - **MUHAMMAD***

* Board members of the family company, Muhammad Humud Al Shaya Co.

ABDALRAHMAN AL SALIH AL SHAYA ESTABLISHMENT

Address head office P.O.Box 4912 Safat
Telephone 431464, 416590
Telex 23480 RAIHAN KT
Activities A company trading as commission agents and dealing in bathroom wares and fittings, hardware and electrical goods.

KUWAIT PREFABRICATED BUILDING CO.

Address head office P.O.Box 5132 Safat
Telephone 438075
Telex 22201 PREFAB KT
Activities Abdullah Abdalatif Al Shaya is the Chairman of this company which is concerned with the design, manufacture and construction of buildings for pre-cast and pre-stressed concrete projects.

MUHAMMAD HUMUD AL SHAYA COMPANY

Address head office P.O.Box 181 Safat
Telephone 442080, 440947
Telex 22322 AL SHAYA KT
Activities This is the original family company founded by Ali and Muhammad Humud Al Shaya. Today it is owned by Salih Ali, Abdalatif Ali and Abdalaziz Muhammad Al Shaya. The Managing Director is Abdalwahab Salih Al Shaya and the executive directors Khalid Abdalatif and Hamad Abdalaziz Al Shaya.
The company represents Komatsu, Lothar Pracht, Asada, Warwick Pumps, Wibau Pumps, Electrolux, Delorme, Frette, Buchtal, Clairot, Gorenje, Sottini and Usha.
They are thus engaged in sanitary ware, electrical appliances, earthmoving equipment, catering equipment, building materials, contractor's plant, industrial tools and supplies, leather goods, footwear, bedroom, bathroom and table linens.

RED SEA IMPORT AND EXPORT CO.

Address head office P.O.Box 2227 Safat
Telephone 441387, 441395
Telex 22322 ALSHAYA ATTN REDSEACO KT
Activities This company is owned by Muhammad Hamud Al Shaya Co and operates as indentors and commission agents.

PAN ARAB COMPUTER CENTRE PACC

Activities A company run by Abdalrahman Salih Al Shaya with associates throughout the Middle East. They provide informative solutions for both business and government, as well as marketing Honeywell, Apple and Philips.

The Family of Al Sidairawi

Originating from Majma'a in Sudair of Saudi Arabian Najd, as their name implies.

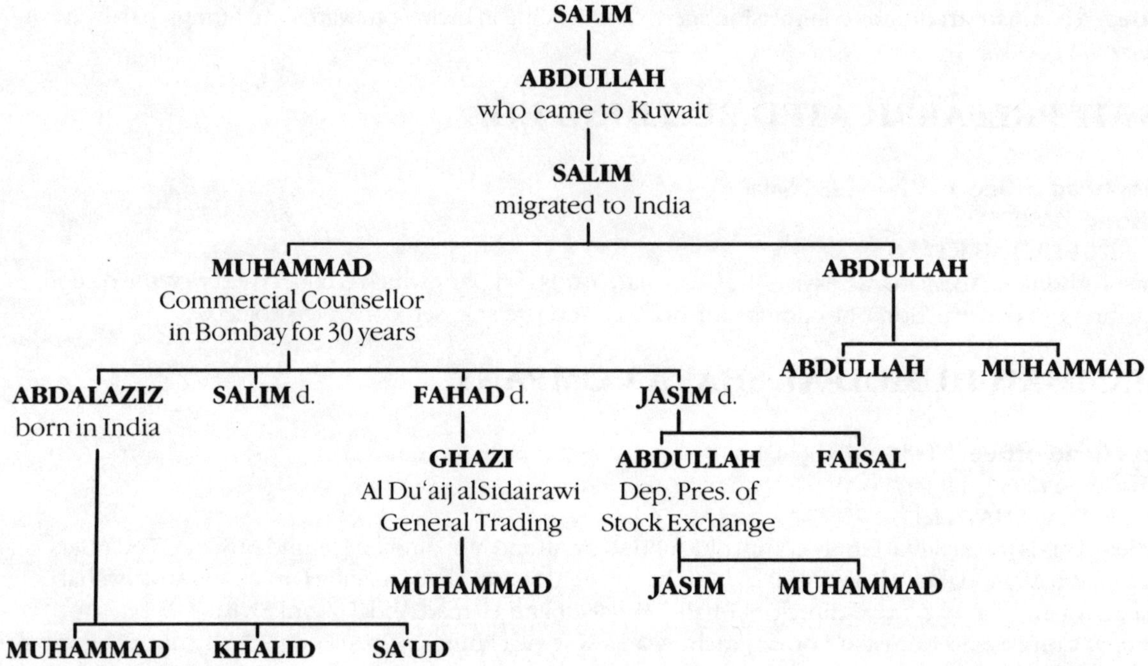

The family began trading horses and dates from Basra, bringing back textiles, foodstuffs and other trade goods from India. Muhammad Salim is, historically, the most famous member of the family, due to his long sojourn in India and his position as Commercial Councillor in Bombay. The family company, the Muhammad Salim Al Sidairawi Establishment, was situated there, and though his sons remained in India until the end of the Second World War it no longer exists as a commercial entity. Abdalaziz Muhammad had an establishment dealing in building materials until his recent retirement, but this too has ceased to exist; though he occupies himself with investment. Salim and Fahad Muhammad did not have actual companies, rather they traded privately in real estate and investment.
Abdullah Salim Al Sidairawi deals in spare parts for vehicles and real estate.
Fahad Muhammad had a partnership in a construction company called Fahad Al Sidairawi and Abdalaziz Al Subai'i Co.

AL DU'AIJ AL SIDAIRAWI GENERAL TRADING AND CONTRACTING CO. LTD.

Address head office P.O.Box 851 Safat
Telephone 738380,1, 749068,9
Telex 22648 SUDAIR KT
Cable ALSUDAIR
Activities This partnership manufactures marble tiles in a modern factory in the Shuwaikh industrial area, and also produces very skilfully carved doors and frames; aluminium windows and doors. They import and export marble chips, marble slabs and white cement. The partnership is between Ghazi Al Sidairawi and Ibrahim Al Du'aij.

AL DU'AIJ AL SIDAIRAWI AGRICULTURAL CO. LTD. (DUSAGCO)

Address head office P.O.Box 851 Safat
Telephone 445439, 447821
Telex 22648 SUDAIR KT
Activities Directored by Ibrahim Al Du'aij and Ghazi Al Sidairawi, the company imports agricultural products and machinery.

SALIM ABDULLAH AL SIDAIRAWI

Address head office P.O.Box 773 Safat
Telephone 547700
Activities Owned by Salim Abdullah, this concern is engaged in real estate and building operations.

The Family of Al Sultan Al Issa of Jana'at

A prominent and respected family with wide and important interests.

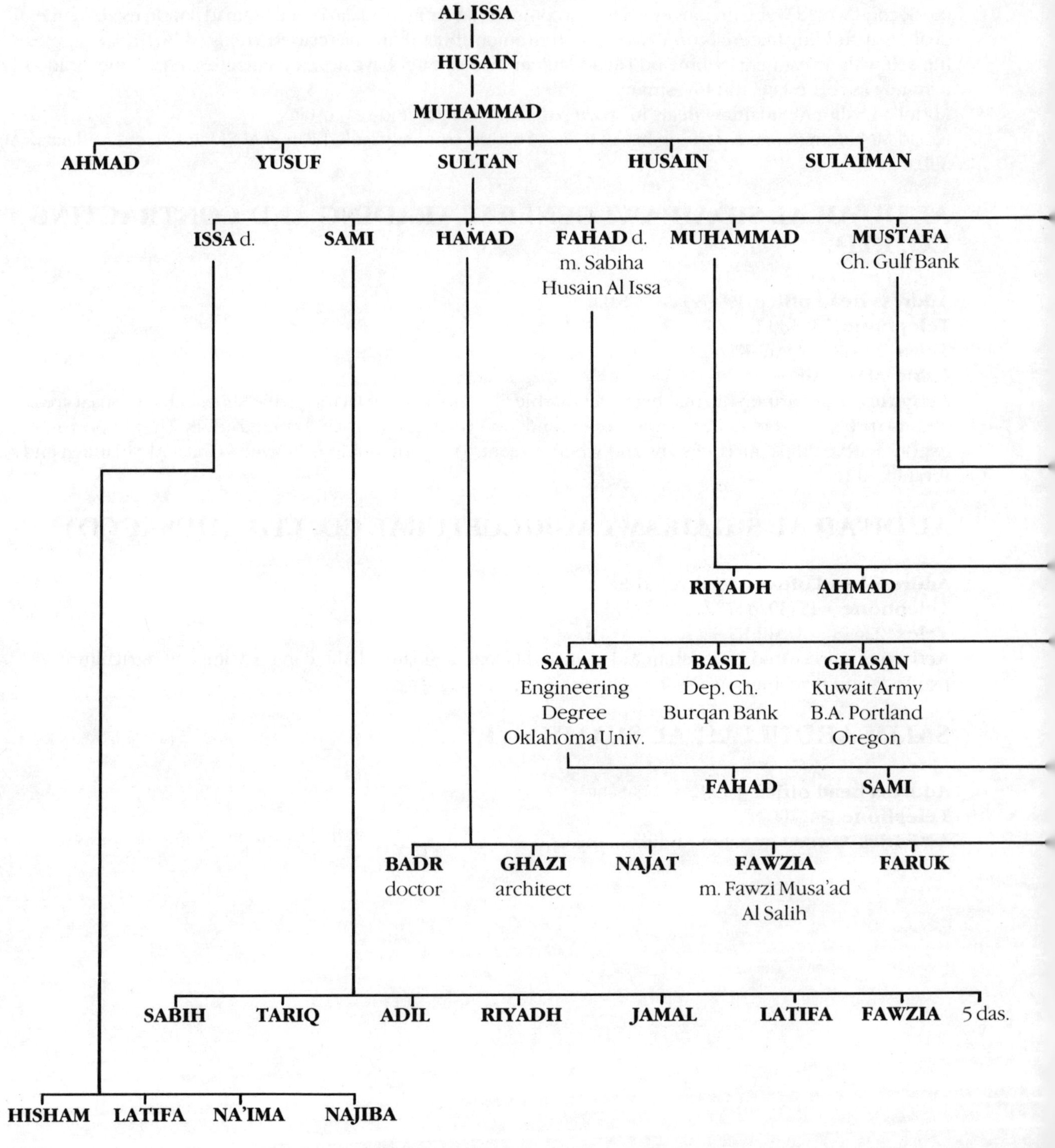

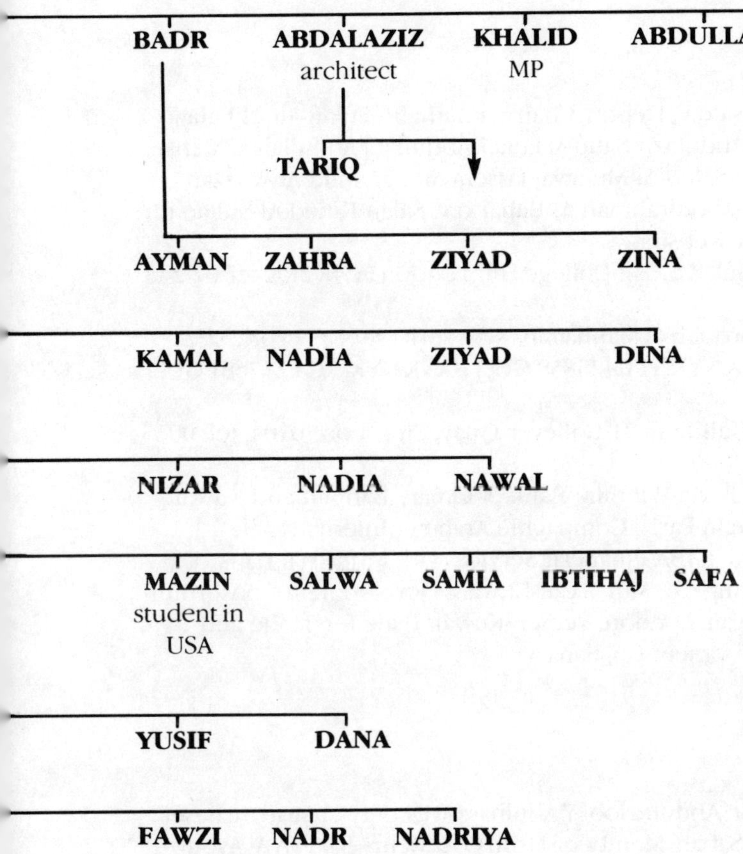
BADR
ABDALAZIZ
architect
KHALID
MP
ABDULLAH
ANWAR
JAMIL
TARIQ
AYMAN
ZAHRA
ZIYAD
ZINA
KAMAL
NADIA
ZIYAD
DINA
NIZAR
NADIA
NAWAL
MAZIN
student in USA
SALWA
SAMIA
IBTIHAJ
SAFA
YUSIF
DANA
FAWZI
NADR
NADRIYA

FAHAD SULTAN SONS AND CO. LTD.

Address head office P.O.Box 208 Safat
Telephone 432714, 417567
Telex 22427 KT
Activities Originally a merchant trading house the company has evolved into a family investment holding company. As such it has been responsible for much very major real estate development, including such projects as the Sharq Commercial Tower, the Fahad Sultan Residential Complex, and Al Mushraqi Project which is currently under development. The family is a prominent one in Kuwait banking and financial circles and it is therefore convenient to include descriptions of relevant institutions under this head.

THE GULF BANK

Address head office P.O.Box 3200 Safat
Telephone 449501
Telex 22001 GULF BANK KT, 22739 GULF BANK KT
Board of Directors Chairman: Mustafa Sultan Al Essa q.v; Deputy Chairman: Khalid Fulaij Ali Al Fulaij; Delegate Member: Daoud Musaad Al Saleh; Members: Abdulaziz Saud Al Fulaij; Abdullatif Abdullah Al Mehri; Faisal Ali Abdul Wahab Al Mutawa; Fayez Abdulaziz Al Saleh Al Mutawa; Jassem Mohammed Al Wazzan q.v; Khalid Abdullah Mohammed Al Mishari; Marzooq Ali Abdulrahman Al Bahar q.v; Salah Fahed Al Sultan q.v; Yacoub Yousuf Al Joua'an; General Manager: Stuart M Webster.
Overseas Branches London Rep. Office: The Gulf Bank K.S.C., 1 College Hill, London EC4R 2RA, tel: 01-248 2843, tlx 887688 GULFBK G.
New York Agency: 520 Madison Avenue 53rd Street, Borough of Manhattan, New York City, New York, USA, tel: 212-715-2300, tlx Western Union 126385 GULFBANK NYK, ITT 425858 GULFBANK NYK, RCA 237681 GULF UR.
Singapore Offshore Branch: 17-01 Hong Kong Bank Building, 21 Colleyer Quay, Singapore 0104, tel: 0065-220-0703, tlx SINGAPORE 22437, 22438.
Affiliates and Subsidiaries Bank of Bahrain and Kuwait, Bahrain; Bank of Oman, Bahrain and Kuwait, Oman; Banque Arabe et Internationale d'Investissement, Paris; Compagnie Arabe et Internationale d'Investissement, Luxembourg; GIBA International Ltd; GIBA Financial Services Ltd; Industrial Bank of Kuwait, Kuwait; Kuwait Reinsurance Co; Kuwait Clearing Co; Moroccan-Kuwaiti Development Consortium, Casablanca; Securities Group Co; United Bank of Kuwait, London; Yemen Kuwait Bank for Trade and Investment, Sana'a; Yemeni Kuwaiti Real Estate Development Co, Sana'a.
The Burgan Bank
Address head office P.O.Box 5389 Safat
Telephone 417100/9
Telex 22730, 22767, 23309 BURGANBANK KT
Board of Directors Chairman and Managing Director: Abdulrasool Y Abulhasan; Deputy Chairman: Basel F Al Sultan q.v; Deputy Managing Director: Ali Jarrah Al Sabah; Members: Jasim O Al Mehri; Salah A Al Ayoub q.v; Abdulatif A Al Duaij; Fahad A Al Hudaib; Faisal S Al Dabbous; Mohamed A M Al Atiqi.
Shareholders' Equity in KD
Total paid share Capital: 1980 - 13,948,993; 1981 - 13,949,034; 1982 - 20,847,353
Statutory reserves: 1980 - 9,373,880; 1981 - 9,806,560; 1982 - 21,876,693
Voluntary reserves: 1980 - 3,503,412; 1981 - 4,161,038; 1982 - 5,064,734
Profit carried forward: 1980 - 78,863; 1981 - 73,067; 1982 - 61,895
Total Equity: 1980 - 26,905,148; 1981 - 27,989,699; 1982 - 47,850,675
Equity participations in associated banks and other companies
1. Kuwait Re-Insurance Co, Kuwait. Capital issued KD5,040,000 - Holding 8.33%
2. Bank of Bahrain and Kuwait, Bahrain. Capital issued BD20,583,333 - Holding 6.75%
3. Arab Hellenic Bank SA, Athens. Capital issued GD555,000,000 - Holding 5.00%

4. United Bank of Kuwait Ltd, London. Capital issued £39,923,259 - Holding 8.30%
5. Arab Co for Trading Securities (ACTS), Kuwait. Capital issued KD6,000,000 - Holding 5.00%
6. Industrial Bank of Kuwait, Kuwait. Capital issued KD20,000,000 - Holding 4.48%
7. United Gulf Bank EC, Bahrain. Capital issued US$250,000,000 - Holding 2.25%
8. Securities Group Co, Kuwait. Capital issued KD50,000,000 - Holding 1.00%
9. Kuwait Clearing Co SAK (Closed), Kuwait. Capital issued KD6,500,000 - Holding 7.69%

HOUSE OF TRADE AND CONTRACTING CO.

Address head office P.O.Box 2518 Safat
Telephone 711039, 711174
Telex 23066 HOMET KT
Activities The Chairman of this company is Khalid Sultan Al Issa and the Managing Director, his brother, Anwar Sultan. The company supplies all local works for heavy mechanical, electrical and instrumentation installations.

KUWAIT WIRE PLANT

Address head office P.O.Box 21719 Safat
Telephone 423748, 423749
Telex 22697 FRSTTRO KT
Activities This company is owned by Faruk Sultan Al Issa and is engaged in the manufacture of bright steel rods and rails for export.

The Family of Sultan

The ancestors of the family were Khojar from India, a group responsible for much Indian trade from the Sudan and the Red Sea to Aden, Hadramawt, Oman and the Arab Gulf.

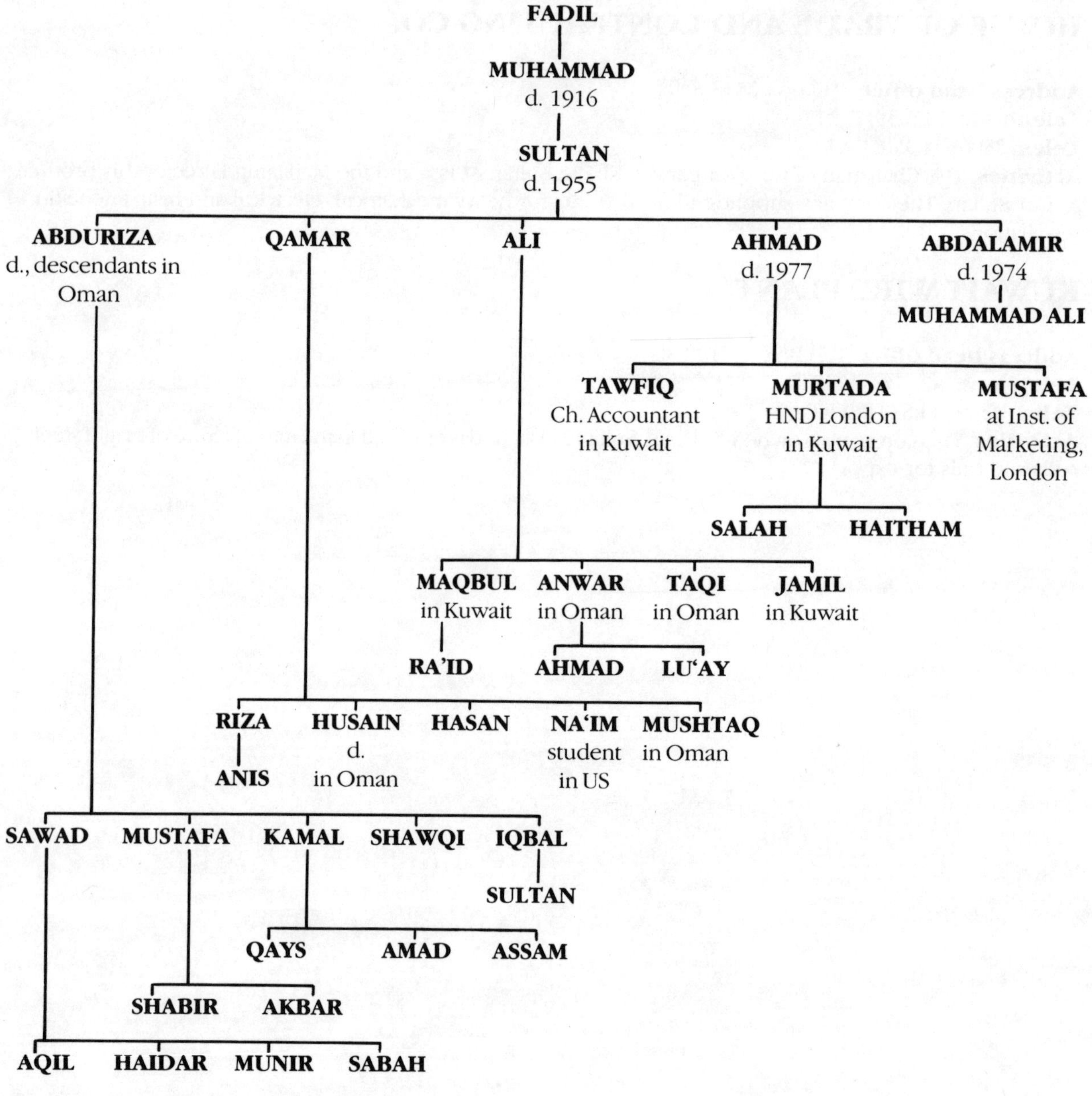

The history of W.J. Towell is one of those stories which brings an air of enchantment to the story of Arabian business. The family concerned, the Sultans, originate from Muscat in the Sultanate of Oman though today, in terms of turnover, the Kuwait branch forms the largest part of their business.

In 1866 an American called Jack Towell landed in Muscat with his wife. No one now knows what made them stay but they did so for thirty years. Mr. Towell was probably a ship's chandler or maybe a sailor, and it may have been that he saw a chance to enter the brisk trade that had grown up in dates to the eastern coast of the United States. Whatever the reasons the Towells established a business employing a Muhammad Fadil as their clerk. In 1880 they also employed a Scotsman named Archibald McKirdy from Rothesay. McKirdy became the American Vice-Consul in Oman and when W.J. Towell left at the end of the century, possibly due to the death of this wife, he also left the business in McKirdy's hands. McKirdy himself left in 1906 and sold the business to Muhammad Fadil for less than £1,000. Muhammad was also by this time Deputy Consul, a post he retained until his death in 1916. By now Muhammad had built up the business and it was a flourishing concern when Sultan inherited it. The mainstay of the business was in the export of pomegranates to the Gulf and India, dried fish to Bombay, shark fins to China and Ceylon, cuttlefish, dried lines and dates of course. The market in these changed from the United States, where dates grown in California took over, to India. These activities were supplemented by the import of kerosene as an agent of the Standard Oil Company and the handling of the agency for the British India and Lloyds of London.

However, over the course of the next three decades, the business declined with the deteriorating state of the Oman economy during those years. It wasn't until they decided to break out of Oman in 1947 that things began to improve. Whilst Sultan had technically run the business it was effectively controlled by his son, Abdalriza, and had been since the late twenties. In 1947 Abdalriza was returning from the Hajj through Kuwait, as at that time there was no direct route to Jiddah from Muscat, and there he met his agent, Ahmad Zaid Sarhan, to whom he sold tyres and tobacco. Ahmad was full of news about oil production and Abdalriza at once saw the business opportunities which would open up.

On his return to Muscat Abdalriza discussed the matter with his brothers and they decided to open an office in Kuwait. When this had been done each brother ran the office in turn until the death of Ahmad in 1977. It is now run by Ali's eldest son, Maqbul.

The first fifteen years or so of the Kuwaiti operation were highlighted by a corner in the ghee market and a successful rice deal with the Al Sabah, but on the whole they were not years of brilliant achievement. The Kuwait business was sustained in a rather ad hoc way by the import of sugar, rice, ghee, Castrol motor oil, films, shirts and perfumes. In short, they brought into Kuwait almost anything they thought might show a profit. However, in 1963 Ahmad Sultan gained the representation for a group of Pakistani merchants dealing in the Pakistani crop of Basmati rice. Hardly before the ink was dry on this agreement there was a dispute and Ahmad was forced to make a bid for 30,000 tons direct to the Pakistani government. This culminated in a highly successful deal and the following year Ahmad was able to bid for the whole crop with a million pounds sterling in hard cash and a letter of credit. This was more hard currency than the entire consortium of Pakistani merchants could muster and so the Sultans were able to win what amounted to a world monopoly in this very desirable commodity. As the years passed the Pakistani government was able to make more and more basmati rice available for export; the 1967 season had produced 90,000 tons, two subsequent seasons produced 150,000 tons, and by 1971 a two-year deal for 210,000 was reached. The rewards were substantial if not staggering, but there was a devastatingly sad and extra price to pay. During the early negotiations with the Pakistani government an Iraqi go-between was employed by the Sultans. It transpired that this man was not, in the event, needed and so the Sultans paid him off handsomely. He was, however, a gambler and spent all this money in Beirut, then at once asked the family for more cash. This was refused and the Iraqi lured the youngest brother, Abdalamir, to the Holiday Inn in Beirut and there murdered him before himself committing suicide.

Before this horrifying event the rice contracts had in fact come to an end, due to the rise in oil revenues enabling all the Gulf States to control food prices and import themselves. This has meant that the merchants have only been able to retain a little over 30% of the market. The Sultans have accordingly diversified into cement, barley for animal feed, building materials, foodstuffs and consumer goods.

TOWELL CONSTRUCTION CO. LTD.

Address head office P.O.Box 2560 Safat
Telephone 436164, 436169
Telex 23494 TOWELL KT
Activities This company is a member of the W.J. Towell Group and is a major construction business with the capability of building and maintaining a very wide variety of projects including: single private houses, apartment complexes, office buildings, schools, clinics and community centres. They can carry out road construction and utility installations, power supplies work and bridge construction, as well as the erection of industrial plant, storage and handling facilities, hangars, laboratories and workshops. The company is managed by the Howe Group of Canada.
The W.J. Towell Group is composed of the following entities:
In Kuwait office's organisation:
1. Banking and Insurance interests include participation in the Kuwait International Finance Co. and the Jordan Insurance Co.
2. Real estate properties include 13% of Beaverton Properties Pte Ltd.
3. Construction interests, apart from Towell Construction, are a 100% ownership of Towell Pre-Fab Housing Kuwait and 70% of Saudi Towell Construction.
4. General Trading embraces the following representations in one or more Middle Eastern country: Mazda cars, Lucas autoparts, Bridgestone tyres, Honda generators, Unilever Exports, Blue Circle Cement Products, R.J. Reynolds Tobacco Co. (covering such brands as Winston, Salem, Camel and More), Elizabeth Arden, Wilkinson Sword, Ray-O-Voc, A and P Foods. This wide range of agency activity is enhanced by the following trading subsidiaries: International Furnishing Co. (50%), Gee Pee and Towell of Singapore (30%), Al Muneer Trading Co. Kuwait (100%), Northern Gulf Trading Co. Kuwait (50%), Middle East Telecommunications Co. Kuwait (50%), Computer Division of W.J.T. Kuwait which is a joint venture with Perkin Elmer Computers.
5. Light industry interests comprise International Foam Co. of Dubai (45%), Terrazzo Tile Factory Kuwait (100%), and Kuwait Snack Products Co. (41%).
The following W.J Towell interests are dealt with from Oman:
1. Banking and Insurance - National Bank of Oman (30%) and a directorship in the Oman Arab African Bank with an agency capacity for the Guardian Royal Assurance Co.
2. Real estate interests include Medinat Qaboos (East) Ltd. (100%), Oman International Developments (29%), Warehousing in Dubai (100%), Hyatt Regency Malaysia (9%).
3. In the construction field W.J. Towell controls 50% of Taylor Woodrow Towell Co. of Oman.
4. General Trading covers the same field as in Kuwait, with the following local interests in addition: Muttrah Cold Stores (51%), General Electric and Trading Co. (50%), Oman United Agencies (12%), W.J. Towell and Co. Ltd. Sharjah (100%).
5. Industrial projects include the Oman National Dairy Products installation (51%).

The Family of Al Thuwaini

This family takes its name from a recent eponym and are Al 'Afra of Jubayr Bani Khalid. The Bani Khalid used to control the area of eastern Arabia before the migration of the Anaiza in the late seventeenth century. The Jubur section is named after Jabir b. Aswad and were the shaykhs of the Bani Khalid before the rise to power of the Al Urayar. The Bani Khalid had sections at Homs in Syria, Ahwaz in Iran, Mafraq in Jordan and on the southern Euphrates in Iraq. The Thuwaini are an eminent and much respected family in Kuwait.

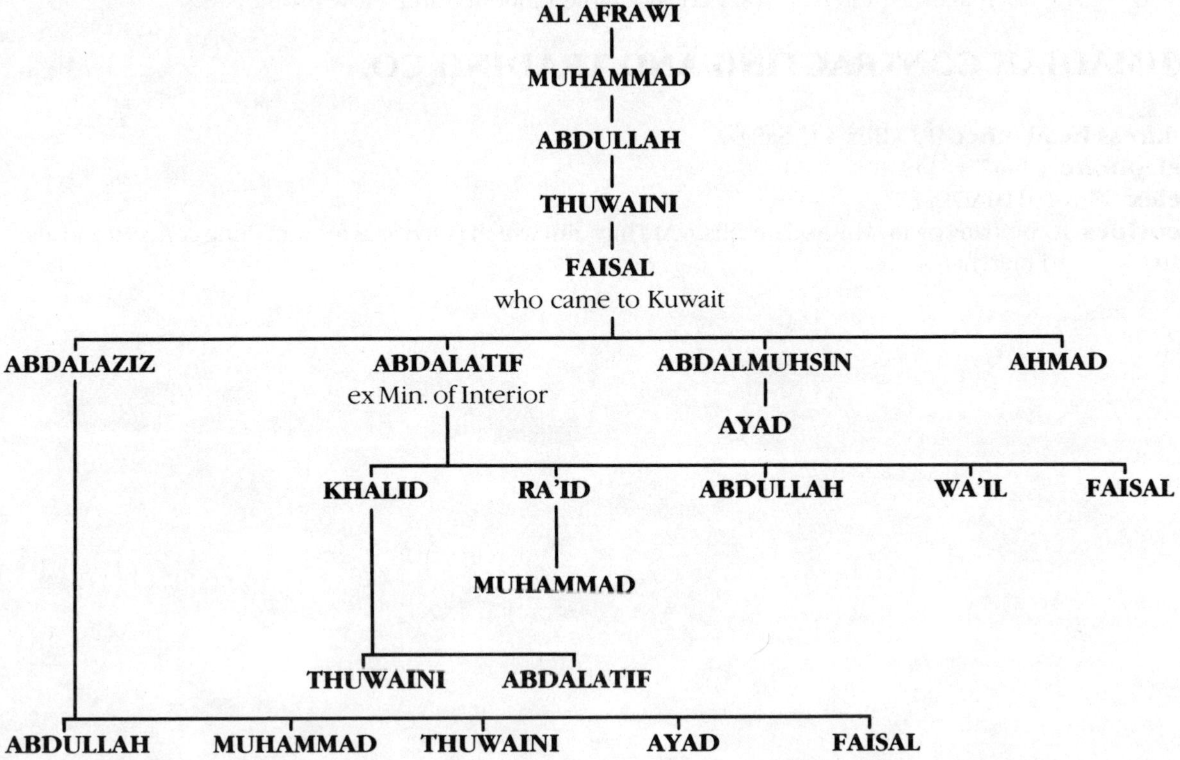

AL THUWAINY TRADING COMPANY

Address head office P.O.Box 171 Safat
Telephone 2460550, 428868
Telex 22253 THUWAINY KT
Cable THUWAINY
Activities The President of the company is Abdalatif Faisal Al Thuwainy and the Managing Director, his brother, Abdalmuhsin. The company is a supplier and stockist for building equipment coming from those companies they may, from time to time, represent. They are also civil, electrical and mechanical engineers. The company has real estate interests, very considerable influence and a low profile.

AHMADIAH CONTRACTING AND TRADING CO.

Address head office P.O.Box 446 Safat
Telephone 814477, 814848
Telex 23314 AHMADIA KT
Activities A company owned by Abdalmuhsin Al Thuwaini which is active as a contracting concern and also as traders and merchants.

The Family of Al Uwaid

A small family illustrating a breakaway from full time participation in business towards professional activity on behalf of another, where the individual thus works for someone else. The circumstances of the family are such that their place as partners in a business is as a consequence of a marriage.

KHALID

- **ABDULLAH** d.
- **KHUDAIR** d.
  m. sister of Ibrahim Muhammad Jasim Al Abdali
  - **KHALIDA**
  - **SABRIYA**
  - **BADRIYA**
  - **NA'IMA**
  - **HASAN**
    in Kuwait National Petroleum
    Ptner Al Abdali General Trading and Arab International Co.
  - **MUNTAHA**
  - **HUSAIN**
    a manager at Commercial Bank
    Ptner Al Abdali General Trading and Arab International Co.
- **NURI** d.

AL ABDALI GENERAL TRADING AND CONTRACTING

Address head office P.O.Box 46208 FAHAHEEL
Telephone 916622, 924614
Activities The company has two main categories of business. The contracting side of its activities concentrates on oil installations and highway construction. The trading side specialises in dealing with carpets, sanitary ware, heavy transport equipment and import export activities.

ARAB INTERNATIONAL CO.

Address head office 7860 Kuwait
Telephone 912995
Activities This concern trades in foodstuffs, acts as a contractor, and is involved in real estate development.

The Family of Al Wazzan

The family in Kuwait originates in Najd in Saudi Arabia. They should not be confused with others of a similar name.

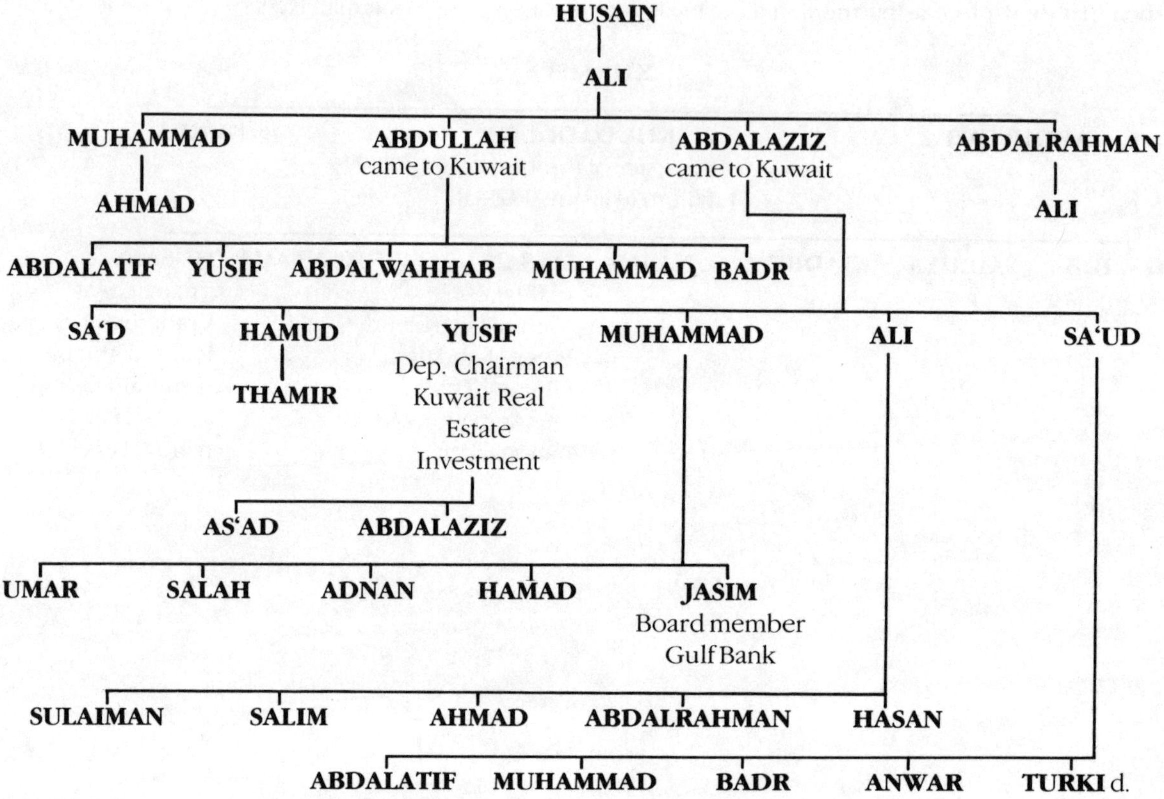

ABDALAZIZ AL ALI AL WAZZAN SONS AND COMPANY

Address head office P.O.Box 1251
Telephone 443911, 443918
Telex 2410 WAZANIAH KT
Activities This, the parent company of the Group, is a major contracting concern which has contributed many buildings to help construct modern Kuwait. The Head Office contains the Land and Real Estate Investment Division and the Stock and Bonds Investment Division. The remainder of the Group's activities are conducted through the medium of the following companies.

BURHAN KUWAITI TRADING AND CONTRACTING CO.

Address head office P.O. Box 20516
Telephone 732715
Telex 3089 BURHAN KT
Formed in 1958 this company specialises in drainage and road construction. It is categorised as a category one company. The General Manager is Hamud Abdalaziz Al Wazzan.

KUWAIT ASPHALT EMULSION CO.

Address head office P.O. Box 5189
Telephone 981153
A fully automatic asphalt plant that produces 300 tons a month. The company started production in 1974 and is under the Chairmanship of Hamud Abdalaziz Al Wazzan.

AL WAZZAN LIFT COMPANY

Address head office P.O. Box 24202
Telephone 526760
Telex 2917 THARWAT KT
A company engaged in electrical contracting and the installation of lifts and escalators. It represents several German manufacturers and its General Manager is Hamad Al Wazzan.

MISHRIF TRADING AND CONTRACTING

Address head office P.O. Box 20516
Telephone 732714
Telex 3089 BURHAN KT
A company founded in 1967 and having a range of activities very similar to the Burhan company. Its General Manager is Hamud Abdalaziz Al Wazzan.

AL WAZZAN STEEL FACTORY

Address head office P.O. Box 20593
Telephone 831816
Telex 4324 BURHANCO KT
The oldest factory for steel construction and fabrication in Kuwait.

THE BURHAN CARPENTRY FACTORY

Address head office P.O. Box 20593
Telephone 818535
Telex 4324 BURHANCO
A large factory making both western and eastern styles of furniture with up to date machinery.

AL ROWDAH TRADING AND CONTRACTING COMPANY

Address head office P.O. Box 23207
Telephone 423927
Telex 2994 RAKAFCO
Established in 1974 this company has special areas of interest including road works, pipe lines, earth moving and construction; aggregate production and sewage treatment projects.

AL MARWAH TRADING AND CONTRACTING CO.

Address head office P.O. Box 23207
Telephone 423000
Telex 2917 THARWAT KT
In association with companies from France, Korea, Germany, India, The United States and Spain, this successful company completed projects worth over twenty five million dinars in the first seven years of it's life. Under the management of Hamid Al Wazzan the company specialises in prefabricated construction and general construction.

AL WAZZAN TRAVELS

Address head office P.O. Box 20508
Telephone 422093
Telex 4769 KITI
A travel agency offering very comprehensive services worldwide.

THE MOWASAT HOSPITAL

Address head office P.O. Box 8323
Telephone 611533
Telex 2056 MUTAL KT
This, one of the largest private hospitals in Kuwait, was founded in 1967 and has a hundred beds. Staffed and equipped to the highest standards, the hospital has established a very high reputation.

AL WAZZAN ELECTRICAL COMPANY

Address head office P.O. Box 26052
Telephone 423000
Telex 2917 THARWAT KT
Under the management of Hamad and Badr Al Wazzan this relatively new company is engaged in electrical contracting.

Address head office P.O. Box 20593
Telephone 831816
Telex 4324 BURHANCO KT
Manufactures doors, windows, furniture framing and general construction products.

SUPPLYING STORES COMPANY

A business formed in 1954 dealing in electrical goods. They are agents for Sony and Sanyo.